THE ROUGH

D1220416

European Football

A FANS' HANDBOOK 2000–2001

There are more than one hundred and fifty Rough Guide titles
covering destinations from Amsterdam to Zimbabwe

Forthcoming titles include
Alaska • Copenhagen • Ibiza & Formentera • Iceland

Rough Guide Reference Series
Classical Music • Country Music • Drum 'n' bass • English Football
European Football • House • The Internet • Jazz • Music USA • Opera
Reggae • Rock Music • Techno • Unexplained Phenomena • World Music

Rough Guide Phrasebooks
Czech • Dutch • Egyptian Arabic • European Languages • French • German
Greek • Hindi & Urdu • Hungarian • Indonesian • Italian • Japanese
Mandarin Chinese • Mexican Spanish • Polish • Portuguese • Russian
Spanish • Swahili • Thai • Turkish • Vietnamese

Rough Guides on the Internet
www.roughguides.com

Commissioning editor: Jonathan Buckley
Editor: Dan Goldstein
Design and layout: Dan Goldstein
Production: Michelle Draycott, Robert Evers, Mike Hancock
Rough Guides Series editor: Mark Ellingham
All photography: Empics, Nottingham, England

....

This fourth edition published November 2000 by Rough Guides Ltd, 62–70 Shorts
  Gardens, London WC2H 9AH.

Distributed by the Penguin Group:
Penguin Books Ltd, 27 Wrights Lane, London W8 5TZ
Penguin Putnam Inc., 375 Hudson Street, New York 10014, USA
Penguin Books Australia Ltd, 487 Maroondah Highway, PO Box 257, Ringwood, Victoria
  3134, Australia
Penguin Books Canada Ltd, 10 Alcorn Avenue, Toronto, Ontario, Canada M4V 1E4
Penguin Books (NZ) Ltd, 182–190 Wairau Road, Auckland 10, New Zealand
Printed in England by Clays Ltd, St Ives PLC
© Peterjon Cresswell and Simon Evans 2000
No part of this book may be reproduced in any form without permission from the
  publisher except for the quotation of brief passages in reviews.
672pp
A catalogue record for this book is available from the British Library
ISBN 1-85828-568-2

....

The publishers and authors have done their best to ensure the accuracy and currency of
  all the information in *The Rough Guide to European Football*, however, they can accept
  no responsibility for any loss, injury, or inconvenience sustained by any traveller as a
  result of information or advice contained in the guide.

THE ROUGH GUIDE TO

European Football

A FANS' HANDBOOK 2000–2001

Written and researched by
Peterjon Cresswell and Simon Evans

Edited by
Dan Goldstein

ROUGH
GUIDES

Contents

Introduction

At times like this, you begin to appreciate what European football is all about – or can be. The season is over, culminating in an adventurous, open, attacking Euro 2000. Another is upon us, spearheaded by an overbearing, money-spinning but at times compulsive Champions' League, reflecting the pomp and power of Europe's major players. A few miles – but another world – away lie the poverty and corruption of the League's poorer Eastern neighbours, most of whom are now reduced to playing ill-attended feeder leagues. Riding second class are the likes of Holland, Belgium, Scotland and Portugal, all with fine footballing traditions, but all trailing so far behind the likes of Spain and Italy that they are scrambling to form their own 'Atlantic League'.

Meanwhile, strewn across this desk lie scores of souvenirs and scribbled names, scrawls on beermats, business cards, ties from FA press offices, fanzines, programmes, pennants, gifts, snippets of information, from first-hand sources from the East to the West of this great continent, diligently gathered in the name of research – the dutiful game. Some items have been provided by press officers; most have been proffered by fans eager to see their club – their team, their identity – given fair representation in this fourth edition of *The Rough Guide To European Football*.

The first edition, published in 1997, broke new ground, spawning three further editions, mini-guides to France '98 and Euro 2000, and a rather dinky version in Japanese. The aim has been simple: to give the new generation of travelling fan all they need to get the most out of a footballing journey to Europe.

This, then, is a city-by-city guide to more than 50 footballing destinations, now incorporating 30 countries. For each city, we've outlined the game's local origins, rivalries, great players and traditions, while also featured are hotel, transport, nightlife and restaurant tips.

A book of this size could not hope to cover every club in the 50-plus countries that now compete in Europe. More modest ones have been sacrificed at the expense of providing comprehensive entries on the major Western nations and the capital cities of the East. Those travelling to Europe's more obscure corners will likely be shepherded round as part of an official tour group, whereas a visit to Paris or Madrid demands more than the provision of an airport, a stadium and a hotel room. For the more obscure provincial clubs, the *Match Practice* sections under each nation, detailing their ticketing systems, tournaments and traditions, should complement any journey.

We've gone to a lot of time and effort to ensure that this fourth edition is accurate and up-to-date. But, with so much changing so quickly in so many cities, your corrections, observations and additions for future editions would, as always, be gratefully received.

Where once it was a closed book, Europe is now an open door. Every week it welcomes a constant traffic of players, agents, promo men, media flunkies, tour operators, UEFA officials, freeloaders... and most of all, fans. A club may derive its profit from TV deals, but its lifeblood remains its supporters. It is their voices, opinions, scribbles and signatures which make this fourth edition of *The Rough Guide To European Football* what it is.

Peterjon Cresswell & Simon Evans, 2000

Acknowledgements

Chief contributors:

John Elliott

Bosnia Arsen Novalija
Croatia Renato Pandza
Denmark Nikolaj Steen Møller, Andrew Spooner
Finland Anne Pötry, Andrew Spooner

Romania Alecs Rîpeanu
Scotland Pete Doyle
Slovakia Ian Hall
Slovenia Greg Davies
Sweden Anders Ljungberg

And with thanks to:

Austria Othmar Loschy
Belgium Chris Feltham
Bosnia Nogometni savez Bosne i Hercegovine (NSBIH), Niall McCann, Dave, Tony and all the crew at The Harp
Bulgaria Kamen Totev (Futbol), Boncho Todorov, Andrei Medintsev (Bulgarian FA), Angel Giaourov, Boleslav, Nick Green, Vladimir Andreyev, Sveto (Studio X), Alexander Kirchev (Bilkova Apteka)
Croatia Alex Dragas, Tomislav Jablan (Rijeka)
Czech Republic Jirí Valín (Czech FA), Will Tizard, Frantisek Bouc (Prague Post), the two Glens
France Gérald Delpierre (l'OM), Chef (l'Euro, Paris)
Germany Gosto Babka von Gostomski (Penguin Bar, Berlin), Martina Weith, Anja Hütter (Hamburg), Róbert Varga, Robert Hollmann (InfoRadio), Nase, Bob and Ulrich, Nick Moody, Tim Graham and all at The Lab
Greece Panos Korkolilos (Greek FA), Daniel Howden, Brian Church, Paris Agiomamitis and all at Athens News, Demetris Nellas (Kathimerini), Harry Karakasis, Vassilios Lagopoulos (To Iero Pou Kaïei, Salonika)
Holland Rob de Leede (Dutch FA)
Hungary Tom Popper, Gábor Ganczer, Krisztina Schuller, DJ Zozo, László Nagy (Vasas)
Ireland Peter Hegarty, Colin Young
Poland Michal Olszasski (Program 3), Michal Pstrucha, Maurice O'Morgan (O'Morgans, Kraków), JasperTilbury (Kraków)
Romania Câtâlin Tepelin (Pro Sport), Marius Mâgârit (Pro Sport), Sorin Cioca and family (Steaua), Christian 'Kiki' Jancu (Rapid), Gabriel Guritâ (Dinamo), Alex Sirbu, Desmond McGrath, Sándor Balaçi (ELTE)
Russia Ken McCargow
Scotland Andra
Slovenia Robi (Maribor)
Spain Nick Eperon (Seville), Tim (Barcelona), Ben Goldstein
Switzerland Thomas Renggli (Neue Zürcher Zeitung)
Turkey Mehves, Evin, Gökman Özdemir (Sampdoria), Erkan Arseven (NTV), Dogan Yildirim, Engin, Erkan Sayin (Bodrum Bar)
Ukraine Stanislav Kournosenko, Sergei Makarevich, Sergei Devyatkin

Further reading

The Encyclopedia of World Soccer, Richard Henshaw (New Republic, 1979)
The Guinness Book of World Soccer, Guy Oliver (Guinness, 1995)
The Secret Life of Football, Alex Fynn and Lynton Guest (Macdonald, Queen Anne Press, 1989)
Out of Time, Alex Fynn and Lynton Guest (Pocket Books, 1994)
Soccer Revolution, Willy Meisl (Sportsman Book Club, 1956)
Soccer Nemesis, Brian Glanville (Secker and Warburg, 1955)
Soccer, A Panorama, Brian Glanville (Eyre and Spottiswoode, 1969)
The Simplest Game, Paul Gardner (Collier, 1994)
Football, Violence and Social Identity, ed. Richard Giulianotti, Norman Bonney and Mike Hepworth (Routledge, 1994)
The Football Grounds of Europe, Simon Inglis (Collins Willow, 1990)
Football, Fussball, Voetbal, The European Game 1956-Euro '96, Colin Cameron (BBC, 1995)
Soccer The World Game, Geoffrey Green (Phoenix House, 1953)
Hockings' European Cups, Ron Hockings (Kenneth Mason, 1990)
Football Against The Enemy, Simon Kuper (Phoenix, 1994)
The European Football Yearbook, ed. Mike Hammond (Sports Projects, annual)

Austria

Österreichischer Fussball-Bund (ÖFB) Ernst Happel Stadion, Sektor A/F,
Meiereistrasse 7, 1020 Wien ☎01/727 180   Fax 01/728 1632   E-mail oefb@asn.or.at

League champions Tirol Innsbruck   **Cup winners** Grazer AK   **Promoted** VfB
Admira/Wacker Mödling   **Relegated** Austria Lustenau

European participants 2000/01 Tirol Innsbruck, Sturm Graz (UCL qualifiers);
Grazer AK, SK Rapid (UEFA Cup); FK Austria, LASK Linz, SV Salzburg (Intertoto Cup)

A dim view – Alex Manninger waits for the next attack

The Austrians have always been keen to distinguish themselves from their neighbours to the East but in football terms, if little else, they are now in the same mire. Without the cash to import talent, Austrian football is dependent on home-grown players and, as the national team have shown for much of the past decade, the country is consistently failing to produce a competitive product.

Those brought in from foreign lands to plug the gaps at club level are generally journeymen from the East happy to pick up some schillings for their mediocre services. Apart from Salzburg's run to the UEFA Cup final in 1994 and Rapid's Cup-Winners' Cup final appearance two years later, Austrian football has done little to suggest that a revival may be on the cards.

In March 1999, the low point was reached when the national side were hammered 9–0 by Spain in a Euro 2000 qualifier in Valencia which effectively ended hopes of qualification for the finals. Later the same year, the Austrian FA's dream of prompting a revival through hosting a major tournament was shattered when its joint bid to host Euro 2004 with Hungary was rejected by UEFA in favour of Portugal. The 'Danube Games' was a nice idea but one which, due to the ill-advised choice of partner, was always doomed to failure.

Hard as it may be to imagine for a country now on the periphery of the game,

the Austrians played a pivotal role in football's development as a Europe-wide phenomenon. They instigated the forerunners of major club and international competitions, eagerly absorbed new tactical ideas, and embraced professionalism at a time when, across much of Europe, football was essentially the province of well-to-do amateurism.

Today they have little to show for their earlier innovation. Austria's national side has never reached the final of a major tournament, and no Austrian club has ever won a modern European trophy. In one of Europe's most affluent countries, many football clubs manage little more than a hand-to-mouth existence, staggering from the arms of one sponsor to the next – and from one unwelcoming town to another – in the hope of finding their niche. The

Victory salute – Grazer AK's double goalscoring hero Igor Pamić after the 2000 cup final

absence of the crumbling stadia, hooliganism and corruption that blights football beyond Austria's Eastern frontier merely means that less attention is paid to the process of slow decline.

Austria's illustrious footballing past was initiated by the work of one man: Hugo Meisl. A Jewish bank clerk enamoured with English culture and a strange new ball game that came with it, Meisl dedicated his life not just to the development of the domestic game in Austria, but to furthering the cause of international football. English workers had founded Vienna's first two football clubs, First Vienna FC and Vienna Cricket & Football Club, at the turn of the century. Meisl became a member of the latter, then in 1911 helped to found a new branch of it, Wiener Amateure-Sportverein, known simply as Amateure and later to become FK Austria. Other clubs quickly sprang up, competing in a series of tournaments open only to teams from Vienna. (Despite early interest elsewhere, particularly in Graz, provincial clubs were not allowed into the Austrian league until after 1945.) On the international front,

Meisl instigated Austria's football rivalry with Hungary, helping to organise the first meeting between the two countries – and the first international match to be played in continental Europe – in 1902. Ten years later he invited the English coach Jimmy Hogan to Vienna. Hogan, who would later coach the Hungarians with such spectacular results, preached his short passing game to a receptive audience, creating what would become known as the Danubian style in which a team's forward line was complemented by wide half-backs and an attacking centre-half.

To these tactical niceties Meisl added the administrator's touch, introducing fulltime professionalism to the Viennese game in 1924. Three years later his knack for football organisation gave birth to the Mitropa Cup and the International Cup, Central European predecessors of the European Cup and the European Championship, respectively.

By the Thirties Austria could boast the most dazzling national team in Europe. The *Wunderteam* lost only twice between 1931 and 1934, beating Germany 5–0 and 6–0,

Basics

EU nationals, Americans, Canadians, Australians and New Zealanders need only their passport to enter Austria.

The Austrian unit of currency is the **Schilling** (ÖS), divided into 100 Groschen. There are coins for 2, 5, 10 and 50 Groschen and 1, 5, 10, 20 Schilling, and notes for 20, 50, 100, 500, 1,000 and 5,000 Schilling. There are about ÖS21 to £1. Exchange rates and commissions vary from bank to bank. **Banks** are generally open Mon–Fri 8am–3pm, Thurs until 5.30pm, with smaller branches closing for lunch. **Post offices** often charge less commission and are generally open until 6pm and early on Saturday mornings. In Vienna there are 24-hour post offices at Fleischmarkt #19 and at the two main train stations, Südbahnhof and Westbahnhof. Cash machines are widespread and credit-card payment is common.

To **call Austria** from abroad, dial 43, then 1 for Vienna, 316 for Graz, 662 for Salzburg. To get an international line from Austria, dial 00 followed by the country code – this may vary at hotels and other businesses which have switched suppliers since deregulation. *Austria Telekom* has cheap rates 6pm–8am weekdays and all day Sat–Sun. **Phone cards** (*Telefonkarten*) cost ÖS50, ÖS100 and ÖS200. **Coin phones** take 1, 5, 10 and 20 Schilling pieces.

Austrian **trains** are clean and efficient; tickets are priced according to the number of kilometres covered. EC, IC and SC services are inter-city trains serving major stations, most incurring a supplement (*Zuschlag*) – indicate which train you are catching when buying your ticket. D trains are fast, E trains slower. You can pay for your ticket with a credit card only if it costs more than ÖS200. An ÖS30 supplement is charged for buying a ticket onboard.

The orange ***BundesBus* network** is really only useful for gaining access to remote mountain locations.

A cheaper way to travel is the **Mitfahrzentrale** service, which links drivers to **hitchers** who pay towards petrol costs (☎01/715 0066, open Mon–Fri 9am–6pm, Sat 9am–1pm). Prices are fixed – Vienna to Graz is ÖS170.

Switzerland 8–1 and Hungary 8–2. Their spirit was typified by their centre-forward, Matthias Sindelar, nicknamed 'Man of Paper' because of his slight build, but whose ball skills could take him past the most physical marker.

Sindelar scored twice to hand Austria the 1932 International Cup, but that was to be the *Wunderteam*'s only honour. In a World Cup semi-final two years later, their subtle skills ran aground in the mud of Milan, and they were beaten by Italy.

Hugo Meisl died soon after Hitler's invasion of Austria, while his players went on to strengthen Germany's World Cup squad of 1938. During World War II, Austrian clubs won both the German league and cup, their bittersweet success a tribute to the flair of Hogan's Viennese school.

In the postwar era, independent Austria made a quick return to international prominence. A new generation of players, led by Ernst Happel, Gerhard Hanappi and Ernst Ocwirk, were determined to make an impact on the modern game without betraying the Danubian tradition. Though nominally deploying the fashionable 'third-back' formation, the Austrians of the Fifties were a fluid outfit in which Ocwirk combined defensive duties with those of an old-fashioned attacking centre-half. Their finest hour was an extraordinary 7–5 defeat of hosts Switzerland at the 1954 World Cup.

By the Sixties, however, the modern European game was beginning to leave such scorelines – and Vienna's incurably romantic approach to football – behind. Neither FK Austria nor the team which had become their greatest city rivals, SK Rapid, were able to compete seriously in the UEFA-backed European club competitions. Domestically, too, their dominance was slipping. Linzer ASK became the first provincial team to win the league in 1965, and Wacker Innsbruck, captained by the fine international sweeper Bruno Pezzey, were Austria's team of the Seventies.

Rapid striker Hans Krankl led Austria to their best modern World Cup in Argentina in 1978, where they beat West Germany 3–2 in the second group stage. Four years later, however, the Austrians drew the vilification of a planet when they allowed their neighbours to beat them 1–0, eliminating Algeria to the two countries' mutual benefit. Hopes of a revival, spurred by Rapid's run to the Cup-Winners' Cup final of 1985, were dented when Josef Hickersberger's much-hyped national team failed to make it past the first round at Italia '90. In September that year came a greater ignominy – a 1–0 defeat by the Faroe Islands in the latter's first-ever competitive international.

Prohaska, a member of the 1978 side who had also starred in *Serie A*, was installed as coach to restore some pride, and the Austrians eventually qualified for France '98, their first major finals in eight years, on the strength of Toni Polster's goals. In addition to Polster, goalkeeper Michael Konsel, central defender Wolfgang Feiersinger and midfielder Peter Stöger were all well into their thirties, and in France Austria would prove a good argument for greater African participation – a highly defensive team had neither the wit not the work-rate to nick a result against Italy in their final game, after last-minute goals against Cameroon and Chile had put them in with a shout of qualifying.

With key members of the Sturm Graz side who had romped to the domestic title in 1998/99, Austria put up a decent show in friendlies and easier Euro 2000 qualifying games before that eventual disgrace in Valéncia. Prohaska was then replaced by Otto Barić, the wily old Croat behind the Salzburg resurgence of the mid-Nineties.

But while Barić may be famed for his motivational qualities, there is clearly a limit to what he can achieve with the current crop of players. Austria's chances of making it to South Korea and Japan in 2002 are slim, and it will take a new generation of players for even a semblance of hope to be restored.

Essential vocabulary

Hello *Grüss Gott*
Goodbye *Wiederschauen*
Yes *Ja*
No *Nein*
Two beers, please *Zwei Bier, bitte*
Thank you *Danke*
Men's *Herren*
Women's *Damen*
Where is the stadium? *Wo ist das Stadion?*
What's the score? *Wie steht's?*
Referee *Schiedsrichter*
Offside *Abseits*

Match practice

Austrian football would starve on turnstile takings alone – many clubs have an improbable string of sponsors in their names, and players' backsides resemble a pair of Grand Prix overalls. Apart from Vienna's Rapid-Austria *Meisterschaftsderby* in the Prater, the other fixtures that raise passions are Rapid's clashes with Linz, Graz and Salzburg, and the *West-Derby* between Salzburg and Innsbruck.

Increasingly popular across the nation are *Wettpunkte*, pub/betting shops which fill up at results time of a Saturday and have rejuvenated the art of communal post-match analysis.

The season runs from mid-July until the end of November, and from the start of March until the end of May. Indoor tournaments fill the winter break. Games are played on Saturdays at 3.30pm and Wednesdays at 7pm, but the live televised game on ÖRF can fall almost any time between Saturday and Monday. Second-division clubs have had to fall in line and kick off at the same fixed 3.30pm time on Saturday.

A different league

There are ten teams in the *max. Bundesliga*, playing each other four times over the course of a season. The bottom club changes places with the winner of the ten-team *Erste Division* which operates on similar lines. Below the *Erste* are three *Regionalligas* – *Ost* (east), *Mitte* (central) and *West* – whose winners take it in turns every year for one to play-off with the one-from-bottom side in the *Erste*.

The bottom club in the Erste swaps places with the winner of a play-off between the winners of the other two *Regionalligas*. The system is further regionalised lower down.

Up for the cup

The *ÖFB Cup* begins with preliminary rounds in July, involving 144 amateur teams. All ties up to and including the semi-final are played at the club first drawn out of the hat and are decided on one game, extra-time and penalties. The ten *max. Bundesliga* clubs enter at the second-round stage in August. The final takes place at Vienna's Prater stadium in May.

Just the ticket

Most Austrian grounds are small, with tickets divided into seats (*Sitzplätze*) and standing (*Stehplätze*), covered (*überdachte*) or uncovered (*nicht überdacht*). At bigger grounds there will be a *Gästesektor* for visiting fans. A stand (*Tribüne*) is generally named after its location, eg *West-Tribüne*, west stand. Tickets for *max. Bundesliga* games are computerised, and queues can build up while each person runs their ticket through the turnstile. Entrance will cost you ÖS200–250 for a prime seat, ÖS150 to stand. Accompanied women are often given an ÖS50–100 discount.

Half-time

All kinds of sausages are scoffed, washed down with beer or wine, all at ÖS30–40 each. In winter mulled wine (*Glühwein*) is popular, as are *Langos* – frisbee-shaped portions of fried dough – in summer.

Action replay

DF1 has pay-per-view games but few viewers, which leaves free-to-air rights to the state ÖRF station, whose rescheduling of plum ties to suit its own demands has driven a wedge between fans and television. 'ÖRF Is Killing Football' demonstrations were commonplace throughout 1999.

ÖRF1 also presents *Fussball*, a goals and highlights show (Saturdays, 6–7.30pm), and has the long-term rights to show Austrian international matches live. The station's Champions' League coverage is excellent, with extended highlights from all matches on any given match-night.

The back page

Two new football publications are on the market: *Sportwoche*, (Mondays, ÖS12) and *Neue Sportzeitung* (Tuesdays, ÖS20), which has all the main European results and tables. The weekly *Wiener Sport am Montag* (ÖS25) concentrates on Viennese football, with details of all the local leagues and a ÖS30 discount token on a ticket for the game of the week in town.

Ultra culture

The commercialism of German fan culture and colourful festivities of the Italian *ultras* are slowly becoming part of the Austrian game, although with such small crowds, they have yet to turn stadia into a replica-shirted mass of noise and colour. The followings who make a noise and travel with it are those of Rapid and Linz – the latter's *Vikings Magazin* (ÖS20) is worth a look. Tirol Innsbruck's *Verrückte Köpfe*, or Crazy Heads, offer fiesta and fireworks despite their club's move to a new stadium.

In the net

The official Austrian *Bundesliga* website is at: www.bundesliga.at. You'll find a wide selection of Austrian football gear, fanzines and the like at: www.folkladen.com. And Europe's – probably the world's – finest stats service is still provided by the Linz-based RSSSF archive at: www.risc.uni-linz.ac.at/non-official/rsssf/results-eur.html.

Vienna

Today's *Wiener Stadtliga*, the Viennese league a flight below the *Regionalliga Ost*, has Slovak, Croatian, Serbian and Turkish teams, reflecting the city's rich ethnic mix. There is a poignant echo here of the time when local football was in its infancy a century ago – Vienna was the centre of a powerful empire, and the game's pioneers originated from across Habsburg Europe, based in Vienna but developing close ties with Hungary and Bohemia.

Today, groundhopping in Vienna – a pastime aided by the #45 S-Bahn line which connects Rapid, Wiener Sport-Club and First Vienna – is a trip into history, to a time when the city's football was as good as, if not better than, any other in Europe. How long the museum can afford to keep running is another matter.

The thrilling fields

FK Austria

Franz Horr-Stadion, Fischhofgasse 12
Capacity 11,800 (5,000 seated)
Colours Violet shirts, white shorts
League champions 1924, 1926, 1949, 1950, 1953, 1961, 1962, 1963, 1969, 1970, 1976, 1978, 1979, 1980, 1981, 1984, 1985, 86, 1991, 1992, 1993
Cup winners 1921, 1924, 1925, 1926, 1933, 1935, 1936, 1948, 1949, 1960, 1962, 1963, 1967, 1971, 1974, 1977, 1980, 1982, 1986, 1990, 1992, 1994

It is now seven years since Austria Vienna last won a league title, and with European campaigns restricted to the early rounds, attendances have fallen away – along with the club's claim to be one of the 'big two' alongside local rivals Rapid. The team's stadium, crouched by a motorway intersection, sums up their peripheral status, yet FK Austria were once a major force in the Austrian and European game.

Having initially been formed as a branch of the Vienna Cricket & Football Club, or Cricketer, who took part in the first-ever Austrian football match in 1894, they won the league as Amateure in 1924 and 1926, becoming FK Austria before the glorious Thirties. During the golden decade of Viennese football, FK Austria always lost out to First Vienna, Admira or their eternal rivals Rapid in the league, but won the Mitropa Cup in 1933 and 1936. The club had no home ground, playing either at the newly built Wiener Stadion or at Rapid's Pfarrwiese. The *Violetten* provided the leading elements of the Austrian *Wunderteam* of the 1930s, in particular the Czech-born striker Matthias Sindelar, whose premature retirement and mysterious suicide in 1939 signalled the sad end of an era.

The club enjoyed a postwar revival based on the passing skills of their attacking half-back and captain Ernst Ocwirk, winning four titles before his departure to Sampdoria in 1956, and keeping the tradition of playing the beautiful game before the financial imperatives of European competition began to loom on the horizon. Ocwirk would return as coach and win two more titles with FK Austria in 1969 and 1970.

Maintaining its links with the past, in 1973 the club absorbed 1915 champions Wiener Athletik Club and built an attractive young side which would win five titles in six years in the late Seventies and early Eighties, reaching the Cup-Winners' Cup final in 1978. Key FK Austria players such as midfielder Herbert Prohaska (who returned as coach in 1999) and goalkeeper Friedl Koncilia also played for Austria at the 1978 and 1982 World Cups.

Hungary's Tibor Nyilasi starred in the three straight title wins between 1984 and 1986, which also saw a young Toni Polster embark on his stint of 120 goals in 145 games. By then the Violets were no longer playing at the Prater, having moved into the modest Franz Horr-Stadion in Sindelar's

Vienna essentials

Wien Schwechat Airport is 19km south-east of central Vienna. Line #7 of the overland railway, the S-Bahn, makes the 30min journey between Schwechat and Wien-Nord and Wien-Mitte stations. There are two trains an hour, 5am–10pm, single fare ÖS38. Two bus services run to town, one every 30mins to the City Air Terminal at the *Hilton* hotel by Wien-Mitte, the other hourly to each main train station, Südbahnhof (S60 and S80) and Westbahnhof (U3/6). Both buses run 5.30am–11.30pm, with a less frequent service through the night, cost ÖS70 and take about 30mins. A taxi is around ÖS400.

Transport in Vienna (5.30am-12.30am) is efficient, consisting of trams, buses, a five-line metro (U-Bahn) and the S-Bahn. Single tickets, valid for all, cost ÖS19 from newsstands and machines at U-Bahn stations. They are valid for an hour from the time you punch them. Tickets bought onboard trams and buses cost ÖS22. A travel pass, *Netzkarte*, costs ÖS60 for 24 hours, ÖS150 for 72 hours, valid from first stamping. Day passes are not valid on the **night bus service**, which has 22 routes running through Schwedenplatz for a flat ÖS25 fare.

Taxi fares start at ÖS27, then ÖS14 per kilometre, plus supplements for nights, Sundays, holidays and luggage. Radio taxis (☎01/31 300 or ☎01/60 160) charge a supplement of ÖS26.

Vienna's efficient main **tourist office** has moved to Albertinaplatz 1 (open daily 9am–7pm, ☎01/513 8892, U1/2/4 Karlsplatz). Listings are comprehensively covered by the German-language *Falter* (Fridays, ÖS28), rather less well by its cheaper competitor *City* (ÖS10).

The main **football store** in town is *Fan-Shop Strobl*, Strozzigasse 18–22 (open Mon–Fri 9am–6.30pm, Sat 9am–1pm, U2 Lerchenfelderstrasse), with shirts and souvenirs from all the main clubs.

home district of Favoriten. The goalkeeping of Franz Wohlfahrt helped FK Austria to three more straight titles from 1991, but regular early elimination from Europe, the rise of Graz and Salzburg and revival of Rapid conspired to leave the Violets with little but a small, dedicated core of fans and a host of memories.

Former national-team coach Herbert Prohaska could manage only fourth place, 23 points behind champions Tirol Innsbruck, in a disappointing 1999/2000 season and was replaced by Heinz Hochhauser. The close-season signing of wideman international Martin Hiden from Leeds United was at least a sign of the ambition that will be needed to restore the club's status.

Here we go!

Take U1 to its southern terminus at Reumannplatz, then tram #67 for three stops to the **Altes Landgut** roundabout. From there, you need to be on the other side of the A23 high-

way – over the pedestrian crossing, past the huge *Ludwig* store.

Just the ticket

There are **ticket offices** above the motorway embankment, behind the *Westtribüne*, and round the other side behind the *Osttribüne*. The cheapest tickets (ÖS150) are for home fans in the covered *West-* and away fans in the open *Osttribüne*. The main *Nordtribüne* is divided into two price ranges, ÖS180 for sectors A and D, ÖS240 for sectors B and C right over the halfway line. The *Südtribüne* (sectors F and G) was reconstructed in 1999, and now boasts a roof.

Swift half

There are plenty of bars along Favoritenstrasse towards the stadium. Try the *Halper*, a beautiful old bar with pub team pictures at #214, or the *Gasthaus zum Kärntnerwirt* opposite at #215. At the Franz Horr itself, the place to be is behind the *Nordtribüne* with its *Sport Buffet*, pennants and pine furnishings inside, tables outside. Right under the stand is the outdoor **Kantine Monika Brosch**, with rows of fans tucking into beer and sausages. Other stands have smaller buffets.

Club merchandise

At the ground, the **Fan Container** is open on matchdays, inside the sector H entrance on the corner of the *West*- and *Südtribune*. In town, FK Austria have their own shop, **FANtastic** (open Mon–Fri 10am–6pm, Sat 9.30am–12.30pm), in a shopping alley at Landstrasser Hauptstrasse 71, bus #74A from U3/4 Wien-Mitte.

Ultra culture

Unless it's derby day, the **Weissviolette Brigaden, Fedayn** and **Bulldogs** will be the ones holding up a few coloured placards in the *Westtribüne*. Fanzine *Veilchen Post* (ÖS15) is available here on matchdays or at the *Folkladen* store in town. **Fanclub 80** are an older fans' group who arrange away trips and social events.

In print

Both the **Austria** matchday programme and the official fanzine **Austria Aktuell** are handed out free with your match ticket.

In the net

The club's **official website** has an extensive English-language area at: www.austria-wien.co.at/fak/.

 ## SK Rapid

Gerhard Hanappi Stadion, Keisslergasse 6
Capacity 19,600 (all-seated)
Colours Green-and-white shirts, white shorts
League champions 1912, 1913, 1916, 1917, 1919, 1920, 1921, 1923, 1929, 1930, 1935, 1938, 1940, 1941, 1946, 1948, 1951, 1952, 1954, 1956, 1957, 1960, 1964, 1967, 1968, 1982, 1983, 1987, 1988, 1996
Cup winners 1919, 1920, 1927, 1946, 1961, 1968, 1969, 1972, 1976, 1983, 1984, 1985, 1987, 1995

If there is a team in Austria that has the potential to join Europe's elite, then it's Rapid. They have a big enough fan base and,

having recovered from near-bankruptcy in the mid-Nineties, they have a modern business structure. Yet they still suffer from a lack of capital which would enable them to hold on to their better players.

The club was founded as 1. Wiener Arbeiter-Fussballklub in 1898 by workers from a hat factory, who changed the name to Rapid under English influence a year later. The club, however, has never lost its working-class roots.

The most successful Austrian team prior to the Twenties, Rapid kept ahead of their Viennese rivals until the introduction of professionalism and the rise of Admira and First Vienna in the Thirties. Matches against FK Austria created the most interest, however, and the rivalry stills flourishes today. At the time all the main Viennese clubs practised the Danubian game, but coach Karl Rappan gave Rapid defensive steel to combat the finer play of their rivals. The arrival of prolific goalscorer Franz Binder should have reasserted Rapid's domination and added to their Mitropa Cup win of 1930, but the Nazi occupation of Austria intervened.

During the war Rapid clocked up German trophies and afterwards provided the impetus for Austria's swift postwar revival. Midfielders Ernst Happel and Gerhard Hanappi would set up wave after wave of attacks, their uncompromising style taking the Austrian league by storm and allowing Rapid to beat both AC Milan and Real Madrid in the home legs of European ties.

With the onset of the Sixties, Rapid's decline mirrored that of the Austrian game in general. But in the early Seventies Rapid commissioned Hanappi, who had become an architect after hanging up his boots, to design a new stadium near their beloved but outdated Pfarrwiese.

Opened in 1977, the Weststadion was to be the perfect stage for the emerging power of striker Hans Krankl, who would lead Rapid back to the top, with championships in 1982 and 1983 and a first European final – in the Cup-Winners' Cup against Everton – in 1985. Hanappi died in

1981 and the arena he designed was renamed after him.

Rapid were floated on the Vienna stock exchange in 1991, but lack of investment by a string of institutional shareholders ended in near-bankruptcy in 1994. A consortium of new sponsors was quickly found, and after an Austrian Cup win in 1995, coach Ernst Dokupil was able to make a string of new signings including midfielder Peter Stöger and Bulgarian defender Trifon Ivanov. The new-look squad reached the final of the Cup-Winners' Cup after stirring wins over Dynamo Moscow and Feyenoord, their surprising European adventure coinciding with a first Austrian title for eight years, sealed with a 2–0 win over Sturm Graz in front of more than 48,000 at the Prater.

Rapid lost their European final 1–0 to Paris St-Germain and performed modestly in the 1996 Champions' League. The TV revenue and an excited new generation of fans should have provided a solid base from which to build, but Rapid sold too many players – Stöger, 'keeper Michael Konsel and striker Carsten Jancker among them – and have not managed a domestic title since the heady days of 1996.

Despite ex-Yugoslav international Dejan Savićević providing 11 goals in 22 games, Rapid were never in serious contention in 1999/2000, finishing a distant third behind FC Tirol and Sturm Graz, and there is little sign of the club making the investments needed to fulfil its potential.

Here we go!

The stadium is right by the U4 western terminus at **Hütteldorf**, where S-Bahn lines S3, S45 and S50 also stop.

Just the ticket

The main **ticket office** (for advance bookings) is on the corner of the *Süd-* and *Westtribüne*; you can buy tickets for the *Ost-* and *Nordtribüne* on the day at smaller windows at their respective sections. The *Westtribüne* is for the younger Rapid element, the *Osttribüne* for visitors (both ÖS150). With the bar nearby, a spot in the *Nordtribüne*

(ÖS200) is the best bet for visiting neutrals, who will more than likely be invited over to a Rapid bar in town after the game.

Swift half

Of the many Rapid bars in town, the **Café Bahnhof** at Felberstrasse 8 by the Westbahnhof is a good start before heading for Hütteldorf. Outside the ground, the most popular bars are behind the *Westtribüne* on Bahnhofstrasse – particularly **Zum Schwarzen Peter** at #3 – and behind the *Osttribüne* on Deutschordenstrasse, where you'll find the **Café Corner** by Keisslergasse. Inside the ground there are **Sport Buffet** stands dotted around the the *Nord-* and *Südtribüne*, with discounts for bringing back your hard plastic glass. Alcohol is not sold at potentially fiery matches. The **Wettpunkt Café** in Hütteldorf station is the perfect spot for that post-match pint.

Club merchandise

The green **Fan Container** (open Tue, Thur, Fri 2–6pm & two hours before kick-off, cash only) is by the main ticket office on the corner of the *Süd-* and *Westtribüne*.

Ultra culture

Rapid is the only Austrian club with a nationwide fan base. **Ultras Rapid** were the first Austrian fans to copy the Italian style in the early Nineties. More traditional groups like the **Green Bulls** have since left the *Westtribüne* to the younger element, and now the *Nordtribüne* is the place for men who have put years into the cause of beer and Rapid Vienna, the stand creaking under the weight of green-hooped bellies of the **Alte Garde**, **Stammtisch Grünweiss** and the like.

In print

A free programme, **Rapid heute**, is handed out with your ticket. The full-colour **Rapid Magazin** (ÖS25, monthly) is also available at the ground and at most newsstands in the city.

In the net

Rapid's **official website** is simple, effective and thorough, but lacks an English-language section at: www.skrapid.at. For an unofficial perspective with an English option, try: www.wu-wien.ac.at/usr/h93/h9350244/eng/rapid.html.

Groundhopping

Vienna's ambivalent attitude to football – adulatory one moment, apathetic the next – is summed up by the fate of the city's minor clubs. Many either folded or were absorbed by bigger teams during the Sixties and Seventies. Yet those that remain continue to cling stubbornly, perhaps foolishly, to their dream of one day rejoining the country's footballing elite.

🟢 VfB Admira/Wacker Mödling

Bundesstadion Südstadt, Johann-Steinböck-Strasse 1, Maria Enzersdorf
Capacity 12,000
Colours Red-and-black striped shirts
League champions 1927, 1928, 1932, 1934, 1936, 1937, 1939, 1947, 1966
Cup winners 1928, 1932, 1934, 1964, 1966

One of the great Viennese teams of the Thirties, when they won seven titles under Hugo Meisl's guidance (only Rapid and FK Austria have won more), Admira committed a fatal error when, after merging with Wacker Wien in 1971, they left the downtown area of Floridsdorf which had provided much of their support.

Admira/Wacker have endured so many mergers since, it seems almost too risky to call them by their latest title. After stints at various suburban and provincial venues, the club has now settled in Maria Enzersdorf on the southern fringes of Vienna. Captured forever on celluloid in Wim Wenders' cult classic film, *The Goalkeeper's Fear of the Penalty*, the Südstadt stadium today has all the atmosphere of its local rival *Shopping City Süd*.

If you plump for football over shopping, the Badner-Bahn, from the opera house at Karlplatz, runs to Maria Enzersdorf every 15mins. Allow half-an-hour from town, and anyone with a city pass will have to pay an extra ÖS19 to go beyond the central zone.

The away fans' entrance is nearest the station, on the corner of the *Süd-* and *Ost-*

tribüne, home fans preferring the *Nord-* (a grassy knoll behind the goal) and the other half of the *Ost*. Behind this latter corner you'll find a **small bar**, under the club badge in the main building. The main covered *Westtribüne* is the opposite side from the station, and houses another bar and the main **ticket outlets**.

All in all, it's an unlikely setting for top-flight football – Admira/Wacker Mödling gained promotion back up to the *Bundesliga* in 2000.

🟢 First Vienna

Hohe Warte, Klabundgasse
Capacity 12,000
Colours Yellow shirts, blue shorts
League champions 1931, 1933, 1942, 1943, 1944, 1955
Cup winners 1929, 1930, 1937, 1943

Hard to believe now, but before the Prater was built, First Vienna's Hohe Warte was Austria's national stadium. As their name suggests, First Vienna were the city's first football-only club, formed by English gardeners on Baron Rothschild's estate. Adopting the Baron's horse-racing colours of blue and yellow, they took part in the first official match ever to be played in Austria, against Cricketer in 1894.

Built against a hillside adjacent to the Rothschild estate, the Hohe Warte hosted all Austria's earliest internationals until a mudslide during a match against Italy in 1923. After the gardeners had helped repair the damage, First Vienna hit peak form in the early Thirties, winning the league twice, the Austrian cup three times and the Mitropa Cup in 1931. By then the Prater had been built, and First Vienna eventually found their natural place floating between the first and second divisions. In 1997, as a second-division side, they beat both FK Austria and Salzburg on their way to a cup final defeat by Sturm Graz.

For an afternoon of gentle football in one of Europe's greenest football grounds,

The Prater

Ernst Happel-Stadion, Meiereistrasse 7
Capacity 49,000

Austria's national stadium is also a UEFA favourite, regularly hosting European finals. Commonly called the Prater after its setting in the city's main Prater park by the Danube, it was commissioned in 1928 to coincide with the tenth anniversary of the Austrian republic. Then named the Wiener Stadion, it was completed in 1931, just in time to see the golden years of the *Wunderteam* before

An atmospheric bowl – Vienna's brightest

Hitler's occupation and the onset of World War II. The bomb damage was repaired by 1945, and the post-war Prater enjoyed full houses and top-class, floodlit international football.

Despite the decline in the Austrian game, the Prater has continued to be improved. Its vast roof was built in 1986, and during the Nineties it hosted matches in Salzburg's and Rapid's European runs – neither club could house such huge crowds at their own grounds. **Rapid**, **FK Austria** and **Salzburg** continue to use the stadium for big domestic and European fixtures.

The Prater has been officially renamed the **Ernst Happel-Stadion**, after the great Austrian international player and coach who died in 1992, after toughing it out on the bench for two World Cup qualifiers while fighting cancer.

Bright, lively, easily segregated and beautifully positioned, the Prater is one of the few modern European super-bowls capable of generating an atmosphere redolent of the past while remaining thoroughly up-to-date. To reach it, take U1 to Praterstern or S3/S7 to Wien-Nord, then a 15min walk down Hauptallee past the Big Wheel, or tram #21 for eight stops to Olympiaplatz.

After a quick one at *Sigi's Sportbeisl*, Nordbahnstrasse 56, across the tramlines from the U/S-Bahn station, many fans take in the pre-match atmosphere in the terrace bars around the Prater amusement park, especially the *Schweizerhaus*, Strasse des Ersten Mai 116, a large beer garden serving vast slabs of roast pork and mugs of Budweiser. The *All Sports* bar nearby shows English Premiership action on Sat, Sun and Mon evenings. In the stadium, you'll find the *Stadionblick* between sectors C and D, and *Zum 11er* buffets dotted all around.

Ticket offices are positioned at regular intervals around the stadium. A higher or lower level (*Oberer/Unterer Rang*) will be designated on your ticket, along with the *Sektor*. The most expensive sectors are red B and green E, over each touchline. Visiting international fans are generally allocated places in sectors A or E.

Entrance to the **football museum** by sector B (open Tue–Fri 9am–12.15pm, 1–4.30pm, Sat–Sun 2–6.30pm) is ÖS25. There are three sections of souvenirs, many from the *Wunderteam* years.

take U4 or S45 to **Heiligenstadt**, then walk straight across 12 Februar Platz, left down Heiligenstadter Strasse, and turn second right up Klabundgasse. Hohe Warte is 100m to the right up the sharp incline. The kiosk by the main entrance sells tick-

ets (ÖS150) plus the free programme *Old Firm Review*. The fan shop, a wooden chalet next-door, sells souvenirs and copies of the fanzine *Division B*. After the climb you'll need a drink – the **buffet** under the main stand opens an hour before kick-off and offers Goldfassl beer and hot dogs – try to get into the small bar section through the double doors under the euphemistically named 'VIP' area.

After your drink, chances are you'll be watching second-flight football – but the atmosphere is worth the effort.

● Wiener Sport-Club

Sport-Club Platz, Hernalser Hauptstrasse 214
Capacity 9,000
Colours Black-and-white shirts, white shorts
League champions 1922, 1958, 1959
Cup winners 1923

Another Viennese club fallen on hard times, WSC are floundering in the *Wiener Stadtliga*, despite a neat, compact stadium in the Hernals district within easy reach of the town centre. Although not a patch on the late Fifties team starring Erich Hof that won back-to-back titles and beat Juventus 7–0 in the 1958/59 European Cup, they were holding their own in the first division until a financial scandal broke in 1994. Club president Herbert Rosenauer was arrested on charges of fraud, and the players went without pay for months.

Now it's Sunday morning football for the boys in white and black, against the local police, post office and bakery elevens. If you can get up early enough after a Saturday night in Vienna, take S45 over to **Hernals,** then a 5min walk up Hernalshauptstrasse away from town. Although the *Café Weinhold*, Hernalshauptstrasse 210, and the *Schweiger* (open from 4pm) nearer the ground on the corner of Kainzgasse are pleasant enough, *Anna Maria's Beisl*, behind the east stand at Frauenfelderstrasse 12, is the real WSC experience, with a front garden for cheap eats and an interior out of *Steptoe & Son*. At the ground, the supporters' bar, *Der Flag*, is by the main ticket windows (flat-rate ÖS60) at the cemetery end – the *Friedhofstribüne* – where souvenirs and the fanzine *Fetz 'N' Laberl* are also on sale.

Eat, drink, sleep…

Bars and clubs

By day the standard Viennese watering hole is the **Beisl**, a neighbourhood pub with a modest menu, serving draught (*vom Fass*) beer in half-litre (*Krügel*) or third-litre (*Seidel*) glasses at about ÖS35 and ÖS25 respectively. Wine is sold by the *Viertel*, a quarter-litre, for about ÖS25 in a **Heuriger**, or wine tavern; these are found just outside town – the Grinzing area is popular with tourists, Stammersdorf with the Viennese.

Nightlife in Vienna has picked up considerably. The *Bermuda Dreieck* area (U1/4 Schwedenplatz) has a more upmarket clientele these days, the younger action having moved to stretches around Salzgries and Burggasse. In summer there are regular parties on the Danube Island.

Café Jetzt, Parhamerplatz 16. Intimate underground bar playing trance or drum-'n'-bass, with a pool room, pinball area and tasty meals served up on breadboards. Tram #9 from U3 Schweglerstrasse or tram #44 from U2 Schottentor.

Chelsea, Leichenfeldergürtel 29–32 – look out for the Guinness sign in the U6 Thaliastrasse metro viaduct, 200m back towards the Josefstädterstrasse stop. Anglophile bar/club with new wave bands in the cellar, a crowded bar area full of spikyheads, crisps, Kilkenny and *Sky Sports* in the entrance bar. Open daily 4pm–4am, occasional cover charge.

Flex, Donaulände/Augartenbrücke. Down the steps from U2/4 Schottenring on the embankment is a dance club adjacent to a café playing underground sounds. If it gets too steamy, chill out by the river as everyone else does.

Krebitz, Salzgries 9. Low-key vibe and decor, with fine sounds. Also check out the **Benjamin** at #11 – table football and candlelit groping.

The Shebeen, Lerchenfelderstrasse 47. Busiest of Vienna's expat pubs, busy for international football and rugby games, offers brunches, lunches and happy hours. Short walk or #46 tram between U6 Thaliastrasse and U2 Lerchenfelderstrasse.

Restaurants

Austrian cuisine, much of it imported from the former Habsburg states of Bohemia and Hungary, is notoriously heavy. The classic main dishes are *Wiener Schnitzel*, cutlet in breadcrumbs, and *Tafelspitz*, boiled beef, usually preceded by a soup and rounded off with a gooey dessert.

Eating out can be expensive, but most **Beisln** will offer a *Tagesmenu*, a two-course lunchtime deal, for under ÖS100. You'll find a **Würstelstand** serving all kinds of sausages on almost every corner.

Greichenbeisl, Fleischmarkt 11. Famous inn behind the Bermuda Triangle where Schubert and Beethoven wined and dined, so a tourist favourite. Garden tables. Expect to pay around ÖS300 all-in. Most credit cards.

Ilija, Piaristengasse 36. Best – and probably cheapest – of the city's many Croatian restaurants, with top-notch seafood served Mon–Sat 11am–3pm, 6pm–1am, most credit cards. U2 Lerchenfelderstrasse.

Krah Krah, Rabensteig 8. The most popular bar in the Bermuda Triangle now does more business as a restaurant – a sign of the times. Main courses ÖS80–150 and a large range of beers.

Radetzky, Radetzkyplatz 1. Big old pub with a terrace overlooking a neighbourhood square, serving lunchtime specials at ÖS58 and ÖS77, and main courses (ÖS80–100) and beers (ÖS30) until 11pm. Just over the canal from Praterstern, short walk from U3/4 Landstrasse.

Salz und Pfeffer, Joanelligasse 8. Cheap diner for nighthawks, offering staple dishes daily 6pm–8am. U4 Kettenbrückengasse.

Tunnel, Florianigasse 39. Large club and café in the university area by U2 Rathausplatz, with breakfasts (daily 9–11am) at ÖS29, set lunches

at ÖS45, and reasonably priced main courses, plus a cellar for discos and concerts.

Accommodation

Vienna is an expensive place to stay, although the worst time for finding a room in the city is the non-football period of June–September. The **tourist office** at Kärntnerstrasse 38 (☎01/513 8892) charges ÖS40 commission for booking a room, as do branches at the airport arrivals hall and at the West- and Südbahnhof.

Myrthengasse, Myrthengasse 7 (☎01/523 6316, fax 01/523 5849) and Neustiftsgasse 85 (☎01/523 7462). Neighbouring hostels, under the same ownership, two #48A bus stops from U2/3 Volkstheater. Reception at Myrthengasse. ÖS165–210 a bed, ÖS40 non-member surcharge, laundry facilities. Advance booking – by fax – essential.

Praterstern, Mayergasse 6 (☎01/214 0123, fax 01/214 7880). One-star hotel in the Prater park with satellite TV and a back garden. ÖS500 a single room with shower, ÖS300 without, doubles ÖS600–700, with breakfast. U1 Praterstern.

Pension Dr Geissler, Postgasse 14 (☎01/533 2803, fax 01/533 2635). Perfectly located for the nightlife of the Bermuda Triangle, a clean pension occupying several floors, all rooms with satellite TV. Singles ÖS450–950, doubles ÖS600–1220. Takes most credit cards. U1/4 Schwedenplatz.

Pension Wild, Lange Gasse 10 (☎01/406 5174, fax 01/402 2168). Near the Ring, behind the university, a pleasant pension with satellite TV and kitchen facilities. Single rooms ÖS450–590, doubles ÖS700–900. U2 Lerchenfelderstrasse.

Hollywood stars, Croatian pin-ups – the glory of Graz

Although football arrived there at the same time as Vienna, **Graz** is an unlikely new power base for the Austrian game. Its two clubs, **Sturm** and **Grazer AK**, dominated the regional Styrian league in the first half of the 20th century, but did nothing for 40 years in the postwar *Bundesliga*. Yet in both 1998 and 1999 they finished first and third in the table respectively, launching their assault on

Euro reality – defeat by United, 1999

Austria's traditional clubs from a new stadium as impressive as any in the country.

In the mid-Nineties Graz's most famous son, **Arnold Schwarzenegger**, who left as a bodybuilding teenager and came back as a Hollywood star, helped finance the building of a new municipal ground on the site of GAK's old Liebenau. Within two years the 'Arnold Schwarzenegger-Stadion' was hosting Internazionale and Real Madrid in Sturm's Champions' League campaign.

Sturm's success story began with the club still at its crumbling Sturm-Platz stadium, when coach **Ivica Osim** persuaded president Hannes Kartnig to ditch Italy's 1990 World Cup star Giuseppe Giannini in favour of Ivica Vastić, a young Croatian-born forward with fresher talents and at least equal potential as a pin-up hero. Together with Hannes Reinmayr and Mario Haas, Vastić formed a 'Magic Triangle' which brought Sturm their first national honour in the ÖFB Cup of 1997, the title 12 months later and another in 1999 – the last despite the revival of Rapid.

While Kartnig arranged for party hats and whistles to be given out before big games to make the Schwarzenegger's 15,000 capacity seem more like twice that, his secretary Heinz Schilcher persuaded Osim to sign a new contract to 2003, putting him out of the running for national-team jobs in Austria and his native Bosnia. A penalty shoot-out win over **LASK Linz** in the 1999 ÖFB Cup final then gave Sturm a league and cup double for the first time.

As Sturm went from strength to strength, the more traditionally minded GAK also flourished under coach **Klaus Augenthaler**, giving themselves a second bite at the UEFA Cup cherry in 1999/2000, and notching a couple of derby wins over Sturm in the process. Sturm lost their title to another provincial club playing at a new stadium, FC Tirol, in 2000, but GAK beat SV Salzburg on penalties to win the ÖFB Cup for only the second time in their history, taking both teams back into Europe for 2000/01.

The Schwarzenegger, on the southern outskirts of Liebenau, is a 10min walk from Ostbahnhof (regular service from Hauptbahnhof). At the tram terminus by the ground, both Sturm and GAK have *Treffbars* and shops (where you can buy advance match tickets), but they all feel like fitted kitchens. Walk back down the main Conrad von Hötzendorf Strasse, towards Ostbahnhof, where at #161 the *White Star Café* is home to the local Eighties pop band of the same name – more flares and medallions than Wigan Casino.

Belgium

KBVB/URBSFA, Av Houba de Strooper 145, B1020, Brussels
☎02/477 1211   Fax 02/478 2391   E-mail footinfo@footbel.com

League champions Anderlecht   **Cup winners** Racing Genk   **League Cup winners** Anderlecht   **Promoted** Royal Antwerp, La Louvière   **Relegated** Lommel, Verbroedering Geel

European participants 2000/01 Anderlecht (UCL qualifiers); Club Bruges, Ghent, Lierse, Racing Genk (UEFA Cup); Standard Liège, Westerlo (Intertoto Cup)

Euro 2000 offered Belgian football the chance of a much-needed boost. Instead, it merely confirmed what the country's frustrated football loyalists already feared. It was not just the disappointing display from the 'Red Devils', who failed to make it past the group stage, that left many wondering it had been worth all the fuss – the lack of enthusiasm from the general public left committed fans contemplating if the home of the European Union will ever return from the periphery of European football.

Next door in Holland, it seemed the whole country had turned orange for a month, with every hosting venue dressed up for the occasion. But those who visited Belgium were often left wondering if the locals knew that the finest footballers in Europe had come to town to on the first big soccer show of the millennium.

The decline of the Belgian national team and the country's major clubs has been ongoing for the past two decades, during which time the game's public image has taken a bashing from match-fixing scandals, the Heysel tragedy and the financial problems that have beset many clubs. Belgium has the most liberal regulations on foreign players of all Europe – but most of the imports are of the cheap East European and African variety, which hardly helps boost the fading sense of identity many have with their clubs. The rivalry between the French and Flemish speaking populations once gave the the league an added edge, but the clubs from French-speaking Wallonia have declined in influence, further weakening the nationwide appeal of the game.

Belgian football has few heroes. Two pillars of local football, coach Raymond Goethals and former national captain Eric Gerets, were implicated in the bribery scandal that swept Standard Liège after their 1982 championship. Anderlecht's 3–0 UEFA Cup win over Nottingham Forest in April 1984 was aided by compliant refereeing – although it wasn't until 1997 that club president Constant Vanden Stock revealed he'd been paying off blackmailers who held de facto proof of the Brussels team's attempt to rig the match. Meanwhile, mystery continues to surround Club Bruges' 1–0 defeat by Marseille in the 1993 Champions' League.

Moreover, the two words most associated with Belgian football in the modern era, Bosman and Heysel, are not pleasant ones for local fans to hear. Administrative negligence significantly contributed to the Heysel stadium disaster of 1985 and cast serious doubt on the country's ability to host major events – something that was tested to the full by Euro 2000. And Jean-Marc Bosman's contractual dispute with RC Liégeois ended in victory for the player at the European Court of Justice in 1995, opening the floodgates of international player trade and, domestically, signalling the decline of many modest semi-pro clubs.

Football first developed in Belgium in the 1860s. English schools in Brussels and

Devil may care – a *Diables Rouges* fan mourns Belgium's early exit from Euro 2000

expatriate workers in Antwerp and Liège introduced both football and rugby to the country, and a handful of clubs were established by the early 1890s. Racing Club de Bruxelles and FC Liégeois dominated the early years of the national championship, inaugurated in 1896, before the rise of another Brussels side, Union Saint-Gilloise. World War I saw Union's power diminish and their mantle taken by Beerschot, the Antwerp club led by the brilliant striker Raymond Braine.

Off the pitch, the Belgians were prime movers behind the setting up of FIFA, a fact which compelled them to take part in the first World Cup in Uruguay in 1930. Up until then, the only experience gained by the 'Red Devils' (*Rode Duivels/Diables Rouges*) had been in friendlies against France and the old enemy, Holland, although they did win a soccer gold medal at the Antwerp Olympics of 1920 – after their Czech opponents walked off the field in the final. On the ten-day boat journey to Montevideo, Belgium's star forward, Bernard Voorhoof, drank so much beer he put on eight kilos in weight. The Devils lost both their games

and failed to score, but Belgium was represented in the final by ref Jean Langenus – cap, plus fours and all. Argentina's defeat led to the Belgians' hotel being attacked by travelling supporters after the game.

Domestically, the post-World War II era belonged to Anderlecht. English coach Bill Gormlie took control of the club and the national side, and Jef Mermans starred upfront for him in both teams. Under another British coach, David Livingstone, Belgium put up a creditable performance at the 1954 World Cup, drawing 4–4 with England. Meanwhile, the domestic game improved with the introduction of semi-professionalism. With Paul van Himst and Jef Jurion in attack, Anderlecht won five titles in a row in the Sixties, and knocked Real Madrid out of the European Cup in 1962. But it wasn't until the Seventies that either the club or Belgium's national side made a sustained impact abroad. Anderlecht won the Cup-Winners' Cup in 1976, the year Guy Thys took charge of the national side. Four years later, his team were the surprise package of the 1980 European Championship in Italy. In the final, a late Horst

Basics

If Belgian football is a game of two halves, Belgian society is a culture of **two tongues**. **French** is the language of Brussels and Wallonia, **Flemish** (Dutch, basically) that of Flanders. Speaking French to a Bruges barman is like adopting a plummy, shire counties accent to a Glaswegian. In Flanders, if in doubt – speak English.

EU nationals and those of the US, Canada, Australia and New Zealand require only a **passport** to enter the country.

The currency is the **Belgian franc** (BF), divided into 100 centimes. There are about 60BF to £1. There are coins for 50 centimes, 1, 5, 20 and 50BF. Notes come in denominations of 100, 200, 500, 1,000, 2,000, 5,000 and 10,000BF. Keep a supply of 20BF coins ready for using the toilet in bars and restaurants. You may be given Luxembourg francs in your change – they are legal but unpopular tender here. Banks are the best places to **change money**, open Mon–Fri 9am–noon & 2–4pm. They charge a 450BF fee for cashing Eurocheques. Note that **credit-card payment** is not as commonplace as elsewhere in Western Europe.

From outside the country, the **telephone code** for Belgium is 32 – for Brussels add a 2 and for Bruges 50. Belgian coin phones take 5, 20 or 50BF pieces, but you can only direct-dial internationally from phones marked with European flags – the access code is 00. Standard *Belgacom* **phonecards** are available from post offices and newsstands (200BF for 20 units, 1,000BF for 105). Cheap international rates are in operation 8pm–8am and all day Sundays and holidays.

Train travel in Belgium is quick, reliable and cheap at 300BF for a 100km journey. You'll get 40 percent discount off return tickets from Friday evening to Sunday evening. There are two trains an hour between Brussels and Bruges, journey time one hour. **Buses** are generally used for short distances in and around towns – bus stations are almost always next-door to the train variety. **Brussels Taxistop** (☎02/223 2231, fax 02/223 2232, open Mon–Fri 10.30am–6pm) is a shared lift service for Belgium and Europe, charging 200BF plus 1.30BF per km.

Hotel accommodation in Belgium is expensive – minimum 1,000BF for a double room. The Tourism Centre in Brussels, Rue Marché aux Herbes 63 (open June–Sept daily 9am–7pm, Oct–May Mon–Sat 9am–6pm & Sun 1–5pm, ☎02/504 0390, fax 02/504 0270) can make free hotel reservations anywhere in Belgium except Brussels. **Bed & Brussels**, Rue Victor Greyson 58 (☎02/646 0737, fax 02/644 01 14, open Mon–Fri 9am–6pm) can book you a room anywhere in Belgium. Leave your details on their answerphone.

Food is more important to the Belgians than it is to the Dutch, although the northern half of the country serves plainer food than the French-influenced south. Buckets of **steamed mussels** in various sauces are a staple diet everywhere. *Waterzooi*, a fish or chicken stew, is a Flanders favourite from Ghent. A **main course** will be around 500BF, but look out for *plats du jour* at perhaps 300BF. If you're on a budget, Belgium is the **home of the chip**, and proud of it.

If Belgians took their football as seriously as their **beer**, Brazil wouldn't get a look-in come World Cup time. A glass of standard **lager** – ordered as a *pintje/chope* – will probably be Stella, Maes or Jupiler, and weigh in at 40–50BF. For twice this, you can usually order any of at least 20 **speciality beers**, often many more. These may be fruit-flavoured; Trappist (such as Chimay, which comes in three different strengths); or *lambic* (aired and matured in production). Wheat beer (*witbier/bière blanche*) is a refreshing option, often served with a slice of lemon. Belgian bar **opening hours** are generous, and clubbing is not nearly as popular as pubbing. Bear in mind that Belgians order in rounds. If you want to leave a club and come back later, tip the doorman 50BF.

Hrubesch goal for West Germany beat a Belgian side which contained Jean-Marie Pfaff in goal, Jan Ceulemans upfront and the ageing but wily Wilfried van Moer in midfield. With Enzo Scifo replacing van Moer, much the same side sprang an even greater surprise at the 1986 World Cup, beating the Soviet Union and Spain before falling to a brilliant Maradona goal in the semi-final – the team's eventual fourth place remains Belgium's best achievement at a major tournament.

As the national team thrived, so the domestic game bounded along with it. Steel millionaire Paul Henrard pumped serious money into Standard Liège in the early Eighties. With industrial dust in the air, Michel Preud'homme in goal and Gerets at the back, Standard were a difficult side to beat. They won consecutive league titles and made the Cup-Winners' Cup final of 1982. In the following two years Anderlecht won and lost successive UEFA Cup finals, while Preud'homme left Standard to star in the rise of another provincial club, Mechelen, backed by wealthy chairman John Cordier. They had an easy run to the Cup-Winners' Cup final of 1988, where they beat Ajax 1–0 – an historic triumph which remains Belgium's last victory in a European club competition.

Guy Thys was still in charge of the Red Devils when they fell to a last-minute goal by England's David Platt in the second round of Italia '90. At the same stage four years later, inept refereeing by Switzerland's Kurt Röthlisberger – later sent home by FIFA – refused the Belgians an obvious penalty which, if converted, would have caused Germany problems in extra time. The evergreen Preud'homme had proved himself the goalkeeper of the tournament, not least with his stupendous performance in Belgium's emotional group-stage win over Holland.

The Dutch gained revenge by twice crushing their neighbours in qualifying for France '98, but a play-off win over Ireland allowed the Belgians to again face their great rivals in their opening match in Paris.

In driving Paris rain, Georges Leekens' Red Devils hung on grimly for a goalless draw against ten men, a feat which should have set Belgium up nicely for a second-place group finish. But in the searing heat of Bordeaux a week later, the side threw away a two-goal lead against Mexico and, needing to beat South Korea by three goals in their remaining match, they failed to capitalise on an early advantage given them by Luc Nilis – they eventually played themselves out of the World Cup with another frustrating draw.

In the aftermath, Nilis became one of many key players to drop out of the national reckoning of their own volition – Enzo Scifo, Franky van der Elst and Lorenzo Staelens were among the others. Without the needing to qualify for Euro 2000, a task which probably would have been beyond Leekens and his team, Belgium embarked on a series of friendly matches. Yet even these proved too much for the increasingly isolated Leekens. Belgium went six successive games without a goal and even contrived to draw away to Luxembourg. With just two wins out of eleven friendlies and less than a year to go before the start of Euro 2000, the Belgian FA finally took the plunge and sacked Leekens, replacing him with 60-year-old former Standard coach Robert Waseige.

Waseige managed to persuade the likes of Nilis, Staelens and Gilles de Bilde to return to the fold and injected a sense of purpose – and a much-needed dose of enthusiasm – into the side. The result was a team transformed, and away wins over Italy and Norway led many to tip the Belgians to at least play a substantial role in Euro 2000. At the same time, the country's most popular club side, Anderlecht, had found their feet again and raced to their first title since 1995, adding to the sense of optimism in Brussels.

Euro 2000 began with a promising 2–1 win over Sweden, and even the 2–0 defeat by Italy which followed was played out with a passion and determination that had been absent two years earlier. But, needing just a point from their final group game against Turkey, Belgium pressed the self-destruct button, with calamitous goalkeeping from Filip de Wilde playing a major role in the team's 2–0 defeat. The illusion was shattered, and when as the competition hit its thrilling quarter-final stage, the only Belgians left playing in the country were Standard Liège…in the Intertoto Cup.

Essential vocabulary
Flemish
Hello *Hallo*
Goodbye *Tot ziens*
Yes *Ja*
No *Nee*
Two beers, please *Twee bier alstublieft*
Thank you *Dank u*
Men's *Mannen*
Women's *Vrouwen*
Where is the stadium? *Hoe kom ik in het stadion?*
What is the score? *Wat is de stand?*
Referee *Scheidsrechter*
Offside *Buitenspel*

French
Hello *Bonjour*
Goodbye *Au revoir*
Yes *Oui*
No *Non*
Two beers, please *Deux demis, s'il vous plaît*
Thank you *Merci*
Men's *Hommes*
Women's *Dames*
Where is the stadium? *Où est le stade?*
What is the score? *Où en sommes-nous?*
Referee *L'arbitre*
Offside *Hors jeu*

Match practice
Although Belgian football is often seen as the poor relation of its Dutch neighbour, it is more accessible and its clubs offer more variety. Away from the executive splendour of Anderlecht, the game's homely, hype-free, beer-heavy atmosphere is capable of refreshing the most jaded football palate. Belgium is very much an industrial society – albeit a rusting one – and a town's

football club plays a valuable role within its local community. Players are expected to meet regularly with fans, and local pride, in this country of two often clashing cultures, is paramount.

The season runs from early August to late May, with a couple of rounds clear at the end of December and beginning of January. Most games are played on Saturdays at 8pm, with a couple on Sundays at 3pm. Plum fixtures, shown live on Canal Plus, kick-off on Fridays at 8pm.

A different league
The Belgian first division has 18 teams, the bottom two of which are relegated automatically to the semi-professional second division, which also has 18 sides. Only the top team goes up automatically, since for the second promotion place, Belgium operates a similar complicated play-off system to Holland – the season is divided into three periods, and each period champion goes into end-of-season play-offs with the overall second-placed team. For this section (*Endronde/Tour Finale*), each team plays each other home and away, and the group winner is promoted to the first. Divisions III A and B, also permanent home of the first division's reserve teams, work on a similar basis.

Up for the cup
The domestic cup competition (*De Beker/La Coupe*) once excited little interest, but is currently undergoing something of a revival. For more than 30 years (1928–53 and 1957–63) it wasn't played at all, but the lure of European competition prompted an increase in attention and the last few rounds are now watched keenly.

Every August, some 120 teams enter the first round, including those from divisions III and IV, and the best from the previous season's provincial cup competitions. First-division sides don't enter until the last 32. Early games are decided on 90 minutes, extra time and penalties. The semi-finals in April are played over two legs, the final on a single game, usually on the last Sunday in May at the Stade Roi Baudouin. It is preceded by the women's final, and tickets are available on the day.

In the past four seasons, first-division clubs have also competed for a League Cup competition, with a place in the following year's Intertoto Cup as dubious reward for the winners.

Just the ticket

The Belgian football authorities have tried to counter a growing hooliganism problem by introducing the same *Club Card* system as their Dutch neighbours – but the system singularly failed to work, and in the summer of 2000, it was unclear whether it would be re-introduced for the season to come. In any case, sellouts are rarely a problem and tickets are always affordable, even though prices rise for the most attractive fixtures (*Verhoogd/Matches de Gala*). If it's a rainy afternoon, then a spot under cover (*Overdektenplaatsen/Places Couvertes*) will keep you sheltered.

Most grounds still offer a choice between a seat (*Zitplaatsen/Assises*) and a place on the terraces (*Staanplaatsen/Places Debout*). A standing ticket (in the cheap *Volksplaats/Populaires*) will cost 300–400BF. The cheapest seats will be in the 400–600BF range, while the most expensive (in the *Eretribune/Tribune d'Honneur*) may run up to 1,000BF.

Half-time

Matches are as much about beer and chips as football. Beer sales are essential to the financial survival of many Belgian clubs and the stadium bar will be busy before, during and after the game. Chip vans (*frituur/friterie*) surround every stadium, while grounds in Brussels and Wallonia also sell snails (*escargots*) and black pudding (*boudin noir*). A surprising number of club bars dispense hot Oxo.

Action replay

Belgium has five Flemish and two French channels, while stations from France, Germany, Luxembourg, Holland and England (including the BBC) are all widely available. The live Friday evening game is on Canal Plus at 8pm, with highlights on terrestial Flemish VTM at 11pm.

The Saturday round-ups are *Goal!* on VTM and *Match 1* on French-language RTBF1, both at 10.30pm. Their Sunday equivalents are *Stadion Sport* (VTM) and *Sport* (RTBF1), both at around 7pm. Flemish station VT4 has English Premiership highlights on Monday evenings, while Canal Plus shows the Monday night Premiership live match, with Flemish commentary, along with selected games from the Dutch, Italian and Spanish leagues.

The back page

There are no daily sports papers in Belgium. Specialist soccer coverage comes from the weekly magazine *Sport Voetbal Magazine/Sport Foot* (Thursdays, 75BF), along with its monthly companion *Voetbal België/Football Belgique* (95BF), both published in two separate language editions.

In Brussels, the French-language paper *La Dernière Heure* (daily, 28BF) offers authoritative sports coverage, particularly in its weekend editions. You'll find an excellent international round-up as well as domestic news and scores.

Ultra culture

Belgium suffers little of the organised hooliganism that afflicts neighbouring Holland. While the local police are keen to show off their riot shields and water cannons, it isn't always clear what they are there for. The main exceptions are clashes between Anderlecht and Bruges – the mayor of Bruges banned Anderlecht fans from his city in 1999/2000.

In the net

The Belgian FA runs an exceptionally thorough site – much more than a mere flag-waving exercise – in English as well as Dutch and French at: www.footbel.com. For general links and stats, try the fine unofficial Verbroedering Geel site at: www.ping.be/kfcvgeel.

Brussels

Soccer city – Racing Genk toast winning the 2000 Belgian Cup final, played in Brussels

Brussels' position in European football went down several notches following the Heysel disaster. Not only was the city's reputation in tatters, it lost its popularity as a venue for European finals (it had previously hosted eight, including the European Championship of 1972). Even the home club who played in the stadium complex, Racing Jet Brussels, moved out to Wavre, 30km away, in 1988.

Whether the Stade Roi Baudouin that was built in Heysel's place will stage as many big matches is open to question. The 1996 Cup-Winners' Cup final between Paris St-Germain and Rapid Vienna, with its potentially explosive mix of fans, passed off without a hitch, but the crowd trouble that involved English, German, Turkish and native Belgian supporters during Euro 2000 wasn't quite such an appetising advertisement for Brussels' ability to soak up a big soccer crowd.

In terms of league football Brussels has always been dominated by one club – Union Saint-Gilloise before World War II, Anderlecht after it. The others folded,

migrated or merged to form the city's poor relation, Racing White Daring Molenbeek. A further merger of RWDM and Union was mooted in 1998, not least thanks to Union vice-president Illi Michielsen being a former member of the RWDM board. But after a series of fan protests, nothing became of the proposed 'Iris FC'. RWDM's link with Feyenoord the following year put a stop to such rumours for the foreseeable future, itself being part of a trend that has seen Belgian clubs increasingly striking 'agreements' with wealthier neighbours to guarantee their survival (viz Antwerp's role as a nursery team for Manchester United and, in the same area, a similar deal between the Germinal Beerschot Antwerp super-club and Ajax).

Anderlecht's facilities and resources put those of all other Belgian clubs in the shade, but this difference is all the more marked in Brussels. When the Mauves were formed in 1908, the city had four other clubs in the first division: Daring, Racing Club, Excelsior Léopold and Union Saint-Gilloise. Now only Union survive

BELGIUM

Brussels essentials

Brussels **airport** is at Zaventem, 14km north-east of town, connected by the Airport City Express train (90BF, every 20mins, 5.30am–11.30pm, journey time 20mins) to all three main train stations. Buy your ticket at the office beforehand as the inspector will ask for a hefty surcharge onboard. There is also an hourly **bus service** to the main bus station by the Gare du Nord, operating from the ground-floor level of the airport's new terminal (70BF, journey time 35mins). A taxi will cost around 1,500BF.

Domestic mainline **trains** all call at Gare du Nord, Gare Centrale and Gare du Midi, but the **Eurostar service** from London's Waterloo International (seven departures a day, journey time 2hrs 40mins) serves Gare du Midi only.

City **transport** is made up of three **Métro lines** – 1A, 1B (both red) and 2 (orange) – which all cross at Arts-Loi. There is also a blue **Pre-Métro** line connecting Gare du Nord and Gare du Midi; the Bourse stop is the most central, serving the city's showpiece Grand Place. A tram system also runs underground, and a network of buses overground. The whole service runs 5.30am–midnight. There is no night transport.

A single **ticket** costs 50BF, a five-journey ticket 240BF and a ten-journey one 340BF – all available from bus or tram drivers, Métro kiosks and STIB offices. A 24-hour pass is 130BF. You're trusted to validate tickets as you enter the Métro stop or bus. To enter some trams, caress the felt strip dividing the two door halves.

Taxis are rarely hailed. Pick one up outside the main train stations or order one by phone – call *Taxis Verts* on ☎02/349 4646 or *Taxi Orange* on ☎02/511 2288. Minimum charge is 95BF (plus 75BF night tariff), plus 38BF per km inside the city's 19 districts (*communes*), 76BF outside.

The TIB **tourist office** in the Grand Place (open daily 9am–6pm, ☎02/513 8940, fax 02/514 4538) is cramped and over-crowded.

Some English-language listings are published by *The Bulletin* (weekly, 85BF), including film and TV information. For club and concert details, get a copy of the French-language *Kiosque* (monthly, 60BF) or the slightly inferior *Bruxelscope* (monthly, 28BF).

intact, and only just, eking out a bare existence on the edge of the forested Duden park, the other side of the Charleroi canal from Anderlecht. RWDM are slightly further north, attracting a few thousand thanks mainly to the marvellous fanfare band that plays all through their matches.

RWDM are a mix of four old clubs. Royal Racing Club de Bruxelles (formed 1891) and Royal White Star AC (1909) merged to become Royal Racing-White Bruxelles in 1963, who in turn merged with Royal Daring Club de Molenbeek in 1973. Racing and Daring won 11 titles between them and both teams made brief appearances in Europe. The classic derby before the war was Union against Daring, a fixture later staged at Heysel.

Until their relegation in 1973, Union were *the* Brussels club, with an identifiable

neighbourhood feel and that sardonic *Bruxelleois* humour in the club bar. The few fans who still shuffle up Rue du Stade do so out of a sense of duty to the club's great name.

The bars and restaurants at Anderlecht have the same executive feel as their plush stadium in the Parc Astrid. It's a pleasant place to see a game of football, but the fact is that many who do so come from out of town. Like Juventus, Manchester United and Real Madrid, the *Mauves* have fan clubs all over the country, and one of many accusations hurled at the club from the provinces is that they do not serve the city they reside in. In Flanders, Anderlecht are loathed because they are rich, can buy the best, propose Dutch-Belgian superleagues and, most of all, because they are French, and snobbish with it (though many of the team's fans are Flemish-speakers).

Ironically, the area of Anderlecht itself is rundown and full of poor Belgian families, whereas Saint-Gilles is mainly residential, boasting some of the city's most beautiful *art nouveau* buildings. Molenbeek is a mixture of both.

RWDM's title win in 1975 could not have been sweeter, coming as it did with a 1–0 victory over Anderlecht. The roles and scoreline were reversed for Anderlecht's championship victory in 1991.

In Belgium, a 'Royal' tag is given to a club after 25 years' existence, but sponsorship does more to keep a team afloat financially, as do outgoing transfers. The sale of young prospect Johan Walem to Anderlecht in 1986 was doubly humiliating, in that Anderlecht met some of RWDM's unpaid bills as part of the deal. It is said they also wanted to buy the fanfare band, but were told they weren't for sale at any price. Some things, even in Brussels, money just can't buy.

operation boasting one of the best medium-sized stadia in Europe. That he was being blackmailed by players' agent Jean Elst for much of this time is a matter which came to light too late for Elst's information – concerning Anderlecht's bribing of referees – to come under the jurisdiction of Belgian law.

All of Anderlecht's three European successes came during the late Seventies and early Eighties, the club's golden period. After that, the money needed to convert the Parc Astrid stadium, as it is known, and to keep Elst quiet, meant that there was less to go round on players. The *Mauves* have thus under-achieved in Europe for most of the Nineties.

Founded in 1908, Anderlecht moved to the Parc Astrid ten years later but did not grace it with first-division football until 1935, by which time a modest stadium, Stade Versé, had been built. Vanden Stock himself joined the club as a boy, but injury

The thrilling fields

 Anderlecht

Stade Constant Vanden Stock, Avenue Théo Verbeeck 2
Capacity 28,000
Colours All white with purple trim
League champions 1947, 1949, 1950, 1951, 1954, 1955, 1956, 1959, 1962, 1964, 1965, 1966, 1967, 1968, 1972, 1974, 1981, 1985, 1986, 1987, 1991, 1993, 1994, 1995, 2000
Cup winners 1965, 1972, 1973, 1975, 1976, 1988, 1989, 1994
Cup-Winners' Cup winners 1976, 1978
UEFA Cup winners 1983

Anderlecht is a one-man empire built by booze. In the 15 years that he was club president before handing over the post to his son Roger in 1996, brewery owner Constant Vanden Stock turned Belgium's most successful club into a professional

Jan the man – *les Mauves* greet a Koller goal

cut short his playing career. He became involved in management and would go on to coach the national team for a decade. The 1942 signing of striker Jef Mermans helped Anderlecht win their first title five years later. Two years after that, an English ex-goalkeeper by the name of Bill Gormlie was appointed first-team coach, ushering in a decade of seven titles that established Anderlecht as the country's biggest club. Europe remained out of reach – during the Fifties, the team lost 7–2 on aggregate to Rangers and 10–0 in a single match to Manchester United, underlining the fact that theirs was still very much a semi-pro outfit relying on local talent.

As Mermans and Gormlie bowed out, however, two inside-forwards came through the ranks to push Anderlecht to greater heights: Paul van Himst and Jef Jurion. Van Himst became the greatest Belgian player of all time, and his class and understanding with Jurion sent shockwaves across Europe. In the early Sixties Real Madrid, CDNA Sofia and Bologna were all beaten, while at home Anderlecht won five titles in a row. In 1964, the Belgian national team that beat Holland 1–0 was composed entirely of Anderlecht players.

In 1970 the *Mauves* beat Newcastle and Internazionale on their way to the Fairs' Cup final, where giving away a late consolation goal to Arsenal in the home leg proved costly, as the Gunners matched Anderlecht's three goals in the second game.

Van Himst retired the year before Anderlecht's greatest triumph – their Cup-Winners' Cup victory of 1976. A new hero had replaced him, the Dutch forward Rob Rensenbrink, fast and supremely gifted. Provided for by François van der Elst and Arie Haan in midfield, Rensenbrink was unstoppable in the final against West Ham, scoring two goals in a powerful 4–2 win. Anderlecht made the final of the same trophy the following year, losing to two late Hamburg goals, then got their revenge by beating the Germans in the second round of the same competition the year after that; they went on to reach a third consecutive final, thrashing Austria Vienna 4–0, with Rensenbrink again scoring twice. Liverpool were duly beaten in the European Supercup a few months later.

Vanden Stock's arrival as president at the start of the Eighties signalled a new era for the club. He brought in van Himst as coach and began the development of the Parc Astrid. Anderlecht unluckily went out to a single goal against Aston Villa in a 1982 European Cup semi-final. But there was to be no mistake in the UEFA Cup a year later, when a team boasting Frankie Vercauteren and Erwin Vandenbergh swept past Porto, Valencia and Bohemians Prague before beating Benfica in the final.

By 1984, a precocious Enzo Scifo was on the scene. But a 2–0 semi-final first leg defeat by Nottingham Forest caused panic in the Anderlecht boardroom. With so much money invested in the stadium – the first in continental Europe to have executive boxes – the team simply had to reach the final. The referee for the second leg, Spain's Emilio Guruceta, has since died in a car crash, so we will never know to what extent Vanden Stock exerted a financial influence over proceedings. At any rate, 3–0 to Anderlecht was the final score, after Forest had had a penalty appeal turned down and a goal disallowed. (The English club continued to pursue its claim for damages against Anderlecht during 2000.) In the final, Spurs equalled Anderlecht's 1–1 home scoreline and won the resulting penalty shoot-out – but the Brussels boxes had been filled one more lucrative time.

A European Cup semi-final defeat by Steaua Bucharest in 1986 and a Cup Winners' Cup final loss to Sampdoria in 1990 have been the club's European highlights since – although quite how Anderlecht contrived to let slip a three-goal lead with 20 minutes remaining at Werder Bremen in the 1993 Champions' League, nobody will ever know.

Anderlecht's coach at that time, Johan Boskamp, was still on the bench come the end of the 1996/97 season. In between times his *Mauves* won the title three times,

The King Baudouin

Stade du Roi Baudouin, Avenue du Marathon
Capacity 50,000

Heysel, Heysel. Memories of the **1985 tragedy** have not gone away but, officially at least, the stadium has. Ten years after the event, the Stade du Roi Baudouin ('King Baudouin stadium') was opened with a friendly match between Belgium and Germany. This time police were quick to stamp out loutish behaviour from a group of German fans whose sense of occasion was warped, to put it mildly.

The big tick-off – Euro 2000 comes to Heysel

A decade earlier it had all been very different. The build-up to the Juventus– Liverpool **European Cup final** of 1985 saw Liverpool fans, many drunk, joined in Brussels by neo-Nazi elements with no interest in football whatsoever. Segregation was poor, local policing disorganised. Parts of the stadium were falling to bits. Shortly before kick-off, a group of English fans stampeded through the supposedly neutral block Z, and 39 (mainly Italian) supporters were crushed to death when a wall collapsed. To avert the risk of further deaths, a match was somehow played out, which Juventus won. English clubs were banned from Europe for five years.

For a time Heysel, which had been built in 1930 in the Parc des Expositions in north-west Brussels, was closed. Then, after much haggling over who should foot the bill for refurbishment, the Belgian FA decided to build the Stade Roi Baudouin in its place – though some parts of the original ground remain. The first part of the renovation was completed in 1996, the second in 1998. By the time the opening game of Euro 2000 came around, the stadium was a 50,000-capacity all-seater.

The Roi Baudouin has its own stop at the end of **Métro line 1A**, 20min from Gare du Midi. This leads you out onto Avenue des Athlètes, with the main entrance around the corner on Avenue du Marathon. Here you'll find the main **ticket office** and a spacious new sports bar, **Extra-Time**, the back wall of which is plastered with shots from classic Belgium-Holland clashes. The beer served here before and during the game is alcohol-free – the real stuff comes afterwards.

Facing the ground on the parallel Avenue Houba de Strooper is the friendly **Corner** bar, while at #264, 5mins towards town by the Houba-Brogmann Métro stop, is **La Coupole**, a shabbily appealing Molenbeek bar.

Inside the ground, the four stands are colour-coded: 1 (orange) has the most expensive seats, 2 (green) and 4 (blue) are behind the goals and 3 (yellow) is along Avenue des Athlètes by the Métro stop.

including a classic double in 1993/94 when the side could boast a commanding Philippe Albert at the back, and a strikeforce of Luc Nilis, Marc Degryse and Johnny Bosman that bagged over 50 goals between them. Boskamp quit for Morocco in 1995, only to return the same year after Vanden Stock had experimented disastrously (and uncharacteristically) with three coaches in as many months, before bowing out with a 4–2 extra-time cup final defeat by Germinal Ekeren. New coach René Vandereycken, despite the return of Enzo Scifo, then lost three home games in a row, and his replacement, Arie Haan, could do little better. By now the bribery scandal was raging, and one man stood above it all – Swedish midfielder Pår Zetterberg, Belgian player of the year in 1997. He was not on hand when the *Mauves* hit an all-time low in September 1998, a 6–0 humbling by Westerlo which, along with defeat by Grasshoppers in the UEFA Cup, saw Haan sacked.

His replacement, Jean Dockx, did a credible job in pulling the club back from the abyss to finish third in 1998/99, giving the incoming Aimé Anthuenis from champions Racing Genk the chance to start afresh. Though his side failed to make much impact in Europe, they comfortably won a 25th league title, big Czech striker Jan Koller providing the firepower in attack with 20 goals, Bart Goor supplying him from the flanks, and Zetterberg again influential in midfield.

Alas, the loss of Zetterberg to Olympiakos in the close season was depressingly familiar, and the club was battling to keep hold of Koller after his impressive showings at Euro 2000. In Belgium, it seems, even the wealthiest club can be made to seem like a pauper.

Here we go!

Take Métro line 1B to **Saint Guidon**, then a 5min walk – around the circular Métro station, with the tower of the church of Saint Pierre et Guidon ahead of you, then left into Rue Saint Guidon.

Just the ticket

The **main ticket office** (Mon–Fri 9am–midday & 2–6pm, Sat 9am–midday) is alongside the main entrance on Avenue Théo Verbeeck. The home end is in Tribune #4, access by entrance #4 or #5. Away fans are opposite in Tribune #1, entrance through gate #1 (it's marked *Bezoekers/Visiteurs*).

Neutrals can go along the side of the pitch in Tribune #3 (entrances #5 and #6) or in the flashier and more expensive Tribune #1. For the time being, the cheapest places are standing ones

at either end or in Tribune #1. All stands have either business seats or lodges.

Swift half

Place de Linde, between the Métro station and the stadium, is full of bars, the best being the *Café Half-Time*, with its framed pictures of classic Anderlecht sides and photo record of a visit from Pelé. The *Extra Time* nearby is a little more staid, while *Au Cheval Blanc*, where the square meets Rue Saint Guidon, is full of *Tintin* memorabilia and can serve a decent meal at 300BF.

Past the stadium, *La Coupe* at Avenue Théo Verbeeck 57 is a modern football bar embellished with team photos from the past and a wonderful multi-coloured league ladder behind the bar.

In the stadium, the *Club House* inside the main entrance is large, modern, tiled and again covered in team line-ups.

Club merchandise

The *RSCA Fan-Shop* is inside the main entrance at the ground (open Mon–Fri 10am–6pm, Sat 10am–5pm and on all matchdays) and acts as a showcase for the club's attempts to turn its staid purple badge into a modern, global sportswear brand. Be warned.

Ultra culture

The hardcore element within Anderlecht's travelling support, the *O-Sector Boys*, are notorious for drinking themselves senseless on away trips, the worst recent scenario being the havoc they caused at Bruges in January 1999.

The atmosphere in the Parc Astrid, meanwhile, is intimate without being intimidating – although the visit of Newcastle for a friendly in 1996 provoked the *Purple Vultures* into some seriously pejorative chanting for 90 minutes.

In print

Anderlecht Sports is the club's fortnightly mauve-and-white publication, cost 50BF.

In the net

The **official website** has got over the attack of indigestion it suffered last season and is now a very complete affair at: www.rsca.be. There are three language options (French, Flemish, English), and the news and match-report section is among the most candid you'll find on an official site, reading as it does more like a fanzine commentary. A full online shopping mall is expected to open during the 2000/01 season.

Among the unofficial offerings, there's an exceptionally slick French-language site, complete with a separate section dedicated to the Parc Astrid, at: www.ibelgique.com/RSCA.

And Anderlecht's Dutch-speaking following have a rootsy, regularly maintained site of their own at: users.skynet.be/sky38118.

Groundhopping

Some of the grand old names of Brussels football may have fled town or faded away altogether, but there's still some soccer to be seen out there in suburbia. You may be pleasantly surprised by the warmth of the welcome, but possibly not by the standard of football.

RWD Molenbeek

Stade Edmond Machtens, Rue Charles Malis 61
Capacity 15,000
Colours White shirts with red and black trim, black shorts
League champions 1975

Are-Vay-Day-Emm started at the top and suffered 20 years of slow decline, before an accord signed with the Dutch club Feyenoord in the spring of 1999 signalled a long-awaited upturn in their fortunes. Behind their formation was Jean Baptiste L'Ecluse, a former chairman of Daring, who persuaded Racing White to merge with his club in 1973, thus ensuring immediate European football through Racing White's final league position of third that year. RWDM duly beat Español of Barcelona before bowing out to Portugal's Vitória Setúbal on away goals.

Better was to follow in 1975, when a goal from international Jacques Teugels against Anderlecht won the club its first and only title. Key player Johan Boskamp

became a local hero – until his move to Anderlecht. Though they were unable to keep their title, the team remained in the top six, and in 1977 they were an away goal from a UEFA Cup final against Juventus.

The club has done little since. With veteran sweeper Guy Vandersmissen and coach René Vandereycken the team made a European place in 1996/97, then beat Anderlecht in the league at the start of the following season – only to be docked three points for fielding three substitutes. Thus began the slippery slope to relegation, at the end of a 1997/98 season dominated by rumours of a merger with Union Saint-Gilloise.

RWDM could do no better than finish mid-table in the second flight in 1998/99 and 1999/2000, but no visit to Brussels would be complete without taking in the club's lively brass band, which plays fanfares in tune with the action on the pitch.

To catch them in full swing, take Métro 1A/B to **Beekkant**, then bus #85 or a 10min walk down Rue Jules Vieujant, followed by a left down Rue Osseghem.

The *Bar Sport* at Rue Osseghem 208 and *Bar à L'Ecu* on the other side of the crossroads at #193 are full of football talk and memorabilia. *Le New Stade*, at the other end of the stadium at Rue des Béguines 186, is sadly closed for evening matches but perfect in the afternoon.

At the ground, visiting fans are allocated a whole end, sections D–F and K–N, while the RWDM faithful are behind the opposite goal, and the *pourtour* A/B in Tribune I is the cheapest spot for visiting neutrals.

Union Saint-Gilloise

Stade J Marien, Chaussée de Bruxelles 223
Capacity 12,000
Colours Yellow shirts, blue shorts
League champions 1904, 1905, 1906, 1907, 1909, 1910, 1913, 1923, 1933, 1934, 1935
Cup winners 1913, 1914
A more romantic ground-hop would be hard to imagine. The Stade Joseph Marien,

named after a former club president, is bordered by the forest of Parc Duden on one side and by a wonderful old club bar on the other.

People crowded up the hillside in their thousands to see Union in their golden prewar days, when this was the biggest club in Belgium. The last decent Union side, that of the late Fifties and early Sixties, made occasional forays into the Fairs' Cup, beating Roma and Olympique Marseille.

Union were too proud to agree to any of the mergers that swallowed up the lesser Brussels clubs in the Seventies, but the club celebrated its centenary in 1997 by being relegated to the third division. This was nearly followed by a further drop in 1999, Union being saved on the last day by Tournai surprisingly losing at home to Hamme, at the same time as they themselves were going down 3–2 at home to Denderhoutem. As the Tournai result came over the tannoy, Union fans were dancing around the club bar with the fanfare band in tow.

The ground is a 5min walk along Rue des Glands from the nearest tram stop at **Van Haelen**, on the #52 line from Gare du Midi or the #18 from Horta.

Once at Chaussée de Bruxelles, *La Brasserie des Sports* at Rue des Glands 80 is a classic old bar, with the clicking of backgammon counters behind the hum of football talk. *Union's Tavern* on the corner of Rue du Stade and Chaussée de Bruxelles is another goodie. But the jewel of Saint Gilles is the **stadium clubhouse** itself. The plaque inside, dedicated to Jef Valise ('Geoff Suitcase'), refers to eternal *Unioniste* Jef van Caelen, who used to carry his uncle Jacques' kit bag to home games and who has followed the yellow-and-blues through thick and much thin ever since.

Eat, drink, sleep…

Bars and clubs

Brussels has neither the hip cachet of Amsterdam nor the fashionable trappings of Paris, but in a lot of ways it's **more fun** than either. For a start, there is more variety to both the beer and the bars serving it, many of which **open late**.

Unpretentious bars full of locals abound – even just 5mins' walk from the bright tourist lights of Grand Place, down Rue du Marché du Charbon or Rue du Midi, or west the other side of Boulevard Anspach.

The area of Ixelles, just south of Trone or Porte de Namur Métro stops, offers further varieties of local colour.

The classic *Bruxelleois* beer is **Gueuze**, which packs a hangover like a drop-kick from local lad Jean-Claude van Damme. The local spirit, served in thimble-full glasses, is a juniper gin, *pèkèt,* of which there is a famous *Van Damme* brand.

À la Mort Subite, Rue Montagne aux Herbes Potagères 7. Possibly the most famous bar in Brussels, it offers the eponymous 'Sudden Death' beer, now served in bars all over town and across Belgium. Smoky and atmospheric, the place has hardly changed since the Twenties. Métro to De Brouckère.

Kafka, Rue de la Vierge Noire 6. Surprisingly unpretentious bar offering a choice of 50 beers, 18 different vodkas, or a cup of hot Oxo. Métro to De Brouckère.

L'Archiduc, Rue Antoine Dansaert 6. Done out like a Fred Astaire movie, with live jazz and a great mellow atmosphere. Civilised opening hours of 4pm–4am. Métro to Bourse.

The Fuse, Rue Blaes 208. First and easily the best techno club in town, with top-name DJs spinning. Open Saturdays only, until 7.30am. Métro to Porte de Hal.

MacSweeney's, Rue Jean Stas 24. Possibly the most convivial of the city's dozen ex-pat pubs, not as overpriced as some, with the usual Sky TV Premiership action. Métro Louise.

Toone VII, Impasse Schuddeveld 6. Unusual bar now firmly on the beaten tourist track, but worth a look-in all the same. Attached to the *Toone* puppet theatre, whose models hang from the ceilings. Just off Petite Rue des Bouchers. Métro to Bourse.

Restaurants

The cosmopolitan mix of the city's inhabitants and continuing demands of the international business community mean that Brussels offers a whole world of **different cuisines**. 'Wide range' simply doesn't do it justice. A lot of places are overpriced, living off their clients' expense accounts, but you can find good-value Portuguese, Greek and North African restaurants around the Gare du Midi. The touristy restaurants around the Ilôt Sacré, east of Grand Place, advertised by all sorts of lobsters and shellfish outside, are often a disappointment once you tuck in; a *plat du jour* around Place Sainte Cathérine will be a better bet. Traditionally, Brussels chefs like to cook with Gueuze beer.

The gent from Genk – Aimé Antheunis, saviour of Anderlecht

Aux Armes de Bruxelles, Rue des Bouchers 13. A far better fish restaurant than the many dotted around the same street, divided into a formal restaurant and a bistro. Great buckets of mussels in various sauces. Main seafood courses around 1,250BF. *Plat du jour* at 495BF. Closed Mondays. Most credit cards. Métro to Bourse.

Chez Léon, Rue des Bouchers 18. As touristy as it gets, but deservedly packs them in with cheap portions of mussels and swift service. Menu at 395BF. Most credit cards. Métro to Bourse. Another branch up at the Roi Baudouin.

In t'Spinnekopke, Place au Jardin aux Fleurs 1. Homely period building with several low-ceilinged rooms. Belgian specialities cooked in beer – the owner has published his own book of beer recipes. Main courses around 800–1,000BF. Most credit cards. Métro to Bourse.

Le Falstaff, Rue Henri Maus 19–25. Famous *art nouveau* café-restaurant serving large portions of main courses until 3am Mon–Fri, 5am Sat–Sun. *Plats du jour* at under 500BF. Covered terrace facing La Bourse. Most credit cards. Métro to Bourse.

Mumtaz, Chaussée de Wavre 64. Unpretentious but tasty and reasonably priced Ixelles curry house, open daily until midnight, cheap lunches and main courses around 700BF. Most credit cards. Métro to Porte de Namur.

Accommodation

Brussels hotels tend to cater for the business community and its Monday–Friday schedule, so always check for bargain weekend rates.

If you're arriving at the airport, the **Destination Belgium** information desk (open daily 6.30am–9.30pm, ☎02/720 5161) has a free hotel reservation service – pay a deposit upfront and have the amount deducted from your hotel bill. The **Belgian Tourist Reservation Service** (☎02/513 74 84, fax 02/513 92 77) can also book a room for you. The **Acotra Travel Agency** at Rue de la Madelaine 51 (open Mon–Sat 10am–5pm, ☎02/512 7078) books

youth hostel accommodation. The cheap
hotels around Gare du Midi and Gare du
Nord can be pretty seedy – watch your
step at night.

Centre Vincent van Gogh, Rue Traversière 8
(☎02/217 0158, fax 02/219 7995, e-mail
chab@ping.be). Youth hostel with no curfew and
single rooms available at 685BF. Doubles
540–570BF a head, dorm beds 330–460BF. All
with breakfast included. Obligatory 120BF for
sheets. Free lockers. Internet access facilities.
Most major credit cards. Métro to Botanique.

Fouquets, Rue de la Bourse 6 (☎02/512 0020,
fax 02/51 9357). Perfectly located pension with
singles at 1,700BF, doubles 2,000BF, breakfast
150BF. Most credit cards. Métro to Bourse.

George V, Rue t'Kint 23 (☎02/513 5093, fax
02/513 4493, e-mail george5@skynet.be). Period
neighbourhood hotel with ornate balconies overlooking a whole mess of bars down below. Singles
at 2,000BF, doubles 2,500BF. All rooms with cable
TV. Bar downstairs. Most credit cards. Métro to
Bourse.

Madou, Rue du Congrès 45 (☎02/218 83 75,
fax 02/217 32 74). Popular, homely hotel near
the cathedral, rooms variable in style, all with a
shower and toilet. Advance booking advisable.
Singles at 1,600BF, doubles around 2,000BF. Most
credit cards. Métro to Madou.

Sleep Well, Rue du Daimier 23 (☎02/218 5050,
fax 02/219 1313). Quality youth hostel with a
bar, cable TV, and currency exchange downstairs.
Single rooms around 700BF, double rooms at
600BF per person, quads 510BF. Near Gare du
Nord. Métro to Rogier.

Bruges

An attraction on its own – the Jan Breydel stadium was massively rebuilt for Euro 2000

Belgium's leading tourist city plays host to its second biggest football team, Club Bruges, and their groundshare neighbours Cercle. 'Club', as they are known to all, represent the pride of Flanders, working class and Flemish-speaking, and gain support from all over the region.

Throughout Belgium, Club are very much the neutrals' favourite, famed for their team spirit and honest endeavour. In Bruges itself, support for the two teams is divided 50–50, but any cross-town rivalry pales next to the mutual hatred of Anderlecht – the chance of Flanders getting one over on the fat cats from Brussels is more important than the local derby match. As Club have won two of the last four titles, and Anderlecht haven't had a look-in, all is well in Flanders, despite the relegation of Cercle in 1997. Bruges is a small town – players of both sides mix socially, and the local football community is refreshingly tight-knit and friendly.

Football was first played in Bruges at the English College in the district of Sint-

Andries west of town, where the Jan Breydel stadium – formerly the Olympiastadion – is now sited. Both clubs were founded in the 1890s, Cercle's players being mainly upper-class Dutch and Englishmen, later local, academic Catholics.

In the early days Cercle had the better of things, but it wasn't until the rise of Club in the late Sixties that Bruges as a city put itself on the football map. The groundshare between the two teams began in 1975. Before then, Club had been playing at the atmospheric De Klokke on Torhoutse Steenweg, while Cercle were at the Edgard Desmedt stadium on nearby Magdalenstraat – both just south of Sint-Andries.

With both clubs experiencing serious financial difficulties, the then mayor of Bruges, Van Maele, had a municipal stadium built at the end of Olympialaan – the Olympiastadion.

It was ready just in time to catch Club's purple patch under Austrian coach Ernst Happel, which included two major runs in Europe – both of them, curiously, ended by Liverpool in the final. Cercle, meanwhile, could only watch and slide.

The teams have met in two Belgian cup finals — the first, in 1986, being the only one ever played at the Olympiastadion. Club won that game, and ten years later they repeated the triumph, at Brussels' newly refurbished Stade du Roi Baudouin, and thus achieved the domestic double; their previous title win meant that both clubs had already qualified for Europe before a ball was kicked on final day.

Neither final was a classic, but plenty of league derbies have been. In 1990/91 Club beat Cercle 10–0, with the Australian Frank Farina scoring four. A year later there were another ten goals — though any comfort Cercle drew from the 5–5 scoreline was tempered by the fact that Club's ninth title was already in the bag at the time.

Club's and Cercle's paths have not crossed for two years, but both are now playing in a ground re-converted to a 30,000-capacity all-seater, which will see Euro 2000 action and plenty else, both before and after.

The thrilling fields

Club Bruges

Jan Breydelstadion, see p.36
Colours Blue-and-black striped shirts, black shorts
League champions 1920, 1973, 1976, 1977, 1978, 1980, 1988, 1990, 1992, 1996, 1998
Cup winners 1968, 1970, 1977, 1986, 1991, 1996

Belgium's most successful provincial side, Club Bruges need to repeat the European form of yesteryear if they are to stay up with the big boys on course for the Atlantic superleague. It's now more than 20 years since Club last made a European final, and domestic success — four titles in the Nineties — in a league as weak as Belgium's

is not enough to keep the top names in the medieval beauty of Bruges.

Although one of the earliest Belgian clubs to be founded (in 1891), the *Blauw-Zwart* ('blue-and-blacks') didn't really come into the frame until around 80 years later, when future Anderlecht president Constant Vanden Stock oversaw the rise of Raoul Lambert and the arrival of Rob Rensenbrink from DWS Amsterdam. The team managed cup wins in 1968 and 1970, and regular, if unsuccessful, European action generated a real buzz around De Klokke. After finishing runners-up five years in six, Club eventually won their first modern title in 1973 and hired wily coach Ernst Happel a year later.

During Happel's four-year reign, the *Blauw-Zwart* became Belgium's top club. The team moved to the Olympiastadion and seemed immediately inspired by their new, modern surroundings. Suddenly, Club were beating European teams of the highest pedigree — AC Milan, Juventus, Real and Atlético Madrid, Roma, Hamburg.

Twice they made a European final, twice they were slightly unlucky to be beaten by Liverpool. In the 1976 UEFA Cup, Club got two goals in the first quarter of an hour in the first leg at Anfield, then conceded three in the space of six second-half minutes; a 1–1 draw was not enough at the Olympiastadion. Two years later Club made the European Cup final for the first and only time, and had to play Liverpool on what was virtually their second home ground — Wembley. The Belgians approached the game suffering an injury crisis, and a Kenny Dalglish goal settled it. Future national coach Georges Leekens played at the back for Club in both ties.

At home, the team's three consecutive titles embraced a league and cup double in 1977. By the time Happel left in 1978, Club had firmly taken their place among a Belgian 'big three', alongside Anderlecht and Standard Liège. With big local hero Jan Ceulemans coming through as the best forward talent since Lambert, the side couldn't match the form of Happel's team in Europe

Bruges essentials

Bruges' **bus and train stations** are south of the town centre, a 15min walk straight up Oostmeers. The city's transport comprises a network of **buses**. Much of the town centre is pedestrianised – most buses stop by Biekorf near the central Markt square.

Buses run 6am–11pm. They're 40BF a ride (tickets available onboard), or 270BF for ten rides, 110BF for a day ticket – all available from the *De Lijn* **kiosk** on Stationsplein. There is no night transport. To call for a **taxi**, dial ☎050/333 455 or ☎050/334 444.

The main **tourist office** is by the Markt at Burg 11 (open April–Sept Mon–Fri 9.30am–6.30pm, Sat–Sun 10am–midday & 2–6.30pm; Oct–March Mon–Fri 9.30am–5pm, Sat 9.30am–1.15pm & 2–5.30pm, ☎050/448 686, fax 050/448 600). There's a smaller branch inside the train station. At either office you can pick up a free copy of the comprehensive, Flemish-language listings monthly, *Exit*.

---

but remained consistent at home, at times featuring the odd foreign star such as Frank Farina and France's Jean-Pierre Papin. With Franky van der Elst solid in midfield, Club twice made further European semi-finals, losing to Español in the 1988 UEFA Cup and Werder Bremen in the Cup-Winners' Cup four years later.

In the mid-Nineties, under coach Hugo Broos (another good old boy who was in the side against Liverpool at Wembley) and with Staelens picking up Ceulemans' mantle, Club continued to succeed at home and frustrate in Europe. The ease of their 1996 double win, which featured 20 league goals from Mario Stanić and only 30 conceded by loyal goalkeeper Dany Verlinden, perhaps said more about the problems at Anderlecht than the quality of the rest of the Belgian league.

The departure of Stanić and Australian sweeper Paul Okon for Italy prompted an inconsistent season in 1996/97, the title being ceded to Eric Gerets' Lierse. After moving across to Club, Gerets led a successful campaign to recapture the championship the following year, helped by the African forward duo of Eric Addo and Khalilou Fadiga. The loss of Staelens to Anderlecht proved too much in 1998/99, however, and a 2–0 defeat at Excelsior Mouscron on the penultimate day of the season let in unfancied Genk.

Gerets left town for PSV Eindhoven, and his replacement René Verheyen failed

to inspire the sort of work-rate and team spirit that had served the club so well in recent seasons. His side finished as championship runners-up, but were eight points adrift of Anderlecht.

In July 2000, Norwegian Trond Sollied, the former Rosenborg boss, was poached from nearby Ghent, where he had enjoyed some success with his brand of Scandinavian route-one football.

Swift half

The *Clubhuis* by blocks 10/11 is a spacious Club bar at the stadium – pay your money at the till before handing your receipt over the counter and picking up your beer.

Club merchandise

The *Clubshop* in the brown building at the end of Olympialaan by the stadium not only features all kinds of Club paraphernalia – including own-brand jeans and board games – but Belgian national gear as well.

Ultra culture

Club fans like a beer and a sing-song, and provided nobody mentions the word 'Anderlecht', everyone's happy. They share an affinity with Feyenoord's faithful (as Anderlecht's do with those of Ajax), and drinking sessions when the two sets of fans meet are the stuff of legend.

In print

Blauw-Zwart Magazine (monthly, 60BF) has been Club's official organ for over 50 years. It's available at the club shop and at newsstands around town.

In the net

An **official website** finally opened its doors during the 1999/2000 season at: www.clubbrugge.be. The content is Flemish-language only and still fairly basic, but expansion is promised soon.

In the meantime, Michel Britte's unofficial site continues undaunted at: www.inconnect.com/~mbritte/club/index.htm. There's plenty of news and stats, and everything's in English.

 ## Cercle Bruges

Jan Breydelstadion, see p.36
Colours Green, white and black striped shirts, black shorts
League champions 1911, 1927, 1930
Cup winners 1927, 1985

The *Groen-Wit-Zwart* ('green-white-and-blacks') are Bruges' second side, one which has seen players from all around the globe, but which has never recovered the form it showed before World War II.

Founded by former students of the Sint-Franciscus Xavelus Institut in 1899, Cercle were the first club from Flanders to win the Belgian championship, in 1911. With regular international Florimond van Halme playing at centre-half, they went on to win the double in 1927 and the title for the last time in 1930, before van Halme retired.

Much of the next four decades were spent flitting between divisions, before the club's move to the Olympiastadion in the Seventies attracted a better class of foreigner. Former Danish international captain Morten Olsen spent a couple of seasons here, but the team's only modern honour has been a cup win in 1985, Cercle beating Beveren on penalties in the final.

Cercle's hero of the early Nineties was Josip Weber, a Croat-born striker who became a naturalised Belgian to play for the Red Devils at the 1994 World Cup. He scored 130 goals in six league seasons

before moving to Anderlecht in 1994/95. Cercle have continued to make the most of cheap East European talent, but in 1996 Romanian internationals Dorinel Munteanu and Tibor Selymes both left, for Cologne and Anderlecht respectively.

The departure of the club's top scorer of 1996/97, Hungarian Gábor Torma, to Roda JC Kerkrade of Holland coincided with relegation – and there's been little sign of a revival since.

Swift half

The *Cercle Pub* in *blok* #12 of the stadium is a friendly bar which is open on Monday, Wednesday and Friday evenings as well as on matchdays. The modest **club shop** is downstairs – open only on matchdays, credit cards politely refused.

In the net

Cercle's **official website** is far longer-established than Club's, and now has a proper URL: www.cerclebrugge.be.

Among the unofficials, Wim van Lancker's long-running effort is always worth a peek at: users.skynet.be/cerclebrugge.

Eat, drink, sleep…

Bars and clubs

Bruges is one of those small tourist towns where the nightlife, such as it is, is best **during the week**. At weekends the cafés around the Markt are packed with coachloads of day-trippers, and 't Zand square is a more bearable option. Locals prefer the **typical Flemish bars** tucked away down side-streets.

't Brugs Beertje, Kemelstraat 5. Friendly pub famed for its huge selection of beers, nearly 200 in all. Open 4pm–1am, closed Wednesdays. Between 't Zand and Markt. All buses to Markt.

Cactus Café, Stint-Jakobsstraat 33. The town's major venue for live acts and DJs, entrance around 150BF for a local band, 300BF for a foreign one. All buses to Biekorf.

De Hobbit, Kemelstraat 8. Popular, studenty bar/club with occasional live music and a full menu. Open late (for Bruges). Closed Mondays and Tuesdays. Between 't Zand and Markt. All buses to Markt.

De Sportcafé, Torhoutse Steenweg/Expresweg. Newly opened sports bar on the main ring road out towards the Jan Breydel stadium, yet to generate a lively atmosphere due to its location, but a large screen and tasty bar snacks may turn the tide. Bus #25.

De Vuurmolen, Kraanplein 5. Rare late-night bar/café, almost always crowded, almost always deafeningly noisy – but a good meeting place, and reasonably priced.

Straffe Hendrik-Huisbrouwerij, Walplein 26. Straffe Hendrik, the most famous Bruges brew, pale in colour and sharp in taste, is the only beer sold here, at the brewery and museum of the same name. A 10min walk from either 't Zand or the station, or if you're feeling lazy, it's on the circular #1 bus route.

The Top, Sint-Salvatorskerkhof 5. The best bar in town, now taken over by dance music buff Karel Lievens, attracting the Cercle fraternity and anyone else interested in listening to some decent sounds until late on. Any bus to Sint-Salvatorskerk.

Restaurants

Like everything else in Bruges, restaurants are geared to the **tourist market**, but that doesn't mean you have to spend a fortune to eat well. If money is really tight, check out the *Bauhaus* or *Passage* hostels, whose restaurants do cheap deals, or the fish stalls by the Vismarkt.

Beware that many Bruges kitchens close early, generally around 9pm; Zuidzandstraat, off 't Zand, has a couple of later options.

Bhavani, Simon Stevinplein 5. Easily beats other local Indian restaurant competition

with its vegetarian and tandoori specialities, its prices (main courses around 600–800BF), its swift service and its stylish decor.

Celtic Ireland Bar, Burg 8. More than just the average Irish pub, along with the usual big-screen TV, Guinness and live music, there's a thoroughly decent upstairs restaurant (open Wed–Sun) serving game and stew, plus daily specials.

Le Chagall, Sint-Amandsstraat 40. Laid-back restaurant with a terrace just off the Markt, also selling snacks. Eel, mussels and shellfish are the specialities. Main courses around 500BF, most credit cards. All buses to Biekorf.

De Hobbit, Kemelstraat 8. Popular bar and restaurant with an extensive menu, famed for its salads and spare ribs – the all-you-can-eat deals can keep you going for a week. Open 6pm–late. Between 't Zand and Markt. All buses to Markt.

High and hopeful – Olivier de Cock throws in for Club

The Jan Breydel stadium

Olympialaan 74, Sint-Andries
Capacity 30,000

The Jan Breydel is Belgium's only major **groundshare**, and a successful one at that. Its recent conversion to a 30,000 all-seater for Euro 2000 – for which the name was changed from Olympia to Jan Breydel, a legendary local war hero – has brought it two new stands at the north and south ends of the ground, a new roof for the main west stand, and new adjacent training areas. Club and Cercle have an equal share of these and all other facilities, and each has its own club bar and office, either side of the VIP/press entrance in the west stand. Naturally, Club's beer is **slightly cheaper** than that of its posher neighbour.

Each club pays an equal share of their takings at the gate to the local council, who built the ground in 1975. However, with Cercle's relegation in 1997, this sum is barely likely to cover the administration costs of keeping the club here.

For most of their two decades together, Club have come out on top. Cercle didn't manage to win a derby match here until 1988, by which time Club had won five titles away from their old De Klokke ground. If ever they meet up again, on derby day Cercle fans occupy the Kirk (church) north end, Club's the Bad (swimming pool) south end; the north is favoured by both for most of the season.

On matchdays, **special buses** are laid on from Stationsplein, in front of the train station, to the ground, a 10min ride away, for the usual 40BF ticket. The buses then wait at the end of Olympialaan until after the game. If you'd prefer to have a little more time on your side, bus #5 or #15 from the station to Sint-Andrieskerk will drop you right by the best bars on Gistelsesteenweg, near the stadium. Allow 15mins for the journey.

Former Club Bruges, Anderlecht and Sheffield Wednesday striker **Marc Degryse** has a stake in *Los Amigos* at Gistelsesteenweg 471, a lads' pub with disco lights and a games room. *De Platse*, on the other side at #536, is more ornate, ideal for the older generation of fans. The perfect mix is at *De Chalet*, #530, full of friendly local character and host to the FC Sint-Andries pub team.

The main **ticket offices** are at diagonally opposite corners of the stadium, one between entrances D and E, the other between A and B. The best (and dearest) seats are in the west stand, the cheapest behind the goals in the north and south.

De Stove, Kleine St Amandsstraat 40. In a quiet street of the Markt, a small, elegant restaurant centred around an old stove and chimney, serving exquisite fish and meat dishes for 700–800BF a main course. Four-course set menus at 1,350BF. Closed midweek.

Accommodation

Central Bruges has bundles of hotels, though none is particularly cheap. Both tourist offices offer an **accommodation service**, whereby they charge 400BF to book you a room, deducted from your hotel bill. The city has a handful of hostels, and some slightly cheaper hotels north of the Markt around the Spiegelrei canal.

Bauhaus International Youth Hostel, Langestraat 135–137 (☎050/341 093, fax 050/334 180, e-mail bauhaus@bauhaus.be). Relaxed youth hostel with dorm beds at 300BF; singles, doubles, triples and quads also available. Cheap restaurant downstairs open until midnight. Most major credit cards. Bus #6 or #16 from the station.

Hotel Jacobs, Baliestraat 1 (☎050/339 831, fax 050/335 694, e-mail hoteljacobs@glo.be). Friendly, comfortable three-star hotel north of the town centre, a 15min walk from the Markt. Double rooms, nearly all with bath/shower, at around 2,500BF. Singles, triples and quads also available. Most credit cards. Buses #4/8 from the station.

The Passage, Dweerstraat 26 (☎050/340 232, fax 050/340 140). Just east of 't Zand, a clean and comfortable hostel with a bed-and-breakfast option next door. B&B doubles at 1,200BF, dorm beds around 350BF, breakfast included. No lock-out or curfew. The restaurant downstairs is a bargain for Bruges – main courses at 250–400BF. Bar open until 3am. Most major credit cards. All buses to Sint-Salvatorskerk.

Le Singe d'Or, 't Zand 18 (☎050/334 848, fax 050/346 628). Clean, simple, centrally located hotel that was a meeting place for Club Bruges players just before and just after World War II. Singles at 1,000BF, doubles 1,500–2,400BF, bathroom facilities in the corridor. Most credit cards. All buses to 't Zand.

Snuffel's Traveller's Inn, Ezelstraat 47–49 (☎050/333 133, fax 050/333 250, e-mail snuffel@skynet.be). Hostel with dorm beds at 325BF, doubles at 450BF per person, breakfast included. No lock-out or curfew. Decent café downstairs. No credit cards. Bus #3 or #13 from the station.

Bosnia

Nogometni savez Bosne i Hercegovine (NSBIH), Sime Milutinovica 10/1,
BH-71000, Sarajevo ☎071/213 881   Fax 071/444 332   E-mail nsbih@bih.net.ba

NSBIH League champions Jedinstvo Bihać **NSHB League champions** Pošusje
NSBIH/NSHB Play-off champions Brotnjo Čitluk **NSBIH/NSHB Cup
winners** Zeljeznicar Sarajevo **FSRS League champions** Boksit Milici   **FSRS Cup
winners** Kozara Gradiska

European participants 2000/01 Brotnjo Čitluk (UCL qualifiers); Budućnost
Banovici, Zeljeznicar Sarajevo (UEFA Cup); Zrinjski Mostar (Intertoto Cup)

f there is a country in Europe
that needs – and deserves – success on the football field, it is
Bosnia-Herzegovina. Ravaged by
Europe's bloodiest conflict since
World War II, the country clung
doggedly to the game, hoping that
one day it would offer not only an
escape route for its talented players, but a source of pride and
recognition for its population.

Football has played its part in rebuilding the shattered morale of the
Bosnian people. FIFA, UEFA and a
number of national FA's have been
involved in projects to help redevelop the national game, while on
the ground soilders and charity
workers have used the game as a
way of breaking down barriers.
While Roberto Baggio's trips to
Sarajevo may grab the headlines,
there are lesser names, like Englishman Scott Lee, coaching kids on
whatever landmine-free space can
be found.

The end of snipers, mortar shells
and air-raid shelters in 1995 meant
that football could come out of its
enforced exile and, almost immediately, clubs sprang back into life. But
Bosnia's integration into the mainstream
of European football has been fraught with
predictable ethnic disputes. The Dayton
agreement, which brought an end to the
fighting, made no direct reference to football, but UEFA adopted its spirit on unified

Stressed out – Dzemaludin Musović, ex-national coach

multi-ethnic governance as a guide to its
policy and demanded that the Moslem,
Croat and Serb football authorities come
together to provide teams for European
competition.

That was never likely to happen – at
least, not overnight. The national FA of

Past times – Faruk Hadzibegić as skipper of Yugoslavia

Bosnia-Herzegovina (NSBIH), based in Sarajevo, is the body UEFA recognises as the main arbitrator of the local game. But its jurisdiction extends only to the main areas of Moslem population around the cities of Sarajevo, Tuzla and Zenica. In 1998, the Mostar-based NSHB, which controls football in the Croat-dominated region of 'Herceg Bosna', agreed to join with the NSBIH in organising a series of play-offs between the top clubs in the two associations' leagues. The top two teams from these then went on to represent Bosnia in Europe in 1998/99, and although they performed poorly, at least the country was on the map.

The train hit the buffers at the end of the 1998/99 season, when another round of play-offs saw Moslem side Velež Mostar due to play a Croat team from the same town, Zrinjski. Mostar is a divided city, and Velež, though affiliated to the NSBIH, is a club with its roots on the other side of the river Neretva, in Croat-controlled territory. Velež officials insisted they should be given the chance to host play-offs at their old Bijeli Brijeg stadium – latterly commandeered by Zrinjski. When the Croats refused Velež permission to return to their pre-civil war home, the club withdrew, along with the rest of the NSBIH contingent. The play-offs were over before a ball had been kicked.

None of this affected the most isolated of Bosnia's three ethnic federations, the Serb-controlled FSRS, based in the major town of the 'Republika Srpska', Banja Luka. They had never shown any interest in the play-offs in the first place, insisting their clubs would not take part unless all games took place on neutral territory.

At the end of the 1999/2000 season, UEFA offered the carrot of a place in the Champions' League qualifiers, as well as the UEFA Cup, if the three ethnic groups could agree on a play-off system. An agreement was duly reached, but the FSRS were again overruled by their political masters, so the Croats and Muslims went ahead without them and their joint efforts were given the nod by UEFA. Brotnjo Čitluk from the Croat area won the summer play-offs, which passed off without the feared ethnic violence, and the Croat and Moslem leagues have now merged to form united league and cup competitions for 2000/01.

The Bosnian Serbs, however, remain isolated. Their major clubs are forced to play against local village teams and the best players make their way to Belgrade to compete in the Yugoslav league in the hope of a foreign deal and a ticket out. It is a scenario which seems certain to leave the teams of the Serbian enclave way behind for years to come. Not surprisingly, no Serb has ever played in the Bosnian national team, although several born in the area, including Savo Milošević, have played for Yugoslavia.

Basics

EU, US and Canadian citizens do not need a visa to enter Bosnia-Herzegovina – though check with your local embassy before travelling. Australians and New Zealanders need a **tourist visa** – as well as the $35 fee, your passport, return plane ticket and letter of invitation also need to be provided. Depending on the political climate, visas may be available at the border for around $50.

The Bosnian currency is the **convertible mark**, KM, fixed firmly to the Deutschmark at a rate of 1:1. Convertible marks come in denominations of KM1, KM2, KM5 and KM10 notes.You may be slipped invalid old Bosnian dinars in your change – beware. The best advice is to bring Deutschmarks in small demoninations, which can be changed at a bank, but which are no longer valid as currency in their own right. In Croatian areas in the west of the country, the **kuna** is used – this is not valid in Sarajevo. Bosnia's is very much a cash economy, with next to no cash machines, although a few of the posher hotels take **credit cards**.

The telephone code for Bosnia-Herzegovina is 387 – add 1 for Sarajevo. The international access code is 00. In Sarajevo, **phone cards** are available from PTT post offices in denominations of KM5, KM8, KM14, KM31 and KM60. Calls to the UK are roughly 2KM per minute, and there are no cheap-rate time periods.

There are currently no direct scheduled **flights** from the UK to Sarajevo – most visitors change planes at Budapest or Ljubljana. The best way to get in and around Bosnia overland is by **bus**, with regular daily services from Dubrovnik, Split and Zagreb to Sarajevo (7–9 hours, KM40–60). There is hardly any train service to speak of.

Never set foot off the pavement anywhere in Bosnia. The country is still heavily mined and injuries are a daily occurrence. Likewise, do not enter any abandoned building – it may still be booby-trapped. Stick to the main streets in Sarajevo, rather than the outlying areas, and you should be fine.

Likewise, a number of ethnic Croat players have chosen to hop over the border to relatively wealthier clubs, and few have been chosen for Bosnia's national team which, like the federation that runs it, remains dominated by Moslems. Until such time as the side that claims to represent 'Bosnia-Herzegovina' gains genuine access to all the ethnic groupings that make up this most tenuous of nation states, it is likely to remain on the fringes of international competition, unable to reflect the strength in-depth which the Bosnian game once had in spades.

Historically, Velež Mostar were the region's last European representatives in the years before Yugoslavia disintegrated. Always a multi-ethnic side, in the late Eighties they were UEFA Cup regulars, their best performance taking them to the third round in 1988. There they were beaten by Hearts, whose striker John Robertson remarked that he 'couldn't believe the way the other side's heads dropped' after they had conceded an away goal – an early sign, perhaps, of ethnic divisions sapping morale.

The Eighties were also a profitable time for the two big Sarajevo teams, Željezničar and FK Sarajevo. Like Velež, Željezničar could trace their foundation back to the Twenties, but took four decades to make much of an impact on the wider Yugoslav scene. Unlike Velež, whose domestic accolades were confined to cup triumphs in 1981 and 1986, Željezničar won the Yugoslav title in 1972, their team going on to provide the backbone for the country's 1974 World Cup campaign. FK Sarajevo were champions twice, in 1967 and 1985, and remained a force to be reckoned with in the league right up until the final 1991/92 season, after Croatian and Slovenian teams had withdrawn in the face of conflict, and as Bosnia was being dragged into its own bloody phase of the war. Like Velež, Željezničar and Sarajevo continued to field multi-ethnic teams until the end. But their traditional tolerance could not survive the waves of hatred that washed over Bosnia in 1992. Those players who could get out, did so. Velež strikers Meho Kodro and Vladimir Gudelj both left for Spain, where they have remained ever since. Sarajevo stopper Risto Vidaković did the same. Željezničar's Mario Stanić and Gordan Vidović found sanctuary in Belgium, while Veldin Karić fled to Italy.

Of those that remained, many were killed in the fighting – FK Sarajevo alone lost nine members of their squad during the city's three-year-long siege.

When peace was restored, the region's footballing goalposts had been moved, perhaps irrevocably. Velež, Željezničar and Sarajevo joined the NSBIH league, along with other occasional members of the former Yugoslav top flight, Sloboda Tuzla and Čelik Zenica. Čelik, their home town emerging relatively unscathed from the conflict, won both the league and the cup in the first post-civil war season of 1995/96, and retained the title the following year.

Since then the Sarajevan clubs have dominated, their resilience drawing deserved praise from beyond the country's borders, their triumphs a welcome boost to the city's morale, if still ringing a little hollow by comparison with those of earlier generations.

Meanwhile, the national team's best young talent is scattered across the continent. Midfielder Hasan Salihamidzić has emerged as a major talent at Bayern Munich, as has Sergej Barbarez at Dortmund. Striker Elvir Baljić, having made his name with Fenerbahçe in Turkey, earned a big-money move to Real Madrid.

National coach Faruk Hadzibegić, captain of Yugoslavia at the 1990 World Cup, was unable to take his developing side to Euro 2000 after they were beaten to second place in their section by Scotland. Having given five years of his career to building his young nation's team, Hadzibegić resigned and joined the foreign legion himself by taking on the task of revitalising his old club in Spain, Real Betis. Miso Smajlović took over and was charged with the task of leading the country to the 2002 World Cup finals. Bosnia's qualifying group is not the toughest, and the progress the side has made in the past four years has been such that a play-off berth – and a possible back-door route to Japan and South Korea – does not look beyond them. Few in the European game would begrudge the Bosnians their chance.

Essential vocabulary

Hello *Zdravo*
Goodbye *Do vidjenja*
Yes *Da*
No *Ne*
Two beers, please *Dva piva, molim*
Thank you *Hvala*
Men's *Muški*
Women's *Ženski*
Where is the stadium? *Gdje je stadion?*
What's the score? *Koji je rezultat?*
Referee *Sudac*
Offside *Ofsajd*

Match practice

Aside from the Sarajevo derby, big cup-ties and the championship play-offs (if and when played), domestic football isn't big news in Bosnia. Crowds of less than 5,000 are common and may even sink to three figures in Republika Srpska.

The season runs from late August to mid-December, then again from March until early June. Sunday is the traditional match-day, with kick-off times varying between 2pm and 5.30pm according to available daylight. Games are also sometimes scheduled for Wednesday and Saturday. Evening kick-offs are rare, as many grounds lack floodlights.

A different league

The concept of a unified premier league for Bosnia was finally agreed by the three local associations during the 1999/2000 season, but with the Serbs having pulled out, the newly formed top flight is comprised only of Moslem and Croat clubs.

There were 22 clubs in this *Premijer Liga* for 2000/01, 11 from each of the former regional leagues, but this will be reduced to a more manageable 16 for 2001/02.

The series of play-offs which had been staged between Moslem and Croat clubs to determine European participation is no longer necessary, but beneath the *Premijer Liga* level, league football continues to be played along ethnic lines, at least for the time being. This remains most obviously the case in isolated Republika Srpska, where the top flight was to be reduced from 20 to 16 clubs for 2000/01.

Up for the cup

The three ethnic federations continued to organise their own competitions until 1999. The FSRS will continue to do so for the foreseeable future, but the NSBIH and NSHB were set to merge their cup competitions into a single tournament for 2000/01. At the end of 1999/2000, the two associations began the slow process of co-operation by organising a six-team play-off group (made up of four Moslem and two Croat sides), which played a single knock-out preliminary round before embarking on a three-team mini-league to determine a joint 'cup' winner.

Just the ticket

You'll have no trouble getting into a game on the day unless it's the Sarajevo derby. Otherwise head for the ticket office (*blagajna*), where prices should be displayed, albeit not always that clearly. You'll pay no more than KM5 to stand (*stajanje*), with a good seat (*sjedenje*) costing perhaps half as much again. On the whole, facilities are poor – don't expect much comfort for your convertible Marks. Each stand (*tribina*) is referred to by its geographical location – *zapad* (west), *istok* (east), *jug* (south) or *sjever* (north).

Half-time

Beer (*pivo*) is almost always available at matches and consumed in some quantity. Snack-wise, fans dig into little bags of sun-flower seeds (*suncokret*), pumpkin seeds (*košpice*) or nuts (*lješnik*), sold by vendors weaving their way through the crowd. The plumes of smoke and appealing smells will be coming from the *čevapčići* grill, another pre-requisite at most matches.

Action replay

In the Moslem-populated areas, state BiHTV will show one league game live every Sunday, with Hayat TV screening another, before BiHTV's league round-up at 8.30pm. In between, BiHTV will screen an English Premiership game live at 5pm on Sundays, a little later if it clashes with a domestic fixture.

Hayat shows live Spanish action, BiHTV the *Bundesliga*, and OBN the *Serie A*. Early Monday evening is the time to catch *Top Goal* on BiHTV, with all the best action from the top five European leagues.

The back page

Sarajevo can boast two sports-dedicated newspapers, *Sport Marker* (daily, KM1) and *Sport avaz* (Tuesdays and Fridays, KM1), the latter being the more comprehensive. The main magazine is the glossy bi-monthly produced by the NSBIH, *Football* (KM4), with lengthy interviews and features. Sarajevo's three main daily papers, *Dnevni avaz*, *Oslobodjenje* and *Večernje novine*, also have comprehensive sports sections.

Ultra culture

Bosnian fans are organising themselves into loud and colourful fan groups, those in Mostar and Zenica being among the most vocal in the provinces. Violence is rare, but trouble can't be ruled out between Moslem and Croat fans in the merged *Premijer liga* during 2000/01.

In the net

The Moslem part of the Bosnian game has a *Flash*-heavy site dedicated to it at: www.bosnia-online.com/nation. For an overview of what's happening across the country, try the excellent *Former Yugoslavia Soccer* stats service at: www.fyusoccer.com.

Sarajevo

First-class football returned to Sarajevo in November 1996, when Italy came to town for an international friendly and were beaten 2–1. The game was played for charity, but Bosnia's opponents in qualifying for major tournaments since then have been less generous. After initially playing 'home' games in Bologna because of security worries, the Bosnians have played all their competitive games in Sarajevo, and have given local crowds little to cheer about. The exception came in August 1997, when Denmark were thrashed 3–0 at the Koševo stadium, sending a 35,000 crowd into ecstacy and prompting a series of street parties that went on until dawn.

To the outsider, this was confirmation that the city's passion for football had survived the war intact. For those on the inside, it never really went away. During the siege of Sarajevo between 1992 and 1995, frustrated players arranged matches against teams of UN 'peacekeepers', while ordinary fans played impromptu games in the streets – risking life and limb from Serb mortar attacks in the process.

Sarajevo's love affair with football dates back to the aftermath of another conflict, World War II, and the Yugoslav civil war that followed it. After their triumph in the latter, the communist authorities merged several local teams together to form FK Sarajevo, a new 'super club' to challenge the established Željezničar. A rivalry was born – the fiercest in any single city of the old Yugoslavia outside Belgrade.

The two teams were not divided along ethnic lines – such a distinction would have been unthinkable in a city which prided itself on its multi-cultural identity. The difference was socio-political, with Sarajevo seen as the team of the establishment, playing in the town's flagship stadium, and Željezničar as the rebellious underdog.

Having two top-flight teams blunted the city's ability to make an impact on national

A tricky place to play – Scotland struggle to see much of the ball in Sarajevo, 1999

competitions – the two clubs managed only three championships between them from 1946 until the old federal Yugoslav league ceased to exist in 1992. With the collapse of federal institutions came the destruction of Sarajevo's precious tolerance – the siege saw the city divided by a sniper-patrolled line, marking out Serb-populated suburbs from the rest of town. FK Sarajevo's Koševo stadium was on the Moslem side, Željezničar's Grbavica on the other. The former bore the brunt of the shelling from Serb positions in the hills above, but before long both would have their pitches turned into makeshift graveyards.

Today both grounds have been refurbished, and their teams are playing competitive football once again. Playing standards have improved over the last three seasons, while support for both clubs – and their mutual dislike of each other – remains fervent.

Alas, you're more likely to see a West African than a Serb playing for either team. Most of the city's Serb population fled after the fighting, fearing reprisals from their former neighbours. Up in the hills at Pale, capital of the self-styled 'Republika Srpska', some of the exiles set up a 'shadow' Sarajevo team, playing under the name Famos. But they finished third bottom of the SRS top flight in 2000, having had the division expanded specifically to accommodate them after 'relegation' the previous year.

The thrilling fields

 ## FK Sarajevo

Olimpijski stadion, Marsala Tita 40
Capacity 48,000 (37,000 seated)
Colours Claret shirts, claret shorts
League champions (Yugoslavia) 1967, 1985
League champions (NSBIH) 1999
Cup winners (NSBIH) 1997, 1998

Twelve months ago, FK Sarajevo appeared in ruder health than their city rivals. Cup winners in 1997 and 1998, and runaway champions of the NSBIH *Premijer Liga* in 1999, the club had a superbly renovated stadium (the Olimpijski, colloquially known as the Koševo after the suburb in which it stands), an experienced squad and a proud history behind it.

Yet the cancellation of Bosnia's 1999 play-offs, victory in which would have given Sarajevo a shot at the Champions' League qualifiers for the first time, was a bitter blow, coming as it did on the heels of a surprise cup final defeat by Bosna Visoko.

Just as seriously, Sarajevo's fans have not yet been able to match the post-civil war support enjoyed by Željezničar, in either numbers or colour. In this respect, having such a big stadium to echo to the sound of only a few thousand handclaps is a hindrance rather than a help.

The team finished third in the NSBIH league in 1999/2000, only a point behind Željezničar and two behind champions Jedinstvo Bihać. Symbolically, however, there was a wider bridge to be crossed.

Here we go!
The Koševo is to the north-east of town, up the incline of Koševo and then Patriotske lige from the centre. Take any bus – the #20b or# 102, for example – marked Park or Jezero, and alight two stops from the terminus at Stajalište 'Koševo'. A taxi will take five minutes, or you could walk it in 15.

Just the ticket
There is a maroon ticket kiosk marked *blagajna*' at the entrance to the main driveway. The cheapest places are in the *tribina sjever D*, with the *Horde zla*, or in the *tribina jug B* with the visiting fans. *Tribina istok C* and *zapad A* are the main stands, where tickets are twice the price, but still very cheap.

Swift half
You'll find a stretch of bars near the bus stop, but the most popular with fans – hence the pictures inside – is the *Bordo*, across the road, 100m further up. Inside the stadium gates, halfway down the driveway to the left, is the *Restoran Stadion*,

Sarajevo essentials

Sarajevo **airport** is 13km west of town, with a sporadic bus service through Novo Sarajevo to the centre. A taxi will cost around KM20. The **bus station** is behind the *Holiday Inn* hotel at Kranjčićeva 9, served by tram #1 or #4.

The city has an **excellent transport system**, comprising trams (6am–midnight, tickets KM1 from a kiosk, KM1.50 onboard), buses and trolleybuses (7am–8pm, tickets KM1 onboard). There is no night transport. Taxis charge an initial fee of KM2, plus a negotiable fare of KM1.30 per kilometre, with extras for luggage and evening rates. To call one, dial ☎071/970 or ☎071/663 555.

The best way of finding accommodation is to seek out the city's **main tourist office** at Ul Zelenih Beretki 22a (Mon–Fri 8am–3pm, Sat 9am–2pm, ☎071/532 606, fax 071/532 281).

A comprehensive range of local football souvenirs can be found at **Kapar Selma**, Baščaršija 6, near the corner with Sarači.

with a goalnet full of football souvenirs that includes a framed gift of Arsenal autographs.

Ultra culture

Formed as the *Pitari* in the mid-Eighties, the **Horde zla** soon changed their name and moved from Koševo's east stand to occupy the north one, just in time to establish enough noise in the old Yugoslav league so that their reputation came before them when a Bosnian one was eventually formed. Few opponents can match them for support – except, of course, Željo's 'Maniacs'.

In the net

You'll find a basic **semi-official website** at: www.bihart.com/fcsarajevo/hz.

 Željezničar

Grbavica stadion, Dinarska 27
Capacity 26,000
Colours Azure-and-white shirts, azure shorts
League champions (Yugoslavia) 1972
Play-off champions (NSBIH/NSHB) 1998
Cup winners (NSBIH/NSHB) 2000

Željezničar's finest hour in post-civil war Bosnia came in June 1998, when a last-minute goal from Hadis Zubanović sealed victory in the play-off championship over FK Sarajevo, at their rivals' Koševo stadium,

and in front of a UEFA delegation that included general secretary Gerhard Aigner. The club, the most avidly followed in the city in recent years, was back on the European map.

Alas, like FK Sarajevo, Željezničar stumbled along the road back to continental acceptance, the team's 2–1 aggregate defeat by Kilmarnock in the 1998/99 UEFA Cup qualifying round being no better or worse than their rivals' 4–1 loss to Belgium's Germinal Ekeren at the same stage.

In 1998/99, 'Željo' lost their way a bit, finishing seventh (outside the mythical play-off places) in the NSBIH *Premijer Liga*, and losing on penalties to Sarajevo in the domestic cup semi-finals. There was further disappointment with a runners-up spot in the league the following season, but the team made up for it by winning the strange play-off mini-league which constituted a combined Moslem/Croat 'cup' competition in June 2000; the 'final', a 3–1 victory over Sloboda Tuzla, was watched by 10,000 in Sarajevo, and was enough to earn the club a return to UEFA Cup action in 2000/01.

Here we go!

From Skenderija, the large shopping complex on the south side of the river, take trolleybus #101, #102, #103, #104 or #105 four stops to the Stajalište Stadion on Zvornička. Be aware that this area was Serb-held during the siege of Sarajevo;

burned-out tower blocks surround the ground, and obscure paths round about may still be mined, so don't go wandering off the main road.

Just the ticket

The Grbavica is a compact ground, with only one main stand and ticket hatches dotted around the north and south sides. There's generally a single, flat rate for admission. The north end is for the meagre away support, the south for the home crew, the 'Maniacs'.

Swift half

The famous *11 Plavih* bar has sadly closed – it's now a Chinese restaurant – so the large, mock baroque **Restoran Plavi Zamak**, right by the bus stop, with its open fire and English menu, might have to do. For something with a more authentic pre-match vibe, try the **Mak** or **Orlando** cafés further down Zvornička on the other side of the stadium. At the ground itself, running along Zvornička, is a string of bars and shops, plus the **Zvono** café above the street-level **Buon Giorno** pizzeria.

Ultra culture

Željo's **'Maniacs'** are the biggest fan group in Bosnia, but perhaps not as fearsome as their name suggests. The club has always enjoyed a lofty reputation in the local game, and the team is a flagship for the city and, in particular, the school of football engendered there. The Maniacs may make a noise – especially against FKS – but many of them know the game inside out.

In the net

You'll find a comprehensive **fan-run website**, with achingly familiar graphics, a history of the club and an English-language section, at: come.to/Bluemania.

Eat, drink, sleep…

Bars and clubs

Café life has returned to Sarajevo. Locals linger for hours over their coffee (*kafa*) or beer (*pivo*) especially along the central, pedestrianised Ferhadija. Imported beers are widely available but there's no reason to pay the premium, as the local *Sarajevsko* is very fine. Domestic wines are also excellent, but beware of drinking too much of the local spirits *rakija*, *šlivovica* and *loza*.

Club life is unsophisticated, but a good time can be had at any of the handful of discos in town.

Bife Aldino, Ul Patke 4. Friendly old family-run downtown local, where the owner's son is a goalkeeper for local second-division club Vrbanjuša, so plenty of football talk and souvenirs on display. Sells beer, unlike the atmospheric **Cardak** round the corner at Safvet-bega Bašagica 4, HQ of another local side, FK Vratnik, with great old black-and-white football photos.

The Bar, Ul Maršala Tita 7. This former Internet Café is now a red cellar of a bar/club, featuring dance music and a wide range of drinks. For something more downbeat, the **Minjon** bar opposite is a classic spit-and-sawdust job.

The Harp, Ul Patriotske Lige bb. Just past the Olympic stadium, by the Jezero bus terminal, is this highly recommended neighbourhood Irish bar, attracting ex-pats and locals alike. Sky Sports, pub menu, a scattering of football scarves and a convivial atmosphere generated by Tony and Dave's careful bar-tending.

Fis, Ul Musala 2. Popular split-level bar/club with an alternative feel, done out in Picasso-style designs, attracting a young, late-night crowd. One block in from the river, round the corner from the friendly, cosy **Marquee**, Obala Kulina Bana 7, which offers pop memorabilia and occasional live acts. Open until late.

Restaurants

Bosnians are big **meat eaters**. The typical dish is *bosanski lonac*, a local stew of meat and cabbage – not for the light-bellied. Street food is widespread, either meaty (*čevapčići*) or cheesy (*sirnica*), but invariably greasy.

The economic climate means locals in Sarajevo do not have the wherewithal to rub elbows with the foreign military or press set, and prefer to eat at home. In consequence, most menus are displayed in English or German, and a main course could set you back KM15 or more. Note that some Moslem-run restaurants will not serve alcohol.

Aeroplan, Sarači 6. Probably the best place in town to try the domestic favourite *bosanski lonac*, served without alcohol but at least with style. Main courses at under KM10, kitchen closes by 9.30pm. Open daily.

Čevabdžinica Sport, Baščaršija 22. Classic old *čevapčići* joint set up by former FKS star Asim Ferhatović, whose legend lives on amid the faded photos. Open 8am–9pm. Also check out the two restaurants nearby, at Kundurdziluk 19 and 20, featuring similar fare and souvenirs from Sarajevo's other team.

Klub Preporod, Branilaca Sarajeva 30. Relaxed, arty feel to this cheap restaurant serving local fare at about KM10 a go. Open 10am–8pm, with a break 3–4pm.

Ragusa, Ferhadija 10. Local delicacies along Sarajevo's busy Ferhadija, with reasonable-sized portions plonked onto heavy wooden tables in the back room, while the front bar is decked out in maritime garb. front of diners gazing at the outside street action. Alcohol served. Open Mon–Sat 10am–11pm, Sun from 6pm.

To Be Or Not To Be, Cizmediluk 5. Tucked in and signposted from Sarači is this small, intimate, two-level eaterie, with a modest menu butswift, attentive service. Open daily, midday–11pm.

Accommodation

Sarajevo's main hotels cater to the international visitor on expenses. A number of *pansions* (at about KM50 per night) are slowly springing up in town, and the **tourist office** (see panel) can book you a private room with a family for around the same price. If you are staying longer than one night, one trick might be to book it

through the tourist office, and negotiate a cheaper rate with the owner for the length of time you're there.

Bosnia Tours, Ul Maršala Tita 54 (☎071/202 206, fax 071/202 207). Private rooms arranged at this friendly agency, all centrally located near the Eternal Flame. Singles at less than KM50, doubles KM75. Office closed Sundays. Book ahead if possible.

Hotel Grand, Ul Muhameda ef Pandže 7 (☎071/205 444, fax 071/205 866). One of Sarajevo's more affordable quality options, centrally located near the train station, with singles at around KM200, doubles KM300, breakfast included.

Pansion Hondo, Zaima Šarca 23 (☎071/666 564, fax 071/469 375). Steep climb the other side of the cathedral, but worth it for the large, clean rooms, all with TVs. Singles at KM80, doubles KM120, including breakfast. Reservations recommended.

Hotel Saraj, Ul Nevjestina 5 (☎071/447 703, fax 071/472 691, e-mail hotelsaraj@bih.net.ba). Another of the city's better mid-range hotels, behind the national library. Rooms around KM200, more for those with city views, breakfast included. All are pleasant and have satellite TV.

Pansion Train, Halida Kajtaza 11 (☎071/200 517, fax 071/200 522). Sleeping compartment of a train moored (if that's the word) in a car park, signposted a short walk from the bus station. Toilets and running water, singles at KM30, twins KM40, breakfast included. Unless you're crazy about trains, could get a little tiring for more than two nights.

Bulgaria

Bulgarian Football Union (BFU), Karingradska 19, 1000 Sofia
☎02/874 725 Fax 02/803 237 E-mail bfu@mail.bol.bg

League champions Levski Sofia **Cup winners** Levski Sofia **Promoted** Cherno
More Varna, Hebar-Iskar Pazardhik **Relegated** Dobrudzha Dobritch, Belasitsa
Petritch, Pirin Blagoevgrad, Shumen

European participants 2000/01 Levski Sofia (UCL qualifiers); CSKA Sofia,
Neftokhimik Burgas (UEFA Cup); Velbazhd Kyustendil (Intertoto Cup)

astern Europe is littered
with countries whose only
connections to footballing
glory are fading black-and-
white photographs pinned to the
walls of bars. But while the Poles,
Russians and Hungarians gaze upon
images captured in the days when
the *politburo* still ruled, Bulgarians'
memories are much fresher and, as
a consequence, the pain of decline
is much more intense. Bulgaria's
golden generation were the fourth
best team at the World Cup in
1994, at a time when the country
was attempting to get to grips with
post-communist realities. Hristo Stoichkov, Emil Kostadinov and Trifon
Ivanov may have emerged from the
communist era, but with their confident swagger and patriotic pride,
they gave those struggling with the
confusion of capitalist transition
something to cheer about.

Follow me – Stoichkov bids a fighting farewell, 1999

Now they have gone, and as the next
generation struggles to live up to their standards, Bulgaria are slipping down the world
rankings. Suddenly, that famous quarter-
final win over the Germans in the United
States is part of history.

Young players *are* emerging, but Stoichkov, who has taken on the role as
assistant coach of the national team, is keen
to point out the difficulties they face in living up to high expectations: 'My generation
were able to learn their trade and mature
as both footballers and men before we
moved abroad. But the young players of

today are leaving too young – because of
the economic situation they take the first
deal that comes along, and won't wait for
the right moment. In this way we will lose
a lot of talented players.'

It is not surprising that players young
and old are swift to accept those moves
to Greece or the German lower divisions.
Domestic Bulgarian football is struggling
to maintain even the most basic levels of
dignity. Barely a weekend goes by without
an accusation of match-fixing, an incident of
serious crowd trouble, or a revelation of
dodgy dealing from the shady characters
at the top of many first-division clubs. The

Basics

EU and American citizens no longer need a **visa** to visit Bulgaria for up to 30 days. Other nationals are advised to check with their Bulgarian embassy as to visa requirements. The dreaded **statistical card** still exists, to write your details and reason for visit, to be kept safe and thrown back at customs upon departure. In practice you can skip it and the official writes the initials *b.k.* in your passport.

The Bulgarian currency is the **lev** – plural leva – made up of 100 stotinki. After drastic devaluation in the late Nineties, the lev has been stabilised and pegged 1:1 to the Deutschmark. Old notes with lots of noughts on the end are no longer legal tender. There are around 3 leva to £1. There are coins for 1, 2, 5, 10, 20 and 50 stotinki, and notes for 1 lev, 2, 5, 10, 20 and 50 leva.. Hotel prices are often quoted in US dollars or DMs. Banks and major hotels charge varying exchange commissions, but there are private **exchange offices** all over Sofia, with rates clearly marked and no commission charged. Keep your receipts for changing lev back into dollars upon departure. Do **not** change money on the black market – you're liable to be stuck with invalid currency.

Credit cards are not widely accepted, and it's wise to bring a certain quantity of US dollars or Deutschmarks in small-denomination notes, secreted on your person. There are a few cash machines dotted around Sofia, mainly *Mastercard* and *Cirrus*.

To call Bulgaria from abroad dial 359, then 2 for Sofia, 32 for Plovdiv, 68 for Lovech. To call abroad from Bulgaria, dial 00, followed by the country code. For local calls, new phones use tokens. For international calls, central Sofia has two kinds of cardphone systems: blue *Betkom* phones and orange *Bulfon* ones. **Cards and tokens** are available at kiosks next to most phones, and are not interchangeable between the two networks. There are no cheap rates – you'll pay just under £1 a minute. Remember that Bulgaria is one hour ahead of Central European Time.

Cross-country travel is best accomplished by **train**, with *intersiti* and *ekspres* services the quickest. Advance booking is compulsory for these, but a *Rila* desk or office at the station can deal with your reservation (*zapazeno myasto*) and ticket (*bilet*) to save on queuing. The regular Sofia–Plovdiv service takes 2–3hrs and costs about $2 first class. For more remote places like Lovech, private **bus companies** like *Etap* and *Group Travel* offer cheap, quick and comfortable services.

Bulgarian FA has been involved in a protracted spat with the government which has seen FIFA and UEFA forced to intervene in an attempt to establish exactly who is in charge of the game.

This swift decline is made all the sadder by the fact that it took the Bulgarians most of this century to reach the top level of international football. For in pure football terms, the country was a late developer. Bulgarian students returning home from Istanbul formed the first team in 1909, and the two oldest surviving clubs, Sofia's Slavia and Levski, were founded shortly afterwards. The Black Sea port of Varna and southern city of Plovdiv also took to the game during what were, in the Balkans as elsewhere in Europe, years of war and turbulence. When the situation was calmer, regional leagues were established, followed by a national championship in 1937. Meanwhile, international games were mainly confined to 'friendlies' against neighbouring states.

With the arrival of Communism in 1945, Bulgarian football remained insular while acquiring a new, rigid domestic structure. From then on teams represented state bodies. The populist Levski became an arm of the Interior Ministry, and an army team was established, to be called CSKA; over the coming decades they were to receive the lion's share of players and funding, while the traditionally bourgeois Slavia, champions in 1941 and 1943, fell out of favour and lost their best players.

Naturally CSKA dominated the league, winning nine titles in a row in the Fifties – a record they share with just three other European clubs, Celtic, Rangers and MTK Budapest. Yet in all this time, the only player of world class they produced was inside-forward Ivan Kolev, who starred in Bulgaria's first appearance in the World Cup finals in 1962; the team managed a goalless draw with England but were eliminated without winning a match.

As the Sixties wore on, the army slowly lost its all-powerful grip on the game, and Levski, with centre-forward Georgi Asparoukhov in his prime, began to pick up the occasional title. Asparoukhov was the finest Bulgarian player of his day, but injury prevented him from showing his best at Bulgaria's next two World Cup appearances, in 1966 and 1970. He died in a car crash in 1971.

For the time being, international success was confined to the Olympics, in a soccer tournament dominated by Eastern bloc 'amateur' sides; Bulgaria won bronze in 1956 and silver twelve years later.

There were to be no more World Cup adventures until 1986 when, in the opening game of the tournament, Nasko Sirakov stooped low to head home a late equaliser against the champions, Italy. It was a false dawn – the Bulgars again went home without a World Cup win. But Sirakov's header would prove a strange pre-echo of events in the 1994 finals.

Throughout the postwar era, Bulgaria had been the Soviets' closest East European ally. In keeping with strict Communist doctrines, Bulgarian players were forbidden from going abroad to earn a living and that, as much as anything, contributed to the national team's poor World Cup showings. One English journalist described the 1986 side as 'a disgrace to football', such was their apathy.

Even then, the cracks were beginning to show. Rival fans from CSKA and Levski became engaged in decidedly non-Soviet bouts of crowd violence. In 1985, fighting between the two sets of players stopped the domestic cup final; in the aftermath, the authorities forced both clubs to dissolve and re-form as Sredets (CSKA) and Vitosha (Levski), while banning several players, including Levski's Sirakov and a young CSKA striker by the name of Hristo Stoichkov, for life.

Neither ban lasted more than a year. Bulgaria's political and sporting climate was thawing. Sirakov was allowed to become one of the first internationals to move abroad, and went to Real Zaragoza. Stoichkov, a headstrong teenager who could sprint 100m in 11 seconds, went on to become top scorer in both the Bulgarian league and the Cup-Winners' Cup in 1988/89. The latter campaign included three goals for CSKA against Barcelona, whose coach Johan Cruyff immediately took out an option to sign him – exercised a year later, after Stoichkov had hit 38 goals for CSKA to earn himself Europe's 'golden boot' as the continent's top scorer. His goals then helped the Catalans to four consecutive Spanish titles and, most symbolically, the 1992 European Cup.

If he was influential in Barcelona, Stoichkov's impact at international level would change Bulgaria's status in the eyes of the world forever. Even after Kostadinov's last-minute goal in Paris had booked the Bulgarians their ticket to USA '94, the team had history against them. This, after all, was the nation that had never won a match in the World Cup finals. When Nigeria took them to the cleaners in their opening game, it looked like being the same old story. But suddenly, after beating Greece, Argentina and Mexico (with Stoichkov on target against each), the Bulgarians were on a roll.

In the quarter-finals, they were 1–0 down against Germany when a Stoichkov free-kick levelled the scores. Three minutes later the bald head of midfielder Yordan Lechkov met a swift cross, just as Sirakov's had done eight years earlier, and the world champions were beaten. Sofia went wild. Players' values soared overnight. Disappointing performances against Italy and Sweden left Bulgaria in fourth place. But Stoichkov, Lechkov, Kostadinov and co bounced back to beat Germany again in a European Championship qualifier in Sofia in 1995. Now we saw a different Stoichkov – a true leader of men, not just a muscular striker with a swagger in his stride and an attitude in his head.

He scored all three Bulgarian goals at Euro '96, but it wasn't enough. The heroes of 1994 looked past their sell-by date, and when coach Dimitar Penev, Stoichkov's old buddy, was sacked, the striker vowed never to play for his country again. He was eventually reconciled with Penev's successor, Hristo Bonev, but both men were powerless to prevent Bulgaria from bowing out of France '98 without winning a match.

Stoichkov, who with a number of other internationals had returned to CSKA Sofia at the end of the 1997/98 season to prepare for the World Cup, spent most of his time in France arguing – with opponents, with officials, with team-mates and with anyone else who would listen.

Dimitar Dimitrov took over the reins for the Euro 2000 qualification campaign, but his mixture of remaining veterans such as Krassimir Balakov and a handful of promising young players was never going to make it to the Low Countries, even with Stoichkov now working as an unpaid assistant coach.

Dimitrov's side finished next to bottom in their group behind England, Sweden and Poland, and the under-fire Dimitrov quit to take on Levski Sofia – who he duly led to both their 21st league title and the domestic cup in 1999/2000.

Stoicho Mladenov was handed the unenviable task of trying to put together a squad that would fare better in the World Cup qualifiers, with Stoichkov carrying on as his assistant despite moving to play for Chicago Fire in the USA. Many feel that Mladenov, who worked as the Under-21 coach before his promotion, is merely a stopgap until Stoichkov finally calls it a day and takes on the biggest challenge of his career – resurrecting the hopes of a nation.

Essential vocabulary

Hello *Zdravei*
Goodbye *Dovizhdane*
Yes *Da*
No *Ne*
Two beers, please *Molya, dva bira*
Thank you *Blagodarya*
Men's *M'zhe* (МѢЖЕ)
Women's *Zheni* (ЖЕНИ)
Where is the stadium *Kude e stadion?*
What's the score? *Kak e igra?*
Referee *Sadiya*
Offside *Zasada*
Most of all, remember that Bulgarians shake their heads for yes and nod for no.

Match practice

Bulgarian league football is a cheap if uncomfortable way of spending a Saturday afternoon. Facilities are poor, crowds low, refereeing decisions often questionable.

The big games are Levski–CSKA and any game involving Sofia clubs against those from Plovdiv – particularly Botev.

The season runs from mid-August to early December and from February to June, with most matches on Saturday afternoons. Some fixtures in the capital are played on Friday night or Sunday afternoon. Kick-off times get gradually earlier as winter creeps in, with games at 6pm until September, 5pm until October, then 3pm and 2pm; in the spring season the trend reverses.

A different league

The Bulgarian league has three main divisions. At the top, the *'A' Grupa* is gradually being reduced in size – from 16 to 14 teams for 2000/01, with the number scheduled to fall again to 12 the following season, during which clubs will begin to play each other four times a year. The second division, the *'B' Grupa*, will remain at 16 teams, while the third division, *'V' Grupa*, is to stay regionalised into four separate 18-team sections.

Up for the cup

The early rounds of the *Kupa Na Balgariya* are played over one leg, with top-flight teams entering at the last-32 stage in late October. Matches are played on a two-leg basis from the last 16, until a one-match final at the Vasil Levski in June.

In the earlier rounds, away goals count double in the case of level aggregate scores, with the 'golden goal' and penalties rule applying if teams are still tied.

Just the ticket

Although your ticket might indicate a row (*red*) and a place (*myasto*), this invariably means any spot you like on a peeling, splintered wooden bench.

Most medium-sized stadia are divided into *sektors* – A, B, V and G. *Sektor A* is generally the main stand, where seats may be a few thousand lev dearer, but where you at least stand a decent chance of being under cover.

There are no matchday programmes at league games, but the Bulgarian FA can normally be relied upon to produce a money-spinning, glossy souvenir for internationals against Western teams.

Half-time

Sunflower seeds are sold in newspaper cones outside grounds. Snacks are otherwise pretty minimal and you'll see no great rush to whatever poor buffet facilities may be on offer.

Action replay

Live domestic action is shared between state channels Kanal 1 and Efir 2, with the former normally getting the plum fixtures, including European matches and Bulgarian internationals.

Highlights shows include Kanal 1's *Sportna Mrezha* ('Sports Network'), at around midnight on Saturday, but most fans agree that Nova TV's *Sporten Syvat*, shown earlier, is superior. Every Saturday night, at 10 or 11pm, Kanal 1 shows *Derbi Ot Evropi*, the leading game of the day from England, Spain or Italy.

Eurosport and DSF are popular across the country, and pirate decoders for Sky Sports are widespread.

The back page

Bulgaria's two sports dailies, *Meridian Match* and *7 Dni Sport* (both 0.50 leva), the latter nicknamed 'Seven Days of Lies' (rather than 'Seven Days of Sport') for its speculative transfer rumours, both offer fine foreign coverage including full Premiership results

Additionally, there are two weekly sports papers – *Evrofutbol*, heavy with stats for the gambling fraternity, and the respected *Futbol*; both are published on Mondays.

Ultra culture

Organised fan culture is slowly raising its head at Bulgarian grounds – as is violence. Small clusters of fan groups have taken it upon themselves to create a mini-Italian style atmosphere with smoke bombs, banners and the occasional explosion.

Derby day between between Levski and CSKA is the most notorious for trouble – in October 1999, Levski fans smashed the seating of CSKA's newly renovated away sector, causing much breast-beating in the press and the possibility of the same fixture being played behind closed doors in the foreseeable future.

In the net

The Bulgarian FA continues to run its own official site, but this is not as regularly updated as it might be at: bfu.online.bg. More reliable is Julian Dontchev's fine unofficial offering, which carries local stats, news stories and many other features, all meticulously maintained. Find it all at: www.helsinki.fi/~dontchev/bulgaria/football.html.

Sofia

Greenery and scenery – but the football could be better in the shadow of Mount Vitosha

Look down Bulevard Vitosha in Sofia's city centre, and your eyes are drawn towards the mountain from which the road takes its name. Sofia and its suburbs feel small in Vitosha's shadow, and indeed this city is home to barely a million people – a moderate fan base, spread thinly over four or five top-flight teams playing second-rate football.

Moreover, Sofia no longer has the prestige of a national stadium, Neftohimik's ground in the Black Sea port of Burgas having hosted most recent internationals. Both the Vasil Levski and the Balgarska Armia stadia are in poor shape. The former's upgrading wasn't finished in time for England's visit in June 1999, forcing the game to be switched to the latter – itself brought up to standard only after CSKA fans volunteered to work round the clock to put in 25,000 seats for their club's 1998 European tie with Servette.

CSKA, based in a large empty space of parkland, draw support from small pockets all over the capital (and indeed Bulgaria, mainly because of their European exploits and Stoichkov's popularity). Rivals Levski have their roots in north-east Podujane, near their original Gerena stadium, renamed the Asparoukhov and another

ground in the process of being restored. Slavia, surprise double-winners in 1996, had to make a few improvements to their stadium in the south-west of town for the subsequent European competition, but still you're likely to see old men tending their goats nearby. Lokomotiv's facilities would put a squatters' festival's to shame, and Septemvri's were so bad the FA refused them permission to play there during their brief visit to the top flight in 1998/99.

The thrilling fields

CSKA

Stadion Balgarska Armia, Bulevard Dragan Tzankov 3
Capacity 30,000 (all-seated)
Colours All red with white trim
League champions 1948, 1951–52, 1954–62, 1966, 1969, 1971–73, 1975–76, 1980–83, 1987, 1989–90, 1992, 1997
Cup winners 1981, 1983, 1985, 1987–89, 1993, 1997, 1999

The most titled team in Bulgarian football history are not the most popular. Nicknamed the *Chorberi* ('soup-eaters') by fans of rivals Levski, CSKA were formed during post-war Communist restructuring as the sports club of the Bulgarian army. The authorities were keen that the club should have the country's best players and facilities, and the team duly won the league on a play-off basis in their first season and, as CDNA, went on to win a remarkable 12 titles in 13 years between 1951 and 1962. Forwards Dimitar Milanov and Ivan Kolev were the big names of the Fifties, Petar Jekov and Dimitar Yakimov those of later years. In 1957 the club had their own ground built next to the Vasil Levski stadium, and in 1964 they became CSKA.

The name change heralded the end of the club's all-powerful position, but a more challenging domestic scene made CSKA more competitive in Europe. Three times CSKA knocked the holders out of the European Cup – Ajax in 1973, Liverpool in 1980 and Nottingham Forest in 1982. They reached a semi-final of the European Cup (against Inter) in 1967, and of the Cup-Winners' Cup (against Barcelona) in 1989.

In Sofia the club remained unpopular, but out in the provinces, a generation of fans was raised on these televised European games. When these new fans came up to the capital, they were invariably faced with a blue wall of Levski support, and the Seventies and Eighties were marked by some serious face-offs on derby day.

Some players thrived on the tension. Hristo Stoichkov was in the thick of the 1985 cup final brawl, which resulted in the club being forced to play under the name of Sredets until 1990. By then Stoichkov had left for Barcelona – for his last match he came out wearing a #4 shirt in recognition of the four goals he had scored against Levski the week before.

Bulgaria's Communists lost power in 1991, and the withdrawal of army influence made the mid-Nineties fallow years for CSKA. In 1997 the team's attachment to *Multigroup*, a vast private enterprise created from the ashes of former sports concerns, won them back some of their political favour. Former Levski boss Georgi

Vasilev coached them to a league and cup double in 1997, but key players then left after *Multigroup* slashed the club's budgets.

The spring of 1998 saw the return of Stoichkov, Trifon Ivanov and Emil Kostadinov, gathering to train for their last World Cup, but a battle of egos between Ivanov and Stoichkov saw the latter off to play for appearance money at Al-Nasr of Saudi Arabia, and then for a real wage at Kashima Antlers of Japan – after ducking out of a 5–0 pasting by Levski in the 1998 cup final.

After that, Bulgaria's 1994 World Cup coach Dimitar Penev took over the reins, leading an inexperienced bunch known as 'The Young Circus' and containing star attacking midfielder Milen Petkov past Servette in the UEFA Cup – much to the delight of the faithful who'd toiled so hard to make the stadium ready in time. A fifth-place finish in the league in 1999 was disappointing, but compensated by victory in the cup final, where Valentin Stanchev's late goal beat champions Lovech and returned CSKA to Europe for 1999/2000.

With another respected former player, Lubo Penev, coming home to become club president, the mood going into the millennium was unexpectedly upbeat. It didn't last. Three months into the new year, the club was unable to pay win bonuses to players following a derby win over Levski, and Dimitar Penev quit. His replacement, Spas Dzhevisov, nursed the team into a runners-up spot in the league, ten points adrift of champions Levski, but was no more than a frustrated spectator when, during the summer, his most precious young talent, striker Dimitar Berbatov, was sold to Leverkusen.

Here we go!

The Balgarska Armia stadium is 500 metres from the Vasil Levski in **Borisova Gradina**, formerly the Park na Svobodata. The same transport information applies – see p.58.

Just the ticket

The **ticket windows** are to the left of the main entrance. The only covered stand is *sektor A*, where league tickets are around 5 leva. Tickets in *sektor V* opposite go for 4 leva, those in *sektor B* and *G*, behind the goals with the CSKA lads, for 3 leva.

Swift half

Halfway up the path from the entrance on the right-hand side is a pleasant, nameless wooden hut with a bar and terrace. You'll find the more prosaic ***Bistro Park*** drinks stand to the left of the main entrance.

In the net

An excellent **unofficial website**, *True Reds*, hit the web in the summer of 1998 and includes a vast amount of content in English, including match reports, stats and links to other Bulgarian football sites, all properly updated. It's at: come.to/CSKA. If this proves elusive, try Daniel Belovarsky's site at: cska.belloweb.com/.

 Levski

Office: Georgi Asparoukhov stadium Ulitsa Todorini Kukli 47
Vasil Levski stadium see panel p.58
Colours All blue with yellow trim
League champions 1933, 1937, 1942, 1946–47, 1949–50, 1953, 1965, 1968, 1970, 1974, 1977, 1979, 1984–85, 1988, 1993–95, 2000
Cup winners 1942, 1982, 1984, 1986, 1991–92, 1994, 1998, 2000

Levski, formed by a group of young enthusiasts in 1914, have always been the team of the people. The problem is that most of their achievements are historical.

Levski's best side is often said to be the one which won four titles immediately after World War II, playing on the site of what is now the Vasil Levski stadium. Aware of Levski's popularity, the Communist authorities attached the club to the Interior Ministry in an attempt to identify the team with government – then made the mistake of changing the club's name to Dynamo Levski. Meanwhile, the favours granted to army club CSKA further angered Levski's support, and set up the Bulgar game's fiercest inter-club rivalry.

After a decade of CSKA domination, and with their old name back, Levski picked up again in the Sixties. They had a new stadium, the Gerena, later to be renamed after the hero of the day, centre-forward Georgi Asparoukhov. His goals helped Levski to three titles between 1965 and 1970, the last after the club's amalgamation with Spartak Sofia. As 'Levski-Spartak' the club enjoyed a halcyon period in the mid- to late-Seventies, after Asparoukhov's death, winning three domestic championships and knocking Ajax out of the UEFA Cup.

Derby games with CSKA became more and more tense – Levski's punishment for their part in the 1985 cup final furore was to be disbanded and reconstituted as Vitosha. After the slow disintegration of Communism, however, the team won their old name back and suddenly appeared well-placed to take advantage of the new market economy, breaking away from the Interior Ministry and attracting the cream of the new local sponsors.

With a team boasting most of the Bulgarian internationals who had not already left for Western clubs – including Emil Kremenliev, Daniel Borimirov and Petar Houbchev – Levski won three titles by large margins between 1993 and 1995. Increasing support meant that all home league games were now taking place at the Vasil Levski, and in 1993 the team were unlucky not to qualify for the Champions' League after beating Rangers and losing narrowly to Werder Bremen.

Bulgaria's poor UEFA ranking deprived Levski of a place in the same competition for a further two years, and the subsequent loss of income led to a sell-off of key players, including all the aforementioned internationals and veteran goalscorer Nasko Sirakov.

The club's Greek-born president, Thomas Laftchis, who'd taken the unprecedented step of offering free entry to home games in the 1997 spring season, became ever more unpopular as 1998 went into 1999. While happy to lavish funds on renovating the Georgi Asparoukhov stadium –

Sofia essentials

Bus #84 runs every 20mins (7am–11pm, tickets 0.25 leva from the kiosk outside and left from the arrivals hall) between Sofia's **airport**, 12km east of town, and central Orlov Most, near the Vasil Levski stadium. A taxi might cost $20 but bargain with the driver first.

Sofia **city transport** consists primarily of buses (5am–midnight), trolleybuses and trams (both 5am–1am). Kiosks sell single tickets (0.30 leva, punch onboard), day tickets (1.50 leva) and five-day passes (6.50 leva) valid from the day of purchase. The city's single-line **metro** between Bul Slivnitsa and Bul Konstantin Velichkov is scheduled to reach central Pl Sveta Nedelya by autumn 2000.

Flagging **taxis** down in town is easy, but be sure to establish the fare to your destination before you move off. To call a cab, dial *Okay* on ☎02/2121 or *Inex* on ☎02/91919 – fares should be under 0.4 leva per km, slightly more after 10pm.

Sofia's main **train station** is the Tsentralna Gara, just north of the centre of town by trams #1, #7 or #15. Buying a train ticket is slightly complicated. Windows 1–8, upstairs at street level, are for destinations in the northern half of the country, while downstairs is for southern cities. Also downstairs is the *Rila* office, where you can make (compulsory) advance bookings for **international journeys** – bring your passport. Dozens of inter-city **bus services** use the car park behind the *Novotel Europa* hotel facing the station. The hotel lobby has secure left-luggage facilities.

The main **tourist office**, *Balkantourist* at Bulevard Vitosha 1 (Mon–Fri 8am–3pm, Sat 8.30am–1.30pm, ☎02/433 331, fax 02/946 1261), deals mainly with upmarket hotels and tours. *Balkan Tour*, at Bul Stamboliiski 27 and 37 (daily 9am–7pm, ☎02/880 655, fax 02/880 795) can book budget accommodation and private rooms.

The English-language weekly *Sofia Echo* (1.5 leva) offers cinema **listings** but not a lot else.

including an expensive new pitch – he declared himself unable to buy any new players, before hiring the costly and snooty Ukrainian coach, Vyacheslav Grozny.

As so often in the past, Levski were saved by good attacking football, with Georgi Ivanov, Doncho Donev and Nikolai Todorov starring in a 5–0 cup final win over CSKA in 1998, and taking the club to within two points of wresting the title from Lovech the following year.

With the squad staying together and fans rallying round to raise the cash needed to make the Georgi Asparoukhov ready for 1999/2000, the club continued to have spirit on its side, if not much else. But before the season began, the club signed a lucrative sponsorship deal with mobile phone company *MobiTel*. Now, not only did they have a renovated stadium and a decent squad, they could afford an impressive new coach, too – Ljupko Petrović. The former

Red Star Belgrade boss had manoeuvred the team into a potentially title-winning position before quitting Levski to take up a lucrative post in China at the turn of the year. His replacement, former national coach Dimitar Dimitrov, had already enjoyed success with provincial sides Neftokhimik Burgas and Lovech, but had supported Levski as a boy. He inherited a confident side in which young playmaker Alexander Alexandrov was outstanding; not only were Levski too good for the rest of the league, they claimed the double with a 2–0 cup final win over Burgas, too.

Here we go!

The Georgi Asparoukhov stadium is next to **Istok bus station**, accessible via Vladimir Vazov (bus #78 or #120 or trolleybus #1 or #9), or via Todorini Kukli (bus #120). For the Vasil Levski stadium, where Levski still play bigger home games, see panel p.58.

The Vasil Levski stadium

Bulevard Evlogi Georgiev 38
Capacity 70,000 (all-seated)

Bulgaria's **national stadium** was built on the site of a much more modest pitch where Levski played until just after World War II. Although renovations are still not complete, the stadium is once more the stage for cup finals, internationals and Levski Sofia's major home games, such as the derby with CSKA.

Named after a 19th century national hero, the Vasil Levski has an ornate entrance which gives out onto a large bowl of a stadium. Apart from a single roof covering the directors' seats, the ground is **open to the elements** – pleasant on a summer evening, bitter in February.

The **view is excellent**, if a little distant from the action across the running track. For club matches the atmosphere is a little one-sided, except for local derbies with CSKA, whose supporters have a reputation for scuttling home quickly from the north end after the final whistle.

The stadium is by Bul Balgaria on the city side of **Borisova Gradina**, formerly the Park na Svobodata. This is a pleasant 15min walk south-east from the city centre, but you could take tram #2, #12, #14 or #19 down Graf Ignatiev to the inner ring road. Bus #84 from the airport stops at Orlov Most on the other corner of the park.

The Vasil Levski is blessed with the city's main **football bar/shop**, the nameless café to the left of the main entrance. Run by *Futbol* editor Karmen Totev, it acts as a meeting point for the football community. If your Spanish, Bulgarian or chess is up to it, you could pass a convivial afternoon talking football with Karmen while players, referees and journalists based in Sofia or passing through town drop by. There's also a selection of **Bulgarian football gear** on sale.

The **ticket office** is also by the main entrance. At Sofia derbies, a ticket in sector B (south side) will put you with the Levski fans, sector G (north side) with CSKA. Sectors A and V are mixed and, depending on the amount of visiting support, reserved for away fans at internationals.

Just the ticket

Like many Bulgarian stadia of its size, the Georgi Asparoukhov is divided into four sectors – A, B, V, G. The main stand is designated as *sektor A* (tickets 4 leva). Many Levski fans congregate here, but the younger hardcore element will be behind the goal in *sektor B* (1 lev). Whatever away support there tends to have its own section at the far end of *sektor A*. The uncovered stand *sektor V* (3 leva) also houses the press and officials.

Swift half

The *Siniya Bar* – or *Blue Bar* – a 5min walk up from the Vasil Levski stadium, is still the main Levski hangout. A small terrace bar just in from the pavement on the corner of Dragan Tsankov and Yevlogi Georgiev, it's an unlikely venue for fans of the country's most popular club to meet

at. At the Georgi Asparoukhov you'll find the *Bivaria Sinyata Lavina*, a bar and restaurant dotted with trophies, next to the Vladimir Vazov stadium entrance. On the other side, through the main entrance on Torodini Kukli, is the *Café Siniyat Klub*.

In print

Levski have two official monthly publications: their eponymous newspaper (monthly, 0.50 leva), with large photo features on star players and classic matches of old; and the more fan-oriented *Siniye Vechna* (3 leva).

In the net

One of the better Levski **unofficial websites** is run from Norway at: www.geocities.com/ Colosseum/Loge/4142.

Groundhopping

Postwar amalgamations have taken their toll on Sofia's minor clubs, but two remain to give the visitor a chance of viewing first-division football away from the big, windswept bowls of CSKA and Levski.

Slavia

Slavia stadium, Ulitsa Koloman 1
Capacity 32,000
Colours All white with black trim
League champions 1928, 1930, 1936, 1939, 1941, 1943, 1996
Cup winners 1996

Slavia are the oldest Bulgarian club still in existence. Founded in 1913 and built with money from the city's new rich, they are nicknamed the Royals because of their early connections.

With a fan base in the west of town, around Ovcha Kupel, Slavia were Sofia's leading club side before the Communist reorganisation of sport that followed World War II. At that point Slavia became Strojtel, the team of the construction union, then Udarnik, before reverting to their original name in 1958.

Throughout this period they were regular top-three finishers but rarely challenged the hegemony of CSKA and Levski. Their only major European run was to the semi-finals of the 1967 Cup-Winners' Cup, where they were beaten by Rangers.

In 1995, the arrival of veteran goalscorer Nasko Sirakov, from Levski via Botev Plovdiv, helped the Royals to their first league championship in more than 50 years. They won the cup that season, too, in bizarre fashion. Slavia were a goal up against Levski with 14 minutes left to play in the final, when Levski president Thomas Slavchis summoned his team from the pitch. They did not return (Slavchis claimed his gesture was meant as a stand against corruption) and Slavia were awarded the match 4–0. The club's 1996 UEFA Cup appearance was brief, and sixth place in the league was as good as the team could manage in 1999/2000.

Alphabet Street – you'll need a crash course in Cyrillic script to work out the latest score here

To get to Slavia take tram #4 or #11 down **Ovcha Kupel** or tram #5 or #19 down Tsar Boris III. Just before the two roads meet, on the site of the Ovcha Kupel marketplace, is the stadium. Between the market and the ground you'll find the **Mekhana Chevermeto** – a typical Bulgarian restaurant offering classic domestic dishes by an open log fire. Next to the main entrance to the stadium's grand two-tier stand is a clean, nameless bar/shop which, along with beer and snacks on matchdays, sells Slavia replica shirts.

🌀 Lokomotiv

Lokomotiv stadium, Bul Rozhen 23
Capacity 25,000
Colours Red-and-black striped shirts, white shorts
League champions 1940, 1945, 1964, 1978

Very much Sofia's fourth club, Lokomotiv actually went out of existence for two seasons while they were merged with Slavia in 1969. The Railwaymen, with international Atanas Mihailov scoring the goals, bounced back with a league title in 1978 and a UEFA Cup run two years later, in which they beat Ferencváros, Monaco and Dynamo Kiev before losing in the quarter-finals to VfB Stuttgart.

Their stadium, with two stands but no floodlights, was rebuilt soon afterwards but has seen little European action since. A fourth-place league finish in 1999, ahead of CSKA, wasn't at all bad, but the following season saw a brief flirtation with relegation before the team consolidated in mid-table. They finished eighth.

The ground is an open bowl up Rozhen, north from the centre. The #11 and #12 trams make a slight turn just before the stadium up Ilyansko Shose, parallel to Rozhen. At the main entrance you'll find the ticket hatch for away fans (5 leva), as well as the new **Chervenoi Cherno** (red-and-black) café. Around the other side of the ground is an area of ramshackle ter-

race bars, some with Lokomotiv line-ups pasted up to hide the cracks in the walls. You'll also find some more ticket huts and a Lokomotiv souvenir kiosk. Football watchers tend to occupy this side of the ground, with hardcore fans of each side (including Lokomotiv's 'Miracle Express' group) frequenting the main stand on Rozhen.

Eat, drink, sleep...

Bars and clubs

Bulgarians are great drinkers of **wine**, even cheaper here than it is in your local Tesco. *Melnik* and *Gamza* are reliable reds (*cherveno vino*), *Misket* and *Euxinovgrad* tasty whites (*byalo vino*). A local beer (*bira*), *Zagorka* or the sweeter *Astika*, will cost around 1–2 leva everywhere, except in flashier discos and hotel bars, which stay open late.

The stabilisation of the Bulgarian economy is best reflected in the range of new bars in the capital, many of them concentrated in a small area of streets between Borisova Gradina (by the Vasil Levski stadium) and the national theatre, particularly on Tsar Shishman.

Biblioteka Klub, St Cyril & Metodius Library, entrance in Oborishte, just off Bul Vasil Levski. Nightclub under Bulgaria's biggest library, with mainstream music and videos. Entrance 3 leva including a beer. Occasional live music, packed at weekends.

Bilkova Apteka, Tsar Shishman 22. Look out for the Astika and Lucky Strike signs just off Gen Gurko, across the park from the Vasil Levski stadium. A buzzing, smoky cellar with decent music and a young crowd, and welcome relief from the false chintz of the nearby *Rock Café* and *Art Club*.

J J Murphy & Co, Ul Karnigradska 6. Large, popular Irish pub just off Vitosha, with a full menu and large screen – but no Sky TV. Diagonally opposite is a nameless local bar for young hipsters, offering drinks at half the price.

Swinging Hall, Dragan Tsankov 8. Probably the best live music venue in town, popular with expats. Large bar, pool room at the back, jazz souvenirs on the walls. Your 3 leva admission includes a beer. Short walk from the Vasil Levski stadium. Tram #2 or #19.

Yalta, corner Tsar Osvoboditel/Bul Vasil Levski. Two-floor blue-lit disco whose name is announced in bright red neon and celebrated with a dominating picture of Churchill, Roosevelt and Stalin. Mainstream dance music, 2–3 leva cover charge Fri–Sat, free Thur.

Restaurants

Bulgarian **cuisine** is heavily reliant on grilled skewered meats (*kebapcheta*) and pork (*svinsko*). Meat stews slowly cooked with vegetables (*gyuvech* or *kavarma*) can be an interesting alternative. Salads are generally simple, fresh and tasty. A **main course** in a traditional taverna (*mekhana*) should be no more than 7 leva. Note that none of the restaurants listed below takes credit cards.

Borsalino, Pl Varazhdane, Ul Chervena Stena 10 (behind the *Orbita* hotel). Excellent 24-hour diner a 4-leva taxi journey from the city centre, offering large portions of local dishes at 6–8 leva. Tables outside in summer.

Eddy's Tex-Mex Diner, Bul Vitosha 4. Steakhouse pub and Mexican joint for expats (open daily midday–midnight), but not overpriced. Useful for picking up English-language info if you've only stepped in for a beer. Noisy even before the live band after nine.

Maistora, Hristo Belchev 9. One block over from Bul Vitosha, a friendly two-floor restaurant offering main courses at 6–8 leva chosen from an English-language menu, Stella Artois at 2 leva, a good selection of salads and a disco downstairs.

Ramayana, Hristo Belchev 32. A short walk from the NDK Palace of Culture, Sofia's first Indian restaurant (daily 11am–3pm & 6–11pm) offers authentic main courses at under 10 leva

from an English-language menu. Popular, so reservations recommended on ☎02/980 4311.

World Sports Café, Angel Kanchev 1. Spanking new downtown sports bar/restaurant, with a mix of Bulgarian and international dishes – many with daft themed names like Romário seafood – a range of satellite TV options, and all kinds of photos and paraphernalia. Separate bar and billiards room.

Accommodation

For decades Bulgarian hotels were filled by pre-booked package tours and prices are still not geared to the independent traveller. The local **star-rating system** is hopelessly optimistic and you won't find many comfortable budget hotels in town.

Most tourist accommodation is at the foot of Mount Vitosha, in villages like Dragalevtsi (tram #12 to terminus then bus #64) or Simeonovo (tram #12 then bus #98). Allow 40mins for either journey, rather less if travelling by taxi.

The best urban alternative is **private accommodation**, which can be arranged at *Balkantourist*, Bulevard Stamboliiksi 27, or at bureaux in the airport arrivals lobby and the upper level of the main station. Cheaper hotels will accept local currency but are happier to see dollars or DMs. Few accept credit cards.

Hotel Baldzhieva, Tsar Asen 23 (☎02/872 914, fax 02/981 1257). Bright, privately owned hotel off Bul Vitosha with four rooms, all with a fridge and shower. About $40 a single, $65 a double.

Hotel Niky, Neofit Rilski 16 (☎02/511 915, fax 02/516 091). Just off Bul Vitosha, a privately run place with its own café/restaurant attached. Small rooms, all with a TV and shower. About $25 a single, $40 a double. Take tram #12 from the station.

Orbita, Bul James Bauchar (☎02/639 3444). Towards Mount Vitosha via tram #9 from town, this is a post-war block with clean rooms at $30/$40 a single/double.

Slavianksa Beseda, Ulitsa Slavianska 1 (☎02/880 441). Privatised but nevertheless gloomy hotel in the centre of town. Still, it's clean and all rooms have a bath. About $40 a single, $65 a double. No credit cards. Tram #12 from the station.

Tsar Asen, Ul Tsar Asen 68 (☎02/547 801, e-mail elena@mbox.infotel.bg). Ideal choice for the budget traveller, a first-floor family-run pension in a quiet area near the NDK Palace of Culture. About $28 a single in a double room, $34 for two, $45 for three. TV and shower/toilet in every room. Ring at the garden gate and walk round to the back door. Advance booking essential.

Croatia

Croatian Football Federation, Ilica 31, HR-10000, Zagreb
☎01/455 4100   Fax 01/424 639   E-mail hns-cff@zg.tel.hr

League champions Dinamo Zagreb   **Cup winners** Hajduk Split   **Promoted** Cakovec,
Marsonia Slavonski Brod   **Relegated** Vukovar '91, Istra Pula

European participants 2000/01 Dinamo Zagreb, Hajduk Split (UCL qualifiers);
HNK Rijeka (UEFA Cup); Cibalia Vinkovci, Slaven Belupo Koprivnica (Intertoto Cup)

Beginning of the end – defeat by Ireland, 1998

Croatia may have been the surprise package of the 1998 World Cup but, with hindsight, their run to the semi-finals now looks like the swansong of the country's 'Golden Generation' rather than the launching pad for great things. The likes of Zvone Boban, Robert Prosinečki, Robert Jarni, Igor Štimac and Davor Šuker strained every sinew to earn Croatia the bronze medal, but the instinctive understanding which underpinned their football came as a result of their having been together since winning the World Youth Cup in Yugoslav shirts back in 1987. There is just no disguising their age – France '98 was their first World Cup, and it will be their last.

All of them had long ago left the Croatian domestic game (Prosinečki alone has returned) but, much more seriously, they have since been followed by hundreds of younger players. Those who remain cannot hope to lift the Croatian league above its mediocrity – not with political interference, rumours of corruption and a messy, post-civil war, post-Communist economy to contend with.

Even the national squad's preparations for the 1998 World Cup were far from ideal. Having flattered to deceive at Euro '96, the Croats had a lot of hype to live up to on the road to France. Yet they allowed Denmark to win their qualifying group, and needed a narrow two-leg victory over Ukraine – aided by a linesman's flag that ruled out an early opposition goal in Kiev – to book their ticket.

Once there, however, Croatia started boldly, an attacking midfield of Boban in the holding position and Prosinečki as the playmaker working brilliantly in their opening 3–1 win over Jamaica. Against a quicker Japan the system was less successful, but Croatia were into the knockout stage with a 1–0 win – after which, ironically, a defeat by Argentina in the last group game gave them the softer option of Romania in the second round. There Boban played a real captain's role, and Croatia could have won by more than Šuker's twice-taken penalty.

The goal set up a quarter-final appointment with Germany, and by now Croatia, eager to avenge their defeat by the same opponents at the same stage of Euro '96, were on a roll. Coach Čiro Blažević took to wearing a lucky French policeman's *képi*, and the team, loudly encouraged by fans who had come over to France, were equally well aware of the massive support at home. While the dismissal of Christian Wörns on 40 minutes undeniably influenced the outcome of that quarter-final, the Germans were already struggling to contain their opponents' quick counterattacking. Once Jarni had put the Croats ahead just on half-time, there was only going to be one winner.

Boban was sadly off the pace in the semi-final with France and it was down to Aljoša Asanović to set up the first goal, for Šuker, just after half-time. Boban then lost the ball to let Thuram through to equalise, and went off injured soon after. Four minutes later, Thuram got a second, and though Slaven Bilić then got Laurent Blanc sent off, Croatia could not break down a ten-man France.

Šuker claimed his sixth, Golden Boot-winning tournament goal, and Croatia their third place, with a 2–1 win over Holland. The team – and the much-criticised Blažević – returned home as national heroes. And the whole world suddenly knew where Croatia was, even if so many of the country's young footballers had already left it.

In truth, Croatia, like the other former Yugoslav republics, has always exported its best talents, both players and coaches. Four key Croat members of the Yugoslav side which entertainingly featured in the three World Cups of the Fifties – Bernard Vukas, Vladimir Beara, Zlatko Čajkovski and Branko Zebec – all played abroad. Josip Skoblar won the Golden Boot with Mar-

seille in 1971, while the Vujović twins, Zlatko and Zoran, were part of the great Bordeaux side of the Eighties. In the dugout, Čajkovski and Zebec both had spells in charge of Bayern Munich in the late Sixties. Tomislav Ivić coached Ajax, Porto and Fenerbahçe. Otto Barić transformed Salzburg in the Nineties. Čiro Blažević earned so much money from his successes in Switzerland, he could go home and *buy* Croatia Zagreb, leading club in the new country's capital city. Before they could get the chance to impress would-be foreign buyers, however, Croat players had to do battle in a Yugoslav league in which the odds were always stacked – by fair means or foul – in favour of Belgrade. Croat teams had held the upper hand before World War II, Zagreb's Gradjanski winning the first and last pre-Tito Yugoslav titles in 1923 and 1940. Split provided 12 of the 24-man squad which took Yugoslavia to the 1930 World Cup semi-finals.

Yet once power shifted to Belgrade in Yugoslavia's postwar, centralised economy, Croatian teams had to make do with little victories, the biggest being Dinamo Zagreb's Fairs' Cup win of 1967 – the only European trophy for a Yugoslav club during the Tito era.

Croatia had four regular representatives in the old Yugoslav first division – Dinamo, Hajduk, Rijeka and Osijek. In the absence of a national team, Dinamo became the symbol for Croatians to rally round, and their title win of 1982 made a local hero of coach Blažević.

When Croatia became independent, these nationalist feelings were duly exploited by state president Franjo Tudjman, a lifelong football fan and former chairman of Partizan Belgrade. A league was quickly set up, chickens were cleared from some of the smaller pitches, and 'Croatia' Zagreb were assured as much favour as politically possible.

That favour continued to be felt, seven years on. An unlikely ending to the 1998/99 domestic season, which saw league leaders Rijeka held to a draw after having a

Basics

EU citizens, Americans, Canadians, Australians and New Zealanders need only a **valid passport** to enter Croatia. Keep your passport on you at all times as the local police often make random checks.

The Croatian currency is the **kuna** (kn), divided into 100 lipa. There are notes for 5, 10, 20, 50, 100, 200, 500 and 1,000 kuna and coins for 1 and 5 kuna, 1, 2, 5, 10, 20 and 50 lipa. There are about 11kn to £1. Banks are generally open Mon–Fri 8am–6pm, often with a two-hour break around noon, and 8am–midday on Saturdays. Credit-card payment is widespread in the main towns. For cash advances, most machines take *Mastercard*, while *Splitska Banka*'s take *Visa*. Many services, such as hotels, calculate payment in **Deutschmarks**, which will always be gratefully accepted as payment.

Phone cards (*telefonske kartice*) are available at newsstands (marked *Vjesnik* or *Tisak*) or post offices, marked *HPT*. The cards come in 25-unit (10kn), 50-unit (20kn) and 100-unit (32kn) varieties. To dial abroad from Croatia hit 00, followed by your country code. There are no cheap international rates. **Post offices** have booths (*kabina*) for international calls – pay for the amount used as you leave.

From outside the country, the **code for Croatia** is 385, followed by 1 for Zagreb or 21 for Split. To call within Croatia, simply add a 0 to the city code in the normal fashion. For local calls, use 1 kuna pieces in payphones. The Croatian telephone service was in the process of changing many phone numbers as this book went to press – if any number given here has changed, you will hear a message giving the new number in English and Croatian.

Buses are the best way to get around the country – efficient and comfortable, with journeys costing around 4kn per kilometre. **Trains** are slower and less frequent, but cheaper. There are three trains a day between Zagreb and Split, the journey taking nine hours and costing around 130kn. Police patrol the corridors of the night service, so safety is assured.

Croatia suffers a general lack of reasonably priced **accommodation**. One way round this is to arrange a **private room** with a family, which should cost no more than 100–150kn per person per night. Bargain for a discount if you're staying for more than three nights or paying in Deutschmarks.

The war savaged Croatia's once-thriving **restaurant trade**, and eating out is considered a luxury. A decent spread of delicious Croatian specialities (especially fish and seafood) will set you back at least 100kn. One exception to this is the commonplace pizzeria, where an excellent home-baked pizza and a beer can often be had for 40–50kn. Takeaway snacks like *burek* (thick pastry with cheese or meat) make for an alternative cheap filler, available from street stalls or holes in the wall.

Draught **beer** (*pivo*), either light (*svijetlo*) or dark (*tamno*), is around 10–15kn a half-litre. *Ožujsko* and *Karlovačko* are the acceptable local brews, but Slovenian *Union* is better. Local red or white **wine** (*crno* or *bijelo vino*) is excellent and cheap.

last-minute goal disallowed for offside while Croatia Zagreb were easily beating Varteks, gave the conspiracy theorists plenty more food for thought, and the culture of political bias drew criticism from sources as diverse as the magazine *Nacional* and the coach of Hajduk Split, Ivan Katalinić. Meanwhile, Čiro Blažević threatened to quit the country (and by extension, the national manager's job) if his mate Franjo Tudjman was voted out of office – a classic case of political blackmail being foisted on the ordinary football-loving fan.

Blažević's tired refrain that his team were the third best in the world was brutally exposed in the Euro 2000 qualifiers. Croatia were still in with a chance of a place in the play-offs as they went into their final game against Yugoslavia (of all teams) – a match which the coach typically claimed would be the 'game of the century'. But despite enjoying vociferous home support and the benefit of an extra man for the bulk of the game, Croatia could manage only a 2–2 draw in Zagreb. Ireland took the play-off spot, while Belgrade celebrated automatic qualification. Boban, who had missed that match through injury, announced his retirement from the international game, and with Bilić's career cut short by injury, the old guard began to break up.

The death of Tudjman in early 2000 and subsequent change of government have left Croatian football uncertain of its future. The communist-style subsidies that the former president ensured for the game are a thing of the past, while the corruption that had riddled the game since independence is slowly being uncovered. Painful as it may be for Croatians to come to terms with, the 'Golden Generation' were the last fruits of the former united Yugoslavia. Only now will football start to see what Croatia is capable of on its own.

Essential vocabulary

Hello *Bok!*
Goodbye *Do vidjenja*
Yes *Da*
No *Ne*
Two beers, please *Dva piva, molim*
Thank you *Hvala*
Men's *Muški*
Women's *Ženski*
Where is the stadium? *Gdje je stadion?*
What's the score? *Koji je rezultat?*
Referee *Sudac*
Offside *Ofsajd*

Match practice

With the exception of clashes between Hajduk, Croatia Zagreb, Rijeka and Osijek, Croatian league football is low-key. There are no real derbies – younger fans have no sense of what it's like to hate Red Star Belgrade and be able to express that sentiment across a stadium at fever pitch.

The season runs from August to mid-December, then again from March until early June. Sunday is the traditional match-day, although it is not unheard of for league rounds to be played on Saturdays. Not all grounds have floodlights, so games kick off at 5pm in August, then half-an-hour earlier each month until December, when kick-off can be as early as 1pm. This trend is reversed through the spring.

A different league

League structure is always a thorny question in Croatia. The current first division, *Prva A HNL*, has 12 clubs, who in 1998/99 were split into championship and relegation groups after March, but who for 1999/2000 reverted to a simpler format, with teams playing each other three times in the course of the season. The bottom two are relegated to the *1.B liga*, the 18-team, semi-professional second division.

Below the *1.B liga* is the *2HNL*, divided into five zones – *središte* (central), *sjever* (north), *istok* (east), *jug* (south) and *zapad* (west). The winners of each play-off in May for the two places available on the rung immediately above.

Up for the cup

The Croatian FA Cup (*Hrvatski Nogometni Kup*) begins in August with 32 second- and third-division clubs playing a two-legged qualifying round for the 16 berths in the first round proper, which sees the arrival of the first-division clubs.

All rounds are then two-legged, with away goals counting double if necessary, until the final in May. If this involves two provincial clubs, then there is a single game at Zagreb's Maksimir stadium. If one team is from Zagreb, as it was in 1999/2000, then the final is played over two legs.

Just the ticket

Head straight for the ticket office (*blagajna*), where prices are usually displayed prominently. The stand (*tribina*) will generally be described by its geographical location – *zapad* (west), *istok* (east), *jug* (south) or *sjever* (north). Standing room is denoted as *stajanje*, a seat as *sjedenje*. A reasonable seat for an average league game should cost no more than 20–30kn, the best in the house about 50kn. For big games, prices tend to be raised about 20%.

There are no programmes, but bigger clubs publish their own monthly magazines.

Half-time

Beer (*pivo*) and *čevapi*, thick grilled meat stuffed into bread, are the order of the day – 25kn will cover both. Before and during the game, vendors pass among the crowd with baskets of pistachios, roasted peanuts, pumpkin seeds and popcorn.

Action replay

State channels HRT1 and 2 hardly touch sport, leaving domestic football to HRT3. Their coverage includes a Sunday afternoon sport show, *Sport Nedjeljom*, which may contain a live league match, or perhaps half of one. This is followed by a highlights show, *Top Sport*, at 10pm. The channel's most popular programme is *Petica* (Mondays, 9pm), which features highlights from around Europe. HRT3 also shows a live English Premiership match on Saturdays at 4pm, a live Spanish game at 8.30pm the same day, and the repeat of an Italian one around 11pm on a Sunday. HRT2 shows Croatia's internationals live.

The back page

Croatia's long-established sports daily, *Sportske Novosti* (5kn), suffered a blow when its respected editor, Darko Tironi, died of a heart attack while attending the Manchester United–Croatia Zagreb Champions' League game in 1999. His passion for completeness is most obviously sustained in the paper's weekend edition, which carries comprehensive match times and line-ups. The paper also issues a fortnightly colour magazine, *Super Sport* (15kn).

Ultra culture

The ultras situation in Croatia is always a political one. For years, Dinamo Zagreb's Bad Blue Boys were locked in battle with the authorities, trying to get their club's name changed from Croatia Zagreb. Now that they have their way, there is still trouble. There were dozens of arrests at both legs of Dinamo's 2000 cup final with Hajduk Split, whose fans used the occasion to demonstrate their anger at the general political influence against their club, and the social situation in Split as a whole.

All of which is a shame, given that Croatia once had one of the most colourful and inventive fan cultures in Europe – nurtured decades ago by Hajduk Split fans copying South American styles, then seized upon by the Italians before a more sophisticated version could be sold back to Yugoslav fans in the Eighties. Matches between Dinamo, Hajduk, and Belgrade's Red Star and Partizan saw ferocious levels of support, until the infamous Dinamo–Red Star clash of May 1990 – a prelude to the war which would split Yugoslavia apart.

Now in independent Croatia, support is often more a case of getting one back on the capital city, Zagreb – as members of Rijeka's *Armada* and Osijek's *Kohorta* could happily testify.

In the net

The Croatian FA has an efficiently maintained website at: www.hns-cff.hr. For a better insight into local club football, however, the English-language *HR Sport* is a better bet at: sport.iskon.hr/en/soccer/index.html. If your Croatian is up to it, there are two further sites with superb news, stats and links – *Nogomet.com* at www.nogomet.com; and *Nogomet Webtree* at: www.webtree.net/cronogomet. For archived stats, try: www.fyusoccer.com.

Zagreb

Zagreb was one of the former Yugoslavia's three main footballing centres and regularly played host to key internationals, including two games in the European Championship finals of 1976. A city of a million people, its modern footballing reputation has been built on the back of one team, Dinamo, themselves constructed from the ruins of the two leading prewar clubs, and until recently playing under the name 'Croatia'.

Zagreb's first club was HAŠK, formed by students and intellectuals in 1903. The city's *Sokol* movement – popular in countries under the Habsburg yoke and dedicated to uplifting the national spirit – helped found smaller clubs soon afterwards. In 1912 Zagreb became home of the football branch of the newly formed Croatian athletics federation. The three main clubs of the day, HAŠK, Gradjanski and Concordia Zagreb, played friendlies in Maksimir park, then took eight of the 17 Yugoslav league titles between the wars, Gradjanski winning five. While most of the Yugoslav national team were provided by Split, inner-city rivalry kept interest in football high, and the *Zagreb* café on Zrinjevec

became a vibrant meeting place for fans and players alike.

With World War II came a brief period of Croatian 'independence' under a Nazi puppet regime. Three national titles were competed for, and Gradjanski won two of them, before merging with HAŠK to form Dinamo under the Communists in 1945.

Although Communist Yugoslavia's President Tito was said to be a Dinamo fan, the balance of power was definitely in Belgrade's favour for most of the postwar era. Such was the importance of Dinamo to the Croatian people, under what they saw as Serb domination, that few other clubs could gather support in the city.

Today, little has changed in this respect. But plenty else has. Croatia's former President Tudjman, having seen the Stade de France in Paris, decreed that his country should have a national stadium of its own, and that it should be based on Croatia Zagreb's home of the Maksimir. But Tudjman did not live to see his dream of turning the city into a major European football capital become reality, and without him, the local game will have to stand on its own two feet.

In a sentimental mood – memories come flooding back for Ossie Ardiles at Old Trafford, 1999

The thrilling fields

 Dinamo Zagreb

Maksimir stadium, Maksimirska 128
Capacity 57,000 (all-seated)
Colours All blue
League champions (Yugoslavia) 1948, 1954, 1958, 1982
Cup winners (Yugoslavia) 1951, 1960, 1963, 1965, 1969, 1980, 1983
League champions (Croatia) 1993, 1996–2000
Cup winners (Croatia) 1994, 1996–98
Fairs' Cup winners 1967

It's official – Dinamo Zagreb are back. After eight years of in-fighting over the name and identity of the country's top club, the fans were finally given the chance to have their say in early 2000, and it was no surprise when they voted to end the career of 'Croatia Zagreb'. Perhaps appropriately, given the level of emotion the debate aroused, the name change was made official on St Valentine's Day.

For a skilled populist politician such as Franjo Tudjman, riding the wave of nationalist euphoria following the successful war of independence from Yugoslavia, the re-naming of his, the capital's and the country's favourite team was a rare misreading of the popular mood. The supporters never accepted Tudjman's argument that Dinamo was a communist name that had no place in the brave new Croatia. For the fans, in particular the hardcore ultras of the 'Bad Blue Boys', Dinamo was the name that earned Croatian football respect in Europe, even when the republic was part of Yugoslavia. Dinamo was a symbol of Croatian identity, and it was for Dinamo that the fans had fought street battles with the Serbs of Red Star and Partizan Belgrade.

But while the fans celebrated the name change by fighting with police at the stadium in early 2000, the death of Tudjman and the loss of power of his political party were set to have another kind of impact.

Tudjman had bankrolled the club, enabling it to bring back Robert Prosinečki on a *Bundesliga* salary and to keep hold of its best players, in turn allowing the team to dominate the domestic league from 1996. Four years on, the cash dried up and all manner of shady goings-on began to be uncovered. With Dinamo in chaos, Tudjman's chosen lackey at the club, president Zlatko Canjuga, was fired in April and a new board, headed by local entrepeneur Mirko Barisić, was appointed. It was time to get down to business.

There is plenty to build on. Dinamo's early successes – three league titles and one cup in the decade after 1945 – were remarkable considering that the Yugoslav army side, Partizan Belgrade, had taken three key international players, Branko Zebec, Stjepan Bobek and Zlatko Čajkovski. But it was the Sixties, and a series of classic European clashes, that set Dinamo's spacious stadium, the Maksimir, buzzing. A Fairs' Cup run in 1963/64, when the team beat Bayern Munich and Ferencváros before finishing as runners-up to Valencia, was no more than a prelude to eventual triumph in the same tournament in 1967, when a Dinamo team without stars beat Juventus and Eintracht Frankfurt before overcoming a full-strength Leeds United in the final.

The club entered something of a decline in the Seventies, when Hajduk took over the mantle of Croatia's flag-bearers in the Yugoslav league. It took the return of mercurial coach Ćiro Blažević to rejuvenate the club. With the goals of Zlatko Kranjčar and sound defending from Velimir Zajec and goalkeeper Tomislav Ivković, Dinamo won the Yugoslav league by five points in 1982.

The Maksimir underwent major improvements for the hosting of the World Student Games in 1987 and, with stars from Yugoslavia's World Youth Cup triumph of the same year, the stage was set for another Dinamo revival as the Nineties approached. It wasn't to be. Before the shine had worn off the medal he'd won as

Zagreb essentials

Zagreb's **airport** is near the village of Plesso, nearly 20km from town. **Buses** (20kn, half-hourly 6am–9am & midday–8pm, hourly 9am–midday, journey time 30mins) run to the city's main bus station on Držićeva, to the south-east of the centre. The main **train station** is nearer town, a 10min walk straight up Praška as you come out. Tram #6 runs from the bus station to the train station and from there into town.

Central Zagreb is criss-crossed by a comprehensive network of **trams** – buses run between the centre and the suburbs. Transport runs 5am–midnight, and night trams #31–34 run regularly along the lines to and from the main square, Trg Bana Jelačića. Tram tickets cost 4.50kn from a newsstand or the driver. Validate them in the ticket punchers onboard. A single ticket is valid for 90mins, regardless of how many transfers you make. A **day ticket** (*dnevna karta*) costs 12kn and is valid until 4am the next day, no matter when you buy it.

Taxis have a 20kn start-up charge, after which it's 6kn per kilometre, plus a 20% surcharge 10pm–5am and all day Sundays. There'll always be a couple outside the train station, but to call one dial ☎01/970.

The main **tourist information office** is at Trg Bana Jelačića 11 (open Mon–Fri 8.30am–8pm, Sat 10am–6pm, Sun 10am–2pm, ☎01/481 4054, fax 01/481 4056). There you'll find copies of the free monthly brochure, *Zagreb Events and Performances*.

Player of the Tournament in Chile in '87, playmaker Robert Prosinečki was poached by Red Star Belgrade. Davor Šuker's arrival from Osijek served only to unite the provincial town against the capital – within months, he was on his way to Spain.

It was another Osijek goalscorer, Goran Vlaović, who moved to Dinamo and helped them win their first Croatian league title in 1993. In the meantime, Blažević had returned (again) to lead a consortium which bought Dinamo – then called HAŠK-Gradjanski – and, assured by Tudjman of as much state support as necessary, took over coaching duties as well.

The coach reduced his involvement, active and financial, when he took charge of Croatia's national team in early 1994. By then, though, the rift over the club's name was beginning to upset team morale, which in turn allowed Hajduk to steal the domestic limelight, albeit only briefly.

Having won the title in 1996 and then retained it a year later with Otto Barić in charge, Croatia Zagreb set out on the search for European glory. A 5–0 win over Partizan Belgrade in the first qualifying round for the Champions' League in August 1997 was political manna from heaven, but

it was also a fine footballing display that set up an extraordinary tie with Newcastle, which the Croats were unlucky to lose after their ten men had fought back to take a 2–1 lead in the Maksimir.

Barić's replacement, Marijan Vlak, had had enough of all the political interference, and former star Zlatko Kranjćar took over to engineer another title in 1998. With Silvio Marić superb in midfield and partnered by the returning Prosinečki, the club finally earned a coveted Champions' League spot after beating Celtic in the qualifiers. A goalless start to the first half of the campaign was turned around by the firing of Kranjćar and the hiring of Velimir Zajec, who led a revived team to surprise wins over Porto and Ajax. It wasn't quite enough for further progress, though, and key players were allowed to leave during the winter – Marić to Newcastle, Viduka to Celtic and Dario Simić to Inter.

Croatia Zagreb still had the talent – and the influence – to win the league again in 1999, but the club's problems were never better illustrated than in the grand opening of the new north stand at the Maksimir in March 1999. In full view of the country's leading politicians, and against

Hajduk to boot, the match was marked by running battles between police and the Bad Blue Boys, leading to dozens of arrests and the ripping up of hundreds of shiny new blue plastic seats.

In a bid to achieve the much-promised European success before their patron's cancer finally caught up with him, the club turned to Osvaldo Ardiles to mastermind their 1999/2000 UEFA Champions' League campaign. Despite some impressive performances, especially in their two games against holders Manchester United, the team finished bottom of their group in the first phase and missed out on even a UEFA Cup consolation prize.

Ardiles was somewhat harshly sacked, although his reported £300,000-a-year salary was a possible motive, and his cheaper Croatian assistant Vlak was given his old job back. Vlak was a wise choice – popular with the fans and known to be in the 'Dinamo' camp on the name issue, he survived the boardroom battles to lead the club to its fifth consecutive title. But it was a sign of the austerity that is likely to come when Prosinečki's Deutschmark contract was terminated and he was given a free transfer. ahead of the club's first full season in the Croatian league as 'Dinamo'.

Here we go!

Take tram #4 from the train station (seven stops, allow 15mins), tram #7 from the bus station (six stops, 10mins) or tram #11 or #12 from Trg Bana Jelačića (seven stops, 10mins) to the stop named **Bukovačka**. The stadium is to your right.

Just the ticket

With the new north stand open and the Maksimir rarely full, buy your **tickets at the ground**. The booths are to the right of the stadium as you approach from the tram stop by the park. The old north end was the traditional home of the Bad Blue Boys, and they continue to occupy it, despite (or probably because of) official warnings not to. The trickle of away fans are opposite in the south end, while older home fans sit in sections of the *Tribina Istok*, opposite the most expensive seats in the *Tribina Zapad*.

Swift half

Bars line Maksimirska Cesta on the way to the stadium. The *HAŠK Café* (at #109) five minutes' walk from the stadium, is as good as any. At the ground, the *Domagoj* restaurant by the ticket office (entrance by the side door inside the stadium gates) has some great old photos of Dinamo's finest moments – waiter service, so at half-time you're best off queuing at its buffet/grill counter outside.

Club merchandise

The *Fan Shop* (open Mon–Fri 9am–4pm, Sat 10am–1pm and 4hrs before kick-off, most credit cards) is to the right of the main ticket office.

Ultra culture

Formed in 1986, the **Bad Blue Boys** are one of former Yugoslavia's Italian-style ultra groups whose activities became more overt as nationalist tensions rose. Their rivalry with Red Star Belgrade's *Delije* spilled over at the Maksimir in the infamous Dinamo–Red Star clash of May 1990, but within two years the BBB would be up against a more insidious enemy. President Tudjman called for the club to be given a new name – HAŠK-Gradjanski, after Dinamo's original founders. The fans couldn't chant it. He thought again. Dinamo had always represented the aspirations of the Croatian people, so...Croatia! Croatia Zagreb!

The BBB saw this as a betrayal of the club's past and continued to chant 'Dinamo', waving homemade scarves and going bare-chested to symbolise their refusal to wear any replica shirt that does not incorporate the old club badge.

Tudjman's death in 1999 has made all that a thing of the past – but the same, alas, cannot be said of the BBB's tendency towards violence.

In print

The monthly magazine *Dinamo Zagreb* (8kn) is available at the ground and at newsstands across the city.

In the net

The club's **official website** is well-maintained and includes a large English-language section incorporating a rolling news service and background information. The URL has, of course, changed to: www.nk-dinamo.hr.

Groundhopping

Croatia Zagreb dominate the city's footballing life. The town's second team, **NK Zagreb**, maintain a discreet presence in the Croatian first division but have never won a thing, while **Hrvatski Dragovoljac**, formed six years ago for the benefit of civil-war veterans and their families, are no longer technically in the city at all...

NK Zagreb

Stadion NK Zagreb, Kranjčevićeva 4
Capacity 18,000 (10,000 seated)
Colours All white

NK are very much Zagreb's second club. Tucked away in the west of the city, they spent decades yo-yoing between the top two divisions of the old Yugoslav league. In the weaker Croatian league, they have regularly finished in the top three without threatening the domination of Croatia Zagreb and Hajduk, or widening their fan base beyond the same shuffling old locals who have been watching them since Tito's day, together with a small huddle of ultras known as the White Angels.

To get there, take tram #3 or #9 from the train station, or tram #12 from Trg Bana Jelačića, to **Tehnički Muzej**. The stadium is on your right.

The **Ozalj** on the corner of Kranjčevićeva and Tratinska is the best pre-match choice for a swift half. The bars behind the terrace, particularly the **Boćar**, are also worth a look-in.

Inside the ground, the tombola bar on the near side of the main stand is less fancy than the **Zagrebački Bijeli** restaurant on the far side.

Their ground, with its impressive main stand, narrow terrace opposite and cycling track ramps behind the goals, is a pleasant venue for a gentle afternoon's football. The atmosphere is relaxed, the nationalist sentiment refreshingly muted.

Hrvatski Dragovoljac

Stadium Inker Zapresić
Colours Blue-and black stripes, black shorts

The 'Croatian Volunteers' were formed in 1994 for the benefit of war veterans and their families, the brainchild of their eccentric president Stjepan Spajić. With his army connections, Spajić hoped to generate popular support lost to the political machinations and hooliganism at Croatia Zagreb. His plan was to site Dragovoljac, who have had to play in so many places their nickname is 'the Palestinians', somewhere in Novi Zagreb.

In 1999/2000, after a spell at NK Zagreb, the Volunteers played at Inker Zapresić's ground, a short distance from Zagreb. Whether Spajic' will ever raise enough funds to build a stadium in the capital remains to be seen.

Eat, drink, sleep...

Bars and clubs

The main area for Zagreb nightlife is behind the market, off main Trg Jelačić, where you'll find two parallel streets jam-packed with bars, Opatovina and Tkalčićeva. There are six in a row down Opatovina, and a couple stay open until 2am. Nightclubs charge admission of around 40kn.

Gjuro II, Medveščak 58. Past Ribnjak north of the centre, the best club in town over the past few years, its reputation built on the quality of its DJs. Closed Mon–Tue. Tram #8 or #14.

Klub Z, Tkalčićeva 16. Large, pleasant bar with a pub feel run by ex-Dinamo star (and former NK Croatia coach) Velimir Zajeć. Football on TV, Stella Artois on draught.

Limb, Plitvička 16. A short walk from the train station – turn left, under the bridge down Miramarska and right down Bednjanska. A designer feel but real drinking underway, and with decent music too.

Točkića, Mesnička 3a. A short walk down Ilica from the main square, a popular bar with football fans, decorated with rock photos and old match tickets. Can get crowded later on, especially for games on the big-screen TV.

Restaurants

Although Zagreb suffers the ills afflicting many Croatian restaurants – overpriced and empty – it offers a reasonable amount of cheap takeaway options. The **Bonita** 24-hour snack bar (Cesarčeva Ulica 3, on the corner of Trg Jelačić) and the **Pingvin** (Nicolae Tesle 7, a minute's walk south of Trg Jelačić) are good spots to know. The latter, above the BP Jazz Club, does huge sandwiches until 2am daily, 3am Fri–Sat.

The row of snack bars between Trg Jelačić and the market are a sound lunchtime option.

Boban, Gajeva 9. Top-class fish restaurant run by you-know-who, just off the main square, with prices matching the top-notch food and service. Popular café upstairs. Open daily until midnight. Most credit cards.

Korcula, Nikolae Tesle 17. Just off the main square, a top-notch seafood restaurant serving Dalmatian specialties for around 50kn. Buffet open from breakfast, restaurant until midnight.

Pivnica Medvidgrad, Savska 56. Popular beer hall and restaurant south-west of the centre, with its own brew stored in vast vats around the walls. Main courses 30–50kn, excellent barbecued meats. Open Mon–Sat 10–midnight, Sun from midday. Most credit cards. Tram #14 or #17.

Pivnica Tomislav, Ul Baruna Trenka 2. Its address belies its prime spot on Tomislav Trg, a minute's walk from the train station. This cheap, friendly wooden cellar bar has a separate restaurant area serving reasonably priced local cuisine. Open until 11pm daily.

Split, Ilica 19. Possibly the best fish restaurant in town for the price, only a short walk from Trg Jelačić. The day's specialities are posted up on a board in the courtyard. Open until midnight Mon–Sat, closed Sun. Most credit cards.

Accommodation

The advice is simple – book ahead. The tourist office (☎01/481 4054) will give you addresses and phone numbers even if they can't actually book you anything. For **private rooms**, try **Evistas** at Senoina 28 (Mon–Fri 9am–8pm, ☎01/483 9545, fax 01/483 9543. e-mail evistas@zg.tel.hr), who'll charge around 180kn a night for a single, 250kn for a double. The office is off Trg Tomislava in front of the train station.

Astoria, Petrinjska 71 (☎01/484 1222, fax 01/484 1212). Centrally located two-star hotel between Trg Jelačić and the train station. Ask for a room with a television. Laundry facilities. Chinese restaurant downstairs. Around 300kn a single, 500kn a double.

Dubrovnik, Gajeva 1 (☎01/455 5155, fax 01/424 451). Overlooking Trg Jelačić, a two-star hotel with TV in each room, air conditioning, laundry facilities and summer terrace café. Around DM120 a single, DM160 a double.

Ilica, Ilica 102 (☎01/377 7522, fax 01/377 7722). Much-needed new addition to the city's lower-price accommodation, two tram stops from the main square. Singles 325kn, doubles 450kn, with bath and breakfast.

Hotel Laguna, Kranjčevićeva 29 (☎01/382 0222, fax 01/382 0035). Handily situated right by NK Zagreb's stadium, a large hotel with gym and sauna. Each of the 100 rooms has air conditioning, bath and satellite TV, for 400kn a single, 550kn a double. Tram #3 or #9 from the train station to Badalićeva.

Omladinski Hostel, Petrinjska 77 (☎01/484 1261, fax 01/484 1269). The only youth hostel in town that's open all year round, so often full. A 5min walk from the train station. Clean and comfortable. Dorm beds are 85kn, singles 160–200kn, doubles 200–275kn. Does not take credit cards.

Split

Split is a footballing Rio de Janeiro in miniature. Its crumbling, graffitied city walls play host to endless games of street football. Its fans, their matchday parades, their torch-bearing, even their very name – *Torcida* – have been borrowed from Brazil. Its stadium, the Poljud, is Croatia's soccer cauldron, a tempestuous bowl of passion and colour, barely a firework's throw from the calm, clear blue of the Adriatic. Small wonder the Croats prefer to play their big international matches here, even if politics has since forced them to move their base to the Maksimir in Zagreb.

The city, for years dominated by one club, Hajduk, has recently seen perennial drifters NK Split launch a serious bid to make the top flight – albeit in front of only a few hundred at the Park Mladeži, a short distance from the Poljud.

But the footballing life of the city still revolves around a small area where the old Hajduk stadium once stood, halfway between the ruined palace of the Roman emperor Diocletian and the Poljud. Although the pitch is still intact – used for youth games – the stands have long gone. Not the spirit, though. The Stari Plac, or *Plinada* ('Gasworks'), where the road leading to the Poljud, Zrinjsko-Frankopanska, meets Matoševa, is a hive of activity on matchdays. From this small square, home of the *Torcida*, their bar and several others, the Split anthem *Ništa Kontra Splita!* ('Don't Dis Split!') thunders out towards the stadium half a kilometre away.

As kick-off time approaches, a huge gathering of supporters sets out on the gentle incline up to the Poljud, along which they are joined by hardcore followers from the nearby Skalice area, and the stadium slowly fills with a drunken revelry which will later spill out over the waterfront and onto dawn.

In recent times, however, the performance of the team has caused these fans to drink more out of desperation than celebration...

The thrilling fields

Hajduk Split

Stadion Poljud, Poljudsko Šetalište
Capacity 50,000 (all-seated)
Colours White with blue and red trim
League champions (Yugoslavia) 1927, 1929, 1950, 1952, 1955, 1971, 1974–75, 1979
Cup winners (Yugoslavia) 1967, 1972–74, 1976–77, 1984, 1987, 1991
League champions (Croatia) 1992, 1994, 1995
Cup winners (Croatia) 1993, 1995, 2000

Thanks to a loyal, passionate fan base and a constant stream of local talent, the oldest Croatian club still in operation has overcome severe difficulties of finance and logistics to establish its position in the contemporary football scene.

The financial burden of maintaining a stadium as magnificent as the Poljud – with its complicated, earthquake-proof roof – is awesome, especially considering the average league crowd in Croatia and the lack of substantial television rights. Hajduk enjoyed a fair run in the 1994/95 Champions' League, finishing as runners-up to Benfica in the group stage and holding the eventual winners Ajax at home before losing in Amsterdam. But it is the sale of players that keeps Hajduk afloat. Five key members of the current national squad were raised here: Aljoša Asanović, Slaven Bilić, Alen Bokšić, Robert Jarni and Igor Štimac.

This export trade is nothing new. Hajduk won three Yugoslav titles in six years in the early Fifties, before goalkeeper Vladimir Beara and forward Bernard Vukas went abroad. The best-ever Hajduk side of the Seventies was actually several sides, the squad rebuilt each year as the stars of the previous season were sold to foreign clubs, among them Zlatko and Zoran Vujović (Bordeaux), Ivica Šurjak (Udinese), Iko Buljan (Hamburg) and Ivan Katalinić

(Southampton), the last returning to coach the side in the Nineties.

Each time Hajduk rebuilt, their fans, the *Torcida*, urged for more. Twice Hajduk reached a European semi-final, twice they lost to an English club by the narrowest margin – to Leeds by the only goal in the 1973 Cup-Winners' Cup, to Spurs on away goals in the 1984 UEFA Cup. Hajduk's sales policy cost them that final push at the highest level, and it continued to work against them in the latter half of the Nineties, as the better-funded Croatia Zagreb usurped the Dalmatian club's position at the top of the domestic tree.

Now accustomed to being second best, in 1999/2000 Hajduk finished behind Dinamo but at least had the consolation of beating their Zagreb rival's in the cup final. The club's perilous financial position had been exposed mid-season and, after a bitter boardroom battle, Sime Luketin took over as director, appointing Pero Nadoveza as coach and promising to put the club's books in order. Sadly, this process began with the sale of popular striker Jurica Vucko to Spain's Aláves, and a number of other players were expected to follow him.

The club was formed by expatriate students in Prague who, after seeing Sparta and Slavia, wanted to see the same in their home town of Split. On returning home, they gathered in the *Troccoli* café and worked out the finer details of their idea, but the team still needed a name. Eventually Hajduk, the name given to ferocious Dalmatian bandits at the time of the Ottoman occupation, was decided on by one of their professors.

Hajduk played friendlies at the military training ground of Kraljeva Njiva and were founder members of the Yugoslav league in 1923. That same year, the team toured North Africa, beating Marseille 3–2 while they were there, and thousands gathered at the port to welcome them home. Football had become an integral part of city life. By 1930 Hajduk had won two titles, had had an operetta (*Kraljica Baluna*, 'The Queen of Football') written in their honour, and

Standing up for Split – Ivan Katalinić

nearly all their team had appeared at international level for Yugoslavia, not least at the inaugural World Cup.

Today Hajduk retain all their traditional assets – a vast Dalmatian catchment area, exemplary youth development and insane local support – but their idealistic approach to football is in danger of being overtaken by the modern world.

Here we go!

Fans walk or rev their mopeds along **Zrinjsko-Frankopanska** to the Poljud. If it's raining, take bus #3 or #17 from the train station.

Just the ticket

With Hajduk's recent dip in form and the national side playing key games in Zagreb, getting a ticket at the Poljud is rarely a problem these days. Buy yours on the day at the *Torcida Shop* (see below) or at any of the small concrete ticket huts along the Kaštelanska side of the ground, the left turn from Zrinjsko-Frankopanska towards the sea. For bigger games, tickets are also on sale at travel agents, particularly the stretch between the train station and the Riva. The *Torcida* occupy the cheaper north (*sjever*) side, while away fans are allocated sector A, in the south-west of the ground. The *Tribina Zapad* (west) has the most expensive seats, along with press and VIP boxes. Average prices for league games are around 30kn, 40kn and 60kn for north, east and west sections respectively.

Swift half

Before the game head for the **Stari Plac**, halfway up Zrinjsko-Frankopanska from town. The official *Torcida bar* is on the first floor at #17 – turn to the stairs immediately to your right as you enter – while the *Café Rossi* downstairs gets into the party mood from mid-morning.

Nearer the stadium, the spacious *Pivnica Du Du Dla* on Poljudsko Šetalište has been busy since its opening just before Christmas 1998, while the *Caffe Bar Hajduk*, under gate F, is your best bet at the ground itself. All sell blue-and-purple cans of *Torcida* beer.

Club merchandise

The *Torcida Shop* (Mon–Fri 9am–midday & 5–7pm, Sat 9am–midday, all day matchdays) has moved from the Riva to a spot right next to the *Caffe-Bar Hajduk* on Poljudsko Šetalište at the stadium. It sells tickets as well as souvenirs.

Ultra culture

Many claim that Hajduk Split's *Torcida* were Europe's first ultras. Looking at the superb photo collection in their bar, you'd be hard-pressed to correlate those eager, dapper Dalmatians in trilby hats with the choreographed groups of modern-day Italy. But back in the Fifties the *Torcida* were the first fans to carry torches, the first to construct large banners, the first to co-ordinate songs – and certainly the first to organise away trips across the land.

They took their lead from South America. Before the main feature, cinemas across Yugoslavia showed newsreel footage of the 1950 World Cup in Brazil, with frequent shots of the crowd. Despite the disappointment of seeing their heroes lose to the host nation, back home fans were so impressed with the atmosphere generated at the Maracaná stadium that they endeavoured to create their own.

A group of Split students based in Zagreb decided to turn a match against Red Star Belgrade into such an event. Two trainloads came down to Split, partying outside the *Park Hotel* to keep the Red Star players awake the night before the game. The next day, 28 October 1950, they sparked off wild support at the Stari Plac, encouraging Hajduk to come back from a goal down, Bernard Vukas scoring the winner in the 87th minute. At the final whistle, the newly named *Torcida* rushed onto the pitch and carried the goalscorer from the stadium into town. A movement was born.

In the net

The club's **official website** is a fair enough effort, with plenty of dramatic pictures of the Poljud to keep visual interest up, but the text is Croatian-language only. It's at: www.hajduk.com.

There are dozens of unofficial Hajduk sites, but the best is the 'official' *Torcida* offering, which has all the latest news and match reports, a history of both the club and its fan culture, and a good links area. Best of all, there's an English-language option throughout. All in all, an outstanding site at: www.torcida.org.

Groundhopping

◖ NK Split

Park Mladeži, Hrvatske Mornarice 10
Capacity 10,000
Colours Blue shirts, white shorts

Wanted – Dalmatian club desperately seeks Arsenal-supporting anarchist to fund promotion and multi-billion kuna stadium development... Split's 'other' team, plain old NK (FC) Split, have high ambitions considering they have only ever spent three seasons up with the big boys, and that in the old Yugoslav league of the late Fifties. They came within a play-off match of promotion to the Croatian top flight in the summer of 1998 and, encouraged by that success, the club nurtured ambitions to

Split essentials

Croatia Airlines run a bus service (25kn) between the **airport** at Trogir, 23km from Split, and their main office on Obala Hrvatskog Narodnog Preporoda (known as the 'Riva') an hour and a half before and after each flight.

The Riva is Split's main drag, stretching along the bay from Diocletian's Palace to Trg Republike. On arrival, as you face the Adriatic from the train or bus station, turn right and the Riva is a 3min walk away.

Most of central Split is **easily accessible on foot**. A bus network covers the rest of the city in four zones – zone 1 is adequate for most visitors' needs. Tickets are sold at blue kiosks or onboard, at 5kn for a zone 1 single, 8kn for two (stamp either end), or 35kn for ten. Buses run 5am–11pm and there is no night transport.

Taxis are generally parked outside the train station or on Trg Republike; they charge 14kn plus 7kn per kilometre. To phone for one, dial ☎021/49 999.

The **tourist office** is on the Riva, at Obala HNP 12 (open Oct–Easter Mon–Fri 7.30am–8pm, Sat 8am–2pm; Easter–Sept daily 7.30am–8pm; ☎021/342 142). There is no city listings guide of note.

---

transform its prosaic Park Mladeži – built for the 1979 Military Games – into a £30million stadium to rival the Poljud.

It sounds, and is, fanciful. But then, NK Split have always attracted dreamers. The team were formed in 1912 by revolutionary management who called them Anarchia Split. This was toned down to Arsenal Split by the Communist authorities in 1950, and the simple 'NK' replaced the Highbury reference two years after that.

Like their close neighbours Hajduk, NK Split have been an excellent breeding ground for young talent – but relegation in 1999/2000 consigned the club to the anonymity of the regional leagues.

Park Mladeži is a 10min walk inland from the Poljud along Hrvatske Mornarice, or take bus #3 from central Tržnica. The modern *Captain's Club* bar sits by the main entrance.

Eat, drink, sleep…

Bars and clubs

By day the cafés along the Riva bustle with custom. By night the narrow maze of alleyways of Diocletian's Palace are a buzzing hive of bars, starting at Mihovilova Širina, the palace entrance. For clubbing, head for the Gripe district and the Koteks centre,

where Matice Hrvatske meets Osječka, and you'll find the *Night Café* and *Metropolis* discos. In summer the action moves down to the shore, a kilometre south-east of the centre, to Uvala Firule or Uvala Zenta.

Dioklecijan, Alešijeva 3. Enter the palace at Mihovilova Širina, turn immediately right into Dosud and at the end you'll find this small, local bar with its rundown terrace and perfect view over the Adriatic. Open daily, 7am–10pm.

Klub Zanatlija, Krešimirova 7. Large cellar bar in the darkest depths of the palace, buzzing with football talk the night before a big match. Enter the palace at Ispod Ure, the far side of Narodni Trg, and walk straight ahead down Krešimirova.

Puls Kavarna, Buvinova 1. Just off Mihovilova Širina, the hippest bar in the palace, with a cool crowd and decent sounds. Open daily until 1am.

Shakespeare, Uvala Zente 3. Down by the marina, a brash and mindless three-level club with a terrace for starlit groping. Bus #10 from Tržnica, or a 25–30kn taxi ride from the station.

Up & Down, Uvala Baluni bb. The most popular centrally located disco, down by the marina past the *Marjan* hotel, with a 20–40kn entrance charge and reasonable music inside.

Restaurants

Dalmatian cuisine is the best in Croatia, a delicious mix of local seafood, fresh vegetables and olive oil. *Dalmat brodet* is a typical dish, but there are many variations. Competition won't bring prices down until the tourist trade picks up again, but you can still eat much more cheaply in Split than in Zagreb.

Central, Narodni Trg 1. Attached to the *Hotel Central*, a large restaurant with tables outside on the square. Daily specials at 25–30kn, otherwise 40–50kn for a main course. Open until 10pm, most credit cards.

Pizzeria Galija, Tončićeva 12. Reasonably priced, centrally located pizzeria serving a variety of pizza and pasta dishes. Separate bar area, air conditioned. Open Sundays, no credit cards. A 5min walk from Trg Republike up Marmontova.

Plava Peka, Poljudsko Šetalište 9. Pricey but polished eaterie near the Poljud stadium, specialising in shellfish, grilled meat and local dishes. Bread baked on the premises. Open until 1am, most credit cards. Bus #17 from Tržnica.

Sarajevo, Domaldova 6. Don't be put off by the tacky pictures outside – this place serves tasty main courses at around 50–60kn, in unusually ornate surroundings. Open daily until midnight, most credit cards. Just off Narodni Trg.

Zlatna Ribica, Kraj Sv Marije 12. Small, friendly, family-run diner by the fish market selling plates of *lignije* (scampi) and other freshly caught delights for 20–30kn. Closed Sundays. A minute's walk from Trg Republike.

Accommodation

Lack of competition will keep hotel prices high in Split until the tourists come back in numbers. A **private room** is probably the best option, arranged through the tourist office (☎021/342 142). Rates are set at 160kn for a single and 240kn for a double including tax, less for long stays. Pay the whole amount to the staff, who will then give you a receipt and point you in the right direction. All hotels listed take credit cards.

Hotel Bellevue, Bana Jelačića 2 (☎021/585 701, fax 021/362 383). Perfectly located by central Trg Republike and the bay, a three-star hotel with TV in every room and a restaurant downstairs. DM100 for a single, DM140 a double. A 10min walk from the train/bus stations.

Hotel Jadran Koteks, Sustjepanski Put 23 (☎021/361 599, fax 021/361 381). Four-star hotel on the far side of the bay by Uvale Baluni, with an outdoor pool and gym. TV and air conditioning in every room. DM110 a single, DM160 a double. Bus #8 from the station.

Hotel Marjan, Obala Branimira 8 (☎021/302 111, fax 021/342 930). A huge hotel overlooking the bay. Outdoor swimming pool, discotheque, restaurant, rooms with air conditioning. Out of season DM110 a single, DM150 a double, in summer DM130 and DM165. Bus #8 from the station.

Park Hotel, Hatzeov Perivoj 3 (☎021/314 755, fax 021/314 567). Pleasant, air-conditioned four-star hotel near the beach with a palm-lined terrace, shower and TV in each room, plus a decent restaurant. Singles at around DM100–150, doubles at DM150–200, depending on season. Bus #3, #5, #8 or #17 from the station, or a short taxi ride.

Prenočište Slavija, Buvinova 2 (☎021/47 053, fax 021/343 567) Slap in the heart of Diocletian's Palace, a comfortable if noisy pension close to the nightlife action. Singles at 170kn, doubles 200–250kn. A 10min from the station, entering the palace via Mihovilova Širina.

Czech Republic

Českomravský fotbalový svaz (ČMFS) Diskarska 100, 16900 Praha 6 Strahov
☎02/2051 3575   Fax 02/352 784   E-mail cmfs@fotbal.cz

League champions Sparta Prague   **Cup winners** Slovan Liberec   **Promoted**
Viktoria Plzeň, FC Synot   **Relegated** FC Opava, Hradec Králové

European participants 2000/01 Sparta Prague, Slavia Prague (UCL qualifiers);
Petra Drnovice, Slovan Liberec (UEFA Cup); Chmel Blsany, Marila Pribram, Sigma
Olomouc (Intertoto Cup)

The Czechs may have been knocked out of Euro 2000 at the group stage, but the national team's performances in Belgium and Holland, coming hard on the heels of an unbeaten qualification campaign, were a reminder that Czech footballing talent remains among the finest the continent has to offer.

The generation of players who reached the final of Euro '96 are still together and still capable. And, unusually for Eastern Europe, the next crop of players offer hope of more good times to come. Prior to Euro 2000, an exciting Czech side reached the final of the European Under-21 championship, where they only narrowly lost to Italy, and players like Marek Jankulovski, who was quickly snapped up by Napoli, are likely to be gradually introduced into Jozef Chovanec's full squad.

These are players who were 10 years old at the time of the collapse of communism, making them the first real products of post-1989 Czech football. And for all the teething problems the game has had in a nascent market economy, their quality shows that even without state support, it is possible for former Eastern Bloc countries to produce good players and good teams.

At club level there are the familiar post-communist complaints of lack of resources, but Sparta Prague were capable of reaching

Crying game – Euro 2000 was hard on the capable Czechs

the second group phase of the Champions' League in 1999/2000, and there are early but encouraging signs of stability at many top-flight clubs.

Euro '96 had been the national team's first major tournament since the 'Velvet Divorce' that broke up the old Czecho-slovakia three years earlier. In 1976, it was

Fan fury – angry Czechs can't hide their contempt for Euro 2000 ref Pierluigi Collina

with a core of Slovak players that Czechoslovakia pipped England to qualify for the knockout stage of the European Championship in Yugoslavia. Having beaten Holland after extra time in the semi-finals, the Czechoslovak team were leading world champions West Germany 2–1 until the last minute, then showed immense character to win a penalty shoot-out with the scores at 2–2. In 1996, under stern-faced coach Dušan Uhrin, it was a purely Czech team in the spotlight. President Václav Havel, a crusading dissident playwright 20 years earlier, was now seen commiserating with his team in their Wembley dressing room. The symbolism could hardly have been stronger.

Yet tough times lay ahead, for players and domestic clubs alike. Within hours of Oliver Bierhoff's flukey 'golden goal' giving Germany victory over the Czechs at Euro '96, the agents were hard at work, setting up deals to sell most of this previously unheralded Central European squad. But some would do better than others. Patrik Berger and Karel Poborský fizzled with inconsistency at Liverpool and Manchester United; Vladimir Šmicer won the

French league with little Lens; Radek Bejbl had a difficult time at a difficult club, Atlético Madrid; midfield dynamo Pavel Nedved became invaluable to Lazio's Italian title challenges of 1998/99 and 1999/2000.

While the stars spread out across the continent, those left behind toiled in a domestic league marked by four-figure crowds, beer, sausages, and poor decision-making by the new investment groups whose backing was supposed to bring the Czech game back to the forefront of European development.

Not that the Czechs have always needed the best facilities to develop their talents. Before World War II, in Prague's footballing heyday, many Czechs learned their quick-thinking skills from České ulice – street football in which beating the man was paramount. Those skills, coupled with a brisk, short-passing style (common throughout the Danube basin but introduced, in fact, by English and Scottish coaches), made Czech sides formidable opposition at both club and international level. Slavia and Sparta, who between them took every prewar domestic title but one, also mustered three wins in the Mitropa

Basics

EU nationals, Americans and Canadians need only a **passport** to enter the Czech Republic. Australians and New Zealanders require a six-month **visa** from their local Czech embassy.

The Czech currency is the **crown**, or koruna česká, usually indicated Kč and divided into 100 haléřů. Crown coins come in denominations of 1, 2, 5, 10, 20 and 50, with 20, 50, 100, 200, 500, 1,000 and 5,000 crown notes. There are around 55Kč to £1. The crown is convertible in the West, but you'll get a far better rate changing back unused crowns in the Czech Republic.

The centre of Prague is littered with **exchange offices**, including a 24-hour one at Staroměstské Náměstí 21, but they generally offer poor rates. Banks (usually open Mon–Fri 8am–5pm) are a better bet. Most major towns have cash machines, but outside Prague, few shops and restaurants take credit cards.

The Czech **telephone system** still leaves much to be desired. From outside the country, the telephone code for the Czech Republic is 420. Dial 00 to call abroad once inside the country. Cheap rates apply 7pm–7am Mon–Fri and all day at weekends – a call to the UK comes down from 23Kč to 14Kč a minute. Internally, the city codes are Prague 2, Brno 5, Ostrava 69 and Olomouc 68.

Most **telephone boxes** now take phone cards (*telefonní karty*), available at newsstands and post offices for 100Kč, 200Kč or 300Kč. There are still some coin phones, for which you'll need 2Kč or 5Kč pieces for local calls.

Travel around the Czech Republic is cheap, if slow. There are three kinds of **train**. The slower they go, the cheaper they are. The fastest are express (*expresný*); then fast (*rychlík*); and finally ordinary (*osobný*). International through trains require a seat reservation (*místenka*). Write down your destination and train time to show the clerk when buying a ticket.

Prague has two main train stations – Hlavní nádraží for trains from the west, Holešovice for the service between Berlin and Budapest. Both are on red metro line C, although Hlavní nádraží is only a 5min walk from Wenceslas Square.

Czech **buses** are even cheaper than trains, run by *ČSAD* and *Čebus*, are even cheaper, and often quicker to country destinations. From Prague, most long-distance buses leave from the station by Florenc metro stop (yellow line B or red line C).

Cup. Goalkeeping captain František Plánička, with seven Slavia team-mates, led the Czech national team to the 1934 World Cup final. They came within eight minutes of winning it. Winger Antonín Puč put them ahead with 20 minutes left against the hosts and favourites Italy, who had the woodwork to thank for not going further behind before Plánička misjudged Raimondo Orsi's cross-shot and the sides were level again. Italy won 2–1 in extra time and Plánička would always blame himself for the defeat.

It was much the same story when Czechoslovakia met Brazil in the 1962 World Cup final, as another hapless goalie, Viliam Schrojf, effectively lost the game for

a different kind of Czech team. Their star was Josef Masopust, midfield leader of the defence-minded army side, Dukla Prague, who would dominate the postwar Czechoslovak championship.

Under communism, Dukla had first pick of the country's most talented players. By the time their power began to wane in the Seventies, Slovak teams such as Spartak Trnava and Slovan Bratislava had the country's real strength in-depth, although Dukla still provided two key players for the 1976 European Championship-winning team – goalkeeper Ivo Viktor and midfielder Zdenek Nehoda.

Dukla were doomed to relative obscurity by the fall of communism. Sparta's domination of the Eighties looked set to keep the team at the top of the new Czech-Moravian league in the following decade, but when they hit a cash crisis in 1995/96, the door was left open for Slavia and to win their first championship since 1947 – old man Plánička lived just long enough to witness it.

Once in England, former Slavia men Berger and Poborský fell out with Uhrin, and the Czechs' failure to reach France '98 prompted the coach's resignation and his replacement with the younger Jozef Chovanec, who had guided Sparta back to the top of the domestic tree. Viewed as 'one of the lads' by his squad, Chovanec healed previous divisions and his newly united team rewarded his faith.

Having waltzed through an admittedly easy qualification group, in which only Scotland were serious challengers, the Czechs were placed in a hellish Euro 2000 section with co-hosts Holland and world champions (and eventual winners) France.

A late penalty controversially awarded by Italian referee Pierluigi Collina resulted in a 1–0 defeat by the Dutch in an opening game which had seen the home side struggling to cope with Czech counter-attacking, after which Chovanec's side won praise for their battling display in a 2–1 defeat by the unstoppable French. The final match against Denmark was meaningless, but a comfortable 2–0 win left many commentators describing the Czechs as the best team not to make the quarter-finals.

Essential vocabulary

Hello *Ahoj*
Goodbye *Na shledanou*
Yes *Ano*
No *Ne*
Two beers, please *Dvě piva, prosím*
Thank You *Děkuju*
Men's *Muži*
Women's *Ženy*
Where is the stadium? *Kde je stadion?*
What's the score? *Jaký je?*
Referee *Rozhodčí*
Offside *Mimo hru*

Match practice

In this age of golden goals and rich agents, most Czechs still get by on the simple pleasures of beer, sausages and *kopaná* – football. Here the game is a cheap, basic form of entertainment, short on modern facilities. Crowds are small, but then, so are most grounds – but perhaps for not much longer. With only Sparta's renovated, all-seater Letná and Teplice's Na Stinadlech currently meet top international standards, the Czech FA has imposed a ruling for all top-flight stadia to meet minimum standards of comfort and safety by June 2003 – or face closure. How most clubs will find the wherewithal for these improvements remains a mystery to most…

The Czech season runs from early August to late November and late February to early June. Sunday is the traditional day for football (Saturday is for ice-hockey), with most games kicking off at 4.30pm. One key game is shown live by TV Nova at 5pm on Friday, and traditionally Žižkov play on Sunday morning, so as not to clash with other games in Prague. In winter and early spring, before the clocks go forward, expect 2.30pm kick-offs at grounds without floodlights.

A different league

The *Českomoravského liga* (Czech-Moravian league) came into being for the 1993/94 season after Slovakia left the old Czechoslovak federation, and its format has not been tampered with since.

The retention of a 16-team top division initially came in for criticism by sages who predicted it would lead to falling standards. However, the rise of provincial sides previously denied access to top-flight football by Slovak clubs has inspired a surge of interest in soccer across the republic, even if not all the football is exactly world-class.

The two bottom-placed sides from the top flight, the *I. fotbalová liga*, change places with the top two from the *II. fotbalová liga*. The semi-professional third division is divided into two groups, one 18-team Czech (ČFL) and one 16-team Moravian

(MSFL). Slavia and Sparta's 'B' teams play in the ČFL, Ostrava's, Olomouc's and Brno's in the MSFL – none of them can be promoted. Otherwise the winners of each section swap places with the bottom two of the second division.

Up for the cup

After a *předkolo* ('preliminary round') for the minnows in late July and a first round in August, the *Pohár ČMFS* starts in earnest when the first-division clubs join at a seeded, second-round stage. Ties are decided over one game, including the quarter- and semi-finals in April. The final takes place at the Strahov in May. After what happened to them at Euro '96, the Czechs seemed unlikely candidates to adopt the controversial 'golden goal' rule – yet three recent cup finals have been decided in precisely that way.

Just the ticket

Prices vary according to the standard of stadium and level of interest. A seat for a big league match at Sparta's comfortable Letná could set you back 200Kč; to see a lesser team visiting Bohemians or Slavia should only cost 50Kč. At most grounds you should be able to get your ticket at the ground a few minutes before kick-off.

Places will be divided into seated (*k sezení*), generally a spot on a bench, and standing (*k stání*). Stands are open (*krytá*) or covered (*nekrytá*). For the Letná and the Strahov, your ticket will indicate a sector (*sektor*), a row (*řáda*) and a seat (*místo* or *sedadlo*). Most clubs issue a programme, on sale at the ticket office, for 10–30Kč. At many games you'll come across a variety of vendors offering an array of old football badges, often very cheaply.

Half-time

Beer (*pivo*) and sausages (*klobása*) or frankfurters (*párek*) keep most fans going of a Sunday. Beer is always within range of the average fan's pocket, rarely more than 20Kč, while sausages are 25Kč with bread and mustard. Service can be painfully slow.

Action replay

Privately owned TV Nova has exclusive rights to screen one live game each round, generally at 5pm on Friday, often preceded by its half-hour weekend preview package, *Penalta*. Its league round-up, *Minipenalta*, is screened on Sunday around 10pm, featuring 20 minutes of highlights.

State ČT1 shows a 15-minute sports news and highlights package every day before 8pm and 11pm, while ČT2 shows brief European highlights at 10pm on Sunday evening, and has the rights to Champions' League and international matches.

The back page

Fans' staple diet is the daily *Sport* (7–11Kč, no issue on Sundays) – classic, print-heavy, advert-free fare which has changed little since communist days. Monday's edition has a round-up of domestic and European results and goalscorers.

The weekly *Gól* (Thursdays, 15Kč) gives equal space to football and ice-hockey, whereas the glossy monthly *Fotbal Sport* (35Kč) is all soccer features and news. The back page of the English-language weekly *Prague Post* (Wednesdays, 45Kč) offers good local football coverage.

Ultra culture

Czech fans are studiously unhip, all denim, beer bellies and greengrocers' haircuts. They are also harmless, unless it's a big game involving Sparta Prague and a club from the provinces with a chip on its shoulder.

Racism, although not as bad as in Hungary or former East Germany, is not unknown – and patently ignored by the authorities.

In the net

The official Czech-Moravian FA website is a good source for stats and news, and promises an English-language section in the future at: www.fotbal.cz.

Otherwise have a look at Milan Šoba's unofficial site at: come.to/fotbal.cz.

Prague

Beer versus wine – Sparta get stuck into Bordeaux in the Champions' League, 1999

Capital of Bohemia in the old Austro-Hungarian Empire, Prague was a prime mover in the early development of soccer in Central Europe. The first game under regular conditions in the old empire took place here, between members of the Ruderklub Regatta Sailing Club and Viktoria Berlin, in December 1893. Within three years, representative teams from Prague and Vienna had begun a series of matches, and an English FA eleven played the Prague team in 1899.

The team was made up of members from the city's two main clubs, Sparta and Slavia, who dominated the first fledgling league, the *Mistrovstvi Čech*, in the late 1890s. The Bohemian FA was founded in 1901, its national team playing a series of friendlies with Hungary before its last international, against England, in Prague in 1908. Games would take place on Letná, the parkland in the bend of the Vltava river, just north of the city centre, where both Sparta and Slavia had their base.

With Bohemia pulling out of the 1908 Olympics, Prague would have to wait until the formation of 'Czecho-Slovakia' after World War I before it hosted another international. At club level, the two Prague giants won every title in the *Mistrovstvi ČSF* either side of the war, before the *Stredočecsky Liga* was formed in 1918; this popular tournament was restricted to teams from in and around Prague, but it was the strongest in the region until the formation of the first Czecho-Slovak league in 1925.

Apart from Viktoria Žižkov's victory in 1928, Slavia and Sparta took every Czecho-Slovak title up to World War II. Now the city boasted a national stadium, the Strahov, high over Malá Strana in the west of the city, while Žižkov, Bohemians and, after the war, Slavia, would have modest grounds within a short range of each other in the working-class wasteland east of town.

By the late Fifties the city's powerbase had become Dejvice, a drab district of north-west Prague dominated by the huge Socialist-Realist *Hotel International*, a backdrop perfectly in keeping with the army team based there, Dukla. A visit to their Na Julisce stadium, a steep walk up Pod

Juliskou surrounded by military buildings, was a daunting prospect. With the pick of the best players, the army side were the most successful team of the era, but by no means the most popular.

Dukla's decline – they would move out of the city entirely in 1997 – followed the fall of communism and the subsequent partition of Czechoslovakia. But other Prague clubs flourished in the new Czech league. Apart from the inevitable domination by Sparta, Slavia and Žižkov both enjoyed revivals in the mid-Nineties.

Eccentric, romantic, anachronistic but above all an essential part of everyday city life, football in Prague is unique and unforgettable – if not always for the most obvious reasons.

The thrilling fields

Sparta Prague

Stadion Letná, Milady Horákové 98
Capacity 22,000 (all-seated)
Colours Claret shirts, white shorts
League champions 1912, 1919–23, 1925–27, 1932, 1936, 1938–39, 1944, 1946, 1948, 1952, 1954, 1965, 1967, 1984–85, 1987–91, 1993–95, 1997–2000
Cup winners 1964, 1972, 1976, 1980, 1984, 1988–89, 1992, 1996

Record title winners, AC Sparta are the biggest club in the Czech Republic. Their huge support has kept them at the top for the best part of a century, and they're still they're today.

Sparta's first golden era was in the Twenties. Founded as Athletic Club Královske Vonobrady – literally 'King's Vineyard' – in 1893 and becoming Athletic Club Sparta the following year, they played their first derby against Slavia on the Letná playing fields in 1896. Sparta attracted working-class support, earning the nickname *železná* ('iron') Sparta. They won the

first Czech league in 1912, seven more titles in the Twenties and the inaugural Mitropa Cup – an embryonic international competition open to Central European clubs – in 1927.

Their prewar star was inside-forward Oldřich Nejedlý, top goalscorer at the 1934 World Cup, but a player whose domestic era was dominated by Slavia. A second Mitropa Cup win in 1935 coincided with the rebuilding of the Letná stadium after it was gutted by fire. (A much later redesign, in 1973, turned it into a perfectly formed, compact ground, converted to an all-seater in the mid-Nineties.)

Although the club was forced into a series of name changes, Sparta did not do too badly out of Communist Czechoslovakia. In contrast to sorry old Slavia, Sparta received some state support, pinching a title every few years from Dukla.

The only low point was relegation in the Slovak-dominated mid-Seventies – after which the club bounced back to take 13 titles between 1984 and 1999, putting them first in line for regular and lucrative participation in the Champions' League, and giving Sparta the chance to set a shining example to Eastern Europe of how to succeed in a post-Communist world.

Things started to go wrong when former car mechanic Petr Mach picked up Sparta for a song in 1992. Mismanagement over the expensive modernisation of the Letná stadium caused near bankruptcy in the winter of 1995/96, forcing a quick sell-off of players and allowing eternal rivals Slavia to take the title in May 1996. That same month, Slovak steelworks *VSŽ Košice* bought the club and its huge debts. The new owners, the Rezes family who were also proprietors of the Slovak club 1.FC Košice, planned to export cheap Slovak players to Prague, and thence to Europe. They pulled off a masterstroke when they appointed former club captain Jozef Chovanec to the post of first-team coach midway through the 1996/97 season – Sparta surged up the table to reclaim the championship they had lost the previous year to Slavia. The following year, Sparta made life awkward for Parma and Galatasaray in the Champions' League, but lost heavily to Borussia Dortmund, by which time Chovanec had taken the job of national coach. Yet with the Rezes clan pumping 70 million crowns into the club that season, Sparta won the title with 12 points to spare over Slavia.

After selling defender Tomás Repka to Fiorentina in the 1998 close season but keeping a formidable attack of Josef Obajdin, Vratislav Lokvenc and Horst Siegl, Sparta were unlucky to lose in the qualifying round to eventual Champions' League semi-finalists Dynamo Kiev. The side got over that disappointment to again dominate in the league – it was March 1999 before they lost a match – but behind the scenes things were going wrong. Facing crippling tax bills, the Rezes family slashed all expenditure not directly concerned with steelmaking. Worse, Rezes senior, Alexander, a former transport minister in the Slovak government, lost his seat in parliament, and lost interest in Sparta. Coach Zdeněk Scasny came back from the winter break to find that key midfielder Martin Cizek had been sold to Munich 1860 without his knowledge

Still, the title was retained with two games to go, and in June 1999, German-owned publishing group *Vltava-Labe-Press* bought the Rezes family out, installing a former team-mate of Chovanec's, Ivan Hašek, as coach for 1999/2000. Hašek's side reached the second group phase of the Champions' League and, while they were unable to outdo Porto and Barcelona, back at home a fourth consecutive title was sealed in perfect fashion with a 5–1 hammering of Slavia. Whether the team would continue to thrive in the absence of towering striker Vratislav Lokvenc, sold to Kaiserslautern in the close season, remained to be seen.

Here we go!

Take green metro line A to **Hradčanská**, then a 5min walk along Milady Horákové. A slower route – red metro line A to **Vltavská**, then tram #1 or #25 – offers a better selection of bars.

Just the ticket

There are two **ticket offices** along Milady Horákové and another on the corner with U Sparty, with seat prices at 50–150Kč – perhaps twice that for European games. Sparta's following gather behind the south goal on Milady Horákové. Away fans are behind the opposite goal, in sections H, I, J and K. Neutrals are best placed in section D1, D2 or D6, near the bar.

Swift half

If you're coming via Vltavská, watch out for the sign marked *Orient Express* at Milady Horakové 5, visible from the first tram stop in the direction of the stadium. It's a comfortable bar with 25Kč Budvar and a hot-dog window on the street that serves until 2am daily. Opposite Hradčanská metro, on Dejvická, there's the *Restaurace Dejvická* at #2, and the *Bruska* bar at #18. Inside the ground, the *Občertsvenó* buffet by block D2 has slow-moving queues shuffling towards Samson beer and sandwiches.

Club merchandise

There are two stores opposite each other by the ticket office at the corner of Milady Horákové and U Sparty. The *Fan Shop AC Sparta* (open Mon–Fri 9am–12.15pm & 12.45–5pm, weekends on matchdays, no credit cards) has a modest selection of shirts, cups, spoons and glasses. *Association Club Sparta* (Mon–Fri 9.30am–12.30pm & 1–5.30pm, Sat 9am–1pm, no credit cards) has pennants, videos and some classic Czech three-coloured horns (*tralalák*).

In town, you'll find an *AC Sparta Praha* shop at Na Perštýne 17 (open Mon-Thur 10am–5pm, Fri 10am–4pm).

Ultra culture

Sparta has the country's biggest fan base, but they look pretty mild on home turf. You'll see the south end wave a few flags and set off the occasional firecracker, but little more than that.

In print

Spartan Letenský Magazin is the A4-sized programme, sold around the ground at 25Kč.

The Strahov

Stadión Evžena Rošického, Olympijská
Capacity 19,600 (all-seated)

The Czech Republic's **national football stadium**, officially named after a well-known victim of Nazi terror, Evžen Rošicky, is commonly called the Strahov after its four-arena sports complex and monastery nearby. High up over Prague, the Strahov has the perfect setting for major events, but its tatty condition has persuaded the authorities to move Czech national games to the Letná.

Athletics are now the Strahov's main *raîson d'être*, but cup finals are still played here, and the stadium also hosts Slavia Prague's big European ties. To get to it, take bus #132 or #217 from Anděl or #176 from Karlovo Náměstí.

The ***Restaurant Bar Strahov*** by gate A3, open until 7pm on weekdays and matchdays, is worth a look-in for its black-and-white photos of Czech football heroes. If it's closed, there's a Staropramen bar by gate C7, or the ***Restaurace Sport***, an old-style cheap Czech lunchtime buffet, with bendy cutlery and a terrace view of the complex, up a flight of stairs above gate D11.

In the net

Sparta finally launched an official website during the 1999/2000 season at: www.sparta.cz. It's slick, quick and efficiently run, but there are no language options beyond the impenetrable-looking Czech.

 Slavia Prague

Eden, Vladivostocká 1460/2
Capacity 16,000 (5,000 seated)
Colours Red-and-white halved shirts, white shorts
League champions 1913, 1924–25, 1929–31, 1933–35, 1937, 1940–43, 1947, 1996
Cup winners 1997, 1999

Since ending their generation-long title drought in 1996, Slavia have fallen victim to the administrative mismanagement endemic among clubs in former Communist Europe in the latter half of the Nineties. And in Slavia's case, the source of the grief has been British. Millionaire Joe Lewis' *English National Investment Company* (*ENIC*) were welcomed with open arms when they acquired a majority stake in the club for £2.3million in October 1997. Yet two years on, and the team have lost their ability to compete seriously with Sparta in

the league, star players have continued to be sold, and the club's rickety wooden home ground, Eden, seems no nearer to being modernised than it did when *ENIC* first arrived. At the end of the 1998/99 season, Slavia gifted the runners-up spot in the league – and a Champions' League qualifying berth – to Teplice, while fewer than 5,000 fans turned up at the Strahov to see Pavel Horvath's 'golden goal' win the domestic cup back against Slovan Liberec, a reflection of the increasingly strained relationship between the club's management and its supporters.

Formed in the late 19th century as a Czech-language literary and debating society, and viewed with deep suspicion by the ruling, German-speaking Habsburg authorities, the Slavia club attracted rebellious young members of Prague's intelligentsia. A sports branch was set up, and the football section opened for business in 1892, taking its colours of red-and-white with a red star after what was then the independent Czech flag.

Slavia first met Sparta in 1896, and the two clubs took it in turns to win the title until the arrival of Communism in 1948. By then two generations of fans had been raised to root for either Slavia or Sparta, Slavia attracting the university-educated,

Prague essentials

Express buses run every 30mins (4.30am–11.30pm) from Prague **airport** into town, first stopping at Dejvická metro stop (15mins, 15Kč), the terminus of green metro line A, then by the Czech airline office on Revoluční (30mins, 30Kč), close to Náměstí Republiky metro stop on yellow line B. Pay the driver. After midnight, night bus #510 runs every 40mins to Divoká Šárka, the terminus for night tram #51 to central Národní – tickets are 10Kč from orange machines inside the airport. A **taxi** should cost around 300Kč but could easily run to 500Kč (see below).

   City transport is cheap and efficient, but ticket dispensing from the orange machines is classic contemporary Czechnology. There are two kinds of tickets, both valid for Prague's metro, trams and buses – an 8Kč ticket is valid for one ride of up to 15mins (stamp onboard) or up to four stops on a metro line (stamp at entrance), while a 12Kč ticket lasts for an hour up to 8pm, 90mins at evenings and weekends. Choose the ticket type you want, hit the button for as many tickets as you want, then press Enter, then insert your coins. Change will be given. It's probably easier to buy a handful from newsstands or *DP* windows at metro stations. There you can also buy a 24-hour pass for 70Kč, a three-day one for 180Kč or a weekly for 250Kč, valid from the time of first stamping. Your full name and date of birth must be filled out on the back.

   Transport runs 5am–midnight, after which there are night bus and tram routes, running every 40mins and requiring the usual 12Kč tickets. Trams stop at the Lazarská crossroads on Spálená near Národní Třida, most buses at the top of Wenceslas Square near Muzeum metro.

   Prague's **taxi drivers** have earned their grim reputation. The cabs standing in Wenceslas Square are there to rip you off. Try to hail a moving one in the street. Once it stops, make sure it is clearly marked as a taxi, with fares prominently displayed and a black-and-white chequered stripe along the side. Ensure the driver does not turn on the meter until you get in, and that it is set to '1' when he does. You should be charged an initial fare of 25Kč, then no more than 17Kč per kilometre. The least disreputable firms are *AAA* (☎02/1080) and *ProfiTaxi* (☎02/1035).

   The main **tourist information office** in Prague is *PIS*, Na Příkopě 20 (☎02/544 444, Mon–Fri 9am–7pm, Sat–Sun 9am–5pm), with other branches in the Old Town square and at Hlavní Nádraží station. None of these, though, can help with accommodation enquiries.

   Prague is woefully short of English-language **nightlife information**. In clubs, look out for the English-language weekly *Think* or the Czech monthly *Navigator*.

Sparta the working-class support. Former Scottish international John Madden guided Slavia through the glory years in the professional era of the Thirties, when the team won six titles and provided eight of Czechoslovakia's World Cup runners-up team in 1934. Goalkeeper František Plánička was the hero, while winger Antonín Puč will go down in history as the all-time top scorer for Czechoslovakia. Slavia won the Mitropa Cup in 1938, by which time prolific forward Pepi Bican had arrived from Vienna. Bican's Slavia dominated the Czech-Moravian wartime championship and took the Czechoslovak title in 1947. Within a year, however, state president (and former Slavia player) Edvard Beneš had resigned to hand full power to the Communists, and Madden had died while still in the Slavia coaching job – and still preaching the short-passing game.

   In the total restructuring of Czech football which ensued, Slavia were renamed Sokol Praha 7 and lost half their squad to the newly formed army side, then called ATK. An ageing Bican moved to Vítkovice. The devastation was completed at the start of the Fifties when the club, by now renamed Dynamo Slavia, were forced from the rebuilt Letná to a working-class area of tower blocks, railway sidings and a large cemetery – 'Eden'.

Slavia slumped to the second division but fought back in the mid-Sixties, winning back their name and their status and clocking up a handful of European appearances. Twenty years later, Slavia players marked the student demonstrations of November 1989 with a pre-match show of support.

After the fall of Communism, the club found itself in the unaccustomed position of having an exciting crop of young players it could actually keep. But Slavia still had a run-down wooden stadium and the club's new owner, millionaire Czech-American Boris Korbel, left after a series of boardroom disputes in 1994.

In the absence of Korbel's cash, key players such as Patrik Berger were sold to balance the books. But Jan Suchopárek, Radek Bejbl and Vladimír Šmicer stayed, to be joined by Karel Poborský from Viktoria Žižkov, and these players were the engine that powered Slavia to a thrilling UEFA Cup run – when Roma were among their victims – and title win in 1996. All four players went west after Euro '96, and a weakened Slavia were crushed by Grasshopper Zürich in the Champions' League qualifying round that summer.

After the title had been lost – but the cup won – in 1997, the arrival of *ENIC* was supposed to give Slavia a new financial platform on which to build. But the new owners put Miroslav Ondříček, best-known for his work in the cinema business, in charge at Eden, and the 1997/98 season ended uneventfully in every sense – no honours, no fresh players, no new stadium blueprints. Striker Karel Vácha was then sold to Austria, playmaker Pavel Novotny (more painfully) to Sparta. After beating Schalke on penalties in the 1998/99 UEFA Cup, Slavia had to go to Bologna with a 14-man squad, their two outfield subs 17-year-olds from the youth team.

Victory in the cup final gave the club a passport back to Europe for 1999/2000, when Steaua Bucharest and Udinese were impressive scalps before Leeds United proved to be one test too far. On the domestic front, Slavia were always going to be second best to Sparta, but at least there was the consolation of a pot-shot at the Champions' League.

Here we go!

There are three ways of finding Eden. Take green metro line A to Náměstí Míru, then tram #4 or #22; red metro line C to I P Pavlova, then tram #4; or red line C to Vyšehrad, then tram #7.

Just the ticket

The **ticket windows** are by the main entrance, with spaces divided between seats in the main stand (covered, *krytá*), seats in the rest of the ground (uncovered, *nekrytá*) and standing places (*k stání*). Expect to pay 50–90Kč.

On the north (*sever*) terrace you'll find the hardcore 'Slavia Fanatics', while the handful of away fan are allocated a small section of the south (*jih*) terrace, down a leafy lane around the corner from *U Slavie* before the railway bridge. A small programme is available with your ticket.

Swift half

The Eden restaurant once attached to the stadium is long gone, replaced by a two-level modernised bar/restaurant. Outside the ground, your best bet is the **Pivnice U Stadiony**, on the corner of Vršovická and Čeljabinská – an unpretentious source of cheap Staropramen.

In the stadium, there are two private bars. **Slavia-Klub** under the main stand is a joy, with team history displayed all over the walls and lavish meals served on matchdays, but can be hard to get into. Around the corner, in the bowels of the main stand, is a tiny **fans' hutch** where you may be more welcome to the modest sarnies curling their edges towards a TV precariously balanced on beer crates.

In the net

Libor Laubacher's once-unofficial website has been adopted by the club and continues to grow, with news, stats, history and multi-media areas, and an increasing amount of English content. It's now at: www.slavia.cz.

Hopping along – the Bohemians kangaroo

Groundhopping

🌐 Bohemians

V D'oličku, Vršovická 31
Capacity 17,000 (3,000 seated)
Colours Green-and-white shirts, green shorts
League champions 1983

Bohemians began the 1999/2000 season with a new lease of life, on the back of promotion back to the first division, a sponsorship deal with insurance company *CGU*, and the promise of a prolonged stay at their beloved if tatty D'oliček ground. A year earlier, facing another season of second-division football, fans were pulling souvenir clumps out of the hallowed turf, after hearing that management were to close the stadium and move home games to the Strahov...

Colloquially known as *Bohemka* and also nicknamed the Kangaroos after a tour of

Australia in 1926, Bohemians are a short hop from neighbours Slavia and have suffered a similarly blighted history. They were originally AFK Vršovice, named after the working-class district of Prague in which they play. The D'oliček ('Dimple') saw hard times and several name changes under communism. At one time the Kangaroos were even known as Spartak Stalingrad.

Under coach Tomáš Pospíchal, the club hit a purple patch in the Eighties, making the UEFA Cup semi-final in 1983, the year they won their first league title. They came within minutes of another in 1985, after which fraud investigators, perhaps tipped off by inscrutable Sparta and Dukla, arrested a club official – Bohemians' good name has been tainted ever since.

After Bohemians were relegated in 1997, the organisation representing all the club's sports departments transferred the stadium rights to a sister company, *Bohemians Real*. Protracted negotiations over use of the ground followed, but didn't stop the players from doing the business on the pitch in 1998/99. Fans, meanwhile, were treated by their new British sponsors to a traditional double-decker bus with which to follow the Kangaroos around the Czech Republic. They were rewarded in 1999/2000 with a seventh-place finish – and one of the club's best seasons in years.

To reach the Dimple, take red metro line C to I P Pavlova or green metro line A to Náměstí Míru, then tram #4 or #22 to Vršovické Náměstí. The *U Tří Soudků*, on the corner of Sportovní and Vršovická, is right opposite the Dimple's away sector, so it can be full of mean Moravians on match day. Worse, the landlord has removed the unique display of scarves.

Passing by the stadium, further up Sportovní, you'll find *U Sokola*, a home fans' favourite, with a terrace and food. For some real local colour, try the *Eva Bistro*, a small corner store where they sell Staropramen from someone's living room. From the tram stop, walk back down Vršovicka, past the stadium, to the corner of K Botiči.

🌑 Viktoria Žižkov

Na Žižkov, Seifertova Třída
Capacity 8000 (1,500 seated)
Colours Red-and-white striped shirts, red shorts
League champions 1928
Cup winners 1994

Ah, Žižkov! Elsewhere in Prague, fan loyalty may depend on your father's persuasion, but Žižkov's is one born of the Prague 3 district, with its rundown bars and staunch Communist loyalties. After decades in the doldrums, the club was rescued in the spring of 1992 by multi-millionaire Vratislav Čekan, who saw it as his mission to rejuvenate his beloved *Viktorka*. Leasing the stadium from the Prague 3 district council, Čekan raised the club from the bottom of the third to the first division in two years, his influence peaking with a Czech cup triumph in 1994.

The bubble burst when the local sports authority realised they had a similar municipal contract signed the year before. Czech bureaucracy then caused Čekan to pull out in the summer of 1996. But although the team have lost faith, the supporters have not, and a visit to Žižkov, with its piped chants and flat caps, is like a taste of milltown England in the 1890s.

The 1999/2000 season looked like being particularly gloomy as the team at one stage dallied dangerously close to the relegation zone, but they pulled themselves clear in the second half of the season to finish a respectable ninth.

To get to Žižkov, take tram #5, #9 or #26 from the Hlavní Nádraží train station along Senovážné Náměstí. It's about a five-minute ride to the ground and the tatty bars that surround it.

If you get tired of gloom and grime, the *Pod Viktorkou*, Seifertova 55, opposite the ground, has discovered the delights of tablecloths and wallpaper. It even sells its own T-shirts, and frames those of the team. Inside the ground, the *restaurace* behind the home goal doesn't sell beer, but a stall around the corner does.

🌑 Marila Pribram

Stadion Na Litavce, Postovni schránka 59
Capacity 10,000
Colours All yellow with claret trim
League champions 1953, 1956, 1958, 1961–64, 1966, 1977, 1979, 1982
Cup winners 1961, 1965–66, 1969, 1981, 1983, 1985, 1990

'Dukla Prague', celebrated in song by Half Man Half Biscuit and Czech football's most famous name, has been consigned to the history books. The club moved out of the capital in 1997 after merging with the local team at Příbram, a small mining town 50km away. Then, in the summer of 2000, the 'Dukla' bit disappeared, to be replaced by the name of the team's latest sponsor.

Although yet to grab the imagination of the Liverpool underground songwriters, Příbram did set the second division alight in their first season, 1996/97, winning it by 19 points and making the cup final, only to lose the latter on a 'golden goal' to Slavia. While life in the first division since then has not been a bed of roses, 'Marila' are in a much better position now than when they were merely paying lip service to the military and playing before a few hundred people in Prague.

Few former Eastern Bloc army clubs had sunk as low as Dukla in the summer of 1994. Having been relegated from the first division after one win all season, the club couldn't afford the professional licence fee to stay in the second division, and management reluctantly volunteered to send their team into the amateur third. How the mighty had fallen.

In line with communist restructuring of the game, the Czechoslovak army was given its own team, ATK, in 1948 – they became Dukla in 1956. The club could call up any player it liked by drafting him into the army, and the generals had wise advisors. Josef Masopust, European Footballer of the Year in 1962, led the team to five titles in the Sixties, along with a European Cup semi-final, against Celtic in 1967.

Of future generations, goalkeeper Ivo Viktor and Zdeněk Nehoda, the most-capped Czech player of all time, starred in Czechoslovakia's European Championship-winning side of 1976. With Nehoda and Ladislav Vízek, Dukla had a successful time of it in the Eighties, and even won the cup – on penalties – as recently as 1990.

But by then there were new forces in charge – market ones – and the army withdrew its support in January 1994. Since then, Dukla have slowly pulled themselves up by the bootstraps under the enterprising leadership of a new owner, Bohumir Duričko. In 1995/96 Duričko bought another Czech side, second-division FC Příbram, and subsumed them into Dukla, who then assumed Příbram's position in the higher division.

After promotion was won in 1997, Duričko moved the club, lock, stock and rusting army barrel, to the modest Na Litavce stadium in Příbram, which the local council offers rent-free.

The **regular bus** #18 for Příbram leaves from Na Knížečí station, near metro line B metro stop Anděl (return fare 45Kč, journey time about an hour). The bus driver can let you down at the nearest stop, from which it's a 15min walk past crumbling Seventies blocks and rows of neat allotments to the ground.

A **ticket** for a seat in the covered stand is 60Kč and there's a small refreshment hatch behind the turnstile block. The Sunday bus service is less frequent, so either get the last bus back at 5pm, take a taxi (about 2,500Kč) or stay at the comfortable *Modrý Hrozen* hotel (☎0306/28901) in the main square.

Eat, drink, sleep…

Bars and clubs

Czech **beer** is the best and the cheapest in the world. In tourist traps near to Prague's major attractions, you may be stung for 50Kč, but otherwise you should be paying 25Kč for a half-litre of the stuff,

either light (*světlé*) or dark (*tmavé*). The **classic brews** are Plzeňský Prazdroj (known as Pilsner Urquell in export markets) and Budvar (the original Budweiser). Beers local to Prague include Staropramen, Krušovice, Měštan and Radegast. The best commonly available **dark beers** are Braník and Purkmistr.

The average beer hall (*pivnice*) will close around 10–11pm. A wine bar (*vinárna*) will tend to close later. The local spirit is *becherovka*, a strong liqueur. Watch out for sanity-stealing absinthe bars. **Nightclubbing** is as good as you'll find east of Vienna.

Caffrey's, Staroměstské Náměstí 10. Best of the Irish pubs, right on the Old Town Square. Full breakfast fry-ups, local and stout brews, back-room screen for Sky Sports. Most credit cards. Open 9am–1am.

Dugout, Týn 1. Clean, modern and two steps from the Old Town Square, a cellar bar with a hipper expat crowd watching Sky Sports and other satellite football. Sports bar menu and happy hour specials. Open until 1am.

Hostinec Fotbal, Kozi 17. In the same building as the branch Czech FA offices, a friendly local football bar with a big screen for match coverage. Cheap beer and open until 2am. Namesake restaurant next door. Short walk from Staroměstská metro.

Roxy, Dlouha 33. Old cinema now the best dance spot in town, thanks to DJs occasionally flown in from the UK and bizarre touches like a bumpy dancefloor. Tearoom until midnight and balcony bar. Metro Náměstí Republiky.

Zelezne Dvere, Jilská 18/Michalská 19. Possibly the best bar in town, in an alleyway in the Old Town, with a lounge feel, top sounds and cocktail specials. Flaming absinthe, flaming blondes, flaming hangovers. Open daily until 4am.

Restaurants

Most beer halls serve hefty portions of pork, dumplings and sauerkraut, mainstays of the Czech high-calorie diet. A restaurants (*restaurace*) will have a slightly more adventurous menu, although the clientèle will probably still be tucking into goulash or **beef in cream sauce** (*svíčková*). Fish also features on most menus. **Lunch** is the main meal of the day, and most restaurants close by 10pm. Expect to pay 250–350Kč for a full spread and surly service.

De Lux, Vácslavské Náměstí 4. Under the *Bata* building at the bottom end of Wenceslas, a spacious, ornate, restaurant-cum-nightclub serving decent Vietnamese food until 4am. Live jazz and DJs on certain nights.

Restaurace Fotbal, Kozi 7. Tastefully presented football-themed restaurant, decorated with atmospheric action shots from the Thirties. Open daily 11am–midnight, most credit cards accepted.

Taj Mahal, Škrétova 10. Standard Indian basement restaurant right behind the national museum with all the usual fare. Around 250Kč a main course, most credit cards.

U Zlatého Soudku, Ostrovní 28. As good as any of its kind downtown, a local hostelry serving huge portions of classic Czech fare, under the watchful eye of portraits of old Soviet leaders. Open daily 11am–midnight, most major credit cards accepted.

Zlatá Hvezda, Ve Smeckách 12. More local and low-key than its huge sports bar competitor, *Jagr*, round the corner at Wenceslas 56, the *Golden Star* has a young clientèle tucking into cheap local dishes over the latest offering from Sky Sports. The *Demijohn* bar at #16 is a dimly lit classic.

Accommodation

Finding a centrally located, budget hotel in Prague can be a problem. The best option may be a hostel bed or a private room arranged through an accommodation agency such as *AVE* (open daily 6am–11pm, ☎02/2422 3521, fax 02/5731 2986, most major credit cards) which has branches at the major train stations and in the Old

Town Square. With the recent upgrading of the city's hotels, any double room for under 2,000Kč is snapped up pretty quickly. Book ahead, whatever the season.

Hotel Coubertin, Atletická 4 (☎02/3335 3109, fax 02/2051 3208). Right next to the Strahov stadium, with stunning views of the city, this is a well-run and modern if functional hotel a racket's throw from the neighbouring sports facilities. Doubles at 2000Kč, singles at 1600Kč. Most credit cards.

Grand Hotel Evropa, Václavské Náměstí 25 (☎02/2422 8117, fax 02/2422 4544). Cut-price luxury at the most beautiful hotel in town, bang in Wenceslas Square. Reserve a room well in advance – they're a bargain at 1,500–2,700Kč for a single, 2,000–4,000Kč a double. The higher rates are for suites with period furniture. Most credit cards.

Hotel Koruna, Opatovická 16 (☎02/2491 5174, fax 02/292 492). Conveniently located budget hotel, whose elegant facade belies the prosaic, Socialist-style rooms. Singles at 2,300Kč, Doubles at 3,300Kč. No credit cards.

U Krále Jiřího, Liliová 10 (☎02/2222 0925, fax 02/2222 1707). Tiny pension in the Old Town above the *James Joyce* pub, with attic rooms and its own bar. You'll pay 2,000Kč a single, 3,000Kč a double. Most credit cards.

Pension Unitas/Cloister Inn, Bartolomějská 9 (☎02/232 7700, fax 02/232 7709, e-mail unitas @cloister-inn.cz). Former prison cells which once held Václav Havel, now converted into a comfortable Old Town basement hostel with three-star inn rooms upstairs. Singles/doubles around 1,000Kč downstairs, 3,000Kč upstairs. Most credit cards.

Denmark

Dansk Boldspil Union (DBU) Idrættens Hus, Brøndby Stadion 20, 2605 Brøndby
☎4326 2222 Fax 4326 2245 E-mail dbu@dbu.dk

League champions Herfølge **Cup winners** Viborg FF **Promoted** Haderslev, FC
Midtjylland **Relegated** Vejle, Esbjerg

European participants 2000/01 Herfølge, Brøndby (UCL qualifiers); AB
Copenhagen, Viborg (UEFA Cup); AaB Aalborg, Silkeborg (Intertoto Cup)

After three comprehensive defeats and not even a goal to cheer up their supporters, Denmark bade farewell to Euro 2000 while their coach, Bo Johansson, packed his bags and went back to his native Sweden. It says a lot about Danish football that at his last press conference as national team coach, the Danish media allowed the likeable Johansson to reminisce about the good times he had enjoyed at the helm, and to suggest that the future looked bright for his replacement Morten Olsen. There were no vegetables on the back page, and no inquest into the team's poor results. Their side having been drawn with France, Holland and the Czech Republic in the group phase, the Danes were honest and sensible enough to have realised – long before the tournament – that their visit to the Low Countries would be brief.

Olsen, who will be assisted by Michael Laudrup, inherits a decent if unspectacular group of players who, as always, are drawn from all over the continent. But at domestic level, the leap in quality promised by the founding of a fully professional *Superliga* has failed to materialise.

Many clubs have been left in limbo by the changes, some of them in Copenhagen itself. But the leading clubs have been the subject of stock-exchange flotations, drawn

Sandwiched by the French – Allan Nielsen loses out

serious money from sponsorship, and been able to carry out stadium improvements to bring Denmark's grounds into line with the best in Europe, in terms of facilities if not size.

At the end of the 1998/99 season, AaB Aalborg's title triumph broke the three-year hegemony of Brøndby, raising interest

Basics

Citizens of the EU, America, Canada, Australia and New Zealand require only a **passport** to enter Denmark.

The Danish currency is the **krone** (plural kroner), divided into 100 øre. There are coins for 25 and 50 øre, 1 krone, 2, 5, 10 and 20 kroner, and notes for 50, 100, 200, 500 and 1,000 kroner. There are around 12kr to £1. Change money at banks – there is a **fixed commission charge** of 25kr regardless of the amount. Banking hours are Mon–Fri 9.30am–4pm. You'll find plenty of cash machines accepting the usual cards.

There are two kinds of **public telephones**. Coin phones take 1kr or 5kr coins, while card phones take cards costing 30kr, 50kr or 100kr – buy them at post offices or news kiosks. The international access code for Denmark is 45 and there are no individual city codes – each customer number has eight digits. To get an international line from inside the country, dial 00. Cheap rates apply Mon–Sat 7.30pm–8am and all day Sundays, but not to every country.

Denmark has an excellent domestic **train network** run by *DSB*, the Danish state railways. Tthere is no discount on return tickets and seat reservations (15kr) are compulsory on *InterCity* trains. Note that the *InterCityLyn* service is aimed at the business traveller and has a 33% surcharge.

Only trips to outlying areas will require you to become acquainted with Danish **buses**, but this is a country with a huge number of islands and you may well find yourself wanting to make use of the odd **ferry**. The cost of this will be included in your train fare if it is part of a DSB service. Otherwise, as a foot passenger you'll pay around 40kr for a short crossing – just turn up and pay at the terminal.

---

levels outside the capital and restoring the spread of strength that had seen five different clubs win the *Superliga* in its first five years in the first half of the Nineties. The pattern continued in 1999/2000, when it was the turn of unsung Herfølge to put Brøndby in the shade.

Like all revolutionaries, the progressives in Danish football had to fight hard to bring about change. There was the conservative sporting establishment to convince but, more importantly, there was an ideological opposition, in what is a deeply social-democratic country, to the commercialisation, competitiveness and personality cults of modern soccer. Yet the national team's surprise success in winning Euro '92 took the sting out of opposition to the new approach. When the Danes beat Germany to be crowned kings of Europe, the sons and daughters of those stern egalitarians were dancing in the streets, their faces painted red and white.

Latecomers to the modern business of football they may have been, but the Danes

were one of the first continental nations to take up the game. Københavns Boldklub (KB) were founded in 1876, long before most of the big English clubs had had their foundation meetings in the local pub. With this head start Denmark performed well in the early Olympic competitions. In London in 1908 they won the silver medal, losing to England in the final after beating France 17–1 in their opening match – a game in which Sophus Nielsen scored ten goals, setting an international record which has not been broken since. (One of Nielsen's team-mates, Niels Bohr, went on to win the Nobel Prize for Physics.)

Four years later, in Stockholm, the Danes were again Olympic runners-up. But by the Twenties, the Danish game was in decline and it wasn't until 1948 that they made any further impression, winning bronze at the London games.

As in Sweden, strict amateurism forced many of Denmark's best players to leave the country. The first Dane to make an impression abroad was Nils Middleboe, who played at Chelsea between 1913 and 1921. Three members of the 1948 Olympic bronze-medal winning side, Karl Præst and Karl and John Hansen, moved to Juventus, and by the Sixties Danes were popping up all over Europe – St James' Park veterans may recall one Preben Arentoft scoring a crucial goal for Newcastle in the 1969 Fairs' Cup final.

The Danish league was dominated by a dozen or so small teams from Copenhagen until the Sixties, when Aarhus and Esbjerg began to make an impact. Meanwhile a Copenhagen Select XI, comprising players from KB, B93, Frem and AB and known as the *Stævnet*, competed without distinction in the Fairs' Cup.

After a silver-medal performance at the 1960 Rome Olympics, the Danish national team failed to qualify for the final stages of either the World Cup or the European Championship for more than two decades. But the seeds of change were planted in 1976, when the Danish FA finally bowed to pressure to include professionals in the side. The man who forced their hand was Allan Simonsen, European Footballer of the Year in 1977, who set a continent alight in the colours of Borussia Mönchengladbach and Barcelona, before ending his career with a bizarre move to Charlton Athletic of the English second division.

Simonsen was to be a role model for a whole generation of Danish players in the Eighties, when the likes of John Sivabæk, Jesper Olsen, Peter Schmeichel and Jan Mølby all moved to England. Liverpool midfielder Mølby, with his perfectly developed Scouse accent and Sunday League beer belly, was the most popular, 'keeper Schmeichel the most successful – a giant rock of a man upon whom Manchester United would build their Nineties legend.

It wasn't just English football which witnessed an influx of talented Danes. Michael Laudrup, probably the best player Denmark has ever produced, enjoyed a glittering career with Lazio, Juventus, Barcelona and Real Madrid. And Flemming Povlsen was a consistent goalscorer with Cologne, PSV and Dortmund before injury forced him into premature retirement in 1995.

Face in the crowd – former national coach Sepp Piontek (centre of picture) at Euro 2000

Perhaps appropriately, it was a non-Dane, German-born Sepp Piontek, who was to bring the country's scattered exiles together and mould them into a world-class national team. His Denmark side beat England at Wembley in 1983 to qualify for the European Championship finals for the first time, and theirs was to be an impressive début – after losing to France in their opening game, the Danes qualified from their group thanks to a 5–0 hammering of Yugoslavia and a thrilling 3–2 victory over Belgium. In the semi-finals they played most of the football against Spain but lost on penalties.

The Spaniards crushed Danish hopes again at the Mexico World Cup two years later. As in France, Piontek's Danes impressed in their group games, defeating Scotland, Uruguay and West Germany in style. But they were destroyed 5–1 by Spain in the second round.

After losing all three group games at Euro '88 and failing to qualify for Italia '90, Denmark looked a fading force. But their greatest moment was yet to come. Having apparently missed the boat to Euro '92, the Danes were handed a last-minute lifeline when Yugoslavia, the team which had topped their qualifying section, were squeezed out of the tournament by the pressure of international sanctions. The Danish squad would be without Michael Laudrup, who wasn't seeing eye-to-eye with coach Richard Møller Nielsen. But other stalwarts such as Schmeichel, Povlsen and Michael's younger brother Brian were happy to cancel their summer holidays in order to represent their country.

Even so, the team were badly underprepared – and looked it after a dull goalless draw with England and a 1–0 defeat by hosts Sweden in their opening games. But an unexpected victory over France earned the Danes a semi-final against the holders Holland which they won on penalties, and suddenly Møller Nielsen's men found themselves in the final against newly united Germany. There, a stunning goal from John Jensen, which was to earn him

an ill-fated move to Arsenal, and a late clincher from Kim Vilfort saw the gate-crashers run away with the prize. Nobody – Danes included – could quite believe it.

Although Denmark failed to qualify for USA '94 and failed to impress at Euro '96, the national team was then usefully reshaped by Bo Johansson, who combined the talents of both Laudrup brothers with the continuing solidity of Schmeichel. At France '98, the Danes made heavy weather of their group matches before playing their most inventive football for a decade in the knockout rounds. They destroyed Nigeria 4–1 in Paris, and had Marc Rieper's header bounced down into the net from the crossbar rather than over it, they'd have taken Brazil to extra-time in the quarter-finals. After the 3–2 defeat, Michael Laudrup, sole survivor from the *Danish Dynamite* side of '86, threw his armband, shirt and boots into the crowd to signal his retirement.

There are not yet any players of Laudrup's quality to replace him and, while not too much should be read into Denmark's results in the 'group of death' at Euro 2000, the side clearly lacked both a dominant personality and star quality. Yet the Laudrup family has a habit of inspiring those around them, and Michael's new role as coach may yet re-ignite the dynamite.

Essential vocabulary

Hello *God dag*
Goodbye *Farvel*
Yes *Ja*
No *Nej*
Two beers, please *To øl, tak!*
Thank you *Tak!*
Men's *Herrer*
Women's *Damer*
Where is the stadium? *Hvor er stadion?*
What's the score? *Hvad staar det?*
Referee *Dommer*
Offside *Offside*

Match practice

Despite the dramatic changes taking place in the Danish game – helped by a huge increase in in sponsorship – few games are sell-outs, and matches are generally played in a laid-back atmosphere, with plenty of humour and English chants.

The season runs from late July to the end of November, breaks for four months, then continues from mid-March until early June. *Superliga* rounds generally take place on Sundays at 3pm, with live TV games on Sundays at 5pm and Mondays at 7pm. Lower-league clubs often stick to traditional match times – Copenhagen's Fremad Amager and B93 have Sunday morning and Saturday lunchtime kick-offs respectively.

A different league

The *Superliga* features 12 clubs, playing each other three times in the course of a season. Clubs are given home advantage before the season starts on a co-efficient system.

The bottom two teams in the *Superliga* are relegated and replaced by the top two from the 16-team first division (*første division*). Four teams swap between the first and second division (*anden division*), and below this are four regional leagues – *Danmarksserien* – which host *Superliga* reserve teams among others.

Up for the cup

The *Landspokalturneringen*, Denmark's main knockout competition, begins in July and finishes the following May, with *Superliga* clubs entering at the fifth-round stage in September. Lower-division sides are automatically given home advantage, and ties are settled on one game, extra-time and penalties if necessary. The semi-finals in April are two-legged, while the final takes place at Copenhagen's Parken at 3pm on Ascension Day; this is again decided on extra-time and penalties if necessary.

Just the ticket

You'll only need to buy advance tickets for the FCK–Brøndby derby, big European games and internationals; otherwise, just pay at the turnstiles. Ticket prices are around 60–80kr for standing space (*ståplads*) and upwards of 90–100kr for a seat (*siddeplads*). If you want to stand with the visiting fans, ask for *udeholdet*. Programmes are around 15kr in the top flight, often free at lower-division grounds.

Half-time

Danish football would be unimaginable without sausages (*pølser*), usually sold with bread and a choice of mustard for about 25kr, and beer – usually an excellent local brew such as Carlsberg, Tuborg or Faxe. If hunger strikes after the final whistle, don't panic – you won't have to walk far to find a *pølser* wagon parked on a street corner. Most grounds have either clubhouses or fully blown restaurants, but arrive early if you want a pre-match meal.

Action replay

Live league games on satellite channel *TV3* are scheduled for Sundays at 5pm and Mondays at 7pm, with a highlights package shown after each. (Sister channel *3+* shows Spanish action on Sunday evenings.)

State *TV2* has the rights for all Danish international games, while *Canal Plus* has the rights to the English Premiership, showing the *Sky* games on Sundays and Mondays all season long, plus maatches on Saturdays during the Danish winter break. The channel also shows two Italian *Serie A* games on Sundays.

The back page

The authorative football weekly is *Tipsbladet* (Fridays, 20kr), whose coverage includes two pages on the English game. It has recently been undercut by *Spil Op* (Tuesdays, 10kr), which has more information for the pools punter.

Such is the rise in football's domestic profile that the quality mainstream press have had to beef up their coverage – look out for heavy Monday morning sports sections in *Politiken* and *Berlingske Tidende*. Tabloids *Ekstra Bladet* and *BT* track the day-to-day transfer rumours.

Ultra culture

Much of Danish fan culture has been imported from England but, unlike their

A very British crowd – AB Copenhagen fans before a local derby with Brøndby, 1999

counterparts in Sweden, supporters here have not been tempted to copy English violence. The Eighties saw the rise of the *Roligans* (*rolig* means peaceful), fans who followed the national side to France in 1984 and Mexico in 1986. They invented the fashion for face-painting, donning red-and-white make-up as well as daft Viking hats, and exuding goodwill. In most cases, they could afford to – these supporters were thirtysomethings happy to flex their credit cards on a potent new hobby.

Thanks partly to the exploits of the *Roligans*, football lost its sad image at home and well-organised supporters' clubs, usually linked to management and with easy access to players, began to flourish, many adopting English names and English terrace anthems. As the Nineties wore on, a younger generation of fans, embarrassed by the *Roligan* style (or lack of it) looked to Germany and Italy for inspiration, bringing flares, firecrackers, flags and the mass wearing of replica shirts to stadia for the first time. Today, although you'll still see *Roligans* at international games, there is

more bite to the chanting at major Danish league matches, even the odd scuffle when FCK meet Brøndby. At the same time, mass travelling support is still the exception rather than the rule, and many provincial games in Denmark have the feel of a village cricket match.

In the net
The Danish FA runs a rather serious, text-heavy official website, with a surprising lack of English-language content, at: www.dbu.dk/ forsiden/index.html. Then again, the DBU also sponsors the excellent online RSSSF stats archive (see Austria), so perhaps we shouldn't complain.

Speaking of stats, Jesper Lauridsen continues to maintain an extensive Danish archive at: www.login.dknet.dk/~rorschak/fodbold.html. The site covers all levels of the Danish game and offers an embarrassment of links to stats sites worldwide.

For Danish football links, there is a further, very wide-ranging one-stop source at: www.fodbold.com.

Copenhagen

You might have to look around for it now, but Copenhagen is steeped in football tradition. The first football club on the continent was formed here – Københavns Boldklub in 1876 – and the city's amateur clubs continued to win Danish league titles right up until the introduction of professionalism in the early Eighties.

Although lesser surburban teams like Lyngby and Hvidovre then began to shine, it was Brøndby, from a grey area of factories and warehouses in the far west of town, who took Danish football into the modern era and spelled the beginning of the end for the amateur clubs. When KB and B1903 merged to form a new force, FC København, Copenhagen at last had a city rivalry born of the late 20th century rather than the 19th.

The new *Superliga*; the complete overhaul of the national stadium, Parken, into an international arena favoured by UEFA; and the sizeable followings enjoyed by Brøndby and FCK have all contributed to Copenhagen becoming a modern football capital – anyone who was here the night Denmark won the 1992 European Championship would have found it hard to imagine the amateur days of 20 years before.

The thrilling fields

Brøndby IF

Brøndby Stadion, Park Allé, Glostrup
Capacity 30,000 all-seated (terracing open for domestic games)
Colours Yellow shirts, blue shorts
League champions 1985, 1987–88, 1990–91, 1996–98
Cup winners 1989, 1994, 1998

In a city full of teams with long histories and proud traditions, it is the youngest club

which has made the biggest impression in the professional era. Encouraged by local mayor Kjeld Rasmussen, who promised to provide a new stadium, *Brøndbyernes Idrætsforening* were formed in 1964 from the merger of two local teams in east and west Brøndby, a drab industrial zone in Copenhagen's western suburbs. Rasmussen was the club's first president.

After 18 years in the lower leagues, the team were promoted to the old first division and turned semi-professional. In 1985 they lifted their first domestic championship and took the decision to become the country's first fully professional club.

The bulk of Denmark's 1992 European Championship-winning side had been with Brøndby in the mid-Eighties – most notably John Jensen, Peter Schmeichel and Brian Laudrup. And it was the Laudrup family who were at the heart of Brøndby's irresistible rise. Brian's and Michael's father, Finn, was a leading player with the historic amateur club KB in the Seventies and had a spell in Austria with Wiener SC. At the end of the decade Brøndby – then in the third division – invited Finn to join them. He surprised everyone when he accepted the invitation and helped plant the first seeds of professionalism at the club before returning for a brief spell at KB. In 1981, at the age of 36, he came back to Brøndby to lead them up to the top flight.

Finn's most important decision was to encourage his son Michael to leave KB as a schoolboy for the more professional (but then second-division) Brøndby. The move revealed the bankruptcy of KB's amateur approach and indicated the growing status of Brøndby. In 1982, Finn retired as a player to become coach, and his #10 shirt was taken by Michael. When Michael left for Italy after a season and a half, younger brother Brian took his shirt in turn.

Finn Laudrup is rightly credited for introducing real scouting, training and overall professionalism to Brøndby, but his pioneering work was so nearly destroyed.

Copenhagen essentials

Kastrup airport, 8km from the centre of Copenhagen, is linked with the city's central station, Hovedbanegården, by a train service (every 20mins 5am–1am, journey time 15mins, fare 18kr). Tickets are sold at the office in the departure terminal, or from a nearby machine. A taxi will cost about 125kr.

Ferries from Norway and Sweden dock at Nyhavn, a 10min walk from the heart of the city centre, while **international trains** arrive at Hovedbanegården, opposite the Tivoli gardens and just a few minutes' walk from the main pedestrian shopping street, Strøget. **North Sea ferries** from Harwich, Hull and Newcastle arrive at the port of Esbjerg on the Danish mainland – a 270km train ride from Copenhagen.

Public transport is made up of buses and *S-tog* suburban trains. Services run 5am–12.30am, after which there are **night buses**. The *Copenhagen Card* costs 155kr and allows free use of the city transport system for 24 hours, plus entry to most museums; a 48-hour version costs 255kr, a 72-hour one 320kr. If you aren't going to visit museums, an all-zone, 24-hour travel card costs 70kr, while a *Rabatkort* strip of ten tickets is 80kr for two zones. For a single journey buy a *grundbillet* (12kr), valid for unlimited transfers within one hour and two zones. Additional zones cost 6kr. On buses pay the driver – night buses charge double – and for S-trains pay at the station, punching the ticket in the yellow timeclock on the platform.

Taxis operate a 22kr standing charge plus 8kr per kilometre (10kr 4pm–7am and at weekends). Those with signs indicating 'fri' can be flagged down – otherwise call ☎3135 3535. Most accept credit cards.

The main **tourist office** (Sep–Apr Mon–Fri 9am–4.30pm, Sat 9am–1.30pm; May–Aug Mon–Sat 9am–8pm, Sun 10am–8pm, ☎3311 1325) is adjacent to the train station at Bernstorffsgarde 1, where you'll find a free copy of the *Copenhagen This Week* listings magazine.

The best shop for local and international **football gear** is *Unisport* (Mon–Fri 10am–6pm, Sat 10am–2pm, most credit cards), Vesterbrogade 45, Vesterbro.

In 1991 the club's ambitious directors, flush with cash from the heavy exporting of playing talent, decided to purchase *Interbank*. The move was a disaster – the bank quickly went into receivership, leaving the club saddled with debts of £35million. Ground development plans were put on hold and Brøndby had no choice but to continue selling players.

Happily, the business failure had little effect on the club's growth. On the field, Brøndby enjoyed a run to the semi-finals of the UEFA Cup in 1991, and dumped Liverpool out of the same competition four years later. Off the field the club increased its stadium capacity and witnessed the rapid growth of a large and well-organised fan base across the country.

The formation of FC København in 1991 completed the picture – now Brøndby fans had someone to hate as well

as love, their view of FCK's support as rootless and middle-class helping to shape their perception of themselves as genuine, working-class fans following a genuinely professional club.

After Eighties coach Ebbe Skovdahl had returned to the club and introduced an attacking 4–4–2 formation, Brøndby won three league titles on the spin from 1995/96. At the third time of asking the team qualified for their first Champions' League campaign in 1998, only to be lumped into the 'group of death' alongside Manchester United, Bayern Munich and Barcelona – they won their first game, 2–1 at home to Bayern thanks to a pair of late goals, then lost the rest.

The European campaign seemed to have a dispiriting effect on the squad, as despite the presence of Mogens Krogh in goal, Søren Colding at the back, John Jensen in midfield and Ebbe Sand in attack, Brøndby then lost their domestic title to AaB. Skovdahl then departed for Aberdeen, but despite being hit with injuries and never really ever hitting peak form, Brondby were in the 1999/2000 title race until the end, yet finished two points behind John Jensen's Herfølge.

Little obvious squad strengthening took place during the summer of 2000 in readiness for the Champions' League qualifying campaign, but fans at least had the consolation that were the team to make it back into the European big time, they would be playing on home soil – Brøndby's stadium redevelopment was finally due for completion in July.

Here we go!

Take *S-tog* B to **Glostrup** station, then bus #131 to the stadium. Allow 30mins for the journey, and be prepared for a serious crush on the bus.

Just the ticket

Only the fixture with FCK sells out, so turn up and pay on the day – seats 90kr, standing 70kr. Stands are named after sponsors, the livelier fans preferring the Faxe end, the quieter ones the OBS end; the latter has one section allocated to away support. The Codan stand, running along the side of the pitch, is probably the best choice for neutrals.

Swift half

Hovsa, Seminarievej 1, is a 5min walk from the ground and has a fine pennant collection, satellite TV and a summer beer garden. Fight your way through the yellow-and-blue shirts ordering glasses of draught Tuborg. Everyone knows this as the pre- and post-match bar so it is always crowded on matchdays, but this is one place in Copenhagen where they don't mind you drinking on the street outside.

Club merchandise

The **official store** (open Mon–Thur 8am–10pm, Fri 8am–7pm, Sat–Sun 9am–6pm) is at Gildhøj-centret, right across the street from the stadium. Souvenir booths are at all corners of the ground, the biggest by Gate C at the south end terrace.

Ultra culture

At the end of 1993 the official fan club, *Brøndby Support*, had barely a thousand members; today it has close to ten times that number, with separate sections all over the country. With their combination of Latin-style flames and flags, this lot are the most passionate supporters in Denmark. The Latin influence even stretches to a thousand-strong choir meticulously co-ordinated by a man with a megaphone.

In print

A bog-standard match programme is produced for all home games and costs 10kr, while fanzine *2 Minutes Left* (5kr) is as irreverent as things get in Denmark.

In the net

The club's **official website** is fast, attractively laid-out and efficient. It includes some English sections, an online shopping area and a history of the club at: www.brondby-if.dk. Meanwhile *Brøndby Support* continue to run their own excellent site at: www.bif-support.dk.

Brøndby bite – Søren Colding takes aim

FC København

Idrætsparken, P H Lings Allé 4
Capacity 41,500 all-seated
Colours All white with blue trim
League champions 1993
Cup winners 1995, 1997

FC København, commonly known as FCK, are a business merger which may yet pay off. Having bought the national stadium, Parken, thanks to a further share issue on the stock exchange, Denmark's richest team have been steadily attracting city support, helped by the high-profile signing of Brian Laudrup in 1998. Sadly, Laudrup's subsequent departure, just six months into a two-and-a-half-year contract, served only to confirm the club's susceptbility to being blown off-course by external events.

In 1996, FCK were the laughing stock of Denmark, facing relegation and bankruptcy. Yet only three years earlier, they were boasting of domestic domination and European success within 12 months of their formation.

With the advent of the *Superliga* in 1992, Copenhagen's amateur clubs could not hope to compete with the suburban professionals of Brøndby and go-ahead provincial clubs like Aalborg, Aarhus and Odense. Two occasionally played at the national stadium: B1903, league runners-up in 1992, who had the players but no infrastructure; and KB, who had the tradition and the support but who hadn't been near the title in over a decade. Harald Nielsen, an ex-1903 star who had played with Bologna in the late Fifties, led a consortium of businessmen and former players intent on merging the two clubs. The result was FC København, a bold new club to play at the newly revamped Parken.

FCK spent a small fortune on bringing in some of the top players from the provinces, and won the championship in their first season, 1992/93, with some skilful, glamorous football. But the instant glory and media attention failed to create a firm fan base. The crowd were happy to cheer Brian Laudrup's Milan when they won 6–0 at FCK in the European Cup the following season, and mismanagement gradually allowed the club to slide into further ignominy. To stave off financial collapse, captain Allan Nielsen – later of Spurs – was sold to rivals Brøndby, and subsequent cup wins only produced more embarrassing performances in Europe.

The appointment of Flemming Østergård as director in 1997 turned things around. He brought with him a couple of players – and no little cash – from Lyngby, and as the team's form picked up, the club was floated on the Copenhagen stock exchange. FCK finished third in 1997/98, but were given a sharp lesson in class when Brøndby beat them 4–1 in the cup final.

With crowds averaging a credible 10,000 and a squad strengthened by the signing of Laudrup (who joined immediately after his goal for Chelsea had knocked FCK out of the Cup-Winners' Cup in Copenhagen), the team were theoretically capable of a title challenge in 1998/99. But it failed to materialise, and after coach Christian Andersen was sacked, Laudrup too decided to leave, his inability to stay the course proving a devastating blow, even to supporters as familiar with the fragility of dreams as FCK's. An eighth-place finish in 1999/2000 served only to prolong the collective hangover.

Here we go!

Take any of several *S-tog* lines to **Døsterport**, then bus #1. Extra buses are laid on for major matchdays. Allow 20mins from the main station.

Just the ticket

As well as FCK's home matches, the Parken also hosts most Danish internationals. Tickets are sold in advance through the *BilletNet* system at post offices, with anything unsold being available on matchdays at the booths behind the B end stand. Hardcore FCK fans favour the lower C stand, the lower B stand is for families, and away fans are allocated the D end. For most FCK games, simply pay on the day at the turnstiles – admission should be around 90kr.

Swift half

Different FCK fan factions meet at various spots around town, generally in the Nørrebro area. The *Fooligans* drink at the **Klovnens Bodega**, Rantzausgade 70, before drifting on to join other FCK fans nearer the stadium at traditional Danish pubs such as the **Trafikcaféen**, **Sankt Hans Torv** and **Café Stadion**.

Club merchandise

The **club shop** (Mon–Fri 11am–5.30pm, Sat 10am–2pm, most credit cards) on the corner of the Parken's C and D stands is large and well-stocked, with all manner of trinkets decorated in the white of B1903 and the blue of KB.

Ultra culture

The *FCK Fan Club* has some 7,000 members from across the city – nothing like as many as Brøndby but dwarfing the 200-strong *Cooligans*, the TV presenters, DJs and ad men in black clothes and shades who have their own section of the C stand at the Parken.

In print

FCK have the most colourful match programme in Denmark (15kr), while the FCK Fan Club also produces its own magazine, *Brølet* (20kr).

In the net

FCK is another example of a club that has turned a fan-run site into an official web presence. The fans responsible are the *Fusionsnipserne*, and their fine work can be seen at: www.fck.dk.

Groundhopping

🔘 Akademisk Boldklub

Gladsaxe Idrætspark, Skovdiget 1, Bagsværd
Capacity 10,000
Colours Green shirts, white shorts
League champions 1919, 1921, 1937, 1943, 1945, 1947, 1951–52, 1967
Cup winners 1999

The scholars of AB – their team was traditionally composed solely of students and

Tangled web – FCK 'keeper Michael Stensgård

professors from Copenhagen university – have enjoyed a surprise revival in the Nineties after years in the wilderness. Successful in the amateur era, when they played at Fælled Park by the national stadium, in 1965 AB were lured to a windswept athletics arena in the northwest suburb of Gladsaxe by the local mayor. There they festered for three decades before a cup run in 1995 – they beat Brøndby but lost to FCK in the final – and promotion to the *Superliga*.

Under the strict coaching of Christian Andersen, AB held their own in the top flight. He brought the best out of striker Chris Hermansen and veteran midfielder Brian Steen Nielsen, while the management raised £10million from a stock-exchange flotation and saw to much-needed ground improvements. To Andersen's dismay, they also sold key players abroad, including left-foot hot shot Peter Knudsen to Bari, and the coach left in a huff for FCK.

After blazing a trail at the top of the league during the autumn, AB found scoring difficult in the second half of the 1998/99 season. Knudsen returned from Italy in April, however, and while AB now had too much ground to make up in the league (they finished a distant third), they did win their first-ever Danish cup, Hermansen's goal proving decisive in a 2–1 win at the Parken that denied AaB the double.

The reconstructed Gladsaxe was unveiled to a disinterested public in August 1999 – not even free tickets got them bums on seats – and as the autumn wore on, shares plummeted and form dropped. The highlights were the signing of Bolton's Michael Johansen, and the promise of young defenders Martin Albrechtsen and Allan Olesen. A third-place *Superliga* finish was enough to get AB back into the UEFA Cup, but AaB got their revenge in the domestic up semi-finals, leaving the trophy cupboard bare.

Gladsaxe is a 20min ride on bus #250S from Hovedbanegården. Unless Brøndby are the visitors, there shouldn't be any queues at the turnstiles.

☕ Hvidovre

Hvidovre Stadion, Sollentuna Allé 1–3, Hvidovre
Capacity 15,000
Colours Red-and-white shirts, blue shorts
League champions 1966, 1973, 1981
Cup winners 1980

'It's not a matter of money,' said Peter Schmeichel on the day in December 1999 that he bought 100% of the shares in Hvidovre Fodbold A/S. 'This club is part of my history.'

Hvidovre are the local rivals to Brøndby, their star having fallen as Brøndby's rose. Many of the club's youth products, such as Schmeichel, have been snapped up by their wealthier neighbours, and the trend showed every sign of continuing until the big man stepped in to buy

the place, lock, stock and barrel. A new sponsorship deal with a Swedish telecoms firm was the first tangible evidence of the Schmeichel takeover, but fans will have to wait at least another year before they see him between the sticks – he's contracted to Sporting Lisbon.

To get to Hvidovre, take *S-tog* A towards Hundige and get off at **Friheden**, a 5min walk from the ground. The official fan club, the *Red Blacksmiths*, meet at *Johnny's Bodega*, Hvidovre vej 256.

☕ Lyngby

Lyngby Stadion, Lundtoftevej 61, Lyngby
Capacity 15,000
Colours Blue shirts, white shorts
League champions 1983, 1992
Cup winners 1984, 1985, 1990

After two league titles and three cup wins in the days immediately prior to professionalism, Lyngby FC are struggling to adjust to Denmark's brave new footballing world. They were weeks away from bankruptcy in the mid-Nineties before being rescued by a consortium led by Flemming Østergård – who then controversially became a director at FCK, taking key players with him. The club is renowned for finding unknown youngsters in the lower divisions and selling them on in order to survive in the *Superliga*, and 1999/2000 was pretty typical. Lyngby old left-winger Carsten Fredgård to Sunderland, but maintained a respectable position in the league thanks to the form of Swedish goalkeeper Per Fahlstrøm, midfielder Martin Johansen and ex-Brøndby winger Christian Magleby.

Lyngby Stadion is a tiny, homely venue surrounded by neatly trimmed hedges. To reach it, take *S-tog* A or B towards Holte or Hillerød, get off at **Lyngby**, then take bus #300S three stops in the direction of Kokkedal station. The family feel of the club is evident in the *Stadion Restaurant*, where members of the *Blue Vikings* fan club chat over a beer with club directors and assorted ex-players.

B93

Østerbro Stadion, Gunnar Nu Hansens Plads 3
Capacity 8,000
Colours White shirts, blue shorts
League champions 1927, 1929–30, 1934–35, 1939, 1942, 1946
Cup winners 1982

Although they play only a few yards away from FCK's Parken, B93 are in another world, that of the Copenhagen amateur era, when the club won a hatful of league titles. Surprisingly promoted to the *Superliga* in 1998, B93 managed only three wins all season (although one was against Brøndby), and were immediately relegated.

Former AB and FCK boss Christian Andersen steered the club into the running for a promotion place out of the first division in 1999/2000, but there was to be no instant return, and his departure in the close season did not bode well for 2000/2001.

The stadium is a 5min ride down **Østerbrogade** by tram #6 from Østerport. There's a typical Danish pub, *Stafetten*, by the main entrance.

BK Frem

Valby Idrætspark, Julius Andersenvej 3, Valby
Capacity 12,000
Colours Red-and-blue shirts, white shorts
League champions 1923, 1931, 1933, 1936, 1941, 1944
Cup winners 1956, 1978

Based in south Copenhagen, Frem is very much a workers' club. Its most famous player, Forties star John Hansen, went on to play for Juventus, but more recent ones (Kim Vilfort, Dan Eggen, Søren Colding) left for Brøndby before being able to help Frem to any honours.

The club actually went bankrupt in 1992 and were relegated to non-league football, but Frem battled their way up the lower echelons of the Danish league, reaching the first division in 1998 while holding on

to a loyal if small fan base. There's even a younger group of fans, gathered under the snappy slogan *Frem Is Cult*, who find the club's tradition an admirable alternative to, say, FCK's transparent modernity. To join them, take *S-tog* A from Hovedbanegården, direction Hundige, to **Ellebjerg**. You'll see the ground from the platform.

Fremad Amager

Sundby Idrætspark, Englandsvej 60, Sundby
Capacity 8,000
Colours Blue shirts, white shorts

Amager is the island which forms Copenhagen's eastern end, site of Kastrup airport. The islanders are an independent bunch, and the symbol of that independence is Fremad Amager. The closest the club has come to an honour in living memory was the cup final of 1972, lost 2–0 to Vejle. Some famous names have appeared in the blue-and-white, however – Søren Lerby, Frank Arnesen and Ivan Nielsen to name but three.

Amager have twice given up their professional status, a move they regretted when they achieved promotion to the *Superliga* in 1994 – only to drop back down again. Since then they've been a first division fixture, but a proud one, refusing FCK's offers of merger – one reason their working-class and bohemian fans keep turning up, generally on Sunday mornings at 10.30 as the ground has no floodlights.

If you're an early riser, take bus #30 from Rådhuspladsen by Tivoli, alighting at **Englandsvej** when the ground comes into view on the left-hand side after about 15mins.

Eat, drink, sleep...

Bars and clubs

Copenhagen is Scandinavia's party town, with liberal opening hours and drinks cheaper than Sweden or Norway. The beer is good too, the local Carlsberg and Tuborg breweries producing clean-tasting nectar (25–35kr). The westside Nørrebro area (bus #5 from Rådhuspladsen) has scores of bars and cafés – clubs charge a 50kr cover for live music.

Bang & Jensen, Istedgade 130. Popular bar/café at the less seedy end of Istedgade, the heart of the city's red light district further along.

Café Osborne, Elmegade 23. Expat without being overbearingly so. Sky TV, Irish motif and beer at 25kr a pint. Fixture list posted outside. In Nørrebro.

Rust, Guldbergsgade 8. Named after the young German pilot who flew into Moscow's Red Square, a combined bar/restaurant in the daytime, a dance club at night – though mildly sterilised by a refit. No dress code, packed at weekends. Nørrebro area.

Stereo Bar, Linnægade 16a. Not the trendy hangout it once was, but all the better for the thirtysomethings who gather here to listen to bearable music, occasionally diving down to the small basement dancefloor. Open until 3am.

Vega, Enghavevej 40. The busiest venue in Copenhagen with two concert halls, in an atmospheric old building. Doubles up as a club, with the ground-floor *Ideal Bar* a kitschy nightspot. In the hip Vesterbro area behind the main station.

Restaurants

Eating out in Copenhagen needn't require an extended overdraft. Look for restaurants – or, better yet, **traditional pubs** (*vinstue*) – serving a *Dagens ret*, a two-course Danish lunch for around 80kr. If you tire of fish and potatoes, the city has plenty of ethnic options, again centred around Nørrebro.

Base Camp, Halvtolv, Bygning 148, Holmen. A huge café/restaurant on Holmen, the historic navy island across the harbour. Substantial weekend brunches attract a good crowd. Doubles as a nightclub later on.

Peder Oxe, Gråbrødre Torv 11. Fair-priced restaurant in an atmospheric old building just north of Strøget, with lunchtime deals, substantial meat main dishes and fine salads.

Pussy Galore, Sankt Hans Torve. Busy and trendy eaterie in Nørrebro. A perfect spot for lunch, with first-rate hamburgers.

Sommersko, Kronprinsensgade 6. Large café in the centre of town, with a reasonably priced menu, generous opening hours (until 2am) and wide range of beers that attract a young crowd.

Accommodation

Staying overnight in Copenhagen is never going to be cheap, but hostels and 'sleep-ins' are all clean and comfortable, and the dearer hotels include an eat-as-much-as-you-like breakfast as part of the package. The tourist office (see *Essentials*) has a separate desk, marked *vørelsesanvisning*, which books rooms at a discount.

Bellahøj, Herbergvejen 8 (☎3828 9715, fax 3889 0210). Most youth hostels in town are open summer months only – this one is closed late Jan and Feb only. 80kr for a dorm bed, 24-hour reception. Bus #2 from Rådhuspladsen to Fuglsangs Allé.

Missionhotellet Nebo, Istedgade 6 (☎3121 1217, fax 3123 4774). Mid-priced hotel in a central location, friendly English-speaking owners. Around 380kr a single, 580kr a double.

Sømandshjemmet Bethel, Nyhavn 22 (☎3313 0370, fax 3315 8570). Good option away from the station, with views of the harbour; 300–450kr a single, 450–600kr a double, breakfast included.

Turisthotellet, Reverdilsgade 5 (☎3122 9839). The cheapest of the options around the station. Singles 250kr, doubles 350kr. Space at a premium.

England

The Football Association 16 Lancaster Gate, London, W2 3LW
☎020/7262 4542   Fax 020/7402 0486   E-mail info@the-fa.org

League champions Manchester United   **Cup winners** Chelsea
League Cup winners Leicester City   **Promoted** Charlton Athletic, Manchster City,
Ipswich Town   **Relegated** Watford, Sheffield Wednesday, Wimbledon

European participants 2000/01 Manchester United, Arsenal (UCL); Leeds United
(UCL qualifiers); Chelsea, Leicester City, Liverpool (UEFA Cup); Aston Villa, Bradford
City (Intertoto Cup)

O n the surface of it, English football approached the new millennium in justifiably confident mood. An English team were champions of Europe for the first time since 1984. The Premiership was the richest league in the continent – and looked set to become richer still thanks to the signing of a record-shattering new TV rights deal. Impressive new stadia were being built the length and breadth of the country. Immense commercial nous, aggressive marketing and a compliant retail culture had made the business of English football the envy of the world. The game had never had it so good.

Look closer, though, and a few hairline cracks can be seen. The Premiership's plethora of foreign talent – and the lack of incentive for homegrown players to expand their horizons by moving abroad – has impoverished the national team, which fell all too clumsily at the first hurdle of Euro 2000, despite the psychological fillip of beating Germany. The huge power wielded by the game's top administrators has led (perhaps inevitably) to accusations of corruption, and there have been high-profile resignations from Premiership, FA and club boardrooms. England's bid to host the 2006 World Cup was plagued by controversy, not least over the proposed redevelopment of Wembley stadium, the game's spiritual home, and by the all too predictable outbreaks of fan violence in the Low Countries which finally sounded the bid's death-knell – though the reality was

that it was probably doomed long before beer glasses were shattered in the squares of Brussels and Charleroi.

Above all, the game is in danger of becoming a victim of its own success. With the earning potential of some clubs now so far ahead of everyone else's, there's a danger that an unbridgeable gap is being created not just between the Premiership and the rest of England's much-envied league pyramid, but between the leading three or four sides and the rest of the Premiership. If current trends continue unchecked, the number of predictable and/or meaningless fixtures will rise, and popular support (as the Spaniards and Italians can testify) will diminish. That's the problem with hype – if the product itself doesn't deliver, it has a habit of backfiring in your face.

The brave new world of English football has always had its critics. Yet while many fans have found the rapid changes to the game hard to stomach, few would deny that something had to be done. By the Eighties, English clubs were banned from European competition because of the thuggery of their fans. Thirty-nine Juventus fans died at the 1985 European Cup final at Brussels' Heysel stadium, as a result of the hooliganism of Liverpool fans. It was by no means an isolated incident – throughout the Seventies and Eighties, English fans had wreaked havoc across the continent and at home.

Ageing English stadia were also a source of concern, particularly after the deaths of

Basics

Visitors arriving in England from the continent often remark that they feel they have **left Europe**. It's not just that cars drive on the left-hand side of the road or that the policemen wear strange helmets; in many important cultural ways, England differs from mainland Europe.

However, this is part of the United Kingdom and, by extension, part of the European Union – so although **passport controls remain** for EU citizens, there are no visa requirements. Visitors from other countries should check with their local British Embassy before travelling. Non-EU residents travelling into the UK are asked to fill out an **entry form**, or landing card if they are flying.

The currency is the **pound sterling**, abbreviated as '£' and divided into 100 pence. Coins come in denominations of 1p, 2p, 5p, 10p, 20p, 50p, £1 and £2; notes in £5, £10, £20 and £50. Most banks are open Mon–Fri 9.30am–3.30pm, though some stay open later and are also open for a few hours on Saturday morning. **Cash machines** can be found throughout all towns and cities, and **credit-card payment** is more widespread here than anywhere in mainland Europe.

From outside the country, the international telephone code for the UK is ☎44. Some of the major English **city codes** are: inner London ☎020 7, outer London ☎020 8, Birmingham ☎121, Manchester ☎161, Liverpool ☎151 and Newcastle ☎191. Public phone boxes take coins of 10p upwards, although many are now for card use only – **phonecards** are available from post offices and newsagents at £2, £5 or £10. There is a reduced rate for international calls between 8pm and 8am weekdays, and also all weekend. For an international line dial ☎00; for the operator dial ☎100. A growing number of public phones take credit cards as well as phonecards.

The local **train network** is certainly not up to European standards, and tickets are expensive to boot. The privatisation of train operating companies means there is no longer a standard fare or ticket structure, and train times can also be hard to get hold of. There is, however, a central rail enquiry phone number – ☎0845/748 4950. If you plan to travel around the country by train you can buy a weekly or monthly *Britrail* pass before coming to the UK – contact your local rail company for details. Inside the country, if you are aged under 24 you can buy a *Young Persons' Railcard*, which gives a 30% discount on fares.

National Express provides express **bus and coach services** between all major towns. The services are much cheaper than their rail equivalents, and popular routes can get booked solid; if you can, reserve in advance.

England is not famed for its cuisine but there are some tasty **traditional dishes**. 'Fish and chips' is unpredictable, generally better in the north of the country (though this is contested by southerners) and on the coasts. Traditional English **casseroles** and **stews** can be delicious in good restaurants and family-owned pubs. The **English breakfast** – a vast fry-up of bacon, egg, sausage, mushrooms and tomato, served with either toast or fried bread – may be a shock to the system of those used to starting the day with a coffee and a croissant, but such is its popularity that many cafés and pubs offer 'all-day breakfast', giving the visitor a chance to try it at lunch.

The **English pub** has been exported around the globe and while many of the imitations may get the design right, few manage to re-create the atmosphere. Some of the best are in isolated villages, but in cities, every suburb has its 'local' – often a community centre with sports clubs and quizzes, as well as food and drink

In many city centres, pubs are being replaced with hideous **theme bars** or trendy cafés which try to imitate the design and atmosphere of a European café – some of the latter are worth a peek inside, most are not.

45 fans in a fire at the Valley Parade ground of Bradford City in 1985, and the Hillsborough tragedy of 1989, when 96 were crushed to death at an FA Cup semi-final between Nottingham Forest and Liverpool.

Unfashionable at home and mocked abroad, English football was at one of its lowest ebbs since the mid-Fifties, when the assumed invincibility of the national team was so brutally crushed by Hungary. Prior to the Fifties, the idea that England could be anything other than the best in the world was unthinkable to most fans. After all, this was the home of football.

The rules of the game were adopted by the Football Association upon its foundation in 1863. (To this day, the FA remains the only federation in the world not to have the name

We'll do it my way – Sir Alf spells it out, 1966

of its country in its title.) In 1871, the world's first cup competition – the Football Association Challenge Cup, later known as the FA Cup – was introduced. The early competitions were dominated by southern teams drawn from public schools and amateur gentlemen's clubs. But the game was spreading fast in the north of England, particularly in Lancashire. Here players were drawn from working-class backgrounds, and many sought – and received – a wage for their efforts.

In 1883, Blackburn Olympic won the FA Cup, defeating Old Etonians in the final. It was a symbolic result – the victors were a workers' team from a mill town, the vanquished a group of former students from one of the country's leading privately run schools. There was no turning back.

In 1885 professionalism was legalised, and three years later the Football League was founded. Although the founding meeting took place in London's Fleet Street, the capital, and the south of England in general, had little to do with the world's first

professional soccer league. The 12 founding members were all from the north and the Midlands. Lancashire made up half the league, with Preston North End, Blackburn Rovers, Accrington, Bolton Wanderers, Everton and Burnley among the county's representatives. Professional clubs were springing up all over the north, strengthened by imports from Scotland. To this day, the north and Midlands remain the dominant regions in English football – the title has only been in southern hands 16 times in more than a century of competition, and ten of those have been won by Arsenal.

In 1892 the League expanded to two divisions, and by 1923 two regional third divisions had been added. That structure remained untouched until 1958, when the bottom two divisions became national. Today England remains the only country in Europe with four fully professional, national tiers of clubs.

The English also pioneered international competition – of a sort. The 1872 goalless draw between England and Scotland in

Morning after – down and out in Charleroi

Glasgow was the first-ever game between two footballing nations. However, while they were quite content to arrange games against other British sides in the so-called 'home internationals', the FA were reluctant to participate in the international competitions that emerged in the decade before World War II. England had toured the continent as early as 1908, playing Austria, Bohemia and Hungary – but they declined to compete in the World Cup until 1950, when they went to the finals in Brazil. They needn't have bothered. Defeats by Spain and (embarrassingly) the USA led to a rapid, first-round exit.

Yet while they were clearly beatable overseas, England remained impregnable at home – until Puskás' Hungary came to Wembley and won 6–3 in 1953. The defeat did more than shatter a record; it finally alerted the English to the fact that the game was now progressing in Europe much more quickly than in its homeland.

When England failed to win a game at the 1958 World Cup in Sweden, coaches began to look to the continent for ideas. England reached the quarter-finals of the same event in Chile four years later, but were still some way short of the finished article when Alf Ramsey, their team manager, began preparations for the World Cup England would host in 1966. It was Ramsey who introduced the 4–4–2 formation to the English game at international level. The press were sceptical of a formation which dispensed with inside-forwards and wingers (traditionally two areas of English strength), and Ramsey's side were labelled 'The Wingless Wonders'. With the exception of the classy West Ham pair of centre-half Bobby Moore and midfielder Martin Peters, Ramsey's side contained few stars. His system was based on hard work and versatility.

Within days of the 1966 World Cup kicking-off, the critics had been forced to eat their words. Mexico, France and Argentina were all arrogantly despatched, setting up a semi-final with Eusébio's Portugal. Bobby Charlton (who, in the absence of the out-of-favour Jimmy Greaves, was England's main flair player) then scored twice in a 2–1 win which was as close as the scoreline suggests.

In the final England met West Germany, against whom – odd though it may seem today – they had never lost. The game was to be a topsy-turvy affair. Haller gave the Germans the lead on twelve minutes. Six minutes later, Hurst headed an equaliser. In the 78th minute Peters looked to have wrapped the game up for England, but in the last minute Weber scored to take the game to extra-time.

Ten minutes in, a shot from Hurst bounced down off the crossbar. Roger Hunt, following up, was so confident the ball had crossed the line that he pointedly failed to do the obvious and knock it into the net. The Swiss referee, after consulting with his Soviet linesman, duly gave a goal. But the Germans were furious, and TV evidence later added some ammunition to their argument. In the last minute, with the opposition gambling everything, Hurst put the game beyond doubt with his third goal, and the World Cup was England's.

Four years later, in Mexico, the Germans would have their revenge – though it seemed unlikely when the quarter-final in Guadalajara stood at 2–0 to England with an hour gone. The fatigue of the English full-backs – wilting under the heat, the altitude and Ramsey's insistence on sticking with 4–4–2 – allowed West Germany back into the game, and they eventually won 3–2 after extra-time.

For the national side, worse was to come. England failed to qualify for the 1974 or 1978 World Cups, leaving the Scots as Britain's sole ambassadors at the game's highest level. English clubs, however, had seized on the post-1966 euphoria – and on Ramsey's tactical innovations – and were finally making their mark in Europe.

Prior to 1966, no English club had made the final of the European Cup. The only glory had been in the Cup-Winners' Cup, with Tottenham lifting the trophy in 1963 and their fellow Londoners West Ham winning it in 1965. But, just two years after the World Cup victory, Manchester United beat Benfica to become the first English side to win the European Cup. In the same year Leeds United won the Fairs' Cup, starting a sequence in which that competition would be won six seasons in a row by English clubs.

Between 1977 and 1982, the European Cup never left England, Liverpool (three times), Brian Clough's Nottingham Forest (twice) and Aston Villa all winning the competition. Had it not been for Heysel and the subsequent ban on English participation in Europe, the hegemony would surely have continued.

It was in 1982, under Ron Greenwood, that England returned to World Cup action. But the squad that travelled to Spain contained two key players, Kevin Keegan and Trevor Brooking, who had sustained long-term injuries. Neither played any part until 15 minutes from the end of the team's

second-round match against the hosts (who, thanks to am absurdly top-heavy competition structure, had already been eliminated). England needed two goals to stay in the tournament; Keegan and Brooking couldn't score them.

Four years later, with Bobby Robson now at the helm, England had the goals of a young Gary Lineker to thank for taking them to a quarter-final against Argentina – in which they were beaten by both 'The Hand of God' and, for Maradona's second goal in a 2–1 defeat, the Feet of God.

At the 1988 European Championship in West Germany, in which England lost all three of their matches to Ireland, Holland and the USSR, it seemed that the enforced absence from continental club action was already having a detrimental effect. But the emergence of Paul Gascoigne to act as Lineker's main supply line coincided with Italia '90 – Robson's swansong as manager, and a World Cup which will forever be associated, at least in English minds, with one man and his tears.

In the early Nineties, Graham Taylor's spell as England boss was characterised by tactical ineptitude (taking off Lineker against Sweden at Euro '92) and the odd slab of bad luck (Ronald Koeman's ability to stay on the pitch to win a World Cup qualifier for Holland in Rotterdam). Terry Venables would be the new broom to sweep away Taylor's flirtation with the long ball, and had it not been for Gareth Southgate's penalty miss at Wembley, Euro '96 might have been for El Tel what the 1966 World Cup was for Sir Alf – not just football coming home, but turning up on the doorstep with some silverware tucked under its arm.

Venables' side, with their 4–1 win over Holland in particular, had won English football the respect of Europe once again. So, too, had English fans – Euro '96 was the most relaxed, trouble-free major tournament to be held in Europe for a generation. Not since Bobby Moore raised the Jules Rimet trophy had English football been in a healthier all-round state. Or so it seemed. It didn't take long for the backlash to begin.

The man who took over as national coach after Euro '96, Glenn Hoddle, was no Venables. Initially hailed as someone who would continue the short-passing revolution of the previous regime, he was unable to command the same respect as his predecessor, either among the players or within England's volatile press corps.

En route to France '98, a series of PR disasters culminated with a poorly handled rejection of Paul Gascoigne and a return of the vision – at least partially obscured under Venables – that England's preparations for major games were still plagued by excess alcohol consumption.

Once the tournament got going, Hoddle's tactical naivety at the top level was also exposed. England gave Romania's playmakers as much time as they wanted to engineer a 2–1 defeat in the group stage, and in the resulting second-round clash with Argentina, the coach made a series of substitutions that deprived his side of almost all their best penalty-takers.

The one bright light to shine in France, that of emerging young striker Michael Owen, burned only fitfully over the following months, as Hoddle's grip on reality became ever more tenuous. The England squad, uninspired by the presence of a faith healer or tales of reincarnation, was slipping beyond the manager's control, and it was no surprise when Hoddle was eventually forced to resign in February 1999.

His replacement, Kevin Keegan, showed his customary indecision in initially accepting the job on only a temporary basis before confirming that he would leave his club post at Fulham. He succeeded in persuading England players to attack the ball again – an underrated attribute under both his immediate predecessors – but Keegan, perhaps more than any England manager since the post was created after World War II, was impotent in the face of the big clubs' reluctance to nurture young home-grown talent, or to release what little they had when he most needed it. His team needed a win by Sweden over Poland to sneak a play-off place on the journey to Euro 2000, followed by an unsatisfactory 2–1 aggregate win over Scotland. At the finals themselves, the gung-ho approach adopted by Keegan backfired disastrously against Portugal, who came from 2–0 down to win 3–2; worked brilliantly against the Germans, who were vanquished in a competitive international for the first time since 1966; then seemed to desert England entirely as an uncharacteristic attack of nerves allowed Romania back into a game that was as good as dead, and win 3–2 with a last-minute penalty.

In the aftermath, Keegan may have reflected that both he and his German counterpart, Erich Ribbeck, had gone into Euro 2000 with their hands tied behind their backs by increasingly successful and self-regarding domestic leagues. But in England, the domination of the big clubs is affecting the game in other ways. Cut off from the supply of transfer money that was once their lifeblood and separated from the upper echelons by an entirely arbitrary division of TV cash, the country's smaller professional clubs are engaged in an increasingly bitter battle for survival.

In the meantime, the growing gap between rich and poor has allowed England's hardcore hooligan element to thrive once more in the lower divisions, where fans priced out of the Premiership, embittered by football's new direction and encouraged by the 'success' of the thugs in France and Belgium have brought about a rise in arrests at matches for the first time since the Eighties.

The hooligans aren't the only ones voicing their concerns. The country's post-Hillsborough stadia may be all-seated and safe, but with their controlled, muzak-infested atmosphere, many of them seem to be football grounds only by accident, resembling instead temples dedicated to retail worship, little different from the shopping complexes they are built alongside and which they are designed to complement.

In a last sounding of the warning bells, the failure of England to come anywhere near the technical level of football displayed

Healing 34 years of hurt – Shearer scores against the Germans at Euro 2000

by the best of the continent at Euro 2000 was matched by the inability of Premiership clubs to attract the best foreign talent across the Channel in the close-season transfer round. England fans, it seems, aren't the only ones to have misgivings about the national game's enduring appeal.

Match practice

The days of turning up ten minutes before kick-off, paying at the turnstiles and grabbing a pie and a pint on the way to the terraces are over. For Premiership football, at least, you need to plan in advance – tickets for big games are a rare commodity and you will pay accordingly. In return you will be treated to some of the best facilities in European football. As well as modern all-seater stands offering unobstructed views of the action, you will find fast food outlets, on-site bookmakers, restaurants and a huge selection of club merchandise.

While the cold pies and smelly toilets have gone, some of the old English match-day traditions remain. For many fans, Saturday wouldn't be Saturday without a

visit to the pub before the game. And with the advent of Sky Sports, the pub has assumed another role – as a venue for watching the game. Rather than pay out for the satellite equipment and subscription, large numbers of fans pop down to their local to watch the top clashes, reviving the fortunes of many ailing pubs and clubs, and creating a new form of support.

Although stadium developments have taken place in the lower divisions as well, at Nationwide League grounds you will find much more of the old scene. Terracing remains, tickets are cheaper and easier to find, and though crowds are smaller, there is often more intensity to the occasion.

The season begins in mid-August and ends in mid-May, with no winter break. There are, however, 'blank' weekends prior to England international matches. Saturday league games kick-off at 3pm. Midweek fixtures – of which there are more in England than anywhere in Europe – traditionally take place on Tuesday or Wednesday nights at 7.30pm or 7.45pm. Kick-off times for live TV matches vary, but Sunday games usually kick-off at 1pm or 4pm, while those on Fridays and Mondays start at 8pm.

A different league

The 20-team Premiership is administered jointly by the Football Association and the Premier League. The bottom three clubs are relegated and replaced by the top two from the first division of the Football ('Nationwide') League, plus the winners of a series of play-offs.

The same system operates for promotion and relegation between the three divisions of the Football League. The bottom side in the third division is replaced by the champions of the Conference, a national semi-professional league, providing the latter have a stadium which meets League regulations.

Up for the cup

The FA Cup is the oldest national cup competition in the world. Unlike in many European countries, the cup can boast serious status (undimmed by Manchester United's decision, itself prompted by the Government and England 's World Cup 2006 bid, not to defend it in 1999/2000)

and attendances are as high as, if not higher than, those at league games.

Around 500 non-league clubs begin the competition in August, fighting to earn a place in the first round proper in November, when they are joined by the second- and third-division clubs. Premiership and first-division sides don't join in until the third round, which is to go back to its former place in the calendar of early January in 2001. Ties are played on Saturdays with the exception of live televised games and replays. The format for all rounds is one-leg games, with a replay in the case of drawn matches. These days there can be only one replay, after which the game goes to extra-time and penalties if necessary. Semi-finals are held at neutral venues and the final, also at a neutral ground, is in May.

A second knockout competition, the Football League Cup, was begun in 1961 and is currently sponsored by Worthington beer. The cup is open only to clubs competing in the Football League and the Premiership, and until the semi-finals all rounds are played midweek. The first two rounds and semi-finals are two-legged affairs. In recent years, the top clubs have

Swiss miss – England's team faces the music after losing the right to host the 2006 World Cup

shown less and less interest in the League Cup, with some fielding virtual reserve teams. At one point UEFA withdrew the European berth offered to the Cup's winners in an attempt to force the Premiership to reduce its size to 18 teams, but the Football League successfully complained that it was being penalised for something over which it had no control. For as long as the UEFA Cup place remains, the tournament's future seems assured.

Just the ticket

For Premiership games you should contact clubs in advance to enquire about availability. All clubs have 'ticketline' numbers dedicated solely to providing information, and in most cases you can book your seat over the phone with a credit card and pick the ticket up at the stadium on matchday. Ticket prices for Premiership matches range from £15 to more than £50. Most clubs offer reduced-price admission for children and pensioners.

Half-time

An English football ground is one of the few places in the world where you can eat a boiled hamburger – avoid them at all costs. That aside, the food and drink on offer inside grounds varies enormously. Some clubs serve draught beer before a game, others don't. Some clubs offer decent hot pies, others stodgy cold ones. In recent years, fast-food outlets offering more varied choice have popped up inside newly redeveloped stands.

But the best bet remains to do your eating and drinking down the road, before and after the game. You'll find a pub on the corner of almost all English grounds except for some of the new, out-of-town stadia, and wherever you go, you'll see fish and chips or pies being consumed with remarkable pace, both before and after a match. Traditional town-centre grounds will have a chippy close at hand, and these are a far better bet than the hamburger and hot-dog stands which line the streets around the stadium.

Action replay

For decades, football on television in England meant *Match Of The Day* – a Saturday night highlights package on BBC 1 which has become a national institution, but whose existence is now threatened by new TV deals struck for the 2001/02 season and beyond. For the time being, the show offers lengthy highlights from three featured games, with goals from all the other Premiership clashes and analysis from studio guests. It goes out at around 10.30pm on Saturdays and is repeated early the following morning.

But although *Match Of The Day* remains the most-watched football show, for those with cable connections or satellite dishes, football on TV means Sky Sports. With three channels devoted to sport, Sky has the rights to live Premiership games, the Nationwide League, the FA Cup, the League Cup and England internationals played at home. The live Premiership action is on Sunday afternoon and Monday evening, but there is a game of some kind on Sky almost every night, as well as chat shows, magazines and highlights packages.

Sky's volume of football programming is unmatched, as is the professionalism of its presentation. It even offers 'Interactive Football' through its digital service, whereby subscribers can choose their own camera angles and view action replays, stats and other options at the push of a button.

It is not having things all its own way, however. The terrestrial ITV network shares live FA Cup coverage with Sky, and has also retained the increasingly lucrative rights to the Champions' League. Two ITV companies, Carlton and Granada, are now using the latter to bolster their own pay-TV service, ONDigital, which screens every UCL match (not just those involving English clubs) in its entirety – although at least one live game involving an English team remains free-to-air on ITV.

In addition, terrestrial operator Channel 5 has scooped the rights to many of England's away games and to selected European ties involving English clubs.

Elsewhere, Channel 4 continues to cover Italian football, though its Sunday afternoon live action, desperately in need of a makeover to lighten up leaden, London-based commentary, is put in the shade by the excellent Saturday morning magazine show, *Gazzetta Football Italia*.

Sky shows live Spanish football on Saturday and/or Sunday nights (again with London-based commentary) and also offers a live Scottish game every Sunday evening at about 7pm. Magazine programmes allow you to keep tabs on both leagues during the week.

Cable and ONDigital (but not Sky) subscribers can also watch 'British Eurosport', a re-branded version of Eurosport which suffers much the same problems as its predecessor – excellent football action marred by woeful presentation.

It will be all change for 2001/02, however, with ITV taking over Premiership highlights from the BBC, ONDigital grabbing live Nationwide action, and cable operator NTL screening selected Premiership games on a pay-per-view basis.

The back page

Strangely, for a country with a huge interest in football and sport in general, England does not have a daily sports paper. The weekly *Sport First*, which appears on Sunday mornings, has little not already offered elsewhere and is best avoided.

Of the broadsheet papers, the *Daily Telegraph* is hard to beat for the sheer scale and weight of reporting, while the *Times* has cornered the market in eye-catching graphics and the *Guardian* boasts the most accomplished columnists.

The mass-market tabloids – the *Mirror, Sun* and *Daily Star* – are more sensationalist but are often the first papers to break transfer stories and other rumours. The mid-market tabloids – the *Daily Mail* and *Express* – are an accessible compromise between sophistication and sleaze.

The magazine market is increasingly dominated by bland one-club offerings, some officially sanctioned, others not. The weeklies *Shoot!* and *Match* remain for kids, while *FourFourTwo* and *Total Football* are the heavyweight monthlies worth peeking into.

The global scene is covered by the increasingly accessible *World Soccer*, while *When Saturday Comes* continues to offer its refreshingly eccentric, fanzine-influenced take on life.

Speaking of fanzines, there is barely a professional ground in the country where you won't see an earthy, locally produced publication on sale.

Ultra culture

In the home of the hooligan, most fans no longer travel to games expecting trouble, happily wearing their replica shirts to matches to make a statement of their allegiance – and spawning an entire industry in the process. Much of the credit for the suppression of hooliganism has gone to improved policing, but there has also been a dramatic change in the attitude of fans themselves.

Sadly, with many of the old 'singing ends' demolished, there is no one area in many modern stadia were noise can be generated. Fans who used to stand together are now dispersed around the ground, in numbered seats assigned by the box-office computer – and matchday atmosphere has suffered as a result.

In the net

The FA was one of the last national football federations in Europe to offer an official website, but there should be one by the time you read this at: www.the-fa.org.

Most of the big media players now offer web versions of their football output, but for more original content, stick with web-only providers. *Football365* is one of the few generic sites to offer an original perspective at: www.football365.co.uk; while the *Total Football Network* acts as a central home for the best unofficial one-club sites and online fanzines, each one individually vetted, at: www.totalfootball.co.uk.

London

Like Paris or Rome, London's importance as a football city bears little relation to the number of national championships its clubs have mustered. Few European cities have as much regular representation in their country's top division – often five or six teams – yet these clubs share just 14 league titles between them.

In terms of its prestigious position as an international venue, only Paris can challenge London. The capital is the seat of the Football Association, the stuffy body of ex-public schoolboys who ran the game until the Football League was founded, and who have been responsible for internationals and the FA Cup ever since.

The FA was formed in 1863 in the *Freemasons' Tavern* in Great Queen Street, where a group of genteel public schoolmasters met to draft a set of rules for the game. Firmly amateur, almost invariably upper class, the game in London and the south-east centred around an annual Challenge Cup played for by teams from the country's highest institutions. Its first final was at Kennington Oval, now a cricket ground. Its first winners were The Wanderers, a team composed of old Harrovians originally based in Snaresbrook, near Epping Forest. Ever since then, London has traditionally performed well in the glamorous cup competitions, but poorly in the long, gruelling league championship.

Arsenal and Tottenham Hotspur form the city's big rivalry, the clubs being three miles apart in the north of the city. Attracting different communities – Arsenal Irish and Greek, Spurs traditionally Jewish – they have famously loathed each other from the day in 1913 when Arsenal moved across the Thames from Plumstead to Highbury. Spurs opposed the move, and ne'er the twain have met.

Like the big north London pair, Chelsea attract a following from across the Home Counties as well as in the capital, all the more so since the club's revival in the Nineties. West Ham are firmly rooted in

the East End, home of London's famous Cockneys, while further south-east, Millwall and Charlton attract a similarly strong local partisanship. QPR, Wimbledon and Crystal Palace draw varying degrees of support, depending on league position and the weather, from the west, south-west and south-east respectively, the latter two now based at Palace's Selhurst Park. Leyton Orient, Brentford and Fulham represent pockets of supporters in east and west London.

A London representative side made the first Fairs' Cup final in 1958, but Greaves and Blanchflower could not prevent Barcelona winning 8–2 on aggregate. Soccer in London would not be at its best until the Sixties and Seventies, when the city's status as the 'Swinging' capital of the world's music and fashion industry seemed to rub off on its football clubs. Spurs and Arsenal won the double, Chelsea and West Ham the FA Cup and European honours. Even QPR and little Fulham drew big crowds. It was a great time to be young, free, single and football-supporting – although by the late Sixties, the cross-town rivalries were spilling into ugly violence.

After the dark ages of the Eighties, today London can again be regarded as a kind of Socceropolis. But while football's version of Swinging London was essentially inward-looking, today the capital is a cosmopolitan centre whose style, services and amusements attract contemporary stars like Jimmy Floyd Hasselbaink, Thierry Henry and Sergei Rebrov.

Meanwhile, the likes of Pelé, Puskás and Maradona occasionally pass through town for some event or other, and the city is packed every weekend with young, footie-loving Europeans on spending sprees – though this traffic has lessened somewhat in the last couple of years because of the strength of the pound sterling against the euro.

Still, as London's show-business community might say – no business, no show.

London essentials

Of London's two main **airports**, Heathrow (25km west of central London) is the world's busiest, while Gatwick (50km south) is mainly for charter flights. The former has four separate terminals, while the latter is divided into North and South, with a monorail linking the two.

From Heathrow, the quickest way to central London is the new *Heathrow Express* **rail service** to Paddington (every 15mins, 5.10am–11.40pm daily, journey time 15mins, £10 single, £20 return). The slower but cheaper **Piccadilly line Tube** to the centre (daily 5.30am–11.30pm, journey about an hour, £3.40) has separate stations for Terminals 1–3 and Terminal 4. **Airbus A1** goes into town via Victoria, while **A2** runs via King's Cross (every 15mins, 5.30am–10.30pm daily, journey one hour, single fare £6, return £10).

From Gatwick, the *Gatwick Express* overground train takes just 30mins to do the journey to Victoria (every 15mins daytime, hourly 1am–4am, single fare £9.50). *Connex South East* and *Thameslink* run slower train services to other London stations.

Forget the idea of getting a **taxi** to or from either airport. In addition to being ruinously expensive, a cab can easily get caught in the city's monstrous traffic.

The colour-coded ***London Underground*** service ('the Tube', 5.30am–midnight, from 7am Sundays) is dirty, infrequent, overcrowded and overpriced. Security alerts, suicides, maintenance and all manner of other horrors may delay you, so always leave as much time as possible. That said, when it is working well, the Tube is still the best way of moving around the city. The **main train stations** (Paddington, Euston, King's Cross, Victoria and Waterloo, whose International terminal is the departure point for the *Eurostar* train service to France and Belgium) all have Tube stops of the same name. The network is divided into six zones: central zone 1 and neighbouring zone 2 are ample for most needs, except for trips to Tottenham and West Ham (zone 3). Tickets are bought at Tube stations – a single fare in zone 1 is £1.50, rising to £3.50 for an all-zone single. A carnet of ten zone 1 tickets is £11.

The red London **bus network** is part of the city's charm. A journey of a couple of Central London stops costs £1 – tell the conductor or driver your desination. The city boasts a big network of **night buses,** most of which pass through or leave from Trafalgar Square – the average fare is £1.50.

If you are venturing south of the Thames to clubs such as Crystal Palace, Millwall or Charlton, you will have to use London's suburban **overground train network**; services are less frequent than the Tube, but the ride is usually more pleasant.

A *One-Day Travelcard* for Tube, bus and train, valid Mon–Fri from 9.30am and all day Sat–Sun, is £3.90 for zones 1–2, or £4.70 for all zones. The cards are sold at stations and newsagents, but are not valid on night buses.

London's **black taxi cabs** are luxuriously roomy, but come at a price. Hail one with the yellow-lit flag showing. A short journey in central London will cost at least £5, with surcharges for extra passengers and travel after 8pm and at weekends. If you need to call a cab, dial ☎020/7272 0272 – the minimum call-out charge is £3.

Minicabs, whose drivers may not be as knowledgeable as their famous competitors, are at least cheaper, and don't baulk at going south of the river. *Addison Lee* (☎020/7387 8888) are as reliable as any. Avoid using **pirate taxi drivers** who cruise London at night, and who also hang around the arrivals halls at Heathrow.

The main **tourist offices** are at the Heathrow Tube station concourse (daily 8.30am–6pm), Victoria station forecourt (daily 8am–7pm), and the *Eurostar* arrivals hall at Waterloo International station (daily 8am–10.30pm). The best **listings information** guide is *Time Out* magazine (Wednesdays, £1.70).

The thrilling fields

Arsenal

Highbury Stadium, Avenell Road, N5
Capacity 38,500
Colours Red shirts with white sleeves, white
shorts
League champions 1931, 1933–35, 1938, 1948,
1953, 1971, 1989, 1991, 1998
Cup winners 1930, 1936, 1950, 1971, 1979,
1993, 1998
Cup-Winners' Cup winners 1994
Fairs' (UEFA) Cup winners 1970

As one English football writer once put it, Arsenal were not put on this Earth to be loved. They are at once Boring Arsenal, Lucky Arsenal, and by far London's most successful club. Prior to the rise of Manchester United, they were England's best-known club overseas, their name evoking a feeling of gravitas and tradition. In fact, Arsenal brought the name across with them when they moved over the Thames from the Royal Arsenal armaments factory in Woolwich, in south-east London.

Formed as Dial Square FC in 1886, the team were at first composed mainly of Scots employed at the munitions works. They were sent a set of red shirts by Nottingham Forest, and the club have worn red ever since. They soon changed their name to Royal Arsenal FC, and were quick to adopt professionalism in 1891. They were promoted to the first division in 1904, but ran into financial difficulties and were relegated nine years later.

Arsenal's owner, Henry Norris, had the idea of moving the club to a part of London that had a greater potential catchment area, with easier access from the city centre – a site was chosen next to Gillespie Road tube station in Highbury, north London. Royal Arsenal became Arsenal FC and, thanks to Norris' influence, were admitted to an extended first division after World War 1 – at the expense of Spurs.

Arsenal have never been relegated since. Herbert Chapman arrived at the club as manager in 1925, and in his nine-year stint, he not only turned a rootless club without honours into the most feared in the land – he altered the game almost beyond recognition (see panel p.123).

Chapman's Arsenal was diverse and quick. With prolific goalscorers Joe Hulme and Cliff Bastin on the wings, and Alex James and David Jack at inside-forward, Arsenal were kings of the counter-attack and the breakaway goal. Their 'Lucky' tag was thus earned.

After beating Chapman's old side Huddersfield to lift the FA Cup and their first honour in 1930, Arsenal then won the title three years in a row. Chapman's untimely death in 1934 prevented him from seeing out Arsenal's treble. Radio commentator George Allison took his place, and with Ted Drake breaking all scoring records, Arsenal retained their superiority.

The postwar period began successfully with two league titles and another FA Cup win. But before long Arsenal hit a trough of mediocrity that was to last until the late Sixties, when a former club physiotherapist Bertie Mee dragged the team into the modern era. Its spine was again Scots, with internationals Bob Wilson in goal, Frank McLintock at centre-half and George Graham as the midfield mechanic. Upfront was Charlie George, a long-haired prodigy and the terrace hero of Highbury's North Bank. His extra-time goal which beat Liverpool in the 1971 Cup final became a legendary strike, sealing as it did a League and Cup double, the former having been won at Tottenham (of all places) five days earlier. The success followed a storming Fairs' Cup final win over Anderlecht the previous season, which saw the Gunners pull back a 3–1 deficit to forge a 4–3 aggregate win in the second leg.

The double-winning side did not go on to dominate the English game, as many predicted it would. Instead, Arsenal ticked over quietly through the Seventies until a crop of Irishmen breathed new life into the

Dignified in defeat – Wenger in Copenhagen

club. Liam Brady was a midfielder with a left boot of precision and elegance, Frank Stapleton a classic centre-forward, David O'Leary a solid centre-half, and Pat Jennings a goalkeeper of immense ability whose shock move from Tottenham all but ripped the heart out of White Hart Lane. Although this side won neither a league title nor a European honour (the closest they came to the latter was a penalty shoot-out defeat by Valencia in the 1980 Cup-Winners' Cup final), they appeared in three consecutive FA Cup finals, winning the 1979 'five-minute final' against Manchester United at the death.

The appointment of George Graham as manager in 1986 ushered in another successful period. Under Graham, the Gunners were never less than tight at the back – the sight of captain Tony Adams for-

ever appealing for offside earning them the 'Boring' tag they struggled so long to be rid of. But they were also a team of fighters, their spirit never better demonstrated than in the last-minute Michael Thomas goal that beat Liverpool at Anfield in 1989, to win Arsenal their first title since 1971.

The title was won again in 1991, with a side that conceded just 18 goals all season. The club put the development of Highbury top of its priority list (above the acquisition of new players), but still the honours kept coming – two domestic cups in 1993, followed by the Cup-Winners' Cup, secured with a typically gritty 1–0 win over Parma in Copenhagen in 1994. Graham prized this European honour above all others, and the team did not let it go until the 120th minute of the following year's final against Real Zaragoza, when the Gunners' big 'keeper David Seaman was left stranded by a remarkable lob from Nayim, a former Tottenham star.

The Graham era ended in scandal when he was forced to resign following the revelation that he had taken cash from the Norwegian players' agent, Rune Hauge. Both Adams and striker Paul Merson then hit the headlines for their abuse of alcohol and drugs. And the team as a whole was mired in disciplinary problems, both on and off the pitch.

The surprise hiring of French coach Arsène Wenger in the summer of 1996 marked a sea-change in the club's thinking, however. While keeping the same defence that had been in place for the best part of the decade, Wenger added international class to Arsenal's traditional conservatism. Dutch star Dennis Bergkamp was coupled with stalwart Ian Wright upfront, while another Dutchman, Marc Overmars, provided extra pace. Frenchmen Patrick Vieira, Emmanuel Petit and Nicolas Anelka conjured classy moves a cut above the regular Premiership thrash, and Arsenal's surprise UEFA Cup exit at the hands of PAOK Salonika – with Bergkamp's absence due to fear of flying a key factor – left them free to concentrate on the league in

1997/98. After winning 13 games on the spin, Arsenal surprised even their own fans by overtaking runaway leaders Manchester United, before completing the club's second double with a 2–0 FA Cup final victory over Newcastle.

Bergkamp's continued European absence remained critical in the subsequent Champions' League campaign, which saw Arsenal outflanked by Dynamo Kiev and out-fought by the French title holders Lens. Domestic competition was equally frustrating in 1998/99, Arsenal finishing runners-up to Manchester United on the last day of the league season, after the title had seemed in their grasp in April. The FA Cup was a heartbreaker, with a classic semi-final also lost to Manchester United after Bergkamp had missed a penalty in the last minute of normal time.

In the 1999 close season, the much-delayed but very necessary departure of the unsettled Anelka to Real Madrid enabled Wenger to bring in Davor Šuker and Thierry Henry, and put some money in the bank for later. With the emerging Nwankwo Kanu providing a new creative dimension, Highbury was set for another season of competing at the top level, with an improved performance in Europe now the top priority for many supporters.

Yet the club repeated its mistake of the previous season in deciding to play Champions' League ties at Wembley, where the wide open spaces were ill-suited to Arsenal's ageing back four and seemed to inspire opponents like Barcelona and Fiorentina. A third-place finish in their group wasn't enough for UCL progress, but it did give the club a back-door pass into the UEFA Cup, and in the latter half of the season – traditionally Arsenal's strongest time – the team capitalised on its increasingly confident domestic form by brushing aside the likes of Deportivo La Coruña and Werder Bremen to reach the UEFA Cup final.

Their opponents, Galatasaray, had taken a similar route via the Champions' League, and the two sides were all too well-matched. A dull game in Copenhagen was goalless after 120 minutes, and the Turks won the resulting penalty shoot-out.

Back home, the Gunners' late burst of form had come too late to wrest the Premiership title from Manchester United, but it was enough to see them into second place and another shot at the Champions' League. With Petit, Overmars and Šuker disposed of and Robert Pires arriving as Wenger's latest French import – and Wembley, as luck would have it, scheduled for demolition – there was a feeling that it might just be third time lucky in Europe's premier competition.

Here we go!

Take either the Piccadilly line Tube to **Arsenal**, which is right behind the North Bank, or the Victoria line to **Finsbury Park**; if doing the latter, exit into Station Place, walk by the *Arsenal World Of Sport* store, cross over into St Thomas' Road, then keep on the right-hand side until you reach Gillespie Road behind the North Bank.

Just the ticket

Highbury's limited capacity of 38,500 means the only way for non-ticket holders to get into league fixtures is by dealing with a tout. Matchday tickets are available for some cup games, however. Visiting fans are placed in the Clock End stand and the adjacent West Stand corner's lower tier. For all ticket enquiries, call ☎020/7704 4040.

Swift half

Arsenal's ground is surrounded by pubs. The most obvious one to head for is *The Gunners*, 204 Blackstock Road – a ten-minute walk from the ground. It is packed with framed programmes, pictures and shirts, and has a pool room at the back. If the security is a tad heavy, try the similarly themed but more laid-back *Arsenal Tavern*, facing you as you enter Blackstock Road from Gillespie Road. The **stadium bar** underneath the North Bank is better than most in London, with a live band and two counters serving beer.

Club merchandise

The obvious first port of call if coming from Finsbury Park is *Arsenal World Of Sport* (open Mon–Sat 9.30am–6pm and on matchdays, most credit cards), which is next-door to the Tube and train station. For those coming via Arsenal Tube, there's the smaller **Gunners' Shop** (open Mon–Fri 9.30am–5pm and on matchdays, Visa and Mastercard only) along Avenell Road behind the East Stand.

Ultra culture

The first-rate facilities of the North Bank stand are a classic example of the gentrification of English football. Gone are the days when Spurs and Chelsea fans would regularly invade it for pitch battles on derby day. Today the clientèle are well-heeled and well-behaved. It remains the end towards which the players prefer to attack, however, and for good reason.

In print

The **matchday programme** is £2, while the official **club magazine** is *Gunners* (monthly, £2.50); both have colourful features about the club, but are nothing special. The most widely-read fanzines are *The Gooner*, *One-Nil Down, Two-One Up*; and *Highbury High*.

In the net

The **official website** cuts no corners and resides at: www.arsenal.co.uk. You'll find superb graphics, up-to-date 'Gunformation' and a stats database which has to be seen to be believed. Arsenal were one of the first clubs to act as an Internet Service Provider, through *AFCi Connect*. As an antidote to all this slickness, try the unofficial **ArseWeb** site at: www.arseweb.com. It's fun, witty and irreverent – all the things, in fact, which the club and its fans are not supposed to be.

 Chelsea

Stamford Bridge, Fulham Road, SW6
Capacity 35,250 (all-seated)
Colours All blue with white trim
League champions 1955
Cup winners 1970, 1997, 2000
Cup-Winners' Cup winners 1971, 1998

Chelsea are London's chic cosmopolitans. Their stadium was built before the club was formed and their glitzy following is

famously drawn from the transient world of stage and screen. The club's location, close to the trendy boutiques and art galleries of the King's Road, was the fashionable place to be in the late Sixties, and Chelsea had a team of swingers to match. The FA Cup win of 1970 was the high point of those pre-Premiership days, but a repeat performance in 1997 marked the dawn of a new era in which the team would become genuine title challengers, while Stamford Bridge, with its *Chelsea Village* complex of hotels, penthouse suites, shops, bars and restaurants, would be transformed into a money-making machine. And all of it the brainchild of controversial chairman Ken Bates, who saved Chelsea from bankruptcy by wresting control of the club from the Mears family in 1982...

It was H A (Gus) Mears who had the stadium built in 1904, with a view to offering it to nearby Fulham. When they refused, a club had to be formed to play in it. Chelsea FC were founded in 1905. Players were hired, including the famous 22-stone goalkeeper Bill 'Fatty' Foulke, from Sheffield United.

Stamford Bridge, with its oval shape and running track, was one of the finest grounds of its day. But it wasn't until former Arsenal star Ted Drake came in as manager in the early Fifties that Chelsea actually won anything. A Peter Sillett penalty beat Wolves in the deciding game to win the championship in 1955, and that remains Chelsea's only title to date – one that would have brought an appearance in the inaugural European Cup that September, had the Football League not viewed the fledgling competition as a joke.

Chelsea's golden era began when Tommy Docherty replaced Drake as manager in 1962. The club had just won the FA Youth Cup for the second year in a row, with a team which included goalkeeper Peter Bonetti, midfielders Terry Venables and John Hollins, and forwards Peter Osgood and Bobby Tambling. With the first team floundering in the second division, Docherty chucked the boys in at the deep end. They won promotion immediately. Docherty then bought the mercurial Scots winger Charlie Cooke to send over crosses for the prolific Tambling and Osgood. These were exciting times. London had become the pop and fashion capital of the world. Film stars, hairdressers, restaurateurs – all would hang around the club, accompanying the players to nightspots after matches.

Docherty got Chelsea as far as the Fairs' Cup semi-final of 1966. He was replaced by Dave Sexton, a graduate of the West Ham academy, who brought in a bargain basement forward, Ian Hutchinson, nurtured the precocious midfielder Alan Hudson, and added some steel to the line-up in the form of Dave Webb and Ron 'Chopper' Harris.

The team's star turn came in the 1970 Cup final with Leeds – a game that pitted chic flamboyance against a 60-game-a-year mean machine. After four hours of football – a muddy draw at Wembley followed by a gruelling replay at Old Trafford – flamboyance triumphed.

Won-nil – Marcel Desailly with the FA Cup, May 2000

It would do so again a year later, when Chelsea beat Real Madrid, after another replayed final, to lift the 1971 Cup Winners' Cup.

On the back of this success, the club began to build a huge East Stand at vast expense. Its completion coincided with relegation. Nearly bankrupt, Chelsea sold their main asset, young midfielder Ray Wilkins, and the team spent much of the Eighties shifting uneasily between the top two divisions. With creditors knocking on the door and an evil racist following in the Shed end, few outside the club would have mourned its demise. But Ken Bates, an outspoken businessman, took it upon himself to save Chelsea from liquidation. He spent ten years making more headlines than the team itself, but made a wise investment in hiring Glenn Hoddle as player-coach in

1993. Under Hoddle, Chelsea made the Cup final and Europe the following year.

Meanwhile, the club's leading shareholder Matthew Harding, though an outspoken critic of Bates, provided the fortune needed to finance the chairman's masterplan for Stamford Bridge's redevelopment. Harding's obvious love of the game brought a human face to the much-maligned club leadership and helped to lure Ruud Gullit to Chelsea, first as a player and then, after Hoddle was named England coach in 1996, as manager.

Gullit brought in Italian stars Gianfranco Zola, Roberto di Matteo and Gianluca Vialli, plus a host of other exotic foreign imports. Harding's death in a helicopter crash heralded a brief pause in the club's extravagant progress, but ultimately there was no stopping them – Zola, di Matteo and veteran striker Mark Hughes were the stars of an easy 2–0 win over relegated Middlesbrough in the 1997 FA Cup final.

Gullit's shock departure midway through the following season gave the more mild-mannered Vialli a shot at the manager's job, and almost immediately Chelsea won another trophy, beating 'Boro again in the League Cup final. Then, with Vialli himself inspired on the pitch and his assistant Graham Rix a key influence off it, Chelsea progressed to the Cup-Winners' Cup final via wins over Real Betis and Vicenza. At the final, against VfB Stuttgart in Stockholm, it was Rix's idea to replace striker Tøre André Flo with Zola, and within 30 seconds of coming on, the diminutive Italian had scored the only goal of the game, rekindling memories of Chelsea's victory in the same competition 27 years earlier.

The chequebook was out again in the 1998 close season, the club buying Marcel Desailly, Brian Laudrup and Pierluigi Casiraghi among others. But the most influential player on the pitch, certainly after Laudrup's surprise move back to Denmark, was the huge Uruguayan midfielder Gustavo Poyet. His injury, and that to Casiraghi, proved a fatal blow to Chelsea's 1998/99 title challenge. Unbeaten for almost half the season, they fell away badly in the spring, dropping too many points against lesser opponents.

Favourites to become the first (and last) club to retain the Cup-Winners' Cup, Chelsea were surprisingly beaten by Real Mallorca in the semi-finals, and finished the league season in third place. The fact that such a campaign could be viewed as a letdown indicated the extent of the club's transformation – from fringe-playing celebrities to habitual challengers for silverware.

Not were the team about to stop challenging anytime soon. With third-place finishers being given the chance to enter the Champions' League for the first time and European experience aplenty at the Bridge, Chelsea stormed into the 1999/2000 edition of the continent's premier club tournament, holding their own against the likes of AC Milan and Lazio and progressing through both group stages before a quarter-final loss to Barcelona in extra time at the Nou Camp.

Aside from an early, morale-boosting 5–0 trouncing of Manchester United, Vialli's imports seemed keener on European games than Premiership ones. But the idea of playing in the last FA Cup final to be staged at the old Wembley stadium held a romantic appeal, particularly to Chelsea's large French-speaking contingent – Desailly, Deschamps, Leboeuf and inspired loan signing George Weah all toasted their 1–0 win over Aston Villa in the final as if they had won the first medals of their careers, although it was again an Italian, di Matteo, who provided the vital goal.

With Weah's loan spell at an end, Casiraghi's career a write-off and record buy Chris Sutton offloaded to Celtic, Vialli brought Dutchman Jimmy Floyd Hasselbaink back to England from Atlético Madrid to lead his line for 2000/01. Would it be the signing Chelsea needed to become true title challengers?

Here we go!

District line Tube to **Fulham Broadway**, then turn left out of the station – the ground is a 10min walk away, on your left.

Just the ticket

As at Arsenal, lack of planning permission to extend Chelsea's home means the ground is basically a sell-out for all Premiership games, though cup-ties and European matches may be a different story. Visiting fans are allocated space in the lower tiers of the East Stand (access gate #6). For all ticket enquiries, call ☎020/7386 7799.

Swift half

The pubs near Fulham Broadway station – the **White Hart**, the **Slug & Lettuce** – appeal to a more sedate clientèle than those right opposite the ground on the Fulham Road. A short walk down Holmead Road is the other hive of activity on the King's Road, with the **Tut N' Shive** on the corner with Holmead Road and Matthew Harding's favoured haunt, the more upmarket *Imperial Arms* at #577.

Stamford Bridge itself has more bars than a Beethoven symphony, but many of them are themed and soulless. The main one is the *Shed Bar*, behind the South Stand, where it's ten-deep to get served.

The Ginola fan club – White Hart Lane, 1999

Club merchandise

The *Chelsea Megastore* (open Mon–Sat 9am–5pm and match-day Sundays, most credit cards) is a main feature of the *Chelsea Village* behind the South Stand, with three floors of merchandise including baby clothes downstairs.

Ultra culture

Chelsea's *Headhunters* were one of England's most notorious fan groups during the Seventies and Eighties, growing more fanatical as Chelsea's football got worse. The Shed, where they gathered, was an uneasy place to be of a Saturday afternoon, a meeting point for violent and racist elements from all over the south-east. The fact that it has since been knocked down to make room for the South Stand and *Chelsea Village* is indicative of the wind of change blowing through not just Chelsea but the whole of English football.

In print

The Chelsea **matchday programme** is thick but pricy at £2.50, while the official monthly magazine (*Chelsea*, £2.95) and newspaper (*Onside*, £2.50) could be better. Fanzine *The Chelsea Independent*, voice of the club's independent supporters' association, is a better read than any of the official stuff, continuing to ask pertinent questions of the Bates regime.

In the net

The **official site** is at: www.chelseafc.co.uk. It long ago dropped its obligatory registration and had already evolved into an excellent all-round site before being facelifted for 1999/2000. Among

the unofficial sites, *Priesty's Chelsea Refuge* has a wicked sense of humour and comprehensive links at: www.btinternet.com/~alexc/ chelsea.htm.

 Tottenham Hotspur

White Hart Lane, 748 High Road, N17
Capacity 36,000 (all-seated)
Colours White shirts, navy-blue shorts
League champions 1951, 1961
Cup Winners 1901, 1921, 1961–62, 1967, 1981–82, 1991
Cup-Winners' Cup winners 1963
UEFA Cup winners 1972, 1984

Glory, Glory, Tottenham Hotspur, runs the song, and the Lilywhites were put specacularly back on the glory trail with a League Cup win in 1999. The first British club to win a European trophy, always renowned for their adventurous football, Spurs had had a mediocre time of it since their last FA Cup win in 1991.

That summer saw electronics millionaire Alan Sugar assume the club's vast debt and attempt to transform Tottenham into an American-style sports operation. After a bitter courtroom dispute with former manager Terry Venables, Sugar seemed comfortable keeping the club ticking over in mid-table, as just another branch of his leisure and communications empire. It has taken him five changes of team manager to convince Spurs fans otherwise, and bring the good times back to London N17.

Tottenham Hotspur Football Club were started by a group of bookish schoolboys who met under a lamp-post near the current ground. They took the name Hotspur from the Shakespearean character Harry Hotspur, nickname of Henry Percy of the Northumberland family whose ancestral home was near Tottenham marshes.

The club moved from Northumberland Park to White Hart Lane in 1899. They won the Southern League in 1900 and became the last non-league club to win the FA Cup the following year. At an official dinner afterwards, the local mayoress tied blue-and-white ribbons to the Cup, instigating a tradition that has endured to this day. With Football League status assured in 1909, a new stand was built with a copper cockerel perched on top – the club's future motif. Spurs flitted between divisions between the wars, winning the Cup in 1921 with the inventive Jimmy Seed running the show against Wolves.

The arrival as manager of Arthur Rowe, a former Spurs player whose career had been cut short through injury, saw the team rise quickly to the top in the early Fifties. Playing a style called push-and-run, in which short passing and quick movement were paramount, Spurs won the second and first divisions in consecutive years. In the team were future England manager Alf Ramsey at full-back, and winghalves Bill Nicholson and Eddie Baily, soon to become the coaching duo who would lead the club into their most successful era.

Two more wing-halves would be crucial to Nicholson's and Baily's plans: Danny Blanchflower, all anticipation and positional sense, and Dave Mackay, tough tackling and inspirational. With inside-forward John White picking up Blanchflower's precise passes, Spurs began an unbeaten league run in 1960 that culminated in their securing the century's first League and Cup

double the following spring. As 1961 drew to a close, the signing of Jimmy Greaves from AC Milan made the team perfectly poised to become English pioneers in Europe. Though they were pipped by the odd goal in seven by Benfica in the 1962 European Cup semi-final, Spurs successfully defended the FA Cup, then destroyed Atlético Madrid, 5–1, in the Cup-Winners' Cup final of 1963. England's first European club trophy was in the bag, and it had Tottenham's blue-and-white ribbons draped around it.

The retirement of Blanchflower, injuries to Mackay and death of White – struck by lightning on a golf course – saw a slight dip in the club's fortunes. But Terry Venables' arrival from Chelsea helped Spurs to an FA Cup final win over his old club in 1967. And the goalkeeping prowess of record Northern Ireland cap Pat Jennings was becoming another feature of the side – as it would remain until his surprise move to Arsenal in 1977.

The Nicholson era had as its swansong three UEFA Cup runs – one of them, in 1972, victorious. Upfront, the wily Scot Alan Gilzean was joined by England internationals Martin Peters and Alan Chivers, while young Steve Perryman showed a cool head as midfield anchor. Between them they had the edge over Wolves in a fiercely contested, all-English final.

Nicholson's surprise resignation in 1974, after nearly 40 years with the club, left a gap which Tottenham struggled to fill. In 1977 the team were relegated, and though they bounced straight back up again, the old Spurs fire was barely flickering.

There were some bright spots, however – the breakthrough of the precocious midfield talent of Glenn Hoddle, and the pioneering signing (at a time when foreign players were a novelty in English football) of Argentines Osvaldo Ardiles and Ricardo Villa after they had starred in the 1978 World Cup. Under the dour but decent managership of Keith Burkinshaw, Spurs kept playing entertaining football, and eventually it paid off with two FA Cup final wins

– the first, in 1981, featuring a classic dribble and goal from Villa.

Although Tottenham again won the UEFA Cup, on penalties at home to Anderlecht in 1984, financial problems overshadowed most of the Eighties. The big-money signings of Chris Waddle and Paul Gascoigne from Newcastle, the refurbishment of the East Stand and the reorganisation of the club as a publicly quoted company nearly conspired to drive Spurs out of business by 1991. After a stunning Gazza free-kick in the semi against Arsenal, and despite the same player's self-inflicted injury in the final against Nottingham Forest, Tottenham won their eighth FA Cup that year.

In 1994, after Venables had departed in acrimony, the unpopular Sugar invited Jürgen Klinsmann onto his yacht in Monte Carlo and offered him the chance to become part of a brave new Tottenham, alongside Romanians Gica Popescu and Ilie Dumitrescu, and coach Ardiles. Klinsmann jumped at the chance, but within a year the rest of the cast had been thrown overboard, and the German decided to follow of his own volition in the summer of 1995.

Ardiles' replacement, the former England captain Gerry Francis, adopted the same safety-first policy as his chairman. The team did little else but avoid relegation, and after a prolonged period of uncertainty Francis was replaced by the Swiss disciplinarian Christian Gross in 1997.

Although there were positive signs, particularly the slow re-emergence of David Ginola as a midfield force and the maturing of Sol Campbell as an international defender of true class, Gross' methods fell foul of striker Les Ferdinand and, once he had returned on a three-month contract to save Spurs from the drop in 1998, the fans' idol Klinsmann.

Enter the former Arsenal manager George Graham, poached from Leeds as Gross' replacement when the 1998/99 season was barely two months old. This was Sugar's greatest gamble of all, yet by the end of the campaign, with the League Cup won, an FA Cup semi-final also reached and Ginola, the footballer of the year, the outstanding presence in a team playing surprisingly attractive football, both chairman and manager had restored their reputations at #748 High Road.

Tottenham couldn't quite maintain their momentum in 1999/2000, with Ginola out of form and increasingly out of favour, and a series of injuries exposing the fragility of Graham's squad. The club dug deep to bring Sergei Rebrov in from Dynamo Kiev during the close season, but when Ginola was finally sold to Aston Villa, fans were offered season-ticket refunds. A sad story, perhaps, but also a sign that Spurs had rediscovered their sensitive side at last.

Here we go!

Victoria line Tube to **Seven Sisters**, then change there for an overground train to **White Hart Lane**; alternatively, you can take the latter direct from Liverpool Street. Allow 30mins for the whole journey from town. Walk right down White Hart Lane, then turn right at the junction with Tottenham High Road. The stadium is 2mins away. Buses #149, #259 and #279 run up the High Road from Seven Sisters.

Just the ticket

A small number of non-member tickets are available in the upper sections of the East and West Stands that run the length of the pitch. Price depends on the category of the fixture – you'll pay £38 or £46 in the West, £31 or £38 the other side. A section of the South Stand is allocated to visiting supporters – entrance in Park Lane. The main **ticket office** is on the corner of Park Lane and Tottenham High Road (Mon–Fri 10am–6pm). For all non-member ticket enquiries call: ☎020/7420 0234.

Swift half

The Park, 220 Park Lane, by Northumberland Park overground train station and *The Victoria* at 34 Scotland Green, are pubs the club recommends to visitors not wearing colours. *The Northumberland Arms*, 102 Northumberland Park, welcomes home and away supporters but can get very crowded. You'll find bagels served at the ground, which can be washed down with alcohol before the game but not at half-time.

Club merchandise

There are stores at either end of the ground, open Mon–Sat 9.30am–5.30pm, and on Sunday matchdays, and club opened a new *Megastore* adjacent to the ground in the summer of 1999.

Ultra culture

These are the calmest of the main London clubs' fans, especially since seating conversion removed The Shelf, the raised standing area along one side of the ground.

In print

The Spurs **matchday programme** is £2, while the monthly colour glossy magazine, one of the better of its type, is £2.50. The main fanzine is *Cock A Doddle Doo*.

In the net

The **official site** is essentially a merchandising operation but the club plans to make it a broader communication platform in the future. See how far they've got at: www.spurs.co.uk. For an unofficial site that actually tells you something about the team, try the smartly designed *SpursWeb* at: members.aol.com/neilv1/index.htm.

 # West Ham United

Boleyn Ground, Green Street, E13
Capacity 26,000 (all-seated)
Colours Claret shirts with sky-blue sleeves, white shorts
Cup winners 1964, 1975, 1980
Cup-Winners' Cup winners 1965

West Ham is best known for being home to the so-called 'Academy of Football' whose rigorously technical approach produced a trio of World Cup winners in the mid-Sixties. But although they have won two FA Cups since, the Irons' stance is traditionally that of the underdog, fighting relegation battles with spirit and guile.

The club were originally the company team of the *Thames Ironworks*, founded in

1895 – hence their nicknames 'The Hammers' or 'The Irons'. They became independent and joined the Southern League in 1900, moving to their present ground four years later. Like any East End family, West Ham kept a tight grip on the purse strings, and the club's youth policy has always been important.

Apart from losing the 'White Horse Final' to Bolton as a second-division side in 1923, West Ham's story starts in earnest in the mid-Fifties. Members of their young squad including Malcolm Allison, Noel Cantwell, John Bond, Dave Sexton and Frank O'Farrell (all of whom would later coach top clubs) would meet after training and discuss tactics. The local game was going through an identity crisis after England's 6–3 thrashing by Hungary in 1953. Jogging endless laps in training wasn't delivering the goods – so what to do instead? Sitting for hours in *Cassetari's Café* near the ground, the young Hammers would plan out moves using salt cellars and vinegar bottles – moves which would culminate in a second-division title in 1958, after years in the doldrums.

With Ron Greenwood in charge (West Ham changed managers every ten years or so, keeping the job in the family), the lessons at *Cassetari's* paid off. Three class youngsters, half-back Bobby Moore, inside-forward Martin Peters and centre-forward Geoff Hurst, were the stars of the show. West Ham won the Cup in 1964, then the European Cup-Winners' Cup at the same Wembley stadium a year later, 2–0 over TSV Munich 1860. A year after that the trio were back to pick up the World Cup for England, Moore as captain, Hurst and Peters as the goalscorers.

In the Seventies, Peters left for Spurs and Trevor Brooking came through the ranks, an Academy player if there ever was one. Billy Bonds was the stalwart in front of the defence, Brooking the provider of the destroying pass. West Ham won the Cup again, then lost the Cup-Winners' Cup final to Anderlecht in 1976. After that the Hammers began to yo-yo unpredictably between divisions. When they reached Wembley again in 1980, for an FA Cup final against Arsenal, it was as a decent second-division side. But they won anyway.

As the Eighties went on they were forced to sell the family silver to survive – Tony Cottee and Paul Ince going to Everton and Manchester United, respectively. Transfer fees still wouldn't meet the expense of making Upton Park all-seater, however, so the board tried to instigate a bond scheme, requiring fans to pay £500 for a lifetime's use of a seat. The proposal saw mass protests, and the scheme was eventually dropped. In the end, Sky's TV money helped towards the impressive renovation in 1995 of the North and Bobby Moore Stands, while former Hammer Harry Redknapp presided over a revival of confidence on the pitch, with an entertaining side built around cultured young defender Rio Ferdinand, Israeli playmaker Eyal Berkovic and big Welsh striker John Hartson.

The Hammers' new hero – cavalier Paolo di Canio

Berkovic and Hartson have since departed, but with new signings Paolo di Canio and Paulo Wanchope, and a return to Europe (of sorts) in the 1999 Intertoto Cup, West Ham were another London side looking ahead, not back. In the event, only di Canio proved a success, and although the Hammers' European adventure lasted longer than anyone dared hope (they got as far as the UEFA Cup second round), it was a ten-game odyssey which appeared to sap the strength from Redknapp's squad as the regular season went on.

The team finished ninth in the Premiership table for 1999/2000, insufficient for another European place in any competition other than the Intertoto – which the club this time declined to enter. The decision deprived fans of the summer fun they'd enjoyed the previous year, but surely increased the likelihood of more consistency in the league.

Here we go!

District line Tube to **Upton Park**. Turn right out of the station, then take a 5min stroll down Green Street – the ground is on the left.

Just the ticket

Upton Park, as the Boleyn Ground is almost always known, is up close and personal. The **ticket office** in the West Stand on Green Street is open Mon–Fri 9am–5pm and on matchdays from 9am. Away fans are allocated a block in the North Stand, with turnstile access from Green Street. Home fans are based in the lower tier of the East Stand, the former 'Chicken Run', and in the Bobby Moore Stand. Neutrals are best placed in the West Stand. The club's dial-a-seat service can be reached on: ☎020/8548 2700.

Swift half

The classic West Ham pub is the *Boleyn Tavern*, down Green Street from the Tube and past the stadium on your left-hand side. It's a large pub with a wooden interior and two spacious bar areas. For food and a slice of history, *Cassetari's Café* is round the corner at 25 Barking Road. In the ground you'll find bars dotted all around, such as the *Trevor Brooking* and *Geoff Hurst* bars in the main West Stand, serving beer up to 15mins before kick-off.

Club merchandise

There's a new, spacious shop (open Mon–Fri 9.30am–5pm, Sat 9.30am–1pm, later on matchdays, most credit cards) at 39–41 Barking Road, just around the corner from the ground past the *Boleyn* pub.

Ultra culture

The conversion of Upton Park to an all-seater ground disbanded the Chicken Run, the standing area in the East Stand and soapbox for so much East London banter. These days you'll hear regular choruses of *I'm Forever Blowing Bubbles* coming from the Bobby Moore Stand, but the atmosphere is more sedate than it was.

In print

The **matchday programme** is £2, while the club magazine, *Hammers News* (£2.75) has recently been redesigned. The main fanzines are *On A Mission*, *Over Land And Sea* and *The Water In Majorca*.

In the net

The **official website** is now run by Britain's ubiquitous *Planet Internet* and looks and feels as if it belongs to someone else. Go if you must to: www.westhamunited.co.uk. For genuine, online East End banter, try: easyweb.easynet.co.uk/~graeme.howlett/contents2.htm.

Groundhopping

At the last count, London boasted 13 teams playing in England's top four divisions. Of these, Charlton Athletic were promoted to the Premiership in 2000; Crystal Palace, Fulham, Wimbledon and QPR kicked off the 2000/01 season in the

first division; Brentford and Millwall were in the second; and Leyton Orient and Barnet in the third.

Charlton Athletic

The Valley, Floyd Road, Charlton, SE7 8BL
Capacity 16,000 (all-seated)
Colours Red shirts, white shorts
Cup winners 1947

South London's Charlton are synonymous with their home at The Valley, and their fans' seven-year struggle to successfully reclaim it. The club had been based at the 70,000-capacity ground since 1922, gaining first-division status in 1936 after a three-year consecutive run from the third. The Valley was packed for the boom period either side of World War II. Charlton reached two successive cup finals, in 1946 and 1947, winning the latter 1–0 over Burnley.

The club lost its first-division status in 1957. A crowd-pleasing attack-minded side in the late Seventies, featuring Derek Hales, Mike Flanagan and Colin Powell, put a buzz back around The Valley, but Charlton were unable to gain promotion.

In 1985 it was announced that the beloved Valley was to be sold for development. While many boycotted home games at Selhurst Park, thousands got behind a boisterous campaign to return to the old ground. Although the club gained promotion in 1986 under tireless manager Lennie Lawrence, crowds remained low, and attention was focused on the Valley campaign. Helped by the local *South-East London Mercury*, fanzine *The Voice of the Valley* and supporters who stood in local elections on a 'Valley Party' ticket, fans won a famous victory in 1992 when the club made an emotional return to the ranch. The ground came in for a thorough overhaul in the summer of 1997 with the building of a new double-decker West Stand.

Meanwhile, manager Alan Curbishley was rebuilding the team, and Charlton surprised many by stealing in on the blind side to win promotion to the Premiership in 1998, after drawing 4–4 with Sunderland in a play-off final at Wembley, and winning the resulting penalty shoot-out. It was, in retrospect, a jump in class too soon, but after relegation in 1999, the club kept faith with Curbishley who, in turn, stuck with the players who had translated Charlton's new-found optimism into real footballing ambition. The consequence was a runaway first-division title win in 1999/2000, and an immediate return to the Premiership where, fans hope, Charlton can make a better go of it this time.

To see if they can, take an overground **train** from Charing Cross, Waterloo East or London Bridge to **Charlton** (journey time 30mins); turn right out of the station and immediately left into Floyd Road.

Of the many **pubs** dotted around the ground, *The Valley* in Elliscombe Road, the other side of Charlton Church Lane, and *McDonnells*, 428 Woolwich Road, are as good as any.

The more vociferous home fans gather in the North Stand by Harvey Gardens, away fans in the South Stand through entrance 4. Advance booking will be essential for Premiership games, and tickets can be booked by credit card on ☎020/8333 4010.

The **club shop** is on Floyd Road behind the West Stand (open Mon–Fri 10am–6pm, Sat 10am–2.45pm, later on matchdays).

Wimbledon

Selhurst Park, Park Road, Norwood, SE25
Capacity 26,000 (all-seated)
Colours All blue with yellow trim
Cup winners 1988

After a famous FA Cup run as a Southern League side in 1975, Wimbledon gained entry to the fourth division in 1977, and climbed steadily up the ladder. Perennial goalscorer Alan Cork stayed with them all

the way until they made the top flight in 1986. This was the era of the Crazy Gang, personified by the impish Dennis Wise and hardman Vinnie Jones. They played a fairly ugly brand of football, but their pub-team humour and collective spirit took them to an FA Cup final win over Liverpool in 1988. England's European ban sadly prevented the club from taking their rightful place in the Cup-Winners' Cup.

Nine years later the team were again denied a European spot – this time, playing a more attractive game under the careful guidance of manager Joe Kinnear, by chronic fixture congestion and the increasingly unplayable pitch at Crystal Palace's Selhurst Park, on which the Dons have been playing ever since their own Plough Lane ground was deemed too expensive to redevelop in the late Eighties.

Kinnear suffered a heart-attack in March 1999, and in the summer was replaced by the former national coach of Norway, Egil Olsen. No sea-change in style or philosophy was expected, and none came. But behind the scenes, popular club owner Sam Hammam finally tired of trying to find an alternative home for the club, and sold his entire stake in Wimbledon to the Norwegian consortium which had brought Olsen across the North Sea. In Hammam's absence, the team's form dipped alarmingly toward the end of the season, and a final-day defeat at Southampton – while fellow relegation candidates Bradford City were beating Liverpool – ended the Dons' 14-year stay in the English élite.

To see whether or not they can bounce straight back, take an overground train from Victoria or London Bridge to **Norwood Junction**, about a 20min ride. Out of the station, walk up to the crossroads ahead, turn left down Selhurst Road, and the stadium is on your right.

Low crowds mean few problems getting a ticket on matchdays – just turn up on the day. The most vocal Dons fans have now settled at the Holmesdale Road end also favoured by Palace. Neutrals are

Day of despair – the Dons are down, 2000

best-placed in the the Main Stand along the side of the pitch. *The Cherry Tree*, 32 Station Road, between Norwood Junction and the ground, is the traditional pre-match watering hole.

Eat, drink, sleep…

Bars and clubs

London's bar scene has enjoyed a real boom of late, radiating from trendy Hoxton, Clerkenwell, Angel and neighbouring areas within easy reach of the City. Many places stay open until at least 1am if not 2am, though some club bars charge a modest admission. Visitors still flock to Soho and Camden Town, although both areas have lost some of their shine.

Many pubs now have **big screens** for televised football, but be aware that wearing football colours on matchday may make

it hard to get served in the West End. As for the **beer**, the Guinness in north London is the best you'll get outside Ireland, and draught Czech lager is becoming justly commonplace – but you could be paying at least £2.50 a pint for either. Northerners complain about the quality of the **bitter** down south, but there are often good deals on cheap pints of it.

When it comes to clubs and concerts, London really excels – there are literally hundreds of events to choose from every night, but beware that top dance clubs charge up to £20 admission, and depending on the venue, snotty doormen may not let you in wearing trainers. If they turn you away, the club probably isn't up to much anyway.

Café Kick, 43 Exmouth Market. Lively table football bar in Clerkenwell, with authentic French tables, a range of beers and Portuguese touches to the soccer souvenirs on display. Open Mon–Sat 11.30am–11pm. Tube to Farringdon.

The End, 18a West Central Street. The West End's leading dance venue, boasting a stupendous sound system, and a first-rate club bar/restaurant next door, AKA, open until 3am. Tube to Tottenham Court Road or Holborn.

Turnmills, 63b Clerkenwell Road. Non-stop dancing all weekend long in this maze of a Clerkenwell club. Many punters have fallen in from *Dust*, at #27, a dance bar *par excellence*. Tube to Farringdon.

Ministry Of Sound, 103 Gaunt Street. Seminal dance club despite its location south of the river. Long queues, hefty entrance of £10–15 and heavy security. The biggest-name DJs spin here, and the Ministry now has its own record label, magazine and shop in Covent Garden. Tube to Elephant & Castle.

Terry Neill's Sports Bar & Brasserie, Bath House, 53 Holborn Viaduct. A good spot if you're after a more down-to-earth pub feel than the tackier sports bars in the West End. Run (and often frequented by) the former Spurs, Arsenal and Northern Ireland manager Neill, whose mementoes cover the walls. Tube to Blackfriars.

Restaurants

No-one goes to England for the food, but London can at least provide as big a variety of **international cuisine** as you'll get anywhere outside New York. The West End is the best stomping ground, Soho in particular being full of cheap Chinese and not-so-cheap Italian restaurants. Brick Lane and Westbourne Grove are full of curry houses, though wherever you are, there's bound to be 'an Indian' nearby. When it comes to English food, **pubs** do the best lunchtime stodge.

Belgo Centraal, 50 Earlham Street. The £5 set lunch here – mussels and chips in true Belgian style – is a surefire winner. Main courses otherwise £10–15, plus an excellent selection of beers. Tube to Covent Garden. Separate branch, *Belgo Noord*, at 72 Chalk Farm Road.

Chor Bizarre, 16 Albemarle Street. Good Indian restaurants are thin on the ground in Central London – this is one of the best. Set lunches £10–15, main courses from £15, food invariably excellent. Tube to Green Park.

Rules, 35 Maiden Lane. This inn, dating back 200 years, knocks spots off themed 'traditional' pubs, with fine touches to its British cuisine and unpretentious decor. Not cheap – wonderful two-course set meals are a shade under £20 – but well worth a visit. Tube to Covent Garden or Charing Cross.

Pollo, 20 Old Compton Street. Classic budget Italian diner, always busy despite there being two floors of tables. Incredibly cheap, open past midnight. Tube to Leicester Square.

Sea Shell Fish Restaurant, 49–51 Lisson Grove. The most famous fish-and-chip place in town, so you may have to wait to get seated. All kinds of fish, grilled or fried, with assorted side dishes. Far more expensive than you'd pay at your corner chippy, but worth it. Closes 10.30pm. Tube to Marylebone.

Accommodation

London is an **expensive city** to stay in. It's virtually impossible to pay less than £60 for a double room, and you could easily be charged twice that, even in a moderate hotel. **Bed-and-breakfasts** might be a better option – you'll find them grouped around the main train stations, but check your room first.

The **London Tourist Board** has a reservation line service (☎020/7932 2020), with a £5 booking fee. There are eight official **youth hostels** in town, for which an IYHF or YHA card is required. Foreign guests can buy an *International Guest Pass* (£1.70) to stay at hostel rates.

City Of London Youth Hostel, 36–38 Carter Lane (☎020/7236 7681). Centrally located, clean and modern, there are rooms with 2–15 beds, with TV, luggage storage, currency exchange and laundry facilities downstairs. Reception open until 11pm, no curfew. Beds £19–25 including breakfast. Visa and Mastercard. Tube to St. Paul's.

Edward Lear Hotel, 28–30 Seymour Street (☎020/7402 5401, fax 020/7706 3766). Former home of the famous limerick writer, a pleasant, central B&B which welcomes children. Singles are £45–55, doubles £65–100 with breakfast. Visa and Mastercard accepted. Tube to Marble Arch.

Oxford House, 92–94 Cambridge Street (☎020/7834 6467, fax 020/7834 0225). Cosy B&B near Victoria coach station, with spacious rooms and a TV lounge. Singles around £35, doubles £45. Triples and quads also available. Visa and Mastercard accepted. Tube to Victoria.

Woodville House, 107 Ebury Street (☎020/7730 1048, fax 020/7730 2574). Pleasant B&B near Victoria in a street full of them. Singles £45, doubles £60–80. No private facilities but breakfast included. Most major credit cards. Tube to Victoria.

Young, gifted and white – the Leeds United revival

Leeds United's promising young team may find it hard to match the club's glory days of 30 years ago, but at least they have restored a great deal of pride to West Yorkshire. European football has returned to **Elland Road**, in tandem with plans for a £50million redevelopment programme, embracing 5,000 new seats in an extended West Stand, a separate smaller sports arena and a new train station, all to be built on the wasteland which surrounds an already impressive modern ground.

Up from down under – Harry Kewell gets stuck in

The club's history really begins in the early Sixties. They had been founded as **Leeds City** in 1904, but were closed down after World War I due to illegal payments. Leeds United rose from the ashes, flitting between the top two divisions from 1920. They were promoted in 1956, as a young, tactically aware half-back by the name of **Don Revie** was lifting the FA Cup for Manchester City. Revie would become Leeds' manager five years later, by which time the club were back in the second. With a young side built initially around Scottish international Bobby Collins and later his compatriot Billy Bremner, Revie's Leeds were promoted in 1964. A year later, they surprised everyone by running Everton close in the title race, and losing to an extra-time goal to Liverpool in the Cup. It would be the start of a decade at the top, marked by tactical innovation, a relentless will to win...and atrocious luck.

Few clubs enjoyed the trip to Elland Road, where tough-tackling Norman Hunter ruled the midfield roost and referees were ruthlessly intimidated by players and fans alike. Yet Leeds were losers far more often than they were winners. They would win the championship only twice – in 1969 and 1974 – while finishing runners-up on five occasions. They were Cup finalists in four times, but winners only once. Twice the Fairs' Cup was won – yet the grand prize, the European Cup, eluded them. They were beaten in a tight semi-final with Celtic in 1970, and in 1975, after Revie had taken the England job and was replaced – after an infamous 44-day stay by Brian Clough – by **Jimmy Armfield**, they made the final only to lose in controversial circumstances to holders **Bayern Munich**, prompting a riot by supporters in Paris.

Under a variety of coaches – often ex-Leeds players – the club spent most of the Eighties in the lower flight. The arrival of **Howard Wilkinson** as manager in 1988 spelled change, and his side were the last pre-Premiership English champions in 1992. Four years later, Leeds rescued **George Graham** from the wilderness, and it was his side that provided the foundation for **David O'Leary**'s young, attack-minded team to make such an impact in 1998/99 and 1999/2000.

On matchdays, regular **shuttle buses** depart from Neville Street, next to the main train station, to Elland Road, where the main **box office** (☎0113/226 1000) is in the new East Stand – tickets are generally available up to kick-off for most fixtures. The away end is in the South Stand, home end the Revie Stand behind the opposite goal. If you find the *Old Peacock* pub behind the South Stand too busy, then try the *Dry Salters*, a 10min walk towards the *White Rose Shopping Centre*, or Peter Lorimer's *The Commercial* in Sweet Street, Holbeck, a meeting place for all the old stars.

Birmingham

Aston Villa *137*
Birmingham City *140*

England's second city in terms of size and population, Birmingham cannot claim to wield the footballing influence of either London or the north-west, but it is proud of its importance in the development of the game. In addition to Aston Villa, the region's major club, and nearby Coventry City, the West Midlands conurbation boasts a number of England's 'sleeping giants' – Birmingham City and, in the adjacent Black Country, Wolverhampton Wanderers and West Bromwich Albion.

All these last three are currently playing Nationwide League football, underlining both the area's potential footballing strength and the extent to which the mod-era era has, so far at least, passed much of the region by.

Aston Villa

Villa Park, Trinity Road, Birmingham B6
Capacity 39,300
Colours Claret shirts with sky-blue sleeves, white shorts
League champions 1894, 1896–97, 1899, 1900, 1910, 1981
Cup winners 1887, 1895, 1897, 1905, 1913, 1920, 1957
European Cup winners 1982

Aston Villa entered the 20th century as the best side in English football and left it as a major club. But for most of the intervening 100 years, they have consistently failed to live up to the high standards set by their Victorian-era successes.

Villa were the first giants of English football. It was no surprise that they were founder members of the Football League – they had won the FA Cup the year prior to the League's inception, and one of the directors of the club, William McGregor, was the man who proposed the founding of the League and became its first chairman. With Scottish-born George Ramsay a vital influence both on and off the field, Villa

dominated in the Victorian era. Their distinctive claret shirts with blue sleeves were copied by Burnley and West Ham United, as clubs in all parts of the country tried to imitate the success of the Birmingham side.

In 1897, Villa became the second team (after Preston North End eight years earlier) to do the League and FA Cup double, and the trophies continued to roll in until World War I. After it, though Villa remained a force in the first division thanks largely to the goals of prolific striker Harry Hampton and later 'Pongo' Waring, they were no longer the mighty power they had once been. Relegation in 1936 seemed an epoch-shattering disaster; in reality it was only a foretaste of what was to come after World War II. Once again Villa found themselves struggling to rebuild after hostilities and, two years after an FA Cup final win over Manchester United in 1957, they were again relegated to the second division.

Wily manager Joe Mercer brought them back immediately, and a year later Villa won the inaugural League Cup. But Mercer's promising side, which included England international forward Gerry Hitchens, failed to develop. Mercer took his coaching skills off to Manchester City, Hitchens went to Inter Milan, and Villa were relegated again in 1967.

In 1970 the unthinkable happened – the club sank into the old third division. For two years Villa Park, one of the premier grounds in the country, played host to small-town football, while across town, Birmingham City were preparing for a flamboyant assault on the top flight. It wasn't until 1975 that Villa won back their first-class status, under the management of Ron Saunders.

Saunders was a stern figure, but his strict discipline and eye for talent helped breathe new life into Villa. They won the League Cup by beating Norwich at Wembley in 1975, and won it again two years later, after a third replay against Everton. In 1981, with Saunders still very much in

The ponderer – David James at Wembley

charge, Villa won their first title for 70 years, finishing four points ahead of a highly fancied Ipswich Town. If few had expected a title, even fewer could quite believe it when Villa won the European Cup the following season – despite the resignation of Saunders following a contractual dispute midway through the season. Anderlecht were beaten in the semi-finals and in the final against Bayern Munich, Breitner, Rummenigge and all were defeated by a goal from Villa's bulky, bearded target man, Peter Withe. The victory was made all the more remarkable by the fact that first-team 'keeper Jimmy Rimmer was injured and had to be substituted by a completely untried youngster, Nigel Spink.

The Villa side of the day had few stars, but Saunders and his successor, Tony Barton, had struck just the right balance of youth and experience, flair and grit. There

was the tough Scottish midfielder Des Bremner, the talented young playmaker Gordon Cowans, flying wingers Tony Morley and Mark Walters, and the burly central-defensive pairing of Ken McNaught and Allan Evans. Above all there was Withe, a man who could make even a tap-in look clumsy – as he did in Rotterdam against Bayern – but whose presence was enough to strike fear into any central defence in Europe.

As Barton was succeeded by Graham Turner and then by Billy McNeill, Villa failed to replace the older players in the side, and were relegated again in 1987. They bounced back within a season under the former Watford manager Graham Taylor, who set about building a younger team that included some of the most exciting players seen at Villa for years – among them the skilful winger Tony Daley and a masterful midfield signing from Crewe, David Platt. After they finished second in the league in 1990, much was expected of Taylor's side. But then the boss made the worst decision of his career – he left his promising young team for the England manager's job.

Since then, the most widely supported club in the Midlands and their chairman, Doug Ellis, have provided no shortage of cash to invest in players. Ron Atkinson took over from the ill-starred Slovak Jozef Vengloš as manager in 1991, and Villa progressed steadily, becoming regular title and European contenders, and winning the League Cup (denying Manchester United a domestic treble in the process) in 1994.

Atkinson's replacement, Brian Little, a hero of the triple-replay League Cup final of 1977, continued to spend millions in the transfer market and kept Villa among the top five clubs in England. Yet another League Cup – now something of a club speciality – arrived thanks to a 3–0 demolition of Leeds in 1996, but within 18 months Little had resigned, to be replaced by another former Villa player, John Gregory. The new regime was rootsier and quicker to raise a smile than the previous one, and Villa's squad responded, rising from the wrong end of the table to claim a UEFA Cup place in 1998.

Further progress was made the following season, with Villa making a particularly impressive start to the Premiership campaign despite the loss of striker Dwight Yorke to Manchester United. Alas, with Stan Collymore and Paul Merson needing various kinds of off-the-field counselling, Villa were over-reliant on Dion Dublin for goals, and as his form faded, so the club's title challenge faded with it. A sixth-place finish wasn't good enough for Europe, and after a similarly stop-start campaign in 1999/2000, the club settled for the Intertoto Cup as a possible route to serious continental competition. The mid-season arrival of Benito Carbone did inject enough flair into Gregory's side for a couple of decent cup runs, but after Leicester had denied Villa at the semi-final stage of the League Cup, an error by David James allowed Chelsea to take the spoils in the last FA Cup final to be played at Wembley.

Gregory and Ellis couldn't agree terms with Carbone to keep the wayward Italian at Villa Park for 2000/01, and as the close season went on, it became clear he hadn't been the only player on the staff to be frustrated at what many fans perceive as the club's lack of ambition. With transfer requests landing on his desk like food orders at a takeaway Balti house, Ellis sanctioned the signing of David Ginola from Spurs in the hope that he alone might make Villa a creative force once more.

Here we go!

The nearest train station is **Witton**, three stops from New Street and a 2min walk from the ground. From Birmingham city centre you can take **bus #7** to the ground – allow 15mins.

Just the ticket

Although big games are sold out weeks in advance, by no means all Premiership fixtures are all-ticket at Villa Park. The view from anywhere inside the ground is excellent. Home fans sit in

the huge Holte End or the nearest section of the Doug Ellis Stand to it. Neutrals are best off in the Trinity Road Stand, but the rebuilding of this fell behind schedule during the summer of 2000 and not all sections may be open. Away fans are allocated the Lower North Stand – turnstiles in Witton Lane, at one end of the Doug Ellis Stand. For all ticket enquiries call ☎0121/327 5353.

Swift half

Favoured spots for a pre-match beer include **The Harriers**, at the junction of Broadway and Davey Road, and **The Witton Arms** by the train station. The spacious *Harriers* has table football, pool and plenty of sport on TV; the *Witton* is shabbier but convenient for fans coming by train.

Club merchandise

The huge **Villa Village** (open Mon–Sat 9am–5.30pm, later on matchdays) set back behind the North Stand has an enormous range of claret-and-blue merchandise, including a particularly fine array of vintage shirts and, from 1999, vintage wine, too. There's also a smaller shop (open matchdays only) behind the Holte Stand.

Ultra culture

The now all-seated Holte End is the biggest end stand in England and, on a good day, it sounds like it. Refreshingly, Villla's hardcore element is renowned for its anti-fascism.

In print

Villa's **matchday programme** (£2) is glossy but has plenty of substance to back up the photography – a rarity in England. The people who produce it, *Sports Projects*, are also responsible for the official club magazine, **Claret & Blue**, which again is one of the better of its type.

In the net

Villa's **official website** is a little graphic-heavy but has all the essentials, including an excellent news archive, a detailed history and comprehensive e-commerce section. You'll find it at: www.astonvilla-fc.com.

Of the unofficial sites, **VillaWeb** was one of the first on the net and is very efficiently run from Denmark by Christian Jahnsen. It's at: www.gbar.dtu.dk/~c937079/AVFC/.

Groundhopping

◉ Birmingham City

St Andrews, St Andrews Street, Birmingham B9
Capacity 24,796
Colours Blue shirts, white shorts

Despite a strong support base, Birmingham have not a single major honour to their name, and have spent most of their life bobbing up and down between the top two divisions.

The club joined the Football League as Small Heath in 1892, but it wasn't until the Twenties that they showed any signs of potential with a sustained spell in the top flight. In 1931 they reached their first FA Cup final, losing to local rivals West Bromwich Albion. After a quiet decade or three, the Blues were selected as England's representatives in the Fairs' Cup – the forerunner of today's UEFA Cup. They reached the final in 1960 and 1961, losing to Barcelona and Roma. Four years later, they were back in the second division.

The Seventies saw Birmingham at their best. From 1972 to 1979 they competed in the top flight, with the likes of Trevor Francis and Bob Latchford wowing the crowds, dressed in a now immortal shirt of blue with a single, white centre stripe. Francis was sold to Nottingham Forest in 1979, becoming England's first £1million player. City were relegated.

They slumped into the third division in 1989, and though promoted in 1992 they have only recently begun to look like a club with serious ambition once more. In 1994 club chairman David Sullivan, owner of the *Daily Sport* newspaper, and his CEO Karren Brady gave an open chequebook to manager Barry Fry. After using a League record 46 players in 1995/96, the club had a massive staff but showed little in the way of progress.

Trevor Francis returned as manager in 1996, and though City were muscled out of the play-offs by Watford in 1998/99 and by Barnsley a year later, there's a sense of purpose about the newly rebuilt St Andrew's that's been lacking here for decades.

St Andrew's is about a mile east of **New Street station**, a 20min walk (follow signs for Small Heath), or take bus #15, #17, #96 or #97. A pre-match pint is best supped near New Street station.

Eat, drink, sleep...

Bars and clubs

Birmingham's nightlife is widely dispersed. Many congregate in trendy pubs and clubs in central Broad Street and Brindleyplace, the student area of Moseley can be lively of a weekend, and there are a few popular Irish pubs in the Digbeth area.

Bonds, Hampton Street, Hockley. On a Saturday night *Miss Moneypenny's* features house and rare grooves for £7–10 admission with occasional visits from big-name DJs. Bus #74 from town.

The Dubliner, 57 Digbeth. Probably the best Irish bar of the many in the area, near the city's main coach station, with decent pub grub and live bands most nights.

Que Club, Corporation Street. A former church, now the biggest club in town. The *Atomic Jam* techno nights are as good as you'll get anywhere, with major international DJs flying in.

Ronnie Scott's, 258 Broad Street. Centrally located live music venue, with jazz, blues and world music plus a separate tapas bar.

The Sanctuary, Digbeth. Spacious club that reopened in 1997 and within a year had won its old crowd back. *God's Kitchen* is essential on a Friday night, with top-name DJs.

Restaurants

Centrally located places cater to the business crowd, but you can find good ethnic eateries in the Chinese quarter at the top

Birmingham essentials

The main terminal of Birmingham **airport**, 12km east of town, is connected to Birmingham International **train station** by a courtesy bus that serves each incoming flight from the arrivals hall. Four trains an hour run from Birmingham International to **New Street station**, journey time 15mins, single fare £2.60. New Street, which serves mainline trains to London and Manchester, is in the city centre.

The main **bus station** is at Digbeth, a 10min walk from New Street. The main city bus company, *Centro*, operates a two-tier fare system, in which off-peak travel (Mon–Fri 9.30am–3.30pm & 6pm–11.30pm, Sat–Sun all day) costs just 90p for any journey; note that many bus stops in central Birmingham have been temporarily moved during rebuilding. A limited night service is run through Friday night/Saturday morning and Saturday night/Sunday morning, between 1am and 4am. Pay your fare to the driver, who can also issue **day passes** at £2.50. For a **black cab**, call *TOA* on ☎0121/427 8888.

Tourist information is available at two offices, equidistant from New Street: at 2 City Arcade, off New Street (open Mon–Sat 9.30am–5.30pm, ☎0121/643 2514,); and at the Central Library, Chamberlain Square (open Mon–Fri 9am–8pm, Sat 9am–5pm, ☎0121/236 5622). The offices issue a free fortnightly listings magazine, *What's On*, also available in major clubs and venues.

of Hurst Street, and in the southern suburbs of Balsall Heath and Sparkhill, home of the Balti. There are further Balti options if you find yourself walking back through Digbeth from St Andrew's.

Calabash, 32–38 Coventry Road, Digbeth. Large West Indian restaurant near the coach station, with tropical décor and fine cocktails. Open Tue–Thur 7pm–10.30pm, Fri–Sat 7pm–11pm, and Sunday lunchtimes.

Celebrity Balti, 44 Broad Street. Centrally located Balti house near the International Convention Centre. Pricy, but the food is great.

Leftbank, 79 Broad Street. Elegantly converted Victorian banking hall serving first-rate *nouvelle cuisine* at around £17 a head. Set menus at £10 and £12.50. Open Mon–Sat until 10pm.

San Carlo, 4 Temple Street. Near St Philip's Cathedral, this is a better bet than the branches of Italian chain restaurants in nearby New Street, if for no other reason than that it serves fresh produce cooked by real Italian chefs.

Accommodation

The B&Bs and cheaper hotels are to be found two miles west of town along Hagley

Road (buses #9, #19, #120, #126, #192, #193 and #292) and at Acocks Green, four miles south-east of the centre (buses #1, #11, #37 and #38). The International Convention Centre **tourist office** offers cheap weekend deals on business-class hotels.

Ashdale House Hotel, 39 Broad Road, Acocks Green (☎0121/707 2324, fax 0121/706 3598). Cosy place with TV in every room. Singles £25, doubles £40. Visa and Mastercard accepted.

Bridge House Hotel, 49 Sherbourne Road, Acocks Green (☎0121/706 5900, fax 0121/624 5900). Clean, comfortable B&B with a shower/bath and TV in each room. Single rooms around £35, doubles £50. Most credit cards.

Kennedy Guest House, 38 York Road (☎0121/454 1284). Downbeat but comfortable B&B just off the Hagley Road stretch of similar establishments. Singles around £30, doubles £50. Most credit cards.

Robin Hood Lounge Hotel, 142 Robin Hood Lane, Hall Green (☎0121/778 5307, fax 0121/604 8686). Guesthouse five miles from the city centre. All rooms with a television, some with bath/shower. Singles at around £30, doubles at £50. Most credit cards.

Manchester

A family affair – Brooklyn Beckham and chums are centre-stage at the 2000 title celebrations

While there is no doubt that the north-west is the stronghold of English football, the two major cities of the region, Manchester and Liverpool, continue to compete for the right to be its capital. After being overshadowed by Liverpool and Everton in the Seventies and Eighties, Manchester – or, more accurately, Manchester United – has dominated the game in the Nineties.

The wider Greater Manchester region, which as part of the old county of Lancashire was the engine behind the growth of professional football, is packed with small-town sides scrapping for a piece of the pie, but arguably only the Manchester clubs have the resources to succeed in the modern era of sky-high salaries and corporate sponsorship.

Both sides, City and United, have enjoyed periods of ascendancy since World War II. But in the Nineties their fates have been very different. United, under Alex Ferguson's coaching and Martin Edwards' business leadership, have re-emerged as the dominant club in the English game. Throughout their barren years in the Seventies and Eighties, they maintained a large support base which spread far beyond the boundaries of the city. Today no club in the country, and quite possibly the planet, matches them for marketing and commercial acumen. City, meanwhile, are struggling in the Nationwide League, scarred by boardroom acrimony, inept coaching and other man-made disasters.

In many senses the two clubs sum up the two sides to the city. United epitomise the industry and wealth which made Manchester the world's first industrial town. City, based in the blighted Moss Side district, attract a young support which identifies with 'Madchester', sometime capital of the UK indie music scene, drugs culture and 'baggy' fashion.

The two clubs' souvenir shops reflect the dichotomy perfectly. United's *Megastore* sells mass-produced tack to visitors from all over the world. City's little hut sells designer gear modelled on the look and attitude of two of the club's current celebrity fans, the Gallagher brothers of Oasis. Yet however much United's loyal support (much of which, contrary to popular opinion, does come from Manchester) feels embarrassed about the crass commercialism, they know that the Japanese tourists buying *Red Devil* teddy bears are helping to pay for the stars their club are able to attract and, more importantly, keep and develop. And the City faithful, set to turn out in even more impressive numbers after a second successive promotion, would happily trade some style for silverware.

The thrilling fields

 Manchester United

Old Trafford, Sir Matt Busby Way, Manchester
Capacity 68,000 (all-seated)
Colours Red shirts, white shorts
League champions 1908, 1911, 1952, 1956–57, 1965, 1967, 1993–94, 1996–97, 1999–2000
Cup winners 1909, 1948, 1963, 1977, 1983, 1985, 1990, 1994, 1996, 1999
European Cup winners 1968, 1999
Cup-Winners' Cup winners 1991

As any Mancunian who has travelled will tell you, to the outside world, United *is* Manchester. How many pidgin English conversations have begun with the words 'Manchester United', quickly followed by the name 'Bobby Charlton'?

Which begs another question – why is the world so besotted with Manchester United? For a start, because they were the first English club to make an impression in Europe, with a talented, young Fifties side playing attractive, attacking football. When that side was tragically destroyed by the Munich air disaster, the sympathy of the world was with the club. And those sympathisers were delighted when, ten years later, United lifted the European Cup. They were the first English side to do so and

won the hearts of uncommitted fans across the country, thanks in part to the presence of some of the brightest stars to illuminate modern English football – Bobby Charlton, George Best and Denis Law.

Like other European clubs with nationwide support, such as Bayern Munich and Juventus, United are also one of the most disliked clubs in their own country. Every committed fan in the land recalls the kid in the playground who, rather than support his local team, wore a red-and-white shirt and dreamed of one day actually seeing a match at Old Trafford.

The team's historic 'treble' of 1998/99 merely polarised public opinion about United further. To those for whom the club has become a symbol of English football's polarisation between rich and poor, it was confirmation of all their worst fears. For the dedicated fan, whether an Old Trafford regular or one of the many thousands now priced out of live games but who watch every second of the action on television, it was a poetic culmination of so many years of yearning. To the uncommitted neutral, it was simply enthralling – a seemingly endless round of spectacular goals, great escapes and last-minute winners, combining to create the most dramatic climax to a season a single club has ever enjoyed, or endured. It could be decades before the English game sees anything to compare with it.

Founded as a railway workers' team, under the name Newton Heath Lancashire and Yorkshire Cricket and Football Club, in 1878, in their early years the club were rarely on a stable financial footing. Newton Heath joined the Football League in 1892 but went bankrupt ten years later, swiftly re-emerging as Manchester United – despite a strong lobby that preferred the name Manchester Celtic.

Between the wars, United were firmly fixed in the shadows of a more popular and more successful Manchester City. Old Trafford was destroyed by bombing in World War II, and there were many who felt the club might not get off the ground in peacetime. Bill Shankly wandered past the ground and saw the wreckage. 'I thought that's it – this is the end,' he recalled.

But United survived, playing their games at City's Maine Road for three seasons while Old Trafford was rebuilt. While at Maine Road they took on a former City and Liverpool right-half by the name of Matt Busby as manager. Just as his fellow Scot Shankly would do at Liverpool, Busby set about building a team that played modern football with style. Initially his personnel were pre-war players, including Jack Rowley, Stan Pearson and skipper Johnny Carey, who led United to the 1948 FA Cup and then the league title in 1952.

Off the field, however, Busby was setting up a matchless scouting system and youth scheme. As his side aged, he plugged the gaps with locally produced youngsters. The policy was so successful that between 1953 and 1957, United did not sign a single player from another club.

The young side which picked up two titles in 1956 and 1957 was dubbed the 'Busby Babes'. Among the many talented young players, the one who stood out was Duncan Edwards, who made his debut for United aged just 16, and who went on to become the youngest man ever to play for England. Although he played many of his games in the centre of defence, Edwards was ahead of his time in that he could, and did, play in most positions on the park.

With Edwards bossing the defence, Bobby Charlton at inside-left, Tommy Taylor at centre-forward and Eddie Coleman the playmaker in midfield, United became the first English team to enter the European Cup in 1956. The Football League was sceptical, but it was another sign of Busby's vision that he saw the importance of European competition and pressured the FA into backing United's adventure 'abroad'. In the first game, Belgian champions Anderlecht were crushed 10–0 in Manchester, then Borsussia Dortmund and Athletic Bilbao were disposed of, before United were stopped by Real Madrid.

The club's second European campaign ended in tragedy. Following a quarter-final, second-leg draw in Belgrade against Red Star, the team plane crashed after attempting to take off from Munich airport. Among the dead were eight United players – Edwards (who fought for his life for 15 days), Taylor, Coleman, Roger Byrne, David Pegg, Mark Jones, Geoff Bent and Billy Whelan. To this day the clock outside the club offices at Old Trafford remains set at 3.40 – the time the plane crashed.

Busby survived to begin the whole process again, but it was four years before the new United took shape. The new side, which won the FA Cup in 1963 and the title two years later, still featured Bobby Charlton, but by then Busby had switched him to a more central role. Charlton's

Manchester essentials

Manchester's **airport** is the biggest in the UK outside London and lies 16km south of the city centre. Trains leave the airport every 15mins (5.15am–10.10pm, with less frequent service through the night) for **Piccadilly train station** in the centre of town. Journey time is around 25mins.

Most *Intercity* trains from around Britain also come into Piccadilly, but those from the north-east and some minor regional trains roll up at **Manchester Victoria**. The two stations are connected by the *Metrolink* – a **modern tramway** which has reduced, though not eliminated, traffic congestion in the city. *Metrolink* runs from Bury, 16km north of the centre, to Altrincham 15km miles to the south. Tickets are purchased from automatic machines at stations, of which there are eight in the city centre. The main **bus station** for services to other cities is at Chorlton Street, close to Piccadilly.

The **tourist office** (open Mon & Sat 10am–5pm, Tue–Fri 9am–5pm) is at the town hall, in St Peter's Square. Best source for **listings** is *City Life* (fortnightly, £1.50).

place on the left flank was filled by a young Irishman, George Best, who acted as the provider for Denis Law, a former Manchester City striker who had been brought back from a miserable year with Torino for a British record fee of £115,000.

In the European Cup quarter-final of 1966, United defeated Benfica 5–1 in the Stadium of Light, but went out to Partizan Belgrade in the semi-finals.

When the Sixties swung – George Best in his boutique

United won another title in 1966/67, when they remained unbeaten at home, and this time there was no stopping them 'abroad'. After coming back from 3–1 down in the last 20 minutes at Real Madrid in the semis, United faced Benfica again, this time in front of 100,000 at Wembley. The game stood at 1–1 and had gone into extra-time when 'keeper Alex Stepney sent an aimless punt upfield and Best ran on to it, danced through, and slotted the ball past Henrique. Young forward Brian Kidd and Charlton then struck twice within six minutes – and ten years after Munich, United had become the first English team to win the European Cup.

A year later Busby moved 'upstairs' to become general manager, but his successors, Wilf McGuiness and Frank O'Farrell, could not sustain the momentum. Charlton retired, Best went to seed, Law went back to City. United were relegated in 1974, their final nail a backheeled goal from Law in the Manchester derby. (Law was devastated and was substituted immediately, but as other results came through he was slightly comforted by the knowledge that United would have gone down anyway, even without his goal.)

United bounced back to the top flight straight away, but over the next two decades they would rarely look like championship material. Tommy Docherty's brash

mid-Seventies youngsters, with Lou Macari upfront and Steve Coppell on the wing, were FA Cup specialists. So were Ron Atkinson's dynamic Eighties side, with England skipper Bryan Robson in midfield, the diminutive Scot Gordon Strachan alongside him and the peerless Irishman Paul McGrath in the centre of defence. In between, former Chelsea manager Dave Sexton kept 'feeling good about the future' but never delivered jam today.

In 1986, when nearly 20 years had elapsed since United's last title, the club turned to a winner, and another Scot, Alex Ferguson. He had led Aberdeen to the European Cup-Winners' Cup in 1983 and, although his job appeared to be on the line on several occasions, his determination finally brought the results United chairman Martin Edwards demanded. In 1990 the team won the FA Cup, and the following season defeated Barcelona to win the Cup-Winners' Cup – England's first European honour since Heysel.

The prize Old Trafford wanted more than any was the championship, and Ferguson duly delivered it in 1992/93, after making what one critic called 'the deal of the decade' to buy Eric Cantona for a pittance from holders Leeds.

Cantona's United did the double in 1994, missed out by a point to Blackburn a year later, then became the first English team to win the double twice in 1996.

Like Busby before him, Ferguson pinned great faith in youth. The policy gave the club precious continuity, and made United less dependent on big-money transfers than their rivals. Ryan Giggs, David Beckham, the Neville brothers, Paul Scholes and Nicky Butt all came through the ranks to take their place in the Theatre of Dreams. Even so, the manager would need to spend nearly £23million on just two players – striker Dwight Yorke and Dutch stopper Jaap Stam – on the eve of the 1998/99 campaign to give his squad the strength in-depth needed to compete successfully on three fronts. The signings seemed to go against the grain but, on the other hand, so did any notion that United's by now obsessive pursuit of the European Cup should come before domestic concerns.

By comparison with 1967/68, entering Europe's premier competition was easier now – United sneaked in as Premiership runners-up, something that would have been impossible in Matt Busby's day. Yet actually winning the competition was infinitely harder. Ferguson's side played 12 matches en route to the Nou Camp, compared with just eight 31 years earlier. They didn't lose a game, and they never gave up – not even when the Barcelona scoreboard said 90 minutes had gone, and time, just as on the Old Trafford clock, seemed to stand still...

Repeating that treble achievement in 1999/2000 was always going to be impossible – not least because United chose not to defend the FA Cup, playing instead in the inaugural World Club Championship in Brazil after pressure from England's World Cup 2006 bid committee. The Brazilian trip was a disaster, yet somehow United bounced back from it to retain the Premiership title with something to spare. Europe was more difficult, with the new second-phase group stage proving a tall order even for Ferguson's large squad to

cope with, and the surprise, if anything, was the team managed to get as far as the quarter-finals, before falling to an inspired Real Madrid at Old Trafford.

For 2000/01, French international Fabien Barthez was recruited as an overdue replacement for Schmeichel, who'd left a year earlier, but the club record signing of Dutch striker Ruud van Nistelrooy was put on hold after an injury scare. United may more money than the rest of the Premiership, but that does not make them immune from football's unpredictability.

Here we go!

Take the *Metrolink* **tram** heading for Altrincham from any city-centre station. Get off at **Old Trafford** and walk down Warwick Road, past the Lancashire cricket ground, and keep heading straight on until you reach Sir Matt Busby Way and the stadium.

Just the ticket

Old Trafford has now been extended to a capacity of 68,000, and United – like all Premiership clubs – have signed up to a charter which will give a guaranteed number of fans access to some seats on the day. Even so, it's best to call the ticket office well in advance on ☎0161/872 0199, and still prepare to be disappointed if your goal is a big Premiership or European encounter.

Swift half

There are a couple of pubs by the crossroads of Chester Road and Warwick Road which you will pass on your way from the tram station. *The Trafford* is packed out on matchdays, but further down Chester Road, the *Gorse Hill Hotel* is a decent traditional pub with a big-screen TV which attracts those unable to strike a deal with the touts outside the ground.

Another option is to get off the *Metrolink* a stop earlier at Trafford Bar – facing you as you leave the station is the *Tollgate Inn* on Seymour Road, where you may actually get served and still meet up with some Old Trafford regulars.

At the ground itself is the *Red Café* in the North Stand which, like the stadium, is booked up in advance for all games. You'll get in during the week (the café is open midday–11pm daily), but don't bother unless you're turned on by the idea of eating burgers while surrounded by videos of Roy Keane injuring himself.

Club merchandise

The large **Superstore** at the corner of the East and South Stands and the even bigger **Megastore** behind the Stretford End (now officially the West End) sell everything from the very latest yellow/green/blue/white/grey away shirt to United all-over body spray. Prices are high, but then, so is the Old Trafford overhead. Both shops are open Mon–Sat 9am–5pm, Sun 10am–4pm, later on matchdays.

Ultra culture

The Stretford End is no more than another feature in United's museum, and although some early Champions' League games in 1999/2000 were eerily quiet (the *After The Lord Mayor's Show* effect, perhaps), Old Trafford can still create atmosphere. The East Stand makes plenty of noise and the West (still the Stretford End to most) is competing hard. United fans have played a major part in the revival of the English football song – the *Marseillaise* was popular during the Cantona era, as was the Gap Band's *Oops Upside Your Head* – and the successful campaign against Rupert Murdoch's takeover of the club owed much to the galvanising of grassroots support.

In print

United Review (£2) is the matchday programme, while the monthly **United** (£2.95) is the most readable of the many official magazines. A clutch of lively fanzines proves there's more to United fan culture than shopping and eating – try **United We Stand** or **Red News**.

In the net

United's **official website** has come a long way since it was run as an area of the *Sky Sports* site. Now it's a fully fledged, slickly designed, with (as you'd expect) a comprehensive e-commerce section. It still lacks depth, however at: www.manutd.com.

Among the unofficials, *Theatre Of Dreams* has the historical context the official site lacks, plus lots of fan input and plenty of multi-media bits, at: mufc.simplenet.com.

Manchester City

Maine Road, Moss Side, Manchester
Capacity 32,000
Colours Sky-blue shirts, white shorts
League champions 1937, 1968
Cup winners 1904, 1934, 1956, 1969
Cup-Winners' Cup winners 1970

An Atlético Madrid, Torino or Munich 1860 fan would understand. Life is hard when your team are constantly in the shadows of more successful city rivals. It gets harder still when the media begin to talk as if there is only one club in town. And as for your heroes having to struggle awkwardly through the second-division play-offs while the other lot are doing the treble, well...

At least, when United were drawing all the accolades in the Sixties, City were able to spoil the party by winning some silverware of their own. At the end of the Nineties, United's glory coincided with the worst spell in City's history. A lethal cocktail of boardroom disputes and embarrassing managerial musical chairs culminated in relegation from the Premiership in 1996, but this was nothing compared with the despair of two years later, when despite winning their last game of the season, City were relegated again, and forced to taste life in the lower half of the league for the first time in their history.

The club certainly have history on their side. City were the first team from Manchester to win the FA Cup when they beat Bolton Wanderers in 1904. They spent part of the Twenties in the second division, won the Cup again in 1934 and the title in 1937, then got themselves relegated just prior to the outbreak of World War II.

In the Fifties, City manager Les McDowall based his team's tactics on those of the great Hungarian side of the era, with Don Revie, later to become a successful manager with Leeds (and an unsuccessful one with England), playing the deep-lying centre-forward's role of Nandor Hidegkuti. Just as England couldn't understand what Hidegkuti was doing inside his own half at

Wembley in 1953, so English sides couldn't work out why Revie, with a #9 on his back, was wandering deep into midfield.

In 1956 the strategy brought City an FA Cup final win over Birmingham – though the game is better remembered for the part played by City's goalkeeper, Bert Trautmann. Trautmann, popular with local fans despite having fought for Germany in the war, discovered after the game that he had played the final minutes with a broken neck.

A fallow decade then followed until 1965, when City appointed Joe Mercer as manager and Malcolm Allison as his assistant. Within a year they had built a completely new team around winger Mike Summerbee, midfielder Colin Bell and striker Francis Lee. In 1968, just two years after winning back their first-division status, City won the title. The campaign ended in dramatic style. City were being chased to the wire by United and needed to win their last game away to Newcastle – they just managed it, 4–3, with two goals from

Good to be back – the Ewood party begins

striker Neil Young. With United winning the European Cup that season, City fans boasted that their idols were not only English champions but *de facto* the best team in Europe as well.

A year later City beat Leicester 1–0 in the FA Cup final, which gave the club a crack at Europe in the Cup-Winners' Cup the following season. The team seized their moment, beating Athletic Bilbao and Schalke 04 on the way to the final against Górnik Zabrze of Poland in Vienna. City won, more easily than the 2–1 scoreline suggests, with goals from their on-song strike pairing of Lee and Young.

It looked as though City would win another title in 1972. But in March of that year, with the team sitting pretty at the top of the table, Allison persuaded Mercer to sign Rodney Marsh from QPR. Mercer's team had succeeded by playing simple, fluid, passing football. Now Marsh, a fancy-dan crowd pleaser, typical of the period, disrupted the rhythm of the side. In the end, City didn't even make the top three.

Mercer left that summer and Allison took charge for part of the next season. There were two other managers before former player Tony Book took charge in 1974 and led the side to a League Cup win over Newcastle, memorable only for Dennis Tueart's unlikely bicycle-kick goal. Under Book, City were prospering. But at the end of the Seventies, the decline set in.

Allison returned as manager in 1979, in a weird arrangement whereby he shared coaching duties with Book. The idea was that of City chairman Peter Swales, a wealthy local businessman who'd decided City needed a dose of glamour if they were to progress. Swales had money to spend and Allison spent it – his £1.5million purchase of the uncapped Steve Daley from Wolves is still rated by many as the worst piece of transfer business in English football history. At the same time, Allison sold two of City's best young players – midfielder Gary Owen and the talented England international winger Peter Barnes. Allison was fired in 1980, but City's long-running comedy act was only just getting into its stride. Tommy Hutchison scored for both teams when City drew 1–1 with Tottenham in the 1981 FA Cup final – and the Londoners went on to win the replay. In 1983 City were seven minutes from first-division safety when they allowed Luton's Yugoslav super-sub, Raddy Antić, to score from outside the box. They spent two separate spells in the second division before Howard Kendall dragged them up by their bootstraps at the end of the Eighties – but the club then let Kendall go back to his beloved Everton.

When Francis Lee finally rode in on a white horse to oust the hated Swales in 1995, he brought in an old friend, Alan Ball, as manager. Ball, a member of England's 1966 World Cup-winning side had a poor track record as a manager, and sure enough, despite the presence of Georgian midfielder Georgi Kinklazde and German striker Uwe Rösler, City were relegated on the last game of the 1995/96 season. In the three years that followed, the club had three managers, witnessed another boardroom takeover (Lee making way for David Bernstein in 1998), suffered a further relegation and, in a climax to the 1998/99 season every bit as unlikely as United's, clambered out of the wrong half of the League after scoring two stoppage-time goals in the play-off final against Gillingham.

The climax to the 1999/2000 campaign was, in some ways, even less likely. Manager Joe Royle took his side into the final game at Blackburn knowing that a win would be enough to secure automatic promotion to the Premiership. City went behind before romping to a 4–1 win, but the euphoria that followed was tempered by the knowledge that, for all their two promotions, the team would need more than Royle's inspiration – and the fans' adulation – to survive among the elite.

Here we go!

Buses #41, #42 #43, #44 and #46 all run from Piccadilly to **Platt Lane**, which is a 5min walk from the ground.

Just the ticket

City could have sold out Maine Road twice over for their return to the Premiership, but the board has insisted on there being some tickets available on the day for all fixtures. The **ticket office** at the ground is open prior to games and during the week, 10am–4pm. The club's ticket information number is: ☎0161/226 2224.

Swift half

One of the most popular pre-match spots is *The Claremont* at 112 Claremont Road. It's a spartan bar, full of fans on matchdays, but can be a bit rough during the week. The *Sherwood Inn* at #417 on the same street is smarter.

Club merchandise

The **club shop** is on the corner of Maine Road and Claremont Road, by the Supporters' Club building, and is open Mon–Sat 9.30pm–5.00pm, later for midweek home games.

Ultra culture

Blue Moon may have given way to *Wonderwall* but nobody sings – or laughs – like the **lads on the Kippax**. City's travelling support is, if anything, even sillier. Once a fairly rough contingent with a reputation for trouble, they invented the Eighties fad for inflatables with their rubber bananas, and remain innovative – how many other sets of fans would react to a drubbing at Grimsby by doing the conga?

In print

The **matchday programme** (£2) is not a bad read, while the official monthly magazine, *City* (£2.25) has improved of late. Heavy sarcasm and anti-United gags are the stock in trade of fanzines *King Of The Kippax* and *Bert Trautmann's Helmet*.

In the net

City's **official website** is a lookalike *Planet*-run horror, though to be fair, its content still has more depth than United's. Find it at: www.mcfc.co.uk.

City have spawned an internet community as vibrant as any in English football. To find your way around it, try *Wookie's Man City Links* at: www.wookie.u–net.com/citylow.htm.

Eat, drink, sleep...

Bars and clubs

Manchester nightlife is among the best in the UK. The **music clubs** pride themselves on being at the cutting edge and as well as traditional **pubs**, the city also boasts many **café-bars** that are packed out at weekends. The scene is constantly changing – listed here are some of the more established venues.

Alaska, Whitworth Street. Snobbish, costly bar/restaurant boasting excellent sounds – mainly drum 'n' bass – and even better breakfasts.

Barça, Catalan Square, Arches 8–9. Owned by Simply Red frontman Mick Hucknall, this spacious café bar has a terrace overlooking a Spanish-style plaza.

Prague V, Canal Street. The main crossover haunt in the so-called 'Gay Village', with a mainly straight crowd enjoying some serious house music. Free entrance for most of the evening, open until 1am.

The Old Wellington Inn, Shambles Square. The oldest pub in Manchester opened in 1378 and has been serving up fine pints of bitter ever since. Very central.

Restaurants

Manchester is the best English city outside London for tasting **ethnic food**. Chinatown is in the centre of the city close to Piccadilly, while the Rusholme district is packed with curry houses, as is Wilmslow Road, close to the Manchester City ground – the latter area is cheaper.

Armenian Tavern, 3–5 Princess Street. Albert Square. Famed for its lavish banquets and its _baklava_, this place also does set menu dishes for a very reasonable £5. With a bit of luck you might even bump into an Ararat Yerevan fan.

Café Istanbul, 79–81 Bridge Street. Extremely popular, well-established Turkish restaurant with far more than kebabs on the menu, plus authentic breads and terrific fresh salads.

Henry J Bean's, 42 Blackfriars Street. Busy with office workers getting tucked into Tex-Mex nosh at lunchtime, and taking advantage of happy hour on cocktails in the evening (5.30–8pm). Chilli, steaks, spare ribs and burgers.

Jewel In The Crown, 109 Wilmslow Road. Unlike many of the Indians in the area, this one is licensed and has a small bar. The Lamb Raan is highly recommended.

Mongolian Barbecue, Chorlton Street. The internationally successful restaurant chain (London, Moscow, Budapest) comes to Manchester. Choose from delicately laid-out slabs of raw meat which the chef will expertly slap onto the grill and produce tasty dishes to go with your side salads in no time. Justifiably popular.

Accommodation

Like many English cities, Manchester has plenty of accommodation for business people and any number of cheap B&Bs, but not much in between. As ever, book in advance if you can.

Burton Arms Hotel, 31 Swan Street (☎0161/834 3455). A traditional B&B above a pub. Close to the city centre but with only eight rooms, so you should definitely call in advance.

The Crown Inn, 321 Deansgate (☎0161/834 1930). Very central B&B accommodation above a traditional pub.

Gardens Hotel, 55 Piccadilly (☎0161/236 5155). Right on Piccadilly Gardens, yet doesn't suffer too much from the noise. This accommodating three-star place offers a bathroom and TV in every room.

YHA Manchester, Potato Warf, Castlefield (☎0161/839 9960). Youth hostel with singles, two-, four- and six-bedded rooms, all en suite. Full catering, 24-hour access, optional breakfast.

Geordie joy and pain – Newcastle in the Nineties

No region in England has produced as many top players as **the north-east**. Almost every school and boys' club in the area has a famous son who has gone on to play for his country and coach at the highest level – the Charlton brothers, Bryan Robson, Bobby Robson and so on.

Back to his roots – Wor Bobby claps hands

Yet until a few years ago the area lacked a club capable of taking the modern game by the horns. By 1999 all three of the major sides were in the Premiership, with the biggest, **Newcastle United**, struggling to maintain its dominant position in the face of fresh challenges from Sunderland and Middlesbrough.

Earlier in the decade, the commercial acumen of millionaire chairman **Sir John Hall** and inspirational coaching of **Kevin Keegan** dragged Newcastle from the brink of relegation to the wrong half of the league into the top two in the Premiership and the European elite. Yet after both men had faded from the scene, the great edifice they had built was shown to have shaky foundations. A new boardroom regime lost the respect of the fans, while new manager **Kenny Dalglish** attempted to plug the gaps in Keegan's adventurous team by building a defensive, overly experienced side which likewise failed to inspire St James' Park.

When Hall took over the club in 1991, Newcastle were struggling in the second division and seemed to have a better-than-evens chance of dropping into the third. Hall and Keegan didn't just keep the club off the scrapheap – they propelled Newcastle into Europe and created one of the new generation of **Premiership super-teams**, bringing the likes of David Ginola, Philippe Albert, Les Ferdinand and Tino Asprilla to the club. In 1995/96 Newcastle **led the Premiership table** for most of the season, but a loss of concentration in the run-in gifted the title to Manchester United.

Geordie disappointment turned almost immediately to joy, when it was announced Newcastle had bought local lad **Alan Shearer** for £15million. Yet six months later Keegan stunned Newcastle by quitting. Newcastle had become a publicly quoted company, and Dalglish had the misfortune to be the manager who inherited a City-inspired tightening of the purse-strings – his team lost the 1998 FA Cup final, 2–0 to Arsenal.

Ruud Gullit, who succeeded Dalglish barely a week into the 1998/99 season, was given more money to spend by the returning Sir John, but the end result – a 2–0 loss in the Cup final, this time to Manchester United – was the same. The Dutchman was sacked with the team bottom of the Premiership four weeks into the 1999/2000 campaign, and his successor, Geordie boy Bobby Robson, needed all his powers of motivation to put a sinking ship to rights. He did so spectacularly, leading the team not only to mid-table security but to the FA Cup semi-finals, where they were unlucky to lose to Chelsea. From Newcastle's main train station, the excellent *Tyne & Wear Metro* will whisk you to **St James' station** right next to the ground. The stadium has been extended, but you'll still need to book in advance for a space on ☎0191/261 1571. To share a jar with the Toon Army, try *The Strawberry* on Strawberry Place, between the *Metro* exit and St James' Park.

Liverpool

Liverpudlians are a proud lot. No other city in England matches Merseyside for local patriotism. And though the city has faced some of the worst social and economic problems over the past two decades, it has also had much to be proud of in the record of its two football teams, Liverpool and Everton.

Alas, neither club had much to shout about in the Nineties, save for the odd victory in cup competitions. Both clubs have been disrupted by internal battles for their soul, Everton at boardroom level, Liverpool at boot-room. And those battles have been fought against a backdrop darkened by the long shadow of the past, for football on Merseyside is recovering from more than just a slump in form. Heysel and Hillsborough had reverberations far beyond Anfield Road, but the feelings remain strongest among those directly affected by the tragedies, and as the *Justice For The 96* campaign continues into a second millennium, Liverpool looked set to be pre-occupied by the less savoury aspects of its football history for some time to come.

As a city, Liverpool offers little for the tourist. Sure, there's the Beatles Museum, and the Albert Dock by the River Mersey has been spruced up to offer a façade of modernity and affluence. But beneath the surface Liverpool remains a city with plenty of problems, not least crime.

Catch an older scouser in a good mood in a pub, however, get him talking about football, and you're in for a good night. This is a city whose supporters have seen the best in Europe – and seen their own boys reign supreme over them. All it wants now is for the good old days, rather than the bad ones, to come rolling back. It has already waited long enough.

The thrilling fields

 ### Liverpool

Anfield Stadium, Anfield Road, Liverpool
Capacity 45,300 (all-seated)
Colours All red
League champions 1901, 1906, 1922–23, 1947, 1964, 1966, 1973, 1976–77, 1979, 1980, 1982–84, 1986, 1988, 1990
Cup winners 1965, 1974, 1986, 1989, 1992
European Cup winners 1977, 1978, 1981, 1984
UEFA Cup winners 1973, 1976

No club in England has ever been able to sustain domestic success for such a long period as Liverpool. And no club in England has a better record in European football. Ever since Bill Shankly took over the reins at Anfield in 1959, Liverpool have been an example of all that is best about the British game. The sides managed by Shankly, Paisley, Fagan and Dalglish may have contained fewer stars than many of

Liverpool essentials

You will probably arrive by train, at **Lime Street station,** which is in the centre of the city. Buses and coaches pull into the station on **Islington Street,** close by. All local public transport is provided by **buses** – the main service runs until around 11.30pm, with a limited night service on some routes after that. For the latest on **fares** and other information, call the 24-hour enquiry service on: ☎0151/708 8838.

There are two major sources for **tourist information.** The *Merseyside Welcome Centre* at the Clayton Square Shopping Centre (open Mon–Sat 9.30am–5.30pm) and the *Tourist Information Centre* in the Atlantic Pavilion at the Albert Dock complex (open daily 10.00am–5.30pm).

Shankly's pride – Liverpool line up at Anfield before the start of the 1969/70 season

their rivals', but they all played by the Liverpool passing method, as taught by the legendary 'boot-room' where coaching staff met to discuss selection and tactics.

The club was founded by John Houlding, the owner of the Anfield ground. Prior to 1892, Everton had been the only professional club in the city and had played at Houlding's ground. But the landlord fell out with his tenants and set up his own team, originally under the name of Everton; on March 15, 1892 he changed the club's name to Liverpool and the team won admission to the League the next year. The club won two titles before World War I and two more between the wars.

In the first post-war championship, Liverpool won the title by a single point from Manchester United. The star of the side was Scottish striker Billy Liddell, but high expectations for the coming decade were not realised, and in 1954 Liverpool were relegated. They spent eight years in the second division, before Bill Shankly's young team climbed back to the top flight in 1962.

Shankly had an astute grasp of the psychology of sport, imbuing his side with a self-confidence that became the hallmark of Liverpool sides down the years. The sign *This Is Anfield* that greets players as they go down the tunnel to the field is a symbol of the man's method and his scouse arrogance – though Shankly, like Matt Busby up the road at Old Trafford, was a Scotsman.

Within two years of taking the club back to the first division, Shankly had delivered the title. The next season Liverpool won the FA Cup and in 1966 they won the league again and made it to the final of the Cup-Winners' Cup, which they lost to Borussia Dortmund. Shankly's side included a strike partnership of England's Roger Hunt and Scottish international Ian St John. Ron Yeats was the hard man in defence and young Ian Callaghan was the creator in midfield.

By 1973, Shankly's boys of the Sixties had obviously aged, but the new generation were, if anything, even hungrier for success, particularly in Europe. In the UEFA Cup that season, they defeated AEK Athens, Dynamo Berlin and Tottenham to set up a final with Borussia Mönchengladbach. Liverpool won the first leg 3–0 with two goals from Kevin Keegan. In the second leg the Germans led 2–0 at half-time but the Reds hung on to claim their first European honour.

Shankly retired a year later, confident that his new side was capable of going on to greater things under his replacement, and former assistant, Bob Paisley. The optimism was well-placed. In Paisley's nine years in charge Liverpool won six league titles, three European Cups and one UEFA Cup. Like his predecessor, Paisley had an exceptional eye for young talent. Some players came through the ranks of the youth system, many others were bought. However, Liverpool rarely signed established players from rival clubs, preferring to bring in promising youngsters from lower down the ladder. Keegan and goalkeeper Ray Clemence came from lowly Scunthorpe,

Beaten by Bradford – Houllier troops off

while classy Scottish centre-half Alan Hansen was spotted at Partick Thistle.

When Keegan left for Hamburg in 1977 (after Liverpool had again beaten Mönchengladbach to win their first European Cup), Paisley brought in Kenny Dalglish to wear Keegan's #7 shirt. Dalglish was the perfect replacement – an effortless edge-of-the-box predator who crowned his first season by scoring the only goal of the European Cup final against Club Bruges at Wembley.

Paisley retired in 1983, and two years later Dalglish took over as player-manager. In his first season in charge, Liverpool did the double for the first time. Dalglish's sides were perhaps the most exciting of all the Liverpool championship teams. Ian Rush was the goalgetter, Peter Beardsley his impish, irrepressible assistant, John Barnes the flamboyant provider from the wing.

But while on the field Liverpool were enjoying the final years of their incredible run of success, away from the action the club had been shaken by two tragedies – Heysel and Hillsborough. The first was the result of hooliganism at the 1985 European Cup final against Juventus, which left 38 dead and 454 injured when a wall collapsed after a charge by Liverpool fans. On April 15, 1989, 96 Liverpool fans died and 170 were injured at an FA Cup semi-final against Nottingham Forest at Sheffield Wednesday's Hillsborough stadium. Prior to the game, a gate was opened admitting Liverpool fans into the packed Leppings Lane end of the ground. Supporters at the front of the enclosure were suffocated in the crush. In the days following the tragedy, Anfield was covered in scarves and floral tributes, among the most poignant of which was a wreath from Juventus. Players and club officials attended the funerals of the victims, and the city closed ranks.

It was partly the stress resulting from those tragedies that led Dalglish to quit in 1991. He was replaced by his former teammate Graeme Souness, whose only achievement in a disappointing three years in charge was an FA Cup win in 1992.

Souness left the club with a host of expensive players who were failing to live up to Anfield's expectations, and the club returned to the boot-room in search of stability, appointing Roy Evans as manager.

Evans put the emphasis back on youth, bringing in Steve McManaman, Robbie Fowler and Jamie Redknapp. At times their football was reminiscent of some of the great Liverpool sides of old, but consistency – once an Anfield watchword – remained elusive. After a string of premature burnouts in the title race and some particularly ignominious exits from Europe, the board appointed the former French national-team coach Gérard Houllier as Evans' co-manager in the summer of 1998. It was a compromise arrangement, seemingly destined to failure from the start, and within months Evans had been moved aside – although former Liverpool captain Phil Thompson was made Houllier's assistant to retain at least a slender link with the old boot-room days.

With the blossoming of young striker Michael Owen making up for the impending departure of McManaman to Real Madrid, by the end of 1998/99 Houllier had an embarrassment of attacking riches but a defence that kept shooting itself in the foot. His response was to spend more than £20million on players in the close season, all of them from Europe. Liverpool were finally embracing the bold new world of the continental transfer market – how well they played it would dictate their ability to compete for serious honours once again.

Ironically, it was a major domestic transfer that seemed to upset the apple cart in 1999/2000. Liverpool had looked solid top-three material for most of the Premiership season, and although injuries to Fowler and Owen left the team short of firepower, Houllier's continental-style defence, with Finnish international Sammy Hyypia outstanding, was as watertight as they came. In March, the board sanctioned the £12million purchase of Emile Heskey from Leicester, hoping to recoup the money through guaranteed Champions'

League football the following year. But Heskey couldn't hold the ball up long enough for Liverpool's safety-conscious midfield to join, and with the ball coming back at them so quickly, the defence began to leak goals at inopportune moments. A 1–0 defeat at Bradford City on the final day condemned Liverpool to fourth place – and left them out of the continental limelight for at least another season.

Here we go!

From the gyratory opposite Lime Street train station hop on a #14, #F4 or #F5 bus to **Walton Breck Road**. Allow 20mins.

Just the ticket

Anfield is basically a sellout for Premiership fixtures, making the away fans' section (an area of the Anfield Road Stand, opposite the rebuilt Kop) the only option for visiting neutrals. You may have more joy in other areas of the ground when it comes to cup ties. The **box office** number is: ☎0151/260 8680.

Swift half

The Arkles at 27 Anfield Road is the most popular of the many pubs in the area around the ground. It's busy both before and after the game – when fans crowd in to check out the day's other results on the big-screen TV.

Club merchandise

The main outlet for Liverpool gear is the **Liverworld** store built into the new Kop Stand (open Mon–Fri 10am–4.30pm and on matchdays with extended hours, ☎0151/263 1760) There's a smaller shop by the **Shankly Gates** at the corner of the Anfield Road Stand and the Main Stand, keeping similar hours.

Ultra culture

The Kop, a 'seething mass of humanity', as one critic described it, is a modern all-seater stand, not the vast terrace of yore. Gone is the surge of fans, running down the terraces after each goal or near miss. Yet the mass choir that turned Merseybeat hits like *You'll Never Walk Alone* into world-famous football anthems remains as one of the most cohesive of its kind within England's post-Taylor Report stadia. Liverpool always look more likely to score when attacking this end.

In print

The **matchday programme** (£2) is regarded as one of the best in the Premiership, but the club's **official magazine** is not as hot as *The Kop*, an unofficial title produced by the city's *Post & Echo* newspaper group. Of the fanzines, try *Red All Over The Land* or *Through The Wind & Rain.*

In the net

The club's **official website** was a long time coming but has been well worth the wait at: www.liverpoolfc.net. It actually has its origins in the former unofficial offering, *Liverpool – The Mighty Reds*, which perhaps helps to explain why it is so effortlessly able to provide a genuine feel of the club.

Among the unofficial sites that remain, *Mersey Reds* concentrates on nostalgia (and why not?) at: members.tripod.com/~merseyreds.

⚫ Everton

Goodison Park, Goodison Road, Liverpool
Capacity 40,200 (all-seated)
Colours Royal blue shirts, white shorts
League champions 1891, 1915, 1928, 1932, 1939, 1963, 1970, 1985, 1987
Cup winners 1906, 1933, 1966, 1984, 1995
Cup-Winners' Cup winners 1985

Everton were the first professional club in Liverpool and were founder members of the Football League. In 1892, after a rent row with the landlord of their Anfield Road ground, they moved across Stanley Park to Goodison Road, their home ever since.

Around the corner from the stadium in those early days was a sweet shop whose owner used to promote his wares by throwing toffees to the crowd before the game – hence the club picked up their nickname, 'The Toffeemen'. The sweet shop has long since gone but the tradition of throwing toffees remains. There is even a black-and-white sweet known as an 'Ever-

ton mint', whose origins date back to the days when the side wore black shirts with a white sash and were known as the 'Black Watch'. It was in those colours that Everton won their first title in 1891. The team switched to royal blue and white ten years later, and in 1905 they won the FA Cup. Another league title was added in 1914, but World War I put paid to hopes of a prolonged spell of success.

In 1925, the club signed William Ralph Dean from their near neighbours Tranmere Rovers. 'Dixie' Dean scored 60 league goals in 1927/28 as Everton won the title. His record still stands today and is unlikely ever to be beaten.

Although Everton were relegated in 1930, they bounced back swiftly, winning the second-division title in 1931 and taking the championship in their first season back. Another title was added in 1939, with a new star in the #9 shirt – Tommy Lawton. Although only 19, Lawton was an England international who had been signed from Burnley. When he arrived at Lime Street station, Dean was there to greet him and make a symbolic handover of power. But Lawton's hopes – and those of Everton – were again to be dashed by gunfire. After the end of World War II, neither Lawton nor Everton would enjoy the same level of success. In fact, it was to be more than a decade before Everton were challenging for top honours again.

In 1961, Harry Catterick began a 12-year stint in the Goodison dugout. In 1963 Everton won the championship with a side inspired by Scottish midfielder Alex Young, who Catterick labelled 'The Golden Vision'. After Everton won the FA Cup and England the World Cup in 1966, Catterick bought England's young midfielder Alan Ball and teamed him up with Colin Harvey and Howard Kendall in the centre of the park; from there they provided the ammunition for striker Joe Royle. Another FA Cup win followed in 1968 and the league was won with style in 1970.

It was Kendall who was behind Everton's next spell of success, taking over as manager at the start of the Eighties, and winning the Cup for Goodison in 1984, when the Scottish strike pair of Graeme Sharp and Andy Gray were on the mark in a 2–0 win over Watford at Wembley.

Both men were to play a key role in Everton's success the following season, when the Blues won the title by a massive 13 points and also gained the first European honour in the club's history. After knocking out Inter Bratislava, Fortuna Sittard and Bayern Munich, Everton defeated Rapid Vienna 3–1 in Rotterdam to clinch the Cup-Winners' Cup.

There was no weak point in the side, which played fast, passing football married with aggression. Welsh international 'keeper Neville Southall had the sound central defensive partnership of Kevin Ratcliffe and Derek Mountfield in front of him. Peter Reid, a bargain buy from Bolton, was a true general in the centre of the park, feeding Irishman Kevin Sheedy on the left flank and Trevor Steven on the right. But the team were not infallible. Three days after winning in Europe, they faced Manchester United in the FA Cup final with a unique treble in their sights – and lost 1–0.

With cash rolling in, the club signed Gary Lineker from Leicester City for the next season. Although few complained about the quality of the football, it was a painful year for Evertonians, as Liverpool pipped them by two points to the title, then defeated them 3–1 in the first all-Merseyside FA Cup final. Still, another title followed in 1987, before Kendall stunned the club by leaving for Athletic Bilbao.

Kendall's assistant Colin Harvey took over, and in 1989, in the emotional aftermath of Hillsborough, the side lost another FA Cup final to Liverpool, 3–2.

Kendall returned in 1990 but his second spell in charge was trophyless. He was succeeded by Mike Walker, who spent a fortune in vain. Joe Royle took over in November 1994, and at the end of that season Everton beat Manchester United 1–0 in the FA Cup final. Royle resigned in March 1997, paving the way for a second

Salvation from the States – Joe-Max Moore

return by his former team-mate Kendall. In the close season club chairman Peter Johnson offered fans a referendum on whether to leave Goodison and move to a new 60,000 all-seater stadium. To the surprise of many, the fans voted for the move.

What they did not vote for was an ongoing soap opera that would soon envelop the Goodison boardroom and which was still running two years later. With Johnson running out of both money and patience – and the fans losing patience with him – his former enemy-turned-co-director Bill Kenwright announced his intention to launch a takeover bid. The sticking point was Johnson's asking price and Kenwright's struggle to attract the necessary funds – a quest which soon reached epic proportions. With the club's financial future uncertain, new manager Walter Smith went bargain-hunting in Europe for 1998/99, bought a series of misfits, and had arranged buyers for most of them by the time Everton had escaped relegation once again at the end of the season.

For 1999/2000 the emphasis was on youth, but only because the club could not afford anything else. Happily, Kenwright finally completed his takeover on Christmas Eve, and almost immediately, the mood at the club changed for the better. Manager Smith coaxed a revival in form from the likes of Nicky Barmby and also got the best from unlikely foreign buys such as Portuguese international defender Abel Xavier and American striker Joe-Max Moore. Everton finished 13th – unspectacular, perhaps, but a definite improvement on what had gone before.

Whether Kenwright could take the club forward another step on the road back to glory would depend on how quickly he could move the club out of Goodison – a development which, if past stories of football politics on Merseyside are anything to go by, could take longer than a plot resolution in *Brookside*.

Here we go!

Take bus #19 from Sir Thomas Street, close to Lime Street train station. Get off at **Walton Lane**, then just stroll down Goodison Road.

Just the ticket

With the exception of games against Liverpool and Manchester United, getting a ticket at Goodison should not cause too many headaches. Visiting supporters are allocated one end of the Bullens Road Stand, where upper-tier seats are worth the extra money for the decent view they provide. Credit-card **bookings** can be made on: ☎0151/330 2300.

Swift half

The *Winslow Hotel* at 31 Goodison Road is the nearest pub to the ground, straight across from the main stand, but a better bet is *The Abbey*, which is popular with away supporters as well as the locals.

Club merchandise

Everton's kitsch 'white castle' *Megastore* (open Mon–Sat 9am–5pm and evenings for midweek games, ☎0151/330 2333) is a 5min walk from the ground in Walton Road.

Ultra culture

Goodison is a tight ground whose Main Stand leans so close over the edge of the pitch that, before the days of fences, goalscorers were in danger of disappearing into it in mid-celebration. The **Gwladys Street boys** never were a match for the Kop in the singing department, but this crowd is as passionate and as fiercely partisan as any in England – and the hecklers will have you in stitches with their one-liners.

In print

As well as the fairly predictable **matchday programme**, there's the official club magazine *Evertonian* and two well-established fanzines, *When Skies Are Grey* and *Speke From The Harbour*.

In the net

Everton's **official website** is steadily becoming a serious endeavour after a slow start. You'll find it at: www.evertonfc.com.

Of the unofficial sites, *ToffeeWeb* stands out from the crowd, at: www.toffeeweb.org. It's informal, approachable and utterly comprehensive – everything the official site isn't, in fact. A lesson to all football webmasters everywhere.

Eat, drink, sleep...

Bars and clubs

Liverpool may no longer be the epicentre of British pop, but it boasts some of the top **dance clubs** in the north and the city centre has a fine mix of traditional pubs and newer café-bars. The last three years have seen an explosion in late-opening bar life, with the area around Hanover Street and Slater Street, the 'Creative Quarter', at its epicentre, and some early-morning chill-out bars on the periphery.

Baa Bar, 43–45 Fleet Street. Close to *Cream* (see below) in the Palace complex, this designer bar attracts a hip pre-club crowd. Reduced prices in the day, resident DJs in the evening.

Cream, Wolstenholme Square. This huge venue attracts busloads of clubbers from across the UK. The three separate dance areas can pack in more than 2,000 guests. Top UK and European DJs perform here regularly. Dress is informal but the doormen can be selective and will not admit anyone in trainers.

Mello Mello, 40–42 Slater Street. Pre-*Cream* venue with a wacky interior, open until 2am Mon–Sat and ideal for star-spotting – if you can make anyone out among the packed crowd.

The Philharmonic Dining Rooms, Hope Street. Don't be put off by the name – this is a genuine Victorian-era pub with all the trappings. Wide range of cask ales and bottled beers.

The Sandon, Anfield Road. Freshly restored pub, easily accessible from both Liverpool's and Everton's grounds, which was once owned by Liverpool founder John Houlding and where Everton players got changed for matches when they used his Anfield ground.

Restaurants

The **Albert Dock** shopping area has plenty of eateries including Italian, French, German and Indonesian, and most of the city-centre pubs serve snacks or bar meals. Liverpool had a Chinese community long before most of the UK and this is reflected in a wide choice of **Chinese restaurants** and takeaways.

Blue Bar & Grill, 17 Edward Pavilion. The big hit on Albert Dock since opening a couple of years ago, with dishes as pretentious as the decor, but slap by the waterfront, with excellent sounds, and the occasional celebrity dining.

Everyman Bistro, 9–11 Hope Street. Popular with students from the nearby University, the *Everyman* offers a broad range of dishes at very reasonable prices, including hearty soups and tasty stews.

Mayflower, 48 Duke Street. Broad-ranging menu featuring Cantonese, Peking, seafood and vegetarian dishes. Busy, central, mid-priced.

Modo, 23–25 Fleet Street. Futuristic sister operation to *Baa Bar* (see above) along the street, *Modo* is trendy without turning you off. Restaurants and bar areas with ever-changing themes on different levels.

Accommodation

Liverpool is not geared up to house vast numbers of tourists but, like all ports, has a history of accommodating a large transient population. The result is a high concentration of **cheap B&Bs** and budget hotels, of admittedly variable quality. If you're turning up on spec, both **tourist offices** (see panel p.152) will book a room for you without charging commission.

Aachen, 89–91 Mount Pleasant (☎0151/709 3477). Small hotel with rooms in the £30–40 range. Centrally located, and with an eat-as-much-as-you-like breakfast.

Britannia Adelphi, Raneleigh Place (☎0151/709 7200). A famous hotel in the centre of the city, made infamous by the recent BBC docu-soap. Rooms in the £50–80 range. Full comfort at decent prices, despite the impression given on the box.

Feathers, 117–125 Mount Pleasant (☎0151/709 9655). In a street full of B&Bs and small hotels, *Feathers* has double rooms from £40 and a bar and restaurant. Excellent value for money, central location.

YMCA, 56 Mount Pleasant (☎0151/709 9516). The most central of the city's youth hostels and up to the usual YMCA standards of cleanliness. Dormitory beds from around £15 a night.

Finland

Finnish Football Union Läntinen Brahenkatu 2, PO Box 179, SF 00511 Helsinki
☎09/701 0101   Fax 09/7010 1098   E-mail maajoukkue@palloliitto.fi

League champions FC Haka Valkeakoski   **Cup winners** FC Jokerit
Promoted United Tampere   **Relegated** TPV Tampere

European participants 2000/01 FC Haka (UCL qualifiers); HJK Helsinki, FC
Jokerit (UEFA Cup); MyPa Anjalankoski (Intertoto Cup)

With the national side coming within 60 seconds of a World Cup play-off and a leading club winning the country's first-ever place in the Champions' League, Finland has seen its footballing profile raised dramatically over the last three years. Several key players are at top-level clubs abroad – defender Sammy Hyypia at Liverpool, forward Joonas Kolkka at PSV Eindhoven, Mikael Forssell at Chelsea and, of course, Jari Litmanen at Ajax and Barcelona. And those stars have continued to influence the development of the national team, who went on to cause a few upsets in their Euro 2000 qualifying group.

But in the cold light of day, once the 30,000 crowds have gone home from the big-name events, the domestic scene is still moribund. With small crowds and modest salaries, it's not just the Litmanens who are seeking their fortune abroad – even journeyman players head for other Scandinavian leagues, particularly Norway. Ice hockey is still the biggest team sport, while Finnish baseball, *pesäpallo*, is another big draw during soccer's short summer season.

Historically, the Finns are footballing makeweights. The national team has not reached the finals of any major competition since losing the semis of the 1912 Olympic soccer tournament, and Finnish clubs have rarely made an impact in Europe.

The first national championship was held in 1908, and the event was dominated by teams from Helsinki until World War II. Postwar, provincial teams came to the fore, especially TPS Turku, Reipas Lahti, KuPS Kuopio and Haka Valkeakoski. Interest was generated by the regular visits of top continental sides in the early rounds of European club competitions. All-time top league goalscorer Kai Pahlman became a folk hero for his stunning goal for HJK against Manchester United in the first round of the European Cup in 1965. That same year, he was the main attraction in the HJK-Haka fixture which drew more than 17,000 to Helsinki's Olympic stadium.

During the Eighties, the game gradually became semi-professional. As standards rose, so the league's top players began to drift abroad, mainly to Scandinavian countries – although Ari Hjelm and Mixu Paatelainen became popular figures in Germany and Britain, respectively.

Despite one legendary win by TPS Turku over Internazionale at the San Siro in 1987 – Mika Aaltonen's goal earned him a brief contract with Bologna – the domestic game attracted scant national attention until the Nineties, and the rise of Finland's only footballing superstar, Jari Litmanen. Snubbing a possibly lucrative career in ice hockey to follow in his father's footsteps at modest Reipas Lahti, Litmanen scored 28 goals in 86 games there to attract the attentions of HJK in 1991. His move to Ajax, where he replaced his hero Dennis Bergkamp in 1993, coincided with the Dutch club's renaissance on the European stage, and Litmanen won a Champions' League medal in 1995.

The forward's presence was crucial to the rise of the national side, as was the

Chasing a lost cause – Hannu Tihinen stretches every sinew against Wales, March 2000

appointment, in 1996, of Richard Møller-Nielsen as coach.

Having guided Denmark to the European Championship trophy four years earlier, Møller-Nielsen would hear no talk of the Finns being no-hopers. In a relatively easy qualifying group for the 1998 World Cup, his team suffered a couple of single-goal defeats, but a draw away to favourites Norway and a win in Switzerland allowed them a shot at second place and entry to the play-offs.

Needing a win in the driving rain in Helsinki against Hungary, the Finns went one-up with a goal from Antti Sumiala. With Møller-Nielsen making late substitutions to run down the clock, the visitors won a corner deep into stoppage time. The ball was swept goalwards into the wind by Vilmos Sebôk, cleared off the line by Sami Mahlio, then rebounded into the Finnish net off the backside of goalkeeper Teuvo Moilanen. There wasn't a Hungarian in sight.

As the Magyars ran aimlessly in celebration (who could they congratulate, after

all?), a deathly hush descended on Helsinki. It was a bitter blow to the Finns, not least to Moilanen, who had just one previous cap to his name and had only been called up from his English club, Preston, because of an injury to Rangers' Antti Niemi...

At home, FC Haka came from the lower division to win the league in 1998 and 1999, a period which also saw the rise of a new Helsinki team, PK35, who were to be re-invented as FC Jokerit the following year, and who have since absorbed FinnPa.

Essential vocabulary

Hello *Hei*
Goodbye *Näkemiin*
Yes *Joo*
No *Ei*
Two beers, please *Kaksi kaljaa, kiittos*
Thank you *Kiittos*
Men's *Miehet*
Women's *Naiset*
What's the score? *Mikä on tilanne?*
Where is the stadium? *Missä on stadion?*
Referee *Erotuomari*
Offside *Paitsio*

Basics

EU, US, Canadian, Australian and New Zealand citizens need only a valid **passport** to enter Finland and stay for up to three months.

The Finnish **currency** is the markka, indicated as FM and divided into 100 penniä. There are coins for 10p, 20p, 50p, FM1 and FM5, and notes for FM20, FM50, FM100, FM500 and FM1,000. There are around FM10 to £1. On arrival in Helsinki, money can be **exchanged** at the airport (open daily 6.30am–11pm), at Katajanokka harbour (open daily 9am–1pm & 3.45–6pm), and at the main train station (open daily 8am–9pm). Ordinary banks are open Mon–Fri 9.15am–4.15pm, and charge around FM15 commission for exchanges. Exchange offices such as *Forex* may offer a better rate. **Credit cards** are widely used in major towns, and even in Helsinki taxis.

Finland is connected north–south as far as the **Arctic Circle** by a reliable if expensive **train service**. A journey between Helsinki and Tampere takes two hours and costs about FM100. Journeys east-west, and travel in the north of the country, are best accomplished by **bus**. Services are run by private companies sharing a common ticket system, with fares calculated according to distance (roughly FM50 per 100km). Return tickets on long-haul journeys work out 10% cheaper.

If you fancy catching some **Estonian football**, which like Finland has a summer season, note that visas are no longer required for EU nationals travelling on the **hydrofoil service** between Helsinki and Tallinn. For more details, call *Tallink* on ☎09/2282 1211 or *Silja* on ☎09/180 4555.

Most **public phones** now take *Tele Cards*, available in FM30, FM50 or FM100 sizes, which can be bought from *R-kioski* stands. Be aware that certain provincial towns, such as Turku, have only their own local card system. Coin phones take FM1 and FM5 for local calls. From outside the country, the **dialling code** for Finland is 358, followed by a 9 for Helsinki. To get an international line inside Finland, dial 990, 994 or 999, depending on the phone company, followed by the country code. Cheap rates apply Mon–Fri 10pm–8am and all weekend.

Remember that for most of the year, Finland is **one hour ahead** of Central European Time, two hours ahead of GMT.

Match practice

If you're looking for real stadium atmosphere in Finland, you'll find it at the ice-hockey rink. Few football fans travel, meaning there is little rivalry between supporters, and this is reflected in the mood of calm which descends on most matches. During the game, the loudest noise you'll hear will probably be the players shouting to each other.

Finland's long, harsh winter means football has to be played over a short season. The first games begin in mid-April and champions are celebrating in mid-October.

Given the short campaign, there are often two rounds in a single week, and games are usually played on Thursdays and Sundays. At either end of the season, kick-off time is 3pm, but this is the land of the Midnight Sun, and during the middle of the campaign, kick-off can be as late as 8.30pm, no floodlights necessary.

A different league

As of 1999, the Finnish premier league or *Veikkausliiga* is made up of 12 clubs. Teams play each other on the usual home-and-away basis, after which the top eight play one further round of matches against each other to decide the championship, the top four gaining home advantage for four of the seven games.

The bottom four teams play each other home and away, with the team finishing bottom being relegated to the first division, *Ykkönen*. The latter is divided into a pair of ten-team sections, southern (*etelälohko*) and northern (*pohjoislohko*). The top five in each go into a nine-game play-off league (*ylempi loppusarja*), with the winners being promoted directly to the *Veikkausliiga* while the second- and third-placed sides play off over two legs with those finishing second and third from bottom of the *Veikkausliiga*.

The lower-placed clubs in the *Ykkönen* have a fiendishly complex system for changing places with sides from the four-pool second division.

Up for the cup

The *Suomen Cup* was first contested in 1955 and has seldom aroused much interest – though as always there is the prospect of European football for the winners. First-division teams enter at the fifth-round stage, *Veikkausliiga* sides in the sixth.

The cup final is traditionally the last game of the season, played in October at the Olympic stadium in Helsinki.

Finland now also has a league cup, really more of a pre-season warm-up, with two groups of six clubs playing each other in February and March, group winners and runners-up playing semi-finals, and a final in the Lahti stadium in mid-April.

Just the ticket

Tickets are sold at the turnstiles – simply ask for '*yksi lippu*' ('one ticket'), and you're in. Should the heavens be threatening to open, you might want to make sure your seat is covered (*katettu*). Uncovered places will be marked *ei-katettu*. A ticket for a domestic game shouldn't set you back more than FM60.

If you want to book in advance for a big game without going to the stadium, there are several outlets (*Lippupavelu*) in Helsinki city centre which sell tickets, including the main tourist office and a desk on the seventh floor of the *Stockmann* department store, on the corner of Mannerheimintie and Pohjoisesplanadi.

Half-time

At half-time people rush to the beer tents, where a half-litre costs about FM15 and a

grilled sausage (*makkara*) with mustard and ketchup around FM8.

Action replay

Canal Plus moved into Finland with much hoo-ha in 1999, then withdrew their live coverage of league games a year later because of a lack of advertising revenue. The company no longer screens English Premiership action, either.

Highlights of Sunday's league round are shown in the half-hour *Futis Forum* show on MTV3 later that evening. State TV2 – which has the rights to Finnish national games – shows Scottish league action and selected FA Cup ties.

The back page

Finland's biggest sports paper is the weekly *Veikkaaja* (Mondays, FM12), which offers coverage of British and European football as well as the domestic game.

For the latest news and results, there is no daily sports press but the general newspaper *Helsingin Sanomat* has stats and other bits and bobs in the *Tulokset* section of the *Urheilu*, or sports pages.

A recent arrival on the newsstands is a monthly football magazine, *Futari* (FM19.90).

Ultra culture

Football matches in Finland have seldom been considered any kind of event, but in Helsinki, at least, hopes are high that the compact new FinnAir Stadium will allow supporters at least a half-decent chance of creating an atmosphere.

In the net

The Finnish FA runs an official website at: www.palloliitto.fi. There are some English-language areas but, even so, it can all be a bit impenetrable at times.

If it's stats you're after, then head for Riku Soininen's site at: sunsite.tut.fi/rec/riku/soccer_html/fin.html. This URL will get you into the Finnish area of Riku's site, which covers most European countries and is a fine source of links.

Helsinki

HJK 166
FC Jokerit 166

With top European action, record crowds, a major new club in town and a new stadium to boot, football has never had it so good in Helsinki.

For decades, the game in the Finnish capital was dominated by one club – HJK. The country's most illustrious side had HPS and the long-established HIFK as early rivals, when the domestic championship was only nominally 'national', effectively being contested by teams from Helsinki and around.

Modern-day opposition did not arrive until the airline-sponsored team FinnPa began to challenge for honours in the Nineties. Affluent and ambitious, FinnPa nakedly poached key players from their city rivals and successfully dented their support base in town.

Derby games between the two sides briefly drew crowds of up to 10,000, but FinnPa couldn't bridge the gap between slickness and silverware, and were relegated in 1998.

Happily for Helsinki, FinnPa's fall coincided with the rise of another local side, PK35, who have since become FC Jokerit. They lost only narrowly to HJK in the cup final, finished six points above their established rivals in the league in 1998, and won the cup a year later.

Both clubs are now playing at a brand-new stadium. For years, Helsinki had been crying out for an arena to suit the local football climate – all-covered, all-seated, and above all compact. The Olympic stadium, used for internationals and bigger club games, was impressive but overpowering, while the Pallokenttä opposite was becoming increasingly outdated despite a series of improvements. Now the Pallokenttä has been demolished to make way for the Töölön Jakapallostadion, better (and more easily) known as the FinnAir stadium – an 11,000-capacity arena of modest intentions but with all mod cons. The ground is used by both HJK and FC Jokerit, the latter having taken over FinnPa.

A bit of a stretch – HJK's 1998 Champions' League was hard work, but worth it

Groundhopping

HJK

FinnAir stadium, see panel p.167
Club office & shop Mannerheimintie 29
Colours Blue-and-white striped shirts, blue shorts
League champions 1911–12, 1917–19, 1923, 1925, 1936, 1938, 1964, 1973, 1978, 1981, 1985, 1987–88, 1990, 1992, 1997
Cup winners 1966, 1981, 1984, 1993, 1998

The relaxed, improvised atmosphere of Finnish football was never better illustrated than in the legend that surrounds the founding of Helsingin Jalkapalloklubi. Apparently the club's founding president, Fredrik Wathen, a former world champion speed-skater, was having a quiet ice-cream when he decided it would be a good idea to set up a football club.

Other teams, notably HIFK, were already established in the Finnish capital, but it wasn't long after their formation in 1907 that 'Klubi' became top dogs, not just in Helsinki but across Finland. They won a Finnish title every two years until World War II, and by the Sixties and Seventies the club's star talent, its reputation boosted by HJK's high profile, was heading abroad for real wages.

Once HJK themselves started paying players properly at the start of the Eighties, a new generation of fans was raised on a combination of domestic and continental success – six titles between 1981 and 1992, plus home-leg wins over Liverpool and Porto in Europe. Key players included Jari 'Jallu' Rantanen, who later scored five goals for IFK Gothenburg on their run to the UEFA Cup in 1987, before moving on to Leicester City – and then defecting to the dreaded FinnPa.

The rise of their airline-backed city rivals coincided with Klubi's worst spell in the modern era. In 1996 they even had to suffer the indignation of playing-off to stay

in the top division. Yet within a year they'd be back with a vengeance under new coach Antti Muurinen.

With Brazilian forward Rafael top scorer in the league and 16-year-old Mikael Forssell, despite making only a handful of appearances, named Finland's young player of the year, Muurinen's HJK ran out easy title winners in 1997.

Jazz Pori snapped up Rafael, but Chelsea at least gave the club another year's use of Forssell after signing him – enough time for Ararat Yerevan and (surprisingly) French league runners-up Metz to be eliminated in the 1998 Champions' League qualifiers.

HJK proved difficult opponents in the Champions' League itself. Only a last-minute PSV Eindhoven goal defeated them in Holland, and they held Kaiserslautern 0–0 at home. A win and a draw against Benfica had the Finnish public dreaming of a miracle, but a record 34,000 then saw HJK lose 3–1 at home to PSV, and the fairy-tale was over.

European duties put Klubi off the pace in the league, but they beat PK35 3–2 to win the cup, and despite the loss of three key players to Norwegian football, morale remained high enough for a strong title challenge in 1999, when the team finished as runners-up just three points behind champions Haka.

FC Jokerit

FinnAir stadium, see panel p.167
Club office Unikkotie 3
Colours All white
Cup winners 1999

FC Jokerit have a bizarre history. The club started out in Viipuri, now Vyborg, one of the oldest cities in Europe, which was incorporated into the Soviet Union during World War II. They were formed in 1935, hence their first name – Pallo-Kerho-35. After the war they relocated to Helsinki, first to Kallio, then to Pakila, and eventually to the suburb of Pihlajanmäki. Despite

The FinnAir stadium

Finnairstadion, Urheilukatu 1
Capacity 10,700 (all-seated)

At last Helsinki has a stadium perfectly suited to its footballing needs – even down to **sauna-heated seats**. The FinnAir, wedged in between the main Olympic and ice hockey stadia, was opened in June 2000 to much acclaim. With easy access – three entrances along the main west stand on Urheilukatu – four ticket outlets, and a quarter of the covered seats nicely heated, no Finnish fan could wish for more comfort in which to watch either HJK or Jokerit, the two teams to feature at the the arena's first match, and who will ground-share here from now on.

The **official inauguration** came with a friendly between Finland and Norway on 16 August 2000. Even the pitch – often a problem area for new stadia – is made from grass especially grown in Joroinen, and transported down to Helsinki.

Home fans are gathered either at the *Etelä* (south) or *Pohjoinen* (north) end, and security is easily maintained as it is impossible to move between sections. Other features include the 1,000-seater *Aeropoli* restaurant, accessible via gate 4 in the main stand, which serves cuisine from around the globe.

Tickets (there are two kiosks in each of the west and east stands) are FM50–80. Transport details are the same as for the Olympic stadium – see p.168.

years of mediocrity, Pihlajanmäki residents took a shine to 'PK35', until local businessman Harry Harkimo bought the club and moulded them in the image of his successful ice-hockey team, 'Jokerit'.

With former HJK star Pasi Rautiainen as coach, PK35 won promotion to the top flight in 1997. Then, while Harkimo was laying out elaborate plans for his club to become a major player in the Finnish football boom, the team surprised everyone with a third-place league finish in 1998, and reached the cup final to boot.

Before the 1999 season, the inevitable happened and, to the extreme annoyance of local residents, Harkimo changed the club's name to FC Jokerit. The colours were changed to all white from PK35's traditional red-and-black stripes, while the team entered Europe for the first time via the Intertoto Cup.

League form in 1999 was mixed, but the team finally broke its trophy duck by coming from behind to beat Jaro Pietarsaari 2–1 in the cup final at Helsinki's Olympic stadium. With Harkimo buying out FinnPa following the latter's relegation and now using the former FinnAir-sponsored club

as a feeder team, hopes were high that Jokerit's move to their new home (ironically, sponsored by FinnAir) would coincide with a serious title challenge in 2000, as well as participation in a 'real' European competition, the UEFA Cup.

Eat, drink, sleep...

Bars and clubs

Although alcohol is by no means cheaper, at least the drinking laws in Finland are more liberal than in Sweden or Norway.

Beer (*olut*) is sold in two main categories: *III-Olut*, available in shops and cafés, and the stronger *IV-Olut*, which can only be bought in *ALKO* stores, restaurants and nightclubs. The *ALKO* stores (open Mon–Thurs 10am–5pm, Fri 10am–6pm, Sat 9am–3pm) offer strong local brews like *Karjala* and *Lapin Kulta Export* at around FM8 a bottle.

Vodka is the most popular spirit, particularly *Finlandia*. Keep an eye out for *Koskenkorva-Viina* (or *Kossu*), a 38% proof vodka distilled from wheat.

The Olympic stadium

Olympiastadion,
Mannerheimintie
Capacity 39,500

Built for the 1940
Olympics, which it even-
tually hosted 12 years
later, Finland's national
stadium is a pleasant all-
seater tucked between
Sibelius park and an area
of **lakes and woodland**
some 2km north of the
city centre. Normally
used for athletics meet-
ings and rock concerts,
the Olympiastadion also
stages a **handful of
football games** every
year, including most of
Finland's international

Towering glory – but will the stadium now be overshadowed?

matches – though there have been recent moves to stage some of these at smaller
provincial stadia in Tampere and Turku – and the domestic cup final.

HJK's Champions' League games in 1998 broke all attendance records for football,
and Finland's recent international progress also bodes well for filling what is one of
Europe's most convivial grounds. Its main feature is a large white tower behind the
main stand, which offers a stunning view of Helsinki and beyond to Finland's
southern coast. If there's nothing going on at the ground, the **tower is open** to visitors,
Mon–Fri 9am–8pm, Sat–Sun 9am–6pm, admission FM10.

To reach both tower and ground from central Helsinki – from the huge *Stockmann*
department store or the *Forum* shopping centre – take tram #4, #7 or #10 north up the
main avenue, Mannerheimintie, for 10mins. Alternatively, you can **walk it** from the
main train station in around 20mins. A taxi will cost FM50.

There are several bars near the stadium. The *William K*, Mannerheimintie 72, is a
cosy local which specialises in beers from around the world; if this is full, try *Chicos* at
#68. The *City Marathon* (nicknamed *Pääty*) at #17 has a more sporting feel, as has
the *Sportticafé*, Savilankatu 1B. There is also a café within the Olympic stadium
itself, to the right as you come in via the main entrance.

The most popular meeting place of all is probably the *Tik Tok* Chinese bar and
restaurant at Toivonkatu 1–3, with its terrace and sports store next-door.

When it comes to buying a ticket for domestic games at the Olympic, simply pay
your FM60 at the turnstiles. For internationals, the **ticket office** is in block A, under
the main stand. This is where the most expensive seats are, at around FM250, with
prices falling to FM120 in block D, and FM80 in blocks B, C, E and F around the
ground.

At one end of the main stand you'll find the **Sport Museum** (open Mon–Fri
11am–5pm, Thur until 7pm, Sat–Sun noon–4pm, admission FM20). The bulk of the
large collection is dedicated to Finland's famous long-distance runners, but there are
some soccer souvenirs, including some natty Finnish kits from the Fifties.

In bars, ask for *tuoppi*, draught beer, and be prepared to part with about FM25. Licensed restaurants and pubs close around midnight or 1am, clubs at 3–4am. Admission for the latter will be FM20–30. None of the venues listed below is more than a short walk from the train station.

Kerma, Erottaja 7. Between the train station and the west ferry terminal is the city's Bermuda Corner, with happening clubs in and around Uudenmaankatu. Kerma is not as pretentious – or as expensive – as others, with Latin and funk downstairs, and a house DJ upstairs. Occasional visits from UK jocks. FM30–50 entrance.

Molly Malone's, Kaisaniemenkatu 1C. Next to the train station, so busy day and night, but the large upstairs bar is ideal for a quiet lunchtime pint. Usual Irish trappings and plenty of sports talk. Open daily.

Soda, Uudenmaankatu 16–20. One of the trendiest places in town, with a young, upbeat crowd. Upstairs a bar with guest DJs, downstairs a regular dancefloor. Entrance FM30–50.

Spårakoff. If you see a pillar-box red tram parked outside the train station, jump on it before it starts moving – it's a pub! Running every hour in summer, 11am–3pm Mon–Sat, the pub tram careers around Helsinki while drinks are served inside – FM30 gets you a ticket and the first beer in your hand.

Sports Academy, Kaivokatu 8. The main sports bar in town, directly facing the train station, with big TV screens mainly for ice-hockey action, but Finnish soccer internationals shown as well.

Restaurants

Eating in Helsinki, as in the rest of the country, isn't cheap, but there is plenty of choice. Fish (*kala*), reindeer (*poro*) and elk (*hirvenliha*) are the mainstays and you'll also find a lot of Russian dishes.

At a typical **pizzeria** you'll pay around FM60 for dinner, providing you don't drink alcohol with your meal. Finnish restaurants and those serving Russian specialities can

be expensive – expect to spend at least FM150 per person.

Restaurants are usually open daily until around 1am, though the kitchens often close at 11pm. If you're watching the pennies, many places offer a fixed-price menu at lunchtime, some for under FM40.

Until early evening you can get a decent dish – and the weakest beer, *I-Olut* – in *baari*, which serve straightforward Finnish dishes for FM35–50.

Kellarikrouvi, Pohjoinen Makasiinikatu 6. Traditional Finnish food served at reasonable prices in this cosy restaurant a stone's throw from the harbour.

Ostrobotnia/Manala, Dagmarinkatu 2. A famous late-night Helsinki spot that offers solid, dependable Finnish home cooking of the meat and potatoes variety until 3.30am. Bar and dancefloor.

Ravintola Lappi, Annankatu 22. A fine, though not cheap, restaurant specialising in real Finnish food like pea soup and oven-baked pancakes, as well as Lappish specialities of smoked reindeer and warm cloudberries. Lunches from FM35. Short walk from the train station.

Saslik, Neitsytpolku 12. Highly rated for its Russian food, served amid lush, Tsarist-period furnishings and accompanied by live music. Closes midnight. Tram #3T or #3B.

Zetor, Kaivokatu 10. Popular restaurant done up in Country & Western style, with tractors, straw, the works. Short walk from the main train station.

Accommodation

Finnish hotels offer sauna, swimming pool and enormous breakfasts, but at high prices – more than FM500 for a double room. At weekends and in summer (which is when the football's on, remember), **prices often fall**, sometimes to as low as FM300 for a double. Always phone well in advance to get the best bargain. **Tourist hotels** (*matkustajakoti*) are more basic, but clean

Helsinki essentials

Helsinki's airport, **Vantaa**, is 20km north of town and is connected to the main train station by frequent bus #615 (journey time 45mins, fare FM16). A **taxi** will be quicker but might cost FM150.

The ferry lines *Viking* and *Silja* have their terminals on opposite sides of the South Harbour (docks known respectively as *Katajanokka* and *Olympic*), a walk of less than a kilometre to town. The train station is in the city centre, next door to one of the two city **bus terminals**. All **trams** stop immediately outside or around the corner on Mannerheimintie. Just across Mannerheimintie and a short way up Simonkatu is the second city bus terminal and the long-distance coach station.

Helsinki is hemmed in on three sides by **water** and all the places you'll want to go are either within walking distance or a few minutes apart by an integrated transport network of buses, trams and metro. A **single journey** on any of these costs FM10 onboard, F8 in advance, and unlimited transfers are allowed within one hour. A multi-trip ticket gives ten rides for FM75. A *Helsinki Tourist* ticket, available in one- (FM25), three- (FM50) or five-day (FM75) versions, allows travel on all buses and trams and can be purchased from *R-kioski* stands and metro stations. Public transport runs 5am–1am and there is no night service.

Taxis levy a basic charge of FM20, with a further FM5 per km, plus a FM10 evening surcharge after 8pm. Phone for one on ☎09/700 700.

The main **tourist office** is at Pohjoisesplanadi 19 (May–Sept Mon–Fri 8.30am–6pm, Sat–Sun 10am-3pm; Oct–April Mon–Fri 8.30am–4pm, Tues–Fri 8.30am–4pm; ☎09/169 3757, fax 09/169 3839). It dishes out free street and transport maps, along with the useful free tourist magazine *Helsinki This Week*.

The free fortnightly paper *City-lehti* can be picked up in record shops, restaurants and metro stations, and has concert and club **listings**, with a section in English.

and comfortable, with doubles around FM200. Again, always book ahead, particularly in summer.

In Helsinki, you can book a room for a FM15–30 fee through the **Hotel Booking Centre** at the train station near the left-luggage office (mid-May to mid-Sept Mon–Fri 9am–9pm, Sat 9am–7pm, Sun 10am–6pm; rest of year Mon–Fri 9am–6pm; ☎09/171 133, fax 09/175 524).

Academica, Hietaniemenkatu 14 (☎09/1311 4334, fax 09/441 201). A well-placed summer hotel with morning sauna and pool. Around FM300 for a double. Hostel-type accommodation is available in another section on production of an IYHF or student card, June–Aug only, for around FM100 per bed. Bus #18, tram #3T, or a 10min walk from the station down Salomonkatu.

Euro Hostel, Linnankatu 9 (☎09/622 0470, fax 09/655 044, e-mail euroh@icon.fi). Comfortable

place with free morning sauna and twin beds (not bunks). FM120 per bed. Single and double rooms also available. Close to the *Viking Line* arrival point; take tram #4.

Satakuntalo, Lapinrinne 1a (☎09/6958 5231, fax 09/694 2226). Handily located summer hotel which doubles as student accommodation. Shared bathrooms. About FM235 for a single, FM330 for a double, FM80 for a dorm bed. Tram #4 or a 10min walk from the station.

Stadion Hostel, Olympiastadion (☎09/496 071, fax 09/496 466). From a football point of view, the youth hostel with the best location in Europe, with an entrance on the far side of the Olympic stadium complex. FM75–150 per person. Own café on site. Open all year. No credit cards. Tram #3T, #4, #7A or #10.

France

Fédération Française de Football 60 bis Avenue d'Iéna, F-75783, Paris Cedex 16
☎01/4431 7300   Fax 01/4720 8296   E-mail info@fff.fr

League champions AS Monaco   **Cup winners** FC Nantes
League Cup winners FC Gueugnon   **Promoted** Lille OSC, En Avant Guingamp,
Toulouse FC   **Relegated** Nancy-Lorraine, Le Havre, Montpellier HSC

European participants 2000/01 AS Monaco, Paris St-Germain (UCL); Olympique
Lyonnais (UCL qualifiers); Girondins de Bordeaux, FC Nantes (UEFA Cup);
AJ Auxerre, Sédan-Ardennes, RC Lens (Intertoto Cup)

'There are still some people who say we only won the World Cup because we were at home. Well, we are going to prove them wrong here – we are the champions of the world.' Thus spake France's Marcel Desailly before the start of Euro 2000. A month later, he was dancing around Rotterdam's Feyenoord stadium with another trophy in his hand, having silenced any of those remaining voices suggesting his team was anything less than the best.

In 2000 France became the first ever country to win the European Championship while world champions. The nation which started European competition after a spat over who had the best club side in Europe had put an end to another argument. It may have needed an injury-time equaliser and a golden goal winner to see off Dino Zoff's Italy in the final, but from the moment the tournament began, it was clear that France were in a different class.

Although the stars who have won the French their two trophies continue to play abroad in what remain Europe's premier domestic leagues, at home the situation is brighter than ever before. Average attendances are on the rise, French teams are appearing in more European finals than at any time since the club trophies were introduced, and almost all French sides now have big private money behind them, shaking off their long-held status as providers of municipal entertainment. More than anything, the French have reached their goal

with few compromises when it comes to style. The finest of all French national teams, featuring Michel Platini, may have fallen to West Germany in two consecutive World Cup semi-finals in the Eighties, but the current generation's attitude to the game is every bit as cultured, and France's coaching expertise is now in demand across the globe.

As well as the building of a new national stadium outside Paris, France's main club grounds also underwent reconstruction for the 1998 finals, some for the first time in 60 years. Then, the French were chosen as World Cup hosts in honour of their contribution to the structure of the world game. After overcoming early problems of oval-ball domination at home and English intransigence abroad, Robert Guérin co-founded world football's governing body, FIFA, in 1904. Another Frenchman, the organisation's president for more than 30 years, Jules Rimet, was behind the introduction of football's greatest trophy, the World Cup, in 1930. Europe's major trophies were also French inventions, Gabriel Hanot founding the European Cup in the late Fifties, Henri Delaunay the European Championship not long after.

Forty years later, the man following in the footsteps of these great historical figures, Michel Platini, may have seemed like a romantic choice as the nation's official ambassador for the 1998 World Cup. But it is not hard to understand why the French put their faith in him. Before Platini's arrival as a player, the French had won none of the trophies their administrators had given the world.

Between the Fifties and the Seventies, only provincial clubs Stade de Reims and St-Étienne came close to lifting a European trophy. Reims lost the first-ever European Cup final to Real Madrid in 1956, then lost the same fixture to the same team three years later. In between, the side provided the core of a high-scoring French national squad that gained third place at the 1958 World Cup, thanks to 13 goals – still an all-time tournament record – from Just Fontaine, and the vision of Raymond Kopa, the greatest French player of his day.

St-Étienne, French champions seven times between 1967 and 1976, featured in some classic European ties, the most memorable a 3–1 quarter-final defeat at Liverpool in the 1977 European Cup, a year after the French side had lost the final of the same tournament to Bayern Munich.

St-Étienne – *Les Verts* – were the first French club to engender a modern fan following. Just as significantly, in the late Seventies they provided a home for the emerging vision of Platini – a vision that would shine not just in French club football, but in three World Cups and one stunning European Championship.

First spotted playing for his hometown team AS Nancy-Lorraine in 1975, Platini scored three goals in four qualifying games to take France to their first modern World Cup finals in 1978. There they were unlucky to be drawn in a tough group alongside Italy and the host nation, Argentina; the French lost to both by the narrowest of margins, and went home.

Misfortune would strike again in Spain in 1982. Coach Michel Hidalgo, a veteran of Reims in the Fifties, had built a midfield of rare talent, with Platini, Alain Giresse and Jean Tigana. Even more than in Argentina, France were a joy to watch. They were 3–1 up in extra-time of an electric World Cup semi-final with West Germany and, despite having lost defender Patrick Battiston to a wild and unpunished challenge by German 'keeper Toni Schumacher, they

continued to attack. The strategy was naïve – leaving gaps at the back, the French allowed the Germans to score twice, then lost the game on penalties.

It seemed the French could not win and entertain at the same time. But two years later, in the European Championship on home soil, they did precisely that. Their midfield now given bite by Jean Fernandez, France were outstanding. Platini scored seven goals in three group games to line up another epic semi-final, this one in Marseille against Portugal. An enthralling game was tied at 2–2 and heading for penalties when Tigana went on a desperate surge down the park in the last minute of extra-time – he got to the byline, crossed low, and there was Platini to sweep the ball home. Delirium at the Vélodrome – a firework atmosphere that Paris couldn't match when France duly won the title in a dour final against Spain four days later.

Platini's last hurrah was at the 1986 World Cup in Mexico. With Luis Fernandez now the dominant midfield force, the French knocked holders Italy out in the second round, setting up a quarter-final against Brazil which featured attacking football of the highest quality; it was to end in another penalty decider, this time in France's favour. In the semi-final the opponents were West Germany again, but by this time French creativity had dried up – Platini played bravely on through injury, but an early German goal obliged France to settle for an eventual third place.

Throughout this buoyant period on the international stage, many French clubs were in a poor state. Bound by a law of 1901, they were not allowed to make a profit or pay high transfer fees. Propped up by local councils, many set up slush funds and secret bank accounts.

Things began to change in the mid-Eighties, when Bordeaux president Claude Bez rejuvenated his club thanks not only to vast municipal loans but also to lucrative deals with the new Canal Plus TV channel. Though the experiment was to end in disgrace and financial ruin, Bordeaux were France's first glimpse of how a football club could be run in the modern era.

Bez opened avenues for his great rival, Olympique Marseille's Bernard Tapie. The archetypal Eighties wheeler-dealer, Tapie pushed *l'OM* to new heights; the team won five straight titles before making history in 1993 by becoming the first French side to win the European Cup. Days after Marseille's 1–0 win over Milan in Munich, however, news broke of the club's domestic match-fixing. Stripped of their fifth league title, *l'OM* were also denied the right to defend their European trophy. One of the great Marseille stars of the era, striker Jean-Pierre Papin, had become a linchpin of the national side, now coached by Platini. The attacking combination of Papin and Eric Cantona made France one of the favourites to win the 1992 European Championship in Sweden. Yet fans saw only glimpses of them – Platini, so adventurous as a player, preached caution as a coach. The ploy backfired, and after France failed to win a match in Sweden, he resigned.

Earlier glory – Platini lifts the Delaunay trophy, 1984

Within 18 months Platini's successor, Gérard Houllier, had also quit. Needing only a point from their remaining two qualifying games to book their tickets to the 1994 World Cup, Houllier's French threw away a 2–1 lead against Israel to lose their penultimate match 3–2. Then, with only a few minutes of their last game against Bulgaria left and the game standing at 1–1, Houllier brought on David Ginola as a replacement for Papin. Ginola gave the ball carelessly away deep in Bulgarian territory, and Emil Kostadinov raced away to score a winning goal that would signal not only Houllier's downfall, but the end of the international road for Papin, Ginola and Cantona.

The latter two would become stars in their own right in England's Premiership,

but would be overlooked by Houllier's replacement, Aimé Jacquet, who eschewed individual flair and put the emphasis firmly on the group. And what a group it was – Youri Djorkaeff, Christophe Dugarry, Zinedine Zidane and Didier Deschamps all starred in the French side that reached the semi-finals of Euro '96.

This same core of players, with a solid defence of goalkeeper Fabien Barthez, Lilian Thuram and Laurent Blanc, and the added Premiership steel of Emmanuel Petit in midfield, were the team on which French hopes were pinned in 1998.

The fact that they were not only able to satisfy those hopes, but expand demand from a core fan base to the nation as a whole – and without an attack to speak of, no Ronaldo or Maradona figure – speaks

Basics

EU nationals and those of the US, Canada, and New Zealand require only a **passport** to enter France. Australians require a visa, but this will be valid not only for France but for all EU countries party to the Schengen agreement on frontier controls.

The French currency is the **franc** (F), divided into 100 centimes. There are F1, F2, F5, F10 and F20 coins, and notes for F20, F50, F100, F200 and F500. There are around F10 to £1. Cash machines for credit cards are widespread, the most popular card being the *Carte Bleu* Visa.

French public phone boxes take only **phonecards** (*télécartes*), available at most tobacco stalls (*tabacs*) and newsagents, in units of 50 (F49) and 120 (F97.50). **International calls** from within France are cheaper between 7pm and 8am weekdays, all day Saturdays and Sundays. French telephone numbers have ten digits, including the area code. The country is divided into five areas – 01 around Paris, 04 around Marseille, and so on. To call France from abroad, dial country code 33, dropping the 0 of the area code afterwards. For all inland calls, re-instate the 0. The **international access code** from France is 00.

The French **transport system** is centralised around Paris, with an excellent rail network run by the state operator *SNCF*. Travelling to and from the capital is quick and comfortable on high-speed **TGV trains**, which serve most major towns and for which you will be charged a modest F20 supplement. A TGV journey to Marseille takes just over four hours and costs F400. Normal *SNCF* express services are slower but still reliable. Remember to validate your ticket before boarding.

Buses are to be avoided unless there is no other choice, but **hitching** is a possibility if money is tight. *Âllo-Stop Provoya* matches drivers willing to share petrol costs with hitchers – the Paris office number is ☎01/5320 4242, e-mail allostop@ecritel.fr.

Accommodation is generally clean, plentiful and affordable; you'll pay around F200 for a basic double room, a little more in Paris.

French **cuisine** is excellent if rarely cheap. Watch out for *menus fixes* lunchtime bargains, posted outside the restaurant – three-course meals can cost as little as F60.

In bars, there are generally three price ranges: one for standing at the bar (*au comptoir*), one for being waited on (*á table*) and one for drinking after 10pm (*tarif de nuit*). The cheap option is **wine**, almost always drinkable. Draught **beer** (*pression*) is sold by the 33cl glass (*demi*), at about F12–15. Light (*blondes*) and dark (*brunes*) beers are available, and sometimes the bitter *rousse*. French beers offer little regional variation, but there are often Belgian or Dutch options. The national **spirit**, particularly popular in the south, is the aniseed-flavoured *pastis*, served with a small jug of water.

Entrance to French **nightclubs** is expensive but usually includes your first drink (*consommation*).

volumes for Jacquet's achievement. For the first time, *les Bleus* had won the Cup and won over the country.

After cruising through a relatively easy first-phase group, without Zidane France struggled in a tense, hot game against Paraguay, settled by a Blanc 'golden goal' in the 114th minute. Zidane was back for the quarter-final with Italy, won on a penalty shoot-out, when a confident Barthez psyched out two of the Italian

penalty takers, ensuring there would be no repeat of his side's exit from Euro '96. By now the French public were well and truly gripped. In the semi-final with Croatia, Thuram atoned for his defensive slip in allowing Šuker to score by immediately equalising, then put France ahead on 70 minutes. Soon after, Blanc was cruelly red-carded and France played out the last 20 minutes with ten men. With Frank Leboeuf taking over Blanc's defensive duties in the final, France took the game to a lacklustre Brazil, Zidane's two headers giving them a 2–0 half-time lead – he later revealed that the team had been working on delivering crosses from set plays ever since the semi-final. Despite having Desailly sent off and Stéphane Guivarc'h missing a remarkable number of chances, France held on. Petit capped a fine tournament with a late box-to-box run which culminated in the third and final goal – and gave France her first World Cup. More than a million people took to the streets of Paris in celebration, as the French finally shook off their traditional ambivalence to the game.

The capital had last seen such adulation when Paris St-Germain won the Cup-Winners' Cup in 1996. With backing from Canal Plus, and domestic superiority following Marseille's post-Tapie decline, PSG revived football in the city and ushered in the new domestic era of slick merchandising and pay-per-view TV. Ironically, the club that took the first steps along the same road ten years previously, Bordeaux, also won through to their first European final the same year, losing in the UEFA Cup to Bayern Munich.

TV money from Canal Plus allowed less glamorous clubs to climb a mountain of debt and take on the big boys: Guy Roux's Auxerre, title winners in 1996, and RC Lens, from a small northern mining community, champions in 1998.

The open, unpredictable nature of the domestic game encouraged more fresh talent to emerge, as David Trezeguet's goals led Monaco to the title in 2000, and Sylvian Wiltord impressed enough at Bordeaux to earn a place in Roger Lemerre's squad for Euro 2000.

In 1998 the French had managed to win the World Cup with only the frail Stéphane Guivarc'h in attack. Now they had a choice of Thierry Henry, Arsenal's leading scorer in England; Nicolas Anelka, who had rediscoverd his form at Real Madrid in the nick of time; plus Wiltord and Trezeguet.

Lemerre left Jacquet's defence untouched, and his only change in midfield was to introduce the maturing Patrick Vieira. From their convincing win in their opening game against Denmark, it was clear that France were even better than they had been two years previously. After a hard-fought win over the Czechs, a reserve team was sent out against Holland and still managed to sparkle in a 3–2 defeat.

In the quarter-final against Spain, Zidane opened the scoring with a beautiful free-kick in the 32nd minute and, after Gaizka Mendieta had equalised with a penalty, Djorkaeff blasted France back into the lead just before the break. Spain's Raul missed a penalty in injury time and France began to sense that it was their year again.

Portugal were next up in a semi-final which ended in controversy. At 1–1 the game went into extra-time and then Portuguese defender Abel Xavier was judged by a linesman to have handled on the line – Zidane slotted home the penalty despite wild Portuguese protests.

There was no doubt that the French were capable of beating anyone in an open contest. But their opponents in the final were an Italy team who had shown that they were back to their negative best – or worst. When Marco Delvecchio gave the Italians the lead, the French struggled to break down a masterful Italian defence until injury time, when substitute Wiltord grabbed a dramatic equaliser. The Italians were distraught, and two more young subs, Robert Pires and Trezeguet ran rings around their opponents to create the golden goal which sent Paris on to the streets again.

With so much talent streaming through the system and with their key player, Zidane, still only 28, it's tempting to believe that they will keep their place at the top of the European tree for some time. Now the challenge is for the domestic game to capitalise on the momentum and rise to the level of its rivals in Spain and Italy. Then, perhaps, the next generation of talented youngsters will stay at home for a few more seasons, rather than pack their bags before their 20th birthday.

Essential vocabulary

Hello *Bonjour*
Goodbye *Au revoir*
Yes *Oui*
No *Non*
Two beers, please *Deux demis, s'il vous plaît*
Thank you *Merci*
Men's *Hommes*
Women's *Dames*
Where is the stadium? *Où est le stade?*
What's the score? *Où en sommes-nous?*
Referee *L'arbitre*
Offside *Hors jeu*

Match practice

Despite encouraging rising attendance figures, the lack of cross-town competition means that French stadia are rarely full for league matches. The exceptions to this are Paris St-Germain and Olympique Marseille, who both boast large followings.

The season runs from late July until early May, with a short winter break between mid-December and mid-January. Games normally take place on a Saturday at 8pm, but clubs involved in European competition often bring their games forward to Friday or even Thursday evening and, as in England, there are some midweek rounds. Live games for Canal Plus are played either side of the main matchday, generally at 8.30pm.

A different league

La Ligue Nationale has two professional divisions. *Division 1* (often known simply as *D1*) has 18 teams, the bottom three clubs changing places with the promoted trio from the 20-club *Division 2*. The bottom three from this swap with the top three from the semi-professional *Division National*.

Beneath this are the four-group *Championnat de France Amateurs 1* and the eight-group *CFA2*. Both *CFA* tiers have their groups organised on a regional basis.

Up for the cup

France has two cups. *La Coupe de France* is the oldest and best-loved domestic cup tournament in continental Europe, and has no fewer than 14 rounds including the final. To encourage unpredictability, all rounds are decided on a single game, then extra-time and penalties if necessary. Progress by modest village teams is common – witness the run by a team of shopkeepers, Calais, all the way to the final in 1999/2000. Alas, mainland visits by teams from former French colonies such as Martinique and Guadeloupe rarely last more than 90 sixth-round minutes. First-division clubs enter at the ninth-round stage. The final is staged at the Stade de France, with the winners qualifying for the UEFA Cup.

The recently introduced *Coupe de la Ligue* is for first and second division clubs, plus the top four *National* teams. All ties are single-game and the competition is played concurrently with the established cup, with a May final at the Stade de France.

Just the ticket

Most French clubs operate a three-level pricing system, with a *match de gala* (against PSG, Marseille, or European opposition) being the dearest.

In general the *virages* behind the goal, which are often standing (*debout*) areas, are for hardcore support; a spot here will cost around F50–60. The *tribunes populaires* also have faithful followers, often from the older generation, happy with their regular spot in the cheap seats, high up over the action, at around F40–60. The side stands (*tribunes latéralles*) are almost always seated (*assis*) and tickets here vary in price according to the view, from F50 to F200.

For big European games, contact the host club well in advance for tickets as many are given out *en masse* to sponsors.

Half-time

At most grounds you can buy beer and sausages (*saucisses*). At northern venues you'll find chips (*frites*), dished up in the Belgian fashion with mayonnaise, while southern clubs will have *mergüez*, North African blood sausage. Note that alcohol is banned from certain grounds, particularly in the top flight.

Action replay

Canal Plus rules the roost – at least for now. The subscription channel whose money transformed French league football currently screens all *D1* matches as part of its pay-per-view *Kiosque* system – each game is given a number next to the letter K to indicate which game the viewer is paying to see. To its non-pay-per-view (but still subscription-paying) audience, Canal Plus screens one live match on Saturdays for both analogue and digital customers, and another on Friday evenings for digital and *Kiosque* users only.

There's also a round-up show, *Jour de Foot*, after 10pm on Saturdays, and a more analytical version, *L'Équipe du Dimanche*, at 10pm on Sundays.

The current TV deal runs until 2001, but the French league, worried that it has undersold pay-per-view rights, has already begun an auction between Canal Plus and rival pay-TV network TPS for the rights after that date.

And while Canal Plus may have all the angles, France's voices of football remain those of terrestrial TF1's Thierry Roland and Jean-Michel Larqué. This popular duo present cup ties, most international matches, certain European games and France's best-loved football show, *Téléfoot*, at around 11am on Sundays.

At the start of the 1998/99 season, the daily sports paper *L'Équipe* launched its own pay-TV channel, broadcasting mainly news but branching out to show French and European highlights daily at 9–9.30am.

The back page

Reflecting the visual age, the country's leading football publication, *France Football*, underwent radical change in 1997. With big colour features and less reportage, and with the focus more on television, finance and marketing than how the Belgian league went last weekend, the relaunch spawned a glossy Tuesday (F12) and a newspaper Friday (F8) editions. For all that, it is still 'La Bible du Football', worthy of the fine French sporting-press tradition. Its sister

Modern moment – Djorkaeff and co, July 2000

daily, the classic *L'Équipe* (F4.90, F6 on Mondays), has also had to move with the times, issuing a weekend colour-supplement edition on Saturdays (F11.50).

Both papers have pioneering backgrounds. After Henri Desgrange, chief of the prestigious sports daily *L'Auto*, instigated cycling's Tour de France at the turn of the century, the French press has taken an active role in sports development. *L'Auto* gave way to the classic all-sport daily *L'Équipe*, whose football editor Gabriel Hanot brooded for 20 years on the idea of introducing a trophy for European champion clubs. When the popular English press proclaimed Wolves 'Champions of Europe' for beating Honvéd of Hungary in a meaningless muddy friendly in 1954, Hanot got to work. Gathering club presidents in the *Hotel Ambassador* on Boulevard Haussmann in April 1955, Hanot and his team hammered out immediate plans for a European Cup, to be introduced four months later.

At a stroke, European football had been dragged out of the dark ages, to be transformed into the lucrative midweek circus we know today. A year later, *France Football* introduced the European Football of the Year award.

Away from all this prestige, younger fans decorate their walls with posters from the monthlies *Onze Mondial* (F27) and *Planète Foot* (F25). Watch out for the monthly *Afrique Football* (F18), which offers fine coverage of the game in Africa.

Ultra culture

The average Frenchman watches a game of football through a love of the sport rather than partisan interest. With notable exceptions – Metz, Marseille, Bastia, Lens – the older generation of supporters have not handed down a singular passion for younger fans to take up and interpret in the modern custom. It was only when the great St-Étienne and Olympique Marseille teams were riding high in Europe that France saw genuine outbreaks of mass fan culture, fireworks and all. This was picked up by followers of Paris St-Germain, a club often criticised in France as manufactured, but whose 1996 Cup-Winners' Cup triumph brought thousands spontaneously onto the streets of the capital.

Crowd violence is rare, but Cannes goalkeeper Sébastian Chabbert was hospitalised after an attack by Nice's *Brigade Sud* in January 1999, and Marseille fans' pitch invasion at Toulouse the same month was one of many incidents involving the club's supporters during the season – and there was further trouble involving them in 1999/2000.

Meanwhile, up in the VIP stands of the major clubs, the game attracts the country's movers and shakers, politicians and captains of industry, for whom football has become a fashionable place to be seen.

Deeper underground, the independent fanzine *Ultras News* (F10) documents French fan culture every month. It's available from Mathieu Garde, Quartier des Fourques, 83520 Roquebrune s/Argens.

In the net

The French FA maintains a simple, logically laid-out official website, divided between a club directory, the latest on the *Coupe de France,* an administrative section and (as you might expect) a substantial archive dedicated to France '98. There's no English but it's easy to find your way around at: www.fff.fr.

The once rather insubstantial football area of the Canal Plus website has evolved into a serious piece of online sports publishing, with stats, news and interviews by the bucket-load, covering all areas including *D1* and *D2*, the national team, European competitions and foreign leagues. There's some English-language info, too, at: www.cplus.fr/html/sports/football.htm.

Stats anoraks will find a French championship archive dating back to 1949 at: oxygene.com/foot/france/.

Paris

The million-plus Parisians who jammed the streets after the 1998 World Cup and Euro 2000 triumphs were not only celebrating France's victory – they were taking brief advantage of the city's position back on the world football stage.

Yet once the bottles have been cleared away, the cold light of day reveals a club scene which continues to stand comparison with the star player at another of the city's major attractions, *Disneyland Paris*. The only lasting monument to the city's hour of glory in 1998 is le Stade de France, the purpose-built arena which had staged the country's finest footballing hour in the northern suburb of Saint-Denis. The rest was looking on shaky foundations.

The dream ticket of two top-class sides playing European football in the city – Paris St-Germain at the Parc des Princes and another, as yet unknown club at le Stade de France – still looks as far away now as it did when the new ground was still being built, if not further.

The only consolation is that things could be much worse. At the start of the Nineties, when PSG were threatened with relegation, they'd looked like going the way of all other major postwar teams in the French capital. Both Racing Club and Stade Français had gone under, while Red Star and Paris FC were playing to three-figure crowds in lower leagues. Even international matches were being moved to the provinces, such was the Parisian antipathy towards football.

Then Canal Plus stepped in to rescue PSG from oblivion, and their gamble paid off. The club clambered back up the ladder to attain domestic success, embellished by serious inroads into Europe. Support grew, particularly in the city's suburbs. Suddenly PSG were no longer a boardroom creation – they were an identifiable way for a suburban kid to get back at those flashy wheeler-dealers from the south. The climax came in May 1996, with PSG's Cup-Winners' Cup triumph sparking wild celebrations on the Champs-Élysées, just as the World Cup would two years later. A combination of money, luck and corporate ambition had created a team out of nothing and thrust them into the European elite.

Perhaps, to become a truly great club, PSG now need a meaningful cross-city rivalry to sustain the passion of their supporters. The problem is that Parisians can't agree on who that rival might be. Out in the suburbs, former Bordeaux president Alain Afflelou has endowed US Créteil with a big transfer budget, a tidy youth scheme and, in 1999, promotion to the second division. Meanwhile, his old sparring partner Bernard Tapie has returned as a 'consultant' to third-division Olympique Noisy-Le-Sec, telling the media that 'a second club in Paris, other than PSG, is a necessity to cool tempers in the suburbs'.

Closer to the city centre, the outlook is less rosy. US Créteil's rise coincided with Red Star 93 dropping out of *D2*, while the grand old names of Paris FC and Racing Club are likewise toiling in France's semi-professional divisions.

Yet Racing still enjoy a special place in the football life of the city, for they were the most prestigious of the handful of Parisian amateur clubs who won the first six French cups after World War I. Indeed, it was in Paris that the game first took root in France. Racing Club de Paris, whose footballing section became an autonomous professional outfit in 1932 were a pre-war legend, with club members from the capital's political elite and a multi-national group of players. Their home, Colombes, hosted five World Cup games in 1938. Today it is little more than a ghostly echo of Paris' former status as football's capital – though at least it is still there.

The game's great leap forward earlier this century had two main venues in Paris. Today, neither shows any sign of history having been made. The former French FA office at 229 Rue Saint-Honoré, in whose backroom FIFA's original members first met in May 1904, is now a house like any other in the 1st *arrondissement*. Meanwhile, after decades at 10 Rue du Faubourg-Montmartre, where the European Cup was dreamed up, the editorial team of *L'Équipe* and *France Football* moved (with great reluctance) outside town to Issy-les-Moulineaux. The old building is now a modern office block, while the shop downstairs which once sold fading pre-war sports papers is a kebab stall. For those keen on seeing some football history, it's worth visiting the *Musée National du Sport* at the Parc des Princes, near the Stade Jean Bouin (open Mon–Fri 1.45–5.15pm, admission F20). Here you'll find two floors of souvenirs from several sports, including French captain Jean Vincent's shirt from the 1958 World Cup and a programme from the France-Italy World Cup quarter-final of 1938.

The thrilling fields

 Paris Saint-Germain

Parc des Princes, 24 Rue du Commandant Guilbaud
Capacity 49,000 (all-seated)
Colours Blue shirts with red centre stripe, blue shorts
League champions 1986, 1994
Cup winners 1982–83, 1993, 1995, 1998
Cup-Winners' Cup winners 1996

If Paris Saint-Germain didn't exist, it would have been necessary to invent them. After Racing Club's demise in the Sixties, 20,000 football-starved Parisian donors founded Football Club Paris in 1970; they would soon join forces with Saint-Germain-En-Laye to climb the league ladder as Paris Saint-Germain.

The move coincided with the complete reconstruction of the Parc des Princes, former home to Racing's football team and the *Tour de France* finale. Rebuilt with only football and international rugby in mind,

the Parc seemed the perfect home for the first serious soccer team in the capital for 20 years.

And so it was. With a team starring Luis Fernandez and expensive imports like Osvaldo Ardiles and Kees Kist, PSG won domestic honours in the Eighties – albeit without generating a real fan base or ever challenging in Europe.

By the time Olympique Marseille were ruling the French roost, PSG were starting to flounder. Having turned down a deal in 1988, pay-TV giant Canal Plus stepped in three years later, bailing PSG out to the tune of around F30million a year. The club, although still receiving financial support from city hall, became a limited company, able to wheel and deal.

With the decline of *l'OM*, fans across the country looked to PSG to fly the French flag in Europe. They weren't disappointed. Between 1993 and 1995 the team made consecutive semi-finals in three different European competitions, while solidly picking up silverware at home. Key players such as David Ginola became nationwide stars. In the Parc des Princes itself, an ultra culture developed, some of it distasteful – Liberian striker George Weah, whose goals had taken PSG to within a sniff of the European Cup final, had to endure a thoroughly unpleasant send-off to Milan, though his signing to the Italian club on the eve of playing against them for PSG hardly helped. Meanwhile, the cruder banners and mob gestures were not always appreciated by the image-conscious Canal Plus management (nor, curiously, were they picked up by the company's camera teams).

The return of former player Luis Fernandez as coach in 1994 gave the side steel to go with its style. While Ginola left for Newcastle, Fernandez became the first French coach to win a European trophy, when PSG beat Rapid Vienna 1–0 in the 1996 Cup-Winners' Cup final. While Paris celebrated in style, the players were flown back from Brussels to be fêted in the Canal Plus offices. Fernandez's departure to Athletic Bilbao soon afterwards – and his

Unpronounceable, unforgettable – PSG skipper Eric Rabrenandratana is mobbed by colleagues

replacement by another former player, the Brazilian Ricardo – led to the realisation that in football, maintaining success is more difficult than achieving it. PSG trailed Monaco in the league, were knocked out of the cup by fourth-division Clermont, and were whitewashed 6–1 at home by Juventus in the European SuperCup. While Ricardo kept his job, club president Michel Denisot launched an unprecedented purge of senior management. Too late, it seemed, for PSG's bold attempt to make history by becoming the first club ever to retain the Cup-Winners' Cup also ended in failure, after Ronaldo's penalty had given Barcelona victory in Rotterdam. Brazilians Raí and Leonardo had been the only highlights of a disappointing season – and the latter was quickly poached by Milan.

Two further mixed seasons were to follow. After their fans voted to stay at the Parc des Princes in December 1997, PSG spent £15million on improving it, while the team plummeted to their lowest league position in a decade, flunked their Champions' League campaign and somehow won both domestic cups.

Behind the scenes, club president Denisot then gave way to the director of sports at Canal Plus, Charles Biétry. Together with new coach Alain Giresse, Biétry promised a bold new era of attacking football, smashing the French transfer record to bring Nigerian playmaker Jay-Jay Okocha to Paris for £10million during the 1998 close season. Within months, both Giresse and Biétry were gone, after PSG were knocked out of the Cup-Winners' Cup by Israel's Hapoel Haifa.

Artur Jorge, returning for a second spell as coach, plugged the gaps in Giresse's defence but fatally blunted the team's attack – his side went two months without scoring a goal and were teetering on the brink of the relegation zone when new president Laurent Perpère sacked Jorge and sought salvation in France's 1998 World Cup-winning goalkeeping coach, Philippe Bergeroo.

At last, the right compromise between attack and defence was struck, and PSG finished the season sitting comfortably in mid-table. With Marco Simone, once an inspirational captain but latterly a disruptive

Paris essentials

Paris has two **airports**, Roissy-Charles de Gaulle to the north, Orly to the south. A free shuttle bus takes you from Roissy to the last stop on the RER (express rail) line B, from where a F45 ticket takes you into town. Journey time is about 45mins. A *Roissybus* (every 30mins, 6am–11pm, F45) runs to Rue Scribe near Place de l'Opéra. From Orly, a 10min high-speed shuttle (F50) takes you to Antony on the RER line B.
Alternatively, a free 5min shuttle takes you to Pont de Rungis on RER line C, while an *Orlybus* (every 15mins, 6am–11.30pm, F30) runs to Denfert-Rochereau on RER line B. *Air France* run buses between the city and both airports, but take account of heavy traffic *en route*.

An increasingly popular alternative to flying is the **Eurostar** high-speed train service from London's Waterloo International. There are at least eight trains a day and the service takes three hours to reach Paris Gare du Nord, which is on RER lines B and D and the *métro*.

The Paris **transport system** is among Europe's best, with 15 *métro* lines intersecting with four RER ones, all running 5.30am–12.45am. Free maps are given out at most stations. Lines are colour-coded, and at transfer stations they are further identified by their end stops (*direction*). A single ticket, valid for one journey within central zone 1 (change lines with your validated ticket), costs F8, so a *carnet* of ten is a bargain at F52. A one-day *Formule 1* ticket, covering travel outside the central zone, costs from F30; F100 to include both airports.

Paris also has a comprehensive network of **buses**, on which tickets are valid according to a complicated zonal system – any journey worth its salt requires two tickets. Three tickets are required on any of the ten *Noctambus* routes which operate from Châtelet during the night.

Paris has 15,000 **taxis** but finding an empty one in rush hour is nigh impossible. At night, watch out for the white light glowing on the taxi roof. Even on a night tariff, a journey in town shouldn't cost more than F60. To phone for a cab, dial ☎01/4241 5050 or ☎01/4585 8585.

For **tourist information**, there are four branches of the *Office du Tourisme* at the Eiffel Tower, the Gare du Nord, the Gare du Lyon and the main one at 127 Avenue des Champs-Élysées (☎01/4952 5354). All are open daily, 9am–8pm, except winter Sundays and holidays, 11am–6pm.

The best **listings information** can be found in the weekly *Pariscope* (Wednesdays, F3), which has an eight-page English-language pullout. More comprehensive clubbing information can be found in the freebie *Lylo*, which is handed out around town every three weeks.

influence, sold to Monaco, Bergeroo's team were dark horses for the title in 1999/2000, their chances enhanced by an unusual (for PSG) lack of European distractions. The side wasn't quite good enough to make a dent in Monaco's big championship lead once it had opened up, but with Okocha justifying his price-tag at last and Eric Rabresandratana a capable new captain, the team guaranteed themselves Champions' League football for the coming year with a runners-up spot. In the summer of 2000, the return of Nicolas Anelka, who had never started a game for the club who first signed him as a teenager and which he had supported all his life, gave the Parc des Princes another shot in the arm.

Here we go!

Take *métro* line #9 to **Porte de Saint Cloud**, coming out at the Côté Boulogne exit.

Just the ticket

There are **ticket offices** dotted all round the ground. Prices – and availability – vary according to whether the game is a *Super Gala* (Marseille and major European ties), a *Gala* (Bordeaux, Lens, Saint-Étienne) or a normal match.

The Parc is divided into colour-coded tiers – red, blue and yellow. The red tier is the cheapest and nearest the pitch. PSG fans go to either end, and the hardcore mob are to be found in the Boulogne red section. The blue and yellow sections are less hectic, particularly the seats in the *Tribune Paris* (G, H, I, J and K), which are accessed from Avenue du Parc des Princes. For international games, away fans are allocated a corner in red *Tribune* F, accessed from Rue Claude Farrere.

Swift half

Les Trois Obus, 120 Rue Michel-Ange, is run by club management. Advance tickets, reasonably priced meals and pitchers of wine are on sale, under the watchful gaze of a huge mirror design of the Parc, but like many bars around Place de Saint Cloud, it's a little soulless. *Café aux Deux Stades*, 41 Avenue Général Sarrail, nearer the stadium, is more like it The bar area is dominated by club pennants and signed photographs of PSG and Brazilian stars.

Club merchandise

The main PSG **superstore** in town, at 27 Avenue des Champs-Élysées (open daily 10am–midnight, most credit cards) has a ticket office upstairs (open until 10pm Sun–Thur, midnight Fri–Sat) and a wider selection of sports goods and souvenirs than the one at nearby 25 Avenue Franklin-Roosevelt (open Mon–Sat 10am–7pm). The store by the stadium, at 30 Avenue du Parc des Princes (open Mon–Fri 9am–6pm and from 2pm on matchdays) does not sell tickets.

Ultra culture

Ten years ago PSG had a crowd but few supporters. Now the club has two sets of committed fans, at the Boulogne and Auteuil ends. The longest-established crew are the *Boulogne Boys*, the most fun are the *Hoolicools* and the most colourful are the *Supras* in the Auteuil end.

In print

The Paris edition of the weekly *Journal du Dimanche* (F6.50) carries a 16-page PSG supplement which is then handed out at the ground

the following weekend. The club publishes a colour monthly magazine, *Paris Go!* (F20).

In the net

The club's **official website** is slick but refrshingly understated at: www.psg.fr. You need to dig deep to find some decent content, but it's all there somewhere, including news, club history and Parc des Princes stadium info.

A quirkier **unofficial option** resides at: www.chez.com/psgonline. Up-to-date match reports and photography are the strong point, but as with the official site, it's all in French language only.

Groundhopping

Red Star 93

Stade de Marville, 51 Avenue Roger-Salengro, Saint-Denis-La Courneuve
Capacity 10,000
Colours All white with green trim

Red Star 93 were formed by Jules Rimet in 1897 – he took the reasoning behind their Anglicised name to his grave. Having dominated the French cup after World War I, the club have had a rough time of it ever since World War II.

Having celebrated their centenary by gathering together a thousand current and former players (many of whom had seen years of potential mergers, liquidation and lower-league football) onto the Stade Bauer pitch, Red Star then left their legendary home ground for the municipal Stade de Marville in the Parc Corneuve in 1998. Soon afterwards club president Jean-Claude Bras, who had taken over the club in 1978, was jailed for misuse of public money, and a promising start to the 1998/99 season ended with a potentially ruinous relegation to semi-professional ranks. There was to be no escape from these in 2000, but the team did at least manage a run to the semifinals of the League Cup, where the prospect of a dream final against PSG in the Stade de France was dashed by FC Gueugnon, the eventual winners.

Although the Marville ground is only 2km from le Stade de France, where Red Star successfully staged a 'home' game with Saint-Étienne in front of 45,000 in 1999, the club's roots are very much back at the Bauer, in postal district 93 (hence the second part of the club's name). The *Olympic* bar opposite is still decorated in Red Star paraphernalia, a short walk from the **Mairie de St Ouen** métro stop.

Until the club can afford to pay for the Bauer's repair, take bus #153 from St-Denis-Porte de Paris métro (line #13) for ten stops to **La Courtille**, by the Marville swimming pool. A little further along Avenue Romain Rolland at #73 is the *Bar des Fleurs*, for disgruntled Portuguese workers and their football souvenirs from home. The stadium is a short walk across the road, with a large bar under the tatty old main stand – home fans are in the Pesages Salengro at one end, away fans in the Pesages Marville.

🏐 Racing Club

Stade Colombes, 12 Rue du Manoir, Colombes
Capacity 30,000
Colours Sky blue-and-white hooped shirts, white shorts

Along with Wembley, the Maracaná and the Azteca, Racing Club's Colombes has staged a World Cup final – in 1938. The stadium also played host to decades of cup finals and internationals, and provided the backdrop to the football action in the cult film *Escape To Victory*.

Before World War II, Racing Club de France attracted both high society and top-class international stars to their exclusive grounds north-west of Paris. Buenos Aires' Rácing, who also play in sky blue and white, are still known as 'The Academy'.

The football section, Racing Club de Paris, was separated when the French league turned professional in 1932. For 30 years Racing remained part of French football's elite, winning the double in 1936 with the help of Austrian *Wunderteam* goalkeeper Rudi Hiden.

Racing were dissolved in 1966. But Pierre Littbarski, Enzo Francescoli and Luis Fernandez all starred in a disastrous attempt to revive the club 20 years later, as Matra Racing. When the sponsors' money dried up, the stars fled and the club soon foundered in the lower leagues.

The latest reincarnation of the football team, Racing 92, nearly went under in 1995. Yet despite the team's failure to win promotion to *D2*, the stadium is enjoying a F5million facelift, new sponsors have been found and the club has even been able to afford ex-PSG star Antoine Kombouaré. Like Red Star, the team has even had a run-out in the Stade de France which they would like one day to be able to call home – they staged a Coupe de France game against Monaco there in 1999/2000.

To reach Colombes, take an SNCF train four stops from Gare Saint-Lazare to **Le Stade**, then a 10min walk. The fabulously tatty **RCF buffet** by gate #1 is a must, but closed on Mondays and Tuesdays. The *Café du Stade*, 67 Rue Nouvelle, opposite, does reasonable food.

🏐 Paris FC

Stade de la Porte de Montreuil, 36 Rue des Docteurs Déjerine
Capacity 5,000
Colours All sky blue

The very embodiment of the dishevelled 20th *arrondissement* in the east of the capital, Paris FC are run by the Bariani brothers, high up in local government. The club have the usual history of adoption and mergers. Their ground, with its two stands, is satisfyingly homely and shambolic, although bigger games, such as the shock cup win over Lorient 1–0 in January 1999, are played at Charléty. This is French

Le Grand Stade

Le Stade de France, Cornillon Nord, La Plaine Saint-Denis
Capacity 80,000 (all-seated)

Rising up over a former gasworks and dominating the depressed suburb of Saint-Denis
was the venue for France's greatest footballing triumph, the 1998 World Cup final.
One transport zone away from central Paris,
le Stade de France, or **le Grand Stade** as
it is popularly known, is France's national
stadium, with nearly twice the capacity of
the last one, the Parc des Princes.

Le Stade has eight levels with four tiers
of stands, the lower one retractable with a
25,000 capacity. The roof, made of filtered
glass and providing sound and lighting, is
suspended on 18 steel needles. The stadium's **elliptical shape** is said to give a
perfect view to all 80,000 spectators, but
especially to the diners in the panoramic
restaurant up on the west side. Construction
was funded partly by a private consortium,
who take the lion's share of the gate
receipts, and partly by the state.

Three colours read – the players' tunnel

What is still to be decided is which club can make le Stade their permanent home.
Paris Saint-Germain are contractually obliged to stay at the Parc des Princes and
have carried out major improvements accordingly. Modest crowds hinder both the natural and geographical candidates, **Red Star** and **Aubervilliers**, from uprooting,
although Red Star's one appearance here in March 1999 against the ever-popular St-
Étienne did pull in a gate of 45,000. Earlier plans to move in an almagamated **Saint-
Denis** and **Saint-Leu-la-Forêt** club have been shelved as impractical. For the time
being, le Stade will have to make do with hosting occasional French internationals and
the two domestic cup finals.

The stadium is served by two *RER* lines, B (**La Plaine-Stade de France** stop,
down Avenue du Stade) and D (**Stade de France-St-Denis**, down Avenue François
Mitterand), both one stop away from the Gare du Nord (fare F23 return).

Several of the tatty **bars** along Avenue du Président Wilson have closed, but not
Café Wilson at #258, with its signed, framed shots of Zidane and fine lunches. Entry
to the **panoramic restaurant**, opposite gate T, is by reservation only (☎01/5593 0440,
restaurant open Mon–Fri lunchtimes except on events days), but the soulless
Planisphère self-service outlet by gate C is open to the public Mon–Fri 8.30am–4pm.

Tickets (☎01/4468 4444) for major events are available from large outlets like
FNAC (Forum des Halles, 1–5 Rue Pierre Lescot, level –3, métro Châtelet-Les Halles)
and *Virgin* (52 Avenue des Champs-Elysées, métro Franklin D Roosevelt).

There are two kinds of **tours** available – *Premiers Regards* (daily 10am–5pm,
F35), with an open itinerary and guides ready to answer your questions every half-hour,
and *Les Coulisses du Stade* (daily, 10am, 2pm & 4pm, F90), a full-works guided tour
lasting 90mins.

And they call this 'manufactured' – PSG fans prove their terrace credentials, March 2000

semi-prodessional football at its muddiest
– but none the worse for that. To see it,
take *métro* line #9 to Porte de Montreuil,
then a short walk down Rue des Docteurs
Déjerine. Nearby, the *Café des Sports* at
111 Boulevard Davout, offers a quiet pre-
match swiftie.

Eat, drink, sleep…

Bars and clubs

The large, well-lit and archetypally Parisian
cafés on the main boulevards tend to
charge outrageous prices for drinking outside. Parisian **districts** quickly fall in and
out of fashion, the latest chic area being
the tenth *arrondissement* around
Oberkampf. **Clubbing** is an expensive
habit, but worth it when the classier world
music and jazz acts pass through town.

Black Bear, 161 Rue Montmartre. Three-floor
former cinema converted into a sports bar/bistro
by a group of sporting personalities from the

Pyrenees, including rugby star Jean-Pierre Rives.
France '98 pushed the accent more towards the
round-ball game, although – fortunately, some
might say – the wine remains firmly from the
south-west. Closed Sun and Mon evenings. Métro
Rue Montmartre.

Cyrano, 3 Rue Biot. Best football bar in town.
The boss, Jacky, a disillusioned Saint-Étienne man,
has regular visits from fans all over the world,
hence the vast collection of pennants. Métro
Place de Clichy.

Le Keeper, 5 Rue Claude Bernard. Run by Pascal Olmeta, once a top-class 'keeper with
Marseille and others, a themed football bar/bistro,
with a signed shirt from Eric Cantona among the
artefacts on display. Giant TV screen. Closed Sunday evenings. Métro Censier Daubenton.

Rex Club, 5 Boulevard Poissonière. Top international DJs regularly pass through the stylish
Rex, mainly thanks to its reputation and first-
rate sound system. Admission around F60, drinks
reasonable, credit cards accepted, open Wed–Sat
from 11pm. Métro Bonne Nouvelle.

Underworld Café, 25 Rue Oberkampf. Taking their lead from London, a host of club bars are springing up across Paris, and this is one of the liveliest. Free admission, and decent sounds thanks to up-and-coming club DJs using this as a warm-up. Open daily 7pm–2am. Métro Oberkampf.

Restaurants

No other city in Europe has a **range of cuisine** like Paris. It can cost a fortune to enjoy it (especially the local variety) but shop around – the city boasts many long-established cheap haunts, and North African, Chinese and Vietnamese food is almost always reasonably priced. In addition, most half-decent bars will lay on some kind of hot food until the evening. All the places listed below take most credit cards.

The Bowler, 13 Rue d'Artois. English-style pub opened in 1996 with a cricketing theme, curries, roast dinners and the daily papers from Blighty. Métro St-Philippe du Roule.

Chartier, 7 Rue du Faubourg Montmartre. Everyone's favourite cheapie, always packed, always filling. Shared tables. Closes 9.30pm. Métro Rue Montmartre.

Chez Mustapha, 46 Rue Volta. Family-run, friendly couscous restaurant with mystic decor. Métro Arts et Métiers.

Le Gambrinus, 62 Rue des Lombards. Hearty portions of favourite French dishes at reasonable prices, right in the Châtelet area. Open until 6am. Métro Châtelet.

Accommodation

Even in high season (when there isn't much football on, anyway) it isn't difficult finding a reasonably priced room in central Paris. The main **tourist office** at 127 Avenue des Champs-Élysées (open daily 9am–8pm, ☎08/3668 3112) charges a varying commission for reserving a room, depending on the hotel category.

If you're arriving on spec, the area around the Gare du Nord will almost always have something, though it may be a little seedy.

The following hotels all charge around F200–300 for a double room unless stated.

Henri IV, 25 Place Dauphine (☎01/4354 4453). Perennial classic budget lodgings with a fine view on the Île de la Cité. Book at least a month in advance. Most credit cards. Métro Pont-Neuf.

Hôtel des Academies, 15 Rue de la Grande Chaumiére (☎01/4326 6644). Cheap, clean one-star hotel in the Montparnasse area. No credit cards. Métro Vavin.

Hôtel Apollo, 11 Rue de Dunkerque (☎01/4878 0498, fax 01/4285 0878). Opposite the Gare du Nord so perfectly located for Eurostar travellers, this is a cut above the seedier competition nearby but in the same price range, around F400 for a double, F200–300 a single. Most credit cards. Métro Gare du Nord.

Hôtel des Sans Culottes, 27 Rue de Lappe (☎01/4805 4292, fax 01/4357 7739). Ideal for those nights out on the tiles around the Bastille, with bright if functional rooms and its own bistrot downstairs. Singles at F300, doubles F350, including breakfast. Most credit cards. Métro Bastille.

Idéal, 3 Rue des Trois Fréres (☎01/4606 6363, fax 01/4264 9701). Comfortable and friendly joint around Montmartre. No credit cards. Métro Abbesses.

Golden goals and glory – the lifeblood of Lens

The little town of Lens is pitched between the coal-fields and World War I battle-grounds of north-east France. Blood and Gold, *le Sang et Or*, are apt nicknames and shirt colours for home team **Racing Club**, whose Bollaert stadium is a can of concentrated football passion like no other in France. This tiny community hit the motherlode in 1998, when it hosted four World Cup games (including France's 'golden goal' victory over Paraguay) and the local team won their first title.

Highbury high – Nouma gives Arsenal a fright, 2000

After their foundation in 1906, the team were forced to seek a new home by complaints from neighbours, and the mine-owning **Bollaert family** offered them land. Later, in 1932, the firm built the club its stadium.

A couple of top-three placings and cup final defeats were as good as it got over the next decades, and before long the club were going the same way as the coal company that ran them. The local council then bought the Bollaert for a nominal franc, and the mayor, **André Delelis**, set about reviving RCL. First he had the stadium upgraded to host games in the 1984 European Championship, then he set to work with incoming club president Gervais Martel.

Their ten-year programme began with promotion back to the top flight in 1990 and the founding of a new training centre, soon to come under the direction of former player **Daniel Leclerq**. Frédéric Dehu was one of the centre's first products, and he would forge a key midfield understanding with Cameroonian Marc-Vivien Foé. In 1997 Leclerq became coach, and built a balanced, attack-minded team with local lad Tony Vairelles, Montenegrin Anto Drobnjak and Czech Euro '96 star Vladimir Smicer leading the line, while captain Jean-Guy Wallemme kept it all on an even keel.

Sixth at the halfway stage in 1997/98, Lens were soon neck-and-neck with Metz at the top, and remained there until the last round, when a draw at Auxerre was enough to give them the title. That night, Delelis ordered the bars to stay open until dawn.

Despite upcoming **Champions' League** involvement, the team broke up. The new batch barely had time to gel before Arsenal were in town in September 1998, yet RCL were still in with a chance of further progress before Dehu's red card gave Dynamo Kiev the space to win the last group game 3–1 in the Bollaert. The European campaign was an unwelcome distraction, yet Lens recovered to win the **1999 League Cup**, beating northern rivals Metz 1–0 at le Stade de France. This triumph was a passport to the 1999/2000 UEFA Cup, in which Arsenal gained their revenge over the the *Lensois*.

The Bollaert is a short walk from the train station – turn left and keep walking. *Chez Muriel* and *Le Bollaert* in Route de Béthune are two of many bars near the ground. The Tony Marek north stand houses the *Sup 'R' Lens* and *Tigers*, with the *Kop Sang et Or* on the corner with the east Delacourt stand. Away fans are allocated a sector in the lower west (Tranin) stand.

Nantes

Thanks to forward thinking, faith in youth and, ultimately, good football, the sleepy city of Nantes has remained at the forefront of the French game for thirty years.

Its team, *les Canaris*, may not have enjoyed the same kind of resources, fan base or European runs as other brasher, provincial outfits, but the FC Nantes Atlantique training school has continued to produce outstanding talent.

It seldom stays long. Trying to compete with the big boys, with only rare lucrative forays into the later stages of European competition, has entailed a constant flow of major players from the Loire estuary. Of the side that won the club's last French title in 1995, Patrice Loko, Nicolas Ouédec and Reynald Pedros had all found alternative employment within two years.

Nevertheless, Nantes always seem to finish in the top six, picking up a title every five years or so, and three decades of entertaining, top-flight football have made local fans knowledgeable as well as partisan.

The team's entertainers were given the perfect stage in 1984, when a boldly designed new stadium was built in time for the European Championship. The construction of the futuristic Beaujoire, set in parkland on the opposite side of the river Erdre from the training school at La Jonelière, has since firmly established Nantes as part of the fabric of modern French football.

Although comfortable and spacious, and a popular venue for international rugby, the Beaujoire has been under-used by the national football team. It was full to the brim for Platini's hat-trick in France's 5–0 thrashing of Belgium in 1984, but then had to wait more than a decade before the next appearance of *les Bleus*, when David Ginola was the first French name on the scoresheet in a 4–0 win over Slovakia.

Driving the midfield that day were Didier Deschamps and Marcel Desailly, a pair of former Nantes team-mates who first met when they were young lads at the training school. They were the star duo of an exceptional crop of players raised at Nantes, finding their feet not just on the pitch but also on the dancefloor at the city's New Way nightclub.

Like so many others, both would be sold on, to star together in Marseille's European Cup win of 1993, then in victories in the same competition for Milan and Juventus, respectively. Their debt to the old school was repaid by their performances as World Cup winners with France in 1998.

The thrilling fields

 FC Nantes Atlantique

La Beaujoire, Route de Saint-Joseph
Capacity 40,000 (all-seated)
Colours Yellow-and-green striped shirts, yellow shorts
League champions 1965–66, 1973, 1977, 1980, 1983, 1995
Cup winners 1979, 1999–2000

Nantes are the third most successful league team in France, with the most modern-looking stadium and an adventurous youth policy second only to Auxerre's.

This is remarkable considering that they had not tasted top-flight football before 1963. Indeed, Football Club Nantes had been founded only 20 years before, as an amalgamation of five local clubs: Saint-Pierre, Mellenet, Loire, ASO Nantes and Stade Nantes. Straight away they won *le Championnat de l'Ouest* and *la Coupe de l'Ouest*, entering the second division in 1945.

Promotion to the first in 1963 allowed for modernisation of the club's Marcel Saupin stadium, which saw the winning of six league titles beginning in 1965. By the time Nantes had made the European

Nantes essentials

From Nantes-Atlantique **airport**, an hourly TANAIR bus (F38, journey time 25mins) takes you to the railway stop at Gare Sud, then on to the main Place du Commerce in the centre of town.

There are **trains** almost hourly between Nantes and Paris Montparnasse, journey time just over two hours. Of the train station's two exits, Nord gives out to the stop on green tramway line #1. The other tramway, red line #2, crosses at Commerce. Tram **tickets** (F8 each, F32 for a *mini-carnet* of five, F58 for ten) are sold only from machines. The same tickets are also valid on the city's extensive **bus network**. A day ticket (*journalier*) covering everything is F20.

Bus and tram services run 5am–midnight. **Taxis** can usually be found at Commerce, but to phone one, dial *Allo Taxi Nantes Atlantique* on ☎02/4069 2222.

The main **tourist office** is also at Place du Commerce (open Mon–Sat 10am–7pm, ☎02/4020 6000, fax 02/4009 1199). The listings publications *Nantes Poche* and *Nantes des Jours et des Nuits* are distributed here.

Cup-Winners' Cup semi-final in 1980, it was obvious that the Marcel Saupin, now home to youth and reserve-team games, was becoming too cramped.

The first team, quietly but effectively bossed by coach Jean-Claude Suaudeau, had great potential, and the prospect of hosting regular European football, together with the imminent 1984 European Championship, provided a perfect opportunity for stadium architect Berdje Agopyan to try something radical. He certainly achieved it – from above, La Beaujoire looks like a particularly testing Scalextric track, with its curving roofs on either side. Once inside, there is a tremendous sense of light and space.

Eight years after the Beaujoire was built, the club found themselves with debts of F60million. They were rescued by biscuit billionaire Guy Scherrer, who gave Suaudeau the opportunity to build the team up over three years to win the title again in 1995.

Despite revenue from a run to the semi-finals of the Champions' League the following season, another sell-off followed, coupled with more boardroom disputes; Scherrer eventually quit in November 1996.

After a calamitous start to their 1996/97 campaign, Nantes went 30 games unbeaten and, with the goals of Chad international Japhet N'Doram, claimed their now customary place in Europe. The long-serving Suaudeau then handed over the reins to youth coach Reynald Denoueix, who found his mentor's act a hard one to follow. But after a relegation scrap was avoided thanks to Jocelyn Gouvennec's goals in 1997/98, Denoueix took another crop of La Jonelière youngsters to the French Cup final in 1999.

Masterfully skippered by the only survivor of the 1995 title-winning side, Argentine midfielder Nestor Fabbri, and with Olivier Monterrubio a live wire upfront, Nantes were fine upholders of their club's educated footballing tradition. They were also exceptionally lucky. A freak combination of results left them as the only top-flight team in the last eight of the 1998/99 *Coupe de France*. And once in the final itself, they were labouring against the ambitious second-division side Sédan Ardennes, before Frédéric da Rocha conned the referee into awarding them a second-half penalty by diving after failing to reach a Monterrubio cross. The latter converted the spot-kick, after da Rocha had added a feigned injury to his insult, and there would be no more goals.

The promise of Denoueix's side was undeniable, and Europe did not appear too big a stage for their emerging talents. But a 1999/2000 season which had promised so much turned into a battle against relegation, won only on the final day of the season when a Manara Vahirua goal gave Nantes a 1–0 win at already relegated Le Havre. Even another Cup win did little to ease the pain, as Nantes ruined the romantic dreams of amateurs Calais with (another) highly debatable penalty, this time from Alain Caveglia, making them unpopular party poopers at le Stade de France, just as they'd been a year earlier.

In the summer, the decision to sell striker Antoine Sibierski to Lens did little to encourage belief that 2000/01 would be a better year.

Here we go!

Take tramway green line #1 to its **Beaujoire** terminus – allow 15mins from the train station.

Just the ticket

The main **ticket offices** are facing you as you walk from the tramway stop. Sell-outs are rarely a problem. For the neutral, the *Tribune Jules Verne* (named after Nantes' most famous son) is a fine if expensive (F85–95) option.

Away fans are generally placed in the *Virage Océan* (F75). Behind the goals are the *Tribunes Erdre* and *Loire* (both F50). For advance tickets, contact the club on: ☎02/4037 2929, fax 02/4037 2921.

Swift half

Down by the train station you'll find **Les Canaris**, 9 Boulevard de Stalingrad, where a number of Nantes supporters gather before getting the tramway up to the Beaujoire.

On the way to the stadium, near Haluchère tramway stop, there's **le Café de la Gare** on Chemin du Ranzay and **Bar la Beaujoire**, 1 Rue de la Petite Baratte.

Outside the stadium by the main ticket office there's a row of **stand-up bars** selling beer, wine and sausages.

Club merchandise

The club has a **new shop** in the centre of town at 7 Rue des Halles (open Mon 2–7pm, Tue–Sat 10am–7pm). On matchdays, on the concourse by the ticket offices, you'll find two yellow vans marked **Allez Nantes**, selling souvenirs.

Ultra culture

The 1995 title win motivated the **Young Boys** in the *Tribune Loire* into noisy action. **Yellow Flight 49** in the *Tribune Erdre* produce their own fanzine, *L'Envol Jaune*. The mainstream Nantes supporters' club, **Allez Nantes Canaris**, was founded in 1945 and speaks for the older generation.

In print

Sportmania, the club's official publication, has been scaled down to a foldover job in the sports pages of the local paper **Presse-Océan** two days before the game; it's then distributed free around the ground on matchdays.

In the net

There's no official site but an exceptionally capable unofficial offering is at: www.fcnantes.com. As well as match reports and news, there's information galore on the club, its history and stadium. Well worth brushing up on your French for.

Embarrassment – Nantes and Calais captains lift the *Coupe*, 2000

Eat, drink, sleep…

Bars and clubs

There is a large concentration of **bars** around la Place du Commerce, but few are particularly inspiring. Locals prefer the old Quartier du Bouffay nearby – easily reached via its own tramway stop.

La Belle Équipe, 10 Quai de la Jonelière. Fine sports bar with a terrace looking out onto the river Erdre near the FCNA training centre. Run by ex-Nantes player Vincent Brascigliano. Full menu. Closed Mondays and Sunday and Tuesday evenings. Bus #51 from Médiathèque, or a pleasant walk from red tramway stop Recteur Schmitt.

La Maison, 4 Rue Lebrun. Immensely successful bar/club playing modern dance music, formerly the *Black Mint* rave club before the local council revoked its licence. Spacious house and garden with a collection of gnomes. Open 3pm–2am Tue–Sat. Bus #21 or #23 to Place Foch.

Le Quai West, 3 Quai François Mitterrand. Large multi-purpose riverside venue owned by ex-FCNA player Jean-Michel Ferri, with a large bar and disco. Open Wed–Sat from 10pm until early.

Le Virgil, 33 Rue de Verdun. Centrally located bar owned by Marcel Desailly, whose picture (in Milan colours, mind) greets the visitor. Three TV sets plus a further huge screen for Canal Plus broadcasts. Short walk from the castle.

Restaurants

Fish and seafood are the main **local delicacies** in Nantes, but you'll also find plentiful Chinese, Vietnamese and African eateries.

La Cigale, 4 Place Graslin. Elegant brasserie inaugurated on April Fools' Day 1895. Specialities include oysters, *fruits de mer* and a variety of fish prepared according to local tradition, but it's the fin-de-siècle decor that grabs the attention. Kitchen stays open until midnight daily. Bus #11 or #24.

Le Djerba, 3 Rue Lekain. Amiable diner offering North African dishes, including couscous at under F65. Near Place Graslin on the #24, #51, #54 and #55 bus routes.

L'Étoile d'Orient, 3 Rue Maréchal de Lattre de Tassigny. Friendly two-floor Vietnamese restaurant with cheap menu deals. Green tramway to Médiathèque.

La Poissonerie, 4 Rue Léon-Maître. Seafood delights at reasonable prices. Considering the quality of the food, the lunchtime menu at F70 cannot be bettered. Green tramway to Bouffay.

Accommodation

For a sleepy French town of less than half a million people, Nantes has a decent number of cheap rooms. A list is available at the **tourist office** in Place du Commerce.

Beaujoire Hôtel, 15 Rue des Pays de Loire (☎02/4093 0001). Two-star hotel by the stadium, cheaper and more modest than the *Otelinn* below. Visiting teams generally stay here when necessary. Most major credit cards. Green tramway to Beaujoire.

Hôtel de l'Océan, 11 Rue du Maréchal de Lattre de Tassigny (☎02/4069 7351). Clean one-star hotel as cheap as you'll find anywhere in town. Green tramway to Médiathèque.

Hôtel Duquesne, 12 Allée Duquesne, Cours des 50 Otages (☎02/4047 5724). A family-run hotel offering affordable luxury, with quiet rooms in the centre of town at around F250 a double. Canal Plus in every room. Red tramway to 50 Otages.

Otelinn, 45 Boulevard des Batignolles (☎02/4050 0707, fax 02/4049 4140). Two-star business hotel/restaurant by the Beaujoire stadium. Sixty rooms, each with a Minitel point and Canal Plus. Most major credit cards. Green tramway to Beaujoire.

Turning second into first – Olympique Lyonnais

France's second city is not one steeped in football tradition. But **Olympique Lyonnais**, not founded until 1950, are not letting this stand in their way. With media money behind them, OL have big plans for the new decade, including their own TV station, business sectors around their **Gerland stadium** and European success. But first, they need to keep their healthy 20,000-plus average gate happy.

Older fans look back fondly on OL's golden days in the Sixties, when a young team featuring goalkeeper Marcel Aubour, defender Jean Djorkaeff (Youri's father) and forward Nestor Combin, all members of **France's 1966 World Cup team**, twice won the French cup and missed a Cup-Winners' Cup final appearance on a play-off in 1964. The star was inside-forward Fleury di Nallo, *le Petit Prince*,

Best hand forward – top scorer Anderson

whose talents sadly came to maturity when both club and country had begun a footballing decline. Di Nallo was still playing when OL won the cup for the last time in 1973, in a team also starring **Bernard Lacombe**, who a decade before had been standing on the platform at Lyon Part-Dieu station to welcome home the winning team.

Though the club festered in the second division for much of the Eighties, young talent from its training centre began to flourish, including **Rémi Garde** and **Florian Maurice**. With old boy Jean Tigana in the dugout, and a team featuring Abedi Pelé and Alain Caveglia, Lyon finished runners-up in the first division in 1995.

OL didn't have the punch for a title push, but with Lacombe replacing Tigana as coach, they starred in a series of spectacular wins away from home in European competition, the most notable being a 2–1 win in Milan over Inter, and a 4–3 victory in Bruges that got them into the UEFA Cup quarter-finals in 1999. By now the club had lost Maurice, but gained three key new players: Vikash Dhorasoo from Le Havre, and Stéphane Malbranque and Frédéric Kanouté, both formed at the club.

Bologna halted Lyon's European progress, but a **third-place finish** at home was good enough for a first crack at the Champions' League. The team flunked this chance, losing to Maribor of Slovenia home and away, but the club's deal with *Pathé* – who own part of BSkyB and Canal Plus – brought the French record signing of **Sonny Anderson** from Barcelona, and his top-scoring display in 1999/2000 gave OL another third-place finish, and the opportunity to make up for their earlier aberration.

The Stade Gerland is in an industrial zone south of the centre, connected by bus #18 from metro Jean Macé or #32 from Perrache station. Once there, you've little choice of bars – *Le Stadium* at Rue de Gerland 202 is as good as any. The *Virage Nord* (F40–60) is home to the *Bad Gones OL* fans, the Jean-Boulin stand alongside the pitch (F70–100) the best for visiting neutrals. Depending on their numbers, away fans are generally placed in a section in the *Virage Sud*.

Bordeaux

Tough at the top – Valéncia were among the teams to expose the Girondins' frailties in 2000

Bordeaux is a city of immediate contrasts. Guidebooks indicate a quiet, *bourgeois* rugby-playing wine town, but your nose quickly guides you to fading riverside bars where the talk is all football.

Lying between the quaint farmhouse territory of the Dordogne and the political powderkeg of the Basque country, Bordeaux has known several spells of soccer fever. There was one in the spring of 1996, when its club, the Girondins, capped an epic 20-game run from the Intertoto Cup by reaching the UEFA Cup final. Defender Bixente Lizarazu celebrated victories at the Parc Lescure by parading the Basque flag; ten years before, he'd been singing with the ultras in the Parc's *Virage Sud*. The local paper, *Sud Ouest*, sold three times more copies after Bordeaux's win over Milan than it did after the death of François Mitterand.

Three years later came an even greater prize, and even greater adulation. Pascal Feiduono's stoppage-time winner in Paris on the last day of the season brought the French title to Bordeaux for the first time

in 12 years – a richly deserved accolade for a team whose footballing attitude was at times recklessly adventurous. The club's Parc Lescure home, a listed building that was given a F50million spruce-up for the 1998 World Cup but saw few goals that summer, had now thrilled to the sight of strikers Sylvain Wiltord and Lilian Laslandes helping the Girondins to an average of more than two goals a game.

As the sole soccer representatives of south-west France, the Girondins have always received official favour from regional government. In the Eighties, millionaire businessman Claude Bez made use of these connections to revive the club – but his under-the-counter deals were to cost everyone dear.

Now a takeover by the giant *CLT–UFA* media conglomerate promises bigger and more legitimate funding, over a seven-year period, to place Bordeaux firmly among the European elite. Watch out for those marine blue shirts and white chevrons – they're going places.

The thrilling fields

 Girondins de Bordeaux

Parc Lescure, 347 Boulevard Wilson
Capacity 36,500 (all-seated)
Colours All marine blue with white chevron
League champions 1950, 1984–85, 1987, 1999
Cup winners 1941, 1986–87

Sixty years spanned the Parc Lescure's opening and its renovation for the 1998 World Cup. In 1938, the stadium had the feel of a grand ocean liner, embellished with a vast concrete arch, a pseudo-classical courtyard and two Olympic towers – but it lacked a football team. For all but 15 of those years, the Lescure served rugby and cycling fans, with football as a side issue. It stood unused for the 1984 European Championship, even though the Girondins had by then acquired an ambitious club president and a star-studded side which, with Jean Tigana, Alain Giresse, Marius Trésor, Patrick Battiston and Bernard Lacombe, had just won the French title under eventual national-team coach Aimé Jacquet.

Club president Claude Bez revamped the Lescure in 1986, nearly doubling its capacity with the removal of the cycle track. European success was surely only just around the corner; in the previous year, 2–0 up after the first leg, Bordeaux had lost 3–0 to Juventus in the European Cup semi-finals (and thus missed out on a date with Liverpool at Heysel). Two years later they lost to Lokomotiv Leipzig on penalties in a Cup-Winners' Cup semi-final.

In anticipation of further progress, Bez made two significant business deals: one, with Canal Plus TV, was tied in with European coverage; the other was the building of an impressive team headquarters in a château, out of town at Le Haillan. The potential gains of the TV contract would inspire Bez's great rival, Bernard Tapie, to bigger things at Marseille; the second deal would prove Bez's undoing, involving as it did the opening of secret bank accounts and the misuse of public money.

By the time his various frauds had been uncovered, Bez was too ill to stand trial. But the club could not escape unpunished. The Girondins were forcibly relegated in 1991, and though they quickly bounced back, they were saddled with a F25million debt bequeathed to them by Bez.

Enter another megalomaniac president, Alain Afflelou. Keen to extract support from the region's wealthy winemakers, he turned the team's shirts from marine blue to claret red. The vineyards didn't want to know. The ultras weren't happy either, as their patch in the *Virage Sud* became all-seated for the 1998 World Cup.

Bordeaux essentials

Buses between the city's Mérignac **airport** and Saint-Jean **train station** run every 45 minutes and cost F35. Trains run hourly between Paris and Bordeaux, taking around three hours.

From Saint-Jean, bus #7 or #8 will take you to Place Gambetta in town, while bus #1 runs along the waterfront to the Esplanade des Quinconces. **Bus tickets**, available onboard for F7.50 and valid for 30mins, also come in *carnets* of ten (F54.50) from *tabacs*. A day ticket is F22. There are no night buses.

You should find a **taxi** around Quinconces. If not, phone *Taxi Blues* (☎05/5651 3994) or *Sud Ouest Taxi* (☎05/5639 7030).

The main **tourist office** is at 12 Cours du XXX-juillet (open Mon–Sat 9am–8pm, Sun 9am–7pm, ☎05/5600 6600). Here you'll find a free copy of the fine fortnightly listings publication, *Clubs et Concerts*. **Maori's Techno Shop**, 30 Rue de la Devise, off central Place St Pierre, is the best source of club and DJ info.

All parties, not least the players, were surprised by the 1995/96 UEFA Cup run. Only 3,000 turned up to watch Bordeaux beat Vardar Skopje in the UEFA Cup first round in September 1995. By December there were 18,000 to see Real Betis vanquished in the third round. A 2–0 defeat at AC Milan in the quarter-final first leg appeared to signal the end of the road. It was anything but – the Girondins' 3–0 win in the return was voted 1996 match of the year by *France Football*, and would earn transfers to Italy for Zinedine Zidane and Christophe Dugarry.

Could Bordeaux repeat the feat against Bayern Munich in the final? Alas, they could not – and, despite a city's devotion, the club wasn't big enough to keep its stars; Afflelou followed them out of the door in the summer of 1996.

While many expected the club's fortunes to wane, the goalscoring of summer signing Jean-Pierre Papin and the quick maturity of young international Ibrahim Ba kept Bordeaux in the top six in 1996/97, and the latter's big-money move to Milan gave a new regime some financial room for manoeuvre. Incoming coach Elie Baup had the forward duo of Laslandes and ain Wiltord at his disposal, as well as a talented midfield including Johan Micoud and, a little later, Ali Benarbia.

The 1997/98 season was full of near misses – a European exit to a last-minute Aston Villa goal, a League Cup final lost on penalties to Paris Saint-Germain. Revenge was to follow, however, when the Girondins beat PSG 3–1 in the first game of the 1998/99 season. Baup's team were soon knocked out of both domestic cups, allowing them to concentrate on the league – in January they whipped Marseille, their nearest rivals for the championship, 4–1 at Parc Lescure.

Like Marseille, Bordeaux would fall to eventual winners Parma in the UEFA Cup. But with Wiltord and Laslandes now the leading two scorers in the French league, the club was closing in on the title. The same night in early May that the Girondins

were digging deep to overturn a 2–1 losing scoreline at Lens to win 4–2, Marseille fell 2–1 at PSG. That left the Girondins a point clear at the top – a margin that would be maintained by Feiduono's late, late winner in Paris, and celebrated across south-west France with feeling.

Alas, with the title in the bag, the club failed to make the necessary investments to mount a serious challenge in Europe. Bordeaux managed to get into the second group phase but were unable to compete with Manchester United and Valencia – although a win at Fiorentina in their final match restored morale.

At home the Girondins finished fourth in 1999/2000, missing out on another crack at the Champions' League. Promising midfield playmaker Johan Micoud was sold to Parma and replaced by Belgian battler Marc Wilmots. With Wiltord also likely to leave, the title-winning squad was beginning to disintegrate, and with it the optimism it had prompted.

Here we go!

Take bus #9 from Saint-Jean station to **Stade Municipal**, or bus #12 or #93 to **Barrière d'Ornano** from Pey Berland in town.

Just the ticket

The two main **ticket offices** are near the corner of Boulevard Leclerc and Rue Albert Thomas, under the giant hoop. Neutrals will find themselves in the *Virage Nord* (F45–55) in blocks H–L, segregated from both home and visiting support. Blocks A–G and S–M are dearer seats (F60–200) in the *tribunes latéralles* along the touchline.

For **advance tickets**, recommended for games against Marseille and PSG, contact the club on: ☎05/5616 1111, fax 05/5657 5446.

Swift half

The *buvettes* at the ground sell only **alcohol-free** beer. The best bet just outside is *Le Rond de Point*, on the corner of Avenue du Parc de Lescure and Boulevard Maréchal Leclerc. Its bar is lined with pennants from various European campaigns, the scores lovingly written above the names of each team. A better bar, though, is *le*

Bar des Sports, 5mins away on the corner of Boulevard Leclerc and Rue Léo Saignat. On offer here are couscous, paella, Amstel beer, darts and football talk until match time.

Club merchandise

There's no shop at the stadium or in town, but a new outlet has opened at the club **headquarters** at Le Haillan – this is some way out of town, but accessible by bus #18 from Jean-Jaurès. You'll find souvenir stalls set out around the Lescure on matchdays.

Ultra culture

The European Cup semi-final with Juventus in 1985 was Bordeaux fans' first encounter with ultra culture. A supporters' group was soon formed, **Collectif Club Ultramarines**, in the traditional home end, the *Virage Sud*, followed by a breakaway group, the **Blue Devils**. Alain Afflelou's changing of the club colours from marine blue to claret red provoked a storm of protest in the *Virage Sud*, and the two groups merged in 1995 to create the **Collectif Virage Sud**, co-ordinating displays and away trips.

In print

Le Scapulaire (F20) is a 32-page colour magazine published by the club for home games. The monthly **Foot Gironde** (also F20) is an independent colour monthly which also covers the quaint football scene in the Aquitaine region.

In the net

The club's **official website** is very smart, with an understated design typical of the French attitude to online publishing. Much of the content is replicated in English, and there's an e-commerce section on the way, at: www.girondins.com.

Also worth a browse is **Girondins Online** at: stuwww.kub.nl/people/rxb/bdx/.

More than a local hero – Sylvain Wiltord

on expensive vineyard excursions. The bars around Place de la Victoire, Cours de la Somme and Rue de Candale are hangouts for young *Bordelais*, while the Quai de Paludate may turn up something less mainstream. For six months of the year, the terraces around the neoclassical centre of town are humming with tourists, but with luck you can wade through the tack and pick up on Bordeaux's music scene.

La Chuchumbe, 6 Rue Causserouge. Named after an old Afro-Cuban dance, a salsa dance club with cocktails, cigars and a wild party atmosphere when it gets going. Centrally located.

Le France, 4 Cours de Verdun. Three-floor bar/restaurant with a giant screen for Bordeaux and French international matches, and special menus. Open Mon–Sat 7am–2am.

Eat, drink, sleep…

Bars and clubs

Bordeaux has a **lively nightlife**, generally unaffected by the visitors who come here

Le Gaulois, 5 Place de la Victoire. Named after a famous – if unattractive – cocktail of beer, Martini and blue curaçao, this is a decent, central spot to watch the game on large screens.

Le Jean Bart, Avenue de la République/Rue de la Liberté. The main football bar in town, done out in club colours, with a huge screen, music, dancing girls and meal deals. Open until 9pm, later on Bordeaux matchdays.

Lollapalooza, 48/49 Quai de Paludate. Large club playing acid jazz and other danceable solutions. Plus point: free entry. Minus point: over-vigilant bouncers. Bus #1.

Nulle Parts Ailleurs, 19 Cours du Maréchal Foch. Belonging to Bordeaux star Christophe Dugarry, this large, pleasant bar behind Quinconces is a hangout for the local sports community.

Restaurants

Bordeaux has a rich **variety of food** on offer, largely on account of its proximity to Spain and the Basque country. Local fish and seafood dishes are well worth trying. The cheapest joints are down in the area by Saint-Jean train station, but life here can get a little seedy after dark.

Café des Arts, 138 Cours Victor Hugo. The big meeting place in town – an institution ever since its inauguration in 1933. *Plats du jour* at F43, with house specialities of rabbit and *coq au vin*. Most credit cards. Bus #3, #4, #5 or #6.

Casa Sansa, 21 Rue Maucoudinat. With all the usual trimmings – huge hocks of ham hanging from the ceiling – this is a decent Spanish restaurant specialising in Catalan dishes. Two-course *menus* begin at F48. Off Cours d'Alsace. Bus #3, #4, #5 or #6.

Chez Georges, 53 Rue des Faures. Cheapest in town for local cuisine, with soup, a main course and a glass of wine for under F45. The decor matches the profit margin. Between Saint-Michel and Cours Victor Hugo. Bus #3, #4, #5 or #6.

Etchecopar, 351 Avenue du Maréchal de Lattre de Tassigny à Caudéran. Large portions of Basque cuisine and a range of *prix fixe* menu options starting at F59. Closed Saturdays, kitchen closes at 2pm and 10pm. Bus #18 past Parc Bordelais.

Accommodation

The best part of town for **cheap rooms** is opposite Saint-Jean train station. Although guidebooks warn people away from this red light area, the hotels are generally safe, clean and friendly. The small **tourist office**, located to the right of the main entrance at Saint-Jean (open Mon–Sat 9am–midday & 1–7pm, Sun 10am–midday & 12.45–6pm, ☎05/5691 6470), can provide hotel information, as can the main office at 12 Cours du XXX-juillet.

Bristol, 4 Rue Bouffard (☎05/5681 8501, fax 05/5651 2406). Every European city has a *Hotel Bristol*. This is Bordeaux's, and it's the cheapest place in town with Canal Plus. Cheapest rooms at F175–230. Most credit cards. Near Place Gambetta. Bus #19, #20 or #21.

De la Boëtie, 4 Rue de la Boëtie (☎05/5681 7668, fax 05/5681 2472). Near the Mairie, a smart but still reasonably priced place whose satellite dish can pick up a host of foreign TV channels. Visa and Mastercard accepted. Bus #26.

Dijon, 22 Rue Charles-Domercq (☎05/5991 7665). A low-budget but perfectly reasonable hotel opposite Saint-Jean station, with optional shower facilities and a bar downstairs. Most credit cards.

Maison des Étudiants, 50 Rue Ligier (☎05/5696 4830). Just west of the Spanish quarter, this student hostel is open for guests of both sexes from July to September (allowing you to catch the first month of the French football season), otherwise it's women only. Bus #7 or #8 from the station to Cours de la Libération.

The royal command performers – AS Monaco

Europe's **smallest country** is home to the most consistently successful yet unpopular team in French football. Monaco is a cliff-top principality overlooking the Côte d'Azur, a 3km-square piece of prize real estate whose banks, casinos and hotels form the familiar backdrop for the annual *Grand Prix*. Of its 30,000 population, only one in five possesses Monaco citizenship, and few care about the local football team.

Title smile – John Arne Riise celebrates a goal

Champions of France for the seventh time in 2000, AS Monaco receive an annual F50million subsidy from the national council, whose president, Jean-Louis Campora, holds the same position at the football club. The money invested in the club is seen as good for the principality's image, and the 18,000-capacity Louis II stadium is one of France's finest.

The team's most famous supporter is **Prince Albert**, and the whole royal family, along with other tax-exile regulars like Boris Becker, turn out for big occasions such as the UEFA Cup run in 1997, which saw Monaco beat Newcastle before going out to Inter Milan in the semi-finals.

The club were founded in 1924, turning professional after World War II and making the top flight in 1953. Prince Rainier poured in enough money for Monaco to strike a winning formula in the early Sixties, with a team that starred future French national-team coach **Michel Hidalgo**. The red-and-whites won the league and cup twice each, then had to wait twenty years before two of the stars of Hidalgo's national team, Manuel Amoros and Bruno Bellone, helped them to a third title in 1982.

The arrival of a young **Arsène Wenger** as coach from Nancy and of Glenn Hoddle and Mark Hateley from England prompted perhaps the club's finest season in 1987/88. Wenger's team was brash and adventurous, with Hoddle in midfield playing the best football of his career. Wenger would stay at Monaco for seven seasons, taking the club to a Cup-Winners' Cup final in 1992.

Jean Tigana took over as coach in 1995/96, when Brazilian Sonny Anderson became the league's top scorer, and an 18-year-old **Thierry Henry** its best newcomer. Tigana's team won the league a year later, and another young sensation, striker **David Trezeguet**, replaced the Barcelona-bound Anderson for the subsequent Champions' League run, past Manchester United, to a semi-final defeat by Juventus.

In 1999/2000, with new signing **Marco Simone** forming a lethal strike partnership with Trezeguet and Marcelo Gallardo and Ludovic Giuly providing the ammunition, Monaco raced to another title. But Trezeguet was tempted away by Juventus after Euro 2000, while 'keeper Barthez, who had clashed with coach Claude Puel throughout the season, left for Manchester United.

Buses #4 and #5 run the short distance from **Monaco train station** to the stadium. Once there, the *Bar L'Équipe*, behind the uncovered Cap D'Ail away end (gates G and H), at 11 Avenue du 3 Septembre, is a favourite. The home end is the *Pesages* behind the Le Rocher goal.

Marseille

Olympique de Marseille 200
SC Endoume 204

The only football club to hold France in its grip, Olympique Marseille are as essential to this bubbling, maritime melting-pot of a city as fish to the local *bouillabaisse* stew. Halfway between Barcelona and Genoa as the firework flies, Marseille enjoys as much excess, colour and passion as any football city in Spain or Italy.

Unfortunately, it also suffers as much corruption. The shadow of one man still darkens those rose sunsets over the hills of Provence – Bernard Tapie. A former club president, boss of *Adidas* and socialist MP, among other things, Tapie used secret bank accounts, shady political connections and a small fortune fraudulently diverted from his business empire to push *l'OM* to four league titles, and a European Cup in 1993. The result was two years in jail for Tapie, and ignominy for the club.

The team's remarkable comeback from second-division football to a runners-up spot in both the UEFA Cup and the French league in 1999 was as much due to its fantastic popular support as to the business expertise of current owner Robert Louis-Drefyus. At a time when so many French cities are becoming increasingly divided by racial tension, Marseille's many ethnic divisions are held together by this one club, the country's most titled team – and the fans' unity is the most potent weapon in the team's contemporary armoury.

The south-east corner of France has always been a small footballing enclave in the morass of rugby south of France's Massif Central. In the first 28 editions of the French cup, from its introduction after World War I to the end of World War II, *l'OM* won six. To accommodate the crowds inspired by this success, and to coincide with France's hosting of the 1938 World Cup, the city's Stade Vélodrome was built. This intimidating arena has since seen some of football's greatest moments, from the Italy–Brazil World Cup semi-final of 1938, to the France–Portugal European Championship semi of 1984, which nearly cost

the BBC's John Motson his voice. Converted to a 60,000 all-seater for France '98, the Vélodrome welcomed more than 35,000 season-ticket holders prior to the start of the 1998/99 campaign – a French record. Olympique Marseille's European nights here are as much about festival as football, the local crowd celebrating in a way the French public normally sees only secondhand on Italian or Spanish TV.

Football has always been part of the city's street culture, in the town and back into the hills beyond. Eric Cantona learned his chops with his brothers on the high plain of Les Caillols, Jean Tigana at Grandes Bastides nearby. That *l'OM* had to buy both stars from other teams says much about the way the club used to be run.

The centenary year of 1999 was the team's most successful since the Tapie era, but that success was achieved with a squad full of big-name signings – and when they fell out of favour a year later, Marseille were almost relegated again. A team based on home-produced stars from the newly built training centre behind the Vélodrome is the next logical step.

The thrilling fields

Olympique Marseille

Stade Vélodrome, Boulevard Michelet
Capacity 60,000 (all-seated)
Colours All white with sky-blue trim
League champions 1937, 1948, 1971–72, 1989–92
Cup winners 1924, 1926–27, 1935, 1938, 1943, 1969, 1972, 1976, 1989
European Cup winners 1993

Their motto may be *Droit au But* ('straight for goal'), but Olympique Marseille's path to success, like that of true love, has rarely run straight at all. On the contrary, the club's recent history is strewn with controversy, honour and disgrace, in about equal measure.

The club have always been first to the ball, competing in the first French cup, the first national amateur championship, and the first professional league. In those pre-war days, fans crammed into the modest Huveaune stadium until, with France's hosting of the 1938 World Cup, a new arena was built nearby. However, the Stade Vélodrome, with the bright cycling track that gave the ground its name, saw little postwar glory until Marcel Leclerc took over the club in 1965.

Leclerc revamped both the club and their stadium, brought in stars from the 1970 World Cup like Brazil's Jairzinho, and led *l'OM* to a league and cup double in 1972. It wasn't to last. By 1980 Marseille were nearly bankrupt and, worse, relegated.

Inspired by both Leclerc and by Claude Bez at Bordeaux, in 1985 new club president Bernard Tapie began the multi-million franc rollercoaster ride that scaled heights and plunged depths never before experienced in French football. Amid all the fireworks of four league titles and three epic European runs, Tapie was near deified. But one prize still eluded him, and the French nation: the European Cup.

Between Marseille and the trophy lay the weight of history. A sleight of hand (an unpunished penalty-box handball by Benfica's Vata) cost them the 1990 semi-final. A sleight of foot (Red Star Belgrade uncharacteristically playing for penalties) cost them the 1991 final. Each time, Tapie swept out one load of stars for another. Jean-Pierre Papin came and went, as did Chris Waddle – *'Waddle Reviens!'* graffiti was daubed over the stadium, begging him to return. Eventually, in the 1993 final, Tapie's Marseille faced Berlusconi's Milan and squeaked it, 1–0. The city erupted.

Only 24 hours later, news broke that the team's previous league match against Valenciennes had been fixed. The scandal dragged on for three years, in the courts and through every newspaper in the land. Tapie's dozens of corrupt dealings, using a whole network of agents and middlemen, came to light. Doubt was cast on other European results, against AEK Athens in 1989, Spartak Moscow in 1991 and Club Bruges in 1993.

Poised to go off – sparklers light up the sky but the Vélodrome still suffers from violence

Marseille essentials

There are **12 trains a day** from Paris to Marseille. The main train station, Gare Saint-Charles, is walking distance from the centre of town and the Vieux Port, and is also the hub of the city's transport system. **Airport buses** (F46) leave every 20mins for the 25-minute journey to Saint-Charles, and the city's two *métro* lines, blue (#1) and red (#2), cross there. Buses and the *métro* run only until 9pm, after which *Fluobuses* run every 15mins until 12.30am. Tickets for all cost F8 (F25 for a day ticket, F41 for a *carnet* of six singles) and are valid for any one journey up to 70mins.

A solitary **tram line** runs from Noailles to Saint-Pierre. For a **taxi**, call either *Tupp Taxis* (☎04/9105 8080) or *Eurotaxis* (☎04/9105 3198).

The **tourist office** is on the city's main drag at La Canebière 4 (open daily July–Sept 8.30am–8pm; Oct–June Mon–Sat 9am–7pm, Sun 10am–5pm; ☎04/9113 8900). The office can book accommodation and provide you with the area's weekly listings brochures, *Semaine des Spectacles* and *L'Officiel des Loisirs*.

For more lively listings information, the *Virgin Megastore* at 75 Rue Saint-Ferréol has a noticeboard with concert information and flyers, and copies of the free weekly listings paper, *Taktik*, which appears on Wednesdays.

Yet, in the recession-hit port, many *Marseillais* blamed Paris for plotting his downfall. Even after he'd almost dragged the club down with him, Tapie remained a popular figure in Marseille, and former Vélodrome stars such as Alen Bokšić came to visit him in jail.

Stripped of the 1993 league title and of the right to defend their European one, Marseille were relegated and eventually placed in receivership. Insolvency denied the club a rightful place in the first division in 1995, but they at last claimed promotion a year later, thanks to the help of top goalscorer Tony Cascarino.

The next stage of the club's renaissance was then plotted at a secret meeting at the *Hotel Costes* in February 1997 between Marseille's new president, Adidas chief Robert Louis-Dreyfus, and the team's new coach, Rolland Courbis. With the club now formed as a limited company and receiving hefty backing from the president's company, Courbis bought stars Fabrizio Ravanelli and Laurent Blanc to challenge for the league title in 1997/98. And although the side's form fell away in the spring, post-World Cup euphoria allowed the coach to invest heavily in the transfer market again, this time picking up French internationals Christophe Dugarry and

Robert Pires for the upcoming domestic and European campaign.

It was to prove a fiery one. After pipping southern rivals Monaco over a bitter two legs in the UEFA Cup third round, the players were involved in a brawl in the tunnel after Laurent Blanc's late penalty equaliser in the semi-final in Bologna. Lacking four key players through suspension, including Dugarry and Ravanelli, *l'OM* fell in their bid to become the first French team to win the UEFA Cup, losing 3–0 to Parma in Moscow.

At home, they ran Bordeaux neck-and-neck for the French title, but lost a crucial game with PSG, 2–1 in Paris – a defeat which signalled not just the end of Marseille's championship challenge, but street battles between the team's travelling support and local police.

Marseille's centenary season should have been one big celebration, but almost became a wake. The team avoided a return to second-division football only on the last day of the season and only on goal difference. Courbis was sacked in March, after the pre-season sale of Blanc to Inter Milan and the mid-season exits of Dugarry and Ravanelli had robbed him of his best players. The club's Champions' League campaign, brightened initially by a home win over Manchester United, ended in disgrace as a shambolic and demoralised team were crushed 5–1 by Lazio in Rome.

With Louis-Dreyfus' honeymoon period clearly over, the president put his faith in Brazilian coach Abel Braga to turn the club around. Robert Pires wasn't impressed and left for Arsenal. With almost a dozen new players brought in during the close season, it was anyone's guess what lay around the corner. But one thing was for sure – it wouldn't be dull.

Here we go!

Take red *métro* line #2 to **Rond Pont du Prado**, leaving by the Boulevard Michelet exit. The Vélodrome will be directly in front of you.

Just the ticket

Although the Vélodrome comfortably holds 60,000 (the biggest in France after le Grand Stade), buying tickets a few days in advance is advised. Central outlets include *l'OM Café* (ticket sales daily 10.30am–6.30pm) at 3 Quai des Belges in the Old Port; at the five *Virgin Megastores* in France including Paris (52 Avenue des Champs-Élysées, métro Franklin D Roosevelt) and Marseille, 75 Rue Saint-Ferréol; the *Musée Boutique* at the eastern end of the Jean Bouin stand at the Vélodrome; and the *Billetterie Ganay*, Rue Raymond Teissere, on the opposite side of the stadium, by the Sainte Marguerite-Dromel métro.

The best seats (F200) are in the Jean Bouin stand nearest Boulevard Michelet, with visiting neutrals best-placed in the facing Ganay stand (F100–150). *L'OM* ultras are to be found in both north (Ray-Grassi) and south (Chevalier-Roze) stands, the most vociferous in the latter. Depending on their numbers, away fans are allocated a section in the Ganay or the north stand, underneath the huge radio tower. For further details, contact the club office on ☎04/9171 4700.

Swift half

No alcohol is on sale in the Vélodrome. The best bars are either side of the Rond Point du Prado and the stadium. *Octopussy*, 231 Avenue du Prado, boasts football souvenirs, old pictures of the city and a good lunch, credit cards accepted.

The *Brasserie Michelet*, 123 Boulevard Michelet, is a perfect pre-match spot down the main road the other side of the stadium, with a large bar, a terrace and plenty of football talk.

Club merchandise

There are a handful of official club shops around town, not to mention dozens of unofficial ones. At the stadium, the *Musée-Boutique* at the east end of the Jean Bouin stand has a whole range of sports gear to complement the souvenirs, plus many other items that are strictly for display only, including Chris Waddle's shirt and a squeezed empty packet of *Belga* cigarettes, courtesy of former coach Raymond Goethals.

Ultra culture

No fan culture in France comes close to this. After territorial disputes during the Vélodrome's pre-World Cup conversion of 1997, the club's various fan groups have clearly marked patches at either end of the ground, the more numerous **Ultras** and **South Winners** in the south side, the **Yankees** and **CCS** in the north.

Each ultra group has its own home bar, some out of town. The *Club des Ultras*, opposite the Vélodrome at 46 Boulevard Michelet, run a small shop, *Le Magasin Virage Sud*.

In print

Droit Au But (F25) is the club's monthly magazine, available from newsstands around the city. A free four-page hand-out has team news on matchdays. There is a general mistrust of any Parisian media, so to earn kudos with your barman, read *Le Provençal* – particularly its Monday sports supplement – over your morning *pastis*.

In the net

Marseille's web presence dwarfs that of any other French club. The **official site** is every bit as smart as you'd expect, with extensive news, history and e-commerce sections, and English areas on the way, at: www.olympiquedemarseille.com.

You'll find an excellent English-language fan site at: www.babasse.com/marseille; and an appealing French 'online newspaper' at: www.multimania.com/nicastro/om.html.

Two for the road – Ravanelli and Pires taunt United

Groundhopping

🔵 SC Endoume

Stade Luminy, Rue Henri Cochet
Capacity 5,000
Colours Red shirts, black shorts

Now firmly tucked away in group E of the *CFA 2* and at the modest Stade Luminy at

the far end of town past the Stade Vélodrome, SC Endoume seem doomed to be forever trailing leagues behind their more famous neighbours. The clubs' paths rarely cross and when they did, for a cup game in 1996, even the Endoume coach seemed reluctant to halt another OM cup run.

The club's finest hour came with a cup win over Cannes, four divisions above, in 1988, and three years later, the red-and-blacks stood 90 minutes away from second-division football. But the 15,000 who had turned up to see the last game of that season against promotion rivals Grenoble at the Stade Vélodrome left disappointed, and in 1999 Endoume even fell out of the *CFA1*, France's fourth division, into the fifth (*CFA 2*).

To see Endoume climb their way back, take **bus #21 or 47** from the Rond-Point du Prado seven stops to Michelet Bonneaude. Match tickets, from the hut by the only bar anywhere near, are F40.

Eat, drink, sleep…

Bars and clubs

Bars in Marseille are far more **down-to-earth** than their Parisian counterparts. During the day, take your pastis and water at any terrace bar down by the Old Port. At night, hit La Pleine, the nickname for Place Jean Jaurès and surrounding sidestreets. In clubs, rap, raga and reggae are the order of the day, mixed with a little techno and African sounds.

Bar des Allées, 45 Allée Léon Gambatta. Base for the Marseille fan club, where away trips are organised for any of the 6,000 members. Fortunately there is a long counter, plenty of bar space and a terrace. Ideal spot for catching a game on TV. Between Saint-Charles and Réformés-Canebière *métro* stops.

Bar Les Flots Bleus, 82 Corniche Kennedy. The most picturesque footie bar in all Marseille, with a huge mural of *that* night in 1993, colourful scarves and a terrace kissing the Mediterranean. Bus #83 from the Vieux Port.

L'OM Café, 3 Quai des Belges. A great success since it opened in 1998, a themed bar by the Old Port, open daily 6am–1am, with a full menu and its own souvenir shop and ticket office.

Titus, 32 Rue Horace Bertin. Vibrant pub/tapas bar off La Pleine with live music, billiards and a huge plastic shark.

Trolleybus, 24 Quai Rive Neuve. Best club to head for down by the Old Port, with four separate areas for different kinds of music and French bowls in the cellar. Open Thur–Sat, F60 cover charge on Sat.

Restaurants
The *Marseillais* eat well and are proud of it, the city's rich ethnic mix never better reflected than in its food. As well as an abundance of **all kinds of stalls** for eating on the hoof, you'll find wonderful fish and seafood restaurants and the best couscous this side of the Mediterranean.

Bar de la Marine, 15 Quai de Rive Neuve. Probably the most famous brasserie in Marseille, still done out in Thirties style, still attracting sailors and fishermen. Set lunches at F75 an excellent bargain, and right in the old harbour too.

Chez Angèle, 50 Rue Caisserie. A real Le Panier favourite, packed at lunchtimes for the *menu fixe* specials. Closed Sat eve, Sun and Aug. No credit cards.

Chez Michel, 6 Rue des Catalans. Said to be the place in town to eat *bouillabaisse*, which comes with all the trimmings, a reasonably heavy price tag, and a seaview from the furthest end of the Vieux Port. Open daily.

Chez Vincent, 2 Avenue des Chartreux. Not cheap, but this was Ravanelli's favourite haunt,

serving fine local cuisine until late. Near Cinq-Avenues Longchamp métro stop.

Une Table au Sud, 2 Quai du Port. A newcomer to fine dining in town, above the famous *La Samaritaine* café with views over the harbour. This is the best Marseille has to offer, and at reasonable prices too – *plat du jour* at F135, two courses at F155. Open daily except Sun and Mon lunchtimes. Most credit cards.

Accommodation
Cheap rooms can usually be found opposite Saint-Charles station — those by the Vieux Port might provide **more than just a bed** for the night. The tourist office at La Canebière 4 has a free **booking service**.

Hôtel Alizé, 35 Quai des Belges (☎04/9133 6697, fax 04/9154 8006). A great find, offering reasonably priced and comfortable rooms, all with showers and TV, some with a balcony overlooking the Vieux Port. Doubles for under F400.

Hôtel Beaulieu Glaris, 1–3 Place des Marseillais (☎04/9190 7059, fax 04/9156 1404, e-mail Hotel.Beaulieu@wanadoo.fr). Right opposite Saint-Charles station. Clean and friendly, but a bit of a climb to the upper rooms. Doubles for around F250.

Hôtel Bearn, 3 Rue Sylvabelle (☎04/9137 7583, fax 04/9181 5498). In a quieter area, a little more expensive but each room has a bath or shower. Métro Estrangin-Préfecture.

Hôtel du Sud, 18 Rue Beauvau (☎04/9154 3850, fax 04/9154 7562). A slightly more pricey establishment by the Vieux Port (double rooms at around F350), but with that priceless commodity in Marseille – air conditioning.

Marseille-Bonneveine (FUAJ), 47 Avenue Joseph Vidal (☎04/9173 2181, fax 04/9173 9123). 185 beds in a youth hostel near the seafront, 6km from the city centre. F120 a bed including breakfast. Bus #44 from métro Rond-Point-du-Prado to Place Bonnefon, in the direction Roy d'Espagne.

Germany

Deutscher Fussball Bund Otto-Fleck-Schneise 6, Postfach 710265, D-60492
Frankfurt-am-Main ☎069/67880 Fax 049/678 8266 E-mail dfb.info@t-online.de

League champions Bayern Munich **Cup winners** Bayern Munich
Promoted 1.FC Cologne, VfL Bochum, Energie Cottbus **Relegated** SSV Ulm, MSV
Duisburg, Arminia Bielefeld

European participants 2000/01 Bayern Munich, Bayer Leverkusen (UCL);
Hamburg SV, Munich 1860 (UCL qualifiers); Kaiserslautern, Hertha Berlin, Werder
Bremen (UEFA Cup); VfB Stuttgart, VfL Wolfsburg (Intertoto Cup)

Despite recent dips in form by the national side, German football is still riding the crest of a popularity wave. Average crowds are the highest in Europe, providing a passionate (and financially lucrative) fan culture, backed by matchless administration that is the envy of the continent.

And although the German game is often reviled for its lack of spontaneity and the unending workrate that has pulled off so many last-ditch rescues, its technical qualities cannot be denied, nor the international class of the players who have used them to their best advantage.

The postwar German revival was kick-started by the shock World Cup win of 1954, and built on by skilled coaching. The introduction of the *Bundesliga* in 1963 coincided with the opening of a coaching academy in Cologne which would soon be churning out trainers gifted enough to nurture the country's prodigious output of footballing talent into players of world class.

In the 30-year period from the World Cup final in 1966, the national side appeared in four World Cup finals, winning two, and five European Championship finals, winning three – a truly awesome record. Perhaps better than anyone else, the Germans, with an even wider pool of talent since unification of their country in 1990, have balanced physical durability with creativity and tactical sophistication.

How ironic, then, that it has been poor midfield creation, the *spiel aufbau*, which has let the national side down at the last two World Cup tournaments. Journeymen sloggers have replaced craftsmen for the simple reason that there aren't any of the latter around – at least for the time being.

Introduced to the northern ports and Berlin in the 1870s by British residents, the game in Germany suffered a slow start, with sports directives from Prussia insisting on a gymnastic programme for schools into which soccer did not fit. The handful of football clubs played in regionalised leagues with an annual play-off, their players lacking the tactical sophistication developing elsewhere. The national team's only early highlight was a third-place finish in 1934, and even when bolstered by Austrian players in 1938, 'Greater Germany' flopped.

At club level, the balance of power, once held by Nuremburg, came to rest in the Ruhr industrial area, especially at Schalke 04 – their lead would later be followed by neighbours Borussia Dortmund and Cologne.

Following the postwar division of Germany, each half of the country was given its own FA, league and national team – both admitted to FIFA in the early Fifties. In the East, never a footballing stronghold, the game was restructured along classic Communist lines, with the top teams representing branches of the state.

Meanwhile, in West Germany, five regional leagues had been set up in 1953, the dominant side being the Walter brothers' Kaiserslautern. Few noticed when West Germany made their World Cup debut in 1954, drawn as they were in the

A long, lonely walk – Matthäus troops off after Germany's 3–0 defeat by Portugal, June 2000

same first-round group as hot favourites Hungary. Wily coach Sepp Herberger deliberately fielded an under-strength side in a 8–3 defeat by the Hungarians, knowing that his team would then easily beat Turkey to ensure their own progress. Moreover, star Magyar Ferenc Puskás limped off during the game, kicked by German defender Werner Liebrich. West Germany then breezed through easy ties to the final, where they would meet a tired Hungary in muddy conditions which favoured the Germans. Within eight minutes, Hungary were two up, but the Germans struck back quickly, Max Morlock and Helmut Rahn grabbing a goal each. Galvanised by captain Fritz Walter, and with 'keeper Toni Turek outstanding, they held out until a late Rahn goal against the run of play made it 3–2. Two minutes from time, a shot from a half-fit Puskás hit the net, only to be dubiously ruled out for offside. West Germany had beaten the Magic Magyars – the celebrations became a national holiday, and the country got on with its economic miracle.

West Germany next made the final in 1966. Herberger's assistant, Helmut Schön,

was now in charge of a team with two key players: Uwe Seeler, a bullish but versatile centre-forward; and Franz Beckenbauer, a precocious half-back. Their clubs, Hamburg SV and Bayern Munich, were now members of a new *Bundesliga*, a single national league, the belated development of which was starting to make an impact on West German teams' performance in Europe. Borussia Dortmund were the first, with goalkeeper Hans Tilkowski and forwards Siggi Held and Lothar Emmerich starring in a Cup-Winner's Cup win in 1966. Two months later, these same players strode out at Wembley to face hosts England in the World Cup final.

Beckenbauer had been the tournament's revelation, but Schön would shackle him to Bobby Charlton in the final, and German invention was stifled as a result. Haller's early goal was soon equalised, and all seemed lost when England went ahead towards the end. But, as the Germans would often prove, it's never over until it's over. A dubious free-kick on the edge of the English box would cause a mêlée transformed into a last-minute equaliser by

Basics

Citizens of the EU, the USA, Canada, Australia and New Zealand need only their **passport** to enter Germany.

The German currency is the **Deutschmark**, divided into 100 Pfennig. There are coins of 2, 5, 10 and 50 Pfennig, and for DM1, 2 and 5; and notes for DM10, 20, 50, 100, 200, 500 and 1000. Basic **banking hours** are Mon–Fri 9.30am–midday & 1.30–3.30pm, although in major cities some banks stay open an hour or two later. There are usually small bank offices in train stations which are open seven days a week, until 9pm or 10pm. You can change money at almost all banks, and they offer a better rate than commercial exchange offices (*Wechselstuben*).

Cash machines are widespread but the use of **credit cards** is not as prevalent as you might expect. Germany has a much less highly developed retail culture than the UK – be aware that if you want to do some last-minute souvenir shopping, most city-centre stores are closed on **Saturday afternoons**.

If you are travelling on from Germany to other countries, particularly to **Eastern Europe**, then it's worth keeping hold of any leftover Deutschmarks – you'll get good rates of exchange or discounted prices when using the German currency.

From outside the country, the **international access code** for Germany is 49. You can call abroad from all telephone boxes in the country except for those marked *National*. Coin phones take DM1 and DM5 coins, phonecards are available at DM12 and DM50, and credit-card phones are becoming more widespread. Alternatively, all main post offices have booths from which you can make an international call, then pay the charge at the desk afterwards. For national calls, commonly used **city codes** are: Berlin 030, Cologne 0221, Dortmund 0231, Hamburg 040 and Munich 089.

Getting around inside Germany, you can't avoid the excellent **rail service**, provided by *Deutsche Bahn* (*DB*). Fares are around DM26 per 100 km, second class, but there are cheaper deals for travel after 7pm. You'll pay a supplement for the 250kph *ICE* trains, and also for *IC* and *EC* services.

An alternative way to travel across the country is to use a **paid-hitching system**. Journeys work out much cheaper than by train, and the absence of *Autobahn* speed limits means they can be almost as quick. The best service is provided by *ADM*, who have offices in all the major cities. Their telephone number is the same in all locations – ☎19440; if you are outside a city, then simply add the city dialling code.

All major cities have **tourist information offices** who will book accommodation for a nominal booking fee. As well as upmarket hotels, you will usually have a choice of B&B in a *Pension* or *Gasthöf*, though these are not necessarily any cheaper than small hotels. German **youth hostels** are good value and graded, like hotels, by a star system.

Germany is a **beer-lover's paradise**. All locally produced brews have to comply with a 450-year-old purity law which prevents the use of chemical substitutes, and there are some superb regional variations in addition to the ubiquitous *pilsener*. Draught beer (*vom Fass*) is poured very slowly, so order a round in advance.

There's more to the **local wine** than *Liebfraumilch*. *Riesling* and *Gewürztraminer* are more interesting whites, and German red wine is also better than you might think.

A football fan can't visit Germany without tasting the sausage (*Wurst*), which comes in a bewildering array of regional varieties. If the somewhat **stodgy local cooking** gets you down, most major cities offer a wide choice of Turkish, Chinese, Italian and 'Balkan' (usually Serbian or Croatian) restaurants.

German rock music is the world's worst, but in recent years the country has produced some innovative dance sounds, and this is reflected in the popularity of the growing number of **techno clubs** in big cities.

Wolfgang Weber. The boot was on the other foot in extra-time, though, when a Hurst shot bounced off the crossbar onto the goalline, and linesman Tofik Bakhramov signalled a goal. Hurst would then finish the job in the last minute; 4–2.

German revenge would come four years later. For the 1970 tournament in Mexico, Schön integrated Seeler as a deep-lying forward paired with Gerd Müller, *der Bomber*, a goalscoring machine at Bayern Munich, the new dominant force in the *Bundesliga*. With Bayern's Sepp Maier between the sticks and Beckenbauer and Cologne's left-footed Wolfgang Overath emerging as midfield players of class, West Germany swept through their group. Substitutes were now allowed, and Schön took to throwing winger Jürgen Grabowski at tiring defences – it was this tactic that turned the quarter-final with England. With the Germans two goals down in the second half, a weak Beckenbauer punt from distance fooled reserve England 'keeper Peter Bonetti, who then also succumbed to a bizarre Seeler backheader. West Germany won the game in extra-time on a classic Müller strike from close range.

A tired German team faced Italy in the semi-final, and were a goal down for almost the entire game until a late equaliser from Karl-Heinz Schnellinger. The period of extra-time that followed has gone down in legend, but its excitement – each side taking the lead, each a high-altitude breath away from the final – was born of weary defensive error. Beckenbauer, his arm in a sling, had little influence, and Italy scraped it, 4–3.

The Seventies would see West Germany dominant at both club and international level, the only dark cloud a *Bundesliga* match-fixing scandal in 1971. The team of the decade were Hennes Weisweiler's Borussia Mönchengladbach, who assumed Bayern's mantle. Their midfield star, Gunter Netzer, could invent the game at will, and Schön chose him over Overath for the European Championship of 1972. This was West Germany in their

prime, Netzer destroying England at Wembley in the quarter-final first leg, 3–1, then running riot over the USSR in the final, 3–0. As well as a victory for German organisation, it was a triumph for 'total football', with Beckenbauer playing as an attack-minded *libero*, releasing players as he moved forward.

The World Cup two years later, hosted by West Germany, left Schön in a dilemma. He fielded Overath for the first two games, then, with his team playing East Germany for the first and only time and the scores tied at 0–0, he brought on Netzer – only for the GDR to win with Jürgen Sparwasser's late goal. The players themselves lobbied for Mönchengladbach's Rainer Bonhof, allied with Overath, over Netzer, and this combination saw West Germany through, albeit after a tricky 1–0 win in the mud over a spirited Poland.

The final pitched Beckenbauer's Germany against Johan Cruyff's Holland, a meeting of two forms of total football. The Dutch were 1–0 up without a German touching the ball, Hoeness bringing down Cruyff in the penalty box within 60 seconds. But a more dubious penalty appeal was given the other way 25 minutes later. Just on half-time, in his last game for his country, Müller produced a typical turn in the box to create a goal out of nothing – 2–1, and that's how it stayed, thanks to some inspired Maier goalkeeping.

The supremacy was soon translated at club level, where Bayern usurped Ajax's prime position on the continent, winning three European Cups on the trot. West Germany provided three semi-finalists for the UEFA Cup of 1979, and all four the year afterwards.

Although the national side suffered the early retirements of Maier, Müller and Overath, it still made the European Championship final of 1976 – only for Hoeness to send his spot-kick into the Belgrade night sky and gift a shoot-out victory to Czechoslovakia. The loss of Beckenbauer the year after proved more critical, and

West Germany made a poor defence of their title in 1978, their last-game defeat by Austria an ill-fitting farewell for Schön.

Under new coach Jupp Derwall, an effective West German side – with Bernd Schuster starring in his only major finals – won a poor European Championship in 1980, the touch of new star Karl-Heinz Rummenigge and the muscle of midfielder Hans-Peter Briegel and forward Horst Hrubesch proving decisive.

After a disgraceful 'agreed' win over Austria in the group stage, the same side minus Schuster then won through to the World Cup semi-finals two years later, to face an adventurous France in Seville. It was a game of the highest drama, partly decided by a horrendous and unpunished challenge by German goalkeeper Toni Schumacher on Patrick Battiston when a fiery game stood at 1–1, the genial Pierre Littbarski having given Germany the lead. With France going 3–1 up in extra-time, all seemed lost until a half-fit Rummenigge was brought on; he sneaked a tap-in goal before a Klaus Fischer overhead levelled the scores. Hrubesch scored the final kick of the penalty shoot-out, and an unpopular

West German side faced old foes Italy in the final, where they would fall 3–1.

For the 1986 World Cup in Mexico, Franz Beckenbauer replaced Derwall, his pedigree waiving any need for a coaching licence. Although Rummenigge was again not fully fit, with a young Lothar Matthäus in midfield, two powerhouses in Briegel and Andreas Brehme, and Rüdi Völler upfront, West Germany won through to another final. There, in an echo of Beckenbauer's own fate at Wembley in 1966, Matthäus' creativity would be stifled by a strict marking job on Argentina's Maradona, giving Valdano and Burruchaga space to score decisive goals. The game saw another famous German recovery, from 2–0 down with five minutes remaining, Rummenigge and Völler the scorers, only for a weary Briegel to play Burruchaga onside for Argentina's stoppage-time winner.

At club level, Bayern's second place in the 1987 European Cup would be their last European final for ten years. While the national side remained strong, German clubs – bound by the FA's strict licence-granting financial guidelines – were unable to challenge the debt-ridden, star-studded

Defeat into victory – bid-team boys Rummenigge and Völler discuss hosting the 2006 World Cup

An invincible machine – Andy Möller at Wembley, 1996

bad-tempered game with Holland, after Völler and Rijkaard were sent off early on. The subsequent narrow win over the Czechs saw the Germans head-to-head with England in the semi-final, another game of extreme drama and memorable images. For most of it, England outplayed the favoured Germans, but then fell behind to a deflected Brehme free-kick. With Lineker equalising, the game went to extra-time, which saw each side hit the post, and Thomas Berthold fall over a Paul Gascoigne tackle, the immediate protest from the German bench enough for the referee to yellow card the tournament's star out of any chance of playing in the final. The Germans then took four perfect penalties against an ageing Peter Shilton, England missed two and, suddenly Gazza's fate was irrelevant, anyway. The final, a repeat of 1986, was dire, remembered only for Argentine indiscipline and German gamesmanship – and Maradona's tears after Brehme converted a late penalty to win the game, 1–0.

To many outsiders Germany had become an invincible machine, while for their public, turning up in ever-increasing numbers to watch a newly unified league, success was expected.

Both illusions would be shattered at the next two tournament finals. Beckenbauer, having won the World Cup as both player and coach, bowed out in favour of his assistant and former 1974 team-mate Berti Vogts. Despite the difficulties of integrating former East Germans into the squad, Vogts' side started favourites for Euro '92. They lost another clash with Holland, 3–1, but recovered to make the final against unfancied Denmark with confidence high. In diminutive Thomas Hässler they had the player of the tournament, in Jürgen Kohler a defender of rare class, and in Matthias Sammer, the brightest prospect from the East. Denmark simply stuck two men on

sides of Italy and Spain, to which many of their stars were now drifting. The saddest dip in fortunes was felt by Borussia Mönchengladbach, who spent the next decade flirting with a relegation that would eventually come in 1999.

Germany hosted the 1988 European Championship, when a defeat by Holland in the semi-final, a Marco van Basten goal settling things at the death, set up a series of grudge matches with the Dutch – the first coming two years later at Italia '90. With Jürgen Klinsmann now partnering Völler upfront, and Matthäus an example-setting captain, West Germany had powered through their group games. Klinsmann's tireless work stood out in the

Hässler, preventing his runs in either direction, scored early, and ran out 2–0 winners.

Worse was to follow at USA '94, when an unconvincing German side allowed Bulgaria to get back into the quarter-final, Yordan Lechkov outjumping Hässler, the smallest player in the *Bundesliga*, to score the winner.

Such tactical indiscipline struck home hard, as did the severe criticism of Vogts, and it was a workmanlike German side that faced the Czechs in the first game of Euro '96. Sammer had become an inspiration as sweeper, Andreas Möller emerging as the main force in midfield. Germany rode over the Czechs, but rode their luck against Italy, Andreas Köpke saving a penalty when he should have been off the field, and against Croatia, who had been reduced to ten men when they were beaten 2–1.

Another semi-final with England was set up, this one equal to that of Italia '90, all the more so because of the new 'golden goal' rule hanging over the knife-edge of extra-time. At 1–1, Germany had a goal disallowed, Gascoigne missed from close range, and it was penalties again. Southgate missed for England, Möller converted for Germany, and the Germans would play the Czechs again in the final. This time, the Czechs were on a roll, and deservedly went 1–0 up. New striker Oliver Bierhoff pulled the score back to 1–1 for Germany, and his flukey 'golden goal' would give them their fifth trophy in 30 years.

Meanwhile, football had taken off back home, big style. Bayern, with Beckenbauer as president, were now a huge industry, the team's winning exploits – seven titles in 12 years – generating a boom in merchandising that would soon be felt across the board – except in the economically depressed East, where fans had little spare cash to spend on club-branded trinkets, and where few teams were capable of sustaining membership of the top flight for very long.

Domestic success, however, had its downside. With the *Bundesliga* increasingly using foreign imports and squashing young

homegrown talent, it was an ageing German squad which Vogts took to France '98. With Matthäus, Kohler and Klinsmann all past their best, Germany stumbled through the group games, the coach unable to work out a tactical formula that could include both Hassler and Möller. Fortuitous comebacks against Yugoslavia and Mexico did not bode well for the quarter-final against a Croatia side bent on revenge. And so it proved, Christian Wörns' red card reducing the Germans to ten men in the first half, and an insipid midfield allowing the Croats to roam at will.

The catastrophic 3–0 defeat raised serious questions about the German game. Amazingly, Vogts stayed in his post, but was forced to resign within weeks, after some more poor displays in friendlies. The lack of an obvious successor – after decades in which national coaches had simply slipped into the job – signalled alarm bells, and Erich Ribbeck's first game in charge was a 1–0 defeat in Turkey, not the best of starts to the Euro 2000 qualifying tournament. Worse was to follow in February 1999, when a full German team were 3–0 down to the USA in 30 minutes, with all goals coming from *Bundesliga* players, and then suffered the ignominy of having to hold on to prevent a massacre.

Not since World War II had the national team sunk so low. Euro 2000 wins over Northern Ireland and Finland in March did nothing to hide the fact that Germany were no longer expected to win through to every major final. Missing out on qualification would be a first since 1968 and, from one of the easier groups, that still seemed unlikely. But another poor display at the Confederations' Cup in the summer of 1999 left the approaching *Bundesliga* campaign not as a celebration of the national team's performances, but as a welcome escape from them.

That theme continued throughout the 1999/2000 season. The bigger the thrills thrown up by the domestic campaign, the darker the mood within the national-team camp. At home, Christoph Daum's highly motivated Bayer Leverkusen pushed Bayern Munich all the way in the title race, before losing their grip on the crown on a final day of high drama, just as it seemed they were destined for a first-ever championship. Rjuvenated Hamburg SV and Werder Bremen sides gave northern Germany something to cheer about, the former finishing third in the *Bundesliga*, the latter enjoying a fine UEFA Cup run that included spectacular comeback victories over Olympique Lyonnais and Parma. And in the east, Hansa Rostock clung doggedly to their top-flight place, while Energie Cottbus, a small-town club coached by the GDR's last national-team boss, Eduard Geyer, defied all the odds to win promotion from the second division for the first time in their history.

But if the *Bundesliga* was a fairytale, the national team was a dour soap opera, mixed with elements of tragic-comedy. Ribbeck's Germany somehow qualified for Euro 2000 without recourse to the play-offs, but the warm-up games which followed were little short of disastrous. While the players, led by veteran sweeper Lothar Matthäus, called for stronger leadership, Ribbeck sacked the one man who seemed capable of providing it, his assistant Uli Stielike. Once the finals had kicked-off, the folly of retaining the 39-year-old Matthäus was brutally exposed, first by a quick-witted Romania who forced a 1–1 draw; then by a hard-tackling England, who defeated Germany 1–0; and finally by what amounted to a Portuguese reserve team, whose 3–0 victory left Matthäus lost for words on his long walk back to the tunnel, and Ribbeck looking for another job.

The future is far from clear. The DFB's chosen successor for the job of national coach, Christoph Daum, is contracted to Leverkusen for another year and is determined to have one last crack at the title. So Daum in turn nominated Rudi Völler, formerly Leverkusen's sporting director, as caretaker boss until the summer of 2001. It seemed a desperate compromise, but the lack of other options was almost tangible.

Essential vocabulary

Hello *Guten Tag*
Goodbye *Auf wiedersehen*
Yes *Ja*
No *Nein*
Two beers, please *Zwei Bier, bitte*
Thank you *Danke*
Men's *Herren*
Women's *Damen*
Where is the stadium? *Wo ist das Stadion?*
What's the score? *Wie steht's?*
Referee *Schiedsrichter*
Offside *Abseits*

Match practice

After what was effectively a product relaunch in the early Nineties, Germany's *Bundesliga* is now continental Europe's most commercially successful league.

As in England, lucrative new TV contracts, the increased business awareness of clubs and intense media and marketing activity have propelled the domestic game into an era of unprecedented wealth and influence. Unlike England, however, Germany also had a range of modern, world-class stadia in which the revolution could unfold – the product of massive construction programmes for the 1974 World Cup and 1988 European Championship, and a firm base from which the Germans have launched their campaign to host the World Cup again in 2006.

There has been no Taylor Report here, and no need for one. Many grounds still have standing areas, assisting in the creation of big-match atmosphere which might otherwise be reduced by the common placement of running tracks between stands and action. And while many of these stadia are out of town, the transport links to them are invariably excellent and, once inside the ground, facilities are second to none.

Prior to games, expect an American approach with a local radio personality taking the field, mike in hand, warming up the crowd with a mixture of team news and naff pop music. When the team sheet becomes available, only the first name of

Eastern promise – Eduard Geyer, last coach of the GDR, talks little Cottbus to promotion

the home-team players is read out – the crowd bellows out each surname. This tradition is also followed for announcements of substitutes and goalscorers – and will also be applied to away teams if there is substantial travelling support.

The *Bundesliga* kicks-off in mid-August and takes a break from late December to late February. The season doesn't end until early June – two weeks earlier if there is a major international tournament in the summer. Many prominent figures in the game are unhappy that the long winter break makes it necessary to bring players back to full fitness from a standing start twice a year, and with UEFA also angling for Germany to shorten its rest period in order to accommodate Champions' League expansion, change may not be far away.

Most league games take place on Saturday at 3.30pm. Live TV games are on Friday nights at 8pm, and on Sunday at 6.30pm. There are a handful of midweek rounds, with games being played on Tuesday or Wednesday at 7.30pm.

A different league
The *Bundesliga* consists of two divisions, with 18 teams in each. All clubs in the top two divisions must be granted a professional licence from the German FA, the *DFB*. Clubs suffering from financial irregularities or insufficient funds can have their licence withdrawn and be consigned to the amateur leagues – this happened to TSV Munich 1860 in the Eighties and to Dynamo Dresden in 1995, and was at one stage threatened to Eintracht Frankfurt during the 1999/2000 season.

It's a straightforward three-up, three-down between the top two divisions. The bottom four from the second tier are relegated to one of four *Regionalligen* which make up the third tier. This level includes some small semi-professional clubs, amateur sides and the reserve teams of the bigger *Bundesliga* clubs which, although called *Amateure*, include many paid young players. Promotion from the *Regionalligen* is achieved via a complicated system of play-offs.

Back in time – low prices and old terracing lend German grounds an old-fashioned atmosphere

Up for the cup

Unlike many domestic cup competitions, the *DFB Pokal* was traditionally organised to maximise the possible embarrassment of top clubs. All matches are still single-leg affairs, with penalty shoot-outs deciding the outcome if the scores are level after extra-time.

However, under pressure from top-flight clubs, the *DFB* altered the competition's structure for 1999/2000, giving the bottom half of the first division a bye to the third round, and the top half direct entry to the fourth. Whether this will impair the tournament's ability to help the game at grassroots level, or detract from its popular appeal, remains to be seen.

The first round takes place in the second week in August, followed by three more rounds until the quarter-finals in November. The semi-finals are in April, and the final is played at Berlin's Olympic stadium in late May or early June – a fixture which has over the past few years has become a real showpiece event to rival Wembley's FA Cup final.

Just the ticket

There are no officially designated all-ticket matches in Germany. If the stadium is not sold out in advance, you can buy tickets at the stadium on matchdays. At Dortmund and Freiburg almost every match is sold out, but most other grounds are big enough to accommodate fans arriving on-spec, unless there's a big derby on.

Tickets are divided into seats (*Sitzplätze*) and standing (*Stehplätze*). Look out for signs showing a *Gästesektor* for visiting fans. The areas behind each goal are *Kürve*, while each stand (*Tribüne*) is normally named according its location – *Süd-Tribüne* is the south stand, and so on. In smaller grounds there will be a *Seitentribüne*, with seats close to the edge of the pitch.

Ticket prices are very reasonable. Adult standing spaces are DM12–16, while seats can be had for as little as DM25 – though you'll pay twice that for the best seats in the house in the *Haupttribüne*.

Most clubs operate a ticket hotline for information on availability and credit-card bookings.

Half-time

Although a number of clubs have banned alcohol inside their grounds, beer is an essential part of the German football experience. At large, out-of-town stadia there are scores of beer stands, with the local sausage (*wurst*) speciality sizzling nearby. At smaller, town-centre grounds, local bars will be packed before kick-off. On any long trip by U-Bahn or S-Bahn out to a stadium, you'll see fans swigging back cans along the journey.

Naturally all this results in a fair amount of drunkenness on the terraces, but remember that police and stadium security have the right to refuse admission.

If there is a beer festival, fairground or *Volks Fest* of any kind going on in town, it will be flooded by fans after the match and terrace chants will roar on into the night.

Action replay

Subscription satellite channel Premiere has the rights to live league games, which are shown Fridays at 8pm and Sundays at 6.30pm. You need a decoder and card to view Premiere, so if there's a game on that you're particularly keen to catch, head for a suitably equipped bar. As in England, the football authorities have ensured that the game retains maximum exposure by insisting that the pay TV companies share highlights packages with a terrestrial channel – in this case SAT 1. Fronted by the showman of German soccer, Reinhold Beckmann, SAT 1's output is lively, colourful and, even if you speak not a word of German, compelling viewing. The main highlights show is *Ran* (Fridays, 10.15pm & Saturdays, 6pm). It features a studio audience of fans, live satellite link-ups around the grounds and interviews, as well as extended highlights of all games played that day. SAT 1 also shows four Sunday games each season, 'as live', on *Ranissimo* (7.15pm). For all other match rounds, *Ranissimo* becomes a highlights show with a very similar format to *Ran*.

Domestic cup matches are shown across all the terrestrial channels – ARD, ZDF, RTL and SAT 1 – while German international matches are normally shown by either ARD or ZDF.

Germany's dedicated subscription sports channel, DSF, has failed to get much of a grip on domestic football. The station has a live second-division game on Monday nights at 8pm, plus live Spanish league action (Saturdays, 8pm) and a live Italian game (Sundays, 8.15pm) – this last being followed by highlights of the weekend's top-flight *Bundesliga* action.

Champions' League coverage is shared between Premiere and free-to-air RTL, with the former showing a Tuesday game live (followed by a highlights package on RTL), the latter a Wednesday one.

The back page

The longest-established and most respected football magazine in Germany is *Kicker*. The brainchild of one of German football's founding fathers, schoolteacher Walter Bensemann, it first appeared in 1920 and has been the staple diet of fans ever since.

Kicker has two weekly editions. Monday's issue (DM3) carries interviews and main features in colour, with weekend results and reports in a black-and-white supplement, which also contains results from the major European leagues. The midweek edition (DM2.30) is a thinner, black-and-white only affair featuring a wrap-up of any midweek action, plus news and previews of all the weekend's games.

For all its thoroughness, *Kicker* can be a bit on the serious side. For a more frivolous read, try the newcomer *Hattrick* (monthly, DM6) with its colour features and irreverent style, or the weekly *Sport Bild*, a tabloid connected to the daily *Bild*, Germany's answer to *The Sun*. Be aware, though, that *Sport Bild* covers more than football and at any one time can be full to the brim with tennis, golf or motor racing.

At the start of the season you'll see special guides to the new campaign, with all the stats and player info you need. *Kicker's Bundesliga Sonderheft* (DM9) is the best of these but *Fussball Sport Extra*

(DM6.90) is also worth a look. British-based fans of the German game have their own fanzine, *Elfmeter* (£1). It has a witty and approachable style, and is available from: 30 Chapel Close, Rainham, Kent, ME8 9TE, UK; e-mail ed@elfmeter.f9.co.uk.

Ultra culture

Nowhere is the German attitude to football as a pastime better illustrated than in clubs' relationship with their supporters. With one eye on their social responsibilities to the communities they serve and another on public relations, most big German clubs have a *Fan Projekt* – a coalition of supporters' groups and local authority-funded youth organisations. Club directors hold regular meetings with their *Projekt*, which usually runs alongside the traditional, officially sanctioned supporters' clubs.

The *Fan Projekt* idea arose as a way of involving fans at grassroots level and cutting out the cancer of hooliganism. But the latter is still a problem in the former GDR, and with extreme right-wing followers of the national team.

On a less serious note, there is a distinctly Seventies look on the terraces, with the most loyal young fans keen to show their commitment with an array of sew-on patches and pin badges stuck to sleeveless denim jackets, layers of scarves tied around the wrist, and *Kiss Me Quick Deutschland* party hats. Some fans have tried to create a more latin feel, but stadium authorities rarely permit smoke bombs or flares.

The terrace tunes will be achingly familiar to a British visitor, but most clubs also have their own rock anthem; it says a lot about German football culture that these are actually quite popular with fans.

There is another side to the fanaticism of German fans. Just as England has the *92 Club*, so Germany has its *Groundhoppers*. Unlike their English counterparts, they do not restrict themselves to their own national boundaries. Armed with that essential accessory, the international train schedule, they travel across Europe and beyond – most serious *Groundhoppers* have attended games at more than 200 stadia.

If you hear German being spoken at a ground somewhere in Europe, there are probably *Groundhoppers* about. Forget your pre-conceptions and approach them for a chat – these people do their research and will invariably know of any other games taking place later that day. Chances are, they will have visited your home ground and sunk a pint in your local, too.

In the net

The *DFB* runs an exemplary, elegant official website at: www.dfb.de. A simple design conceals a huge depth of content underneath, together with a section dedicated to Germany's (successful) 2006 World Cup bid.

Old Walter Bensemann would have been proud of *Kicker Online*, Germany's best generic football website, accessible at: www.kicker.de/. Easy to navigate with its smart, innovative graphics, the site is a treasure trove of news, stats, interviews and features – no substitute for the paper itself, but an excellent site all the same.

Bernd Timmerman, the doyen of German soccer stattoes, runs an extraordinary online stats archive at: www.informatik.uni-oldenburg.de/~bernd/ soccer.e.html.

Munich

Brazilian beat – Giovane Elber and Paulo Sérgio hail another goal on the way to the double

Bavaria, with all its clichéd images of shaving brush hats and *Lederhosen*, occupies a huge area of southern Germany, stretching from the Swiss to the Czech border, and as far north as the outskirts of Frankfurt. It is no wonder then, that Bavaria has seen more titles come its way than any other *Land*, especially as its capital, Munich, is home to the country's richest and most powerful club, Bayern.

Although sports associations had been founded in Munich quite early on – TSV in 1860, MTV in 1879 – they were governed by the gymnastic creed of the *Turnvater Jahn* movement, and Bavarian schools banned the game until 1913. Nevertheless, breakaway members had already formed football clubs by then, MTV's becoming Bayern in 1900.

Bavarian teams played in a South German regional championship, whose winners would enter the national play-offs. Of these, the most successful were Nuremburg, a club so dominant they simply became known as *der Club*. Meanwhile, Munich's two main clubs, TSV and Bayern, only got the occasional look-in at regional level, although Bayern sneaked a national title in 1932. Bayern's original stadium was in Leopoldstrasse, Schwabing, the club's traditional fan base north of the city centre, and at that time a bohemian home to both Hitler and Lenin.

Meanwhile, 1860 were more working-class, their supporter base south of the Ostbahnhof around Giesing. Here the city's main football stadium, Grünwalder Strasse, was built, and would become home to both clubs until the Olympiastadion was unveiled in 1972. Initially it was 1860 who packed in the crowds at the Grünwalder, and they became Munich's sole representatives in the first *Bundesliga* of 1963. They won the German cup in 1964, and reached a European final a year later. But Bayern were slowly catching up, and joined them in the *Bundesliga* in 1965. Bayern were also putting together a team of locally produced stars – Beckenbauer, Maier and Müller – whose exploits would change football's status in Germany forever. With a professional management team, and scouting and coaching networks that put their rivals' to shame, Bayern slowly gained the local ascendancy. After winning the cup in 1966 and the Cup-Winners' Cup the following year, the club developed a fan base across the whole region, Bavarians being keen to get one over on the liberals and Socialists from the north.

Meanwhile 1860, in slow decline after their *Bundesliga* win of 1966, retained the same hardcore fans of old, but could not add to them. So while Bayern, now way ahead of their former rivals, comfortably slipped into the Olympiastadion (half their team played in the West German side that inaugurated it in 1972), 1860 played in front of meagre crowds for a couple of seasons, then went back home to Giesing.

The Olympic stadium radically altered Munich's national footballing status. Prior to its opening, Germany's third largest city had staged a grand total of four internationals – three in peacetime – and certainly none since World War II, hence the locals' excitement at international success. After the 1972 Olympic Games, with the decline of Berlin's old Olympiastadion, Munich became the nearest Germany had to a national stadium. It witnessed West Germany's World Cup win of 1974, and a handful of European finals.

With Bayern's three-time European Cup success in the mid-Seventies, the club's stars became the focus of tabloid attention, their fans spread in their tens of thousands across the country and beyond. Meanwhile 1860 dropped down to the lower leagues, almost fading out of existence altogether. Beer salvaged them, incoming club president Karl-Heinz Wildmoser owning hostelries all over Bavaria, and ploughing his millions into the club from 1992 – at the same time as coach Werner Lorant arrived on the scene. Together they brought the club up through three divisions in as many seasons, culminating in a return to the *Bundesliga* in 1994. Their decision to move from Giesing back up to the Olympiastadion was unpopular, and while crowds remain healthy for both

clubs, today neither team is happy there. Still, derby day in November 1998 could not have been better staged. For the first time in 30 years, the two Munich clubs were first and second in the league. While 1860 fans won the singing hands down, their former hero Jens Jeremies broke the deadlock on the hour, and sent Bayern fans home to Baden-Württemberg, Thuringia and Westphalia happy.

In 1999/2000, Munich 1860 beat Bayern in a competitive match for the first time in 21 years, then repeated the feat in the second half of the season, to leave their rivals' grip on the title hanging by a thread. But it all ended happily ever after – for *all* the characters – with Bayern doing the double, 1860 finishing fourth for a crack at the Champions' League, and little Unterhaching stunning the nation with their well-earned, mid-table finish.

The thrilling fields

FC Bayern

Olympiastadion, see p.224
Club office Säbener Strasse 51
Colours Red with black trim
League champions 1932, 1969, 1972–74, 1980–81, 1985–87, 1989–90, 1994, 1997, 1999–2000
Cup winners 1957, 1966–67, 1969, 1971, 1982, 1984, 1986, 1998, 2000
European Cup winners 1974–76
Cup-Winners' Cup winners 1967
UEFA Cup winners 1996

Although FC Bayern München ('Bavaria Munich') were formed in 1900, it was to be 60 years before they made a lasting impression on German football. Today, with more than 70,000 club members and a vast casual supporter base which buys a million replica shirts every year, Bayern can attract the best players Germany has to offer.

Perhaps not surprisingly, 'FC Hollywood' have also become the country's most reviled club. Their many critics consider their players overpaid actors, their fans football tourists, and their management a Bavarian football mafia. But since Bayern's move into the moneyed echelons of the European elite after former captain Franz Beckenbauer and his old team-mates took over the club in 1994, the club are in a different league from any in Germany.

Before World War II, Bayern defeated Eintracht Frankfurt to win the national championship in 1932, but didn't win another trophy for 25 years. The club did not gain admittance to the first season of the *Bundesliga*; the *DFB* were keen to have only one representative from each city, and chose TSV 1860 as Munich's side. But club president Wilhelm Neudecker insisted on introducing professionalism anyway, and within two years Bayern had gained promotion to the top drawer – they finished their first season in it, 1965/66, with another domestic cup win. A year later they retained that trophy and, more significantly, also won their first European honour – the 1967 Cup-Winners' Cup. The final of that competition against Rangers drew plenty of local support, as the pre-selected venue was Bavaria's second city, Nuremburg. An extra-time winner from Franz 'Bulle' Roth made for a beery train journey home for the fans.

The European win made the rest of West Germany sit up and take notice of Bayern, who until now had been regarded as no more than a middle-ranking club. The cup-winning sides of the Sixties were dominated by three gifted youngsters – goalkeeper Sepp Maier, anchorman Franz Beckenbauer and striker Gerd Müller. Under their Yugoslav coach, Tschik Ćajkovski, Bayern played fast, adventurous and free-flowing football, with a team spirit second to none in the *Bundesliga*.

When Ćajkovski was replaced by his fellow countryman Branko Zebec in 1968, the team became better disciplined and, as a consequence, much harder to beat. They dominated the 1968/69 league campaign from the start, won the title by eight

points, then completed a domestic double with a cup final win over Schalke.

In March 1970, Zebec was replaced by a former assistant coach to the West German national team, Udo Lattek. His arrival coincided with the start of an unbeaten home record which would stretch for more than four years and 73 matches. During that period, Bayern would win three titles in a row from 1972.

By 1973 Bayern were supplying no fewer than six regulars to the West German national side – Maier, Beckenbauer, Müller, defenders Paul Breitner and Georg Schwarzenbeck, and midfielder Uli Hoeness. For both his club and his country, Beckenbauer had withdrawn from midfield into a sweeper's rôle – though his interpretation of that position was so liberal that he could sometimes be the furthest Bayern player forward.

Beckenbauer had been influenced by the 'Total Football' of the Ajax side of the early Seventies, and it was the Amsterdam club that stood between Bayern and the European domination Lattek craved. In 1973, the Germans were thrashed 4–0 in Amsterdam in a European Cup quarter-final – a defeat which prompted 'keeper Maier to throw his gloves out of his hotel window. But a year later, with Ajax eliminated, Bayern met Atlético Madrid in the final and, after an equaliser from Schwarzenbeck in the last minute of extra-time earned them a replay, they demolished the Spanish champions, 4–0.

Bayern had become the first German club to win Europe's premier club competition, and while their position of pre-eminence in the league was usurped by Borussia Mönchengladbach, the club had been bitten by the European bug. They retained their crown with a 2–0 win over Don Revie's Leeds in Paris, and in 1976 they followed Real Madrid and Ajax into the record books, becoming the third club to win three consecutive European Cups when they beat Saint-Étienne in Glasgow.

One by one, the Beckenbauer generation left Bayern. One of the last to quit was Maier, his career ended prematurely by a horrific car crash in 1979. His departure from the scene signalled the end of an era – and the start of a new one. Under the flamboyant Hungarian coach Pal Csernai, who insisted that his team approach every fixture with the same game-plan, no matter what the opponents, Bayern won the title in 1980.

They retained it a year later, with Karl-Heinz Rummenigge in irrepressible form, and in 1982 they reached two cup finals, winning the domestic version against Nuremburg, but losing in the European Cup to Aston Villa. In 1984 Rümmenigge was sold to Inter Milan. His replacement was a young Mönchengladbach forward by the name of Lothar Matthäus. With Lattek back in the dugout and Matthäus adding some much-needed creativity to the team, Bayern won the title in 1985 – the first of five championships in six seasons. They also reached the 1987 European Cup final, where they lost to two late FC Porto goals.

Much of the Nineties proved to be a more frustrating time for Bayern. The once famous youth policy failed to produce the talent fans had come to expect, and the club looked to the international transfer market to fill the gaps, with mixed success.

A returning Beckenbauer took over the coaching reins and led Bayern to the title in 1994. The following year, the club's first-ever Champions' League campaign ended with a semi-final demolition by Ajax in Amsterdam – an unwelcome echo of times past. By this time, Beckenbauer had been elected club president and appointed the Italian-born Giovanni Trapattoni as coach. 'Trap' made two big-name signings, Jean-Pierre Papin and Emil Kostadinov, who spent most of their time on the bench. In the league, Bayern finished sixth.

After Trapattoni had departed, Otto Rehhagel was lured away from his beloved Werder Bremen for the 1995/96 season. Rehhagel inherited a squad with several malcontents and an ongoing public row

Munich essentials

Munich's **Franz-Josef-Strauss airport** is at the terminal of S-Bahn line #8, 30km from the central train station (Hauptbahnhof). The train terminal is under the airport's arrival and departure lounges. Trains leave every twenty minutes for the centre, the journey taking forty minutes. A single ticket is DM14.

City transport consists of S-Bahn trains, the U-Bahn metro, trams and buses. All U-Bahn lines run through the three central stations of Marienplatz, Karlsplatz and Hauptbahnhof. **Tickets** can be bought from the blue machines at stops and stations, or from tram or bus drivers. The **fare** you pay depends on the number of zones you cross. Providing you are travelling in the same direction within the zones for which your ticket is valid, you can change as many times as you like within four hours. A one-zone single journey (*Einzelfahrtenkarte*) is DM3.70, a two-zone DM7, and so on. A short journey of up to four stops (*Kurzstrecke*) is DM2. An inner-zone day ticket (*Innenraum Tages-Karte*) is good value at DM9; an all-zone version (*Gesamtnetz*) is DM18; both are valid from the time of stamping until 6am the next day.

Transport runs Sun–Thur 5am–12.30am, Fri & Sat 5am–1.30am. Night buses and trams run every 30mins Fri and Sat, 1.45am–3.45am, mainly from the Hauptbahnhof and Karlsplatz. **Taxis** (☎089/21610) charge DM3, then DM2.50 per km.

The two main **tourist offices** are in Marienplatz (open Mon–Fri 10am–8pm, Sat 10am–4pm, ☎089/2333 0272); and at the Hauptbahnhof (open Mon–Sat 9am–8pm, Sun 10am–4pm, ☎089/2333 0256, fax 089/2333 0233). There's a smaller branch at the **airport** (open Mon–Sat 8.30am–10pm, Sun 1–9pm, ☎089/233 0300).

The monthly German-language **listings magazines** *Prinz* (DM5) and *Münchener Stadtmagazin* (DM4) have excellent bar, club and concert information.

between his two most senior players – Matthaus and Jürgen Klinsmann. Beckenbauer, though clearly preferring his dual role as club president and TV pundit, ousted Rehahgel before the end of the season and took personal control with just a handful of games left in the title race. It was a gamble which didn't pay off. Bayern lost to Bremen and Schalke; and Dortmund ran off with the title.

Bayern's consolation was a superb UEFA Cup run, culminating in a two-leg final win over Bordeaux. The competition was a personal triumph for Klinsmann, who scored in every round, and the victory also got the club into the record books again – as a member of the select group of teams to have won all three European trophies.

Beckenbauer moved back upstairs in the summer of 1996, to plan the club's privatisation, then made the extraordinary decision to recall Trapattoni. It was to prove one of the *Kaiser*'s more inspired decisions. While he could not stop the internal feuding, Trap at least took time out to learn some rudimentary German and engaged the support of most of the players. An early UEFA Cup exit proved a blessing in disguise, allowing Bayern to concentrate on the *Bundesliga* which, in the end, they won with something to spare.

The next season looked even more promising, with the arrival of Brazilian Giovane Elber and Carsten Jancker upfront – but 'FC Hollywood' got the better of the Italian this time. Losing patience with his lazy stars – his pidgin German outburst at a post-match press conference was sampled onto a rap record – Trap fined Thomas Strunz, Mehmet Scholl and Mario Basler, while a vengeful Rehhagel led his surprise Kaiserslautern team to the title.

Trapattoni bowed out with a cup win in 1998, to be replaced by the former Dortmund coach Ottmar Hitzfeld. With new signings Stefan Effenberg and Jens Jeremies, Bayern stormed ahead in the league, winning their first six games on the trot, and had the championship pretty much sewn up by Christmas.

They were less impressive in a tricky Champions' League group, having surprisingly lost the first game to Brøndby on two late goals. But they gradually improved as the campaign went on, helped by Hitzfeld's total (yet always dignified) intolerance of internal dissent. Bayern beat Barcelona home and away, and drew twice with Manchester United to secure a place in the quarter-finals, where Kaiserslautern were brushed aside. The team then brilliantly exploited Dynamo Kiev's defensive frailties to come back from 3–1 down in Ukraine and take the semi-final tie comfortably – setting up a reunion with United in the final at the Nou Camp.

It said much about the manner of Bayern's defeat in Barcelona that, in its immediate aftermath, players and management alike could only praise United. They were still in a state of shock – what team could concede two goals in stoppage time to lose the European Cup and be otherwise? The time for calm reflection would come later, during the close season, after the German cup final had also been lost (to Werder Bremen on penalties, Matthäus missing the vital spot-kick) and Hitzfeld had signed Paulo Sérgio and the teenage Paraguayan striker, Roque Santa Cruz, to bolster the squad further.

During the 1999/2000 campaign, Beckenbauer and his general manager Uli Hoeness abandoned plans to privatise the club, deciding that Bayern had enough money to do everything it wanted, and that the club 'should be run by football people, not investment bankers'. It sounded like a nostalgia trip, but the team's form reflected the boardroom's bullish mood. With Elber, Jancker, Paulo Sérgio and Alexander Zickler providing a feast of goals, Bayern could afford the mid-season losses of Basler (to another temper tantrum) and Matthäus (to Major League Soccer in the US). Hitzfeld's side were unlucky to lose to Real Madrid in semi-finals of the Champions' League, but fortunate that their near-neighbours Unterhaching beat Leverkusen on the final day, thereby gifting Bayern a 15th *Bundesliga* title. Add cup final revenge over Werder Bremen and a rare atmosphere of calm and unity within the squad, and the club seemed perfectly prepared for 2000/01 – when, perhaps, the emphasis would be on Europe, first and foremost.

Just the ticket

The sheer size of the Olympiastadion means you stand a fair chance of getting into a run-of-the-mill league clash simply by turning up and buying a ticket at the door. For big games, however, advance booking is advisable. Tickets are available a week ahead at the office on the first floor of the **club's headquarters** at Säbener Strasse 51 (☎089/699 310, fax ☎089/644 185, open Mon–Fri 8.30am–5pm, Thur until 6pm, Sat 9–11am unless a matchday).

On the day, tickets are sold only at the ground. **Admission prices** are kept reasonably low. The cheapest seats (DM20–30) are behind the goals – Bayern fans in blocks S–V of the *Südkurve*, away fans E2–H1 in the *Nordkürve*, or slightly further along in I2–J1. Tickets for the *Hauptribüne* (blocks A–B, Y–Z) are in the range DM30–60 – choose from covered or uncovered, middle or side seats. The *gegengerade* opposite is a little cheaper. Black-market dealing takes place at the bridge nearest the U-Bahn station.

Club merchandise

For all the club's merchandising muscle, the *Bayern Fan House* at Säbener Strasse 51 (open Mon–Fri 9am–5pm, Thur until 6pm, Sat matchdays 9am–1pm, most credit cards) is quite modest, cramped even. It does, however, sell jars of mustard, bottles of champagne, sets of playing cards and even the odd football shirt, should you be perverse enough to want one. The club's merchandise catalogue, *Trends Für Fans*, is the size of a small telephone directory.

In town there are **smaller stores** at central Orlandostrasse 1 (open Mon–Wed, Fri 10am–6.30pm, Thur until 7pm, Sat 10am–2pm) and in the lower level of the Hauptbahnhof (open Mon–Fri 10am–8pm, Sat 10am–4pm).

Ultra culture

Bayern have more than 1,250 registered supporters' associations. As well as hundreds in Germany, there are official Bayern Clubs in Japan, Kenya, Venezuela and Ireland.

While the club happily mail copies of *Trends Für Fans* to all these places, local fans are less impressed, particularly by the diluted atmosphere that the so-called 'terrace tourists' bring to the Olympiastadion.

Bayern's number one fan group are the **Red Munichs** – a likeable collection of a hundred or so hardcore fans who even travel away to watch the club's women's and amateur teams. At the Olympiastadion, they try to sneak fireworks past the fun-loathing security staff and do their darndest to create something approaching a genuine atmosphere.

In print

The matchday **Bayern-Magazin** (DM2.50) is crammed with stats and information as well as the usual glossy posters and the inevitable ads for Bayern products. Fanzines to watch for include **Red News** and **Final Attack**.

In the net

Bayern's **official website** has had a couple of uncharacteristic false starts but is now run by *Sportal*, the European equivalent of England's *Planet Internet*. It's very efficient, as you might expect, with a large English-language section including a rolling news service. Read for yourself at: www.fcbayern.de.

There's a no-nonsense, text-led **unofficial site**, also with complete English and German sections and no end of news and information at: www.object-factory.com/Bayern/.

🌐 Munich 1860

Olympiastadion, see p.224
Office Grünwalderstrasse 114
Colours Blue-and-white shirts, white shorts
League champions 1966
Cup winners 1942, 1964

TSV 1860 München are everything Bayern are not. Bayern have won the European Cup three times; 1860 have only ever entered it once. Bayern have supporters the length and breadth of Germany; 1860

The Olympic stadium

Olympiastadion, Olympiapark
Capacity 63,000 (56,000 seated)

Bayern fans complain that too many people watch their team. Munich 1860 fans want their side to play somewhere more in keeping with their small crowds. While the wrangling goes on, the Olympiastadion remains as one of Europe's classic sports arenas.

Built for the **1972 Olympic games**, the ground is best known for its extraordinary, tent-like grass roof – actually best seen from the top of the Olympic tower, which is part of the same complex. Unlike more recent designs, the roof covers only a percentage of the seating, but while the wind and rain take their toll in cool weather, the design at least ensures that everybody has an excellent view.

After the Olympics, the stadium was the venue for West Germany's **World Cup win** two years later, and the scene of **Holland's victory** over the Soviet Union in the 1988 European Championship final. **Trevor Francis** will never forget his diving header which won the European Cup for Nottingham Forest against Malmö in 1979 – he ended up face down on the concrete shot-throwing area, just to the side of one goal. Despite such failings, the stadium has remained **a UEFA favourite**, hosting Marseille's European Cup final win over Milan in 1993 and, most recently, Dortmund's unlikely victory over Juventus in the 1997 edition of the same competition.

The **German national team** are regular visitors here, too, and the ground played a pivotal role in the country's bid to host the **2006 World Cup**, for which it will be extensively refurbished – although precisely who will foot the bill for this has yet to be decided.

Take U3 to **Olympiazentrum**, 10mins from Marienplatz, then walk 10mins across Olympiapark. Allow 30mins from the Hauptbahnhof including a change at Scheidplatz.

There are two **popular bars** near the stadium – turn right out of the metro, and follow the red piping up to the *Ladenzentrum*. Opposite each other in the shopping centre are the *Dorfkrug* and the *Olympia-Imbiss*, both packed with fans on matchdays.

Of the many stalls dotted around the ground, the *Biergarten* behind the north end is a popular spot for a sit-down beer. Inside the stadium, the large cafeteria in the lower level of block Y is where many fans stay to view the second half, watching the game on one of the TVs over a Weissbräu and a Wurst.

There are groups of grey **ticket booths**, from the Nord entrance nearest the U-Bahn station, all around to the Süd-West.

cling to a loyal, local fan base. Bayern are sponsored by *Opel*, German wing of the multi-national *General Motors* corporation; 1860 wear the logo of a local brewery, *Löwenbräu*. The commercial tie-up is appropriate because 1860 are nicknamed *Löwen* ('Lions'). The trouble is, they only seem to roar every few decades or so.

They might claim more local support than Bayern, but on the field, there is no longer any doubt that Munich 1860 are the city's second team. While the club are proud of their heritage, only recently have the team begun to show any sign of living

up to it, having emerged from a decade of gloom in Bavarian regional leagues.

Before World War II, 1860 competed (not very successfully) with Nuremburg for dominance in the south of Germany. When the *Bundesliga* kicked off in 1964, they were given a place in the first division. They justified that decision by winning the West German Cup in 1964.

In the following season's Cup-Winners' Cup, and helped by the goals of striker Rudi Brunnenmaier, 1860 powered their way past Porto and Legia Warsaw in the early rounds, before meeting Torino in the semi-finals. The Germans lost 2–0 in Turin, then won a thrilling second leg 3–1. In those days away goals did not count double and games level on aggregate went to a replay – which the Lions duly won 2–0.

In the final, 1860 were at an obvious disadvantage as the venue had been pre-selected as Wembley, at that time almost a home from home for some members of the opposing side, West Ham United. Two goals from Alan Sealey gave the Hammers the silverware.

If the club were dispirited by that loss, they didn't show it. They began the 1965/66 season with a 1–0 derby win over Bayern, and finished it three points clear of Dortmund at the top of the *Bundesliga* table. The championship, which remains 1860's only league win, was a tribute to the attacking 4–2–4 formation favoured by their coach, Max Merkel. Prior to the start of the season he had poached striker Timo Konietzka from Dortmund to partner Brunnenmaier in attack, and that year 1860 scored eighty goals. But the real hero worship was reserved for the team's Yugoslav goalkeeper, Petar Radenković. *Radi* had arrived in Germany with no job, nowhere to live and two suitcases carrying all his worldly goods – but convinced he could become a professional footballer. He was quickly signed by 1860 and stayed with them until 1970, going on some legendary excursions outside his penalty area, and even cutting his own top-ten single.

With Bayern winning the cup in the same year as 1860 won the league, Munich looked as if it might defy the 'one city, one team' logic of the *Bundesliga* and sustain two top-class sides. It wasn't to be. By Christmas 1966, Merkel had resigned after falling out with some of his key players, and the club never recovered.

The Seventies were a decade of utter mediocrity. The Eighties were worse. In 1981 they were relegated from the first division. A year later the club had its professional licence revoked due to financial instability, and the team were relegated again. Among the players to desert the sinking ship was a young Rudi Völler. Nine grim years in the amateur ranks followed.

In 1991, the club won back their professional licence and, under coach Werner Lorant, gained promotion to the second division. With Karl-Heinz Wildmoser providing the cash, the team had clawed all the way back to the top flight by 1994.

The club's years in the wilderness had altered the character of their support. The German amateur leagues have always attracted fans who are turned off by the commercialism and impersonal nature of the big clubs, and 1860 attracted many fans with an alternative view of life. Punks and ravers took their seats next to older *Münchener* who could remember the days of Wembley and Radenković.

Today these fans have a hot-and-cold relationship with president Wildmoser. When his money talked and 1860 won promotion back to the big time, he was the hero. But he quickly turned villain when he uprooted the club from their old Grünwalder ground to the Olympiastadion – repeating a similar move which had backfired spectacularly two decades earlier.

After qualifying for Europe through the back door in 1997 – club captain Manfred Schwabl was sacked for organising a rival celebration party – 1860 sadly blew their first international appearance for nearly 30 years with a poor display at Rapid Vienna in the first leg of the UEFA Cup second round. In fact, the club's *Bundesliga* survival was sealed with a 1–0 win over a nine-man Schalke only in the season's penultimate match, and with key midfielder Jens Jeremies controversially sold to Bayern before his appearance in a Germany shirt at the World Cup, fans held out little hope for success in 1998/99.

But with new signing Gerard Vanenburg as attacking libero, and established strikers Bernard Winkler and Austrian Harald Cerny scoring the goals, 1860 got off to a flying start. They were clinging on to Bayern's coat-tails in second place when the city rivals met in November – and a Jeremies goal broke the tension after an hour's play, paying the way for a 3–1 Bayern win. Depleted and demotivated, the team lost their way either side of the winter break, and finished mid-table.

Time for another rethink on behalf of Lorant, who signed Thomas Hässler from Dortmund and Germany's supreme goal-poacher, Martin Max, from Schalke during the close season. The new recipe didn't always taste great, but it worked well enough for 1860 to beat Bayern not once but twice in the league, and to finish on top of a whole rabble of clubs chasing fourth place in the *Bundesliga* table – and a coveted spot in the Champions' League qualifying rounds.

Just the ticket

Tickets can be bought **in advance** at the Grün-walder, on the corner of Candidstrasse and Grünwalderstrasse, or on the day at the Olympiastadion. Either way, prices are lower than for Bayern. TSV fans occupy the *Nordkurve*, blocks E–H, away fans the *Südkurve* S2–U2.

Swift half

Fans still meet by the old Grünwalder stadium in Giesling (U1 to Wettersteinplatz), if possible at the stadium bar itself – when the junior or reserve teams play on Saturday morning – or at one of two bars nearby. The *Wirtschaftswunder*, Giesinger 9, is a basic, popular *Kneipe* among 1860 fans on matchdays. The *Sängerheim Gast-stätte*, 500m nearer town at Tegernseer Landstrasse 131, is more convivial, with team pics and blue-and-white trimmings – but its own-ers close up on Saturdays.

Club merchandise

There is an official **club shop** in the centre of town at Orlandostrasse 8, and another at the old Grünwalder stadium.

Ultra culture

The revival of the club has been accompanied by a rapid growth in **supporters' organisations**. There are now more than 300 organised fan groups, and as the fans are keen to point out, most of them are based in Munich – although there is a branch in Tobago.

New lease of life – 1860's Thomas Hässler

In print

The matchday magazine **Löwen News** (DM2) is every bit as glossy and statistically comprehensive as Bayern's – without so much of the sales pitch.

In the net

The **official website** is a bit like the club itself – straightforward and unpretentious, but good-looking nonetheless. It's at: www.tsv1860.de.

Groundhopping

SpVgg Unterhaching

Sportparkstadion, Am Sportpark 1
Capacity 10,000
Colours All red with blue trim

Hidden away in Munich's quiet suburbia are Spielvereinigung Unterhaching, founded in 1925 and unlikely *Bundesliga* newcomers in 1999/2000. With two top-flight teams

Backing Haching – 'keeper Jürgen Wittmann

already in the city, the club once struggled to pull in the crowds, relying on local residents to make up their average gate of around 3,000 – easily the worst in the *Zweite Bundesliga*.

But with kick-off times switched to allow as many Bayern or 1860 fans as possible to make the S-Bahn trip out to the ground, 'Haching' surprised the nation by setting one of the best home records in the *Bundesliga* in 1999/2000 – so good, in fact, that Bayer Leverkusen could do no more than wilt on their day of destiny, allowing the home side to win 2–0.

To see Haching, take S2 to **Fasanenpark**, then a 15min walk through the underpass and on to the stadium in the distance. The Sportspark's best feature is the *Sportsadl* clubhouse, with its view

over the pitch, Guinness on draught and full menu. Match tickets will be around DM25 to sit in the *Haupttribüne*, DM15 to stand elsewhere.

Eat, drink, sleep…

Bars and clubs

Bavaria is synonymous with beer. Munich alone has six labels, including *Augustiner*, *Hacker-Pschorr* and *Löwenbräu*, all with their own **beer halls** – large, noisy affairs which close around midnight. A large litre-glass is called a *Mass* (around DM10), a half-litre a *Halbmass* (DM6). Wheat beer, called *Weizenbier* in the rest of Germany, is called *Weissbier* here and is extremely refreshing. The big booze-up is, of course, the *Oktoberfest*, which runs from the last Saturday in September to the first Sunday in October, at the Theresienwiese fairground.

The main area for nightlife is **Schwabing** (U3/U6 Münchener Freiheit), with its flash, glitzy discos. Further south, behind the university (between U2 Königsplatz and U3/U6 Odeonsplatz) you'll find things cheaper and less overbearing. The alternative district is across the river towards the Ostbahnhof in **Haidhausen** (most lines to Rosenheimer Platz).

55 Bar, Schillerstrasse 19. Classic cellar bar near the train station, a favourite with male fans because of its 55 kinds of beer (only three on draught) and its buxom barmaids. Football graffiti over the walls, scarves over the bar. Open until 3am. All lines to Hauptbahnhof.

Atomiccafé, Neutrumstrasse 5. Popular city-centre club with Seventies decor playing mainstream dance and Britpop, techno every other Sunday. DM10 entrance. All lines to Marienplatz.

Nachtcafé, Maximiliansplatz 5. Great all-night haunt with live jazz, blues and funk bands after midnight, small glasses of beer at DM10, breakfast served after 3am. All lines to Karlsplatz.

Nachtwerk-Club, Landsberger Strasse 185. Huge warehouse disco playing house, funk or trance, depending on the night. DM10 entrance, half-litre beers at DM7, open until dawn. All lines to Donnersberger Brücke.

Restaurants

Bavarian cuisine is designed for Bavarians – big, straightforward and **hearty**. Munich's *Gaststätten* serve honest regional fare, generally large portions of roast pork and dumplings to go with your beer, at around DM30–40. The local delicacy is *Weisswurst*, a white sausage made from veal and herbs, whose discovery is marked by a plaque on Marienplatz. Bavarian meatloaf, *Leberkäs*, is also popular.

For lunch, the *Viktualienmarkt* by Marienplatz has dozens of **stand-up options**. In the evening, the area around Türkenstrasse (just north of U3/U6 Odeonsplatz) has cheap **diners**.

Café Schiller, Schillerstrasse 3. Spacious, comfortable sports bar/restaurant near the train station, run by former champion boxer Fritz Hals. Framed autographed shirts of German football heroes amid the boxing souvenirs. Premiere TV. Open until 4am, kitchen open until 1am, night tariff from 10pm. All lines to Hauptbahnhof.

Gaststätte Engelsburg, corner of Türkenstrasse and Schellingstrasse. Reasonably priced Bavarian dishes, including daily three-course lunchtime specials at around DM16. Open until 1am. No credit cards. U2 Theresienstrasse.

Hundskugel, Hotterstrasse 18. The oldest tavern in Munich dates back to the 15th century and is as Bavarian as it could possibly get. No credit cards. Open daily 10am–midnight. All lines to Marienplatz.

Straubinger Hof, Blumenstrasse 5. Opposite the Viktualienmarkt, a famous old tavern with a beer garden where, following the tradition of eating it only before noon, the *Weisswurst* is served from 9am. Closed Sat eve, all day Sun. No credit cards.

Accommodation

Munich can be a pig of a city to find a cheap room in. Always book weeks before you travel, and for the *Oktoberfest*, months in advance. The cheapest **pensions** are to be found near the Hauptbahnhof, but make sure you're looking around in daylight.

The **tourist office** at the station will book you a room for DM5. The *EurAide* desk nearby opposite platform 11 (☎089/593 889, fax 550 3965) provides a similar service.

Haus International, Elisabethstrasse 87 (☎089/1200 224, fax 089/1200 6251). Youth hostel with a disco, cafeteria and swimming pool on site. Dorm beds from DM 40, singles DM55, with shower DM85, doubles DM100/135, and some larger rooms available. Over-26s allowed. No credit cards. A 5min walk from U2 Hohenzollernplatz.

Hotel Eder, Zweigstrasse 8 (☎089/554 660, fax 089/550 3675). Between the station and Karlsplatz, a quiet, clean, efficiently run hotel. Singles DM65–95, doubles DM75–100, most rooms with showers, breakfast included. Most credit cards.

Hotel-Pension am Markt, Heiliggeiststrasse 6 (☎089/225 014, fax 089/224 017). With a perfect location near Viktualienmarkt, this old pension has fading photos of celebrity guests and a grand piano in the lobby. Singles DM65, DM110 with shower, doubles DM110/160. Reserve at least two months in advance. No credit cards. All lines to Marienplatz.

Pension Agnes, Agnesstrasse 58 (☎089/12 93 061, fax 089/129 1764). Basic pension with spacious double rooms and shoebox singles. DM50–60 for a single, DM85–90 a double, breakfast not included. No credit cards. U2 Hohenzollernplatz.

Pension Frank, Schellingstrasse 24 (☎089/281 451, fax 089/280 0910). Come-as-you-are pension which charges DM45 per person to share a double, DM60 for a single and DM85–90 for a double, showers and breakfast included. No credit cards. U3/U6 Universität.

Cologne

Poor-weather friends – Cologne continued to pull in the crowds in the second division

Perched picturesquely on the river Rhine, Cologne is a major industrial centre which happens to have spawned some of the most successful and effective teams to have graced the *Bundesliga*. The town's big club, 1.FC Cologne (in German '1.FC Köln', meaning 'the first football club of Cologne') won the first-ever *Bundesliga* title and have been there or thereabouts ever since.

In recent years, though, the club have sunk into the mid-table mire, seeing their position as the region's major player usurped by others – notably Leverkusen, a ten-minute train ride to the north-west, whose backing from the chemicals giant Bayer allows them to spend more freely in the transfer market than their more illustrious neighbours. There is also a strong traditional rivalry with nearby Borussia Mönchengladbach.

Next to these threats, the presence of little Fortuna, stuck in the lower rank for more than 25 years, hardly seemed to matter until both sides had to face each other in the *Zweite Bundesliga* in 1998/99, 1.FC having been relegated for the first time in their history the previous season. Each club had an ex-international and former 1.FC player as coach, Bernd Schuster at 1.FC –

poached from their new *Zweite* city rivals in the close season – and Toni Schumacher at Fortuna. The teams played ducks and drakes with each other in mid-table the whole season, 1.FC finishing tenth, Fortuna three points clear of the trap door to the *Regionalligas* in 14th.

Twelve months on, and the picture couldn't have been more different. While 1.FC under new coach Ewald Lienen raced to the second-division title at breakneck speed, Fortuna headed in the opposite direction – with all too similar alacrity.

The thrilling fields

1.FC Cologne

Müngersdorfer Stadion, Müngersdorf
Capacity 54,000
Colours All red with white trim
League champions 1962, 1964, 1978
Cup winners 1968, 1977–78, 1983

1.FC Cologne are a product of postwar reconstruction. Just as the devastation of their major cities allowed the Germans to rebuild their infrastructure in a logical way, so the re-organisation of football gave Cologne a chance to create a team worthy of one of the nation's major cities.

Before World War II, Cologne had two major teams: Kölner Ballspiel-Club (KBC) and Sülz 07. Neither of them had made it to the final of a German championship or cup. Sülz had a strong tradition in a number of sports, while KBC were well-organised and had stronger finances. The city already had an excellent stadium – the Müngersdorfer, built as part of a huge sports complex in 1923 – so a merger to create a team worthy of such facilities made sense.

1.FC Cologne were born on February 13, 1948, and took the field four months later in the *Oberliga West*. It didn't take long for the new club to make an impact. There was a place in the final of the West German cup in 1954, and after competing in the latter stages of the qualifiers for the national title, Cologne made their first championship play-off in 1960, losing 3–2 to Hamburg. In 1962, they went one better, beating Nuremburg 4–0 in the Olympic

stadium, Berlin, with a team inspired by the international full-back Karl-Heinz Schnellinger.

The club sold Schnellinger to AS Roma a year later, but there was no question that they would be founding members of the *Bundesliga*. They began the inaugural, 1963/64 season as favourites and lived up to expectations, winning the title by six points, thanks largely to the influence of Wolfgang Overath. A hard-grafting midfielder with tremendous shooting power, Overath was to stay with the club throughout his career, during which he clocked up 81 caps for West Germany.

The title gave Cologne their second tilt at the European Cup. In their first appearance in 1962/63, they'd suffered a humiliating defeat by Dundee, losing 8–1 in Scotland. In 1965 they fared better, reaching a semi-final against Liverpool. A pair of goalless draws against England's champions typified Cologne's gutsy, fighting spirit; they lost the replay 2–0.

A domestic cup win in 1968 ended Cologne's run of success, and it wasn't until

Cologne essentials

Cologne's **airport**, Köln-Bonn, which it shares with the former German capital, is connected with the city's central crossing point, Dom/Hauptbahnhof, by bus #170 (every 15mins, 6am–11.45pm, 5.30am–11pm from town, journey time 20mins, DM8.90). The bus station is directly behind Cologne's busy main **train station**, which is served by the comfortable *Thalys* rail service from Paris, Amsterdam and the *Eurostar* terminal at Brussels Midi.

The city's **public transport system** (5.30am–11pm) – buses and S-Bahn trams, which run underground in the centre – is also shared with Bonn, hence a complicated ticket system. A short journey, in *tarifzone K*, costs DM2.20, a longer one, in *tarifzone A*, DM3.90. A better bet may be to buy a 24-hour pass, *T1*, for DM9.50, or a three-day pass, *T9*, for DM23. Tickets are sold from coin-only machines onboard or on platforms – stamp the latter in the smaller red devices by the main doors of the bus or tram. Through Friday and Saturday nights, ten main **tram routes** run every hour through the city's main crossing points on the same ticket system. **Taxis** line up outside the Hauptbahnhof. To call one, dial the central office on ☎0221/2882.

The main **tourist information office** is opposite the Hauptbahnhof at Unter Fettenhennen 19 (open Mon–Sat 8am–9pm, Sun 9.30am–7pm, ☎0221/221 3345, fax 0221/23320). They charge DM5 commission for booking you a room, but it's worth it – they can often get discounted prices. The office also publishes a monthly guide to entertainment and cultural events, but better **listings magazines** are *Kölner* (DM2) *Prinz* (DM4.50).

the late Seventies that the fans at the Müngersdorfer had cause to celebrate once more. In 1977, with Hennes Weisweiler, architect of the great Mönchengladbach side of the early Seventies, in charge, and with Overath playing his last season, they won the cup. The following year they won it again, and also lifted the title to become only the third West German team to do the double (Schalke in 1937 and Bayern in 1969 were the other two). The last round of the *Bundesliga* title race was nothing if not bizarre – Cologne were level on points with 'Gladbach, but their goal difference was so massively superior that if they won, Weisweiler's men knew their rivals would have to score twelve to overhaul them. 'Gladbach duly beat a strangely under-strength Dortmund side by exactly 12–0, but Cologne were not to be denied – they beat St Pauli 5–0 on the same day.

Weisweiler's side, skippered by West German international Heinz Flohe and with the prodigious Dieter Müller upfront, reached the European Cup semi-finals in 1979, where they lost to eventual winners Nottingham Forest. In the Forest side that faced them was England international striker Tony Woodcock. The striker must have made quite an impression as the following season he moved to Cologne, where he enjoyed three seasons before being sold to Arsenal. Woodcock returned to the city to play and later coach Fortuna Köln, and still lives in the area.

Cologne's best run in Europe came in 1986, when they made it all the way to a UEFA Cup final against Real Madrid. After taking the lead in the first leg at the Bernabéu, the Germans went down 5–1 and could not recover. Supporters, however, often cite this team as the most attractive seen at the Müngersdorfer, with the wayward but magical talents of Klaus Allofs and Pierre Littbarski in the final third.

There have been no honours since. Cologne finished as *Bundesliga* runners-up in 1989 and 1990, but more recently they have drifted dangerously in mid-table. The club's leadership are far from popular with the fans, who have become frustrated with what they see as a lack of ambition – exemplified by an absence of adventure in the transfer market. The 1995/96 season saw two coaches fired as the team slipped close to the drop zone, before recovering to finish twelfth. The following campaign was little better, the club surviving in tenth place off the meagre pickings delivered by their ageing strikeforce of Bruno Labbadia and Toni Polster.

Much wrse was to follow in 1998, when the club were relegated for the first time in their *Bundesliga* history. The mid-season purchase of Iranian Khodadad Azizi belatedly gave the forward line some pace, but to no avail. One game from the end of the season, in the drizzle of Bielefeld, former Cologne striker Uwe Fuchs scored twice to consign his former employers to the drop. To add injury to insult, the formality of relegation was completed the following weekend, when next-door neighbours Leverkusen came to the Müngersdorfer and went home with a 2–2 draw under their belts. Some of the visiting fans weren't so fortunate – trams carrying them from the stadium were attacked by Cologne hooligans, and police made nearly 300 arrests.

After poaching coach Bernd Schuster from Fortuna, 1.FC started 1998/99, their first season in the *Zweite*, full of high hopes, but despite some occasionally excellent performances from Romanian midfielder Dorinel Munteanu, lack of self-confidence led to their mediocre mid-table finish.

Munteanu then departed for Wolfsburg, but new 1.FC coach Ewald Lienen, appointed in the summer of 1999 to add some much-needed realism to the squad, had few problems motivating a workmanlike but ambitious team. Cologne were promoted before April was out, and crowned *Zweite Bundesliga* champions long before a loss of form, in meaningless games, cut their winning margin to four points.

Here we go!

Take S-Bahn line S1, direction Junkersdorf, to **Stadion**. The journey, which takes around

20mins including one change from the Haupt-bahnhof, is free to ticket-holders on matchdays. From the S-Bahn station, the Müngersdorfer is a short walk across the park, past the multi-storey car park.

Just the ticket

The **ticket offices** are at opposite ends of the stadium, one by the main entrance a short walk from the tram-stop, the other, which sells tickets for visiting fans, on Junkersdorfer Strasse at the far end. The home end is the *Südkurve*, blocks 1-4, with standing tickets at DM15, seats in the *Oberrang Süd* at DM27. Away fans are allocated blocks 37-41 in the *Nordkurve* at the same prices. Visiting neutrals may be best placed in one of the sides at DM35–40; the most expensive seats in the *Oberrang West* or *Ost* run to DM50.

Swift half

For a pre-match drink, your best bet is to get off one tram-stop before Stadion at **Alter Militärring**, where there are two terrace restaurants either side of main Aachener Strasse – the **Stadt Waldgarten** and the **Müngersdorfer Garten-Restaurant**, the latter with old sports pics inside.

There are *Kölsch* vans dotted around the stadium, and **alcohol-free beer**, sold in toothbrush mugs, inside.

Club merchandise

Souvenirs are available from the **1.FC Köln Geissbock** shop (Mon–Fri 10am–5.30pm, Sat or Sun matchdays 11am–2pm) at the club headquarters in the *Sportpark des 1.FC Köln*, a 10min walk from the #18/19 tram stops at Klettenbergpark. Advance match tickets can also be purchased here. The sports complex, tucked away in the woods, is signposted on the junction of Militär-ringstrasse and Berrenrather Strasse.

Ultra culture

The *Südtribune* is home to the most enthusiastic and noisiest of the local support, particularly the bottom tier. The fans have a friendship with supporters of St Pauli which dates back to 1978, when Cologne won the title in Hamburg and spent the night partying around the Reeperbahn with the Pauli crowd.

You may also see a group parading a banner declaring **Arsenal Cologne**. Although the origins of this bizarre sect are not clear, it's believed they may originally have been a Tony Woodcock fan club who continued to follow the permed one after his move to Highbury.

In print

Geissbockecho (DM2) is the official and rather dull match programme. The most popular fanzine is named after a former coach, **Hennes**, and copies are usually on sale outside the entrance to the *Südtribune*.

In the net

The club's **official website** is at www.fc-koeln.de. It includes a full online shopping service, still a relative rarity among German clubs, though otherwise it's unremarkable. Sadly, many of Cologne's unofficial fan sites faded along with the club's *Bundesliga* fortunes.

Groundhopping

⚽ Fortuna Cologne

Südstadion, Am Vorgebirgstor
Capacity 15,000
Colours All white with red trim

Like 1.FC Cologne, Fortuna were formed in 1948. Like 1.FC Cologne, Fortuna came about from the amalgamation of prewar clubs – in their case Victoria, Bayenthaler and SV Köln. But there the similarity ends.

Fortuna have had just one season in the top flight – 1973/74, with Irish international Noel Cantwell in the side. But the season was spoilt for many loyal fans by the fact that the team had to groundshare with 1.FC Cologne.

Two years later the club left their old Radrennbahn ground behind for good, and moved to the newly built Südstadion. The ground was upgraded in the summer of 1994 when the north end was redeveloped, but the stadium is a disappointment – a

Smiling through the pain – Hans Krankl

characterless arena typical of the cheap Seventies mini-bowls that can be found across western Germany and Austria.

The club's finest hour came in 1983, when they made the final of the West German cup. Even then, 1.FC were there to steal the limelight, defeating the 'southsiders' 1–0 with a goal from Littbarski.

Mediocre or not, Fortuna had at least been consistent, having notched up more than two decades of *Zweite Bundesliga* football before the calamities of 1999/2000 – which included the sacking of coach Schumacher while he was giving a half-time teamtalk and his replacement by the former Austrian international striker Hans Krankl – culminated in a 16th-place finish, and relegation to the *Regioinalligas*.

In its new lowly position, the club will need all the support it can get from its loyal band of colourful supporters. The *Fortuna Eagles* are the main fan group, and they can be found singing away in the *Stehplatz Mitte*

– the terracing opposite the main stand. If you fancy singing along with them, take **tram #12** from the Hauptbahnhof, direction Zollstock, to Südfriedhof. The ground is on your left as you get off the tram. Match **ticket prices** are maximum DM30 for the *Tribüne West* main stand, DM15 for the *Stehplatz Mitte* and DM10 for either *Kurve* – away fans occupy the *Nordkurve* at the scoreboard end.

The beer at the ground is alcohol-free. Next-door to the club offices at Am Vorgebirgstor 1, just down the road from the stadium, is ***Bacchus***, a friendly pub/restaurant owned by the club. Dark and smoky inside, during the week it does a fair trade serving business lunches. On matchdays, however, it fills up early with young Eagles preparing to fly.

Eat, drink, sleep…

Bars and clubs

Packed with bars and restaurants of all varieties and boasting an exceptionally varied nightlife, Cologne won't make you look far in your search for a pint and a bite.

The traditional local beer is *Kölsch* – a light but bitter ale which is served in a tall, thin *Stange* glass. The locals love it but the rest of Germany considers it to be the equivalent of **drinking halves of shandy**.

The traditional setting for sipping a glass of *Kölsch* is the *Brauhaus* – a large bar or beer hall owned by a local brewery, which will often also be an ideal place to try out some local cooking at a reasonable price. There are scores of *Brauhäuser* dotted all over the city, but some are a little tacky and touristy. For **nightlife**, try the areas around Brüsseler Platz (for an alternative feel) or Zülpicher Strasse – the latter has its own U-Bahn stop and is busy with a young crowd at weekends.

Alter Wartesaal, Johannisstrasse 11. Centrally located club/disco with a varied programme of electronic and soul party nights. Admission fee (DM10–25) varies according to the quality of DJ.

Brauhaus Sion, Unter Taschenmacher 5. Popular Alstadt *Brauhaus*, but slightly further from the Cathedral than more well-known spots like the *Früh am Dom* at Am Hof 12–14, so not as touristy. Both serve their own versions of *Kölsch* and offer large portions of local cuisine.

Heimspiel, Zülpicher Strasse 10. Deep in the trendy Kwartier-Lateng, a cocktail bar with themed drinks such as the 'Elfmeter' and 'Golden Goal', and silly drinking games encouraged after the TV game is over. Open daily 5pm–1am.

M20, Maastrichtstrasse 20. Packed designer bar near Brüsseler Platz, with fewer pretensions than the equally popular *Hallmackenreuther* on the square at #9. Both are fine examples of what Germans call a 'scene bar', a pre-party meeting point and informal nightlife info centre.

Restaurants

Tired with their reputation for stodgy meat, cabbage and dumpling dishes, German chefs and restaurant owners are busy trying to reconstruct the *Deutsche Küche*. The result is *Neudeutsch*, a **lighter, modern German cuisine**, and Cologne is one of the best places to try it.

Alt-Köln, Trankgasse 7–9. A central *Brauhaus* with a reputation for good, solid, local food, served in large portions and to be washed down with freshly poured beer. Not quite *Neudeutsch* but a good winter warmer. Open Mon–Sat 12 noon–12 midnight, Sun until 11pm.

Chicago Meatpackers, Hahnenstrasse 37. Don't come here unless you're hungry. Monster-sized (even by German standards) burgers and steaks, piles of chips, great fresh salads, chilli – and loads of footie on TV. Open daily midday–11pm.

Lesar, Mozart Strasse 39. A friendly little tavern serving fine *Neudeutsch* dishes. Also does an excellent breakfast buffet. Open until 1am Mon–Sat, 10pm Sun.

Neumarktstube, Neumarkt 13. Friendly hostelry by a central crossing point offering large portions of local specialities at around DM15. Kitchen open until 10.30pm.

Zum Geissbock, Cluballee 1-3. Located at 1.FC Cologne's HQ, overlooking the training pitch, a terrace restaurant offering lunchtime daily specials at DM15, and evening meals from 6pm. Closed Mon, early Sun eve. Signposted from the junction of Militärringstrasse and Berrenrather Strasse, a 10min walk from the Klettenbergpark stop on tram #18/19.

Accommodation

Cologne gets plenty of tourists in summer but most of its hotels are geared towards the business community – the city has a vast *Messe* trade-fair centre and the almost fortnightly events between September and June can mean a doubling of room rates. Many of these business hotels do, however, offer **cheap weekend deals**, the only disadvantage being that they can be a good way out from the city centre.

The resumption of the German football season in early spring often coincides with **Carnival time** in Cologne, when spare rooms fill up quickly.

Hotel Cristall, Ursulaplatz 9–11 (☎0221/16300, fax 0221/163 0333). Small, fairly upmarket hotel, five minutes from the train station and the *Dom*; 85 new rooms, hotel bar. Doubles from DM160.

Hotel Rheingold, Engelsbertstrasse 33–35 (☎0221/924 090). Good value at DM65 per person in a double room, with en-suite bath/shower and colour TV. Central location.

Im Kupferkessel, Probsteigasse 6 (☎0221/135 338, fax 0221/125 121). Central, unpretentious place with singles at DM55–70, doubles from DM120. Location ideal for clubbing.

Jugendherberge Deutz, Siegestrasse 5a (☎0221/814 711). Just over the river, this is a basic youth hostel, with surly and unhelpful staff who must have been trained in the GDR. Still, it's only 10mins by U-Bahn from the centre and offers a decent continental buffet breakfast Dorm rooms from DM15.

Giving their rivals a headache – Bayer Leverkusen

The decline of traditional Rheinland giants Borussia Mönchengladbach and 1.FC Cologne has coincided with the rise of the works team of the country's largest chemical plant, *Bayer*, based in a small town a short drive from Cologne, Leverkusen.

So near yet so far – despair is the order of the day

The company inaugurated its sports club in 1904, shortly after the launch of its **headache tablet**, *Aspirin*. Although a football section was introduced three years later, it did not enjoy the same success as the small white pill. Playing at the modest Sportpark, Leverkusen made the *Oberliga West* in 1951, flitting to and from the regional leagues.

Despite this, Bayer saw fit to invest in the building of a new stadium near the Sportpark in 1958, which was eventually named after a former company director, Professor Ulrich Haberland. With its 25,000 capacity, the **Ulrich-Haberland stadium** was hardly a hotbed of footballing passion, but Leverkusen won promotion to the top flight in 1979, and have stayed there ever since.

It was under future German national-team coach **Erich Ribbeck** that things started to move. After hs appointment in 1985, the club began to make regular UEFA Cup appearances, culminating in a surprise run to the final in 1988, when the team came back from losing the first leg 3–0 to **Español** in Spain to win the tie on penalties on their own patch. Despite a succession of top coaches, however, the club were unable to build on this success, save for a domestic **cup victory** over Herth Berlin's amateur side in 1993.

The arrival of **Christoph Daum** in the dugout in 1996 transformed the club. A south stand was built in 1997, a precursor to the *BayArena* of today, with its hotel, panoramic restaurant and crêche. On the pitch, money was made available for Daum to pepper his solid 3–5–2 formation with Brazilian talent, including Paulo Sérgio and Jorginho. Coupled with this creativity was the decade's most prolific *Bundesliga* scorer, Ulf Kirsten. In Daum's first season, Leverkusen finished runners-up to Bayern in the *Bundesliga*, then invested £11million in new players before their first appearance in the **Champions' League**. There they overcame a 4–0 defeat at Monaco to qualify for the quarter-final stage, before losing 4–1 on aggregate to Real Madrid. In the 1998 close season the club lost defender Christian Wörns to PSG, but kept Kirsten and playmaker Stefan Beinlich. The team were no match for Bayern in 1998/99, but should have beaten their rivals to the title a year later when, needing only a point in their final game of the season at little Unterhaching, they were beaten 2–0.

The *BayArena* is a short walk from Leverkusen-Mitte Stadtbahn station – special *Löwenlinie* buses are provided on matchdays. Near the ground on Bismarckstrasse are the fans' *Sportivo* bar at #230, and right opposite the stadium is the *Mobs-Biergarten* at #127. Advance tickets are sold at the *Bayer Kaufhaus*, Wiesdorfer Platz 2 in town. Visiting fans are allocated places in the *Südtribüne*, standing in blocks G1–G3, sitting in F4. The home faithful are to be found in block C between the east and north stands.

Berlin

For most of the Nineties, Berlin was a foot-balling orphan. Unlike Paris, it had had no superteam artificially thrust upon it to win league titles and compete with Europe's best. Unlike Paris, few national-team games were regularly played there. But, also unlike Paris, it has always had a genuine football culture, rooted in the city's international mix and a close working relationship with the game that dates back a century.

Berlin was quick to take to football in the 1870s. While other German boys were forced into gymnastics, the new English sports fad was all the rage here and in the north German ports. The first inter-city match took place in 1896 between Berlin and Hamburg (won 13–0 by the former), and Berlin sides won German titles in 1905, 1908 and 1911. Yet Hertha's championship of 1931 was Berlin's last.

The building of Hitler's vast, all-seated Olympiastadion for the 1936 Games kept Berlin in the football spotlight, with record crowds drawn to the new annual cup final – until World War II, that is.

In the aftermath of the conflict, Berlin was governed by the four Allied powers, with the Soviet authorities taking the east-ern part and sealing it off from the rest. As the east and west sides of town devel-oped separately, so did their football.

In East Berlin, now capital of the GDR, football was remodelled in the classic Com-munist mould, with each team representing the army, the police, and so on. ASK Vor-wärts Berlin were the army side, receiving the usual political favours and star players, of whom there weren't that many. East Germany, whose main cities never featured strongly in the old regional play-offs before the war, spent two decades in relative international obscurity, while Vorwärts notched up a handful of titles in the Fifties and Sixties.

After that, the reorganisation of the GDR's domestic game favoured provincial factory outfits like Carl Zeiss Jena and Dynamo Dresden, and Vorwärts fell from

grace, eventually being moved to Frankfurt an der Oder in 1971.

Meanwhile, the game in what was now West Germany was also reorganised, with Berlin being treated as a separate regional entity among four more powerful others, mainly due to logistical difficulties, travel being possible only through a 'corridor', a single road, rail and air route, which ran from the East–West border, 150km away, to the city. In 1961, the city itself had a wall built through it.

Hertha, who had been suffering from the lack of local competition and were totally outclassed when it came to the regional play-offs, moved from their ground at Am Gesundbrunnen by the Wall, to the Olympiastadion way out west. When the *Bundesliga* was formed in 1963, each of the five regions received a quota of entries for the new national 16-team league – Berlin got one.

The history of West Berlin clubs in the *Bundesliga* is beset by abject defeat and notoriety. The four clubs to play in the top flight – Hertha, Blau-Weiss, Tennis Borus-sia and Tasmania – were all quickly relegated, Tasmania's effort in 1965/66 being an all-time Bundesliga low. When Hertha did begin to enjoy the kind of suc-cess the custodians of the Olympiastadion should merit – European runs and bumper crowds – they were brought down to earth by a bribery scandal in 1971.

Over the next two-and-a-half decades, Hertha were rarely able to attract decent crowds, their working-class fans failing to move with the club to the Olympiastadion. Hippies, pinkos and punks of every hue drifted to Berlin to avoid national service, and the few that could be bothered with football began to support Blau-Weiss, who would later also become popular with nightclubbers shunning sleep the morning after, cheering them on when they ground-shared with Hertha. In the meantime Hertha's fan base attracted a reactionary element, and support for either team became a political rather than a sporting choice.

Throughout this period, Berlin was not for the career-minded young footballer. Its junior leagues could produce players of the quality of Pierre Littbarksi and Thomas Hässler, but both had to go to other cities to seek their fortune, having to work twice as hard to prove themselves. The West German FA deliberately kept football interest in the city going by locating the cup final there on a permanent annual basis from 1985 – yet Hertha spent most of the Nineties in the lower flight.

On the other side of the Wall, a football culture developed – of sorts. While Hertha's results were eagerly devoured by disillusioned Easterners, 1966 saw a year of change in the capital's football. A modest outfit called SC Dynamo Berlin became the police team, Berliner FC Dynamo, while obscure Oberschöneweide became 1.FC Union Berlin.

While Union drew working-class support, Dynamo were despised, primarily because their club president was Erich Mielke, head of the Communist state secret police, the *Stasi*. (The fact that you could see the West from the main stand of their Friedrich Ludwig Jahn stadium didn't help.) Mielke ensured that Dynamo Berlin won – every year. Daft penalties, curious disallowed goals, you name it, Dynamo got it. The club's ten-year stay at the top of the East German *Oberliga* was a standing joke, although the team were not without talent, and players like Thomas Doll and Andreas Thom would later make their fortune in the West.

The fall of the Wall in 1989 ended Dynamo's hegemony. As FC Berlin they began to attract a violent, right-wing following, while a now impoverished playing staff failed to lift them above the *Regionalliga Nordost*, adopted home for the city's many obscure teams, the ethnic sides SD Croatia Berlin and Turkyimspor among them.

Soon after the fall of the Wall, in the spirit of reunification, a Hertha–Union

friendly at the Olympiastadion attracted a crowd of 50,000. A few months later, it was back to normal – low crowds and mediocre football. Even Blau-Weiss sadly foundered after losing their professional licence.

The game in the city was relauched by Hertha and their backers, the media giant *UFA*, in 1994. Commercially, the *UFA* move followed Canal Plus' example in Paris. But the development was also political. *UFA* was the pre-war film studio responsible for the classic city images which brought in the tourists, and had since become the audiovisual branch of Germany's huge *Bertelsmann* media empire.

The *Bertelsmann* powerbase was in the SPD stronghold of Rhine-Westphalia, while the company's great rival, Leo Kirch, was based in conservative Bavaria. For years *Bertelsmann* had been looking for a high-profile city to challenge Kirch's Munich, and Berlin would be the obvious choice if it were to have a flagship club. Hertha was chosen to be that club, and *UFA* put in manager Robert Schwan – the man behind Bayern's transformation in the Sixties – to relaunch them.

Hertha's promotion to the *Bundesliga* in 1997 duly attracted big crowds back to the Olympiastadion, and since then crowds have rarely dipped below 30,000, rising to twice that as the team marched towards a first-ever place in the Champions' League qualifiers at the tail-end of the 1998/99 campaign.

Progress on the pitch should soon be matched by rebuilding off it, as Germany's federal government, having made Berlin its capital once again, has pledged to refurbish the Olympiastadion as part not just of the city's reconstruction but of the country's hosting of the 2006 World Cup.

Berlin is back on the football map, albeit as a pawn between media giants. And if it all goes up in smoke, then its local leagues are as colourful and competitive as any in Germany, documented in the weekly *Fussball Woche* (DM3) and bi-monthly fanzine *Berliner Sport-Echo* (DM3.50).

The thrilling fields

 Hertha BSC Berlin

Olympiastadion, see p.243
Colours Blue-and-white-striped shirts, blue shorts
League champions 1930, 1931

The revival of Hertha Berlin is one of the great German football success stories of recent years. Now that the team have bounced back, they're attracting the kind of crowds not seen at the Olympiastadion since the early Seventies.

Now that there are bums on the seats again, the aim is to create a major team in the capital which will challenge Bayern's hegemony on the *Bundesliga* and grab a lucrative slice of the nationwide merchandising pie. To achieve this, Bayern's old manager Robert Schwan is in charge of strategy, while Dieter Hoeness is sport director – in direct competition with his brother Uli down in Munich. Yet, historically at least, winning the title is not something Hertha have found easy.

Founded as Hertha '92 in 1892, it was after a merger with Berliner BC '99 (hence Hertha BSC) in 1923 that the club were able to win the then regional championship with regularity. With inside-forward Hanne Sobek as the lynchpin, Hertha BSC had a great side, but victory in the regional play-off final – in effect the German national championship – proved elusive, the team being runners-up four years in a row before their luck changed. In 1930 Hertha pipped Holstein Kiel 5–4, and the following year they beat TSV Munich 1860 3–2.

These were to be the last honours Hertha would win. Yet despite their lack of success, they enjoyed a decent level of working-class support at Am Gesundbrunnen, their ground (nicknamed the *Plumpe*, because of its awkward appearance) squeezed between the Wedding and Prenzlauer Berg areas. By the Sixties, this

Capital kid – Michael Preetz goes all out

awkwardness became even more apparent – the Berlin Wall was put up next-door. When they moved to the Olympiastadion, Hertha lost two crowds – the faithful from Wedding, many of whom refused to make the trip out, and thousands of East Berliners who would listen out to the sound of the crowd at the *Plumpe*.

When Hertha became Berlin's sole representatives in the inaugural *Bundesliga*, they were thrown out in 1965 for financial irregularities. To their credit, they bounced back up – although how is another matter, since they earned a further identical punishment for their part in the match-fixing scandal of 1971.

They at last had a decent side by the mid-Seventies, featuring internationals Norbert Nigbur in goal and the prolific Erich Beer upfront. But still the title proved out of reach, with a second place in 1975 and a third in 1978. The year after, Hertha lost out on the chance to play compatriots

Borussia Mönchengladbach in the UEFA Cup final when Red Star Belgrade pipped them on away goals in the semi.

In 1980, Hertha were relegated from the *Bundesliga* as a result of their performance on the pitch for the first time. They would climb back up only twice, both times for just one season, before *Bertelsmann* launched its grand scheme in 1994.

Promotion was paramount, of course. With only old hand Axel Kruse and a bunch of enthusiastic youngsters at his dis-

posal, coach Jürgen Röber turned around a mid-table position in autumn 1996 into a regular top-three spot by the spring. The key game, against fellow promotion hopefuls 1.FC Kaiserslautern, drew 75,000 to the Olympiastadion, and Hertha won 2–0.

To prepare for the top flight, the club signed eight new players in the 1997 close season, including Norwegian Kjetil Rekdal and Dutchman Bryan Roy. Yet they initially struggled to cope with the gap in class, and relegation looked likely until striker Michael

Berlin essentials

Berlin's main **airports** are Tegel, Tempelhof and Schönefeld, the last formerly serving East Berlin. City buses (4am–midnight or 1am) connect the airports to the nearest U- or S-Bahn stops, or the city centre – tickets (DM3.60) are valid for two hours for the onward journey. From **Tegel**, take bus #109 or #X9 to central Zoologischer Garten ('Zoo') station (every 20mins, journey time 25-40mins), or change at U7 Jakob-Kaiser-Platz onto the underground system; a taxi into town is about DM30. **Tempelhof** is just south of the centre, the terminal a short walk from U6 Platz der Luftbrücke, or take bus #119 to Zoo. **Schönefeld** is in the far south-east, connected to S9 Flughafen Berlin-Schönefeld by bus #171. Alternatively, you can stay on the #171 until U7 Rudow. Allow 40mins for the journey into town; a taxi will be DM60.

International **train services** from the west arrive at Zoo station, a major U-Bahn crossing point; those from the east arrive at Lichtenberg (U9, S5, S7, S75). The central **bus station** is by U2/S4 Kaiserdamm.

Berlin city transport is divided into three zones – central A and B are adequate for most visitors' needs – and made up of the U-Bahn, S-Bahn and buses. Tickets are available from orange machines at stops and platforms, and must be validated in the red ones next to them. Single tickets are also sold onboard buses. There are two types of singles (*Einzelfahrschein*) – the short-distance (*kurzstreckentarif*, DM2.50) allows journeys of up to three stops by U- or S-Bahn, six stops by bus, no transfers; the *Normaltarif* (DM3.90) allows two hours' travel between two zones (three zones DM4.20), with any number of changes provided you do not return by the same route. Better value is the day ticket (*Tageskarte*, DM7.80, DM8.50 for three zones), valid until 3am the day after validation.

The network runs 4am–midnight/1am, with the U9 and U12 lines running all night Fri–Sat. A comprehensive network of night buses and trams run 1am–4am, generally every 30mins through Zoo, on the same ticket system as daytime. The modest daytime **tram network** operating mainly in the east, has its own ticket system – tickets are available from machines onboard.

A taxi hailed from the street will charge a DM4 start-up fee, then DM2.10 per km, DM2.30 at night. You can also ask for a *Kurzstrecke*, a journey of 2km or 5mins for DM5. For a **radio taxi**, dial ☎030/261 026 – the standing charge is DM6.

The main **tourist office** is at the *Europa-Center*, Budapester Strasse, by Zoo station (open Mon–Sat 8am–10pm, Sun 9am–9pm, ☎030/250 025, fax ☎030/2500 2424), with branches at Tegel airport, Under den Linden and the Brandenburg Gate.

The two main **listings guides** are the comprehensive German-language *Zitty* (DM3.50) and *Tip* (DM4), which come out on alternate fortnights.

Preetz arrived from MSV Duisburg. With his nose for goals, and the conversion of Rekdal to sweeper, Hertha picked up 16 points from six games to climb up the table, finishing comfortably out of the relegation zone.

By now Hungarian goalkeeper Gábor Király had earned the status of folk hero, and with the arrival of international midfielder Dariusz Wosz from Bochum, better things were expected in 1998/99. They came, too. With Preetz still in the scoring mood and Király keeping frequent clean sheets, Hertha began strongly, symbolically beat Bayern 1–0 with a Preetz goal in November, and by the end of the season had made third place – and a Champions' League qualifiying berth – their own.

To the surprise of many in Germany, Hertha did more than hold their own in Europe's premier club competition, young playmaker Sebastian Deisler inspiring them to a place in the second group phase. But at home the team's form suffered, and it wasn't until they'd been eliminated from Europe – and Preetz had recovered from injury – that Röber's men put together a run of form good enough to secure sixth place and, with it, Germany's last remaining UEFA Cup berth for 2000/01.

Swift half

There are dozens of bars in town where Hertha fans meet before heading off to the Olympiastadion. The *Maskottchen*, Grolmanstrasse 59 (corner Goethestrasse, all lines to Savignyplatz) caters to a more sedate clientele.

Club merchandise

The *Hertha Fanshop* (Mon–Fri 9am–5pm, no credit cards) is a short walk up from the Olympiastadion, down Rominter Allee (right out of the U2 stop) and up Hanns-Braun-Strasse. There's an advance **ticket office** in the main entrance, and the shop – bicycles, rubber rings, umbrellas, wheelchair blankets – is well-stocked.

Ultra culture

Although there is a significant group of traditional older fans – the kind who produce the fanzine *Der Hertha-Freund* (monthly, DM1.50) – and a bigger number of younger ones who have joined in with the Hertha revival, among the club's hardcore followers is a reasonably nasty right-wing element, many of whom reacted against the trendy nature of Hertha's city rivals Blau-Weiss in the Eighties.

In print

Wir Herthaner (DM2) the club's glossy A4 match magazine, is as good as any on the market.

In the net

The club's **official website** is smart and commercially astute, with each main area having its own sponsor. A full e-commerce section now, too at: www. herthabsc.de/.

For a fan's-eye view, try the busy **unofficial homepage** at: www.bz-berlin.de/bz/hertha/hertha.htm.

Groundhopping

⚽ Tennis Borussia Berlin

Mommsenstadion, Waldschulallee 34–42
Capacity 14,500 (1,700 seated)
Colours Lilac shirts, white shorts

With money pumped in from the *Göttinger Gruppe* insurance group, Te-Be looked like becoming Berlin's second club. But towards the end of the 1999/2000 season, the club's expensively assembled team – including former Manchester City striker Uwe Rösler in their ranks – began to realise that something was badly wrong. Then, at the end of a season in which Te-Be had finished a disappointing 13th in the *Zweite Bundesliga*, came the bombshell. *Göttinger* was being investigated for fraud, and with the club's financial lifeline effectively cut, the German FA had no option but to relegate them to the *Regionalligas*.

It's hard to see how the club will be revived. Stuck out in leafy Charlottenburg, only 2km from the Olympiastadion, the

Violets have no fan base to speak of, their only rivals until recently being SC Charlottenburg in the regional leagues.

Formed from the fusion of a social club and the *Berliner Tennis- und Ping-Pong Society* in 1902, Te-Be moved into their current Mommsenstadion after the war. Named after a local Nobel-prize winning historian, Theodor Mommsen, the modest ground hosted a handful of matches in the 1936 Olympic soccer tournament, but has seen top-flight football for only two seasons since, Te-Be's only spell in the *Bundesliga* having come in the mid-Seventies.

After winning promotion to the *Zweite* in 1998, Te-Be performed creditably, staying in the race for promotion and beating Hertha 4–2 in the cup. But despite the efforts of players like Macedonian Toni Micevski and Dietmar Hamann's brother Matthias, *Göttinger* went through three coaches during the season, and the resultant disruption saw the club miss out on a top-flight place by four points come the final day. In retrospect, that was probably just as well…

To get to the Mommsen from Zoo, either take S5 or S75 to **Eichkamp**, or U2 six stops to **Theodor-Heuss-Platz** – the latter involves a slightly longer walk. Once there, the *Kleine Kneipe* 100m from the ground is perfect for a pre-match beer. Inside, the *Engelhardt* is a reasonable club bar on the first floor of the stand, where the home fans either sit (DM25) or stand (DM15). Away fans occupy block F of the *Südkurve* opposite.

I.FC Union Berlin

Alte Försterei, Oberschönewalde
Capacity 25,000
Colours Red shirts, red shorts
Cup winners (East Germany) 1968

The 'Schalke of the East', 1.FC Union, were formed from TSC Oberschönewalde, an area of parkland by the river Spree, in 1966. In contrast to their East Berlin rivals

Dynamo, they had a popular following, acquiring the nickname *Eisern* ('Iron'), a hangover from one of their former factory sponsors, SC Motor Berlin. They enjoyed one cup final win, over Carl Zeiss Jena in 1968, but the Soviet invasion of Prague that year put paid to the club's participation in Europe.

Hard times fell on Union after unification, but when the German FA threatened to withdraw their licence in 1993, fans blocked the streets, 15,000 signatures were gathered almost overnight, and TV crews filmed supporters gathering in bars under 'Save Union!' banners. Sponsors flocked to the club.

Having gained promotion to the *Regionalliga Nord-Ost* in 1994, Union have since come bitterly close to the elusive top spot that would grant them admittance to the professional ranks, while developing their merchandising, public relations and fan activities. Getting Nina Hagen to sing the club song at the start of 1998/99 was, perhaps, taking things a little too far…

To see a Union game, take the S3 seven stops from Ostbahnhof to **Köpenick**, follow the railway back for 5mins along Am Bahndam, and turn left at the railway bridge into Hämmerlingstrasse. At #80–88 you'll find the big clubhouse bar, *Abseitsfalle* ('Offside Trap'), easily the best in Berlin.

The stadium itself is a bowl of stone terracing cut into the forest. Union fans occupy the *Haupttribüne* and the forest goal, *Seite Wald*, while visiting fans are behind the opposite Köpenick goal – seats DM25, standing DM10.

Dynamo Berlin

Sportforum, Hohenschönhausen
Capacity 15,000 (2,000 seated)
Colours White shirts with red trim
League champions (East Germany) 1979–88
Cup winners (East Germany) 1959, 1988–89

Few European clubs have a history as notorious – or 'successful' – as this one.

The Olympic stadium

Olympiastadion, Olympischer
Platz 3
Capacity 67,000 (all-seated)

The Olympiastadion is a totalitarian triumph in limestone and
granite. It's also **falling to bits**.

Apart from a couple of World
Cup matches in 1974, which saw
the building of two roofs, and
every cup final since 1985, the
place was sorely under-used until
Hertha's recent revival. When
Germany beat Bulgaria here in
their final **European
Championship qualifier** in

Crumbling edifice – it's not as nice as it looks

November 1995, it was the stadium's first international game for seven years. 'The
crowd,' said Berliner **Thomas Hässler**, 'was our twelfth man.' The atmosphere that
night forced the German FA to reassess Berlin's importance in the national setup, and
the stadium was an essential part of the nation's successful World Cup 2006 bid.

In 1936, the arena hosted **Hitler's Olympics**. It had been built at huge expense on
the site of a former racecourse, with Albert Speer part of the architectural team. The
result was an imposing, grandiose arena set against the Marathon Gate and a clock
tower offering a stunning view of the whole complex.

After World War II, the only time the Olympiastadion was regularly full was when
Hertha enjoyed a brief revival in the late Sixties – the **88,000 crowd** for a game
against Cologne in 1969 is still a *Bundesliga* record. By the time the 1974 World Cup
came to town, Hertha had sunk out of the top flight and into ignominy. The stadium
played no part in the 1988 European Championship, and there followed years of meagre crowds, either Hertha's, or Tasmania's or Blau-Weiss's, but meagre all the same.

Now plans are on the drawing board for the stadium's DM600million transformation,
scheduled to begin in the summer of 2000 and to last three years, during which time its
capacity will be reduced to 52,000. The main new feature will be an 11,000-capacity
stand area which, over the course of half a day, can be withdrawn. This will allow for a
77,000 crowd at football – enough to host a **World Cup final** – and 66,000 for Berlin's
popular and lucrative athletics meets.

The Olympiastadion has its own metro station on the U2 line (eight stops from Zoo),
which gives access to its east end, over Rossitter Platz and down Rossitter Weg past a
host of grills and beer stalls. Those arriving at the south end by S5 or S75 (six stops
from Zoo) are greeted not only by the original bell which sounded the start of the '36
Games, but by the only two bars around the ground. Facing each other across
Coubertinplatz are *Am Olympiastadion*, a small, friendly *Imbiss* bar with pennants
and a jukebox, and the more upmarket *Stadion Terrassen*, with a superb display of
Thirties prints of the stadium.

Ticket offices are to be found by Süd- and Osttor. Neutrals can enjoy the action in
blocks B–E and M–N. Block O is traditionally Hertha's, although P–S are also full
these days. Tickets in block T are the only ones sold on the day in the Hertha end, with
away fans allocated F–H. **Advance tickets** are also on sale from *Berlin Ticket*,
Potsdamer Strasse 96 (☎030/2308 8230), but they charge a hefty commission.

Formed as an offshoot of Dynamo Dresden in 1954, they had the reputation as cup fighters in the old East German setup before becoming Berliner FC Dynamo in 1966. With the departure of the army side ASK Vorwärts from the city, East Germany's capital needed a prestige team and found it in the otherwise modest Dynamo Berlin, who had the good fortune to represent the Ministry of the Interior Police, the hated *Stasi*. He may have had his faults (spying, torture, false arrest) but the head of the Ministry, Erich Mielke, loved his football and Dynamo were his personal entertainment – the secret policeman's ball, as it were.

Apart from gathering the nation's best players – goalkeeper Bodo Rudwaleit, forward Andreas Thom, midfielder Thomas Doll – the club were also able to influence the game in other ways. Legend has it that a provincial stadium tannoy once announced: 'Today we would like to welcome the players of Dynamo Berlin and their referee.' Dodgy penalties, disallowed goals, generous time-keeping, all allowed Dynamo to win the title an incredible ten years running, a European record. Dynamo were the *Schiebemeister*, the 'Cheating Champions'. And all in front of a few thousand people, the *Stasi* not being the most popular organisation at the time.

Progress in Europe was rather less spectacular, for obvious reasons. The club's best effort was their first, a run to the semi-finals of the Cup-Winners' Cup in 1972, where they lost to Dynamo Moscow – the *KGB* against the *Stasi*, no less.

Dynamo quickly changed their name after the Wall fell – to FC Berlin – and moved from the imposing Friedrich-Ludwig-Jahn Sportpark to the smaller Sportforum in Hohenschönhausen. Here, by the stench of the *Schultheiss* brewery, in front of a few hundred skinheads, they play out games against old foes 1.FC Magdeburg, Dynamo Dresden and Carl Zeiss Jena, in the *Regionalliga Nord-Ost*, the regional third division critics like to call the modern-day GDR *Oberliga*. And there is

where many would like them to stay. There is one successful Dynamo side at the Sportforum, the Berliner Eisbären ice-hockey team, whose **Arena** bar near the football pitch is a far better option than the rock-festival toilet masquerading as a bar behind the main stand. Perhaps in the hope of emulating the hockey team's success, the football club changed its name back to Dynamo in 1999.

To reach the Sportforum, either take tram #23 from S8/S10 **Frankfurter Allee** or tram #5 or #15 from S8/S10 **Landsberger Allee**, both a distance of about 2km – the latter will drop you at the sports complex entrance nearer to the *Arena* bar.

Eat, drink, sleep…

Bars and clubs

Legally, bars in Berlin must close for one hour in 24, but even this law is flouted. Basically, anything goes.

The classic Berlin bar is the **Eck-Kneipe**, full of locals supping bottomless glasses of *Berliner Kindl*, spouting on while their dogs howl along to Roy Orbison tunes on the jukebox.

The bars and clubs of Kreuzberg (around U1 Kottbusser Tor) and Schöneberg (U1/2/4 Nollendorfplatz) have been attracting misfits, dropouts and boozehounds for decades, but if the city has a nightlife centre, it's Mitte, just north of Friedrichstrasse, around U8 Rosenthaler Platz or U6 Oranienburger Tor. Pick up a copy of the fortnightly **Flyer Berlin Up-Date** for the latest clubbing information.

Delicious Doughnuts, Rosenthaler Strasse 9. Constantly changing Mitte club famed for its doughnuts and music policy of rare groove and acid jazz; all done out in ferocious red and black. U8 Weinmeisterstrasse.

Holst am Zoo, Joachimsthaler Strasse 1. Turn right out of Zoo station for Germany's premier soccer bar. Opened in 1977 by Wolfgang Holst, the place is a shrine to the game, and has seen scores of players – and politicians – pay homage. The prize display is a pre-war collection of Hertha pictures. Full menu, daily specials at DM6.50.

Tresor/Globus, Leipziger Strasse 126a. Seminal techno club short on innovation but still able to draw a crowd with a name DJ. Open Weds-Sun, cover DM5–10, U2/S1/S2 Potsdamer Platz.

Wiener Blut, Wiener Strasse 13–14. A Kreuzberg classic, with a diner feel, jukebox and table football, DJs at weekends. Closed in the daytime. The *Morena* café at #60 is also popular. U1/12 Görlitzer Bahnhof.

Restaurants

Although the local cuisine, available at most **corner bars**, is the usual hearty German mix of pork, cabbage and potatoes, Berlin has every kind of food imaginable, reflecting the city's ethnic mix. If you've no time to sit down and eat, there's an *Imbiss* on every other street corner.

Altberliner Bierstube, Saarbrückerstrasse 16. Classic old Berlin restaurant, justifiably busy. Open daily midday–2am. U2 Senefelderplatz.

Gugelhof, Knaackstrasse 37. Busy, occasionally cramped but reasonably priced eaterie with lunchtime specials at around DM40–50. U2 Senefelderplatz, by Kollwitzplatz.

Konnopke's Imbiss, Dimitroff Strasse/Schönhauser Allee. Tradtional family-run *Imbiss* with homemade wurst, under the U-Bahn tracks in Prenzlauer Berg. U2 Eberswalder Strasse.

Kellerrestaurant im Brecht Haus, Chausseestrasse 125. Pretentious, touristified cellar in the basement of Bertolt Brecht's old house, with literary readings upstairs. Excellent food all the same, for around DM25 a main course, some recipes invented by Brecht's wife. Open 5pm–2am daily. U6 Oranienburger Tor.

Accommodation

During trade fairs and festivals, it can be nigh impossible to find a cheapish room on the day, and reserving a place is recommended at all times of year.

The **tourist office** (see *Essentials*) charge a nominal fee for their booking service, although the rooms are often in the moderate category and above. The best bet is to fax them with details of when you intend to stay, and how much you're prepared to pay – don't expect to find much under DM70 a single, DM100 a double. Most places include breakfast in the price.

None of the establishments below take credit cards unless stated.

Artist Hotel-Pension Die Loge, Friedrichstrasse 115 (☎030/280 7513). Solid old Friedrichstrasse flat converted into a pension, ostensibly for artists, but artisans welcome too. Singles around DM75, doubles DM110. All rooms with TV, but showers and toilet in the corridor. U6 Oranienburger Tor.

Circus Hostel, Rosa Luxemburg Strasse 39–41 (☎030/2839 1433, fax 030/2839 1484). A godsend, if you can deal with the backpackers. No curfew. Singles at DM40, doubles DM60, dorms at DM25. Laundry and internet facilities. U2 Rosa-Luxemburg-Platz.

Hotel Märkischer Hof, Linienstrasse 133 (☎030/282 7155, fax 030/282 4331). Comfortable but modest hotel in Mitte, all rooms with TV, some with showers and toilets. Singles around DM125, doubles around DM150. Visa cards accepted. U6 Oranienburger Tor.

Hotel Transit, Hagelbergerstrasse 53–54 (☎030/789 0470, fax 030/7890 4777). Clean, friendly place in Kreuzberg, singles at DM90, doubles DM110. U6/U7 Mehringdamm.

Pension Silvia, Knesebeckstrasse 29 (☎030/881 2129, fax 030/885 0435). Classic, fading Berlin pension, but cheap and clean. All rooms spacious and with bathrooms. Singles at DM55, doubles from DM100. All lines to Savignyplatz.

Canny Kaiserslautern – Germany's Red Devils

The hottest football atmosphere in Germany is in neither Dortmund nor Gelsenkirchen, and certainly not in Munich. The Betzenberg at **Kaiserslautern**, home of *die Roten Teufel*, the 'Red Devils', is as legendary as the Wagnerian myths of the surrounding Rheinland-Pfalz forests.

The Betzenberg is now renamed after the club's most famous player, local boy **Fritz Walter**, who arrived here as an 18-year-old in 1938. Sixteen years later, after running the PoW football team on Mamara Island in the Ukraine, he was lifting the World Cup. These were **Kaiserslautern's golden years**, when five members of West Germany's 1954 side – Fritz and brother Ottmar Walter, Kohlmeyer, Eckel and Liebrich – made five national finals in seven years, winning two. Samples of radio commentary from the 1954 World Cup final still play as post-goal jingles at the Betzenberg.

Gritty battlers became the club's stock in trade, typified by current coach **Otto Rehhagel** and **Hans-Peter Briegel**. The latter would star with **Andreas Brehme** in the early Eighties side that played regularly in Europe – including a 5–0 thrashing of Real Madrid in 1982 – but neither featured in a team free of stars that were surprise *Bundesliga* champions in 1991.

Brehme then returned, only to be seen crying in Rüdi Völler's arms when the Red Devils were relegated in May 1996 – Fritz Walter listened on the radio, heartbroken. Incoming coach Rehhagel, just sacked by Bayern, sat his players round in the *Da Rosario* pizzeria outside town and told them: 'A year from now, we'll be here celebrating promotion.' Two years later, they were there celebrating the German title – the only newly promoted team ever to win it.

Rehhagel's motivation, Brehme's spirit and **Olaf Marschall**'s goals had gained the *Lauterer* promotion, after which they faced Bayern on the first day of the 1997/98 *Bundesliga* season. Revenge was sweet for Rehhagel – a 1–0 win. The season would soon see Swiss midfielder **Ciriaco Sforza** make a brilliant return to the club, Czech libero **Miroslav Kadlec**, a member of the 1991 side, come into his own, and Marschall earn Germany qualification for the World Cup. After running neck-and-neck with Bayern, Kaiserslautern came back from two down to beat Mönchengladbach 3–2 on a last-minute Marschall goal – one fan died of a heart attack – and the title was theirs.

In 1998/99, with former Manchester City striker **Uwe Rösler** added to the ranks, the team won through the easiest of the Champions' League groups to face Bayern in the quarter-finals. Without the injury-prone Marschall, they lost the away leg 2–0, before Hungarian defender János Hrutka was sent off for an early foul, and Stefan Effenberg converted the subsequent penalty – the first of four Bayern goals.

Meanwhile Kaiserslautern had started tentatively in the league, and on the season's final day they lost out to Borussia Dortmund on goal difference in the race for a Champions' League qualifying position. The **UEFA Cup** would have to do for 1999/2000, but at least the unexpected close-season arrival of **Youri Djorkaeff** allowed skipper Sforza to quit creative duties and devote himself full-time to the Red Devils' often fragile defence.

The **Betzenberg** is high up behind Kaiserslautern's main **train station**. Either take bus #2, or from the underground passage, walk up to the far end of Malzstrasse, then up the steps to the stadium. Ticket info is on ☎0631/318 8222. Home fans are in the *Westtribüne*, blocks 7–9; away fans in the opposite *Osttribüne*, blocks 1–2.

The *Kiebitz* is the club bar in the car park, the *Zick-Zack* near the station at Richard-Wagner-Strasse 88 hasn't changed since Fritz Walter's day, the *Hannen-Fass* at central St Martin Platz 1 is the main fans' bar and the *Wladi Rock Stock* at Weberstrasse 14 provides the alternative version.

Dortmund

The Ruhr is Germany's industrial heartland and in many respects it is the hotbed of the nation's football scene – the Teutonic equivalent of the north-west of England. There are top-drawer clubs scattered across the area, among them Schalke 04, VfL Bochum and MSV Duisburg. All have had their moments – Schalke, in particular, in the years before World War II.

But in recent years it is Borussia Dortmund who have emerged as the major force. Their two *Bundesliga* titles in the mid-Nineties earned them successive places in the Champions' League, and their 1997 victory in that competition cemented their reputation further still.

Dortmund have ridden the *Bundesliga* boom as well as anybody, and today only Bayern can get close to matching them for off-the-field commercial success.

The fortunes of the football club have risen as those of the region as a whole have declined – the Ruhr is suffering a string of post-industrial problems, and the cliché that the team has put the city 'on the map'

certainly rings true for Dortmund. Visitors come here for one thing only – a game at the Westfalen stadium.

The Westfalen is proof that a state-of-the-art stadium can still provoke a pounding atmosphere, and that attracting wealthier fans and families need not mean alienating traditional working-class support. While the team's fluorescent shirts were becoming a consumer fashion accessory (since masterfully re-invented by *Nike*, who have re-instated Dortmund's traditional amber), the club backed striking steelworkers by offering them free seats in the ground and allowing players to take part in street demonstrations.

Dortmund's 1997 European Cup final triumph over Juventus was greeted with bemusement by many. But Schalke's UEFA Cup final victory over Inter Milan, just seven days earlier, gave Dortmund all the impetus they needed – the rivalry between the two clubs (Schalke are based in Gelsenkirchen, just a few kilometres away) is one of the most intense in Germany, and

Not a great year – Dortmund are beaten by bottom club Bielefeld, April 2000

Dortmund essentials

From Dortmund **airport** the SB47 bus (hourly, Mon–Fri 6am–9.30pm, Sat 7.15am–2pm, journey time 30mins, fare DM3.20) runs to the main **train station**, the Hauptbahnhof. Many air passengers use Cologne instead, an hour away by regular trains. The train station, a short walk from the main Markt square, is also a hub for local S-Bahn and U-Bahn **train networks** which go beyond the city boundaries to cover neighbouring towns such as Bochum.

Dortmund city centre is easily covered by foot, with the rest of the town, including the Westfalen stadium, served by U-, S-Bahn, trams and buses (5am–11pm). Tickets are available at platform machines. Short journeys or *kurzstrecke* are DM2.10, longer *A tarif* trips such as that to the Westfalen DM2.90. Day tickets are DM9.50. All tickets must be stamped onboard. There is a limited night service Fri–Sat. **Taxis** queue at the Hauptbahnhof, or can be phoned on a central number – ☎0231/144 444.

The city's **tourist office** is facing the Hauptbahnhof at Königswall 20 (open Mon–Fri 9am–6pm, Sat 9am–1pm, ☎0231/502 5666, fax 0231/163 593). There you can find copies of three free **listings publications**, *Heinz*, *Coolibri* and *Lokalführer*.

derby games between the two are an unforgettable occasion.

The thrilling fields

 Borussia Dortmund

Westfalen-Stadion, Westfalenpark
Capacity 69,000
Colours Amber shirts, black shorts
League champions 1956–57, 1963, 1995–96
Cup winners 1965, 1989
European Cup winners 1997
Cup-Winners' Cup winners 1966

BVB ('Ballspiel Verein Borussia') Dortmund were formed out of a merger of several local clubs. The original players were a 'rebel group' who left the sports club Trinity in 1909, after constant rows with Chaplain Derwald, the head of the club. They teamed up with members of two other clubs, Rhenania and Brittania, to compete as BVB in the regional leagues. August Lenz was one of the players who came through from the ranks of the then popular street football competitions to become Borussia's first international. In 1936, Lenz led the side into the competi-

tive *Gauliga* which covered the region, and where their derby rivalry with Schalke 04 began to take off. Yet before World War II, it was Schalke who dominated, winning six German championships. The very presence of Schalke in the region ruled out any chance of Dortmund making the national play-offs.

In the post-war era, it was all change. In 1947 Borussia defeated Schalke 3–2 to become Westphalian champions for the first time and enter the national play-offs. Two years later they made the finals but lost out to VfR Mannheim. They finally got their first national title in 1956, when they defeated Karlsruhe 4–2. The team, coached by Helmut Schneider, retained their title a year later with a 4–1 win over Hamburg.

A few years later, Dortmund looked well set to make an impact in the new *Bundesliga*. They won the last title to be decided by the play-off system, in 1963, then in 1965 finished third in the league and won the West German cup.

While a *Bundesliga* title eluded them, Dortmund concentrated on the 1965/66 European Cup-Winners' Cup. CSKA Sofia and Atlético Madrid were defeated on the way to the semi-finals, where they met holders West Ham United. The other semi-final saw Liverpool meet Celtic and the British press were licking their lips at the prospect of an all-British final. But West Ham were defeated 2–1 at Upton Park and 3–1 at the Westfalen – Dortmund were in the final, against Liverpool.

Dortmund's side included four players who would be part of West Germany's squad in that summer's World Cup – Tilkowski, Held, Emmerich and Paul. The Germans took the lead through Held on 62 minutes, but Roger Hunt levelled the game six minutes later. Then, in extra-time, midfielder Reinhard 'Stan' Libuda got the winner.

It was the first time a German side had won a European competition. More significantly, Dortmund's victory demonstrated that, just three years after its foundation, the *Bundesliga* was producing a standard of club football that was just as high that of the West German national team.

The triumph should also have heralded the arrival of Dortmund as a major power in West German and European football. Instead BVB faded, finishing third in the league in 1969, but not getting their hands on any more silverware for thirty years.

In 1972 they were relegated from the first division, and did not return there until 1976. For a decade Dortmund struggled to escape from mid-table, and in 1986 they needed an epic three-game play-off with Fortuna Cologne to avoid the drop again.

Tortuous though it was, the relegation scare provoked large-scale reorganisation of the club's off-the-field activities and a renewed effort to improve its finances. For the 1986/87 season the club signed a sponsorship deal with Dortmund-based insurance company *Die Continentale,* and visionary new president Gerd Niebaum appointed a full-time commercial manager – then a novelty in the German game. Two seasons later, BVB lifted the West German cup and were back in Europe.

The Nineties saw Niebaum's Dortmund revival plan finally come to full fruition, with consecutive *Bundesliga* titles under Ottmar Hitzfeld's coaching in 1995 and 1996. The team's success was based on a series of players bought from Juventus. In 1992, Ger-

man international defender Stefan Reuter was brought back to his homeland from Turin. Twelve months later, a Juve side including Brazilian Júlio César and Germans Andreas Möller and Jürgen Kohler hammered Dortmund, 6–1 on aggregate, in the final of the UEFA Cup.

Within a year, BVB had signed both César and Möller. Kohler joined in 1995, and another former Juventus man, Portuguese playmaker Paulo Sousa, signed in 1996. Meanwhile, two other former *Serie A* exiles, striker Karl-Heinz Riedle and anchorman Matthias Sammer, were signed from Lazio and Inter respectively.

In the space of four years Dortmund had recruited almost all the German internationals who had fled the *Bundesliga* for Italy in the early Nineties. Kohler and Reuter had both been expected to return to Bayern when their Italian contracts were up – Dortmund's coup in signing them signalled a shift in the balance of *Bundesliga* power from Bavaria to the Ruhr.

Hitzfeld's *coup de grâce* was delivered at the Olympic stadium in Munich in May 1997. Four years after watching his team taken to the cleaners by Juventus in the UEFA Cup final, he now fielded many of those ex-Juve stars in Dortmund yellow. They did not let him down. Riedle scored twice in the first half, and Lars Ricken added a spectacular third in the second period, just as the Italians were beginning to look dangerous – 3–1 to BVB, and Europe's highest footballing accolade was theirs.

After that, Hitzfeld's decision to move upstairs deprived his side of the continuity it needed, and the appointment of an outsider, Nevio Scala, as his successor further disrupted the team's rhythm. Midfielder Andy Möller, in particular, was not amused by the Italian coach's tactical tinkering. Meanwhile, the club doctors were busy with Sammer's career-threatening series of knee operations, and other long-term injuries to Lars Ricken, Heiko Herrlich, Stefan Reuter and Steffen Freund.

In the 1997/98 Champions' League, Dortmund did enough to finish top of their group above Scala's former club, Parma. An extra-time win over Bayern then moved them into the semi-finals, but by this time they had lost two of their most influential players, Paulo Sousa (to Inter Milan) and Paul Lambert (to homesickness). The *Schwarzgelben*, once the archetype of togetherness, were falling further apart by the week – European defeat by Real Madrid the inevitable consequence.

While Niebaum was taking the club out into the big wide world of a stock-market flotation, the departure of Scala and Hitzfeld allowed the football side to go back to its roots – Michael Skibbe, former coach of Dortmund's amateur and youth sides, took charge of the first team for 1998/99.

Little older than Möller and new signing Thomas Hässler, Skibbe initially struggled to impose his authority. The midway point in the season saw Dortmund in mid-table, but the spring signings of goalkeeper Jens Lehmann and midfielder Miroslav Stević

Badge boys – Dortmund fans are a proud lot

proved inspired, and the team eventually finished fourth, enough to earn a Champions' League qualifying berth.

In the 1999 close season, the troubled Hässler was offloaded to Munich 1860, while Victor Ikpeba, Christian Wörns and Fredi Bobić were all high-profile arrivals. Yet still the team did not gel, and Skibbe was dismissed just one game after the winter break. Newcomer Bernd Krauss then took charge for eight disastrous, winless games, during which Dortmund tumbled headlong towards the relegation zone. In April Krauss too was dismissed, to be replaced by a 65-year-old Udo Lattek. More significant, though, was the appointment of Matthias Sammer as Lattek's assistant; once the veteran had steered the club to safety, the way seemed clear for Dortmund's former European footballer of the year to call an end to his injury-stricken playing career, and take over as first-team coach for 2000/01.

Meanwhile, the cash from sponsorship and merchandising has continued to flow, and has been ploughed into the Westfalen stadium. Built for the 1974 World Cup (the club's pre-1974 ground, Rote Erde, is still functioning next-door), the ground has been gradually upgraded since 1986, and new tiers have now been added to all four stands, to create an overall capacity just shy of 70,000.

The Westfalen now boasts Europe's largest covered Kop, the *Südtribune*, capable of holding 25,000 alone. In order to save the character of this stand while still meeting UEFA regulations for European games, the club has installed removable seats, so that fans can sit for Champions' League games and stand up for the *Bundesliga*. Now Dortmund want to go one stage further and install a new pitch that will double as a stadium roof. As well as allowing the Westfalen to host 'indoor' events such as concerts, this might solve the problem of the ground's over-shaded turf, which has been repeatedly re-planted, and which many fans blamed for the team's troubles in 1999/2000.

Here we go!

The Westfalen is well out of the centre but easily reached by U-Bahn line U45 from the Hauptbahnhof to its end stop, **Westfalenstadion**. The journey takes 15mins.

Just the ticket

Advance tickets for most games – excepting the visits of Bayern, Schalke and big European clubs – are available from various spots around town, including the *Sporthaus Gelhar*, under the *Carlton Hotel* at central Lütge-Bruckstrasse 5–7.

For run-of-the-mill league fixtures, tickets can be bought at the **green huts** which surround the stadium.

The *Südtribune* is firmly the home end, while the lower section of the *Nordtribune* is for visiting fans – both have standing ticket prices of DM16.50. The cheapest seats (DM35.20) are in the lower-numbered, pitch-level sections of the east and west stands. A DM40–50 ticket in sections 20–25 of the west or 40–49 of the east will afford an excellent view.

Swift half

The main Hohe Strasse from town, which edges the popular Kreuzviertel as it approaches the stadium junction, is littered with bars, which either close up or become a *Sport-Treff* for fans on matchdays. The *Gildenschänke* at #139 is one of the latter.

The stadium area is full of beer and wurst stands, with popular meeting spots being off Strobelallee in front of the riding stables and in the *Ardeyblick* gardens restaurant. You'll also find fans gathered behind the *Nordtribune* by the old stadium, the concourse buzzing with *DAB* beer dispensers in yellow space suits with hosepumps on their backs.

Inside the ground, beer is DM7, of which DM2 is refunded when you take back your glass to a separate kiosk.

Club merchandise

The *BVB Megastore* is at Felicitasstrasse 2, Dortmund-Hörde (Mon–Fri 10am–6pm, Sat 10am–2pm, Sun matchdays 10am–4pm), just the other side of a steelworks from the Westfalen stadium on the #457 bus route. It sells advance match tickets as well as merchandise.

You'll find a smaller shop and ticket office in the club building by the old Rote Erde stadium.

In print

Borussia Magazin (DM2) is a high-quality colour glossy produced for every home game. The monthly *Borussia Live* (DM4.50) is aimed at a younger, TV audience. *Der Reporter* (DM1.50) is a regional sports magazine with coverage of handball and other sports as well as football. The local daily paper is the *Ruhr Nachrichten,* which carries a well-informed sports page in its Dortmund edition.

In the net

Dortmund were one of the first German clubs to host their own **official website**, and they now lead the way in the use of multi-media, with internet radio among the features on offer at: www.borussia-dortmund.de/. You'll also find a brief history and profile of the club in English.

Most of the **unofficial sites** are strictly German only. There's a comprehensive, text-led site at: www.object-factory.com/dortmund; and a glitzier, less accessible but more ambitious alternative at: www.borussenweb.de/.

Eat, drink, sleep...

Bars and clubs

Dortmund isn't the best night out in Germany but there's still plenty of choice for eating, drinking and dancing. The **local beer** is *DAB*, best-known for the five-litre barrels of the stuff which Germans take home for their summer garden parties.

All around town, unpretentious BVB bars overflow with fans, while the beer halls around the central Markt are a little more sedate.

BVB Fanhouse, Borsigplatz 5b. Now incongruously plonked in the Turkish quarter the other side of town from the Westfalen stadium, the *Fanhouse* is a bar, souvenir shop, diner and meeting place, complete with an illustrated history of the club. Tram #404 from Kampstrasse.

Come In, Olpe 33. How can you walk past a place with a name like that? Good little bar, with seating outside in warm weather. Inside there's table bowling and that strange German invention, the electronic dartboard. Cheap menu of sausages and soups.

FZW, Neuer Graben 167. Disco given a new lease of life with its *Club Trinidad* Saturday nights – two floors of dance action with international DJs, DM6–10 entrance. On the S5 and S47 lines from the Hauptbahnhof.

Im Keller, Geschwister-Scholl-Strasse 24. Centrally located cellar nightspot open Wed, Fri, Sat, with a young clientele and either dance or underground music. DM10 entrance, two floors.

Max Café, Kuckelke 14. Ideal central meeting spot, with club info, food and good sounds. Open until 2am weekends, 1am otherwise.

Restaurants

Avoid those restaurants obviously geared for the expense-account business trade; Dortmund is a **workers' city** and there's no need to spend a fortune on keeping yourself fed. Look out for excellent *Tages-menu* lunchtime deals.

Brinkhoffs No.1, Markt. The cooks make use of the market opposite to serve up traditional German food to the masses. Seats for 120 inside, capacity doubles when the terrace opens in spring. The steaks and salads are excellent and there is a lunchtime *Tagesmenu* for around DM15.

Juffure, Lange Strasse 117. Late-opening West African restaurant in the Kreuzviertel, also with Jamaican specialities. Main courses around DM15, open until 2am, closed Tue. On the #453 bus route.

Kaktus Jack, Weissenburger Strasse 35/37. Mexican and American restaurant/bar with steaks, burgers, spare ribs, cocktails and a wide range of tequilas. Often has special deals midweek such as happy hours and 'eat-all-you-can'. Open Mon–Fri 5pm–1am, Sat 6pm–3am, Sun 6pm–1am.

Pfefferkorn, Hoher Wall 38. Old-fashioned atmosphere to this fine brewery-run *Gaststätte* near the city centre, open Mon–Sat 11am–1am, kitchen until midnight. Local specialities.

Accommodation

Finding a room is rarely a problem in Dortmund. The tourist office (see *Essentials*) runs a **BVB Special** deal for fans staying at three-star hotels and above, with rates in the range DM130–180 for a double, depending on location. They will also have details of cheaper options.

Hotel Carlton, Lütge-Brückstrasse 5–7 (☎0231/528 030, fax 0231/525 020). Slap bang in the centre of town, just a 5min walk from the Hauptbahnhof. Sports shop downstairs, with an owner who will happily chat about BVB's latest form. Rooms from DM45 including a good cold breakfast.

Parkhotel Westfalenhallen, Strobelallee 41 (☎0231/12 04 555). Ideal if you are just going to the game and aren't planning a night out in the city, as it is located in the same park as the stadium. Wide range of room prices with doubles from around DM100.

Pension 'Cläre Fritz', Reinoldstrasse 6 (☎0231/571 523, fax 0231/579 623). Cheap and friendly guest house in the centre of the city with rooms from DM45. Only ten rooms, however, so check avalability in advance.

Holiday Atlanta, Ostenhellweg 51 (☎0231/557 0750, fax 0231/586 0054). Centrally located, mid-price hotel with singles and doubles at around DM75 per person. All rooms with TV. Most major credit cards.

From coalmines to the continent – Schalke 04

Traditionally the Ruhr industrial region is Germany's footballing powerhouse, and its engine is **Schalke 04** from Gelsenkirchen, a small town 40mins by local *Stadtbahn* train from Dortmund.

Although *die Königsblauen* have never won the Bundesliga, indeed have not won a league title for more than 40 years, they hold a legendary status in the German game, built on a pre-war side that won six championships, and the huge populist fan culture it generated which remains loyal to this day.

Formed in 1904 as FC Westfalia 04, the club merged with TV 1877 Schalke, then became Schalke 04 in 1924. Essentially a miners' team, they came into their own in the Thirties. With Fritz Szepan, Ernst Kuzorra and Ötte Tibulski, Schalke 04 made **nine national play-off finals** in ten years, winning six. Their intimate Glückauf Kampfbahn home was the most passionate ground in Germany.

Banging the drum – Schalke style

By the Sixties both the ground and the team it played host to were obsolete. With the rise of Borussia Dortmund nearby, and the awarding of the 1974 World Cup to West Germany, a plan was hatched to build a 100,000-seater super-stadium for the Ruhr area. Due to the rivalry involved, there was room for only one winner. Gelsenkirchen won the contract – and the funds – to build the 70,000-capacity **Parkstadion** in no man's land, north of town, with easy access to the motorway.

A **match-fixing scandal** all but broke the club in 1971, until they came back with Erwin Kremers and Klaus Fischer upfront six years later. In a remarkable season, they beat Bayern 7–0 in Munich – the only clean sheet they kept. Conceding almost as many goals as they scored, Schalke kept pace with league leaders Mönchengladbach, but finished one point off the title.

It would prove the club's best-ever run in the *Bundesliga*. By the early Eighties they were relegated, prompting a yo-yo decade which culminated in a return to the top flight in 1991. With a huge fan base, Schalke then rode the *Bundesliga* boom with ease, but it took the appointment of a Dutch coach, **Huub Stevens**, to revive the team's form in 1996/97. With an international line-up, including World Cup '90 star **Olaf Thon** and Dutchman **Youri Mulder**, Schalke enjoyed an almost totally unheralded run to the UEFA Cup final, where they beat **Internazionale** on penalties in the San Siro. A year later, they faced the Italians again in the same competition, only to lose 2–1 on aggregate in extra-time.

The 1999/2000 season was disappointing, but the record signing of Emile Mpenza cured the team's goal drought midway through, for a secure, mid-table finish.

Now the club now wants to build a modern, multi-functional arena, *Auf Schalke*, at a cost of more than DM350million. To get to the Parkstadion while it's still there, take S-Bahn #302, direction Gelsenkirchen-Buer, A-zone ticket DM2.80 – the journey is free with a match ticket. There are no bars, or indeed anything at all, around the Park, so check out *Auf Schalke*, Uechtingstrasse 98, near the old ground.

Hamburg

If any city can claim to be the home of foot-ball in Germany, that city is Hamburg. While southern and eastern regions of the country reacted with scepticism or out-right hostility to the game's popularity at the turn of the century, Hamburg – always, like any major port, more tolerant of out-side influences – embraced soccer with open arms.

Germany's first dedicated football club, SC Germania Hamburg, were founded here in 1887. Subsequently the city also pio-neered the idea of competition between representative sides from different towns, at a time when the game was still very much confined to regional competitions.

Today Hamburg's two football teams couldn't be more different. Hamburg SV are a famous old club, well-established in the top flight of the *Bundesliga* and playing at a big, purpose-built, out-of-town sports arena. FC St Pauli are the outsiders who have spent most of their life in the regional leagues and play at a tiny ground cramped into the city's famous red light district.

Recent years have seen the relation-ship between the two clubs change. St Pauli have enjoyed a spell in the top flight and pulled in crowds that almost equal those of HSV, who have been struggling to live up to a long tradition of success at both national and European level. True, St Pauli were relegated (not for the first time) in 1997. But the club's management are boldly going ahead with plans for a new stadium, indicating a confidence of purpose which has been lacking at HSV for years.

It's not just the contrasting stadia and histories that distinguish the two clubs – it's their support. HSV are followed by the traditional working-class fan, while St Pauli attract a mix of anarchists, punks and weirdos that seem totally out of place at a football match.

It's a fascinating clash of football cul-tures, and regardless of whether you prefer the leather and attitude of St Pauli's 'Happy Fans' or the commitment and loyalty of

the HSV boys, a football weekend in Ham-burg can count among the best in Europe.

The thrilling fields

 Hamburg SV

Volksparkstadion, Hamburg-Altona
Capacity 50,000
Colours White shirts, red shorts, blue, black and white trim
League champions 1923, 1928, 1960, 1979, 1982–83
Cup Winners 1963, 1976, 1987
European Cup winners 1983
Cup-Winners' Cup winners 1977

Hamburger Sport-Verein are members of an elite group that have never been rele-gated from the top drawer of the *Bundesliga*. But it's more than 15 years since HSV last won a league title, more than ten since their cup win of 1987.

The club were formed in 1919. As with most German cities there were several amateur clubs competing in the regional leagues prior to World War I. Three of them – Germania, Falke and Hamburger SC – merged to form the new club after the end of hostilities. Four years later, HSV won their first national championship, defeating Union Berlin 3–0 in the play-off final.

In 1953, HSV left their historical home of Rothenbaum, in the centre of the city, to move out to the newly reopened and redesigned Volksparkstadion ('People's Park stadium') several kilometres outside the city in the district of Altona. While the supporters were less than happy with hav-ing to make the long journey out of the city every other Saturday, these were good times on the field. HSV reached two West German championship finals in the late Fifties and lifted the title in 1960, with a side including the legendary West German international striker Uwe Seeler.

In the following season's European Cup, HSV were involved in a remarkable quarter-final against the English champions, Burnley. At a packed Turf Moor, the Germans were outplayed and lost 3–1. But in the second leg Hamburg pulled out all the stops, and a 4–1 win took them through to play Barcelona in the semis, where they lost out after a replay.

In April 1961, Seeler was approached by Inter Milan who tabled the impressive sum of £600,000 for him. With salaries in Italy soaring way above those in (still semi-professional) West Germany, the club were not going to stand in his way. But Seeler, whose brother Dieter also played for HSV, turned Inter down. He never left the club, playing with them until 1971. Today he is the club president. He went on to lead HSV to the final of the Cup-Winners' Cup in 1968, where they lost 2–0 to AC Milan.

It was to be nine years before HSV got another crack at the same competition. They got to the final after defeating Atlético Madrid in the semis, again despite losing the first leg 3–1. In the final against holders Anderlecht in Amsterdam, goals from Georg Volkert and Felix Magath inside the last twelve minutes clinched the prize.

Within weeks of winning that first European honour, HSV pulled off a major coup in the transfer market when they persuaded Kevin Keegan to leave Liverpool. His first season in Hamburg was mixed – the team's rigid formation stifled his creativity, and some team-mates were envious of his reportedly massive salary cheques. He also took severe stick from the Kop after Liverpool licked HSV 6–0 at Anfield in the second leg of the European SuperCup.

Everything changed, however, when HSV appointed the former Bayern Munich coach Branko Zebec as team boss in the summer of 1978. Under Zebec, the team abandoned man-for-man marking and played with greater fluidity. It suited Keegan perfectly. In 1979, *Mächtige Maus* ('Mighty Mouse') led HSV to their first *Bundesliga*

Back to his best – Tony Yeboah in full flow

title. They finished runners-up the following year, while Keegan himself was voted European Footballer of the Year two seasons in a row.

Keegan returned to England, but Hamburg continued to dominate the German game. After Zebec's alcohol addiction had forced him to quit, Ernst Happel took over the coaching reins and HSV won the title again in 1982. In the same season they made the final of the UEFA Cup, but were surprisingly beaten by IFK Gothenburg, their cavalier style swept aside by canny Swedish counter-attacking.

Any disappointment vanished the following season, when HSV defeated Juventus 1–0 in the final of the European Cup. The side, which also retained the *Bundesliga* title, included Magath (who scored the winner), international sweeper Manni Kaltz, anchorman Wolfgang Rolff (who marked Michel Platini out of the game) and the colossal striker Horst Hrubesch. A West German cup win in 1987 has been the only honour since Europe was conquered, and after several disappointing seasons, in 1997 the club came dangerously close to dropping out of the *Bundesliga*.

President Uwe Seeler knew all too well the high expectations of the club's support. In the summer of 1997 he sacked his old team-mate Magath from his position as coach and brought in the relatively inexperienced Frank Pagelsdorf.

Despite the signings of Tony Yeboah (who was a success) and Martin Dahlin (who wasn't), lack of punch upfront proved HSV's undoing in the mediocre seasons of 1997/98 and 1998/99, when the main focus of attention lay off the field – on the conversion of the Volkspark into a 50,000-capacity, multi-function arena.

Seeler himself took a back seat prior to the 1999/2000 season, but coach Pagelsdorf, nicknamed 'The Chocolate Bull' for his sweet tooth and gruff demeanour, was getting Hamburg playing the right kind of

football at last. With Croatian midfielder Robert Kovac now doing the midfield prompting, goalkeeper Hans-Jörg Butt scoring effortlessly from the penalty spot and Yeboah reeling in the years upfront, HSV were never less than fun to watch.

A leaky defence prevented the team from sustaining a credible title challenge, but a third-place finish was enough to secure a first-ever Champions' League berth – no less than what the rebuilt Volkspark deserves.

Here we go!

The quickest and cheapest way to get to the Volksparkstadion is to take S3 or S21 to **Stellingen**. Your ticket is valid for the #380 shuttle-bus transfer (*Shuttle-Verkehr*) on to the stadium from there. Allow yourself a good 40mins for the trip.

Just the ticket

The main **ticket offices** in town are at Eppendorfer Weg 234 (U3 Hoheluftbrücke) and Mundsburger Damm 33 (U2 Mundsburg). At the stadium, the *Ticket Center*, Sylvesterallee 7, is

Hamburg essentials

There are two ways to get from Hamburg's **Fuhlsbüttel airport** into the city centre, 10km away. The *Airport-City-Bus* runs every 20mins to the city's Hauptbahnhof (6.30am–10.30pm, journey time 30mins, DM8), while the *HVV-Airport Express* (bus line #110, DM3.40) runs every 10mins to Ohlsdorf S- and U-Bahn stations, about 15mins from Hauptbahnhof. A taxi into town will cost you DM30.

Most inter-city **trains** also arrive at the Hauptbahnhof, the meeting point for seven S-Bahn and U-Bahn lines. The city's **bus station** is just behind. **North Sea ferries** from Harwich and Hull arrive at St Pauli Landungsbrücken, a short U-Bahn journey into town.

Hamburg's **city transport** comprises S-Bahn, U-Bahn and buses. The network runs 5am–midnight, after which night buses leave every hour from the Rathaus Markt. Ordinary **single tickets** cost DM2.40 for a short journey, DM3.90 for longer trips of about six stops or more. A **day pass** is good value at DM7.50, a three-day version even better at DM20; both are valid Mon–Fri 9am–midnight and all day Sat–Sun. All tickets can be bought from the orange machines at stations or from bus drivers. For a **taxi**, dial ☎040/666 666 or ☎040/221 122. The standing charge is DM3, plus DM1.60 per km.

The main **tourist information office** is at the exit from the Hauptbahnhof into Kirchenallee (open daily 7am–11pm, ☎040/3005 1201). You'll find another, smaller one at St Pauli Landungsbrücken, between landing stages #4 and #5 (open daily 9.30am–5.30pm, ☎040/3005 1200).

For **listings information**, the monthly magazines *Szene Hamburg* (DM5) and *Prinz* (DM4.50) are the best of the bunch.

open Mon–Fri 10am–6pm, but closed on match-days, when there is a kiosk open by the free bus stop from Stellingen.

Home fans gather in the *Nordtribüne,* blocks 23–27, where there are also standing places. Away fans are allocated two blocks, 14A and B, in the corner of the *West*- and *Südtribüne.* The most expensive seats are in the new *Osttribüne,* those in the *West* the best for the visiting neutral.

Swift half

The first port of call is the *Hunger & Durst* (?!) bar, at Stellingen S-Bahn station, which answers both questions. At the stadium itself, the much-promised *Fankneipe,* between the *Nord*- and *Osttribüne,* has yet to materialise, although it may see the light of day during the 2000/01 season. In the meantime, you'll find stalls dotted all around the ground, especially in the car park behind the *Südtribüne.*

Ultra culture

It's hard to generate an atmosphere in a half-empty superbowl, but HSV's **organised fan groups** (of which there are more than 60) do their best, and make a fair amount of noise.

In print

HSV Live (DM2) is the official monthly maga-zine, while the official fan club produces its own monthly, *Supporters' News* (DM3.50).

In the net

There's a slick if rather bland and predictable **official website** at: www.hsv.de. It's good for the latest news and team information but real depth of content is lacking. For the **unofficial view**, try Stefan Erichsen's regularly updated homepage at: talk4fun.de/hsv_fanpage.

 St Pauli

Wilhelm Koch Stadion 'am Millerntor', Auf dem Heiligengeistfeld
Capacity 20,000
Colours White shirts, brown shorts

Depending on your politics, lifestyle and washing habits, you will be either enchanted or alienated by FC St Pauli and their fans.

Visit the Wilhelm Koch stadium (known to all and sundry as the 'Millerntor'), and you could have the time of your life, wak-ing up next morning with a much sought-after brown-and-white scarf and a hangover that's actually worth having. On the other hand, you might find the whole experience has little to do with football as we know it, and is just an excuse for a bunch of lefty slackers to drink and sing away the dole cheque.

St Pauli were founded in 1910, but the team didn't make the top flight of the *Bundesliga* until 1977. They finished bottom of the table at the end of their first season, and were unable to clamber back up again until 1988. Since then it's been up and down (but mainly down) all the way, the team's latest relegation from the top flight coming in 1997.

In truth, little attention is paid to the team, either in Hamburg or elsewhere in Germany. There are no superstars or boardroom personalities making the head-lines here – the focus is on the terraces.

The St Pauli district is home not only to scores of brothels and seedy strip-joints, but also to cheap housing attracting stu-dents, anarchists and the 'alternative lifestyle' brigade. In most cities this crowd spend their Saturdays walking dogs on strings, hanging around in alternative record shops, or sleeping. In Hamburg, for some reason, they've acquired an interest in foot-ball. St Pauli, ignored and unfashionable, forever scrapping it out in the lower leagues, fit the bill – the small community fighting the eternal struggle against corpo-rate capitalism.

St Pauli fans pride themselves on their anti-racism – the slogan *St Pauli Fans Gegen Nazis* is present on badges, posters and T-shirts – and they also proclaim their internationalism. Some St Pauli fans actually celebrated Denmark's win over Germany in the 1992 European Championship final.

But while the punks and anarchists may make the headlines, there are genuine

World weary – Pauli coach Willi Reimann looks on

football fans at the Millerntor who have followed the team from their days in the *Oberliga Nord*. Alongside them are a good number of fair-weather HSV fans who've become tired of the long trip out to the soulless superbowl in Altona. For them, St Pauli is how football used to be – a small, packed ground in the centre of town, with a friendly atmosphere and none of the hype and crass commercialism that has taken over the *Bundesliga*.

Alas, the 'used to be' tag may also soon apply to the Millerntor, for St Pauli are considering moving to a purpose-built stadium of their own within the next few years. The 20,000 capacity of the current ground prevents the club from competing at the highest level – as the 1997/98 season showed. It remains to be seen whether the 'Happy Fans' (as the media have dubbed them) will still cheer the team on in different surroundings, and whether the football they will be watching is first or second division – or lower.

In the spring of 1999, the club was even threatened with having its professional licence withdrawn and consequent forced relegation to the *Regionalliga*. It didn't happen but, in a curious way, it would have been exactly the kind of imposition from

society that St Pauli's self-styled rebels enjoy rallying against.

Here we go!
Take U-Bahn 3 to **St Pauli**, no more than 15mins from the Hauptbahnhof, then cut across the fairground to the stadium.

Just the ticket
Standing tickets are a snip at DM12, while seats (of which there are only a few thousand) are much more expensive at DM60–120. The St Pauli *Kartencenter* hotline number is: ☎040/319 1893.

Swift half
Of the many bars around the ground, the 24-hour *Zum Lustigen Clocha* (corner of Simon-von-Utrecht Strasse and Detlev-Bremer Strasse) is the most typical, with scarves, old record sleeves, pictures of the regulars and a small yappy dog called Carolina. You'll find more football talk further up at Detlev-Bremer Strasse #21 inside the *St Pauli Treff*, while *Zum Kicker*, at the corner of Clemens-Schulz-Strasse and Rendsburger Strasse, has a more Irish theme.

The *St Pauli Clubheim* is inside the ground but has an entrance on the street. It's still full of serious drinkers, old punks and Bing Crosby fans, while the trophy cabinet is crammed with cups so irrelevant, nobody ever asked for them back.

Ultra culture
The once vibrant fan scene has faded somewhat along with the team's recent form. Sure, you'll still find spiky-tops in the *Clubheim*, but many of them lack real match practice.

In print
The match magazine, *Pauli* (DM1), faces competition from a number of fanzines, the best of which is *Der Übersteiger* (DM3.50).

In the net
The official FC St Pauli website is typically quirky, some would say all too predictably so. The homepage presents an image of a large wooden

door which you click on to reveal a virtual locker-room. Move the cursor around to the various images (which include a crate of *Holsten* beer bottles and a naked footballer making good use of the urinals), and you'll find links to the expected squad and club info, news and history. All in German at present, alas, at: www.fcstpauli.de.

Eat, drink, sleep…

Bars and clubs

Hamburg has the best nightlife in Germany after Berlin. The heart of it is the Reeperbahn in St Pauli. Although it is better known for its bordellos, the Reeperbahn has a great bar scene, along with a number of techno and trance clubs which open late and close at noon the next day. **U3 St Pauli** or **S1/S3 Reeperbahn** are the jumping-off points. A more sedate drink can be had in the student bars around Grindelallee (U1 Hallerstrasse). For a quiet lunchtime pint, try the Grossneumarkt (S1 or S3 Stadthausbrücke). The local Hamburg beer is the very quaffable *Astra*.

Café Treibeis, Gaustrasse 25. Up in Altona, a convivial bar for the underground and alternative crowd, particularly after a St Pauli game, with excellent sounds and atmosphere. A short, sharp climb uphill from S1/S3 Altona.

Golden Pudle's Club, Max-Brauer-Allee 201. Bizarre bar/club in the harbour area, popular with the Hamburg in-crowd, happily entertained by DJs and cabaret artists. S1, S3 or U3 St Pauli Landungsbrücken.

Osborne, Friedrichstrasse 7. One of three city-centre bars around Hans-Alberts-Platz that are particularly popular pre- and post-match. The other two are the **Kölsch Pub** (Silbersacher-strasse 3) and the **London Pub** (on the square itself); the latter has Sky Sports.

Irish Harp, Reeperbahn 36. Best of the many Irish bars in town, popular with HSV fans and open until late. S1 or S3 Reeperbahn.

Mojo Club, Reeperbahn 1. Excellent, imaginative mainstream club, with acid-jazz, rare grooves and cabaret. Generally a DM10–15 cover charge. Jazz café next door. U3 St Pauli.

Rosi's, Hamburger Berg 7. Legendary Hamburg bar/club, whose owners have seen everything come and go since the days when the Beatles were making nuisances of themselves. *Lunacy* at #25 is a little smaller, and a good place for club flyers.

Restaurants

Fish plays an important part in the diet of this port city. The classic sailor's dish is *Labskaus*, a cheap mix of mashed potatoes, herring, pickled cucumber and a fried egg. Spicy eel soup (*Aalsuppe*) is also a local favourite.

Hamburg has plenty of **cheap eats**. The streets around the university and the area further south towards Altona, either side of Schanzenstrasse (S21/31 or U3 Sternschanze) offer a particularly wide choice, while the dock area has tasty lunchtime fish bars (S1/3 or U3 St Pauli Landungsbrücken) and, a little further down, a clutch of unpretentious Spanish and Portuguese diners (U3 Baumwall).

Arkadasch, Grindelhof 17. Friendly, romantic and reasonably priced restaurant in the university area with main courses at DM20 and hearty soups at DM6. Most major credit cards. U1 Hallerstrasse.

At Nali, Rutschbahn 11. Popular Turkish restaurant with an extensive menu, open until 2am. Most credit cards.

Fischerhaus, St Pauli Fischmarkt 14. Popular and reliable establishment with efficient service, fresh fish a speciality. No credit cards. Open daily 11am–11pm. S1, S3 or U3 St Pauli Landungsbrücken.

Klett, Grindelallee 146. Student haunt which tries a bit too hard to be cool, but pleasant nonetheless. No credit cards. U1 Hallerstrasse.

Sagres, Vorsetzen 46. Busy Portuguese diner, full of regulars from the dock area. You may have to wait for a table, but the prices are right and the food is tasty. No credit cards. U3 Baumwall.

Accommodation

Hamburg is one of Germany's **most expensive cities** to stay in. Most hotels cater for the business community, which does at least mean they bring their prices down at weekends. The very cheapest hotel room you'll find will be around DM60 for a single room, DM80 for a double.

The area just north of the Hauptbahnhof, around Steindamm, Bremer Weg and Bremer Reihe, has many cheaper pensions, some used for purposes other than rest.

The main **tourist office** (see *Essentials*) provides a room-booking service for DM6, as does the office in the terminal 4 arrivals lounge at Fuhlsbüttel airport (open daily 8am–11pm, ☎040/3005 1240).

The *Tourismus Zentrale* office in town is not open to visitors but can reserve a room for you on ☎040/3005 1300, fax 040/3005 1333.

Annenhof, Lange Reihe 23 (☎040/2434 2618). Basic but clean hotel, not far from the Hauptbahnhof, with shared bathrooms and kitchen facilities. DM50–60 for a single. Breakfasts DM8 extra. No credit cards.

Hotel Kochler Garni, Bremer Reihe 19 (☎040/249 511, fax 040/280 2435). Large, comfortable single, double, triple and quad rooms, right next to the Hauptbahnhof. Kitchen facilities available. Singles around DM55–70, doubles DM90–100, triples DM120, quads DM140. Breakfast DM10. No credit cards.

Jugendgästehaus Horner Rennbahn, Rennbahnstrasse 100 (☎040/651 1671, fax 040/655 6516). A fair way out in the east of town, this is Hamburg's friendliest youth hostel. Open March–December, reception 7.30am–9am, 1pm–6pm & 12.30pm–1am. Dorm beds for under DM30, excellent buffet breakfast included. U3 Horner Rennbahn, then a 10min walk.

Pension Helga Schmidt, Holzdam 14 (☎040/280 2119, fax 040/243 705). Pleasant and comfortable pension near the Hauptbahnhof with spacious rooms, all equipped with a shower and a television. Singles around DM70, doubles DM115. No credit cards.

Greece

Elliniki Podosferiki Omospondia Syngrou Avenue 137, GR-17121, Athens
☎01/931 1500   Fax 01/935 9666   E-mail none

League champions Olympiakos   **Cup winners** AEK Athens   **Promoted**
Athinaikos, Ioannina   **Relegated** Kavala, Proodeftiki, Apollon, Trikala

European participants 2000/01   Olympiakos (UCL); Panathinaikos (UCL
qualifiers); AEK Athens, PAOK Salonika, Iraklis Salonika, OFI Crete (UEFA Cup);
Kalamata (Intertoto Cup)

The Ancient Greeks had a word for it: pandemonium. Modern Greece has seen its football suffer internecine chaos ever since violent scenes marred a match between representative teams from Athens and Salonika in 1906, and little has changed in the last nine decades.

The only difference has been that, over the past 20 years since the introduction of professional club football, various millionaires have flaunted their egos over their favourite football teams, usually one of the big Athenian three of Panathinaikos, AEK or Olympiakos. But, while only four league titles have escaped these clubs since World War II, European success has eluded the Greeks – even under the guidance of a string of expensive foreign coaches.

Internationally, too, Greece can look back on only a handful of modest achievements, the first of which was qualification for the European Championship finals of 1980. The team travelled to Italy as rank outsiders and promptly finished bottom of their group, but under coach Alketas Panagoulias they played some smart football, giving the Dutch a fright in their first match and holding West Germany to a goalless draw in their last.

Fourteen years later, after a sanctions-struck Yugoslavia had conveniently been forced to withdraw from their qualifying section, Greece made it to the World Cup finals for the first time. Panagoulias, now aged sixty, had returned as coach after a spell in America and used images from Greek mythology to bolster his pre-match

Hooked on classics – support is colourful

rhetoric. The stories might have been colourful but they had an unhappy ending. Panagoulias' team of seasoned veterans such as Tassos Mitropoulos, Savvas Kofidis and 37-year-old 'keeper Antonis Minou were no match for the bright young things of Bulgaria and Nigeria; they lost all three of their matches at USA '94 and failed to score a goal.

Since then, Greece have failed to qualify for both Euro '96 and France '98, a frustrating goalless draw at home to a Schmeichel-inspired Denmark putting paid to play-off hopes in the quest for a place at the latter.

A new forward partnership of Vitesse Arnhem's Nikos Machlas and AEK's Demis Nikolaidis, under the expensively recruited Romanian coach Anghel Iordanescu, suggested a bright start to Greece's Euro 2000 qualifying campaign. But the Greeks got anything but, and after two goals from Ole Gunnar Solskjær had given Norway all three points in Athens in March 1999, Iordanescu resigned. His replacement, former Panathinaikos coach Vassilis Daniel, promised a more attacking approach, but his first game in charge, played just four days after the Norway defeat, was a dull goalless stalemate away to Latvia. The same opponents then ended all hope of a place in the Low Countries by winning 2–1 in Greece in June.

Nonetheless, the Greek Football Association, the *EPO*, is pressing ahead with a controversial proposal to mount a bid to co-host the Euro 2008 finals with the country's next-door neighbour, Turkey – relations between the two national federations having thawed as a consequence of the earthquakes which disupted the footballing life of both during 1999/2000.

In the meantime, while basketball now brings Greece her international glory, football is still in the blood. A shame, then, that so much has been spilled in its name. Fan violence in its modern, callous, organised form has ruined the domestic game as a family spectacle, prompting the *EPO* to come up with a four-point plan to combat trouble in the summer of 2000.

The imbalance of power between the big Athens sides and the rest means that few matches attract more than 10,000 fans — and many clubs are in serious debt. Two league rounds were delayed in January 1999 because clubs were demanding a greater percentage of pools revenues from the government.

While a handful of Greek stars have left for Premiership riches – Nikos Dabizas at Newcastle for example – quality foreign players are no longer interested in wasting two years of their career in what is becoming a violent football backwater. The result has been a huge influx of cut-price imports from Yugoslavia, Romania, Russia and even Albania. At club level, the big three of Olympiakos, AEK and Panathinaikos continue to dominate, but while Olympiakos made a reasonable go of their Champions' League appearance in 1999/2000, all three Greek participants were knocked out of the UEFA Cup at the third-round stage.

For the visiting football fan, however, the very chaos and sectarian passion of the Greek game make it as attractive a reason to grab a cheap flight to the country as any naturist beach or desecrated monument.

Essential vocabulary

Hello *Khérete*
Goodbye *Adío*
Yes *Néh*
No *Ókhi*
Two beers, please *Dhyo bires, parakaló*
Thank you *Efharistó*
Men's *Andron*
Women's *Gynaikon*
Where is the stadium? *Pou ine to yipedo?*
What's the score? *Ta apotelesmata?*
Referee *Dietitis*
Offside *Offside*

Match practice

Unless the game you're going to is an international or involves one of the big three clubs playing each other, chances are you'll be spending your Sunday afternoon with a few thousand other souls. Whatever the occasion, if you avoid the cheapest seats behind the goal in the *pedalo*, or 'horseshoe', you'll be safe enough. Refereeing decisions may favour the home side to a laughable extent. If you're in Salonika for a game against a side from Athens, take a crash helmet. As many grounds still have primitive stone seating, most spectators

Basics

Citizens of the EU, the USA, Canada, Australia and New Zealand require only a **passport** to enter Greece – but be prepared for a certain amount of hassle at customs if yours contains a stamp from an earlier visit to Turkey.

The Greek unit of currency is the **drachma**, or Dr. There are around Dr470 to £1. You'll find coins for Dr5, Dr10, Dr50 and Dr100, and notes for Dr100, Dr500, Dr1,000 and Dr5,000. **Credit cards** are generally accepted in major towns, but watch for a high commission charge on cash advances at travel agents and *bureaux de change*.

From outside the country, the international telephone code for Greece is 30; Athens is 1 and Salonika 31. Greek **coin phones** take Dr10 pieces, but most machines are now **cardphones**, for which cards are available at most newsstands for Dr1,700, Dr7,000 or Dr11,500. For international calls, dial 00 followed by the country code and number. The cheap rate is between 10pm and 6am. Note that Greece is one hour ahead of Central European Time. You will often find a couple of phones at **newsstands** for public use, though these are slightly more expensive than those in phone boxes. Simply pay the amount clocked up on the vendor's meter.

Buses are the most commonly used form of transport around Greece, since many towns do not have a rail link and trains are pretty slow, anyway. However, the national rail company, *OSE*, offers eight **inter-city trains per day** between Athens and Salonika – the journey takes around six hours and costs about Dr15,000.

Western-style **bars** tend to be more expensive than the traditional coffee houses (*kafenia*) or ouzo dens (*ouzeri*); they also attract a younger crowd, whose favourite tipple is iced coffee – *frappé*.

The *ouzeri* is the place to head for if you're taken by the idea of gambling on **green baize tables** while the waiter serves up snacks (*mezhédes*) such as cheese on toast (*sagnaki*) or meat in vine leaves (*dolmádhes*). The *ouzo* itself costs around Dr200 and, like its French cousin *pastis*, comes with a small glass of water as a mixer.

Dining takes place in *tavernas*, at their best with simple food, simple furniture and a roof-top setting under the olive trees. The whole caboodle, with half a bottle of resinated wine (*retsina*), shouldn't cost more than Dr2,000. *Moussaka* (meat and egg-plant) and *souvlaki* (lamb kebab) are the mainstays of any tourist menu.

You should find reasonably-priced **accommodation** even in the height of summer. The Greek National Tourist Organisation categorises hotels according to facilities and quality of service, but you may find a 'B' hotel better than an 'A' one. 'L' is the top of the range. For 'D' class hotels, a single room will cost about Dr5,000, a double Dr7,000, with a shower in the corridor. If you're paying a bit more – perhaps Dr20,000 for a 'C' or 'B' class double – ask about **air conditioning**.

buy a small sheet of polystyrene pillow, a *maxilari*, for a nominal sum – even the toughest-looking fan can be seen incongruously wielding their *maxilari*. Few grounds offer much cover from the elements, so remember to protect yourself against the Greek sun in late spring and early autumn.

Apart from a short break at Christmas, the season runs between late August and late May. With the exception of live TV matches, league games are on Sunday after-noons, with kick-off at 5pm in early autumn and late spring, 3pm in winter. Televised games are on Saturdays at 3pm, Sundays at 7pm or Mondays at 6pm.

European games can kick-off as late as 9.30pm, so make sure you can catch the last metro back from the stadium.

A different league

The Greek first division, *A' Ethnikis*, has been reduced to 16 teams for 2000/01. Two teams go down automatically, while as many as four others can also be involved in play-offs, depending on the margin of points between them at the end of the season. The second division, *B' Ethnikis*, was also reduced to 16 teams and operates on a similarly bewildering basis. The third tier, *G' Ethnikis*, is divided into north (*vorras*) and south (*potos*) – two go up from each division and six go down into the regionalised fourth division.

Up for the cup

Following four two-legged rounds, the cup final akes place in the Olympic stadium in May. All too often in recent years, the game has been just another excuse for a riot between rival gangs. If both teams happen to come from northern Greece, then the final switches venue to the Kaftantzogliou in Salonika.

Just the ticket

Hardcore fans tend to enter the stadium early, so unless you're going to a major international, you won't find long queues at the ticket office (*isistiria*). As systems are not computerised, tickets only go on sale a few days before the match.

The more expensive seats are in the middle numbered section, *arithimena elbigieli*. These are designated according to gate number (*fyra*), sector (*tmima*), row (*seira*) and seat number (*fesi*).

The big three in Athens increase prices for derby games, when you might find yourself paying about Dr6,000 for a ticket, or haggling with a ticket tout (*mavragorites*). There are no matchday programmes, but the bigger clubs have their own magazines.

Half-time

Alcohol is generally not available at major league games, so half-time is accompanied by the nervous twirling of worry beads and quick hits of coffee. Have a beer beforehand on your way to the ground, when you'll also see trays of pistachio nuts, almonds, sunflower seeds and monkey nuts in bags. Fleshy smoke bellows from grills of kebabs (*gyros*) or sausages (*lukánika*),

both around Dr500 a throw, and generally sold lukewarm to suit the Greek palate.

Action replay

Pay channel *Supersport* shows one game live on Saturdays, Sundays and Mondays, followed by full highlights. It also shows the Monday English Premiership game live, with commentary in Greek and English. State TV shows live European and national games, but note that the *Mega* channel has a separate deal with Panathinaikos. The best round-up is ET1's *Athletiki Kiriaki* at 10pm on Sundays. Sky Sports can be seen in many bars in main towns and resorts.

The back page

On any newsstand, particularly on Monday mornings, you'll see a confusing number of colourful sports papers. Of these, the daily *Sportime* (Dr200) is well laid-out and, for the non-Greek speaker, has results and fixtures which are easy to work out. The most authoratitive read is the *To Vima* sports section in the national paper *Ta Nea* on Monday mornings. *Athens News* also has comprehensive coverage of the Greek football scene, in English, every Tuesday.

Ultra culture

Ultras tend to meet at their own fan clubs, then march to the stadium *en masse*, rarely without a police escort for derby matches. Despite thorough searches (you may find heavy coins confiscated), fireworks are somehow sneaked into the ground, helping to create one of the most colourful atmospheres in Europe, and probably the loudest.

In the net

The *EPO* now has its own official site, but with Greek-language content only, at: www.epo.gr. *Takis Online* provides a good stats, facts and news service, regularly updated and with a choice of English and Greek language, at: takis.simplenet.com/Greece/greece_data.htm.

Athens

🏴 Panathinaikos 266   🏴 AEK 267   🏴 Olympiakos 270   🏴 Athinaikos 272
🏴 Ethnikos Asteras 272   🏴 Ionikos Nikea 273   🏴 Panionios 273

Rising to the occasion – the Olimpiako stadium is home to two clubs, for now at least

Athens, a cosmopolitan capital city of four million people, often feels like a Middle Eastern madhouse of ten times that. Yet, while its transport system might be hopelessly inadequate, its taxi drivers stubborn and its air pollution the stuff of legend, for a major game Athens can still rise to the occasion and has become a justifiably popular venue for European finals.

As for domestic football, despite dwindling attendances, people talk of little else in the *kafenia* and *ouzeri* around town. The great pity, given the natural passion for the game and the millions of drachma poured into it every year, is that that these drinkers have raised a glass to international success so rarely. In place of national flag-waving, victories over traditional club rivals have had to suffice.

In town, AEK enjoy the most passionate support, while down in the port of Piraeus, Olympiakos are the team to be seen supporting. Panathinaikos fans, from their traditional base high up in Ambelokipi, north-west of central Athens, tend to look down on the rest. With Panathinaikos and Olympiakos currently building new stadia, both teams ground-share at the national Olimpiako stadium, where Greece play their main international fixtures. Only hardcore followers make trips from the capital up to Salonika for club games against Aris, Iraklis or PAOK.

Generally there will be five or six Athenian clubs in the Greek top flight in any given season, the lesser lights traditionally playing on gravel pitches alongside a row of stone steps that wouldn't pass muster at the most modest non-league game in England. However, the current crop are doing what they can to improve both their image and their facilities – with some success.

Despite their dangerous reputation, most Greek fans you meet will be friendly and will talk knowledgeably about football until the stars come out. You'll find stands selling football souvenirs on practically every central street corner, but be careful on matchdays if you're proudly wearing your new AEK scarf, especially around Omonia Square, the city's main crossing point.

The thrilling fields

 Panathinaikos

Stadium Olimpiako, see p.271
Capacity 76,000
Club office Karelas Paiania
Colours All green with white trim
League champions 1930, 1949, 1953, 1960–1962, 1964–65, 1969–70, 1972, 1977, 1984, 1986, 1990–91, 1995–96
Cup winners 1940, 1948, 1955, 1967, 1969, 1977, 1982, 1984, 1986, 1988–89, 1991, 1993–95

In 1984, Panathinaikos moved home (but not heart) from their old stadium, the intimate Apostolos Nikolaidis, the other side of Athens' Licabettus hill. From the heights of Ambelokipi – and with the weight of his-

Skipper and striker – PAO's Warzycha

tory behind them – Pana fans still view their club as the elite. Originally formed as Panhellenic by English gentlemen at the turn of the century, the club adopted their Greek name in 1908, but stuck to their foreign roots by featuring a shamrock on the team badge – an idea suggested by one of their athletes during World War I.

It wasn't until the Sixties, however, that Pana began to challenge Olympiakos for domestic supremacy, their most successful period coming under the stewardship of former Hungary and Real Madrid star Ferenc Puskás. Double-winners in 1969, league champions again in 1970, Panathinaikos then surprised Everton and Red Star Belgrade to reach the European Cup final at Wembley in 1971. With stars such as centre-forward Anton Antoniadis – scorer of ten European goals that season – and midfielder Mimis Domazos, the Greeks were holding the great Ajax team of the era to a single-goal lead until a late own-goal sealed their fate. Later that year, they replaced Ajax in the World Club Championship, losing 3–2 on aggregate to Nacional of Uruguay.

Like most Greek teams, Pana didn't turn fully professional until the end of the Seventies – five years before their move to the then newly built Olimpiako. Once established there, they resumed their continental adventures, losing to Liverpool in the 1985 European Cup semi-final.

The club had to wait until 1996 to reach the same stage again, when once more Ajax were their opponents. Polish international striker Krzysztof Warzycha scored a shock late goal to win the first leg in Amsterdam, 1–0. But a Jari Litmanen strike, early in the second leg, then silenced the capacity crowd in the Olimpiako. A more confident and experienced side, under less pressure from their home fans, might have responded differently to such a setback. Pana lost 3–0.

Although Pana won the Greek title that year, the only achievement since has been Warzycha's in becoming top goalscorer in the club's history, surpassing Antoniadis' record of 181 in 1998. His team-mates, meanwhile, contrived to lose to Rosenborg Trondheim in the qualifying round for the Champions' League in 1996/97, but gave a reasonable account of themselves in the group stage of the 1998/99 version. Coach Vassilis Daniel's men – including influential Norwegian Erik Mykland and class right-half Stratos Apostolakis – were the only team to beat Dynamo Kiev, but lost twice to Arsenal.

After Daniel quit to take charge of the national team, Yannis Kyrastas stepped into the dugout and his side ran Olympiakos close in the 1999/2000 championship race. Their runners-up spot was enough for a Champions' League qualifying berth, but club president George Vardinoyiannis, the longest-serving in Greece with 21 years under his belt, would not be around to oversee that campaign – he resigned in June 2000 to concentrate on the rebuilding of the Alexandras stadium, where Pana's fanatical following still meet.

Swift half

You'll find PAO bars near club's old stadium along Leof Alexandras – take bus #230 from Syndagma to Agias Sabbas.

Club merchandise

The **PAO store** (open Mon, Wed and Sat 9am–3pm, Tue & Thur 9am–2pm, Fri 5–8.30pm, most credit cards accepted) can also be found on Odos Tsokha around the old stadium, a short walk down the hill from the ticket gate.

Ultra culture

Athens Fans Pana, an umbrella organisation embracing 13 ultra groups, produces a monthly magazine, *Skizofrenia,* available for Dr300 on matchdays. The most likeable group are the *Mad Boys,* who meet in Ambelokipi under a huge banner proclaiming *'In Green God We Trust'.*

In the net

The club's **official website** has a large area in English covering news, club history and online shopping at: www.pao.gr. The *Mad Boys* also have a fine English site at: users.hol.gr/~madboys/.

AEK

Nikos Goumas stadium, Perissos
Capacity 15,700 (see text)
Colours All black with yellow trim
League champions 1939–40, 1963, 1968, 1971, 1978–79, 1989, 1992–94
Cup winners 1932, 1939, 1949–50, 1956, 1966, 1978, 1983, 1996–97, 2000

Athletiki Enosis Konstantinopoulos were formed in 1924 by Greek refugees who had fled Constantinople, now Istanbul. Having chosen a Byzantine double-headed eagle as their emblem, they built the rough and ready Nea Filadelfia (now Nikos Goumas) stadium in 1936, three years before winning their first Greek title.

Once regarded as the club with money, AEK today have, if anything, the rootsiest support in the city. In the postwar era the team have enjoyed several spells of domestic domination, but have achieved little in Europe save for a run to the semi-finals of the UEFA Cup in 1976/77, when their progress was halted by Juventus.

AEK won three consecutive titles from 1992 and earned themselves a place in the 1994 Champions' League, where they were unlucky to be drawn in the same group as both the eventual finalists, Ajax and AC Milan. The man who took them there, Bosnian Serb coach Dušan Bajević, controversially moved to Olympiakos for a better salary in the summer of 1996. More than a thousand policemen were on duty for the AEK-Olympiakos clash in January 1997, and while AEK won that game, 2–0, the ease with which Olympiakos went on to take the Greek championship that year enraged the AEK faithful.

A run to the quarter-finals of the 1996/97 Cup-Winners' Cup and a cup final win over Panathinaikos did nothing to stem and neither has the acquisition of an 80% stake in the club by the British investment vehicle *ENIC,* completed in 1997.

The new owners put pay-TV boss George Leotsindis in charge, only for him to resign after a sad Cup-Winners' Cup

Athens essentials

Athens' **airport**, Ellenikon, has three termini, East, West (for *Olympic* flights only) and a charter terminal. There is a shuttle bus service between the two main termini. Blue express bus #091 runs every 30mins between Amalias 4, by central Syndagma square, and the termini; the journey takes 30–45mins, depending on traffic, and costs Dr250, or Dr500 after 11.30pm. The service runs hourly in the early hours. A **taxi** to or from the airport should cost around Dr2,000, but Dr5,000 rip-offs are not unheard of. Note that a new international airport is scheduled for completion in 2001; this will be connected to town by a metro extension from Ethniki Amyna.

The city's two main **train stations**, Larissa (northbound) and Stathmós Peloponníssou (southbound) are adjacent to each other. Trolleybus #1 goes to Larissa, bus #057 to Peloponníssou, both from Venizelou, between Syndagma and Omonia squares. The main **bus stations** are at Odos Kifissou 100 (bus #051 into town) and Odos Liossion 260 (bus #024).

With the Acropolis high over the city and the surrounding area of Plaka as its heart, orientation isn't a problem, but transport is. There are two new **metro lines**, running east to west and south-west to north-east, and meeting at a new split-level station at Syndagma. The original north-south metro line continues as before, bypassing Syndagma. **Tickets** are Dr150 for the original line, Dr250 for the new ones; they're available at stations, and should be validated in the orange box as you enter. The service runs from 5.30am to midnight. All the main football stadia are near a metro stop.

A system of allowing odd and even number-plated cars into town on alternate working days has alleviated some of Athens' traffic chaos, but even so, the city's blue **buses** and yellow **trolleybuses** can be painfully slow. Tickets (Dr100) are available at newsstands. Stamp them onboard. Route numbers change frequently and no transport map is available. There is a limited service after midnight on Sat, but no daily or weekly pass.

Official **taxis** are yellow with red number plates. You should hail a cab as you would hitch a lift, making sure to stand in the right direction for your destination. Do as the locals do and shout your destination from the pavement through the passing car window. It is normal for the driver to pick up other passengers along the way. The meter should start at Dr200, or Dr400 between midnight and 5am, plus an additional Dr50 per item of luggage. To dial a cab call **Parthenon** (☎01/581 4711), **Kosmos** (☎01/420 0042) or **Hellas** (☎01/643 3400).

For **tourist information**, dial 171 for the 24-hour English-speaking service. The main **tourist office** is at Odos Amerikis 2 (open Mon–Fri 9am–7pm, Sat 9am–2pm, ☎01/331 0437).

Of the English-language information sources, *Athens News* (daily, Dr250) is the best, although the Greek-language *Athinórama* (Fridays, Dr500) has by far the most complete bar, club and restaurant information.

quarter-final loss to Lokomotiv Moscow and a disastrous home defeat by Veria in the spring of 1998. The duo of Nikolaou Pantelis and Patrick Komninos took over the presidency, overseeing a couple of coaching changes before settling on Oleg Blokhin in the late autumn of 1998.

The one bright spark in all this upheaval has been the striking skills of Demis Nikolaidis, the perfect foil for Nikos Machlas in

the national team. With Nikolaidis' help, AEK finished second in the Greek league in 1999, a full ten points off the title-winning pace of Olympiakos, but enough for a passport to the Champions' League qualifiers. There the club got a favourable draw against AIK Solna of Sweden, but flunked their chance and had to be content with a modest run in the UEFA Cup of 1999/2000. At home, AEK were even further off the title pace, finishing in third, a full 26 points behind champions Olympiakos. A Nikolaidis goal set them on their way to a 3–0 Greek cup final victory over Ionikos Nikea, but the big news, sadly, was off the pitch. AEK's stadium was severely damaged by the earthquake that struck Athens in September 1999, with one stand being completely destroyed and the capacity being slashed to less than 16,000 as a result. The Greek government has agreed to pick up a quarter of the £2.5million it will cost to rebuild the ground, but the irony is that the club had already been planning the construction of a new stadium, 5km from the current site in the Nea Ionia area. Work is expected to start by 2001.

Here we go!

Take the metro to **Perissos**, 15mins north of Omonia. The stadium is a 5min walk away. Beware buildings around the ground which have been daubed with red crosses – these have been condemned as a result of the 1999 earthquake.

Just the ticket

The well-stocked **AEK shop** on the corner of Odos Fokon and Kappadokias (open Mon & Wed 9am–midday, Tue, Thur, Fri & matchdays 9am–2pm & 5–8.30pm, credit cards accepted), sells tickets for the following weekend's fixture. Domestic matches are given three categories: A (against the big two), B (against PAOK, Aris, Iraklis and OFI Crete) and C (all the others).

The cheap spots behind the goals (gates #9–11 and #21–23) are for AEK's radical faithful. Away fans are allocated a section through gates #1–2.

Swift half

At the **555** bar on the corner of Kaplinoleas, with tables outside and food served before and after the match, you'll be sharing a Heineken with the average thirsty fan. Nearby at Fokon 59 is the *Ideal*, a kebab and beer joint with AEK pictures on the wall.

Club merchandise

In addition to the **official store** (see *Just the ticket* above), there's a smaller, family run shop

Defending the faith – Gordan Petrić clears

nearer the metro station on Odos Ignias, open matchdays only.

Ultra culture

AEK's following may not have the numbers of Panathinaikos', nor the tradition of Olympiakos', but they make up for this with passion, commitment and a much-tested sense of humour. The younger, partying element occupies the south end between gates #9 and #11, while those entering gate #21 are more wayward, their antics celebrated on local radio show *Original 21*.

In print

Dikefalos is a weekly fan paper available on matchdays.

In the net

AEK loyalists continue to run an excellent website at: www.aek.com. A focus for the campaign to oust hated club president Mihalis Trochanas before the *ENIC* takeover of 1997, it has become a little more mainstream since but is still the best AEK site on the web.

Olympiakos

Stadium Olimpiako, see p.271
Capacity 76,000
Club office Ipsilantou 170
Colours Red-and-white striped shirts, white shorts
League champions 1931, 1933–34, 1936–38, 1947–48, 1951, 1954–59, 1966–67, 1973–75, 1980–83, 1987, 1997–2000
Cup winners 1947, 1951–54, 1957–58, 1960–61, 1963, 1965, 1968, 1971, 1973, 1975, 1981, 1990, 1992, 1999

With an original support base of blue collar workers, joined in modern times by bikers and heavy metal fans, Olympiakos are Greece's most popular and most decorated club. Greek champions for four years running since 1997, they were lifted from an extended period of stagnation by coach Dušan Bajević and the club president who poached him from AEK in 1996, mobile-phone millionaire Sokratis Kokkalis, one of the ten richest men in Greece.

The club are known as *Thrylos* (or 'legend'), after their founders and original five-man forward line, the Andrianopoulos brothers. After helping the team win four of the first six Greek titles, the brothers persuaded the Greek Olympic Committee to convert an old velodrome used for the 1896 Games into an athletics ground of international standard. The ground was the Karaiskakis, and work began on converting it in 1936. After that, the dockers, fishermen and ferrymen were to see their favourites win 16 further titles, including six on the trot before 1960.

In the modern era, Olympiakos continued to win the occasional Greek title without making serious progress in Europe, before the club's financier president George Koskotas was embroiled in a £13million embezzlement scandal in 1988 – the effects of which would be felt for the best part of a decade.

Incoming chief Kokkalis refloated the club in 1993, then snapped up star coach Bajević from AEK in the summer of 1996. With Serbs Ilija Ivić and Sinisa Gogić upfront, Olympiakos won the title by 12 points over AEK in Bajević's first season. The coach subtly reshaped the team to

Troubled star – Zlatko Zahovic in UCL action for Olympiakos against his former club, Porto

The Olympic stadium

Stadio OAKA 'Spiros Louis', Irinis
Capacity 76,000 (all-seated)

The Olimpiako, Greece's first national stadium since the one built in Athens for the inaugural modern Games of 1896, is a pleasure to visit. It is set to be the main athletics venue for the **2004 Olympics**, and its official title, OAKA 'Spiros Louis', stems from those 1896 games, when Louis was the Greek winner of the first modern Olympic marathon.

Currently host to **Panathinakos** and **Olympiakos** domestic fixtures, cup finals and major international ties, the Olimpiako, built in the early Eighties, comes into its own for the big occasion, an open bowl of noise and colour. Your seat, whether in the upper or lower tier, will afford you **an ideal view** of the action, played out on the lushest sporting surface in Greece.

The stadium is a short walk across across the concrete from the **Irinis metro stop**, indicated by the Olympic symbol on the metro map, 30 minutes from Omónia. You'll see the angled floodlights loom enticingly as the underground train's journey takes it overland.

There are no bars around the stadium, but you'll see groups of **beer and sausage stalls** by the metro entrance and main car park, where the **ticket offices** are also indicated in both Greek and English.

If you're here for a Panathinaikos game, in the stadium itself, there's the **Kafeneio Thyra 3**, covered in PAO pictures and articles, including three freeze-frames from the shock late goal that beat Everton to take the club into the European Cup final of 1971.

retain the crown in 1997/98, forging a midfield in which balding ball-winner Grigoris Georgatos and yet another Serb, playmaker Predrag Djordjević, were a cut above the domestic opposition.

In 1998/99 they proved they could cut it in Europe, too, winning their Champions' League group over Ajax, Porto and Croatia Zagreb, before rather unluckily going out to a late Antonio Conte goal for Juventus in Athens.

Failure to reach the last 16 of the Champions' League in 1999/2000 resulted in a falling out between Kokkalis and Bajević, and the latter quit in November, his place taken by the former Napoli coach Alberto Bigon. The latter succeeded in healing a rift between the club's big foreign signings – Brazil's Giovanni and Slovenia's Zlatko Zahovič – and the rest of the squad, and duly led Olympiakos to a fourth successive domestic title. But with Zahovič, at least, determined to leave Greece after Euro 2000, it remained to be seen whether Bigon could maintain the momentum.

Off the field, meanwhile, the club abandoned plans to redevelop its atmospheric old Karaiskakis ground, of which the Greek Olympic committee had refused to relinquish control, and are instead building a new 40,000-seater arena in the otherwise underdeveloped area of Redis. Work is expected to be finished in time for the 2004 Olympics at which, ironically, it is due to host part of the football tournament.

Just the ticket

The Olympiakos **ticket office** (Mon–Fri 9am–5pm, Sat 10am–3pm, most credit cards) is in a shopping alley by a parking lot at Kointouriotou 138, a road parallel to the club headquarters at Ipsilantou, a 15min walk from the Pireaus metro stop. Olympiakos' famous gate 7 **ultras** now find themselves in the lower tier behind one goal at the Olimpiako, in sections #15, #17 and #19, while away fans are allocated upper sectors #30, #32 and #34. Visiting neutrals should head for the even-numbered sectors #20–28. On matchdays, tickets go on sale at the Olimpiako itself (see panel).

Swift half

The bars around the **Karaiskakis** are still where fans congregate. The nameless café on the corner of Karaoli Dimitriou and Diamanti, on the side of the stadium furthest from the **Neo Faliro** metro stop, is the best of these.

Club merchandise

The small but well-stocked **Olympiakos shop** (Mon, Wed & Sat 9am–3pm, Tue, Thur & Fri 9am–2.30pm & 5.30pm–8.30pm, major credit cards accepted) is under the club's headquarters at Ipsilantou 170 in Pireaus.

Ultra culture

The various *Karaiskakis Gate 7* groups – *Legenda Gate 7, Bad Boys 7, Byron City Boys* – are the ones making the noise at the Olimpiako.

In the net

The club's **official website** is well-designed and melodramatic-looking. It includes an extensive English-language area and, like many Greek football sites, also includes sections on the club's various other sports branches, such as basketball and volleyball. It's all at: www.olympiakos.gr.

Groundhopping

Athens' minor clubs could occupy a chapter of their own, such is their diversity and unpredictability – abandoning their derelict grounds one year, boldly reconstructing them the next. For 2000/01 there are four of these smaller teams in the Greek top flight, Apollon and Proodeftiki Piraeus having been relegated, while Athinaikos moved in the opposite direction. A further team, Egaleo, finished just one point behind Athinaikos but failed to make it through the promotion play-offs.

Ethnikos, the team who have traditionally played in the shadow of Olympiakos in Piraeus, sank even further into the third division, but the emergence of another team bearing a similar name, Ethnikos Asteras, has kept the city's statisticians and groundhoppers busy.

Athinaikos

Ethniko Stadio Verona, Neas Efessou 6
Capacity 6,000
Colours Red-and-yellow shirts, yellow shorts

Founded in 1917, Athinaikos are one of Athens' oldest clubs, the pride of Veronas in the south-east of the city. The team have troubled the historians only once, when they made the 1991 Greek cup final. They were hammered 5–1 by Panathinaikos, but since Pana did the double that year, the red-and-yellows sneaked into the Cup-Winners' Cup, where they met Manchester United. Having managed a goalless draw at home, Athinaikos came close to taking the lead at Old Trafford before ultimately losing in extra-time.

Relegated in 1998, Athinaikos won Greece's second-division championship in 2000, the only team to win automatic promotion in what was a year of league restructuring. The club's grandly named stadium comprises one main stand, two sides of rock and a cemetery. The cemetery, **Nekrotafeio**, also lends its name to the **bus stop** by the ground – two from the terminus of the #204 that runs hourly from Syndagma. The more frequent #214 runs from Syndagma to Formionos, with a stop at Dimitriou which is a 10min walk to the stadium, up Arch Chrisostomou, where you'll find the *To Eteki* bar.

Ethnikos Asteras

Ethniko Stadio Kessarianis, Ethnikis Andistaseos 226
Capacity 4,700 (all-seated)
Colours Red shirts, white shorts

Athens' newest up-and-coming side have been a long time coming. Formed in 1927, this team from the eastern district of Kessarianis did next to nothing for 60-odd years until the arrival of Nikos Papadopoulos as club president. Papadopoulos saw his investment gradually rise, from the fourth, to third to second divisions, until the biggest day in the club's history, 5 May 1998, when a 2–0 home win over Larissa guaranteed Ethnikos a spot in the top flight.

Since then the team have finised creditably mid-table two seasons running, thanks mainly to the dedicated coaching of Spyros Livathinos. 'Red Star' Ethnikos will need further investment to challenge for a top-ten position, but the construction of a new 700-seater stand is a step in the right direction.

From Anfield to Athens – Ronnie Whelan mulls it over

The team play at the local council stadium, the Ethniko Stadio Kessarianis, by the terminus of the **#223** and **#224** buses, both of which stop at the *Hilton Hotel* in central Athens.

The club's spiritual home, however, is at its old stadium five bus stops into town, at 9th Karisarianis, where you'll find the ***Ethnikos Asteras Café*** nearby at Leof Ethnikis Andistaseos 198. There's also a small bar on Odemisiou, with pictures, scarves, *Panini* stickers and caged budgies.

Ionikos Nikea

Karaiskakis stadium, Neo Faliro
Club office Panayi Tsaldari 128
Capacity Variable (see text)
Colours All blue with white trim

Few clubs relish a visit to Ionikos. The team's consistent ability to finish in the top half of the table is based on their home form, aided by a fiercely loyal crowd which continues to make a noise, despite being temporarily moved to Olympiakos' old home of Karaiskakis while Ionikos' own Neopolis ground is overhauled. Look out for the hardcore *Blu Leone* huddled between gates #3 and #5, unless you're at a derby game against one of the Athens giants, when more areas of the stadium are

opened. The nearest metro stop to the Karaiskakis is **Neo Faliro**, 20mins south from Omonia. Turn right out of the station, then walk through the underpass to the ground.

Panionios

Nea Smyrni, Iannou Xrysostomou 1
Capacity 15,000
Colours All blue with red trim
Cup winners 1979, 1998

Panionios hail from the southern Athenian district of Nea Smyrna. The club was founded in Smyrna – now Turkish Izmir – in 1890. Eighty years ago, members and their families had to flee a burning city and set up camp in Nea ('new') Smyrna, Athens. Greece's oldest operating football club then saw some creditable finishes in the league and the occasional European highlight, before a remarkable cup final win over Panathinaikos in 1998.

That summer, president Loukas Siotropos sank a small fortune into ground improvements and hired former Liverpool midfielder Ronnie Whelan as coach – and former Manchester United star Mark Robbins as striker, together with a handful of other journeymen professionals from the English game.

The idea was to lay the foundations for a serious challenge to Athens' big three, but it didn't work out that way. Whelan's side were soundly beaten by Lazio in the quarter-finals of the Cup-Winners' Cup, their run to which proved an almost fatal distraction in the league. The club escaped relegation only by virtue of having scored more goals in their two meetings (one lost, the other won) with Panelefsinaikos, who went down in 16th place.

In October 1999, the atmosphere at this tight-knit family club was soured when fans set light to the cars of team captain Antonis Sapoutzis and star player Milinko Pantić, after a 4–1 home defeat by OFI Crete.

On matchday, the place to be is still **O Nikos**, a top-notch football bar and cheese-pie shop on the corner of Aidreou and K Palaiougou (near Ag Aidreou church), with its mural of a fantasy European Cup final win over Juventus. Trolleybus #10 runs from central Stadhíou, south down the main Syngrou avenue to **Nea Smyrna** – a journey of at least 30mins. A taxi to do the same trip will cost about Dr750.

Eat, drink, sleep…

Bars and clubs

At last Athens has a downtown nightlife centre – the **Psyrri** area radiating from Pl Iroon, once home to rundown shops and market stalls. Scores of new bars, clubs and cafés have sprung up here almost overnight. Nearby **Thissio** is also worth dipping into for nightlife. Clubs tend to be overpriced, their clientèle overdressed, especially in Glyfada along the Apollo coast.

Athinaikon, Themistokléous 2. On the corner with Panepistímiou, near Omónia metro, a beautiful old *ouzerí* which has lost none of its character since recently moving. Good lunchtime option.

Flying Pig, Filonos 131, Piraeus. Ex-pat pub near the docks, with Boddington's and Bud on draught, a huge range of whiskies, a full menu of pub grub and satellite TV.

Inoteka, Platía Avisynnias 3. Intimate bar in the flea market, with excellent dance sounds and friendly clientèle. Impromptu busking outside, guest DJs inside. Decent sounds until 5am weekends, 2am weekdays. Monastiráki metro.

Privilege, 130 Piraeus Avenue. Hippest place in town, a bar/lounge/restaurant in blue, blue, blue, the design attended to by wonder-boy Babis, the music by DJ Vasili Tsilichristos. Enough space for a couple of thousand of Athens' trendiest movers and shakers. In summer it all moves down to St Kosmos Beach at Elliniko.

Thirio, Lepenioutou 2. Probably the best bar in Psyrri, with a dark, wooden, candlelit feel, and fine sounds. Look out for the bongos and pomegranates in the window. The nearby **23**, on the corner of Ogygou and N'chou Apostoli, is also worth a look-in.

Restaurants

Plaka, the crumbling area of narrow streets and market stalls in the shadow of the Acropolis, is the best area for *tavernas;* food is surprisingly authentic, but most of the live music will be tourist mush. On the other side of Ermou, around Pl Iroon, you'll find locals tucking into cooking that is at least as good, without the tourist trappings.

Archaion, Kodratou 22. Newly opened restaurant with a menu based on dishes that were prepared at the time of Ancient Greece. Seafood, pork, goat – but no forks to eat it all with. Main courses around Dr3,000. Near Pl Karaiskaki.

Kouklis, Tripodhon 14. Acceptable tourist venue in the heart of Plaka. Main dishes at Dr1,000. Grab a balcony table, order another bottle of wine and let the afternoon take its course.

Taverna Kostoyiannis, Odos Zaími 37. Arrive early for a terrace spot at this bustling, friendly *taverna* behind the National Archaeological Museum. Closed Sundays, no credit cards.

Taverna Tou Psyrri, Odos Aischíylou 10. Just off Pl Iroon, and justifiably popular despite the range of options nearby, with half-a-dozen traditional dishes of the day all laid out and ready to choose from. The *Platía Iroon* at Karaiskaki 34 is also worth a look.

Vithos, Platía Asomaton 9/Adrianhou. Pricy but delicious fish restaurant near Thissio metro, with excellent salads. Open daily until 1am, most major credit cards.

Accommodation

If you arrive on spec, the small **tourist office** in the *National Bank Of Greece* in a corner of Syndagma square (Odos Karagheorghi tis Servias 2, 323-7193, Mon–Fri 8.30am–1pm, Sat 9am–12.30pm) will be able to help, but don't leave it until late in the day.

Remember that although a room in central Plaka or Omonia will solve transport problems, these areas can also be **extremely noisy** until the early hours. Out of season (ie. when there's football on), some places drop their rates, so try and strike a bargain.

Amalia, Leoforos Amalias 10 (☎01/323 7301, fax 01/323 8792). For luxury at half the price of the *Hilton*, and convenience to boot, the *Amalia* is just off Syndagma square, right by the airport bus stop. The upper back rooms have a view of the Acropolis, most others a view of the National Gardens or Lykavittos Hill in the distance. From Dr30,000 a double, most credit cards accepted.

Athens Gate Hotel, Leoforos Syngrou 10 (☎01/923 8302, fax 01/325 2952). Well-furnished rooms, most with balconies and televisions, for around Dr20,000 a double. Sun deck and roof-garden restaurant. Just across from the temple of Olympian Zeus. Most credit cards.

Attalos, Athinás 29 (☎01/321 2801, fax 01/324 3124, e-mail atthot@hot.gr). Slightly upmarket option near Monastiráki metro, but clean, comfortable and generally free of backpackers. Dr10,000 a single, Dr15,000 a double with breakfast. Most credit cards.

Hermes, Apollonos 19 (☎01/323 5514, fax 01/323 2073). Good value 'C' category hotel, where all rooms have a TV and bath/shower. Doubles around Dr25,000, including a great breakfast spread. Triples also available. Short walk from Syndagma.

Pella Inn, Ermou 104 (☎01/325 0598). Cheap, clean and conveniently situated by the Monastikiri metro stop, opposite the flea market and taverns of Plaka, this place is ideal for the budget-conscious traveller. Dr8,000 for a double room, some with balconies overlooking the Acropolis – the higher you go, the better the view.

Salonika

Greece's second city, the port of Salonika, has a turbulent multi-cultural history and current status as capital of Greek Macedonia. Occupied by the nearby Turks for 500 years, the place only became part of modern Greece after the Balkan Wars of 1912–13.

When British sailors brought football to Salonika in the 1880s, the then Ottoman rulers frowned upon what they viewed as a sinister new Western invention. In this repressive climate, the game took root. Greek students, some returning from all over the Ottoman Empire, took up football with a passion that has hardly diminished in over a century.

Alas, much of this passion has been misplaced. At the 1906 Intermediate Olympics, the football tournament, the first of its kind to be organised in Greece, saw serious fighting between sets of players and fans from Athens and Salonika. Within 20 years Salonika's three main clubs, PAOK, Aris and Iraklis, had been founded, Aris having the gall to win the first national championship in 1928. The die was cast. So polarised was the game's development in Greece that it wasn't until the Sixties that other towns were allowed to compete in an overall national league.

Traditionally fierce local pride, coupled with modern-day hooliganism, has produced some horrendous scenes, both on and off the pitch. Like some three-headed Tasmanian devil, Salonika's clubs are always being cautioned, fined or thrown out of Europe for crowd trouble.

PAOK, traditionally seen as the club of the workers and, like AEK Athens, formed by Greek refugees from Turkey, have the most notorious following. When a PAOK-Olympiakos game was stopped for crowd trouble in November 1998 – only two months after the mayor of a nearby town was hit on the head by a bottle in the Salonika derby – 10,000 locals went on a pavement-beating demonstration around regional government buildings.

The local hooligan phenomenon is at odds with Salonika's generally wealthy, cosmopolitan atmosphere. To most residents' relief, however, all three main stadia are in the east of the town, a fair way from the city centre.

The thrilling fields

Aris

Stadium Harilaou, Yanni Angelou 146
Capacity 27,000
Club office Vas Olgas 99
Colours Yellow and black
League champions 1928, 1932, 1946
Cup winners 1970

Although most of their honours are pre-civil war, Aris Salonika at least have the one honour of having won the first-ever Greek league title in 1928.

In modern times, Aris have been thereabouts but never really there. The club's last outstanding side was that of the 1979/80 season. With internationals Kostas Kouis and Georgias Semertsidis in the forward line, Aris knocked Benfica out of the UEFA Cup and finished equal top in the league, losing 2–0 to Olympiakos in a championship play-off.

Since then, Aris' followers have attracted more press than the team. The heavily-graffitied Harilaou resembles a set from *West Side Story*, with home fans occasionally facing off against each other during a lull in the game.

After being elegated for the first time in 1996/97, Aris bounced straight back the following year. A good early start to the 1998/99 season – including a 4–1 win over PAOK which saw some of the worst crowd violence in living memory – culminated in a sixth-place finish and a return to the UEFA Cup, but after finishing level on points with Iraklis in 1999/2000, Aris were beaten by their neighbours in a subsequent play-off and missed out on Europe for 2000/01.

Here we go!

The blue #10 bus runs from the train station, stopping right outside the **Harilaou**. Allow 20mins' journey time.

Just the ticket

The main **ticket booths** are on Odos Alkminis, by the entrance to the main stand. From there, gate #5 allows the neutral a safe view from the concrete terraces, above the halfway line where the press and VIPs sit. There is no protection, however, from the chilling *Vardaris* wind that blows over the ground from the north hills.

The entrance to gate #3, home of the Aris faithful by the west goal, is from the main Papanastassiou road from town, where the fans also have a *Super 3* kiosk open matchdays.

Visiting fans are bussed in and heavily policed in a small section to the east end of the ground.

Swift half

Bar action can be found along Papanastassiou. The *Maze*, by the town-bound bus stop at #165, is a pleasant gamblers' bar with plenty of football talk.

In the net

For English-speakers, the best website is run by the *Aris Fan Club Of Melbourne*, Australia, at: arisau.cjb.net. There's properly updated editorial content and a large bank of video action and still images, among many other things.

 PAOK

Stadium Toumba, Ethnikis Anistassis 32
Capacity 41,000
Club office Ethnikis Aminis 30
Colours Black and white
League champions 1976, 1985
Cup winners 1972, 1974

The biggest Greek club outside Athens, PAOK are the bad boys of the nation's football. Around the criss-cross of streets leading up to the chilling Toumba from the main Egnatía road from town, every scrap of concrete is smoked with the soot-coloured letters, PAOK. Panelikos Athletikos Omilos Konstantinopoulos were formed by Greek refugees fleeing Istanbul in 1926, and they have a nickname to live up to: the Black Devils.

The club is regularly banned from Europe, and games against major clubs from Athens are often either interrupted or postponed altogether by police. The resultant disruption has consistently prevented PAOK from mounting a major challenge to their rivals in the league. In November 1998, a pitch invasion during a game against Olympiakos prompted a five-match home ban, and slim title hopes faded into the inevitability of a UEFA Cup place.

A shame, because PAOK are the one club who could break the capital's hegemony. In 1976 they became the first provincial club to win the title for 30 years — since local rivals Aris, in fact. Five cup final appearances were followed by another title in 1985. During this time, PAOK held their head high in Europe, losing on penalties to both Bayern Munich and Eintracht Frankfurt, and going out on a solitary goal to Maradona's Napoli. A two-year European ban, following a riot against Paris St-Germain in 1992/93, prevented any further progess in that arena, at least for the time being.

Yet five years later, PAOK stunned Arsène Wenger's Arsenal with a 2–1 aggregate win in the UEFA Cup, before losing out to Atlético Madrid in the next round by the odd goal in 17 over two legs. Coach Angelos Anastassiadis, who took PAOK to fourth place in the league that season, was thought to lack enough international experience to tackle Rangers in the 1998/99 UEFA Cup – but his replacement, Oleg Blokhin, was then sacked following a 2–0 aggregate defeat.

It was as business as usual, too, in 1999/2000, when PAOK finished in fifth position – higher than their two city rivals

Pleading their innocence – PAOK's players get into almost as much trouble as their fans

(who were sixth and seventh), but way off the Champions' League pace. Off the pitch, too, little had changed: dozens of fans were injured and scores arrested at the PAOK–Aris derby game in March 2000.

Here we go!

The #12 bus marked **Toumba** makes the 15min journey from Egnatía to the stadium, then goes back to the centre via Tsimiskí, nearer the bay.

Just the ticket

The main **ticket office** is by gate #3, the entrance for press and neutrals. Graffitied ticket bunkers are dotted behind gate #4, home of the PAOK ultras, to the north end. Away fans will find themselves surrounded by a police cordon towards the south goal, through gates #7–8.

Swift half

The *Kafe Aupsiktigio* on the corner of Malakopis and Dardanelion is an upmarket café for frappé-sipping. On the north side of the ground, on the Kleanthou/Souanidi intersection, is the more convivial and refreshingly downmarket *Oasi*, with a terrace and small menu.

Club merchandise

Metal skip-shaped souvenir kiosks marked *PAOK Authentics* are dotted around gate #3, with a more regular **store** a short walk away at Grig Lambraki 82.

In the net

A very complete **fan-run website**, with a range of different language areas, resides at: www.paok.com. The English content is limited to a rolling news service, however.

Iraklis

Stadium Kaftantzoglio, Basileos Georgiou 33A
Capacity 45,000
Club office Pavlou Mela 38
Colours Blue and white
Cup winners 1976

Salonika's third and oldest team, known by fans of the other two as the 'Old Ladies' because of their alleged genteel background, have the honour of playing in the

Salonika essentials

Bus #78 makes the 16km, 40min journey from the **airport** to the main **train station** every 40mins (6.30am–11.30pm, tickets onboard Dr140). A taxi will cost around Dr2,000. Salonika's train and bus stations are to the west of the city, a 10min walk from the main thoroughfare, Odos Egnatía.

City transport consists of orange downtown buses and blue or red suburban ones, many of which run from Platía Eleftherías, from 5am to midnight. Tickets for most journeys in town are Dr100 – pay the conductor at the back, or throw a coin into the machine. Kiosks also sell individual tickets, which should be stamped onboard, or books of 12 for Dr1,100. There is no night bus service, but you'll find taxis in all the main squares. **Radio taxi** firms include *White Tower* (☎031/214 900) and *Alexander The Great* (☎031/866 866).

The main *EOT* **tourist office** is at Platía Aristotélous 8 (Mon–Fri 8am–8pm, Sat 8.30am–2pm, ☎031/263 112). The main **listings guide** is *14 Meres & Nykhtes*, a fortnightly Greek-language publication freely available in many bars and cafés.

town's main stadium, the impressive Kaftantzoglio, venue for the odd Greek international and the infamous Milan-Leeds Cup-Winners' Cup final of 1973.

Yet apart from derby games – there was a pitch invasion when Aris visited in the 1995/96 season – all is quiet in this residential area near the university. With its wide running track and flat appearance, the Kaftatzoglio gives the impression it can hold more than 45,000 people, but is rarely called upon to host half that number.

Most fans gather around the north goal or the east side to catch the last of the day's sun before it sets into the gulf, just visible from the top of the entrance steps. Such a great panorama deserves a great team, but there have been precious few of those in the club's 90-year history.

Despite finishing above Aris in the 1999/2000 Greek table, Iraklis were forced to play off with the former and the Athens club Panionios for a UEFA Cup berth, but came through unscathed, winning the vital game against Aris 2–0 at home.

Here we go!

Buses #17 and #37 run from Egnatía along Agiou Dimitriou and stop by the stadium – allow 10mins. If you're on the seafront, near the White Tower, the stadium is a pleasant 15min hike up Tritis Septemvriou past the exhibition grounds and *DEF* radio tower.

Just the ticket

Crumbling stone **ticket booths** line Agios Dimitriou, from where steps lead up to gate #4 for a spot over the halfway line. The Iraklis hardcore, *IRA 13*, are named after the gate number that leads to to their section behind the north goal.

Swift half

The only bar (sort of) in sight is the *Perasma*, tucked away on the corner of Politehniou and Agiou Dimitriou, 200m along the main road away from town. There's a **snack bar** inside the ground between gates #1 and #17, facing the training pitch.

In the net

There's a surprising amount of Iraklis activity on the web, and the best way of navigating around it is via Kostas Simeonidis' links exchange page at: egnatia.ee.auth.gr/~ksym.

Eat, drink, sleep...

Bars and clubs

Salonika is a **party town**, and in hot weather thousands flock to the fashionable cafés along the seafront, the scent of perfume and buzz of mopeds as entrancing as the lights across the gulf. The area radiating from Platía Morhovou, between Tsimiskí and the customs house, offers warehouses converted into tacky bars and clubs. Information on more authentic DJ events can be picked up at *Noïse*, Lóri Margaríta 4/6, a block inland from Níkis.

Isalos, Níkis 43. Best bar on the seafront, designed with style but not over-extravagance. Blue feel, good music too.

Kentriki Stoa, Irakliou 31. A great bar space and popular meeting spot directly above the town's main meat market – listen out for the bass speakers rattling the window panes.

Mylos, Andreou Ghiorghíou 56. A converted flower mill which now houses a rock club and a jazz and blues bar. In the dilapidated harbour streets past Ladhádhika, parallel to 26 Oktovriou.

To Iero Pou Kaïei, Koromilá 47. Best bar on a street once full of them, just inland from Níkis, a two-level affair with good sounds and friendly service.

Baxtse Tsflik, Vogatsikou 4. Packed out since opening in October 1999, this upstairs bar/club has more of a pub feel, thanks to the decor and huge range of spirits.

Restaurants

Greeks in Salonika enjoy a higher standard of living than Athenians and much of this disposable income is lavished on the town's **cosmopolitan restaurants**, either around Ladhádhika or along the seafront near Platía Aristotélous. For something rootsier, the area around **Platía Athonos** near the market is full of reasonably priced, family-run eateries which fill up quickly at lunchtime.

Bechtsinar, Katouni 11/13. Friendly *ouzerí* with a decent atmosphere in the heart of Ladhádhika, full of locals rather than out-of-towners dressed up for the night.

Brotos, Mitropolitou Gennadiou 6. *Ouzerí* near the market place with a wide selection of eats served on outside tables.

Megas Alexadandros, 26 Oktobriou 10. The friendliest of a string of late-opening establishments opposite the law courts, where for little more than Dr1,500 you can have a main course, salad and a carafe of wine.

Ouzeri Leonardos, Pl Emporious/Odos Aghiou Mina. Family-run *ouzeri* with home cooking and friendly service. Ideal before a night's bar crawling around nearby Ladhádhika,

Tsaroukhas, Olymbou 78. Celebrated for its *patsas* (the local speciality of tripe), an unpretentious favourite near the Roman market close to Platía Dhikastiríon.

Accommodation

Although Salonika is more expensive than Athens, its cheaper hotels are full of absurd hustlers and flotsam and jetsam from all over the Balkans. Keep your valuables safely hidden. The main drag, Egnatía, a 10min walk from the train station, is full of hotels, but if you need somewhere quieter, the *EOT* office at Platía Aristotélous 8 (see *Essentials*) can reserve free of charge.

Bill, Syngróu 29/Amvrossíou (☎031/537 666). Tranquil option just north of Egnatía, with doubles around Dr10,000 and singles at Dr7,000 – but bargain off-season.

Ilios, Egnatía 27 (☎031/512 621). A reasonable choice along Egnatía, if not entirely hustler-free. Individual bathrooms and a TV in every room. Some cable sports channels available. Dr7,000 a single, Dr9,000 for a double.

IYHF Hostel, Svólou 44 (☎031/225 946). The only hostel in town for both men and women, just south of the Galerius Arch. Bus #10 from the train station. Operates an 11pm curfew.

Tourist, Mitropóleos 21 (☎031/270 501, fax 031/226 865). Between busy Egnatía and the seafront, so a little quieter, the recently restored *Tourist* has doubles from around Dr12,000 and a couple of singles at Dr8,000. Advance reservations recommended.

Holland

KNVB Woudenbergseweg 56–58, PO Box 515, NL-3700 AM, Zeist
☎0343/499 211 Fax 0343/499 189 E-mail none

League champions PSV Eindhoven **Cup winners** Roda JC Kerkrade
Promoted NAC Breda, Groningen, RBC Roosendaal
Relegated Den Bosch, MVV Maastricht, Cambuur Leeuwarden

European participants 2000/01 PSV Eindhoven, SC Heerenveen (UCL);
Feyenoord (UCL qualifiers); Vitesse Arnhem, Ajax, Roda JC Kerkrade (UEFA Cup);
RKC Waalwijk (Intertoto Cup)

The year 2000 was to be the year when Total Football came home. Frank Rijkaard, a European champion as a player in 1988, was to lead his country to a second title, this time as a coach and this time on home turf. Young PSV Eindhoven striker Ruud van Nistelrooy would be the top scorer of the tournament, while the sight of Edgar Davids powering through the midfield with his Lenny Kravitz dreadlocks and wraparound shades would be the enduring image of a summer when everything went orange.

Total Football did indeed rule the day in June 2000, but it was the French who proved that they had truly mastered the fluid, modern game. Van Nistelrooy missed the tournament with a knee injury, but while his absence and Holland's semi-final defeat by Italy meant that the orange bunting was taken down before the final of Euro 2000, the performances of Davids and his support band lived up to expectations in every other way – the Dutch team entertained a continent, and the fans put on a party.

It is impossible not to like Dutch football. The precise, visionary passing, the perceptive movement on and off the ball, the explosive free-kicks and the belief that

When the lenses matched the shirt – Edgar Davids provided Euro 2000 with an enduring image

a victory is only a real victory if it is accomplished in style – all these things made Holland not just the bookmakers' favourites at Euro 2000, but those of many neutral fans.

In fact, the Dutch have been the purist's choice for three decades now. The period has been marked by three generations of awesomely talented players, each of which won a European Cup in its prime: Cruyff's Ajax in 1971–73, van Basten's and Gullit's AC Milan in 1989–90, and coach Louis van Gaal's young Ajax prodigies in 1995. Rijkaard, the third of Milan's Dutch trio, bridged the generation gap with his European swansong with Ajax in 1995. The three of them were essential to the Dutch national team's European Championship win of 1988.

Holland has a modest league dominated by three teams and draconian tax laws which force most Dutch stars to leave home early. Yet somehow there always seems to be another generation of teenage talent to replace those who have left.

The country's reward will come in 2000, when it co-hosts its first major international tournament, the European Championship, with Belgium. Not bad for a nation whose football was still amateur when Italy and West Germany had already won three World Cups between them...

Thanks to Holland's proximity to England, Dutch football was the second fastest on the continent to develop, after Denmark. English textile workers first played the game here in the mid-1860s. In 1879, Haarlemse Football Club were the first club to be formed and modest league and cup competitions were inaugurated ten years later. English clubs made regular tours and Holland enjoyed a brief reign among Europe's amateur elite. The Dutch were quick to propose an international football association in 1902 (which became FIFA two years later) and won two bronze medals in early Olympic soccer tournaments. But those semi-final appearances in 1920 and 1924, in what were effectively the World Cup finals of the amateur era,

were the last time the national side, *de Oranje*, would feature at international level for 50 years.

Professionalism left Holland behind. Of 26 internationals played between 1949 and 1955, *de Oranje* won two and lost 22. Defeats by Luxembourg and Northern Ireland kept them out of the latter stages of the 1964 European Championship and 1966 World Cup. It wasn't until the departure of leading goalscorer Faas Wilkes for the high salaries of Valencia in 1956 that professionalism was officially sanctioned and a proper national league created.

The new era saw the rise and eventual domination of the *eeuwige rivaals*, 'eternal rivals', Ajax and Feyenoord. Both were blessed with a remarkable crop of young players. Young Ajax forward Johan Cruyff became Dutch football's first modern superstar, his talents honed by the strict coaching of Rinus Michels. Ajax won three straight titles from 1966, and have scarcely looked back since. But it was Feyenoord, with the intelligent Wim van Hanegem in midfield, who won Holland's first European Cup, beating Celtic 2–1 in the 1970 final.

Ajax responded by taking Europe apart for three years. An almost tentative win over Panathinaikos in 1971 was followed by a confident stride through the competition in 1972 and 1973, with the forward-thinking Romanian coach Stefan Kovács at the helm. On paper, Ruud Krol and Wim Suurbier were defenders, Johan Neeskens, Arie Haan and Gerrie Mühren ran the midfield, while Cruyff, Piet Keizer and Johnny Rep led the line upfront. On the pitch, the players constantly interchanged in a flowing 4–3–3 system which left *catenaccio*, quite literally, standing. 'Total Football' had arrived.

With Michels in charge, Holland were the punters' dark horses for the 1974 World Cup. Within a few games they had become the neutrals' favourite, too, their popularity soaring still higher after they had beaten a deeply negative Brazil team, 2–0. That result set up a final encounter with the hosts West Germany – pairing

The solitary honour – Holland still waits for an achievement to match that of winning Euro '88

Cruyff with Franz Beckenbauer, two inter-pretations of Total Football. The Dutch were ahead within a minute through a Neeskens penalty, but once the Germans had won a (slightly dubious) spot-kick of their own, Holland's *wanderlust* got the bet-ter of them. After Gerd Müller had put the hosts ahead, Holland created few chances.

By 1978, the Ajax stars, including Cruyff, had gone abroad, allowing Bayern Munich to dominate Europe and PSV Eind-hoven the domestic league. It was PSV's van de Kerkhof brothers, Willy and René, who were at the heart of the *Oranje* side which travelled to the World Cup in Argentina that year. Cruyff refused to make the trip, apparently in protest against the Argentine military junta. His replacement was Rob Rensenbrink, who had been forced to leave the 1974 final through injury and who, while less flamboyant, was also less prone to go walkabout.

With a slightly more direct approach and an awesome display of long-range shooting, Holland made their way to the final, where for the second successive

World Cup, they found themselves up against the hosts. There, a hostile atmos-phere provoked some abonimably weak refereeing, and when Rensenbrink struck a post in the last minute of normal time, the Dutch knew it wasn't going to be their day – Argentina won 3–1.

It was to be ten years before the Rijkaard/Gullit/van Basten triple act, an adventurous formation kept on course by a returning Rinus Michels on the bench, got Holland back to the top. In the 1988 European Championship, just two years after a humilliating play-off defeat by Bel-gium had denied them a place at the Mexico World Cup, Holland were playing their best football since 1974. A van Basten hat-trick destroyed England, then a single touch from the same player three minutes from time gained the Dutch their revenge over West Germany in the semi-final. In the final, a thunderbolt header from Gullit and an extraordinary far-post volley from van Basten were enough to beat a Soviet Union side who had been weakened since themselves beating Holland earlier in the

Basics

EU citizens and those of the USA, Canada, Australia and New Zealand require only a **passport** to enter the Netherlands.

The Dutch **currency** is the guilder, abbreviated to f, divided into 100 cents. There are coins for 5c, 10c, 25c, f1, f2.50 and f5, and notes for f10, f25, f50, f100, f250 and f1,000. There are around f3.3 to £1.

Banks offer the best **exchange rate**, and are open Mon–Fri 9am–4pm, with occasional late Thursday opening in the main cities. *GWK* offices are open much later, and can give cash advances on credit cards. Payment by credit card is widespread.

Phonecards, in f5, f10, f25 and f50 sizes, are sold at post offices and tourist information (*VVV*) offices. From outside the country, the code for Holland is 31; for Amsterdam add 20, Rotterdam 10 and Eindhoven 40. Add a 0 before the city code if you're calling inland. From inside Holland, the international access code is 00, and the reduced rate period for European calls is Mon–Fri 8pm–8am, all day Sat–Sun.

Holland is a small country and few **journeys** take more than three hours. **Trains** are comfortable and efficient, and fares, calculated by the kilometre, are reasonable. A journey of 50km costs around f15, with a 10% discount on return fares if you come back the same day on a *dagretour*. Buying a ticket onboard incurs a hefty supplement.

Bus stations are nearly always located next to train termini, and local services are equally cheap and efficient. Like all public transport in Holland, buses run on the *Nationale Strippenkaart* system, in which a ticket strip is divided into numbered bars, which the bus driver then stamps according to the length of your journey. Simply tell him your destination when you board. On **city trams** and **metros**, it's up to you to stamp the ticket in the machine by folding the strip to include sufficient bars. Few urban journeys require more than two. The driver can sell you strips of two, three or eight bars onboard; more economical 15- (f11.75) and 45-bar (f34.50) strips are sold at train stations and newsstands.

For all the efficiency of the transport, **cycling** is often the best way to get around. There are bike hire offices at most train stations; they charge about f10 a day, but require a form of ID and f200 deposit. Be sure to use a sturdy lock wherever you park.

Hotels in Holland are not particularly cheap but there is a **national reservation service**, *Nederlands Reserverings Centrum* (open Mon–Fri 8am–8pm, Sat 8am–2pm, ☎070/419 5500, fax 070/419 5519, e-mail info@hotelres.nl). Large towns have a *VVV* tourist office at or near the train station, where you can book a room for f3.50 commission per person. In a two-star hotel, expect to pay around f100–130 for a double room with a bath/shower. Pensions are about f50 per person, youth hostels f30.

Dutch **cooking** is high on protein, low on variety, relying on fish, meat and dairy produce. *Eetcafés* provide a good-value version of it – look out for the *dagschotel*, the dish of the day, at around f20, or three-course tourist menus at f25–30. The Dutch tend to dine early, so restaurants normally only stay open until 11pm. Most towns have a fair ethnic selection, especially Chinese, Surinamese and Indonesian. Restaurant bills are subject to a 17.5% tax surcharge and 15% service charge.

The traditional Dutch bar is the *bruine kroeg*, or **brown café**, cosy and tobacco stained. These places serve food until early evening and lager (*pils*) in small glasses with a large head theatrically skimmed off by a plastic knife. *Heineken, Amstel, Oranjeboom* and *Grolsch* are the most common brews, but more adventurous Belgian varieties should also be available. The national spirit is *jenever*, a gin made from molasses and juniper berries. Most bars stay open until 1am, 2am at weekends.

Note that the renowned liberal attitude to **smoking marijuana** in Holland applies only to designated **coffee shops**.

competition. The *Oranje* had won a major tournament at last.

The Germans would figure prominently in the Dutch bid to win the next two big international events. At Italia '90, Holland's tempestuous defeat by West Germany featured the ugly sending-off of Rijkaard and Rudi Völler. Revenge came at Euro '92, with an easy 3–1 win for the Dutch in a first-round group encounter, but subsequent celebrations and complacency in the semi-final against Denmark proved Holland's undoing.

Euro '92 would mark van Basten's last top-level international appearance before injury. In the run-up to the 1994 World Cup, Gullit withdrew at the last minute, and there was further (now familiar) dissent in the ranks during the tournament itself. Holland went out in the quarter-finals – though not without a fight – to the eventual winners Brazil.

The squad was again divided as it approached Euro '96, with several members of the young Ajax contingent openly at war with coach Guus Hiddink. After a 4–1 crushing by England at Wembley, elimination duly came at the quarter-final stage, in a penalty shoot-out against France.

Yet the same players, under the same coach, produced a marked contrast at the 1998 World Cup. Of all the players to have won honours that season for their respective foreign clubs – Dennis Bergkamp and Marc Overmars for Arsenal, Clarence Seedorf for Real Madrid, Winston Bogarde and Michael Reiziger for Barcelona – it was Juventus' Edgar Davids who commanded coach Hiddink's attention. He'd flown to Turin to make his peace with a player who had been sent home from the Euro '96 camp, and his gesture was rewarded as Davids produced dynamic peformances throughout the tournament. Quite apart from his late winner from distance against Yugoslavia in the second round, it was Davids' tireless work-rate in the later stages that inspired Holland.

For the quarter-final against Argentina, Kluivert returned from suspension while Bergkamp was lucky to have avoided it after disgracefully stepping on a floored Mihaijlović in the previous round, the two forwards combined for an early first goal, and three touches of Bergkamp genius from a long Frank de Boer pass sealed the game 2–1 at the death.

Bergkamp's fitness deserted him in the semi against Brazil, however, and it was left to Kluivert to miss several chances before levelling the scores, again at the death. But, as at Euro '96, Holland's penalty-taking let them down, although this time it was Clarence Seedorf who would console the unfortunate Ronald de Boer – a gesture no Dutch player had afforded Seedorf after his own penalty miss two years earlier.

The new-found unity was strengthened by the appointment of Rijkaard as coach. Still only 37, he had played with most of the ex-Ajax boys and, as the son of a Dutch mother and a Surinamese father, he was perfectly placed to maintain dressing-room harmony – although his team's form in the run-up to Euro 2000 was mediocre.

Once the tournament had kicked-off, in front of massed ranks of orange Rijkaard's Holland needed a controversial late penalty to get a barely deserved three points in their opening group game against the Czech Republic. But a 3–0 romp over Denmark was more like it and, while qualification was already assured, Holland's 3–2 win over a second-string French team whetted the appetite for what many felt would be the eventual final.

Yugoslavs with revenge on their mind were next in the quarter-finals, but whereas the Serbs had stifled the Dutch midfield at France '98, this time they were simply swept aside. Kluivert scored a hat-trick in a scintillating 6–1 victory in which Davids and Overmars were outstanding.

Having witnessed the massacre, Italy coach Dino Zoff decided that old-fashioned *catenaccio* was the only way to deal with Holland in the semi-final. When Gianluca Zambrotta was sent off in the 33rd minute it was backs against the walls for Italians, yet the Dutch had only themselves to blame for failing to find a gap – Frank de Boer saw a penalty saved by Francesco Toldo, then Kluivert hit the post with another spot kick. So it was penalty shoot-out time again and, just as in the last two tournaments, Holland's nerve failed them.

Rijkaard quit his post, but the appointment of Louis van Gaal, freed from his torture at Barcelona, as his successor should ensure that the Ajax generation will have one last chance of glory at the 2002 World Cup.

In contrast, meanwhile, the constant flow of players abroad means that at club level, the Dutch seem further away from success than ever.

Essential vocabulary

Hello *Hallo*
Goodbye *Tot ziens*
Yes *Ja*
No *Nee*
Two beers, please *Twee bier, alstublieft*
Thank you *Dank u*
Men's *Mannen*
Women's *Vrouwen*
Where is the stadium? *Hoe kom ik in het stadion?*
What is the score? *Wat is de stand?*
Referee *Scheidsrechter*
Offside *Buitenspel*

Match practice

The first thing to know about domestic football in Holland is that you can't see any of it without a *Club Card* (see *Just the ticket* below). To counter the rise of hooliganism, this membership scheme was introduced for all Dutch premier-league grounds in 1996/97, and modified slightly by the top clubs the following year.

The system did not prevent some horrendous off-the-ball incidents between Ajax and Feyenoord nutcases in the spring of 1997, but most high-risk matches are so heavily policed, you won't see any trouble at the ground.

The top stadia were all improved for Euro 2000, and even the minor top-flight grounds are now all-seaters. Yet scratch this impressive veneer, discount the big three, and you'll find the average premier-league crowd to be under 8,000. Unless you manage to get into *de klassieker*, Ajax-Feyenoord, or a game between either of those and PSV, you'll be watching a match in surroundings not far removed from those of an English lower-division fixture.

The season runs from mid-August to the end of May, with a one-month break between Christmas and the end of January. Premier-league games take place on Saturdays at 7.30pm or Sundays at 2.30pm. Live televised games are scheduled for 7.30pm on Fridays and 6pm on Sundays. There are a handful of midweek rounds, and Dutch city mayors – who have the right to postpone games unilaterally if they fear crowd trouble – can play havoc with the calendar, causing a pile-up of fixtures at the end of the season.

A different league

Holland has two professional divisions, the premier (*Eredivisie*) and the first (*Eerste Divisie*). Both have 18 teams. At the end of the season, the bottom of the premier swaps places with the top of the first. Other promotion and relegation places are decided in June's *Nacompetitie*, which comprises two play-off groups of four teams each, playing each other home and away.

The first-division season is divided into four periods, and the most successful team in each is known as the period champion. These four sides, the clubs finishing second and third from bottom in the premier and the clubs finishing second and third in the first go to make up the two *Nacompetitie* groups. In practice, the play-offs also involve teams finishing fourth or fifth, as invariably period champions finish in the top two or three of the *Eerste Divisie*. The winners of each six-game play-off group go into the next season's *Eredivisie*.

At present, no professional club can be relegated to the amateur leagues, though this may change at some point over the next couple of years to encourage movement between the professional and amateur sectors. The latter is strictly divided into Saturday and Sunday leagues, from the days when Christian clubs refused to play on a Sunday. The identity of Holland's top amateur club is decided when the Saturday and Sunday champions play each other – on a Saturday.

Up for the cup

The *KNVB Beker* involves 60 amateur and professional clubs. The cup winners and top three league teams from the previous season are exempt from the qualifying group matches in August, when the other 56 are divided into 14 pools of four teams each. These pools are seeded, with one premier, one first and two lower-first or amateur clubs. After three group matches per team, the top two of each pool join the four exempt teams in the first round proper. The four rounds (November, January, February, April) to the final are decided on one match, extra-time with sudden death, and penalties. The final is always played on Ascension Day in May, and always at Feyenoord's de Kuip, irrespective of who the finalists may be.

Just the ticket

To buy a ticket for an *Eredivisie* game, you must have a *Club Card*, designating you as a member of any of the 18 clubs. With the help of the cards, a computerised seat allocation system and Dutch national lottery outlets, 80% of tickets are automatically allocated to the home club, 5–10% to away fans and 10–15% to neutrals.

If there are tickets available – and for Ajax, Feyenoord and PSV, there probably won't be – neutrals can buy a token for f10 on the day to allow them to buy a ticket in. Alternatively, you can simply enrol as a member of a lesser-supported club (f10 for two years), which will enable you to see more regular football without any hassle beforehand.

For Holland internationals, members of the official *Dutch Supporters' Association* (f25 for two years) get first priority on tickets, then *Orange Club Card* holders (f10 for

Face of failure – defeat by Italy, June 2000

two years), then regular *Club Card* holders. Standing tickets (*staanplaatsen*) have now been phased out at most premier-league grounds. Seats (*zitplaatsen*) are either covered (*overdekte*) or open (*onoverdekte*). The sector (*vak*) marked *bezoekende* is for visiting supporters. *Verhoogd* matches are the choice games, for which prices are raised.

The cheapest places will be f30–40, a decent seat f50–70. The best view can be had from the *Hoofdtribune*, the main stand. Prices drop dramatically for first-division games, for which f20 will get you the best seat in the house.

Most clubs issue a matchday programme, but don't expect a work of art.

Half-time

The beer on sale at the main Dutch grounds is *malt*, without alcohol, but is still sunk in great quantities. Snacks include *patat met frietsaus* – chips with mayonnaise; if you want them without, just say '*zonder*'.

Sandwiches (*broodjes*) come with various fillings, including herring (*haring*). You'll also find waffles (*stroopwafels*) and frankfurter sausages (*fricandel*).

Action replay

The most popular TV show is *Studio Sport*, a highlights package of the day's league games screened at 7pm on Sundays by state channel NOS, which also shows Italian action at 10pm that evening.

Subscription channel Canal Plus, formerly Supersport, has the rights to show 68 live premier league matches per season – generally on Fridays at 8pm and Sundays at 6pm – while the commercial station SBS6 shows live cup matches and English and Dutch league highlights on Saturdays at 6.15pm and 10pm, and Sundays at 6pm and 11pm. SBS6 also screens a *Match Of The Week*, a first-division game, on Monday evenings. BBC and the main German and Belgian channels are easily available all over Holland.

The back page

The main football publication is the authoritative colour weekly *Voetbal International* (Wednesdays, f4.95), which has fair foreign coverage as well as all the local features, gossip and stats. There are two football-only monthlies, *Voetbal Magazine* (f5.95) and *elf Magazine* (f6.95), which appeal to a younger readership with more pictures than text.

Hard Gras (quarterly, f16.90), a *Granta*-style, pseudo-literary booklet with in-depth interviews and philosophical meanderings on the game, is printed in both Dutch and English.

Of the dailies, the populist *De Telegraaf*, a tabloid dressed as a broadsheet, has all the juicy transfer rumours, and as Holland has no Sunday papers, its *Telesport* supplement on Mondays is pretty much essential.

Ultra Culture

Much has been done in Holland to counteract the country's hooligan problem: security fences, strict segregation, the *Club*

Card system for buying tickets, and an increase in police powers to allow them to inflitrate supporters' groups and tap their telephones.

The bitter Ajax-Feyenoord rivalry has always overshadowed the fan scene in Holland. It first saw light of day in the mid-Seventies when groups, modelling themselves on English hooligans and calling themselves *Sides* after the section of terracing they occupied, began to arm themselves every weekend. The violence escalated until the FA were forced to take action.

At national level the picture couldn't be more different – so long as the opposition aren't German. Dutch fans are renowned for their oompah bands (*The Orange Hooters* in particular), good spirit and friendly drinking.

In the net

An official FA website was launched prior to Euro 2000 at: www.knvb.nl. It includes extensive English-language areas, including an excellent news section devoted to the national team.

There is a sponsor-run homepage for the *Eredivisie* at: www.kpn-telecompetitie.nl. This has club-by-club news and stats, and although there is no English, the Dutch signposting is easy enough to understand.

Among the unofficial sites, the first port of call must be Joost Schraag's homepage at: soccer.boa.nl/aftrap.html. It contains a stats archive and details of the current season to help you work your way through Holland's usual fixture chaos. It's also a great source of links, a selection of which take you to the online version of *NOS Teletekst*, a first-rate news source which can be hard to navigate otherwise.

Elsewhere, the flashy online edition of *Voetbal International* is at: www.vi.nl. It's been considerably expanded and, like the magazine, covers the latest news in both the Dutch and Belgian domestic games.

Amsterdam

Fans visiting Amsterdam find it strangely bereft of football culture. Sure, they love its peaceful vibe, its canals, bars and coffee shops, but...where's the footie?

The answer is at a futuristic superdome on the city's south-eastern edge. Ajax's new stadium, the Amsterdam Arena, was opened in August 1996 with a friendly against AC Milan. Queen Beatrix did the Mexican wave with 51,000 other spectators, all season tickets were quickly snapped up and, despite justified criticism of the turf and lack of atmosphere, plans were laid for an entertainment complex to complement Europe's newest major football venue.

It looked like Amsterdam had a ground to challenge favoured Feyenoord's in the international stakes, but Rotterdam city council outbid their cautious rivals for the right to stage the Euro 2000 final. With Ajax going off the boil, average gates have dipped below 45,000, and Arnhem has stolen a lot of the Arena's thunder with its novel Gelre Dome stadium.

Still, Amsterdam city council and the corporate investors who ploughed some f250million into the project are happy. The Arena is regularly hired out for shows, while the museum, shop and guided tours bring in daily revenue.

Yet still visitors beg the question, where's the football? The Jordaan area, where Gullit and Rijkaard played together in the street, has been yuppified. Amsterdam is a one-club town, with none of the tension and colour that a big inner-city rivalry can provide.

It hasn't always been this way. Many local clubs have fallen by the wayside, including RAP Amsterdam, who won the first Dutch title in 1898 and the first double a year later. Ajax's three former cross-town rivals – Blauw Wit, De Volewijckers and DWS – merged to form FC Amsterdam in 1972 (and beat Internazionale in the UEFA Cup two years on), then went their separate ways to operate as amateurs ten years later. The stadium they used, the Olympic, venue for the 1928 Games, was rescued from property developers by a campaign group who raised f5million from donors happy to have their name inscribed on a brick of the restored ground. Although due to re-open in October 1999, it will be used mainly for athletics meets and junior football. Even in the days when Ajax used it for European ties, residents limited top-class games at the Olympic to six per year due to the noise.

Holland's first football ground, the Oude Stadion, was demolished to make way for the Olympic in 1928. Almost 60 years later, Ajax's own de Meer was knocked down to make way for housing. Yet this blunt fact covers a multitude of history. De Meer not only saw Ajax rise from a modestly successful club side to a major European power – half the players who achieved this grew up within a two-mile radius of the ground. Johan Cruyff's mother, who used to wash the team's shirts, still uses the club shop opposite where de Meer once stood. Fans still drink in the bar next door. Sure, it could barely hold 30,000, and most league matches barely pulled in a third of that. But these people were Ajax through-and-through – not least the F-side mob opposite the scoreboard end. The fact that these people are still drawn to de Meer's locale indicates the unease many feel about the move to the Arena.

The club have not been insensitive to fans' feelings. Some have taken their old de Meer seat from the ground and plonked it in their living rooms, so that instead of watching home matches from it, they can now use it to sit back and enjoy away games on the box. Other fans have had their ashes scattered on pieces of de Meer turf donated to a special plot, designed in the shape of a football pitch and planted in the city's Westgaarde cemetery.

Ajax can't help being fashionable. The Arena now attracts media personalities, businessmen, hot shots, people who wouldn't have been seen dead in de Meer – or in Westgaarde cemetery, for that matter. The atmosphere in the Arena, with five times the average gate of the old de Meer, has been subdued not because of the stadium's design (without a wire fence or running track, it's as intimate as a 50,000-seater stadium can get) but because a fair few spectators simply don't know what you should do at a football match.

The ground has not brought promised employment to the otherwise economically depressed area of Bijlmer, to which white city workers have been drafted when so much of Ajax's successful modern image has been in bringing young black talent to the fore. But the development has brought Ajax's famed soccer school superb new facilities in an area known as de Toekomst ('The Future'), a part of the Arena complex. And the future, as Ajax will tell you, is what it's all about.

The thrilling fields

 Ajax

Amsterdam Arena, Arena Boulevard 1
Capacity 51,500 (all-seated)
Colours White shirts with thick red stripe, white shorts
League champions 1918–19, 1931–32, 1934, 1937, 1939, 1947, 1957, 1960, 1966–68, 1970, 1972–73, 1977, 1979–80, 1982–83, 1985, 1990, 1994–96, 1998
Cup winners 1917, 1943, 1961, 1967, 1970–72, 1979, 1983, 1986–87, 1993, 1998–99
European Cup winners 1971–73, 1995
Cup-Winners' Cup winners 1987
UEFA Cup winners 1992

That thick red stripe on Ajax's white shirts is a symbol of technical excellence, of faith in youth and, ultimately, of success. The club's soccer academy, a production line of prodigious teenage talent, is the envy of Europe. Ajax's new stadium, the Amster-

dam Arena, is one of the finest on the continent. And yet, despite a high-scoring league and cup double in 1998, since the departure of Louis van Gaal and much of his team for Barcelona in the summer of 1997, Ajax have hit a hiatus.

Almost the whole of the team who so brilliantly took on Europe's best – and won – in 1995 has gone. Kluivert, Bogarde, Reiziger, Overmars, Kanu, George, Davids, Seedorf and the de Boer twins have taken with them a football education second to none, and a confidence born of constantly having proved their worth through those early years of development. Behind them they have left a club which, though commercially healthy, has been stung by the implications of the Bosman ruling and is, temporarily at least, having to break with tradition by signing established internationals from foreign clubs.

The last time there was an exodus on this scale, when Johan Cruyff followed coach Rinus Michels to Barcelona in 1973, it took a decade for the team to recover. For many fans, Cruyff still embodies much that is forever Ajax: flair, versatility, vision and a genius bordering on arrogance. At his peak he led a team which stands alongside Europe's all-time greats.

The Ajax story really begins with Cruyff's debut and the appointment of Michels as coach in 1965. Until then the club, formed by businessmen meeting on Sunday lunchtimes in 1900, had been a medium-sized fish in a small pond. The Dutch league was of mediocre standard and Holland's international status was on a par with that of Norway. In the Thirties, de Meer stadium was built and the club won five titles under English coach Jack Reynolds. But few outside Holland took much notice.

Even by the mid-Sixties, Ajax were scarcely a name to be conjured with in the wider picture of European football. Michels, a disciplinarian who encouraged freedom of spirit on the pitch, changed those perceptions for good. He introduced a 4–2–4 system, with a young Cruyff moving

Meeting of minds – Total Football practitioners Beckenbauer (Bayern) and Cruyff (Ajax), 1973

between midfield and centre-forward. With Piet Keizer on the wing, it began to rain goals at de Meer. Ajax easily won the Dutch title in 1966, then beat Liverpool 5–1 in the European Cup. In 1966/67, Cruyff scored 33 goals in 34 league games.

Ajax were not quite ready to conquer the continent – they were hammered 4–1 by AC Milan in the 1969 European Cup final. It needed Johan Neeskens, Horst Blankenburg, Gerrie Mühren, Arie Haan and Ruud Krol to raise the club's game to another level. In 1970/71, Ajax beat Celtic and Atlético Madrid in a European Cup run that culminated in a 2–0 victory over Panathinaikos at Wembley in 1971.

Michels then left for Barcelona. His successor, Romanian coach Stefan Kovács, adapted Michels' attacking *catenaccio* to form a fluid 4–3–3 system which required all outfield players to improvise their positions with constant movement off the ball. Everyone was aware of each other's presence, and could anticipate runs from deep positions, not least by the attacking

sweeper. Like an orchestra, it was complicated but, when in full flow, was unbeatable. Like an orchestra, it required a high degree of technical skill and an inspired conductor – Cruyff.

This *Totaal Voetbal* swept aside much of the negativity of the previous decade. In 1972 and 1973 Ajax were simply unstoppable, achieving two European Cup wins over *catenaccio*-driven Inter and Juventus, before Cruyff followed Michels south to Barcelona.

Without their conductor, Ajax floundered – and Franz Beckenbauer's Bayern Munich assumed their mantle. Neeskens also left for Barcelona and soon Haan, Blankenburg and young goalscorer Johnny Rep were gone, too.

It took more than ten years, and the return of Cruyff as coach, for Ajax to regain their strength. As a player, he had come back to lead Ajax to a Dutch league and cup double in 1982/83 – a season during which he'd been substituted by a gangly 17-year-old striker, Marco van Basten, who

Closing time – the Arena with its roof on

would make a goalscoring debut. By the time van Basten's five-year career at Ajax was over, he had scored 128 goals in 133 league games. His last strike was the winning goal against Lokomotiv Leipzig in the 1987 Cup-Winners' Cup final – not just van Basten's swansong in an Ajax shirt, but also Cruyff's finale as coach.

Also on the pitch against Leipzig were Frank Rijkaard (who would join van Basten at AC Milan but return to lead van Gaal's prodigies), Dennis Bergkamp and Aron Winter. Before leaving for Italy, the latter two would star in Ajax's UEFA Cup win five years later – the first success of the van Gaal era.

A former youth and reserve team coach, van Gaal relied on Ajax's technical chief, the influential Co Adriaanse, to produce a new generation of players. Adriaanse's graduates were a joy to behold: a group of raw, skilled, committed youngsters who took on the millionaires of Milan in the 1994 Champions' League and beat

them – twice. When the two teams met again in the final of the competition in May 1995, it was a 19-year-old, Patrick Kluivert, who scored the late winner – his lively opportunism a fitting tribute to the Ajax philosophy.

Yet by the time the side had lost the following year's European Cup final to Juventus on penalties, storm-clouds of uncertainty were gathering. In 1996/97, Ajax gave up their Dutch title with less than a quarter of the season gone, and after a European Cup quarter-final win over Atlético Madrid, they were destroyed by Juventus in the semi – making the campaign (van Gaal's last) their first without a trophy in five years.

In 1997/98, without the pressure of the Champions' League, Ajax surprisingly swept all before them under van Gaal's replacement, Morten Olsen. They won their first 11 league games straight, often by large margins, eventually scoring 112 league goals in 34 games, even beating PSV 5–0 in the cup final. But, aside from the goalscoring prowess of Litmanen and new signing Shota Arveladze, the cracks were there if you looked hard enough. Spartak Moscow took Ajax apart in a UEFA Cup quarter-final tie at the Arena. Players were showing their discontent with Olsen's methods, not least the de Boers, slowly sulking their way to a dual transfer to Barcelona.

The following season, Ajax got off to their worst league start in 40 years, and finished bottom of what had looked a relatively easy Champions' League group. A bitter Olsen was replaced by Jan Wouters, less experienced as a coach, but an Ajax man to the core.

After discarding some of Olsen's less successful signings, Wouters got the team playing the 'right' way again, and his reward was a comfortable Dutch cup final win, 2–0 over Fortuna Sittard. Yet this proved a false dawn. In 1999/2000, Ajax's UEFA Cup campaign ended with a 3–0 aggregate defeat by Mallorca in the third round, while the club could finish no higher than sixth in the league – the worst finish in living memory.

Wouters was dismissed and replaced by Co Adriaanse for 2000/01. Van Gaal's former right-hand man was under no illusions about the size of the task ahead, but the impression, at least, was that things could only get better.

Here we go!

Metro line #54, direction Gein, runs from Centraal through three zones (stamp four bars) to **Bijlmer**. Allow 15mins. The Arena is ahead of you as you turn left down the stairs from the platform.

Just the ticket

Most games at the Arena are a sellout, but not all. If a less attractive team is in town, there'll be tickets on sale (f45–55) at a small office round the corner from *Soccer World* towards Bijlmer metro. If you're visiting for the first time, you'll also have to buy a temporary club card, for which

you'll need f25, your passport and a photograph. The stadium is colour-coded in two tiers. The most expensive seats are in the yellow upper tier of the *Hoofdtribune*, through entrances D, E and F, the cheapest in the pink lower tier alongside the touchline, sectors #119–122. Visitors are generally allocated 1,600 tickets, and enter by gate K to sectors #415–416 in the corner of the red *Noord* end.

Swift half

By the metro entrance you'll find three soulless, upmarket bars, incongruously spilling out drunken football fans on big matchdays. Of the three, the *Klein Arena*, right out of the metro exit, is the most convivial.

A better bet is *Soccer World*, by the stadium entrance, a two-floor bar/restaurant part-owned by the de Boer twins, Frank Rijkaard and Danny Blind. The TV screens and walls depict football's legends, while spirits hang from the

Amsterdam essentials

A fast train service (every 15mins daytime, hourly at night, journey time 20mins, single fare f6.25) connects **Schiphol airport** with Centraal station, hub of Amsterdam's transport network and a short walk from Dam square. Many trains go on to other cities after calling at Amsterdam Centraal – don't miss your stop.

The seven-and-a-half hour *Eurostar* journey from London Waterloo International (change at Brussels Midi) terminates at Centraal. *Eurolines* buses terminate at Amstel station, a metro journey from Centraal.

Most of central Amsterdam is accessible by foot or bicycle, but **buses, trams** and a three-line **metro** network run on the *Strippenkaart* system. Most journeys you'll make will only take in one zone, so stamp two bars – the stamp is valid for one hour. Transport runs 6am–midnight, after which five hourly **night bus** routes take over. A day ticket (*dagkaart*, f10) also covers night buses. A two-day ticket is f15.

Taxis can be ordered from a rank, or by phoning ☎020/677 7777 – you can't hail them down. Cabs are expensive – f5.80 initial charge, then f2.85 per km, rising to f3.25 midnight–6am – and often slow in Amsterdam's crowded streets.

If you want to travel in style, hop aboard the *Canal Bus* (daily 10am–6pm, f22 for a day ticket), which serves Centraal station, Leidseplein and Westerkerk every 30mins.

If you want to rent a **bicycle**, *Take-A-Bike* at Centraal station charge f8 per day and require a f200 deposit, while *Bike City* at Bloemgracht 70 charge f12.50 per day, f50 and your passport as deposit.

The *VVV* have four **tourist offices** in town: one inside Centraal station (Mon–Sat 8am–7.30pm, Sun 9am–5pm); one just outside it (daily 9am–5pm); another on the Leidsestraat/Leidseplein corner (Mon–Sat 9am–7pm, Sun 9am–5pm) and one at Stadionplein (Mon–Sat 9am–5pm).

The *VVV* produces an English-language **listings guide**, *What's On In Amsterdam* (monthly, f4). The free Dutch-language monthly *Uitkrant* has more information.

goalnet behind the bar. A small beer counter operates by the door for the pre-match rush.

At the stalls inside the ground (where the only beer on sale is low-alcohol), you'll have to pay for things with an *Arena Card*, available by charging your credit card in the machines, or by exchanging for guilders at a till.

Ultra culture

The *Ajax F-side*, born of de Meer's south-east end terrace, were the fans who pick up on some Jewish influences in the club's history and wave Stars of David as a means of identity. They spray-painted their end with graffiti and had running battles with police during celebrations on the Leidseplein. The early Nineties saw fans slowly drifting away from this terrace culture, even before de Meer closed. Many, brought up on clashes with Feyenoord through the Seventies and Eighties, had simply grown out of it – not least when an Austria Vienna goalkeeper was hit by an iron bar thrown from the crowd in 1989, and Ajax were banned from Europe for a year.

In moving to the Arena, the club made no provision to keep the *F-side* together, and this was a major factor in the lack of atmosphere at early games in the stadium. Now other season-ticket holders have been moved from the *Zuid* end and *F-siders* shifted in. The Arena management have even allowed fans to spray-paint images across the advertising hoardings.

Club merchandise

The official *Ajax Fanshop* is by the main entrance (open Mon–Fri 9am–6pm, Sat–Sun 10am–5pm, most credit cards), with aftershave and clogs on sale in a designer atmosphere. There's also an entertaining **club museum** (open daily 9am–6pm except on events days, f12.50), and **tours** of the Arena are available (f12.50).

The main official Ajax shop **in town** is at Kalverstraat 86 (Mon midday–6pm, Tue–Sat 10am–6pm, Sun 10am–5pm, most credit cards).

In print

A colour programme, *Kick Off*, is issued free for every Ajax home game. The club also publishes *Ajax Magazine* (f8.50), a men's lifestyle glossy, and the official fan magazine *AjaxLife* (f8.50) – both eight times a year.

In the net

The club's **official site** has big online shopping and English-language areas at: www.ajax.nl. It's smart and well-organised, but a bit uninspired.

More like it is *AjaxMania*, a very thorough fan-run site with plenty of English and a wide range of correspondents contributing reports, gossip, historical features and other titbits. It's also quicker with news than the official site. There are dozens of other unofficial Ajax webpages, but there's really no need to go anywhere other than: www.ajaxmania.com.

Eat, drink, sleep…

Bars and clubs

Visitors to Amsterdam cluster around three main patches. The red light district (out of Centraal station, go straight up Damrak and turn left at the *Grasshopper* coffee shop), full of lads on beanos; the Rembrandtplein, neon, tacky and over-priced; and the Leidseplein. **Bars** fall into three categories: the designer variety; dirty old *bruine kroeg*, brown cafés; and coffee shops, or 'smokings', which attract tourists.

Nightclubbing is also concentrated in the centre – check out the flyers at *Midtown Records*, Nieuwedijk 104.

Bobby Haarms, Utrechtstraat 6. Just off Rembrandtplein, a bar for older-generation fans run by ex-player Haarms. Packed with souvenirs. Closed Sun. Tram #4 or #9 from Centraal.

Café Hendrik VIII, Prins Hendrinkstraat 83. Ajax fans' bar diagonally left out of Centraal, with framed posters, scarves, badges and a big screen for TV games. Full menu.

El Paradiso, Weteringschans 6–8. A former church that's the best venue in town to see a live band. Tram #1, #2, #5 or #11 from Centraal.

Escape, Rembrandtplein 11. Large, popular techno club with a varied selection Tue–Sun, top foreign DJs invited to the *Chemistry Club* on Sat. Admission f15–35. Tram #4 or #9 from Centraal.

Meerzicht, corner Middenweg/Brinkstraat. Opposite where de Meer stadium once stood, a friendly, local football bar with a signed pic of former neighbour Johan Cruyff. Tram #9 to Brinkstraat from Centraal.

Restaurants

The large concentration of non-Dutch nationals in Amsterdam means the city has as wide a **variety of cuisine** as almost any in Europe. This doesn't make the Dutch version more exciting, but heavy competition ensures more bargains and better quality here than elsewhere in Holland.

Balraj, Binnen Oranjestraat 1. Indian restaurant off Haarlemerdijk with vegetarian options. Open until 10pm. A 10min walk from Centraal.

Bojo, Lange Leidsedwarsstraat 51. Fine-value Indonesian in the tourist-oriented Leidseplein area. Invariably crowded, open until 2am, 4am Sat–Sun. Tram #1, #2, #5 or #11 from Centraal.

Keuken van 1870, Spuistraat 4. One-time soup kitchen, now a cheap, popular, centrally located eaterie serving Dutch standards. Tram #1, #2 or #5 from Centraal.

Van Beeren, Koningstraat 54. Excellent lunchtime choice in the red-light district, with large portions of *stamppot*, a traditional dish of mashed potato and cabbage which is better than it sounds. Metro to Nieuwmarkt.

Accommodation

Hotels in Amsterdam are an expensive proposition. Prices for a double room, with breakfast, start at around f100. During holiday periods and Queen's Day (30 April), make sure you book in advance.

Amstel Botel, Oosterdokskade 2–4 (☎020/626 4247, fax 020/639 1952). Large floating hotel moored to the left of Centraal station with a late bar. Be sure to get a room looking out onto the water. Shower and TV in every room. Singles at around f125, doubles f140, triples f190.

Flying Pig Palace, Vossiustraat 46 (☎020/400 4187, fax 020/400 5159). Good-value hostel near Leidseplein with kitchen facilities and no curfew. Tram #2 or #5 from Centraal.

Globe Hotel/Sports Café, Oudezijds Voorburgwal 3 (☎020/421 7424, fax 020/421 7423). Two- to six-person rooms (f40–60 each) and dorms (f30 each), many with canal views, 24-hour pub downstairs with Sky Sports, pub grub, English breakfasts and pints of Heineken at f7. No credit cards. Short walk from Centraal.

International Budget Hotel, Leidsegracht 76 (☎020/624 2784, fax 020/626 1839). Great canalside location, free lockers and showers, video lounge. Doubles f110, dorm beds f35. Tram #1, #2 or #5 to Prinsengracht.

Rotterdam

The football passions burning in Rotterdam are simply explained. Everyone hates Amsterdam. While Rotterdam works, Amsterdam dreams – that's how the Rotterdammers see it. And that's how they see the football, too – honest, workmanlike Feyenoord against flashy, arrogant Ajax.

Getting one over on Amsterdam has been the priority ever since the city's main stadium was opened in 1937. A favourite with UEFA for staging European finals, *'de Kuip'* ('The Tub') has seen a lot of classic football in a fervent atmosphere. But by the end of the Eighties it was falling to pieces, and Rotterdam city council had to step in to give it a complete overhaul, putting up the Maas building for VIPs and sponsors, and making the site more attractive to the business community.

Yet the surrounding Feijenoord area, unlike so much of Amsterdam, still feels like it belongs to the game, its rundown bars embellished with tatty pictures of its beloved soccer-playing stars. This is a football patch *par excellence*, a rare part of Holland where you feel as if football, and doubtless much more, is still being practised in the street. Many outside Holland were surprised that Feyenoord's home was chosen above the Amsterdam Arena to host the final of Euro 2000, but there was a certain poetic justice about the decision.

Feyenoord attract fans from all over the Brabant and Zeeland regions, which is more than can be said for their city rivals Sparta, who barely attract people from the street next door. On the other side of the Maas river from Feyenoord, conservative Sparta have seen demographic change in their Spangen district reduce their average gate to one of the lowest in the *Eredivisie*. The club's laid-back management is generally credited with having allowed Feyenoord to reverse Sparta's once clear dominance in the town.

Rotterdam's third club, first-division Excelsior, are stuck out east of the centre near Erasmus university.

The thrilling fields

Feyenoord

Stadion Feijenoord, Van Zandvlietplein 1
Capacity 51,000
Colours Red-and-white halved shirts, black shorts
League champions 1924, 1928, 1936, 1938, 1940, 1961–62, 1965, 1969, 1971, 1974, 1984, 1993, 1999
Cup winners 1930, 1935, 1965, 1969, 1980, 1984, 1991–92, 1994–95
European Cup winners 1970
UEFA Cup winners 1974

Holland's most passionately supported club celebrated their 90th anniversary in 1999 by winning their first league title after six lean years in the shadow of Ajax and PSV Eindhoven. Feyenoord, the first Dutch club to win the European Cup and the UEFA Cup, had had a sparse time of it until the arrival of coach Leo Beenhakker in 1997. But there was nothing really new in that – without the financial resources of *ABN-AMRO* or *Philips*, backers of the other two members of the big three, *Feije* have always made their way with a handful of modest sponsors, hard work and honest football.

Photos in the club museum show fans partying in Lisbon before the 1963 European Cup semi-final with Benfica, and the townsfolk out on the streets after the club's European Cup win of 1970. Yet for all their pioneering spirit, Feyenoord have had a tough time of it in the era of sponsorship, marketing and pay TV.

The club's inferiority complex was first fed in the Sixties. Feyenoord had honest left-winger Coen Moulijn; Ajax had Cruyff, the ultimate maverick trickster. Feyenoord coach Ernst Happel came up with a fluid form of *catenaccio* in 1970; Ajax's Rinus Michels adapted it, called it 'Total Football' and Ajax won the next three European Cups with it.

Only twice since then have Feyenoord fans enjoyed supreme moments of oneupmanship. The first was Wim van Hanegem's superb season in 1973/74, which culminated in a championship and a UEFA Cup triumph (marred by crowd trouble) over Spurs. The second was Johan Cruyff's shock transfer from Ajax before the 1983/84 season – during which, at the age of 37, Cruyff played some of the best football of his life and won Feyenoord their last double.

The club's rise was a gradual one. Founded by a mining millionaire in 1908, the club played in the lower divisions while Sparta won five early titles, until promotion to the top drawer in 1921. It was at this point that Feyenoord had the advantage of Holland's greatest pre-war soccer star, left-half Puck van Heel, who led them to a handful of league titles. This success persuaded president Leen van Zanvliet to build a stadium worthy of champions, with van Heel himself appearing in the ceremony to begin the construction of de Kuip.

After miraculously surviving World War II, de Kuip saw little success until the arrival of Coen Moulijn in 1954. A team was gradually built around him, and Feyenoord won three titles in five years, enjoying Holland's first European run in 1962/63.

It was Ernst Happel's team, later in the decade, that really earned the club its continental reputation. First, with Europe very much in mind, the club's name was changed from Feijenoord to Feyenoord to ease foreigners' pronunciation. Happel then brought in Swedish goalscorer Ove Kindvall, sweeper Rinus Israel and a young van Hanegem. Fans who queued all night for tickets for the team's second-round European Cup clash with holders AC Milan in 1969 were rewarded with a 2–0 win, and an easy passage to the final against Celtic. There, Israel and Kindvall were the goalscorers in an extra-time victory that few outside Rotterdam had expected.

Suddenly, Feyenoord were up there with the Madrids, Milans and Manchesters. Then, just as suddenly, they fell – stumbling out of the following year's competition, on

Face of the future – Feije's Paul Bosvelt

away goals, to Unirea Tricolor Arad of Romania.

Since then, van Hanegem's triumph, Cruyff's year of magic and the arrival of a young Ruud Gullit from Haarlem have all given the fans something to cheer about. Feyenoord have become known as cup specialists in Holland, while 50,000 fans crammed into de Kuip to watch a live transmission of the game at Groningen that won the title in 1993.

A decent challenge to PSV in Ronald Koeman's last season, 1996/97, promised a revival in Feyenoord's fortunes, but a 5–1 thrashing by Juventus in the Champions' League and a 4–0 domestic defeat by Ajax – as well as some disgracefully indisciplined tackling against Manchester United – saw cautious coach Arie Haan on his way by November 1997, and Leo Beenhakker take over. The following summer Beenhakker bought modestly but wisely, bringing two British flops, Jon Dahl Tomasson (from

Newcastle) and Peter van Vossen (from Rangers), into the attack, and covering the left side with free-kick specialist Patrick Pauwe from Fortuna Sittard. More midfield responsibility was given to the often hotheaded Jean-Paul van Gastel and Paul Bosvelt, and suddenly Feyenoord were off on a dozen-game unbeaten streak, ironically ended by Wim van Hanegem's adventurous AZ '67 side.

With Ajax traumatised and PSV rebuilding, Beenhakker's Feyenoord were champions by April 1999, their final winning margin of 15 points by no means flattering them. It was a victory which, for all his experience, Beenhakker could not build on. Although Feyenoord made it into the second phase of the Champions' League, they were unable to progress beyond a group containing Lazio and Chelsea, and European distractions were breeding inconsistency at home. After a 2–1 home defeat by Utrecht, Beenhakker quit. The team finished third in the *Eredivisie*, good enough only for a Champions' League qualifying berth.

Here we go!

On matchdays a **special train service**, the *Voetbaltrein*, runs every 20mins from Centraal station to Stadion, opposite the ground – about a 10min journey. There are strict controls at the gate, so be sure to stamp your *Strippenkaart* on the third bar. If you miss the train, **bus #49** also runs from outside Centraal to Olympiaweg.

Just the ticket

The main **ticket office** is at the corner of the *Stadiontribune* (immediately facing you from the station) and the *Maastribune*. De Kuip is rarely full for games against minor opposition, so tickets can be bought on the day with a *Club Card*. The cheapest tickets are in sectors W, X, Y and Z, at pitch level behind the goals and along the sidelines, around f20–40.

The four stands are colour-coded: yellow for the *Stadiontribune*, home of the Feyenoord boys in sector S and around; orange for the *Maastribune*, with the press and VIP rooms; green for the *Marathontribune* behind the goal, with visiting

fans in sector GG; and blue for the *Olimpiatribune*, where more tickets are generally available in the range f30–70.

Swift half

Many bars just across the river have the atmosphere of old Feijenoord. One, on the corner of Roetgenstraat and Oranjeboomstraat by the first #49 bus stop over the bridge from town, is actually called **Café Oud Feijenoord**. Nearer the stadium, on the #77 bus route towards it, is the **Café Schuyer** on the corner of Slaghekstraat and Beijerlandse. The best of the lot is **Café Boulevard Zuid** nearby, where Laantjesweg and Beijerlandse meet – pin-ups of Feyenoord's old stars line the counter.

Inside the ground, the **Brasserie de Cuyperij**, on the first floor of the Maas building, has a ollection of memorabilia. On matchdays it's open by reservation only, so try during the week.

Club merchandise

Despite 1994's major stadium renovation, the **Feyenoord Fanshop** is little more than a hut by the main entrance, open during training sessions and on matchdays only – no credit cards. There is however, an excellent **Home Of History** museum (open Wed–Thur midday–5pm, Sat 10am–5pm).

Ultra culture

The vicious off-the-field wars with Ajax hooligans have soured the memory of the fans who followed Feyenoord peacefully across Holland and Europe in the Seventies and Eighties. The Feyenoord roar was the first of its kind in Holland, and these days the stadium atmosphere, still the best in the country, is generated by foot-stamping and daft songs.

Alas, hooliganism is nothing new at de Kuip. The violent scenes which marred Feyenoord's 1974 UEFA Cup final win over Spurs acted as a grim catalyst, the antics of the visitors later being copied by the **sector S hardcore**, who organised increasingly violent away trips.

Most recently, hundreds of thugs 'celebrated' Feyenoord's 1999 title win by going on the rampage through the streets of Rotterdam – the street battles with police went on into the night, and dozens of fans were arrested.

In print

Feyenoord Sport Nieuws (f2) is on sale outside the *Stadiontribune*. Also available is *de Krant van Feyenoord* (weekly, f3.25), the club's official newspaper.

In the net

The **official website** was still unaccountably 'under reconstruction' during summer 2000 but might be worth a try at: www.feyenoord.nl.

As an alternative, try the Dutch-only fans' homepage at: www.xs4all.nl/~chagoi/.

Groundhopping

⚫ Sparta Rotterdam

Het Kasteel, Spartastraat 7
Capacity 12,000 (8,000 seated)
Colours Red-and-white striped shirts, black shorts
League champions 1909, 1911–13, 1915, 1959
Cup winners 1958, 1962, 1966

Sparta are keepers of a crumbling castle whose base support of old locals who shuf-fled out of their doors up to the ground has long gone. The rebuilding of Holland's oldest stadium, het Kasteel ('The Castle'), which unlike the proposed Wembley development was completed with the old twin towers intact, was meant to usher in a brave new era for the club. Instead, Sparta 'celebrated' by coming perilously close to being relegated from the *Eredivisie* for the first time.

Sparta are the fifth most titled club in Dutch history, but the last of those honours was won 30 years ago, during a brief period of success – itself 40 years after the last one – that saw a handful of European appearances. The most recent of the latter, in 1985, featured a win on penalties over Hamburg SV.

Since then Sparta have had to knock down parts of their grand old pile and man the drawbridge whenever one of the Big Three visit. Low crowds forced the sale of the de Nooijer twins, and despite a 2–0 win over Ajax in October 1998, coach Hans van der Zee was replaced by former Dutch international Jan Everse at Christmas. There was no miraculous recovery, and after finishing second from bottom of the *Eredivisie* table, Sparta were forced to

Kings of their own castle – Sparta Rotterdam line up for the derby against Feyenoord, 2000

play off for their top-flight survival, beating city neighbours Excelsior (see below) home and away before securing their position with a 3–0 win at Groningen.

The outlook brightened considerably in 1999/2000, with a comfortable 13th-place finish and, more importantly for the Sparta faithful, a first victory away to Feyenoord in 19 years. With stability in the boardroom and some bright young faces on the pitch, new coach Dolf Roks had a rare wave of optimism on which to build in the summer of 2000.

Spangen is west of Centraal station. **Buses #38** and **#45,** and **trams #7** and **#17** all run between the two, or catch the metro to **Marconiplein** and take **tram #6** from there.

At Hooftplein 17, where the trams stop, is the *Café Biljart*, with a huge football mural. Nearer the stadium are *het Doelpunt* on Spartastraat and the *Sparta cafeteria* on the corner of Coornherstraat and Spartastraat. Inside the ground, you'll find a bar by the main entrance.

☕ Excelsior

Woudestein stadium, Honingerdijk 110
Capacity 8000 (1000 seated)
Colours Red-and-black striped shirts, red shorts

Excelsior are a feeder club for Feyenoord, their big neighbours just across the Maas river. The pair met at the 1930 cup final, Feyenoord winning 1–0, but since then they have been as far apart as the narrow constraints of the Dutch league system allow. Things have picked up recently with new sponsorship money and the arrival of skilful forward Ellery Caïro, and Excelsior finished opening period champions in the 1998/99 *Eerste Divisie*. This entitled them to compete in the promotion play-offs, where they were heavily beaten away from home by Sparta and Groningen.

The team reached the play-offs again in 1999/2000, but finished third in their group behind FC Zwolle and surprise package RBC Roosendaal. The ground is about 15mins from Centraal, by **tram #3** or **#13** via Blaak station. The pleasant club bar, behind the goal nearest the tram-line, with its window overlooking the pitch, would put a lot of *Eredivisie* clubs' to shame.

Eat, drink, sleep…

Bars and clubs

Without the tourists, there is a sharper, more determined pace to nightlife in Rotterdam than in Amsterdam. Early evening, the harbour area between Blaak and Willems bridge, Oudehaven, is ideal for a quiet *pils*.

By night, the streets Nieuwe Binnenweg and Witte de Withstraat, either side of Eendrachtsplein metro stop, are packed with bars; the former is street level, rather seedy at one end, while the latter attracts an artier crowd.

Café t'Haantje, Bierens de Haanweg 12. If you want an afternoon in the heart of Feijenoord, this football bar is the one for you. Ernst Happel spent many a card session here with his players in the Seventies. Full menu. Bus #47 or #48 from Zuidplein metro to Spinozaweg.

De Vlerk, Westblaak 80. Former premier punk haunt now more techno or retro, but still a decent venue for a night out, f10–20 cover. Eendrachtsplein metro.

Nighttown, West-Kruiskade 28. Varied disco and concert venue. For DJ nights, expect a f15–25 door charge. The *Café Popular* next door has jazz and underground music concerts. A 5min walk from Centraal station.

Rotown, Nieuwe Binnenweg 19. Multi-purpose restaurant and live music venue in an old Rotterdam townhouse, surrounded by late-night bars. Open until 2am, 3am weekends. Lunchtime specials at f15. Concerts at 10pm. Tram #4 from Centraal station.

Rotterdam essentials

Bus #33 runs from Rotterdam's small **airport** into town, but since flights are much cheaper to Amsterdam, many visitors arrive via **Schipol**, which is connected to **Rotterdam Centraal station** by an hourly train service (journey time one hour). Centraal is a short walk from Rotterdam's imposing modern centre.

City transport consists of buses, trams and metro, run on the universal *Strippenkaart* system – two bars will take you to anywhere central. There is an extensive night bus network at weekends; tickets are f5 and all routes call at either Centraal station or Zuidplein, where **taxis** should be available. If not, simply phone ☎010/462 6060. The *VVV* **tourist office** (☎010/402 3234, fax 010/413 0124) is a 10min walk from Centraal station at Coolsingel 67.

For **listings information**, the monthly *R'uit* (f2.50) offers tips on high- and low-brow culture. For techno and dance events, check out the flyers at the *Midtown*, Nieuwe Binnenweg 79.

Restaurants

As well as the usual mix of Chinese, Indonesian and Surinamese restaurants, **cosmopolitan Rotterdam** has a decent range of other options. Cheap lunchtime sitdowns can be found around the Lijnbaan shopping centre, with *dagschotels* around f13. Unless otherwise stated, the places below take most major credit cards.

De Mosselman, Mariniersweg 74a. Reasonably priced, family-run fish restaurant with decor to match – the walls are covered in fishermen's artefacts. Metro to Blaak.

Midnight, 1e Middellandstraat 57b. Late-night, early-morning diner within walking distance of the city's main bar areas, open until 4am Sun–Thurs, 6am Fri–Sat. Tram #1, #7 or #9 from Centraal station. No credit cards.

Restaurant Engels, Stationsplein 45. Multi-restaurant setup opposite Centraal station, with Tokaj (Hungarian), Beefeater (English), Don Quijote (Spanish) and Brasserie all in one place.

Schieland, Schiekade 770. Mainstream sports café with Feyenoord memorabilia, a giant TV screen and a full menu. Tram #3 or #5 from Centraal station.

Accommodation

The *VVV* office (see *Essentials*) offers a room-booking service for f2.50. If you're stuck, the area a kilometre or so south-west of Centraal station has a number of reasonably priced options close together.

Astoria, Pleinweg 203–205 (☎010/485 6634, fax 010/485 4602). One-star, no-nonsense but friendly joint the other side of the river near the Maastunnel. Late bar, TV room with a massive screen and a former Miss World serving breakfast. What more do you want? Singles f50, doubles f95. Tram #2 from Maashaven metro.

Hotel Bienvenue, Spoorsingel 24 (☎010/466 9394, fax 010/467 7475). Small hotel a short walk north of Centraal station. Ten rooms, all with a telly. Singles at f65 without bath/shower, f70 with. Doubles also available.

Hotel Wilgenhof, Heemradsingel 92–94 (☎010/425 4892, fax 010/477 2611). Medium-sized, comfortable three-star hotel with 80 rooms, each with a television. Restaurant downstairs. Singles at f75 without bath/shower, f105 with. Tram #4 from Centraal station.

NJHC City Hostel, Rochunssenstraat 107–109 (☎010/436 5763, fax 010/436 5569). Rotterdam's only youth hostel is 3km from the centre of town. Eight-bed dorms, kitchen facilities, 2am curfew, lockout 10am–3pm. IYHF members f30, non-members f35. Metro to Dijkzigt.

Eindhoven

Eindhoven is a peculiar town. It is home to Holland's third most successful football team and the huge Philips industrial and research plant that finances it – and little else. Nearly one in five people are employed by the electrical conglomerate and many of these are regulars at the football club.

PSV are the richest team in the land and have a stadium to match. Until the renovation of de Kuip in 1994 and the construction of the Amsterdam Arena, the Philips Stadion was the best in Holland. It still is a very comfortable place in which to see a football match, with superb facilities for the business crowd and rooftop gas heaters warming everyone else down below. Walking around the stadium – the ground level is dominated by a huge *Toys R Us* store – reveals four floors of business lounges and sponsors' restaurants.

For Philips, this expense is an investment – the chance to send the company name around the globe. In any case, PSV is a profit centre in its own right, the club's management having made a serious surplus from the sale of Ruud Gullit, Ronald Koeman, Gica Popescu, Romário and Ronaldo (Gullit in particular was not happy with having to pose for all kinds of company commercials), and more recently from that of Jaap Stam to Manchester United.

The club's enormous financial clout also means that the team are the most unpopular in Holland. Ajax and Feyenoord may hate each other, but everyone hates PSV. For this reason, many of the club's younger fans have a chip on their shoulder, and the atmosphere surrounding a big game at PSV can be at best boisterous, at worst downright menacing.

The stadium is a short walk from the train station, so many footballing visits are of the flying variety. Diehard groundhoppers have to cross town to get to the city's other professional football club, EVV Eindhoven, out on the residential southern fringes of town.

The thrilling fields

 PSV

Philips stadion, Mathildelaan 81
Capacity 30,000
Colours Red-and-white striped shirts, black shorts
League champions 1929, 1935, 1951, 1963, 1975–76, 1978, 1986–89, 1991–92, 1997, 2000
Cup winners 1950, 1974, 1976, 1988–90, 1996
European Cup winners 1988
UEFA Cup winners 1978

Philips Sport Verenigeng were formed in 1913 after a sports event organised by the company to celebrate Holland's independence. They joined the Dutch league a year later and the first division in 1921. Although the club have been relegated just once, in 1925, Philips didn't see any return on their investment until PSV broke the Ajax-Feyenoord duopoly in the mid-Seventies.

Keeping players away from the bright lights of Amsterdam or Rotterdam proved difficult until coach Kees Rijvers came to the club and built a successful team from 1972/73. With Jan van Beveren saving goals and left-winger Willy van der Kuylen scoring them, PSV bided their time until the break-up of Cruyff's Ajax.

A 6–0 cup final romp over NAC Breda in 1974 led to a run in Europe the following year, PSV losing a semi-final to eventual winners Dynamo Kiev. Domestically, with the van de Kerkhof brothers, Willy and René, bought from Twente Enschede, PSV made no such mistake in the league, beating Feyenoord by two points. They won it again, by a one-point margin, in 1976.

The club were twice knocked out of the European Cup by Rijvers' old team Saint-Étienne, but went on to win the UEFA Cup in 1978, overcoming Barcelona in the semi-final, and Bastia in the final. A league title that year proved to be the last until the arrival of Ruud Gullit in the mid-Eighties. Gullit ushered in a new and golden era, one of six league titles in seven seasons, a European Cup, and a team of highly paid superstars at odds with each other. Running the show was Hans Kraay, a controversial coach who applied the simple principle that the club should sign players directly from their title rivals, Ajax and Feyenooord, so that the stars would not be playing against them.

Knee deep – van Nistelrooy takes a tumble against Valéncia

After Gullit's and Kraay's departure in 1987, Guus Hiddink took charge of the team and Wim Kieft was left to score the goals, equalling the club record of 28 in 1987/88. With Hans van Breukelen in goal and Ronald Koeman and Soren Lerby providing passes for Kieft and Gerald Vanenberg, PSV crept through Europe. Almost before anyone knew it, they had reached the 1988 European Cup final against Benfica, which they duly won on penalties. Outside Eindhoven, theirs was not a popular win – they'd averaged only a goal a game through the tournament and hadn't actually won a match beyond the second round.

At the end of the decade, Romário arrived to bring flair and more than 100 goals in five seasons. Hiddink left the whole circus to Bobby Robson in 1990, but though the former England manager won the title for PSV two years running, the team's failure in the potentially lucrative new European era frustrated club management. With Romário gone to Barcelona and Robson to Portugal, PSV gazumped all-comers to capture the nineteen-year-old Ronaldo for £3million in 1994. Yet even his goals could not bring the title back to Eindhoven in a 1994/95 season which saw three managerial changes. It took coach Dick Advocaat to steady the ship, steering

Ronaldo, Wim Jonk, Phillip Cocu, Jan Wouters and top scorer Luc Nilis to a cup win in 1996, then riding the upset of the Brazilian's departure and capturing the title, for the first time since Robson, in 1997.

Advocaat had less good fortune the following season, and resigned at the end of it, taking defender Arthur Numan with him to Rangers. His successor, Bobby Robson, returning for a year while long-term replacement Eric Gerets – captain of the 1988 European Cup-winning team – served out his contract at Club Bruges, inherited a squad decimated by the loss of Numan, Stam, Philip Cocu, Boudewijn Zenden and Wim Jonk. Expectations were low, and after Robson's side had toiled in the 1998 Champions' League, they were desperately fortunate to make it into the quailfying tournament for the following year's event, scoring three lucky goals in the last ten minutes to win their final game.

Robson bequeathed Gerets a decent squad, with top Dutch goalscorer Ruud van Nistelrooy, class Russian sweeper Yuri Nikiforov and Finnish forward Joonas Kolkka all looking the part. Although PSV finished bottom of their first-phase group in the Champions' League, van Nistelrooy's goals at home were attracting the attention of scouts from across the continent and propelling PSV towards the title. There was a stutter just before the winter break, with a home defeat to challengers Heerneveen and an unscheduled exit from the cup at the hands of Vitesse. But in the *Eredivisie*, PSV ended the season 16 points clear of the pack.

Van Nistelrooy's subsequent knee operation put his big-money transfer to Manchester United on perhaps permanent hold, and also ruled him out of the first half of the 2000/2001 season – when all eyes would be on prodigious young Yugoslav striker Mateja Kezman.

Here we go!

Either a 10min walk as you turn right out of the **station** down Mathildelaan, or take bus **#12, #13** or **#14**.

Just the ticket

The PSV **ticket office**, *Hoofdkassa*, by gate #24 is open Mon–Sat 10am–5.30pm and two hours before a match. You'll need to have a *Club Card*, and expect bigger games to be already sold out. The stadium is sectioned into north, south, east and west stands. The east (*Oost*) end, alongside Stadionplein, gates #12–#21, is with the PSV boys behind one goal. Away fans are herded into *Noord*, along Mathildelaan. The class seats are in the *Hoofdtribune*, through gate #8, in *Zuid* along

Frederiklaan. Prices range from f40 in the *Oost* and *West*, to f50–70 in the *Noord* and *Zuid*, rising to f100 in the *Eretribune Noord/Zuid*. The bigger the fixture, the more you'll pay.

Swift half

The younger element head for **D'N Berk**, on the corner of Gagelstraat and Mathildalaan, a minute's walk from the stadium. There'll be a couple of bouncers on the door, loud music from the DJ and a crowd three deep at the bar.

The **Supportershome**, up a flight of stairs decorated with PSV murals at gate #12 of the ground, is a better bet. A large bar area has two counters and there's sport on TV, Grolsch beer and pictures of Ronaldo.

Club merchandise

The **PSV Souvenirshop** by gate #12 is open Mon–Fri 9am–5pm, Sat 10am–middays, two hours before kick-off and an hour afterwards.

Ultra culture

PSV's young *Oost Side* fans are notoriously brash and away support is carefully manoeuvred in from the train station. Security equipment is, naturally, ultra-modern and troublemakers are quickly singled out and dealt with in a special rehabilitation scheme run by the club.

Windows on the world – the stadium's owners got yet more welcome publicity from Euro 2000

Eindhoven essentials

Eindhoven has a small **airport** 6km west of the centre. Bus #8 runs to and from the train station (7.30am–6pm, journey time 30mins). There is also a regular train service connecting the city with Schipol airport and Amsterdam Centraal.

Eindhoven is part of the *treintaxi* scheme, whereby rail travellers who have paid an extra f7 can take a taxi anywhere in town for free when they get to their destination. Otherwise the station is a 5min walk from the centre of town, much of which is pedestrianised. A network of **city buses** runs 7am–11pm, with fares operating on the *Strippenkaart* system. The main routes run after midnight Fri–Sat. To call a **taxi**, phone ☎040/252 5252.

Eindhoven's *VVV* **tourist office** (☎040/297 9100, fax 040/243 3135) is right outside the train station. Here you'll find the Dutch-language **listings** publication, *Uit-CultuurKrant*. The local daily, *Eindhovens Dagblat*, also has entertainment information and a good sports supplement on Saturdays.

The average PSV fan is otherwise pretty happy with his lot, the company organising a variety of social events through the year. While some 20–25,000 season tickets are sold every year, PSV's travelling support is pretty sparse.

In print

Programmes (f2.50) are produced each matchday. The club magazine, **PSV Inside** (monthly, f4.95) is also available at newsstands in town.

In the net

The **official website** is at: www.psv.nl. It's businesslike and matter-of-fact, just like the club, but nothing special. More comprehensive is the **PSV Supporters' Homepage** which offers news, gossip and a livelier attitude, with plenty of English content, at: www.supver-psv.nl.

Groundhopping

◖ EVV Eindhoven

Jan Louwers Stadion, Charles Roelslaan 1
Capacity 5,000 (2,000 seated)
Colours Blue-and-white striped shirts, black shorts
League champions 1954
Cup winners 1937

The huge floodlights and superstars at PSV leave little EVV Eindhoven in the shade.

Nevertheless, for a mid-table *Eerste Divisie* club pulling crowds of around 2,000, EVV's Jan Louwers Stadion is well-equipped. All it needs is a team like the one which won the club's solitary title in 1954, two places ahead of PSV. When the two sides met again in the quarter-finals of the Dutch cup in 1999, PSV walked it, 5–0.

If you've picked the wrong weekend to be in town, take **bus #171** or **#172** from the train station to Florialaan, or **bus #7** to Alterweg. Either way, allow 20mins.

The **EVV Corner** bar under the main stand along Charles Roelslaan, was being renovated along with the rest of the stand in the spring of 1999. The **Amstel** bar in the nearby indoor sports centre on Theo Koomenlaan is also a pre-match option in this leafy residential area.

Eat, drink, sleep…

Bars and clubs

Eindhoven's affluence is reflected in the number of **fashionable bars** to have opened in the last couple of years. All are concentrated in the centre, in the streets of Kleine Berg and especially Stratumseind. There are six in a row in one stretch of the latter.

As for **clubbing**, you have to wonder what poor Romário and Ronaldo did during their spare time here, except lie back and think of Brazil...

Baloo's Blues, Kleine Berg 60. Accessible rockers' bar with a bit of spirit to it. Pool table, loud music and Baloo the Bear memorabilia. Short walk from the station.

de Dans Salon, Stationsplein 4. The town's main disco, across from the station, open Thur–Sun. Free entry before 11pm, f5–10 thereafter.

Effenaar, Dommelstraat 2. Left-field culture centre which puts on anything from Belgian hardcore to R&B. Live music f10–20 admission, DJ nights f5. Just across from the train station.

O'Sheas, Jan van Lieshoutstraat 9. Main Irish bar in town with Sky Sports, weekend breakfast specials at f15, and all the usual trappings.

Trafalgar, Dommelstraat 21. Just across from the train station, an English-style pub with a friendly atmosphere, half-decent music and a restaurant section. Guinness on draught.

Restaurants

Eateries are concentrated down a couple of streets of **central Eindhoven**, especially Kleine Berg. There aren't many late-night options. All places listed are a short walk from the station.

Ajdanski, Stratumseind 81. Russian and Balkan specialities in this sizeable restaurant at the end of Stratumseind, run by ex-PSV player Petar Ajdanski. Open daily 4–11pm, special prices on Balkan dishes Mon–Thur. Mastercard and Amex accepted.

Charlie's Pub, Dommelstraat 36. Small *eetcafé* where a main course will set you back no more than f20–30. Terrace in summer. Closed Mon–Tue. No credit cards.

Grand Café Berlage, Kleine Berg 16. Most popular diner in town, with a summer terrace and two side bars. Free live jazz in the evenings. For the price – f20–30 a main course – and the

tasteful surroundings, very good value. Open daily noon–11pm.

Touch Of India, Geldropseweg 22. Only Indian restaurant in town, buffet specials and main courses f25–40. Open daily, evenings only, most major credit cards.

Accommodation

There are precious few cheap centrally located **hotels** in town, but the *VVV* (see *Essentials*) can book you a room on the spot – pay them for your first night, plus f4 commission.

de Bengel, Wilhelminaplein 9 (☎040/244 0752). Modest but pleasant hotel behind the Philips complex and near the PSV stadium. Singles at f85, doubles f125. Most credit cards.

Corso, Vestdijk 17 (☎040/244 9131). One-star hotel along the main drag that runs from the station through town. Singles, doubles or triples at f65, f95 and f130 respectively. Most credit cards.

Oud Eindhoven, Stratumseind 63 (☎040/244 4559). Perfectly located if you're living it up for the weekend, annoyingly noisy if not. One-star hotel slap bang in the area of bars and clubs. Singles at f70, doubles f100. Most credit cards.

Mascotte, Tramstraat 5b (☎040/246 0056). Small pension near the station offering bed and breakfast at f50 per person. No credit cards.

de Zwaan, Wilhelminaplein 4 (☎040/244 8992). Family-run pension which offers B&B at f45 per person. Near the PSV stadium. No credit cards.

Stealing Amsterdam's thunder – Vitesse Arnhem

The most futuristic stadium in Holland – indeed in Europe – houses a club determined to muscle in on the country's traditional Big Three, **Vitesse Arnhem**. Formed by members of the Vitesse cricket club in 1892, the football team was run along amateur and, at best, semi-professional lines before **Karel Aalbers** rescued it from bankruptcy in 1985.

Promoted to the *Eredivisie* in 1989, Vitesse have never left the top six since. But, along with this success on the pitch, for much of the last decade Aalbers had another dream: the **Gelre Dome**. Legend has it that the idea came to him when opening a box of matches to light one of his famous cigars – not only a movable roof (the Amsterdam Arena has that), but a movable pitch, which could be rolled away after the match and the venue rearranged for other entertainment, that very evening if necessary.

Tough at the top – cup defeat in 2000

Enlisting the help of German architect **Joseph Wund**, and drawing strength from the city council's rejection of a reconstruction plan for Vitesse's old **Monnikenhuize** ground, Aalbers spent years convincing the powers-that-be that such an arena would be worth its £43million investment.

Meanwhile Vitesse were hovering under the top three, with never enough firepower for further progress. In the summer of 1996, forward **Nikos Machlas** arrived from OFI Crete. Teaming up first with Rob Mackaay and then with Dejan Čurović, in 1997/98 he got more than half Vitesse's 85 goals, becoming Europe's top scorer in the process.

The Gelre Dome was also taking shape. An 11,000-tonne concrete slab was built to slide along steel strips that would **roll the pitch away** in four hours. As well as hydro-electric motors, energy would be provided by solar panels, while the 26,600 bucket seats – expanded to 30,000 for Euro 2000 – would be constructed from **recycled products**.

Sited in south Arnhem, near the German border, the Gelre Dome has an ideal catchment area. It was opened in March 1998 and has since staged several Dutch internationals. As for Vitesse, they were second to Feyenoord for almost the whole of the 1998/99 season, yet slumped to fourth at the end, overshadowed by Willem II's brilliant late run to the runners-up position, and edged out of the Champions' League qualifiers by PSV's freak last-match result. It was an almost identical story a year later, when not even a 25-goal haul from new arrival **Pierre van Hooijdonk** could squeeze Vitesse into the top three. Off the pitch, the club's failure to get its hands on Champions' League cash resulted in the resignation of Aalbers and a much-needed rescue package being put together by local energy firm *Nuon*.

Regular **special buses** are laid on from various spots in town to the Gelre Dome on matchdays – otherwise take bus #7 or #43 from the station to Batavierenweg. Vitesse operates a *Seizoenkaart* system, for a whole or half season, but holders are entitled to buy an extra match ticket for a friend (details on ☎026/880 7337). The *Noord* and *Zuid* sectors have the cheapest seats. Fans still enjoy a pre-match drink near the old stadium, at *Papillon*, Weverstraat 34a and *de Schoof*, Korenmarkt 37.

Hungary

Magyar Labdarúgó Szövetség Istvánmezei Ut 3–5 Népstadion, Toronyépület Pf 106
H-1581 Budapest ☎01/222 0343   Fax 01/222 0344   E-mail mlsz@hungary.net

League champions Dunaferr FC   **Cup winners** MTK Hungária
Promoted Videoton, Matáv Sopron   **Relegated** Siófok, Diósgyor, Vác

European participants 2000/01 Dunaferr FC (UCL qualifiers); MTK Hungária,
Vasas (UEFA Cup); Tatabánya (Intertoto Cup)

It simply cannot get any worse. After being threatened with a ban from international football because of political interference, and having failed in an audacious bid to co-host the finals of the 2004 European Championship with Austria, Hungary then failed to qualify for Euro 2000, while its league tottered on the edge of total collapse.

The new century started with a humiliating 3–0 home defeat by Australia for the national side in a friendly. After that, the first week's league action after the winter break took place with two top-flight clubs gone forever. Szeged folded after cash problems left them with only five registered players and a transfer ban prevented them from finding another six. To add farce to the tragedy, Gázszer were bought by a second-division club, Pécs, and had their name and home ground changed to the latter, in a business deal which effectively saw the lower-flight team buy themselves a mid-season promotion.

Surviving somehow – national boss Bertalan Bicskei

It's all a far cry from the glory days of the Fifties, when the likes of Ferenc Puskás and József Bozsik made Hungary the most respected football nation in the world. Today, even the mid-Eighties seem like a golden age to many. Yet the time when teams like Videoton could beat Manchester United to reach the final of the UEFA Cup, and players such as Lajos Détari were sought-after by Europe's elite clubs, now seem as far away as that famous night at Wembley in 1953, when Hungary crushed England 6–3. And while poor results, poor teams and poor players are things that Hungarians have become used to in the past decade, what is really worrying them now is whether professional football can survive in their country at all.

The game is caught in a vicious circle – poor football means low crowds, meaning ticket prices cannot be raised to cover increased costs without driving away the

Basics

Citizens of the EU, America and Canada require only their **passport** to enter Hungary, and while Australians and New Zealanders need a 90-day **visa**, this can be obtained easily enough from the local Hungarian embassy or consulate.

The Hungarian currency is the **forint** (Ft or HUF), currently Ft375 to £1. Forints come in notes of Ft200, Ft500, Ft1,000, Ft5,000 and Ft10,000. There are also coins of Ft1, Ft2, Ft5, Ft10, Ft 20, Ft50 and Ft100. In Budapest and major towns, cash machines are widespread, as is credit-card payment in shops, hotels and restaurants.

Most **public telephones** take cards, Ft800 for 50 units or Ft1,600 for 120, available at most newsstands. Some coin phones still exist, taking coins of over Ft20 value, the price of the cheapest local call.

From outside the country, the international code for Hungary is 36, the city code for Budapest 1. From Hungary, there is no cheap time for international calls – dial 00, followed by the international code. For town-to-town calls inland, dial 06 followed by the code. To call Budapest from the provinces, for example, dial 061.

Train and bus services are generally cheap, clean and punctual. Main-line **trains** leave from the three central Budapest stations of Nyugati, Keleti and Déli, all of which have metro stations. Fast trains are labelled *gyorsvonat* on timetables; *személyvonat* are stopping services which should be avoided at all costs. Reservations are obligatory on some express and international trains.

The fast *InterCity* service requires a modest supplement (*pótdíj*), as do international trains within Hungary – many between Budapest and Győr, for example. Indicate which train you are taking when buying your ticket, or pay a little extra onboard. Prices for return tickets to former Eastern Bloc destinations are reduced by 30–50%.

International **buses** leave from Budapest's central Erzsébet Tér, main domestic services from Árpád Híd.

few diehard fans who still turn out at the nation's dilapidated stadia. Multi-national companies that have arrived in Hungary in droves since the borders were opened in 1989 are hardly lining up to sponsor teams. As one forthright executive at a major Budapest advertising agency put it: 'Who wants their product to be associated with that crap?'

Football came early to Hungary. The three main Budapest teams, MTK, Ferencváros and Újpest, were formed soon before the national football association and the league in 1901. A year later Hungary took part in the first full international in continental Europe, against Austria – a fixture which was to become an annual tradition. Budapest, Vienna and later Prague became a new, Central European sphere of influence in the development of the international game. Public interest in early matches was low, however, and the style

of play in Hungary lacked tactical subtlety. Lancastrian Jimmy Hogan was the man who changed all that. A former player with Bolton Wanderers, Hogan arrived in Budapest from an internment camp in Vienna at the end of World War I to coach MTK, bringing with him the short passing game from English league football. Thanks to Hogan's revolutionary methods – soon to become known as the Danubian style – MTK won seven consecutive league titles between 1919 and 1925. Interest in the game had risen to such a level that in 1926 Hungary launched a fully professional league. The foundations were laid for an excellent national team which showed their progress by reaching the World Cup final in 1938, where they were unlucky to lose 4–2 to hosts Italy.

After World War II, Hungarian sport, and football in particular, benefited from unprecedented state backing. Additionally, an extraordinary crop of talented players emerged such as Puskás, Bozsik and Sándor Kocsis, clubmates in the newly formed army side Honvéd. That trio was to become the backbone of a free-scoring national team which would remain unbeaten for four years. Having arrived at Wembley on a foggy November afternoon in 1953 for a friendly against England, the Magic Magyars gave the old masters a lesson in football. Hogan, having returned to England to take charge of Fulham, was in the stands to witness the bittersweet fruits of his labour.

The final scoreline of 6–3 barely did Hungary's dominance justice. Faced with opponents to whom perfect close control and precise passing seemed to come naturally, England above all just couldn't fathom how to deal with the visitors' deep-lying centre-forward Nándor Hidegkuti who, unmarked for much of the game, helped himself to a hat-trick.

The bitterness came the following year, only a month after Hungary had repeated the dose in Budapest, destroying England 7–1. Hot favourites to win the 1954 World Cup in Switzerland, but with Puskás playing

through an injury in muddy conditions, the Magyars suffered a shock 3–2 defeat to West Germany in the final. Long after the names of the victorious Germans were forgotten, however, the Hungarians would be remembered as a prime example of top-level football at its best. As Tom Finney put it: 'The 1954 Hungarian soccer masters did not go into the record books as the champions of the world. But they went into my personal memory file, and that of millions of other football lovers, as the finest team ever to sort out successfully the intricacies of this wonderful game.'

Within two years, the magic had gone. The 1956 Hungarian uprising and subsequent invasion of the country by Soviet troops prompted several players, including Puskás and Kocsis, to flee to the West. Worse, most of Hungary's youth team, on tour at the time of the invasion, decided not to return to their homeland. Two generations of soccer talent were lost – and the Hungarians never fully recovered from this decimation of their ranks.

After the Soviet crackdown, large crowds were still drawn to the big club games. Újpesti Dózsa and Ferencváros had

Ready and waiting – police have their work cut out when Újpest meet Ferencváros

occasional runs in Europe, the latter lifting the Fairs' Cup in 1965. Hungary maintained a respectable presence in international football, winning Olympic titles to add to the gold Puskás and company had won in 1952. At the 1966 World Cup, they reminded the English football public of their quality with a fine 3–1 win over Brazil at Goodison Park, with Flórián Albert an enduring star performer. Yet by the early Eighties it was becoming clear something was going badly wrong. A series of match-fixing scandals reduced public confidence in the game, and a humiliating 6–0 defeat by the Soviet Union at the 1986 World Cup was the final straw for many fans.

Hungary have not graced the finals of a major tournament since. The last attempt at qualifying for the World Cup ended in shame: 7–1 and 4–0 play-off defeats by Yugoslavia in 1997. In the aftermath of that debâcle, Bertalan Bicskei took over as national coach and turned to youth, promoting almost the entire Under-21 squad which had qualified for the 1996 Olympics in Atlanta. Victories over Austria and Switzerland and impressive displays in draws against Romania and England offered some encouragement. But another tournament passed without the Hungarians after defeats by neighbours Romania and Slovakia ended any chance of qualification for Euro 2000.

Bicskei survived calls for his head – thanks largely to the absence of any alternative – but the election of a new, reformist president of the Hungarian FA, Imre Bozoky, offered some hope of progress. Bozoky secured a peace deal with the country's sports minister, Tamás Deutsch, whose desire to shake-up the FA had led to him suspending its board and earning the wrath of UEFA and FIFA in the process.

A one-off injection of funds from the state now looks on the cards, and the cash from a new £8million television deal, if handled wisely, could offer a new lease of life to those clubs that remain in the top flight, wisely reduced in size to 16 teams for 2000/01.

Essential vocabulary

Hello/goodbye *Szia*
Yes *Igen*
No *Nem*
Please *Kérem*
Thank you *Köszönöm*
Two beers, please *Két korsó sört, kérek*
Men's *Férfi*
Women's *Nõi*
Where is the stadium? *Hol van a stadion?*
What's the score? *Mennyi az állás?*
Referee *Bíró*
Offside *Les*

Match practice

Hungary is a refreshing taste of how football used to be. For Sixties prices you can stand on the terraces, drink and swear to your heart's content, with little worry of offending the nuclear family next to you.

With a three-month winter break, the Hungarian campaign is split into autumn (late July to late November) and spring (late February to mid-June) seasons.

Most games are on Saturdays at 5pm, with winter kick-offs at 1–2pm for clubs without floodlights. Kick-off times can change at short notice, so buy Friday's or Saturday's *Nemzeti Sport* for the latest news.

A different league

In June 2000, the Hungarian FA surpassed itself in complicating the arrangements for reducing the size of the nation's footballing top flight. The aim is to have a 12-team division in place by 2001/02. With this in mind, the top 14 in the 1999/2000 *PNB*, Hungary's premier league, plus the top two from the league below, were divided into two groups of eight, called *NBI A* and *B*, for 2000/01. Each team will play each other twice, home and away, in an autumn season finishing in late October. The top six from each group will then join to form a 12-team league, carrying bonus points over from the autumn season matches. These sides will play each other twice, home and away, and the 12-team league will remain in place, so that the bottom two teams change places every year with the top two from below. Teams in the 12-team league will play each other three times in future seasons.

The second division, which in 1999/2000 contained an unwieldy 20 teams, will be composed of four groups of eight for 2000/01, with the best teams from the third tier making up the numbers. The top five from each group, plus the bottom four dropping out of the *NBI A/B*, will then form an even more unwieldy second division of 24 clubs.

Up for the cup

The *Magyar Kupa* is a drawn-out non-event. It starts in the summer break with qualification at county level. First- and second-division clubs join in mid-July to make up 16 groups of four teams, seeded to ensure there are one first, one second and two lower-division clubs in each. Teams play each other once, generally on Sundays and Wednesdays, the top two qualifying for the knockout stage.

The rest of the competition consists of straightforward two-legged games, with low crowds and generally low interest until the quarter-finals. From then on ties are decided on a single game, including the final in mid-May.

Just the ticket

For all matches, buy your tickets (*belepő*) from the ticket office (*pénztár*) – usually a small hole in the wall by the main entrance. There's little worry of a sellout, even with prices down in the Ft500 range. For costlier (but still affordable) internationals and the Ferencváros–Újpest derby, buy your ticket in advance.

For a seat (usually a bench) ask for an *üllőhely*; a standing ticket is *állóhely*. The word *tribün* on a sign or ticket generally refers to the main stand, with *lelátó* indicating a superior view. In bigger stadia, your ticket may also indicate an entrance (*kapu*), section (*szektor*), right (*jobb*) or left (*bal*), a designated row (*sor*) and a seat number (*szék*). There are few match programmes, but with your ticket you may be given a copy of the colourful freebie *Stopli* ('Stud'), strangely reminiscent of the *Football League Review* in days of yore.

Half-time

With the exception of Ferencváros and some of the other big Budapest clubs, you can buy a drink at most Hungarian grounds. In November you can warm up with mulled wine (*forralt bor*). On the way to the ground you will be met by scores of people selling toasted sunflower seeds (*szotyi*), or orange-coloured pumpkin seeds (*tökmag*) – Hungarian football is played to the sound of crackling shells, which carpet the terraces once their contents have been consumed. Food at stadium snackbars is generally restricted to salami sandwiches and savoury scones (*pogácsa*). Ferencváros do sausages (*virsli*), while a spicy cold meatball sandwich (*fasir*) is the nearest thing you'll find to a hamburger.

Ultra culture

Expect to see plenty of banners hung over the fences – these will announce the presence of terrifying-sounding hooligan and ultra groups with names like 'Green Monsters' and 'Viola Kaos'. In many cases the groups consist of nothing more fearsome than a bunch of schoolkids, complete with satchels and sandwiches.

Serious ultra culture has caught on at some clubs, however – Újpest and Debrecen in particular pride themselves on their smokebombs and banners. Sadly, another foreign import, terrace racism, is also on the rise, with African players and gypsies the targets of boo-boys and skinheads. The problem is widespread and particularly prominent at Ferencváros, but there are few signs of anything being done about it.

Despite the fact that Hungary is not exactly a huge country, with the honourable exceptions of Debrecen and Haladás, few fans from the provinces follow their team to the capital. Unless your match is one of the many Budapest derbies, whatever atmosphere is created will be a little one-sided.

Action replay

After interminable arguments over TV rights, live televised football has returned to the domestic game. State MTV1 or 2 carry one top league game on a Saturday afternoon, with the kind of dull delivery usually reserved for flower shows. Pay station Duna TV has a more imaginative approach, modelling its presentation on Sky Sports. Its live Sunday afternoon game breaks the staid state TV mould.

The main highlights package is TV2's *Gól, gól, gól!*, on Sundays at around 10.30pm, with goals from the Italian and Spanish leagues. TV3 shows the previous weekend's English Premier and Spanish *Liga* highlights early on Saturday afternoons.

The back page

The daily sports paper *Nemzeti Sport* (Ft68) is a national institution and deserves its status. Its back pages carry results and scorers from all European leagues, with weekly reports from around the region and half-pages dedicated to England, Italy, Spain and Germany. Goal times and line-ups for the weekend's domestic games obviate the need for match programmes, but beware a heavy leaning towards Ferencváros to boost provincial sales.

For all its status, however, *NS* now has competition in the form of *Színes Sport* (Ft67), a new all-colour sports daily which launched in May 2000 with a fair number of staff journalists poached from the established title.

No-one has yet found the ideal weekly or monthly to place on the newsstands. The weekly *Foci Világ* (Ft148) is too stats-heavy, *Sport Plusz Foci* is good for scandal and transfer rumours but little else, and others like *Bravo Sport* are for decorating school desks with.

In the net

The Hungarian FA's official website is at: www.mlsz.hu. There's no English content but the rolling news service is kept bang up-to-date, and the depth of content is pretty fair.

The people behind *Színes Sport* are also responsible for a wide-ranging sports news site at: www.asport.hu. Again, there's no English to be seen, but match reports and photos are all present and correct, and the Hungarian is surprisingly easy to navigate.

For links to various Magyar football sites both official and unofficial, try: www.telesport.hu.

Club loyalty is spread thinly around Hungary's capital. This means that although you can't fail to catch at least two matches in town on any given weekend, invariably you will be one of 3,000 people shouting at demotivated players across an echoing stadium. The Budapest season's main fixture is the Ferencváros–Újpest clash, a city derby whose ferocity has recently spilled over into serious violence. At Ferencváros' comfortable modern all-seater ground, the event is easily policed; at Újpest's crumbling Megyeri Út, it's a security nightmare.

The thrilling fields

Ferencváros

Üllői Út stadium, IX Üllői Út 129
Capacity 18,000 (all-seated)
Colours Green-and-white striped shirts, white shorts
League champions 1903, 1905, 1907, 1909–13, 1926–28, 1932, 1934, 1938, 1940–41, 1949, 1963–64, 1967–68, 1976, 1981, 1992, 1995–96
Cup winners 1913, 1922, 1927–28, 1933, 1935, 1942–44, 1956, 1972, 1974, 1976, 1991, 1993–95
Fairs' Cup winners 1965

Ferencvárosi Torna Club (FTC) are Hungary's biggest club. They are the most loved, the most hated, the most talked about. There are Ferencváros bars all over town, and every other taxi driver's mirror has a green-and-white pennant hanging from it. Based in the suburb of Ferencváros in the city's ninth district, the club is known as *Fradi* – a shortened version of its German name, Franzstadt.

The most successful Hungarian team before World War II, under Communism *Fradi* became the unofficial team of the opposition. The anti-Communist pride of the fans was not surprising, since Stalinist dictator Mátyás Rákosi had personally

forced the club to play under the name Budapest Kinizsi, after a medieval Magyar hero adopted by the new regime, and wear red – as punishment for the fact that they were the favoured team of the Nazi Arrow Cross, who ruled the country towards the end of the war. The working-class area where the stadium sits was at the centre of the 1956 uprising, and the following year the club won back their name and famous green-and-white shirts.

Due to their marginalised position in the Fifties, the club had few representatives in the Golden Team, although *Fradi* fans never tire of pointing out that a number of the Honvéd side of the period were stolen from them by the military. By the Sixties, though, the club were back at the top. Led by Flórián Albert, they won the Fairs' Cup in 1965, becoming the only Hungarian club to win a European trophy when they defeated Juventus in Turin. Three years later they finished runners-up to Leeds United in the same competition, and that December Albert was named European Footballer of the Year, the only Hungarian ever to win the award. In 1975, inspired by their latest star Tibor Nyilasi, Ferencváros reached the final of the Cup-Winners' Cup, where they lost to Dynamo Kiev.

With easily the broadest fan base in Hungary, the club successfully courted private capital in the post-Communist era. With Nyilasi as coach and a team starring András Telek as sweeper, Tibor Simon a tough-tackling defender, Péter Lipscei and Flórian Albert's namesake son in midfield, *Fradi* won back-to-back titles in the mid-Nineties. Stadium improvements and abusive racist chanting – Ajax coach Louis van Gaal nearly pulled his team off at half-time – marked a subsequent Champions' League appearance in 1995.

Yet despite the breakthrough of precocious talent Krisztián Lisztes in midfield, and a remarkable win over Newcastle in the home leg of the 1996/97 UEFA Cup,

Budapest essentials

Private bus firm *LRI* runs a service between Budapest's Ferihegy **airport** and the *Kempinski* hotel, Erzsébet Tér 7–8 (daily every 30mins, 5.30am–9.30pm, pay Ft600 onboard, journey time 30–40mins). Cheaper is the city bus #93 from the airport to its terminus at Kőbánya-Kispest, the start of blue M3 metro line into town. A taxi will be Ft4,500 to downtown Pest, Ft5,000 to Buda.

The city's efficient **transport system** is made up of buses, trams and trolleybuses, running 4am–11pm. Night buses (indicated by É) cover the main routes 11.30pm–4am, using the same ticket system. Buy your ticket from the orange machines at stops, or from *BKV* kiosks at major stations. A ticket (*jegy*) for a single journey with no changes is Ft90, to be stamped onboard. The three-line metro (M1 yellow, M2 red, M3 blue, all crossing central Deák tér) has three kinds of tickets, explained in English at kiosk windows – you'll find stamping machines on the platform. More economical, and valid for all transport, are books (*gyűtojegy*) of ten (Ft900) or 20 (Ft1,750) tickets – stamp each ticket, without removing it from the book, for each ride. Also available are day passes (*napijegy*) at Ft740 and three-day passes (*három napra*) at Ft1,500. The most reliable **taxi** firms in town are *Főtaxi* (☎061/222 2222), and *City Taxi* (☎061/211 1111).

The best place for **tourist information** is *Tourinform*, next to central Deák Tér, at V Sütő Utca 2 (open Mon–Fri 9am–7pm, Sat–Sun 9am–4pm, ☎061/317 9800).

There is currently no good English-language source for **listings**, although the freebie weekly *Pesti Est*, distributed in bars and cafés, has a regularly updated list of clubs and concerts.

Note that Budapest addresses start with the Roman numeral of their district (*kerület*) – V is downtown, VI the neighbouring nightlife area.

FTC slowly floundered under the weight of corrupt mis-management. After a takeover by the *IMG* marketing group fell through, the board revealed that some of the club's Champions' League revenue could not be accounted for, and became the target of street demonstrations by fans.

Hungary's populist agriculture minister József Torgyán took over as club president in 1999 and, after seeing Marijan Vlak return to Dinamo Zagreb, he appointed another Croat, the hapless Stanko Poklepović. The outcome was a sixth-place finish in 1999/2000, another season's absence from Europe, and a major rebuilding job for incoming boss Janos Csank in 2000/01.

Here we go!

Blue metro M2 to **Népliget**; take the FTC exit. Allow 15mins from Deák Tér.

Swift half

At the top of the exit stairs in one corner of the stadium is the *Fradi Vendéglő*, with a busy terrace, a restaurant and a bar area. Next to it, downstairs, is the *Fradi Söröző*, a dark wooden bar with black-and-white action shots around the walls.

Occasionally these bars are closed for potentially fiery fixtures (the away fans' entrance is nearby). If so, walk away from Népliget metro, keeping the stadium to your left, down Üllői Út to Nagyvárad Tér metro, and cross the underpass to the **Bacskai Borozó** at #121.

Club merchandise

The **Fradi Ajándék Bolt** (open Mon–Fri 10am–4pm and matchdays, no credit cards) is hardly Bayern Munich's supermarket, but in Hungarian terms it's a treasure trove. You'll find it just around the corner from the bar/restaurant.

Ultra culture

Crowds have dropped below 10,000, and the atmosphere at *Fradi* has been a flat one in the last couple of seasons. The green mob can still cause trouble away – as seen by the scenes in and around the Újpest ground at the 1998/99 fixture – but many are staying away.

In print

The *FTC Újság* is a colour-covered newsletter (Ft50) available at home games in the club shop or from vendors near the metro exit.

In the net

Emre Zsoldos hosts an onofficial homepage at: www.ferencvarosi-tc.hu. It offers a rich statistical database in English, plus a Hungarian-language archive of match reports and a number of other features.

MTK Hungária

MTK Stadion, VIII Salgótarjáni Út 12–14
Capacity 18,000 (6,000 seated)
Colours Blue-and-white shirts, blue shorts
League champions 1904, 1908, 1914, 1917–25, 1929, 1936–37, 1951, 1953, 1958, 1987, 1997, 1999
Cup winners 1910–12, 1914, 1923, 1925, 1932, 1952, 1968, 1997–98, 2000

The richest man in Hungary, *Fotex Holding* boss Gábor Várszegi, has been able to buy success for MTK, inviting guests to the executive boxes above the attractive new blue plastic seating in the club's main stand. What he can't do is buy the club a new identity or fan base. The MTK crowd – an average 3,000 for one of the best teams in the land – consists largely of elderly men and a smattering of enthusiastic young Jewish kids, easy targets in the current local climate of anti-Semitism.

That climate was hardly different in 1888, when MTK was formed by liberal and Jewish defectors from a pro-Habsburg former national gymnastics club. An intense rivalry with Ferencváros began early on, exacerbated when star player Imre Schlosser moved the short distance from Fradi to MTK during World War I. Once coach Jimmy Hogan had arrived after the end of hostilities, MTK became the dominant force in Hungarian and Central European football.

The team were to pay dearly for their Jewish origins during World War II, when the Nazi Arrow Cross took power and banned the club, sending president Alfred Brüll, one of the founding fathers of Hungarian football, off to his death in a concentration camp along with hundreds of the team's Jewish fans.

Peer group – MTK are a successful team in need of their own bedrock of support

After the war the club became Vörös Lobogó ('Red Banner'), team of the hated ÁVO Communist secret police. Following the 1956 uprising, the team achieved independence from the henchmen and led a quiet and dignified existence, surfacing briefly in 1964 to reach the final of the Cup-Winners' Cup, which they lost to Sporting Lisbon after a replay.

Today MTK are the first Hungarian club to have replaced the old Communist sports club structure with a modern, European-style business setup. After buying goalscorer Béla Illés and midfielder Gábor Halmai from Kispest, and defender Zoltán Molnár and forward Ferenc Orosz from BVSC, MTK won the double in 1997.

The club then improved its stadium but pushed admission prices beyond the average fan's pocket, and European progress did not follow domestic success. MTK were head and shoulders above the rest of the league and coasted to another title in 1998/99, but coach Sándor Egervári was then surprisingly allowed to take over at provincial club Dunaferr, and took several leading players with him.

Dutchman Henk ten Cate, Várszegi's choice as replacement coach, coaxed MTK to more silverware thanks to a 3–1 win over Vasas in the 2000 cup final, but was powerless to prevent Egervári's upstarts from waltzing off with the title.

Here we go!

Red trolleybus #75 runs from **Népliget** (blue metro M3) to **Népstadion** (red metro M2), with the MTK stadium halfway in between.

Swift half

In the **main stand** you have a choice of slipping though the blue sliding doors at the top to the convivial sponsors' corner bar, or clambering along to the middle of the stand to join the punters heading for the *büfé* in the main building.

In the net

The club now as its own site at: www.mtk.hu. No English to be seen, but again the local signposting is easy enough to follow.

⬤ Újpesti TE

Megyeri Úti stadium, IV Megyeri Út 13
Capacity 32,000 (12,000 seated)
Colours All white with lilac trim
League champions 1930–31, 1933, 1935, 1939, 1945–47, 1960, 1969–75, 1978–79, 1990, 1998
Cup winners 1969–70, 1975, 1982–83, 1987, 1992

Based in the north Budapest port district of Újpest, the once mighty Lilacs have fallen on hard times. The loss of interior ministry funding after the end of Communism sorely weakened the club's spending power, and even a comeback title win in 1998 resulted only in the departure of key players due to unpaid salaries.

Founded in 1885 as Újpesti Torna Egyelet, Újpest did not emerge as a real force until the Thirties, when they replaced MTK as the big rivals to *Fradi*. But the club's golden era came under their Communist-era name of Újpesti Dózsa. Just prior to embarking on a magnificent run of seven straight title wins, a side packed with internationals such as Ferenc Bene and Antal Dunai met Newcastle United in the 1969 Fairs' Cup final, losing 6–4 in a thrilling, two-legged battle.

During the Seventies Újpest produced one of the last true stars to emerge in the Hungarian game: international winger András Tőrőcsik, whose light-footed trickery prompted the crowd to shout 'Dance Tőrő!' whenever he got the ball. Along with Ferencváros star Tibor Nyilasi, Tőrőcsik was sent off while playing for Hungary against Argentina at the 1978 World Cup. It was a typically controversial moment in a career which would be prematurely ended by drink.

Having reverted to their previous name, the club were almost relegated in 1993, but enjoyed a revival when István Kozma, once of Liverpool reserves, returned to the club in 1997. With lively midfielder György Véber and classy sweeper Vilmos Sebők, UTE improved on their runners-up spot of 1997 by sweeping past Győr in the league, going through the spring season unbeaten to claim their first title in eight years. The club then prepared for the Champions' League by signing no-one over the summer of '98, and having coach Péter Varhidi plead with the players not to strike for pay. Kozma left for Videoton, Sebők for Bristol City, and UTE were duly thrashed by Sturm Graz and Club Bruges in Europe.

A cash crisis almost saw the club go out of business in 1999, but a last-minute takeover by a consortium of local businessmen ensured that the Lilacs were at least able to complete the season, although an 11th-place finish was UTE's worst since 1993. Having stabilised the club's finances and smartened up the stadium, Újpest's new owners were hoping new coach István Kisteleki would at least manage to conjure a European placing in 2000/2001.

Here we go!

Take **blue metro #3** to its terminus at Újpest-Központ, then bus #96 or #104 four stops to Megyeri Út. Allow 30mins for the journey.

Swift half

Near Újpest-Központ, along Árpád Út, is a string of bars including the *Primo Söröző* at #85. Inside the metro station itself is the *Gold-Metro* bar, a small but popular meeting place. In the stadium under the main stand you'll find the *Fán Fán*, a recently renovated bar and restaurant decked out in lilac-and-white tiles with a huge banner from the time when ÚTE was Dózsa and had a little red star above the classic 'D' symbol.

Ultra culture

The *Ultra Viola Bulldogs*, having adopted fellow purple-wearers Fiorentina as their twin club, behave accordingly, trying hard to create a Latin atmosphere on their crumbling terraces. Twice-yearly pilgrimages to Florence, to stock up on memorabilia, reveal the extent of the fans' friendship with the *Collettivo Autonomo Viola*.

In the net

In theory there's an official website at: www.ute.hu. But it's only available sporadically, and there are no fan-run alternatives.

Groundhopping

If you thought some of the bigger names in Budapest football seem to have fallen on hard times, try taking a tour of the smaller grounds. There are plenty to choose from. Among the lesser lights, 1997 domestic cup runners-up BVSC, for whom Lajos Détari played in his swansong season in 1998/99, are based by Mexikói út, terminus of the #1 metro line, while III Kerület, literally Third District, represent Old Buda, and are at the end of the #1 tram line. Both clubs were relegated at the end of the 1998/99 season and have not yet resurfaced.

☕ Kispest-Honvéd

Bozsik Stadion, XIX Újtemető Útca 1–3
Capacity 15,000 (6,000 seated)
Colours Red-and-black striped shirts, black shorts
League champions 1950, 1952, 1954–55, 1980, 1984–86, 1988–89, 1991, 1993
Cup winners 1926, 1964, 1985, 1989, 1996

The former village of Kispest is where Ferenc Puskás learned his football. But the stadium is named after another member of the Fifties 'Golden Team', captain József Bozsik, who won a record 100 caps for his country, and to whom a commemorative plaque now stands before the clubhouse.

Honvéd were the Hungarian army side which, as well as providing the backbone of the Golden Team, also romped to five championships in the first half of the Fifties. After a lean couple of decades in the aftermath of the 1956 Hungarian uprising, they bounced back in the Eighties, winning seven titles between 1983 and 1993, the last as Kispest-Honvéd – the name the club adopted after Communism to reflect their pre-World War II existence as Kispest AC. Between 1991 and 1994, an ambitious group of Belgians led by players' agent Louis

The Nép stadium

Népstadion, XIV Stefánia Út 2 (☎061/251 1222)
Capacity 70,000 all-seated

Built by the people for the
people, Népstadion, 'The
People's Stadium', was the
flagship of Hungary's
Communist, postwar
reconstruction. The
Olympian statues behind
it are a testament to the
Socialist-Realist style of
the era.

Today, however, the
stage for the national
team's legendary games of
the Fifties is filled only
for rock concerts.
International football
games rarely attract more
than 20,000 – mostly

Making an entrance – the impressive gateway to the Nép

Ferencváros fans holding up a wall of flags in the southern end. Visiting support can
usually be found to the right of the tunnel.

In the glory days, with no club grounds big enough to hold a 70,000 crowd, the
Hungarian football federation would put on double-bills of Ferencváros-Újpest and
Vasas-Honvéd clashes here. Újpest fans would arrive early to cheer on Vasas, forging a
friendship which remains strong to this day.

The lighting and press facilities were improved for the 1998 European Athletics
Championships, and a roof is expected to be put on – probably leaving small sectors by
each scoreboard uncovered – by 2003.

The Népstadion has **its own metro station** on red line M2 – take the left station
exit after leaving the train. Allow 10mins from Deák Tér.

Outside the stadium, the *Félido* at Kerepesi Út 24, near the metro exit, has framed
black-and-white photos of Flórián Albert and Tibor Nyilasi, while the *Tücsök* is a
pleasant wooden bar at Stéfánia Út 29.

You can buy **tickets** for Hungary internationals at major outlets in town, such as
the *MCD* store at Jókai Utca 40, near Nyugati. There are also stone **ticket huts** around
the stadium walls on Ifújság Útja, below the walkway leading from the metro, and on
Dózsa György Út.

de Vries bought into the club, investing a
small fortune in nostalgia and the hope of
a regular place in lucrative European competition. It was not an entirely foolish
venture, but since de Vries took his cash
home, the business side of the club has
collapsed and the team with it. The bulk
of the promising 1993 championship squad
was sold to Belgian clubs, and today the
only surviving legacy of this bold but ultimately doomed first attempt at Western
investment in Hungarian football is a VIP
bar under the main stand. Now Kispest-
Honvéd are very much Budapest's
also-rans, with a fan base of young urchins
from this forgotten dusty suburb, who have
less to play for than old Puskás – probably
asleep in the stands – ever did at their age.

To get the man's autograph on matchday, take **blue metro line M3** to Határ

Út, then tram #42 six stops to Tulipán Utca, one stop before the terminus. Allow half-an-hour from central Deák Tér. Those getting off the tram will be heading for one of two bars: the *borozó* 150 metres back along the tram line – look out for the Bor and bunch of grapes sign – at Ady Endre Út 115; or the **Arena** bar between the railway line and the ground at Hofherr Albert Utca 27.

● Vasas

Fáy Utcai stadium, Fáy Utca 58
Capacity 18,000
Colours All red with blue trim
League champions 1957, 1961–62, 1965–66, 1977
Cup winners 1955, 1973, 1981, 1986

Traditionally the team of the iron workers, Vasas are nestled in the district of Angyalföld ('Angel Land'), which produced three-time Olympic champion boxer László Papp and was described by the late Communist leader and Vasas fan János Kádár as 'the beating heart of the Hungarian working-class movement'.

The team have almost always played in the shadow of the bigger clubs but, after winning the title in 1957, they reached the semi-final of the European Cup the following season; having thumped Ajax in the quarter-final, they lost out to Real Madrid. In the Sixties, factory whistles would blow early for workers to catch another great Vasas team which included 1966 World Cup stars Kálmán Mészöly and János Farkas.

Today's side is some way off that standard, but Peter Kabat's goals got Vasas to the cup final in 2000, and although that was lost to MTK, a third-place finish in the league and a UEFA Cup berth in 2000/01 put some of Budapest's more illustrious clubs in the shade.

Fáy Utcai remains one of the most pleasant grounds to visit in Budapest. Take blue metro line M3 to Forgách Utca, then walk towards the floodlights down Fáy or parallel Forgách Utca, which houses the **Gol!** Kisvendéglő at #30. Inside the ground, you'll find the pseudo-Mexican **Santa Fé** bar/restaurant, an executive box for the masses behind one goal, with the front table overlooking the pitch generally reserved for the Mészöly clan. There is also a beer pump behind the main stand, with scarves and shirts sold alongside, opposite the **Vasas Pirates** making merry next to the players' tunnel. Behind them is the clubhouse with its **Vasas Mini Büfé**.

Eat, drink, sleep…

Bars and clubs

Budapest is a party town. Places open and close every week, but you'll find plenty of bars around Liszt Ferenc Tér (M1 Oktogon) and the shabbier area downtown (between M3 Kálvin tér and M3 Ferenciek tere). Closing times are refreshingly flexible.

Wine (*bor*) is the opium of the Magyars, guzzled in cheap abandon in seedy wine cellars (*borozó*) which open before dawn. The younger generation prefers **beer** (*sőr*), often Dutch or German lager, at Ft200–300 for a half-litre or *korsó*. Of the cheaper local brews, *Borsodi* is acceptable. The traditional beer hall, *söröző*, is giving way to the more expensive and tackier pub or theme bar.

Club life is unsophisticated fun, but don't mess with the gorillas on the door. DJ info can be picked up at *Trance*, VI Révay Köz 2 (M3 Arany János Utca).

6:3 Borozó, IX Lónyay Utca 62. A typical wine bar whose walls sing the praises of *that* game, featuring three large, framed sepia photographs. M3 Ferenc Körút.

Darshan, VIII Krúdy Gyula Utca 7/8. A Gaudiesque bar with ambient sounds, coupled with a bar/café courtyard opposite, playing more adventurous music at later hours. M3 Kálvin Tér.

Garage, V Arany János Utca 9. Large downtown bar/restaurant/disco, with a big screen for Sky and Champions' League matches. Popular with trendy young Magyars. M3 Arany János Utca.

Pótkulcs, VI Csengery Utca 65B. Brought to you by the management of the legendary *Sixtus*, the 'Spare Key' takes you through a gate into a secret courtyard, to an old building housing a bar/restaurant frequented by just about every swinging Magyar and ex-pat in town. Open until midnight Mon–Thur, 1am Fri–Sat. M3 Nyugati Pu.

Ráckert, I Hadnagy Utca 8–10. This bar garden next to the Rác baths is *the* summer spot in town, with big-screen football every two years, live music and food otherwise. Open until dawn, closed Sun, May–Sep. #7/7É bus.

Restaurants

Hungarian food is not as spicy or exotic as its reputation suggests, but portions are hearty and cheap. The average local eaterie – *vendéglő* or *étterem* – will have a menu (*étlap*) dominated by meat dishes, either beef (*marha*) or chicken (*csirke*) The world-

famous goulash turns out to be a hearty soup rather than the paprika-laden stew you may be expecting; for the latter, ask for *pörkölt*. A main course should be under Ft1,000, perhaps a little more at one of Budapest's many international-class establishments.

Fatál, Váci Utca 67 (entrance in Pintér Utca). Busy downtown Hungarian restaurant, serving huge portions of domestic dishes on wooden trays. Open midday–2am daily, no credit cards. A 10min walk from M3 Ferenciek Tere.

Kétballábas, VI Teréz Körút 36 (entrance in Dessewffy Utca). The 'Two-Left Feet' is owned by former MTK midfielder György Bognár, whose 50-cap international career is illustrated among the football kitsch. Occasional special guests for major games on TV. Mid-range menu, open daily midday–midnight. M1 Oktogon.

Simon Pince, XIII Hegedűs Gyula Utca 2. Owned by Tibor Simon, the short-cropped, tough-tackling ex-*Fradi* full-back. His bar is tamer than his tackling ever was, with a restrained display of team photos. Where Ferencváros players come to celebrate a big win. M3 Nyugati Pu.

Marble majesty – Budapest's football grounds are full of crumbling relics of the past

Söröző Szent Jupat, II Retek utca 16. Open daily 24 hours, a perennial late-night favourite offering vast portions and great foaming glasses of beer. No credit cards. M2 Moszkva Tér or night bus #6É.

Tütü Tangó, VI Hajos Utca 2. A great success since opening in the winter of 1999/2000, this comfortable two-floor space for dining, drinking and dancing has won over Budapest's trendily alternative set. Main courses average Ft750, with the attraction of live music – genuine folk or gypsy sounds without the tourist trappings – downstairs, and DJs thereafter. Open until midnight Sun–Tue, 2am Wed–Sat. M1 Opera.

Accommodation

Cheap accommodation is plentiful in Budapest thanks to the large number of private *panziós*, or bed-and-breakfasts, and private rooms offered by old ladies waiting at Keleti station.

Beware though, that many cheaper options are stuck up in Buda, so you may be spending the price difference on taxi fares at night. A clean double room should be around Ft8,000 a night.

Citadella, XII Citadella Sétány (☎061/466 5794, fax 386 0505). Youth hostel with a splendid view of Pest from the top of Gellért Hill. From Ft1,500. Bus #7 to Móricz Zsigmond Körtér, then #27.

City Panzió Ring, XIII Szent István Körút 22 (☎061/340 5450; fax 061/340 4884). Slick, modern pension bang in the heart of the city, a short walk from Nyugati station. Around DM80 per single room per night, DM100 for a double, breakfast included.

Hotel Stadion, Ifjúsági Útja 1–3 (☎061/251 2222, fax 061/251 2062). Purpose-built by the Népstadion for visiting sports teams, with a sauna, swimming pool and solarium, all rooms with satellite TV and private facilities. From DM99 for a single, DM124 a double, DM145 a triple.

Mohácsi Panzió, II Bimbó Út 25/a (☎061/326 7741). Pleasant, family-run pension. Some rooms

with an excellent view of the town from the balcony. Breakfast optional. No credit cards. Bus #11 from M2 Batthyány Tér or a 10min climb up from the main #4/6 tram line, Mechwart Liget stop.

Travellers' Hostel Diáksport, XIII Dózsa György Út 152 (☎061/340 8585, fax 061/320 8435). Quality youth hostel with 24-hour bar and reception, rooms with up to four beds or dorms, washing and internet facilities. Around Ft2,000 a single, Ft3,000 a double, Ft15,00 a dorm bed. No credit cards. M3 Dózsa György Út.

Ireland

Football Association of Ireland 80 Merrion Square, Dublin 2
☎01/676 6864   Fax 01/661 0931   E-mail info@fai.ie

League champions Shelbourne   **Cup winners** Shelbourne   **Promoted** Bray
Wanderers, Longford Town, Kilkenny City   **Relegated** Sligo Rovers, Drogheda
United, Waterford United

European participants 2000/01 Shelbourne (UCL qualifiers); Bohemians, Cork
City (UEFA Cup); UCD (Intertoto Cup)

The achievements of Jack Charlton's national side at the 1990
and 1994 World Cups have
changed the status of football in
Ireland forever. For those two barmy, balmy
summers, Irish sports fans the world over
were transfixed by their team's extraordinary progress. Ireland's politicians and
business community were soon in on the
strange new phenomenon, and before long
soccer was *the* game to be involved with.

Charlton bowed out in December
1995, his team having been outclassed by
Holland in a play-off for a place at Euro '96.
His successor, Mick McCarthy, just failed
to take an ageing squad to France '98, but
can look to an Irish Under-18 squad that
won the European Championship almost
unnoticed in the summer of 1998 as a sign
of hope for the future.

McCarthy's team missed out on Euro
2000 after losing to Turkey in a qualification play-off. In the first leg in Dublin,
Ireland took the lead with 11 minutes to
go through a superb finish from young
striker Robbie Keane, but in the dying seconds midfielder Lee Carsley needlessly
handled in the penalty area to gift the Turks
an equaliser. That away goal became even
more significant when McCarthy's men

No luck of the Irish – getting tripped up by Turkey, November 1999

Lean and green – David O'Leary, 1979

were unable to break down Turkey in Bursa and the Irish went out on away goals, amid chaotic and violent scenes as Turkish fans clashed with Tony Cascarino as they invaded the pitch.

But while Ireland can count themselves unlucky to have missed out on the last two major tournaments, the sense of disappointment merely reflects the increased expectations of this emerging football nation.

Prior to the Charlton era, the typical Irish soccer fan came from Dublin's working class, gathering with a couple of thousand kindred spirits on rundown terraces before a Sunday afternoon pint. Today international football brings Ireland's new business class to Lansdowne Road, the national rugby stadium hired out for the round-ball game. Tomorrow they will all be gathering at an all-purpose, all-seater arena to be built in Citywest, outside Dublin, by the end of 2001. The task facing the League of Ireland in the meantime is to bridge this two-tier system and attract

new fans, and their families, to regular weekend games.

In 1994, the Football Association of Ireland (FAI) allowed BSkyB to beam English Premiership action throughout Ireland via cable. In return, Sky stumped up around IR£1.5million towards equipping league grounds with floodlights. The consequent scheduling of domestic games on Friday and Saturday evenings increased attendances, allowing fans to turn up for local action while still following Ireland's three most popular teams – Liverpool, Manchester United and Celtic – on the box. FAI grants from smaller sponsorship deals have gone towards ground improvements at Shelbourne's Tolka Park, Bohemians' Dalymount and St Patrick's Athletic's Richmond Park.

The progress is not confined to Dublin. A soccer museum is being built in Galway and the best crowds of all are to be found at Cork and at the Brandywell, home of Derry City, across the border in Northern Ireland.

Sectarian violence caused Derry to withdraw from the northern Irish League in 1972. The club joined the south's League of Ireland fifteen years later, and did the Irish double in 1989. But the Derry story was beginning to turn sour until the appointment of Felix Healy as manager in 1995. Under Healy's guidance, Derry won the league again in 1997.

None of this would have been conceivable before Big Jack. Soccer in the Emerald Isle had traditionally been based in industrialised Belfast. Before the north-south split in 1923, only Dublin's big three of Shelbourne, Bohemians and Shamrock Rovers competed in all-Irish football, mustering just four cup wins in 40 years between them.

In the south, the Gaelic Athletic Association promoted the traditional Irish sports of Gaelic football and hurling. Schoolboys were beaten for indulging in the 'foreign' game of soccer and the GAA enjoyed the lion's share of state funding and favour. Rugby, unaffected by the events of 1923, remained all Ireland's premier international sport.

For much of the postwar era, the League of Ireland was little more than a breeding ground for the English and Scottish leagues. Only record title-winners Shamrock Rovers could pull in reasonable crowds, thanks to stylish football and, in the Sixties and Seventies, some regular European action.

At international level, the game was scarred by administrative incompetence and the reluctance of English and Scottish clubs to release key players. Ireland had the talent – Johnny Giles and Liam Brady to name just two examples – but needed a strong character to bind it together. That character was Jack Charlton. After pipping Bob Paisley to the post of national-team manager in 1986, Charlton made sure Ireland's players did the simple things right: they closed opponents down, and got the ball forward, fast. Frustrating opponents in Lansdowne's long grass, and displaying a unique team spirit, they were hard to beat. With only a small pool of Irish-born talent to choose from, Charlton encouraged players to exercise their parental – or even grandparental – right to choose the Irish first team over occasional England squad membership. Neither Glasgow-born Ray Houghton nor his then Liverpool teammate, John Aldridge, had set foot in Dublin before Charlton's first game in charge.

It was Houghton who set Ireland alight with an early winning goal against England in the 1988 European Championship, Big Jack's – and Ireland's – frst major tournament. After drawing 1–1 with the Soviet Union, Ireland went out against the eventual winners Holland to a late, lucky Wim Kieft goal. But the team had made its mark, as had its supporters – an exuberant Green Army whose easygoing attitude contrasted so starkly with the ugly demeanour of their English counterparts, and who gleefully carried the green, white and orange tricolour on to Italia '90.

In sometimes dour but always indefatigable style, the Irish progressed to the World Cup quarter-finals in Italy despite failing to win a single match, a David O'Leary penalty beating Romania in the second round and sending Ireland football crazy. Even the staid BBC coverage could not help but be brightened by Liam Brady's

Basics

EU nationals and citizens of the United States, Canada, Australia and New Zealand need only their **passport** to enter the Irish Republic.

The Irish currency is the **Irish pound**, or punt (indicated IR£), divided into 100 pence. Credit-card payment is generally accepted and automatic cash machines are widespread. Many shops and businesses also accept payment in pounds sterling, and the two currencies are of broadly equivalent value. Banks are open Mon–Fri 10am–4pm, with many open until 5pm on Thursdays.

The international **telephone code** for Ireland is 353. Once inside the country, Dublin is 01, Cork 021 and Galway 091. From Ireland, the international access code is 00. Cheap rates are after 6pm weekdays, all day weekends. Coin phones take 10p, 20p and 50p pieces, while **phonecards** come in units of IR£2, IR£3.50, IR£8 and IR£16.

Travel around Ireland is slow but reliable, and centralised on Dublin. **Trains** from Dublin to Belfast run from central **Connolly** station, to Cork and Galway from **Heuston** in the west of town. An off-peak return train ticket is almost the same price as a single – around IR£25 between Dublin and Galway.

Buses, operated by the state concern *Bus Éireann*, are often cheaper than trains, but slow and infrequent; a *Boomerang* ticket, valid from Tuesday to Thursday, allows a return journey for the price of a single. Private operators run **alternative services** on many routes – they're cheaper and usually busier than the state-run buses.

emotional commentary. Although they went on to lose 1–0 to the host nation, Ireland and Charlton were clearly enjoying their spell in the international football limelight, and the stage was set for another thrilling episode.

It could not have been scripted better. For their first game of the 1994 World Cup, the Irish again faced Italy, this time in New York. It was to be the scene of Ireland's finest hour, an early Ray Houghton goal winning the day, just as it had in Stuttgart eight years earlier. Although the team would later wilt in the Florida heat against Holland, history had been made.

Match practice

A number of Irish grounds have been improved in recent years thanks to the influx of lottery cash, but all the same, the scene is pretty low-key. Crowds are generally in four figures, but friendly with it. Any talented youngster will stand out and no doubt be spotted by someone significant in the crowd – scouting is a cottage industry here.

The season begins in late July or early August with lucrative friendlies against English and Scottish clubs. The league generally starts on the last weekend of August, continuing right through until late April, leaving early May free for the cup final and promotion play-offs.

Major games kick-off at 7.45pm on Fridays and 7.30pm on Saturdays, with lesser Dublin Premier Division teams and some First Division sides playing instead on Sunday afternoons. Some fixtures are also played on Thursday evenings.

A different league

Ireland's National League has two divisions, both of which contain semi-professional clubs. The Premier Division's 12 sides have a 33-game season, playing each other home and away and, as far as relegation allows, home and away every other season.

The First Division has ten clubs, playing 27 games in a similar fashion to the Premier. The bottom and top two

automatically swap places between Premier and First, while the third-bottom and third-top are involved in a two-legged play-off. The bottom two of the First must apply for re-election to the League at the end of the season.

Up for the cup

The FAI Cup has six rounds, though the first is the sole province of 20 non-league clubs. All Premier and First Division clubs join at the second-round stage. Level scores after extra-time in the first match force a replay, at which there will be both extra-time and penalties if necessary. Home advantage for the semi-final is decided the same way as in the previous three rounds – on the luck of the draw. The final takes place midweek in early May, traditionally at Lansdowne Road, although the last two have taken place at Tolka Park.

As in England and Scotland, there is also a League Cup to be played for. This takes place in the autumn and involves six groups of four teams – the 22 National League sides plus two non-league sides. The winners of each group plus the best two runners-up go through to a knockout stage, where ties are decided on one game, extra-time and penalties, before a two-legged final in November or December; level aggregate scores lead to extra-time and penalties in the second leg.

Just the ticket

League football is cheap in Ireland. A typical standing price is IR£5, a seat IR£6. Simply pay your money at the turnstile. For international games at Lansdowne Road, prices range between IR£35 for the best seats and IR£15 for the so-called 'bucket' seats behind the goals. Tickets are only officially available from the FAI. Almost all clubs issue a matchday programme, usually available for about IR£1.

Half-time

Many Irish clubs survive on bar takings alone. The supporters' club usually has a social function during the week as well as performing its important role serving drinks on matchdays. Chocolate is consumed in almost as great a quantity as Guinness, and vendors will regularly come round with baskets crammed full of gum-threatening goodies.

Action replay

Televised football has improved of late. State channel Network 2's *Soccer Show* on Friday evenings is the major league preview programme, and the same channel shows a highlighted game the next day at 10.30pm. Network 2 also has the rights to Irish internationals, but refused to stump up the millions asked by the Turkish FA for live coverage of the Euro 2000 play-off second leg – forcing bar-owners across the land to point their satellite dishes hopefully in the direction of a Turkish station.

When it comes to English action, Network 2's *The Premiership* on Saturday evening has highlights, analysis and heavyweight guests such as Johnny Giles, Liam Brady and Eamon Dunphy.

Irish-language channel TG4 has ambitious plans to show a range of European action.

The back page

Unless there's an international match looming, at least five times more newsprint is dedicated to the English Premiership than to its Irish counterpart. Most fans read the Irish edition of *The Star* and the Tuesday edition of the *Irish Times*. There is a comprehensive sports section in *Ireland On Sunday*, while the *Sunday Tribune* is also hot on weekend analysis.

The monthly *Irish Soccer Magazine* (IR£1.50) offers perhaps the most comprehensive coerage of the game north and south, while various fanzines crop up every now and then.

In the net

The FAI launched its official website in October 1998, and although it can be a bit leisurely, there's no arguing with the depth of the coverage, which includes youth, schoolboy and women's football, as well as the full national side and the Premier Division. The site is at: www.fai.ie.

For a more irreverent take on the Irish football scene, try *Soccer Central* at: www.soccercentral.ie/index.htm.

Dublin

🏐 Shamrock Rovers *330* 🏐 Bohemians *332* 🏐 Shelbourne *332*
🏐 St Patrick's *333* 🏐 Bray *335* 🏐 Home Farm *335* 🏐 UCD *335*

Provincial sides such as Derry and Cork may attract their loyal followings, but the epicentre of football in the Republic has always been Dublin...

The thrilling fields

Shamrock Rovers

Stadium Morton Stadium, Santry
Club office Spawell Leisure Complex, Templeogue, Dublin 6
Colours Green-and-white hooped shirts, green shorts
League champions 1923, 1925, 1927, 1932, 1938–39, 1954, 1957, 1959, 1964, 1984–87, 1994
Cup winners 1925, 1929, 1930–33, 1936, 1940, 1944–45, 1948, 1955–56, 1962, 1964–69, 1978, 1985–87

Ireland's biggest club are both everything that was wrong with domestic football and everything that could be put right. Shamrock Rovers, after a decade in nomadic wilderness, have pinned their future on a new all-seater ground on the outskirts of town. The Tallaght stadium, near Rovers' traditional fan base in south Dublin, has suffered a host of bureaucratic problems since the first proposals were published in 1996. Work finally began on building the first phase, including a 3,000-seater main stand, in May 2000. For the time being, Rovers are playing their home games at the Morton Municipal Stadium in Santry.

When finished, Tallaght should finally lay to rest the ghost of Milltown, Rovers' beloved old stadium which witnessed the best football in the league over a 60-year period before its site was sold to developers in 1987.

Formed in the Ringsend area, Rovers became Dublin's leading club soon after the League of Ireland's inauguration in 1921/22. Their rivalry with nearby Shel-

bourne attracted record crowds, obliging the club to lease some land in the Milltown area from the Jesuit community, and to build a stand there in 1928.

The Hoops continued to chalk up league and cup wins, but it was the work of player-coach Paddy Coad that won over a generation of fans in the 1950s. 'Coad's Colts', as the young side became known, not only won honours, they played a stylish, passing game that had not been seen in Irish club football before. Pioneers in Europe as well as at home, the team famously restricted the Busby Babes to a 3–2 win at Old Trafford in 1957.

Rovers became cup specialists, winning six straight Irish finals between 1964 and 1969. Yet the Jesuit landlords were unhappy about such craven innovations as floodlights and half-time music, and the team were forced to play their lucrative European games at Dalymount Park.

The Kilcoyne family bought a controlling interest in Rovers in 1972, but invested little money in the club until the arrival of former Leeds United star Johnny Giles as manager in 1977. By then, Rovers were fielding virtually a junior side – they had had to apply for re-election in 1976. Giles' ambition was to build a winning team capable of attracting large crowds to a redeveloped Milltown, raising the profile of the domestic game as a whole. But his slow passing game floundered on bumpy, provincial pitches, while business interests in North America kept him away from Dublin for extended periods.

While Giles' dream faded, the Kilcoynes maintained a steady trade in selling players across the water and buying up all the best Irish ones cheaply. The 'four-in-a-row' title team of the mid-Eighties had the pinpoint accuracy of future coach Pat Byrne in midfield, but the success of that era was brought to a dramatic end when the Kilcoynes sold Milltown. A subsequent groundshare with Shelbourne at Tolka Park proved disastrous, with more Rovers fans on the picket-line outside than on the terraces. A move to the Royal Dublin Society Showgrounds in the early Nineties was no more than a costly half-solution, and a new-look board of directors began work on the Tallaght plan in 1994 – the year the club last won the league. The star of that side, Stephen Geoghegan, was soon sold to Shelbourne, with whom the Rovers again groundshared in the late Nineties.

If the move to Tallaght is a success, Rovers may lose their reputation as a selling club, and the domestic game could emerge from the dark ages for good.

Here we go!

Buses #41 and #16 make the journey to Santry from central Eden Quay, although the #16 takes

a less roundabout route. Get off at the *Omni Shopping Centre* stop. When Tallaght is ready, special buses will run fans the 8km from town on matchdays – until then, take bus #49, #54A, #56A or #77A from Eden Quay.

Swift half

A bar and clubhouse will be in place at Tallaght for the big kick-off in 2001. Until then there is a modest bar at the Morton Stadium, but Rovers fans tend to have a swiftie at various spots in town before heading to the match.

In the net

There are no unofficial Rovers sites any more, but the club recently launched its own official homepage, typically down-to-earth but detailed with it at: www.shamrockrovers.ie.

Dublin essentials

If you're arriving at the **airport**, the Airlink express bus makes the seven-mile journey south to Dublin's central bus station, Busáras (every 20–30 minutes, 6.40am–11pm, single ticket IR£3). Alternatively, a normal city bus #41A, #41B or #41C will take you to central Eden Quay in around 30mins for IR£1.10. A taxi will cost IR£12–15 to do the same trip.

A more relaxed alternative to flying is provided by two **ferry companies** offering a twice-daily Dublin service from Holyhead in north Wales. The ferries are modern and comfortable, and crossings take around three-and-a-half hours. *Irish Ferries* sail to **Dublin port**, where a bus service awaits for the 15min journey to Busáras – pay the driver IR£1.50. *Stena Sealink* sail to **Dún Laoghaire**, a 20min journey into town on Dublin's fast overland electric rail line, **DART** (fare IR£1.30). The DART runs every 5–15mins, north to south via the city's central train stations, Pearse and Connolly, Mon–Sat 6.30am–midnight, Sun 9.30am–11pm. A one-day unlimited DART travel pass costs IR£3.20.

Dublin's **bus network** comprehensively covers the city, running Mon–Sat 6am–11.30pm and from 10am on Sundays. A bus into the centre will be marked 'An Lár'. Tickets, in the range 55p–£1.10 depending on the length of journey, are sold at newsagents, or onboard provided you have the right change. A one-day bus pass is IR£3.30, or IR£4.50 for a combined DART/bus one-day pass. A four-day DART/bus Explorer pass is IR£10, valid Mon–Fri from 9.45am, all day Saturdays and Sundays.

A **night bus service**, *Nitelink*, runs on the half-hour, Thurs–Sat, 12.30–3.30am, from College Street, D'Ollier Street and Westmoreland Street to a range of suburban destinations for IR£2.50 – pay the driver.

Taxis are hard to find and even harder to flag down. St Stephen's Green and O'Connell Street are the most likely parking spots. Otherwise call *Metro* on ☎01/668 3333.

Dublin's **Tourism Centre**, at the restored former Church of St Andrew in Suffolk Street (Mon–Sat 9am–6pm, Tues from 9.30am, ☎01/605 7799), is friendly and efficient. For entertainment information, *In Dublin* (fortnightly, IR£1.95) is by far the best listings source.

Bohemians

Dalymount Park, Phibsborough, Dublin 7
Capacity 14,500 (2,000 seated)
Colours Red-and-black striped shirts, black shorts
League champions 1924, 1928, 1930, 1934, 1936, 1975, 1978
Cup winners 1928, 1935, 1970, 1976, 1992

The Bohs are the oldest club still in existence in the Republic, and their rivalry with Shamrock Rovers is Dublin's biggest. Fenced in by terraced housing in the wide catchment area of Phibsborough, the Bohs have been playing at Dalymount Park since 1901. They appeared in six pre-1923 all-Irish cup finals, winning one in 1908, and after the separate FA of Ireland was formed, Dalymount Park became the Association's home ground. All internationals and cup finals were played here until the Lansdowne deal was struck in 1971.

Now four new stands are being built, starting with the replacement of the oldest, wooden one, to give an eventual overall capacity of an all-seated 16,000.

It's 22 years since Bohs last won the title, thanks to the goalscoring of striker – and future manager – Turlough O'Connor. In 1999 the club even had to endure the ignominy of a play-off match with Cobh Ramblers to ensure top-flight football would remain at Dalymount into the new millennium. But within a year, Bohs were playing arguably the most attractive football in Ireland, finishing a deserved third in the league and reaching the FAI Cup final, which they lost to Shelbourne after a replay.

Here we go!
Take bus #19 from O'Connell Street or #18 from Phoenix Park. Allow 15mins for the journey, alighting where Phibsborough Road, North Circular Road and Dalymount meet. Head through any narrow alleyway toward the floodlights.

Swift half
Two favoured haunts are the *Sir Arthur Conan Doyle*, on Doyle's Corner, with its open fire, cinema memorabilia and substantial lunches, and the neighbouring *Hut*, 159 Phibsborough Road, which has a preservation order on its mahogany bar fittings. The *Bohemian House*, on the corner of Phibsborough and the North Circular, has a large black-and-white photo mural of classic Irish internationals of the Fifties and Sixties. There are three bars inside the ground.

In the net
For all the latest Bohs news, including match reports and collated features from newspapers and other media, look no further than the unofficial site at: www.isfa.com/server/web/bohs.

Shelbourne

Tolka Park, Richmond Road
Capacity 10,500 (9,500 seated)
Colours All red with white trim
League champions 1926, 1929, 1931, 1944, 1947, 1953, 1962, 1992, 2000
Cup winners 1939, 1960, 1963, 1993, 1996–97, 2000

The Shels play in Dublin's most pleasant soccer ground, Tolka Park. Shelbourne have always suffered from their reputation as a big-money club, but much of this money has been wisely invested in an all-seater ground that has since become the prototype for other Irish clubs to follow.

The biggest Dublin team before the north-south division – Shelbourne won three all-Irish cups – the Shels went through some bleak times in the Seventies and early Eighties before the current influx of new money. Although Tolka Park is a short bus ride from Dalymount's terraced housing in Phibsborough, Shelbourne's traditional fan base is in the quiet southern district of Harold's Cross, where the club played for most of the Eighties while Tolka was being refurbished.

Since then the club has acquired a reputation as a cup team, denying both St Patrick's and Derry City the double by scoring late goals in the finals of FAI Cup 1996 and 1997. The boot was on the other foot in 1997/98, when the Shels were in the running for three trophies – and came second in them all. The following season, under new coach Dermot Keely, and having to play their home tie at Tranmere for fear of crowd trouble, the Shels went 3–0 up against Rangers in qualifying for the UEFA Cup, before losing 5–3.

Mediocrity followed in the league that year, but in 1999/2000 all the club's investments paid off. Shelbourne's rock-solid defence, with Welsh 'keeper Steve Williams outstanding, ensured there were only two defeats all season and enabed the team to finish 11 points clear of free-scoring Cork City. Just to put the icing on the cake, the Shels added the FAI Cup to their haul, beating Bohemians 1–0 with a goal from Pat Fenlon in a replayed final, after the first game had finished goalless.

Here we go!

Bus #3, #11 or #16 from O'Connell Street. Allow 15mins and alight in Drumcondra just by the narrow Tolka river.

Swift half

The *Cat & Cage*, 74 Upper Drumcondra Road, a ten-minute walk from Tolka Park, is a fans' pub with its own soccer team and a huge pull-down TV screen for Sky Sports. Dramatist Sean O'Casey was a regular here. *Fagan's*, on the corner of Botanic Avenue and Lower Drumcondra Road, is more rough and ready but nearer the ground. The **supporters' bar** by the main entrance to Tolka Park is open evenings and matchdays.

In the net

The club's **official website** remains one of the best in Ireland – nice and quick but regularly updated and with great depth, the links section being particularly comprehensive. The site is at: www.connect.ie/users/shels/shels.htm.

St Patrick's Athletic

Richmond Park, 125 Emmett Road, Inchicore
Capacity 7,000
Colours Red-and-white shirts, white shorts
League champions 1952, 1955–56, 1990, 1996, 1998–99
Cup winners 1959, 1961

The recent success of this family-run club has been a popular one. Three titles in four years, ambitious plans for an all-seater

Trim and proper – like a lot of Dublin grounds, Shelbourne's Tolka Park has been improved

Friendly fire – St Pat's meet Lazio, 1999

'Stadium of Light' across the road from their current home at Richmond Park, all at a club that nearly went bankrupt the year they won the title in 1990, when they were playing at a greyhound stadium in Harold's Cross. A committed squad of players and a small, dedicated staff dug in, moved back to the club's home ground Richmond Park at Inchicore, and won the title again in 1996 – then twice more.

Behind much of this progress has been former player Pat Dolan who, as commercial manager, wrote and distributed influential documents on how to improve Ireland's league scene. Team boss Brian Kerr went on to work wonders with Ireland's Under-20 side, so Dolan himself took over in the dugout in 1997.

St Pat's then won the league in consecutive seasons, both times on the last

day. In 1997/98, trailing Shelbourne in the league, they came to the final game knowing that even a win might not be good enough. News that the Shels were 2–0 down to Dundalk spread to Kilkenny, where St Pat's had taken an early lead. Kilkenny then drew level, which would have given Shelbourne the title, only for captain Eddie Gormley to hit a late shot which deflected off a defender to give Dolan's boys the title.

By 1998/99 Liam Buckley had replaced Dolan, who had moved up to become managing director. After a narrow defeat to Celtic in Europe, St Pat's concentrated on the league, in which Cork were their nearest rivals. The strikeforce of Trevor Molloy and Ian Gilzean proved the difference, the title being won by a goal from Canadian Jeff Clarke to seal the vital three points against doomed Bray.

Alas, indifferent form in the first half of the 1999/2000 season prompted Buckley's departure in December and the return of Dolan to the dugout. A sixth-place finish was disappointing for a team that had threatened to dominate the domestic game for a sustained spell, and with Molloy decamping to Bohemians in the close season, Dolan has some work to do again.

Here we go!

Take bus #51B or #78A from O'Connell Bridge to the stop outside the stadium, allowing 15mins. A taxi from Heuston Station would take less than half that and cost IR£4.

Swift half

As well as being Ireland's leading club, St Pat's can boast Dublin's best football bar. The friendly, intimate *McDowell's*, right by the main turnstiles at Richmond Park, has old club photos dating back to 1911/12, Sky Sports on the television and free sandwiches after the game.

In the net

The club runs an excellent **official website**, with graphics and layout that would not be out-of-place on an English Premiership site, at: homepage.tinet.ie/~saints/.

Groundhopping

With the bigger clubs switching home matches to Friday or Saturday evenings, visitors to Dublin often get the chance to sample a game at one of the city's smaller grounds on a Sunday afternoon. It may not be the perfect antidote to the previous night's excesses, but it will be different...

🌣 Bray Wanderers

Carlisle Grounds, Bray, Co Wicklow
Capacity 6,500 (2,500 seated)
Colours Green shirts, white shorts
Cup winners 1990, 1999

The most appealing groundhop is to the end of the DART line down by the sea. Here you'll find a team as eccentric as their location – FAI Cup winners in 1999 after an epic three-game marathon that ended with a 2–1 win over Finn Harps, Bray Wanderers were also relegated after only a season in the top flight.

Relegation was a double blow considering the much-needed improvements that had been made to their modest ground, with a new stand on the railway side and a School of Excellence run in conjunction with Newcastle United. Happily, the team responded to adversity by bouncing back at the first attempt, winning the first-division title in 1999/2000, and also reaching the semi-finals of Ireland's League Cup competition.

There are plans for a new clubhouse but, for the time being, visitors have to make do with the authentic trappings of provincial Irish football – ladies dispensing apple cake in the tea hut and the smell of *Ralgex* and cheap tobacco. Bray's 1990 appearance in Europe, against Trabzonspor after their domestic cup win that year, is documented in Kodak form in the hut.

The Carlisle Grounds are a short walk from the southern terminus of the DART line, about 30mins from the centre.

🌣 Home Farm Fingal

Whitehall, 97A Swords Road, Dublin 9
Capacity 3,000
Colours Blue shirts, red shorts
Cup winners 1975

This former nursery club for Goodison Park was known briefly as Home Farm Everton until 1999. Despite a long-standing tradition of turning out good young players, the club was unable to produce the goods, either on the pitch or for export, during its four-year association with the Merseyside outfit. (Ironically, the most famous player produced here is still Ronnie Whelan, who starred for Liverpool.)

Home Farm played at Tolka Park until 1990, when they moved up to Whitehall in the far north of Dublin. The bleak surroundings – narrow stone terracing, one crumbling main stand – are in tandem with the mid-table, lower-flight football the team have been playing of late.

Buses #3, #16, #16A, #41 and #41A run from the city centre via Whitehall in the direction of Dublin Airport. Allow a good 20mins. As there are no pubs in the immediate vicinity, fans tend to drink in the *Cat & Cage*, near Tolka Park. You'll find a social club bar in the main stand.

🌣 University College Dublin

Belfield Park, Stillorgan
Capacity 5,500 (800 seated)
Colours All sky blue
Cup winners 1984

Formerly called Catholic University FC, this team of students plays League of Ireland football of varying quality, depending on the footballing skills of the season's intake. Pressure is not a watchword in the UCD changing room. Still, the club won the FAI Cup, 2–1 in a replayed final against Shamrock Rovers, in 1984. That autumn, the eventual Cup-Winners' Cup victors Everton were held to a goalless draw in

Dublin and a 1–0 win at Goodison. Prior to 2000/01, this was UCD's solitary European performance.

Another decent season in 1998/99 encouraged the club to take steps to generate more support on the campus. Five hundred bucket seats were put in, and home fixtures moved to Friday nights. There are further plans to move to the Belfield Bowl, a natural amphitheatre the other side of the university.

General manager Dr Tony O'Neill, who had done so much to maintain UCD's top-flight status over the years, died at the start of the 1999/2000 season, but the team he helped to build finished fourth in the league, earning themselves a place in the Intertoto Cup. 'A'-Level students contemplating their university application forms should note that not many campus teams offer the prospect of playing in Europe.

Belfield is a fair way from Dublin city centre – take **bus #10** from Phoenix Park and allow 30mins. Once it drops you on the Stillorgan Road by the main entrance, you'll see the **Montrose Hotel** on the other side of the pedestrian bridge from the college, with its bar offering set lunches and Irish cabaret.

Eat, drink, sleep…

Bars and clubs

The **pub** is at the centre of Irish life and Dublin has over a thousand. Some are large, ornate places, others are binge holes, many serve food, a fair number have live music – but all will slowly serve thick, creamy pints of Guinness, where it tastes best, at around IR£2 a pint. Beamish and Murphys are its competitors, Smithwicks a popular bitter, while lagers are normally limited to Harp, Heineken or Carlsberg. Irish whiskeys such as Jameson's are served in larger measures than in the UK.

Pubs are generally open Mon–Sat 10.30am–11.30pm, and from 12.30pm on Sundays, when doors close 2–4pm,

although you can probably stay drinking through. Between October and April, pubs close 30mins earlier.

In Dublin, the Temple Bar area by the Liffey has a lively pub atmosphere, perhaps a little trendy for some tastes.

Note that clubs cannot sell alcohol past 2am, and generally close by 3am.

All Sports Café, Fleet Street. Lively pub in the Temple Bar area, with plenty of big TV screens, Tex-Mex pub-grub, and regular happy hours. Open until 12.30 am Fri–Sat, 11pm Sun–Thurs.

Kehoe's, 9 South Anne Street (off Grafton Street). Smoky old bar slowly filling with shoppers, workers and drinkers of all shapes, ages and sizes, with rows of snugs for that intimate drink. Above all, Niall Quinn's favourite hostelry.

The Kitchen, East Essex Street. U2's expensively furnished nightclub, with designer decor and decent sounds. Downstairs from the *Clarence Hotel* in Temple Bar.

Mulligan's, 8 Poolbeg St. Said to serve the best Guinness in Dublin, this traditional pub has two floors and no fewer than four bar areas. You may be asked if you want your Guinness cold – you don't. Near Tara Street station.

Ri Ra, Dame Court. The hottest club in town, with revival nights during the week and serious dance action at weekends. Attached to the *Globe* pub, which provides clubbers with a much-needed chill-out room. Admission IR£5–8.

Restaurants

The Nineties have seen a huge variety of restaurants spring up in Dublin, especially in the Temple Bar and St Stephen's Green areas. If you're staying in a B&B, a huge Irish breakfast and a late, cheapish pub lunch will probably keep you going for the rest of the day. Seafood and vegetables should be deliciously fresh.

Beshoff's, 14 Westmoreland St. A tiled palace of fish and chips, with various similar combinations.

The national stadium – Lansdowne Road

62 Lansdowne Road
Capacity (for soccer internationals) 34,000 all-seated

Until Ireland's football team finds its own place at a new national arena (and in 2000 there were rival plans to build an 80,000-seater, all-purpose stadium and a 45,000-seater dedicated to football), it has to pay its dues on rugby's home turf, Lansdowne Road.

Through the gloom – Lansdowne shows off its lights

The FAI's rental arrangement with the Rugby Football Union has been a successful one for both parties since the former moved from Dalymount Park in 1971. Even at Irish soccer's lowest ebb, Dalymount had become too rough and too cramped for international matches. Lansdowne Road was spacious but homely, and an impressive new east stand – built before the Charlton boom years – gave the stadium a grandeur worthy of the major occasion.

Lansdowne was also handily located near Dublin port and right on the DART line for supporters arriving from Dún Laoghaire. Alas, the ground's convenience was cruelly exposed when right-wing English fans eluded security cordons, ripped up seats and hurled debris on their compatriots below, stopping a friendly international in 1995.

That match had been an evening kick-off under Lansdowne's new floodlights. In 1990, a European Championship qualifier involving the same potentially abrasive sets of fans had taken place without incident in Lansdowne's convivial afternoon atmosphere. Those were the days when the ground would be full even for a friendly, when it was party time and everyone wanted to join in. Now the party is simmering down and all the lights are on – and it might take something more than new seats to generate the same kind of atmosphere.

Lansdowne Road is three DART stops from central **Connolly station**. The train service is suspended for 20mins before and after kick-off to allow pedestrians across the tracks. North Terrace ticket-holders should arrive via Havelock Square, those for the South Terrace via Lansdowne Road.

The immediate area around the stadium is usually fenced off, so the best pubs are around a 10min walk from the ground – **Slattery's**, 62 Grand Canal Street, is the best known. You're almost bound to spot a player after the game here. **Paddy Flaherty's** at 51 Haddington Road and **Brett's** (otherwise known as the *Lansdowne Bar*), 14 Bath Avenue, are old favourites, the latter covered in soccer souvenirs.

Inside the ground the **Lansdowne Pavilion**, behind the east stand, is open before and after the game. You'll find a large, bare bar downstairs, with hot beef rolls sold in the hallway, and a carpeted bar upstairs whose walls illustrate the history of Irish rugby.

Cheap, central, spacious late-night dining. Open until 11pm Sun–Thurs, 3am Fri–Sat.

Bewley's, 78–79 Grafton St. Classic weekend round-the-clock breakfast haunt, now transformed into a very reasonable spot for set lunches and dinners as well. Open Sun–Thurs 8am–1am, Fri–Sat 7.30am–5am.

Elephant & Castle, 18 Temple Bar. Low-key, popular and unpretentious eaterie with daily specials. Open from breakfast time until midnight, from noon on Sundays.

Gallagher's Boxty House, 20–21 Temple Bar. Beer stew, potato pancakes and other hearty traditional fare, served in Irish country kitchen decor. You'll be sharing one of the long tables with complete strangers.

The Old Dublin, 90–91 Francis St. Tucked away among the junk shops in the Liberties area. An atmospheric place replete with open fireplaces, its speciality is a strange but excellent combination of fresh Irish fish done in Russian or Scandinavian styles. Pricey, but try the set menu at IR£10 per head between 6pm and 7pm. Open Mon–Fri 12.30–2.30pm, Mon–Sat 6–11pm.

Accommodation

For a reasonably cheap, centrally located room in Dublin your best bet is to try one of the better hostels. Hotels are either expensive or very expensive, while bed & breakfasts tend to be out of town, or centred in the Ballsbridge area.

Whichever option you go for, be sure to book a room well in advance. Most places charge a little more in summer and over rugby weekends. Dublin's **Tourism Centre** in Suffolk Street (details on p.331) and tourist offices at Dublin Airport and Dún Laoghaire can all book you a room for 10% deposit by credit card, deducted from your bill at the end of your stay.

Avalon House, 55 Aungier Street (☎01/475 0001, fax 01/475 0303). Friendly hostel near St Stephen's Green with singles at IR£20, twins

IR£30 and dorm beds IR£13. Modest breakfast included. No curfew. Decent café downstairs.

Berkeley Court, Lansdowne Road (☎01/660 1711, fax 01/668 6033). The place to stay and be seen when there's an international, although rooms in this elegant, period hotel will cost you some IR£185 a double, IR£165 a single, breakfast not included. Non-residents welcome in the luxurious bar. Short walk from Lansdowne Road DART station.

Isaac's Hostel, 2–5 Frenchman's Lane (☎01/855 5660, fax 01/855 6524). Well-organised, comfortable and friendly hostel just around the corner from the main bus station. Single rooms at IR£19, twins IR£32, dorm beds IR£9. No curfew, but room lockout 11am–5pm. Self-catering kitchen and restaurant. No credit cards.

Lansdowne, 27 Pembroke Road (☎01/668 2522, fax 01/668 5585). Comfortable hotel within shouting distance of Lansdowne Road stadium, popular with visiting sports fans. Satellite TV and bath/shower in every room. Doubles around IR£80 including breakfast. Most credit cards.

Wellington Hotel, 21–22 Wellington Quay (☎01/677 9315, fax 01/677 9387). Ideal place to plonk yourself in the Temple Bar area, overlooking the Ha'Penny Bridge. Perfect for bar-hoppers, en with the Fitzsimmons next-door for a late, last nightcap. IR£50 per person midweek, IR£60 weekends.

Italy

Federazione Italiana Giuoco Calcio Via Gregorio Allegri 14, CP 2450, I-00198 Roma ☎06/84911 Fax 06/849 1256 E-mail none

League champions Lazio **Cup winners** Lazio **Promoted** Vicenza, Atalanta, Brescia, Napoli **Relegated** Torino, Venezia, Cagliari, Piacenza

European participants 2000/01 Lazio, Juventus (UCL); AC Milan, Internazionale (UCL qualifiers); Parma, Roma, Fiorentina (UEFA Cup); Perugia, Udinese (Intertoto Cup)

Nowhere in Europe does football matter as much as in Italy. Every Sunday the fate of the nation – not to say billions of lire and civic pride – hangs in the balance. The Italian game, *calcio*, is a weekly celebration of noise and colour, fed by a media hyberbole which would put an American presidential campaign to shame.

Leading politicians, captains of industry, Mafia bosses – all have used the game's exaggerated importance for their own ends. Football's remarkable niche in Italian life sealed Mussolini's popularity in the Thirties. More recently, it allowed media mogul Silvio Berlusconi to climb to the top and become Italian prime minister. The most popular club, Juventus, are as important to the Agnelli family as the wheels on their Fiat cars.

For most of the postwar era, the Italian league has been world soccer's shop window, the stage where the greatest talents parade their skills every Sunday. The transfer market is a twice-yearly week of trading in one of Milan's grand hotels, as frenetic as Wall Street, the commodity being not futures or trusts, but footballers.

In Italy, football really can be a matter of life and death, as sadly proved by occasional fatal incidents which raise serious questions about Italy's ultra gangs – the fans

Bright new hope – Stefano Fiore, hero of Euro 2000

who provide much of the noise and colour essential to every match, and who receive official favour (including match tickets) from many of the biggest clubs. In fact, the ultra phenomenon harks back to the beginnings of the Italian game in sixteenth century Florence. Now played out for tourists

Only the lonely – Alessandro del Piero rues his misses after Italy had lost the Euro 2000 final

every summer, this original *calcio* was a bright, loud and bloody carnival involving fifty Florentine aristocrats violently rucking for a ball, originally a decapitated head.

When the modern version was introduced by English sailors and traders four hundred years later, it was to become the people's art, the aristocracy being left to conduct their business off the pitch. The English influence can be still be seen in the three north Italian cities where the imported game first developed: Genoa and AC Milan carry Anglicised club names, while Juventus of Turin play in a black-and-white striped shirt originally derived from that of Notts County.

Genoa dominated the first annual Italian championships, played for at the turn of the century. Their mantle was soon taken by AC Milan and that club's rival off-shoot, Internazionale. The championship was decided on a north/south/central play-off until the formation of a national league in 1929. Behind the new league lay the workings of a man who did much to hasten football's development in Italy between the wars – Vittorio Pozzo.

Pozzo transformed Italian football. From his early experience in England he brought tactical know-how to Italy, then far behind the Danubian game of their Central European rivals Austria, Czechoslovakia and Hungary. An innovative coach of the national team, the *azzurri*, he couped his players up in regimented training camps, *in ritiro*, away from the trappings of city life. On the field, he introduced the attacking centre-half, a creator and destroyer, a concept embodied in Luisito Monti, an Argentine of Italian extraction whose rugged talents were a prime factor in Italy winning the World Cup they hosted in 1934. If Monti was the anti-hero, then the hero was Giuseppe Meazza, a fast, delicate forward who starred for both Milan clubs. A likable rogue, the popular *Peppino* would receive the posthumous accolade of having the San Siro stadium renamed after him.

At the World Cup, the first to be held in Europe, neither the Austrians nor the Czechs could overcome the awesome Monti, nor cope with his fellow Italo-Argentine wingers, Guaita and Orsi; with a goal from each, Italy beat Austria 1–0 in

Basics

EU citizens require only a **passport** to enter Italy, as do Americans, Canadians, Australians and New Zealanders.

The Italian currency is the **lira** (plural lire), abbreviated as 'L' or 'Lit'. There are L50, L100, L200 and L500 coins, and notes for L1,000, L2,000, L5,000, L10,000, L50,000, L100,000 and L500,000. There are around L3,000 to £1.

Italy is still very much a **cash economy**. Major cities have *Bancomat* machines for cash advances, but credit-card payment for goods and services is relatively rare. Banks are the best places to **change money**, open Mon–Fri 8.30am–1.45pm & 3.30–4.30pm, with restricted working hours before a public holiday.

By law you must **take your receipt** for every purchase. In your change you may find a *gettone* – a token worth L200 for jukeboxes and phone calls from bars. Other coin phones take L100, L200 and L500 pieces. Most public phones will only accept **phonecards**, L5,000, L10,000 or L15,000 from newsstands and *tabacchi* stores designated by a blue 'T' sign. Break off the corner of the card before use.

Calling abroad from Italy is expensive – off-peak times are Mon–Sat 10pm–8am and all day Sunday. To get an international line from inside the country, dial 00. To call Italy from abroad, dial 39, then the city code, which must now have a zero prefixing it: Rome is 06, Milan 02, Turin 011, Florence 055, Genoa 010 and Naples 081. The codes are the same inland.

The first thing to know about Italian **trains** is that you must validate your ticket in the orange machines by the platform before you board. Services are cheap, frequent and comfortable. *Pendolino*, *Eurocity* and *Intercity* trains connect major towns and require both a reservation and a supplement.

Italian **accommodation** is more expensive than its French or Spanish counterpart. In most towns a double room in a two-star hotel (*albergho*) will cost about L100,000. A cheaper option is a *pensione* – a family-run guesthouse where a nominal fee is charged for use of the shower in the corridor. Most of these places will ask guests to be in by around 1am, but a double should run to no more than L60,000.

Italian **cuisine** is claimed by many to be the best in the world. It is certainly not cheap. A stand-up *pizzeria* will charge around L7,000 for a basic slice and up to L10,000 for anything fancier. A *trattoria* – usually slightly cheaper than a *ristorante* – will have first pasta courses at L10,000, with the main meat course weighing in at L15–20,000. You will also be charged *pane e coperto*, bread and cover charge, and *servizio* of 10%.

Bars are generally clean, chrome affairs, not designed for passing time in. Standing in a bar for hours is as senseless to an Italian as standing in a hardware store. Alcohol is consumed in good taste, as part of a meal, and wine is (deservedly) the most popular drink. Excessive beer drinking, even if carried out with decorum, is frowned upon. Let none of this deter you. Go to the cash desk (*cassa*), order your drink and pay, then slap your receipt (*scontrino*) on the counter to attract the barman's attention.

Ask for a *birra alla spina* ('beer on draught') and you'll be given a choice of *piccolo*, *media* or *grande* sizes. Of the local brews, **Peroni** and **Nastro Azzurro** are fairly bland but **Moretti**, from the north-eastern region of Friuli, has a distinctive flavour. The national spirit, *grappa*, made from wine-making residues, must be taken in the knowledge that it will leave you a babbling wreck.

Italian **nightlife** is generally dear, derivative and disappointing. Even if you avoid the L5–15,000 entrance fee by negotiation at the door to a club, you may be charged for membership (*una tessera*), not to say twice usual bar prices inside.

the semi-final and Czechoslovakia 2–1 after extra time in the final.

The event was a propaganda victory for Fascist leader Benito Mussolini, but it also left a legacy of first-class, modern municipal stadia in many of Italy's major cities.

By the time of the 1938 World Cup in France, Pozzo had discarded most of the 1934 squad, recruiting their replacements from his country's 1936 Olympic gold medal-winning team. His masterstroke was to pair Meazza with Silvio Piola, the Lazio striker who would score five goals in the tournament, including a brace in Italy's 4–2 win over Hungary in the final.

World War II saw the rise of a great Torino side, five times title winners, and captained by their chief goalscorer, Valentino Mazzola. All the team would perish in the Superga air disaster of 1949, when a plane carrying Torino back from a friendly in Lisbon crashed into the side of the Basilica overlooking Turin. The dead were accorded a state funeral.

It would take the Italian national team years to recover from the loss at Superga, but there were other factors at work, not least an influx of star foreigners which accompanied the country's postwar economic boom. When Sweden won Olympic soccer gold at the 1948 Games, AC Milan went out and bought their entire forward trio. To counteract their talents and those of John Charles, Juan Schiaffino, Kurt Hamrin and others, Italian defences of the Fifties adopted the rigid *catenaccio* defensive system of strict man-to-man marking with a *libero* or sweeper behind.

League games became low-scoring affairs, dominated by strong defences and quick counter-attacking. After the demise of the great Real Madrid of the late Fifties, Italian discipline would bring European Cup success for both Milan clubs. It was the Internazionale coach Helenio Herrera who perfected *catenaccio*, his strategies aided and abetted by the brilliant overlapping fullback Giacinto Facchetti and by training methods as strict as any in Pozzo's day. Herrera constructed an infernal defensive

trap to frustrate the home side, but the new generation of fans who followed *la Grande Inter* across Europe didn't care.

A fourth successive poor World Cup showing by the *azzurri* in 1962 led to a ban on foreign imports to the Italian league two years later. For the national side, worse was to follow with defeat by North Korea at Ayresome Park in 1966 – causing a World Cup exit as ignominious as any in the competition's history, and the team to be met by a hailstorm of rotten tomatoes on their return to Italy.

Domestically, however, the ban on foreigners allowed home talents to flourish, like those of Gianni Rivera and Sandro Mazzola in the midfields of Milan and Inter, respectively. Mazzola, son of Valentino who had perished in the Superga crash, would play a key rôle in the event which signalled Italy's return to the top drawer of the international game – victory in the 1968 European Championship. As at the World Cup 34 years earlier, Italy's win (over Yugoslavia in the final) owed a little to luck and much to their hosting of the tournament. But the point had been made – the *azzurri* were a force to be reckoned with once again.

Both Mazzola and Rivera would be used in Italy's run to the final of the 1970 World Cup. In the heat and altitudes of Mexico, each would play for 45 minutes. With the powerful, prolific Luigi Riva (whose goals had helped Cagliari to a surprising league title that year), the Italian side were Europe's best in the tournament, but still no match for the incomparable Brazil of Pelé, Tostão and Jairzinho.

As the Seventies went on, the absence of foreign stars from the domestic game began to have negative as well as positive side-effects. Italian clubs lost the creative edge they needed to compete in European competition, and at the 1974 World Cup, the *azzurri*, with their rigidly defensive formation, had no answer to the fluid 'Total Football' of the Dutch and West Germans.

Juventus, nine times title winners between 1972 and 1986, were Italy's silver lining. The team provided the core of the *azzurri* side who came good under Enzo Bearzot at the 1978 and 1982 World Cups. Paolo Rossi, Roberto Bettega, Franco Causio, Gaetano Scirea and Marco Tardelli were the keys to a fourth-place finish in Argentina in 1978, and to an exhilarating run to the 1982 final – after a stultifyingly slow start – in Spain. After gaining revenge over Brazil in a heart-stopping 3–2 win at the second-round group stage, Italy sealed their third World Cup with a 3–1 victory over West Germany in Madrid. Rossi, who in the mid-Seventies had served a two-year ban for his involvement in a betting scandal, emerged as the tournament's top scorer with six goals.

By then, foreign imports had been allowed back into Italy, and two in particular dominated the Eighties – Frenchman Michel Platini at Juventus and Diego Maradona at Napoli. Platini's remarkable goalscoring prowess from midfield kept the 'Zebras' at the top in the middle part of the decade, not just in Italy but in Europe, where they mounted a serious challenge to the then-dominant English game and its prime exponents, Liverpool. The face-off between the two clubs for the 1985 European Cup turned into disaster, however, as English hooligans, Italian ultras and Belgian disorganisation combined in the death of 39 (mainly Italian) fans before the match, then played and almost irrelevantly won by Juventus.

If Platini's skills were mesmerising, Maradona's success with Napoli was no less than the stuff of fantasy. His team's title win in 1987 marked the first time the Italian championship had been won by a team from the deep, impoverished south – a historical footnote given added potency by the regional rivalry that had characterised the game in Italy from its very earliest days.

Napoli's success (they won the title again in 1990) was all the more extraordinary considering the contemporary strength of the two Milan clubs. Media mogul Silvio Berlusconi had bought a bankrupt AC Milan in 1986, ostensibly as a tool with which his Canale 5 TV station could challenge the state monopoly of televised football. But the kind of money he made available exceeded expectations, attracting the Dutch trio of Ruud Gullit, Frank Rijkaard and Marco van Basten to the club. Berlusconi didn't just want results – he wanted his viewers entertained. Under coach Arrigo Sacchi, Milan played a fast, attacking style that took the game to the opposing side. Their great *libero*, Franco Baresi, played in front of the defence rather than behind it, while their full-back Paolo Maldini made incisive runs down the flank. In the 1989 European Cup, Milan beat Real Madrid 5–0 in the semi-final and Steaua Bucharest 4–0 in the final. Italy had seen nothing like it in 40 years.

Under Milanese influence, zonal marking slowly replaced *catenaccio* and goals

Gentleman's agreement – Dino Zoff quit 'as a matter of honour'

New boss, old ideas – Giovanni Trapattoni

While Sacchi's *azzurri* prepared for the USA, Capello's Milan won the Italian title three times between 1992 and 1994 – their 4–0 whitewash of Barcelona in the 1994 European Cup final an awesome demonstration of the chasm in class that existed between the Italian league and the rest of Europe. Every year between 1989 and 1995, there were at least two Italian clubs in the three European finals. In 1996 there was only one – and although Juventus won the Champions' League, the two stars who had helped them win it, Gianluca Vialli and Fabrizio Ravanelli, were playing in England's Premiership within months of their victory in the final over Ajax. Despite the vast sums earned from Europewide TV rights and sponsorship, Juve could no longer afford the high-figure salaries demanded by Italian stars – England could. In the summer of 1996, Sacchi made a string of unforced team changes which caused Italy to lose to the Czech Republic and ultimately depart England before the knockout stage of the European Championship. Less than a year later, with the *azzurri* showing signs of revival under Cesare Maldini, not one of Europe's club competitions was won by an Italian team.

In 1997, changes in Italian law obliged clubs to turn themselves from informal associations into limited companies, the first to float on the stock exchange being Sergio Cragnotti's Lazio, whose fine league performance and Cup-Winners' Cup triumph in 1999 proved that the days of the Italian soccer mogul were far from over.

Lazio's rise was accompanied by a decline in the fortunes of some of Italy's bigger names, Juventus and Inter among them, too many of their stars – both Italian and imported – burnt out after the exertions of the 1998 World Cup. Italy's performance in France had been disap-

flowed in the Italian league. It made great television, and coincided with Italy hosting the 1990 World Cup, the preparations for which saw billions of lire spent on renovating the stadia used in 1934, while all-new grounds were built in Turin and Bari.

Italy began as favourites, and played like them – with rising star Roberto Baggio, a surprise find in goalscorer Totó Schillaci, and Baresi sublime in defence. It was Maradona who stopped them, in a tense semi-final in Naples, of all places. Just as Baresi and Baggio would do in the 1994 World Cup final, Roberto Donadoni missed in the penalty shoot-out, his unlucky number 17 shirt splashed across the front page of every morning paper, sinking into the turf in grief.

The 1994 side was coached by Sacchi, who had quit Milan, leaving former international Fabio Capello to take charge.

pointing, a half-fit Alessandro del Piero and half-used Roberto Baggio failing to inspire a team which, for all Maldini's promises before the tournament, withdrew into its defensive shell once the serious business got underway – a penalty shoot-out defeat by the hosts in the quarter-finals was the seemingly inevitable consequence.

Dino Zoff took over after the finals, and did a decent enough job in getting Italy through the Euro 2000 qualifiers. But Italian clubs had their worst season in European competition for 13 years in 1999/2000, prompting the *Gazzetta dello Sport* to run a two-week long series of articles on *il crisi di calcio*. Its verdict was familiar – too many foreigners, too much emphasis on fitness rather than skill and, above all, too much money.

So it was that Zoff's side went to Euro 2000 with the lowest expectations of any Italian squad in living memory. Some of the team's pre-tournament displays had been dreadful, yet an opening win over Turkey gave some cause for cautious optimism, and when Belgium were despatched in Brussels, the Italians found a new idol in the Udinese playmaker Stefano Fiore, scorer of what turned out to be the goal of the tournament.

In the quarter-finals, an under-strength Romania were comfortably beaten 2–0, setting up a semi-final against Holland in Rotterdam. This was where the Italians were meant to say their farewells, return home with their heads held high, and leave the world to enjoy a France–Holland final. But Zoff and his players had not read the script. Following the dismissal of defender Gianluca Zambrotta for two yellow cards, Italy played for 87 minutes with ten men, and kept most of them behind the ball, for most of the time. Goalkeeper Francesco Toldo saved Frank de Boer's penalty to keep the score at 0–0, then saved three more Dutch spot-kicks in the shoot-out to make himself a national hero – and book his team a place in the final.

Against the French, Italy produced a more attacking performance than their catenaccio-inspired semi-final display. They took a deserved lead through Marco Delvecchio, and would have added to it had Alessandro del Piero shown more composure in front of goal. Then, in the last minute of stoppage time, an uncharacteristic defensive lapse allowed Sylvain Wiltord in to equalise, and there was a certain inevitability about David Trezeguet's 'golden goal' winner for France in extra time.

As the French danced in jubilation, Italian bodies slumped to the turf. But the tale which unfolded that night in Rotterdam was only the first act in a very Italian saga. On the day the squad arrived back home, Silvio Berlusconi criticised Zoff's tactics and the following morning, an indignant Zoff resigned. Italian FA officials tried unsuccessfully to get the coach to change his mind, before appointing Giovanni Trapattoni as his successor. The soap opera, it seems, must go on.

Essential vocabulary

Hello/goodbye *Ciao*
Yes *Sì*
No *No*
Two beers, please *Due alla spina, per favore*
Thank you *Grazie*
Men's *Uomini*
Women's *Donne*
Where is the stadium? *Dovè lo stadio?*
What is the score? *Come siamo?*
Referee *Il arbitro*
Offside *Fuori gioco*

Match practice

The first week of September is the big kick-off for a league season that lasts until the first week of June, with a short break for Christmas and New Year – although note that the start of the 2000/01 was put back to early October because of Italy's involvement in the Olympic football tournament in Australia. A round of league matches (*giornata*), takes place on Sunday afternoons, with kick-off time usually 3pm. One match will be at 8.30pm for live television coverage, while teams involved in upcoming midweek European action play on the preceding Saturday evening, usually also at 8.30pm.

The build-up to each Sunday's match starts on the previous Monday. While the media are awash with rumour and counter-rumour concerning the upcoming fixtures, fans dutifully swamp the training grounds before heading off to rehearse their stadium routines back in town.

The grounds begin to fill up from late on Sunday morning. For derby games, the gates may be opened four or five hours before kick-off to allow fans time to put up their banners.

At the turnstiles, security is often tight. Coins and cigarette lighters may be confiscated, and you'll catch your first glimpse of Italy's much-maligned *carabinieri*, the branch of the police responsible for keeping public order. Turnstile searches aren't the only reason to leave yourself plenty of time before kick-off – whatever the quality of the match, you'll be treated to a veritable pageant in the stadium that will live with you long after the details of the game itself have faded from memory.

Remember that Italian football is as exaggerated as everything else in Italy. Outbreaks of violence aren't unknown, but it's easy for the visitor to misinterpret aggressive gestures as provocation – when in fact all you're witnessing is an uncontrollable outburst of local pride.

On full-time (and often sooner), fans of the losing side will take their frustrations out on their mopeds, and are quickly home to watch the highlights on TV. Another Sunday is over – at least until Monday morning.

A different league

The top drawer of Italy's *Lega Calcio*, *Serie A*, has 18 teams. The one that wins the title earns the right to wear *lo scudetto*, the green, white and red shield, on their shirt for the whole of the following season, and the championship itself is often referred to simply as *lo scudetto*. Those who are crowned champions ten times are awarded a gold star above their badge – Juventus are the only team with two stars.

The bottom four clubs change places with the top four from the 20-team *Serie B*. Teams level on points have their position determined by goal difference, but promotion, relegation and European berths cannot be decided this way – a play-off (*spareggio*) being used in these circumstances. These play-offs are normally two-legged affairs, but at the end of the 1999/2000 season, to avoid fixture congestion ahead of Euro 2000, Inter and Parma played a single game to determine Italy's remaining Champions' League qualifying berth, and this format could be repeated in the future.

From *Serie B*, four teams go down to the third division, *Serie C1*, which is divided north-south into two groups, *Girone A* and *B*. The top two from each 18-team *Girone* go up automatically, while those finishing second to fifth play off against each other for one place each. Three teams from each *Girone* drop down, to be replaced by six teams rising from the three-section *Serie C2*. The next rung down is for amateur clubs, known as *dilettanti*.

Up for the cup

La Coppa Italia is a half-hearted affair. Following restructuring in 1999/2000, the competition begins with a group phase involving 32 clubs from *Serie B* and *C*, played in August and September. Lower-placed *Serie A* teams enter at the second-round knockout stage, while the top eight *Serie A* clubs do not enter until the third round.

The quarter-finals, semi-finals and final are all played over two legs, with away goals counting double. As a rule, *la Coppa* generates reasonable crowds only when one of the teams involved in the latter stages has been starved of honours – such as Fiorentina's successful run of 1996 and Lazio's two years later.

Just the ticket

Ticket prices vary widely in Italy. It is possible to stand behind the goal at many

Spectacular displays of fan worship are not confined to the big clubs – this is Bari

grounds with the *ultras* for less than L25,000, while top half-way line seats at the big stadia can cost up to ten times that amount. The major grounds are divided into rings (*anelli*) with varying prices and you should be able to get a decent seat between the *curva* and the middle of the stand for around L50,000. Ticket prices for all games are listed in the day's sports press – worth checking, as clubs frequently reduce prices for unattractive European or Italian cup games, and for end-of-season matches when little is at stake.

For an average *Serie A* game, the sheer size of the stadia means you should be able to buy a ticket at the ground on the day. If you want to make sure in advance, all major clubs now have credit-card ticket phone lines and an increasing number are offering purchase via their official internet sites. You can book via either from abroad, and pick up your tickets once in Italy.

Big derby games will often be declared a sell-out days in advance, but there are *always* tickets available on matchdays. It is always worth going to the official ticket office, as often there are several hundred tickets which have not been claimed or have been returned. If you have no luck there, then it's time to do battle with the touts (*bagarini*) who will have probably already approached you. Haggling is the order of the day, but be wary if the ticket you are offered seems surprisingly cheap – it could well be a fake. The mark-up can be huge at some matches, but rather than accept the first ticket you're offered, get an idea of the going rate first. If you can, avoid the touts who are first up at bus stops and metro stations – they work the football tourist market and most locals will ignore them, preferring instead to do business with the more 'reliable' characters nearer the stadium.

Half-time

No beer is on sale at Italian grounds. Fans get high instead on *caffè borghetti* – small yellow-topped canisters of heavily sugared, spirit-strengthened coffee. There'll be no queue for the hot dogs, either. At half-time Italians either smoke nervously or unwrap sandwiches lovingly packed by their mothers, while vendors selling plastic bottles of soft drinks pass through the crowd.

Action replay

The advent of pay-per-view television means many Italians are having to watch their Sunday games in a bar for the first time. Be warned that *calcio al bar* is a distinctly different experience from the match down the pub, and a million times more complicated. For a start, at most bars the customers eat an ice-cream or drink a coffee while sat in neat rows in front of a giant screen. There will be waiter service and it is generally considered out of order to stand at the bar with a pint and a cigarette while watching the match. Instead you can expect a cover charge of between L5,000 and L10,000 to enter a back room specially assigned to viewing games.

Pay-per-view football is split between two satellite channels, Tele Piu and Stream, each of which has deals with individual clubs for home games. Tele Piu has the rights to Inter, Milan and Juventus, while Stream has Lazio, Roma, Fiorentina and Parma. As you need a separate decoder for each service, few bars will have both Stream and Tele Piu. A Milan supporters' bar may have a subscription for all San Siro fixtures, but will probably not have access to an away match at Lazio, say.

The Sunday night live game is screened by Tele Piu to all its subscribers, regardless of whether they have taken a pay-per-view package.

Mercifully, highlights from all *Serie A* games are available free-to-air from state broadcaster RAI. *Novantesimo Minuto* (90th minute) on Rai Uno at 6.15pm has the goal round-up, while extensive highlights are on *Domenica Sprint* at 8pm on RAI Due, and *Domenica Sportiva* at 11pm, also on RAI Due, has fuller highlights with pundits and scantily clad models adding their opinions to the mix.

Silvio Berlusconi's Mediaset now has the rights to the Champions' League, but most games are expected to be shown on

Stream, with some higher-profile fixtures will be shown on Mediaset's free-to-air channels, Italia Uno or Canel 5. Rights to UEFA Cup matches are sold on a game-by-game basis although RAI tends to end up with most of the matches. Check the morning's press for up-to-date info.

Tele Piu usually has a live English Premiership game on Saturdays at 4pm, with another of the day's games shown 'as live' at 8pm. There is also a goals round-up from the Premiership, Spain and Germany after Tele Piu's Sunday night game. Sky's Monday night match will also be shown on Tele Piu, albeit sometimes delayed.

If you are bored in your hotel room, then a flick through the channels will enable you to find one of scores of late-night football highlights and chat shows on both national and local stations throughout the week. Expect lots of arm-waving and replays of dodgy penalties given to Juventus.

The back page

While all Italian daily newspapers carry a decent-sized sports section, most football fans opt for one of the three daily sports papers, all of which have sizeable readerships, but are prone to defend the region they represent.

La Gazzetta dello Sport (L1,400) is the best-known paper, its pink pages containing both the most reliable information and the best writing. Although based in Milan and devoting extensive coverage to the two teams at the San Siro, the paper offers daily news on every *Serie A* and *Serie B* team, but international news is almost ignored unless it involves a player who has been linked with a move to Italy. You'll find the results of the major European leagues, but that's about it.

Corriere dello Sport (L1,400) is based in Rome but has a northern edition (red masthead as opposed to green) which gives more detailed coverage of Juventus and the Milan duo. *Corriere* has slightly better international coverage and does what it can to out-manoeuvre *Gazzetta* when covering the transfer market.

Tuttosport is based in Turin and its coverage is ludicrously biased towards Juventus – don't believe any of its transfer stories, which would not be out of place in a British tabloid.

The weekly magazine *Guerin Sportivo* (Thursdays, L4,500) has results and standings from across Europe, a full review of the previous week's Italian action and plenty of posters, while *Calcio 2000* (monthly, L7,500) has a well-earned reputation for quality writing – even if you don't have enough Italian to read the lengthy features on the history of the game and tactics, it is packed with stats and has plenty of pull-out posters; the pre-season edition is well worth picking up for its squad lists and team photos.

Rigore (Thursdays, L2,000) is an attempt at a literary look at the game, while *Il Nuovo Calcio* (monthly, L7,500) is a magazine for coaches which is attempting to broaden its appeal.

Finally, if you want to check on the fortunes of Reggiana in *Serie C,* then the new monthly *Calcio di C e D* (L5,900) has all the news on the lower divisions.

Ultra culture

Italy is the home of ultra culture. The movement evolved during the early Seventies and had become an integral part of the game within a decade. The choreography, the colour and the noise of Italian ultras remain unmatched anywhere in the continent, though their fashions have been copied all across Latin America and Southern and Eastern Europe.

Unfortunately, the rise of the ultras has come hand in hand with occasional violence, and the next fan death may push the Italian parliament into taking action to prevent organised gangs travelling to matches. The ultra scene is covered every month in *Supertifo* (L5,000), available at newsstands.

In the net

There is a limited official FA site at: www.figc.it. And the Italian league, the *Lega Calcio*, runs a more than useful site at: www.lega-calcio.it – each *Serie A* and B club has its own area with information on the team, their stadium, and links to their own official sites.

There are now scores of commercial sites offering news and features on the Italian game in English as well as Italian. *GoalNetwork* has editorial contributions from the Rome-based *Irish Times* and *Guardian* correspondent Paddy Angew at www.goalnetwork.com; while *OneFootball* has decent news coverage of all *Serie A* clubs at: www.onefootball.com.

For Italian-language news, the online version of the *Gazzetta* is worth a look despite a rather basic visual design at: www.gazzetta.it. For transfer news, *Calcio Mercato* is fast, covers the market in extraordinary detail, and also carries injury and team news. Some English content is promised soon at: www.calciomercato.com.

Milan

Milan is a true football capital. Its stadium, the San Siro, is one of the world's great arenas, shared by opposing city giants AC Milan and Internazionale, who between them have won nearly 50 European and domestic titles.

The rivalry dates back to 1908, when members of Milan FC formed a breakaway team in protest over the British influence prevalent at the club, which had been founded as Milan Cricket and Football Club in 1899, by Englishman Alfred Edwards. The club became the domain of English sportsmen and well-to-do Milanese, who would meet over cocktails at the *American Bar*. On March 9, 1908, an Italian and Swiss rebel faction met in a backroom of the *Orologio* restaurant near the Piazza del Duomo, intent on breaking away. They decided to call their club Internazionale Milano, after the multi-national nature of their group.

The rivalry began in earnest with five straight wins for Milan FC, a series interrupted when Internazionale romped to a 5–0 victory in 1910. In time, it would be Inter, as they became known (*never* Inter Milan) who would attract the upper crust, while Milan FC (later AC) appealed to the working class. These criteria have shifted again in the Eighties and Nineties, making the rivalry hard to define. Support for either the *nerazzurri* (the blue-and-black stripes of Inter) or *rossoneri* (the thinner, red-and-black stripes of Milan) has never been a matter of geographical location. Arguments are won and lost over the family breakfast table, making the derby more a domestic tug-of-love than a civil war.

Before the breakaway, Milan FC won three Italian championship play-offs, the last in 1907. Within three years the upstarts of Inter were champions, and two decades later, as Ambrosiana-Inter, they would become the first winners of the all-Italian league. Playing at the Arena behind Sforzesco castle, the *nerazzurri* kept one step ahead of their rivals, who by now

were playing in a newly built stadium in the west of the city – the San Siro, whose construction was financed by a former *American Bar* regular from the turn of the century, tyre millionaire Pieró Pirelli.

Never mind that Milan had the stadium – Inter had the players, among them top goalscorer Giuseppe Meazza, who played for his country at the 1934 and 1938 World Cups and, at a time of increasingly overbearing Fascist authority, became a symbol of the city's brash individuality. Ironically, the Arena where Meazza gave spectators so much pleasure was used by the Nazis during World War II to round up and shoot local partisans.

After World War II, Inter moved out into the suburbs to share the San Siro with Milan, leaving the Arena, the oldest surviving stadium to have staged first-class football, to fall into disrepair. (It was renovated in 1996, its main function today being the staging of junior athletics.)

Inter and Milan both won league titles in the early Fifties, and the San Siro crowd witnessed some tense derbies – the legendary 6–5 game of 1949 was the first that current Inter president Massimo Moratti was taken to as a young boy.

Two key figures helped to turn Milanese football into the modern, multi-million pound business it is today. The first was Inter coach Helenio Herrera, a man who manipulated not just his players but also the press and, by extension, the public. During the Sixties his controversial Italo-Spanish rants made football the main talking point and kept the city buzzing, while on the pitch, Inter's European Cup win over Real Madrid in 1964 proved a turning point in the history of the European game – never again would a Spanish giant overshadow its Milanese counterpart.

Now the city would come alive for big nights of European action, and the San Siro on derby day was a place for high society to be seen. The rivalry between the clubs' two inspirational inside-forwards, Milan's

Double trouble – it took two referees to sort out the derby in the 1999/2000 *Coppa Italia*

Gianni Rivera and Inter's Sandro Mazzola, gave the fixture added spice.

The second crucial figure was Silvio Berlusconi. After taking over an ailing AC Milan in 1986, Berlusconi put the club on an entirely different commercial footing from the rest of the Italian game. 'Milan' shops, bars, restaurants and clubs were opened across the city, and star players were contractually tied to give them their blessing. The game, and its prime exponents, became a high-profile commercial tool in Italy's business capital. A Martian could visit Turin and not know the city played football. Not so Milan.

In 1989, the trio of Gullit, van Basten and Rijkaard who'd helped Holland win the 1988 European Championship brought AC Milan their first European title for 20 years. That same year, the trio of Klinsmann, Matthäus and Brehme who would lead West Germany to the 1990 World Cup won the title with Inter – the club's first for a decade. Milan was indubitably

Europe's football capital. The San Siro, renamed the Giuseppe Meazza after the popular figure's death in 1979, was given a hundred billion lire refit in order to host the opening ceremony and five other matches of the 1990 World Cup.

Not long after Italia '90, the *rossoneri* pulled away and won three straight Italian titles. Inter couldn't hold a candle to their rivals' earning power from media and merchandising, and while Berlusconi ruled supreme at Milan, boardroom power struggles crucially weakened Inter. In 1994, Milan won the European Cup in supreme style, with a 4–0 win over Barcelona, while Inter, after a season struggling against the threat of relegation, also won in Europe, beating Salzburg to lift the UEFA Cup. Both sets of supporters celebrated in the traditional way, parading around the Piazza del Duomo – but the chasm in class between the two teams was hard to ignore.

Within three years it was Inter who were back in the spotlight, with the signing of Ronaldo part of Massimo Moratti's grand design to recreate *la grande Inter* of his father's Sixties heyday. While Milan sank ignominiously into mid-table, the *nerazzurri* were the city's sole title contenders for two straight seasons, picking up the 1998 UEFA Cup in the process. Yet the roles were reversed in 1999, when Moratti's Inter sunk without trace and Milan came up on the rails to take the title. The following year, while neither side was capable of keeping up with Lazio and Juventus in the title race, both earned spots in the Champions' League qualifying rounds, offering the prospect of almost weekly European football in the city during the autumn of 2000.

The thrilling fields

 AC Milan

Stadium San Siro, see p.354
Club office Via Turati 3
Colours Red-and-black striped shirts, white shorts
League champions 1901, 1906–07, 1951, 1955, 1957, 1959, 1962, 1968, 1979, 1988, 1992–94, 1996, 1999
Cup winners 1967, 1972–73, 1977
European Cup winners 1963, 1969, 1989–90, 1994
Cup-Winners' Cup winners 1968, 1973

For all the criticism that can justifiably be laid at his door, Silvio Berlusconi has revolutionised European football. He has transformed his boyhood favourites, AC Milan, turning them from a shambolic, debt-ridden wreck into world-beaters. Along the way his coaches, Arrigo Sacchi and Fabio Capello, rid Italian football of interminable, defence-first goalless draws. And the president's need to be guaranteed top-class European action for his TV interests has led directly to the creation of the Champions' League and its subsequent expansion. The arguments surrounding this

modern offspring of the European Cup are beside the point. Berlusconi has pushed the game into another financial league and this new money – and the need to make more of it – has given us some breathtaking football, the like of which many in Europe thought they would never see again.

Almost incidentally, Berlusconi, a former cruise-ship singer, used both his football club and his media interests to assist him in becoming prime minister of Italy – albeit briefly – in the early Nineties.

Whether his ambitions have been in broadcasting or politics, Berlusconi's vehicle has been AC Milan. Yet in taking the club relentlessly forward, he has remained true to tradition – even before his arrival in 1986, the *rossoneri* had a reputation for buying the best and attacking with it.

After their formation as Milan Cricket and Football Club in 1899, Milan became the first club to break Genoa's early stranglehold on the Italian game. They won three titles, two as Milan FC, and enjoyed a flow of cash from one of their founding members, car tyre magnate Pieró Pirelli. Progress was halted when half the club left to form Internazionale.

Pirelli put his money behind the building of a new stadium, the San Siro, in 1926, but although it saw regular international action, its home club floundered. With their English influence, Milan were out of political favour with the Fascist authorities that held sway in Italy in the Thirties.

After World War II, the purchase of Swedish stars Gunnar Gren, Gunnar Nordahl and Nils Liedholm (the so-called *Gre-no-li* trio) helped lift Milan back into the upper echelons of the Italian game. Between 1948 and 1966, Milan finished in the top three of *Serie A* every year but one.

With the inception of the big European club competitions, more foreign stars came to Milan – Uruguayan Juan Schiaffino and Brazilian José Altafini among them. Milan lost to Real Madrid in the 1958 European Cup final, 3–2 after extra time. But there was to be no let-down five years later, against Benfica at Wembley, when two

Altafini goals put paid to Eusébio and co. In the Milan ranks that fine May evening in 1963 was a young inside-forward from Alessandria, Gianni Rivera, who would become the club's figurehead for fifteen years. Alongside him were two men who would make an even greater impact as coaches – Cesare Maldini, later Italian national-team boss, whose son Paolo would star in three European Cup finals, and Giovanni Trappatoni, seven times a *scudetto* winner from the dugout in the Seventies and Eighties.

With Nereo Rocco calling the shots from the sidelines, Rivera running the midfield and two more imported stars, Swedish winger Kurt Hamrin and German full-back Karl-Heinz Schnellinger, spicing up the mixture, Milan won one *scudetto*, two more European trophies and a World Club championship in 1968 and 1969.

Only Rivera remained in the side that beat Leeds in the 1973 Cup-Winners' Cup final – a match tainted by strange refereeing decisions, and one which would give Milan their last European trophy for sixteen years.

Rivera bowed out by helping the club to a star-winning tenth *scudetto* in 1979, but behind the scenes, all was far from well. During the lowest period of the club's history, president Felice Colombo was found guilty of match-rigging during the 1978/79 campaign, and Milan were sent down to *Serie B*. After promotion, they played their way back down again – and Colombo's successor, Giussy Farina, fled to South Africa reportedly owing a fortune in back taxes. British players Mark Hateley, Luther Blissett, Joe Jordan and Ray Wilkins all had the misfortune to be part of Milan during this low ebb.

Milan essentials

Milan has two **airports** – Linate, 7km east of the centre, and Malpensa, 45km northwest. Both are connected by bus to the main **train station**, Stazione Centrale. From Linate, buses leave every 20–30mins, 5.40am–9pm (L4,500, journey time 20–25mins). City bus #73 also runs between Linate and Piazza San Babila, 5.30am–midnight. From Malpensa, airport buses leave every 30mins, 7.30am–12.30pm, and every hour 12.30pm–5.30pm (L18,000, journey time 75mins).

The city has a fast, efficient **metro system** with three colour-coded lines: red (line 1), green (line 2) and yellow (line 3). Lines 2 and 3 cross at the Stazione Centrale, lines 1 and 3 at the city centre, Piazza del Duomo. Lines 1 and 2 cross at Cadorna, near the main **bus station** in Piazza Castello. There is also a blue line underground railway between Bovisa Nord station and Porta Venezia, Via Garibaldi. Buses and trams augment the transport network.

Tickets, available from newsstands and vending machines, cost L1,500 each and are valid for 75mins on any tram or bus, and for one metro journey. Punch the ticket onboard or when entering the metro. **Carnets** of ten tickets are available, as are **passes** for 24 hours and 48 hours. Transport runs 6am–midnight, with **night buses** following metro routes 1 and 3 until 1.30am.

Yellow **taxis** can be found outside the main train station or by Piazza del Duomo. To call for one, dial Radiotaxi (☎02/5353) or Autoradiotaxi (☎02/8585).

The two main **tourist offices** are at the Stazione Centrale (open Mon–Sat 9am–7pm, ☎02/7252 4360) and at Via Marconi 1, by Piazza del Duomo (open Mon–Sat 8.30am–7pm, Sun 9am–12.30pm & 1.30–5pm, ☎02/7252 4300).

Milan has no **listings magazine**, but the Thursday edition of the daily newspaper *La Repubblica* includes *Tutto Milano*, with details of restaurants and concerts.

There is no one decent football store, but a fair sports bookshop, *La Libreria dello Sport*, at Via Carducci 9, near Cairoli metro (open Mon 3–7pm, Tue–Fri 9am–1pm & 3–7pm, Sat 9am–12.30pm & 3.30–7pm, most major credit cards).

The San Siro

Stadio Giuseppe Meazza, Via Piccolomini 5
Capacity 85,500 (all-seated)

The Meazza, usually still known by its original name of San Siro, is as rectangular as the day it was first planned. Its pitch is up close to the advertising hoardings, giving the stadium an **intimacy** few others of its stature or grandeur can match. Noise booms around the ground, and smoke hangs in the air with the Milanese mist.

From its **inauguration in 1926**, San Siro has seen three major overhauls, culminating in a £50million redevelopment for the 1990 World Cup. This gave the stadium a third tier built on a series of cylindrical towers, a plexiglass roof supported by steel girders – and **an overshadowed pitch** which can be about as playable as the trotting track next door. Another £500,000 was spent on drainage and irrigation during the summer of 1995, but the roof, twice-weekly use and **foggy Milanese weather** still play havoc with the playing surface.

San Siro is the name of the district in the west of the city. It was here that Peiro Pirelli built the stadium for his beloved **Milan FC**, its strictly rectangular shape offering no scope for a running track to kill the ambiance. It soon became the leading venue in Italy, the local climate helping the *azzurri* to a muddy semi-final victory over Austria at the 1934 World Cup.

The postwar boom saw another tier added, giving the stadium its **distinctive candy-twist appearance**, in time for the modern age of European competition and televised matches. The San Siro became a household name across Europe before the stands started crumbling in the Eighties. Suitably refurbished for Italia '90, the stadium hosted the tournament's opening ceremony, followed by Cameroon's surprise 1–0 win over holders Argentina. It also hosted a second-round game between West Germany and Holland, in which the teams fielded three players each from Inter and Milan respectively – and all of them playing 'at home'.

The **easiest route** to the stadium is to take the M1 metro line (Molino Dorino branch) to Lotto (fifteen minutes from Duomo), where **stadium buses** will be waiting. In daylight the ten-minute walk alongside the San Siro hippodrome is a pleasant one; after dusk the Viale Federico Caprilli is lined with prostitutes and kerb crawlers.

Getting off the bus, the **Bar Stadio** by the *biglietteria nord* has Forst beer on draught. The **Bar Nuovo Trotto**, by the trotter track on Via dei Rospigliosi 42, is a better bet, recently expanded into a sit-down bar/restaurant, and with a diplomatic pennant display of both host teams. Inside the stadium, the beer is alcohol-free.

As well as the shops and bars listed in the club sections, the Meazza has two main **ticket offices**: *biglietteria nord*, by gates #36/#37, nearest the stadium bus stop from Lotto metro; and *biglietteria sud* by gates #26/#27 opposite, in Piazza Axum.

Apart from big European ties, the Milanese derby, games against Juventus and internationals, **ticket prices** never vary. They are coded in four colours: *rosso* (red, the best tickets, over the halfway line with the press and VIPs); *arancio* (orange, opposite); *blu* (blue, south goal with the Milan fans) and *verde* (green, north goal with the Inter crew).

The *3 anello* (third tier) has the **cheapest seats**, with the poorest view from high up. The middle *2 anello* is more expensive, while the *1 anello* nearest the pitch is the dearest of the lot.

Milan diehards enter through gates #17–#22, the **Inter** lads through gates #41–#46, and away fans (regardless of the opposition), tucked in a corner of the south end, through gates #13–#14.

Facing the music – Alberto Zaccheroni (centre) after his team were eliminated from Europe

Berlusconi took over the club in 1986. And while his emphasis on developing the business side of Milan has been well documented, not all of his innovations were driven by the dash for cash. Berlusconi expanded the club's youth structure and invested heavily in the training centre at Milanello, making it the best equipped in Italy. Even more courageously, he entrusted his £20million investment in the hands of a little-known coach of then unknown Parma, Arrigo Sacchi.

It was Sacchi who bought Dutch stars Marco van Basten and Ruud Gullit, the latter for a world record fee. It was Sacchi who instigated the tactic of 'pressing' the game into the opposition half, attacking the man with the ball instead of falling back. It was Sacchi who laid the groundwork for Milan to pip holders Napoli to the Italian title in 1988.

With another Dutchman, Frank Rijkaard, sweeper Franco Baresi, overlapping full-back Paolo Maldini and midfield creator Roberto Donadoni all maturing into players of world class, the Milan of 1989 were simply irrepressible. Their 5–0 European Cup semi-final thrashing of Real Madrid was the best Europe had seen since their opponents' heyday 30 years before. The 4–0 final win over Steaua Bucharest was a formality – albeit an impressive one.

The work rate involved in the pressing game, and the fact that most of his players were involved in the 1990 World Cup, took Milan off the boil before Sacchi's appointment as Italian national-team coach in 1991. After a less convincing European Cup win in 1990, the team made an ignominious exit from the 1991 event. Having refused to take the field after a floodlight failure at Marseille, Milan didn't just lose the tie – they were banned from Europe for the following season.

Sacchi's replacement was a former Juventus star, Fabio Capello. In his first season, 1991/92, Milan won the league without losing a single game, starting an unbeaten run which would last for 58 games until March 1993 – an Italian record. Before the 1992/93 campaign, Berlusconi bought in bulk. His critics claimed many of the purchases – Gianluigi Lentini, Jean-Pierre Papin, Zvone Boban and Dejan Savićević among them – were made simply to keep the players out of his opponents' clutches. But few neutrals were complaining: that autumn, Milan won 5–4, 7–3, 5–3 and 5–1. Marco van Basten became Italy's all-time highest-scoring foreigner, before sustaining the ankle injury that would eventually – and prematurely – end his career. Clearly unfit, the flying Dutchman was substituted and Milan missed a string of chances in losing the 1993 European Cup final to Marseille.

With the loss of their Dutch trio, it was a solid rather than inspiring Milan that won *lo scudetto* a third consecutive time in 1994. Their head-to-head clash with Barcelona at the European Cup final in Athens that year was billed as a contrast in styles – hadn't Cruyff's team scored nearly three times more goals that season than Milan? Capello's answer was emphatic. Contrary to all expectations, his team attacked from the start, the final 4–0 scoreline barely reflecting their superiority. Marcel Desailly, recently acquired from Marseille, was outstanding in midfield, Savićević simply sublime.

Crucially, the Montenegrin magician was injured in training before Milan's defence of their European title a year later. Without him, the team retreated into their defensive shell, and were deservedly beaten, 1–0 by Ajax in Vienna.

In the meantime Berlusconi had entered politics, leading his right-wing *Forza Italia* party (named after a football chant) to victory in the 1994 Italian general election. Much of his campaign had been fought using football imagery.

But while Berlusconi's political star rose, that of his football club was starting to fall. In the summer of 1995, Roberto Baggio arrived from champions Juventus, and another new signing, George Weah, got the goals that brought another title to the San Siro. Both men played poorly, however, as Milan were knocked out of the UEFA Cup by Bordeaux, a struggling French side who had entered the competition through the Intertoto Cup.

At the end of the season, Berlusconi hesitated before offering Capello a new contract, and his coach departed for Real

Madrid. Under Capello's replacement, the mild-mannered Uruguayan Oscar Tabarez, Milan's players began to see a little too much of the good life around town. On the pitch, Baresi had lost at least a yard, Maldini was neglecting his defensive duties, and a string of new signings were failing to gel. And, ironically thanks to TV overkill, crowds in the San Siro were down.

After a series of poor league results, Milan needed a draw at home against Rosenborg of Trondheim to set up a meeting with Juventus in the Champions' League quarter-finals. Berlusconi panicked. In the middle of the night he phoned Arrigo Sacchi, who duly appeared back at Milanello, relieved at being given an easy way out of his increasingly untenable job in charge of the *azzurri*. Three days later, Rosenborg won 2–1 and the San Siro fell silent.

Worse was to come. Milan continued to flounder in mid-table as Sacchi's tactical turnarounds confused the players – a 6–1 home defeat by Juventus said it all.

Despite Capello's return as coach in the summer of 1997, and major signings such as Patrick Kluivert, Winston Bogarde, Ibrahim Ba and Leonardo, Milan suffered another mediocre season of awesome salary bills and fan discontent. Berlusconi then looked for inspiration from the bright Udinese side which finished third in 1997/98, signing its adventurous coach Alberto Zaccheroni, German striker Oliver Bierhoff and Danish midfielder Thomas Helveg. Under Zaccheroni, Milan rediscovered their sense of adventure but were giving the ball away too easily before the coach altered his favoured 3–4–3 formation to suit what was still essentially Capello's squad. Players like Weah and Boban revived almost overnight, and as the leaders Lazio stumbled, Milan held their nerve, sealing the title with a last-day win at relegation-threatened Perugia.

Yet the limitations of Zaccheroni's side were ruthlessly exposed in European competition during 1999/2000. Despite the addition of lively Ukrainian striker Andriy Shevchenko, Milan finished bottom of what looked a relatively easy Champions' League group including Chelsea, Galatasaray and Hertha Berlin. A last-game defeat by the Turks cost Milan their consolation place in the UEFA Cup and almost cost Zaccheroni his job. After that, the introduction of youngsters Massimo Ambrosini and Rino Gattuso, along with the goal poaching of Shevchenko, pushed Milan up to third place in the *Serie A*, but even so, it was clear that some fresh talent was needed if Zaccheroni was to achieve the kind of European success this club has come to expect.

Club merchandise

This is the club with the biggest commercial enterprise in Italy. **Milan Point**, Via Pietro Verri 8 (M1 San Babila, entrance in Via San Pietro all'Orto, open Mon 3–7pm, Tues–Sat 10am–7pm, most major credit cards), has two floors of class gear, including perfume, Zippo lighters, jewellery, aftershave, long johns and jeans. There's a **ticket desk** upstairs.

There are smaller sales outlets behind all four stands at the San Siro, and a new club shop is expected to open in the near future.

Ultra culture

The *Lions' Den*, as the lower level of the San Siro's *Curva Sud* has become known, is home to any number of ultra groups, including some of the most feared in Italy – *Fossa del Leoni*, *Commandos Tigre* and *Brigate Rossonere*.

In print

The substantial *Forza Milan!* (monthly, L4,000) boasts a circulation of 100,000, an average of 70 for each of the team's 1,400 supporters' clubs nationwide.

In the net

The club's **official site** is at www.acmilan.com. Among its many features are an outstanding news service in English and a virtual tour of the San Siro, in addition to the expected shopping, squad and historical information areas. Of the unofficial sites, one of the best remains that of the Maltese AC Milan fan club, now residing at: www.forzamilan.com. Again, plenty of English content and efficient news delivery. Another unofficial site resides at: www.milanmania.com. It features a particularly lively messageboard in English.

 # Internazionale

Stadium San Siro, see p.354
Club office Via Durini 24
Colours Blue-and-black striped shirts, black shorts
League champions 1910, 1920, 1930, 1938, 1940, 1953–54, 1963, 1965–66, 1971, 1980, 1989
Cup winners 1939, 1978, 1982
European Cup winners 1964–65
UEFA Cup winners 1991, 1994, 1998

As AC Milan fans are reminded twice a year, Internazionale have never been relegated. That aside, however, there is little ammunition with which to dispute the view that Inter are effectively Italy's third club, and always will be unless either Milan or Juve seriously flounder. It is more than a decade since Inter last won the *scudetto*, and despite spending millions of his family fortune each summer, club president Massimo Moratti has been unable to get a taste of the success his father enjoyed when at the helm of the club.

Inter's reputation was built on great sides from two different eras, responsible for six of the club's thirteen titles between them. One man dominated each era: striker Giuseppe Meazza in the Thirties, coach Helenio Herrera three decades later.

Formed by a breakaway group of disgruntled cosmopolitan members of Milan FC in 1908, Inter won their first title two years later almost by default. Their opponents in a title decider, Pro Vercelli asked for the game to be postponed as their best players were involved in a military tournament. When this was refused, they sent a junior team instead. Inter won 10–3.

After a second title ten years later, Inter had to wait until the Fascist era before they again rose to prominence. Ironically their star player, Meazza, was the very opposite

Dejected in defeat – Ivan Cordoba (left) and Luigi di Biagio after the *Coppa Italia* loss to Lazio

of the Fascist ideal – a dedicated man about town who also happened to be a fast, delicate and prolific forward. After his debut against the US Milanese club with whom Inter would merge in 1928, his lifestyle would be curtailed by Inter president and Fascist party representative Ferdinando Pozzani. It was to be the first of many interventions. Not only was a strict routine forced on the club, but so was a change of name. The authorities disliked the Leninist implications of 'Internazionale'. So the team became 'Ambrosiana-Inter', after Ambrosio, patron saint of Milan, and under that guise spent the Thirties in a dogfight with Juventus over *lo scudetto*. Matches between the two, which featured several World Cup winners, became known as *il Derby d'Italia*.

Three titles, one cup, 247 Meazza goals and a world war later, Inter got their old name back. They lived up to it with a post-war attack composed of a Dutchman, Faas Wilkes ('The Flying Tulip'), a Frenchman of Hungarian origin, Stefano Nyers, and a Swede, Lennart 'Nacka' Skoglund. In

1950/51 the team hit 107 goals but won nothing. Inter were conceding goals as well as scoring them, until their coach, 1938 World Cup winner Alfredo Foni, devised a solid defensive strategy. In 1952/53 Inter scored 46 goals and won the championship – and a reputation for dour football.

The combination of Foni's discipline and the forward line's spirit kept the title at Inter for another year, often thanks to the considerable talents of the much-loved Skoglund, whose most tenacious opponent was a bottle of *grappa*.

In 1955, Angelo Moratti became Inter president. A man who had spent his working life in the lubricant oil business and his free time at Inter, his skills were not immediately obvious. Inter fell away in the league and, in an eerie precursor to what would happen in the Nineties, few paid attention to their efforts competing for valueless silverware like the Inter City Fairs' (later UEFA) Cup. Moratti recognised brass from muck. After a high-scoring defeat by Barcelona, he persuaded Barça's mercurial coach, Helenio Herrera, to leave behind his battle royal with Real Madrid and make Internazionale great again.

With Moratti's millions to oil the wheels, Herrera created an infernal machine. From Barcelona he brought midfield schemer Luis Suárez for a world record fee. In Chile he tracked down the Brazilian Jair, a right-sided winger to play alongside Inter's demon left-winger Mario Corso. To meet their crosses was the precocious young talent of striker Sandro Mazzola, whose father Valentino was the biggest footballing loss in the Superga tragedy of 1949. In defence, a junior champion sprinter at overlapping full-back, Giacinto Facchetti, was deployed alongside two henchmen, Armando Picchi and Tarcisio Burgnich. Behind them was Giuliano Sarti, a goalkeeper of rare composure.

Vacuum-tight, man-to-man marking with a solid *libero* and an attack ready to counter – this was *la Grande Inter*. And on the sidelines sat Herrera, *il Mago*, 'the sorcerer', a wizard of hyperbole and sports psychology. He had players chant slogans, he bound the team like a close-knit family, ruled over by a strict Godfather. He introduced the cult of the manager. Above all, he instigated two concepts still relevant today: *ritiro*, a prison-like, three-day training camp far from players' loved ones, and *tifosi* – trainloads of flag-waving fans who would follow Inter's progress around Europe.

The latter were particularly significant. In his early days in Milan, Herrera had missed the atmosphere of the Nou Camp and he persuaded Moratti to encourage organised supporters' clubs. Suddenly, the San Siro was an intimidating place to visit – all the more so when you consider the presence (in the background) of general manager Italo Allodi, Herrera's Mr Fixit, the exact nature of whose dealings with middlemen and referees will probably never be known...

Inter won the league in 1963, then made their way through the European Cup to a final against Herrera's old rivals Real Madrid. Thanks to the *tifosi* the match, held

in Vienna, inspired the first mass movement of fans to a major European club game. Past their sell-by date but still potent, Madrid's stars were shackled by Inter's gritty man-markers and Inter won the European Cup at their first attempt, 3–1. They beat Independiente in the World Club Championship later in the year.

In 1965, things got even better. Inter won the league, the European Cup (1–0 at a rainy San Siro against Benfica) and the World Club Championship for a second time. Herrera was the most talked about man in world football.

Although Inter earned their gold star with a tenth title win in 1966, their luck couldn't last. In the European Cup final of 1967, Inter faced Celtic. Without the injured Suárez and Jair, they fell to a superb team performance by the Scottish champions. Liverpool manager Bill Shankly, still smarting from a questionable semi-final defeat by Inter in 1965, took pleasure in taunting Herrera at a post-match dinner.

A few days later, a rare slip by Sarti let in a decisive goal to allow Juventus the title. The magician's spell was broken. Both Herrera and his paymaster Moratti left in 1968.

With a team modified from Herrera's – Facchetti at left-back, Mazzola as midfield playmaster – Inter regained their domestic title in 1971. But Europe was beyond them this time. Their road to the 1972 European Cup final was rocky enough (a 7–1 defeat by Borussia Mönchengladbach was nullified by a beer can thrown from the crowd at an Inter player), but in the final they were swept aside by the exciting Total Football of Ajax.

The 1971 side featured Roberto Boninsegna, a centre-forward in the classic mould. Nine years later Inter would have another, Alessandro Altobelli, to help them to the 1980 title. Again, though – and despite the presence of West German international Karl-Heinz Rummenigge – Inter's European progress was limited.

With further influence from Germany in the shape of Lothar Matthäus, Andreas Brehme and Jürgen Klinsmann, Inter won the title again in 1989, and the UEFA Cup two years later. But the pressure was on to keep pace with Berlusconi's Milan, and Inter just couldn't keep up. Debts rose, further expensive imports flopped, and the club's catering millionaire president Ernesto Pellegrini lost interest.

A UEFA Cup win in 1994 looked good on paper, but served only to disguise a season of boardroom struggle and near relegation in the league. The following year was no better, and Pellegrini sold the club for a mere $25million to Angelo Moratti's son, Massimo.

A 90th-minute goal in the last game of the 1994/95 season kept Inter in Europe. Moratti put Facchetti, Mazzola and Suárez on the payroll. But after Inter lost to Lugano of Switzerland in the 1995/96 UEFA Cup, he hired Englishman Roy Hodgson as 'technical director'. With Hodgson in charge, midfield destroyer Paul Ince's game improved no end, and Inter again qualified for the UEFA Cup.

To bolster Inter's challenge, Moratti spent prodigiously, recruiting another galaxy of foreign stars including the spectacular French striker Youri Djorkaeff and his spectacular goals. Hodgson tried manfully to work the ingredients into a convincing mixture, but without success – Inter never seriously challenged for the title in 1996/97, and in what should have been the season's saving grace, their third UEFA Cup final appearance of the decade, they were beaten on penalties by Germany's Schalke – a team that cost a fraction of Moratti's star-heavy squad.

Hodgson jumped before he was pushed, and his departure would have far-reaching consequences. While Moratti provided the funds to make Ronaldo the world's most expensive player in the summer of 1997, the man he put in charge of the team, Gigi Simoni, lacked any experience of managing top-name players. While Ronaldo's goals steered the team to the 1998 UEFA Cup, Inter were edged out of the title by a fortunate Juventus. In 1998/99, with Ronaldo struggling to recover from

the World Cup and the remainder of the squad wrecked by disharmony, no fewer than four coaches endured spells in the dugout – Simoni, Mircea Lucescu, Luciano Castellini and the returning Hodgson. All were stopgaps while the club waited for Marcello Lippi to arrive from Juventus; none could prevent Inter from slipping out of the European places in the *Serie A*, while the club's first-ever Champions' League campaign ended at the feet of Manchester United.

Upon his arrival in the summer of 1999, Lippi was presented with Christian Vieri, Moratti having spent £30million to prise the big striker away from Lazio. Veteran French stopper Laurent Blanc was brought in to replace Giuseppe Bergomi, who had finally hung up his boots after almost two decades in the Inter defence, and on the eve of the campaign, Roma playmaker Luigi di Biagio was added to the midfield mix. Costly it may have been – but Inter's squad could have been younger, and with Ronaldo missing most of the season while undergoing two knee operations and Vieri also troubled by injuries, the team never had enough firepower to be considered serious title contenders.

The prospect of compensation in the *Coppa Italia* lingered until the second leg of the final against Lazio at the San Siro, when Inter failed to score the one goal that would have brought them the cup, but the team did at least make it into the Champions' League qualifiers after beating Parma 3–1 in an end-of-season *spareggio*.

With a seemingly bottomless pit of cash available, the only question is whether Lippi, with a season's experience under his belt, is capable of re-creating the success he enjoyed at Juventus. His paymaster Moratti demands nothing less.

Club merchandise

The **Inter shop** by gate #21 of the San Siro is open only on matchdays. At other times head for *Football Team*, Via Rubens 26 (M1 Gambara, open Mon–Sat 9.30am–12.30pm & 3.30–7.30pm, most credit cards).

In print

The glossy *Inter Football Club* (monthly, L5,000) can be found at most newsstands.

Ultra culture

Of the big clubs, Inter's ultras have featured least in unsavoury incidents over the last 20 years. The *Interisti* are traditionally on the right-hand side of the political sphere, with no few skinheads in their midst. Split into groups like the *Forever Ultras Inter* and the *Irrudicibili*, they occupy the *Curva Nord* of the San Siro.

In the net

By comparison with Milan's, the official Inter website has a more individual feel and more attractive design, but less actual content. Still, there's plenty of English and some good multi-media elements at: www.inter.it.

For more English-language news and comment, try the Swedish Inter homepage at: internazionale.8m.com.

Eat, drink, sleep…

Bars and clubs

Drinking in Milan need not be as exclusive as its big-business image would have you believe. The city *does* have its fair share of upmarket joints for the mobile phone brigade, but can also offer unpretentious **pubs** and reasonable **live music**.

In a hangover from the 19th century, *aperitivi* are taken in the early evening, when many places keep the tradition of providing selections of free snacks on their bar counters. Remember – Campari is a Milanese invention.

The best, and most atmospheric, area for **nightlife** is south-west of the centre, alongside the city's canals (*navigli*), near Porta Genova train and metro station.

Bukowski, Via S Sofia 21. Themed after the American literary boozehound and covered in football scarves, this offers a decent menu and evening beers in liberal company. M3 Crocetta.

Hollywood, Corso Como 15. The place to go if you fancy a dance with a Milan player – Paolo Maldini met his future bride here, and stars passing through town often stop by. Prices to match. In the same building around the corner is the **Loolapaloosa Pub**, an Irish-style pub with a decent selection of whiskies, popular among the sporting fraternity, closed Sun. M2 to Garibaldi.

Osteria del Pallone, Viale Gorizia 30. Atmospheric football bar overlooking the canal. San Miguel and Guinness on draught, framed front pages of *La Gazzetta* from after each World Cup victory, and a huge line drawing of Tardelli's manic celebration after scoring in 1982. Downstairs, framed poems dedicated to the 4–3 semi-final win over West Germany in 1970. Closed Mon. M2 Porta Genova.

Pogue Mahone's, Via Salmini 1. The most popular of the Irish bars scattered across the city, this one at least has Irish beer and a decent collection of Irish and Scotch whiskies. Sky Sports expected for the 2000/01 season. Closed Mondays. M3 to Porta Romana.

Racaná Pub, Via Sannio 18. The best of the city's pubs, its genuine atmosphere engendered by simple furniture and regular clientele. Cider and darts available. M3 to Porta Romana.

Restaurants

Lunchtime sees Milanese office workers swarm around the multitude of **fast-food joints** in the city centre. Join them only if you must.

Many restaurants close in the afternoon, before the relaxed tradition of cocktails and an evening meal. Milanese **specialities** include *risotto giallo* (rice with saffron) and *cotoletta alla Milanese* (veal cutlet in breadcrumbs).

Collina Pistoiese, Via Amadei 1. Once owned by the father of Inter star Sergio Gori, and a haunt for the football community of the Sixties. You still might find a few old stars in here. Fish specialities at L25,000–30,000, *piatti espressi* at L25,000. Closed Fri. M3 Missori.

Ibiza, Corso Garibaldi 108. Part-owned by Milan players Sebastiano Rossi and Alessandro Costacurta, this is where the team celebrates major victories. Large, simple interior, starters at L15,000, main courses at L30,000. Guinness on draught and 30 types of cocktails. Evenings only. M2 Moscova.

Milanese, Via Santa Marta 11. Tucked away down the back streets near the bourse, this is one of the better options for tasting traditional local dishes such as *risotto milanese*. M1 Cordusio.

Stalingrado, Via Biondi 4. Former haunt of disaffected left-wing youth, now a bustling two-floor Irish tavern serving Guinness, Tennants and main courses at L18,000. Open until 2am. Closed Sun. Near Piazza Firenze.

Trattoria Bagutta, Via Bagutta 14. One of the oldest restaurants in the city, with a large and diverse menu containing some international dishes as well as Milanese and popular Italian standards. Upmarket feel, midrange prices. Reserve a table in the garden on ☎02/7600 0902. M1 S Babila.

Accommodation

Milan gets booked up quickly so reserving a room in advance is always advisable. The tourist offices will check for vacancies, but **Hotels Milano Central** can reserve a centrally located hotel room for you on ☎02/805 4242, fax 02/805 4291).

Hotel Nettuno, Via Tadino 27 (☎02/2940 4481). Quiet pension near the main train station, with showers in the corridor and the usual 1am curfew. A bit scruffy, but cheap. Singles around L60,000, doubles L80,000. No credit cards. M1 Lima.

Hotel San Tomaso, Viale Tunisia 6 (☎02/2951 4747). On the third floor of a building halfway between the main train station and the centre. On the sixth floor is the **Hotel Kennedy**, which is more comfortable but has a midnight curfew. Both places L50–65,000 a single, L80–100,000 a double. No credit cards. M1 Porta Venezia.

Hotel Cervo, Piazza Principessa Clotilde 10 (☎02/2900 4031). Centrally located three-star establishment, ideal if you are planning to eat and drink in the central Brera district. Offers a football deal including a ticket to the San Siro, which could be handy for derbies and other big matches. Singles from L170,000, doubles from L280,000.

Ostello Pietro Rotta, Viale Salmoiraghi 1 (☎02/3926 7095). Best hostel in town, out near the San Siro. IYHF members L24,000 for a dorm bed, annual membership L25,000. Lockout 9am–3.30pm, curfew 12.30pm. Laundry facilities. No credit cards. A 10min walk from M1 QT8.

Hotel Serena, Via Boscovich 59 (☎02/2952 2436). Not far from the main train station and close to the metro line, this is one of the better budget hotels in the area. Singles L120,000, doubles L180,000.

Florence

Florence exudes both calm and affluence. The narrow streets of the old city are filled with treasure houses of art, and in summer are flooded with tourists heading for the galleries and popping into town from cottages in the Tuscany countryside. Without serious local rivals (the nearest major city is Pisa, whose team have spent most of their life in the lower divisions), the local football club, Fiorentina, and the ground at which they play, the Stadio Comunale, might be expected to have an easygoing atmosphere, reflecting that of their surrounding environment.

Nothing could be further from the truth. Belonging to neither the north nor the south of Italy, rather than be ignored Fiorentina find themselves in the position of being disliked by almost every other supporter in the land. The relative geographical isolation of the club has created a strong local patriotism, which finds an outlet in the stadium. A series of controversies involving Juventus and Fiorentina over the past 15 years has created a new derby in Italy, at which tensions often boil over into violence. Crowd trouble has continued to be a major problem in Florence, with the club suffering a series of fines and punishments – the latest, forced elimination from the 1998/99 UEFA Cup, coming partly as a result of the previous one. Obliged to play 'home' ties away from Florence after earlier misdemeanours, Fiorentina played Grasshopper Zürich in Salerno, only for a firecracker to be thrown from the crowd – almost certainly by a fan of Salernitana who have a long history of antagonism towards the *Viola* – at an assistant referee, and the tie to be awarded to the Swiss.

Yet the fanaticism of support here has a positive side. Local stars are idolised to extremes, and the ultras produce some outstanding firework and choreographed displays. On its day, the Stadio Comunale can provide one of the most intense experiences in football – its atmosphere, like the match itself, poised on a knife-edge.

The thrilling fields

Fiorentina

Stadio Comunale Artemio Franchi, Campo di Marte
Capacity 47,000
Colours All lilac with red and white trim
League champions 1956, 1969
Cup winners 1940, 1961, 1966, 1975, 1996
Cup-Winners' Cup winners 1961

Florentines will tell you that theirs is a club on its own – always producing sides with flair, often ignoring trends pursued by the rest of Italy, and following a tradition of attacking football. Take a trip to a game in Florence and you will understand why the defensive, slow-motion football that dominated Italy for so long never had the chance to establish itself here. This is a city where the fans don't just shout and sing – they roar their team on with the passion, and the impatience, of a Spanish or English crowd.

Although Florence was the birthplace of the original game of *calcio*, the region was slow to pick up on the English rules which first became popular in Europe in the late 19th century. Lacking the industrial and cosmopolitan influences of northern Italy, Tuscany had only three teams competing in the early series of regional play-offs for the national championship – Livorno, Pisa and Lucca. Florence itself had two minor clubs which had failed to make much impact – Palestra Ginnastica Libertas, founded in 1887, and Club Sportivo Firenze. A British expatriate team known as Firenze Football Club had also been founded, but achieved little.

Enter Luigi Ridolfi, a local aristocrat from a grand old Tuscan family, who had fallen in love with the game he had seen on his travels to England. A young man of 31 committed to developing sport in the region, he persuaded the two major clubs,

Libertas and Club Sportivo, to merge and form a team capable of competing in the newly formed Italian championship. On September 19, 1926 the new club was founded, and the team quickly worked their way up the football pyramid, finding themselves in *Serie A* after just five years.

The timing couldn't have been better – Florence's new stadium, designed by the respected architect Pier Luigi Nervi, had just been completed. The Stadio Comunale Giovanni Berta (named in honour of a local Fascist leader), a breakthrough in stadium design with its functional, modernistic approach, was inaugurated on September 13, 1931 with the visit of Austrian side Admira Wacker. The game also marked the début of the first of Fiorentina's many South American stars, Uruguayan striker Pedro Petrone, known as *l'Artillero* – 'The Gunner'. Petrone's scoring record was outstanding, but he had a poor relationship with the club's management and was released in 1933.

Problems both inside the club and on the field came to a head in 1938/39 when the *Viola* were relegated to *Serie B*. They bounced back at the first attempt and then, in 1940 and with most of Europe at war, they won their first silverware, lifting the *Coppa Italia* after hammering Milan, Lazio and Juventus before beating Genoa 1–0 in the final. At last, President Ridolfi had something to show for twenty years of effort in building up the club.

The cup win didn't just put Fiorentina on the map – it established the club's reputation as innovators. The success of the 1940 side, coached by Beppe Galluzzi, was based on a radical change in tactics, Fiorentina (along with their fellow cup finalists Genoa) being the first to abandon Italy's favoured *Metoda* formation of 2–3–5 in favour of the 'WM' system developed by Herbert Chapman at Arsenal.

With the help of what become known in Italy as the Sistema formation, Fiorentina hoped to increase their power base within the game. But World War II intervened, and after it, the club had to start again.

The stadium had been damaged by bombing, but care was taken to repair the

Florence essentials

Florence's small **airport**, Vespucci, is 5km west of town in Peretola, connected by two bus services to the main **Santa Maria Novella** train station – *Sita* from outside the arrivals terminal (hourly, 9.45am–10.35pm, L6,000 onboard); and city bus #62 from the airport gate (every 20mins, 6.30am–10.45pm, L1,500 from the machine by the exit). A taxi will cost around L25,000.

You are more likely to arrive at **Pisa airport**, 80km west of Florence, which offers only an irregular train connection to Santa Maria Novella. It may be quicker to get a taxi (L12,000) or bus #7 from the airport to **Pisa Centrale**, then get a train from there. On returning, if you get the Pisa airport train from Florence, you can check your flight luggage in at platform 5, 15mins before train departure.

Santa Maria Novella is a 10min walk from central Florence, itself best crossed on foot. **Buses** (5.30am–9pm) cover the city and surrounding areas – tickets are dispensed from machines by main bus stops. Sixty-minute tickets (L1,500) allow any number of transfers once stamped onboard; three-hour (L2,500), 24-hour (L6,000) and three-day (L11,000) tickets are also available. Route #70 runs all night between Santa Maria Novella and Campo Marte – pay L3,000 onboard. For a **taxi**, call ☎055/4242 or 4798.

The main APT **tourist information office** is at central Via Cavour 1 (open Nov–Feb Mon–Sat 8.15am–1.45pm, Mar–Oct Mon–Sat 8.15am-7.15pm, Sun 8.15am–1.45pm, ☎055/290 832). They cannot book accommodation, but can provide copies of the annual English-language *Concierge* info brochure and *Firenze Spettacolo*, a monthly Italian cultural guide.

ground in keeping with Nervi's original design and the Fascist name was dropped from the ground's title. Enrico Befani took over as president in 1951 and Fiorentina became regulars in Italy's top five. In 1955/56, they won their first *scudetto*, going 33 matches without defeat and losing only in the last game of the season, when the title was in the bag – the *Viola* finishing twelve points clear of their nearest rivals, Milan. Coach Fulvio Bernardini's side was outstanding in defence, conceding just six goals at home all season. But Fiorentina's fans still cared for goals above all else. Among the heroes who were greeted in the Piazza della Repubblica (to this day a meeting point for *Viola* fans) was the title-winning strike partnership of 21-year-old Beppe Virgili and Miguel Montuori. The latter, nicknamed *Pecos Bill* because of his obsession with cowboy comics, was born in Argentina to an Italian mother. Despite his mixed parentage, he spoke no Italian and during Bernardini's lengthy tactical discussions, he would simply stare, uncomprehending, into space. He went on to score 72 goals in 162 appearances for the club, before injury cut short his career at the age of 29.

Providing the ammunition for the front two was Brazilian winger Julinho Botelho. As a player with São Paolo he had earned a place in the Brazilian national team and was a star of the 1954 World Cup side. Bernadini spotted him there and for the next twelve months, Fiorentina tried to persuade him to leave Brazil. He finally arrived in the summer of 1955 and was an instant hit in the #7 shirt. Homesickness led him to return to Brazil in 1958, but his three seasons of magical wing-play had earnt him an eternal place in the hearts of all *Viola*. The picture of Julinho leaving the field after his last game, against Padova in 1958, tears streaming down his face, is tucked away in scrapbooks across Tuscany.

In truth, Fiorentina's title-winning side was packed with stars. Six of the *azzurri* side which played against West Germany in Rome in 1955 came from the Florence

club, and against Yugoslavia in 1957, there were no fewer than nine *Viola* in Italy's starting line-up. Yet European success eluded them. In the 1957 Champions' Cup, Fiorentina beat Grasshoppers and Red Star Belgrade but lost 2–0 to Real Madrid in the final. The penalty award with which Alfredo di Stéfano gave Madrid the lead 20 minutes from time – given by a visibly nervous Dutch referee in front of 125,000 in the Bernabéu – still raises voices in Florentine cafés.

Fiorentina's championship side quickly fell apart. Bernadini left in 1958, after which there would be four coaches in as many years, former Hungarian international Nandor Hidegkuti among them. Julinho was replaced by Swedish international winger Kurt Hamrin, who would go on to Milan and Napoli after nine years at the Stadio Comunale. It was Hamrin, a remarkable goalscoring winger, who was the most influential figure in the *Viola* side which, in 1961, won the club's only European honour to date. In the Cup-Winners' Cup they defeated Lucerne and Dinamo Zagreb, before beating Rangers home and away in the final, Hamrin scoring the last of four Fiorentina goals in the tie.

A year later the *Viola* defeated Újpesti Dózsa in the semi-finals of the same competition, then became the first in a long line of clubs to just fail to retain that particular European crown, losing out in a replay to Atlético Madrid.

Contenders rather than champions during the mid-Sixties, Fiorentina held their own under the stewardship of Giuseppe Chiapello while never remotely threatening another *scudetto*. All that was to change in 1968/69, when Bruno Pesaolo was brought in as coach and immediately abandoned Chiapello's caution and fielded four strikers. Widely criticised as naïve, Pesaolo's tactics worked – not just because of the team's instinct for goal, but because their attacking movements were co-ordinated from the back, by the brilliant sweeper Giuseppe Brizi. It was a unique combination, good enough to win Fiorentina their second Italian title. Yet within two years, Brizi would be a hero in entirely different circumstances – his goal against Inter saving Fiorentina from relegation to *Serie B*.

Once again, the club had allowed a successful squad to break up before it had had a chance to leave a lasting impression on the game – and the consequences were serious. For Fiorentina, the Seventies were a decade of frustrating mediocrity, relieved only by the artful playmaking of international midfielder Giancarlo Antognoni, drafted into the ranks of the *azzurri* by old boy Bernardini, by now coach of the national team.

For the 1981/82 season, Giancarlo de Sisti, Fiorentina's former Italian international, was brought in as coach by new president Ranieri Pontello. To play alongside the ageing but still capable Antognoni, de Sisti blooded fresh talent in the formidable shape of stopper Pietro Vierchowod and target man Daniele Massaro – future Milan players both. The new-look team led the Italian table for most of the season but on the last day of the campaign, Fiorentina were level on points with Juventus. 'The Old Lady' had to visit Catanzaro while the Lilacs were at Cagliari. At half-time both games were scoreless and the Italian championship was heading for a rare play-off. But in the second half two events occurred which determined the outcome of the title. Bertoni scored for Fiorentina but his goal was disallowed. In the other game, Juventus were awarded a disputed penalty in the 75th minute. The title went to Turin, and Florence all but exploded with rage.

Ask anyone in the town today about that season and you will hear any variety of conspiracy theories – the most popular being that both referees had been bribed by Juve officials. The protests, official and unofficial, went on for weeks, but the Italian FA stood by the results and the *Viola* had been denied a third title.

The city's loathing of Juventus began with that season and only intensified in the coming years. In 1985/86, Fiorentina signed a promising youngster by the name of Roberto Baggio from Vicenza. Baggio, along with resourceful Brazilian Dunga, was the inspiration in a side that reached the final of the 1990 UEFA Cup, where they were to meet Juventus in an all-Italian clash. Juve won the first leg in Turin, 3–1, but there was an outbreak of violence from the travelling support, and the Italian FA were ordered by UEFA to play the second leg at a neutral ground. The site chosen was Avellino – a town without a major team but, according to Fiorentina, with a large traditional support for Juve. Again the club protested, but to no avail. The second leg finished scoreless and Juve lifted the trophy.

Within weeks, even that ignominy would seem irrelevant. On the eve of Italia '90 Juve announced they had signed the darling of the *Viola* – Baggio – for a world record transfer fee of £8million. The city went wild with anger. Baggio, along with fellow international Nicola Berti (who had left Fiorentina for Inter the previous season) were targeted by local fans when the Italian team came to their training camp at Coverciano, close to Florence. Not only had Juve 'stolen' a *scudetto* and a major European trophy – now they had nicked Fiorentina's star, too.

The fans launched a successful campaign to oust president Lorenzo Righetti, who was replaced by film producer and businessman Mario Cecchi Gori.

During the following season, 1990/91, Baggio's return to Florence in a black-and-white striped shirt required a massive police mobilisation. With Fiorentina ahead, Juve were awarded a penalty. Baggio, who had been taking penalties all season, turned his back. In the incredibly hostile atmosphere, he dared not score against his old club. As a Juve team-mate of the time, Thomas Hässler, put it: 'For the first time in my life I felt we were playing not against another team, but against an entire city.'

Intimidating the fans may have been – the team were anything but. Despite high-profile signings like Marius Lacatuş, Stefan Effenberg and Brian Laudrup, Fiorentina could not mount another challenge for the title, and in 1993 they were relegated to *Serie B* for the first time since World War II. The following year, President Mario Cecchi Gori died, leaving the post to his son, Vittorio.

With their backs against the wall, the men in purple hit out, returning effortlessly to *Serie A* at the first attempt, with Argentinian striker Gabriel Batistuta their leading scorer. The long-haired goal-poacher, nicknamed *Batigol*, was the man who finally buried the memory of Baggio. His dedication was admired – he had resisted lucrative offers from elsewhere and stuck by the club in *Serie B*, determined to help get them back where they belonged. And his instinct for goal was lauded not just in Florence but the length and breadth of Italy.

On Fiorentina's return to the top flight in 1994/95, Batistuta scored 26 goals, including one in each of the first eleven games – a *Serie A* record. It was Batistuta's goals, coupled with the understated but intelligent coaching of Claudio Ranieri, which brought Fiorentina victory in the *Coppa Italia* in 1996, and an excellent run in the Cup-Winners' Cup a year later.

In the semi-finals of that tournament, however, Florence's inability to lose gracefully was again thrown into sharp relief. Barcelona coach Bobby Robson was hit by a bottle, and the referee threatened to abandon the match.

The result? A hefty UEFA fine, a ban on staging European ties, suspensions for key players who insulted the match officials. With Ranieri gone, Batistuta restless and Cecchi Gori increasingly preoccupied by his media interests, the Fiorentina ship appeared to be sailing close to the rocks. But the appointment of Giovanni Trapattoni in the summer of 1998 prompted the club's best title shot in a decade. Rather than sign strikers, as had been the *Viola* habit, 'Trap' bought defenders Jörg Heinrich, Moreno Torricelli and Tomas Repka. With Batistuta motivated again alongside his Brazilian strike partner Edmundo, the team were four points clear at the top of the table come Christmas.

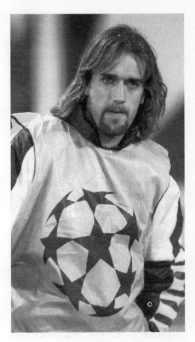

The star's last year – *Batigol* in UCL garb

It all went wrong one February afternoon at home to Milan, when Batistuta pulled up lame and Edmundo galloped off to party at the Rio carnival as a prelude to a court case for manslaughter. Pictures of him partying in a tuxedo were sent around the world, while at home Fiorentina went six hours without scoring a goal. The *Viola* ended up finishing a distant third to Lazio and Milan in the league, and also lost the *Coppa Italia* final, to Parma on away goals.

With *Batigol* back to full fitness and Edmundo packed off back to Brazil, Trapattoni strengthened his attack with the addition of Enrico Chiesa from Parma and Pedja Mijatović from Real Madrid. A majestic performance in a win over Manchester United opened up the prospect of a place in the Champions' League quarter-finals, but European progress was coming at the expense of league form – Trap's team couldn't win away from home in the league until March. After that, defeats in Valéncia and Manchester put paid to the European dream, and a mid-table finish persuaded Trapattoni to quit.

Worse was to come. Batistuta finally decided he had sacrificed enough of his career in Florence and left for Roma, prompting predictable street protests against a floundering Cecchi Gori as the *Viola tifosi* erupted in anger.

Turkish coach Fatih Terim, who had just won the UEFA Cup with Galatasaray, seemed an unlikely choice as Trap's replacement, and the signing of young Portuguese striker Nuno Gomes, while not a bad piece of business, was hardly replacing Batistuta. With rumours stirring of financial problems in Cecchi Gori's media business, the passion of the Florence supporters may be directed in protest rather than celebration for some time to come.

Here we go!

Take one of the four **trains** an hour (journey time f5mins, L1,750) from Santa Maria Novella one stop to Campo di Marte station, a short walk to the stadium over the railway bridge. Of the city **buses**, #52 runs match ays only from Santa Maria Novella, bus #17 takes a similar route, and the #10 drops you close. Allow half-an-hour, plus waiting time.

Just the ticket

With a stadium capacity of only 45,000 and a large number of season-ticket holders, arriving in town without a ticket can mean problems.

A good start would be the **ticket stand** in town at Piazza della Repubblica, where Già Chiasso di Borghese meets Pellicceria, but they tend to sell out fast. The one at the stadium is open Mon–Fri 10am–4pm, and for away fans there is a green ticket office on the corner of Viale Maratona and Viale Pasquale Paoli, selling seats for L35,000 between the Nervi tower and the scoreboard end.

Viola fans occupy both ends, so neutrals are best, if expensively, placed in the main Nervi stand (L150–200,000). Both the *Marisa* and *Stadio* bars also sell tickets.

Swift half

Just opposite the main stand, on the other side of Via della Manfredo Fanti, are the two traditional meeting places for *Viola* fans. The **Bar Marisa** is a must, any day of the week. It attracts an elderly clientèle with nothing else on their minds than the next game and the last 600. There's bottled beer as well as the usual coffee concoctions, and in fine weather the football forum moves out on to the street. If this self-appointed purple parliament drags you outside to join them, don't miss the interior – the photos on the wall, including team line-ups of both title squads, old shots of the Comunale and stars of past and present, amount to a free Fiorentina museum.

At the crossroads, the **Bar Stadio** has less character but better coffee, live football on TV and doughnuts to die for. It also attracts a younger crowd, including women. Creamy cappuccino, fresh doughnuts and plenty of *la bella figura* in lilac – *sempre!*

Ultra culture

Collettivo Autonomo Viola, founded in 1978, are the boys gathered in the *Curva Fiesole* behind the goal. They were responsible for the stunning 1991 choreography which displayed a silhouette of the city's outline in lilac; their symbol is an American Indian.

In print

The newspaper **Noi Viola** and colour programme **Fiorentina News** are distributed free on match-days, along with various unofficial fan sheets.

In the net

The club has redesigned its official site at: www.acfiorentina.it. English-language content is limited, but the site is well-designed and easy to get around.

Eat, drink, sleep…

Bars and clubs

Avoid the **tourist traps** and Florence is a fine place to drink in. Most of what you want is in the centre, and with its small-

FLORENCE

town feel and thousands of visitors a week, clubbing here can be a lot more fun than in, say, Milan or Turin.

Chequers, Via della Scala 7/9. Just off Piazza Santa Maria Novella, a good venue for watching live games on the big screen. Pre-match happy hour 6.30–8pm with – unusually for Italy – half-price drinks. A busy and lively boozer.

Lidò, Lungarno Pecori Giraldi 1. On the city bank of the Arno by Ponte San Niccoló, a club that uses the river to great advantage, with a terrace and table football. Inside, reasonably priced drinks, excellent sounds, unpretentious but hip clientele, free entrance.

Lion's Fountain, Via Borgo Albizi 34. The best of the pubs with TV football, this one is packed for Italian games. Of the others, only the inferior *Fiddler's Elbow*, Piazza Santa Maria Novella, has Sky TV. *The Public House*, Via Palazzuolo 27, is the liveliest and least pretentious of them all – no TV but decent music and decor.

Totocalcio 'Viola Club', Piazza Salvemini 3. Where Via Verdi and Via Fiesolana meet, a small daytime betting bar decked out in *Viola* memorabilia with plenty of football talk. Closed weekday lunchtimes.

Restaurants

Traditional **Tuscan cuisine** is a fresh mix of meat and vegetables, often served as stews and with the emphasis on fine ingredients. However, Florence's restaurants mostly cater to tourists, so dull **pizza** and **pasta** predominate. If you really want to pig out, head for the suburbs.

Antico Noé, Volta di San Piero 6. In a seedy alley, near Piazza dei Ciompi, a reasonably priced restaurant, with a signed pic of Fiorentina's '56 side on the wall. Fixed menu at L15,000. Open Mon–Sat 11am–8pm, no credit cards.

Caffè Richi, Piazza Santo Spirito 9. Perfect lunchtime spot, main dishes L10–15,000. Tables overlooking a busy square with other options.

I Latini, Via dei Palchetti 6. A classic Tuscan-style trattoria tucked away amid city-centre back streets. The menu is a 'greatest hits' of Tuscan cuisine. Worth booking ahead on: ☎055/210 916.

Osteria dei Benci, Via dè Benci 13. Locals enjoy this imaginative restaurant with its daily specials and excellent array of Tuscan specialities to go with the various kinds of toast. Closed Sun. Most credit cards.

Trattoria Casalinga, Via del Michelozzi 9. Traditional Tuscan dishes in this neighbourhood *trattoria*, with local wines and olive oils. Main courses L15–20,000, most credit cards, closed Sun. Between the Pitti Palace and the river.

Accommodation

Florence has a longer **tourist season** than most Italian football cities. Anytime between April and October, there could be a serious shortage of places to stay. There is an *ITA* hotel booking office at Santa Maria Novella train station.

Alessandra, Borgo Santi Apostoli 17 (☎055/283 438, fax 055/210 619). Classy, upmarket two-star hotel but reasonably priced. From around L120,000 for a double. Most credit cards.

Archi Rossi, Via Faenza 94 (☎055/290 804, fax 055/230 2601). Modern, clean youth hostel near the station, L25,000 per person with breakfast, big-screen TV, curfew 12.30am, no credit cards.

Azzi, Via Faenza 56 (☎055/213 806). In a street full of small hostels and pensions, this is in a block jam-packed with accommodation. Checkout 10am, curfew 2am, breakfast included. From L65,000 per person. Most credit cards.

Hotel Villa Fiesole, Via B Angelico 35 (☎055/599 133). If you want to wake up in the morning, stroll out onto a terrace, order an *espresso* and look down on a view of the city, then this is the place. Located in the hills above the stadium – you'll need a L40,000 taxi ride to get to the village of Fiesole. L170,000 for a single room during the football season.

From Scarborough to Scala – the Parma story

Parma were *the* Italian club of the Nineties. For a club with no record before 1990, their nine consecutive top-seven finishes – interspersed with three European trophies and two Italian cups – was remarkable.

Founded as **Verdi FC** to celebrate the centenary of the composer's birth in 1913, Parma FC, as they soon became, were the first love of club president Ennio Tardini. On New Year's Eve 1922, Tardini laid the first stone of the club's new stadium which now bears his name, although he died before its comple-

Sudden lapse – beaten by Bremen, March 2000

tion. Parma then flitted between divisions, rarely the top one, until bankruptcy in 1969 saw the club re-emerge as Parma Associazone Calcio a year later.

A host of famous coaches – Sacchi, Maldini, Zeman – helped the club move up the league, but it was the arrival in the late Eighties of **Nevio Scala** and millionaire **Calisto Tanzi** that changed Parma's fortunes. Tanzi's dairy firm *Parmalat* had been sponsoring clubs across Europe; now he decided to pump a decent amount of money into the local club.

In 1990, Scala boosted a freshly promoted team with World Cup stars Claudio Taffarel of Brazil in goal, Georges Grun of Belgium in defence and Tomas Brolin of Sweden upfront. Two respectable league finishes and a *Coppa Italia* win over Juventus were the fruits of Scala's adventurous labour, and Parma found themselves in Europe.

Previous continental appearances had been limited to a narrow win over **Northwich Victoria** and defeat by **Scarborough** in the Anglo-Italian Cup of 1976. But with the arrival of unconventional Colombian striker **Faustino Asprilla**, Parma swept all before them in the following season's Cup-Winners' Cup, beating Antwerp at Wembley 3–1. Before long Dino Baggio and Gianfranco Zola would join the ranks, and the 1994/95 season saw a battle royal with Juventus, Parma falling just behind in the league and cup, but beating Juve in the UEFA Cup final, 2–1 on aggregate.

A **well-organised club** free of hype and inner-city rivalry, Parma have always been able to concentrate on the task at hand. Their forward line alone – Enrico Chiesa, Argentines Hernán Crespo and Abel Balbo, and a returning Asprilla – would have made them a major threat in 1998/99, but added to that was a world-class defence featuring French World Cup '98 hero **Lilian Thuram**, the playmaking skills of Argentine **Juan Veron**, and the introduction of solid coaching by **Alberto Malesani**. For a while Parma looked like they could go all the way and win a first *scudetto*. In the end, they had to settle for a mere *Coppa Italia* and the UEFA Cup. The 1999/2000 campaign was trophyless, with an uncharacteristic lapse against Werder Bremen in Europe and a play-off defeat by Inter preventing a quick return to the Champions' League. More serious, perhaps, may be the sale of **Crespo** to Lazio in the summer of 2000.

Buses #8 and #9 run from the train station to the **Ennio Tardini stadium**, taking 10–15mins (tickets L1,300 from orange machines), arriving either side of the ground. By the #8 bus stop at Viale Duca Alessandro 13a is the *Bar Tardini*, with flags and the floodlights reflected in the windows. The grand main entrance and **ticket office** are on Piazzale Risorgimento.

Turin

The heart of Turin's football culture lies at the opposite end of the city from the Stadio delle Alpi currently shared by the town's two big clubs, Juventus and Torino. Built at awesome expense for the 1990 World Cup, the delle Alpi is a white elephant, bereft of both atmosphere and decent transport links. While the most recent plans suggest a modified, smaller stadium with hotel and a Juventus museum, for most of the last half-decade, both Juve and Torino have been threatening to go back to their roots at their Comunale and Filadelfia stadia.

These two grounds face each other across the Corso Unione Sovietica which leads south from town, dividing the vast Fiat car plant from the Mirafiori housing estates opposite. The Fiat factory employs some 50,000 workers in Turin, many of whose families live on the Mirafiori estates. Behind Fiat lie the Agnelli family who have been financing Juventus since 1923. Their club are the most successful in Italy, with seven million supporters, two million of them in the south. Many of their hometown fans are also originally southerners, economic migrants who, like the team's coach of the late Nineties, Marcello Lippi, came to Turin for work.

The rest of Agnelli's employees, however, are loyal Torino folk, supporting the working-class club across the road whose five years of football fame were cruelly ended by the Superga air crash of 1949. The scene of that disaster, the Basilica, looks down over the city from its 700m-high vantage point on the other side of the river Po.

Torino FC had been formed in 1906 by disgruntled members of Juventus, and by the fusion of two teams who had featured in the finals of the first three Italian championships: Internazionale Torino and FC Torinese. The former had been Italy's first football club, founded by noblemen two years after local Edoardo Bosio had come back from London with a football in 1887.

It was Genoa who won those first three titles, but when the Italian Football Federation was set up in 1898, its headquarters were in Turin.

Behind Torino FC (later simply Torino) was Vittorio Pozzo, who was born nearby. Coach of Italy's World Cup winning sides of the Thirties, Pozzo also worked for many years behind the scenes at Torino. He would see the club win just one prewar title, in 1928, Juventus having conspired to nullify one the year before; Agnelli's club claimed Torino officials had tried to bribe Juve defender Luigi Allemandi, and the Federation, by then moved to Rome, came down in Juventus' favour. A great soccer rivalry was born.

With Agnelli's financial backing, Juve left their neighbours firmly behind in the years to World War II, winning five titles in a row with the best players money could buy. Oddly, though, during the war Torino's emerging side was nurtured not only by wise old Pozzo but by the Agnelli family, who gave the players nominal jobs at Fiat to keep them out of the Italian army.

It was a generosity of spirit the Agnellis would regret, for Torino would win five titles between 1943 and 1949, and would surely have gone on to dominate the city's footballing life had the Superga crash not intervened. After the disaster, Juve reasserted their old dominance, but clashes between the two sides in what had become known as *Il Derby della Mole* were always closely fought, not least after Toro came good again in the Sixties.

The mercurial talents of Torino's exceptional young forward, Gigi Meroni, had the crowd on their feet many times on derby day, before he was killed by a car while crossing the city's busy Corso Re Umberto in 1967. For the derby game a few days later, Toro refused a Juve offer of another player in his place. Before the match, as the colours of each team were entwined all around the Comunale, flowers were laid where Meroni would have stood.

In 1976, when Torino won their first and so far only post-Superga title, it was Juve who were pushed into second place – not least thanks to two derby-day defeats. The following year the positions were reversed, in what would be the last post-war Turin one-two.

Torino managed to do the double over Juve again as recently as 1994/95, but by that time the club were in deep trouble; a year later the team would be relegated, in the same season as Juventus, under Lippi, were winning both the *scudetto* and the *Coppa Italia*.

If the two clubs have been poles apart in terms of league status in recent years, they are at least united in their desire to return 'home'. Torino's beloved Filadelfia stadium, which last saw *Serie A* action in 1963, is overgrown with weeds, ivy and faded Toro banners – walking around it is like exploring a shipwreck. Yet fans still share memories in the bars opposite the ground, and 25,000 of them would be able to fit into the Filadelfia were it to be rebuilt, 75 years after its initial construction was funded by Count Cinzano.

Juve's Stadio Comunale is in better shape – after all, the two clubs shared it for 25 years until the eve of the 1990 World Cup. Currently used for Juve training sessions, it can still hold 65,000 at a pinch. But, like the Filadelfia, the ground still needs serious work before it is fit to host top-class *calcio*.

In the meantime, and with their nation-wide appeal, Juventus could, and do, play major games anywhere in Italy...

Turin essentials

Caselle **airport** is 12km north of Turin. A *Sadem* bus service (L6,000) runs into town, calling at the two **train stations**, Porta Susa and Porta Nuova, every 45mins, 6.30am–11.30pm, journey time about 40mins. A **taxi** will cost about L50,000 to do the same journey.

Porta Nuova is the main train station and lies at the crossroads of two of Turin's main avenues, Corso Vittorio Emanuele II and Via Roma, the latter leading on to central Piazza San Carlo and Piazza San Castello; Vittorio Emanuele leads to the main **bus station** at Corso Inghilterra 3, 1.5km away, and down to the river Po, 1km in the opposite direction.

The city is laid out on a grid system, criss-crossed by a network of buses, trams and fast trams, running 6am–midnight, with no night transport. Free **route maps** are available from the information offices at Porta Nuova and Porta Susa. You can buy **tickets** there, and at *tabacchi* designated by an 'ATM' sign, and also from automatic machines at main tram stops.

A single ticket (*ordinario urbano*) is L1,400, valid for 70mins – stamp one end in the yellow box onboard, then the other end if you're continuing your journey on another route within the 70mins. A book of ten costs L13,500; a one-day ticket (*giornaliero*) is L4,200; and a 'shopping' ticket, allowing four hours' travel between 9am and 8pm, is good value at L2,400.

You should find taxis parked either side of Porta Nuova on Via Nizza or Via XX Settembre, or in the main square by the river, Piazza Vittorio Veneto. To phone for one, dial ☎011/5737 or ☎011/5730. Standing charge is L5,000, after which it's L1,300 per km, with a L3,500 night tariff and L1,500 surcharge on Sundays and public holidays.

The new central **tourist office** is at Piazza Castello 161 (open daily 8.30am–7.30pm, ☎011/535 181, fax 011/530 070), with smaller branches at Porta Nuova station (☎011/531 327) and at Casale airport (☎011/567 8124).

The Turin daily *La Stampa* has a high-brow **entertainment section** on Thursdays. In town, look out for the free weekly pamphlet *Spettacolo News*, which has comprehensive bar and club **listings**.

The thrilling fields

 Juventus

Stadium Delle Alpi, see p.375
Club office Piazza Crimea 7
Colours Black-and-white striped shirts, white shorts
League champions 1905, 1926, 1931–35, 1950, 1952, 1958, 1960–61, 1967, 1972–73, 1975, 1977–78, 1981–82, 1984, 1986, 1995, 1997–98
Cup winners 1938, 1942, 1959, 1960, 1965, 1979, 1983, 1990, 1995
European Cup winners 1985, 1996
Cup-Winners' Cup winners 1984
UEFA Cup winners 1977, 1990, 1993

Italy's biggest club is inevitably the country's most unpopular. Juventus' record 25th *scudetto* in 1998 set the bulk of the Italian footballing public against them, such was the favouritism thought to be given by referees to the Zebras in their title run-in with Inter. This despite Alex del Piero and Pippo Inzaghi scoring more goals than any Juve forward duo for over three decades, and all in the club's centenary season to boot.

On November 1, 1897, pupils from the well-to-do Massimo d'Azeglio Grammar School formed a sports club, settling on the name Football Club Juventus two years later. Twenty-fiver titles, two European Cups and dozens of other trophies later, the bench the boys were said to have met on stands, battle weary, in front of the club's heavily guarded offices on Turin's Piazza Crimea.

Juventus – literally 'Youth' – mean many things to many people. For their thousand supporters' clubs worldwide, they are a point of contact with the *calcio* they see on satellite TV. For the Agnelli family, whose Fiat car company bankrolls the club, they have been a fantastic showroom but a 75-year loss maker. For seven million Italian fans, many from the south, they are *La Vecchia Signora* – 'The Old Lady', a symbol of devotion. For everyone else, *La Juve* are a callous hussy, buying their way up the ladder to worldwide fame.

Juventus won their first Italian title in 1905, but lost players to the newly formed Torino the following year and had to wait for the Agnellis' funds to kick in before they won another one. Then, just as now, talented players were attracted by a huge signing-on fee, a decent wage and a new Fiat car. Argentines Raimundo Orsi and Luisito Monti, Italians Luigi Bertolini and Giovanni Ferrari – all to win the 1934 World Cup with Italy – were teamed with goalkeeping captain Giampiero Combi and a goal-a-game youngster by the name of Felice Borel. It was a setup not unlike

How the mighty fall – defeat by Celta Vigo, 2000

today's, and millions of fans followed their progress to five straight titles from 1931.

The Juve years set the newly shaped Italian league alight. The Zebras, nicknamed after their black-and-white striped shirts, were loved or hated by all. As this great side aged, however, their neighbours Torino rose, and it was not until the season after the Superga disaster that Juventus won their next title, with further expensive imports in the shape of Danish forwards John Hansen and Karl Præst.

The club stayed in the hunt all through the Fifties, with striker Giampiero Boniperti as the figurehead. Boniperti would subsequently lead the club into the modern era, as its managing director from 1972 to 1994. As a player he scored a goal every other game for more than a decade. But his playing career was coming to an end when a complementary striking pair were imported to bring Juventus three more titles between 1958 and 1961: John Charles, the Welsh gentle giant who cost a record British transfer fee to buy from Leeds; and Omar Sivori, a brilliant but temperamental Argentine. Over five years, Charles became a folk hero in Turin, famed for his power, bravery and subtle ball skills. Sivori was a magician, European Footballer of the Year in 1961. Each topped the league's scoring charts for one season.

But when Charles left and Sivori faded, for once the Bank of Agnelli could not find a winning return on their investment. Juventus were overshadowed by the Milan giants in the league, and were no more than also-rans in the emerging European competitions – they reached two UEFA Cup finals in 1965 and 1971, but lost them both, to Ferencváros and Leeds respectively. Unusually, Juve were out of the limelight, and Italy's ban on foreign transfers prevented the club from buying their way back into it.

At the start of the Seventies Juve learnt to buy wisely in safe Italian stock: José Altafini, a European Cup-winning goalscorer with Milan in 1963; a 1968 European Championship winner, Pietro Anastasi, as his partner upfront; and another 1968 gold medallist, Dino Zoff, in goal.

With their help, the team carved out a narrow title win over Milan and Torino in 1972. The victory encouraged Juventus to nurture a core of players who would go on not just to dominate the domestic game, but to represent a regenerated Italian national team. Wily forward Roberto Bettega and midfield creator Franco Causio may have been on the losing side when Ajax beat Juve in the 1973 European Cup final, but they would still be around four years later, as part of the team that lifted the 1977 UEFA Cup – Juve's first European silverware.

That same year saw the arrival of coach Giovanni Trapattoni – *Il Trap* – a former canny wing-half with AC Milan who set about constructing an iron defence and tightly sprung attack which would bring Juve six titles in ten years. Italy's national-team coach, Enzo Bearzot, used practically the entire Juve team for the 1978 World Cup, and seven of them were still there to win it for him in 1982 – including the old-warhorse Causio, brought on as a late sub in the final against West Germany.

At various points in the Seventies and Eighties Juventus could call on Antonio Cabrini, Gaetano Scirea and Claudio Gentile in defence, Romeo Benetti and Marco Tardelli in midfield, and a rejuvenated Roberto Boninsegna in attack, later replaced by Italy's hero of 1982, Paolo Rossi. When foreigners were allowed back into the Italian game, Juve imported flair – men like Liam Brady, scorer of a late penalty in his last game in 1982 which won Juve two stars for their 20 *scudetti*; the rapid-fire Pole, Zbigniew Boniek; and the matchless Frenchman, Michel Platini.

Platini's contribution was awesome. In three successive years between 1984 and 1986 he was Italy's top scorer – from midfield. More than anyone else, he spearheaded Juve's quest for the European Cup. In 1983 they had been outwitted by Ernst Happel's Hamburg. In 1985, having won the Cup-Winners' Cup in between,

The Stadio delle Alpi

Strada Altessano 131
Capacity 71,000

Expensive, unwanted and unloved, the delle Alpi stands in Turin's northern outskirts, home to two football clubs who desperately desire not to play in it. Its construction, for the 1990 World Cup, cost three times the originally estimated L60billion. But to Juve and Toro, the real cost has had to be borne since – the company that built the ground, *Acqua Marcia*, had a contract with the Turin city council, which administers it, to take three-quarters of stadium advertising revenue. Since then, *Acqua Marcia* have gone bust, and the council must now decide what to do with the site.

Torino want to move back to their beloved Filadelfia, but don't have the money to do so – although the 2000 boardroom takeover may provide just that. **Juventus** want a 99-year lease so that they can make the arena smaller and build a vast sports and leisure complex around it; if they don't get it, they have threatened to move out of Turin altogether, and build a new stadium near the village of **Borgaro**, which has granted them planning permission to build whatever they like on a greenfield site. The Turin city council's reaction was to threaten not to build road or public-transport links which would be necessary to take fans from the city to the site, and with the prospect of such a deadlock, both sides of the debate were expected to compromise during 2000.

For the time being, however, nothing has been signed, so the atmosphere at the stadium is as cold as the wind that howls through it. With the running track (which remains unused), there is **a 20m gap** between spectators and players, who complain that they cannot hear the crowd at all. The stadium *is* accessible, but only if you're coming by car from out of town. The journey from the city centre is fertile ground for pickpockets who eagerly fill the tram as it slowly winds its way through Turin's dark streets for what seems like an eternity.

Ironically, given that the decision to build the delle Alpi was taken in an atmosphere of post-Heysel paranoia, security is another complaint laid at the stadium's door. The exits are too narrow, and segregation is not as tight as it could be.

On matchdays, **tram #9** runs every 10mins directly to the stadium from Porta Nuova station; at other times it takes a circuitous route, terminating at Piazza Stampalia, a 10min walk from the ground down Strada Druento. Leaving the ground, you'll find the tram waiting on Corso Grande Torino, along the west side of the stadium.

Before and after the action, many fans head for the **Self-Service delle Alpi**, Strada Altessano 146 (facing the east side of the ground), a large, soulless cellar serving three-course lunches, with a bar on one side and a TV in the corner. Further along, at Strada Altessano 55, *L'Elite* is indeed a far classier option. It has a lively bar area, which sells match tickets and cans of Boddingtons, and a self-service restaurant behind. For a genuine football bar, *Italia '90*, Strada Altessano 42, has colour pictures of the stadium under construction and noisy card games going on in the background.

The *Stadio Service* behind the south end, at Via Sansovino 229 (open Mon–Fri 9am–noon & 2.30–5.30pm, ☎011/455 9691), sells **advance tickets**, as do the club shops. On matchdays the stadium has eight ticket gates and can suffer from dreadful queueing. Many deal with touts merely because they can't be bothered to wait.

There are **three tiers**, the highest (*3 anello*) far too high, the lowest (*1 anello*) too low. The *tribune est* and *ovest* are over the halfway line, the most desired place to be for the neutral, especially the middle tier. If you're willing to spend a reasonable amount of money for a reasonable view, *distinti centrale* seats are the best. You'll find Toro fans in the *Curva Maratona*, behind the north goal; Juve's are in the *Curva Scirea*, opposite.

Still seeking success – coach Carlo Ancelotti

they set up a long-awaited head-to-head with Liverpool – but the match was to be rendered irrelevant by the Heysel stadium disaster. Platini accepted the cup after his penalty had given Juve a hollow win. 'He never talks about it,' his wife said later. 'In his head was the fact that a Frenchman, who died at Heysel, had come to see him play. That broke Michel in two. He wanted to give everything up.'

As Platini faded, Juve disintegrated. The club moved to the Stadio delle Alpi, having crowned the Comunale era with a UEFA Cup win over Fiorentina in 1990. But they did not get a sniff of the title for ten years.

As the Nineties unfolded, it was clear Juve would have to buy bigger than ever to match the Milanese. Italian internationals Roberto Baggio, Gianluca Vialli and Dino Baggio, plus Germans Jürgen Kohler and Andreas Möller, were in the side that won the UEFA Cup in 1993. Like Boniperti before him, Roberto Bettega then moved

upstairs to direct affairs, and within months coach Marcello Lippi was in the Juve dugout after performing miracles at Napoli. Journeyman striker Fabrizio Ravanelli came through to earn his place alongside Vialli, and while Kohler and Möller had gone back to Germany, Juve were blessed by the arrival of a prodigious young playmaking talent, Alessandro del Piero, from Padova.

This was the backbone of the team that did the Italian double in 1995, and though Parma beat them in the UEFA Cup final that year, Bettega and Lippi had their sights set on higher things – the laying to rest of the ghost of Heysel. A year later their goal was achieved, thanks to a penalty shoot-out win over Ajax in Rome – an untainted European Cup was Juve's for the first time.

That summer, with old Gianni Agnelli demanding belt-tightening, Bettega and Lippi bought and sold wisely, surprisingly selling Ravanelli and Vialli to England. In came Nicola Amoruso, Christian Vieri Croatian Alen Bokšić and Frenchman Zinedine Zidane, a new breed of players with an average age of 24.

The move worked perfectly – up to a point. Juve comfortably won back a *scudetto* that had been lost to Milan in 1996, but after playing some magnificent football in the 1996/97 Champions' League, their ambitious bid to retain Europe's premier footballing honour failed at the feet of Borussia Dortmund's super-sub, Lars Ricken, in Munich's Olympic stadium.

Within weeks of that European Cup final defeat, Bokšić and Vieri had been off-loaded, and Lippi again went for comparatively modest signings like forward Filippo Inzaghi from Atalanta and full-back Alessandro Birindelli from Empoli. But it took a while for the team to gel, the turning point coming with the mid-season arrival of Edgar Davids, discarded by Milan and with a point to prove, as both a destroyer and a creator in midfield.

With Davids' prompting, club captain Antonio Conte returning from injury and Inzaghi and del Piero forging a profitable goalscoring duo upfront, Juve hit four apiece past Dynamo Kiev and Monaco to reach the European Cup final, while overhauling Inter with a series of single-goal victories in the league. With the media ranged against them at home, the club won their 25th *scudetto* with a 3–2 win over Bologna, Inzaghi scoring all three goals.

In Europe, however, an injury to del Piero proved crucial and Juventus could find no answer to Real Madrid once the Spaniards had gone ahead in Amsterdam. The match would prove a curious pre-echo for the 1998/99 season to come. Just as he was returning to full fitness, del Piero sustained a further injury in a league game at Udinese, and Juve's defence of their title collapsed when coach Lippi's agreement to take charge of Inter the following year became public knowledge. The team somehow qualified for the knockout stage of the Champions' League, once again at the death after failing to win any of their first five games, but before the quarter-finals, with the players' respect for him draining away, Lippi resigned.

The new coach, Carlo Ancelotti, took Juve past Olympiakos but ran into the brick wall of Manchester United in the semifinals. The only route back into Europe was now in the league, but even this seemed barred when Udinese beat Juve in a play-off for a UEFA Cup place on away goals. That left the Intertoto Cup as a back-door road to continental competition, and Juve's squad full of internationals were forced to cut short their holidays and make trips to Romania and Russia in order to tread it. Having made such a sacrifice, it was strange that Ancelotti should then choose to field a second-string side for much of the 1999/2000 UEFA Cup campaign – a humiliating 4–1 defeat at Celta Vigo, with Zidane left out of the team, was the result.

The coach's excuse for protecting his players from the extra demands of European competition was that Juve were on course for the title at home and couldn't afford to be deflected from it. By comparison with their championship rivals Lazio, Ancelotti's teams weren't pretty to watch

– nine of their 21 victories bore a 1–0 scoreline. But at one stage Juve were nine points clear, and it seemed their safety-first tactics would win the day when, on the season's penultimate weekend, Parma had a late equaliser at the delle Alpi inexplicably ruled out, leaving the Zebras with the relatively simple task of winning at lowly Perugia on the final day to claim their 26th *scudetto*. Then the gods – or at least, heavy rain – intervened. Juve lost a much-delayed game 1–0 on a bog of a pitch, and with Lazio winning at home to Reggina, the title went to Rome…

Club merchandise

Near the ground is the *Juve Shop*, Strada Altessano 57 (open Tue–Sat and matchdays 9am–9pm, Mon 2–9pm). In town your best bet is the *Kappa* store, Via Giolitti 2 (Tue–Sat 9.30am–12.30pm & 3.30–7.30pm, Mon 3.30–7.30pm).

Ultra culture

Lo Juventus Club were one of the earliest ultra groups to be founded in Italy, during the early Seventies. Splinter groups like the *Black & White Supporters* brought drums and rattles to the old Stadio Comunale, but it wasn't until the post-Heysel formation of the *Drughi* that ultra culture became a lively issue. Competition became fierce with the foundation of *i Viking*, especially when the rival groups had to scrap for territory at the new Stadio delle Alpi. Now you'll see the *Black & White Supporters* and *Drughi* in the *Curva Scirea*, and *i Viking* at the other end.

In print

Two monthly magazines can be found on most Turin newsstands: *Hurrá Juventus!* and *Forza Juve!* (both L5,000).

In the net

Clearly designed and maintained by the same firm responsible for the AC Milan site (*Sportal*), Juve's **official website** resides at: www.juventus.it. Like its *rossoneri* counterpart it boasts a particularly strong English-language news area.

For a comprehensive, fan-run Italian-language site, try the Lugano, Switzerland supporters' club offering at: www.pubblinet.com/juve/juve.htm.

🌑 Torino

Stadium Delle Alpi, see p.375
Club office Corso Vittorio Emanuele II 77
Colours Claret shirts, white shorts
League champions 1928, 1943, 1946–49, 1976
Cup winners 1936, 1943, 1968, 1971, 1993

The fact that Torino are part of the four-team, twin-city triumvirate that has won all but ten Italian titles since World War II does not hide the fact that the club is in sorry shape now. Shifting between first and second divisions, their faithful fan base barely covering the *Curva Maratona* of the Stadio delle Alpi, forever selling their best players, Torino have all the trappings of a small club from Italy's southern provinces.

Fewer and fewer fans have been coming to see the team since *Il Grande Torino*, product of the coaching genius of Vittorio Pozzo and the business acumen of agriculture millionaire Ferruccio Novo (and perhaps the greatest club side in Italian football history), were cut down in their prime by the 1949 Superga air disaster.

Pozzo, who helped found the club from the 1906 merger, had kept a close watch on his beloved *Toro* for 40 years even though occupied with the affairs of the national team. Very much in the shadow of successful city rivals Juventus, Torino had won one title and one cup before Pozzo began to mastermind the assembly of a new side in the early Forties. He persuaded Novo to snap up Venezia's inside-forward partnership which had won them the cup in 1941, Ezio Loik and Valentino Mazzola. The duo's mutual understanding had curious origins – both were born on the same day, 26 January, 1919. A bullish but light-footed inside-left, Mazzola would become the hero of the era, something great and good to look up to while Italy were losing the war after 20 years of Mussolini's Facism. The pair duly helped *Toro* win the double in 1943.

With Pozzo's organisation, and with much of Italy still in disarray after the war, Torino won another title in 1946. By 1947

they were unstoppable, with a ten-point winning margin over Juventus in the league and providing all the outfield players for Italy's 3–2 defeat of Puskás' Hungary in Turin that May. In 1948 the winning margin was 16 points over Milan. The Filadelfia, including the team mascot, Valentino's son Sandro, saw 19 wins in 20 home games.

Towards the end of the 1948/49 season, chasing a fifth title, Torino were just ahead of Inter, with a difficult away game to come at the San Siro. On 4 May 1949, the team were flying back from Lisbon after fulfilling a testimonial fixture as a favour to Mazzola's retiring friend Francisco Ferreira. The plane carrying the entire Torino squad, journalists and officials, crashed into the side of the Basilica on top of Superga Hill outside Turin. The pilot's decision not to land at Milan Malpensa and fly on to Turin has never been explained in half a century. When the plane hit the cathedral, it was flying in the wrong direction to its destination at Torino Caselle airport. The team bus stood waiting at Malpensa. Vittorio Pozzo had to identify the bodies.

With the city in mourning, Torino's junior team played out their last league fixtures against their club counterparts and a fifth title went to a grieving Campo Filadelfia.

The shadow of Superga lay heavy over the postwar period until the form of *La Granata* ('the clarets') slowly picked up in the Sixties. An unlikely striking partnership between Joe Baker and Denis Law was responsible for a few goals – and no few beers – in 1961/62, until it ran aground after a post-party car prang.

Not long after, the club moved from Campo Filadelfia to share with Juventus at the Stadio Comunale. There was no lack of atmosphere – the arrival of coach Nereo Rocco from Milan, and his signing of the genial prodigy Gigi Meroni, saw to that. In 1965, a play-off defeat by Munich 1860 was all that separated the club from a place in the European Cup-Winners' Cup final against the eventual winers, West Ham. Meroni's death in a road accident two years later saw the city in mourning once more. It was to be a decade before his ghost and those of the Superga victims were finally laid to rest, after coach Gigi Radice had taken hold of a side featuring the goalscoring partnership of Paolo Pulici and Francesco Graziani. Winning all but one of their home games, Torino took their first and only post-Superga *scudetto* in 1976.

The best Torino team since then emerged in the early Nineties. With the right blend of foreign (Belgian Enzo Scifo, Brazilian Walter Casagrande, Spaniard Martín Vázquez) and Italian (Gianluigi Lentini) influences, the side looked anything but an outfit that had just scrambled out of *Serie B*. Lentini was the key – a tricky young winger who had come through Torino's junior squads. In 1991/92 Lentini was at his sublime best, taking Torino to the only European final in their history (a UEFA Cup showdown with Ajax, lost on away goals) and third place in the league.

Then the fans took to the streets. President Gianmauro Borsano was selling Lentini! The very symbol of the new Torino had become no more than a multi-billion lire bargaining chip, eventually going to Milan for a world record £12.8million. The sale provoked near-riots, a fans' boycott of home fixtures, and a miserable exit from Europe at the hands of Dynamo Moscow.

Without Lentini, Torino still managed to win the 1993 *Coppa Italia*, on away goals after a remarkable 5–5 aggregate draw with Roma – their first trophy since 1976. The following season they narrowly lost to Arsenal in the quarter-finals of the Cup-Winners' Cup. But by then, despite the proceeds from the Lentini sale, the club was heavily in debt. The team, further weakened by outgoing transfers, were finally relegated in 1996 and never looked likely to bounce straight back.

In the summer of 1997, the appointment of Graeme Souness as coach and the return of Lentini – after a lean spell at Milan, a near-fatal car crash and a revival at Atalanta – prompted a new optimism among fans. Souness departed within weeks, but his team looked like winning promotion in 1997/98 until a last-day defeat at the only team who could stop them, Perugia, whose fans had kept the Torino players awake the night before. The result meant a play-off between the two sides at neutral Reggiana, and after a 1–1 draw, former England full-back Tony Dorigo missed the vital penalty that saw Torino condemned to another season of *Serie B* football.

Happily, the combination of Lentini with Marco Ferrante upfront ensured there was no mistake in 1999, as Torino finished runners-up to Verona. But there was no cash for new players, and in 1999/2000, Torino struggled from the outset. A prolonged boardroom takeover battle was finally won by an outside consortium led by local industrialist Franco Cimminelli in April, but it was too late. The transfer deadline had passed, and Torino went straight back down to *Serie B* without so much as a fight.

Brief revival – Lentini returns to the *Serie A*

During the close season, the new board brought former Inter star Sandro Mazzola, son of Superga victim Valentino, to the club to run football affairs and appointed the much-travelled Gigi Simoni as coach, as the *Granata* looked to pull themselves back up to *Serie A* – and stay there this time.

Swift half

Campo Filadelfia (bus #14 from Piazza Solferino) is the Toro fans' old stomping ground. Close to the stadium, **Sweet Bar**, Via Filadelfia 31, has a huge colour picture of *Toro* fans and old men playing cards in the back room.

Club merchandise

The **Toro Store** near the old stadium, at Via Spallanzani 20B (Mon–Fri 9am–12.30pm & 3–6.30pm, match weekends Sat 9am–midday, Sun 9–11am, no credit cards) is a modest souvenir shop with a *biglietteria* next door. In town, the **Toro Shop** in tiny Via Nino Costa 3 (next to Piazza P Le V Fusi, open Tue–Sat 9am–12.30pm & 3pm-7pm, no credit cards) is more like a gents' outfitters.

Ultra culture

A rainy, windswept game against lowly opposition in *Serie B* can be a thoroughly depressing experience – a fact not lost on the **Ultras Granata**, whose choreography, particularly in derby games against Juventus, was once among the best in Italy.

The vast 12million lire *bandierina* exclaiming *'From Here To Eternity'*, with two bulls' heads and a heart, was a classic of its time. The day these boys can make the rebuilt Filadelfia come alive like the Comunale of old, the better for Italian football culture.

In print

Alé Toro (L5,000) is the club's full-colour monthly publication, available around town.

In the net

Fan-run sites are thin on the ground, but the official website is well worth a look at: www.toro.it. Though in Italian only, it's a finely detailed site with properly updated news and match reports, together with a tastefully designed area dedicated to the great side of 1949.

Eat, drink, sleep…

Bars and clubs

Turin is picturesque rather than lively. The main area for nightlife is the Murazzi, a quay of lock-up warehouses alongside the Po, under the far edge of Piazza Vittorio Veneto (tram #15 from Porta Nuova), but it only gets going after midnight. If you can avoid the occasional presence of the *carabinieri* and blag your way in to places without paying a hefty membership fee, you can have a fair time club-hopping.

On the other side of the Po are a row of cheap(ish) bars, less pretentious than those in town. If you're on a real budget, nip into a *vineria* – a cheap wine bar. As in Milan, early evening is *aperitivi* hour, when better establishments stack their counters with free snacks to go with your vermouth, an invention of 18th-century Turin.

Alcatraz, Lungo Po Murazzi 37–41. Popular and spacious two-floor nightclub in the Murazzi with alcove tables overlooking the Po, a vague prison theme and bearable music. Tram #15.

Bar Baspas, Corso Casale 16. Down-at-heel *Totocalcio* bar opposite the Murazzi and overlooking the Po, with faded team line-ups on the wall and lively conversation on a Sunday night. Closed Wed. A walk across Emanuele I bridge from town, or buses #61 or #66.

Caos, Corso Francia 229. Without doubt Turin's top dance club, with foreign DJ's popping in regularly at the weekend. House, techno, jungle and the rest. Open Thurs–Sat only.

Mulassano, Piazza Castello 9. If you fancy going native, this is as fine a place as any for sitting down and enjoying a coffee and a cake. Bottled beer if you must.

Tetley Huntsman, Corso Vittorio Emanuele II 43. Large boozer five minutes' walk right out of Porta Nuova station, opened at the start of the 1998/99 season. The history of Tetley beer and the visit of Athletic Bilbao's fans decorate the walls.

Restaurants

Turin cuisine is heavy on polenta – a corn-meal porridge, covered with butter and cheese or meat sauce – risotto and *farinata* (fried corn batter). Everything here is fried in butter, not olive oil, and many restaurants have a distinct French influence. The local pasta dish is *agnolotti* – ravioli with lamb and cabbage. To help digest the starch, the local red wines, Barbera and Barbaresco, are excellent.

Many places close mid-afternoon and before 10pm. For something cheaper, you'll find plenty of takeaway snack-bars around Via Nizza, near Porta Nuova station.

Corner House, Corso Sebastopoli 230. Friendly, modern operation near the Comunale stadium specialising in fish. Main courses around L30,000. Open Tue–Sun midday–3pm & 6.30pm–2am, most major credit cards. Bus #17.

Osteria del FIAT, Via Biglieri 2/corner with Via Nizza. Piedmontese specialities at this friendly, family run hostelry, lunch and dinner menus from L16,000, main courses L20,000. Closed Sun. Most major credit cards. Bus #35 from Porta Nuova.

Pizzeria Bochicchio Rodolfo, Via Monferrato 7c. A rarity in Turin – an excellent, reasonably priced pizzeria, near the Piazza Gran Madre on the far bank of the Po, also serving a decent range of pasta dishes. L15,000 should cover you for a pizza and a beer. Closed Thur. Bus #61 or #66.

Taverna Fiorentina, Via Palazzo di Città 6. Centrally located, reasonably priced Florentine cuisine at around L15,000 for a main course. Closed Sat. Tram #4 or #12.

Trattoria Toscana, Via Vanchiglia 2. Near Piazza Vittorio Veneto, moderately priced diner with basic decor but decent cuisine, popular with students. Main courses at L20,000, no credit cards. Open midday–2.30pm & 7–10pm. Tram #15.

Accommodation

Both tourist offices can provide hotel and pension information. If you're turning up on spec, the streets to the right as you come out of Porta Nuova station are full of one-star hotels, but after dark this area can be a little seedy. Opposite, around Piazza Carlo Felice, is safer if a little more expensive. The area west of Piazza Castello also has a few reasonably priced rooms. Note that the skiing crowd passes through Turin in mid-winter.

Albergo Versilia, Via San Anselmo 4 (☎011/657 678). Pleasant, clean pension around the corner from Porta Nuova station, with a bar downstairs and a decent café a couple of doors down. L45,000 a single, L65,000 a double, L70,000 a double with a shower. No credit cards. Tram #9.

City Hotel, Via Juvarra 25 (☎011/548 188). Just by Porta Susa railway station is this modern hotel, part of the *Best Western* chain, near to many of the better drinking holes and ten minutes from the delle Alpi stadium by car or cab. Single rooms L130,000.

Hotel Bellavista, Via B Galliari 15 (☎011/669 8139). Round the corner from the station, spacious rooms, each with a TV and radio. Singles at L65,000, doubles L110,000, or L140,000 with shower. Triples available on request. No credit cards. All transport to Porta Nuova, then turn right down Via Nizza – you want the second street on the left.

Magenta, Corso Vittorio Emanuele 67 (☎011/542 649, fax 011/544 755). A little pricier than most around Porta Nuova, all rooms in this two-star hotel have a TV and telephone. Bar downstairs. Singles without shower L60,000, with L90,000; doubles without L75,000, with L110,000. Most credit cards. Left out of the station or tram #1, #9 or #15.

Ostello Torino, Via Alby 1 (☎011/660 2939, fax 011/660 445). Tidy and comfortable youth hostel with dorm beds at L18,000 for members, L23,000 for non-members. No credit cards. Bus #52 from Porta Nuova – get off after Piazza Crimea over the bridge, turn right up Corso Giovanni Lanza, then up Viale Enrico Thouvez. Via Alby is the narrow road to the right.

Back where they belong – Bologna

Bologna celebrated their 90th anniversary in 1999 with a UEFA Cup semi-final and another top ten finish in *Serie A*. But these seven-time Italian champions have spent most of the last two decades in lower-division obscurity, even sinking down to *Serie C*.

A club of Bolognese football lovers was formed in the ***Birreria Ronzani*** in Via Spaderie on 3 October 1909. By the Twenties, with **Angiolio Schavio** leading the line, they had an exciting young team which broke the northern domination of the championship. Their title win of 1925 coincided with the building of a new stadium, in the classic municipal design of the times. With Schavio netting 29 goals – he would score the winning one for Italy in the 1934 World Cup final – Bologna won another title in 1929. But the golden era of *il rossoblu*, the red-and-blues, would be the Thirties. Textile mer-

European return – flying high against Anderlecht

chant **Renato dall'Aria** became club president in 1934, and with Uruguayan Miguel Andreolo as the lynchpin, Bologna broke Juve's stranglehold on the *scudetto*, and won four in a five-year period up to 1941.

The most popular figure of the post-war period was **Ezio Pascutti**, a centre-forward who would throw his balding head at anything wingers Giacominio Bulgarelli and Helmut Haller could throw at him. The team were neck-and-neck with Herrera's Inter in 1963/64, when *il Mago* pulled another masterstroke of gamesmanship, accusing Bologna players of doping. The FA docked Bologna three points, which were restored after much furore, and *il rossoblu* finished level with Inter at the top. The strain was too much on dall'Aria, who died of a heart attack only days before his beloved Bologna faced a play-off match for the title – which they won 2–1. Bologna's stadium, renovated for the 1990 World Cup, would later be named after him.

Bologna then trod water in the *Serie A* before relegation for the first time in 1982. The club was saved from bankruptcy in 1993, but it was the astute coaching of **Renzo Ulivieri** that saved them on the pitch. After he had taken them from the third to the first divisions in two seasons, it took the inspired signing of **Roberto Baggio**, the bargain of the 1997/98 pre-season at £1.7million, for Bologna to regain the limelight.

Alongside Swede **Kennet Andersson** and Russian **Igor Kolyvanov**, Baggio rediscovered his true form, finishing third top scorer in the league and booking his ticket for the 1998 World Cup. Moreover, Bologna were back in Europe, where only a lapse of concentration in the semi-final second leg against Marseille would stand between them and an all-Italian UEFA Cup final against Parma in 1999.

Regular **bus #21** from Stazione Centrale takes 15mins to reach the stadium. The ivy-clad ticket offices are opposite the main entrance on Via Costa.

Genoa

Sea ports, with their big immigrant communities and working-class populations, often create vibrant football towns, and Genoa is no exception. A cramped, messy city with buildings crawling over hills and crowding into valleys, it barely seems to have any space in which to kick a ball about. No surprise, then, that there is room for only one stadium. Yet history has blessed the city with two big football clubs, each with its place in Italian soccer history.

The Genoa Cricket and Athletic Club were formed in 1893, exclusively for British expatriates. Four years later, locals were allowed into the club and the football team met a select eleven from Turin in the first inter-city game ever played in Italy.

Genoa dominated the early Italian league competitions but soon faced a local challenge from Andrea Doria and Sampierdarenese – the two teams who would later merge to become Sampdoria.

In the modern era Samp have become one of the elite in *Serie A*, boasting a long line of foreign stars and with a record of making astute buys in the domestic transfer market. Meanwhile, Genoa have bobbed up and down between the top two divisions, occasionally promising a revival but usually failing to deliver.

Yet despite the presence of more glamorous neighbours – perhaps because of it – Genoa have managed to hang on to their support throughout the barren years. Naturally there is a competitive rivalry between the two clubs, but it has rarely spilled over into violence, and in recent years there has been a suspicion that a large number of fans are actually watching both teams. Nonetheless, the local *Derby della Lanterna* ('Lighthouse Derby') remains a passionate affair – when it is played.

Sadly, in 1999/2000 it was to be played in *Serie B*, Sampdoria's relegation the previous season and Genoa's inability to travel in the other direction condemning both clubs to life in Italy's second division, where they will remain for at least one more year.

The thrilling fields

Genoa

Stadium Luigi Ferraris, see p.387
Club office Via Roma 7/3
Colours Red-and-blue halved shirts, blue shorts
League champions 1898–99, 1900–04, 1915, 1923–24
Cup winners 1937

There are two plaques outside the Stadio Luigi Ferraris. One is in tribute to Dr James Spensley, one of the founders of the Genoa club. The other is to Genoa fan Vincenzo Spagnolo, who was stabbed to death by Milan hooligans in 1995. Between them, they sum up the two Genoas. The first is a reminder of the long-gone era when Genoa dominated the Italian championship, the latter of more recent times when there have been little but bad memories.

It would be easy to dismiss Genoa as dinosaurs. Easy, but unfair. It may be more than sixty years since they last won a trophy, but Genoa are survivors. Plenty of European clubs enjoyed success in the early days of organised league football but vanished in the era of professionalism or in the face of fresh local competition. Thanks largely to the loyalty of their supporters, Genoa are not a footnote in the history books, but a major organisation – albeit one that has a lot to do to recapture its long-lost status.

With the good Dr Spensley in goal, Genoa won six of the first seven Italian championships, although at that stage the competition consisted of a series of regional play-offs, rather than a national league. After World War I the club won two more titles – in what was now a much more competitive championship. The first of those post-WWI campaigns was particularly impressive, seeing Genoa unbeaten throughout the season. The side included several of the early Italian national team – notably goalkeeper Giovanni de Prà and striker Aristodemo Santamaria.

In 1929 the club were forced to change their name. Italy's Fascist authorities did not take kindly to the English sound of 'Genoa', and until the end of World War II the team played under the name Genova 1893. Psychologically, the name change could scarcely have come at a worse time, for the club were already beginning to fade from the limelight. In 1934, the unthinkable happened and the mighty *Grifone* ('griffins') were relegated. The fans could scarcely believe it, but over time their children and grandchildren would become accustomed to yo-yoing between divisions.

A cup win in 1937 seemed to show that the club were still capable of matching the best, but today it remains Genoa's last piece of silverware.

After World War II the club got their old name back, but struggled to establish themselves in *Serie A*. The Fifties saw a string of relegations and promotions, and Genoa spent the whole of the period between 1965 and 1973 outside of the top flight, enduring a year in the amateur ranks of *Serie C* in 1970. Throughout the Seventies and Eighties the club's existence revolved around the fight against relegation from *Serie A* – a battle joined with varying degrees of success.

In 1989, a promising young side won the *Serie B* title and there was optimism that a genuine revival might be around the corner. It proved justified.

In 1990/91, with Osvaldo Bagnoli as coach, midfielder Stefano Eranio pulling the on-field strings and a colourful Italia '90-inspired strikeforce of Czech Tomáš Skuhravý and Uruguayan Carlos Aguilera, Genoa had their best season for half a century, finishing fourth in the league.

Typically, their local rivals Sampdoria stole the show, winning the title. But fourth place was enough to earn Genoa European qualification for the first time in the club's history. The following year's UEFA Cup campaign provided enough memories to sustain another generation of supporters. Wins over Real Ovideo and Dinamo Bucharest were followed by an impressive victory over a strong Steaua Bucharest side, to set up a quarter-final with Liverpool. Anfield fans may have long since forgotten the tie, but the Genoa *tifosi* consider their team's 4–1 aggregate win the club's greatest postwar success. Skuhravý in particular

Genoa essentials

Genoa's **Cristoforo Colombo** airport is 6km west of the centre at Sestri Ponente, connected by a *Volabus* (half-hourly, 6.15am–10.30pm, 5.30am–9.30pm from town, ticket L4,000), which calls at the main train station, Principe, on Piazza Acquaverde before going on to its terminus at Brignole train station on Piazza Verdi. The stations are either side of the old town centre, Centro Storico.

Public transport (5.30am–midnight) consists of ATM **buses** and local FS **trains**. Single tickets (L1,500), available from ATM kiosks and stations, are valid for 90mins from stamping in the machines, for any amount of changes but only one ride by train. A 24-hour tourist ticket (L5,000) allows journeys on all transport up until midnight. Two infrequent weekend night bus services, #601 and #602, serve the city's outskirts via central Piazza de Ferrari. To call a **taxi**, dial *Radiotaxi* on ☎010/5966 or *Cooperativa Taxista Genovesi* on ☎010/594 690.

The main **tourist office** is at the Palazzina Santa Maria by the old port (open Mon–Sat 8.30am–6pm, ☎010/24 871, fax 010/246 7658), with branches at the main train station (☎010/246 2633), the maritime station, Crociere Terminal (☎010/246 3685) and the airport (☎010/601 5247).

The local daily newspaper *Il Secolo XIX* is a decent source of **nightlife listings**, and the tourist office also puts out occasional free 'what's on' pamphlets.

terrorised the Merseysiders' defence, earning his team copious praise in the Italian sports press, while their opponents were dubbed 'Little Liverpool'.

The victory earned Genoa a semi-final date with Ajax. With Sampdoria heading for the final of the European Cup, the city's football heart was beating as never before. Genoa were looking forward to the prospect of an all-Italian UEFA Cup final, against their old northern league rivals Torino. But Ajax, themelves showing the first signs of their great Nineties revival, hadn't read the script – Genoa were out, and the party was over.

Within a few years it was back to the old struggle. Bagnoli was sacked, and by 1995 Genoa were facing a relegation play-off against Padova, in which an overweight Skuhravý, shambling around the park in a desperate hunt for the goal that would avoid a penalty shoot-out, seemed to symbolise the decay that had set in. The shoot-out duly came, Genoa lost it, and while Padova were themselves relegated the following year, that was scant consolation for the proud Genoa club and their unswervingly loyal supporters.

That loyalty has since been tested by an extended spell of second-division football that has brought half-a-dozen managerial changes, but not a sniff of promotion. Indeed, for two-thirds of the 1999/2000 campaign Genoa were flirting with the unthinkable – relegation to *Serie C* – prompting fan protests and yet more rumours of a takeover. Survival was assured and the team finished a decent sixth, five points below Sampdoria, and playing a brand of football that did not suggest the 2000/01 season would be much better.

Club merchandise

Genoa Point, Galleria Mazzini 57r, 50m from the club's office at Via Roma 7/1, sells souvenirs and tickets.

Ultra culture

The *Fossa dei Grifone* voted to disband in 1993. With the death of Vincenzo Spagnolo in 1995

and the club's lack of success since then, no particular group has replaced them in the *Gradinata Nord*. The only two groups to speak of are the thirtysomethings in the *Vecchi Orsi* ('Old Bears'), and the teenagers in the *Genoa Club Ottavio Barbieri*, dabblers in sixth-form politics.

In print

Genoa News (L5,000) is a glossy monthly produced for the club. Programmes are sold outside the stadium on matchdays.

In the net

Smart graphics, a decent club history and a well-maintained stats archive, alas all in Italian only, are the strong points of the only Genoa website currently active, an unofficial affair that can be found at: dns.promix.it/genoa.

🟢 Sampdoria

Stadium Luigi Ferraris, see p.387
Club office Via XX Settembre 33/1
Colours Blue shirts with white, red and black hoops, white shorts
League champions 1991
Cup winners 1985, 1988–89, 1994
Cup-Winners' Cup winners 1990

Although most Italian clubs managed to survive Fascism and World War II, and the post-war Italian league contained many of the same names as the prewar championships, the city of Genoa had a new club around for peacetime.

In 1946, two of the clubs who had been struggling to compete with Genoa merged to form Sampdoria. Andrea Doria and Sampierdarenese had had their moments – both had played in *Serie A*, Sampierdarenese had come close to winning the title in 1922, and Francesco Cali of Andrea Doria was the first captain of Italy.

In 1927 the two clubs decided to unite, under the grandiose name of Dominante, in an attempt to dislodge the Anglophiles of Genoa from their seat of power in the city. But in their first season Dominante were

Waiting in the wings – the Luigi Ferraris is not the cauldron of a stadium it once was

relegated. The club changed their name to Liguria (the region of which Genoa is the capital) and finished fifth in *Serie A* in 1939. But in the last championship before World War II, the team finished in bottom place.

Immediately after the war the two clubs re-emerged under their original names and with separate structures, but on August 1 1946, they united once more, choosing the name which has survived to this day, Sampdoria Unione Calcio, and moving in to share the Stadio Luigi Ferraris with Genoa.

The new club could boast nothing like Genoa's level of support, but in their first season 'Samp' won both city derbies, setting a pattern for the coming seasons in which the upstarts would regularly finish above their more illustrious neighbours in the *Serie A* table.

One of the stars of the early postwar sides was striker Adriano Bassetto – 'The Dwarf' – who despite his lack of height notched 93 goals in seven seasons with the team that had become known as the *Blucerchiati* – literally 'blue-and-hoops', after their

distinctive blue shirts with white, red and black hoops. (The strip was a compromise between Sampierdarenese's blue-and-white and the red-and-black of Andrea Doria.) The other favourite of the Fifties was Argentinian international Tito Cucchiaroni, whose name lives on in the title of Sampdoria's main ultra group.

Although they enjoyed a successful year in 1961, when they finished fourth thanks largely to 27 goals from striker Sergio Brighenti, Samp suffered from instability for much of the early Sixties, and in 1966 they were relegated to *Serie B*. They bounced back within a season but were down in *Serie B* for half of the Seventies, and the dream of a fresh football force in the city seemed to be fading. All that changed in the Eighties with the appointment of oil magnate Paolo Mantovani as club president. Mantovani didn't just bring cash to Samp – he also brought a rare (for a sporting entrepreneur) insight into the game he was financing. In 1982 he made his first inspirational signing – Roberto

Mancini. The arrival of *Mancio* coincided with the club's return to the top flight. He was the archetypal Italian attacking midfielder, with style, imagination and the ability to score goals – especially from set pieces.

All he needed was a striker to feed – and in 1984 he got that when Mantaovani signed 20-year-old Gianluca Vialli from Cremenose. Vialli, whose wealthy Lombardian family background gave him a relaxed air perfect for situations demanding a cool head in front of goal, soon struck up a lethal forward partnership with England international Trevor Francis. With Scottish

midfielder Graeme Souness signed from Liverpool and the massive Pietro Vierchowod marshalling the defence, Mancini now had all the supporting cast he needed.

In 1985 Samp earned their first piece of silverware, defeating Milan in the final of the *Coppa Italia*. Veteran Brazilian Toninho Cerezo was signed from Roma in 1986 and another cup win followed two years later.

By this time the team were playing to a tune orchestrated by Vujadin Boskov, an unassuming Yugoslav coach who turned out to be another of Mantovani's shrewd investments. Boskov's ability to change his

The Luigi Ferraris

Stadio Luigi Ferraris, Via del Piano 9
Capacity 42,000 (all-seated)

There has been a football stadium on this site in the **Marassi** district, some way northeast of the city, since Genoa began playing here in **1910**. It has been rebuilt three times since then, and was renamed 'Luigi Ferraris' after a former Genoa centre-half killed during World War I.

The last remodelling was by **Vittorio Gregotti** for the 1990 World Cup. It included the construction of four brick-red towers which stand at each corner of the ground, and from which fans get a dramatic if rather eccentric view of proceedings on the pitch.

The ground is by no means the biggest in Italy, but it is certainly one of the easiest to **fill with atmosphere** – as Ireland supporters discovered when their team played Romania here at Italia '90.

Buses #37 and #47 go from **Stazione Principe** to the ground. On matchdays these are augmented by a special bus service, beginning around two hours before kick-off; this latter ride takes around 20mins and deposits you at the ground for L3,000. If you take either of the regular city buses, get off at Marassi and head down Via Giuseppe Bertucioni – it's a 5min walk to the stadium.

With Genoa and Sampdoria currently in different divisions, ticket prices vary depending on which team is at home. For **Genoa** games, the cheapest seats in one of the *Curvas* behind the goals are around L20,000, with prices rising to L100,000 for the best seats in the house. For **Sampdoria** matches, these prices go up to L25,000 and L150,000, respectively.

To check on seat availability in advance, call one of the two **ticket hotlines**: Genoa's is ☎010/540 547, Sampdoria's ☎010/564 880 or 585 343.

There are plenty of opportunities for passing an hour with a **pint** or a **cappuccino** close to the stadium. The *Bar Stadio*, slightly isolated at Via Tortosa 3, gets packed before games and is also a popular midweek meeting point, for supporters of both clubs. This being Genoa, the debates are usually friendly, but the regulars appear to wield some influence – one former Genoa coach blamed the patrons for his sacking.

The *Football Pub* on Via Piano itself fits the disappointing chrome-and-neon norm, but there are a few other options nearby. Popular with older fans is the small *Bar Vittorio*, directly facing the *Gradinata Sud*.

team's formation to suit the occasion was particularly useful in Europe, and in 1988/89 reached their first continental final, in the Cup-Winners' Cup against Barcelona in Berne. The Italians were stunned by a fourth-minute strike from Salinas, however, and when Recarte struck eleven minutes from time, the trophy was Barça's.

Boskov was undaunted, and the pain of defeat was eased immediately in the same competition the following year, when Samp beat Grasshoppers and Monaco on the way to a final with Anderlecht in Gothenburg. Playing a less open game than in Berne, Sampdoria took the match into extra time, in which two goals from Vialli were enough to give the club their first European title.

Ever ambitious, Mantovani continued to augment the squad, adding balding wide man Attilio Lombardo and tough-tackling Slovenian midfielder Srećko Katanec to the mix before an all-out assault on the Italian title in 1990/91. With Katanec acting as Boskov's eyes and ears on the pitch, Vierchowod an unbreachable barrier at the back, and Mancini and Vialli netting more than 30 league goals between them, Samp's first *scudetto* was duly won with something to spare. Almost 200,000 fans gathered in the Genoa streets to celebrate.

Sampdoria found themselves in the European Cup just as it was beginning its transformation into the Champions' League. After edging past Kispest-Honvéd by the odd goal in seven, they entered group one of the new mini-league system. They lost just one game (against Anderlecht away) and finished top of their group above holders Red Star Belgrade, who were defeated home and away.

The final at Wembley pitted them against Barcelona again. There were plenty of chances for Samp, but the game went to extra time and in the dying minutes, Ronald Koeman's epic free-kick allowed Barça to foil the *Blucerchiati* once again. Vialli departed for Juventus, and in 1992/93, Samp failed to hold on to their title.

Recent years have seen stars come and go. Boskov was replaced by another canny foreign coach, Sven Göran Eriksson. For 1993/94 Ruud Gullit was brought to the Luigi Ferraris, along with two former Red Star Belgrade stars, Siniša Mihajlović and Vladimir Jugović, while the club broke their transfer fee record to lure David Platt from Juventus. The result was another *Coppa Italia*, followed by a run to the semi-finals of the Cup-Winners' Cup where Samp lost out on penalties to Arsenal. To add to the disappointment, Vierchowod, Jugović and 'Popeye' Lombardo all joined Vialli at Juventus at the end of the season, while Platt returned to England.

Following the death of Paolo Mantovani in October 1994, the club passed into the hands of his son, Enrico. One of his first acts was to bring young striker Enrico Chiesa back from loan, to see him score 22 goals in 27 games in 1995/96. They weren't enough to lift Sampdoria back into the European frame, though, and Chiesa was sold to Parma in the summer of 1996.

The subsequent arrival of Argentine coach Luis César Menotti and Jürgen Klinsmann were too much of a shock to the established team, who were knocked out by Athletic Bilbao in early stages of the UEFA Cup in 1997. Boskov returned to replace Menotti and began playing with a libero, only to lose five straight games, including a 4–0 home defeat by Lazio after which Mancini received a huge ovation.

Boskov eventually steered Samp into an Intertoto place, before being replaced by 39-year-old Luciano Spalletti. Influential midfielder Alain Boghossian was sold to Parma, a loss compensated by Ariel Ortega's arrival from Valencia. Declaring his aim as a top-six place prior to the 1998/99 season, Spalletti fielded an audacious 3–4–3 side which thrilled the crowd but leaked goals.

By December the coach was on his way, surprisingly replaced by another old boy, David Platt – who could not even formally be called 'coach' because of his lack of qualifications. His inexperience soon told and, in a sad admission of his error, Mantovani asked Spalletti back. By now

Samp were facing a relegation battle – one they were destined to lose before the final round of matches was over.

Relegation meant the departure of the remaining quality players, with striker Vincenzo Montella moving to Roma and Ortega taking the now familiar route across to Parma.

With a young side, Samp were in contention for promotion from *Serie B* until the end. On the final day of the season they needed to win and hope that Brescia or Atalanta slipped up. Samp had a ding-dong 3–2 win over Alzano, but it was in vain – both their rivals won and another season of second-class football loomed.

Club merchandise

Sampdoria have two official *Solo Samp* shops – one in the club's traditional stronghold in the western district of Sampierdarena, at Via Antonio Cantore 150r, the other in the centre of town at Largo XII Ottobre 45.

Ultra culture

With the current downturn in the club's fortunes, Samp's *Ultras* agreed to split up in 1998, leaving space in the *Gradinata Sud* for a host of other minor groups such as the long-established *Fedelissimi* and the *Hell's Angels* from the Sampierdarena area and points west. They may not have to learn the words of *Siamo L'Armata Blucerchiata* or *Se Deserte Son Le Strade*, but they sure as hell need some encouragement.

In print

The club's official quarterly publication is titled simply *UC Sampdoria* (L12,000), while a programme, *Noi Sampdoriani*, is distributed free on matchdays.

In the net

The official site is at: www.sampdoria.it. It contains a very complete English-language area, but some of the news is in Italian only. Meanwhile, Tamás Kárpáti's *CyberSamp*, once purely a historical archive, has now evolved into a fully fledged unofficial homepage boasting detailed team information and excellent links, among other things, at: pernix.bke.hu/~snobil/sampd.htm.

Eat, drink, sleep...

Bars and clubs

A potent mix of students and immigrant dock-workers gives Genoa a varied nightlife, concentrated into three main areas: the centre (radiating from Piazza de Ferrari); Foce (the seafront area past the Fiera Internazionale); and the Lido discos around Passeggiata Anita Garibaldi. In clubs, live bands still outnumber DJs.

Brittania Pub, Vico Casana 74–76. The main pub in town, off Piazza de Ferrari, which naturally attracts more locals than expats. Guinness, Tetley and the usual pub grub. Closed Sun.

La Goletta, Marina Molo Vecchio, Magazzini del Cotone, Modulo 3. Ideal afternoon spot, with cocktails, a good choice of imported beers, relaxed conversation and a seaside feel. Down by the congress centre.

Mako, Via Podgora 17/Corso Italia 28r. Popular disco in Foce, playing rare groove and funk. Seventies nights on Thurs, occasional live bands, L10–20,000 cover.

Quaalude, Piazza Sarzano 46r. Mixed clientele in a loud, smoke-filled environment, central enough to be a good stop-off point on a bar crawl.

Senhor do Bonfim, Passeggiata Garibaldi. Best of the seafront clubs, a Brazilian-style disco with samba nights and capirinhas a go-go. The nearby **Agua** is a reasonable alternative. Take a local train to Nervi there, night bus #602 back.

Restaurants

The Liguria region is famed for *pesto*, a basil sauce made with pine nuts and parmesan. It is most often used as a pasta sauce but finds its way into many other dishes. Chill out – dining is much less formal in Genoa than in many Italian cities.

Corona di Ferro, Vico Inferiore del Ferro 11, off Via di Macelli di Soziglia. In the centre of the

the old town, this unassuming place serves up straightforward pasta dishes and seafood, all at a reasonable price.

Ristorante Amadeus, Via P E Bensa 40r. Centro Storico eaterie with a *menú turistico* and regionally influenced main courses. Closed Sat lunchtimes. Most credit cards.

Ristorante Pesce d'Oro, Piazza Caricamento 65r. Seafood and Genoese specialities in the Centro Storico, menú turistico around L25,000. Closed Sun eve. Most credit cards.

Trattoria del Molo, Via del Molo 87–89r. Down by the congress centre on the seafront. Genoese cuisine at around L20,000 a main dish. Closed Mon. Visa cards accepted.

Accommodation

There's no shortage of affordable hotel rooms in Genoa, but many are pretty seedy. If you turn up on spec, then Via XX Settembre, near Brignole train station, is as good a place as any to start. Note that the tourist office (see *Essentials*) will provide phone numbers but cannot book a room for you.

Brittania, Via Balbi 38 (☎010/246 2942). One of the few quality hotels in the centre of town charging reasonable rates. A smart, four-star operation with singles at L150,000, doubles from L195,000.

Della Posta Nuova, Via Balbi 24 (☎010/246 2005). One of dozens of options in Via Balbi, which stretches from Piazza Acquaverde by Principe station towards town. Two-star hotel, singles L40–90,000 doubles L60–130,000. Most credit cards.

Ostello Genova, Via Constanzi 120 (☎010/243 3457). New hostel which provides a stunning view of the city. From Stazione Principe, take bus #64 up the hill. Don't even think about walking.

Hotel Iris, Via Gabriele Rossetti 5 (☎010/376 0703). One of the better hotels close to the har-

bour. Comfortable and perfectly located for an easy return after a night out, with no curfew and friendly staff. Singles L140,000, doubles L180,000.

Rome

Southern comfort – Lazio's Latin American contingent celebrate the 1999/2000 double

'Rome is now the capital of Italian football,' declared Lazio president Sergio Cragnotti as he announced the £35million signing of Hernán Crespo from Parma. It was a bold statement and, like all those of Italian club presidents, it was aimed at the terraces. But, coming as they did after Roma had signed Gabriel Batistuta and Lazio had won the domestic double for the first time, his words were not without foundation.

Historically, Rome has always trailed behind the northern giants from Milan and Turin. Lazio's 1999/2000 championship was only the fourth time the *scudetto* has come to Rome. But a rare spell of stable management, coupled with immense purchasing power, is enabling Italy's political capital to challenge the traditional dominance of the north at the start of the new millennium.

Like Milan and Turin, Rome is a two-club, one-stadium city. Lazio and Roma share the Stadio Olimpico, built for the 1960 Games. Across the river Tiber is the Flaminio, venue of *Serie C* minnows Lodigiani, and home to the big boys during the

political upheavals either side of World War II.

Italian Fascism was centred on Rome. Mussolini wanted to re-create the city in its ancient imperial image and football was too important in the public consciousness to escape involvement. *Il Duce* was a Lazio man, taking his kids to games when the club were based at their Rondinella stadium, at the base of the heights of Pairoli, a leafy, residential area of northern Rome which is still firm Lazio territory today.

An abandoned Stadio Nazionale stood near the Rondinella, and this was to be the site for Mussolini's Stadio del Partito Nazionale Fascista, or PNF. After staging a friendly with Hungary in 1928 – Italy's first home game south of Bologna – the PNF would be the venue for Italy's (and Mussolini's) triumphant 1934 World Cup final.

Lazio were also based at the PNF by then, having left the Rondinella three years previously. Shortly before then, local patriot and Fascist politician Italo Foschi had been behind the merger of four clubs to form

Roma, a club intended to represent the city in name and colour.

Foschi died after being taken ill while watching a Lazio game. His beloved Roma made their home at a wooden stadium, Campo Testaccio, in Via Zabaglia. The district of Testaccio is everything Pairoli is not – shabby, urban, and still Roma through and through.

Reasonable success on the pitch led to a huge rise in Roma's popularity at their overcrowded stadium, and they joined Lazio at the PNF as war broke out in 1940. Mussolini needed to promote Rome as the capital of a new, rationalised Italy, football included. When Roma were topping the league in 1941/42, authority favoured the leaders. In the vital Lazio–Roma game that January, some strange refereeing decisions and a weird last-minute own goal went Roma's way – as did the title in May.

Without political interference – save for the bungling and backhanders that got the Stadio Olimpico finished and improved upon 30 years afterwards – Rome saw its footballing role reduced to that of a big events venue and little else.

The Eighties saw a rise in the local ultra movement, some of it developing into violence as bored Roma youth from the Fascist-built housing project at EUR clashed with their disaffected counterparts from Lazio. The divisions were political as well as geographical – Lazio fans being predominantly suburban right-wing, Roma's inner-city left.

The violence has lessened, but first-time visitors shouldn't be surprised to see losing fans attempt to burn down their section of the ground before the final whistle of *Il Derby Capitale*. Preparation for the ever more ostentatious ultra choreography starts months in advance, donation boxes appearing at either end for materials to be gathered for the big day.

For years, the colours and passions of the Rome derby have carried little significance outside the capital. Yet the Olimpico is becoming a central arena in determining the destiny of the Italian title. In 1999/2000, Lazio's Cragnotti was finally rewarded for his huge investment in foreign talent, as a team inspired by the dynamic midfield presence of Argentina's Juan Verón pipped Juve to the *scudetto* on the last day of the season. Roma president Franco Sensi responded by splashing out £20million to prise Gabriel Batistuta from his beloved Fiorentina, and Lazio replied by signing his Argentine team-mate Crespo. The summer transfer *mercato* had been won by Rome, hands down. Would the city also dominate on the field of play in 2000/01?

The thrilling fields

 Roma

Stadium Olimpico, see p.397
Club office Via di Trigoria
Colours All burgundy with yellow trim
League champions 1942, 1983
Cup winners 1964, 1969, 1980–81, 1984, 1986, 1991
Fairs' (UEFA) Cup winners 1961

It is 17 years since Roma were last champions of Italy – a point vocally made by the sky-blue half of the city as Lazio celebrated their title in May 2000. But Roma president Franco Sensi, though he may not be popular among the country's footballing elite, is making a serious attempt to get his club back to the top. The summer of 1999 saw former AC Milan and Real Madrid boss Fabio Capello recruited as coach, and although he was unable to manage more than a UEFA Cup spot in his first season, there is a genuine feeling that big things may be around the corner, with a team rich in foreign talent but which, thanks to the presence of homegrown striker Francesco Totti, has also kept its identity.

Formed from the Alba, Fortitudo, Roman and Pro Roma teams in 1927, the club soon earned a loyal fan base in the poor, tatty Testaccio area of the city. Roma boasted two members of Italy's 1934 World Cup-winning team – right-winger Enrico Guaita and half-back Attilio Ferraris IV – and were virtually unbeatable at their cramped home, Campo Testaccio. Goalscorer Rodolfo Volk, whose century-plus of strikes for Roma was bettered only in the Eighties by Roberto Pruzzo, was the club's first folk hero, nicknamed *Siggefrido* ('Siegfried') because of his Wagnerian appearance. In their first seven seasons at the Testaccio, Roma never failed to finish in the top six of *Serie A*.

The move north to the PNF was a practical but unpopular one, sweetened by centre-forward Amadeo Amadei, who hit 100 goals for the club and helped Roma

win their first title in 1942. *I Lupi* ('the wolves') fell away after that, even going down to *Serie B* at one point, despite signing Alcide Ghiggia, scorer of Uruguay's winning goal in the 1950 World Cup. Cup football was the fans' biggest cheer – two Argentine forwards, Antonio Angelillo and Pedro Manfredini, gained the club the Fairs' Cup of 1961 and the *Coppa Italia* in 1964.

Two men changed Roma's fortunes around after Italy's ban on foreign imports was lifted in the Seventies. Brazilian Falcão, he of the immaculate shoulder dummy in the 1982 World Cup game against Italy, ran a busy midfield, engineered by Swedish coach Nils Liedholm. Aided by winger Bruno Conti and Roberto Pruzzo, three

Rome essentials

Rome has two **airports**, one for scheduled flights, the other for chartered. The former, **Fiumicino**, also known as Leonardo da Vinci, is 30km south of the city, and connected to Rome's main train station of Termini by an hourly direct express rail service (L15,000, daily 7am–9.15pm, journey time 30mins). A more frequent stopping service runs until midnight (L7,000, journey time 40mins) and calls at Ostiense, by Piramide metro. An overnight bus (L7,000 from automatic machine) runs to Tiburtina metro station, almost hourly from opposite the arrivals hall entrance. A taxi will set you back some L70,000.

The other airport, **Ciampino**, is 15km south-east of the city, connected by a half-hourly *COTRAL* bus to Anagnina metro station (L1,500, daily 7am–11pm).

Rome has **buses**, **trams** and a two-line **metro**, all running 5.30am–11.30pm. Metro lines A (red) and B (blue) cross at Termini. Tickets must be bought in advance from the machines at major stations or from *tabacchi*. A single ticket ('BIT', L1,500) is valid for 75mins from validation on all orange buses, and for one metro journey. A day ticket ('BIG', L6,000) is valid for all city transport until midnight of the day it is stamped. For the city's 27 night bus routes (marked N), you can buy a BIT ticket onboard.

Licensed **taxis** are either yellow or white. Make sure the meter is switched to zero when you pick one up from a rank, which will be marked with a blue taxi sign. As you set off, the meter should indicate the minimum fare (currently L4,500) for the first 3km or 9mins of the journey, followed by L1,200 per km. There are various surcharges at night, on Sundays and holidays, and for pieces of luggage. To call a cab, dial ☎06/4994 or ☎06/3570, giving your whereabouts. You will be given a taxi code-name, a number and a time. The meter will start running from the time of your call.

The main EPT **tourist office** is at Via Parigi 5, by the *Grand Hotel*, diagonally left out of Termini (open Mon–Fri 8.15am–7.15pm, Sat 8.15am–1.45pm, ☎06/4889 9253, fax 06/4889 9255). This can be chaotically understaffed, so a better bet might be the *Enjoy Rome* office at Via Varese 39 (open Mon–Fri 8.30am–1pm &3.30–6pm, Sat 8.30am–1pm, ☎06/445 1843, fax 06/445 0734), which offers a free accommodation booking service and left-luggage facilities.

The best listings publication is the Italian-language *Time Out Roma* (monthly, L4,500).

Leading from the back – Roma's Aldair

farewell to Giannini, and within a year, incredibly, Liedholm was back in charge, now in his seventies, as a stopgap before the arrival – from Lazio, of all places – of new coach Zdeněk Zeman. The Czech manager's reputation for pragmatism seemed perfectly suited to a star-studded squad that included the Brazilians Cafú and Paulo Sérgio, midfielders Luigi di Biagio and Eusebio di Francesco, and homegrown striker Totti.

Yet Roma have continued to under-achieve, unable to finish higher than the UEFA Cup places in the past three seasons, and failing to get past the quarter-final stage in Europe. Now, with Sensi's wallet and Capello's expertise, a long-awaited place in the Champions' League is the least the *Romanisti* expect.

Club merchandise

The **official shop** at Via Paolina 8 (open Mon–Sat 9am–1pm & 3.30–7.30pm, most credit cards) sells tickets and souvenirs. To reach it, take metro line B to Cavour, then a short walk up Via Cavour to Piazza Esquilino. Other club outlets can be found at via 7 Chiese 133 and at Via Sampiero di Bastelica 12.

Ultra culture

Only five years ago, Roma's ultras were among the fiercest in all Italy. The main bunch, the **CUCS** (*Commando Ultras Curva Sud*), were an imposing and colourful presence at any Italian stadium. Derby day became something akin to standing on the launchpad of Cape Canaveral at take-off.

Since the CUCS' heyday, **Boys Roma** and sympathisers of the neo-Fascist *Movemento Sociale Italiano* have infiltrated the ranks, creating minor pockets of havoc.

In print

LaRoma (L5,000) is the glossy club monthly, sold at newsstands across town.

In the net

The club's official site is at: www.asromacalcio.it. It has a nice, clean design with the bare minimum of intrusive Java or other distractions. Sadly, it also lacks an English-language area.

times *Serie A* top scorer, Roma had their best side since the Thirties. Back-to-back cup wins at the start of the Eighties were followed by a first postwar title in 1983.

Alas, the team froze on their big night – the 1984 European Cup final on home turf against Liverpool. It was a poor game, lost on penalties to Bruce Grobbelaar's wobbling knees. Almost as quickly as it had arrived, Roma's moment had gone.

During the last decade Roma's fans have enjoyed watching some star names upfront – Rudi Völler, Daniel Fonseca, Abel Balbo – and sustained a long love affair with mid-fielder Giuseppe Giannini, *Il Principe* ('the Prince'). The latter's presence wasn't enough to turn things round in the club's last European final, a 2–1 aggregate defeat by Inter in the 1991 UEFA Cup.

That year Roma lifted the *Coppa Italia* again, but there has been no sniff of silver-ware since then. In 1996 the club said

Lazio

Stadium Olimpico, see p.397
Club office Via U Novaro 32
Colours Sky-blue shirts, white shorts
League champions 1974, 2000
Cup winners 1958, 1998, 2000
Cup-Winners' Cup winners 1999

The *biancocelesti* (literally 'white-and-skies') were founded as a multi-sports club in 1900 on stout Victorian principles by Luigi Bigiarelli, a military man who chose the club name from that of the region surrounding Rome, and whose choice of club colours was inspired by the Greek flag.

Among Lazio's handful of early venues was a military parade ground, and their core fan base is still in the quiet, green-belt northern outskirts of Rome, now pestered by the revving-up of sports car engines and the bleeping of mobile phones.

For all their early ancestry, Lazio were also-rans until the modern era. Before World War II, rare highlights included moving from their Rondinella ground to the then sumptuous PNF stadium in 1931, and the arrival of 1938 World Cup hero Silvio Piola – the most prolific striker in *Serie A* history with 290 goals to his name. Generally, though, Lazio were overshadowed in the league by new boys Roma.

A cup win in 1958 and an occasional promotion from *Serie B* kept fans hungry until the arrival of Giorgio Chinaglia from Swansea Town in 1969. A big, affable lunkhead of a forward, Chinaglia had been born in Italy but raised in South Wales. He was delighted to be given the chance to move back to his homeland, and certainly made the most of it. Diving in bravely where Italian defenders trod – and most local forwards dared not – he was idolised by the fans.

By now Lazio were being coached by Argentine Juan Carlos Lorenzo, who learned his football with the notorious Estudiantes side of the Sixties. His win-at-all-costs attitude saw Lazio improve their derby record and qualify for Europe for

the first time, but at a cost to club discipline. A fiery home Fairs' Cup clash with Arsenal ended in a fight between players at Rome's *L'Augustea* restaurant – some say engineered by Lorenzo. The coach left but the malady lingered on. Fans now began to occupy the *Curva Nord* in serious numbers, and Rome derbies became ferocious.

When Ipswich Town came for a UEFA Cup game in 1973, leading 4–0 from the first leg, Lazio went 2–0 ahead on the night before they had a penalty refused. One was then given to the English, duly converted, and the match finished 4–2 in Lazio's favour. No favours were done afterwards, as fans rained anything they could get their hands on down on the departing players, who began to set upon each other in the tunnel. Lazio were banned from Europe for a year – which just happened to follow their solitary Italian title.

Chinaglia was top *Serie A* scorer in that championship season of 1973/74, partnered by Renzo Garlaschelli upfront, provided for by midfielder Mario Frustalupi, and guided by the team's Darlington-born captain, Pino Wilson. Chinaglia was practically chained to the Fiumicino runway when he left for New York Cosmos two years later.

Without Chinaglia, Lazio declined further into tragi-comedy. Young midfield prodigy Luciano Re Cecconi was shot dead in a jeweller's store in 1977, when he walked in disguised as a robber and pretended to heist it for a joke. Two years later a Lazio ultra was slain by a firework at a derby game.

The club began the Eighties by being relegated for their part in the Milan match-fixing scandal, came back up, then went down again. In 1986/87 Lazio had one foot in *Serie C1*, maintaining their second-division status only with a 1–0 play-off win over a village side, Campobasso.

By the time Paul Gascoigne arrived in 1992 – after a year on the operating table – Lazio's fans were desperate for success. Gazza's three seasons in Rome were the usual mixture of controversy and injury off the pitch, wayward genius on it. But he was surrounded by great players, thanks to financier Sergio Cragnotti's millions, which brought Alen Bokšić, Karl-Heinz Riedle, Thomas Doll and Aron Winter to the club.

The fans' favourite was 'Beppe' Signori, his little legs running like dynamos, his mind constantly devising new attacking ideas. He and Czech coach Zdeněk Zeman had both come from Foggia. With Signori's goals – 49 in his first two seasons from 1992/93 – and Zeman's adventurous, three-upfront formation, Lazio became regular top-five finishers for the first time in their history.

Such was Signori's popularity that fans swarmed Rome's Piazza del Popolo to prevent Cragnotti from selling him to Parma in the summer of 1995. Two years later Signori was still a Lazio man, but Riedle, Doll, Winter, Gazza and Zeman had all gone, and Italy's 1982 World Cup goalkeeping hero, Dino Zoff, was caretaker coach, pending the arrival of Sven Göran Eriksson – the latest to take on the task of turning Lazio from nearly men into a team of winners.

It was Eriksson who finally sold Signori to cure ego problems upfront, as a switch was made to a rigid 4–4–2 formation. But while the new line-up launched a brilliant comeback in front of a packed Olimpico to win the 1998 *Coppa Italia*, 3–2 on aggregate against Milan, the gulf in class between Lazio and the big boys was exposed only a week later, when Ronaldo's Inter beat them 3–0 in the UEFA Cup final in Paris.

Enter the likes of Vieri, Salas and Sérgio Conceição as Cragnotti spent £70million in a single close season. Often wonderful to watch, the star-studded team waltzed through to the 1999 Cup-Winners' Cup final to become the last victors in the competition, beating Mallorca 2–1 thanks to Pavel Nedved's clever late strike. Alas, by the time Lazio had made their little piece of history at Villa Park, the title was already lost to Milan.

That summer, the sale of Christian Vieri to Inter for £30million led some to question whether Cragnotti had the staying power to continue funding his dream. But

it turned out to be a masterstroke. Eriksson used the cash to bring Argentine playmaker Juan Verón from Parma – arguably the best midfielder in the world, he gave Lazio a new, more combative dimension. With Nedved and Conceição formidable on the flanks and Simone Inzaghi and the returning Bokšić taking turns to partner Salas in attack, Lazio were impressive in Europe until an inexplicable 5–2 defeat at Valéncia in the quarter-finals.

But the real progress was being made at home, where the team were in a two-horse race with Juventus throughout the season. A Diego Simeone header gave Eriksson's side a crucial win over Juve in Turin, and on the final day of the season Lazio comfortably defeated Reggina at home, and 50,000 fans waited for almost an hour inside the Olimpico for the result of the rain-delayed match between Juventus and Perugia. Then news came through that Juve had somehow contrived to lose – and the title was Lazio's.

Cragnotti celebrated by spending £35million on Hernán Crespo, effectively replacing Vieri a year late. Other signings, such as goalkeeper Angelo Peruzzi from Inter and Italy Under-21 midfield star Roberto Baronio. were a clear signal that Lazio were not prepared to wait another 26 years for their next title.

Club merchandise

The main *Lazio Point* is at Via Farini 34 (open Mon 3.30–7.30pm, Tues–Sat 9am–1pm & 3.30–7.30pm, most credit cards) and sells both tickets and souvenirs. Take metro A to Vittorio Emanuele, then walk up Via Napoleone III. There is a Monteverde branch is Via Portuense 544, and a Prati one at Via Cipro 4/1.

Ultra culture

Lazio fans started hanging around the *Curva Nord* in groups in the early Seventies, fired by the political tensions of the day and by the bullish success of Chinaglia's champions of 1974. The movement became focused on one main group, *Eagle's Supporters*, who copied a lot of English fashions, not all of them good. The arrival of the

The Stadio Olimpico

Viale dei Gladiatori
Capacity 82,000 (all-seated)

Italy's **national stadium** will be a multi-purpose, seven-day-a-week, American-style
leisure centre before the end of the year 2000. Chains of shops, pizzerias, bars, restaurants… What would poor Benito have made of it? Put them in uniform and stop them
eating pasta had been Mussolini's motto.

A sports complex, the so-called *Foro Mussolini*, had been constructed in the
leader's honour during the Thirties – an obelisk announcing a grand, marble, tree-lined
walkway leading to a fountain and, it was planned, a 100,000-seater modern-day
Colosseum. The latter was never built, but the grand **Fascist entrance** still stands.
Behind it lies the modern Stadio Olimpico, begun in 1952. It was then that the area,
and the smaller sports stadia around it, became known as the *Foro Italico*. The complex played host to the Olympic Games in 1960, the Olimpico staging athletics events,
the nearby Flaminio some of the football.

Home to Roma, Lazio, every third Italy home game and various European finals
(including two Liverpool victories in 1977 and 1984), the Olimpico has a **tremendous
setting**. With the sun sinking over Monte Mario, the Tiber and the Eternal City as the
backdrop, the stadium's vast open bowl presents a picture not easily forgotten.

To host Italy's intended march to the **1990 World Cup final**, the Olimpico needed a roof and individual seats. After the usual politics and doubling of estimates, a
translucent roof was added and space made by extending each end nearer the pitch.
Now the *azzurri* had their stage. Nobody who went to one of Italy's games in 1990 will
forget the wall of **noise and colour** at the Olimpico – it was as if the opposition were
being fed to the lions, the kind of spectacle that had them going in Nero's day.

To reach the stadium, take **metro line A** to its terminus at Ottaviano, and on leaving the station, turn away from the Vatican into Via Barletta, with the #32 bus stop in
the middle of the street. Head towards **Maresciallo/Cadorna**, and the Olimpico will
be on your left after about 10mins.

For **tickets**, your best bet is to get an advance (*prevendita*) ticket from an individual
club outlet – although around L3,000 dearer, it will save you a lot of headaches on
matchday. At the stadium, Lazio's office is in the *Curva Nord*, Roma's in the *Curva Sud*.
You'll pay around L25,000 to sit at either end. Away fans are placed in the *distinti* section opposite the home boys. For neutrals, the *Tribuna Tevere laterale* are fair value at
around L60,000, while the better-placed *centrale* cost around L90,000.

For a pre-match beer, the tiny **Roma '90** snack bar is the other side of the
Lungotevere from the main entrance, by the river. Alternatively the **Bar del Tennis** is
by the tennis courts behind the *Curva Sud*, at Viale dei Gladiatori 31.

Irriducibili, predominantly Fascist, swung the
club's support firmly to the right.

In print
Like Roma, Lazio publish their own glossy club
magazine, *Lazialità* (monthly, L5,000).

In the net
The design of the official website is a bit flashy
for its own good, but there's still a lot going on at:

www.sslazio.it. For a simpler but still very
impressive offering, try the fan-run version,
sadly in Italian only, at: www.lazionet.com

Eat, drink, sleep…

Bars and clubs
Away from *la dolce vita* of Via della Pace,
the once glamorous Fifties hangout which

still attracts film stars, Rome lacks a real nightlife centre. If anything, it's Testaccio (Metro B to Piramide), full of popular, reasonably priced clubs, although Trastevere and San Lorenzo also have a decent range of unpretentious bars. Well-organised large squat clubs, *Centri Sociali*, are a cheap source of live entertainment, generally in former municipal buildings. Elsewhere is a morass of disco bars and Irish pubs.

Bar San Calisto, Piazza San Calisto 3. The jewel in Trastevere's crown, serving cheap beer which you can buy at the bar and take to the terrace. Inside are old shots of both teams. Classy it ain't, but a visit here and you've definitely been to Rome. Closed Sundays. Any bus to Trastevere.

Dome Rock Café, Via D Fontana 18. Don't let the name put you off. This is a very popular, very fun disco and bar. Bands on most weekends, DJs nightly, playing a mix of dance and indie sounds. Unusually for an Italian club, posing is not essential. Open until 3am daily. Any bus or tram to Piazza San Giovanni.

The Drunken Ship, Piazza Campo de Fiori 20. Long-time hangout of Rome's expatriates but plenty of local lads and lasses as well. Heavy on the motif, as usual, but a good bet if Italian bars are not to your liking. Happy hour 6–9pm daily.

Villaggio Globale, Lungotevere Testaccio. Set in the old slaughterhouse of Mattatoio, this *Centro Sociale* features live bands on Fri, DJs on Sat. The *Mattatoio* bar opposite opens at dawn. Metro B to Piramide, then tram #13 down Via Marmorata.

Restaurants

Roman food is traditionally reliant on offal, brains, tripe and such – a hangover from ancient times when commoners lived on leftovers. Traditional Italian mainstays are also available, but prices are high.

Pizzeria la Pappardella, ia degli Equi 56, off Via Tiburtina by Piazza le Tiburtino. Cheap, wood-oven *pizzeria* in the San Lorenzo area. Crispy, thin pizzas at L8–12,000. Closed Mon.

No credit cards. Out of Stazione Termini and immediate right down Via Marsala.

Da Giovanni, Via della Lungara 41a. Busy, cheap two-room diner near the Tiber in Trastevere. Roman dishes at L15–20,000. Closed Sun. No credit cards. Bus #23, #41, #65 or #280.

Myosotis, Vicolo della Vaccarella 35. In the heart of the *centro storico*, a friendly, modern restaurant that gives classic Roman dishes a modern twist. Booking advisable on: ☎06/686 5554.

Perilli a Testaccio, Via Marmorata 39. Straight out of a Fellini film, a family-run *trattoria* serving huge portions of local delicacies. Closed Wed. Metro B to Piramide.

Accommodation

Rome has a shortage of mid-price hotels. Always try to reserve a place well in advance, and allow for the possibility of it not being available for the length of time originally agreed.

Ariston, Via F Turati (☎06/446 5399). No more than 50m from Termini train station, this four-star hotel is a rarity in offering a full American buffet breakfast as opposed to the usual continental fare. Singles L150,000, doubles L200,000.

Foro Italico, Viale delle Olimpiadi 61 (☎06/324 2571, fax 06/324 2613). Rome's main youth hostel is right up by the Stadio Olimpico. Dorm beds for IYHF members at L25,000 (L5,000 extra for non-members), breakfast and showers included. Midnight curfew. No credit cards. Metro A to Ottaviano, then bus #32 to Cadorna.

Fawlty Towers, Via Magenta 39 (☎06/445 0374). Pensione-cum-hostel with no curfew, terrace and sitting room with satellite TV. Dorm beds at L35,000, doubles at L75,000, with bath L100,000. No credit cards. Turn right out of Termini.

Hotel Onella, Via Principe Amedeo 47 (☎06/488 5257). Close to Termini train station, a quality three-star option with single rooms from L130,000, doubles from L200,000.

Football in Naples must be seen in a different context from the rest of Italy, probably from the rest of Europe. Naples is one team, 70,000 season-ticket holders against the world. Naples, of course, *was* one man, whose seven seasons here are almost the stuff of fiction. From the hysteria of his arrival to the ignominy of his departure, Diego Maradona took this benign madhouse to the top and back down again. Whether the club, Napoli, can ever take the city back to the top of the Italian football tree is a subject as hotly debated here as the date of the next eruption of Mount Vesuvius, the volcano which dominates the city.

The thrilling fields

 Napoli

Stadium San Paolo, Piazzale V Tecchio
Capacity 72,000 (all-seated)
Colours Azure-blue shirts, white shorts
League champions 1987, 1990
Cup winners 1962, 1976, 1987
UEFA Cup winners 1989

The history of Napoli can be divided into 'am' and 'pm' – before and after Maradona. Before his arrival in 1984, the club had relied on the occasional European run to appease Italy's most manic support.

It was a Cunard sailor, William Poths, who organised the first football team here at the turn of the century. Poths' Naples FC had a rival, Internazionale, but over pizza and wine at the city's *d'Angelo* restaurant, the two agreed to merge in 1926.

The newly formed Internapoli, later Napoli, had a poor start in life. Their first season in the southern regional division was so disastrous, fans turned the city's symbol of a proud horse into the club's unofficial one of a little donkey. The club

moved grounds up to the tranquility of Vómero, but crowd disturbances soon had the place closed and the authorities sought to build a secure venue where Neapolitans could vent their passions. They chose a spot in the west of the city, outside an area of toxic gases and extinct volcanoes known as Campi Flegrei.

With the backing of shipping magnate Achille Lauro, a huge bowl, the Stadio San Paolo, was built in 1959. Lauro, *Il Comandante*, bought the South American strike partnership of José Altafini and Omar Sivori from Gianni Agnelli's Juventus, in a deal which gave Fiat the contract to motorise Lauro's ocean liners.

At last, Naples had a team to challenge the north. Napoli won the *Coppa Italia*, their first major honour, in 1962, made second place to Milan in the league in 1968, and the following year went out to Leeds in the Fairs' Cup on the drawing of lots. In 1975 they lost a title decider to Juventus on a last-minute goal – scored by the team's former hero, Altafini.

By this time Corrado Ferlaino was Napoli president, and it was he who brought Diego Maradona to the club. The transfer of the little Argentinian from Barcelona was fraught with difficulties, not least a $1 million shortfall in the fee, overcome in one day after the club appealed to fans to make personal donations, and people queued round the block, savings books in hand. Maradona was flown into a packed San Paolo by helicopter; everyone in the crowd paid L1,000 to attend.

Diego's arrival made little immediate impact on the team. But in 1986/87, after his triumphant World Cup in Mexico, Maradona was on top of his game and Napoli's first-ever *scudetto* seemed within reach. With ex-player Ottavio Bianchi, a strict disciplinarian, as coach, Ciro Ferrara at the back, the gritty Fernando de Napoli in midfield and Brazilian Careca partnering Maradona upfront, Napoli kept ahead of the pack and the city prepared to party.

Naples had waited sixty years for this moment. When it came, with a 1–1 draw against Fiorentina on May 10, 1987, hundreds of donkeys were let loose around the town, no-one slept for a week, let alone went into work, and Maradona himself partied as hard as anyone – a prelude to the drugs-and-prostitutes hell into which he would sink within four years.

In 1989 Maradona's Napoli beat Jürgen Klinsmann's Stuttgart to win the UEFA Cup, and a year later they were champions again, thanks to a two-point award after another of their South Americans, Alemão, was struck by a coin at Atalanta – TV cameras caught Napoli's masseur shouting to the Brazilian: 'Keep down on the ground!'

In many Italian eyes, this incident tarnished Napoli's reputation. Their 1987 *scudetto* had not been unpopular elsewhere in the country, but now the honeymoon was over, and divorce seemed the only possible outcome after Maradona's Argentina knocked Italy out of the 1990 World Cup. Before the semi-final between the two teams at the San Paolo, Diego had

exhorted Neapolitans to cheer for his side as the underdogs against an Italian line-up comprised almost entirely of northerners. The plea did not go down well, either in Naples or elsewhere.

Less than a year later, after testing positive for cocaine, Maradona took a privately chartered plane to Buenos Aires and never set foot in Naples again. Without him, the club stumbled from one financial crisis to another and were unable to hang on to the prodigious talent the Argentinian had left behind – players like Ferrara, Careca, Uruguayan striker Daniel Fonseca, and Diego's understudy, Gianfranco Zola. As Napoli's coach of the mid-Nineties, Marcello Lippi, explained: 'We played without salaries for six months and with lawyers in the dressing room.'

In 1997, the San Paolo drew its first capacity crowd in years for the first leg of the *Coppa Italia* final against Vicenza. Napoli won 1–0, but lost the tie overall. Far worse was to come. In 1997/98, the club endured its worst season ever, finishing bottom of *Serie A* after managing only two wins all

Naples essentials

Naples' Capodochino **airport** is 4km north-west of town. Bus #14 (L1,500) calls at both international and domestic terminals and then runs on to Piazza Garibaldi, the square outside the main **train station**, Stazione Centrale. Buses run every 15mins, 6am–midnight, journey time 30mins. A taxi will cost at least L20,000.

The best way around Naples' narrow streets and back alleys is to **walk**. Towards the bay, the Stazione Centrale is a 20min hike across Piazza Garibaldi and down Corso Umberto. Otherwise there are five modes of **transport**: buses, trams, metro, a high-speed suburban train and funiculars up to Vomero. A single ticket for an inner-city journey on any of these is L1,500, from transport offices and *tabacchi* – stamp it onboard or before entering the train or metro; it is valid for 90mins. An **all-day ticket** is L4,500. Transport runs 6am–11pm, and a few night buses leave from Piazza Garibaldi or Parco del Castello.

Taxis (☎081/570 7070) are yellow, and some of them are metered. Either barter first or watch the meter like a hawk. Journeys should cost L3,000 plus L500 per minute, with supplements for night-time, Sundays, holidays, and items of luggage.

There are EPT **tourist offices** at the station (open Mon–Sat 9am–8pm, Sun 9am–1pm, ☎081/268 779), in town at Piazza dei Martiri 58, Scala B, 2nd floor (open Mon–Fri 8.30am–2.30pm, ☎081/405 311), and at the airport (daily 8.30am–2pm & 5–7.30pm). All should be able to provide free copies of the monthly *Qui Napoli*, which offers reasonable **entertainment** details. The daily *Il Matino* has a **listings guide** every Thursday.

term, and going through four different coaches. Ferlaino's manifold debts made any takeover a legal nightmare, but in 1999 he finally persuaded a consortium of local businessmen to clear them and, with a solid financial foundation at last, the team won promotion back to the *Serie A* at the end of the 1999/2000 season.

It was clear, however, that the side which had fought their way out of *Serie B* would have to be strengthened. Controversial former Lazio and Roma coach Zdeněk Zeman was brought in to add top-flight experience, while some modest moves in the transfer market, including the signing of Portuguese midfielder José Vidigal, offered the prospect of a little more than mere survival in *Serie A* in 2000/01.

Here we go!

Take the Gianturco-Bagnoli branch of the 'FS Metropolitana' train line from Garibaldi (inside the central train station), seven stops to **Campi Flegrei**. The stadium is a short walk between the palm trees of Piazzale Tecchio.

In Maradona's shoes – Gianfranco Zola, 1991

Just the ticket

Since the post-Maradona decline, gaining entry is no longer an issue at Napoli. Apart from the club's outlets in town, there are **ticket offices** immediately facing you as you approach the San Paolo. Napoli ultras are in *Curva B*, and visiting fans are placed in the *distinti* furthest from them. The *tribuna laterale* is a reasonably priced spot for neutrals, with tickets at L30,000; the *tribuna Posillipo* is for press and dignitaries.

Swift half

The best bar is the tiny *Caffè Cumana* on the traffic island between the station and the stadium, with a table outside if you're there early enough. At Via Giambattista Marino 13a, to the right of the stadium as you approach from the station, is the *Caffetteria degli Azzurri*.

Ultra culture

For the decisive game with Fiorentina in May 1987 that won Napoli their first *scudetto*, the **CUCB** (*Commando Ultra Curva B*) organised a banner of such size it made the *Guinness Book Of*

Records. Still fiercely loyal, they put out a monthly ultrazine, *UltrA'zzurro* (L5,000).

In the net

Judging from the official website, you'd never know the club had been in such dire straits. It's a slick, sponsor-friendly but still very worthwhile affair at: www.calcionapoli.it. The unofficial *Club Napoli Internet* can still be found at: www.x4all.nl/~elio/napoli.htm – with its unique choice of English, Spanish, Italian and Neapolitan dialect as preferred language.

Eat, drink, sleep…

Bars and clubs

Start the day with the finest **coffee** in Italy – Neapolitan bar owners warm their cups in special machines under the counter. In the city's **maze of streets**, anything could be around the next corner, a devil's head or an oasis of football talk in a bar.

Be-Bop Bar, Via Ferrigni 34. Hip, intimate late-night bar with cool sounds and a cosy back room, just round the corner from the inevitable pub, the *Irish Joyce*, at Vico dei Sospiri 12. All buses to Piazza Vittoria.

Green Stage, Piazza San Pasquale 15/16. Sympathetic designer bar with a young clientele and big screen for satellite TV action. All buses to Piazza Vittoria.

Maschio Angioino, Via Martucci. One of Naples' many pub/discos, with reasonable prices, heavy clouds of dope smoke and old-fashioned music. Popular with *tifosi*. Metro to Amedeo.

Oasis Pub, Via Giovanni Bausan 30. Incredibly friendly bar with big wooden tables and a decent selection of music. Metro to Amedeo.

Restaurants

Naples is the home of the **pizza** – wafer-thin crust, fresh local tomatoes and lashings of mozzarella cheese. You'll find street stalls serving up **slices** at L1,500 a throw, and you won't want to walk inside your local chain of pizza restaurant ever again.

Although the best spots to dine are at the pricy end of Mergellina **on the bay**, take the metro to Mergellina and it will drop you just inland in a neighbourhood full of reasonably priced *trattorie*.

Avellinese da Peppino, Via Silvio Spaventa 31/35. Piazza Garibaldi is full of pricy, mediocre diners for tourists; its side-streets are full of marvellous, moderately priced places for locals – such as *Peppino's*, with outdoor tables and outstanding *spaghetti alle vongole*. Open daily until midnight. No credit cards.

Dora, Via Ferdinando Palasciano 30. Down a narrow alley, between Piazza Amadeo and la Riviera di Chiaia, a fine seafood restaurant with main courses L20–40,000, grilled fish a speciality. No credit cards. Closed Sun.

Europeo, Via Vespucci 9. Large, reasonably priced restaurant with good service, subtle decor and excellent fare. Most credit cards. A 15min walk from Piazza Garibaldi down Corso Arnaldo Lucci.

Osteria Castello, Via S Teresa a Chaia 38. Cosy restaurant with a literary feel and two courses for under L15,000. Open mid-afternoon. Most credit cards. Tram #1 or #1B to Via Acton, then cross Piazza del Plebiscito by Palazzo Reale.

Pizzeria da Michele, Casale Sersale 1/3. A local institution which sticks by a menu of two varieties of pizza, *margherita* and *marinara*, at L4,000 each, L5,000 with extra mozzarella. Closed Sun. Short walk from Piazza Garibaldi.

Accommodation

Although Naples has the cheapest accommodation of all major Italian cities, it pays to **splash out** a little on comfort and safety. There are many cheap *pensione* around Piazza Garibaldi, but some are hired out by the hour and it can get noisy. The area near the university, between Piazza Dante and the cathedral, is a better bet.

Albergho Colombo, Via Nolana 35 (☎081/269 254). Just 5mins from the main train station, this is one of the cleaner and quieter of the small hotels in the area, which has itself benefitted from recent pedestrianisation. Singles L50,000, doubles L80,000.

Albergho Le Orchidee, Corso Umberto 7 (☎081/551 0721, fax 081/554 4390). Down towards the Piazza Bovio end of the Corso, in *scala B* on the fifth floor, great rooms for the price, with showers and modest balconies, some with sea views. Doubles at L90–130,000.

Ostello Mergellina, Salita della Grotta 23 (☎081/761 2346). Comfortable youth hostel with two-, four- and six-bed rooms, all with bath. L20,000 for IYHF members, L5,000 extra non-members. Curfew 11.30pm. Metro to Mergellina.

Pensione Margherita, Via Cimarosa 29 (☎081/556 7044). Away from the chaos downtown, a smart place up in Vomero by the *funiculare centrale* stop. Singles at L50,000, doubles L90,000. No credit cards. Midnight curfew.

Norway

Norges Fotballforbund Ullevål Stadium, Sognsveien 75, PO Box 3823, N-0805 Oslo
☎022/024 500   Fax 022/951 010   E-mail none

League champions Rosenborg   **Cup winners** Rosenborg   **Promoted** Haugesund, Bryne, IK Start   **Relegated** Kongsvinger, Skeid, Strømsgodset

European participants 2000/01 Rosenborg (UCL qualifiers); Molde, SK Brann, Lillestrøm (UEFA Cup); Stabæk (Intertoto Cup)

In a tournament that delighted many with its open, attacking football, Norway's rather basic long-ball game looked rather out of place at Euro 2000. Yet it is a sign of the elevated status of Norwegian football that the national team's inability to qualify from a group containing Spain, Yugoslavia and Slovenia was considered a let-down by their supporters. The days when a victory over England was regarded as a major upset have long since gone. Norwegian players ply their trade across the continent, highly regarded by their fellow professionals for their fitness and determination.

The key to Norway's arrival at the top table of international football can be traced back to 1984, and a long-term state plan to produce sporting excellence. When the so-called *Elite Sport* venture began, it focused mainly on track and field athletics. The results were impressive: Olympic and European championship medal hauls doubled, and a huge increase in grassroots participation.

Part of the *Elite Sport* philosophy could be summed up as 'win at all costs' – then something of a novelty in a country where so much sporting activity was still strictly amateur. The philosophy was transferred to team games, including football. If the previous generation of Norwegian players were content to travel to Benfica or the Bernabéu as lambs to the slaughter, *Elite Sport* ensured that the next one would not.

In 1990, Egil Olsen was installed as coach of the Norwegian national squad. Nicknamed 'Drillo' after his ability to drill low passes around the midfield, as a player,

Going out after the final whistle – Euro 2000

Olsen took the *Elite Sport* teachings a stage further and incorporated them into what he called 'effective football'. Olsen, a controversial figure who claimed to make more money from playing poker than coaching soccer, told his players to chase every lost cause and get the ball forward early. It was, in effect, a refinement of the long ball game, and was immediately criticised by fans.

But effective it was, and in 1994 Norway appeared in their first World Cup finals

When all seemed well – Ole Gunnar Solskjær believes Norway are in the quarter-finals

since 1938, after finishing top of a qualifying group that included Holland and England – neither of whom could beat Olsen's side. Graham Taylor's England, in particular, were completely nonplussed by Norway's limitless running during a vital defeat in Oslo in the summer of 1993.

At USA '94, Norway beat Mexico, lost to Italy and drew with Ireland. It was a respectable performance, but not one that won many plaudits. In truth, the heat in America had made it impossible for the Norwegians to play the game as they wanted, and without any back-up plan in the locker, they simply wilted in the sun.

Norway needed another tactical string to their bow, and the mass export of players to the English Premiership looked as though it would provide it. Now a little more flexible in their approach, Olsen's team got off to a flier in their qualifiers for the 1996 European Championship. But a late equaliser by Jan Suchopárek for the Czech Republic in Oslo, with the Norwegians just three minutes from the finals, proved a telling blow; after away defeats

by both the Czechs and the Dutch, Norway missed the boat to Euro '96. While the exodus of key players had produced some positive results, Norway needed a more sophisticated domestic game to give Olsen the strength in-depth he needed. The club that provided that sophistication were Rosenborg of Trondheim – tough, efficient, professional, forward-looking, all the things, in fact, which up until now had been anathema to Norwegian club sides.

With Rosenborg and SK Brann of Bergen both reaching the quarter-finals of European club competitions in 1997, the national team were very much back on track when they beat Brazil 4–2 in Oslo in a pre-World Cup friendly.

With practically the whole squad earning their living from the English Premiership or the *Bundesliga*, Norway proved tough opponents again come France '98. Plonked in a tricky group with Morocco, Scotland and Brazil, after two draws the Norwegians needed an unlikely win over the holders to get through the group stage. But win they did, with two remarkable last-

Basics

EU, US, Canadian, Australian and New Zealand citizens require only a valid **passport** to enter Norway for up to three months.

Like other Scandinavian countries, Norway has a reputation for being one of the most expensive European destinations. The Norwegian currency is the kroner, one krone (crown, indiactated here as Nkr) being divided into 100 øre. There are notes for 50Nkr, 100Nkr, 200Nkr, 500Nkr and 1000Nkr, while the coins in circulation are 50 øre, 1Nkr, 5Nkr and 10Nkr. There are around 12Nkr to £1.

The best places to **change money** are banks, savings banks and major post offices, which all offer competitive rates. On arrival, you will also be able to change foreign currency and travellers' cheques at airports, harbours, train stations and hotels, but expect a less generous rate and higher commission charges. **Credit cards** are widely accepted in major towns.

Norwegian cities are connected by the train services of *Norges Statsbaner* (*NSB*), the efficiently run state rail company. In places, the rail network is extended by a train-bus service, with connecting coaches continuing on from train stations. A one-way train ticket from **Oslo** to **Trondheim** costs around 670Nkr for the seven-hour journey. Special **discount fares** are available for long-distance journeys if booked at least one day in advance; enquire about any other special deals before booking. If you have more time to spare and the geography allows, travelling by **ferry** or coastal steamer can be a relaxing alternative.

Norway's **telephone service** is likewise efficiently run by *Telenor* and you'll have no problem making international calls from public phones. These take 1Nkr, 5Nkr, 10Nkr and 20Nkr coins, or phonecards (*TeleKort*) which can be bought from shops and kiosks and come in three sizes: 35Nkr, 98Nkr and 210Nkr

From outside the country, the **dialling code** for Norway is ☎47; city codes are part of the customer number. From Norway, the dialling prefix for international calls is ☎00 followed by the country code; reduced call rates, offering a 15 percent discount, apply from 10pm to 8am daily.

gasp goals, one an apparently dubious but correctly awarded penalty, that took them through to a knock-out meeting with Italy. In a disappointing game in Marseille, Drillo's solitary sweet memory would be the farewell cheers of Viking-helmeted fans after a 1–0 defeat.

The end result of his period in charge – 44 wins, 16 defeats in 87 games – has been Norway's permanent elevation in status from minnows to feared challengers. The knock-on effect is £10million handed out to clubs in share issues and a lucrative trade in players, perhaps more to the benefit of controversial agents than to the domestic game as a whole. Olsen's 4–5–1 approach may have been ruthlessly systematic, but it changed the face of Norwegian football forever.

His replacement, ex-international winger Nils Johan Semb, found Drillo a hard act to follow. But after briefly experimenting with new systems, the coach went back to basics and saw his side cruise through to the Euro 2000 finals as winners of an admittedly mediocre qualifying group.

Norway's Euro 2000 campaign began with a shock 1–0 win over Spain, delivered by a classic piece of Olsen-esque route-one football, headed home by Steffen Iversen. That victory put Semb's team in the driving seat at the head of their group, but they were beaten 1–0 by Yugoslavia in their next game. While the Yugoslavs won few friends with their diving and nasty challenges as they clung on to a seventh-minute lead, their goalscorer Savo Milošević touched a nerve with his post-match comment which questioned whether any neutral supporter would be sorry to see Norway out of the competition. In the last round of games, while Spain and Yugoslavia were offering up a seven-goal thriller, Norway and Slovenia played out a goalless stalemate, the Norwegians suddenly fearful of opponents they had beaten twice in qualifying, and believing that a draw would be enough to see them through. What they did not envisage was that it was Spain, with two stoppage-time goals, who would win the other match – eliminating Norway after the latter's game had finished.

For all the embarrassment of that setback, there is no doubt that Norwegian football is on the move. All that remains is for the last vestiges of the amateur code to be swept away from the domestic game.

In truth, there is still some way to go, for cultural, historical and geographical reasons. Skiing and other winter pastimes have always dominated the sports calendar in Norway, and football, with its necessarily short summer season, didn't get a national championship until 1937 – a year after the national side had beaten Germany in front of Hitler at the Olympic Games in Berlin. Even then, the title was decided by a series of play-offs; a fully fledged league didn't start up until 1963.

Matches in that first league season were watched by an average of 8000 fans, which delighted the Norwegian FA. But the game's popularity wasn't sustained. The modern TV era, combined with the departure of star names such as Rune Bratseth and Erik Thorstvedt, made European football, and the English game in particular, more attractive than the domestic variety. Meanwhile, Norway's terrain and long distances between cities deterred travelling support. And the inability of Oslo to generate an influential club (locals blame a lack of training facilities in the capital and the cosmopolitan distractions of the big city) has deprived football of its biggest natural catchment area of support.

Assuming that a challenger from Oslo (probably Vålerenga) can be found to com-

pete with Rosenborg, Brann and Molde for honours, then the future looks bright for Norwegian football. The exodus of star names shows no sign of letting up, but at the same time, neither does the flow of fresh talent from the clubs' excellent youth policies – a lasting legacy of the *Elite Sport* programme.

And if Norway's men need any further inspiration to make future progress, they need look no further than their women-folk. Football is far from being a single-sex sport here – there are more than 50,000 girls' clubs up and down the country, and in 1995, Norway won the Women's World Cup for the first time.

Match practice

Like their Scandinavian neighbours, Norwegian fans have been brought up on a diet of overseas football. Their long winters are illuminated by live television coverage from England and other countries, and most Norwegian fans have a favourite English club. No surprise, then, that with the exception of Rosenborg, Norwegian fans ape the songs of British supporters.

The Norwegian season begins in mid-April and finishes towards the end of October. By the time most of Europe is approaching its halfway stage, Norwegians are raising a glass to their newly crowned champions. Most league games are played on Sunday evenings at 8pm, with live TV games on Saturdays at 6pm, and occasionally on Sundays at the same kick-off time.

A different league

Norway's 14-team premier division is known as the *Tippeliga*. Below this comes the first division, also a 14-team competition, from which the top two teams gain promotion each year, swapping places with the bottom two of the premier. The club placed third from bottom in the *Tippeliga* is dragged into a two-leg play-off with the third-placed team in the first division. Further down the ladder, the second division is regionalised, with eight groups of 12 almost entirely amateur teams.

Up for the cup

Like all Europe's long-established knock-out tournaments, Norway's is a mammoth competition and is entered by all clubs within the league structure. The tournament remains regionalised until *Tippeliga* clubs enter, normally at the third round but perhaps a round or two later if the national team is involved in a major tournament. The action starts in May and all ties are single-match affairs, with extra-time and penalties if necessary. The tournament ends in October with a single-game final at Oslo's Ullevål stadium.

Just the ticket

Outside of big domestic games involving Rosenborg and/or Brann, you should have no difficulty just turning up on-spec and buying your ticket immediately before the match. Admission prices vary, but the average standing place is around 100Nkr, while a decent seat will cost up to 200Nkr.

The back page

Football competes with skiing for media attention. Norway's leading newspapers, *Aftenposten* and *Dagbladet* both offer decent coverage of the local game, but curiously, it is Norway's ephemeral-looking tabloids that carry the in-depth soccer features.

For a round-up of what's going on both locally and abroad, try the weekly magazine *Bladet Fotball*.

Action replay

State channel NRK shows a live *Tippeliga* match on Saturday evenings, and sometimes one on Sunday too, although the broadcast time of 6pm has not found favour with fans. NRK also shows a live English First Division game every Saturday afternoon. Subscription channel Canal Plus shows live English Premiership action over the weekend, while another pay channel, TV3, has the Champions' League rights.

Ultra culture

Crowd behaviour tends to be very disciplined, with good-natured singing but otherwise a rather refined appreciation of the game.

There are few organised fan groups in Norway outside of officially sanctioned supporters' clubs. With so few fans able to travel to watch their team and only a handful of local derbies in the calendar, there's little potential for trouble.

With typical fair-mindedness, clubs and supporters' groups have always acted together to supress any hooliganism that may surface from time to time. When a few coins were thrown at a Lillestrøm match, there was a major outcry – an indication of how unused Norwegians are to living with the spectre of soccer violence. More recently, a small minority of Vålerenga supporters have tried to emulate other European thugs, but in the main, their antics thus far have been pretty lame.

In the net

The offiicial Norwegian FA site is at: www.fotball.no. It's a lot newsier than you might expect from such a site, though sadly in Norwegian only.

Elsewhere, Lars Aarhus runs a reliable and very extensive Norwegian football server at: www.unik.no/~larsa/football.html. The site contains an extraordinary stats archive embracing international, amateur and women's football, and the news section is regularly updated in English. Also lively is the online football paper *Nettavisen* at: www.nettavisen.no/sport/tippeligaen.

Trondheim

With the capital Oslo continuing to lag behind the pace of Norwegian football, it falls to the northern city of Trondheim to act as the nation's soccer hotbed. This is the place where Norwegian Kings are brought for their blessing, and it is also the home of the country's kings of football – Rosenborg BK. Their dominance in recent years has completely overshadowed the city's other clubs, of whom only Nardo, Strindheim and Byåsen play above the regional leagues.

Trondheim celebtrated its millennium in 1997, but the city has become used to letting its hair down and having a party – the success of Rosenborg has seen to that.

The thrilling fields

 ### Rosenborg BK

Lerkendal Stadion
Capacity 28,000
Colours White shirts, black shorts
League champions 1967, 1969, 1971, 1985–86, 1988, 1990, 1992–99
Cup winners 1960, 1964, 1971, 1988, 1990, 1992, 1995, 1999

When Rosenborg Boldklub were founded in 1917, much of Europe was in the grip of new political teachings. In keeping with the spirit of the times, they extolled the virtues of a people's club. Yet in the Nineties, while they continue to enjoy close links with the local community in Trondheim, the club are also in the forefront of the push towards full professionalism in the Norwegian game.

The team first earned their share of the limelight around the time that Norway began a league championship for the first time, winning two titles and two cups in the Sixties. They remained leading contenders domestically through much of the

following two decades, but in European terms, RBK were an obscure footballing backwater, even less well-known than the amateur sides of Oslo and Bergen.

The arrival of coach Nils Arne Eggen in 1990 acted as the catalyst for change. Eggen had led unfashionable Moss to the title in 1987, and his methods soon paid dividends at Rosenborg. Like his national-team counterpart Egil Olsen, Eggen emphasised teamwork, discipline in defence and the long, aerial pass as a means of bypassing the opposition. He also instigated a clearout of the squad, favouring young players for their superior fitness.

At home RBK quickly became near-invincible. They have won all but one of the championships to be decided during the Nineties, and today no team in Norway can match them for organisation or commercial know-how.

Rosenborg's reputation began to spread to European competition when they appeared in the Champions' League for the first time in 1995. They beat England's millioniare champions, Blackburn Rovers, at the Lerkendal stadium, and while they failed to progress to the knockout stage, they had served notice of their intentions.

Just 12 months later they were back, beating IFK Gothenburg to affirm their position as Scandinavia's strongest club, then taking their greatest scalp so far with a 2–1 win over the Italian champions, AC Milan, in the San Siro. They then pushed European champions Juventus to the limit in the quarter-finals, despite having lost several key players to foreign clubs during the long winter break.

Norwegian players have almost become a fashion accessory in Britain, and a sizeable percentage of the incoming players are from Rosenborg. Steffen Iversen, Stig-Inge Bjørnebye, Bjorn Kvarme and Øyvind Leonharden all hail from the Lerkendal academy. But, happily for Rosenborg, there seem to be plenty more where they came from.

The gloves are on – orchestrated singalongs are *de rigueur* at the Lerkendal before UCL games

In addition to money from transfers and Champions' League sponsorship, Rosenborg's crowd figures alone (11,000 people watch home games at the Lerkendal, compared with a *Tippeliga* average of less than half that) give them a competitive advantage over those who would usurp their crown in Norway.

That advantage was confirmed with repeat title wins in 1997, 1998 and 1999. But Europe was, as always, a different league. In 1997, having won the title with 48 goals between Sigurd Rushfeldt and Harald Brattbakk alone, RBK won their three home ties in the Champions' League, only to be let down by their away performances, not least in a crucial game at Olympiakos.

In 1998 it was a similar story. With Trond Sollied taking over as coach from Eggen, RBK overhauled Molde in the domestic league by going 18 straight games without defeat. They then enjoyed a solid start to the next Champions' League campaign, drawing 1–1 at Athletic Bilbao. But then Solleid was tempted away by Belgian club Ghent. Eggen, who had stepped up to a general manager's role, was put back in charge of the first team, and a superb hat-

trick by Rushfeldt, so often the saviour, against Galatasaray put Rosenborg within a sniff of elusive qualification from their group. As usual, away form let them down. A 2–0 defeat at Juventus, followed by a 2–2 draw at Olympiakos, put paid to their hopes for another year.

The 1999/2000 Champions' League campaign saw Rosenborg in more impressive form. The team finished top of a first-phease group including Feyenoord, Borussia Dortmund and Boavista, due in no small part to the goals of giant striker John Carew. The reward was a second-phase group containing Bayern Munich, Real Madrid and Dynamo Kiev – an altogether tougher proposition, and one from which Rosenborg could plunder only a solitary point, from a home draw with Bayern. The sale of Carew to Valéncia was confirmed shortly afterwards, reminding fans that, for all its attributes, there is a limit to how much even a bright and ambitious Norwegian club like Rosenborg can achieve.

Here we go!

Buses #5, #7, #20, #36, #60, #66 from the town centre run to the Lerkendal.

Swift half

The classic Rosenborg bar in town is the *Bakdøra & Bajazzo* at Søndre Gt 15, just up from the main train station. The *Norsk Rock Café* over the bridge is now the favoured haunt of the *Kjernen* ultras (see below), while *Bobby's Bar* nearby offers cheaper drinks and live action on its big-screen TV.

Ultra culture

While the rest of the country is happy to crash its way through British terrace standards, Rosenborg's *Kjernen* have a vast repertoire of their own to call upon, despite rejecting the official club songs written by composer Dag Ingebrigtsen.

In the net

The official Rosenborg website is at: hwww.rbk.no. Its English-language news service can be rather intermittent, so try the English pages of the ultras-run alternative site at: www.kjernen.com/english. Another well-run unofficial site resides at: come.to/rbk.

A big loss – towering striker John Carew

Eat, drink, sleep...

Bars and clubs

As in other Scandinavian countries, alcohol is **heavily taxed**, rationed almost, in Norway – a half-litre of beer costs around 35Nkr, and the distribution of wines and spirits is strictly controlled by a state-run monopoly. Beer (*øl*) is sold in supermarkets at about half the price you'd pay in a bar. The strongest (class III) beer can only be purchased from state-controlled shops, known as *Vinmonopolet* (open Mon–Fri 10am–4pm, Sat 10am–1pm). The best brands are *Hansa* and *Ringsnes*. The favourite spirit is Aquavit, 40 percent proof and served in ice-cold glasses. In Trondheim, you'll be able to keep drinking in bars until at least 1am, or as late as 4am in some places – but you'll probably **run out of money** first.

The city's large student population ensures a lively (for Norway) nightlife scene with the pick of the bars and clubs along Dronningens gate, around the Britannia hotel.

Bør Børsson Jnr, Nordre gate 28. Centrally located entertainment complex with a bar, restaurant and live music all in one.

Carl Johan Møteplass, Olav Tryggvasons Gate 24. Stylish bar, packed at weekends and a good place to meet with celebrating RBK fans after the big match.

Dirty Nelly, Prinsens Gate 27. Trondheim's inevitable Irish pub, popular with football fans, with the usual range of beers and the atmosphere they induce.

Frakken, Dronningens Gate. On the corner with Nodre Gate, so right in the centre of what passes for Trondheim nightlife, this bar and nightclub appeals to a rock-oriented crowd – but a lively and friendly enough place.

The Dubliner, Nordre Gate 23. An alternative 'Irish' pub. Don't come here for the Guinness.

Trondheim essentials

Trondheim **airport** is 35km northeast of the city at Vaernes, and airport buses (every 30mins, Sun–Fri 5.15am–9pm, Sat until 5.45pm, 50Nkr) run to the main train station, Sentralstasjon, in the city centre, a 45min ride.

Transport in town is by **buses** and **trams** (flat-fare tickets 19Nkr), but you can just as easily walk around the city. However, if you're planning to venture outside the centre, the unlimited 24-hour public transport ticket, *Dagskort*, is worth having (45Nkr from the tourist office – see below); it is valid on all local buses and trams. For a **taxi**, call ☎7350 5073.

The city **tourist office** (open daily until 4pm, 8pm in summer; closed winter weekends, ☎7392 9400, fax 7351 5300, e-mail touristinfo@taas.no) is at Munkegate 18, on the corner of the city's main square, Torvet. They can assist you with accommodation in private houses and sell maps and other guides. The office also issues the free *Trondheim Guide*, the only local source of entertainment and nightlife **listings**.

Restaurants

Those on a tight budget have problems eating out in Norway and Trondheim is no exception. However, there are mobile fast-food stalls, concentrated around the Sentralstasjon and on either side of Torvet, which are a good bet if you're peckish and penniless.

At lunchtime, take advantage of cheaper set menus or the *koldtbord* (Norway's answer to the *smörgåsbord*) where for around 120–170Nkr you can eat as much as you like during the three or four hours that the food is on the table.

Bryggen, Øvre Bakklandet 66. First-class seafood specialities are the order of the day here, fresh and delicious, although not cheap at upwards of 200Nkr a main course. At the far end of Bybrua.

Havfreun, Kjøpmanns gate 7. A great fish restaurant near the cathedral. Good-value main courses from 180Nkr. If it's too busy, try the *Breiflabben* jazz bar downstairs.

Hos Magnus, Kjøpmannsgata 63. Just along the road from Havfreun and worth a look if the latter is full. Fish are again the speciality, with the herring especially recommended.

Ni Muser, Bispegata 9. Modern European cuisine in a relaxed, fashionable café atmosphere, with a terrace bar out the back and a contemporary art gallery upstairs. Reasonable prices. Open until midnight. Closed Mon.

Trubadur, Kongens gate 34. Traditional food, with bargain daily specials such as fishballs and reindeer at lunchtime, right by St Olavs gate.

Accommodation

Norwegian hotels are of the highest standard – neat, clean and efficient and offering huge breakfasts – but they don't come cheap. There are, however, budget alternatives such as youth hostels, guest houses (*gijestgiveri*) and private rooms which could keep you from bankruptcy. Discounts are also offered in summer, which is handy for the visiting football fan.

Pensions (*pensjonater*) charge around 350–450Nkr for a single room and 450–550Nkr for a double, while youth hostels start from 100Nkr for a bed and 50Nkr for breakfast. In Trondheim, **private rooms** are good value, although many of them are a fair way out from the centre; book them at the **tourist office**, where the rate is fixed at 350Nkr per double per night, plus a 30Nkr booking fee.

Britannia, Dronningens Gate 5 (☎7353 5353, fax 7351 2900). Bang in the middle of town and with magnificent *Art Nouveau* architecture. Comfortable rooms, but pricey – around 900Nkr for a double. Summer discounts.

Jarlen, Kongens Gate 40 (☎7351 3218, fax 7352 8080). Basic pension, bargain prices. Central location. Less than 500Nkr for a double.

InterRail Centre, Elgester Gate 1 (☎7389 9538). Basic B&B accommodation in a large house with a couple of hundred rooms. Operated by the university's student society, and open only from late June to mid-August. Curfew from 1am, 105Nkr per person per night. Take bus #41, #42, #48, #49, #52 or #63 along Prinsens Gate and ask for the *Studentersamfundet*.

Rainbow Trondheim, Kongens Gate 15 (☎7350 5050, fax 7351 6058). Popular chain hotel in an attractive old city-centre building. Reasonable value, lively bar. Around 700Nkr for a double room. Sizeable summer discounts.

Poland

Polski Zwiazek Pilki Noznej Al Ujazdowskie 22, PL-00478 Warsaw
☎022/827 1211   Fax 022/827 0704   E-mail none

League champions Polonia Warsaw   **Cup winners** Amica Wronki   **League Cup winners** Polonia Warsaw   **Promoted** GKS Katowice, Slask Wroclaw   **Relegated** ŁKS Łódź, Lech Poznań

European participants 2000/01 Polonia Warsaw (UCL qualifiers); Ruch Chorzów, Wisła Kraków, Amica Wronki (UEFA Cup); Zaglebie Lubin (Intertoto Cup)

Suffering from familiar post-Communist blights – rising corruption and hooliganism, dwindling crowds and insufficient finance – Polish football needs another decade to find the right ingredients for a healthy domestic game and international success.

Today's Polish game seems a long way from the thriving industry that fostered three notable World Cup campaigns between 1974 and 1982, a golden era which had its roots in the gifted side that were crowned Olympic champions in 1972. That was the team which, in the qualifiers for the 1974 World Cup, shocked group favourites England with a home win, then came to Wembley on 17 October, 1973, needing only a draw to deny Alf Ramsey's men a place at the finals. Goalkeeper Jan Tomaszewski confounded the critics – including TV pundit Brian Clough, who had described him as a clown – by somehow keeping the ball from crossing the goal line until it was too late. At the other end, the most capped goalkeeper in English history, Peter Shilton, flopped weakly to a Domarski shot – 1–1 and Poland were through.

Pointless exercise – Poland failed to get the draw they needed in Sweden in October 1999

Eternal flame – passion for football burns on

Kazimierz Deyna, Robert Gadocha, Grzegorz Lato and Andrzej Szarmach would then emerge as world stars of the side that made the semi-finals a year later, losing out to eventual winners West Germany in atrocious playing conditions. Deyna and co were joined four years later by the most successful Polish player of modern times, Zbigniew Boniek, and had it not been for Argentine striker Mario Kempes' punch off the line in their opening second-phase match, the Poles might well have gone on to play in the final instead of the host nation.

Boniek was back at the next World Cup in Spain 1982, but was suspended for the crucial semi-final against Italy; the Poles, as in 1974, would have to be content with victory in a meaningless third-place play-off, where the veteran Szarmach was

among the goals against France. In those halcyon days of the Seventies and Eighties, Silesia, Poland's footballing heartland, could boast packed stadia and the most popular team in the land, Górnik Zabrze. Since then the region's heavy industry has severely declined and, with it, the subsidised entertainment (like football) which once kept the workers happy. Górnik have faded, and even the national stadium in Chorzów was closed following a crowd riot and subsequent UEFA investigation in 1993.

Two sides dominated Polish league football in the Nineties: Legia Warsaw and Widzew Łódź. Legia were involved in a comical match-fixing scandal at the climax to the 1992/93 season, when both they and their co-table toppers LKS Łódz won their final matches by daft scorelines, against teams who were clearly content to provide no more than token opposition. The belated PZPN (Polish FA) decision to award the title to Lech resulted in a grudge between hardcore Legia fans and the rest of Poland, and the more volatile element of Widzew's support was quick to take up the fight. The two sets of fans created havoc at Poznań and Wrocław respectively one black Saturday in October 1996, raising public order questions in parliament, bringing security cameras into first-division grounds, and causing both home stadia to be declared out of bounds for the remainder of the 1996/97 season.

The hooliganism problem continues to haunt the Polish game, but during 1998/99 it faced another crisis – at administrative level. By and large, the FA was manned by the same bureaucrats who were in charge two decades ago. Sports minister Jacek Debski wanted them out, as did the majority of clubs, some of whom boycotted matches in the early rounds of the league season.

But Debski's intervention, as such political interference always does, raised the spectre of Poland's suspension from international competition by FIFA and UEFA, which regard the independence of their member associations as sacrosanct.

Basics

Americans and most EU nationals now need only a **passport** to enter Poland. Australian, New Zealand and Canadian nationals still require a visa, valid for 90 days. Check with your Polish embassy for details.

The Polish currency is the **zloty**, divided into 100 groszy. The current exchange rate is around 6zł to £1. Coins come in denominations of 1, 2, 5, 10, 20 and 50 groszy, and 1, 2 and 5 złoty; notes in denominations of 10, 20, 50, 100 and 200 złoty. Exchange booths (*kantors*) are everywhere and give better rates than the banks. In Warsaw, you'll find a 24-hour *kantor* at the airport and main train station.

In general dollars and Deutschmarks are preferred, but most places will accept **sterling**. In the main cities, credit-card payment is accepted in better shops and restaurants, but most places prefer cash. Cash machines are widespread, and most banks will give cash advances on credit cards.

The international **telephone code** for Poland is 48. The city code for Warsaw is 22, Kraków 12, Łódź 42 and Poznań 61. As usual, add a '0' to these codes if dialling inland. To make an international call from Poland, dial 00, then the country code.

Phonecards come in units of 25 (7.32zł), 50 (14.64zł) and 100 (29.28zł). There is no cheap time for international calls – a 50-unit card should get you just over a minute of calls to Western Europe.

Transport in Poland is cheap. Inter-city **trains**, marked in red on timetables, are reasonably comfortable and should have a buffet car. Seat reservations are compulsory. Leave yourself plenty of time for queueing at the ticket office, and specify the train you're catching once you reach the window. The two **bus** companies are the older, cheaper *PKS* and the newer *Polski Express*. *Orbis* tourist offices dotted around major towns can help with all transport enquiries.

Poland suffers a lack of budget **accommodation,** which tends to be either dilapidated, overpriced, or both. Arranging a private room with a family – you'll find old ladies waiting at train stations or outside tourist offices – is a cheap way round the problem, but check that the room is near the town centre.

Eating out is inexpensive. The mainstay is the milk bar (*bar mleczny*), where you're guaranteed a soup, a slab of pork and potatoes for under 5zł. Main cities now have the full range of international cuisine, but restaurants tend to close early.

Yet the longer the time-servers cling to power, the more intractable the country's footballing problems will become. Poland still has no national stadium to speak of, while provincial grounds are starved of cash by local-council owners who refuse either to refurbish them or to sell them to outside investors.

There were some signs of improvement from the national team during the qualifying phase for Euro 2000, but Poland's inability to get the point they needed for a play-off place from their last game in Sweden resulted in the sacking of coach Janus Wojcik and the appointment of former Polonia Warsaw boss Jerzy Engel in his place. Time for another new beginning…

Essential vocabulary

Hello *Dzień dobry*
Goodbye *Do widzenia*
Yes *Tak*
No *Nie*
Two beers, please *Proszń dwa piwa*
Thank you *Dziekuje*
Men's *Dla Panow*
Women's *Dla Pań*
Where is the stadium? *Gdzie stadion?*
What's the score? *Jaki jest wynik?*
Referee *Sędzia*
Offside *Spalony*

Match practice

Poland is a fundamentally Catholic country – players touch the turf like Italians and cross themselves while stepping out into bleak, empty, Communist-built stadia. But, unlike most Catholic nations, the Poles prefer Saturday to Sunday as the day for league action. The season runs from the end of July to the end of November, then from the beginning of March until the end of June. Only a handful of grounds have floodlights, so kick-off times can be as early as 11am or noon at some grounds either side of winter, 3pm or 4pm at other times. Live TV matches are on Saturdays or Sundays at 2pm or 6pm, depending on lighting availability, with a few on Friday at 6pm.

Security has been tightened at many grounds, especially Legia, Poznań and Widzew Łódź. Football is an easy excuse for Poland's jobless youth to vent their frustration against a rival town and/or its police force. Whether beer is available or not – depending on the club's security rating – you'll see plastic bottles of clear liquid passed around the terraces. More romantically, flowers are often exchanged between teams before matches. As in Russia, every ball-boy has his own ball to keep the game in constant play whenever there's a throw, corner or goal-kick. Stadium commentators follow the match vigorously, trying to raise enthusiasm among home supporters.

A different league

Despite threats of a ten-team breakaway Premier League during the FA dispute in August 1998, the Polish league remains in place – for now. The first two divisions are fully professional. Two teams go down automatically from the 16-team *I liga*, to be replaced by the top two from the *II liga*, which also has 16 sides after being created from the merger of two regional divisions in 1999. Four teams from the *II liga* drop down into the regionalised *III liga*, to be replaced by the latter's four divisional champions.

Up for the cup

The *Puchar Polski* begins in July, with ties decided over one game, extra-time and penalties. First-division clubs enter at the fourth-round stage, with ties taking place at

Hard hat area – security has been tightened at many grounds after a wave of hooliganism

the lower-ranking club's ground to allow for cup surprises. The final takes place at a neutral venue in June.

Just the ticket

At better stadia, there'll be a covered stand (*trybuna kryta*) and an open one (*trybuna otwarta*). At Legia, the most expensive example, you'll pay 30zł for a plastic seat under cover, 20zł for a spot on a wooden bench in the open. At grounds with no cover, tickets will generally be divided into *bilety normalny* (a spot on a wooden bench) for 10–15zł, and *bilety na miejsca stojace* (a standing space on concrete terracing) for 5–10zł. Most clubs issue a free programme which will be given to you with your ticket.

Half-time

The traditional match snack is the *kiełbasa* – a long sausage cooked on the grill, served with bread, mustard or ketchup for 5zł. Alcohol is available only at certain grounds. Tea (*herbata*) is a bearable substitute, but coffee (*kawa*) is generally undrinkable.

Action replay

Poland's two most popular clubs, Wisla Kraków and Legia Warsaw, have signed separate pay-per-view deals with the TVN and Wizja Sport channels respectively. This has dented the subscription monopoly previously enjoyed by Canal Plus, which nonetheless still screens one league game live on a Saturday afternoon, and occasionally another on a Friday evening or Sunday afternoon. Their round-up shows are *Liga Plus* after 10pm on Saturday, and *Z Pierwsej Pilki* at 6.30pm on Monday. State channel TVP is limited to short highlights with its *Gol* programme, at around 7.30pm on Saturdays and Sundays on channel 2.

The back page

Two of the three sports dailies, Warsaw-based *Przegláid Sportowy* (1.50zł) and Kraków's *Tempo* (1.50zł) have gone colour, with new, reader-friendly layouts. Their provincial rival, *Sport* (1.50zł), which concentrates on news from around its Silesian base of Katowice, is still text-heavy, but at least you don't get your hands covered in newsprint these days. All have decent international results coverage on Mondays, and all have weekend editions with a free colour supplement.

Poland has two colour weekly magazines: *TopGol* (2.40zł) and *Piłka Noźna* (2.40zł); the latter publishes a thicker monthly edition, *Piłka Noźna Plus* (3.80zł), a rival to *Hat-Trick* (3.80zł).

Ultra culture

Polish fan culture is more about sporadic violence than organised support. Widzew Łódź–Legia games are the most notorious, and any match between Legia and a Silesian team is liable to provoke tension of some kind.

At international matches, the main problem is fighting between rival gangs of Polish fans. Until parliament sorts out a workable public order act, violence will continue to erupt outside stadia. Inside, meanwhile, the poorly paid, demotivated police force have their own axes to grind.

In the net

Pawel Mogielnicki runs a generic site at vlo.waw.ids.edu.pl/~mogiel/index.html. Stats are the strong point, but there's English and Spanish signposting, plus news stories and match reports in Polish. Other highlights include transfer-market updates and a huge number of links to one-club sites in Poland, only some of which will actually be functioning at any one time.

Unlike many East European countries, Poland boasts a good spread of top-flight clubs throughout its territory. But, thanks to Polonia's revival and the continuing strength of Legia, the capital, Warsaw, remains the best bet for an introduction to Polish football.

The *Derby Stolicy*, the capital's clash of rivals Legia and Polonia, had been dormant for most of the post-war era. Polonia, out of favour with the Communist regime, spent four decades away from top-flight football before gaining promotion in 1993. But they were the first Warsaw club to win a league title – in 1946 – and even in their lean years they still attracted grass-roots support from the Zoliborz and Praga areas of town.

During the Fifties, Legia were named the Central Army Sports Club, but the army was never a popular role model for

young Poles, and Warsaw's flagship team were as despised as the other main club from the capital, Gwardia, the police team who've played five seasons in Europe but achieved little in recent memory. Warsaw's image took a further tarnish when its national stadium, the Stadion Dziesieciolecia, started falling to bits. The ground has been home to Europe's biggest flea market since it staged its last international in 1991, but even that lucrative pleasure might be denied to the sorry place now that new import laws with former Soviet republics threaten to destroy this ramshackle cottage industry altogether, and possibly the stadium with it.

Still, the Dziesieciolecia is easier to police than crumbling Polonia on derby day – the club's 1998/99 clash with Legia took place behind closed doors for fear of fan violence.

Bleak house – Legia's stadium wasn't too welcoming during the club's 1995/96 UCL campaign

The thrilling fields

 Legia

Woiska Polskiego stadium, Ul Łazienkowska 3
Capacity 25,000
Colours All green with red and white trim
League champions 1955–56, 1969, 1970, 1994–95
Cup winners 1955, 1956, 1964, 1966, 1973, 1980, 1981, 1989, 1990, 1994, 1995, 1997

Legia Warsaw are the archetypal Communist army side, still led by steadfast generals whose stern portraits gaze down from the club's 80th-anniversary display on the main stand wall. Inside the ground you'll find a heavy following from modern Warsaw's economically depressed suburbs.

It's a meeting of the old and the new – a contrast thrown into sharp relief whenever those generals are obliged to face the music after another rumpus by Legia's lads.

The match-fixing scandal of 1993, and subsequent title-stripping decision by the

PZPN, has set Legia's following on a collision course with the Polish football authorities and their power base down in Silesia. Regular outbreaks of hooliganism have forced Legia to up ticket prices and have driven away the floating fan.

Meanwhile the sponsors, whose heavy investment refloated Legia's sinking ship when the team faced relegation in 1990, fell out with the generals and left in acrimony. The subsequent financial woes saw half of Legia's team leave immediately after the club had done the double in 1995, yet the goals of Jerzy Podbrozny and Cezary Kucharski were still enough to propel the team past Rosenborg and Blackburn Rovers to a Champions' League quarter-final berth in 1996.

Partly as a result of their European exertions, however, Legia lost their title – and subsequent potential earnings in Europe – to Widzew Łódź later in the year. Twelve months later they were again involved in a head-to-head with Widzew. Two up against 'the enemy' in a six-pointer one round from the end of the 1996/97 season, Legia contrived to concede three

Warsaw essentials

A 2zł ticket (plus a further 2zł per suitcase) will get you from Okęcie **airport** to Warszawa Centralna train station in 20mins – the service is run by bus #175 in daytime and #611 at night. Alternatively, *Airport City* buses run every 20mins from the airport to major city centre hotels; tickets are available at 5.60zł onboard, luggage free. A taxi will fleece you for at least 40zł.

Municipal transport tickets (*bilety*) are available from the *Ruch* kiosks scattered about everywhere. A *normalny* ticket is 2zł and should be validated in the ticket puncher onboard. A **24-hour pass** is fine value at 6zł. Night buses (#601–611), which run from beside the Palace of Culture every half-hour, charge 4.20zł, tickets available onboard.

In town, **taxi** drivers can only charge 3.60zł for the first kilometre, then 1.60zł per kilometre thereafter, though rates rise by 50% after 10pm and at weekends. *MPT* (☎022/919) accept credit cards for longer journeys; *Nowa Taxi* (☎022/9687) and *Sawa Taxi* (☎022/644 4444) are also generally reliable.

The main **tourist office** in the old town, at Pl Zamkowy 1/3 (open Mon–Fri 9am–6pm, Sat 10am–6pm, Sun 11am–6pm, ☎022/635 1881, fax 022/831 0464), can help with hotel reservations. *Orbis*, at Ul Bracka 16 (open Mon–Fri 8am–9pm, Sat 9am–3pm, ☎022/826 0271), can help with booking bus and train tickets.

Warsaw is blessed with an excellent English-language **city guide**, the monthly *Warsaw Insider* (4zł), by far the best source for tips on entertainment and nightlife.

goals in the last four minutes, and another championship chance had slipped through their fingers.

That defeat sparked yet another wave of trouble on the terraces. Yet the sad thing is that Legia, founder members of the Polish league in 1916 and still the nation's most popular club, also have among their following a generation raised during the Deyna era. Under Kazmierz Gorski, later coach to Poland's 1972 Olympic team and 1974 World Cup semi-finalists, Legia were Poland's first modern-day footballing heroes. With Kazimierz Deyna in midfield and Robert Gadocha on the wing, they won the league in 1969 and 1970, the year they also made the European Cup semi-finals. Deyna and Gadocha both ended up in America, via Manchester City and Nantes respectively, but the older fans in the main stand still remember them.

Further disputes between the players, the management, the club's new sponsors *Daewoo* and coach Miroslav Jablonski saw Legia fail to make Europe in 1998, and although a third-place finish a year later was more like it, Polonia's title triumph in 1999/2000, a season in which Legia could finish no better than fifth, threatened to undermine the former army club's position as the capital's premier team.

Here we go!

Legia's base, Łazienkowska, is just south of the city centre, below the Armii Ludowej highway. Several buses go there including #159 (four stops from Pl Konstitycji) and #155 or #166 from Nowy Swiat.

Swift half

No alcohol is allowed in the ground and security is strict. One of the many popular pre-match places for the older or neutral fan is the *Blues Bar*, by Łazienkowski park, where Al Ujazdowskie meets Agrykola. Nearby is another pleasant watering hole, the *Pub Rozdroze*, while in the park itself you'll find the *Café Agrykola*. After the game, you'll find journalists and players consuming beer and fine cheesecake in the nearby *Garaz*, Mysliwiecka 1.

Club merchandise

While the club attempts to tart up its tatty shop, your best bet is to grab your Legia souvenir from a green kiosk marked *Upominki*, behind the west stand.

Ultra culture

Scowling at the Lazienkowska end of the ground are the *Zyleti*, their name a reference to the Gillette ad hoarding under which they used to stand, rather than the weapons they carry. Such is the hatred of Legia around Poland that they and their club-mates the *Warriors* are forever hitting the headlines for all the wrong reasons.

In print

The weekly *Nasza Legia* magazine (2.50zł) is available at most newsstands. The bog-standard *Legiagol* is issued free with your match ticket.

In the net

The official Legia homepage is only sporadically available, but there is at least one excellent unofficial site, properly maintained and with a small English-language area, at: come.to/legia/.

Groundhopping

If the tension of Legia gets too much, both the city's other professional clubs offer a more relaxed environment in which to watch a game…

Polonia

Polonia stadium, Ul Konwiktorska 6
Capacity 15,000
Colours Red shirts, black shorts
League champions 1946, 2000
Cup winners 1952

Across the former Eastern Bloc, the Commnist approach to football resulted in a handful of teams being given the lion's share of resources in order to concentrate the best players together and boost each country's chances in European club football. To that extent, the policy worked. But its inevitable side-effect was that many grand old clubs were left to wither and die. In many cases, the clubs the authorities chose to ignore were those which had strong pre-war links to working-class organisations. Polonia Warsaw were, and are, just such a club.

Like Rapid in Bucharest, Polonia were the team of their city's railway workers and, like Rapid, Polonia were overshadowed for decades by neighbours who enjoyed the backing of the local military. Rapid won their first domestic title for 22 years in 1999, and a year later, Polonia followed suit by winning their first Polish championship since 1946.

Polonia's achievement was all the more remarkable given that they had only returned to the top flight in 1996, with a team largely composed of Legia rejects. Coach Dariusz Wdowczyk, once a full-back at Celtic, led them to a runners-up spot in the league in 1998, and with the able guidance of technical director Jerzy Engel, Polonia continued to build on over the following two seasons.

Engel left to take charge of the Polish national team in November 1999, but the team went on to take the title thanks to the pace and goal-poaching of Nigerian striker Emmanuel Olisadebe. For those Polonia fans who had endured years of third-division football as a result of the uneven distribution of state resources, the championship couldn't have been claimed in a sweeter manner – a 3–0 win over Legia, prompting predictable rioting from Legia fans, and some equally predictable vodka sessions from the long-suffering railwaymen. Just to make sure Legia knew their status in Warsaw was now under threat from a team they had barely considered rivals under Communism, Polonia then beat their neighbours 1–0 in the final of Poland's new League Cup competition.

Olisadebe, meanwhile, had been so impressive that the man who had signed him, Engel, asked the national government to rush through his claim for Polish citizen-

ship in order to make him available for the forthcoming World Cup qualifying campaign. If successful, the application would make Olisadebe only the second black player to play for an East European national side, following in the footsteps of his fellow Nigerian Thomas Sowumni in Hungary.

Polonia crowds are still low, but pleasant to share an afternoon with. A **Hey Polonia** programme will be handed out with your 10zł match ticket.

To get to the ground, take tram #2, #4, #15, #18, #31 or #36 along Gen Wł Andersa, up to the crossroads with Z Słominskiego.

Beer is on sale at the **Restauracja Remis**, straight on from the main entrance, which also offers a full menu and Polonia scarves and pennants.

Gwardia

Racławicka stadium, Ul Racławicka 132
Capacity 12,000
Colours Blue shirts, white shorts
Cup winners 1954

Perhaps the club's most famous export in recent years, former Celtic star Dariusz Dziekanowski, relates the day when the Gwardia crowd surprisingly swelled and chanted perfectly in unison around the otherwise deserted, crumbling Racławicka stadium. The Gwardia players looked around confused, then realised that the club management, the Warsaw police department, had dragged in a hundred prisoners, perfectly trained to groan 'Gwardia Gwardia' as one.

That was in the days when Gwardia were still claiming the occasional UEFA Cup place. Now they are festering in the regional third division. Their matches kick off at noon on Saturdays. Admission is 3zł, and the **Bufet Gwardia** is in the main building behind the goal. The Racławicka is near the Zolnierzy Radzieckich cemetery, down Żwirki i Wigury by bus #114, #136, #175 or #188.

Eat, drink, sleep...

Bars and clubs

Not that long ago, Poles had a serious drink problem: they wanted vodka by the bucketful but there weren't any places to drink it in. Everyone drank at home.

Now everyone's still thirsty, but at least there are bars. Many are cheap dives with greasy food, but a reasonably lively, modern bar culture has developed. It's still fairly cheap, too. Expect to pay about 4zł for a **beer**, of which Okocim, EB and Żywiecki are acceptable local brands. **Vodka** still rules, however – neat, chilled and downed in one. Zwykla, Wyborowa or Polonez are all too drinkable, as is the flavoured Żubrówka.

Warsaw nightlife is slowly improving but has yet to find its focus. In the autumn, Ul Krakowskie Przedmieście can boast a range of bars, sadly depleted by the loss of the excellent *Blue Velvet* club.

Metal Bar, Rynek Starogo Miasta 8. Easily the best option in the old town, great outdoors in summer, designer feel indoors. Highlights include a full cocktail menu.

Morgan's, Ul Okólnik 1. Packed pub run by the ever-popular Ollie, who does impromptu turns with the pick-up band. Sky Sports soccer and GAA memorabilia. Entrance on Ul Tamka – follow the music and you'll find it.

Piekarnia, Ul Młocinska 11. Best dance sounds in town, centrally located near the Powazkowski cemetery. Smart without being oppressive. Back terrace. Open Thur–Sun, 20zł cover.

Tam Tam, Ul Foksal 18. African themed club/bar, but the music veers more towards hip-hop, house and disco. Centrally located and open daily until at least 1am.

Underground, Ul Marszałkowska 126–134. Buried deep opposite *McDonald's*, a traffic-light coloured cellar bar/club with good dance music. Cover charge Fri–Sat after 10pm.

Restaurants

Many of the capital's **milk bars** have given way to modern snack cafés open mainly for lunchtime custom. The old town has a reasonable choice of upmarket eateries at Western prices. The area by the Palace of Culture, along Ul Marszałkowska and Al Jerozolimskie, is dotted with dirt-cheap Chinese and Turkish food stands, some with tables and chairs.

Champions, Al Jerozolimskie 65-79. Opposite Centralna station, a large sports bar/restaurant with the usual autographed momentoes and dozens of TVs switching from ESPN to Eurosport to Sky Sports. Decent burgers with all the trimmings. Open 10am–2am with happy hour 11pm–midnight, most credit cards.

Pod Barbakanem, Mostowa 27/29. Milk bar by the Barbican in the Old Town, clean and with outdoor seating. Give your order to the cashier and take your receipt to the hatch, where your food will be served a couple of minutes later. Dirt cheap but far from nasty. Open daily, closed evenings.

Restauracja Polska, Ul Nowy Swiat 21. Traditional Polish cuisine prepared with care in elegant surroundings along the Royal Way. Main courses around 40–50zł. Open daily, most major credit cards. The sister establishment to the *Dom Polski*, Ul Francuska 11, which is of similar sophistication.

Tandoor Palace, Ul Marszałkowska 21–25. Newest Indian restaurant in town with an extensive menu of reasonably priced Asian dishes. Main courses 20–30zł. Open daily 11am–11pm. Most major credit cards. A 10min walk from Legia's stadium.

Accommodation

This can be a problem in Warsaw. For low-budget travellers, the city's few youth hostels have early curfews, and cheap hotels are generally a fair way from the centre. The private room option can be arranged with the *Syrena* office at Ul

United we fall – Steve Bruce puts paid to Legia's European ambitions, Warsaw, 1991

Krucza 17 (open Mon–Sat 9am–7pm, Sun 9am–5pm, ☎022/628 7540) which offers single rooms for 50–60zł, doubles for 75–90zł. Be sure to check your room's location on the map before you sign up.

For those with more to spend, even mid-range accommodation is overpriced and often fully booked. *Orbis* hotels, generally soulless but functional, may be the best bet.

Dom Literata, Ul Krakowskie Przedmieście 87/89 (☎022/635 0404). A handful of reasonably priced double rooms are rented out on the top floor of this Old Town house, some with an excellent view. Bar and restaurant downstairs. No credit cards.

Harenda, Ul Krakowskie Przedmieście 4/6 (☎022/826 2625). Good budget deal, just south of the university. Rooms with or without a bath, student bar at the back. Most credit cards.

Polonia, Al Jerozilimskie 45 (☎022/628 7241, fax 022/628 6622). Ideally located near Centralna station, a once grand hotel built before World War I, now frequented by Poland's less well-to-

do business community. Clean, comfortable rooms, with the bonus of a fine breakfast. Singles 140–200 zł, doubles 200–340zł, suites and apartments available. Most credit cards.

Praski, Al Solidarności 61 (☎022/184 989, fax 022/185 314). Just over the bridge from the Old Town, clean, basic accommodation with a Lebanese restaurant downstairs. Around 140zł a night for a double. Most credit cards.

Saski, Plac Bankowy 1 (☎022/620 4611, fax 022/620 1115). Centrally located, budget hotel with an elegant façade. Rooms at 100zł a single, 130zł a double, none with a private bathroom, but breakfast included. Amex accepted.

Derby day in the realm of king cotton...

Prior to the re-emergence of genuine rivalry in Warsaw, it was up to the grimy textile centre of Łódź (pronounced 'woodge') to provide Poland's only real derby. To add spice in recent times, the participants in said derby, ŁKS and Widzew, claimed all three league titles between them from 1996 to 1998.

European action under the lights – but for how much longer?

The fact that it was ŁKS, backed by marketeer benefactor **Antoni Ptak**, who took the last title from their cash-strapped city rivals is significant. For much of the Nineties, Widzew were running Legia neck and neck in the race to be the nation's top team. Widzew had previously won two titles with their all-time star **Zibi Boniek** in 1981 and 1982, before losing him to Juventus. It was successful European football – ironically played under the lights of ŁKS – which spread the club's popularity beyond the working-class area of Widzew in the east of the city.

A decade later Widzew were again winning titles and competing in Europe, finishing a creditable third in their **Champions' League** group behind eventual winners Borussia Dortmund. Yet even then, the players were not receiving regular salaries. When Widzew headed the league halfway through the 1997/98 season, it became known that championship bonuses for 1996/97 had not been paid. The FA slapped a ban on Widzew signing any new players, and star coach **Frantisek Smuda** left for Wisla Kraków.

Meanwhile, having been rescued from insolvency by Ptak in 1994, ŁKS were coming up on the rails, and looking at their first title win for 40 years. Although they had lost a bitter derby in November 1997, a dubious late penalty giving Widzew a 3–2 win, the signing of **Marek Saganowski** from Feyenoord and **Rodrigo Carbone** from Brazil's Belo Horizonte eventually paid off, and ŁKS won the title – something they had failed to do when Polish World Cup goalkeeping hero **Jan Tomaszewski** was playing for them. With Carbone stuck in a pay dispute, ŁKS were flattered by a 2–0 aggregate loss to **Manchester United** in their 1998/99 Champions' League qualifier. Coach Marek Dziuba, a key local figure who has played for both local clubs, then saw Monaco take his team apart in their subsequent UEFA Cup tie. Much worse was to come in 1999/2000, however, when ŁKS were relegated and the derby show was put on ice – at least for the time being.

The regular **train service** from Warsaw takes two hours, arriving at central Fabryczna station. Tram #10 runs along Al Mickiewicza/Marsz Pilsudskiego south of Fabryczna between the city's two clubs, either side of the centre. ŁKS are by the other train station, Kaliska.

Widzew's European nights are celebrating in the form of commemorative urns around the club bar, *Kawiarna u Basi*, upstairs in their main building. ŁKS can boast the *Bar Kuba* opposite the train station, the *Trampek* by the club office in the main stand, and the splendid *Bar Karol* over the Bandurskiego highway onto Ul Karolewska.

Kraków

Kraków is both the cradle of Polish football and the face of its future, albeit a scarred one. Whereas football on present-day Polish soil was first played by British engineers in Lodz, it was in the university city of Kraków – then part of Austria – that the first club, Cracovia, was formed in 1906. Wisla, wearing the white star (*Biala Gwiazda*) of Polish independence, followed soon after, the first derby finishing 1–1 on 20 September 1908. Aberdeen were the first British side on Polish soil when they thrashed Wisla over two games in 1911.

This pioneering spirit has earned Kraków a special place in Polish sporting mythology. After the nation's independence, it was fitting that Cracovia should win the first national title, in a play-off between the northern and southern champions in 1921.

Kraków clubs won five of six titles as soon as a national league was formed in 1927. The city rivalry lay either side of Park Jordana, Wisla attracting support from the city's middle class, Cracovia from small businessmen and shopkeepers, earning themselves a Jewish tag.

Kraków was the only major Polish city whose buildings survived the war, and while the rest of the country was rebuilding, Cracovia and Wisla picked up four straight titles between them from 1947. But while the city's buildings may have been left intact, its population was devastated. Members of the bourgeoisie and the Jewish community were thin on the ground in post-war Communist Poland, and football soon withered in Kraków. Poor Cracovia, the Pope's beloved team from boyhood, all but fell to pieces, doomed to lower-league football alongside local ne'er-do-wells Hutnik. Their support is now mainly hoolies rather than holies, from the south-eastern areas of Prokocim and Wola. Wisla's young gangs come from the north and west of the city.

Apart from a solitary title in 1978, Wisla were flirting regularly with second-division football until a recent revival sparked by investment from *Tele-Fonika*,

which saw huge potential in the city's booming tourist economy and burgeoning middle class.

Having built a new team, *Tele-Fonika* set about elaborate plans for a new stadium on the existing site, despite being told – with no little irony – to keep the old ground's Stalinist entrance columns due to a preservation order. Banking on European riches following inevitable domestic success, *Tele-Fonika* almost withdrew their funds after a Wisla fan instigated a one-year UEFA ban from international competition – while the city folk clucked over UEFA's decision and went about with their daily business, the police were scouring southern Poland for the kid who threw a knife at Parma's Dino Baggio.

The international image of a revived Kraków, its legend as large as its potential, had been scarred.

The thrilling fields

Wisla

TS Wisla stadium, Reymonta 22
Capacity 18,000
Colours Red and blue
League champions 1927–28, 1949–51, 1978, 1999
Cup winners 1926, 1967

The oldest club currently in the Polish top flight is also its most celebrated. Wisla won the national championship for the seventh time in 1999, breaking a 21-year title drought in the process. Having first shone in pre-World War I days, when Poland was divided, by the time a single national league had been set up in 1927, Wisla were the strongest team in the land. Under the coaching of their star player Imre Schlosser, and with the Reyman brothers upfront,

Wisla won back-to-back titles, scoring nearly 200 goals in 50 games.

Following a brief era of glory immediately after World War II, Wisla had to wait until the late Seventies to shine again. Star of the side was World Cup striker Andrzej Iwan, whose goals helped them to the 1978 title, but his career was washed up amidst drunken wrong-doings in a hotel bar.

After a spell in the second division, Wisla celebrated their 90th anniversary with promotion in 1996. This attracted an ambitious team of local investors, who hatched a ten-year plan to make the club the market leaders in Eastern Europe.

Having bought a substantial stake in Wisla on New Year's Eve 1996/97, the three-man telecommunications concern *Tele-Fonika* put up enough money to buy 14 new players. Some were Poles who had gone abroad, learned good training habits, and were keen to go home if paid a real wage: Ryszard Czerwiec (Guingamp), Krzysztof Bukalski (RC Genk), Kazimierz Wegrzyn (SV Ried) and Grzegorz Kaliciak (St Truiden) were the key elements. Eighth at the winter break, Wisla won seven out of eight games in the spring, beating champions Widzew 6–0 and earning an eventual third place.

Along with developing the team, *Tele-Fonika* were building two new stands as part of a plan for an all-seater 30,000 stadium by the year 2001. Alas, out in the real world, 30 fans were injured, three blinded, when Wisla and Ruch Chorzów hooligans clashed at the end of the season.

In the summer of 1998, Wisla surprisingly swapped pragmatic coach Wojciech Lazarek for Widzew's more adventurous Frantisek Smuda, and bought prolific forward Tomasz Frankowski from Japan. Smuda deployed an attacking 3–5–2 formation which looked risky on paper, yet his team beat Legia 4–1, Polonia 3–1 and Widzew 3–1. The stage looked set for the best season in the club's history until a fan threw a knife at Parma's Dino Baggio during a UEFA Cup match. Worse, Czerwiec threw the knife away to distract officials. Wisla received a one-year UEFA ban from European competition, and *Tele-Fonika* threatened to withdraw their funds.

Come the end of the season, however, and Wisla's title, secured with a winning margin of 17 points over runners-up Widzew, was still a cause for celebration, not just in Kraków but for fans throughout Poland with a sense of footballing history. Though they failed to retain their title in 1999/2000, a second-place finish behind Polonia at least ensured that Wisla would have a place in the UEFA Cup when their European ban came to an end.

Here we go!

Tram #15 or #18 down Al 3 Maja from the ring road around the old town, or take a 15min walk from the centre going west.

Just the ticket

It's wise to go the day before to the ticket windows, on either the Ul Reymonta (*sektor* B) side or the Al 3 Maja (*sektor* A) one. The queue can be painfully slow-moving before kick-off, and the

Architect of a championship – Wisla boss Frantisek Smuda

wait is often charged with baiting between fans and riot police. Note that the current lack of floodlights means that all Wisla's games are afternoon kick-offs.

Swift half

You'll find the plain buffet *U Wislaków* up the stairs in the main entrance to the sports hall behind *sektor* B, the *restauracja* of the same name on the ground floor.

Club merchandise

On matchdays, Wisla shirts and scarves are sold out of a **large red tent** under the *sektor* A main stand, no credit cards.

Ultra culture

Despite the attempts by the club to generate a family atmosopher, the visitor's abiding memory of Wisla is *sektor* C, where a choirmaster with his back to the action stands on a tall gantry co-ordinating the *Armia Bialej Gwiazdy* songs with those of the *Fanatycy Z Grodu Kraka* behind the goal in *sektor* B.

In print

Biala Gwiazda monthly magazine is on sale at every home game. Occasionally a simple programme comes with your match ticket.

In the net

As befits the club's status in Poland, the **official website** is exceptionally well laid-out, at: www.wisla.krakow.pl.

Groundhopping

Cracovia

Cracovia stadium, Ul Józefa Kałuzy
Capacity 12,000
Colours Red and white stripes
League champions 1921, 1930, 1932, 1937, 1948

Shocking mis-management has reduced the sixth most honoured club in Polish history

to a sorry meeting place for the wild boys of Nowy Prokocim and Nowy Biezanów. When games are played simultaneously, you can even hear the Wisla cheers from the other side of Park Jordana vibrating around the undulations of the Cracovia cycle track and over the ghosts of this once fine club. The plaque by the ticket booths on Ul Józefa Kałuzy tells all – a list of Cracovia players who fell in World War II, some having left behind their championship medals from the Thirties.

Whether their most famous fan, Pope John Paul II, can follow their results in *III.Liga Grupa Krakówska* from the Vatican is as doubtful as the prospect of any Cracovia resurrection to match that of their neighbours' across the park.

To catch Cracovia, either walk west out of the centre for ten minutes, or take bus #152 or express bus B or D to the stop where Al Marsz Ferdinanda Focha splits with Al 3 Maja. On Focha by the stadium you'll find the **Alga Cafe Bar** next to the **Sheriff's Whisky Bar** with its meat grill. A match ticket at the ground around the corner will set you back 6zł.

Hutnik

Hutnik stadium, Ul Ptaszyckiego 4
Capacity 14,000
Colours Blue and white

Nature abhors a vacuum. The workforce of vast *Nowa Huta* steelworks, built in the early Fifties in the far east of town, needed a football team. Hutnik Kraków were that team. While the workforce added to southern Poland's huge pollution problem, the football clubcould barely raise enough steam to crawl out of the lower leagues.

Ironically it was after Communism, when the factory was slowly being run down, that Hutnik hit a bizarre run of form that led to promotion to the top flight in 1995. Moreover, in their best season ever, they finished third behind Widzew and Legia in 1996, dragging their attendance statistics into four figures along the way. To see if Hutnik can climb out of the lower divisions to repeat that success, take tram #15 or #20 east from the centre along Al Jana Pawla II. The **Kawiarna Gol** by the club office is a more convivial bar than either Wisla or Cracovia can boast. Tickets are 15zł at the turnstiles round the corner to the right. Across the car park is the **Fans Souvenirs** shop, with all kinds of scarves and pennants – including Hutnik's.

Eat, drink, sleep…

Bars and clubs

Trendy downtown Kraków can boast more bars per street than any other Polish city, many of them loud, crowded, smoky cellars, where the atmosphere is jovial, perhaps because many punters practise the laudable habit of drinking through thin plastic straws. Clubbing can be fun, but rarely musically adventurous.

Black Gallery, Ul Mikołajska 24. Probably the best of the popular central cellar bars, buzzing and friendly, where care is taken over the music – funk to house and back again – and the clothes worn are generally…black.

Insomnia, Ul Szeroka 10. Probably the best club in Kraków, a warren of bar, dance and chill-out rooms, with half-decent dance music too boot. Open past dawn at weekends, closed Mon.

O'Morgans, Ul Garncarska 5. Opened in 1999, the latest in a chain of homely Irish bars run by Ollie of Warsaw fame. Friendly cavern featuring live music, a full menu and all the usual Gaelic trappings. Open from midday until last guest daily.

Pod Jemiola, Ul Florianska 20. Not easy to spot – look out for the *Sex Shop*, *Tattoo* and *Wedding Dresses* signs – but once inside 'Under The Mistletoe', you'll find ambient and trip-hop sounds in a dark, barely candlelit wooden bar.

Uwaga, Maly Rynek 3. 'Attention' draws a trendy clientèle down a dangerous staircase to its many dark rooms, highlighted by French and Chinese decorations, a TV and a pinball machine. Open daily 2pm–2am.

Restaurants

Nothing better reflects Kraków's recent rapid growth in tourism than its restaurants, which offer as wide a range as any in the old Eastern bloc. And not expensive, either – you can easily find a decent two-course meal in town for under 20zł.

Kraków essentials

Kraków's renovated **Balice** airport is 15km west of the city. Bus #208 and express bus D take 45mins and 30mins respectively to reach the central train station, tickets 3zł for either.

Much of central Kraków is accessible **on foot** – even the main stadia to the west are only a 15-minute stroll. Outside of the centre, you'll need the city's trams, buses or express buses, which run 6am–11pm. You'll pay 1.20zł for a single ticket, 1.80zł for the express, 3zł for one of the 600-numbered hourly **night services** that pass by the train station. Tickets are available from kiosks near stops, or from the driver for a small supplement. Day tickets (*bilet dziennych*) and weeklies (*tygodiowych*) are also available, at 5zł and 14zł respectively. Punch tickets in the machine onboard.

Reliable **taxi** phone numbers are ☎012/422 2222, ☎012/9625 and ☎012/9661. All firms increase their rates by 25% after 10pm.

Dexter Travel (open Mon–Fri 9am–6pm, Sat 9am–1pm, ☎012/421 7706), in the middle of the Old Town's market square, is a friendly, efficient source of **tourist information**. For bar and club listings, pick up the latest edition of the bi-monthly *Kraków In Your Pocket* (5zł).

Chechowa, Ul Jagiellonska 11. Genuine cheap Polish fare in pleasant surroundings, with a limited but properly prepared selection on the menu. Kraków herring a speciality. Most major credit cards.

C K Browar, Ul Podwale 6. Wisla Kraków chose wisely when they were looking for a venue for their Monday evening fans' get-togethers. This bar/restaurant has four kinds of beer brewed on the premises, and a menu of regular pub fare.

Pod Aniolami, Ul Grodzka 35. Historic cellar restaurant, re-opened in 1998, serving traditional local delicacies at not unreasonable prices. Barbecue in summer. Kraków's most atmospheric dining experience. Reservations recommended on: ☎012/421 3999.

U Szkota, Ul Mikoljaska 4. Just off the main square, a Scottish restaurant designed in good taste – if you disregard the waiters in kilts. Trout in almonds, salmon and haggis among the main course options. Open daily until midnight.

Accommodation

The city's mid-range hotels have yet to catch up with the recent rise in tourism. Many are in need of repair, in some cases being slowly carried out. For all that, Kraków has a far broader choice of hotels – and more centrally located – than Warsaw. To arrange a private room, either go to *Waweltur* opposite the station at Ul Pawła 8 (open Mon–Fri 8am–8pm, Sat 8am–2pm, ☎012/422 1921) or check with the old ladies outside.

Dom Turisty PTTK, Ul Westerplatte 15 (☎012/422 9500, fax 012/421 2726). Cheap hostel in the centre, still bleakly Socialist-Realist despite a change of management. No curfew, 24-hour reception. A dorm bed will cost you only 25zł, and the cafeteria grub is tasty and cheap.

Hotel Logos, Ul Szujskiego 5 (☎012/632 3333, fax 012/632 4210). Newest hotel in town, its glass front incongruous next to the surrounding old town, but with sauna and suntan facilities. Around 200zł a double with breakfast. Most credit cards.

Hotel Warszawski, Ul Pawła 6 (☎012/422 0622). The cheapest of three places by the station (the other two are the *Polonia* and the *Europejski*), comfortable and a 10min walk from town. Singles with breakfast at 110zł, doubles at 145zł. Most credit cards.

Polski, Ul Pijarska 17 (☎012/422 1144, fax 012/422 1526, e-mail rezerwo@ podorlem.com.pl). Recently renovated three-star hotel dating back to 1815, situated right by Florianska Gate in the old town. All rooms have a TV and a bathroom. Singles $62, doubles $95, triples $115.

Portugal

Federação Portuguesa de Futebol, Praça de Alegria 25, CP 21 100, P1250-004
Lisbon ☎01/342 8207 Fax 01/346 7231 E-mail dep@fpf.pt

League champions Sporting Lisbon **Cup winners** FC Porto **Promoted** Beira Mar,
Aves, Paços Ferreira **Relegated** Vitória Setúbal, Rio Ave, Santa Clara

European participants 2000/01 Sporting Lisbon (UCL); FC Porto (UCL qualifiers);
Benfica, Boavista (UEFA Cup)

Portugal will host the next big European football party in 2004, and it is going to be a lot of fun. But while the engaging locals and cheap eating and drinking may be the attraction for the fans, for those in Portuguese football, hosting the European Championship in four years' time will be an opportunity to give the domestic game a badly needed cash boost.

For while Portugal may continue to produce exciting individual talents like Luis Figo and Rui Costa, and a national team that almost lives up to its billing as the 'Brazil of Europe', the domestic league is struggling. Most stadia are long overdue a facelift, and the promised government grants and loans for Euro 2004 should ensure that they, as well as the infrastructure that links them together, are brought bang up to date.

Portugal's bid to host the finals focused unashamedly on the need to help football in a country which has provided the European game with so much talent and entertainment over the years. The romantic argument was enough to convince UEFA to overlook the political appeal of the joint Austro-Hungarian bid and the commercial commonsense of the Spanish option. But while there will be money to be made from the hosting of Euro 2004, it is debatable whether the event will enable the country to address the more deep-seated problems of the domestic game.

With the exception of Sporting Lisbon and Porto, Portugal's top-flight clubs are struggling to deal with years of neglect and

Summer love – the party will go on in 2004

mounting interest on bank loans. And even the top two cannot hang on to their talent, as the departure of Sporting's José Vidigal and Porto's Mário Jardel in the summer of 2000 proved. Figo's world-record move to Real Madrid from Barcelona may have shocked most of the continent, but Portuguese fans will have found it particularly painful to read that one of their own players was generating enough cash to keep half-a-dozen clubs going for another year.

A £40million corner – Figo prepares to fire one in for Portugal against France at Euro 2000

It was, of course, the nation's rich footballing past which made Portugal's cry for help impossible for UEFA not to heed. The country's footballing reputation was built on the riches of its former colonies – predominantly African rather than Latin American. It was Africans, particularly the incomparable Eusébio, who were the stars of Portugal's golden era. Eusébio's club side, Benfica, won the European Cup in 1961 and 1962, and the national team made a stunning competitive debut at the 1966 World Cup finals.

Top scorer of that 1966 tournament, Eusébio still dominates the Portuguese game, in spirit if not in fact. His statue stands outside Benfica's Stadium of Light, his reputation as football's endearing ambassador still shining. Fans not only remember his speed and ferocious shot, they revere him for having led cavalier teams whose free-scoring approach surprised the established opposition of the day. Benfica's European Cups were won 3–2 and 5–3 against Barcelona and Real Madrid respectively, and Portugal's adven-turous style saw them knock reigning champions Brazil out of the 1966 World Cup, 3–1.

Having broken Spain's stranglehold on the European Cup, then Brazil's on the World Cup, the way was open for Eusébio and his colleagues, among them fellow Mozambican and national-team captain Mário Coluna, Angolan forward José Augusto and centre-forward José Torres, to be crowned kings of the footballing world. In the World Cup quarter-finals, North Korea scored three shock early goals before Eusébio scored four, Portugal's 5–3 win setting them up for a semi-final clash with the hosts, England. At Wembley, Portugal's hopes were dashed against the rocks of Nobby Stiles' brutal marking job on Eusébio, sterling performances by England's defence and two remarkable goals by Bobby Charlton – 2–1 to England, Eusébio's famous parting tears and an eventual third place for Portugal.

Alas, the generation of '66 quickly waned. Portugal failed to qualify for the World Cup in either 1970 or 1974.

Basics

A passport is sufficient for citizens of the EU, the USA, Canada, Australia and New Zealand to gain entry to Portugal.

The Portuguese currency is the **escudo**, divided into 100 centavos. A $ price sign is normally used to delineate escudos from centavos. There are around 300$ to £1. You'll find coins in denominations of $50 (50 centavos), 1$ (one escudo), 2$50, 5$, 10$, 20$, 50$, 100$ and 200$. Notes come in denominations of 500$, 1,000$, 2,000$, 5,000$ and 10,000$. Credit-card cash machines are widespread and generally charge less exchange commission than the banks.

Telephones take 10$, 20$ and 50$ coins. Most bars will have a phone – simply pay the barman for the number of impulses used. **Phonecards** come in 50-unit (880$) and 100-unit (2,100$) denominations. For international phone calls, cheaper between 10pm and 8am and at weekends, dial 00 followed by the country code. From outside the country, the code for Portugal is 351, followed by a new nine-digit number – there are no more city codes..

Most **trains in Portugal** are classed as *regional* – they're cheap but stop everywhere. Faster and more expensive are the *intercidades*, while the fastest of all are the *rápidos*, such as the **Alfa service** which runs between Lisbon and Porto. A ticket for the Alfa, including a compulsory reservation, costs around 4,000$ return. There are four Alfas a day and the journey takes just over three hours. **Buses** can be a good alternative to trains – the network is more extensive and fares are competitive. In contrast to rail services, most major inter-city bus routes are run by private companies.

Accommodation is cheap and plentiful. **Pensions** (*pensões*) are fine value and are graded according to a star system; a double room in a two-star pension will cost between 4,000$ and 5,000$.

Drinking, dining and clubbing are similarly cheap. **Fish**, **seafood** and **pork** are the mainstays of Portuguese cooking, which can be a little on the bland side – though the portions are never less than generous. **Wine** is invariably tasty, either red (*tinto*) or white (*branco*). The slightly sparkling *vinho verde* from the Minho region is justifiably popular everywhere. **Port** (*vinho do Porto*) and **madeira** (*vinho da Madeira*) are cheap, strong, and served in a bewildering variety of ages and colours.

Beer, probably either *Super Bock* or the sweeter *Sagres*, is served in a small glass (*fino*), a medium glass (*imperial*) or a half-litre (*caneca*). In most bars a *fino* will set you back no more than 150$.

Coffee is the classic pick-me-up, served either black, espresso-style (*bica*), or with a dash of milk (*garoto*). Tea (*chá*) is also popular and is better in Portugal than anywhere else in southern Europe.

Eusébio's emigration to America in 1975 coincided with revolution at home, and the subsequent independence of former Portuguese colonies in Africa slowed the influx of talent from that region into the domestic game. Portugal had to turn towards Europe in an attempt to rediscover its old glories. Clubs queued up to import players and coaches to take on the continent's big boys who, by then, had bigger bank accounts than most Portuguese teams could ever aspire to.

An entertaining revival in the Eighties centred on a squad which seemed to contain the perfect mix of experience (in the shape of Rui Jordão and the veteran striker Nené, a former team-mate of Eusébio's) and youthful exuberance (from the likes of Diamantino and Paulo Futre). Portugal danced their way to a classic semi-final with France at the 1984 European Championship, and though that game was ultimately lost to the genius of Platini, hopes soared of a new Portuguese dawn.

They were swiftly dispelled. Two years later, in what would become known as the Saltillo Affair, Portugal's squad for the 1986 World Cup gathered in a Mexican mountain retreat to demand extra appearance money from federation officials. Some of the demands were met, but after a 3–1 defeat by Morocco brought the team's campaign to a premature end, eleven of the squad were suspended by federation president Silva Resende, who claimed their lack of discipline had contributed to the team's poor performance. The remainder of the players withdrew their services from the national side in protest and Portugal competed (unsuccessfully) for a place at the Euro '88 finals with what amounted to a third-choice team.

On the club front, a European Cup win by Porto in 1987, followed by appearances in the continent's premier final by Benfica in 1988 and 1990, kept Portugal in touch with the elite without ever threatening full membership of it. From time to time during the Nineties, Porto have successfully humiliated some of the greatest names in the European game, only to fall flat again within a few months.

The country continues to produce great natural talent, its Under-20 side having won the World Youth Cup in 1989 and 1991 – the latter in front of 120,000 at the Stadium of Light. Turning that talent into a senior team capable of taking on the world's best remains a circle Portugal have still to square, but the national side came within a hand's breadth of doing just that at Euro 2000.

Two goals down against England in their opening game, and it looked like a familiar story of under-achievement. But the majestic Figo prompted a revival with an effortless individual goal, and by the end, few could deny Portugal were not worth their 3–2 win. A hard-fought 1–0 victory over Romania secured the side's passage to the knockout phase, and even though coach Humberto Coelho picked what amounted to a second-string team for the final group game against Germany, the Portuguese ran riot, Sergio Conceição scoring all the goals in a 3–0 romp.

Turkey were beaten with similar ease, 2–0 in the quarter-finals, setting up a semifinal against the world champions France. There was a growing feeling in the Low

Last act of the drama – Nuno Gomes (right) puts Portugal ahead against the French

Countries that Coelho's team might just pull off an upset, and when Nuno Gomes stole in to give Portugal a 1–0 lead in the 19th minute, the country's colourful travelling support briefly rode a wave of optimism. But Thierry Henry poached a second-half equaliser, and two minutes into the second period of sudden-death extra time, Abel Xavier handled a goal-bound shot on the line. Even after Zinedine Zidane's spot-kick had put them out, a number of Portuguese players continued to argue their case with the match officials, prompting a series of hefty fines and bans from UEFA – a sad note for the team, and coach Coelho, to bow out on.

Domestically, meanwhile, the staid three-club domination of Porto, Benfica and Sporting continues. Yet Portugal's domestic football, played out every Sunday in huge, echoing theatres, holds an enduring, eccentric appeal to foreign visitors – even if increasing numbers of local fans prefer to watch action from Spain or Italy, where the likes of Figo, Conceição and Gomes enjoy the grand stage their instinctive, one-touch football deserves.

Essential vocabulary

Hello *Olá*
Goodbye *Adeus*
Yes *Sim*
No *Não*
Two beers, please *Duas cervejas, por favor*
Thank you *Obrigado/Obrigada*
Men's *Homens*
Women's *Senhoras*
Where is the stadium? *Onde esta o estádio?*
What's the score? *Como esta o jogo?*
Referee *Árbitro*
Offside *Fora de jogo*

Match practice

Although the current downturn and corruption scandals have forced many fans away from grounds, interest in the game itself has not wavered. Every Sunday, you'll see Portuguese menfolk in the bars, radios pressed to their ears.

Inside grounds, the sense of discontent is still palpable. Even when their team's winning, the slightest incident will force grown men to hang their heads and groan theatrically or bark madly at their neighbours. Much of this frustration gets directed at the referee, inspiring chants of *'Gatuno!'* – 'Bandit!' As in Spain, an outstanding piece of play – or a poor performance – brings out the waving of the white handkerchief, a custom borrowed from bullfighting.

The season runs from September to May. Most games take place at 5pm on a Sunday afternoon, with kick-offs brought forward to 3pm in winter. There'll be at least one live TV game at 9pm on both Saturday and Sunday, and occasionally on Monday or Friday, too.

A different league

Portugal's top flight is the *I Divisão* which has 18 teams, as has the next rung down, the *II Divisão de Honra*; teams are promoted and relegated on a three-up, three-down basis. Three teams are relegated from the *II Divisão de Honra* into the *II Divisão B*, itself divided into three regional 18-team zones – the winners of the *Zona Norte*, *Zona Central* and *Zona Sul* are promoted. The *III Divisão* has six zoned leagues, from each of which two clubs are promoted to accommodate the four bottom teams dropping down from each zone of the *II Divisão B*.

Up for the cup

La Taça de Portugal has three *eliminatória* rounds, decided on a replay if necessary, before top-flight clubs enter at the fourth-round stage in October. Thereafter ties are decided on one game, with extra-time and penalties if required. The semi-finals are over by February, leaving a long wait to the final, which is played as near to the traditional date of 10 June, Portugal Day, as possible – although sometimes this can be late May. The venue is the otherwise underused Estádio Nacional just outside Lisbon, which also hosts any replay that may be necessary.

For an average league match, a ticket in the *tribuna central* will cost you around 4,000$; in the *bancada lateral*, 2,500–3,000$; and in the *superiores*, 1,500–2,000$. Expect to pay 2,000$ more for big matches.

Half-time

The Portuguese have a tradition of socialising around steaming concessions vans heaving under the weight of pork, salt cod and beer. If you can distinguish them amid the smoke, *bifanas* are pork steak sandwiches, *entremeadas* fatty pork sandwiches and *coiratos* fried pigskin – all at about 200–300$.

Most big clubs do not sell alcohol at matches, so fans are assaulted by a plethora of beer vendors at the entrance. Smaller snacks come in the form of roasted chestnuts (*amendoins*), peanuts (*amendoins torrados*), butter beans (*tremoços*) and sweet cakes such as *queijadas*.

Flag days – Eusébio's statue outside the Stadium of Light

Just the ticket

Portugal's larger clubs are multi-disciplined sports organisations. Benfica alone can boast more than 150,000 members (*socios*) who get the first pick of tickets for major games. There will usually be a special window for members at the ticket office (*biheteiria*). In practice, given the huge size of the major Portuguese stadia, sellouts are rare.

Best seats will be in the *tribuna central*, which offers the clearest view overlooking the halfway line. The benches alongside, the *bancada lateral*, are the next dearest. The cheapest places, confusingly called *superiores* or *topos*, are behind the goal; if there are any hardcore fans, this is where you'll find them. *Coberta* indicates covered accommodation, *descoberta* open.

Action replay

The north-south civil war in the Portuguese game is perfectly summed up by the battle for TV rights. The first salvo was sounded by the Oporto-based Oliveira clan – Joaquim, his son Roland and his brother, ex-Porto coach António – and their company *Olivedesportos*. The current contract between Olivedesportos and the Portuguese FA was signed in 1997 and is valid until July 2004, covering live league action of all top-flight clubs except Benfica and their ex-nursery team Alverca.

Benfica had a deal with *Olivedesportos* for this period, but the club president João Vale e Azevedo broke it after his election in 1997. On the eve of the 1998/99 season, Benfica signed a separate deal with *SIC* for half-a-dozen league games to be screened live during the season, with the remainder being shown pre-recorded. At the same time, *Olivedesportos* and state RTP launched their pay-per-view channel SporTV, which screens three live games per round, at a cost of 3,000$ a month to the viewer.

While Benfica and *Olivedesportos* fight it out in the courts, fans can tune into live evening games on RTP Internacional on Friday, Saturday or Sunday, and RTP1 on a Monday. RTP1 also screens a highlights show, *Domingo Desportivo*, at 7.30pm and 10.30pm on a Sunday, but this is bettered by RTP Internacional's two-hour *Futebol* review at 9pm on Mondays.

RTP2 has English Premiership action at 5pm on Saturdays and 4pm on Sundays, and previews the upcoming Portuguese weekend at 9.30pm on Thursdays.

The back page

The leading sports paper is Lisbon's well-established *A Bola* (daily, 120$). Although its domestic content leans heavily on the comings and goings at Benfica, its international coverage is excellent.

A Bola also publishes an eponymous colour monthly magazine (350$), and an excellent season preview special, *Cardernos* (400$).

There are two other sports dailies. *O Jogo* (120$) publishes separate Lisbon and Oporto editions, and fans in the north tend to prefer the latter above all other papers. *Record* (120$) is the paper to have lifted the lid on most of the Portuguese game's recent scandals.

Ultra culture

Fan culture is as dependent on the three main clubs – Porto, Benfica and Sporting – as the league title has always been. Games involving these three, especially between Porto and one of the two Lisbon giants, can often spark something off.

Groups are known as *claques*, and all clubs have at least one, the phenomenon having been first imported by Sporting or Académica Coimbra from over the border in Spain. In any case Sporting, whose last league title dates back further than the birthdate of many in the *Juventude Leonina* group, have the most passionate ultras, with scars to prove it. They are also the best organised when it comes to publications and marketing.

As in Spain or Italy, ultras spend their week working out their routines and making flags (*faixas*) and banners (*bandeiras*). The scene is well-documented in the recently relaunched fanzine, *ultra* (monthly, 400$)

In the net

The Portuguese FA runs a well-maintained and very comprehensive official website at: www.fpf.pt. You'll find details on all levels of the domestic game, and this is also the place to turn to for the latest information on Euro 2004.

For match reports and club news, point your browser to *InforDesporto Online* at: www.infordesporto.pt. This is a wide-ranging site covering a lot of different sports, but the football section alone is a goldmine of info, updated daily and easy to understand despite being in Portuguese language only. Detail is the site's strong point – from the tiniest match fact to the Belenenses goalkeeper's date of birth, you'll find it all here.

Lisbon

It may lack the smooth machinations of Milan, the partisan frenzy of Barcelona and London's strength in depth, but Lisbon is one of Europe's legendary football capitals, its fame spread by Benfica's glory years in what was once the continent's largest venue, the Stadium of Light. Though the football legends may have faded, Lisbon itself is still a great city for a weekend's entertainment, like a jumble-sale version of Barcelona – full of the cheap, the weird and the exotic, and now (thanks to Expo '98), with a modern transport system too.

Lisbon has no real football centre as such. Both Benfica and Sporting moved home several times around the Campo Grande, Benfica and Alvalade areas in the far north before both settling on their current neighbouring homes on the highway near the airport. Four bus stops, along the #33 and #50 routes, are all that stand between the city's two giants, Benfica's Estádio da Luz referring to its location in the Luz area rather than the brightness of the stadium's floodlights. In social terms, Benfica are traditionally the team of the people. Sporting, although with a strong young following, have always had links with the government and attract a more upwardly mobile breed of supporter.

Lisbon essentials

The **Aerobus** makes the 30min journey between Lisbon's **Portela airport** and central Praça do Comércio, also calling at Rossio train station. The service runs every 20mins, 7am–9pm, and costs 450$ – which also covers a day's transport use in the city, except for the metro. A taxi will cost you 1,500–2,000$.

The main **Santa Apolónia** train station, point of arrival for trains from Oporto, Madrid and Paris, is linked to the city centre by the *Linha da Gaivota*, one of four colour-coded metro lines.

Most of the modern city centre, the **Baixa**, which runs down to the river Tagus, is pleasantly walkable. The steep twists and turns up to the old town, the **Alfama**, are negotiable by century-old trams #12 and #28 – a thrilling way to see the city. Lisbon's transport system – all except the metro run by *Carris* – specialises in glorious anachronisms. In addition to the trams, there is a giant lift (*elevador Santa Justa*) and a funicular (*elevador da Glória*), either of which will take you up to the former main area for nightlife, the **Bairro Alto**, from the centre of town below.

Carris tickets are 160$ for a single journey, available onboard or from newsstands. A **three-day pass**, again covering everything except the metro, is 1,000$. Night transport (*rede da madrugada*) sets off from Cais do Sodré, every 30mins throughout the night, tickets 300$ onboard.

The **metro system** (6.30am–1am, 100$ for a *bilhete simple*, 800$ for a *caderneta* of ten, 260$ for a day pass) covers both main stadia. Stamp your ticket at the escalators.

The minimum **taxi** fare is 250$, with a night tariff between 10pm and 6am and at weekends. All cabs have meters and no journey in the centre of town should run to more than 800$. Call ☎218 155 061 or ☎/218 152 076 if you can't see a cab near a main square.

The main **tourist office** is at Palácio Foz, Praça dos Restauradores, near Rossio station (open daily 9am–8pm, ☎213 463 314). Of the various **listings publications**, easily the best is *Flirt*, in English and Portuguese, distributed free in bars and clubs.

Match tickets for either Benfica or Sporting are available for 10% commission at the *ABEP* kiosk on Restauradores, on the corner of Rua do Joaquim do Regedor (☎213 475 823). The main ultra gear store is at *Loja 44* in the Lusíadas shopping centre, Rua dos Lusíadas 5, Alcântara, on the #15 tram route.

Lisbon's third team, Belenenses, are based in Belém to the far west of the city, home to diplomats and ambassadors.

The thrilling fields

 Benfica

Estádio da Luz, Avenida General Norton de Matos
Colours Red shirts, white shorts
Capacity 85,000 (all-seated)
League champions 1936–38, 1942–43, 1945, 1950, 1955, 1957, 1960–61, 1963–65, 1967–69, 1971–73, 1975–77, 1981, 1983–84, 1987, 1989, 1991, 1994
Cup winners 1930–31, 1935, 1940, 1943–44, 1949, 1951–53, 1955, 1957, 1959, 1962, 1964, 1969–70, 1972, 1980–81, 1983, 1985–87, 1993, 1996
European Cup winners 1961–62

Crossing the Norton de Matos airport highway to Benfica's Stadium of Light is like coming across a lost empire. The vast eagle over the entrance, Eusébio's statue in kicking action on a grass plinth, the club motto *E Pluribus Unum* and the museum inside – it's a treasure trove from another age.

In the summer of 1961 Portugal's most popular team, nicknamed the Eagles, were set to grab the mantle of the legendary Real Madrid as Europe's team of the new decade. After surprisingly beating Barcelona 3–2 in the European Cup final that May, Benfica then signed Eusébio from under the noses of their city rivals, Sporting.

The scene was set – an arena worthy of worldbeaters in the expanded Estádio da Luz, a master coach in Hungarian-born Béla Guttmann, and a 20-year-old African prodigy who could outshoot Pelé. Eusébio it was who scored the last two goals to beat Real Madrid 5–3 in a classic European Cup final of 1962.

But then it all started to go wrong. A dispute between the Benfica management

and Guttmann over bonus payments, and the coach who had built the team was gone. His departure, coupled with scene-stealing displays by Milan's two *catenaccio*-based European Cup-winning sides (AC Milan in 1963, Inter in 1965), took the red carpet out from under the Eagles' claws. Benfica's dream of European domination was over.

From now on, there would be only heroic defeats in Europe – Alex Stepney's late save for Manchester United in the 1968 final, Celtic's coin toss the following year – though Benfica continued to dominate at home, winning the title 12 times in 15 seasons. Even so, when he left for America in 1975, Eusébio must have been reflecting on what might have been.

After a string of European flops, Benfica's management decided to act. The club had been formed in 1904 by a group of rich kids from Belém, headed by the Anglophile Cosme Damião, from two separate organisations; one had a club with an eagle emblem but no ground, another had the Benfica village football pitch but not enough players to use it. Damião laid down the rule that Portuguese nationals only should play for his *Sport Lisboa e Benfica* – a rule subsequently bent to include stars from the colonies such as Eusébio. Some time after Portugal lost its colonies following the 1974 revolution, Benfica turned to Swedish coach Sven Göran Eriksson to bring European stars to the club. It was Eriksson's side that did the double in 1983 and narrowly lost the UEFA Cup final to Anderlecht the same year. This was followed by European Cup final appearances in 1988 and 1990, although both games were lost.

Benfica's management became progressively less astute as the Nineties wore on. In 1993 the club sold its TV rights to buy Paulo Futre, but were then unable to pay his or other stars' wages. A year later there was a repeat performance, when only a last-minute intervention by Benfica's then sponsors *Parmalat* enabled Claudio Canigia to be bought and paid for one, desperately disappointing, season. In the meantime, Porto kept clocking up the titles and the lucrative Champions' League appearances. It was more than members could bear when, in 1997, president Manuel Damásio shored up the club with a loan from *Finibanco* on the proviso that the almost sacrosanct João Pinto would be sold, for at least £20million, should Benfica fall late with repayments.

In October 1997, fans voted in a new president, lawyer João Vale e Azevedo. Assuming the club's massive debts and paying salaries out of his own pocket, Azevedo negotiated a new TV rights contract for the club and recruited Graeme Souness as coach. With most of the transfer budget already spent on the unsuccessful Brazilian Paulo Nunes, Souness was forced to bring in bargains from the Premiership dump bin – Scott Minto, Karel Poborský and Brian Deane the first of them. With former Boavista striker Nuno Gomes hit-

ting the goal trail bang on schedule, Benfica managed a runners-up place in 1998 and a Champions' League berth for the following season, when further reinforcements – Dean Saunders, Michael Thomas and Mark Pembridge – arrived from England.

The fans were unhappy at the lack of Portuguese stars in the team, and their discontent seemed justified after a disastrous loss to HJK Helsinki put paid to Benfica's European ambitions, and Porto and Boavista were gradually allowed to pull away in the domestic league.

In March 1999, Vale e Azevedo sacked Souness for misconduct, amid suspicions that the charge was trumped up to obviate the need to pay the coach for the remainder of his contract. One by one the imports left Lisbon, some before their initial transfer fees had been paid, others owed months' worth of back wages.

Under German coach Jupp Heynckes, Benfica's depressing European form continued in 1999/2000, with an embarrassing 7–0 defeat at Celta Vigo in the UEFA Cup. And there was failure on the home front, too, as the team finished third in the league, eight points behind champions Sporting. To add insult to the injury of their local rivals winning a first title in 18 years, crowd favourite João Pinto was sold to Sporting in order to balance the books and, after impressing at Euro 2000, young striker Nuno Gomes packed his bags for Fiorentina. Could it possibly get any worse in 2000/01?

Here we go!

Metro to the terminus **Colegio Militar**, 15mins from central Restauradores. As you exit, the stadium is visible on the other side of the highway.

Just the ticket

Ticket windows are to be found on the other side of the highway from the giant *Colombo* shopping centre, although for minor games you might find *socios* milling around there trying to sell their match voucher.

Those *socios* attending will be occupying most of the first and second ring (*anel*) on the east

Played but not well-paid – Michael Thomas

The Estádio Nacional

Avenida Pierre de Coubertin, Caxias
Capacity 60,000 (all-seated)

It was here, at this bizarre
amphitheatre cut deep into the
pinewoods 10km out of Lisbon, that
Bill Shankly turned to Jock Stein
and said: 'John, you're immortal!'
The occasion was Celtic's European
Cup win over Internazionale, the two
Scots managers hailing the first
British team to win Europe's premier
trophy.

Woodland walk – fans stroll to the cup final

Even for those not there that
sultry May evening in 1967, a visit
to the Portuguese **national stadium** can be a
moving occasion – it was also the venue for the great Torino's last game before the
Superga air crash of 1949. The stadium had been inaugurated five years earlier, a
testament to then leader Salazar's strict monetary policies – perhaps the reason for
its only being three-sided – and fascist pretensions. Still, it's a landscape garden
compared to Mussolini's Stadio Olimpico in Rome.

For most of the year, all is quiet on the western front, beyond the city limits of
Lisbon along Pierre de Courbertin avenue. The only sporting events that take
place here now are the **Portuguese cup final** and minor athletics meetings,
although plans are afoot to make better use of the arena in the future. All around
are sports facilities, and the only disturbance during the short walk from the tram stop
to the ground is the rush of air caused by the occasional passing jogger.

Once you're through the old-fashioned turnstiles, the stadium spreads out in a
horseshoe shape, rows of simple, stone benches gradually rising up to a marble
rostrum dominating the far, western, side. The changing rooms, toilets and *Bar
Saida* nearby are overgrown with weeds.

Down below, however, the **stadium office**, with its huge picture of Eusébio in
classic '66 form, is in full working order, as is the small **refreshments stand** by
the reception area. Shankly, Stein and Valentino Mazzola have a rightful place
among football's immortals, and a celebratory beer with their ghosts in the
peaceful forest of Caxias is a rare pleasure.

To get to Caxias, ride the rickety wooden **#15 tram** to its terminus from
Sodré (30mins) or Belém (15mins). Stamp both sides of your ticket. From the terminus, cross the stone bridge away from the shanty huts and keep walking along
the main road into the woods. The stadium, away to your left, is a 15min walk.

side of the stadium, leaving the west side and
some of the dearer *bancada lateral* free. The
cheaper third ring (*terceiro anel*), with the poorest view, is used by neutrals if it is occupied at
all. The hardcore Benfica mob can be found in
the *topo sul*, behind the south goal. If their numbers are substantial, or to comply with UEFA
regulations for international fixtures, their opposite numbers will be in the *topo norte*.

Swift half

There are no bars around the stadium complex
but quite a few inside it – though note that they
can now only sell alcohol up to two hours before
kick-off. *Ponto Vermelho*, opposite gate #8, is a
bar/restaurant, the bar section having a colourful
collection of pennants. Pay at the cash till first.
Credit cards are accepted at the restaurant
which, like the bar, is open every day.

The bar/cafeteria *O Benfica*, between gates #10 and #11, is more down-to-earth, but the best of the lot is probably the *Sala de Convívio* next door, with original framed pictures from the glory days and red billiard tables.

Club merchandise

The *Loja do Benfica* (open Wed–Sun and matchdays 10am–8pm, most credit cards) is by gate #11. Souvenirs include tins of Benfica biscuits called *Benficookies* and cassettes of the club anthem, *Orfeão do Sport Lisboa e Benfica*.

Ultra culture

Benfica's ultras are the *No Name Boys* and the older *Diabos Vermelhos* from whom they split. The former are the most notorious fan group in Portugal. A new element are the *Grupo Manks*, who occupy a section of the *topo norte*.

In print

The weekly newspaper is *Benfica* (Wednesdays, 120$). Produced by the club, it has a stablemate in the colour monthly *Benfica Ilustrado* (500$).

In the net

Benfica's **official website** can be found at: www.slbenfica.pt. It's well-designed and meticulously updated, but covers all the club's various sports sections, and with so much going on, it can be hard to find what you want. For an **unofficial site** try: www.megabenfica.com.

 Sporting

Estádio José Alvalade, Rua Francisco Stromp
Capacity 52,000 (all-seated)
Colours Green-and-white hooped shirts, black shorts
League champions 1941, 1944, 1947–49, 1951–54, 1958, 1962, 1966, 1970, 1974, 1980, 1982, 2000
Cup winners 1923, 1934, 1936, 1938, 1941, 1945–46, 1948, 1954, 1963, 1971, 1973, 1974, 1978, 1982, 1995
European Cup-Winners' Cup winners 1964

The long wait is over. After a break of 18 years, Sporting Clube of Lisbon finally became champions of Portugal again in 2000. With local rivals Benfica showing no signs of a revival, Sporting have a real chance of becoming the major footballing force in the capital – a status they haven't truly enjoyed since World War II.

With the help of disenchanted former Benfica members, the Viscount of Alvalade founded Sporting in 1906, on land owned by his family. Sporting then spent fifty years moving around the Campo Grande area, until the Alvalade fortune built the stadium which still bears the family name in 1956.

Yet the Lions were at their most successful just before, winning seven titles in eight years from the end of World War II – their last a year before the inauguration of the European Cup. The era of pan-European football coincided broadly with the club's decline. Sporting's only European success has been a Cup-Winners' Cup trophy in 1964 – won on a lucky corner in a replayed final against MTK Budapest.

Prior to 1999/2000, the last domestic title arrived under Malcolm Allison's fiery rule in 1982. Since then there had been promises aplenty from a string of ambitious club presidents, and the club continued its tradition of nurturing young talent in the shape of Jorge Cadete and Luís Figo, among others. Sporting were also, arguably, more astute in signing players from outside Portugal's former colonies than Benfica.

Mineral-water millionaire José de Sousa Cintra made a great show of his election at the start of the decade, carving his name over garish monuments like the huge lion and cascade of water that now guard the main entrance. Cintra was also the first club president to sack Bobby Robson, when Sporting were leading the league in December 1993. Robson headed north to guide Porto to a cup final win over Sporting five months later and to the Portuguese title in 1995 – leaving Cintra's lion to keep a sad and solitary watch over the bulldozers, shacks and shanty huts which still litter a neighbouring plot of land, cleared for a hotel complex which has yet to be built. In 1996 Sporting passed back into the family, albeit only briefly. New president José Roquette, grandson of old Alvalade, quickly announced that Sporting would be the first Portuguese club to be floated on the Lisbon stock exchange.

Yet the success of that plan was dependent on Sporting breaking out of the confines of Portuguese football and grabbing a slice of the increasingly tasty UEFA Champions' League pie. In the summer of 1999, Danish 'keeper Peter Schmeichel chose Sporting as his retirement home and Italian coach Beppe Materazzi was brought in to replace the Croat Mirko Jozić. After just five games of the new season, Materazzi was axed and António Inacio took charge on a caretaker basis. Yet under Inacio, things started to click. Porto led the table at the midway stage, but with Argentine midfielder Aldo Duscher in sparkling form, Sporting snuck ahead, and went into the final game of the season a point clear of the reigning champions. While their rivals fell 2–1 at Marítimo, Sporting sealed the title with a stylish 4–0 win at Salgueiros, with two of the goals, fittingly, coming from Brazilian centre-half André Cruz, who had been outstanding throughout the campaign.

Porto's long domination of the league was over, and for the first time in a generation, it was the green half of Lisbon that took to the streets in celebration. While tough-tackling midfielder José Vidigal was sold to Napoli in the summer, Sporting pulled off a coup by persuading João Pinto to join them from Benfica, then teamed him up with his international team-mate, controversial striker Ricardo Sá Pinto – former fans' favourite at the Alvalade, who would now return from Real Sociedad to spearhead the next phase of the revival.

Here we go!

Metro to **Campo Grande**, 15mins from Restauradores. The stadium will appear as you approach the modern metro station complex.

Just the ticket

The main **ticket office** is by gate #15 at the north end of the stadium nearest the metro stop.

Knee-jerk reaction – Sporting's latest hero

After Sporting's movers and shakers have taken their *socio* seats, the most expensive left are generally the *bancada poente* at 4,000$, followed by the *bancada nascente*. The *superior norte*, at 2,500$, is for the older Sporting fan, except for the far end, through gate #9, which is reserved for visiting supporters. The cheapest spots are with the *Juventude Leonina* and the *Curva Stromp*, through gates #10, #12 and #14, in the *superior sul*. If the queues are painfully slow-moving, often the case, a man sells tickets at a 10% mark-up out of an old shack between the stadium and the *Tipe-Tope* bar.

Swift half

The bars by the corner of Rua Antonio Stromp and Almeda das Linhas de Torres, *O Difícil*, *O Magriço* and the *Tipe-Tope* on the next corner, are popular but unremarkable. The *Boia Verde*, Rua Cipriano Dourado 18, facing the main ticket office, is small and cramped, but the action tends to spill out onto the street.

In the stadium, above gate #8a, is a spacious and unpretentious **supporters' bar**.

Club merchandise

The *Loja Verde* (open Mon–Fri 10.30am–7pm, Sat 9am–1pm & on matchdays, most credit cards) is by gate #2. It offers a modest range of merchandise but is a treat for furry lion collectors.

Ultra culture

Sporting's is the most passionate and organised fan support in Portugal. As the speakers strike up James Brown's *I Feel Good* at every Sporting goal, it's the *Juventude Leonina* who go as bananas as the Godfather of Soul himself.

Meanwhile the other occupants of the *superior sul*, the **Torcida Verde**, have produced the first one-claque fanzine in Portugal, *Curva Stromp*, and a very professional job it is too.

In print

The weekly newspaper, *Sporting* (Tuesdays, 120$), is available at most newsstands in the city.

In the net

The **official site** swaps URLs with impunity, but was last spotted at: www.sportingcp.com. Unlike the Benfica effort, this is a mainly-football site with the latest match reports and photos where they should be – on the homepage.

For a fans' perspective, try the unofficial offering at: members.xoom.com/m3ndonca.

 "Os Belenenses"

Estádio Restelo, Avenida do Restelo, Belém
Capacity 42,000 (all-seated)
Colours Azure blue shirts, white shorts
League champions 1946
Cup winners 1927, 1929, 1933, 1942, 1960, 1989

Belenenses are the only club outside the country's 'Big Three' ever to have won the Portuguese championship. Their one-point victory of 1946 is remembered by only a

tiny minority of today's fans, yet it still reverberates through the residential district of Restelo, overlooking the magnificence of Belém in the far west of the city.

The walk from Belém station up the hill to the club's stonewashed denim-coloured stadium leads you past the finest building in all Lisbon, the Jerónimos monastery. Looking down from the stadium restaurant, the monastery is merely a blip in the panorama of the river Tagus and opposite shoreline – the backdrop for Vasco da Gama's men as they set sail for India five centuries ago. The suspension bridge is a recent but still poetic addition.

As for the compact stadium, two grandstands cover the side terraces. The lower seats are stone slabs, the superior *bancada* blue plastic ones. By the main office is a large carving in a stone wall of José Manuel Soares, the idol of Belenenses. His glory days were shortly before the introduction of the national league in 1934, but his goals took Belenenses to three Lisbon titles before he died in mysterious circumstances in 1931. Blue and white flowers embellish the large dedication, while a much smaller plaque marks the pope's visit in 1991.

There have been no honours for "Os Belenenses" to celebrate since the Pontiff came and went, but an occasional UEFA Cup appearance – along with the odd derby victory over Benfica or Sporting – has kept spirits high, and the relegation of 1997/98 was immediately reversed the following season.

After a season of consolidation in 1999/2000, the appointment of Brazilian coach Marinho Peres and the signing of his compatriots Guga and Fabio Cosme raised hopes of a return to European competition in the not-too-distant future.

Here we go!

Take the suburban train from Cais do Sodré to **Belém**, a 7min journey. Trains run every 30mins and a return ticket is 210$. Cross the pedestrian bridge over the rails, cut by the park along Rua de Belém towards the monastery, then hike up Rua dos Jerónimos. Allow a good 10mins – it's a steep old hike.

Just the ticket

The main **ticket offices** are on each corner behind the goal facing the river. There are only two types of ticket – one for the main stand (*bancada*), the other for the terrace opposite.

Swift half

The bars along the Rua de Belém are geared up for the groups of package tourists visiting the monastery. *Os Jerónimos*, at #78, is the best bet, with fair-priced food. Nearer the ground, *A Rampa*, Rua dos Jerónimos 22b, has pennants, paintings and seafood. Inside the ground, the *Restaurante Varandazul* under the main grandstand has *that* view from its far window, but entrance on matchdays is by reservation only. There is a more modest **bar** nearby.

Ultra culture

Despite, or perhaps because of, their club's recent dip into a lower league, the *Furia Azul* have been more furious than ever lately. Flash choreography brightens the riverside goal and the group's fanzine, *Azulão*, brightens half-time reading.

Club merchandise

The *Loja Azul* below the *Restaurante Verandazul* (open Mon–Fri 10am–1pm & 2–5pm and on matchdays, no credit cards) does a nice line in Belenenses ties, mirrors and watches.

Eat, drink, sleep...

Bars and clubs

The party is slowly winding down in the centre of Lisbon nightlife, the **Bairro Alto**, high up over town. Local residents have suffered 365 Saturday nights a year for decades and would like to get some sleep now, so the local council is encouraging establishments to move to the expanding scene by the docks, ideally near the 25 de Abril bridge by Alcântara station. Before

someone turns off all the lights, take an *Elevador* to the Bairro Alto, an area crisscrossed with bar-filled streets, before making your way down to the docks. The last Cais do Sodré–Alcântara train leaves at 2.30am.

For daytime drinking, try one of the half-a-dozen *miradouros*, open-air bars with panoramic views over the city – there are four on the #28 tram route. Flashier discos have a dress code, and charge anything from 3,000$ admission, the entrance ticket valid for one drink.

To pick up on the ex-pat pub and beach football scene, take the regular train from Cais do Sodré to **Cascais**.

Beefeater Bar, Rua Visconde da Luz 1a. Best expat watering hole in Cascais, offering Sky Sports, pub grub and football chat.

Estádio, Rua São Pedro de Alcântara 11. Beautiful old bar in the Bairro Alto with framed paintings of the Estádio Nacional, vintage local pop tunes on the jukebox and friendly service.

La Lisbona, Rua da Atalaia 196. In a quieter stretch of the Bairro Alto, a checked-tiled bar dominated by football scarves and pictures of Marilyn Monroe.

Lux, Avenida Infantil do Henrique. Reflecting Lisbon's mood swing to the docks, the former owners of the seminal *Frágil* club in the Bairro Alto poured an ocean of money into designing this brash new club, throwing a grand opening bash in late 1998. Near Santa Apolónia station.

Portas Largas, Rua da Atalaia 105. Possibly the best bar in all the Bairro Alto, announced by a huge neon *Record* sign outside. Autographed tiled walls, old transistor radios, great Brazilian music, and hectic bar staff mixing *mojito* cocktails.

Restaurants

For a capital city, Lisbon is a remarkably cheap place to eat out. Apart from the **Bairro Alto**, there are dozens of inexpensive places within five minutes of

Rossio station, especially along the Rua San José/Portas de Santo Antão stretch. **Cacilhas**, by the ferry stop on the opposite shore of the Tagus, has a string of cheap fish restaurants.

Adega do Ribatejo, Rua Diário de Notícias 23. *Adegas* are places with local specialities and fado music. Most are to be avoided, but the *Ribatejo* is probably the best fado house in the Bairro Alto, and certainly the most reasonably priced. Open until midnight. Most credit cards.

Cervejaria Trinidade, Rua Nova do Trinidade 20c. Gorgeous old fish restaurant/beer hall decked out in local *azulejo* tiles. Kitchen open until 1.30am. Most credit cards. Baixa Chiado metro.

Galeto, Avenida da Republica 14a. Atmospheric nighthawks' diner straight out of the Fifties, open until 3am. Prices increase slightly after 11.30pm. Known by every taxi driver. Metro Saldanha.

Sol Nascente, Rua de São Tomé 86. In the old Alfama quarter, under ancient São Jorge castle, a reasonably priced restaurant with a perfect view of a sandy five-a-side pitch and, beyond that, the huge sweep of the Tagus estuary. Tram #12.

Solar dos Presuntos, Rua das Portas de Santo Antão 50. Autographed shirts line the walls of this fairly pricy restaurant, popular with the football community. Namesake pub next door, open evenings only.

Accommodation
Conveniently, the central **Rossio** area is the best for cheap pensions. You may have to shop around in peak season, but the **tourist office** in Palácio Foz by Rossio station can book you a room at no extra charge if it's priced at more than 5,000$ per night.

Residencia Campos, Rua Jardim do Regedor 24 (☎213 462 864). Perfectly located, clean, cheap pension, immediately opposite the Benfica club office and within a minute's jog of Rossio station.

Part of a family-run chain which has three other centrally located places if this one is full. Around 4,500$ for a double.

Hotel Eduardo VII, Avenida Fontes Pereira de Melo 5 (☎213 530 141, fax 213 533 879). If you're going to splash out, this three-star hotel might just be the place to do it. Cable TV and bath with every room, panoramic view from the rooftop restaurant. Around 15,000$ for a double, most major credit cards. Rotunda metro.

Pensão Globo, Rua do Teixeira 37 (☎213 462 279). Efficiently run, in a quiet part of the Bairro Alto near the *elevador da Glória* terminal. Around 4,500$ for a double with a shared bathroom, nearer 7,000$ for your own shower and a view.

Pousada de Juventude de Lisboa, Rua Andrade Corvo 46 (☎213 532 696) The city's main youth hostel has 24-hour reception and double rooms available at around 7,000$, breakfast included. Picoas metro.

Pensão Ninho das Aguias, Costa do Castelo 74 (☎218 867 000). Just below the castle, a bright pension with a fantastic panorama from the terrace. Some rooms with private facilities, about 5,000$ a single, 8,000$ a double. Book ahead. Tram #12.

Oporto

Consolation prize – Porto fans celebrate their cup final win over Sporting in May 2000

The quaint city of Oporto is a strange setting for the new power base in Portuguese football. The first-time visiting fan gets none of the immediate sense of grandeur and football history served up by Lisbon – the main footballing areas are tucked far from the old centre's narrow streets.

To the north, along Rua da Constituição, is where you'll find FC Porto's roots. The Campo da Constituição is where the Dragons played for 30 years. The other side of a huge white wall dotted with plaques, signs and badges is the dusty training pitch once used in earnest by Portugal's first trophy winners. (Porto won both the inaugural cup competition in 1922 and the first national league title in 1935.) The club's youngsters now play there, and a small shop, *A Loja do Dragãozinho*, sells souvenirs to the Young Dragons. The club was formed not far away back in 1906.

A kilometre or so to the east is Porto's modern home, the Estádio das Antas. The affluent setting for a five-year title monopoly and a series of runs in the Champions' League at the end of the Nineties, it is a hive of activity in an otherwise sleepy district, and rapidly becoming a regular fixture in the calendar of Portugal's national team.

To the west is Bessa, enticingly run-down, whose club, Boavista, are Porto's poorer relations. Support in the city itself is polarised and barely affected by tiny Salgueiros, the town's third club.

Local rivalries are nothing, however, compared to the strength of feeling against Lisbon. Many fans in the city regard the media revelations of possible corruption involving their club's ex-coach, António Oliveira, as a sideshow deliberately set up by a vengeful capital to distract attention from Porto's successes.

The *ipso facto* declaration of a media war by Benfica president Vale e Azevedo in 1997 did nothing to dispel the ill feeling. By the same token many *tripeiros* – tripe-eaters, the nickname for those from Porto – tend to overlook the fact that the influential daily *O Jogo* is owned by Porto's Mr Football, Joaquim Oliveira, António's brother. The brothers' *Olivedesportos* TV and sports marketing agency is as much a part of Porto's commercial future as the

European journey – a UCL quarter-final against Bayern was as far as Porto got in 1999/2000

refurbished das Antas stadium and the office complex slowly being built around it – home to the most successful club side in Portuguese league history.

The thrilling fields

 FC Porto

Estádio das Antas, Avenida Fernão de Magalhães

Capacity 76,000

League champions 1935, 1939–40, 1956, 1959, 1978–79, 1985–86, 1988, 1990, 1992–93, 1995–99

Cup winners 1922, 1925, 1932, 1937, 1956, 1958, 1968, 1977, 1984, 1988, 1991, 1994, 2000

European Cup winners 1987

World Club champions 1987

Portugal's team of the Nineties, FC Porto are set upon building a football empire

reminiscent of Benfica's nearly 40 years ago – after decades of living in the shadow of their great Lisbon rivals. Like Benfica and Sporting, Porto moved from their traditional home during the Fifties – to a new stadium, das Antas – as the era of European competition was about to dawn.

Yet the Sixties were to be lean times for the Dragons, without a domestic trophy or a European run of any note. It wasn't until former player José Maria Pedroto took control of the side in the late Seventies that things picked up. Under Pedroto, two title wins and a UEFA Cup final appearance were notched up, while the das Antas got a new stand and extra sports facilities. A key factor on the pitch was the goalscoring prowess of Fernando Gomes, twice Golden Boot winner as the top scorer in Europe, a Porto player since signing as a 15-year-old apprentice in 1971, and a member of the side which lost the Cup-Winners' Cup final to Juventus in 1984.

The team's star performance came three years later, under the inventive coaching of Artur Jorge. Surprise European Cup finalists against Bayern Munich in Vienna, Porto conceded an early goal, then packed their midfield to soak up over an hour of pressure before hitting back with two late strikes to win the game 2–1. Algerian-born Rabah Madjer and Paulo Futre were the stars, and Madjer stayed on, combining with Mendes in the Tokyo snow to help beat Peñarol of Uruguay 2–1 in the World Club championship. Add a European Supercup win over Ajax, and the team had notched up a hat-trick of international honours unique in the history of the Portuguese game.

Still dominating at home, Porto were now carving serious (and increasingly lucrative) inroads into Europe, first under Tomislav Ivić, then under Bobby Robson, who arrived as coach in February 1994, embittered at his shock dismissal from Sporting. Not only did his new charges beat his former employers in that year's cup final, they hammered Werder Bremen 5–0 in Germany to qualify for a Champions' League semi-final. They lost that match to Barcelona, but would run away with the league for the next five seasons.

After Robson left for Barça in the summer of 1996, former national coach António Oliveira stepped in to keep Porto top of the domestic heap.

When Oliveira's successor, Fernando Santos, took over for 1998/99, all the talk was of the *penta*, the record-breaking fifth successive title, subsequently achieved thanks to Brazilian Mário Jardel's third consecutive year as top league goalscorer.

Jardel celebrated a fourth year as the country's best marksman in 1999/2000, averaging more than a goal per game for a final haul of 38. But his club was not celebrating a sixth successive title, Sporting having surprisingly pipped Porto to the championship. If there was a difference between the two teams, it was that Porto had enjoyed another extended European campaign, going through both group phases

Porto essentials

Bus service #56 runs makes the 30min journey between central Praça de Lisboa and the city's **Francisco Sá Carneiro airport** twice an hour (6.30am–midnight, fare 160$). Taxis charge about 3,000$ to follow the same route.

Oporto has two main train stations. **Campanhã** is for mainline trains, while the central **São Bento**, gorgeously decked out in *azulejo* tiles, is for local ones. All trains from São Bento stop at Campanhã, but not vice versa. Bus #35 runs between the two.

Buses (5.30am–1am) are the mainstay of the city's transport system. Tickets, available at *STCP* kiosks, cost 80$ for a central-zone 'T1' single, 750$ for a strip of ten. Stamp the ticket onboard, where otherwise the charge is 160$. A day pass (*bilhete diario*) is 370$, a four-day *turístico* 1,900$. Tickets for the last surviving **tram**, #18, which runs through Boavista, cost 85$.

Taxis have a standing charge of 125$, but no journey in town should cost more than 500–750$. Phone ☎225 073 900 for a *Radiotaxi* if you can't see a cab nearby – although if you have time on your side the city, with its winding, cobbled streets and imposing bridges, is best explored on foot.

The city's new **tourist office** is just off central Avenida dos Aliados at Rua do Clube dos Fenianos 25 (open Mon–Fri 9am–7pm, Sat–Sun 10am–5pm, ☎223 393 470). The *ICEP* office, Praça Dom João I 43 (open Mon–Fri 9am–7pm, Sat–Sun 9.30am–3.30pm, ☎222 057 514), deals with regional information.

Minimal **entertainment information** can be found in the free monthly pamphlet *No Porto 12*, available in bars and cafés. *Casa dos Bandieras*, Rua São João 16–18, just down from São Bento station, is a small store with a decent range of football gear.

of the Champions' League before unluckily losing a quarter-final to Bayern Munich, who scored their second-leg winner in stoppage time. Only a minute earlier, Jardel had silenced Munich's Olympiastadion by scoring to level the aggregate scores at 2–2. It would be the Brazilian's last European goal for the club, Porto's board being unable to turn down a huge £20million offer for his services from the Turkish club Galatasaray during the summer. Part of that fee would be used to sign two new Latin American strikers: Paraguay's Carlos Paredes and Argentine Juan Pizzi.

And despite the loss of both the title and Jardel, the money Porto have earned during their years of domestic and European success has financed a major overhaul of the das Antas stadium, which boasts a new club headquarters and a hi-tech office complex – the sort of development the Lisbon giants can only dream of.

Here we go!

Das Antas is in the far east of town. On matchdays, *STCP* now lays on **special bus services**, free if you can show a match ticket, from the Rotunda da Boavista (Praça Mouzinho de Albuquerque) or Praça Liberdade, passing by Campa 24 Agosto. They leave every 20mins up to an hour before kick-off. Buses leave to go back by the same routes until an hour after the game.

Regular bus #21 from the Rotunda, or #78 from Avenida dos Aliados, operate on the same free system for ticket-holders. If you have to pay, you'll need a two-zone 'T2' bus ticket at 120$.

Just the ticket

Tickets are available a week in advance from both the stadium and city outlets. The biggest of the latter is on the ground floor of the shopping centre at Rua Santa Catarina 326 – look out for the blue and white football-shaped kiosk (open daily 10am–11pm, most credit cards accepted). At the ground, the two main **ticket offices** are the *bilheteiria norte* and *sul*, either side of the *bancada maratona* furthest from the main Avenida.

The most expensive tickets after the *socios* have had their fill are in the *bancada lateral* and *arquibancada*, at 3,000$ and 5,000$ respectively.

Entrance to the *superior norte*, through odd-numbered gates #5–17 around the north goal, are 2,000$; gates #1 and #3 are for visiting fans. Tickets for the *superior sul*, if there are any places left (the *Super Dragões* ultras head through even-numbered gates #4–10), go for around 1,500$.

Swift half

There are a number of bars along the main road from town, Avenida Fernão de Magalhães. *O Braseiro das Antas* at #1532 is a cheap, friendly place for a beer and a bite, specialising in tripe *à la Porto*. *Cafeteria Satelite*, at #1556, has footie on cable television.

At the *Restaurante Azul e Branco*, nearer town at #1227, blue and white cover everything, including the toilets, and on the wall sits a caricature of the 1987 European Cup-winning team.

Right behind the stadium's *superior norte* is the *Cafeteria Pião*, recently modernised, with Porto souvenirs on sale behind the bar.

Club merchandise

The *Loja Azul* by gate #10 (open Mon–Fri 10am–7pm and on matchdays, most credit cards) sells small bottles of port in presentation boxes bearing the club badge, and a range of crockery in the local *azulejo* style.

You can also buy Porto bicycles, Porto pagers, a Porto television or a Porto CD hi-fi system.

Ultra culture

Complacency has set in around the *superior sul* as the main ultra gang, the *Super Dragões*, have lost their fire. To keep the flame alive, on the opposite side of the ground the *Colectivo Curva Norte* have begun to come up with some inventive choreography, as have the *Movimento Portuense*.

In print

The club's matchday programme (100$) is available at the ground, its full-colour monthly, *Dragões* (500$), at newsstands throughout town.

In the net

The official Porto website has good depth of content but is a bit graphics-heavy for its own good at: www.fcporto.pt.

Boavista

Estádio do Bessa, Rua O Primeiro de Janeiro
Capacity 20,000
Colours Black-and-white chessboard shirts, black
shorts
Cup winners 1975–76, 1979, 1992, 1997

Regular if unsuccessful performers in
Europe, and without a league title in their
entire history, Oporto's second team,
Boavista Futebol Clube, command a passionate local following.

English bosses and Portuguese work-
ers of *Graham's* textile factory began kicking
a ball about in Ciríaco Cardoso off Avenida
da Boavista in 1903. By 1905, they had
moved to a site nearer the current do
Bessa stadium, and given themselves a
name: Boavista Footballers. This happy
union lasted four years, until natives and
expats fell out over which weekend day to
play on. A general meeting on 30 April
1909 decreed that the now renamed Boavista Futebol Clube would play on Sundays
– and they have been drawing their support from the surrounding factories and
farms ever since.

The team achieved nothing for decades,
but not long after the homely Estádio do
Bessa was built in 1972, Boavista began to
take on the big boys. Three cup wins in
quick succession – the black-and-whites
missed out on the double by two league
points in 1976 – pointed to a bright future
in the Eighties but, despite the arrival of
João Alves, the black-gloved Portuguese
international, the club were always playing
in the shadow of the Big Three.

João Pinto, the striker who captained
Portugal to victory in the World Youth
Cup of 1991, had joined Boavista eight
years earlier at the age of 12. He led them
to a 2–1 cup final win over Porto in 1992,
before departing for Benfica.

The team which next won the cup in
1997 was dismantled when Nuno Gomes
and Erwin Sánchez were sold to Benfica,
and Jimmy Floyd Hasselbaink to Leeds. But
Sánchez would return to line up alongside
club captain Ion Timofte, defender Hélder
and Ghanaian striker Ayew to launch a

Check mate – Boavista played some good football in their first Champions' League appearance

creditable shot at the title in 1998/99. Under personable coach Jaime Pacheco, the *Axadrezada* ('Checks') went the first dozen games unbeaten, including a memorable 2–0 win at Porto. Dropped points against mediocre opponents put paid to championship ambitions, but a second-place finish was enough to give Boavista a first-ever crack at the Champions' League.

Meanwhile, the transformation of the Bessa into a 30,000 all-seater stadium continued apace, with a new 'Dallas' stand opening in time for the 1999/2000 season, its construction overseen by Olimpia de Magalhães – long recognised for his efforts in building the original Bessa by a plaque there in his honour.

The new stand witnessed Boavista giving a decent enough account of themselves in the Champions' League, but at home a fourth-place finish, 24 points off the title pace, was disappointing after the progress of recent seasons. At the end of the campaign, coach Pacheco announced an end to the club's policy of importing cheap foreign talent and promised a renewed focus on homegrown players.

Here we go!

All routes, it seems, lead to Boavista. Romantics should take tram #18 from Rua do Ouro by the river. More prosaically, modern buses include the #3, #19 and #24 from central Praça da Liberdade, #78 from central Avenida dos Aliados or #21 from as far as Porto's das Antas stadium.

Swift half

The unnamed **club bar** by the *bilheteiria*, decked out in black-and-white tiles, has the feel of a fish-and-chip shop. Pay for your order at the till first. There's *Golden Beer* on draught, though not on matchdays. Nearer the Avenida da Boavista, *Pavihão Dr Acácio Lello*, Rua de O Primeiro de Janeiro 278, on the corner next to the club shop, has an impressive pennant collection and framed team pics behind a long bar counter.

Club merchandise

The *Loja Axadrezada*, Rua de O Primeiro de Janeiro 278 (Mon–Fri 10am–1pm & 3–7pm and

matchdays, most credit cards), has a small array of striking Boavista gear as well as more general leisurewear items.

Salgueiros

Estádio Vidal Pinheiro, Rua Álvares Cabral
Capacity 11,000
Colours Red shirts, white shorts

Gaze around Salgueiros' humble home, its corrugated shack of a stand showering rust over any visiting VIPs, its floodlights with half the bulbs missing, set against a background of washer women, barking dogs, car repair sheds and encroaching tower blocks, and ask yourself – how on earth does this club compete with the rest of Portugal's top flight, let alone the big three?

But compete they do, as the graffiti (*'Ten Years Of Love'*) proudly proclaims. This club from the working-class Paranhos area have managed to stay afloat since gaining promotion in 1990, coming close to a UEFA Cup place for the last three seasons running. Their only previous European appearance, when they went out on penalties to Cannes in the 1991/92 UEFA Cup, is best noted for being Zinedine Zidane's first match in European competition.

Patching up their stadium every summer while continually drawing up plans for a new one between the Cintura Interna highway and Rua de Monsanto, a kilometre away, like the washer women Salgueiros roll up their sleeves and get on with the job. With Brazilian Dito as coach and his compatriot, new signing Celso upfront, and midfielder Abílio as the team's lungs, the team produced some more excellent performances in 1998/99, not least a 2–1 win over then unbeaten Sporting in December.

Sporting returned to Salgueiros to claim the championship on the last day of the 1999/2000 season, leaving their hosts in 14th place. It was an indication of the club's modest status that its board spent the following summer trying to persuade Porto to allow Hungarian Miki Feher to remain at Salgueiros on loan for another year.

On the rare occasions when TV cameras visit for an evening game, as they did for Sporting's championship-claiming fixture, matches are played at the Estádio Prof Dr Vieira de Carvalho in Maia, 10km north of Porto on the A3/A4.

Here we go!

Bus #79 from central Avenida dos Aliados to Rua do Augusto Lessa. Bus #6 also runs within walking distance of the ground.

Swift half

The best bet near the stadium is the **Bufete Gondalães** at Rua do Augusto Lessa 253. *Patrocina* bars stand at diagonal corners inside the stadium.

Just the ticket

The **ticket windows** are along Rua do Augusto Lessa. Visitors are allocated a spot through gate #3a, otherwise take your pick. The programme *Vozes do Salgueiros* is handed out free.

Eat, drink, sleep…

Bars and clubs

The two main areas for nightlife are to be found either side of the Douro, in the **Ribeira** (north bank) and **Vila Nova de Gaia** areas. From under the seedy scaffolding that props up Ribeira, the bright, expensive lights of Vila Nova de Gaia entice you across the Dom Luis I bridge. The port wine company names dominate the hillside in Hollywood-sized letters, but while many wine lodges offer free samples during the day, their cafés charge a fortune at night. In contrast Ribeira, especially Rua Fonte Taurina, is a dank hive of cheap bars and artful dodgers.

The **Foz** area down by the ocean (bus #78 from Avenida dos Aliados, or about 1,500$ in a taxi) is the main disco area; some places have a dress code, and may charge 1,000–1,500$ entrance which includes a drink.

Agua Boca, Rua Prof Augusto Nobre 451. Brazilian disco bar off Avenida da Boavista with live music Wed–Sun. Brazilian drinks and snacks. Four bar areas, jeans OK, entrance fee Fri–Sun.

Cosa Nostra, Rua S João 74. Between São Bento station and Ribeira, the best of three popular neighbouring clubs. Two floors without any real dance area, but plenty of smoky alcoves. Free entry, 400$ a beer. Your drinks are run up on a slate which you'll have to settle before staggering out at dawn.

Encontro dos Amigos, Rua Fonte Taurina 78/80. Genuine football hangout in the heart of Ribeira, embellished with scarves, cheap food and local colour.

"Os Ribeirenses", Rua Cimo do Muro da Ribeira 62/63. Atmospheric setting for this modest football bar, home to Ribeira FC, above the waterfront overlooking the Douro.

Ryan's, Rua do Infante D Henrique 18. Just inland from Ribeira, the city's main Irish pub has football on TV (not Sky) and fine dinners. Open daily 9pm–2am.

Restaurants

Fourteenth-century legend has it that Porto's residents gave away all their meat to feed the lost expedition to Ceuta, now Spanish Morocco. The **tripe** could not be transported, and the local cuisine has been based around it ever since. Fish – particularly cod (*bacalhão*) – is also a staple, popularly sampled in the row of tourist restaurants along Cais da Ribeira.

Café Luso, Praça Carlos Alberto 91. Atmospheric café serving cheap snacks and lunches, in an area packed with daytime workers' caffs.

Casa da Filha da Mãe Preta, Cais da Ribeira 40. Busy place overlooking the Douro, perfect for an early evening bite before plunging into

Ribeira. Good-value tourist menu at 1,600$. No credit cards.

Galiza, Rua do Campo Alegre 55. Just west of the centre, Campo Alegre has several late-night eateries. This is probably the cheapest, with a tourist menu at 1600$. Cod a speciality. Open until 2am. No credit cards.

Terreirinho, Largo do Terreirinho 7. Fish restaurant tucked away in Ribeira and owned by Porto club president Pinto da Costa. Cod and salmon are the specialities. Most credit cards.

Accommodation

Invariably the cheapest rooms are near **São Bento** train station, but be sure to have a look at yours first. You'd be better off, warmer and probably safer spending a little more money either side of **Avenida dos Aliados**.

Hotel Antas, Rua Padre Manuel Nóbrega da Costa 111 (☎225 503 008, fax 225 500 503). A stone's throw from Porto's das Antas stadium, this three-star hotel charges 11,500$ for a twin – 1,000$ less for a single and out of high season, breakfast included. Most major credit cards.

Pensão Estoril, Rua de Cedofeita 193 (☎222 002 751, fax 222 005 152, e-mail estoril@ iname.com). Good-value single, double, triple and quadruple rooms at 4,500–8,000$, all with private bath and TV. Cafeteria and billiard room downstairs. A 10min walk from the Torre dos Clérigos. Visa accepted.

Pousada da Juventude, Rua de Rodrigues Lobo 98 (☎226 177 257, fax 226 177 247). The city's only youth hostel is 4km west of the centre – take bus #35 from Campanhã station or Avenida dos Aliados. Clean rooms, curfew at midnight, around 1,500–2,000$ a bed.

Hotel Peninsular, Rua Sá da Bandeira 21 (☎222 003 012, fax 222 084 984). A slight climb from São Bento station, a former monastery building with a decent range of rooms from 4,000$ including breakfast.

Romania

Federatia Română de Fotbal, Bd Poligrafiei 3, Sector 1, R-71556 Bucharest
☎01/224 2983   Fax 01/224 0661   E-mail frf@com.pcnet.ro

League champions Dinamo Bucharest   **Cup winners** Dinamo Bucharest
Promoted Foresta Fălticeni, Gaz Metan Medias   **Relegated** Farul Constanta, Onesti,
CSM Resita, Extensiv Craiova

European participants 2000/01 Dinamo Bucharest (UCL qualifiers); Rapid
Bucharest, Universitatea Craiova (UEFA Cup); Ceahlaul Piatra Neamt (Intertoto Cup)

'There could have been a revolution that night,' was how one Steaua Bucharest supporter reflected on the celebrations which followed his team's triumph in the 1986 European Cup. For the first time in decades, thousands of people filled the streets of the capital, singing, drinking and revelling in success, without the presence of Nicolae Ceauşescu and his cronies pushing them into line and telling them how lucky they were to be Romanian. It was spontaneous. It was liberating. For a few hours, the people of Bucharest controlled the streets – and there must have been more than a few nervous generals wondering whether the success of their own army team would end in tears.

In the end, there was no need for tanks or show trials – the celebration of Steaua's victory remained just that, and it was to be another three years before the army had to decide which side it was on.

The Romanian revolution of 1989 allowed the nation's footballers to pack their bags and cross the once strictly-guarded borders into the world of sports cars, luxury villas and agents' commissions. The generation of Gheorghe Hagi, Gica Popescu, Dan Petrescu and Marius Lăcătuş moved abroad *en masse*. Even with the dictator dead and buried, life was hard in Romania and there was no way the likes of Steaua could stop their stars from going West. After parading their talents at Italia '90, these players had a chance not only to boost their bank balances but to develop their skills, tactical awareness and profes-

Beating England again – Dan Petrescu, 2000

....

sional mentality. The results were plain for the world to see four years later, as the Romanians, along with their Bulgarian neighbours, turned the World Cup form book on its head with display after display of fluent, attacking football. With Yugoslavia in crisis, USA '94 signalled a shift in power in the Balkan footballing world, and the former grand old hotels of Bucharest,

Basics

Post-Communist, post-Ceauşescu Romania, is **corrupt** and **chaotic**, with places opening and closing almost overnight, and 'customer service' a contradiction in terms.

This will become abundantly clear if you have to visit your local Romanian embassy to arrange your visa. EU, Canadian, Australian and New Zealand citizens are charged between $30–40 for a 30-day visa, which as of January 2000 can no longer be purchased at the border. The Romanian embassy in the UK is at 4 Palace Green, Kensington, London, W8 4QD (☎020/7937 9666, fax 0209737 8069). American citizens need only fill out an immigration form on arrival. Along with your passport stamp, you will be given a *talon de lesire* to slip in with it – do not lose this under any circumstances.

The Romanian **currency** is the leu, plural lei. The rate at the time of going to press was around L30,000 to £1. Most hotels accept payment in hard currency only, but payment for everyday items is in local currency. The only coins you're likely to see are for L100 and L500, after which there are notes for L1,000, L5,000, L10,000, L50,000 and L100,000. Take US dollars or Deutschmarks in small denominations, as you may have problems changing leftover lei back into foreign currency. Do not change money on the **black market**, but shop around for the best rate at one of the many private exchange offices – banks are laughably slow and rarely open after noon. Keep your receipts, as you may have to show them when paying for accommodation or long-distance transport tickets in lei. Upmarket hotels, shops and restaurants accept credit cards, otherwise this is a cash economy. Cash machines can be found around Bucharest, but are pretty rare elsewhere.

To call Romania from outside the country, the international code is 40; add a 1 for Bucharest. Around Bucharest you'll find **orange phones** for international calls – **phonecards** at L20,000 and L50,000 are sold from metro station machines and at main post offices. The international access code is 00, and calls to Western Europe cost around L18,000 a minute, with no cheap-rate period. Blue **coin phones**, accepting L100 pieces, are best for local calls.

Trains are cheap and the best way to get around Romania, but anything less than an *InterCity* or *Rapid* will be painfully slow. For a small supplement, you can book in advance up to a day before your journey at railway (*CFR*) offices, or at the station an hour before departure at specific windows.

TAROM deals with domestic **flights**, with fares fixed at the lei equivalent of $40–70 for foreigners – book 36 hours in advance.

which once attracted traders from across the continent, were suddenly filled with the cigar smoke of players' agents.

Like other Balkan leagues, the domestic Romanian competition has suffered as a result of these defections to the West, but despite all the problems, the talent just seems to keep on coming through. To a working-class Romanian lad, a career in football offers much more than a decent salary – it holds out the possibility of the kind of lifestyle even the highest state official in the land could not imagine. Perhaps that explains why, like their counterparts

in Belgrade or Istanbul, Bucharest kids kick a ball around on any spare patch of land they can find – coats-for-goalposts stuff.

Attendances for Romanian league games may be low and match-fixing may still be endemic, but public interest in the game is high and the careers of foreign-based players are closely chronicled by a number of new sports papers and TV shows that have sprung up in recent years.

This corner of the Balkans, then, differs from much of post-Communist Eastern Europe. In Russia, Poland, Hungary and Slovakia, the local footballing greats are

Never can say goodbye – Hagi's red card seems bow out of Euro 2000, but is he gone for good?

captured in fading photos and appear only for cheesy team reunions. In Romania the legends are living, and international matches draw huge crowds keen to get re-acquainted with their heroes.

It's not just the power of the present that reduces the need for nostalgia – there isn't much of a past to speak of. Until the emergence of the Hagi generation, Romania had rarely produced players of note. While East European football was booming in the days of Stalinism, Romania sat on the sidelines, and it wasn't until the era of *glasnost* (which passed Romania by) that the country began to make an impression on the international scene.

Which is not to say that Romania has no footballing tradition. The game arrived at the turn of the century via British workers who, while developing industry in Western Romania and commerce in Bucharest, demonstrated football to the locals. In 1908 the Romanian FA was formed, and two years later a national competition was begun. Bucharest teams dominated from the start, but in the early years the oil town of Ploieşti and the indus-

trial cities in and around Transylvania could boast teams capable of challenging the capital's supremacy. Between the wars, Bucharest had four major teams (Olimpia, Colentina, Venus and Juventus), Ploieşti produced United (later Prahova), and Timişoara had two successful clubs, Ripensia and Chinezul, the latter winning seven titles in a row in the Twenties. The spontaneous growth of clubs across the country created some fascinating local derbies, while the diverse ethnic nature of pre-war Romania saw the creation of Jewish, Hungarian, Serbian and German sides.

Sadly, few of these teams survived World War II and the subsequent Communist restructuring of football. The Soviet-backed authorities wanted each provincial city to be represented by only a single team, and created giant, centralised ministry sports clubs in the capital. The consequences were predictable. Barring occasional successes for UT Arad, Petrolul Ploieşti and Universitatea Craiova, the Romanian championship became the preserve of Steaua Bucharest (backed by the military) and their city rivals Dinamo (supported by the interior ministry). And, by and large, it has remained so ever since.

In the international arena, the Romanians have tended to plot their own idiosyncratic path. The national team did not take the field until 14 years after the founding of the FA, and even then they rarely ventured further than the Balkans. By the early Thirties, however, Romania was keen to embrace international competition, and King Carol gladly accepted an invitation to send a squad to the inaugural World Cup in Uruguay in 1930, even picking the players himself. Yet the Romanians failed to get past the first round in Montevideo, and suffered the same fate in Italy in 1934 and in France four years later.

Romania's Communist authorities were less enthusiastic about testing their footballers' mettle. Between 1947 and 1955 the national side played only against other Communist states, and though they reached the quarter-finals of the inaugural European Championship in 1960, they did not enter the 1962 World Cup at all.

After finishing top of their qualifying group for the 1970 World Cup in Mexico, Romania were drawn in a tough section alongside reigning champions England, the eventual winners Brazil and a strong Czechoslovakia. There was never any hope of progressing but the Romanians beat Czechoslovakia and lost their other two games by only a single goal.

It was to be 20 years before they made the final stages of the World Cup again. In between, Romania made a brief and generally rather ugly appearance at the 1984 European Championship finals in France. But at Italia '90, despite again being drawn in a tough group, they began to show another side to their game. Inspired by the diminutive Hagi, the Romanians beat the Soviet Union with two goals from Lăcătuş in their opening game, then bounced back from defeat by Roger Milla's Cameroon to draw 1–1 with Maradona's Argentina. That took them through to the second round, where Hagi's creativity was stifled by the strong-arm tactics of the Irish midfield; the game finished goalless and Romania went out on penalties.

If their football in Italy had been tasty, it turned out to be only an appetiser for what was to come. Four years later, in the USA, Romania were simply the most attractive side in the competition. They attacked from the start in their opening game against one of the favourites, Colombia, winning 3–1 thanks to two goals from Florin Răducioiu and an extraordinary long-distance curler from Hagi. A 4–1 defeat by Switzerland in the next game might have knocked earlier Romanian sides out of their stride; but under the astute coaching of Anghel Iordănescu the squad regrouped, and a 1–0 win over the host nation took them through to the second round – and a rematch with Argentina which would prove the game of the tournament. The score was 2–1 to Iordănescu's men after just 18 minutes, with left-winger Ilie Dumitrescu having scored both Romanian goals – the first a Hagi-style lob, the second the outcome of a stunning, length-of-the-field counter-attack. In the second half, Hagi made it three and though the Argentinians fought back with a goal from Abel Balbo, Romania held on for a famous win.

The team's quarter-final with Sweden was similarly packed with incident. With his side trailing by the only goal, Răducioiu scored with just two minutes left to take the game into extra-time, and five minutes into the extended game he scored again. Alas, Romanian 'keeper Florin Prunea suffered a rush of blood to the head, seven minutes from time, to allow Kennet Andersson to equalise and force another shoot-out. All the world bar Sweden were hoping for a Brazil–Romania semi, but reckoned without the acrobatics of Swedish 'keeper Thomas Ravelli, whose grinning face still haunts fans in Bucharest.

Despite the disappointment, the Romanian team returned home to a heroes' welcome. Politicians and press alike lapped up the international tributes – Romania had attained the status of a major footballing power.

While still showing sparks of magic, Romania were disappointing at Euro '96 and France '98. The side had aged, and not all the players' individual careers had gone as planned. Răducioiu and Dumitrescu went off the rails after unsuccessful spells in England. Hagi and the team's elegant sweeper-cum-anchorman, Popescu, were playing out their careers in Turkey.

Yet coach Iordănescu, a national hero who'd earned himself the rank of honorary colonel in the Romanian army, oversaw a bright qualifying path to a third consecutive World Cup finals, with the team back to their spirited, indulgent, almost arrogant best.

Once in France, Romania were coolly impressive, shutting out Colombia to win 1–0 thanks to Adrian Ilie's deft strike, then beating England 2–1 with Hagi's prompting and goals from Viorel Moldovan and Dan Petrescu. Revelling in their unexpected early qualification for the knockout phase, the Romanians dyed their hair blond, but an under-strength team could then only scrape a draw with Tunisia.

Against Croatia in the second round, the blond hair remained but Romania were no longer relaxed. On a hot afternoon in Bordeaux, Hagi and his fellow veterans were out-run and out-thought by opponents favouring a similar counter-attacking stance. The penalty that gave the Croats the lead may have been controversially awarded, but Romania, looking uncomfortable when asked to chase the game, had no answer to it. Hagi was substituted, and bowed out. Iordănescu did likewise, having been lured away to take charge of Greece.

His replacement was Victor Pițurca, once imprisoned by the Ceaușescu regime and by no means a universally popular choice. Part of the problem was his long-term involement with Steaua Bucharest, champions for the third year running in 1998 thanks to a series of murky results on the last day of the season.

The Romanians started their Euro 2000 campaign brightly enough, beating Liecht-

enstein 7–0 and Portugal, with a last-minute strike in Oporto, 1–0. But the draws that followed, 1–1 in Hungary and 0–0 at home to Slovakia, put qualification – and Pițurca's job – in jeopardy. Hagi's decision to come out of retirement to help the side to a 2–0 win at home to Hungary, Romania's first-ever against their oldest footballing enemy, was the cue for a resurgence in confidence, effectively securing a Euro 2000 place. But Hagi and Popescu then led a player *putsch* against Pițurca, who was replaced by the veteran Emerich Jenei before the team travelled to the Low Countries.

Jenei, who had led Steaua to that 1986 European Cup triumph and the national team to Italia '90, was a politically astute choice, able to command the respect of the Iordănescu generation while introducing the new blood the squad so badly needed. Fresh from their UEFA Cup success with Galatasaray, Hagi and Popescu were determined to end their international careers on a high, yet their lingering presence led many pundits to write them off as an ageing team with little chance of making an impact at Euro 2000.

The pundits were wrong. Romania deserved more than a 1–1 draw against Germany in their opening game, and managed to stifle Portugal's effortless creativity for 95 minutes before conceding a goal in stoppage time. Defeat in that match in Arnhem meant that Romania faced an England side needing just a point to make it into the quarter-finals – and without the suspended Hagi. Romania outclassed England from start to finish, the absence of Hagi liberating younger players such as left-back Christian Chivu and attacking midfielder Adrian Mutu. Chivu's cross-shot opened the scoring in the 21st minute, and although England fought back with two goals before the break, Dorinel Munteanu crucially pulled Romania level just three minutes after the restart, seizing on Nigel Martyn's goalkeeping error. When, two minutes from time, Phil Neville brought down another young star, Ioan Ganea, in the penalty area, Ganea simply held on to

Crowd pleasers – Romania's travelling support is growing in numbers and in confidence

the ball, selected himself to take the spot-kick, and fired his country into the quarter-finals. The 3–2 win triggered mass street celebrations across Romania, but it came at a price. Petrescu, Cosmin Contra and Adrian Ilie were all suspended and would miss the next game against Italy, as would the injured Popescu. Hagi returned for another farewell, and ended his international career with a red card after a disgraceful late challenge on Antonio Conte. Romania lost 2–0.

It was a sad ending to a great personal footballing story, but the tournament had shown Romanian fans – and the wider European game – that the country had a new generation capable of better things. Jenei handed over the reins to Ladislau Bölöni, a member of Romania's Euro '84 squad, and while the new man made the expected plea with Hagi to reconsider his international 'retirement', some critics wondered if the national side would be better off without him.

Bölöni had spent more than a decade coaching in French football, and returned to a domestic game which, while still pro-

ducing young talent, was still awash with stories of suicide, murder and embezzlement – colourful, perhaps, but far from the ideal in a country in love not just with football but with its most idealistic incarnation.

Essential vocabulary
Hello *Salut*
Goodbye *La revedere*
Yes *Da*
No *Nu*
Two beers, please *Două beri vă rog*
Thank you *Mulţumesc*
Mens' *Toaletă bărbati*
Women's *Toaletă femei*
Where is the stadium? *Unde este stadionul?*
What's the score? *Cît este scorul?*
Referee *Arbitru*
Offside *Ofsaid*

Match practice
The predictable nature of the Romanian championship is slowly breaking up, with the emergence of Rapid, Naţional and Rocar in Bucharest and provincial teams such as Arges Piteşti, FCM Bacău and Oţelul Galaţi to take on the Communist-era

giants, Steaua and Dinamo. Alas, stadium facilities in Romania are predictably poor. Many of the grounds are in an advanced state of disrepair. Crowds are low, but the big derbies in Bucharest can pull in over 20,000, while any major international will probably sell out. Romanian economic development in general has been much slower than in many former Communist countries, and there has been little growth in football-related business such as merchandising. The flip side of this is that ticket prices remain incredibly cheap.

The Romanian season follows the classic East European model, beginning in mid-August, taking a break in November, then restarting in early March to finish in late May or early June.

Kick-off times vary (check the day's sports papers) but are usually 3pm and 5pm on a Saturday afternoon. A couple of matches in each round are rescheduled for Saturday evening and Sunday to be shown live on television.

A different league

Romania's top flight (*Divizia A*) was reduced from 18 to 16 teams in 2000. The *Divizia B* is still divided regionally, east and west, both with 18 teams each, and the champions of each swap places with the bottom two of *Divizia A* at the end of each season. *Divizia C* is further regionalised, with six leagues of 18 teams each.

Up for the cup

The *Tuborg Kupa României* begins with a series of preliminary rounds in July before the first round in August, matches being decided on one game, extra-time and penalties if necessary, until two-leg quarter-finals in December. The semi-finals, also two-legged, take place in April, followed by the final in May, usually played at the Lia Manoliu stadium. A regionalised League Cup takes place in May and June, at least taken seriously by Universitea Cluj director Ion Maja in 1998, when he refused to let his team accept their silver medals after they lost the final on a golden goal to Bacău.

Just the ticket

Few games sell out, so join the local punters at the kiosks. Smaller grounds simply offer *intrare generală*, an across-the-board entry, at L10-15,000. At the larger ones in Bucharest, the cheapest places are the *peluze*, behind the goals, costing around L15,000; a place in the stand, sometimes divided into *tribuna 2* (opposite main stand) and *tribuna 1* (main stand), will cost L30–40,000. *Tribuna 0* are the best seats, possibly even plastic ones, and run from L50,000. For derby games, go to the stadium and buy your ticket in advance.

Half-time

Sunflower seeds (*seminţe*) are hawked around grounds by gyspies, who seem to have a monopoly on the pet-food-for-fans service sector in the former Eastern Bloc. Better stadia will have a kiosk selling simple sandwiches and soft drinks, and you might find a street trader grilling up Turkish-style meatballs. Local snacks include *gogosi*, Romanian doughnuts, and *covrigi*, pretzels, both wolfed down in great quantities.

Alcohol is banned from all football grounds, although the police usually turn a blind eye to a hip flask; watch closely and you will often see the police passing one among themselves.

There is no tradition of fans drinking together in bars before matches, but local restaurants attract a brisk trade after the final whistle.

The back page

Of the three main sports dailies, *Pro Sport* (L2,500) is the best, especially its excellent weekend edition, which carries full transport and ticket details for every game. (Its glossy sister weekly, *Pro Sport Magazin* (L6,000), is more downmarket, full of interviews and chat.) *Gazeta Sporturilor* (L2,000) has done a fair job of shedding its text-heavy image from the old days with splashes of colour and reasonable international coverage. *Sportul Românesc* (L2,000) does a similar job. The other weekly is *Fotbal Plus* (L2,500), very much from the old school, but with everything the domestic fan might need.

Action replay

State channels TVR1 and TVR2 show one live league game every Saturday, plus Romanian internationals and the big European club games. Another league game is shown at a different time live on Antena 1. The best highlights and analysis show is Pro Sport's *Procesul Etapa*, at 11pm on Sundays, after a brief look at the day's goals following the evening news at 8pm.

Of the foreign coverage, Prima occasionally shows English Premiership action on Saturdays at 5pm, while Acasa has one Italian and one Spanish game on Sundays, plus a round-up of German *Bundesliga* action on Sunday afternoons.

Ultra culture

The idea of independent fans' organisations, like the idea of independent organisations in general, was anathema to the old Communist regime. Since the revolution loose fan groups have sprung up at many clubs, and away travel has become much more popular. Ultra groups do exist at Steaua and Rapid, but they are very loosely organised and some amount to little more than a big banner.

There have been waves of hooliganism, however. Steaua fans cut up rough in 1998, first wrecking buses in Craoiva, then attacking coach Mihai Stoichiță's house with a water cannon. Stoichiță then revealed to the press that he carried a gun at all times, at which point every other important figure in the game revealed likewise.

Derbies involving Steaua often attract trouble, and L10million worth of damage was caused to the stadium after the Steaua–Dinamo game in November 1998.

On the up side, Romanian fans are extremely knowledgeable about the European game and large numbers of young people speak foreign languages – a quick word with the lad in the scarf on the tram should provide you with an expert commentator for the game and, more than

likely, a companion for post-match drinking and analysis.

To get up to date on the latest gossip, take a trip to Cişmigiu Park in the centre of Bucharest, close to Eroilor metro stop. Here you will find old men playing chess, drinking coffee and arguing furiously about players and tactics. As many as a hundred old-timers gather at a time in what for decades has been the unofficial open-air forum of Romanian football.

In the net

The Romanian FA has an official site, but its scope is rather limited thus far. Check its progress at: www.frf.pcnet.ro.

Alex Tóth's long-running *Romanian Soccer Page* is the best unofficial generic site, at: www.webcom.rom/~timis/soccer.html. There's a feast of stats and historical info, and each top-flight club gets a miniature homepage of its own. You'll also find the latest transfer news courtesy of the Timişoara paper *Fotbal Vest*, soccer stories (in Romanian) from the daily *Ziua*, and an audio link to Radio Bucharest, along with recent additions such as news from neighbouring Moldova and a separate section devoted to European competition.

Alex himself is a long-suffering Politehnica fan who inscribes his site with the words: 'You do not support your team because they are the best, or because they are successful, but because you have grown up with them and they are part of you.'

Bucharest

It may no longer live up to its Twenties nickname of 'the Paris of the Balkans', but neither is modern Bucharest the living nightmare it was under the Ceauşescu regime. And, despite the obvious poverty of most of its clubs, it remains a city where football is taken seriously, and where the long tradition of a resourceful and flamboyant style of play is studiously upheld.

The thrilling fields

 Steaua

Stadionul Ghencea, Bdul Ghencea 35
Capacity 30,000
Colours Red with blue trim
League champions 1951–53, 1956, 1960–61, 1968, 1976, 1978, 1985–89, 1993–98
Cup winners 1949–52, 1955, 1962, 1966–67, 1976, 1979, 1985, 1987–89, 1992, 1996–97, 1999
European Cup winners 1986

Post-Communist reality has caught up with Steaua Bucharest. The first East European club to win the European Cup back in 1986, they were the favoured team of Romania's politically powerful armed forces. For several years after the revolution they maintained their position as the *de facto* team of the still influential army, and state cash and facilities remained available to them. The neo-Communist regime of Ion Iliescu, who took control of the country after the 1989 revolution, was happy to maintain the *status quo* with regard to the army, and Steaua continued to have the pick of the nation's best players and coaches – they maintained their domestic dominance with five consecutive titles.

But now the army has NATO integration on its mind rather than the Champions' League, and the government has the IMF demanding public spending cuts. Try telling General Wesley Clark and

the World Bank that Steaua need a new centre-half, and you're unlikely to get a sympathetic fax by return.

In the last three years Romania's pro-market reformers have forced Steaua to compete on the same terms as everyone else, and in the struggle to adjust, the club has seen its closest rivals Rapid and Dinamo take honours while Steaua have struggled to muster as much as a UEFA Cup spot.

The club were formed as Armata in 1947 but two years later changed their name to CSCA, subsequently shortened to CCA. They became Steaua in 1962. Although successful in the late Fifties and early Sixties, they played second fiddle to Dinamo from the mid-Sixties on – a change which, according to some local observers, reflected a shift in the balance of power between Romania's army and the interior ministry, which ran Dinamo.

It was a totally different story in the Eighties. But, while many fans might have predicted that Steaua's league and cup double win of 1985 would be the launchpad for an era of prolonged domestic domination for the club, few foresaw the scale of the glory that would come the team's way only a year later. Almost unnoticed, Steaua beat Rangers and Anderlecht on their way to a European Cup final rendezvous with Terry Venables' Barcelona in Seville. With 70,000 Spaniards baying for their blood, Steaua set their stall out early, and concentrated on defence. An ethnic Serb, Miodrag Belodedici, swept up calmly at the back, while an ethnic Hungarian who just happened to be Romania's most-capped international, Ladislau Bölöni, sacrificed his usual role as a forward to snap at the heels of the opposing midfield.

Even so, a Barça side containing Bernd Schuster and Steve Archibald was beginning to make inroads until, in the second half, Steaua coach Emerich Jenei brought on Anghel Iordănescu as a substitute. Iordănescu was a 36-year-old veteran who

Bucharest essentials

Bucharest's Otopeni **airport** is 16km north of the city centre. Bus #783 (about every 30mins, 5am–11pm, journey time 30mins) runs from outside the arrivals terminal to major hotels in town, terminating at Piaţa Unirii. Return tickets (L12,000) should be bought from the small *RATB* booth outside the old terminal. If you pay the driver, he may pocket the money and leave you as fair game for inspectors. A **taxi** could cost $30 or more, so avoid the cartel that operates at the arrivals gate by heading up to the departure lounge and haggling a price with a driver dropping someone off.

If arriving after dark, remember that although Bucharest is safer than most will tell you, it is ill-lit, pickpockets haunt its main stations, and stray dogs its streets. If you're bitten, go straight to the emergency hospital, *Spital de Urgenta*, at Calea Floreasca 8, near Ştefan cel Mare metro stop, or phone the English-speaking *Medicover* operation on ☎092/310 4066.

The main train station, **Gara de Nord**, is on the M1 and T1 metro lines. Piaţa Unirii is a metro intersection for the main M1 (red) circle line and M2 (blue/black) north–south line. There is also an M3 (yellow) heading west, and smaller lines T1 and T2 (green). The service runs 5am–11pm. Magnetic strip tickets are L5,000 for two journeys, L22,000 for ten rides, L8,000 for a day pass, all available from vendors at the top of the stairs, and inserted into the turnstile slot.

City transport is augmented by trams, trolleybuses and buses (5am–midnight) with tickets, to be punched onboard, for all three sold at *RATB* kiosks marked *bilete* near main stops – it's L2,500 for one ride, or L8,000 for a day pass (*una ziua*) from kiosks marked *bilete si abonamente*. Express buses (L8,000 single, L12,000 return) run between the main points in town. There is no night transport.

You'll find **taxis** all over the centre, but bargain on a price before you set off – around L50,000 should cover you for most journeys in town, L75,000 to most stadia. To call one, try ☎092/953 or ☎092/945.

The city's *ONT* **tourist office** at Bdul Magheru 7 (Mon–Fri 8am–6pm, Sat 9am–1pm, ☎092/314 8441), near Piaţa Română metro, is state bureaucracy at its worst, although it can provide a list of hotels and private rooms. For a modicum of service, try *Marshall Turism* down the street at #43 (open Mon–Fri 9am–5pm, Sat 10am–1pm, ☎092/223 1204), one of dozens of private agencies in the centre.

For well-researched, practical entertainment information, pick up a copy of the English-language bi-monthly **Bucharest In Your Pocket** (L20,000) from most major hotel reception areas. The free weekly *Şapte Seri*, available in bars and clubs around town, has a more comprehensive list of names and addresses, with short reviews in English and Romanian.

---

had played for Romania at the 1970 World Cup. Barcelona thought he had retired – after all, he hadn't featured in any of the previous rounds in the European Cup, and he was listed on Steaua's team-sheet as an assistant coach. But he was still registered as a player, and now on he came to ensure there would be no slip-ups at the back until the game was safely taken to extra-time and penalties.

With the home crowd now tensed into a nervous silence, there was a certain inevitability about the shoot-out. Barça missed every one of their spot-kicks, while Marius Lăcătuş and Gavril Balint made no mistake. Steaua were champions of Europe. It was the first time that a team from a Communist country had lifted the top prize in European club football, and to this day it remains the greatest achievement of any Romanian team.

That summer, Steaua strengthened their squad with the signing of Gheorghe Hagi – an ethnic Macedonian whose size-five left boot was the sweetest in the Romanian league – from Sportul Studenţesc. He promptly led them to the first of three consecutive league and cup doubles, and in 1989 Steaua were back in the final of the European Cup. There they had the misfortune to meet the AC Milan of Gullit and van Basten in their prime, and were destroyed 4–0. Yet this Steaua was a better side than that of 1986. Jenei had moved on to coach the national team, and been replaced by Iordănescu, who introduced a more attacking approach, based around the creative genius of Hagi. On their way to the final Steaua had been electrifying, defeating Sparta Prague 5–1, Spartak Moscow 3–0, IFK Gothenburg 5–1 and Galatasaray 4–0.

Following the departure of several of their star players immediately after Italia '90, Steaua staggered, failing to win the title for three seasons. But it wasn't long before the club was back to winning ways. During the Nineties Steaua participated in four Champions' League group stages, without really threatening to come close to winning a second European title.

Like most successful clubs, Steaua are the most loathed as well as the most loved in their country. Supporters of other Romanian clubs are full of tales about how their star player was 'conscripted' for Steaua during the Eighties. And even now, a full decade after the death of the dictator, Rapid fans still refer to Steaua as the *Ceauşeii* – 'Ceauşescu's Kids'.

Ironically, it was the man who masterminded Steaua's greatest moment, Emerich Jenei, who did most to threaten their position in Romanian football when, in his new role as the country's sports minister, he proposed ending all state support for clubs. That has meant the gradual severing of the link between the army and Steaua, and has forced the club to compete for sponsors and players in the same way as other teams. The prospect of seeing his beloved Steaua opened up to such competition was too much for coach Dumitru Dumitriu, who quit in a fit of pique at the end of the 1996/97 season – casting a shadow over the team's double win that year.

Dimitriu's assistant Mihai Stoichiţă was left to pick up the pieces, without Iulian

East End mission – a UEFA Cup win at West Ham was the highlight of Steaua's season

Filipescu and the Ilie brothers, all transferred abroad in the close season. Veteran forward Lăcătuş was made assistant coach, but Steaua couldn't qualify for the Champions' League, a failure they repeated in 1998, after Lăcătuş had become both player-coach and club vice-president.

The club appeared in total confusion and soon fell off the championship pace at home, but Jenei's return as technical director in November ushered in some stability, and a cup final win over champions Rapid, secured on penalties after another veteran, Belodedici, had scored in the 90th minute to level the scores at 2–2, also restored some pride.

A chaotic 1999/2000 campaign ended with Victor Piţurca, another veteran of the 1986 side, returning from his job as national manager, bloodied but unbowed, to become coach again, and striker Ioan Vladoiu also coming back to one of his former clubs. Whether Steaua's continued obsession with the past would enable the club to plan for a better future remained to be seen.

Here we go!

Yellow metro M3 to Gorjului, then tram #41 to the stadium. As you emerge from the metro you need a tram heading right.

Just the ticket

The superiority of the Ghencea over other city stadia is perfectly illustrated by its *Zona Fotolii* ('Armchair Zone'), 700 comfortable seats in an enclosed space, with air conditioning and a reasonably priced bar to hand. Tickets here are L100,000 for a domestic fixture. Next best are the seats in *Tribuna 0*, directly underneath and covered, at L50,000. *Tribuna 1* is to be found either side of this with seats at L40,000. *Tribuna 2* is opposite the whole caboodle, and open to the elements at L30,000. For the *Peluze* behind either goal, it's L20,000.

Swift half

Traffic signs in Ghencea warn drivers to beware of drunks staggering out into the road, and staying around here late on after the match may not

be a good idea. Beforehand, it's cheap and cheerful enough. The best place for a beer is the *Do-Meri*, haughtily calling itself a 'restaurant' but in fact a wooden bar, with a terrace, right by the bus and tram terminal.

Club merchandise

Steaua have a **souvenir shop** in the centre of the city at Str Brezoianu 15 (open Mon–Fri 10am–6pm). It's a dark, dusty place that attracts scant custom and seems to offer little more than a few scarves and hats.

In the net

The only consistent Steaua web presence at time of going to press was the unofficial offering at: www.geocities.com/Colosseum/Field/1559/Steaua -home.html. The site has few frills, but it offers the latest match results with some stats detail and JPEG images from each game for you to download.

 Dinamo

Stadionul Dinamo, Bdul Ştefan cel Mare 7–9
Capacity 18,000
Colours All red with white trim
League champions 1955, 1962–65, 1971, 1973, 1975, 1977, 1982–84, 1990, 1992, 2000
Cup winners 1959, 1964, 1968, 1982, 1984, 1986, 1990, 2000

Dinamo, like most clubs in Eastern Europe carrying that name, were the team of the interior ministry and the police. The connection remains, even though the ministry's brutal *Securitate*, one of Eastern Europe's most notorious secret-police units, have been disbanded. For the average Romanian fan, Dinamo, more than Steaua, were the team of the repressive Communist-era state. Somehow, despite their Ceauşescu connections, Steaua were viewed as a people's team, while Dinamo and their *Securitate* friends were the enemy.

The club were formed in 1948 from the merger of prewar clubs Unirea Tricolor and Ciocanul. Unirea Tricolor had won the last title before the war in 1941 and

Lia Manoliu – the national stadium

Stadionul Lia Manoliu, Parcul de Cultură şi Sport
Capacity 30,000 (all-seated)

Recent improvements at the Lia Manoliu, renamed after a famous Olympic athlete, previously known as the Naţional and before that as the August 23, could not have come at a better time. Its rotting wooden benches have been replaced by **plastic seats in national colours**, high-quality turf has been laid and the floodlights changed, just as national-team players had had enough of being jeered at within the confines of Steaua's up-close-and-personal Ghencea.

The stadium's main feature is the pavilion in the *Tribuna Oficiala*, where Ceauşescu used to speak to **the assembled masses** on May Day and, of course, August 23 – a holiday commemorating a local uprising against Romania's former alliesin World War II, Germany.

The arena has **great natural acoustics** and a capacity crowd can create a great atmosphere with the sound 'trapped' inside the ground. Further renovation is proceeding apace, with the Romanian FA hoping to increase the capacity during the year 2000.

Three **buses** terminate at the Lia Manoliu – the #104 from Piaţa Unirii, the #86 trolleybus from Piaţa Română and the #90 trolleybus from Piaţa Universitatii, all heading toward Vatra Luminoasă. Alternatively, from **M1 metro station** Piaţa Muncii, turn right outside the station and head towards the park – the ground is a 15min walk.

Behind the east stand is the *Teraca Stadionul*, a small bar with a terrace serving snacks and bottled beers.

appeared in two Romanian cup finals. The new club were given a prime venue for their stadium – an area of parkland off the busy Ştefan cel Mare boulevard.

Although Dinamo lifted their first title in 1955, it was not until the Sixties that they established themselves as the second force in Romania. From 1962 they won the title four years in a row, doing the double in 1964. In the late Sixties the club produced three of Romania's top internationals – Cornel Dinu, who made 75 appearances for the national team and is now club president; prolific striker Florea Dumitrache; and Mircea Lucescu, who went on to forge a successful career as a coach with the national team and the Italian club Brescia, for whom he signed Gheorghe Hagi.

Dinamo won three titles in the Seventies, during which their undisputed star was frontman Dudu Georgescu. In 1975 he became the first Romanian to be placed top ten in the voting for European Footballer of the Year, and on three occasions he won the *Golden Boot* award as top scorer in Europe – including the 1977/78

season when he scored 47 goals in the Romanian league. The precise role played by the *Securitate* in elevating Georgescu's goals tally – and that of another Dinamo *Golden Boot* winner, Rodion Cămătaru, in the Eighties – may never be known.

Dinamo's titles in 1982 and 1983 paved the way for a decent European Cup run (Romania's first) in 1983/84. In the second round they defeated the holders, Hamburg, and then squeezed past Dynamo Minsk in the quarter-finals. They ran up against the brick wall of Liverpool in the semis, and lost both legs.

The title was retained that summer, but after that Dinamo had to take a back seat to Steaua. Many Dinamo fans argue that the late-Eighties side, with Florin Răducioiu upfront, was one of their best ever, but that the strength of Steaua ruled out any hope of silverware. That view is strengthened by Dinamo's run in the 1989/90 Cup-Winners' Cup, in which Panathinaikos were hammered 6–1 in Bucharest and Partizan Belgrade were dismissed with almost equal ease. Alas, Dinamo lost both legs of their semi to Anderlecht, and Steaua's record as the only Romanian team to reach the final of a European competition stayed intact.

In the aftermath of the Romanian revolution, Dinamo briefly changed their name back to Unirea Tricolor, and saw their much-maligned nursery club, Victoria, disbanded by the new authorities.

After a title win in 1992, Dinamo became tainted with controversy as the club slowly eased its way out of the clutches of the interior ministry. Virtually all the stars were sold to foreign clubs, generating revenue which fans believed had been squandered by the bureaucrats in charge of the club. Sure enough, in the spring of 1999 former club president Vasile Ianul was up for trial on charges of embezzling £1.5million during his three years in office. At the same time, director Petre Buduru was arrested for falsifying documents as part of a cigarette smuggling operation – he submitted his letter of resignation from jail.

Meanwhile Dinamo announced the appointment of a new president, Nicolae Badea, the first to be elected in the club's history, and the first civilian one to boot. On the pitch, the team were enjoying their best season in years. After the ignominy of European defeat by KR Reykjavík in 1997 and a sixth-place finish in the league in 1998, the squad came to life with the arrival of internationals Ioan Vladiou and Ioan Lupescu from Germany.

With Cornel Dinu now operating with confidence as coach, and half-a-dozen players making the national squad – including top goalscorer Adrian Mihalcea – Dinamo led the league in the autumn, beating nearest rivals Rapid 4–1 away. They were eventually overtaken by Rapid, but not before some fans began to make match-fixing allegations against the eventual title winners.

There was to be no need for such talk in 1999/2000, when Dinamo were simply unstoppable. They stormed to the title, finishing a full 12 points clear of second-placed Rapid, then secured the double with a 2–0 win over Universitatea Craiova in the cup final. The achievements were even more impressive given that Adrian Mutu, who had scored 18 goals before the winter break, had been sold to Internazionale in January.

Here we go!

Red M1 metro to Ştefan cel Mare – a 15min ride from any central station.

Just the ticket

Dinamo's stadium is unpretentious and so is its pricing policy – L50,000, sit anywhere you want.

Swift half

The most conspicuous evidence of Dinamo's image overhaul in 1999/2000 is Bucharest's only themed football bar, the **Red Dogs**, by the stadium entrance – a modest but pleasant sports pub, with a full menu, great old Dinamo photos around the walls and friendly service. Copies of the club's free matchday progamme, *Echipa Tuturor*, should be lying around.

Club merchandise

The **Red Dogs** shop, with the same image as the bar of the same name nearby, has all the Dinamo gear anyone could wish for. Open 10am–11pm Mon–Sat, no credit cards.

Groundhopping

☼ Rapid

Stadionul Giuleşti, Calea Giuleşti 18
Capacity 23,500
Colours All white with claret trim
League champions 1967, 1999
Cup winners 1937–42, 1972, 1975, 1998

East European dictatorships were not renowned for providing choice. But while you can have a one-party state, you can't have one-team football. Soccer was one of the few areas of life where people could exercise freedom of choice. And for football fans in Bucharest opposed to the Ceauşescu regime, there was one simple outlet for frustrations – Rapid Bucharest.

A hangover from the pre-war era, Rapid somehow avoided being merged into a police or army side and were therefore seen as disassociated from the party state. *'Hai Rapid!'* was one of the few slogans that could be shouted without a dictate from above. Rapid were, are and always will be a genuine workers' team, with their traditional support base coming from railwaymen (*feroviarii*) who live in the Giuleşti district and work at the Gara de Nord down the road.

Although Rapid never won a championship before World War II, they were cup specialists, winning the competition six times in a row between 1937 and 1942. The Communists got their hands on Rapid in 1950, when the ministry of transport took over the running of the club. Choosing a new name wasn't difficult – until 1958 they played under the predictable title of Locomotiva. Having won their name back, Rapid enjoyed their most successful post-war spell – they finished runners-up in the league three times in a row from 1964, and in 1967 won the title.

Although there were cup wins in the Seventies, Rapid quickly faded and even spent a couple of spells in the second division. As anyone who has ever driven in Romania will testify, the ministry of transport was not one of the biggest spenders in the country and they certainly lacked the resources to outbid the army and the *Securitate* for players.

Yet despite the lack of success, Rapid maintained their popular support. After the 1989 revolution, politicians of all colours, including President Iliescu, rushed to associate themselves with the club.

Local businessman George Copos, head of the *Samsung* company's Romanian operation took control of the club in the early Nineties, and the clarets established themselves in the top half of the league. Copos' cash provided a new stand at the south end of the Giuleşti, ending the three-sided 'horseshoe' appearance of the ground.

In 1997/98 former Brescia coach Mircea Lucescu, who turned down a post at Dinamo to take over the reins, created a young and ambitious team. With a cast-iron defence bolstered by Romania's Under-21 'keeper Bogdan Lobonţ, Rapid were ahead of Steaua at the top of the table with two games to go. It wasn't to be. Rapid went down 1–0 at FCM Bacău, a game refereed by Marcel Savaniu, an official previously fined for earlier 'defficiencies'. Level on points with Steaua going into the last game, Rapid found the goalposts had been moved again at Universitatea Craiova, when a Lucian Marinescu shot came down over the goal-line from the crossbar. No goal. And no title. Marinescu's revenge was to convert a penalty for the only goal of the cup final, again against Craiova, to earn Rapid their first trophy for 20 years.

The feelings of bitterness over the fate of the title remained, however, and it was a very determined Rapid that went into the 1998/99 season. Their brisk start was briefly halted after Lucescu was whisked off to Inter in December, but Dumitru Dumitriu brought striker Ionel Ganea in from Gloria Bistriţa, and when Lucescu returned from his Italian nightmare in April, it was to mastermind the overhauling of Dinamo and the winning of the championship with one game to spare, after Rapid had beaten Craiova 1–0 with a suspiciously offside goal by Adrian Iencsi, and Dinamo had gone down by the same score at Ceahlaul Piatra Neamt.

Steaua spoiled the celebrations by grabbing a last-minute equaliser in the cup final and ending Rapid's hopes of a double by winning the game on penalties, raising accusations that the two clubs had conspired to share out the honours between them.

Ganea then headed off to Stuttgart, and Rapid failed to make the Champions' League after conceding two late goals to Skonto Riga of Latvia. It was a setback from which the team never really recovered, Dinamo leaving them trailing in the race for the 1999/2000 championship. When the season was over, Lucescu went on his travels again to team up with Hagi and Popescu at Galatasaray. But the appointment of former national-team boss Anghel Iordănescu, though not popular with Rapid fans who remember his past at Steaua, should ensure the club stays in the headlines for 2000/01.

Follow the workers from Gara de Nord train station on **tram #44** to the ground – the journey takes around 10mins. Before the match, the **Tonady**, at Calea Giuleşti 49, is a decent spot for a swift one, while the **Nemecu Billiard Restaurant** on 9 Mai, just off the main road, offers pool, pints and pizza.

At the ground, the club operates a simple admission structure – *Tribuna 1* seats at L50,000, *Tribuna 2* at L15,000 or L10,000 for the *Peluze*.

FC Naţional

Stadionul Cotroceni, Strada Dr Lister 37
Capacity 16,000 (all-seated)
Colours White shirts, blue shorts
Cup winners 1961

The home of FC Naţional is an example of what can be achieved in Eastern Europe if the cash is there. A modern, all-seater (with seats, not benches) arena, the Stadionul Cotroceni is flanked by an equally impressive tennis centre. The ground development was financed by the Romanian national bank, who are the major backers of the club.

FC Naţional were formed as Lafayette in 1934, became Grafica in 1948, and two years later were renamed Spartac. They adopted the name Progresul in 1954, and stuck with it until after the 1989 revolution. Like many Romanian clubs in the postwar period the team were linked to the trade unions, but Progresul had the unusual distinction of being the team of the Romanian hairdressers' association! Well trimmed they might have been, but

they seldom cut a dash on the field. They finished third in the league in 1955 and 1962, and won the Romanian cup in 1961. Throughout the first two decades of Communism, the club enjoyed a decent level of popular support as, like Rapid, they were clearly not a favoured team of the regime.

But in the mid-Eighties the heart was ripped out of the club by a familiar figure. Between 1984 and 1989, a large area of central Bucharest was demolished to make way for Nicolae Ceauşescu's grotesquely impressive Victory of Socialism Boulevard, a giant road lined with huge tower blocks and terminating at the massive House of the Republic – the third largest building in the world. This ludicrous project saw the demolition of 9,500 houses, 15 churches and the Stadionul Republica – the charming, downtown home of Progresul.

The Republica was a pre-war stadium, with an English feel and a grand main stand, and for the older generation of Progresul fans, going to a game was like being transported back in time to a Bucharest where there was no Ceauşescu, no Communist Party and no ration coupons. Perhaps that was why the tyrant razed it to the ground.

For much of the rest of the Eighties, Progresul played in the lower divisions, sharing grounds wherever they could and playing bigger games at the national stadium. In the mid-Nineties, with a superb ground, a healthy bank balance and a team capable of rivalling Steaua and Dinamo, FC Naţional seemed to be emerging as the club of the future. They entered Europe via the UEFA Cup for the first time in 1995/96, and finished runners-up to Steaua in both the league and the cup in 1996/97.

Alas, coach Florin Marin was not able to capitalise on these achievements, and was sacked after a 5–0 defeat at Rapid in November 1998. Former Craiova coach and ex-Spain international José Alexanko was brought in, but couldn't turn things around – the team eventually finished seventh in the league, way off the title pace, and declined an invitation to enter the 1999 Intertoto Cup.

If Romania does develop into a healthy capitalist nation, then no football club will better symbolise the transtition than FC Naţional. And yet, with their traditional support dying out and crowds remaining low in the absence of that elusive first title, you wonder whether – as with MTK in Budapest – the nascent capitalists have chosen the right target for their investment.

The appointment of former Steaua skipper Marius Lăcătuş as coach after an eighth-place finish in 1999/2000 seemed like a last, desperate throw of the dice.

To get to the Cotroceni, take **yellow metro M3** to Eroilor (from the centre, take trains heading for Industrillor). From the metro stop, cross the road and head down Strada Dr Lister – the stadium is on your left.

The **nearest bars** are a row of cheap, nameless terrace affairs, leading up to the military academy from the Eroilor bus stop. **Match tickets** are between L35,000 and L75,000.

Eat, drink, sleep…

Bars and clubs

Romanian bars are where men go to get drunk, either in dank dives or in loud, overly lit, flashy affairs. Hotel bars and nightclubs tend to be overpriced and full of dancing girls.

Beer, generally the home-produced *Bergenbier* or *Ursus* although foreign brands are available, will be around L12,000 in a local bar, twice that anywhere smarter. Spirits – generally fruit brandy, *ţuică* or *palinca* – are cheap and strong.

Bucharest can at least offer some variety. Bars along the north-south axis from Piaţa Victoriei, past Piaţa Universităţii and down to Piaţa Unirii, tend to appeal to the **business and expat community**, whereas the area around metro stops Semănătoarea and Grozăveşti offers cheaper **student nightlife** in term time. With places opening and closing so fast, anything else is pot luck.

A Club, Strada Blanari 14. Short walk from Piaţa Universităţii, a term-time bar/club with live music or DJs, nominal admission at weekends, closed Mon. Football on TV by the entrance.

The Harp, Piaţa Unirii 1. Two-storey Irish pub with a big screen for TV football and a great view of the square. Open from noon until the last guest leaves. Owned by the same team behind *The Dubliner* (Bul Titulescu 18, near Piaţa Victoriei) – both accept credit cards and will have Sky Sports on the box if the weather conditions are right.

Karma, Strada Academei 35/37. Near Piaţa Revolutiei, a new angle on the city's tacky discos, this one playing mainstream techno and attracting a fashionable young clientèle.

Terminus, Strada Gheorghe Enescu 5. Packed, centrally located cellar bar, down a tricky rope staircase, popular with expats and well-to-do locals. Open 10am until last guest. Near the *Hotel Bucureşti* on Calea Victoria.

Restaurants

After years of rationing and black marketeering, **Romanian cuisine** is enjoying a comeback. Dishes to look for include *sarmale* (cabbage stuffed with rice and spiced, minced meat) and *muşchi poiana* – beef filled with mushroom and peppers and served with a tangy vegetable-and-tomato sauce. **Soups** and **stews** are especially good, but if you want something a little less rich, most place's will serve simple grilled meats with salad. The local wine is excellent.

Tourist-oriented restaurants will have a DJ or gypsy band and will probably overcharge. If you can't find anywhere open, most hotels have a restaurant attached.

Carû cu Bere, Strada Stavropoloeos 3/5. A historic restaurant founded in the last century, 'the Beer Cart' is a pleasant Saxon-style tourist haunt in the old town with traditional dishes around L40,000. Avoid weekend evenings if you can't face the folk show.

Count Dracula Club, Splaiul Independenţei 8a. Daft themed restaurant near Piaţa Unirii, with half-a-dozen rooms and a menu featuring Transylvanian and fish specialities. Pity the poor waiters dolled up in medieval drag.

Hanul lui Mamuc, Strada Iuliu Maniu 62. The city's other major tourist spot, a former travellers' inn with a huge courtyard for outdoor dining and drinking. Luxurious hotel attached.

Pescarul, Bul Bălcescu 9. Opposite the *Intercontinental Hotel* near Piaţa Universităţii, a fine fish restaurant despite the silly decor, with main courses around L40,000. Closed Sun.

Sahib, Strada Teodosie Rudeanu 3. Authentic Indian cuisine served daily midday–midnight. Reasonably priced and friendly. Between Piaţa 1 Mai and M1/T1 Basarab.

Accommodation

The city's hotels tend to be extremely expensive and you don't always get what you pay for – always inspect the room before agreeing a price. The *ONT* and other tourist offices (see *Essentials*) can arrange hotel rooms for around 10% commission, as well as private rooms at around $15 per night for a double.

Batistei, Str Dr E Bacaloglu 2 (☎01/314 0880/fax 314 0887). One of three-dozen former Communist Party hotels in the city, set in a quiet area behind the National Theatre. Rooms simple but equipped with cable TV, fridge and balcony. Singles $60, doubles $70, spacious apartments also available.

Carpaţi, Strada Matei Millo 16 (☎01/315 0140, fax 01/312 1857). Cheap, centrally located hotel with rooms ranging from bathless singles ($12) to doubles with private facilities on the upper floors ($35). Also has two apartments available for rent.

Cerna, Strada Golescu 29 (☎01/637 4087, fax 01/311 0721). Cleanest option for the money near Gara de Nord – turn right as you come out of the station. Singles from $10, doubles from

L20, a three-person room with bath $35. Modest breakfast included.

Hotel Triumf, Şos Kiseleff 12 (☎01/222 3172, fax 01/223 2411). Comfortable hotel set in parkland, 1km north of Piaţa Victoriei metro. Singles and doubles, with shower or bath, at around $60–70, most credit cards accepted. Laundry service. Advance booking advised.

Villa Helga, Strada Salcâmilor 2 (☎01/610 2214). Clean and friendly youth hostel with kitchen facilities, free use of washing machine and cable TV in the communal lounge. Two-, four- and six-bed rooms, at just over L100,000 a bed. Bus #79, #86 or #133 from Piaţa Română, east along Bul Dacia to Strada Lascăr; turn right down Lascăr, first left down Viitorului, then right down Salcâmilor.

Russia

Russian Football Union, Luzhnetskaya Naberezhnaya 8, 119 270 Moscow
☎095/201 0834   Fax 502/220 2037   E-mail root@unfootball.msk.ru

League champions Spartak Moscow   **Cup winners** Lokomotiv Moscow
Promoted Anzhi Makhachkala, Fakel Voronezh **Relegated** Zhemchuzhina Sochi,
Shinnik Yaroslavl

European participants 2000/01 Spartak Moscow (UCL), Lokomotiv Moscow (UCL
qualifiers); CSKA Moscow, Dynamo Moscow, Torpedo-Luzhniki Moscow (UEFA Cup);
Zenit St Petersburg, Rostselmash Rostov (Intertoto Cup)

S occer in Russia is up for sale. Shabby market stalls occupy many of Moscow's main grounds, forcing teams to share stadia, while players raise their game only in the shop window of European football. Corruption is rife. In the new 'market' economy, the balance of football power shifted away from Moscow to the provinces, where Rotor Volgograd and Alaniya Vladikavkaz played to packed houses in modern arenas that put the capital's marketplaces to shame – and nobody questioned where the money for the new grounds came from. In pure footballing terms, Moscow has since re-asserted its supremacy, but the ability of provincial club presidents to bank-roll a rise through the ranks remains, as witnessed by the appearance of Uralan Elitsa and Saturn Ramenskoe in the top flight.

Meanwhile Spartak, the people's team, are the only club to attract reasonable custom in the capital. Young Muscovites remember little and care less about the days of exciting domestic football in the old Soviet league, the break-up of the USSR having deprived them, and the older generation of fans, of classic battles between Moscow sides and top Ukrainian and Georgian teams such as Dynamo Kiev and Dynamo Tblisi. A contemporary indoor tournament, held in Moscow every January and involving the champion teams of all the former Soviet republics, does history scant justice.

After its introduction by English mill-owners in 1887, football slowly developed

Impressive façade – Moscow's Luzhniki

in Moscow and St Petersburg, with neither help nor hindrance from the ruling tsars. City teams played each other in representative fixtures, but Russia's vast distances and long, harsh winters stood in the way of nationwide growth – the Olympic team lost 16–0 to Germany in 1912.

After the 1917 revolution, the Communist authorities saw organised sport as a cheap way of keeping workers fit, disciplined and entertained. Although yet to be established on the factory floor, football had been part of the sports curriculum in

Basics

To enter Russia you need a **visa**, pre-arranged with considerable hassle at your Russian embassy back home. For those on **package tours**, this will be sorted out by the travel company. For individual travellers, there are three choices: a **tourist visa**, valid for a specific number of days providing you have pre-booked accommodation for that period; a **business visa**, valid for up to 60 days through a letter of invitation from a Russian company; and an **individual visa**, which requires a private letter of invitation and up to four months of bureaucratic hassle. Your local Russian Embassy will have details of visa applications and costs. The UK office is at 5 Kensington Palace Gardens, London, W8 (☎020/7229 8027).

On arrival in Russia, you will have to fill out a **currency declaration form** stating how much money you have with you. On departure you will have to fill out a similar form, declaring how much money you are taking out.

The Russian currency is the **rouble**, divided into 100 kopecks. There are coins for 5, 10 and 50 kopecks, and 1, 2 and 5 roubles, and notes for 5, 10, 50, 100 and 500 roubles. At the time of writing, the rouble-dollar **exchange rate** was fluctuating wildly, varying from 10 to 25. The best advice is to bring dollars and Deutschmarks in small denominations, although sterling is accepted at some exchange offices. You must show your passport for each transaction.

By law you can only pay for goods and services in roubles, although most shops and bars will accept dollars in small denominations. Smarter businesses accept credit cards, and there are **cash machines** in most major cities.

For local **phone calls**, buy a handful of brown plastic tokens (*zhetoni*) at 300 roubles each from metro station ticket offices. Nearby you'll see a row of old-style telephones (*taksofoni*) – dial your number first, then drop in the token as soon as you hear someone's voice. For **international calls**, main metro stations have card phones; the lowest denomination of phonecard on sale is 50 roubles. In Moscow, these will be for blue *MTTS* phones, which require you to press the *otvet* button on hearing the other person's voice. More upmarket bars and restaurants will have orange access phones, with cards on sale at the bar (125 units for 80 roubles, 250 for 160, 500 for 320).

To dial out of Russia, dial 8 (pause)10, then the country code. Calls are cheaper after 10pm and on Sundays. Remember that Moscow is two hours ahead of Central European Time. To call into Russia, dial 7, then 095 for Moscow, 812 for St Petersburg and 8442 for Volgograd.

Visitors are no longer restricted to the Russian cities listed on their visa form. **Flying** is the best way the cover the vast distances between major cities, but tickets for both planes and trains carry inflated prices for foreigners, and must be bought from official agencies such as *Intourist*.

Moscow's better schools and colleges. The Moscow clubs Dynamo, Spartak, CSKA, Torpedo and Lokomotiv were quickly formed in the Twenties, and the first all-Soviet league was organised in 1936.

Even then, football in this part of Europe was rarely 'clean'. So-called agreed (*dogovorni*) matches, in which the outcome was little more than a formality, were a familiar trait under Communism, and two key figures, Spartak founder Nikolai Starostin and Torpedo star Eduard Streltsov, spent time in gulag camps for refusing to buckle under the authoritarian might of the KGB (represented by Dynamo Moscow) and the Red Army (CSKA).

International appearances were not encouraged until after World War II, when Stalin hoped to capitalise on the propaganda victories of Dynamo Moscow's tour of Britain in 1945, and the Olympic team's debut in 1952. After Stalin's death, the USSR won soccer gold at the 1956 Olympics, encouraging the new Soviet leader, Nikita Khrushchev, to allow the full national team, the *sbornaya*, to play in the World Cup finals of 1958. Under captain Igor Netto, the Soviets bowed out at the quarter-final stage, but progress was clearly being made.

Two years later, the team won the first-ever European Championship by beating Yugoslavia in Paris – although the scale of their achievement was undermined by the non-participation of the likes of England, Italy and West Germany in a tournament then seen as having little potential by the European football elite. The Soviets' hero in Paris was their goalkeeper, Lev Yashin, a six-foot-plus giant dressed in black who would become his country's most enduring footballing legend. A veteran of the 1958 World Cup, Yashin was still in goal when the Soviets finished as European runners-up in 1964 and as semi-finalists at the 1966 World Cup.

After the Sixties, however, the USSR would earn a reputation for being under-achievers at international level, perennial 'dark horses' who faded before the final hurdle. Bad luck certainly played its part – shocking refereeing denied them in 1986, and the team travelled to Italia '90 with an unfeasibly long injury list. But lack of support also took its toll. In those days, whatever voices could be heard in the world's stadia urging the *sbornaya* forward were those of diplomats and spies.

At club level, meanwhile, Moscow's domination was being challenged by clubs outside the Russian republic. Khrushchev's favoured team, Dynamo Kiev, became the first non-Moscow side to win the Soviet title in 1961. And while Russian clubs could only muster one appearance in a European final, the Ukrainians of Kiev and their Georgian counterparts, Dynamo Tblisi, would both win the Cup-Winners' Cup during the Seventies and Eighties, and make an impact on other European competitions.

Ukrainian players such as Oleg Blokhin, Igor Belanov and Oleg Protasov formed the backbone of the *sbornaya* until the squad was effectively disbanded by the break-up of the Soviet Union in the early Nineties. After competing under the CIS ('Commonwealth of Independent States') banner at Euro '92, many top non-Russian players chose not to play for the newly independent nations of their birth, reasoning they would have a greater chance of honours if they represented Russia. While the players' decision reduced the Georgian and Ukrainian national sides to the status of European minnows, Russia duly qualified for the 1994 World Cup – but seven players, Ukrainian-born Andrei Kanchelskis included, then refused to play after a row with team management.

The Ukrainians appeared to get the last laugh by beating Russia – including Kanchelskis – 3–2 in the first meeting of the two sides in September 1998, at the start of qualification for Euro 2000. Acrimony – as seen amid the intriguingly creative squad under Oleg Romantsev which flopped at Euro '96 – was not a problem that day in Kiev, but preparation was. New coach Anatoly Byshovets, who had done a sterling job of reviving the moribund Zenit St Petersburg into serious title challengers before his attention became divided, was given precious little time to work with a squad shorn of Spartak players thanks to a row with their club coach, Romantsev.

Ironically, it was Romantsev who would take over from Byshovets barely three months later, at the end of the worst year in Russian football history. Further defeats by France and Iceland had left the Russians way off the Euro 2000 qualifying pace. But Romantsev, motivating not just his own Spartak players but selected exiles as well, masterminded a rapid revival that included a revenge win over the French in Paris in June 1999 – a display of free-flowing football that left the world champions standing, and reminded Europe of what the Russian game is capable of, given the right sort of encouragement.

In the end, the issue of Euro 2000 qualification would not be resolved until Russia's final game, at home to the old enemy Ukraine. With three minutes to go, Russia were 1–0 up and heading for the play-offs thanks to a 75th-minute goal from Celta Vigo midfielder Valery Karpin. Then disaster struck. Andriy Shevchenko's curling free-kick seemed harmless enough, but Russian 'keeper Alexander Filimonov somehow managed to punch the ball into his own net, and hand Ukraine the point which allowed them to leapfrog his team.

With none of the Russian clubs making the slightest impact on European competition, 1999/2000 was a black year, darkened further by a shocking rise in violence at matches across the country. The Russian game is a mess. But then, given the the backdrop against which it is played, it would be a miracle if it were anything else.

Essential vocabulary

Hello *Zdravstvuyte*
Goodbye *Do svidaniya*
Yes *Da*
No *Nyet*
Two beers, please *Dva piva, pazhalysta*
Thank you *Spasiba*
Men's *Muzhskoy* (МУЖИ)
Women's *Zhenskiy* (ЖЕНЫ)
Where is the stadium? *Gde stadion?*
What's the score? *Kak schyot?*
Referee *Sood*
Offside *Nye igri*

Match practice

The Russian season runs from early March to early November, with a break in June if the national side are involved in the finals of a major tournament. Games generally take place on Saturdays at 5pm, but with Spartak and Lokomotiv sharing grounds, there is invariably a Friday or Sunday game in Moscow.

Security is tight for certain Moscow derbies. Otherwise, the loudest noise you'll hear all afternoon is laughter. Outside the stadium you'll see a swift trade in badges, scarves and old programmes.

Some teams still proudly stride out to the *Footbolniy March*, a rousing Soviet pre-match theme dating back to the Thirties.

A different league

The Russian league is made up of three main divisions. The premiership (*Vysshaya Liga*) has 16 teams, the bottom two being replaced by the top two of the 22-team first division (*Pervaya Liga*). Five or six teams drop from the first into the six-zone second division (*Vtoraya*); the winners of each zone have their season's records matched with each other, only counting games with the top six clubs in their league. The zone winner with the weakest record must play off with the 17th-placed *Pervaya* team, while the other five are promoted automatically. As in Italy, teams finishing on equal points in the premier division must play off if a championship, UEFA Cup place, or relegation are at stake.

Up for the cup

To allow for the huge number of participating teams, preliminary rounds for the Russian cup take place just before the previous year's cup final in May. These early ties are decided over one game, extra-time and penalties if necessary, and can attract vast crowds to provincial grounds.

Premier-league teams join two rounds before the quarter-finals, which take place over two legs the following April. The semi-finals are decided over one game on neutral grounds, while the final in Moscow, at the rebuilt Luzhniki stadium, is decided over a single game.

Just the ticket

A ticket (*bilyet,* displayed as БИЛЕТ) should cost between 30 and 60 roubles and grant you access to any spot on a tatty wooden bench in the sector of your choice. In most grounds, sectors are indicated by north, south, east or west. Unless the fixture is a Moscow derby, visiting fans are rare, so the only seating problem is cured by taking along that day's newspaper as a precaution against any embarrassing splinters.

Beware that prices can increase as much as five-fold for big European ties, especially those at the Luzhniki.

Half-time

Most drinking is done before the match at a stand near the ground – a hangover from the Soviet era when bars were practically non-existent. You'll see supporters sharing a bottle of vodka between three (*na troyom*, about 30 roubles all in) or knocking back beer at 5 roubles a time.

At half-time, follow the plumes of smoke to the nearby kebab (*shashlik*) grill, where some 20 roubles should see you OK. Risk the *khot dogs* (5 roubles) if you must.

A newspaper cone full of sunflower seeds is the essential accoutrement to a summer evening's entertainment. Most stadia will have a small buffet van for sandwiches (*butterbroti*), filled with either ham or caviar.

Action replay

The Russian FA's three-year, £6million sponsorship deal with chewing-gum firm *Stimorol* allows for one league match a week to be televised live throughout the country, on national station ORT, either channel 1 or 2. This is at the same time as most other matches, Saturday at 5pm – hardly conducive to filling empty stadia.

To make life more interesting, Spartak have cut a deal with Moscow's commercial channel NTV, giving the latter exclusive live rights to their games.

Late on Sunday evenings, ORT shows a round-up of the previous day's league highlights, *Footbolnaya Obrazrynyie*; RTR's *Footbol Byez Granitsi* ('Football Without Frontiers'), on Sunday afternoons, is more analytical. RenTV, free in Moscow and St Petersburg, shows a Saturday English Premiership game the following afternoon. *Futbol Klub*, on NTV early on Monday evenings, has a smattering of other European action.

The back page

The launch in 1992 of the daily *Sport Express* swept the red carpet from under the feet of the staid *Sovyetski Sport*, the classic old-style Communist daily put out by the Olympic Committee. The best journalists went straight across to the *Express*, which now boasts a circulation of almost a million. Its bumper Tuesday edition (neither daily comes out on Sundays or Mondays) has excellent foreign coverage if someone can help you out with the Cyrillic. Variable prices will be displayed from vendor to vendor – some 3–4 roubles should cover you. The thinner *Sovyetski Sport* goes for 2 roubles.

For analysis – not *Sport Express'* strong point – the black-and-white weekly *Futbol* (Saturdays, around 10 roubles) is excellent, but a little text-heavy. Its rival, *Futbol Review* (Tuesdays, around 10 roubles), is easier on the eye. The only quality monthly is *Sport Express' Zhurnal* (around 15 roubles), with colour features.

Ultra culture

Russian ultras have been enjoying a revival since the late Nineties, after battling for half a decade with the newly inflated costs of travel and materials. Inevitably, the activity has its ugly side – Moscow clubs CSKA and Dynamo are known allies, Spartak their sworn enemies. Even so, unless you're at one of the overly policed derbies, the only fan culture you might pick up on is the Russian version of *The Whirl*, in which a dozen lads grab each other by any loose item of clothing and quickly whirl around, flailing and kicking, like a bunch of Tasmanian Devils.

In the net

The Russian FA's official site is at: www.feesmg.ru/rfu.htm. It's fairly basic but well laid-out and, thankfully, all in English. It also has links to the official Belarussian and Ukrainian FA sites, run by the same firm.

Meanwhile, Oxana Smirnova's superb site continues at: www.quark.lu.se/~oxana.football.html. There's a full archive for the national teams of both Russia and the USSR, a Lev Yashin photo gallery, the latest international news and excellent links.

MOSCOW

Thin crowds, dilapidated grounds, second-rate players…why would anyone come to Moscow to watch football? There are all sorts of reasons. The game here is steeped in history, while the football itself will never have anything less than a cultured aim, even if it is sometimes clumsily executed.

Above all, though, Moscow is the biggest, most exciting football city in Europe to play its football in the summer – which, as any local will tell you, can be a surprisingly warm and inviting time to be in Russia's capital.

The thrilling fields

 Dynamo

Dynamo stadium, Leningradski Prospekt 36
Capacity 51,000
Colours All blue with white trim
League champions (USSR) 1936 (spring), 1937, 1940, 1945, 1949, 1954–55, 1957, 1959, 1963, 1976 (spring)
Cup winners (USSR) 1937, 1953, 1967, 1970, 1977, 1984
Cup winners (Russia) 1997

Still stuck with the same Communist-era management structure and a general director, Nikolai Tolstykh, who seems more interested in his personal feuds than with improving his club's circumstances, Dynamo have not coped well in the post-Soviet era. A single cup win in seven years hardly reflects the club's golden years either side of World War II, nor their remarkable earlier history.

Although the club were officially named Dynamo in 1923, they have links going right back to the very beginnings of the game in Russia. In 1887, Blackburn Rovers fans Clement and Harry Charnock, whose family ran the *Morozov* cotton mills in Orekhovo Zuyevo outside Moscow,

formed a factory team and kitted them out in their beloved blue-and-white. As the Russian game expanded at the turn of the century, the *Morozovtsi* won the Moscow league five years running before being renamed Orekhovo Klub Sport and relocated to Moscow itself. Once there the club quickly became a front for anti-tsarist activities, and it was these that attracted the attention of Felix Dzerzhinsky, the man who, after the 1917 revolution, would become leader of Lenin's secret police – the forerunners of the KGB.

In 1923 Dzerzhinsky changed the team's name to Dynamo Moscow, affiliating the club to the electrical trades' union. But the VIP box at the open, functional and all-bench Dynamo stadium, built in 1928, played host not to an elite band of electricians but to the hierarchy of Stalin's secret police – among them his soon-to-be chief henchman, Lavrenti Beria. A keen Dynamo fan, Beria watched his team share pre-war Soviet league titles with the Spartak side of his sworn enemy, Nikolai Starostin. Beria would subsequently be fundamental in arranging Starostin's exile to the gulags.

After World War II the club would become the role model for secret police ('Dynamo') teams across the former Eastern bloc, from Berlin to Bucharest. Just as importantly, it was Dynamo whom Stalin sent to Britain in November 1945, for a four-match tour cloaked in fog, mystery and fast-flowing football. The team returned to Moscow in triumph, having won the first leg of Russia's propaganda war with the West.

Star of the tour was goalkeeper Alexei 'Tiger' Komich. Four years later, Tomich was idly watching Dynamo's ice-hockey team when his eye was caught by a promising goal-minder called Lev Yashin. Yashin was promptly converted to football, and would become the hero of the postwar Soviet soccer era, the very embodiment of success and sportsmanship. Over two decades he played in three World Cups and two European Championship finals for his country, and led Dynamo to five titles and three cup wins. He was named European footballer of the year in 1963 – the first and so far only goalkeeper to attain the honour. A one-club man, Yashin played his farewell match (between Dynamo and a FIFA World XI in front of 100,000 at the Luzhniki) in 1971.

After that he worked 'upstairs' at the club, even after he'd had a leg amputated as a consequence of a long-held knee injury in 1986. He died four years later, still a Dynamo employee.

Ironically, it was a year after Yashin's retirement that Dynamo became the only Russian side to take part in a European club final, losing a Cup-Winners' Cup clash to Rangers in 1972. After that there were two fallow decades before the dissolution of the Soviet Union in 1992.

The peeling Dynamo stadium was finally given undersoil heating in 1997. The installation proved a mixed blessing – the heat scorched the grass and the team suffered a string of injuries. This did not prevent a cup win and runners-up place in the league that year, thanks to goals from Oleg

Terekhin and class defending by Yuri Kovtun. But even with the addition of Nigerian forward Lucky Izibor, Dynamo were struggling again a year later, managing a lame fifth place behind the four other big Moscow clubs.

Prior to the 2000 season, crowd favourite Terekhin was sold to Lokomotiv, but the return, after a seven-year absence, of former coach Valery Gazzayev, who had worked wonders at Alaniya Vladikavkaz, promised better things to come.

Here we go!

Green metro line 2 to **Dynamo** – the station interior is richly adorned with sporting figurines.

Just the ticket

The ticket windows are on the stadium side of the forecourt, parallel to Leningradksiy Prospekt. Tickets, 40–50 roubles, are divided into the four main stands. The main entrance is around the corner in Teatralnaya. Dynamo's blue-and-white faithful occupy the west stand.

Swift half

Supporters gather in the modernised bars on the large forecourt between the metro station

Thin smiles and outdated fashions – Dynamo at the turn of the millennium

and the stadium ahead. The **Bar Penalti** there has a terrace serving bottles of vodka, plates of dried fish and *Beck's* beer to wash it all down with. Inside the stadium, the **Restoran Dynamo** by sektor #11 has wonderful shots of Yashin in its entrance, while the **Cafe-Bar Dynamo** above gate #2 through the main entrance has a *Wurlitzer* jukebox, a pool table and *Baltika* beer on draught.

Club merchandise

You'll find a small shop inside the **club museum** (open Mon–Fri 10am–5pm), but there'll be more choice on matchdays among the many souvenir sellers on the concourse in front of the ticket office and the north stand. Also open will be a **kiosk** just inside the main gate selling videos, magazines and badges.

Ultra culture

The **Blue-White Dynamite** were officially formed in 1994 and forged an alliance with CSKA's **Red-Blue Warriors** a year later – an anti-Spartak force which sadly often sees Moscow derby matches turn to violence.

In print

The club publishes **Park** magazine, on sale at the ticket office for 6 roubles.

In the net

Both the club's official site and the former unofficial home of the *Blue-White Dynamite* ultras have vanished, leaving Sergei Ukladov's fan's-view offering as the club's major web presence at: www.soccer.ru/dinamo. There's an efficient news and stats service in English.

Moscow essentials

Arriving at Moscow's international **airport**, Sheremyetevo 2, is a sharp introduction to the realities of life in Russia. Don't pack any valuables in your hold luggage, and watch your bags at all times.

Once through customs and with roubles in your pocket, from the airport you have three choices: go with one of the **taxi sharks** hassling you as soon as you pass through customs (cost $70–100 for the 28km journey south-east into town); step outside the airport concourse and **strike a bargain** with someone going into town anyway (around $30 is reasonable); or take bus #551 to its **Rechnoi Vokzal** terminal, where green metro line 2 starts (4 roubles, ticket available onboard, stamp both sides in the puncher machine afterwards). The bus runs half-hourly 8am–10pm; at night, the shark option is safest.

If you're coming in by train from Berlin or Warsaw, you'll arrive at the city's Belarus **train station**, served by Belorusskaya metro where the circle line connects you with ten of Moscow's 11-line metro system, possibly the world's finest – buy a handful of green plastic tokens (*zhetoni*) from any station at 3 roubles each. At the metal gates above the escalators, throw a *zheton* into the slot – it is valid for any journey until you come back above ground.

The **metro** is clean and fast, and runs 6am–1am. Stations are marked with a large letter 'M'. Get a Russian-language metro map from a newsstand to follow the station names, which are indicated only in Cyrillic letters.

The city's **buses**, **trams** and **trolleybuses** take tickets (*taloni*) at 4 roubles each, available from newsstands. A single ticket is transferable from one route to the next during a single journey – stamp your ticket in the puncher every time you board.

Two reliable **taxi** firms are *Central Moscow Taxi Bureau* (☎095/927 0000) and *Moscow Taxi* (☎095/238 1001), both with a similar call-out charge ($4/$3) and flat rate per km (50/60c). Agree a price before the driver sets off, especially to the airport.

Moscow has no tourist office. For **listings information**, the staid English-language press, the *Moscow Times* and *Moscow Tribune*, are pretty hopeless; wait for your fortnightly *eXile* every other Thursday, with its irreverent coverage of the expat scene and incisive bar and club listings. All these publications are free at expat watering holes.

Spartak

Club offices 1st Koptelsky Pereulok 18/2
Stadium Lokomotiv, see p.484
Colours All red with white trim
League champions (USSR) 1936 (autumn),
1938–39, 1952–53, 1956, 1958, 1962, 1969, 1979,
1987, 1989
Cup winners (USSR) 1938–39, 1946–47, 1950,
1958, 1963, 1965, 1971, 1992
League champions (Russia) 1992–94,
1996–99
Cup winners (Russia) 1993, 1998

Rare sight – a Spartak goal in the 1999 UCL

Far ahead of the domestic game, having won all but one of the league titles in the post-Soviet era, Spartak have thus far been prevented from matching this success internationally by the economic and political conditions at home. Still playing their home games at Lokomotiv's ground, they earned the wrath of populist Moscow mayor Yuri Luzhkov by not moving back to their former home at the Luzhniki stadium, whose reconstruction formed part of Luzhkov's blueprint for the city's regeneration. Having been refused permission by his city council to build a new stadium in Moscow, Spartak turned to regional authorities to see if one could be built out of town – but the knock-on effects of the 1998 economic crisis put those plans on ice.

Meanwhile, Spartak keep winning league titles, and are the only Moscow side with their own football school, complemented by a huge network of talent scouts. The club have their own magazine, their own town-centre store, their own TV contract, even their own brand of cola. More than anything, they have their own substantial fan base.

The people's team do not belong to one class of Moscow society, nor to any particular area, nor even to one home ground, but to the memory of the most dedicated figure in the history of Russian football.

It was the vision of Nikolai Starostin that the city should have a team which could operate independently of political interference. Having helped to create Spartak from the Moscow Sports Club that had been based in the Luzhniki park since the early Twenties, Starostin then coached the team, and even managed to play one match in the club's first Soviet championship win in the autumn of 1936. His three footballing brothers, Alexander, Andrei and Pyotr, also played for the team and for the USSR.

Officially the club was affiliated to the Moscow food producers' co-operative, but Starostin ensured that Spartak's relationship with the authorities was, at best, ambivalent. He would spend much of the next six decades combing the country for young talent and coaxing it away from other, more politically favoured, clubs.

Starostin's resolute stance against the KGB (represented by Dynamo) and the Red Army (CSKA) cost him dear – he spent ten years in Stalin's gulags after being charged with 'the promotion of bourgeois sport', and was released only after the intervention of the dictator's son, Vasily.

Nikolai Starostin died in February 1996, shortly before his 94th birthday. But his legacy lives on. Spartak's nationwide popularity, reputation for attractive football and freedom from any rusting state authority have helped them face the modern age.

Backed by *Gazprom*, the huge state gas and oil company, Spartak won the first three Russian titles after the break-up of the Soviet Union, and took part in three consecutive Champions' League campaigns. In 1995/96, under coach Oleg Romantsev (now the club's president), Spartak shocked everyone by taking maximum points to top their group, only to sell four key players – Stanislav Cherchesov, Viktor Onopko, Vasily Kulkov and Sergei Yuran – in the winter break and fall at the quarter-final stage.

A cut in sponsorship funds from *Gazprom* had forced Spartak to hit the selling trail. But for once, the club found political influence operating in their favour when, just before their Champions' League exit, mayor Yuri Luzhkov issued a decree enabling the team to sign players from outside the city without paying local tax. Their squad suitably reinforced on the cheap, Spartak won back their Russian title from Alaniya Vladikavkaz, beating the provincials 2–1 at a play-off in St Petersburg in 1996.

After an easier title win the following year, and out of action during the Russian winter, Spartak roared back in the spring of 1998 to knock Ajax out of the UEFA Cup quarter-finals, their swift counter-attacking game rewarded with goals by Alexandr Shirko and Valeri Kechinov in Amsterdam. In the semis, Spartak were unlucky to fall to a Ronaldo-inspired Inter, and the same club would stand between the Russians and progress from their Champions' League group in 1998/99.

All four of the country's last players of the year – Ilya Tsymbalar, Andrei Tikhonov, Dimitri Alenichev and Yegor Titov – have come from Spartak's ranks, and the return of Yuran to the club for the 1999 season raised hopes that Spartak might manage a decent run in the Champions' League. But it was not to be. In a relatively easy group, the team managed just one win, against Holland's Willem II Tilburg and suffered a 5–2 hammering from Sparta Prague in their final game. 'Relegated' to the UEFA Cup, Spartak didn't last long there, either, going out on away goals to Leeds United.

At home the club picked up a seventh title in eight years, but the season was blighted by dressing-room rows which saw Yuran depart once again, this time for Sturm Graz, while Tsymbalar chose the calmer changing room down the corridor with 'Lokomotiv' written on the door.

For 2000, the surprisingly successful Brazilian striker Robson was joined by two compatriots from Fluminense, midfielder Marcão and defender Alesandre, in the hope that they would strengthen the next bid for European success.

Here we go!

Turn left out of **Cherkizovskaya** metro (red line 1), where you'll be 2mins from the ticket office and Lokomotiv's main gate.

Just the ticket

The **ticket windows** are to the right of the main entrance. The stands are divided north, south, east and west, with tickets 40–50 roubles each. The covered east stand is best suited to visiting neutrals, the south (especially sectors #5 and #7) for the Spartak faithful, who also occupy far corners of the west and otherwise deserted north stands.

Swift half

The market halls either side of Cherkizovskaya metro have **stand-up bars**. Inside the stadium, there's a **buffet** between sectors #1 and #2, selling sandwiches and beer from under the counter. Promise to keep your can hidden from the passing *militsia*, and you'll be sold one for 8 roubles.

Club merchandise

Although the new **Spartak store** off the Garden Ring near Kursk metro (Ul Stariy Basmannaya 15, open Mon–Fri 10am–7pm, Sat 10am–5pm, no credit cards) looks impressive, inside it's tiny, with a small selection of shirts (250 roubles) and publications. At the Lokomotiv stadium, you'll find two red huts on the path from the main entrance selling merchandise at lower prices.

Ultra culture

Spartak fans earned their hard reputation with away trips to non-Russian republics in the old Soviet days, and became more organised in the post-Communist era. Choosing a name from Robert Louis Stevenson's *Treasure Island*, **Flint's Crew** (a reflection of their drunken revelry rather than any literary leanings), the group burst onto the scene in 1994. Since then, thousands have joined the cause and, considering the economic and geographical circumstances, the *Crew* take decent numbers away with them, some 2,000 travelling to Amsterdam in 1998.

In print

A **colour programme** (5 roubles) is on sale at the ticket office for every Spartak home game. The club also put out an eponymous monthly magazine (20 roubles), available at the ground and the club shop in town.

In the net

The club's **official site** is the most comprehensive of its kind in the country, but is currently Russian-language only at: www.spartak.com.

For a superb **unofficial site** offering the latest news, match reports, a club history and squad details in English, try Oleg Komlyakov's homepage at: www.geocities.com/Colosseum/7326.

 ## Torpedo-Luzhniki/ZiL

Luzhniki stadium, Luzhniki Park, and **Stadion 'Torpedo' E Streltsova**, Avtozavodskaya
Capacity 85,000/20,000
Colours Green shirts, white shorts
League champions (USSR) 1960, 1965, 1976 (autumn)
Cup winners (USSR) 1949, 1952, 1960, 1968, 1972, 1986
Cup winners (Russia) 1993

A club whose roots are in a working-class district of south-east Moscow, Torpedo are named after the first Soviet-built production car, and until recently were sponsored by *ZiL* – erstwhile purveyors of Fifties-style limousines to the politburo. In 1996, as Russia's new political class exercised its right to choose a Mercedes over the home-grown product, *ZiL* found they could no longer support the club and for a few months Torpedo faced extinction.

Salvation arrived in the form of the owners of Moscow's Luzhniki stadium, itself privatised in 1992. After gaining permission from the city council, which retained a 49% stake in the Luzhniki, the entrepreneurs took control of Torpedo and set about transforming the club from a post-Communist relic into a modern sporting organisation.

One of their first actions was to move the team from their modest ground on Avtozavodksaya to the Luzhniki itself – even though the national stadium was undergoing massive refurbishment and when ready would accommodate the average Torpedo home crowd tenfold and more.

As for Torpedo themselves, the squad has been rebuilt following the collapse of *ZiL* and, like Lokomotiv, the club have placed the emphasis on nurturing new talent – a policy that bore fruit earlier in the decade, when the club knocked Manchester United out of the UEFA Cup in 1992.

A sister club, Torpedo-ZiL, continue to operate in the Avtozavodskaya stadium, winning promotion to the game's second level via a play-off in 1998. Despite their given name, Torpedo-Luzhniki also tend to switch home games back to this ground, now named after the most famous – and infamous – player in the club's history: the Russian 'Pelé', Eduard Streltsov.

Like Spartak's Nikolai Starostin in an earlier era, Streltsov fell foul of Soviet authority. On the eve of the 1958 World Cup he was 'invited' to join either CSKA or Dynamo. His refusal to leave Torpedo led to his expulsion from the national team, and he was subsequently charged with 'criminal behaviour' and sentenced to seven years in the gulags.

After his release, Streltsov led Torpedo to the Soviet title in 1965 and a cup triumph three years later. Even had he not returned from the camps, his name would have lived on among the fans – his trademark back-heel pass is still known as a 'Streltsov' in Russia.

Here we go!

For the Luzhniki, take red metro line 1 to **Sportivnaya**, then follow the exit signs to Stadion I Lenina. The stadium is a 5 min walk immediately ahead of you. For the Avtozavodskaya, take green line 2 to **Avtozavodskaya** metro, walk up Ul Masterkova to Vostochnaya, and the ground is ahead on your left.

Swift half

At the Luzhniki, there's a **restaurant** in green stand D behind one goal and **shashlik stands** outside blue stand B behind the other.

Before you get to the Avtozavodskaya, at Ul Masterkova 2, is the classic old *Pelmelnnaya Danilovsky*, a sight straight out of a Vissotsky song, where dumpy toothless dinner ladies serve steaming bowls of *pelmelnnyi*, Russian ravioli, accompanied by cheap beer and raucous prison slang.

Groundhopping

● CSKA

Club office Leningradski Prospekt 39
Stadium CSKA, Ul 3-ya Peschanaya
Colours Red shirts, blue shorts
League champions (USSR) 1946–48, 1950–51, 1970, 1991
Cup winners (USSR) 1945, 1948, 1951, 1955, 1991

CSKA are traditionally considered Moscow's third club, with a reputation based on a post-war side said to have been the greatest team of the Soviet era. The club's board is still run by the Red Army which has overseen the team since the club's official formation in 1923. Originally known as the Society of Ski Sport Enthusiasts (1901), the club went through several changes – OPPV, CDKA, CDSA, CSKMO – before settling on the CSKA in 1960.

The club's golden era – when they were known as CDKA – was the six-year period immediately after World War II. With a team which had enjoyed the luxury of playing together during the war, CDKA won five titles and provided all but one of the players for the USSR's first international competitive appearance at the Olympic football tournament of 1952.

Since then, honours have been few. The defensive strength of international captain Albert Shesternev helped CSKA win the league in 1970, and the team also won the last Soviet title in 1991. A year later, they knocked holders Barcelona out of the European Cup with an away-leg comeback which silenced the Nou Camp.

After recovering from a row with ex-coach Alexander Tarkahanov – who took key players with him to form a rival team, now lowly FC CSKA '97 – and taking advantage of a renovated if roofless CSKA stadium, the club celebrated its official 75th anniversary with an encouraging 1998 campaign under mercurial coach Oleg Dolmatov. A dozen straight victories – including a remarkable 4–1 win over Spartak – pushed the army club into a runners-up spot and a place in the qualifying round of the revamped Champions League' for 1999/2000. With key players Vladimir Kulik upfront and captain Sergei Semak in the midfield, CSKA had the perfect opportunity to improve on an otherwise dire European record.

It was an opportunity they flunked, failing to make the group phase of the Champions' League after a humiliating 4–0 defeat by Norway's Molde. In the league CSKA finished in third place, 17 points behind Spartak, but coach Oleg Dolmatov had other things to worry about prior to the start of the 2000 season – his wife Natalya was abducted, almost certainly by a criminal gang.

The CSKA stadium lies behind the main army sports complex on the odd-numbered side of Leningradskiy Prospekt, a 10min walk along leafy Viktorenko from **Aeroport** (green line 2) metro station.

The **7x7 Bar** at Leningradskiy Prospekt 37, near the sports complex, is decorated with sports pictures, including a large photo of Pelé with Bobby Kennedy.

🏐 Lokomotiv

Lokomotiv stadium, B Cherkizovskaya 125a
Capacity 30,000
Colours Red shirts, white shorts
Cup winners (USSR) 1936, 1957
Cup winners (Russia) 1996, 2000

Moscow's railway workers' team boast a wonderfully kitsch stadium decorated with train motifs in the north-east of the city. Currently also used for Spartak home games, this well-maintained ground, extensively used in the *Coca-Cola* 'Eat, Drink, Sleep Football' TV commercials, has seen a decent amount of European action over the last couple of years.

Lokomotiv seldom troubled the statisticians during the Soviet era, but in the Nineties the club proved themselves smart spotters of young talent. Four of the new breed of Russian internationals have cut their footballing teeth beneath the sign of the diesel engine – defender Igor Chugainov, midfielders Alexei Kosolapov and Andrei Solomatin, and goalkeeper Sergei Ovchinnikov, the latest man to earn the 'new Yashin' tag and beneficiary of a (theoretically) lucrative move to Benfica in the summer of 1997.

A season earlier, these four were at the heart of an enterprising side which beat Bayern Munich in Germany in the first leg of a UEFA Cup tie, then won their first post-Communist domestic honour by lifting the 1996 Russian cup.

Despite having Chugainov tested positive for drugs after the match – the sample later went missing – Lokomotiv qualified for the Cup-Winners' Cup where they got through easy early-round draws to face a depleted AEK Athens side in the quarter-finals. Borrowing Spartak's keeper Ruslan Nyigmatulin for the occasion, Lokomotiv managed to take a 0–0 result to Moscow, and there, with the last kick of the game, it was Chugainov who made the scoreline 2–1. The semi was lost to Stuttgart, but a creditable third place in the league – with goals from the tricky Georgian Zaza Dzhanashiya – coincided with another run in the Cup-Winners' Cup in 1998/99, the club again reaching the semi-finals before losing to Lazio on a narrow 1–0 aggregate.

Loko continued to progress in the 1999 domestic season, staying within touching distance of Spartak throughout before finishing second. A 7–1 aggregate walloping by Leeds in the UEFA Cup put paid to the club's European ambitions, but a string of new signings helped the club to a 3–2 cup final win over CSKA in 2000, and that long-awaited first title may not be far off.

Falling over backwards to score – Zaza Dzhanashiya

Form an orderly queue – empty seats in Russian grounds are often filled by soldiers

Eat, drink, sleep…

Bars and clubs

Moscow survives on a dollar economy and can be as expensive as Tokyo. When it comes to nightlife it is certainly ten times as tacky. The average **nightclub** can cost anything from $30 to $100 admission and will probably feature gorillas on the door, mafia flunkies at the bar and ladies of ill repute on the dancefloor. Keep your wits about you at all times, not least when staggering out of any club and into a taxi.

There *are* decent **bars** in town, charging around $5 for a foreign beer, slightly less for a Russian one – *Baltika* is the most acceptable home brand, *Tverskoe* if you prefer dark beer. Beware that counterfeit liquor abounds.

Chesterfield's, Zemlyanoi Val 26. From the same people that brought you the *Hungry Duck* (see below), a huge bar with a billiard area, a stage, Sky 2 and Channel 5, and other side rooms.

Admission 50 roubles. Look for the neon sign opposite Kursk station/Kurskaya metro.

Khaos, Ul Timirgazevskaya 17. Perhaps Moscow's best underground club, attracting the best local DJs and a young crowd there for what they're spinning. Could do with a quiet bar area to calm everybody down, though. Open until 6am. Timirgazevskaya metro.

Ofsaid, Hovoslobodskaya Ulitsa 14/19. The only football bar in town, signposted on the side of a building by Mendeleevskaya metro. Walk up a lawn-green set of steps to a small room packed with scarves, shirts, framed pictures and a goal-net dominating the bar. Open 11am–11pm daily.

Propaganda, Bolshoi Zlatousinsky Pereulok 7 (off Maroseika Ulitsa). Bar for young Bohemian locals, transformed when the tables are removed at 10pm and a real nightclub atmosphere is generated. Entrance 40 roubles after 10pm Fri–Sat. Kitai Gorod metro.

Respublika, Ul Nikolskaya 17. Very popular new bar/disco with a mixed crowd. Full menu. Not a particularly adventurous music policy, but busy, cosy and fun. Open daily 6pm–6am. Lubyanka or Pl Revolutsiyi metro.

Restaurants

Moscow's eateries reflect the city's economic extremes. Few locals can afford to eat out, but those who do spend a small fortune doing it. If you're on a budget, or into social observation, the *stolovaya* – a **cheap slop** for the masses – is the place for you. Otherwise, expect to pay $15 upwards before drinks, for a two-course meal which will probably include an excellent soup and a meat-heavy main dish. None of the places listed below takes credit cards unless otherwise stated.

Café Margarita, Malaya Bronnaya Ulitsa 28. Intimate eaterie with imaginative decor. Russian specialities. Mayakovskaya metro.

Moscow Bombay, Glinishchevsky Prospekt 3. Best Indian deal in town – tandoori dishes a speciality, vegetarian options, lunchtime bargains. Most major credit cards. Pushkinskaya metro.

Starlite Diner, Ulitsa Bolshaya Sadovaya 16. Serious heaps of Americana on a plate, 24 hours a day. Best breakfasts east of Vienna. Mayakovskaya metro. *Starlite II* is at Ulitsa Koroviy Val 9, Oktyabrskaya metro.

Tiflis, Ulitsa Ostozhenka 32. If you're going to try ethnic cuisine, the moderately priced, moderately spiced fare on offer here is your best option. Being Georgian, every other dish features walnuts. Split-level, but avoid the atrocious Irish bar downstairs. Park Kultury metro.

U Babushki, Ulitsa Bolshaya Ordynka 42. Genuine Russian cuisine at inflated but bearable prices. Theatrical surroundings. Most credit cards. Tretyakovskaya metro.

Accommodation

The type of **room** you find depends on the kind of **visa** you have arranged; those coming on a business visa will do best to opt for private or hostel lodgings, easily arranged with little old ladies at the main train stations. Unless your trip has been organised through a package deal, you'll find most hotels laughably overpriced.

Moskva Hotel, Okhotniy Ryad 7 (☎095/292 1100, fax 095/292 9214). Reasonably priced, classic Communist hotel block within sight of the Kremlin – ask for a west-facing room. Sauna facilities. Visa and Mastercard accepted. Okhotniy Ryad/Teatralnaya metro.

Nasledie Hotel, Ulitsa Kosmonatov 2 (☎095/975 3501, fax 095/975 3619). Spartan but secure hostel with doubles at $20 per person, four-bed dorms at $15 per person, breakfast included. 11pm curfew. Visa and Mastercard. Metro VDNKh.

Prakash Guest House, Profsoyuznaya Ulitsa 83, korpus 1, entrance 2 (☎095/334 8201, fax 095/334 2598). Comfortable hostel on the third floor of a block, 20mins from the city centre. Clean rooms, plus the bonus of a small restaurant serving Indian food. Prices vary according to facilities, but $40 should see you tucked up safe and sound. Belyayevo metro.

Rossiya Hotel, Ul Varvarka 6 (☎095/232 6046, fax 095/232 6283). Recently revamped hotel, one of the most famous in the city, with more than 3,000 rooms. $150–250 for a double. Ideal riverside location just off Red Square, and with an excellent round-the-clock restaurant, *Moscow Time*, worth the journey there alone. Kitai-Gorod metro.

Travellers' Guest House, Bolshaya Pereslavskaya Ulitsa 50 (☎095/971 4059, fax 095/280 7686). A godsend in a wilderness of dodgy, service-free central accommodation, the *Travellers'* can not only sort you out a single room for $40 or a double for $50, but will also help with your visa, your laundry, train tickets and lodgings in St Petersburg for a small service charge. Four-bed dormitories also available. Visa and Mastercard accepted. Short walk from Prospekt Mira metro.

Scotland

Scottish Football Association, 6 Park Gardens, Glasgow, G3 7YF
☎0141/332 6372   Fax 0141/332 7559   E-mail info@scottishfa.co.uk

League champions Rangers   **Cup winners** Rangers
League Cup winners Celtic   **Promoted** St Mirren, Dunfermline Athletic
Relegated none (see text)

European participants 2000/01   Rangers (UCL qualifiers); Celtic, Hearts,
Aberdeen (UEFA Cup)

Long before the establishment of a
Parliament in Edinburgh, football –
along with the legal system and
education – was one of the few
areas of Scottish life independent from English rule. The sense of independence is
more than merely administrative. While
the English may have invented the modern
game, it was the Scots who provided much
of the manpower for their early professional clubs. Take a look at any English
line-up from the early part of the century,
and you'll find plenty of Scottish names.
And the Scots did more than simply supply
personnel – they developed the tactics, the
skills and techniques that transformed the
sport from 'hacking and punting' into a
sophisticated game of short passing and
dribbling.

The Scots were also keen missionaries,
their players and coaches travelling across
Europe to spread the word at the turn of
the century. The enormous influence of
Scottish coaching on the English game has
continued to this day, yet despite the
stream of talent constantly heading south,
and the near total dominance of the Glasgow clubs, the Scottish league remains well
supported.

Perhaps all this goes some way to
explaining the intense pride taken in the
achievements of the national team and of
Scotland's club sides in European competition – though there has been precious
little of the latter in recent seasons.

The Scottish Football Association was
founded in 1873, and a year later a national
cup competition was launched. Few of the

clubs which dominated those early amateur years thrived once professionalism
was given the nod in 1893. Queen's Park of
Glasgow are a surviving remnant of those
early years, but have spent decades in the
lower reaches of the league. Others, such
as Third Lanark and Vale of Leven, have
long since departed from the scene.

The first year of the professional league
saw Glasgow's Celtic lift the title, finishing
just one point ahead of neighbours Rangers.
The battle between the 'Old Firm', with
Celtic representing Irish Catholics and
Rangers the Protestant community, has
dominated the domestic game ever since –
between 1905 and 1947, the title went to
another team only once. The sectarian and
often violent character of the Glasgow
rivalry is one of the most unattractive
aspects of Scottish football but, arguably,
the dominant position of the two teams
on the field has been more damaging.

The Scottish national team took part
in the first-ever official international game
when they drew 0–0 with England in 1872.
They won the first Home Championship,
the annual competition between the four
nations of the United Kingdom.

But it wasn't until 1929 that Scotland
played a continental side. Like England, the
Scots also ignored the pre-war World
Cups, making their first appearance in the
finals in 1954 – they lost 1–0 to Austria
and were hammered 7–0 by Uruguay.

It was at club level that the Scots made
their mark on the international scene. In
1967, Celtic defeated Inter Milan in Lisbon
to become the first British side to win the

London lament – Scots fans have a 'morning after' feeling following play-off defeat by England

European Cup. A week later Rangers lost out in extra-time to Bayern Munich in the final of the Cup-Winners' Cup. And Scotland so nearly fielded a trio of finalists in Europe that year, as little Kilmarnock made it to the semi-finals of the Fairs' (now UEFA) Cup – their performance an indication of the strength in-depth of Scottish club football at the time.

But with the exception of the 'Lisbon Lions', Scotland has been known for its outstanding individuals rather than its great teams – players such as Denis Law of Manchester United, Kenny Dalglish of Celtic and Liverpool, John Robertson of Nottingham Forest. A remarkable percentage of English championship sides have included a Scottish midfield general – George Graham at Arsenal and Billy Bremner at Leeds in the early Seventies; Graeme Souness in the great Liverpool side of the early Eighties; and Gary McAllister, also at Leeds, in the early Nineties.

The list of great managers is equally impressive – Bill Shankly of Liverpool, Matt Busby of Manchester United, Jock Stein of Celtic, and in the modern era the three most successful managers in the English game – Graham, Dalglish and, of course, Alex Ferguson. In recent years the tide of talent flowing southwards has slowed. English clubs can now find cheaper players of equal or higher standing from the continent, and there has been less talent emerging from Scotland's Boys Clubs and junior teams.

Yet still the Scottish national side defies the prophets of doom by keeping its head above the international waterline. The Scots qualified for five World Cups in a row between 1974 and 1990, and though they failed to advance beyond the group stage in any of them, they provided English fans with a surrogate team to 'support' – and a lot of vivid memories. Like Archie Gemmill's solo goal against Holland in 1978, David Narey's toe-poke against Brazil four years later, and Jim Leighton's vain attempt to keep out Careca's late strike for the Brazilians at Italia '90.

The Scots turned in what some regard as their best-ever performance at an international tournament at Euro '92, yet still failed to make it past the first round. They

Basics

If travelling from England, little changes in terms of practicalities once you arrive in Scotland. Customs **entry requirements** are the same, as is the **currency** – although you will be given Scottish £5 and £1 notes; both are legal tender throughout the UK, but few shops in England will accept the latter, so spend them before you head south.

The **telephone code** for Glasgow is 0141, for Edinburgh 0131.

The best way to get from one Scottish city to another is by **train**, although, as in England, the equivalent buses and **coaches** can be substantially cheaper.

The most attractive legal difference between the two 'countries' is the pub opening hours: Scottish pubs are not tied by restrictive **English licensing laws** and most stay open until midnight, some well beyond that.

did not qualify for USA '94 at all. But two years later all those battling qualities of discipline and team spirit were on show again, at Euro '96 – and once more Scotland somehow contrived not to qualify for the knockout stage, Patrick Kluivert's late consolation goal for Holland against England saving Dutch bacon while the Scots could only beat Switzerland 1–0 and went out on goal difference.

At France '98, Craig Brown's men lost out by a wider margin. Feisty in their opening 2–1 defeat by Brazil, carefully controlled in a 1–1 draw with Norway, they lost the plot completely in their last match to go down 3–0 to Morocco.

Subsequent performances in the Euro 2000 qualifiers were typically disciplined but often uninspiring, though they were enough to land the Scots a play-off against England – a two-legged affair which tested to the limit the Tartan Army's ability cheerily to dismiss defeat. Two first-half goals from Paul Scholes in the first leg at Hampden had left Scotland searching for a miracle, yet it so nearly came. Don Hutchison gave the visitors the lead at Wembley, and a complacent England were fortunate to hang on to their aggregate advantage.

Failure to qualify for Euro 2000 resulted in Brown facing calls for his dismissal, yet the majority of fans believe the former schoolteacher has done well to achieve respectable results with a team sadly lacking the quality of past generations.

With English Premiership clubs no longer looking north of the border for

young talent and other SPL teams following the lead of Rangers and Celtic into the European transfer market, the Scottish game is stagnating in more ways than one.

Small wonder that the two Glasgow giants have expressed an interest in the 'Atlantic League' project which would see the leading clubs in Scotland, Portugal, Holland, Belgium and perhaps Scandinavia leaving their domestic leagues in order to play a higher standard of football – for commensurately higher financial rewards. The initial reaction to the idea among Scotland's lesser teams was fearful, but there are those who believe their game would actually benefit from the removal of the Old Firm's domination.

Match practice

The days of whisky bottles being passed around the terraces are gone. Alcohol is banned from many grounds, police and stewards will eject drunken supporters, and most Scottish stadia have been upgraded to all-seaters with modern facilities – clubs here having been quicker to modernise their grounds than their counterparts in south of the border.

Weekend games are played on Saturdays at 3pm, with live TV matches generally on Sunday evenings. Midweek fixtures kick-off at 7.30 or 7.45pm.

A different league

The Scottish League has gone through various mutations over the years. In 1975, in a bid to increase the number of competitive games played by the top clubs, the Scottish Football Association introduced an elite ten-team Premier Division. In 1994 the League was restructured from top to bottom. A new Third Division was created, and all divisions were reduced in size to ten teams. Three years later, the top-flight teams broke away to form the Scottish Premier League (SPL), capable of negotiating its own TV rights and modelled on the English Premiership.

Promotion and relegation between the SPL and the First Division remains, however, and the former was increased in size to 12 teams for the 2000/01 season. At the end of the 1999/2000 campaign, the team finishing top of the First Division (St Mirren) gained automatic promotion, while the second- and third-placed sides (Dunfermline and Falkirk) were due to enter a play-off mini-league with the team finishing bottom of the SPL (Aberdeen). However, Falkirk's facilities did not meet stringent criteria laid down by the SPL, so the play-off group was abandoned – Dunfermline went up automatically, while Aberdeen retained their top-flight status.

The 12 SPL clubs now play each other three times between the end of July and early April, with a short break in January. After 33 matches, the table divides in half; the top six play five games to decide the title and European places, while the bottom six play five games to decide relegation. The bottom team swaps places with the top one from the ten-team First Division, ctieria permitting.

There are now three ten-team Divisions below the SPL, the two new clubs coming into the Third being Elgin City and Peterhead – both from Scotland's emerging football region of the Highlands.

Up for the cup

The Scottish Cup began in 1874, two years after the English FA Cup, but the Scots preceded the English in developing a second knockout competition when their League Cup began in 1946. Unlike their English

counterparts, the two Cups do not run simultaneously.

The first round of the League Cup is in the first week of August and involves 16 clubs, excluding the SPL sides and 14 other sides who receive a bye. The second round in mid-August includes SPL teams. All games are single-leg and there are no replays, results being decided on the day by extra-time and a shoot-out if necessary. The final is played at a neutral ground in November.

The Scottish Cup kicks off with a first round proper in mid-December, although non-league sides begin qualification in August. SPL sides join the competition in the third round, traditionally in the last week of January, and the final takes place in the last week of May at Hampden Park. All ties are single-leg with one replay, after which it's extra-time and penalties.

Just the ticket

Football is a tad cheaper here than in England. Ticket prices range from £10 to £30 and for big games should be bought well in advance. The major clubs operate telephone credit-card booking services.

Half-time

No alcohol is served at most grounds, so fans make do with *Irn Bru* or low-alcohol lager. Scotch pies are scoffed by the dozen, as well as the snacks familiar at English grounds.

The back page

Scotland has a long tradition of serious football writing. At the turn of the century magazines such as *The Scottish Referee* and *Scottish Sport* featured intelligent discussion on the development of the game. Today, alas, there is no exclusively Scottish football publication.

The *Daily Record* is Scotland's daily tabloid, *The Scotsman* and *The Herald* the national broadsheets. Each, in its own way, offers comprehensive coverage of the game in Scotland. In recent years, the London-based tabloids such as the *Daily Mirror* and *The Sun* have produced more local soccer material for their Scottish editions. As with players, Scotland has exported many of its best sportswriters to England. Perhaps the most respected football writer in Britain today is Hugh McIllvanney, of the *Sunday Times*. McIlvanney's fellow Scot, Patrick Barclay, is also well worth reading in the *Sunday Telegraph*.

Action replay

The SPL's deal with BSkyB gives the satellite broadcaster the rights to show a live game most weekends, usually on Sundays at around 6pm. Sky also carries Scottish Cup games, including the final, and the League Cup final live. An excellent round-up programme, *Scottish Football Review*, is broadcast midweek, with highlights of all SPL and First Division matches, plus news and interviews.

Terrestrially, the BBC has a Saturday night highlights show, *Sportscene*, usually shown around 10pm, which in addition to extended highlights and goals from the day's SPL and First Division games, includes a selection of English matches.

Ultra culture

The absence of drink and bottles has meant that the hooligansim which once blighted the Scottish game has all but disappeared – although the assault on referee Hugh Dallas by Celtic fans during the decisive Old Firm game in 1998/99 raised all the old fears of a resurgence of trouble.

As Dallas and his fellow officials would no doubt testify, the Glasgow and Edinburgh derbies remain tense, hostile affairs, but with few visiting supporters now allowed in to such games, you are more likely to see violence on the pitch than in the stands, even if the Catholic and Protestant communities remain bitterly divided.

Strangely, football unites those groups as well as dividing them, since Celt and Ger alike stand proud in their support of the Scottish national team. In contrast to the right-wing thug element which has infiltrated followers of England, the Tartan Army are renowned for their gregarious-ness, good-natured drinking and ability to laugh in the face of footballing tragedy.

After a World Cup qualifying defeat by Yugoslavia in Zagreb in 1989, a lone Scottish piper stood on his hotel balcony to play a lament, and soon found he had a crowd of hundreds listening to him in the square below. A year later, Scots cheerily joined in an all-night samba party alongside fans of the Brazil team which had just knocked their heroes out of Italia '90.

At France '98, the Scots were voted the best-behaved visiting fans by the people of Bordeaux.

In the net

The Scottish FA's official website is a fair offering, with an efficient if somewhat staid layout, the minimum of graphical fuss, the latest national-team news (all levels) and links to club sites (official ones only). You'll find it at: www.scottishfa.co.uk.

The SPL also has its own website, at: www.scotprem.com. This is run by the *Planet Internet* company, responsible for so many English official club sites, and is really nothing to write home about, with little information unavailable elsewhere.

Far better is the D C Thomson company's generic site at: www.scottishfootball. com. Slightly reminiscent of *Football365* south of the border, it lacks that site's wit but its coverage is similarly comprehensive, everything is thoroughly updated and a true Scottish identity comes across loud and clear.

Glasgow

There is no club game in Europe that arouses as much passion and hatred as the Old Firm clash.

Its roots lie in the violent Irish political struggle whose divisions and loyalties were transferred to Glasgow with the large emmigration of Irish workers to Scotland in the late 19th century. Rangers are the team of the city's Protestant community, Celtic represent the Roman Catholics. Rangers were the first to be formed in 1873, with Celtic setting up some 15 years later.

Celtic, formed from an amalgamation of Catholic Boys' Club sides at the prompting of Brother Walfrid of the Marist Order, made no attempt to hide their affiliations – although the club was originally set up to help the poor of Glasgow's East End, regardless of religious background.

Likewise in their early years Rangers had not shown a great deal of interest in religion – yet the foundation of Celtic made them the focus of Protestant support. It was Rangers' unwritten rule of not signing Catholic players, or indeed employing Catholics in any position, that made them the object of so much criticism, as Scottish authorities struggled to tackle the increasingly violent clashes at derby games

between the two teams. The term 'Old Firm' refers to the profitable nature of the rivalry. The sectarian divide intensified a local rivalry and ensured huge crowds – and revenues – whenever the two sides met. With today's SPL structure, the two are all but guaranteed to meet four times in the league season and, given their domination, they usually meet in one or both of the cup competitions.

Violence at Old Firm games long preceded the worst of the British hooligan era but, following a series of incidents in the Seventies and a particularly gruesome riot after the 1980 Cup Final, pressure mounted on the clubs to at least reduce the tension, if not renounce their identities. Still Rangers continued to refuse to sign any Catholics, and Celtic, though they had always signed Protestant players, refused the counterdemand that they remove the Irish tricolour from their ground.

Today, although the Old Firm games are still a focal point for sectarians, with extremist political pamphlets on sale and religious and political songs much in evidence, they are no longer the dangerously violent encounters they once were. Glasgow is no longer divided into Catholic and

Glasgow essentials

Glasgow **airport** is 14km west of the city; *City Link* buses make the 25min journey to the central **bus station** at Buchanan Street (fare £3 single, £5 return).

There are two main train stations, Queen Street and Central. Trains to and from Edinburgh come in to Queen Street while those from England terminate at Central.

There are plenty of **city buses**, but beware that you have to put the exact change into the slot on entrance – no change will be given. Buses run until around 11.30pm, after which there is a skeleton network of night buses. Glasgow also has a local **train service** (known colloquially as 'Low Level') and a one-line circular **underground** (the 'Clockwork Orange', flat fare 80p single, £1.60 return). A day pass for the latter, valid Mon–Fri after 9.30am, all day Sat–Sun, is £2.50, £3.50 when combined with the train.

Glasgow is well served by a fleet of **black cabs**. To call one, dial ☎0141/204 4400.

The main **tourist information centre** is at the corner of George Square near the top of Buchanan Street (Mon–Sat 9am–6pm, ☎0141/204 4400, fax 0141/221 3524).

Information on **nightlife** can be found in *The List* – an excellent fortnightly listings magazine covering Glasgow and Edinburgh, it costs £1.95. The same staff also produce an annual eating and drinking guide to both cities (£3.95).

Protestant districts, and many Rangers and Celtic fans are now neighbours. Officials of both clubs now denounce bigotry, and face stiff penalties if they seek to perpetuate it.

These days, more controversy is generated by the clubs' apparent aspirations to leave the Scottish domestic game altogether than by their mutual rivalry.

The thrilling fields

 ## Rangers

Ibrox Stadium, Edmiston Drive
Capacity 50,500 (all-seated)
Colours Blue shirts, white shorts
League champions 1891, 1899, 1900–2, 1911–13, 1918, 1920–21, 1923–25, 1927–31, 1933–35, 1937, 1939, 1947, 1949–50, 1953, 1956–57, 1959, 1961, 1963–64, 1975–76, 1978, 1987, 1989–97, 1999–2000
Cup winners 1894, 1897–98, 1903, 1928, 1930, 1932, 1934–36, 1948–49, 1950, 1953, 1960, 1962–64, 1966, 1973, 1976, 1978–79, 1981, 1992–93, 1996, 1999–2000
Cup-Winners' Cup winners 1972

Forty-eight titles and counting. Rangers are Scotland's most successful club, period. In recent years, they have become a wealthy business, too – the first club in Scotland capable of bringing in players from England and Europe. Yet two things still rankle at Ibrox: Rangers have never managed to lift the continent's premier club trophy, the Champions' Cup, and after losing the title to their rivals in 1998, they equalled – but not bettered – Celtic's record of nine successive Scottish championships.

While always among the front-runners from the early days, Rangers firmly established themselves as Scotland's top club in the inter-war years when they won 15 league titles, with sides featuring goalscorers such as Bob McPhail, who scored 233 goals between 1927 and 1939, and Sam

English, who hit 44 in 1931/32 alone. This was also a period of massive crowds, and the club's record attendance of 118,567 was set at an Old Firm game in 1939.

Following World War II, Rangers faced a stronger challenge from Edinburgh than from Celtic, but with a side marshalled by the big centre-half George Young, they won three of Scotland's first four post-war championships.

The Sixties saw the Gers begin to make an impression in Europe. In 1961 they reached the final of the Cup-Winners' Cup, losing out to Fiorentina. Defeat in the final of the same competition in 1967 was more painful, however. A week before, Celtic had lifted the European Cup and Rangers had the perfect opportuniy to keep the gloating to a minimum – but an extra-time goal by Bayern Munich ended hopes of an Old Firm double in Europe.

In 1971, Ibrox Park had its second tragedy. Fifty years earlier it had been the scene of the world's first football disaster, when a wooden terrace collapsed, killing 26 people. On 2 January 1971, 66 fans leaving Ibrox by Stairway 13 at the end of an Old Firm derby were crushed to death, and 145 were injured. It was the worst tragedy in Scottish football history and one which united Rangers and Celtic fans in mourning.

A year after the disaster, Rangers had their greatest moment, finally getting their hands on the Cup-Winners' Cup. Revenge was gained over Bayern in the semi-final and two goals from Willie Johnstone helped win the final against Dynamo Moscow, 3–2, in Barcelona's Nou Camp. Though the club's masterful midfield playmaker Jim Baxter had retired, this Rangers included Alfie Conn, Willy Henderson and full-back John Greig in its ranks.

Greig went on to manage the side in the early Eighties, during a lean spell in which the club failed to win a title between 1978 and 1987. The era was brightened by cup wins, the exciting wing-play of Davie Cooper and the emergence of talented striker Ally McCoist. But the Rangers of the Seventies and Eighties was an institution in decline. Ironically, for a club which had been a strident campaigner against old-fashioned amateurism at the turn of the century, Rangers had become conservative and unprofessional.

Their policy of not employing Catholics was increasingly under fire from the media and politicians. Aside from the moral and political aspects of the unwritten rule, it just did not make footballing sense. Rangers missed out on two of Scotland's key players of the late Seventies and early Eighties – Celtic and Scotland full-back Danny McGrain, a Rangers-mad youngster who many believe was ignored simply because of his name, and Kenny Dalglish, another schoolboy Rangers fan who was snapped up by Celtic. Something had to change.

The elderly board received a shake-up when millionaire entrepeneur David Murray and manager Graeme Souness arrived on the scene in the mid-Eighties. While Murray set about transforming Rangers' business practices, Souness made it his mission to reverse the pattern of transfer trade with England, end the club's title drought and make Rangers a competitive

force in Europe. Souness was not a Rangers man. Unlike Greig, he had never played for the club; indeed he had never played in the Scottish League. He started out as player-manager and his own tough tackling, along with those of imported hatchet men such as Englishmen Graham Roberts and Terry Hurlock, gave a brief impression of a team of cloggers. Yet the cash provided by Murray also allowed Souness to bring in more creative English players such as Trevor Francis, Mark Walters and Trevor Steven. The strategy paid off – Rangers won the title in 1989, and would go on to dominate the Scottish game throughout the Nineties.

Yet the European success demanded by Murray did not follow. After Souness' departure for Liverpool in 1991, Rangers continued to look outside Scotland for playing talent under the management of Walter Smith. In 1992/93, they qualified for the quarter-final group stage of the Champions' League, thanks to a memorable two-leg 'Battle of Britain' victory over Leeds United.

Rangers managed to stay unbeaten in the Champions' League. Their 2–2 home draw with Marseille was a classic, played

Day of delight – Tugay Kerimoglu, the first Turk to wear a Rangers shirt, at the 2000 Cup Final

in a frenzied atmosphere, and throughout the campaign the Scottish champions, often with key players missing through injury, and with the three-foreigner rule also depleting their squad, performed with enterprise and guts. Ultimately, Marseille beat them to a place in the final by a single point, gained in their last match against Club Bruges – a game which has since been the subject of a UEFA match-rigging inquiry.

Needless to say, expectations were high for greater things in the following seasons. But despite continued domination on the home front, Rangers flopped in Europe, performing poorly when they managed to gain entrance to the Champions' League, often not qualifying at all.

The 1997/98 season saw the spotlight shift back to Scotland, where Rangers' attempt to win a tenth successive title foundered amid another injury crisis and a collective attack of nerves. With the championship heading back to Celtic Park and the cup final also lost, to Hearts, Smith's last season in charge ended trophyless.

The new boss, Dutch coach Dick Advocaat, disposed of troubled veterans such as Ally McCoist, Brian Laudrup and Paul Gascoigne, and built a new team around a core of Dutch and Italian players. Their style was not always attractive, and some Gers fans muttered that the team had lost its local appeal. Yet it was the mid-season signing of a Scotsman, midfielder Neil McCann, from Hearts that kick-started Rangers' 1998/99 campaign and laid the foundations for a domestic treble, the title being sealed with a win at Celtic Park, the Scottish Cup against the same opposition at Hampden three weeks later.

The club had also enjoyed its best European run in years, beating Leverkusen and falling narrowly to the eventual winners Parma in the UEFA Cup. Revenge for that defeat was to follow within months, Rangers when beat the Italian side 2–1 on aggregate to qualify for the 1999/2000 Champions' League. There, unlucky not to beat Bayern Munich at home and unlucky,

also, to be up against the quality of Hector Cúper's Valéncia, Advocaat's side finished third in their group. Luck continued to desert them in the UEFA Cup, where they were beaten on penalties by Borussia Dortmund in Germany, but at home Rangers were as classy as ever, winning the SPL title by a 21-point margin from Celtic, and crushing Aberdeen 4–0 in the Scottish Cup Final at Hampden.

A clearout of some of the club's underachieving imports – Marco Negri and Daniel Prodan among them – was expected in the close season, but Advocaat seemed unlikely to reverse his policy of looking abroad for new signings. Why change a successful formula, after all?

Here we go!

Take the **underground** from St Enoch's Square to **Ibrox**. Allow 15mins.

Swift half

Right opposite the Ibrox underground station is **Stadium**, an attractive pre-match venue with plenty of Gers stuff to gaze at while downing a pint. The **Stadium Chip Shop** opposite is a popular meeting place, as the piles of greasy newspaper wrapping floating their way up to the ground testify.

Club merchandise

The **Rangers Shop** at 21 Trongate in the centre of town is open Mon–Sat 9.30am–5.30pm, Sun midday–5pm. At the ground, the **1873 Superstore** has a bigger range. It's open Mon–Sat 9.30am–5.30pm.

In print

As well as the **Gers** matchday programme, the club produces **Rangers News** (weekly, £1.50) and the glossier **Rangers** (monthly, £2.50). The fanzine **Follow, Follow** (£1) is the established voice of the Ibrox faithful.

In the net

The club's **official website** is every bit as slick as you'd expect, though not too heavy on the graphics and quick to navigate as a result, at: www.rangers.co.uk.

Celtic

Celtic Park, 95 Kerrydale Street
Capacity 60,000 (all-seated)
Colours Green-and-white hooped shirts, white shorts
League champions 189–94, 1896, 1898, 1905–10, 1914–17, 1919, 1922, 1926, 1936, 1938, 1954, 1966–74, 1977, 1979, 1981–82, 1986, 1988, 1998
Cup winners 1892, 1899, 1900, 1904, 1907–8, 1911–12, 1914, 1923, 1925, 1927, 1931, 1933, 1937, 1951, 1954, 1965, 1967, 1969, 1971–72, 1974–75, 1977, 1980, 1985, 1988–89, 1995
European Cup winners 1967

Nowhere is the transformation of a football club from central component of a working-class community to a multi-million pound business more evident than in the East End of Glasgow, home of Celtic Football Club.

Not so long ago, the area around the ground was home to shipbuilders and factory workers, who on a Saturday afternoon would pour out of the terraced houses and corner pubs to make their way to Celtic Park. Today, the shining plastic and steel of the redesigned stadium stands in the middle of an area of extreme social problems. Boarded-up houses blight the nearby streets, while inside the ground, the terraces have been replaced by new stands and executive boxes.

Disturbing though Celtic Park's environment might be, the new stadium also symbolises the revitilisation of one of Britain's most famous clubs. After a decade of decline, discontent and defeats by Rangers, Celtic are at last in shape to launch a serious challenge on the hegemony of their rivals.

As Celtic fans are keen to remind themselves, Rangers' run in the Nineties was the second time that one of the Glasgow clubs enjoyed a decade of domination. From 1966 on, Celtic lifted nine consecutive titles – a record equalled by Rangers in 1997. But it was the European title they won during this era which is most fondly remembered. In 1967, Celtic reached the

final of the European Cup for the first time, where they met Inter Milan. Inter were clear favourites – with the defensive *catenaccio* system mastered by their coach Helenio Herrera, they had won the competition in 1964 and 1965 and had narrowly lost in the semi-finals in 1966. Celtic manager Jock Stein was determined that the game would be a battle of styles. Before the game, he told *Observer* reporter Hugh McIlvanney: 'We want to win it playing good football, to make neutrals glad we've done it, glad to remember how we did it.'

How they did it was to go at Inter and give a display of passionate, attacking football allied with the traditional ruggedness of Scottish sides. Little red-haired winger Jimmy Johnstone, with his jinking runs and pace, provided the creativity, while Bertie Auld in midfield and Tommy Gemmell at left-back typified the graft and effort that Stein inspired. Celtic's 2–1 victory made them the first British side to lift Europe's premier club trophy, but the 'Lisbon Lions' were acclaimed across a continent delighted to see the death of Inter's dull tactics.

Three years later, in the semi-final of the same competition, Celtic defeated Don Revie's Leeds United – a side as unpopular as Herrera's Inter – in front of 136,000 at Hampden. But the elation of victory in the 'Battle of Britain' was soured when the Bhoys lost in extra-time to Feyenoord in the final.

Within a year, Stein had dismantled the squad and begun creating a new side for the Seventies, including forwards Kenny Dalglish and Lou Macari, who were to go on to lengthy careers at Liverpool and Manchester United respectively.

The departure of Dalglish in 1977, and Stein's resignation a year later, marked the end of the Celtic glory years. One of Stein's old charges, Billy McNeill, created a championship-winning side in the early Eighties, but financial problems were beginning to have an impact. Top players such as Charlie Nicholas, Brian McClair and Maurice Johnston were lured away by English clubs.

In the late Eighties and early Nineties, the club had a string of unsuccessful managers and an ongoing boardroom battle. A takeover bid by former director Brian Dempsey, who had wanted to take the club to a new stadium in the Robroyston district, divided the board. The club's need to redevelop or move their stadium in the wake of the Taylor Report was one of the points of conflict, but while the arguments were raging, Celtic were slipping further and further into debt.

In March 1994, the *Bank of Scotland* announced they were ready to call in the receivers – but at the eleventh hour, the club was sold to a Canadian businessman, Fergus McCann.

The new chairman kept his pledge to redvelop the existing stadium and to provide cash to spend on imported players, recognising that to try to conquer Europe as Jock Stein did three decades ago – with what was essentially a team of Glasgow Boys' Club players – was impossible in the modern era. But McCann's sacking of coach Tommy Burns before the end of Celtic's trophyless 1996/97 campaign divided fans, and led to the acrimonious departure of

the very stars the chairman's money had brought to the club – among them the popular Italian, Paolo di Canio.

Burns' replacement, Wim Jansen, fulfilled the dream of every natural born Celt by winning the title (and preventing Rangers from making it ten in a row) in 1997/98. Yet the glory was to be painfully short-lived. Jansen resigned within days of Celtic's triumph, after failing to agree the terms of a new contract with McCann and his unpopular general manager, Jock Brown, who took an eternity to appoint a successor before settling on the veteran Slovak Dr Jozef Vengloš, barely a week before the club's first-ever Champions' League quailfying campaign. With the players now going head-to-head with Brown over bonus payments, Celtic were knocked out of the qualifiers by Croatia Zagreb. And though the attacking football encouraged by Vengloš, the goalscoring of Henrik Larsson and a five-goal demolition of Rangers in the autumn Old Firm game all had the critics purring, squad morale was too fragile to last the championship pace.

Off the pitch, Brown finally bowed to the pressure and resigned, but McCann's

All smiles – Celtic's new-look management team, before the rot set in

avowed intention to quit the club in the summer of 1999 succeeded only in encouraging takeover talk, some of it involving a consortium led by Dalglish and the Simple Minds singer Jim Kerr. The takeover got nowhere, but Dalglish did indeed return to Parkhead, in what seemed a highly suitable role as director of football.

But eyebrows were raised when Dalglish his former Anfield team-mate John Barnes as first-team coach, while the respected Venglos̆ was shunted into a vaguely defined job as European advisor. Barnes had no experience in management, and his comment that Celtic was the perfect place to learn his trade was both laughably naïve and an ominous sign of things to come.

Barnes' team soon fell behind Rangers in the title race, and bowed out of Europe with a 2–0 UEFA Cup loss to Olympique Lyonnais – a game in which key goalscorer Henrik Larsson sustained a knee injury which he would need the rest of the season to recover from. Worse was to come. A 3–1 defeat by Inverness Caledonian Thistle in the Scottish Cup, amid tales of dressing-room rows, was too much for either the club or its fans to take, and Barnes' lesson in Scottish football was cut painfully short. Dalglish took direct charge of the first team and at least managed a Scottish League Cup win, but at the end of the season he, too, was on his way.

The appointment of former Northern Ireland captain and Leicester City boss Martin O'Neill as manager was well received, but whether his intelligent if slightly idiosyncratic approach to the game would transfer from the Premiership to the Old Firm remained to be seen. One thing was for certain – there would be no shortage of emotion while O'Neill was in charge at Parkhead.

Here we go!

From **Argyle Street** in the centre of town, take one of **buses #61s, #62b** or **#62c** down London Road, getting off at Springfield Road. The journey takes around 15mins.

Swift half

There are a couple of rough pubs on Springfield Road but most fans looking for a pint head for the **Barrowlands area,** which is along the bus route to the ground or a 10min walk from Argyle Street. **Baird's Bar**, next door to the market at 244 Gallowgate, has football from Sky Sports and Celtic videos on the TV screens and features live music at weekends. You could even catch Jimmy Johnstone in post-match discussion. Johnstone and his team-mates are the theme at **Bar 67** across the road at 257 Gallowgate – a tribute bar to the Lisbon Lions. If you're sick of the sight of shamrocks, try **McChuills** at 40 High Street.

Club merchandise

There are three official outlets for green-and-white merchandise. The **Celtic Shop** at 21 High Street is the most central (open Mon–Sat 9.30am– 5.30pm), but there is also a fair-sized shop by the stadium at 95 Kerrydale Street (open Mon–Sat 9am–5pm, later on matchdays) and a smaller store at 40 Dundas Street (open Mon–Sat 9am–5pm).

In print

As well as the matchday programme, the club produce **Celtic View** (£1.80), a long-established monthly newspaper. The latter's conservative approach explains the title of the most popular Celtic fanzine, **Not The View** (£1).

In the net

You no longer need to register to get the best from the official website, though if you do you're entitled to the dubious pleasure of having club press releases e-mailed to you automatically. Otherwise, this is now an excellent site, with an unusual layout that works, an extensive multimedia archive and a proper site map, all at: www.celticfc.co.uk.

Eat, drink, sleep...

Bars and clubs

In recent years, Glasgow nightlife has gained a strong reputation for its **dance clubs**. Irish theme bars have popped up all over

The roar returns – Hampden Park rebuilt

Hampden Park, Mount Florida
Capacity 52,000 (all-seated)

New era, new look – the stadium today

Scotland's national stadium **returned to action** in style in May 1999, hosting the Scottish Cup final between Rangers and Celtic in front of a capacity all-seated crowd of 52,000. The match itself was no classic, but history was being made – the ground that had hosted the classic 1960 European Cup final between Real Madrid and Eintracht Frankfurt was back in the big time as an arena of international class. Some 130,000 souls watched Madrid win that match 7–3, reflecting the fact that prior to the Fifties, this was the **largest football ground in the world**. Almost 150,000 people paid to see Scotland play England here in 1937 – still a record for any European game, and one unlikely to be surpassed.

Safety restrictions imposed following the Ibrox disaster saw Hampden's capacity reduced to little more than 70,000, and with modern stadia appearing across Britain during the Eighties and Nineties, scruffy old Hampden had lost its appeal.

Its refurbishment has been expensive (£65million at the last count) and controversial – Glasgow already had two modern all-seater stadia in Ibrox and Parkhead, while over in Edinburgh the home of Scottish rugby union, Murrayfield, remains under-used. But now that it has opened its doors again, Hampden has the chance to rebuild its reputation. The spectacular **south stand** houses restaurants, astroturf warm-up areas for the teams, six dressing-rooms, a sports injury clinic and 126 executive boxes. Its seven glass-fronted floors will also be home to a football museum and, in time, the offices of the Scottish FA and Premier League.

Sadly, Scottish League football is no longer played here, the ground's owners, Queen's Park, having moved fixtures to Lesser Hampden next-door. (The club was forced to call in administrators during 1999/2000, after refusing Scottish FA help in solving a cash crisis triggered by Hampden's redevelopment.)

For internationals and cup finals, take **bus #45** or **#57** from the centre of town – the journey takes around 20mins. There is a **lack of pubs** in the area around but along the bus route you'll pass the **Brazen Head** at 1–3 Cathcart Road, which proclaims itself to be Europe's only Irish-Italian bar. The theme is illustrated on the walls with a collection of Italian soccer shirts and Gaelic football memorabilia.

the city, along with European-style **café bars**. But the traditional **Glasgow pub** survives in the suburbs, serving malt whisky, Scottish bitter 'heavy' and the traditional bar snack of stovies and meat pies.

McNeill's, 106 Torrisdale Street. Twice manager of Celtic (and one of the many who tried and failed at Maine Road), former Bhoys centre-half

Billy McNeill has followed the familar career path into pub management. Masses of memorabilia, along with a full menu and wide choice of whisky. Open until 11pm midweek, midnight weekends.

Sub Club, 22 Jamaica Street. Packed out on sweaty Saturdays but busy throughout the rest of the weekend as well, a friendly club with respected resident and guest DJs.

The Horseshoe, 17 Drury Street. Classic traditional bar next to Central station, perfect for football watching, with an upstairs lounge for lunches. Couldn't be any friendlier if it tried.

The Arches, Midland Street (off Jamaica Street). Popular dance club with guest DJs from all over the UK and Europe popping in for weekend sessions of house and techno.

The Mitre Bar, 12–16 Brunswick Street. Intimate ittle bar just off Argyle Street with football on TV downstairs. Upstairs is a comfortable lounge. Open until midnight.

Restaurants

Long gone are the days when eating out in Glasgow meant a hot haggis or else. These days the city prides itself on being Scotland's **culinary centre** although, that said, you could still do a lot worse than the local fish and chips.

The Buttery, 652 Argyle Street. Renowned Scottish restaurant specialising in game, venison and salmon, with a wide range of vegetarian options and excellent country soups. Three-course lunch deal for around £16. Closed Sunday.

Crème de la Crème, 1071 Argyle Street. Glasgow has plenty of quality Indian restuarants to choose from, but this one differs in that it is located in a converted cinema, meaning plenty of room. Full range of Asian dishes. Open daily until midnight.

The Rogano, 11 Exchange Place. Classic art deco diner serving mainly fish and seafood dishes. The café downstairs is cheaper and more laid back than the elegant restaurant upstairs, but both boast excellent service and superb cuisine. Not cheap, but memorable.

The Ubiquitous Chip, 12 Ashton Lane. If you're going to splash out on a taste of Scotland, then do it here at Glasgow's most famous restaurant. Haggis, steak, salmon, stews and game. Expect to pay £25 for a three-course lunch during the week, but there are Sunday lunch deals for

around £15. *Upstairs At The Chip* is a smaller, more affordable bistro version, offering variations on the same theme. Closes 11pm.

Walfrid Restaurant, Celtic Park, 95 Kerrydale Street. A stadium restaurant that has been given the seal of approval by Glasgow's culinary reviewers. Traditional Scottish menu with three-course lunches for £10 and three-course dinners for £15, served in a room with tasteful and restrained memorabilia. Open until 9pm. Closed Sun. Book in advance if you want a post-match meal or the Saturday cabaret and meal in the adjacent Jock Stein Lounge: ☎0141/551 9955.

Accommodation

Glasgow has plenty of low-cost B&B options plus some more upmarket places aimed at the business community which do good **weekend deals**.

Albion Hotel, 405–407 North Woodside Road (☎0141/339 8620, fax 0141/334 8159). Small hotel offering B&B for £42 a single, and £52 per person in a double/twin. Just a mile from the city centre. Underground to Kelvinbridge.

Town House Hotel (☎0141/332 9009, fax 0141/353 9604). Recently renovated pair of houses form a comfortable, stylish and reasonably priced B&B. Singles from £25, doubles around £50, most credit cards.

Hampton Court Hotel, 230 Renfrew Street (☎0141/332 6623). Small B&B in the centre with a fixed price of £17 per head. Just three single and four double rooms, so book ahead.

Holiday Inn Garden Court, 161 West Nile Street (☎0141/352 8305, fax 0141/332 7447). Opened in 1995 and in the theatre district, next to the Royal Concert Hall and the Theatre Royal. Pricey but comfy. Around £90 per room for a twin, with deals at weekends.

IYHAF Youth Hostel, 7–8 Park Terrace (☎0141/332 3004). Handily placed in the West End of the city, and open all year round, curfew 2am. Non-YHA members £1.50 extra.

Edinburgh

The Scottish capital boasts the nation's largest and most impressive stadium, but the 65,000-capacity Murrayfield is the home of Scottish rugby union. The arena is filled every year for Five Nations rugby championship games, while Edinburgh's two round-ball teams – Hibernian and Heart of Midlothian – both struggle to fill their two grounds. Not since the Fifties, when both clubs won titles, has Edinburgh been a real force in Scottish football.

The two clubs both have ambitions to become Scotland's third force, behind the Old Firm. It was a status they took turns to hold until the early Eighties, when Aberdeen and Dundee United emerged as new challengers from the north. But although those two clubs faded in the Nineties there has been no real resurgence in Edinburgh.

The rivalry between Hibs and Hearts is nowhere near as intense as that of the Old Firm, but has a similar background. Hibs preceded Celtic as being the club of Scotland's Irish Catholic immigrants, but in the modern era, the club's owners have sought to distance themselves from their origins. Likewise, though Hearts are labelled a Protestant club, today you are unlikely to hear much in the way of Loyalist chants or see union jacks at Tynecastle.

Today's Edinburgh rivalry has more to do with location. Hearts draw their traditional support from Gorgie in the west, Hibs from the port of Leith to the east of the city. Nor, contrary to many English misconceptions, do fans of the Edinburgh clubs automatically have sympathies for their Glasgow equivalents. Hearts have lost many good players to Rangers down the years, and Hibs to Celtic. If anything, a strong anti-Glasgow feeling binds Edinburgh's football fans together.

Until recently there was a third club in the capital. Meadowbank Thistle emerged out of the works team Ferranti Thistle but never managed to get anywhere near worrying the traditional two. In 1995 they gave up, moving out of the city to become Livingston FC, and have done rather well for themselves in their new location.

Edinburgh's football scene was almost radically altered in 1990 when the Hearts chairman, Wallace Mercer, announced his intention to take over and then close down Hibernian. The attempt provoked fierce opposition from Hibs supporters who rallied to save their club from extinction. It wasn't only at Easter Road where the plan was opposed – the idea of losing the derby didn't appeal much to Hearts fans, either.

Although neither club can hope to compete with the Old Firm in the transfer market, Edinburgh fans hope they may yet see a return to the *status quo* of the Sixties, when Europe's finest travelled regularly to the city with justified trepidation.

The thrilling fields

 Hibernian

Easter Road Stadium, Albion Road
Capacity 16,000
Colours Green shirts with white sleeves, white shorts
League champions 1903, 1948, 1951
Cup winners 1887, 1902

Hibs are the original club of Scotland's Irish Catholic community. Formed in 1875, they took their name from the Roman word for Ireland and it was stated in their constitution that all players must be practising Catholics. So close were their Irish connections that the club were actually barred from the early Scottish competitions.

In recognition of their status, Hibs were invited to be the opposition for the opening of Celtic's ground. But the fraternal relations between the two clubs did not last long. When Celtic poached half of Hibs' players, the team never recovered and after a few struggling seasons, the club folded in 1891. Two years later Hibs were re-formed (without the sectarian clause in their constitution), and the new team continued to play at the old club's Easter Road ground.

Hibs' golden era came after World War II. They lifted the title with a young side in 1948, then again in 1951 and 1952. The team included a frontline tagged *The Famous Five* – Gordon Smith, Bobby Johnstone, Lawrie Reilly, Eddie Turnbull and Willie Ormond. It was a team that played the Scottish game at its best – positive, attacking football full of flowing passing and neat, swift movement off the ball.

The cotton-wool king – Hibs' Dirk Lehmann

In 1955 Hibs became the first British side to enter the European Cup, reaching the semi-finals where they lost to the French club Stade de Reims. It would not be the club's last continental adventure – indeed, Hibs' performances in Europe have been impressive for a club that have won so little on the domestic front.

In 1961 they reached the semi-finals of the Fairs' Cup, after a thrilling 7–6 aggregate win over Barcelona. In the same competition seven years later they defeated Porto home and away, then played one of the most memorable games in the club's history – trailing 4–1 down to Napoli from the away leg, Hibs destroyed the Italians in Edinburgh, putting five goals past a visiting 'keeper by the name of Dino Zoff.

There has been little joy for the Hibees since the early Seventies. Badly managed at both boardroom and dugout level, the club entered a deep decline which resulted in relegation for the first time in 1980. They bounced back after a season, but it took the hostile takeover bid from Hearts in 1990 to truly awaken the club. Faced with the prospect of their team's extinction, dormant fans came crawling out of the woodwork in order to ensure the club survived. The protests and fundraising gave Hibs an unlikely boost, and in 1992 they won their first trophy for almost 20 years, clinching the League Cup. But that team, created by manager Alex Miller, failed to develop and by the mid-Nineties the club was flirting with relegation again.

The drop finally came in 1998, ironically the year when Scotland's top-flight clubs broke away to form their own Premier League – a development passionately advocated by Hibs chairman Douglas Cromb. Alex McLeish, the former Scottish international stopper who took over as manager too late to prevent relegation, ensured another instant return to the elite, and his side, bolstered by attractive imports such as Franck Sauzée, Russell Latapy and Dirk Lehmann, managed a creditable sixth place at the end of an important year of consolidation in 1999/2000.

Yet without the finances to strengthen the squad, Hibs may yet be one of the clubs fighting relegation as a result of the SPL's restructuring – a case of recent history repeating itself, perhaps.

Here we go!

Bus #1 from the Royal Mile will take you to Easter Road; **bus #6** makes the journey back. Alternatively, from Princes Street take **bus #75, #106** or **#108** along London Road, getting off at Easter Road. After walking down Easter Road take a right down Albion Road to the ground.

Swift half

Easter Road is almost as famous for bars as for its football ground. *Middletons* at #71 has a big-screen TV and fading black-and-white Hibs photos. The *Royal Nip* (#171), on the corner of Albert Street, has the Hibernian logo built into its bar.

The area also boasts *The Chocolate Shop*, 28 West Norton Place, on the corner of Easter Road and London Road, serving all kinds of traditional boiled sweets, magnificent fudge and handmade chocolates.

The club's **Forthview Restaurant** in the new north stand is open for lunch during the week and Sundays (midday–2pm) and Friday and Saturday evenings for dinner (7.30–10.30pm). If you fancy a post-match nosh-up, then reservations are recommended: ☎0131/661 3618.

Club merchandise

The store at the stadium (open Mon–Fri 9am–5pm, Sat 9.30am–5.30pm) has all the essential Hibee fashion.

In print

The matchday programme costs £1.80. There are two fanzines, *Hibees Here, Hibees There* and *Mass Hibsteria*.

In the net

Ignore the awful green 'turf' background on the club's **official homepage** and scroll down the list of options – there's plenty here and it's all properly updated, although the site does lack some of the multi-media niceties found elsewhere. See for yourself at: www.hibs.co.uk.

 # Heart of Midlothian

Tynecastle Park, Gorgie Road
Capacity 18,000
Colours Maroon shirts, white shorts
League champions 1895, 1897, 1958, 1960
Cup winners 1891, 1896, 1901, 1906, 1956, 1998

Heart of Midlothian were named after the dance hall in which the club was formed. The name springs from the nickname for an old prison by St Giles' Cathedral, which was taken as the title for a novel by Walter Scott and was adopted by several civic organisations. Today, three of these remain – a swimming club, a budgerigar lovers' club, and the football team.

Hearts made an immediate impact, winning two league titles and two cups around the turn of the century, when Bobby Walker emerged as one of the early stars of the Scottish league. Yet it was just as Walker was hanging up his boots that Hearts wrote their name into history. At the outbreak of war in 1914, the entire team, then top of the league, volunteered for the armed forces – a move which encouraged many of their supporters to follow suit. Seven of the squad were killed in action and their names are honoured at a memorial at the Haymarket, where supporters gather to pay their respects every Armistice Day.

In the seasons immediately after World War II, Hearts attracted record crowds across the country to watch their attractive and attacking football. Titles followed in 1954, 1957 and 1959 – the club's best post-war period. Tommy Walker's side included Dave Mackay, who went on to captain Tottenham and Derby County. Mackay was the classic hardman, powerfully built with a fearsome tackle, yet also with the ability to distribute the ball.

The Jam Tarts, as Hearts are known, lost their way in the Seventies, bobbing up and down between the top two flights. After returning to the elite in 1983, the club built a new-look team behind the

Derby daze – Hearts 'keeper Antti Niemi (right) recovers after Hibs fans threw a missile at him

instinctive goalscoring of striker John Robertson. This was to be the side which, in 1986, had a league and cup double in sight but ended with nothing after losing their last two games of the season. Robertson and defensive lynchpin Dave McPherson left for Newcastle and Rangers, respectively, though both subsequently returned to see out their careers at Hearts.

Robertson, in fact, became the club's record goalscorer, and was still in Jim Jeffries' 1997/98 team which pushed Celtic and Rangers most of the way in the title race, and which ended the club's 35-year trophy drought by beating the Gers 2–1 in the Scottish Cup final at Celtic Park. Though the striker would get a feel of the trophy at the presentation ceremony, he did not play on the day – leaving the heroes' accolades to playmaker Neil McCann and the club's two unpredictable Frenchmen, goalkeeper Gilles Rousset and goal-poacher Stéphane Adam, who scored the second.

Alas, McCann's sale to Rangers and a lack of new signings in the close season rendered the 1998/99 campaign one of

anti-climax. Hearts lost to Mallorca in the Cup-Winners' Cup, and spent much of the league season looking in danger of swapping divisions with Hibs. Relegation was avoided in the end, but squad rebuilding was the order of the day at the rebuilt Tynecastle in 1999/2000, when a much-changed side finished third – still 26 points behind Rangers, but crucially back into Europe.

With outside investment coming from the Scottish Media Group, fans continue to hope that their club can become a strong 'third force' in the SPL.

Here we go!

From the Waverley Centre on Princes Street, take **bus #3, #3a, #21** or **#33** to Tynecastle. The journey takes about 20mins.

Swift half

The *Tynecastle Arms* at 1 McLeod Street is the nearest pub to the ground and as a result gets packed on matchdays. A better bet is the *Athletic Arms* at 1–3 Angle Park Terrace; until a few years ago, the 13 pumps here were reserved exclusively for Eighty Shilling, and while concessions

Edinburgh essentials

Edinburgh **airport** is 14km west of the centre. Airport buses provide a frequent service into town, around the clock – the journey takes around 30mins. *Edinburgh Airport Taxis* (cover every flight in and out of the airport, and charge around £12 for the 20min journey into town, depending on the number of passengers.

Travelling from England by train, you'll come into the **main station**, Waverley, which is slap bang in the centre with Princes Street and the castle on either side.

At St Andrews Square you'll find the **bus terminal** for both local and inter-city services. The city is well-covered by **local buses**. As in Glasgow, make sure you have exact change for the slot on entrance as no change is given. Also available from the driver are *Day Saver* tickets – £2.50 for unlimited travel for a day. Services run until around 11.30pm, and there are a few night buses after that, running daily until 4am.

The main **tourist information centre** is above Waverley Shopping Centre at 3 Princes Street (open winter Mon–Sat 9am–6pm, Sun 10am–6pm, summer Mon–Sat 9am–7/8pm, Sun 10am–7/8pm, ☎0131/473 3800). There is another, smaller branch at the airport.

have been made to lager and Guinness drinkers, you can still just ask for 'two' and the bar staff will know what you mean.

Also worth visiting, and right near the ground on Gorgie Road, is John Robertson's bar, *Robertson's*, which is packed with all the expected memorabilia.

Club merchandise

Hearts now have a **modern superstore** under the south stand, accessible from the Gorgie Road, open Mon–Fri 9am–8pm, Sat matchdays from 9am until after the final whistle.

In print

As well as the well-produced matchday programme and *Hearts* monthly (£2.50), there are a couple of fanzines – *Always The Bridesmaid* and *No Idle Talk*.

In the net

The club's **official website** is located at: www.heartsfc.co.uk. Like most Scottish club sites it eschews elaborate graphics in the cause of greater speed, and is much the better for it. It also includes fine links to unofficial sites, of which two in particular are worth looking at. There's *UHH* at: www.heartsfootballclub.freeserve.co.uk; and the *No Idle Talk* fanzine at: web.ukonline. co.uk/members/grant.thorburn/.

Eat, drink, sleep…

Bars and clubs

While it may not enjoy quite as high a reputation as Glasgow for its nightlife, Edinburgh is a **good night out**, with an increasingly cosmopolitan scene. As with Glasgow, check out *The List* magazine for the latest on clubbing.

Carwash, 11 North Bank Street. The lilac exterior makes this a must for Fiorentina and Újpest fans. Inside you'll find kitsch Seventies decor, cocktails and American snacks. DJs most nights make this a good warm-up spot before clubbing. Open until 1am.

City Café, 19 Blair Street. Now famous as the venue for the pub fight scene in *Trainspotting*, the café offers excellent coffee and hot or cold club sandwiches.

Doric Tavern/McGuffie's, 15–16 Market Street. Near Waverley Station, a cosy upstairs bar sits above a busy pub, both serving food but to different clientèle. Closed Sun.

Iguana, 41 Lothian Street. Popular bar with DJs at weekends, attracting the sleek and the stylish, open daily until 1am. Continental menu. Near George IV Bridge.

Mathers, 25 Broughton Street. Offering good guest ales along with the usual Scottish bitter, this is one of the more down-to-earth of Edinburgh's central pubs – the sport on TV is a rarity in this part of town. Open until midnight.

Restaurants

Eating-out **standards are high** in Edinburgh, but many restaurants are geared heavily toward the tourist trade, and during the International Arts Festival in late August and early September, anywhere around the Royal Mile will be intolerable. If you can't avoid hitting town at this time, try to eat somewhere suburban...

Alfredo's, 109 Hanover Street. Unpretentious Italian place with plenty of fish dishes on the menu. Good-value lunchtime deal gets you a three-course meal for around £5.

Dubh Prais, 123b High Street. Cosy diner on the well-worn tourist trail. An imaginative menu makes the occasional wait for a table worthwhile – ostrich, pan-fried haggis, superb soups and salads. The set lunches at under £10 are not to be missed. The name is Gaelic for 'black cooking pot'. Closed Sun–Mon.

Jackson's, 209 High Street. Most of Edinburgh's Scottish restaurants target the business and tourist markets and their prices reflect this. *Jackson's* offers the oysters, salmon, haggis and lamb at more reasonable prices. The daily lunch menu is excellent value at around £6, but set dinners are around three times that.

Mussel Inn, 61–65 Rose Street. Centrally located, stylish fish restaurant offering all manner of shellfish, oysters a speciality. Excellent service, bright interior, nothing could be better. Open until 10pm, closed Sun.

Accommodation

The advice is simple – avoid Festival time. Though it may be tempting to try to catch some **footie before autumn** takes a hold, you've got no chance of finding anywhere to stay. Rest of the year, you should have little difficulty.

Ailsa Craig, 24 Royal Terrace (☎0131/556 1022, fax 0131/556 6055). Great views of the Forth from this comfortable, friendly hotel, and not dear either – singles around £40, doubles £60, including breakfast. The *Greenside* at #9 is its sister hotel.

Apex International Hotel, 31–35 Grassmarket (☎0131/300 3456, fax 0131/220 5345). Stylish new hotel with rooms for £70–80 in comfortable surroundings, with a great view of the Castle. The *Apex European Hotel* at 90 Haymarket Terrace also comes highly recommended.

Edinburgh Backpackers Hostel, 65 Cockburn Street (☎0131/337 1120). £10.45 a head in four- to eight- bedded rooms, in the city centre. Price includes breakfast. Closed December.

Royal Circus Hotel, 19–21 Royal Circus (☎0131/220 5000) Quiet but central location, offering B&B from £26 and good deals on single rooms. Easy walk to all the major sights.

Travel Inn, 1 Morrison Street (☎0131/228 9819, fax 0131/228 9836) Functional but reasonably priced hotel by Haymarket station. Rooms around £40. Most credit cards.

Slovakia

Slovensky Futbalovy Zvaz, Junácka 6, SK 83280 Bratislava
☎07/4924 9150   Fax 07/4924 9554   E-mail none

League champions Inter Bratislava   **Cup winners** Inter Bratislava
Promoted Matador Puchov   **Relegated** VTJ Senec, ZTS Dubnica, HFC Humenné,
Nitra, Dunajska Streda, Banská Bystrica, Baník Prievidza

European participants 2000/01 Inter Bratislava (UCL qualifiers); Slovan
Bratislava, 1.FC Košice (UEFA Cup); OD Trencín (Intertoto Cup)

Since gaining statehood in 1993, Slovakia has struggled to make much of an impression on the European game. The national team have yet to reach the finals of a major tournament, and no Slovak club has ever progressed beyond the first group phase of the Champions' League. Yet it would be wrong to dismiss Slovakia as another small, former Eastern Bloc republic with little hope of ever competing at the highest level. Before the 1993 'Velvet Divorce' with the Czech Republic, Slovak players had more than played their part in Czechoslovakia's national team – especially its most triumphant one, the 1976 European Championship-winning side – while Slovan Bratislava had likewise provided Czechoslovakia with its only European club success in 1969.

Independence created a number of headaches for the local game, however. A national league had to be set up in a country where little more than half a dozen clubs had spent any length of time in the top flight of the old Czechoslovak league. And a national team had to be thrown together in time for the Euro '96 qualifiers.

The upheavals caused by these changes should not be under-estimated but, after fears that the game might lose support and

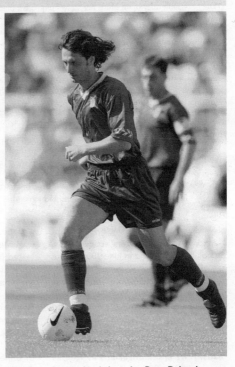

Tragic loss – international playmaker Peter Dubovsky

that there wasn't the strength in-depth for a competitive domestic league and a strong national team, Slovak football is on the up. Attendances are rising, the quality of football has improved and the national team have gelled into a respectable side – albeit one robbed of one of its biggest stars when

Basics

Americans, Canadians and EU nationals need only a **passport** to enter the Slovak Republic. Australian and New Zealand citizens require a **visa**, available for $21 and two passport photos at their local Slovak embassy or at border crossings.

The Slovak currency is the **crown** – or Slovenská koruna, abbreviated as Sk. Coins come in denominations of 1, 2, 5 and 10, with 20, 50, 100, 200, 500, 1,000 and 5,000 crown notes. There are about 65Sk to £1.

The Slovak crown is not convertible in the West, so **keep your receipts** to change currency back when you leave.

Banks give the best rates for **currency exchange**, at the desk marked *zmenáreň*. They are generally open Mon–Fri 8am–5pm. Cash machines and credit-card payment are both fairly widespread in major towns.

The **telephone code** for Slovakia from abroad is 421; add a 7 for Bratislava, 95 for Košice. From inside Slovakia, add the customary '0' to city codes, and dial 00 to call abroad, followed by the country code. There is no cheap time to make an international call – talking to the UK will cost about 60Sk per minute.

Most public call boxes now take **phone cards**, available at newsstands and post offices at 150Sk for 50 units or 300Sk for 100. Coin phones are only really useful for local calls and take 2Sk or 5Sk coins.

When it comes to travelling around the country, Slovak **trains** are cheap, reliable and generally preferable to **buses**, though still a tad sluggish. International *Euro-city* (EC) and *Inter-city* (IC) services require a supplement, if not a reservation, best purchased beforehand – indicate which one you are catching when buying your ticket. A *rýchlik* is the faster and more expensive type of train between towns; an *osobný* will stop everywhere.

SAD buses are more expensive than trains, but cover mountain areas more fully. In major towns, bus and train stations tend to be together.

---

playmaker Peter Dubovsky, once of Real Madrid, was killed in a diving accident while on holiday in Thailand in June 2000, at the age of only 28.

Prior to World War II, in the first Czechoslovak republic, Slovak teams failed to make any impact on the nationwide league between its establishment in 1925 and the outbreak of hostilities. Bratislava, then a cosmopolitan city made up of Germans, Jews and Hungarians as well as Slovaks, had a number of teams based on ethnic lines, such as the Hungarian club Pozsonyi TE. With the exception of PTE, which went on to become Petržalka, none of these minority clubs survived the war and the 'Slovakisation' of Bratislava. This took place during the period of Slovak 'independence' between 1939 and 1945, when the country was ruled by the Fascist dictator Jozef Tiso and was little more than

a puppet state of Nazi Germany. A national league was briefly played for and was dominated by Slovan, then playing under the name of ŠK Bratislava. The Slovak national team played 16 games in this period, the bulk of them against Nazi allies Croatia, Romania and Germany; they won only three times.

After the war, the Communists reunited Slovakia with the Czech provinces of Bohemia and Moravia. In the second Czechoslovak league which then emerged, Slovan became a respected force, winning three titles in the immediate postwar period. By the Sixties, 1.FC Košice and Spartak Trnava had also become Slovak clubs to be reckoned with. Between 1968 and 1975, the championship trophy never left Slovak soil. Indeed, in 1973 the top three clubs were all Slovak. This dominance was reflected in the make-up of the

Czechoslovak national team, and the Czechoslovakia squad which won the 1976 European Championship was dominated by Slovak players. Little wonder, then, that when the Czech Republic reached the final of Euro '96, supporters in both Bratislava and Prague were wryly describing it as Czech football's best-ever achievement.

Today, having initially struggled under the idealistic leadership of the former Czechoslovak national-team coach Jozef Vengloš, the modern Slovak national side are beginning to at least punch their own weight – although qualification for a major finals still feels like a long-term project. Landed in Europe's toughest qualifying group for France '98, alongside Spain, Yugoslavia and the Czech Republic, Slovakia had the pleasure of beating their former compatriots 2–1, after being a goal behind in Bratislava, but lost the return fixture 3–0 – by which time both nations were out of the running.

After the national team suffered a poor run of results in the autumn of 1998 – including a 3-0 home defeat by Portugal in their Euro 2000 qualifying group – a few club sides took to the field the following weekend wearing black armbands, signalling the death of Slovak football, as part of a club presidents' campaign to oust the FA management.

Under a new coach, former World Cup '62 star Jozef Adamec, in the new year Slovakia earned a creditable 0–0 draw in Romania, only for a similar scoreline at home to Hungary a few days later and a 5–1 home defeat by the resurgent Romanians to scupper chances of receiving a Euro 2000 invite.

Yet just prior to the main event in the Low Countries, a bright Slovak side finished fourth in the European Under-21 Championship on home soil, claiming wins over England and Turkey and a draw with eventual winners Italy, before losing narrowly to Spain. The performance was enough to earn Slovakia a place in the soccer tournament of the Sydney Olympics, at which the youngsters looked set to

cement their position as the public's favourites, enjoying a popularity the full national side could only dream of. Players such as Leverkusen left-back Vratislav Greško and his former Inter Bratislava team-mate, striker Szilard Németh, head this lively new generation which, if properly managed, could yet be capable of matching the achievements of their neighbours in Prague.

With Inter Bratislava finding a new role as a producer of young players, Slovan slowly sorting out their messy financial situation, and Spartak Trnava and 1.FC Košice offering a serious provincial challenge, there is no reason why Slovakia's newly trimmed-down top division can not become a competitive championship to act as a feeder to a decent, mid-ranking national side. With substantial foreign investment starting to find its way into the local economy, such developments could soon get a financial shot in the arm, too.

Essential vocabulary
Hello *Ahoj*
Goodbye *Do videnia*
Yes *Áno*
No *Nie*
Two beers, please *Prosím si dve pivá*
Thank you *D'akujem*
Men's *Páni*
Women's *Dámy*
Where is the stadium? *Kde je štadión?*
What's the score? *Aký je stav?*
Referee *Rozhodca*
Offside *Mimo hry*

Match practice
Crowds for the first two seasons of the Slovak league were dreadful, with few games attracting more than 3,000 and a depressing number failing to pull in four figures. It was a stark contrast to the days when matches against the big Prague teams (Sparta, Slavia or Dukla) would attract 30,000 or more Czech-baiting Slovaks.

More recently, however, matches between Slovakia's own big three – Slovan, 1.FC Košice and Spartak Trnava – have brought in crowds of over 20,000, fuelling hopes that those who turned their backs on football after independence can be persuaded to return to the game they love.

Slovak football takes a long winter break. The first half of the season starts in the first week of August and runs until the last week of November. The second half kicks off in the first week of March, and the final round of games is not played until the end of June.

Matches are usually played on Saturday afternoons; kick-off times vary throughout the season but are usually around 4–5pm, except in November when many games start at 1.30pm to avoid expensive floodlight use. One game from each round is usually played on a Sunday afternoon for TV purposes, while some smaller clubs play on Sunday mornings in an attempt to maximise crowds.

The bigger Slovak stadia are better than most in Eastern Europe, but facilities in general are limited. Don't come expecting executive boxes, wheelchair access or sophisticated half-time 'entertainment'.

A different league

The Slovak top flight, or *Superliga*, was reduced in size from 16 to 10 clubs at the end of the 1999/2000 season. To facilitate the change, the bottom seven teams were relegated, while only the champions of the *II.liga* were promoted. A similar process took place in the *II.liga*, to accommodate those clubs relegated from the *Superliga*. The third level, *III.liga* remains split into four regional groups – West, Central, East and Bratislava, each with 18 clubs – and the champions of each division will continue to be promoted to replace the bottom four in the *II.liga*. The fourth tier consists of district leagues.

Up for the cup

Slovakia had its own cup competition as long ago as 1970. Between then and the break-up of Czechoslovakia, the winner of the Slovak Cup played off against the winner of the Czech Cup to decide the overall

Czechoslovak Cup, which was known as the *Interpohář*.

These days the first round of the *Slovenského pohár* takes place in early September. These early ties, played in midweek, are decided on penalties if the scores are level after 90 minutes. Teams then play each other over two legs according to the draw from the second round in late September. The semi-finals are also two-legged, and with extra-time if necessary. The final takes place on a neutral ground in the first week of June, with extra-time and penalties if needed.

Just the ticket

As there is rarely danger of not getting in, tickets are bought at the stadium. A standing ticket (*statie*) should not cost more than 20Sk, a seat (*sedadlo*) in the stand (*tribuna*) 50Sk top whack. The wording on your ticket will be, for the bigger stadia, *sektor* (sector) and *rad* (row). The home fans' section will be signposted *Vlajkonosiči Domaci*, away fans' *Hostá Vlajkonosiči*. Most clubs now issue matchday programmes, either free or for a nominal cost.

Half-time

No surprises here – it's that staple of Central European football cooking, beer and sausages. Both tend to be good, though. If you're lucky the beer will be Czech, though Slovak brands aren't a bad second best. Sausages come in two main varieties. The *klobása* is a chunky affair that can be boiled or grilled – the latter is better. The *párky* is a thinner, boiled, frankfurter-style number.

Popcorn is catching on, as are potato crisps; nationalists among the crowd enjoy *Slovakia Chips*, surely the only bag of crisps to be named after a nation state. If you need perking up before the game and a cup of espresso coffee won't do the trick, then try *Semtex* – the Czech hi-energy drink.

Action replay

Slovak state TV now has a monopoly on league action, mainly shown on STV2, which offers one live game every Saturday.

Field of play – half-time 'entertainment' at Slovan's stadium in Bratislava

It also has the highlights show, *Tango*, at 8pm on Sundays, repeated 5pm Mondays. *Euroligy*, 8.30pm Mondays, is its European round-up. The presentation is primitive – and adjust your contrast button for the lurid suits.

Eurosport is widely available in bars, as are Czech, German and Austrian channels. You'll find the Hungarian-language station Duna TV in towns with large Magyar communities, and Hungarian state television is also available in bars – walk into one on a matchday and you'll most likely be rubbing shoulders with a group of Ferencváros fans looking up at the screen.

The back page

Slovaks may not have had their own state but throughout the Communist years they had their own sports paper, *Dennik Sport* (Mon–Sat, 10Sk). The paper's support for the Slovak cause once carried a hint of subversion, but today it is a typically dry East European read, and the lack of a Sunday edition means you have to wait until Monday morning for a full round-up of the league programme.

Futbal Magazin (25Sk), is the glossy monthly, with pin-up pics and syndicated foreign features.

Ultra culture

Organised fan groups were once almost non-existent in Slovakia, but the recent vogue for travelling to away games – instigated by Slovan fans but now taken up enthusiastically by followers of Spartak Trnava and Košice – has brought supporters closer together. Even so, there is little in the way of well-developed ultra gangs.

Sadly, Slovak football has also attracted a racist skinhead element. Trouble at the team's home games is rare, but Slovan fans have been involved in several violent incidents away from home.

In the net

There's no official FA site and only one generic site dedicated to Slovak football on an unofficial footing. It is one of the best of its kind, however, at: www.geocities.com/ Colosseum/Track/7080. Run from the US by exiled Inter Bratislava fan Michael Vana, the site is all in English (there's a Slovak-language chat-room), and each club is given its own homepage, detailing past players and achievements, its contemporary squad, latest news and links. There are also areas dedicated to the Slovak national team, league and cup stats, transfer news and other matters.

Bratislava

 Slovan 514   Inter 517
 Petržalka 518

Literally just across the river from Austria and a mere 15km north of Hungary, the capital of Slovakia is somehow not quite the heaving melting-pot of a metropolis that its location suggests. It has few splendours to match those of its great rival Prague, yet from a football point of view, Bratislava can claim to have at least as rich a heritage as the Czech capital. The old Czechoslovak national side was always cheered more enthusiastically here, and when full, the city's Tehelné Pole stadium can still be one of the most raucous in Central Europe.

The thrilling fields

Slovan Bratislava

Štadión Tehelné Pole, Junacka 2
Capacity 32,000
Colours Blue-and-white shirts, blue shorts
League champions (Czechoslovakia) 1949–51, 1955, 1970, 1974–75, 1992
Cup winners (Czechoslovakia) 1962–63, 1968, 1974, 1982
League champions (Slovakia) 1994–96, 1999
Cup winners (Slovakia) 1994, 1997, 1999
European Cup-Winners' Cup winners 1969

With the possible exception of Croatia Zagreb, no team in Europe is so closely identified with the nation it belongs to as ŠK Slovan. They wear the Slovak national colours of blue and white, their club badge is almost indistinguishable from the national emblem, their ground is the *de facto* national stadium and the headquarters of the Slovak FA are based just next door in Slovan's sports complex. Add to all this the fact that the first Slovak national team was made up almost entirely of Slovan players, and it is little surprise that the club helped themselves to the first three Slovak championships after independence.

Bratislava is the only major city in Slovakia and Slovan are the only major team in town. For much of the Communist era, they were the Slovaks' only hope of stopping the big Czech clubs, and benefited accordingly. Assured of serious financial support from local industry and government authorities, they were able to take their pick from the best players in the land.

The club were founded in 1919 as First Czechoslovak Sports Club Bratislava (I.CŠK Bratislava). When the first Czechoslovak state was dismembered by the outbreak of World War II in 1939, the club shortened their name to ŠK Bratislava. The official name was altered several times under Communism but the team have been popularly known as Slovan since 1953.

From 1945, Communism brought with it organisation, resources and a determination to create a truly 'national' competition in Czechoslovakia. In contrast to the prewar years, in which the team never progressed beyond amateur leagues, Slovan made a real impact – winning the Czechoslovak title three years in a row from 1949 under the guidance of coach Leopold Štastný.

After the Soviet invasion of Czechoslovakia in 1968, Štastný defected and went on to coach the Austrian national team for seven years. But a year after his departure his old club had their greatest moment, winning the Cup-Winners' Cup and becoming the only Czechoslovak team to win a major European club competition.

In the wake of the Soviet invasion, UEFA had attempted to separate the early rounds of the Cup along East/West lines. The Soviets called for an Eastern Bloc boycott of the competition in protest, and only Slovan and Dinamo Bucharest disobeyed. In the second round, Slovan defeated Porto 4–1 on aggregate, and in the quarter-finals they caused another upset, defeating Torino home and away before sneaking past Dunfermline Athletic to set up a final with Barcelona in Basle, where a 3–2 win gave a demoralised nation a much-needed boost. Slovan ended Trnava's run of titles with championship wins in 1974 and 1975. It was this side, now coached by Jozef Vengloš, which formed the basis for the Czechoslovak squad who were crowned European Champions in 1976; indeed six of the team who beat West Germany in the final in Belgrade came from Slovan, with two more on the bench.

From the mid-Seventies onwards, however, the club entered a decline as the Czechs regained their dominant position in the league. Slovan won the penultimate Czechoslovak title in 1992, but all they'd had to show for the previous 17 years was a solitary cup win in 1982.

When Slovakia woke up to find itself a new football nation in 1994, it did so with only Slovan capable of making any sort of impression in Europe. To add to the frustration of fans bored by the domestic league, however, UEFA did not rate the new republic of Slovakia worthy of a place in the qualifying round for the Champions' League, ruling out a possible source of excitement and revenue for the club.

The loss of some key players to foreign clubs during the 1996/97 season caused Slovan to slip behind Trnava and Košice in the championship race for the first time since independence. Things got worse in 1997/98, with only two players staying on from the 1997 cup-winning side. Slovan finished fifth in the league, and lost their cup after a defeat by second-division Senec.

Something needed to be done, and the man to do it was new club president Jan Ducky, head of the country's richest state-owned business, *Slovak Gas*. In the summer of 1998, Ducky brought in talented young Trenčín coach Stanislav Griga, and gave him four new players to work with: Tibor Jančula, Milan Timko, Stanislav Varga and Jozef Majoroš. Despite this, it was Spartak Trnava who were leaders at the winter

Bratislava essentials

Bratislava's Ivánka **airport** is for short-hop flights only. Bus #24 runs between it and the Sportová hala in Nové Mesto, near the Slovan and Inter stadia. Vienna's Schwechat, 45km away, is the nearest major international aiport. An hourly bus runs to it from the main **bus station** at Mlynské Nivy, east of central Bratislava which can be reached via trolleybus #211. Trolleybus #210 connects the bus station to the main **train station**, just north of the centre, from which you can take tram #1 into town.

Bratislava has three forms of **transport**: buses, trolleybuses and trams, running 5.30am–11pm. Single tickets are now run on a timing system – 6Sk for up to ten minutes, 12Sk for up to 30, 18Sk for up to one hour, from the time of validation on board. Heavy luggage requires an extra 3Sk per piece.

The *MHD* kiosk in front of the train station sells 24-hour (*24-hodinový lístok*, 45Sk), 48-hour (80Sk), three-day (*3 donvý lístok*, 100Sk) and seven-day (*7 donvý lístok*, 150Sk) passes. The clerk time-stamps your ticket upon purchase. There is an hourly **night bus service** (20Sk or two 10Sk tickets) from central Námestie SNP to various points in the outskirts.

Taxis can be found at the station and in Námestie SNP. Alternatively, dial ☎07/5477 7577 or ☎07/5477 7477. The old town (Staré Mesto) is pedestrianised and outside of this, the centre is too small for you to spend more than 200Sk on a cab ride.

The English-speaking ***Bratislava Information Service*** (open Mon–Fri 8am–5pm, Sat 8am–1pm, ☎07/5443 3715, fax 07/5443 2708) is at Klobúčnícká 2, with a smaller branch in the main train station. They can sell you a copy of *Kám V Bratislave* (11.60Sk) a Slovak-language monthly with cinema and concert information. English-language newspaper the *Slovak Spectator* (Mondays, 30Sk, but free at most hotels) has a less ambitious but easier-to-decipher **listings** section.

True faith – Slovan's travelling fans still believe

break, and Ducky, having lost his government position after general elections, made some scathing pronouncements about what he called 'the Trnava privatisation mafia'. Soon afterwards, masked gunmen shot him dead at home.

Perhaps inspired by the tragic loss of their mentor, Slovan hit a run of form in the spring, were top by April, and were crowned champions with a game to spare. They then comfortably beat Dukla Banská Bystrica 3–0 in the cup final to seal their first Slovak double since 1994.

Hopes of a place in the 1999/2000 Champions' League were dashed when Slovan contrived to lose to Anorthosis Famagusta in the qualifying rounds, and despite the appointment of Stanislav Jarabek as coach, a distant third was all that was that could be achieved in the league. In the close season, the club received a much-needed cash injection when defender Varga was sold to Sunderland for £1 million – giving Jarabek at least a theoretical chance of rebuilding his squad.

Here we go!

Tram #2 takes you from the main train station to the stadium, while trams #4, #6 and #10 all make the ten-minute journey from the city centre along Vajnorská.

Just the ticket

The Tehelné Pole is divided into sectors. Those behind each goal, *CS* and *DS* (both 25Sk), have their entrance on Bajkalská Ulica. The main stand, *AS*, and the *BS* opposite are accessed from Junácka Ulica. Tickets for the lower level of the *AS* are 25Sk, for the higher, covered level, 50Sk.

The Slovan faithful tend to congregate at the *DS* end, while away fans are allocated the part of the *CS* sector nearest the *BS* stand.

Swift half

Slovan's hardcore following meet at the **Pohstinstvo**, known by all as the *Gemer* because of the house beer, at Moskovská 15, with pennants, scarves, drums – and heavy right-wing overtones. Nearer the ground, the **Vajnorská Viecha**, near the tramstop at Vajnorská 35, is a good spot for a quiet pre-match beer. For a loud one go to the bar/restaurant **Hysteria**, Odbojárov 9.

Sadly the **Hostinec Štadión**, by the bus station on Bajkalská, closes Sat from 3pm and Sun, but is good for midweek.

The **Bufet Slovan** under the *AS* sector is one of many hatches offering beer and sausages inside the ground.

Club merchandise

There are two **Suveníry ŠK** hatches, at opposite ends of the ground, open on matchdays only, selling a small range of scarves and pennants – no credit cards.

Ultra culture

Few clubs have a 'home' end so dominated by skinheads as Slovan. You'll see row upon row of youths with black bomber jackets, short-cropped hair and black leather boots. Their chants reveal a predictable dislike for gypsies, Jews and Hungarians, while 'Pressburg' emblems on their sleeves reveal their political preferences – Pressburg was the German name for Bratislava during World War II. **Belasi Fanatici** ('Light Blue Fanatics') is the name of the most prominent ultra group, but all are probably worth going out of your way to avoid.

In print

Slovanista, the club's modest A4-format programme, is 5Sk from the ticket kiosks.

In the net

There's no official website just yet, but a fan-run effort has surfaced at: www.elf.stuba.sk/~ordognor. It's in Slovak only but you'll have few problems navigating around history, news, squad details and other areas.

Groundhopping

◖ Inter Bratislava

Pasienky stadium, Vajnorská 100
Capacity 15,000
Colours Yellow-and-black striped shirts, black shorts
League champions (Czechoslovakia) 1959
League champions (Slovakia) 2000
Cup winners (Slovakia) 1995, 2000

Literally overshadowed by their next-door neighbours Slovan, AŠK Inter Slovnaft are a club that have never truly found an identity or a support base. Five name changes, including a spell in the Fifties as Red Star Bratislava, haven't helped; nor has the lack of success or link to any particular district of the city.

They won their only Czechoslovak title as Red Star in 1959, with a side that included international striker Adolf Scherer, who later moved to Slovan. In the following season's European Cup they beat Porto home and away before losing out to Rangers in the second round.

Inter's best run in Europe came in the 1975/76 UEFA Cup, when they defeated Real Zaragoza and AEK Athens before unexpectedly falling to Stal Mielec of Poland in the third round.

After merging with ZTS Petržalka to become Internacionál ZTS, they enjoyed a mini-revival in the late Eighties, winning the Slovak Cup in 1988 and in 1990, the year they also finished third in the Czechoslovak league.

Having demerged from Petržalka and returned to their own stadium, in the new Slovak championship they finished runners-up in 1994 and third in 1995, but on both occasions they were a long way off Slovan's pace and never seriously threatened to win the title. The revival of Slovakia's provincial clubs pushed Inter even further out of the frame in the mid-Nineties, and with little cash, the club were struggling to regain past glories.

All that began to change in 1998/99, when Inter were the dark horses in a three-way title race. With internationals Juraj Czinege and Vratislav Greško in midfield, Inter recovered from a UEFA Cup loss to Slavia Prague and two 1–0 derby defeats by Slovan, to lead the league for the first time in six years come March. They finished as bridesmaids again, but only two points behind Slovan.

Greško left for Bayer Leverkusen in the summer of 1999, but the rest of the squad stayed together and, with Czinege outstanding and striker Szilard Németh notching up 16 goals, a first Slovak title finally came Inter's way, with a nine-point winning margin over Kosice. A penalty shoot-out win over the same opponents in the cup final emphasised the club's domestic dominance, but the real icing on the cake came after the season was over, when Inter players formed the backbone of Slovakia's successful Under-21 side at the European Championship. Indeed, so great was the Inter influence that the team chose to play their matches at the Pasienky, rather than next-door at Slovan.

The back entrance to Inter is a hop across Bajkalská from Slovan, but the main entrance on Tomašikova Ulica, served by buses #38, #103, #113 and #118, or a short walk from Nové Mesto train station.

The stadium is an all-bench affair, with one main stand, divided into left and right sectors, and boasting the Seventies-flavoured

Elvid café-bar downstairs. There are open buffets either side of the main stand, with stand-up tables. The away fans} section is under the leopard-skin floodlight nearest the main entrance, the home area closer to the main stand.

Petržalka

Ihrisko Petržalka, Krasovského I
Capacity 9,000 (5,700 seated)
Colours Green-and-black shirts, black shorts

Slovakia's first professional football club were founded in 1892 as Pozsonyi Torna Egyesület ('Bratislava Gymnastics Club' in Hungarian). Bratislava was then part of Hungary and the team played in a Hungarian regional league before the creation of Czechoslovakia between the wars, when the club became Polgári ('Citizen'). During this period the team became the subject of a long-running dispute between Hungarians and Slovaks, but in 1938 Hitler's Nazi authority ended the argument.

In 1945, with Czechoslovakia once again on the map as an independent, unified state, the club became ZTS Petržalka, after the area to the south of the city centre – the team has been playing next to the Starý Most ('old bridge') on the south side of the Danube since 1900. The club survived a 1986 merger with Inter Bratislava, and ten years later, as 1.FC Petržalka, they gained promotion to Slovakia's expanded top tier.

Today Petržalka are enjoying a revival. Why, they even led the league in September 1998 – only to lose seven in a row and finish in their customary mid-table position. They play on Sunday mornings in front of a congenial crowd, many of whom are here as much to cure their hangover as for any partisan reason. There are no floodlights, but you've a choice between two covered stands behind the goals, one of which has a booze warehouse underneath.

Bus #52 from the other side of Starý Most, by the Kácacia fountain, stops right outside the stadium. Alternatively, **bus #23** from the train station stops a two-minute

Hoarding it – the European Under-21 Championship stirred local passions in Bratislava

walk away. The **Anita**, just behind the ground, is a friendly old wooden bar with a summer terrace. Also popular is the **Corgoň Piváreň**, right by the bridge, with beers consumed outside.

Eat, drink, sleep…

Bars and clubs

Slovakia is unpretentious. Bars are cheap – you should pay no more than 25Sk for a **beer**, which will usually be a tasty local brew on draught, with a pricier popular bottled Czech beer also available. The average pub (*pivnica*) will close around 10pm, a wine bar (*vináreň*), a couple of hours later. A thousand years of Hungarian rule have given the Slovaks, particularly the older generation, a taste for **wine** – *Furmint* is just one of many decent local whites. The locals are also big on **shorts**, the favourites being *slivovica* and *borovička*, strong plum and pine-nut brandies. **Tacky discos** are the meat and potatoes of Slovak nightlife, but Bratislava can offer a few more interesting alternatives.

Charlie's Pub, Špitálska 4. Mainstay of Bratislava nightlife, a late pub and disco in a leisure complex next to the *Hotel Kyjev*. Weekends 30Sk entrance fee, open until 4am Sun–Thur, 6am Fri–Sat.

The Dubliner, Sedlarská Ulica 6. Irish pub in the old town with a large menu, Sky Sports on a big screen, and occasional singing turns by the owner. Open daily until 1am, Sun midnight, kitchen 11am–11pm, 75Sk a Guinness, 35Sk a domestic beer.

KGB, Obchodná 52. The initials stand for *Krčma Gurmánov Bratislavy* ('Bratislava Beer Guzzlers' Club'), but there are busts of famous old Commies inside this popular cellar bar downtown. *Smädný Mních* beer, full menu, open until 2am, 3.30am Fri–Sat.

U-Club, NAG Ludvíka Svobodu. An old air-raid shelter underneath Bratislava castle turned hard-core techno haunt of Bratislava's body piercers and weirdos. Near SNP bridge, open until 2am, later on Fridays and Saturdays.

17's, Hviezdoslavovo Námestie 17. On a long square before SNP bridge, a crowded bar manned by Pedro, half-Slovak, half-Real Madrid. Buzzing at midnight, closed by 2am, 3am weekends.

Restaurants

Slovak specialities suffered under 40 years of collective cooking and today a *reštaurácia* menu will differ little from its Czech counterpart – in other words, dumplings (*knedle*) with everything.

Hungarian spices still feature, though, especially in soups (*polievky*) and meats (*masá*). In most places you'll pay no more than around 250Sk for a two-course meal with drinks.

Lunch is the main meal of the day, and dinner is eaten early, so finding a kitchen open past 10pm is pushing it – whatever the opening hours say.

Arkádia, Zámocké Schody. Elegant restaurant halfway up to the castle, where you can dine for around 400–600Sk, with a view overlooking the Danube, St Martin's cathedral and the SNP bridge. Open daily 10am–10pm, most major credit cards.

Bistro Magda, Panenská 24. Excellent, friendly, cheap lunchtime venue near the *Hotel Forum*. Only room for a handful of people, so get there early. Open Mon–Fri 10am–5pm.

Mamut/Stará Sladovňa, Cintorínska 32. Once the pride and joy of the Bratislava beer industry, now slowly being converted into a bingo parlour – but for the time being it serves large portions of meat and dumplings to go with your beer. A 5min walk from the *Hotel Kyjev*.

Vináreň Velkí Františkáni, Františkánské Námestie 10. Bratislava's most famous wine cellar, in the Old Town with beef and pork specialities. Cover charge for the gypsy violinists, but not as expensive as it looks – around 400Sk all in. No credit cards.

Accommodation

Accommodation in Slovakia is cheap but not luxurious. Hotels are slowly being privatised, but poor service is the norm, and foreigners pay more than Slovaks. *Satur* travel agencies can help with private rooms and hostels – in Bratislava their office is at central Jesenského 3. Alternatively, try the *BIS* offices listed under *Essentials*.

Club Hotel, Odborárov 3 (☎07/4425 6369). Reasonably grim Socialist-style hotel, but cheap and perfectly located for the Slovan and Inter stadia – although it's an ice-hockey team whose picture dominates the entrance. Singles 480Sk, doubles 740Sk, no credit cards. Tram #2 from the train station, #4 or #6 from town.

Gremium, Gorkého 11 (☎07/5413 1026, fax 07/5443 0653). The best cheap option in town, clean and friendly, but with only a few rooms so book ahead. Singles at 890Sk, doubles 1,290Sk, breakfast included, Mastercard and Visa accepted.

Hotel Dukla, Dulovo Námestie 1 (☎07/526 9815). Semi-renovated Communist-era hotel overlooking a quiet square. Around 2,200Sk for an old double, 3,200Sk for a new one, breakfast included. All rooms have baths, most have a TV. Most credit cards. Bus #23 from the station.

Hotel Kyjev, Rajská 2 (☎07/322 041; fax 07/326 820). Tower-block hotel which dominates the centre of Bratislava. Rooms with satellite TV and bathroom. The girls at the bar are friendly for a reason. Singles from 1,550Sk, doubles 1,700Sk, depending on type of room and season, breakfast included. Fantastic views. Most credit cards.

Slovenia

Nogometna Zveza Slovenije, Cerinova 4, PP 3986, SI 1001 Ljubljana
☎061/530 0400   Fax 061/530 0410   E-mail nzs@nzs.si

League champions NK Maribor   **Cup winners** Olimpija Ljubljana
Promoted Koper, Tabor Sezana   **Relegated** Pohorje Ruse, Potrosnik Beltinci

European participants 2000/01 NK Maribor (UCL qualifiers); Olimpija Ljubljana,
HIT Nova Gorica (UEFA Cup); Primorje Ajdovščina (Intertoto Cup)

Favourite underdog – Katanec bids farewell

veryone's favourite underdogs at Euro 2000, the Slovenes still have a fair way to go before their parochial football scene can match the levels of inspiration attained by the national side in the Low Countries With a great tradition in skiing and other Alpine sports, not to mention a passion for basketball, this tiny former Yugoslav state had for years shown a palpable indifference to football, while all around it were entranced by the beautiful game. But the events of the last couple of years – the national team's exploits and those of the country's leading club, NK Maribor, in the Champions' League – have changed all that.

In the former Yugoslav setup, a handful of Slovene clubs played each other as part of a regional division in the federal league's third tier. Clubs from Maribor and the state capital, Ljubljana, dominated proceedings, but there were also pockets of football enthusiasm close to the Italian border in Koper, on the Adriatic coast, and in Nova Gorica. Winning the state title would give the champion club – usually NK Maribor or are their eternal rivals, Olimpija Ljubljana – access to the Yugoslav second division, perhaps leading to a spell in the top flight for a season or two. There was also a state cup competition, separate from the federal Yugoslav tournament.

But by comparison with footballing hotbeds such as Croatia, Montenegro, Bosnia and Serbia, soccer in Slovenia rarely captured the public's imagination. The state produced only two players of real note: Brane Oblak, who played for Yugoslavia at the 1974 World Cup and went on to star for Bayern Munich; and Srečko Katanec, whose career as a gritty midfielder took him to VfB Stuttgart and then to Sampdoria, with whom he won a *Serie A* championship in 1991, and who likewise represented Yugoslavia at a World Cup finals, in 1990.

Basics

Citizens of the EU, America, Canada and New Zealand need only a **full passport** to stay in Slovenia for up to three months.

The Slovene currency is the **tolar** (SIT), divided into 100 stotini. Coins come in denominations of 50 stotin, 1, 2, 5 and 10 tolar, notes in 10, 20, 50, 100, 200, 500, 1,000, 5,000 and 10,000 tolar denominations. There are about SIT275 to £1. Banks are open Mon–Fri 8.30am–5pm, Sat 8.30–11am, and charge varying commissions for exchanging money. The tolar is not yet fully convertible, and you will be unable to obtain any before arriving in the country. Credit-card payment is widespread, although cash machines can be a little scarce, even in Ljubljana. Hotels often quote their prices in Deutschmarks.

Phone cards (*telekartice*) are available at newsstands and post offices, costing SIT700 for 25 units, SIT1,700 for 100 units. There are no cheap rates for international calls; one to the UK will cost around SIT1,000 for three minutes. The international access code from Slovenia is 00. To call Slovenia from abroad, dial 386, then 61 for Ljubljana, 62 for Maribor; as usual, add a 0 when dialling inland. The Slovene telephone service was in the process of changing many phone numbers as this book went to press – if any number given here has changed, you will hear a message giving the new number in English and Slovenian.

Slovenia is a **small country**, and getting around it takes no time at all. **Trains** are cheaper than buses, the fastest being the *InterCity* and *Zeleni Vlaki* – note that return tickets work out 20% cheaper than two singles. A single from Ljubljana to Maribor is just over SIT1,000. The **bus network** is more extensive, and travelling this way can be quicker than rail. Pay the driver or, if travelling from Ljubljana at the weekend, buy your ticket from the bus station at Trg OF in advance.

It was Katanec who returned home from Italy to give the national team a feeling of self-belief which had been all too obviously lacking since independence from Yugoslavia was achieved in 1991. Slovenia entered their first international tournament alongside neighbours Croatia and Italy in a qualifying section for Euro '96. They held the Italians 1–1 at home, but were well beaten by the Croats home and away. After that it was downhill – the Slovenes finished bottom of their qualifying group for the 1998 World Cup.

Taking over the coaching reins from Bojan Prašnikar, a successful manager at club level who had failed to translate those gifts to the bigger stage, Katanec adopted the thorough, professional approach to the game he had learned in Germany and Italy. His Slovenia team may not have been the most talented in their Euro 2000 qualifying group, but they were nobody's fools. A well-earned 2–2 draw in Greece was followed by hard-fought 1–0 wins over Latvia (twice), Georgia and Albania – nothing special, but good enough for second place in the section behind Norway.

If the group draw had been kind to Slovenia, the play-off lottery was not – Katanec's side faced Ukraine, arguably the toughest of the eight teams involved, and few expected them to win over two legs. But with playmaker Zlatko Zahovič hitting a rich vein of creative form and his teammates in bullish mood, Slovenia deserved their 2–1 win in the first leg in Ljubljana – secured by Milenko Ačimovič's absurdly speculative 40-yard lob over stranded goalkeeper Alexandr Shovkovsky.

The away leg was played in a snowstorm – familiar territory for both teams. Ukraine took the lead with a dubious penalty, but Miran Pavlin's late free-kick was deflected in past Shovkovsky, and Slovenia had managed the unthinkable. Thousands gathered at Ljubljana airport to greet their heroes as their plane touched down at 2am, but after a meeting with the national president, the fuss died down until the rest of Europe saw an unlikely name on the board for the finals draw. Slovenia? Wasn't that in *Duck Soup*?

Drawn alongside Yugoslavia, Spain and Norway, the Slovenes began the finals with a game against their former masters – against whom they had fought a ten-day war before independence. Both sides played down the political connotations of the match, but it was Slovenia who were the more relaxed, racing into a three-goal lead before an hour's football had been played. Yugoslavia's Siniša Mihajlović, furious at having given away Slovenia's third, then got himself sent off, and the Slovenes fatally took their collective foot off the gas. Yugoslav substitute Savo Milošević inspired an improbable comeback, and Katanec's team were left hanging on for a 3–3 draw.

No such complacency was allowed to creep in against Spain, who took the lead through Raúl but were then pegged back by a goal from Zahovič – his third of the tournament, cementing his reputation as the star of the finals thus far. But the Spaniards snatched a barely deserved winner midway through the second half, leaving Slovenia needing to beat Norway in their final game to stand a chance of further progress. In the end, the game was a goalless anti-climax, not helped by the Norwegians' mistaken belief that a draw would take them through to the quarter-finals at Spain's expense. Yet the very fact that Norway now treated the Slovenes with so much respect, despite having beaten the same team twice during qualifying, said much about the progress the squad had made under Katanec.

So Slovenia's fans went home, as expected, after three games. Their team had entertained a global audience, Zahovič had become a household name across Europe, and never again would Slovenes take to the ski slopes without first checking their sports pages for the latest football results.

Green day – the Slovenes go three-up against Yugoslavia at Euro 2000

Essential vocabulary

Hello *Živjo*
Goodbye *Na svidenje*
Yes *Ja*
No *Ne*
Two beers, please *Dve pivi, prosim*
Thank you *Hvala*
Men's *Moško*
Women's *Žensko*
Where is the stadium? *Kje je štadion?*
What's the score? *Kakšen je rezultat?*
Referee *Sodnik*
Offside *Offside*

Match practice

Regardless of the exploits of the national team, domestic football in Slovenia is still a pretty low-key affair. Crowds are in the low thousands, less when the occasional league round is played out on a Wednesday afternoon – a hangover from the time when factory workers finished early for the day. The traditional kick-off time is 3pm on a Sunday, with one game taking place on a Friday or Saturday afternoon. The season runs from early August to early December, and then from March until May.

A different league

The top Slovene league, *Prva SNL*, was expanded from 10 to 12 teams in 1998/99. Each club plays each other home and away, and then once more, with the venue decided on the teams' league standings after 22 rounds. The bottom two teams are automatically relegated to the 16-team second division, *Druga SNL*, from which the top two teams go up. Below the second division are a network of regionalised amateur leagues.

Up for the cup

The *Pokal Slovenije* begins in July, *Prva SNL* clubs and all. The first two rounds are decided on one game, extra-time (no golden goal) and penalties if necessary. The quarter-finals, semi-finals and final are all played over two legs, with extra-time and penalties if necessary. The final takes place in early May.

Just the ticket

With crowds so low, getting a ticket is never a problem – simply turn up shortly before kick-off. The Slovene FA maintains high standards for ground facilities, but seats are never numbered, so sit where you like. Admission will be around SIT1,000, perhaps twice that for international matches. The stand (*tribuna*) will be either covered (*pokrita*) or open. Standing areas (*stojisce*) will generally be indicated by their geographical position – north (*sever*), south (*jug*), east (*vzhod*) or west (*zahod*).

Half-time

Alcohol is not generally served inside Slovene grounds, although clubs do a fair trade in low-alcohol (*brezalkoholne*) beer, either Union's *Uni* or Laško's *Gren*. Food is generally limited to a grill serving up *pleskavica*, a big, steaming, and often delicious Balkan-style burger; you'll pay around SIT1,000 for one of these and a no-beer beer.

Action replay

Live domestic games are either shown on SLO 2, the second state channel, or on TV Koper, the regional Italian-language station in the west of the country. The best round-up programme is SLO 2's *Sportna scena* which, although not exclusively dedicated to football, does show all the weekend's goals, plus those from the major European leagues. It's generally on before 10pm on Sundays. Croatian channel HRT3 is widely available throughout Slovenia, while Italy's RAI and Austria's ÖRT are also on the airwaves near the respective borders.

The back page

The main sports paper is the daily *Ekipa* (SIT110), offering comprehensive coverage of both the domestic and foreign football scenes. Its weighty European round-up on Mondays makes up for the lack of a Sunday edition. The main national daily *Delo* (SIT110) offers full previews and match reports over a weekend.

Flying the flag – Euro 2000 was as much about asserting nationhood as playing football

The leading magazine is *SNL Revija* (SIT500), a monthly produced in conjunction with the Slovene FA, with full fixture details, club information and feature stories. The Croatian daily *Sportske novosti* (SIT110) carries a section dedicated to Slovene football and is justifiably popular here.

Ultra culture
A few Slovene fan groups were just beginning to copy ultra fashions picked up from Zagreb, Split and Belgrade when the Yugoslav conflicts erupted at the start of the Nineties. Today, despite low crowds and a low-key independent league, Maribor's *Viole* and Olimpija Ljubljana's *Green Dragons* can still make a noise, especially against each other.

Violence is rare, however, and the atmosphere is generally a good-natured one – followers of the national team made many friends in the Low Countries with their unassuming friendliness, their colourful support and their surprisingly large numbers.

In the net
The Slovene FA runs an official website at: www.nzs.si. It's Slovenian-language only and can be slow to access, but you should be able to find up-to-date results and tables from the top two divisions, the latest from the domestic cup, national-team news and the customary bureaucratic small print.

Maribor

Ljubjlana may be Slovenia's capital, but Maribor is most certainly its footballing centre. Maribor's Ljudski vrt, the 'People's Garden', is the country's most prestigious sports complex, and certainly its finest footballing arena. The team that play there, NK Maribor, have dominated the Slovene championship since the mid-Nineties, and have generated the country's most colourful fan group, the *Viole Maribor* crew. Participation in the Champions' League in 1999/2000 – after shock wins over French and Belgian opposition – put this unassuming town firmly on the European footballing map.

The thrilling fields

NK Maribor

Štadion Ljudski vrt, Mladinska 29
Capacity 10,000
Colours All violet with yellow trim
League champions (pre-independence)
1961, 1976, 1982, 1984, 1986
Cup winners (pre-independence) 1965–66, 1968, 1973-74, 1978, 1980, 1982, 1984, 1986–87, 1989–90
League champions (post-independence)
1997–2000
Cup winners (post-independence) 1992, 1994, 1997, 1999

The emergence of Slovene football during 1999/2000 was due to two main events: the performance of the national team at the European Championship, and the participation of NK Maribor in the Champions' League. Few neutrals batted an eyelid when the Violets won the Slovene championship by a whisker at the end of the 1998/99 season. But when they went on to provide the shock of the Champions' League preliminary rounds by overcoming the champions of Belgium and an expensively

assembled Lyon team that summer, it was time for Europe's footballing elite to get their atlases out.

The first team to be formed in Maribor were SSK, founded in the *Jadran* café in 1919. After World War II they became FD, then later Branik, playing in the local Slovene league at the People's Garden. A rival club, NK Maribor, came into being in 1960. They played mainly in the old Yugoslav second division, but enjoyed five seasons in the first from 1967 to 1972. But Branik were relegated to the regional third division in 1985, and the two clubs amalgamated three years later, following a bribery scandal.

As Maribor Branik, the club played only a handful of seasons in the Yugoslav league before Slovene independence. In the new national league that was established after 1992, they initially played second fiddle to Olimpija Ljubljana, before the balance of power shifted away from the capital.

What made the difference was the sponsorship of *Pivovarna Laško*, one of the country's big two breweries. The company used the club to promote a brand of iced tea, *Teatanic*, which was becoming popular with young Slovenes, and the team became known as NK Maribor Teatanic. And just as the HIT casino chain had poured enough money into the Nova Gorica club to bring them the national title in 1996, so the brewery gave Maribor the funds they needed to attract the best – including young coach Bojan Prašnikar, who'd been dismissed by Olimpija a year earlier after masterminding their early dominance of the Slovene league.

Prašnikar's Maribor went on to win the league four years in a row, their star rising as Olimpija's fell. The club also dipped a toe into European waters, although early adventures were far from successful – a 9–1 defeat by Ajax in the first round of the 1997/98 UEFA Cup was particularly embarrassing. Yet within a year, Maribor were beating another Dutch side, Bobby Robson's PSV Eindhoven, 2–1 at home in the first leg of a Champions' League qualifier. In Holland they lost in extra-time, 4–1, after leading the Dutch club for more than two hours of football.

Happily for Prašnikar, Europe's scouts and agents ignored the progress being made by his side. Midfielder Dejan Djuranovič, Albanian striker Kliton Bozgo (both brought over from Olimpija) and Croatian forward Dalibor Filipović all remained on the roster for another crack at the Champions' League 12 months later.

The Belgians of Racing Genk were first to fall, 5–1 in Maribor after going in at half-time a goal apiece. In the return in Liège, Genk went 3–0 up, but the Slovenes held on for an aggregate win despite having wing-back Amir Karič sent off on the hour. Olympique Lyonnais were the next victims. The French club's new £9million signing, Brazilian Sonny Anderson, was worth more than the entire Maribor team put together. But Filipović ran up the field to score the only goal of the first leg in France, then the whole town went bananas as the Violets beat Lyon 2–0 in the return – the first Slovene team in the Champions' League.

Maribor were a bizarre but rather charming antidote to the increasingly commercial world of European club football – a team from a place nobody had heard of, playing in purple and yellow shirts, and named after Slovenia's answer to *Irn Bru*

(the club had become known as Maribor Pivovarna Laško domestically, but remained 'Teatanic' in Europe). Dynamo Kiev, the club's first UCL opponents, didn't get the joke. They too were beaten 1–0 at home, by Ante Šimundža's late goal, and Maribor briefly topped their group.

There was a limit, however, to what Prašnikar's brisk, breakaway football could achieve. Lazio put four past his team home and away, and Maribor didn't pick up another point until their final match, a goalless draw with Leverkusen in Germany.

Meanwhile, awesome form in the league – only two defeats in 33 starts – saw the Violets on their way to another domestic title. As Europe again beckoned, club president and local MP Joza Jagodnik promised the proceeds would be invested in better stadium facilities and the youth team. But after a surprise Slovene cup defeat by Korotan Prevalje, Prašnikar resigned and was replaced by his assistant, Matjaz Kek. In the close season, as their former coach returned to his old stomping ground of Ljubljana, it looked like being a move the regulars at the People's Garden might live to regret.

Here we go!

The Ljudski vrt is just west of the town centre, a 10min walk from the train and bus stations straight along Partizanska cesta, which passes by the main Grajski trg, becoming Slovenska ulica,

Maribor essentials

Although Maribor does have its own **airport**, at Skoke, 10km south-east of town, most visitors will fly in to **Ljubljana**, 150km away. The two cities are linked by 15 trains or buses a day.

Maribor's huge **bus station** is on Mlinska, just east of the main square, Grajski trg; the **train station** is nearby on Partizanska cesta. The modest centre of town is easily walkable, while a network of 25 buses runs through town to the surrounding areas. There is no night transport.

Taxis can be found outside either the bus or train stations – to phone one, call *Radiotaxi* on ☎062/27755.

The **tourist office** in the main square at Glavni trg 15 (open Mon–Fri 9am–6pm, Sat 9am–midday, ☎062/211 262, fax ☎062/25271) offers the monthly calendar of events, *Koledar Prireditev*.

Beer meets Aspirin – taking on Leverkusen in the UCL

and making a noise at an otherwise unmemorable match with Spartak Subotica. Originally called the **Marinci**, they renamed themselves after the setting-up of the Slovene league in 1992. Easily the most colourful and noisiest fan group in the country, the *Viole* have one sworn enemy, Olimpija Ljubljana's *Green Dragons*. This being forward-looking, fair-minded Slovenia, one of their splinter groups is the *Viole Girls*.

In the net

The **official website** is a riot of lilac and yellow at: www.nkmaribor.com. There's plenty of English content alongside the Slovene, with stills and video images of the team's greatest recent moments to download, a club history, latest stats and, perhaps most intriguingly of all, a link to the official site of the club's brewery sponsor, *Laško*.

The *Viole* ultras have an **unofficial site** of their own, but this seems to be almost permanently under construction at: www.come.to/viole.

then Gospovetska cesta. Turn right at Strossmayereva and the stadium is on your left.

Just the ticket

Tickets are available on the day, or in the case of European games, a few days in advance, from the office by the main entrance. Home fans gather under the scoreboard in the south stand (*tribuna jug*), away ones in the north (*sever*). Tickets for domestic fixtures are under SIT1,000, a little more than that for a spot in the impressive 4,000-seater main stand (*pokrita tribuna*).

Swift half

Fans meet at the *Viola* kiosk at the train station, just outside the main door. You'll find several cafés and bars along ulica Slovenska, but the main bar at the stadium itself is currently being rebuilt.

Ultra culture

The *Viole Maribor* were founded in 1989, the heyday of Yugoslav fan culture, setting off flares

Eat, drink, sleep…

Bars and clubs

Outside of Ljubljana, **nightlife** in sleepy Slovenia is pretty tame, although quality and tradition are the keynotes of the local **drinks**. Wines, either red (*cviček*) or white (*šipon*) are excellent, while the beers, generally *Union* or *Laško* (look out for the latter's dark brews as well as lagers) are likewise very drinkable. A traditional wine cellar is a *vinarna* while a beer hall is a *pivnica*, but there are also general-purpose bars which serve everything, as well as Viennese-style cafés. Spirits include fruit brandy (*žganje*) and schnapps (*špička*).

In Maribor, bar life such as it is can be found along the Drava river, in an area known as Lent, although a daytime visit to the vast network of wine cellars underneath Trg Svobode shouldn't be missed.

Vinag, Trg Svobode 3. Wine cellar dating back two centuries, open to the public until 7pm, where they serve Slovenia's finest from huge oak barrels, kept at constant temperature. You'll also find a shop and a reception area for tours of the wine tunnels.

Klub Gurman, Mainstream downtown bar/nightclub which at least gives the 24-hour clock a decent shot. Open evenings only from 6pm, until 2am, or 4am Fri–Sat.

Martin Krpan, ul Šaranoviča 27. Tucked away in Melje, the other side of the train station from town, is this club with a more alternative feel, taking its lead from similarly radical establishments in Ljubljana. Open Fri–Sat, until early.

Paradiso, Čurfarjeva cesta 21. Nightclub on the other side of the Drava from the town centre, offering nothing more adventurous than the latest dance hits, but fun all the same. Open daily except Sun until 4am.

Restaurants

Slovene cuisine borrows heavily from the Austrian, Hungarian, Italian and south Slav neighbours. There's an emphasis on meat, usually either pork (*svinjina*) or veal (*teletina*). The locals like their soup (*jota*), a mixture of beans, potatoes and pork. Fish (*riba*) is also popular.

Formal sit-down meals are taken in a *restavracija*, cosier ones in a *gostilna* or a *gostišče*. Wherever you go, you shouldn't need to quibble with the bill – many places offer a set lunch (*dnevna kosilo*) at under SIT1,000 for three courses.

Ranca, ul Vojašniškova 4. Riverside location for this basic eaterie offering grilled specialities such as *čevapi* and other Balkan-style delights. Filling main courses for well under SIT1,000.

Ribja, Hotel Slavija, ul Vita Kraigherja 3. One of the *Slavija*'s main attractions is its well-to-do restaurant, open to non-residents, with set lunches at under SIT1,000 that bring in the local business community.

Pri Treh Ribnikih, ul Ribniška 3. Situated in a nice waterside setting in the middle of the City Park, this pleasant *gostišče* offers a fair selection of meat dishes, as well as fish. Open until 10pm.

Zimski vrt Zamorc, Grajski trg 3. The 'Winter Garden' is as smart as it gets in Maribor, with a stylish, elegant feel thanks to its hanging gardens and sleek design. The food is more than reasonable, the service fine. Open Mon–Sat until 11pm.

Accommodation

Most hotels away from the tourist areas in Slovenia are drab, three- to five-star affairs, clean but bland and overpriced. This is particularly true in Maribor. A popular budget option is a **private room** (*zasebna soba*) – the Maribor branch of Kompas Travel, at Trg Svobode 1 (open Mon–Fri 8am–5pm, Sat 8am–midday) will help you find one.

Hotel Orel, Grajski trg 3 (☎062/26171, fax 062/28497, e-mail orel@termemb.si). Functional three-star hotel in the centre of town. Singles at SIT10,000, doubles SIT14,000, apartments also available.

Hotel Piramida, ul Heroja Slandra 10 (☎062/215 971, fax 062/215 984, e-mail piramida@termemb.si). Recently renovated four-star by the main bus station. Singles at SIT15,500, doubles SIT17,000, apartments also available.

Hotel Slavija, ul Vita Kraigherja 3 (☎062/213 661, fax 062/222 857, e-mail slavija@eunet.si). Modern downtown high-rise three-star, with the attraction of the *Ribja* restaurant (see above). Singles at SIT10,500, doubles SIT14,200, apartments also available.

Garni Hotel Tabor, ul Heroja Zidanška 18 (☎062/104 224; fax 062/100 842, e-mail garni.tabor@amis.net). The other side of the Drava from town is this bargain three-star, built in the mid-Nineties, offering singles at SIT6,500, doubles at SIT9,940 triples at SIT 12,900, all with showers.

Green with envy – Olimpija Ljubljana

Olimpija Ljubljana, representing the country's pretty capital, were always likely to be the club to dominate the newly independent Slovene league. However, after **four straight title wins** from 1992, mostly achieved under mercurial coach Bojan Prašnikar, Olimpija have fallen away following his depature to their hated rivals in Maribor. The coach's return in 2000 could yet prompt a climb back to the top for the men in green-and-white.

Safe as houses – the dressing rooms are protected

Historically, Olimpija were the only Slovene club to feature with any prominence in the old Yugoslav league. They can trace their roots back through numerous name changes and mergers to 1911, and **SK Ilirija**, Slovenia's first football club. Ilirija was merged with SK Primorje in 1936 to form **SK Odred**, and in in 1962 Olimpija were officially founded after the Communist-inspired merger of Odred with **Enotnost**.

The new club won the Slovene title at the first attempt, and continued to progress swiftly up the former Yugoslav league pyramid, winning promotion from the federal second to the first division in 1965. They survived a brush with relegation two years later, after beating the mighty Hajduk Split 1–0 at home. Three years later they were docked three points for the **attempted bribe of a Sarajevo goalkeeper**.

In 1970, Olimpija got as close as they would come to Yugoslav silverware, when they held **Red Star Belgrade** 2–2 at home in the first leg of the cup final. They were beaten only by a goal in the last minute of extra-time in the return.

After that the club enjoyed a handful of **top-ten finishes** in the Yugoslav league, that of 1982/83 featuring a young Srečko Katanec, before his move to Dinamo Zagreb and subsequent stardom with Stuttgart and Sampdoria.

With independence came a string of easy title wins, but poor displays on the new stage of Europe. Just as Olimpija were starting to generate a thriving fan culture in the **Green Dragons**, the team lost its position of power to Maribor. By 1998, losing again to the Violets was more than the fans could take, and the *Green Dragons* staged a strike in protest at the club's lack of ambition and incompetent management.

Olimpija won the Slovene cup in 1999/2000, but only 2,000 souls watched the second leg of their 3–2 aggregate win over Korotan Prevalje. Construction company SCT withdrew its sponsorship soon afterwards. Ironically, it is the club's **Centralni stadium**, also known as the Bežigrad after the suburb in which it stands, which is most in need of rebuilding since renowned architect Jože Plečnik designed it in 1925.

Despite the Bežigrad's modest facilities (renovation plans are afoot), most of **Slovenia's home games** take place here. To see either green-and-white outfit, take bus #6, #8 or #21 from town to the 'Stadion' stop. From the train station, either take a short taxi ride, or turn right out of the exit, and walk for 5mins until you come to the junction on Dunajska cesta. Turn right there, and the stadium is 750m to your left. Until renovation is completed, there is no bar or restaurant to speak of.

Spain

Real Federación Española de Fútbol, Calle Alberto Bosch 13, 28014 Madrid
☎91/420 1362   Fax 91/420 2094   E-mail webrfef@sportec.es

League champions Deportivo La Coruña   **Cup winners** Espanyol
Promoted Las Palmas, Osasuna Pamplona, Villarreal
Relegated Atlético Madrid, Sevilla, Real Betis

European participants 2000/01 Deportivo La Coruña, Barcelona, Real Madrid
(UCL); Valéncia (UCL qualifiers); Espanyol, Real Zaragoza, Deportivo Alavés, Rayo
Vallecano (UEFA Cup); Celta Vigo, Real Mallorca (Intertoto Cup)

At the start of the 1999/2000 season, the English media, basking in Manchester United's Champions' League triumph, debated whether the Premiership had now overtaken *Serie A* as the top league in Europe. Less than a year later, Real Madrid beat Valéncia in the final of the Champions' League, having brushed United aside in the quarter-finals and Bayern Munich in the semis. Valéncia had thrashed the eventual Italian champions Lazio to produce an all-Spanish semi-final against Barcelona. Suddenly it was *La Liga*, not the Premiership, that was perched on top of the European game.

The performances of Spain's club sides in European competition and the sparkling football from *La Liga* seen on satellite TV channels across the globe raised expectations of a strong Spanish challenge at Euro 2000. That failed to materialise as José Camacho's side bowed out at the quarter-final stage, but in a sense that was no disgrace. The Spaniards are not alone in having their league dominated by foreign stars, and it's doubtful whether not just they, but also the national teams of England, Italy or Germany, would stand a chance against a representative XI picked from their cash-rich domestic games.

In 1999/2000, the prevailing influence over the Spanish game continued to be largely a foreign one. An Argentine coach, Hector Cúper, masterminded Valéncia's remarkable run in Europe, with his compatriot Claudio López the team's star striker. The bulk of the Barcelona team had achieved far more in the Champions' League in the past under their previous name of Ajax. And Real Madrid became champions of Europe with an English right-winger and a Frenchman upfront.

But that is looking at Spanish football from the outside. From the inside, 1999/2000 was a revolutionary year in a far more dramatic sense. Deportivo La Coruña, from the north-west province of Galicia, won the title ahead of Barcelona, becoming only the 14th team since the war to breal the Real-Barça hegemony. Valéncia, who finished third, had been in the race throughout, while Real Zaragoza finished above Real Madrid in fourth place. Indeed, at one stage in mid-season, the top five consisted entirely of teams from outside the traditional strongholds of Madrid and Barcelona. If *La Liga* needed a dose of unpredictability to add to its rich tapestry of playing talent, then it certainly got it in 1999/2000.

The bold new era may not last long. While Valéncia were powerless to stop the ravaging of their squad when the season was over, Barça and Real offered their customary response to a challenge – they opened the chequebook. And the politically charged clash between Real, representing the Castille region, and Catalonia's Barcelona remains the game the world wants to see.

A match between the two great rivals is the highlight of the Spanish footballing calendar, more thrilling and eagerly anticipated

Real disappointment – the Madrid trio of Raúl, Casillas and Salgado bid farewell to Euro 2000

than any fixture involving *la selección*, the long-suffering national side. In fact, the overwhelming power of the club game in Spain has contributed to its national team's continued lack of success over the years. Club rivalries may be between two sides from the same city (Real Madrid-Atlético or Sevilla-Betis) or, more potently, between regions (Real-Barça). Many of the ethnic tensions that surround the latter are tied up with the Civil War and its aftermath, the country's postwar Francoist regime having suppressed regional identities and forbidden the open use of Catalan and Basque. This in turn helped to create Spain's first football boom in the Forties and Fifties, as huge crowds rallied round their team as an identifiable local cause.

Before Franco, the picture couldn't have been more different. A professional national league wasn't set up until 1928, but at international level, Spain regularly beat France and Portugal in friendlies, and in 1929 became the first continental team to beat England in a full international.

Football had come to Spain via British mining workers in the Basque country,

from where the game spread to Madrid, Barcelona and Valencia. In a regionalised cup competition whose play-off winners were regarded as national champions, Basque flagship side Athletic Bilbao won one in every three pre-war tournaments, earning their reputation as cup fighters.

The hero of the day was goalkeeper Ricardo Zamora, whose acrobatics won Spain a silver medal at their first international appearance in the 1920 Olympics, and who scarcely missed a match for his country until 1936. He might have been able to prevent Italy from winning the 1934 World Cup, but injury ruled him out of the replay his acrobatics had earned when Spain drew 1–1 with the hosts. After a successful playing career with Barcelona and Real, and postwar, title-winning management at Atlético Madrid, Zamora died in 1978, a hero in both cities.

Rare is the player who has earned such an honour. In the hothouse atmosphere which prevailed in the Spanish game of the Forties, Fifties and Sixties, players were Barça or Real, never both. Argentine footballing maestro Alfrédo di Stéfano had to

Basics

Citizens of the EU, USA, Canada, Australia and New Zealand require only a **passport** to enter Spain.

The Spanish unit of currency is the peseta (pta), of which there are around 250 to £1. Coins are named in units of five, a *duro*. A silver 25-peseta coin is five *duros*, useful for phone calls. There are coins for 1, 5, 10, 25, 50, 100, 200 and 500 pesetas, and notes for 1000, 2000, 5000 and 10,000.

Spain has the most advanced **credit-card system** in Europe, but plastic payment is not as widespread as in the UK. Cash can be advanced from machines just about anywhere, and most machines take all kinds of cards. Banks and savings banks (*cajas de ahorros*) are the best places to **change money**. Hours are Mon–Fri 9am–2pm.

After the Expo and the Olympics of 1992, transport in the country has been greatly improved. **Buses** are comfortable, air-conditioned and charge around 1,000ptas per 100km, while the pride of the **train fleet** is the *AVE* high-speed link between Madrid and Seville, a luxury journey of two-and-a-half hours costing around 8,000ptas. The Barcelona–Madrid trek is three times as long for about the same price, and if you're in a hurry you'd be better off taking the air shuttle service – Spain has some of the **lowest domestic air fares** in Europe. On trains, there are a range of discount fares on so-called **blue days** of the calendar.

Coin phones take 5, 25 and 100 peseta coins, and most bar-owners won't mind you using their phone without buying a drink – look for the **yellow telephone sign** outside. Otherwise, telephone cards come in 1,000- 2,000- and 5,000-peseta units.

From outside the country, the code for calling Spain is 34, and all numbers now include an initial 9, whether calling from abroad or in the town itself. Therefore the major **city codes** are now Madrid 91, Barcelona 93, Bilbao 94, Seville 95 and Valencia 96. To call internationally from Spain, dial 00 before the country code. While local calls are cheap, phoning abroad is not, so stick to the off-peak times – 10pm–8am during the week, then 2pm on Saturday until 8am on Monday.

Accommodation is very reasonably priced. In almost any town you can get a double room for under 4,000ptas and a single for 3,000ptas. The most basic lodgings are *hospedajes*, then *pensiones*, then *hostales* – which must offer at least a sink in each bedroom. An English-language accommodation information service (daily 10am–8pm) is available by calling ☎901 300 600 from anywhere in Spain.

Spanish **food** is rich in regional variety. The mainstays include *paella*, a rice and seafood dish originally from Valéncia, and *tortilla*, potato omelette. A set menu (*menú del día*) should be around 1,000ptas. Lunch is the main meal of the day.

Social life revolves around the **local bar**, which serves reasonably priced alcohol for unfeasably long hours. Draught beer will generally be served in a 250ml glass (*una caña*) for around 150ptas. A longer glass is *un tubo*, 250 ptas. The most popular brews are *Mahou* (Madrid), *Estrella Damm* (Barcelona) and *Cruzcampo* (Seville). **Wine**, either red (*tinto*), white (*blanco*) or rosé (*rosado*), will cost around 150ptas for a glass.

On the bar will be a selection of *tapas*, hot or cold snacks for around 300–500ptas a plate, although these are given free in some regions – wait a while before ordering your food, just in case. A larger portion is *una ración* at 500–1,500 ptas. The **drinking and snacking time** (*el tapeo*) finishes around midnight, after which you'll be drinking *copas* – spirits liberally poured over huge ice chunks in tall glasses. The biggest problem with bars in Spain is **leaving them**. Stick around for breakfast, hot chocolate and fritters (*chocolate y churros*), and the smell of the new day's football press.

Streets in Spain are indicated with c/, short for calle. The floor number of an apartment or office is shown with a degree sign (°).

choose, opting for Madrid over Barcelona in 1953. Real president Santiágo Bernabéu's friends in high places may have influenced the decision process, because Barça, with the classy Ladislav Kubala, had by far the more successful team prior to then.

The national side produced their best-ever World Cup form in Brazil in 1950, finishing fourth. With Barça's Ramallets in goal and Bilbao's Zarra upfront, Spain brushed aside the England of Finney, Milburn and Matthews, and drew a thriller, 2–2 with the eventual winners Uruguay. Drained of both strength and ideas, they were then hammered 6–1 by the hosts.

Back home, football was becoming more popular than bullfighting – and would remain so. Real Madrid and Barça both had outstanding teams, but Bernabéu's poaching of di Stéfano would prove the

masterstroke. Bernabéu built his team around di Stéfano, built a great stadium around the team – then added the Hungarian Ferenc Puskás to the mixture. Real won the European Cup five times with a side that would go down as one of the finest in football history. At home, they dominated the league but were by no means the only class act – Spanish clubs won 13 of the 25 titles contested in the first ten years of European competition.

Though neither was Spanish, both di Stéfano and Puskás travelled to the 1962 World Cup in Chile for their adopted country. In the event, only Puskás would actually play – and there was nothing he could do prevent the Spaniards exiting at the first round, having lost to Czechoslovakia and Brazil.

Two years later, it was a very different *selección* which won the European Nations' Cup, forerunner of the modern European Championship, in Madrid. The final pitted Spain against a Soviet side Franco had refused his team permission to meet in the same competition four years earlier. Now he was in the stands along with 120,000 others at the Chamartín (now Bernabéu) stadium to see Spain win comfortably, 2–1. Stars of the victory were forwards Luis Suárez and Amaro Amancio; missing was the speedy, evergreen Real left-winger Francisco Gento, equally among the candidates for the accolade of finest postwar Spanish player.

The next major tournament Spain staged was altogether less successful, in terms of both organisation and the home side's performance. Visiting teams cursed the 1982 World Cup for its blistering heat and tortured logistics (the Spaniards used 16 stadia

Top that – Sergi and Cañizares after the win over Yugoslavia in 13 different cities), while local fans, desperate for a victory that would confirm the country's post-Franco renaissance, imposed a burden of pressure that Spain's modest side could not cope with.

They drew with the rank outsiders, Honduras, in their opening game, took advantage of some imaginative refereeing to beat Yugoslavia in their second, then lost to Gerry Armstrong's breakaway goal for Northern Ireland in their third. Defeat by West Germany and a goalless draw with England drew the whole unhappy chapter to a close.

Within two years there was to be a surprisingly upbeat sequel. At the 1984 European Championship in France, an almost identical side to that which had hosted the World Cup seemed to be heading for its customary early exit when, in injury time in the last group game against West Germany, Maceda launched himself at a cross from Señor and gave Spain an unlikely 1–0 win. The Spaniards then beat Denmark on penalties in the semi-finals, and were making a decent fist of the final against the host nation until their goalkeeper and captain, Luis Arconada, allowed Michel Platini's curling free-kick to slip out from under his body and crawl over the goal line. The match finished 2–0 to France.

The addition of Real Madrid striker Emilio Butragueño, *El Buitre* ('The Vulture'), allowed Spain to build on their progress of 1984. At the Mexico World Cup of 1986, four goals from *El Buitre* beat a much-favoured Denmark team but, having done all the hard work, Spain then surprisingly went out to Belgium after a shoot-out in the quarter-finals.

At club level, meanwhile, Spanish teams had long since ceded their domination of Europe. Like the Italians, the Spaniards banned foreign imports from their domestic game for a while. But in 1973 the ban was lifted as local teams struggled to keep pace with clubs from Holland, West Germany and, towards the end of the decade, England. After a brief reign by hard-tackling Basque teams in the early Eighties,

which put paid to the challenge of Maradona's Barcelona, Butragueño's Real Madrid won five titles on the trot. Terry Venables and Bernd Schuster won Barça the championship in 1985, but the club then lost the subsequent European Cup final on penalties to Steaua Bucharest, and the chance to build a new European power had gone.

Barcelona would have to wait until 1992, 40 years after losing di Stéfano, to finally lift the European Cup. Dutchman Johan Cruyff, whose exploits as a player under Rinus Michels had given Barça an emphatic and stylish title win in 1974, came back as coach in 1988. His influence would transform Spanish club football and spark a second post-war boom in the domestic game's popularity.

Cruyff assigned equal importance to home-produced players and top foreign stars. The success he attained with an arrogantly adventurous side – four titles in a row, two European trophies including the European Cup – encouraged other club presidents to hire attack-minded trainers, who in turn were urged to raise cheap local talent.

The outcome of all this has been that football has become a fashionable pastime, attracting the major players of modern, democratic and economically buoyant Spanish society. In the early Nineties, three nail-biting title finishes, one featuring the perennial underdogs of Deportivo La Coruña, made great TV and helped to arrest the growth of basketball. Today TV companies are effectively underwriting the game, allowing debt-ridden clubs like Real Madrid to spend millions on the finest playing and coaching staff money can buy. In Real's case, the reward was a much-awaited seventh European Cup triumph, sealed with a 1–0 win over Juventus in 1998.

Perhaps inevitably, there has been a reaction against all this conspicuous consumption. When Barcelona coach Louis van Gaal filled his team with Dutchmen, Barça fans put out 'No More Tulips' banners. But, equally inevitably, their sourness was

Peaceful party – Madrid and Valéncia fans watched the European Cup final side by side in Paris

subsequently sweetened when the team won the Spanish championship at a canter in 1999. Meanwhile, neutrals applauded the achievements of Luis Fernandez's Basque-only Bilbao side (Spain's third Champions' League representative in 1998/99), with its accent on football rather than transfer rumours or tiffs between overpaid stars.

At the same time, one Basque in particular was not so popular. National-team coach Javier Clemente became Public Enemy #1 for his team selection and media-unfriendly attitude at France '98.

Before the tournament, Spain had been considered backable dark horses, after an unbeaten qualifying campaign. Many of the side had been unlucky to bow out of the 1994 version to Italy, a late goal from Roberto Baggio settling the quarter-final before Mauro Tassotti, unseen by the referee, broke Luis Enrique's nose. And poor officiating at Euro '96 had refused Spain a clearly onside goal by Julio Salinas against hosts England, who went through to the semi-final on penalties.

Essentially the same side, now with Real Madrid prodigy Raúl leading the line, strode out confidentally for their first game in France, against Nigeria. They would be walking back with their tails between their legs, after Raúl had missed an easy chance to put Spain 3–1 ahead, and veteran 'keeper Zubizarreta let through a weak shot for the Africans to equalise. From being comfortably in control of the game, Spain had lost their confidence and their shape – and any share of the spoils after Sunday Oliseh's unstoppable 25-yard drive.

Worse was to follow in the next game against Paraguay, when Clemente panicked, and fielded too many forwards against a massed defence. Going into the last game with Bulgaria with only a point from a goalless draw in the bag, Spain at last found the winning formula, with Real's Morientes and Betis' Alfonso upfront, and the team scored six – but it might as well have been 60, as a second-string Nigeria were losing to Paraguay in the other game.

Clemente had relied on his old guard, deploying some of them, such as the sluggish Hierro in midfield, out of position. He tried it again in the Euro 2000 qualifying opener in Cyprus. Spain lost 3–2, and the coach his job. His replacement, José Camacho, simply fielded in-form players in position, came away from a tricky tie in Israel with a 2–1 win, then stood back as Raúl ran riot in the next match against Austria, scoring four in a 9–0 whitewash.

Camacho's buoyant *selección* have silenced those calling for regionalised national teams, although four such selections (representing Catalonia, the Basque country, Galicia and Andalucía) now play annual friendlies against international opposition in the run-up to Christmas. Spain's 2–1 defeat by France in the quarter-finals of Euro 2000 may have been disappointing, not least after Raúl had squandered a chance to take the game into extra-time by fluffing a last-minute penalty.

But at least the Spaniards surpassed their achievement of 1998 in reaching the knockout stage, something that seemed unthinkable when they were 3–2 down to Yugoslavia with 90 minutes played of their final group match. Gaizka Mendieta's 93rd-minute penalty and Alfonso's smartly taken winner two minutes later were the perfect finale to the game of the tournament – dramatic, emotional, unlikely and thoroughly entertaining. Exactly what we have come to expect from Spanish football, in fact.

Essential vocabulary

Hello *¡Hola!*
Goodbye *Adiós*
Yes *Sí*
No *No*
Two beers, please *Dos cañas, por favor*
Thank you *Gracias*
Men's *Caballeros*
Women's *Señoras*
Where is the stadium? *¿Dónde está el estádio?*
What's the score? *¿Cómo va el partido?*
Offside *Fuera de juego*
Referee *Árbitro*

Match practice

Spanish football is a celebration of noise, colour and alcohol – though the latter is no longer available inside grounds themselves. Sunday is when football provides the excuse to eat, drink and be merry. Across the land, corner bars fill with wide-eyed kids in nylon shirts; fans (*hinchas*) devour copious afternoon beers and *tapas*; and old men press their ears to *Carrusel Deportivo* on the radio, cursing quietly to themselves.

Traditionally, women prepared dinner at home while all this was going on. But Spain's *fútbolmania* is attracting a wider audience. In the stadia, crowds are more mixed than ever before, and the first duty of the head of any family is to buy club membership cards for the wife and kids. Today's Spanish game is a family affair.

Inside the grounds, cushions (*almohadillas*) and white handkerchiefs (*pañuelos*) are the pre-requisites. The former are thrown onto the pitch to express displeasure at a refereeing decision or a particularly inept display by the home side. The latter, in a tradition borrowed from bullfighting, can be waved to express either exasperation or satisfaction after a stunning goal or move.

Regional tensions can make for a cracking atmosphere, which rarely spills over into violence – though expect Spanish nationalist chants wherever Barcelona are the visiting side. The natural Spanish sense of fun rarely lets pride stand in the way of a good party. High tackles, hilarious refereeing and flashy latin antics all add to the ambience. Ace foreign stars (Spain imports more than any country in Europe) almost invariably win the top goalscorer title, *el Pichichi*, providing the icing on the cake.

The league season runs from early September until mid-June, with a short break for Christmas and New Year. Most top-flight games take place at 5pm on Sundays (7pm in late spring and early autumn). Some matches – those at Rayo Vallecano in Madrid, for example – kick-off at midday so as not to clash with those of bigger rivals across town.

One top game will kick-off a couple of hours later for live coverage on pay TV, while another is brought forward to Saturday night at 9pm for free-access regional TV channels. There are no more Monday evening games, but one second-flight match is televised live on Saturday afternoons.

Note that match posters often list the away side first. Line-up information is distributed in handouts at some clubs, while others issue a free programme.

A different league

The 20-club first division, *la Primera*, will be scaled down to 18 teams – one day. Until that time, the bottom three teams swap places with the top three from the 22-team *Segunda División A*, Spain having abandoned its play-off system in 1999/2000. A number of reserve teams sometimes get as far as the *Segunda A* but cannot be promoted any higher. In 2000, Atlético Madrid's 'B' team was forcibly relegated from the *Segunda A* after the first team's demotion from the top flight.

Not for nothing do Spaniards call their lower divisions *El Pozo* ('The Well'). Below the *Segunda A* lurk the depths of the semi-professional *Segunda B* – four leagues of 20 teams each, roughly divided geographically, from which it is almost impossible for former big-name clubs to emerge. Only one team from each section gains promotion, via play-offs between each group's top four teams.

Four drop from each *Segunda B* down to the fourth tier, *Tercera División*, which is divided into 17 impenetrable zones.

Up for the cup

La Copa del Rey was initiated by King Alfonso XIII in 1902. For nearly 30 years it was Spain's only tournament, and it continued to be held in high esteem until the fixtures started piling up in the Eighties.

Currently *La Copa* is decided on eight two-legged rounds. Fifty teams from the *Segunda B* and the *Tercera* kick things off, followed by those from the *Segunda A* and the *Primera*, except for clubs involved in European competition who are allowed a bye until the last 16.

The single-game final is at a neutral venue, decided when the finalists are known. It is always played as the last game of the season, in late June or a little earlier if there is a major international tournament in the summer. Extra-time and penalties decide drawn games throughout.

Just the ticket

At big clubs, members (*socios*) often number nearly as much as the stadium capacity. However, all clubs put aside at least 10% of tickets to go on sale a few days before the match, so for a major fixture, go to the club office as early as possible. Bear in mind that prices vary according to the class of opposition.

On the day, tickets are bought at ticket offices (*taquillas*). The cheapest, around 3,000ptas, are standing on the seats behind the goal in the *fondo*, normally either north (*norte*) or south (*sur*). Some grounds still have ordinary standing tickets – *de pie*.

Alongside the pitch, there are various kinds of *tribuna lateral* tickets: lower (*baja*), higher (*alta*) and, in larger stadia, the topmost *anfiteatro*, these last going for up to 6,000ptas. Numbered (*numerada*) seats with the best view are known as *preferencia* and weigh in up to 9,000ptas. Contrary to popular myth, it does rain in Spain, and in wet weather a place which is covered (*cubierto*) is obviously preferable. On your ticket, *puerta* is the gate, *sección* the sector, *fila* the row and *asiento* the seat.

Half-time

Bars outside the ground will be packed before and after matches, but at half-time, the beer on sale inside will be alcohol-free. Some bars have hatches that sell *minis* – plastic mugs of booze, either beer or mixed spirits, for glugging down outside the ground before kick-off. Inside, you may see a *bota* – a large pouch made out of hide that squirts wine down the throat of the uninitiated drinker – being illicitly passed around the crowd.

By the stadium, you'll find sunflower seeds (*pipas*) or dried fruit (*fruta seca*), being sold in different-sized bags decorated in club colours. Snacks include sausages (*salchichas*), hot dogs (*perritos*) and the self-explanatory *hamburguesas*, all on offer for around 500ptas.

Action replay

The 1998/99 season saw a pay-per-view battle begin between the private (and more popular) Canal Satélite and the government-backed Via Digital. The impasse suited Spain's bar owners perfectly, as few individual customers can justify subscribing to both services.

Conventional, non-pay-per-view Canal Plus subscribers get to see the live Sunday evening match at 9pm, while the Saturday night game is shown by free-access terrestrial stations, either the local regional network or state TVE 2.

Of the highlights shows, the most popular is *El Día Después* (Canal Plus, Mondays, 8pm), featuring former Liverpool striker Michael Robinson as presenter. The same channel's *El Tercer Tiempo* (Sundays, 11.30pm) is also a must, with action from the top two flights, plus highlights of one game each from the English, German and Italian leagues. The Monday night English Premiership game normally follows in its entirety at 1.30am. *Estudio Estadio* (TVE 2, Sundays, 10.30pm) is the inferior but still watchable highlights offering from state TV.

TVE also screens international games live, along with Champions' League and selected other European club matches.

Title smile – La Coruña upset the big boys in 2000

The back page

There are four main sports dailies. *Marca* (125ptas) is Spain's biggest-selling daily paper, and clebrated its 60th anniversary over Christmas 1998. It now sells more than half-a-million copies a day, but it is heavily geared towards the two Madrid teams, and nobody is seen dead with a copy in Barcelona. Its foreign coverage is also only average. *Marca*'s nearest competitor is *AS* (125ptas), with a similar feel.

Their equivalent in Catalonia is *El Mundo Deportivo* (125ptas) which, naturally, has its first few pages dedicated to news from Barcelona. Its international coverage is more balanced, and while it is Catalan-run, the paper is printed in Spanish and is on sale throughout the country. There's also the Catalan-language *Sport* (125ptas).

Around the regions, *Marca* offers a Seville edition to challenge the city's daily *Estadio* (125ptas) and *El Mundo Deportivo* has a Bilbao edition to challenge *El Correo*'s strong sports section.

Don Balon (Mondays, 350ptas) is the leading weekly, appealing mainly to a younger readership but with the occasional serious feature. Its competitors, *Solo Góles* (395ptas) and *Equipo Líder* (375ptas), are glossy colour picture jobs. *Marca* publishes a matchless season preview magazine, *Guía Marca Liga*, every August.

Ultra culture

Supporters in Spain are organised in clubs called *peñas*, which organise tickets, away trips and social gatherings. In any town, the *peña* bar will be a place to hang out and catch up with all the soccer gossip.

Alongside and occasionally overlapping with the *peñas* are the *ultras*, similar to their Italian counterparts – although the fashion took off in Spain much later. In Madrid, Atlético and Real ultra groups were set up around 1982.

If there is one factor mitigating against further development of the ultra concept, it is the vast distances between clubs which make away travel so difficult in Spain. The fans' choreography also tends to be less ambitious than in Italy, although the big boys can still put on a serious show.

Outbreaks of violence, mainly away from grounds, were becoming more frequent when the Spanish FA decided to ban alcohol at grounds in 1990, and fireworks in 1992. The situation had calmed down considerably until the death of a Real Sociedad fan outside Atlético Madrid's stadium in December 1998, an incident which shook the nation. The dailies splashed the story over their front pages, *El País* running a harrowing picture of the last attempts to revive the victim.

As an antidote to this sensationalism, the monthly fanzines *Super Hincha* and *Jugador #12* (both 300ptas) have the inside ultras info.

In the net

The Spanish FA offers up probably the most informal-looking official site you will see from a national federation at: www.sportec.com/www/rfef/main.htm. It's in Spanish only but the various areas (league cup, national team and so on) are easy to find your way around.

The daily *Marca* runs a *Digital* version at: www.marca.es. It's been completely redesigned and is now much quicker to surf, although the plethora of other sports options (basketball, cycling and so on) can't help but get in the way at times. In addition to the expected news, there's a big fantasy-football section, and the paper has cleverly opened its own online merchandise shop at: www.tiendamarca.com.

Away from all this hurly-burly, the *ServiFútbol* site offers a wealth of useful Spanish soccer links, including scores of individual club sites and areas dedicated to the transfer market and the pools. This mix has now been augmented with a regular news service, a big stats archive and a redesign – the site is still not much to look at, but that in itself is no bad thing. Head for: www.servifutbol.es.

Madrid

Real Madrid *542* Atlético Madrid *548*
Rayo Vallecano *551*

To say there were contrasting moods in Madrid in the summer of 2000 would be to take understatement to new limits. While Real Madrid celebrated their eighth European Cup triumph by breaking the world transfer record to steal Luis Figo away from Barca, their neighbours Atlético were facing their first season outside the top flight since World War II. Atletico's relegation, at the end of a season which saw government administrators appointed to run the team while maverick president Jesús Gil almost lost both control of the club and his liberty, means there will be no derby in Madrid in 2000/2001.

While the clash between the two sides from the capital has always had emotion, for Real fans, the game with Barcelona is *the* derby. Not without justification, they have always considered themselves to be in a different class from their neighbours – ever since Don Santiágo Bernabéu, *los Meringues'* most famous president, took the club from relative mediocrity to European superstardom, building an arena which would go on to host a World Cup final, a European Championship final and three European Cup finals. Today, the Bernabéu stadium's position on one of the city's main avenues befits the club's regal name and status in the game – Bernabéu was one of the prime movers behind the founding of the European Cup.

If you're an ambitious club president, it helps to have friends in high places. The role of Spain's dictator General Franco in Real's rise could be overstated, but it is said he could reel off old line-ups like any good statto. Don Bernabéu was one of his associates, and

used the situation to his advantage – Barcelona were always wealthier, but Real were Franco's pet.

The area around the Bernabéu is one of elegant plazas and palaces. A little to the south is la Plaza de Cibeles, where Real fans go and celebrate, a major city landmark that saw half a million converge upon it on the night of the Champions' League triumph of 1998 – although Atlético fans threatened to paint it black the night their team won the Spanish title in 1996.

The Mattress Makers (*los colchoneros*), as Atlético are known, have almost always lived in the shadow of their wealthier neighbours. Their urban, working-class support have followed them from Vallecas in

Rooms with a view – fans watch Vallecano from Madrid flats

the rough guide 541 european football

the south-west of the city, to Reina Victoria in the north-west, then down to their present home at Manzanares in the industrial south-east.

The club, an offshoot of the Madrid FC team that would become Real, first played their former team-mates in 1905; the game finished 1–1. Atlético had the audacity to win a couple of titles the Forties and early Fifties. But from the day Bernabéu signed Alfredo di Stéfano in 1953, Real were on a different plane. By the end of the decade, they didn't even deign to give Atlético the status of rivals – that position had been taken by Barcelona.

Atlético's best crack at taking Real down a peg or two was the European Cup semi-final of 1959. Both won their home leg by the odd goal, and it took a play-off at Zaragoza for Real to edge it over their neighbours, 2–1.

For *Atléti*, further ignominy was to follow. Jealously coveting Real's palace up the road, Atlético planned to build one of their own, raising money – as Bernabéu did – by membership subscription. While negotiating the sale of their old Metropolitano stadium, Atlético's scheme hit the rocks when funding dwindled, and the club were forced to go cap in hand to Real and play their home games there for a season.

Yet it was around this time that Atlético hit a rare patch of consistency, beating Real in consecutive domestic cup finals in 1960 and 1961. They won the Cup-Winners' Cup of 1962, made the final of the same tournament a year later, then fell to Juventus in the 1965 Fairs' Cup semi.

Atlético eventually moved into their new stadium at Manzanares in 1966. Since then, only the public outbursts of Jesús Gil have kept Real from dominating the headlines – though the historic title win of 1996, black fountains or no, was still a moment for the Mattress Makers to savour.

Madrid's third team have until now been Rayo Vallecano, from the working-class neighbourhood of Vallecas. The club regularly exercise their right to be relegated and promoted, the movement being back up to the *Primera* in 1999, thanks to a play-off win over Extremadura. Rayo are propped up by the eccentric Rivero family, far out on the south-western edge of the city, attracting a small but loyal following of supporters in search of something different. They certainly got that in 1999/2000, as Rayo enjoyed their best-ever season. They were in the top half of the league throughout the campaign and although they faded at the close to finish ninth, the relegation of Atlético leaves them enjoying new-found status as the second-ranked club in the city.

The thrilling fields

Real Madrid

Estadio Santiágo Bernabéu, Avenida Concha Espina 1
Capacity 87,000
Colours All white with violet trim
League champions 1932–33, 1954–55, 1957–58, 1961–65, 1967–69, 1972, 1975–76, 1978–80, 1986–90, 1995, 1997
Cup winners 1905–8, 1917, 1934, 1936, 1946–47, 1962, 1970, 1974–75, 1980, 1982, 1989, 1993
European Cup winners 1956–60, 1966, 1998, 2000
UEFA Cup winners 1985–86

Spain took the field at the 1978 World Cup wearing black armbands. Don Santiágo Bernabéu, club president at Real Madrid, had passed away, and the national team's gesture was much more than a token one.

It was Bernabéu who pulled Real Madrid from post-Civil War austerity up to the rank of aristocracy. For five years in the second half of the Fifties, Real dominated Europe as no other ever team will again, their white strip becoming as feared as any in the game's history.

Those white shirts also came to represent the repressive right-wing regime of the day. For Catalan and Basque alike, General Franco's favoured team of international all-stars were the Castillian overlords, while Bernabéu himself was reviled as an out-and-out Francoist. Catalans would claim that the one player instrumental to Real's rise, Alfredo di Stéfano, was kept away from Barcelona by political manoeuvering.

For the neutral, though, Real Madrid will always mean class, a bastion of attacking football whose finest hour, their 7–3 destruction of Eintracht Frankfurt in the 1960 European Cup final, is etched into the consciousness even of fans who were born after it was played...

Don Santiágo and his brother Marcelo played for Madrid Football Club as teenagers, when games were played by a rubbish tip at a ground known as Campo O'Donnell – now the site of a Walt Disney theme park. Madrid FC had been formed by students at the turn of the century. They moved from ground to ground, at one point playing next to a bullring and changing in the toilets of the bar next door.

Eighth time lucky – McManaman and co with the big one

The club regularly topped the regional *Campeonato del Centro*, which qualified them for the *Copa del Rey*. Madrid celebrated four straight victories in the cup from 1905 – before the Bernabéus had begun their playing career. King Alfonso XIII gave Madrid his royal (*Real*) blessing in 1920, and the club turned professional with the inauguration of the Spanish league in 1929.

By now the team had found a permanent home, the purpose-built Chamartín stadium, south of the station of the same name. Don Santiágo was on the board, and it was he who decided to splash out a world record transfer fee on goalkeeper Ricardo Zamora in 1930. Zamora's Real proved a hardy defensive unit, and the club won their first two titles in 1932 and 1933.

The Spanish Civil War interrupted the run, and when Bernabéu took over as club president in 1943, his first task was to rebuild Chamartín, which had been all but destroyed by fighting. At this time, *la liga* was dominated by Real's two biggest rivals, Barcelona and Aviación Madrid, later to become Atlético. After a brush with relegation, Bernabéu vowed to make Real the best in Spain, playing in a new Chamartín. Raising money from a bond issue among supporters – and with possible state assistance – Bernabéu built a stadium worthy of champions, between the old ground and Avenida del Generalísimo Franco, today's Castellana.

To help hire these champions, there was club treasurer Raimundo Saporta and Bernabéu's political connections. Saporta's first task was to draw up a contract with

Millonarios of Colombia for forward Alfredo di Stéfano, formerly of River Plate in the Forties – a team considered by his fellow Argentines to be the greatest in their football history.

Di Stéfano had learned his trade by dribbling with the ball at speed down Buenos Aires' grid-pattern streets. Direct, gifted and ambitious, he was football's complete player. Money had lured him to Colombia's breakaway league, and $50,000 brought him to Spain in 1953. Barcelona had also drawn up a contract – but with River Plate, not the Colombians. Amid the confusion, the Spanish FA decided that di Stéfano should play for Madrid and Barcelona in turn, each for a season at a time. The ruling pleased nobody. Saporta manoeuvred with the powers-that-were, and after the player had spent six weeks with Real, Barcelona dropped their option. A day later, Di Stéfano scored four against them in Real's 5–0 win.

Alongside di Stéfano were Héctor Rial from Uruguay and former Santander winger Francisco Gento. Behind them as the team's engine was Miguel Muñoz, who would become coach before the decade was out. Real won four titles in five years. But it was the European Cup that made them. Bernabéu had been behind the competition from the start, meeting in Paris with Gabriel Hanot when the blueprint was drawn up. The first of his club's five consecutive victories in it began in 1956, with a difficult win over Stade de Reims in Paris. The French had scored two in the first ten minutes, and it took a surprise run and strike from centre-back Manuel Marquitos to level the scores, before Madrid went on to win 4–3.

Bernabéu duly bought Reims' Raymond Kopa, di Stéfano dropped a little deeper, and three more Cups were won. Uruguay's José Santamaría anchored the back, former Betis striker Luis del Sol buzzed upfront, Brazil's Didi came and went. But it was the arrival of Hungarian exile Ferenc Puskás that completed the best-loved Real line-up. Although he only played in one

winning final, that of 1960, it was in a display so exquisite that the scoreline alone has come to suggest Madrid's showcase football – 7–3 to Real, four to Puskás, three to di Stéfano. "We were scoring goals and they stood and watched us," said Puskás of the opposition, Eintracht Frankfurt. Also standing and watching were 135,000 fans at Glasgow's Hampden Park, every one of them entranced by what they saw.

The 'Galloping Major', who had starred in another scoreline milestone, Hungary's 6–3 mauling of England in 1953, had been exiled from his homeland since the 1956 uprising, drifting round Europe before assuming a role complementary to di Stéfano's at Real. It took a special Barcelona team to beat Madrid in the following year's tournament, and an even better Benfica to edge the 1962 final 5–3 – a game in which Puskás scored a hat-trick in 20 minutes yet finished on the losing side.

The turning point came in 1964, when Puskás and di Stéfano, both 38, weren't quick enough to slip Internazionale's tight marking. Their era had given way to *catenaccio* and the cult of the manager.

Gento stayed on to captain the team to a record sixth European Cup win in 1966. He was still there five years later, when Real lost the Cup-Winners' Cup final to Chelsea after a replay.

Throughout the Seventies and early Eighties, Real's Spanish players were good but not great – Pirri, Camacho and Amaro Amancio in midfield, Juanito and Carlos Santillana upfront. Their expensive imports were patchy – Bernd Schuster was under the thumb of his domineering wife, while Lawrie Cunningham's dragged him around Madrid's nightclubs when he should have been at home nursing an injury. But Mexican Hugo Sánchez regularly topped the league goalscoring list, while Argentine forward Jorge Valdano and German anchorman Uli Stielike both played with conviction.

In the mid-Eighties, *la quinta del Buitre* – 'the Vulture Squad' – rose through Real's competitive ranks to win the club five

Madrid essentials

Madrid's Barajas **airport** is 16km east of the city. The new M8 metro connection runs to M4 Mar de Cristal, journey time to the centre 30mins. Airport buses leave from all terminals (every 15mins, 5.15am–2am, 385ptas, journey time one hour) and make six stops on the way to their underground terminus at Plaza Colón. Walk up to street level to find Colón metro station on line M4. A taxi costs around 2,500ptas – only use those from official ranks outside each terminal.

The city has two main **train stations**. Chamartín (M10) serves France, northern Portugal, Catalonia and northern Spain; Atocha (M1 Atocha Renfe) serves the rest of Spain, Lisbon and the high-speed *AVE* trains to Seville. Confusingly, some trains call at both. International and long-distance **coaches** terminate at Estación Sur de Autobuses (M6 Méndez Alvaro).

Madrid's **transport system** (6am–1.30am) is excellent. The colour-coded, **11-line metro** is quick, clean and safe. Its only drawback is the long pedestrian tunnels at major station interchanges, which can add ten minutes to your journey time. A single ticket (130ptas) should be inserted into the turnstile machines at the top of the escalators. The city bus network (6am–11.30pm), for which single tickets (130ptas) are sold by drivers, is also extensive. *Metrobús* tickets (680ptas), sold at metro stations, *EMT* kiosks and newsstands, are valid for ten journeys on either network. Tickets are the same for the 20 night bus (*búho*) routes, which run from Plaza de Cibeles every half-hour midnight–3am, then hourly until 6am.

Taxis are white, with a diagonal red stripe on the door. The minimum fare is 180ptas, then it's 85ptas per km, with supplements 11pm–6am, at holidays, for luggage and for journeys to the main stations or the airport. Cabs can be flagged down, found at ranks marked with a blue T-sign, or booked on: ☎91/445 9008 (*Tele-Taxi*, Visa card accepted) or ☎91/547 8200 (*Radioteléfono Taxi*, Amex and Visa accepted). Give the name of the bar, restaurant, hotel or street corner, and your name – the **meter starts running** when the call is answered.

The main city **tourist information office** is at Plaza Mayor 3 (open Mon–Fri 10am–8pm, Sat 10am–2pm, ☎91/588 1636, M1/2/3 to Sol). There are branch offices at Duque de Medinaceli 2 (open Mon–Fri 9am–7pm, Sat 9am–1pm, ☎91/429 4951, M2 Banco de España), at the international arrivals hall of Barajas airport and near platform #14 of Chamartín station. None can book hotels but all will provide names, addresses and phone numbers.

The best **listings magazine** is *In Madrid*, an English-language monthly available in clubs and bars. Otherwise, there's the weekly *Guía del Ocio* (Fridays, 125ptas), while the Friday editions of dailies *El País* and *El Mundo* have leisure supplements. For a city-run telephone information line, dial ☎010 (☎91/366 6605 from outside Madrid, open Mon–Fri 8am–9pm). You may have to wait for an English-speaking operator.

The city's main **football store** is *Fútbol Total*, c/Cardenal Cisneros 80 (open daily 10.30am–2pm & 5–9pm, most credit cards, M2 Quevedo), with replica kits from all over Europe.

straight titles. Butragueño, Michel, Sanchis, Martín Vázquez and Gordillo became first-team regulars for the best part of a decade which, in addition to a bulging trophy room, also saw major renovation to Bernabéu's stadium. Behind the glossy exterior, however, Real were being subjected to scandalous financial mismanagement. In the early Nineties, president Ramón Mendoza all but bankrupted the club, spending money that wasn't in the bank, then forging a series of disadvantageous marketing deals which robbed the club of huge potential earnings when they entered the Champions' League in 1995. That was the year when, having gifted two consecutive titles to Barça by losing the last match of their season at Tenerife, Real won a long-awaited title with the thoughtful Valdano as coach.

The Argentine's premature dismissal midway through the 1995/96 season saw the club miss out on Europe altogether the following year. So new president Lorenzo Sanz went for broke – investing in Davor Šuker, Clarence Seedorf, Roberto Carlos, Christian Panucci, Predrag Mijatović and coach Fabio Capello.

It worked for a season, explosive teenage prodigy Raúl voted Spain's player of the year with his 21 goals to complement Šuker's 24, but Capello's swift departure back to Milan left his replacement Jupp Heynckes with one outstanding task – win the 1997/98 Champions' League. In the group stage, Real were efficient away, effusive at home. They lost just once, to Rosenborg in Trondheim, and scored 13 goals in three games at the Bernabéu. With the previous season's strike partnership of Šuker and Mijatović misfiring, it was left to Fernando Morientes, an unheralded close-season signing from Zaragoza, to lead the line. No matter – with Roberto Carlos, Seedorf, Hierro and Panucci, Madrid could score goals from anywhere.

During the winter break, Heynckes bought Brazilian forward Sávio from Flamengo and, after much wrangling, Christian Karembeu from Sampdoria. His team's progress through the European Cup knock-out stage began with an easy win over Bayer Leverkusen, then a trickier one over holders Borussia Dortmund, the home leg held up when Real's ultras moved the goalposts. Although extra-cautious away from the Bernabéu in previous ties – Rosenborg had been the only one of five teams to get past their defence – in the final against Juventus in Amsterdam, Real were first to find their rhythm, first to the ball and first to score, through Mijatović's cutely finished poached goal. After that, the team rarely looked troubled by a Juventus side that was apparently waiting for disaster to strike.

As the final whistle blew, Spain erupted. Nearly 200 were injured when police over-reacted to the sheer size of the crowd at the Cibeles fountain, but nothing could take the edge off the triumph or the sense of history accompanying it. This, after all, was la séptima, the seventh European Cup success the club and its followers had been waiting for since 1966.

From a footballing point of view, Real had played a classic percentage game, more Italian than German – which was no surprise, as the side was essentially the creation of Heynckes' predecessor Capello. Small wonder that Capello's name was first in the frame when Heynckes departed the scene but, after a brief appearance by old boy José Camacho, it was Guus Hiddink who took over as coach.

In a more subdued but safer Bernabéu – the notorious Fondo Sur ultras section was now all-seated after the Dortmund fiasco – Real set about defending their crown and gaining back the Spanish title they had let slip while concentrating on Europe. They flunked both. Hiddink was dismissed after a 3–0 defeat at Barcelona in the league in early 1999, and John Toshack, arriving for a second spell in charge of the club, could not prevent the team's elimination from Europe at the hands of Dynamo Kiev, or their subsequent humiliation in the Copa del Rey by Valéncia.

During the close season, Toshack somehow kept his job, signing Steve McManaman for free and Nicolas Anelka for more than £20million. The former Liverpool man settled in reasonably well, but the Anelka signing was a disaster, the young French striker apparently even more homesick in Madrid than he had been in London. At one point he was even sent back to Paris 'to recover', while Toshack was dismissed after a public spat with Sanz, and replaced by Vicente del Bosque, a man who many saw as a stopgap while the president set about grabbing another big name – not least after Real suffered their worst-ever home defeat, 5–1 at the hands of Zaragoza in December.

Yet there was gradual improvement both at home and in Europe. Anelka returned to the fold, anxious to prove his fitness for Euro 2000, and del Bosque's team ran rings around Manchester United in their Champions' League quarter-final second leg at Old Trafford. Anelka then scored the first headed goal of his career to help eliminate Bayern Munich in the semis, and set up an all-Spanish European Cup final with Valéncia. In a fiesta atmosphere at the Stade de France, Real's opponents froze, leaving McManaman to run the midfield show and inspire a 3–0 win.

A season that had threatened to become one of the club's least memorable had ended in triumph. The problem was that nobody could quite work out how, and Sanz was unexpectedly defeated in the presidential elections that followed the club's record eighth European Cup success. His successor as president, Florentino Pérez, had built his campaign around an outlandish promise to bring Barcelona's Portuguese winger Luis Figo to Madrid. Pérez kept his word, and Real's reported £150million debt was increased by another £40million or so. But nobody at the Bernabéu was complaining.

Here we go!

The Estadio Bernabéu now has its own **metro stop**, on line 10, right by the stadium.

Just the ticket

For most games, tickets go on sale two days before the match, 5–8pm, at gate #42 on the Concha Espina side of the stadium, and 11am–2pm on the day of the game. The other ticket offices around the stadium open two hours before kick-off, with the cheapest seats (2,500–3,000ptas) behind the goal in the *fondo sur* and in the *tribuna superior baja* and *alta*, on sale at taquilla #3 by gate #34. Taquillas #4–6 by gate #24 sell tickets for the *anfiteatro lateral*, the uncovered main stand, divided into two tiers with prices scaled accordingly, 4–6,500 ptas.

The most expensive seats, in the covered *anfiteatro preferencia* or *tribuna preferencia*, are sold at taquillas #7 and #9, by gate #9 on the Avenida Castellana. Visiting fans are heavily policed into the upper tier of the *fondo norte*.

Swift half

The Bernabéu is **ringed with bars**. Many fans hang out down c/Marceliano Santa Maria, the second street on the right down Avenida Concha Espina, either swigging wine on the street, or drinking beer in the *Chiquifru* (#8) with its superb collection of match tickets, or the quieter *Mr Raf* (#9) opposite.

OK Madrid, c/San Juan de la Salle 5, has a great wall of black-and-white Madrid pictures, while *Birrä*, Concha Espina 8, is an upmarket bar full of Forties Americana, with table football (Real–Atlético!) and a good selection of beers.

Club merchandise

The official shops on three corners of the stadium are rather modest kiosks (open Mon–Fri 10am–1.30pm & 4.30–8pm, Sat 10am–1.30pm and on matchdays). The *Tienda Estádio* by gate #61 (open Mon–Fri 10am–1.30pm & 5–8pm and on matchdays, most credit cards) is equally unimpressive for a club of Real's stature. The *Todo Fútbol* van, parked at the corner of Concha Espina and Castellana on matchdays, has a better selection of shirts and souvenirs.

Ultra culture

The **Ultras Sur**, a permanent fixture in the *fondo sur* since 1982, are the most notorious in Spain and probably the loudest, too. Unlike many Spanish fan groups, this lot have always travelled widely. Throughout the Eighties, tensions rose whenever the *Ultras Sur* came to town, while at home, Real have often been fined for their activities – the heaviest penalty coming after certain members damaged the goalposts before the 1998 European Cup semi-final first leg against Dortmund. High barriers and a wider area to the touchline now divide the troublemakers from the action.

n print

A *Programa Oficial* is issued free of charge, available all around the ground. The club also produce a glossy magazine, *Real Madrid Monthly*, 500ptas from newsstands.

In the net

The official website was a long time coming, but is now a fully fledged commercial affair run by *Sportal*. There's plenty of English-language news and information, but it's not as impressive as it should be at: www.realmadrid.es.

For a thorough unofficial offering, try Gonzalo San Martín's long-running effort at: www.yrl.co.uk/~gonzalo/rm/rm.html.

 Atlético Madrid

Estádio Vicente Calderón, Paseo Virgen del Puerto 67
Capacity 57,000 (all-seated)
Colours Red-and-white striped shirts, blue shorts
League champions 1940–41, 1950–51, 1966, 1970, 1973, 1977, 1996
Cup winners 1960–61, 1965, 1972, 1976, 1985, 1991–92, 1996
Cup-Winners' Cup winnners 1962

'Be with us for a season in hell,' was the slogan Atlético Madrid chose for their season ticket campaign for the 2000/2001 season. But could life in the second division really be any more hellish than the year the regulars at the Calderón had just endured?

Atlético had been threatened with bankruptcy, seen two of their best players sold mid-season, and then been relegated for the first time since World War II. Oh yes, and just to add torture to the pain, neighbours Real went and won the Champions' League again.

All of this had come just four years after Atlético had won the Spanish title for the first time in almost two decades, and president Jesús Gil y Gil had promised his team would overtake Real as the city's premier club in time for the new millenium. Gil is a cartoon version of the southern European football president. The mayor of the coastal resort of Marbella, he was jailed for criminal negligence in the Sixties (a building his company constructed had collapsed with fatal results) but released after the personal intervention of General Franco. He has faced, and survived, charges of corruption and nepotism throughout his political, business and football career, and has been involved in hilarious punch-ups with his critics on live television. In his 14 years in charge at Atlético, he has brought the joy of the title and the despair of relegation, not to mention sacking more than 30 coaches along the way.

Among that legion of former managers, Gil has one soft spot, and his name is Raddy Antić. Best remembered in Britain for scoring a goal that kept Luton Town in the old first division and which prompted their manager David Pleat to race across the turf at Manchester City's Maine Road to hug him, Antić was a modest player who became a master motivator once he made the move into coaching. He had taken Real Madrid to the top of *La Liga* in 1991, and got the sack for his trouble. He then turned modest Oviedo into one of the most attractive club sides in Spain, before ignoring everyone's advice and taking the top job at Atlético in 1995.

While planning a new-look team for Gil, Antić had seen a fellow Yugoslav, playmaker Milinko Pantić, on TV. The same under-achiever he had brought from third-division Jedinstvo to Partizan Belgrade in 1985 scored a hat-trick that day for Greek club Panionios. Just half-a-million dollars secured his transfer. Valéncia's third-choice goalkeeper, Francisco Molina, was another cheap acquisition. Bulgarian striker Ljubo Penev came with him on a free, and Antić urged existing players like striker Kiko and midfielders José Luis Caminero and Argentine Diego Simeone to give their all.

In the 1995/96 season, Atlético stayed top of the league from the first game to the last. Before the final whistle was blown on their decisive 2–0 win over Albacete, Gil was bathing in champagne. Outside, the stadium, so rarely full over the preceding last ten years, made up for lost time. The double was then won with an extra-time Pantić goal beating Barcelona. Fans of *los colchoneros* – the 'Mattress Makers' – had never slept so soundly.

Anguish at the end – Jimmy Floyd Hasselbaink's goal came too late in the 2000 cup final

After attaining domestic glory, Gil promised the same in Europe. A confident breeze to the top of their 1996/97 Champions' League group, which included a win over the eventual winners Borussia Dortmund, earned Atlético a classic quarter-final pairing with Ajax. With the aggregate score tied at 2–2, a Pantić penalty looked to have given his side a semi-final meeting with Juventus. But on 100 minutes Ajax equalised and, with chances going begging at either end, sealed the tie with a goal a minute from the end of extra-time.

Gil had gambled that the 1996 double-winning side was good enough to take on Europe. He quickly owned up to the error, signing Juninho, Christian Vieri and Jordi Lardín for £25million in the 1997 close season. Between them they scored a hatful of goals, but Juninho's broken leg scuppered a serious assault on the title.

In the UEFA Cup, after defeats of Leicester City and Aston Villa and an extra-ordinary win over PAOK Salonika, Atlético fell to a single Vladimir Jugović goal in the semi-final with Lazio. Antić then bade farewell to the club, parting amicably with Gil (perhaps the first coach to do so), and leaving his post to Italian Arrigo Sacchi, who would bring ten *Serie A* players with him – including Jugović. It was to be an incident-filled autumn off the pitch, with the sudden sale of Vieri to Lazio after an argument with Sacchi, the fatal stabbing of a Real Sociedad fan outside the Calderón, and the jailing of Gil for misuse of public funds. On the pitch – nothing happened. Sacchi resigned in February 1999, as the team went through the worst run on the club's history.

Gil called up his old mate Antić to save the day – but he had been in charge for only a week when he saw his team outclassed by Parma in a UEFA Cup semi-final. Out of Europe and struggling in mid-table of the league, Atlético made the *Copa del Rey* final but were well-beaten by Valéncia, Gil then using the post-match press conference to announce that the victors' coach, Claudio Ranieri, would be in charge at the Calderéon for the 1999/2000 season – or at least, the start of it.

Almost from the word go, however, Ranieri's team struggled at the wrong end of the table – despite the instinctive goalscoring of Dutchman Jimmy Floyd Hasselbaink. With Gil's axe poised to fall, Ranieri called it a day, and was replaced (inevitably) by Antić. However, rumours of serious financial irregularities at the club were now surfacing in the press, and in January, Gil and his directors were removed from office by the courts, who appointed administrators to run Atlético in their absence. The men with the clipboards sold two of the team's key players – experienced Argentine defender José Chamot and Spanish Under-21 striker José Mari – to AC Milan in an attempt to balance the books, and their loss proved fatal.

Atlético lost their second successive cup final, this time to Espanyol, and were then relegated. Antić offered to work for free as players lined up to leave, despite Gil's uncharacteristic promise – issued from police custody – that those who stayed would not be forgotten.

There was clearly a rocky road to be trodden ahead, but it would not be the first in the club's epic history. Atlético earned their nickname because of their red-and-white striped shirts, originally borrowed from Athletic Bilbao when the club was formed by disgruntled members of Madrid FC in 1903. Initially a subsidiary of the Bilbao club, 'Athletic de Madrid' were drifting into obscurity when the Civil War came along. Relegated then promoted by default, the club were merged with the Spanish air force team, Aviación, with backing from the authorities. Former star goalkeeper Ricardo Zamora was put in charge, and as Atlético Aviación the team won back-to-back titles in 1940 and 1941.

Another star coach, Helenio Herrera, was responsible for two further titles ten years later, but the newly named Atlético de Madrid received no further favours from General Franco. Real Madrid did them few favours, either. The first time the poor relations got a sniff of continental glory, in the semi-finals of the 1959 European Cup, Real brushed them aside in a replay. Few clubs could have lived in such a shadow as Real's over Atlético. Even the team's single European success, in the 1962 Cup-Winners' Cup, slipped by almost unnoticed, their victorious replay against Fiorentina coming four months after the first game.

At around this time, Atlético's prospective move from the cramped Metropolitano to Manzanares at the other end of the city became bogged down in debt. The club's hard-working president, Vicente Calderón, bailed them out after they had spent a season grumpily ground-sharing with Real. The team returned briefly to the Metropolitano and the club's last season there fittingly saw the title won in 1966.

The new stadium, built over a ring road on the banks of the Manzanares river, by an old gasworks and surrounded by the smells of the *Mahou* brewery, saw some brutal football. First, Austrian disciplinarian Max Merkel instilled a tight, defensive game. Then, to add insult to inflicting injuries, Juan Carlos Lorenzo took control. The Argentine was known the world over for producing teams in the style of the Estudiantes side he played for in the late Sixties: vicious and unrepentant. Three of his players were sent off against Celtic in the 1974 European Cup semi-final, yet Atlético won the tie, and came within a minute of lifting the trophy itself. At the final in Brussels, a speculative long-range shot by Bayern Munich defender Georg Schwarzenbeck in the last minute of extra-time tied the final at 1–1, after Luis had given the Spaniards the lead four minutes earlier. Bayern easily won the replay, 4–0.

Calderón, rewarded for his efforts by having the stadium named after him, would live only to see one more Spanish title, attained by a single-point margin over Barcelona in 1977. One wonders if Jesús Gil might yet suffer the same fate...

Here we go!

Take **M5 metro** to Pirámides, cross the large roundabout of Glorieta de las Pirámides, then walk downhill towards the river for 5mins.

Just the ticket

Tickets go on sale at **gate #6** two days before the match (11am–2pm & 5–8pm) and two hours before kick-off, with another set of ticket windows open on the opposite corner, the other side of the underpass.

The **most expensive tickets** are the *preferencia*, above the highway that runs under the stadium, colour-coded blue. On the other side is the *lateral*, colour-coded orange. Behind the goals are the *fondo norte* and *sur*, the latter home to the *Frente Atlético*.

Visiting fans are allocated sections 405/6 and 505/6 in the *tribuna superior* of the *preferencia* (gates #3 and #4), and sections 417/8 and 517/8, opposite in the *lateral* (gates #31 and #33).

Swift half

The Paseo de los Melancólicos, parallel to the river, is where you'll find the main bar action, with many fans sinking minis outside where Melancólicos meets c/San Epifanio by the *Mahou* brewery. **Bar Resines** has a main branch there and a couple just round the corner. In between, the **Bar el Parador** has live TV coverage of the game going on across the street. On the north side, at #49, the **Bar Alegre** has a proud display of pub team trophies. Curiously, the best of the bunch, the **Alvaro** at #43 is, in fact, a friendly Sporting Gijón bar.

Club merchandise

The main club shop, **Tienda Estádio Oficial** (open Mon–Fri 10am–2pm & 4.30–8pm, Sat 10am–2pm, and matchdays) is by gate #10 of the Calderón. There's a **smaller store** on the corner of Paseo Virgen del Puerto and c/del Duque de Tovar, open the same hours.

Ultra culture

El Frente Atlético, are one of the country's best-organised ultra groups. Their colourful choreography is certainly among the top three in the land and their away support is, for Spain, impressive.

Their reputation was soured, however, by the fatal stabbing of Real Sociedad fan Aitor Zabaleta outside gate #6 of the Calderón in December 1998, after which *el Frente* came in for the justified ire of both the Sociedad club –

Zabaleta was a personal acquaintance of two players – and the nation as a whole.

In print

Atlético Madrid's eponymous magazine (monthly, 300ptas) is available at their club shops. You'll also see a fanzine, **Super Atléti** (300ptas), being sold at the ground on matchdays.

In the net

The club's official website has extensive English and Spanish language areas, with an e-commerce operation, history and fan surveys among other things. The site is at: www.at-madrid.es.

For a simpler, fan's-eye look at life, with excellent links to other Atlético fan sites, try: www.geocities.com/Colosseum/9890.

Groundhopping

◎ Rayo Vallecano

Nuevo Vallecas, Payaso Fofó
Capacity 19,500
Colours White shirts with red sash, white shorts

Madrid's third club had the best season in its history in 1999/2000. With a young and determined side coached by the inspirational Guande Ramos, and led on the field by the brilliant Spanish Under–21 midfielder Jordi Ferrón, Rayo were top of the table for much of the first half of the season, while Real and Atlético were floundering near the relegation zone.

Although Rayo faded to finish ninth, they were rewarded by a place in the UEFA Cup under UEFA's 'Fair Play' bonus place scheme. That in itself was just reward for María Teresa Rivero, Spain's only female football club president, who has fought hard to get the club out of the constant revolving door between first and second divisions.

Until Ferrón, without doubt a star of the future, the biggest name to play here was the Mexican international and former

Unlikely setting – outside the Vallecas ground

Real Madrid striker Hugo Sánchez, who averaged a goal every other game in 1993/94. Nigerian goalkeeper Wilfred Agbonavbare was a popular mainstay until his departure in 1996 – his place between the sticks was occupied by the USA international Kasey Keller in 1999/2000.

The immediate environs of Rayo's ground, with their Maoist graffiti and bingo halls, are about as unlikely a prelude to a big football team as you can get. But with the ambition of the Rivero family and the loyalty of coach Ramos, who agreed to stay on for another season despite tempting offers in the summer of 2000, Madrid may yet have another serious football force about which to boast.

To watch the latest relegation struggle unfold, take **M1 metro** to Portazgo, two stops from the terminus. The metro stop is right next to the stadium.

Along c/Teniente Muñoz Diaz, which runs from the Portazgo metro exit round

to La Colonia Virgen del Castañar, you'll find a host of bars, including the **el Castañar**, brimming with old *Vallecasos*, surrounded by the fug of cheap tobacco and faded old football pictures. By the metro on the other side of Avenida Albufera is the **Meson Carlos** at #139, seat of many Rayo *peñas*. Opposite is the main **ticket office**, with another around the corner by the white gates on c/del Payaso Fofó.

The **club shop** (open Mon–Sat 10am–2pm & 5-8.30pm and matchdays, most credit cards), at the corner of Albufera and Fofó, puts Real Madrid's to shame, its many wares on view through its transparent floor.

Eat, drink, sleep…

Bars and clubs

Madrid is nocturnal. Its streets start buzzing from midnight on, and bars and clubs are at their busiest between 2am and 4am. Despite various city council rulings to close bars earlier, no-one pays any attention, a hangover from the hedonistic *movida* days of the Eighties.

The sheer volume of **bars and clubs** matches anything in Europe. With the metro running until 1.30am, barhopping is easy between the touristy Huertas, earthier Malasaña and sexually ambivalent Chueca areas, broadly covered by Sol, Sevilla and Atocha metros. **'Discobars'** don't charge admission but full-blown **clubs** will demand around 2,000ptas cover.

Big Bamboo, c/del Barquillo 42. Popular reggae discobar with cocktails. M4/5/10 Alonso Martínez.

Finbar's, c/Marqués de Urquijo 10. One of a dozen pubs in the city, this one with Sky Sports, live music and expat teams. M3/4/6 Argüelles.

Davai, c/Flor Baja 1, corner Gran Vía 59. Mainly drum 'n' bass or house at this once seminal club,

Seventies nights not unknown during the week. Cheaper cover than most. M3/10 Plaza de España.

Amnesia, Popular, occasionally adventurous dance club situated in a marketplace, with varied dance sounds Wed–Sun until 5am. M5 Puerta de Toledo.

Viva Madrid, c/Manuel Fernández y González 7. Ideal starting point for a night around Santa Ana, a large, popular tiled bar which buzzes with anticipation. Open 8pm–3am. M1/2/3 to Sol.

Restaurants

Madrileño cuisine is traditionally heavy, reliant on **stews** and **offal**. *Cocido Madrileño* is a classic dish – a chickpea stew with chorizo sausage – as is *caldereta de cordero*, lamb stewed with tomatoes and peppers.

Eating out here isn't cheap, but look out for a lunchtime *menú del día* at around 1,500ptas. *Tapas* bars are popular, but a few *raciones* during an evening can be surprisingly dear. Local favourites include potatoes in spicy pepper sauce (*patatas bravas*), pig's ear (*orejas*) and tripe (*callos*).

El Botín, c/Cuchilleros 17. Eighteenth-century tavern which has seen many famous visitors pass through its doors. Castilian roasts a speciality, 3,500–4,000ptas a main course. M1/2/3 Sol.

La Farfalla, c/Santa María 17. Late-night/early-morning Huertas eaterie serving platefuls of Argentine meats to revellers. M1 Antón Martín.

Museo del Jamón, c/de Alcalá 155. A Madrid institution (with six similar branches around town), a *tapas* bar and restaurant decked head to trotter in ham hocks, which dangle enticingly from the ceiling. Set lunches at 1,000ptas. No credit cards. M1/2/3 Sol.

Nueva Galicia, c/de la Cruz 6. One of Madrid's many Galician restaurants, this one serves an excellent (and cheap) *caldo gallego* – vegetable and ham soup, Canal Plus on TV and endless football chat. The bar is open long after everything else around Sol has closed. M1/2/3 Sol.

Viuda de Vacas, Cava Alta 23. Traditional *Madrileño* cooking in authentic surroundings, at reasonable prices. Closed Thurs, most credit cards. M5 La Latina.

Accommodation

Madrid is still a fairly **cheap city** to stay in, with most of the budget accommodation conveniently centred around the main nightlife areas.

Puerta del Sol and Plaza Santa Ana (M1/2/3 Sol) and c/Fuencarral (M1/5 Gran Vía) are all good stomping grounds, where you can expect to pay 5,000ptas or less for a double room in a *hostal* or *pensión*.

The *Brújula* accommodation agency, c/Princesa 1, 6th floor (open Mon–Fri 9am–7pm, Sat 9am–1pm, ☎91/559 9705, M2/3/10 to Plaza de España), can book you a room for a 250ptas fee. They also have branches at the airport bus terminal in Plaza de Colón, and at Atocha and Chamartín train stations.

Albergue Juvenil Santa Cruz de Marcenado, c/Santa Cruz de Marcenado 28 (☎91/547 4532, fax 91/548 1196). Modern, quiet youth hostel in the university area, dorm beds at 1,300ptas including breakfast. Three-day maximum stay. Curfew 1.30am. M3/4/6 Argüelles.

Hostal Sud Americana, Paseo del Prado 12, 6th floor (☎91/429 2564). With a great location by the Prado museum, this small *hostal* has elegant fittings and high ceilings. Singles around 3,000ptas, doubles 5,000ptas. M2 Banco de España.

Hotel Monaco, c/Barbieri 5 (☎91/522 4630, fax 91/521 1601). If you've a little extra to spare and have a sense of humour and history, this is the place for you – a former celebrated bordello now frequented by pop video directors and lifestyle photographers. In spite of this, very reasonably priced. M5 Chueca.

Pensión Poza, c/Nuñez de Arce 9 (☎91/522 4871). Basic *pensión* two steps from all the nightlife action, with another floor of rooms a few doors down. No credit cards. M2 Sevilla.

Seville

Arguably the fiercest cross-town rivalry in the Spanish game, the 2000/2001 Seville derby will take place in the second division, after both teams were relegated at the end of the most miserable season in the city's footballing history. Sevilla have been traditionally the stronger of the two clubs in this fiery Andalucian city, but the Nineties witnessed a temporary rise in the fortunes of ambitious Betis, until they got carried away and wasted £21.5million on Brazilian winger Denilson, and ploughed cash badly needed for squad building into stadium development. Now, after a single season back together in the *Primera*, the two clubs face at least a year of playing glorified village teams.

In the city's huge construction boom, Sevilla's impressive Sánchez Pizjuán stadium is now ripe for sale to developers, a fact not lost on Rafael Carmona, the man responsible for the building of the new Olympic stadium which hosted the 1999 World Athletics Championships in the north of the city. Carmona, part of a team behind Seville's bid to host the Olympics in 2008, regularly urges both clubs to share the new venue, and leave their old grounds behind.

This is unlikely to happen while Betis is owned and run by Manuel Ruiz de Lopera, who has invested a small fortune in the reconstruction and expansion of his club's ground – which now carries his name despite still being some way short of its promised future capacity of 85,000.

Andalucía first saw football being played even before the Basque country in the far north. Recreativo Huelva, the first club to be formed in 1889, are the oldest one in Spain still in operation, and their debut game was played against a Seville select XI consisting mainly of British employees of the Riotinto mines. It was these employees who formed Sevilla Football Club in 1905, their directorship taken from the native land-owning classes that ruled Andalucía. When one director refused to

hire a local factory worker at the club, there was a revolt and Betis were founded by the dissident members.

Betis merged with Sevilla Balompié in 1914, and made King Alfonso XIII their honorary president. They became Real Betis Balompié, taking their new title from their royal patronage and the old Spanish name for football, and met Sevilla for the first time on New Year's Day, 1916. Against a political backdrop of disputes over land reform and Andalucían autonomy, the first derby game, which finished 2–2, saw flare-ups of violence all over Seville. The next 80 years saw Sevilla generally holding the upper hand, until the Betis revival of the mid-Nineties.

Although both clubs have moved around town since their early days at the Prado de San Sebastián, their deep divisions are typified by their current respective geographical locations. Sevilla's Sánchez Pizjuán is in the commercial district of Nervión, surrounded by fast highways and a brand-new shopping mall; Betis' stadium is in working-class Heliópolis, south of town on the 'wrong' side of the river Guadalquivir.

Both grounds were originally named after their area, then renamed after influential club presidents. Both underwent renovations for the 1982 World Cup. And both will long be remembered for the games they hosted: Betis' for David Narey's toe-poke for Scotland against Brazil; Sevilla's for the epic semi-final between France and West Germany.

Until recently, both grounds were also used regularly for Spain's international matches. The tradition began with a bizarre 12–1 win over Malta in late 1983, which enabled Spain to qualify for Euro '84 above Holland on goals scored. Playing in Seville became known as *un talisman*, a lucky charm, the team apparently galvanised by the raucous atmosphere and fervent flamenco handclapping. Free from any of the ethnic tensions felt elsewhere in Spain, the

Andalucían crowd was solidly behind *la selección*. After Malta, Spain won 20 out of 23 qualifying matches in Seville. But it was a thin, frustrated crowd which witnessed a narrow 1–0 win over Armenia in June 1995, causing the Spanish FA to rethink and stage important games elsewhere.

Sevilla fans accused Betis of plotting to get their club relegated by 'going easy' against another struggling side, Sporting Gijón, in 1997. But when Sevilla finally did go down that summer, nobody worried more than Manuel Ruiz de Lopera, who knew the derby was good for business – he had, after all, been the first to stand behind his counterpart when Sevilla were threatened with relegation by the FA over bureaucratic irregularities in 1995.

Sadly, the derby games of 2000/01 are set to be played in a division in which neither club can afford to spend too much time.

The thrilling fields

 Sevilla FC

Estádio Sánchez Pizjuán, Avenida Eduardo Dato
Capacity 68,000
Colours All white with red trim
League champions 1946
Cup winners 1935, 1939, 1948

The grand mosaic which once dominated the entrance to the Sánchez Pizjuán stadium, incorporating badges from teams who have visited the ground, has been turned around to face the huge *Nervión* shopping centre next-door. For the lucky fans who flocked here for the epic France-West Germany World Cup semi-final in 1982, the Sánchez Pizjuán would have been on the edge of the town. With the Santa Justa train station since built nearby and massive development going on for miles yonder, the stadium is now in the city centre – and Sevilla's wretched form over the past five years is not going to pay for its upkeep.

While the club's management considers the option of selling up and moving into the newly built Olympic stadium, the fans can look forward to top-flight football again, and at least the possibility of their team living up to its illustrious past, both ancient and modern.

The club's early progress, after their foundation in 1905, was halted by half the team leaving to form Betis two years later. Seville was the first city to fall to Franco in the Civil War, and Sevilla took advantage of their stadium staying open by winning the cup in 1939, their only league title in 1946, and the cup again two years later. While Betis declined, Sevilla kept their passionate home crowd happy by taking the occasional big scalp at the Sánchez Pizjuán. Their only major European victory, however, was a 3—1 win over Benfica in the pre-Eusébio days of 1957.

There has been much endeavour but little to show for it since. Like so many Andalucían workers, Sevilla's homegrown players have tended to leave for the bright lights as soon as they've been given the chance. Yet until recently the club was not without resources, and in the Eighties and Nineties recruited a series of expensive foreigners to the Sánchez Pizjuán.

Their fortunes were decidedly mixed. Russian international 'keeper Renat Dasayev settled in well, staying on to run a sports shop in town. Toni Polster, Daniel Bertoni, Bebeto and Ilie Dumitrescu all flitted in and out. Perhaps the saddest of all was Diego Maradona, brought here by his fellow Argentine, coach Carlos Bilardo, partly to cure his cocaine addiction, and partly to keep world attention focused on Seville after the Expo had finished at the end of 1992. Unfit and unsettled, Maradona proved an expensive flop. His 26-game stay resulted in five goals, two red cards – and an awful lot of shoe leather on the part of the private detectives hired by the club to follow him around the city's nightclubs and bordellos.

Much more successful was Davor Šuker, the Croatian striker who scored more than 60 goals in four seasons at the Sánchez Pizjuán. Towards the end of the 1995/96 camnpaign, Šuker signed a pre-contract with Real Madrid. But the Sevilla faithful refused to turn against him. In his last game for the club, he scored a hat-trick against Salamanca to keep the team in the top flight and was carried head-high from the field, a modern-day flamenco hero.

Sevilla received around £7million for Šuker, but all it did was pay off old debts. When the club tried to buy another Croa-

tian, Robert Prosinečki, from Barcelona later in the summer of 1996, their cheque bounced.

It was Sevilla's inability to secure bank guarantees that almost led to their automatic relegation in 1995; thousands took to the streets in protest, and the club's reinstatement gave rise to an unwieldy 22-club first division.

By June 1997, however, Sevilla had done the FA's job for them, after a season which saw three coaches come and go, a series of bad-tempered boardroom squabbles, and relegation.

Seville essentials

Expo '92 in Seville brought fast, new transport links with the rest of Spain. The city's San Pablo **airport** is 12km northeast of town, connected by a bus service (hourly, 30mins' journey time, 750ptas) to central Puerta de Jerez. A taxi will come to about 3,000ptas.

The main **train station**, Santa Justa, east of the centre, is where the luxury high-speed *AVE* train arrives from Madrid Atocha. The service is expensive – about 15,000ptas return – but takes just two-and-a-half hours. Other trains cost two-thirds as much to do the same journey, taking around six hours. To get into town from Santa Justa station, take bus #20 to Plaza Nueva.

Five trains and nine buses a day run from **Málaga** to Seville, taking between three-and-a-half and four-and-a-half-hours each. From Málaga airport, take the electric train to the main RENFE train station, one before the terminus at Guadelmedina (journey time 25mins). Málaga's bus station is nearby.

Seville's main **bus station** is at Plaza de Armas, on the river opposite the former Expo site at La Cartuja, connected by circle line buses C3/4, and bus #43, which runs to Plaza de la Magdelena, near central Plaza Nueva. City *TUSSAM* buses run from the central squares (6am–11pm in winter, until midnight in summer) to the outskirts. Outer circle lines C1/2 and inner circle lines C3/4 loop the city. *TUSSAM* tickets are 125ptas onboard, or 625ptas for a *bonobus* of ten with transfers, available from orange machines by busstops. They also issue three-day (1,000ptas) and seven-day passes (1,500ptas). A limited **night bus service** runs from Plaza Nueva at midnight (winter only), 1am and 2am, tickets (125ptas) issued onboard.

Official **taxis** are white with a blue stripe. The driver will prattle away in fluent *Andaluz*, a lifestyle away from your GCSE Spanish, and will charge around 800ptas for a journey from Santa Justa to somewhere central. Officially the flat fare is 120ptas, plus 60ptas per km, with supplements according to time, luggage and mood. To call a cab, dial ☎95/462 2222.

The **tourist office** is near the cathedral at Avenida de la Constitución 21 (open Mon–Fri 9am–7pm, Sat 10am–2pm & 3–7pm, Sun & holidays 10am–2pm, ☎95/422 1404, fax 95/422 9753). The staff are friendly but practical information is thin on the ground.

You'll find Seville's only **listings publication**, the free monthly *El Geraldillo*, woefully short on concert and nightclub info, but *The Tourist*, a free monthly issued by the tourist board, has a reasonable selection of pub and restaurant information.

The fans stuck with the club in the second division, 40,000 turning out for Sevilla's first game outside the top flight in more than 20 years. Greek striker Vassilis Tsartas was the goal hero in the play-offs against Villarreal that earned promotion at the first attempt.

But the club failed to invest in badly needed new players, and in February 2000 president Rafael Carrion resigned as the club's debts continued to mount. Tsartas went back to Greece, coach Marcos Alonso resigned in March, and the club's technical director Juan Carlos Alvarez took over as caretaker, with little chance of

Setting sons – Gazza and Diego in Seville, 1992

saving the club from an immediate return to the *Segunda*.

With no cash available, Joaquin Caparros, whose experience is entirely in the lower divisions, arrived as coach well aware that a swift return to the top flight was far from guaranteed.

Here we go!

Several buses pass down the highways surrounding the Sánchez Pizjuán. The #24 and #27 run from central Plaza de la Encarnación to the ground, the #21 from Plaza Nueva. The #32 goes from Encarnación via the Santa Justa train station, a couple of stops away from the stadium. And the #23 runs from Plaza Nueva via Avenida de Eduardo Dato, stopping a little closer to the ground and ideal for the bars of *Nervión* opposite. Allow 15mins from town.

Just the ticket

The **ticket office** is by the main entrance, open two days before kick-off, 10am–2pm. Cheapest places are in the *Baja Gol Sur* and *Norte*, while the *Fondo* is a little pricier and the best seats in the house are in the *Preferencia Tribuna*. Visiting fans are placed in the *Grada Alta* of the *Gol Sur*. Note that Sevilla will play five home games at the

city's Olympic stadium in the course of the 2000/01 season as part of a financial arrangement. What happens the season after has yet to be decided.

Swift half

There are two main areas for a pre-match drink. There are a couple of traditional fans' bars on c/Luis Montoto, near Puerta Carmona, a 10min walk from the stadium. The local *peña* bar at #52 is officially members only, but these are generally sympathetic old men playing cards. The **Bar Jota** next door is a tiny stand-up drink counter, with Cruzcampos, cod sticks and serious football talk.

Nearer the ground, the three streets parallel to Eduardo Dato, on the south side of the stadium, throng with activity. The **Peña Sevillista Al Relente** at c/Aznalcazar 6 is again for older supporters, but has a superb display of photos.

Nearby, the **Bar Buenos Aires**, Divino Redentor 10, run by ex-player Acosta, has a good selection of *tapas*.

Club merchandise

The **Tienda Oficial** (open Mon–Fri 11am–2pm & 5.15–8pm, Sat 10am–1.30pm and matchdays,

Visa cards only) is by the main entrance. In among the usual paraphernalia, you'll find Sevilla-badged lingerie for those hot Andalucían nights.

Ultra culture

The **peña Biri-Biri** are named after an African player who was with the club in the Seventies. The group is divided into *Norte* and *Sud*, and the two sections indulge in choreographed chants which echo around the Sánchez Pizjuán The *Norte* section count among the most fervent fans in Spain – videos of their activities are on sale in the club shop, and they produce their own fanzine, *Mágico Nervión*, available at the ground on matchdays.

In print

An independent weekly newspaper, **Blanco y Rojo** (100ptas) came out in 1998 to challenge the club's monthly *El Sevillista* (300ptas). Both are available at most newsstands in town.

In the net

There's supposed to be an official Sevilla website at: www.sevillacf.es. But, like the team's form, it can play hard to get. A more reliable friend is fan Javier Gayán Guardiola's unofficial site, with it news, history, and multi-media areas at: ibgwww. colorado.edu/~gayan/futbol/sevilla.html.

Real Betis

Estadio Manuel Ruiz de Lopera, Avenida de Heliópolis
Capacity 52,000
Colours Green-and-white striped shirts, white shorts
League champions 1935
Cup winners 1977

For years a club in Sevilla's shadow, Betis have once again become a laughing stock thanks to their overambitious owner/president Manuel Ruiz de Lopera. The summer of 1998 saw the arrival of the world's most expensive player, the Brazilian Denilson, while three coaches came and went before the season had even started. By Christmas, the massive redevelopment of the club's homely Benito Villamarín stadium was nowhere near finished as planned, and the £2million-a-year Denilson had failed to score in 15 games. The most reviled coach in Spanish football, Javier Clemente, had been hired to lift the expensive flops out of the relegation zone. Meanwhile, shareholders were voting on whether to rename the stadium after their president.

A shame, because *Er Beti* as they are known in the local rapid-fire, swallow-all dialect, had been the most popular Spanish provincial team of the Nineties. This mini-boom was instigated by Lopera, who turned a debt-ridden second-division club into a profitable, fashionable but still down-to-earth outfit capable of taking a few big scalps both at home and abroad.

Apart from a narrow title win in 1935 and a cup final triumph on penalties over Athletic Bilbao in 1977, Betis have spent much of their 90-year history in relative obscurity. Some 30 years have beeen spent in the lower divisions, and the club nearly went under altogether in the Fifties.

Historically, Betis were not designed to shine in the Franco era. Born of the social prejudice of turn-of-the-century Andalucía by a breakaway group from Sevilla FC, the club have always attracted left-wing sympathy. That solitary title win came on the eve of the Civil War and the killing of Andalucían republican poet Federico García Lorca; fans of the *verdiblancos* should have known the glory wasn't to last.

The main star the club produced in the Franco era was Luis del Sol, and it is significant that his finest hour came not in green and white but while playing for Real Madrid in their 7–3 win over Eintracht Frankfurt in 1960. By comparison, Betis themselves were non-entities in Europe, their only win of note coming over AC Milan in the Cup-Winners' Cup in 1977.

Such a lack of big-time experience did nothing to deter coach Lorenzo Sarra Ferrer, nicknamed *El Brujo* ('The Wizard'), who came from Real Mallorca in 1994, gained the club promotion, then kept them in and around the UEFA Cup placings for three seasons. In addition to expert coaching, the club's easygoing nature and passionate support kept star names eager to stay and compete. In 1996/97, Nigerian World Cup star Finidi George and Croatian wing-back Robert Jarni provided the service that allowed striker Alfonso to stay just behind Ronaldo in the *Liga* scoring charts. – all three were in tears as Betis lost the final of the *Copa del Rey* to Barcelona after extra-time at the end of the season.

The following year, former Sevilla boss Luís Aragonés failed to keep the momentum going – Betis were all too easily knocked out of the Cup-Winners' Cup by Chelsea, and returned to Europe only thanks to Real Madrid's Champions' League win at the end of 1997/98.

Prior to the 1998/99 campaign, both Aragonés and his replacement António Oliveira walked out, Chilean coach Vicente Cantatore was hired at the last minute and Jarni, crucially, was sold to Real Madrid after a majestic World Cup with Croatia. Alfonso was injured in Spain's fiasco in Cyprus, Denilson couldn't cope with the pressure of his price-tag, and after a UEFA Cup exit at the hands of Bologna, Cantatore was on his way. It was as much as Javier Clemente could do to instill some discipline and save Betis from the drop. He managed it, but the results weren't pretty, and Clemente himself made way for Carlos Griguol during the summer of 1999.

Come January 2000, and Lopera sacked Griguol with the team languishing in 15th place. Guus Hiddink failed to inspire a demoralised dressing room, and Betis slumped into the bottom three; the Dutchman had already quit by the time the club was relegated.

In the close season, Alfonso was sold to Barcelona and Denilson was packed off to Brazil, with an option to return should Betis make it back to the top flight. Former Betis player and Bosnian national team coach Faruk Hadzibegić was given the job of ensuring the Brazilian gets such a chance – but the odds were by no means stacked in his favour.

Here we go!

Take bus #34 or #35 from Plaza Nueva toward the Heliópolis district – both stop just short of the ground. Allow a good 25mins from town.

Just the ticket

The main **ticket office** is between gates #5 and #25. The Betis ultras go behind *Gol Sur*, away support with the cheaper tickets in *Gol Norte*. The most expensive seats are in the *Anfiteatro Numerado*; the *Tribuna Numerada* is slightly cheaper but still offers a decent view.

Swift half

There are cheap bars all the way down c/de Reina Mercedes on the way to the stadium, some offering set lunches for as little as 600ptas. The *Chani* at #19a has the best atmosphere, though the *Metropolis* at #5 and the *Barro* at #9 are equally lively. The *Bodeguita Castulo* at Terejo 17 is a classic Betis bar, cramped and hotter than an Andalucían launderette, but full of team photos and bullfighting graphics.

Gone for now – £21million flop Denilson

Club merchandise

Al Real Betis (open matchdays and theoretically Mon–Fri 9am–2pm & 5–8.30pm), is a small shop between gates #1 and #2 on c/Dr Fleming. There is also a general soccer store, *Market Fútbol*, nearby at Terejo 9.

Ultra culture

There's a family atmosphere at the Benito Villa-marín, and the *Supporters Gol Sur* do little more than let the odd green-and-white painted rabbit onto the pitch. Other fan groups cluster behind the *Gol Norte* to bait whatever visiting support is occuping the area between their territory and the *Fondo*.

In print

El Mundo Bético (monthly, 300ptas), is the club's glossy mag available at newsstands.

In the net

Betis were a bit slow off the mark with an official website, but are making up for lost time with a comprehensive site that offers a choice of 'Shocked' and 'Unshocked' versions. No English, but plenty to see at: www.realbetisbalompie.es.

Eat, drink, sleep…

Bars and clubs

The Andalucían summer takes no prison-ers. The only way to survive from April to September is by knocking back a glass of draught *Cruzcampo*, the excellent **local beer**. The average bar is run by some shuf-fling old *Andaluz*, who'll chalk a running tab on the counter. Service will be desperately slow, but friendly.

That said, Sevilla is a tourist city and the places in central Barrio Santa Cruz can be pricy. Just across the river from here is Triana, a more down-to-earth district full of *tapas* bars, a Betis stronghold. The places along c/Betis by the river's edge are lively.

Discos, many located on the former Expo site at La Cartuja, are too dear for many, so people organise *botellonas* –

improvised open-air parties with cheap rum sold out of car boots.

The only people you'll see in the city's **Flamenco clubs** are tourists willing to part with up to 3,000ptas for a show.

Aduana, Avenida de Bonanza, by Avenida de la Raza. Decent dance club by the customs house of the old riverside port, playing house and break-beat, to a young crowd. Open from midnight, 1,000ptas admission.

Blanco Cerrillo, c/Dr Jiménez Díaz 16. A bit out of the centre, but a great football bar with caricatures of the pub team on the wall, signed pix of old Betis stars and a crowd for games on Canal Plus. The regulars know their football. Bus #11 or #12 from central Encarnación.

La Carbonería, c/Levies 18. Atmospheric tra-ditional flamenco bar which operated illegally in Franco's time, with a terrace and patio. Tucked away near Santa Cruz church.

P Flaherty, c/Alemanes. In a tiny street by the cathedral, the best Irish bar in town, with a TV room showing English Premiership action on Sat-urdays at 4pm, and Spanish games on Canal Plus. Kitchen midday–midnight daily, bar open until 3am if there's a crowd.

Sopa de Ganso, c/Pérez Galdós 8. Popular music bar with live bands on Thursdays and an original range of *tapas*. Gets crowded, so grab a table early. Open until 2–3am. Just off lively Plaza Alfalfa in the centre.

Restaurants

Andalucía is the home of *tapas* – small snacks to go with your drink – and a full restaurant meal is generally reserved for special occasions here. There are *tapas* bars on virtually every street, offering small platefuls of meat or fish for 300–500ptas, or larger *raciónes* for 500–700ptas; a cou-ple of the latter is a meal in itself, washed down with beer, wine or *fino* (dry) sherry.

Andalucían cooking is fresh and light. Seafood is prominent, being used in zarzuela (fish stew) and arroz marinero, the local fish paella. But a set menú del día three-course lunch (around 750–1,000ptas) will probably feature meat for main course.

The other local delicacy is the famous gazpacho – cold tomato, pepper and garlic soup, served in glasses clinking with ice.

El Aragonés, c/Juan Manuel Rodríguez Correa 15. Just up from the Red Cross building on the circular C1 and C4 bus routes, notable for serving the best patatas bravas in town and some of the cheapest tapas. No credit cards.

Kiosko de las Flores, Plaza del Altozano. Classic seafood eaterie and bar overlooking the river with outdoor tables, in operation for nearly 70 years. A little pricy but worth it for the atmosphere. Closed Mon. Tucked into Triana bridge – circle line C1/C2 buses run nearby. If full, the **Casa Mejias**, c/Reyes Católicos 25 on the opposite side of Triana has a lunchtime menu at 1,400ptas.

La Albahaca, Plaza Santa Cruz 12. All the romantic trimmings in this converted mansion slap bang in the middle of Seville, with tables outside, three dining rooms inside and great variety on the menu. Expect to pay 5,000ptas for the full splurge, but the menú at 4,000ptas can be money rather well spent. Closed Sun. Most credit cards.

Mesón La Barca, c/Santander 6. Small, reasonably priced restaurant serving decent portions of fish and venison dishes, near the Torre del Oro. Open until midnight, closed Sat. No credit cards. If you feel like splashing out, the **Bodegón Torre del Oro** at #15 has superb set meals with wine at 3,000ptas.

Accommodation

Seville is not cheap to stay in at any time of year. If you're thinking of coming during Semana Santa, the festival between Palm Sunday and Good Friday, or the April Fair, book yourself a room months in advance – and be prepared to pay double. For the rest of the year, the area around the old train station, particularly c/de San Eloy, is the best hunting ground for reasonably priced accommodation. The Barrio Santa Cruz is a little more expensive, but equally reliable. At any time of year, **air conditioning** is a luxury worth paying extra for.

Hostal Goya, c/Mateos Gago 31 (☎95/421 1170). Reasonably priced, clean pension, with other options down the same street if full.

Albergue Juvenil Fernando el Santo, c/Isaac Peral 2 (☎95/461 3150). Comfortable youth hostel out towards the Betis stadium, with no lockout or curfew. Beds at 1,200ptas for IYHF members under-26, 1,400ptas those over-26 and 3,000ptas for non-members. Three-day maximum stay. Bus #34/35 from Plaza Nueva.

Hotel Murillo, c/Lope de Rueda 7 (☎95/421 6095, fax 95/421 9616). Simple but comfortable hotel in a restored mansion. Doubles at 12,000ptas with a shower, 7,000ptas without. Most major credit cards. In the heart of Barrio Santa Cruz.

Hostal Plaza Sevilla, c/Canalejas 2 (☎95/421 7149, fax 95/421 0773). Designed by Aníbal González, the architect of the Ibero-Americana Exhibition held in the city in 1929, this comfortable hotel has a splendid façade, air-conditioning and an on-site hairdresser. Doubles at 12–18,000ptas. No credit cards. Within a stagger of the bars of c/San Eloy.

Hotel Simón, c/García de Vinuesa 19 (☎95/422 6660, fax 95/456 2241). A bargain out of season, the Simón is in a restored 18th century mansion with a fabulous courtyard and dining room. Double rooms at 6,000ptas, 9,000ptas with bath. Breakfast extra. Laundry service available. No credit cards. Off Avenida de la Constitución, near the cathedral.

Beyond the beach – the rise of Real Mallorca

The rise of Mallorca, Spain's most improbably successful side of 1998/99, was down to two men: top TV doctor **Bartolomé Beltrán** and gritty Argentine coach **Hector Cúper**. Before their involvement, football on the island meant the beach, pre-season visits by English teams, or fan-club trips to Barcelona.

In the summer of 1995 Beltrán, who had founded TV channel Antena 3 after starring in a hit medical radio show, was a guest at a party in Marbella. Also there was the town's mayor **Jesús Gil y Gil**, spouting off about the riches in TV rights for his football club, Atlético Madrid. At the time, Antena 3 were losing the ratings war with a schedule dominated by bullfighting, and Beltrán's home team of Mallorca were going to the wall. Gil's words struck a chord. Beltrán and Antena 3 president Arsenio Asensio decided to buy the club on the cheap, and found a loophole in the law which allowed them to sign the team exclusively to their channel.

With 100million pesetas from his company, Beltrán hired a load of new players, including **striker Dani** from Real Madrid, and several coaches – only to see Mallorca miss out on promotion in a play-off with **Rayo Vallecano** in 1996. Former Barcelona star Victor was then brought in as coach in 1996, and a steelier Mallorca again made the play-offs, again faced Rayo – and won.

Needing to strengthen the squad that summer of 1997, Beltrán found a little-known Argentine coach, Hector Cúper, who had won the 1996 Conmebol title with Lanús, and picked up half-a-dozen players from Valéncia. Cúper in turn brought his goalkeeper, **Carlos Roa**, over from Buenos Aires, and formed the so-called *Cúperativa*, a strict defensive unit. It wasn't pretty but it was effective. Moreover, Antena 3 screened games with the big boys, and the goals of Gabriel Amato broke viewer monotony.

Despite three saves (and one goal) in a penalty shoot-out from Roa, Mallorca lost the 1998 Spanish cup final to double-winners Barcelona – but at least managed to get into the Cup-Winners' Cup. A boardroom row saw Beltrán leave the running of the club to architect Guillermo Reynes, and almost the entire team (including Amato) was sold. But Cúper got on with the job, hiring three more Argentines from his old Lanús side, and leading Mallorca to a brief stay at the top of the *Primera División* in 1998, thanks to an uncanny ability to win 1–0, both home and away.

With Dani scoring from every chance that came his way, Mallorca maintained their form to finish third in the league, and also progressed to the **Cup-Winners' Cup final** at the expense of Hearts and Chelsea, among others. At Villa Park, they were a shade unlucky to lose 2–1 to Lazio – although, in the long term, the loss of Cúper to Valencia would prove more significant.

Cúper was replaced by another Argentine, Mario Carlos Gómez, and Mallorca began the 1999/2000 season with no fewer than seven of his countrymen on the playing staff. But Dani had been sold to Barcelona and defensive lynchpin Marcelino to Newcastle, while goalkeeper Roa had hung up his gloves to find God. Gómez's side, looking ill-at-ease in their new home of the **Son Moix stadium** on Palma's northern outskirts, were beaten by Molde of Norway in the Champions' League qualifiers, and finished a mediocre tenth in the league – their worst finish since promotion.

At the end of the season, Reynes sold Cameroonian midfielder Lauren to Arsenal, and another summer of squad upheavals looked to be on the cards.

With cheap flights from both England and mainland Spain, Mallorca is the perfect football weekend destination. Bus #17 runs from the airport to central Plaça Espanya, and from there bus #8 goes to the Lluis Sitjar. There, around Plaça Barcelona, the *Bar Deportivo Mallorca*, c/Bonaventura Serra 7, remains popular despite the move north to Son Moix.

Barcelona

FC Barcelona 564
RCD Espanyol 569

If you're young, free and football mad with it, there is no better destination in the whole of Europe than Barcelona. After forty years of subjugation from Madrid, Catalonia, with Barcelona as its capital, now has a degree of autonomy unthinkable in Franco's day. Barcelona feels independent, and wants the whole world to know. And one of the ways in which it expresses that feeling is through its football club, FC Barcelona.

This last decade has seen the city strike more than a few blows against the old empire. On the football field, Johan Cruyff's Barcelona team won four titles in a row and captured a previously elusive European Cup in 1992. The celebrations in the city's Plaça Sant Jaume were as much for a triumphant Catalonia as for a victorious Barça. Away from football, the staging of the 1992 Olympics sealed Barcelona's century-long love affair with sport, and legitimised the city's status as one of Europe's great capitals – albeit one that is still without a country.

Times change; nationalist sentiment doesn't. Between World War II and the dictator's death in 1975, Franco's regime suppressed the use of the Catalan language and the show of identifiable Catalan symbols. Barcelona was Catalonia's flagship team, and games against the Franco-favoured Real Madrid became statements of national intent, an excuse wantonly to fly the Catalan flag. FC Barcelona was, in effect, an empire in opposition, a huge structure built up around a palace of a stadium, the Nou Camp.

Catalonia is also Spain's most industrial province, with a businesslike attitude that contrasts with the *mañana* culture of the rest of the country. In the postwar era, the region attracted thousands of migrant workers from Andalucía and elsewhere. To earn brownie points with their colleagues and neighbours, many joined Barça as club members, during Spanish football's boom years of the late Forties and Fifties. Those

workers whose sympathies were more inclined to Madrid (either through their status as employees of public companies or because they were on the winning side in the Civil War) supported Barcelona's rivals, Español – literally, 'Spanish'.

Both clubs were formed at the turn of the century. Barcelona owe their formation to a Swiss national, Joan Gamper. In October 1899, he placed a classified ad in the paper *Los Deportes* – desperately seeking 'Foot-Vall'. A team called FC Barcelona were duly gathered and dressed in blue and grenadine (*azúlgrana* or *blaugrana* in Catalan), the colours of Gamper's native Swiss canton of Ticino. They lost 1–0 to an English select XI at the Bonanova velodrome. Still with Gamper playing upfront, they enjoyed their first victory when they beat Català 3–1 on Christmas Eve, 1899.

Local students then formed another club, naming it Español in mockery of Barcelona's Swiss connections, and *soel derbi barcelonés* was born.

Playing in grounds at the Hotel Casanovas, both teams competed in the Catalan championship until it was interrupted by the Civil War. By then, Barça and Español had already happily scrapped it out on the pitch itself. In 1912, the two clubs severed relations for the first time after a brawl between players in a cup match. Within ten years both had settled in stadia a kilometre apart – Barça at Les Corts, Español at Sarrià. Barça's modern home, the Nou Camp, is in this same square mile of the city, just north of Sants train station.

Although Español rarely challenge for honours, derby matches between the two are traditionally tense and unpredictable. Scores of fans were injured in 1952 when the crowd surged forward after an Español goal. In March 1973, with Barça and Español first and second in the league, a dubious penalty was enough for the underdogs to beat the leaders at home, and let Atlético Madrid in to win the title. It was a similar story in 1982, when Barcelona lost 3–1 at home to Español, and effectively lost the championship.

The changing political climate has drawn some of the sting from the occasion. With a rampant Catalan renaissance going on all around them, Español have had to move with the times, in more ways than one. They are now known by the Catalan version of their name, 'Espanyol', and have moved from Sarrià to the Olympic stadium at Montjuïc. The last derby at Sarrià, in 1997, ended in a win for the home side – a bittersweet finale for the ground's loyal supporters, and the end of 75 years of football concentrated in the north-west of the city.

The thrilling fields

FC Barcelona

Camp Nou, Avenida Arístides Maillol
Capacity 118,000
Colours Blue-and-grenadine striped shirts, blue shorts
League champions 1929, 1945, 1948–49, 1952–53, 1959–60, 1974, 1985, 1991–94, 1998–99
Cup winners 1910, 1912–13, 1920, 1922, 1925–26, 1928, 1942, 1951–53, 1957, 1959, 1963, 1968, 1971, 1978, 1981, 1983, 1988, 1990, 1997–98
European Cup winners 1992
Cup-Winners' Cup winners 1979, 1982, 1989, 1997
Fairs' (UEFA) Cup winners 1958, 1960, 1966

Barcelona are the biggest and – no matter what the accountants' reports about Manchester United might say – richest football club in the world. Few teams mean as much to their city as this one. Though the club's membership of more than 100,000 is spread all over the world, it was the vast local contingent who put up the where-

withal to build Europe's biggest football stadium, the Nou Camp.

It is a venue whose grandeur befits the cosmopolitan adventure of Barcelona's football. It is also a monument to Catalan pride and business sense. The Nou Camp is effectively the national stadium of Catalonia, and its trophy cabinets have been filled by the world's best: Diego Maradona, Johan Cruyff, Ladislav Kubala, Sándor Kocsis, Romário, Hristo Stoichkov, Johan Neeskens, Luis Suárez, Ronald Koeman and Ronaldo. Foreign influence has been the key to Barcelona's success. The club were formed by a Swiss national, Hans Gamper (he later changed his first name to the Catalan 'Joan'), in 1899, and their first president was an Englishman, Walter Wild. Of the club's 50-odd managers, more than half have come from abroad. All the coaches who have won Barcelona a title in modern times have been foreigners: Helenio Herrera, Rinus Michels, Terry Venables, Johan Cruyff and Louis van Gaal.

Yet although the motto for the club's 1999 anniversary celebrations was *El Centenari de Tots*, 'Everyone's Centenary', foreign involvement had by then become a vexed question with Barça fans, as coach van Gaal practically re-formed his old Ajax side in Barcelona colours. Even Jordi Pujol, president of the *Generalitat* of Catalonia, protested about the lack of Catalan influence at the Nou Camp.

Barcelona were without question the best team in pre-championship Spain. In the Twenties they were regular cup winners, with Ricardo Zamora in goal, Josep Samitier and Philippino-born Paulino Alcántara up front. As supporters' membership crept into five figures, Barcelona moved to the Estadi Foixarda at Montjuïc from their cramped quarters at Carrer de la Industria. When Foixarda became too small, Gamper bought land around Les Corts and built a stadium that was to be the club's home either side of the Civil War. Hungarian Franz Platko replaced Zamora in goal, and would become a folk hero during a decade of playing service and two spells

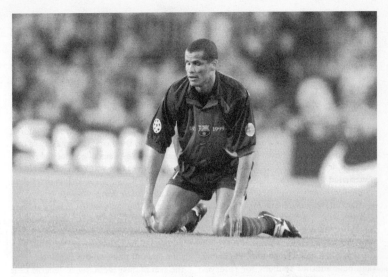

End of an era – Rivaldo is on his knees after Champions' League defeat by Valéncia

as coach. He later died in desperate poverty in Chile, his last years sustained by handouts from his former employers.

Barcelona became the first Spanish club to turn professional and were winners of the inaugural Spanish championship in 1929. But Spain's economic recession in the Thirties forced Barça to sell key players, Samitier going to Real Madrid, and the subsequent Civil War nearly destroyed the club completely. Many players stayed abroad after a tour of North America in 1937, and the Spanish FA named a Francoist, Enric Piñeyro, as club president in 1940. He immediately changed the name to the Castillian 'Club de Fútbol Barcelona' (as opposed to the Catalan 'Futbol Club Barcelona') – and so began 40 long years of football in opposition to the totalitarian régime in Madrid.

For these four decades, Catalonia existed for 90 minutes every other Sunday. This was fine when Barça had a team as stunning as that which won five titles in eight years from 1945. With Antoni Ramallets in goal, Estanislao Basura and Ladislav Kubala upfront, Catalans could satisfy their desire for nationhood through support of the *blaugrana*. For much of the 30 years that followed, however, that desire remained unfulfilled – Madrid not only ruled by law, but also by football, constantly humiliating Barcelona on the field of play.

The arch-rivalry between Barça and Real Madrid was at its peak in the Fifties, when both clubs had their most talented sides. Fate (and Franco) favoured Madrid, not least after Alfredo di Stéfano had opted out of a 50-50 agreement with both clubs and stayed with Real from 1953 onwards. Barça had Kubala, signed after touring Spain with a team of Hungarian exiles in 1950, but he contracted tuberculosis in the year of di Stéfano's transfer.

From then on, Barça were always one step behind. Their attack included Hungarian stars Kocsis and Czibor; Real had Puskás. From South America, Barça had Brazilian Evaristo; Real had di Stéfano. Barça won the first two Fairs' Cups; Real won the first *five* European Cups. When Barcelona finally got a crack at the continent's premier club trophy in 1960, they lost to Real in the semi-finals. Coach Helenio Herrera was chased out of the club by furious fans. When he went to Inter, he took with him Luis Suárez, Barcelona's greatest young prospect – and together, they would take the European Cup to Italy.

A diving header from Evaristo put Real out in 1960/61 – their first elimination from the European Cup. Here was Barça's chance to get even, drawn against an inexperienced, almost unknown Benfica side in the final. It was superb end-to-end stuff, punctuated by slips from Ramallets – 3–2 to Benfica.

Backed by prosperous local industry and the deep pockets of all those loyal members, Barcelona continued to throw serious money at their inferiority complex. They added a new tier to the Nou Camp (and built another stadium, for reserve-team games, alongside it). Yet still the Bernabéu was grander. In the Seventies they paid a world record transfer fee for Johan Cruyff, having already established his old Ajax boss Rinus Michels as coach. In the early Eighties they paid another record fee for Diego Maradona, getting in his old boss, César Menotti, as coach. Then they got an English coach, Terry Venables, and British forwards, Steve Archibald, Gary Lineker and Mark Hughes. *Still* no European Cup – not even when they were playing the final in Spain, against little-fancied Steaua Bucharest, in 1986.

Behind the scenes, Basque-born Barcelona chief José Luis Núñez wielded an authority that antagonised star players and coaches alike. Such was the political scenario after Franco's death that the club president of Barcelona became the biggest civilian post in all Catalonia.

All along, there were small crumbs of comfort for the fans. Like a Cruyff-engineered 5–0 win at the Bernabéu in 1974; a cup final victory over Real, conjured by Maradona and Bernd Schuster in 1983; and a handful of Cup-Winners' Cup triumphs, the last of them under Cruyff, who had come back as coach in 1988.

Cruyff recognised that giving home-grown players the same attention as the foreign stars raised the game of both. As Barcelona progressed inexorably to the 1992 European Cup final, young midfield orchestrator Josep Guardiola was as creative as Michael Laudrup or Hristo Stoichkov, José-Maria Bakero as solid as Ronald Koeman.

For the final against Italy's Sampdoria, London was transformed into a city of carnival, Wembley a sea of continental colour. In truth, the game was not a classic. But a rocket of a Koeman free-kick in extra-time was all it took for a 40-year itch to be scratched. Joy at Wembley, ecstasy at Plaça Sant Jaume.

At home, with Koeman's boot safely encased in the club museum, the team won four Spanish titles on the trot – three by the skin of their teeth. Twice Tenerife beat Real on the last day to hand the title to Barça. Then, in 1994, a last-minute missed penalty by Miroslav Djukić cost Deportivo La Coruña the championship

The Nou Camp was no longer the place for nationalists with an axe to grind. Cruyff's Barcelona had won everything. The fans grew tired of the daily grind of competing for domestic honours, but any notion that an era of European domination might be beckoning was swiftly disabused by AC Milan's 4–0 thrashing of Romário, Stoichkov and company at the 1994 European Cup final in Athens.

Cruyff fell out with Núñez; everyone fell out with Romário. Barcelona was a dull place to be until Ronaldo came along in the summer of 1996. The young Brazilian not only scored fantastic goals, he made football fun again and gave the city a fresh appetite for the game. He also won them silverware – the Cup-Winners' Cup and the *Copa del Rey* of 1996/97.

After Ronaldo's long drawn-out transfer to Inter, and with van Gaal taking over from Bobby Robson, Barcelona suffered a tempestuous autumn with a players' revolt – neither Rivaldo nor Ronaldo's replacement, Sonny Anderson, were happy, and nor was Luís Figo, Robson's favourite. The evidence of disharmony was clear as two thrashings by Dynamo Kiev put Barça out of the Champions' League. Yet despite rumblings amid fans as well – the anti-Núñez group *l'elefant blau* were increasingly volatile in their opposition to the recently re-elected president – the team gradually gelled on the pitch. Rivaldo and Figo picked up, Anderson started scoring, and 22-year-old Albert Celades directed the midfield traffic with a confidence that belied his age. With Real Madrid concentrating on the

Champions' League, Barça won the league with a month to spare. The double was achieved with a penalty shoot-out win over Mallorca in the *Copa del Rey* final.

The summer of 1998 saw a huge clearout of players – mainly homegrown ones. De la Peña, Ferrer and Amor were transferred abroad, key defenders Popescu, Blanc and Couto also, and fans wondered how Barça would make a serious assault on the Champions' League, the final of which was due to be played at the Nou Camp in the club's centenary year. Their

Barcelona essentials

Although the official language of Barcelona is firmly **Catalan**, everyone understands and many people speak ordinary Castillian **Spanish**.

From El Prat de Llobregat **airport**, 12 km south-west of the city, there's a half-hourly rail service to the main train station, Estació de Sants, (6am–10pm, journey time 20mins, 305ptas). There's a welcoming little *tapas* bar on the platform if you've just missed one. Some trains run on to the metro stop of the main square, Plaça de Catalunya. An *Aerobús* (6am–10pm, every 15–30mins, journey time 30mins, 450ptas) calls at Plaça de Catalunya, Sants and Plaça Espanya. A **taxi** will cost around 3,000 ptas. The other main **train station** is Estació França, close to Barceloneta metro.

The **city transport system** is made up of buses, the *TMB* metro and the *FGC* suburban railway. Free maps are given out at most stations. A single ticket, *billlet senzill* (145ptas) is valid for one journey on any of the five metro lines (Mon–Thur 5am–11pm, Fri–Sat 5am–1am, Sun 6am–midnight), or the two main *FGC* rail lines (daily 5am–1.30am), but transferring between the two requires a new ticket. There are two kinds of ten-trip *targetes* – *T1* (795ptas) for the bus and metro but not the *FGC*, and *T2* (790ptas) for the metro and *FGC* but not buses. A day ticket, *T-Dia* (600ptas) covers all transport, the three-day (*3-dies*, 1,450ptas) and five-day (*5-dies*, 2,150ptas) passes only cover metro and buses. Tickets are available from metro stations, some newsstands and *Servi-Caixa* banks. Pay onboard for single tickets on buses, and for the extensive *nitbus* system, numbered N1–14, with most buses running from 10.30pm through Plaça de Catalunya – normal *targetes* are not valid on these. There are also cablecars and funiculars, mostly serving Montjuïc.

The city's yellow-and-black **taxis** are quick and cheap. If his cab is free (*Lliure*), the driver uses a set of lights on the roof to indicate how far he will travel – a green light means anywhere in the city limits. Each zone carries a 300ptas minimum charge, plus 150ptas per km, and there are night and holiday tariffs on top of this. To call a cab, dial *Barna-Taxi* on ☎93/357 7755 or *Fono-Taxi* on ☎93/300 1100.

The are regional **tourist offices** are at the airport, and at Palau Robert, Passeig de Gràcia 107 (open Mon–Sat 10am–7pm, Sun 10am–2.30pm, ☎93/238 4000). The main city office is at Plaça Catalunya (open daily 9am–9pm), with branches at Ajuntament, Plaça Sant Jaume and Sants. City information is also available 24 hours by dialling ☎010 – ask for an English-speaking operator.

The weekly **listings magazine**, *Guía del Ocío* (Thursdays, 125ptas), is the best for cinema and restaurant information. For concert and club action, pick up a free copy of *AB* or *Mondo Sonoro*, both distributed around the city's bars.

Unmatched moment – beating Real, 1999

expanding the club's retailing and TV operations, did not have enough cash in the
bank to pay off the remainder of his contract and recruit a replacement.

For the second season running, though,
a lack of European distractions would aid
Barcelona's cause. Crucially, too, the team
welcomed back 'Pep' Guardiola from the
injury that had ruled him out of France '98.
Here was a player who could pull van
Gaal's overly adventurous formation back
together – and he was Catalan to the core.
League leaders at the Christmas break,
Barça never relinquished that position
before the end of the season, eventually
finishing 11 points clear at the top.

The team endured another poor start
to the season in 1999/2000, and this one
effectively cost them their title, try as they
might to play catch-up on Deportivo. But
the real focus of attention was Europe,
where it seemed van Gaal's attacking game-
plan might finally earn Barça a return to
the European Cup final, particularly after
a magical 5–1 win over Chelsea at the Nou
Camp in the quarter-finals. But that set up
an all-Spanish encounter with Hector
Cúper's canny Valéncia, whose 4–1 home
win in the first leg effectively killed the tie.
Barça's moderate 2–1 victory in the return
sparked a final and successful attempt from
van Gaal's many opponents to remove him
from the club. President Núñez, also on
the receiving end of protests, likewise
decided to call it a day, prompting a bitter
election campaign which looked set to
dominate the summer headlines in the city.

That was until Luis Figo left for Real
Madrid, instantly turning from hero to villain in the eyes of the Catalan nation. The
fans would have been happy to see van
Gaal's Dutch colony quit the club, but the
loss of Figo left a huge chasm to be filled.
Former vice-president Joan Gaspart won
the elections and promised plenty of big-
name recruits, as well as revenge on Real
for poaching Figo. With Llorenc Serra Ferrer confirmed as coach for 2000/01, the
drama looked like having a more resolutely
Catalan cast for its latest instalments.

worries were hardly eased with the signings
of Dutchmen Phillip Cocu, Boudewijn Zenden and Patrick Kluivert – the last too late
to be eligible for European competition.

Two single-goal defeats by Bayern
Munich severely dented Barça's European
hopes, and a 3–3 draw at home to Manchester United – despite a world-class
performance by Rivaldo – effectively ending the campaign, four days before the
centenary celebrations at the Nou Camp.
The team then lost the league game that
followed the over-the-top razzmatazz, 1–0
to Atlético Madrid, and Van Gaal hardly
helped his diminishing popularity with the
fans when he secured the signatures of two
more Dutchmen, the de Boer twins, from
Ajax. At one point, rumours were rife that
the coach had only kept his job because
the Barça board, having spent millions on

Here we go!

Metro to **Collblanc, Maria Cristina** or **Les Corts**, all about a 10min walk from the stadium, depending on where you're sitting.

Just the ticket

With nearly as many *socis* as seats in the stadium, the small percentage of tickets available for each match are sold pretty quickly. The black market trading along Travessera de les Corts can get pretty fevered before a big occasion.

The main **ticket office** is where Les Corts meets Avenida Aristides Maillol (open Mon–Fri 10am–1pm & 4–8pm, and two hours before kick-off). The cheapest seats are behind *Gol Sud* (gates #16–19) and *Nord* (gates 1–8), where 4,500ptas should get you a decent view. Another couple of thousand and you've a place in the *Lateral* (gates #20–21), while the best seats are in the *Tribuna* (gates #9–15). The details on your ticket will be printed in Catalan – *seient* is seat, *fila* is row, *boca* is section, *acces* is gate. *Entrades generals* are for non-members.

Swift half

The two best bars near the stadium, **Gent del Barri** (c/Arizala 53) and the **Bar J Tous** (c/del Comte de Güell 29), have both sadly been renovated, but are still used by fans. Also popular is the c/Riera Blanc, parallel, with the spacious **El Cargolet Picant** at #7 as good as any of the handful of hostelries on offer.

At **the ground**, the beer on sale is non-alcoholic Damm. The most popular snack is *butifarra*, Catalan blood sausage on bread spread with *sofregit* – tomato and garlic – at 500ptas.

Club merchandise

Barcelona sell more merchandise than any other club in Spain, virtually doubling their turnover since signing up with Nike and introducing a special centenary shirt for 1999.

At the stadium, the main store is **La Botiga** (open Mon–Sat 10am–8pm, Sun 10am–3pm, later on matchdays, most major credit cards), recently expanded and reached via *accès #7*.

Ultra culture

Although there are hundreds of Barça *penyas* all over the world, some visitors have returned home disappointed about the lack of atmosphere at the Nou Camp. 'The loudest noise you'll hear is the sandwiches being unwrapped at half-time,' complained one Scottish regular in the early Nineties.

Recently the stadium has been brought back to something like its fiery self, but for all that, after some ritual pre-match singing of the *Himne del FCB*, a cinema hush falls over the crowd, broken by the odd ripple of occasional, knowledgeable applause.

However, if you're standing with the **Boixos Nois** or the younger, more flamboyant **Penya Almogavers** behind either goal, you'll be made more than aware of the kind of passion that has kept alive European football's greatest arch-rivalry. The **ICC** (*Inter City Culés*) are Barça's travelling support, their name deriving from the days when fans would sit with their backsides (*culés*) sticking out over the edge of the wall at the club's old Carrer de la Industria ground.

In the net

The official Barcelona website is everything you'd expect it to be – smart, fast and full of panache. You've a choice of Spanish, Catalan and English language, and you can take a virtual your of the Nou Camp and have a peek inside the club's TV channel, Canal Barça. By comparison with the best, however, the site could still do with a bit more depth. Find it at: www.fcbarcelona.com.

For a livelier fan-run site, in Spanish and Catalan only, try **BarçaWeb** at: www.fut.es/~amab/welcome3.html. Alternatively, an English-language site that promises a ticket-finding service for matches is at: members.tripod.com/~cule.

⚽ RCD Espanyol

Estadi Olimpic, Montjuïc
Capacity (for football) 30,000
Colours Blue-and-white striped shirts, blue shorts
Cup winners 1929, 1940, 2000

Espanyol are firmly Barcelona's second club. While they have often snapped at the heels of their wealthier neighbours, their history is one of almost total failure. They entered the new millennium having had to change name from their proud Castillian 'Español' to its Catalan equivalent, despite their student founders' intention of winding up the 'foreigners' at FC Barcelona.

Worse, the club had to sell their beloved, intimate Sarrià stadium to make way for developers. Apart from the epic Italy–Brazil tie in the 1982 World Cup, sorry old Sarrià had seen precious little top-level excitement since its opening in 1923. But that wasn't the point. To the club's traditional inner-city support, Sarrià was home – a shabby but unpretentious antidote to the hyperbole of the Nou Camp down the road.

Among the Sarrià memories that have since been blurred by the bulldozers, perhaps the most precious is that of goalkeeper (and national hero) Ricardo Zamora. He reluctantly left Español for Real Madrid in 1930, but not before leading the Barcelona club to a 2–1 cup final win over his future employers. Apart from another narrow win over Real at the 1940 cup final, Los Periquitos ('The Parakeets') have had little to squawk about since Zamora's day – although each decade has produced at least one half-decent team.

In the mid-Seventies, under former Real star José Santamaria, Español twice made the UEFA Cup and played good football in the process. A decade later, with a young Javier Clemente as coach, the club came desperately close to a European honour. With Cameroon's Thomas N'Kono in goal and Dane John Lauridsen upfront, they beat Borussia Mönchengladbach and both the great Milan clubs on the way to the 1988 UEFA Cup final, where they met Bayer Leverkusen. In the first leg at Sarrià, the Parakeets were on song, and won 3–0. Yet their domination was so total that they could have scored more, and their profligacy would prove costly when the Germans won the second leg by the same score. Español lost the shoot-out, and the players left the pitch in tears, knowing a lifetime's opportunity had been blown.

The 1988 side was so pre-occupied with Europe that they almost got relegated, and there were several more battles against the drop – not all of them successful – in the early Nineties. But with José-Antonio Camacho in charge, the team bounced back in 1994/95, their first season as 'Espanyol'. With Spain's Olympic gold medallist Toni in goal, Romanian Florin Răducioiu upfront and young talent Jordi Lardín pulling the midfield strings, they even approached derby games in a higher league position than their city rivals, and a return to European action duly came the following season.

In the meantime, the club wiped out their £45million debt by selling the prime Sarrià site and moving up to the otherwised under-used Olympic stadium at Montjuïc. Built for the 1929 International Exposition and a venue for the Alternative Olympics of 1936, it was completely overhauled for the 1992 Games. It is a huge arena, and Espanyol began by dedicating the areas behind the goals to advertising hoardings, halving its normal capacity to 30,000.

The first season at Montjuïc was a reasonably successful one, under the charge of a returning Camacho, and with striker Juan Esnaider in fine form. Camacho left for Real and was replaced by Argentine Marcelo Bielsa, who in turn made way for his compatriot Miguel Ángel Brindisi after taking the national job on the eve of the 1998/99 season. Dismissing the club's stars – Esnaider left for Juventus – Brindisi brought in a bunch of youngsters, some of whom had played in that year's Intertoto Cup. Although hardly setting the league alight, Brindisi's boys put together a solid ten-match unbeaten run to finish mid-table – enough for a return to Intertoto action in the summer of 1999.

Meanwhile, the Montjuïc was full for one game – a charity match between a Catalan select XI and Nigeria, at which local *ultras* invaded the pitch, destroying the turf, the goalposts, and any feeling Espanyol might have nurtured of being at home.

But a year is a long time in the history of this club, and Espanyol ended up celebrating not just their centenary in 2000, but their first silverware in 60 years, thanks to a 2–1 Spanish Cup final win over Atlético Madrid. The league campaign had been a mediocre one, Brindisi departing as coach mid-season and being replaced by Paco Flores – an internal appointment which helped stabilise the club during a rocky spell when the relegation zone was beckoning.

Flores stuck kept faith with his young crop, among whom the brightest was dumpy, bespectacled striker Raúl Tamudo. And while the team's improvement in form was sufficient for a safe 14th-place finish in the league, the semi-finals of the *Copa del Rey* were shaping up nicely, with the last four being the big two from each of Madrid and Barcelona, and the draw keeping each set of city rivals apart. A single goal from Martín Posse was enough for Espanyol to beat Real Madrid over two legs, but in the other semi, Barcelona failed to turn up for their return leg after losing 3–0 at Atlético Madrid.

The *Copa* clearly meant little to the Nou Camp, but after Tamudo and Sergio González had given Espanyol a 2–1 win over Atlético in Valéncia, defender Nando Muñoz, who had seen it all as an Espanyol player through the Nineties and had been sent off for two yellow cards in the final itself, couldn't have expressed the emotion of the occasion better when he called it: 'The greatest day in the history of Espanyol. This is for all those fans and everyone else who can remember the bad times – all those dire moments.'

Here we go!

On matchdays the club lays on **free buses**, which leave regularly from a designated stop, *Servei Especial*, at Plaça Espanya, from 90mins before kick-off.

Otherwise, many come by the **Funicular de Montjuïc** (215ptas single, 375ptas return), which runs from Paral.lel metro – although the service only runs until 8pm Oct–May, and it's a 10min walk to the stadium from the Montjuïc terminus.

If you have some extra time, there can be few more spectacular journeys in European football than the **cablecar** across the harbour from Torre de Sant Sebastià (midday–5.30pm, 1,000ptas single, 1,200ptas return, from L4 Barceloneta) to the Miramar terminus, a steep 15min walk away from the Olympic stadium. **Bus #50** from Espanya to the Anella Olímpica is the most prosaic way of reaching the ground on non-matchdays.

Just the ticket

The main **ticket offices** (open two days before the match 10am–1.30pm & 5-8pm, matchdays from 10am) are outside gate #2 of the stadium, opposite the club shop. The club sensibly issues a *carnet* (*Socigol*) for all 19 home games in a season, so the section through gate #8 for Espanyol fans is always full. Vistors are allocated

Centenary smile – Sergio González with the *Copa del Rey*

Bitter legacy – fans' graffiti decorates former club offices before the bulldozers flatten Sarrià

the neighbouring section, accessed through gate #9. Prices are divided into *general* at 3,000ptas (uncovered) and *tribuna* at 7,000ptas (covered). Tickets are also on sale at the *El Corner del Perrico* stall at *El Corte Inglés*, Plaça Catalunya, and its branches at Av Diagonal 471–473 and 617–619.

Swift half

The *Bar Sarrià 82*, Avinguida Sarrià 129, is now full of workmen on their lunchbreaks from the construction site that was the old stadium – although a couple of old regulars still meet there before an Espanyol game at the Montjuïc. There, the *Bar Marcelino*, right by the funicular terminus, is a popular pre-match spot, with a restaurant area upstairs.

Nearer the ground, there is a small terrace bar just the other side of the roundabout from the main entrance. Inside the stadium, the bar upstairs from the main entrance has a good view of the action – but only serves soft drinks.

Club merchandise

La Tienda de l'Espanyolista (open Oct–Mar Mon–Sat 10am–6pm, Apr–Sep until 8pm, Sun

10am–midday, later on matchdays, most major credit cards), outside gate #2 stocks a far wider range of gear than the old shop at the Sarrià could ever boast.

Ultra culture

The relegation battles of the early Nineties caused the rowdier elements of Espanyol's support to give vent to their feelings, and a nasty right-wing element still lurks in their midst. The *Brigada Blanquiazules*, with their hardcore subsection, *Los Irreductibiles*, can still offer a mean show of strength.

In the net

The club's official website is hosted by *ServiFútbol* at: www.servifutbol.es/espanyol. Spanish language only, but a good history, stats archive, penya information and links are all here present and correct. For a fan's eye view on Espanyol's centenary, try: usuarios.iponet.es/jmblanco/index.htm.

Eat, drink, sleep…

Bars and clubs

Measure for measure, Barcelona is as lively as any city in Europe. Champagne bars, cocktail lounges, designer clubs, down-and-out harbour dives – this town has it all.

The economic boom of the late Eighties was one big party in Barcelona, and no-one has turned the lights off yet. The pulse of the city can be taken along the **Ramblas,** the main drag which by day sings with the sounds of street performance and caged birds, but which by night becomes the domain of the strange, the deranged – and the innocent backpacker. The nearer you get to the lap of the Mediterranean, the seedier it gets. Keep your wits about you. The **Barrí Gótic**, just off the Ramblas, is crammed full of bars and small restaurants, as is the Ribera area nearby.

Along Carrer de Balmes the scene is more upmarket, and further west in the Eixample you'll find designer bars and clubs where serious money gets spent on fun. The Port Olimpic also buzzes all summer long. Flashier venues have a strict dress code and an entrance charge of up to 5000ptas. However, bar prices, while the most expensive in Spain, are bearable. Estrella Damm is the local beer.

Apolo, Nou de la Rambla 113. Bright, noisy dance club in an old theatre with a balcony for sorting out a spot for your next bop. Reasonable admission prices. Music is either pounding and electronic, or latin and funky. Open Thurs–Sat from 1am. Metro to Paral.lel.

Distrito Marítimo, Moll de la Fusta. Ideal starting place for a night's clubbing in either direction, this large terrace bar overlooks the harbour, heaving with anticipation. Metro to Drassanes.

Glaciar, Plaça Reial 13. A former haunt of punks, junkies and bikers in an off-Ramblas square which is a springboard into the Barrí Gótic. These days the *Glaciar* is much calmer – pleasant, even. Out-door tables, decent music, and all the concert information you need. Metro to Liceu.

Ovisos, c/Arai 5. In the vibrant Plaça George Orwell, a designer squat bar playing excellent sounds to a hip clientèle. Food available. Open daily, until 3am Fri–Sat.

Les Tapes, Plaça Regomir 4. A welcome alternative to the dozen or so pubs in town, run by a Scottish-Catalan couple, this place combines the best of a tapas bar with a feel for what's needed to watch English Premiership action on the box. Metro to Jaume I.

Restaurants

Dining out is as expensive here as anywhere in Spain. If you baulk at the cost of a full blowout, don't panic – the Barrí Gótic and Port Olimpic are dotted with little *tapas* bars, where you'll find bread coated with tomatoes, oil and garlic – *sofregit* – also used as a sauce in many Catalan dishes.

In restaurants, most **specialities** are pretty meaty, bloody affairs, like *butifarra amb mongetes*, sausage with haricot beans, and *escudella*, a meat-heavy casserole. These are best washed down with the local 'black' wine, from Penedès.

Barcelona also has plenty of seafood – *bacallà a la llauna*, salt cod with tomato and garlic, is the most popular dish.

Las Caracoles, c/Escudellers 14. Possibly the best-known restaurant in town, its two floors plastered in photographs of famous guests like Ingrid Bergman and Edward G Robinson. For all that, it is reasonably priced for the superb quality of the food on offer. Snails (*caracoles*), *paella* and mussels are the specialities. Open daily 1pm–midnight. Most credit cards. Near Plaça Reial, metro to Drassanes.

Sports Bar, Ronda Sant Pere 3. Beautiful old bar converted into a sport-themed restaurant with 40(!) TV screens (all Sky channels available) and wall-to-wall memorabilia. Lunchtime deals at 1,100 ptas Mon–Fri. Open until 1am Sun–Wed, 3am Thur–Sat. Metro to Catalunya.

Euskal Etxea, c/Montcada 1–3. Friendly, low-key Basque tapas bar and restaurant, best enjoyed at busy lunchtimes. Another branch nearby, **Txakolín**, c/Marquesa de l'Argentera 19, is more upmarket.

El Xampanyet, c/Montcada 22. Classic *tapas* and champagne bar, often deservedly crowded. Blue tiles on the walls, sawdust on the floor, and fridges packed with *cava*, the local sparkling wine. Plus a range of tasty eats. Metro to Jaume I.

Accommodation

Barcelona is the most expensive city in Spain for accommodation, the clean-up for the 1992 Olympics having cleared a lot of the town's rundown old pensions. If noise isn't a problem, then anywhere just off the Ramblas will be adequate and affordable – beware that the nearer to the sea you go, the seedier it gets.

Ultramar Express, in the hallway of Sants train station (open daily 8am–10pm, ☎93/491 4463), can book a room for 200ptas – they take a deposit which will then be chalked off your final hotel bill. The main tourist office at Plaça Catalunya (see *Essentials*) will do the same.

Albergue Kabul, Plaça Reial 17 (☎93/318 5190, fax 93/301 4034). Perfect if you're out late in Barri Gòtic and not too fussy about sleeping conditions – although the Kabul is clean, the dorms can get a little crowded.

Hostal Dalí, c/Boqueria 12 (☎93/318 5580). Perfectly located a few paces off the Ramblas, a perennial favourite cheapie with singles around 3,000ptas, doubles 4,000ptas. Booking advisable. Most credit cards. Metro to Liceu.

Hotel Jardí, Plaça del Pí 5 (☎93/301 5900, fax 93/318 3664). Pleasant, slightly upmarket pension in a quiet market square. Bit of a climb up to the higher rooms, but nice and airy inside. Most credit cards. Metro to Liceu.

Hotel Ambassador, c/Pintor Fortuny 13 (☎93/412 0530, fax 93/302 7977). Chic hotel

with excellent facilities, where a double can be had for under 20,000ptas. Terrace pool, jacuzzi, panoramic sun lounge, gym and sauna. Most credit cards. L3 Liceu.

Hotel Rey Juan Carlos I, Avenida Diagonal 661–672 (☎93/364 4040, fax 93/364 4082, e-mail hotel@hrjuancarlos.com). If you can afford its luxury, this hotel, just past the Nou Camp, is the place for player-spotting when there is a match on. Built for the officials of the 1992 Olympics, each room has a different decoration. Doubles around 50,000ptas, singles 40,000ptas. L3 Zona Universitária.

Bilbao

Bilbao is the home of Spanish football. Its team, Athletic, are both a throwback to the British influence on the game's introduction a hundred years ago, and the figurehead of contemporary Basque national pride.

Unlike their near neighbours Real Sociedad, from San Sebastián, Athletic have never signed a non-Basque. The arrival of French international defender Bixente Lizarazu from Bordeaux in the summer of 1996 raised eyebrows – his was the first transfer of a foreign-national Basque, and the move suggested that the club may yet adopt a more open policy in the future. Yet it was still a small and motivated squad, under Cádiz-born coach Luis Fernandez, that claimed a Champions' League place over moneyed rivals Real and Atlético Madrid in Athletic's centenary year, 1998.

The British influence in Bilbao is still apparent, in both the club's anglicised name (although Franco had it changed to the Spanish 'Atlético' during his dictatorship) and their red-and-white striped shirts. English foundrymen and mining engineers working in the Basque country during the industrial boom at the turn of the century introduced the name and the shirt, the latter taken from the greatest English side of the era, Sunderland. They began playing alongside local merchants' sons who had been sent to school in England and learned the game there.

In 1902, a Bilbao select XI were invited to participate in a tournament organised in Madrid by King Alfonso XIII, which they duly won. Today, no team in Spain have won more *Copas del Rey* than Athletic de Bilbao – 23 to date. The 1902 win sealed not just Bilbao's position as leading exponents of the game, but that of the Basque country as a whole. Ciclista San Sebastián, Racing and Real Union Irún, and Bilbao's city rivals Arenas Getxo all won the cup in the early days, and a Basque cup is still competed for in earnest every summer. Athletic were ahead of the game in many ways. Their

San Mamés stadium was such a revelation when it was built in 1913 that it immediately earned the title *La Catedral*, a name which has stuck. It was laid with English turf and staged Spain's first home international in 1921.

One of Athletic's leading strikers, Rafael Moreno, nicknamed *Pitxitxi*, died young, and as well as a street running alongside the San Mamés, Spain's top goalscorer award, *El Pichichi*, is still named after him.

Perhaps because of the influence of their other national game, pelota, Basques have provided generations of great goalkeepers, including José Iríbar and Andoni Zubizarreta, who amassed 175 Spanish caps between them. Iríbar is now goalkeeping coach at the club, but whether the straitjacket of the Basque-only policy will produce another like him in modern-day competition is another matter.

The thrilling fields

⚽ Athletic Bilbao

San Mamés, Avenida Alameda Mazarredo 23
Capacity 46,500 (all-seated)
Colours Red-and-white striped shirts, black shorts
League champions 1930, 1931, 1934, 1936, 1943, 1956, 1983–84
Cup winners 1903–4, 1910–11, 1914–16, 1921, 1923, 1930–33, 1943–45, 1950, 1955–56, 1958, 1969, 1973, 1984

The new millennium has not started well for Athletic Bilbao. The excitement generated by a run into the Champions' League in 1998 has quickly evaporated. After finishing 11th in *La Liga* in 1999/2000, the club faces a second season without European football. The Basque region's representative in the UEFA Cup in 2000/2001 will be, embarrassingly for Athletic, little Alavés, who finished sixth.

It was too much for coach Luis Fernandez, who many felt could usher in a new era at the club. At the end of the campaign he decided to call it a day and the task of bringing the best out of Athletic's all-Basque team has fallen to a Basque – the highly regarded Txetxu Rojo, poached from Real Zaragoza.

Fernandez was not hounded out of Athletic. His achievement in getting the club into the Champions' League earned him the respect of supporters and although the team finished bottom of a tight group, the coach had shown there was a chance of joining the big boys without following the trend of expensive foreign, or even Spanish,

signings. Yet for all that Fernandez attained, for all the enormous pride associated with the club and for all its still relevant heritage, the fact remains that Athletic Bilbao haven't won a thing in more than ten years and haven't put together a decent European run in 20.

The fact that Athletic are finding it hard to compete with the money men of *La Liga* is not surprising. What is extraordinary is the way they kept on winning titles, well after the end of their domination of the early amateur era. The team's cup form was never in doubt, but to win the professional league eight times, finishing in the top three every third year, in a league in

Bilbao essentials

The language you'll hear on the streets of Bilbao is **Basque**, but most people here are bi-lingual and will easily (if sometimes grudgingly) switch to Spanish if that's all you can muster. From Bilbao's **airport** at Sondika, 9km from town, the A-3247 *Bizkaibus* runs to the **bus station** on c/Sendeja, alongside the river next to the Puente del Ayuntamiento (every 40mins, 6am–10.30pm, 40min journey time, 150ptas). You can get off the bus on its way through town, at the Plaza de España by the main **train station** of Abando. A taxi will take 20mins to do the journey and cost around 2,000ptas.

Coming **overland** into Bilbao can be confusing. Most major train lines arrive at Estación de Abando. Local services from San Sebastián use the Estación Atxuri (Achuri) on the other side of the river, south of the Casco Viejo. *FEVE* services, along the coast from Santander, stop at Estación Concordia, on the riverbank below Estación de Abando.

Most long-distance and international **bus routes** are covered by *ANSA*, c/Autonomía 17, with a bus-station entrance around the corner at Alameda de Recalde 73, south of the centre in the new town. There are at least half-a-dozen other bus stations in town run by various private companies.

The *P&O* **ferry** from Portsmouth docks at **Santurtzi**, across the river from Getxo. Local trains run from nearby Portugalete, or you can cross over the hanging bridge which transports cars and passengers every 10–30mins to Las Arenas, site of a zone B metro station. Bilbao's recently built **metro** (Sun–Thur 6am–11pm, Fri–Sat 6.30am–1.30am) has just one line, running from the Casco Viejo through the new town and up to the coast. Zone A covers any travel in town – 125ptas for a single ticket, 800ptas for a strip of ten (*metro bonoa*).

The metro is augmented by the *Bilbóbus* network (daily 6am–11.30pm); tickets are 135ptas, payable onboard, or 700ptas for a *bonobus* of ten, available at newsstands. There is no night service, but you'll probably find a **taxi** by Plaza Arriaga; if not, call for a *Tele Taxi* on ☎94/410 2121 or *Radio Taxi Bilbao* on ☎94/444 8888.

The main **tourist office** (open Mon–Fri 9am–2pm & 4–7.30pm, Sat 9am–2pm, Sun 10am–2pm, ☎94/479 5760) has moved to Paseo del Arenal 1, to the left of the Arenal bridge as you cross into the old town. There you'll find a free copy of the city's bi-monthly, tri-lingual *Bilbao Guide*, with better listings information than the weekly *La Ría del Ocio* (Thursdays, 125ptas).

which seven clubs have played in European finals, was a remarkable achievement.

What is also remarkable is the way the club have been able to hang on to their Spanish international midfielder Julen Guerrero – though perhaps the tax advantages of living in the Basque country have made their job easier. Guerrero's historical counterpart, and the first modern-day Athletic star to take the national side by storm, was Telmo Zarraonandia, or 'Zarra' – still the fifth highest scorer in a Spanish shirt, and hero of the 1950 World Cup campaign.

Like so many Bilbao stars before and especially since, Zarra was part of a team that played a rugged, English style, on a pitch well-watered by the local heavy rain or, in times of drought, by canny groundstaff. Both style and surface have occasionally troubled European opponents. After knocking Honvéd out of the European Cup in 1956, Bilbao beat Manchester United's Busby Babes 5–3 at home, before falling 3–0 at Old Trafford. Liverpool were beaten 2–1 at San Mamés in the Fairs' Cup in 1968, Rangers 2–0 a year later.

The only time Bilbao ever made a European final was in the UEFA Cup against Juventus in 1977. En route, with little Dañi upfront and the veteran Irríbar in goal – and the weight of the Basque country behind them at San Mamés – Athletic beat AC Milan (4–1!) and Barcelona in home legs. But another home win, 2–1, in the second leg of the final wasn't enough to counter Juve's 1–0 victory in Turin, and the Italians won the trophy on away goals.

The political terrorism in the Basque country after Franco's death in 1975 led to a tense atmosphere at some domestic matches. That tension, coupled with the iron discipline and attention to detail of a young Javier Clemente as coach, brought Bilbao the title in 1983 and 1984. Clemente's side was fearsomely aggressive, with a hatchet man, Andoni Goikoetxea, who was nicknamed *The Butcher of Bilbao*.

The 1984 cup final between Athletic and Barça ending in a free-for-all fight in front of King Juan Carlos and millions of

Respect due – former coach Luis Fernandez

TV viewers. Bilbao won the match – and their last piece of silverware to date.

Since then, while the Basque-only policy has been rigidly enforced among the playing staff, a selection of foreign coaches have passed through San Mamés with varying degrees of success. Dragoslav Stepanović and Guus Hiddink flopped; Jupp Heynckes and Jean Fernandez performed well under the circumstances; Howard Kendall was unsuccessful but well-liked, famously rejecting the penthouse apartment he was offered by the club in preference for a more spartan one that overlooked Athletic's training ground.

The big change was to come in 1996 with the arrival of Luis Fernandez, a World Cup hero with France in 1986 even though he had spent his childhood in Andalucía. Two key elements were already in place, the gifted young Guerrero and his partner upfront, Joseba Etxeberría, whose transfer from Real Sociedad had sparked a huge diplomatic row. Although Athletic finished only sixth, domestic wins over Real Madrid and Barcelona restored lost pride, and a European place. Roberto Ríos from Betis was added to bolster the defence, but an injured Guerrero missed the subsequent UEFA Cup defeat by Aston Villa.

In Guerrero's absence, Ismael Urzáiz and Bittor Alkiza came into their own, and by the spring of 1998 Athletic were in the bunch behind runaway leaders Barcelona. A 1–0 win at San Mamés over Zaragoza sealed Bilbao's first Champions' League qualifying spot and earned Fernandez hero status. He and his players took to the streets with everyone else, knocking back the *kalimotxo* and dancing with the Basque flag. It was a treble celebration, for not only was it the club's centenary, but they had pipped Real Sociedad to second place…

Here we go!

San Mamés has its own **metro stop**, three stops from Abando. Coming out of the metro, the ground is a short walk down Luis Briñas.

Just the ticket

The San Mamés has been all-seated since 1997. Its main ticket booths, *txarteldegi ofiziala*, are between gate #1 and #40, on the corner of the *tribuna iparralde* and *ekialde*, at the far end of Luis Briñas from the metro stop. Neutrals are best placed in the lower east stand, *beheko ekialde*, through gate #10 on Luis Briñas. The more expensive seats next-door through gate 9, *ekialdeko aurrekaldea*, are usually allocated to away fans, as are the *iparraldeko aurrekaldea*, through gate #35 in the north stand. The most expensive seats are in the main *alboko aurrekaldea*, accessed through gate #30.

Swift half

C/Licenciado Poza, which leads to the stadium, and its surrounding streets boast more than 50 bars. Three have a particular appeal: the modern *Gales* at #49, the old-style *Mugi* at #55, with its beautiful old pictures, and the *Atharratxe* opposite at #48, is typical *peña* bar.

Just before the ground, the **Bar Gol** on the corner with Avenida Sabino Arana is dominated by a huge photo of Zamora, Iribar and Yashin

together. Facing the stadium, the **Bar Flower** (#3) has a framed pic of Atlético Bilbao, Euskal Hintxak fan souvenirs, and a fantastic shot of the San Mamés.

Club merchandise

The new *denda ofiziala* (open Mon–Fri 10.30am–1.30pm & 5pm-7.30pm, all day matchdays, most credit cards) is near the ticket booths by gate #2. There is also a kiosk by gate #9.

Ultra culture

In the stadium, the two main *ultra* groups are the **Herri Norte** in the lower north stand and the **Abertzale Sur** and the **Tripustelak** in the south stand. In 1996/97, a firecracker thrown from one *Grada* group hit Real Zaragoza goalkeeper Otto Konrad, briefly closing San Mamés and forcing the introduction of $750,000 worth of closed circuit TV equipment.

In the net

The official Athletic website offers a choice of Basque, Spanish and English content but is still a bit on the flimsy side at: www.athletic-club.es. An excellent unofficial site, in Spanish only but with a nice tidy layout and great links, is at: www.geocities.com/Colosseum/Dome/8580.

Eat, drink, sleep…

Bars and clubs

The best place to start in Bilbao is between the San Mamés stadium and the next metro stop towards town, Indautxu – an area known as **Pozas**, packed with bars and popular during the day.

For a relaxed drink in the early evening, head for the outdoor tables in Plaza Nueva, Plaza de España or c/Ledesma.

The Casco Viejo is perfect for exploration deep into the night, by which time quick shots of the local spirit, *pacharrán*, will be doing the rounds. There's plenty of clubbing action, but most of it out of town – pick up flyers at *Teknopolis*, Avenida Universidades 3, the other side of the river from the Guggenheim museum.

Bordatxo Taberna, c/Ramon y Cajal 24. Local *peña* bar across the river from the San Mamés, between Deutso metro and the bridge, with occasional exhibitions of its fan culture and plenty of football talk.

Café Pinkerton, c/Dr Arielza 37 (corner with c/Simon Bolivar). Designer bar, but designed with feeling, with football knick-knacks, ads and artefacts from the Fifties. Metro to Indautxu.

Crazy Horse, Avenida Universidades 5. The other side of the river from the Guggenheim museum, an English music pub happily obsessed with rock 'n' roll history, played out against the clack of the pool balls.

Distrito 9, c/Alameda Recalde 18. The only half-decent dance club in town, in a gallery of shops a 5min walk from Moyua metro, with a young, well-heeled clientele.

Gauxtxori, c/de la Pelota 5. Casco Viejo bar with team shots and pennants in the front area, cheap lunches out back – next to the local *peña* branch.

Restaurants

Basque **cooking** is the most sophisticated in Spain, varied and tasty, and Bilbao is the best and cheapest place in the whole region to dine. The most enjoyable way to eat is to move from **bar to bar**, snacking on *tapas*. Casco Viejo is the best area to head for, with almost wall-to-wall places on c/Santa María and c/Barrencalle Barrena.

For a full meal, *bacalao a la vizcaína*, salt cod in tomato sauce, and *chipirones en su tinta*, cuttlefish in its own ink, are the local **delicacies** to seek out.

Aji Colorado, c/Barrencalle 5. Bilbao's only Peruvian restaurant, and a good one, if a little pricy. Specialities include raw fish and peppered chicken. Closed Sun. Metro to Casco Viejo, then a 10min walk.

Café Iruña, Colón de Larreátegui 11/13. Walk through the revolving door to find a historic turn-of-the-century café with statues decorating the walls. The place to lunch in style. *Menú del día* at 1,400ptas. Separate bar area serving Guinness. Abando metro end of Larreátegui.

Taberna Aitor, c/Barrencalle Barrena 16. Lovely old *tapas* bar with football trimmings, in the Siete Calles area down by the river. Metro to Casco Viejo, then a stroll across the cathedral square.

Accommodation

You should have no problem finding a reasonably priced place to stay. The best places are almost all in the **Casco Viejo,** especially along c/Bidebarrieta, which leads from Plaza Arriaga to the cathedral, and in the streets around it.

Hostal Roquefer, c/Lotería 2, 2nd and 4th floors (☎94/415 0755). Don't be put off by the dingy building – the rooms inside are fine, and some have a view of the cathedral square. Doubles around 4,500ptas, singles 4,000ptas. Most credit cards. Metro to Casco Viejo.

Hotel Ripa, c/Ripa 3 (☎94/423 9677, faax 94/423 1816). Newly modernised one-star hotel, by the waterfront a short walk from Abando station. All rooms with bath and TV, singles around 6,000ptas, doubles 8,000ptas. Most credit cards. Metro to Abando.

Pension Mendez, c/Santa María 13, 4th floor (☎94/416 0364). Centrally located pension in the Casco Viejo by the *Bolsa* building, clean and reasonably priced. Metro to Casco Viejo.

San Mamés, c/Luis Briñas 15 (☎94/441 7900). Three-star *hostal* conveniently located near the stadium, doubles 6,700ptas with bathroom, singles 4,700ptas without. The two-star *Estadio* hotel is nearby at c/J A Zunzunegui 10, but more upmarket.

Singing and dancing in the rain – Celta Vigo

The rainswept coast of the north-western province of **Galicia** produced a Spanish champion for the first time in 1999/2000. But while Deportivo La Coruña's title may have been warmly welcomed by neutrals anxious to see an end to the Real–Barça duopoly at the top of the domestic game, it is their neighbours **Celta Vigo** who continue to have the connoisseurs purring with their instinctively elegant football.

Talking a good game – coach Victor Fernández

It's just four years since Celta were saved from the drop only by the Spanish FA's decision to extend the first division to 22 clubs. Indeed, Celta have been the top flight's permanent also-rans, their sixth-place finish in 1996/97 their best since 1948.

Founded in 1923 by the merger of the town's Fortuna and Sporting clubs – the name Celta reflects **Galicia's Celtic links** – the club made the first division just after the Civil War, and lost the *Copa del Rey* final to Sevilla in 1948.

Celta then flitted between divisions – although generally winning battles against local rivals Deportivo La Coruña – until another cup final appearance in 1994. There they were faced by an adventurous Real Zaragoza side coached by a young college graduate, **Víctor Fernández**. Zaragoza took the trophy on penalties and went on to win the Cup-Winners' Cup the following year.

Meanwhile, Celta nearly went bust. Fans took to the streets to protest against the club's relegation to the third division by the FA for the board's failure to produce bank guarantees. With the club having been saved at the last minute, a young industrialist, **Horacio Gomez Araujo**, took over as president. In 1998 he appointed Fernández as coach, and the team's resurgence took serious shape. Fernández's adventurous approach allowed existing stars such as Brazilian **Mazinho** and Russian midfielders **Alexander Mostovoi** and **Valery Karpin** to express themselves. The coach also brought in a steady Argentine defender from his Zaragoza days, Fernándo Cáceres. More than anything, he transformed the team's only Galician, **Michel Salgado**, from a local journeyman into a defender of international class.

In 1998/99, it was Celta's performances in the UEFA Cup that had Europe talking. Fernández's side came from behind to beat both Aston Villa and Liverpool. Then, in the quarter-finals, they restricted **Marseille** to a 2–1 win in France but then, despite dominating the game, could not break them down in the return. A year later, and despite the sale of Salgado to Real Madrid, the European adventures continued. Celta put **seven past Benfica** and, even more remarkably, **four past Juventus** at home, before rather surprisingly losing to RC Lens of France, again at the quarter-final stage.

Araujo, meanwhile, is drawing up plans to expand the intimate Estadio Balaídos to a 40,000 capacity. To reach it, take any bus carrying the destination board Balaídos from central Vigo – a 15min ride. Once there, the *Don Balon* and *Soto* bars in c/Alexandre Bóveda and *O Canizo* and O Luar in c/Manuel de Castro are popular pre-match spots. Home fans make a noise in the *Marcador* behind one goal, and in the Rio stand by the river Lagares. Away fans are allocated the corner of the *Preferencia* section under the main stand, by the opposite goal.

Valéncia

The vibrant fiesta city of Valéncia was one of the first to pick up on football after the game filtered south from the Basque country. Its main club, Valéncia CF, are the fifth most-titled in Spanish history, with three European honours to their name.

The club were formed by foreign residents and students in 1902, then reformed with local players in 1919, but didn't make the first division until 1931, and only won their first honour, the *Copa del Rey*, ten years later.

Valéncia's stadium, La Mestalla, was used for the host nation's three group games at the 1982 World Cup. It had been intended that Spain would remain in Valéncia for the second-round group, too, and *la selección* played no fewer than six warm-up friendlies here to acclimatise themselves to the atmosphere. But in their last group match, Gerry Armstrong gave Northern Ireland a 1–0 win which pushed the Spaniards into second place in the table – and packed them off to Madrid for the second stage.

Since then, Valéncia has hosted matches in the 1992 Olympic soccer tournament, but has only occasionally been used by the national side and as a neutral venue for the Spanish cup final.

Former club president Paco Roig, big-talking and publicity-hungry in the Jesús Gil y Gil mould, was the man who tried to take the city's football onto the elite plane occupied by Barça and Real Madrid. Having renamed the stadium long after it had first been called the Luis Casanova after one of his illustrious predecessors, Roig unveiled elaborate plans to expand the Mestalla to a 75,000-capacity footballing palace, with the obligatory shops, offices and executive boxes. These plans have since been put on ice after local residents complained to the council that the planned extra tier of seating would block their daylight.

Daylight and other such trivia are not matters which concern Valéncia's most famous fan, 'Manolo', the fat drummer on whom the cameras focus at every World Cup, whose bar by the ground is a living testament to how far a man can go with a drum, a football shirt, a hat and a beer belly.

Valéncia's other team, Levante UD, decked out in Barça colours as if deliberately to annoy their richer neighbours, have their stadium north of La Mestalla, on the outskirts of town. The two teams met in the fourth round of the cup in January 1999, and 25,000 gathered at Levante's Estadi Nou to watch Valéncia CF give their lower-league ne'er-do-wells a 3–0 tanning, on the way to lifting the trophy itself five months later.

The thrilling fields

Valéncia CF

La Mestalla, Avenida Aragón 33
Capacity 53,000
Colours White shirts, black shorts
League champions 1942, 1944, 1947, 1971
Cup winners 1941, 1949, 1954, 1967, 1979, 1999
Cup-Winners' Cup winners 1980
Fairs' (UEFA) Cup winners 1962–63

Nobody who caught a glimpse of Valéncia during their run to the Champions' League final of 2000 could fail to have been impressed by a side playing modern football at its best. Although they froze in the final against Real Madrid, a team which league form had shown they were well capable of beating, Hector Cúper's men offered a timely preview of the style fans were to be treated to at Euro 2000 – fast and fluid football, with the emphasis on attack.

But the modern game doesn't allow clubs like Valéncia to get away with surprising people for long. Italian champions Lazio, who had been destroyed by Cúper's

Young generation – Valéncia's Champions' League run captured the whole city's imagination

team in the Champions' League quarter-final, stole away the man who had inspired that victory, Argentine Claudio López, for £20million in the summer of 2000. Young midfielder Gerard López, a Barcelona reject who had scored a hat-trick against Lazio and impressed throughout a domestic campaign that saw Valéncia finish third, was tempted back to the Nou Camp.

If Cuper's side now failed to maintain their momentum, it would not be the first time that the club's rapid progress has been equally swiftly halted. Valéncia have won something in every decade since World War II, but aside from one spell in the early Sixties they have never managed to sustain their success.

Valéncia were late developers – the club's first title came a full 25 years after their recognised foundation in 1919. But regular European football has come to be expected here, following a tradition which began when the club reached three consecutive European finals between 1962 and 1964. *Los Ches* won a European trophy at their first attempt, with Brazilians Chicão and Waldo and inside-left Vicente Guillot in

their side. Guillot got a hat-trick in the 6–2 home win over Barcelona in the first leg of the Fairs' Cup final, and the trophy was successfully defended the following season against Dinamo Zagreb. The 1964 final was decided on one match in Barcelona against Real Zaragoza, with the 2–1 scoreline going against the holders.

In those days Valéncia's football was crisp and cavalier in the style of the great Real Madrid team of the era. When one of the key members of that Madrid side, Alfredo di Stéfano, coached Valéncia to their only title in modern times in 1971, they were playing a dour, defensive game; after finishing level on points with Barcelona, their low 'goals against' total earned them the championship – hardly the stuff of which legends are made.

Valéncia have scarcely had a sniff of the title since, and Europe has also been an unhappy hunting ground, save for a Cup-Winners' Cup triumph in 1980. In what was the first European club final to be decided on penalties, a side containing 1978 Argentine World Cup hero Mario Kempes and the 1974 tournament's influential German, Rainer Bonhof, beat Arsenal after 120 tense, goalless minutes. Goalkeeper Carlos Pereira saved Graham Rix's final penalty (he was in good company – both Kempes and Liam Brady failed to convert), and the *Recopa* was Valéncia's.

International defender Miguel Tendillo wasn't asked to take one that night in Brussels, but it was his penalty which saved Valéncia from relegation three years later – and prevented Real Madrid from winning the title.

Though there have been no similar scares, mediocrity has been the keynote since. In the *Copa del Rey* final of 1995, 10,000 *Valéncianos* travelled to Madrid to see just 14 minutes of football, after the initial game had been abandoned in torrential rain – it was just long enough for their opponents, Deportivo La Coruña, to net the winning goal.

Knocking holders Bayern Munich out of the 1996/97 UEFA Cup was a major achievement, but it did not disguise the fact that the club had some serious rebuilding to do on the pitch as well as off it. Roig's money prompted the arrival of Brazilian striker Romário, against the wishes of coach Arsenio Iglesias. The club may not have been uppermost in Romário's mind when he was heard to say 'the night is my friend', and he was constantly at odds with Iglesias, whom he unsuccessfully tried to have sacked. Iglesias eventually left of his own free will, and Romário survived the short reign of his replacement, Jorge Valdano, before leaving Valéncia – and Europe for good – in October 1997.

Former Fiorentina boss Claudio Ranieri was left to pick up the pieces with the Argentine attacking duo Ariel Ortega and Claudio López, French international

Valéncia essentials

The official **language** of Valéncia is a local brand of Catalan, which is being fiercely promoted by the regional government, but Spanish is used and understood everywhere.

Valéncia's **Manises airport** is 15km south-west of the city. *Cercanías* trains run from here to Estación del Nord (Mon–Fri every half hour, Sat–Sun hourly, journey time 30mins, 165ptas). It's a short walk from the train station down Avenida Marqués de Sotelo to central Plaza de Ayuntamiento. A *CVT* bus runs to the main **bus station** at Avenida Menéndez Pidal 13 (hourly 6am–8pm, journey time 30mins, 250ptas), which is across the river by bus #28 from town.

From **Mallorca** and the other Balearic Islands, **ferries** connect with Valéncia's Estación Marítima, from which bus #4 goes to the Plaza de Ayuntamiento.

Valéncia has a four-line **metro system**, part of which runs overground as the *tramvia*. A single ticket, *billlet senzill*, is 125ptas for the central *AV* zone (165ptas in other zones, then 285–425ptas when crossing zones). A better bet might be a *bono-metro* at 700ptas for ten journeys in *AV* only. Alternatively, a *T1* ticket allows a day's travel in *AV* for 500ptas. A *B10 bono* (820ptas) also allows use of the city's *EMT* buses. Tickets are sold at machines in metro stations and on *tramvia* platforms, to be stamped in another nearby, and valid for 90mins.

Tickets for the *EMT* bus network cost 110ptas onboard or from newsstands, or 690ptas for a *bonobus* of ten. Both the metro and buses run 6am–10.30pm, after which there is a limited **night bus service** through Plaza de Ayuntamiento every 40mins, 11pm–1.20am only.

Taxis are generally found in Plaza de Ayuntamiento, or call ☎96/370 3333 or ☎96/357 1313.

The main **tourist office** is at Plaza de Ayuntamiento 1 (open Mon–Fri 8.30am–2.15pm & 4.15–6.15pm, Sat 9.15am–12.45pm, ☎96/351 0417). The best publication for **nightclub and concert details** is *¿Qué y Dónde?* (Mondays, 175ptas).

defender Jocelyn Angloma and mid-season signing Adrian Ilie. The team had plenty of punch, but lacked the discipline needed to hang onto a lead.

That was precisely what Argentine coach Hector Cúper provided when he took over in the summer of 1999, after proving his worth at Mallorca. While the sizzling 5–2 win over Lazio in the Champions' League quarter-final first leg and even more satisfying 4–1 drubbing of Barcelona in the semi were the games that made Europe sit up and take notice of Valéncia, they had been consistent throughout the tournament, unbeaten at home against teams of the calibre of Bayern Munich, PSV Eindhoven, Manchester United and Fiorentina. At home they had been among the front-runners in a wide open title race, and finished joint-runners up level on points with Barcelona.

Cúper's side had youth in midfield with Gerard and Francisco Farinos, and experience in attack with Claudio López and Romanian Adrian Ilie. But the key man in the team was Basque skipper Gaizka Mendieta, whose performances throughout the season made him one of the first names on Spain's squad list for Euro 2000.

The departure of Gerard and Claudio López, along with that of Farinos to Internazionale, left fans wondering whether Cúper could continue to work miracles with youngsters and bargain buys. One thing was for sure – nobody would be complaining if he did.

Here we go!
La Mestalla is the other side of town from the dried up Turia river, along Avenida de Aragón, a 25min walk from Plaza de Ayuntamiento. The nearest metro is **Facultats**, a 10min walk away, but perhaps worth it as buses #10, #12, #89 and #90 can get stuck in heavy traffic.

Just the ticket
The main **ticket office** is on the corner of c/Artes Gráficas and Avenida Suecia. The *Palco Preferiente* has the most expensive seats, the *Tribuna Numerada* is best for the neutral, and the

Fondo Sur behind the goal is dirt cheap, with standing spaces still available. **Visiting fans** are allocated seats in sector 27, the highest part of the *Tribuna* overlooking the sideline.

Swift half
On Plaza Valéncia CF by the stadium, the main attraction is Manolo's *Museo Deportivo de Manolo el del Bombo*, a shrine to the dumpy drummer's career in the beautiful game. The meeting of King Juán Carlos and the great man is illustrated over the bar, and there are dozens of other snaps of stars posing with football's answer to *Zelig*.

Club merchandise
The *tienda oficial* (open Mon–Fri 10am–2pm & 5–8pm, Sat 5–8pm, matchdays from 10am, most credit cards), right across from the bar action in Plaza de Valéncia CF, has two levels of Valéncia gear, with sportswear at the back.

Ultra culture
Los Yumos in the *Fondo Norte* like a beer. Formed in 1983, they were the first fan group in Spain to choreograph with coloured cards, and their originality is widely recognised. Their sworn enemies are Barcelona, the empathetic groups the *Gavnas Sur* from Logroñés and the *Ultra Boys* from Gijón.

In the net
The official website is at: www.valenciacf.es. Click on the appropriately coloured swooping bat (the club's symbol) for your choice of English, Spanish or Valéncian Catalan.

Groundhopping

◖ UD Levante

Estadi Nou, c/Vicente Paúl 44
Capacity 30,000
Colours Blue-and-red striped shirts, blue shorts

The *blaugrana* are very much Valéncia's second club, yo-yoing between the second and third divisions. The ground, like the team in its prime in the Sixties, is now surrounded by the *Parque Orriols* development – new shops and houses encroaching on the established allotments and Marxist graffiti.

The club have enjoyed two moments of glory – in 1963/64, when they finished in the top half of the first division, and in the early Eighties, when Johan Cruyff turned out for them for a spell.

There have been three changes in divisional status in the last four seasons, the last move being up into the *Segunda* for 1999/2000, when the club consolidated with a creditable seventh-place finish.

To see the team in some kind of action, take **bus #11** from Plaza de Ayuntamiento de c/Santiago Rusiñol, where you'll find the bar *Torre Levante* at #26, the exploits of its proud indoor football team dominating the conversation rather than the team across the road. For that unusual souvenir, the *Levantemania* stall is by the entrance to the *tribuna* (gate #8) and *grada* (gate #10). The ticket offices are by gate #19.

That silver medal feeling – Angloma in Paris

Eat, drink, sleep…

Bars and clubs

Valéncia has some of the **best nightlife** to be found in mainland Spain – no idle boast. Another plus is that there are few tourists here outside *Fallas*, the week-long festival (March 12–19) of fireworks and processional floats. The central area around the cathedral is quite dead after dark and can give the false impression that nothing goes on in town. In fact, the action is taking place around Plaza del Carmen and Plaza San Jaime.

Drinks-wise, **cocktails** (*combinadas*) are particularly popular, with *Agua de Valéncia* (orange juice, champagne and vodka) the locals' favourite.

Cervecería de Madrid, c/de la Abadía de San Martín 10. Just below Plaza de la Reina, an old-fashioned bar with walls full of paintings, where they serve the orthodox *Agua de Valéncia* and lay on jazz and literary evenings.

Easy Love Café, Paseo Neptuno 30. Has taken over as the most popular venue in the line of cafés along Playa de las Arenas, with DJ sessions at 2pm and 10pm, terrace lunches, and a good crowd. The *Vivir sin Dormir* at #42 is still rocking further down the strip (tramvia Les Arenes).

Fox Congo, c/Caballeros 35. The newest place to be in the old town, designed in a bizarre but cool style by local whizz-kid Nacho Moscardó. Open every night from 7pm for house, garage, trip-hop and techno. *Johnny Mardcas* at #39 in the same street is also worth checking out.

Noupernildolo, c/Juristas 4. Late-night weirdness in the old town, in a theatrical bar run by a former star ballerina and her Romanian barman. Fried eggs cover the wheelchair she has used since a tragic accident ended her career, while the seats are embedded with pagers. Very Lynch, very friendly.

Restaurants

Valéncia is the home of *paella*, a dish traditionally eaten at midday, which means that it is sometimes difficult to find after dark. Paseo Neptuno is lined with small hotels, all of which have their own *paella* and *marisco* **restaurants**. The city beach, Playa Levante, also has plenty of possibilities. For *tapas* and **budget eating**, head for the Barrio del Carmen.

Barbacoa, Plaza del Carmen 6. Serves a wonderful *menú del día* including barbecued meat for 1,500ptas. Be prepared to wait as it's small and very popular.

Bar Pilar, c/Moro Zeit. Just off Plaza del Esparto, a traditional place for *mejillones* (mussels). They serve them up in a piquant sauce and you throw the shells into buckets under the bar.

Ben Fet, New and traditional Valéncian cuisine in a historic building in the old town, off Plaza Reina, part of a training school for hoteliers, who also run the international pub/restaurant *Phileas Fogg* in the same building. Both change their menu every day – presumably to keep the students on their toes.

Casa Mundo, c/Don Juan de Austria 7. Run by a former member of Valéncia's legendary *Delantera Eléctrica* ('*Electric Forward-line*') and in a central, pedestrianised shopping street, this is a perfectly themed football *tapas* bar with decent variety on the menu.

Gargantua, c/Navarro Reverter 18. Fine Valéncian restaurant serving regional specialities. Closed Sun evening and all day Mon.

Accommodation

Valéncia is not a tourist city, so there are plenty of **cheap rooms** all year round except during the *Fallas* festival in March.

Budget accommodation is centred around the train station, in c/Bailén and c/Pelayo, parallel to the tracks off c/Játiva. C/Pelayo is the quieter of the two streets, but the area is not exactly charming.

For nicer and not much more expensive places, head for the centre of town, around the market and out near the beach. You'll find an **information point** with a hotel reservation service at the main train station.

Hospedería del Pilar, Plaza Mercado 19 (☎96/331 6600). Safe and central pension, crumbling, but you won't find cheaper. Doubles under 3,000ptas, singles 1,500pts.

Hostal Moratín, c/Moratín 15 (☎96/352 1220). Just off c/Barcas from the Plaza de Ayuntamiento, a good-value *hostal* with clean and comfortable rooms, and excellent *paella* served in the dining room. Singles at 2,000ptas, doubles 3,500ptas, Most credit cards.

Hotel Alkazar, c/Mosén Femades 11 (☎96/351 5551, fax 96/351 2568). Dependable town-centre hotel, near the post office. All rooms with shower. Doubles around 4,500ptas. Most credit cards.

Hotel La Marcelina, Paseo de Neptuno 72 (☎96/371 3151). Comfy hotel in a lovely spot near the sea, all rooms with bath. Around 5,000ptas a double. Most credit cards.

Penalty, c/Artes Gráficas 44 (☎96/362 3158). Perfectly located alongside Valéncia's Mestalla stadium, albeit small and quite expensive for a pension at 4,000ptas for a single, 6,000ptas a double. A 5min walk from Facultats tramvia stop line 3.

Sweden

Svenska Fotbollförbundet PO Box 1216, 17123 Solna
☎08/735 0900   Fax 08/275 147   E-mail svff@svenskfotboll.se

League champions Helsingborgs IF   **Cup winners** Örgryte IS   **Promoted** GIF
Sundsvall, BK Häcken, GAIS   **Relegated** Djurgårdens IF, Malmö FF, Kalmar FF

European participants 2000/01 Helsingborgs IF (UCL qualifiers); Örgryte IS,
Halmstads BK, Norrköping, AIK Solna (UEFA Cup); Västra Frölunda (Intertoto Cup)

The Nineties saw the standard-bearers of Scandinavian football arrive in the modern world. After decades of patient and carefully planned effort, Sweden finished third at USA '94 and a nation that had long considered football to be just one of many athletic pursuits began to take the game seriously. Now Swedish business has finally realised the benefits of backing football, TV companies are starting to compete for rights and the bigger clubs can offer salaries which at least tempt key players to stay at home.

Yet despite the interest generated by the national team's successes and the improved performance of Swedish clubs in European competition, the domestic league, the *Allsvenskan*, remains a low-key affair. There are no full-time professional clubs (although some are edging towards this status), league crowds rarely top 5,000 and football culture is under-developed. For adults, it is simply entertainment; for a growing number of kids it is a chance to act hard.

Football arrived relatively early in Sweden, with the game taking root in Gothenburg in the 1870s thanks to the usual missionaries – English engineers and railway workers. But the game didn't begin to take off until pioneer Victor Balck,

Rubbing their noses in it – Euro 2000 was one big let-down for Sweden's travelling support

founder of the Swedish National Sports Federation, travelled to England in the 1880s. On his return he penned a book, *Sports Illustrated* – his description of English football as 'not a game for the weak and timid' proving to be a prophecy for the future style of Swedish football.

Initially the game met with opposition from the austere gentlemen of Sweden's Gymnastics Federation, a body dedicated to developing fit, healthy young men. They saw football as a dangerous phenomenon and were willing to accept it only on the understanding that when players kicked the ball they alternated between their left and right feet, in order to ensure balanced physical development.

Under the auspices of an unofficial FA, a national championship, in knockout format, began in 1896, and the game found a place in the 1912 Stockholm Olympics – at which Sweden were knocked out in the early stages. A league began in 1925, dominated by Örgryte, from near Gothenburg, and by the Stockholm clubs AIK and Djurgårdens.

It wasn't until the end of World War II that Sweden began to make an impact on the international scene, a 3–1 victory over Yugoslavia winning them gold at the 1948 London Olympics. Sweden's success, with a side managed by Englishman George Raynor, resulted in a number of players being lured away from the strictly amateur Swedish league for the seriously professional *Serie A*. Indeed, the entire front three of the Olympic side – Gunnar Gren, Gunnar Nordahl and Nils Liedholm – was snapped up by AC Milan in 1949. The Milanese nicknamed them the *Gre-no-li*, making an Italian-sounding word from the beginnings of their surnames, and they went on to bag a collective 329 goals for their club – even though only Liedholm chose to remain with Milan for the whole of the Fifties.

With the departure of others such as Kurt Hamrin, who played for five Italian clubs, and Lennart Skoglund, who went to Inter, the Swedes banned professionals

from the national team and went into the 1950 and 1954 World Cups without their top players. Despite this self-imposed handicap, they managed third place in Brazil. But when Sweden hosted the 1958 World Cup, the FA was pressured into recalling the pros. Ten years after they last appeared in national colours, the veterans of the Olympic side gave local fans a taste of what they had been missing. After dismissing the USSR in the quarter-finals, the Swedes drew a capacity crowd to Gothenburg's then new Ullevi stadium to witness a highly physical 3–1 crushing of West Germany. The 1958 Swedes were a great side, but their opponents in the Stockholm final – the Brazil of Didi, Garrincha and a 17-year-old Pelé – were on another plane and hammered the hosts 5–2.

Attendance records were smashed at the World Cup, which saw the Swedes use a number of small provincial grounds in order to create a close-knit, 'family' atmosphere. In 1959, the local FA switched the club programme to a summer season in an attempt to keep the fans who had turned out in such force the previous year, but the move failed. With the retirement of the *Gre-no-li*, the national team faded and the Sixties were a barren time for Swedish football.

In the Seventies the national team maintained their consistency in qualifying for the final stages of major competitions but, save for an epic 4–2 defeat by the hosts at the 1974 World Cup in West Germany, they failed to make much impact.

Club sides were making more progress. In 1979, Malmö FF finished as runners-up to Nottingham Forest in the European Cup. In 1982 came the big breakthrough – IFK Gothenburg slaughtered Hamburg to lift the UEFA Cup, becoming the first Swedish club to win a European competition. They won the same trophy five years later, 2–1 on aggregate over Dundee United.

Swedish fans got another chance to see top-class football when the country hosted Euro '92. Stadiums across the land were upgraded and the finals coincided with the

Basics

A full, valid **passport** is sufficient for EU citizens and those of the US, Canada, Australia and New Zealand to gain entry to Sweden.

The Swedish currency is the **krona** (plural kronor) or crown, divided into 100 öre; the exchange rate is roughly 13kr to £1. There are coins for 50 öre and 1, 5 and 10kr, and notes for 20kr, 50kr, 100kr, 500kr, 1,000kr and 10,000kr. Prices are generally rounded off to the nearest 50 öre. All banks change money and standard opening hours are Mon–Fri, 9.30am–3pm, but beware that exchange rates can vary widely. *Forex* exchange offices are open late in the cities and charge a commission of 20kr on cash, 15kr on travellers' cheques.

Sweden has a fast and reliable **public transport** system. Swedish state **railways**, SJ, cover the country; second-class trains cost 25% less on Fridays and Sundays. There is a maximum fare of 610kr for all journeys over 815km. The exception to this rule is the new **X2000** high-speed train, which links Sweden's major cities much faster than the previous *InterCity*. By early 2001, it will also link Stockholm to Copenhagen via the Öresund Bridge. Prices are higher – Stockholm–Gothenburg is 920kr compared with 540kr – but at weekends and during holidays, including summer school holidays, prices fall to *InterCity* levels. Rail passes are valid with a 50kr supplement.

The domestic **bus** system, run by Swedbus, is cheaper than its rail equivalent. For weekend city-to-city travel the company's *Expressbuss* services are your best bet.

You can make **international phone calls** from public kiosks. Dial 009 to get an international line. All payphones are now card-only. Cards (*Telefonkort*) are available from newsagents (*Pressbyrån*), priced 40kr, 60kr and 100kr. All operators speak English and both domestic (07975) and international (0019) directory inquiry services are fast. From outside the country, the international code for Sweden is 46. From within Sweden, the code for Stockholm is 08, while Gothenburg is 031.

As elsewhere in Scandinavia, **eating out** can be an expensive business. Stoke up at breakfast time, then take advantage of a *Dagens Rätt* (set lunch) on offer in many restaurants, and often including bread, salad, coffee and a drink in a price of around 45–60kr. Local specialities include reindeer, elk meat and wild berries. Open sandwiches (*Smörgåsar*) are a good-value snack but the celebrated self-service *Smörgåsbord* cold buffet can be costly.

If food is expensive, **drink** is positively prohibitive. **Beer** is divided into three classes according to its strength. All are available in bars but beware that Class I is virtually non-alcoholic. Class I and Class II beer is sold in supermarkets, Class III only in state-run off-licences (*Systembolaget*), where you will need to be over 20 and show ID to get served. Expect to pay 40kr for a glass of beer or wine in a bar, perhaps a little less during a *Happy Hour*. The local spirit is *Akvavit*, a form of schnapps.

Accommodation is also dear, but many **hotels** drop their rates at weekends, and the country's youth hostels (*Vandrarhem*), are widespread and almost hotel-like in their amenities. An average hotel room, with a TV and bathroom, runs to 350kr for a single, 500kr for a double, with a good breakfast included.

emergence of an attractive national team coached by Tommy Svensson. The side performed well, reaching the semi-finals before the Germans gained revenge for '58. The damage to national pride was increased when Sweden's neighbours Denmark, whom the Swedes had beaten in a group game, won the final.

Two years later, at the World Cup, Svensson's side at last fulfilled its potential. Traditional physicality was complemented by the verve of target-man Kennet Andersson, the guile of midfielder Tomas Brolin and the eccentricity of 'keeper Thomas Ravelli. Again, it was only the Brazilians who could stop them – this time in the

Barely fit – Henrik Larsson at the end

careers, while former golden boy Brolin struggled to lose the pounds with Crystal Palace before throwing in the towel altogether in the summer of 1998.

Yet Sweden qualified comfortably for Euro 2000, with a new generation of players quickly finding their international feet. Arsenal's Fredrik Ljungberg became established as the link man between midfield and attack, while Henrik Larsson emerged as a top-class striker. But after England, Poland and Bulgaria had all been dismissed with some aplomb, Larsson broke his leg playing for Celtic and, although he recovered just in time for the finals, he was far from the livewire who had given Sweden's opponents such problems during qualifying. One of the leftovers from the Svensson era, towering forward Kennet Andersson, was also short of match-fitness, and experienced midfield general Stefan Schwarz was ruled out of the entire event.

A 2–1 defeat by Belgium in the opening game of Euro 2000 made life even more difficult, especially as another key man, Patrik Andersson, was sent off nine minutes from the end and missed the second, decisive game against Turkey. Sweden badly needed a win against the Turks to maintain hope of progress, but were found desperately lacking in ideas in the goalless draw which many critics marked down as the worst game of the tournament.

Sweden then had to beat Italy in their final game to have any chance of making the quarter-finals, and although they provided their best display against Dino Zoff's team, a 2–1 defeat meant it was all over.

Back home there was disappointment, but not disillusion. The Swedish public accepted that their squad had been stricken by injuries, and with more young talents continuing to emerge, the overall outlook remains bright. In particular, Helsingborg's domestic title win in 1999 confirmed that the Swedish league has much greater strength in depth than in, say, neighbouring Norway, as well as giving one of the country's best-supported clubs a long-awaited first postwar championship.

semi-finals. Few people remember third-place play-offs, but in Los Angeles, the Swedes trounced Bulgaria 4–0 in a performance which ensured they returned home to thousands of cheering fans in Stockholm's Ralambshovsparken.

As in 1948, the bulk of the squad swiftly departed for more lucrative leagues, leaving the domestic competition starved of stars. The national team failed to qualify for either Euro '96 or France '98 and, after some initially promising displays by IFK Gothenburg in the Champions' League, performances in the European club competitions have been disappointing.

An era had come to an end in October 1997, when Tommy Svensson stepped down as national team coach after watching a poor 1–0 win over Estonia. His successor, former Under-21 coach Tommy Soderberg, knew he had some rebuilding to do. Skipper Jonas Thern, stopper Roland Nilsson and goalkeeper Ravelli were all nearing the end of their international

Essential vocabulary

Hello *Hej*
Goodbye *Adjö*
Yes *Ja*
No *Nej*
Two beers, please *Två öl, tack*
Thank you *Tack*
Men's *Herr/Herrar*
Women's *Dam/Damer*
Where is the stadium? *Var ligger stadion?*
What's the score? *Vad står det?*
Referee *Domare*
Offside *Offside*

Match practice

If you brought a book and opened it after five minutes of a Swedish game, no one would look at you twice. Sit down. Pull a tartan rug over your legs. Open a flask of coffee. Apart from the rowdies – usually behind the goals and burdened with a ridiculous gang name – the Swedish football experience is sedate and relaxed.

People don't argue about football in the pub, wives don't curse their husbands' domination of the remote control and you won't catch Ace of Base in the stands. With an upbringing like this, it's no wonder Lennart Johansson, Swedish president of UEFA, has a vision of football as nicely packaged, family entertainment.

But things *are* changing. Just as Swedes brought the idea of pubs and bars back from holidays outside Scandinavia, fans have got a taste of what supporting a team means from abroad. Fans of IFK Gothenburg and AIK Solna have travelled all over the continent in Champions' League campaigns, and Europe came to Sweden in 1992. All this has resulted in a growth in supporters' clubs and, alas, in a sad fad for hooliganism.

Sunday and Monday are the most popular days for league games. Kick-off time for evening games tends to be 7pm, with afternoon games at 5pm.

The Swedish football season begins in April and runs until the start of July, when it breaks for a month. It restarts in August and, including the play-offs, continues into late October, with another week or two tacked on for play-offs.

A different league

The *Allsvenskan* is Sweden's 14-team premier league. Teams play each other home and away. Between 1982 and 1990, the title was decided in a two-leg play-off between the top two sides in the table.

Below the *Allsvenskan* is the new 16-team *Superettan*. At the end of the campaign its top two teams change places with the bottom two of the *Allsvenskan*. The third- and fourth-placed *Superettan* clubs play off over two legs with the 11th- and 12th-placed teams in the *Allsvenskan*.

Because Sweden's league campaign doesn't end until after the main European competitions have begun, Swedish teams book their places in Europe by their position in the previous year's season.

Up for the cup

The *Svenska Cupen* is traditionally low-key, but since AIK reached the quarter-finals of the Cup-Winners' Cup in 1997, there has been a surge in interest.

Preliminary rounds begin in late May with around 500 clubs involved. The first round proper is in August, with *Allsvenskan* clubs joining in the second round except those in European competition, who get a further round's grace. The tournament runs right through to the end of the league season, beginning again the following spring with a last-16 round in March.

The final is played in May and is now, contrary to all other games, decided over two legs. The winners go straight into the UEFA Cup the following autumn.

Just the ticket

With a few exceptions (Hammarby, local Stockholm derbies, the *Skåne* derby between Helsingborg and Malmö), domestic games rarely sell out. On average they cost 100–300kr for a seat in the stand (*långsida*) and 60–150kr behind the goals (*kortsida*). A seat is a *sittplats* while a spot on the terraces is a *ståplats*.

Half-time

You'll find hot dogs, coffee, light beer and soft drinks, and confectionery at the stadium. In recent years, more and more fans have adopted the habit of going to a bar before the game. Most of them drink beer, but don't hesitate if you are offered a sip of *Vargtass* ('*Wolfpaw*') – homemade vodka mixed with lingonberry juice.

Action replay

During the domestic season, state channel STV1 has its main football programme, *Fotbollskväll*, on Mondays at 10pm, with highlights of the weekend's games plus goals from the main European leagues if they are being played. Subscription channel Canal Plus shows live games from the *Allsvenskan*, and during the English season a couple of Premiership games every week, plus some *Serie A* action. Independent free-to-air TV3 has the rights to the Champions' League.

The back page

Sweden has no daily sports paper, but as of April 2000, the tabloid *Aftonbladet* has published a daily pink-papered supplement, *Sportbladet*. Provincial papers tend to be more involved in the comings and goings of the local side than what's going on in Stockholm. The free weekly *FotbollExtra* offers club-by-club news and a stats round-up. Look out for the new quarterly *Offside* (59kr), a Swedish version of *Perfect Pitch*, in which famous football writers get long and literary about their passion.

Ultra culture

All teams have their 'Fan Club' or 'Support', usually with an official or semi-official relationship to the club. These groups are generally well-organised and often run souvenir shops as well as arranging away travel.

Hooliganism is still a problem in Sweden, but a minor one. Though the tabloids love to paint it black, it's mostly when Stockholm clubs visit IFK Gothenburg that there's real tension in the air. The supporters of the three Stockholm clubs are sworn enemies, but of late police have been successful in keeping them apart. As a general rule, AIK and IFK have the most notorious 'firms'.

In the net

The Swedish FA runs an excellent one-stop site at: www.svenskfotboll.se. It feels more like a rolling news, stats and features service from the commercial sector than a federation flag-waver, and that's no bad thing. Much of the content is in Swedish but you'll find introductory pieces on the national team and domestic club competitions in English.

Stockholm

AIK 593   Djurgårdens 595
Hammarby 596

Traditionally, Gothenburg is the heartland of Swedish football. It was there that the first game was played and where most championship titles have gone since then. But its status has been challenged in recent years – by Stockholm. Not only is Sweden's capital the official centre of Swedish football, the masses have been returning to its football stadia. In 1998, an exceptionally good year in which both AIK and Hammarby challenged for the title, there were two sell-out derbies at the national arena, the Råsunda – and you have to go back 20 years to find crowds higher than 30,000 for domestic fixtures there.

Naturally, no-one in Gothenburg would ever agree that Stockholm has taken over. For them, the capital is still a backwater in footballing terms, where everyone seems to be more interested in ice hockey or its outdoor equivalent, bandy.

One thing is certain. Stockholm has the liveliest football scene, consisting of three almost equally big clubs, and little else. Even if you have a deep involvement with some minor club in the region, you are expected to support one of the big three. And when you do, hating the other two is obligatory.

The resident club of the Råsunda, AIK, were one of the first teams to be formed in Sweden and have remained an influential, if not consistenly successful force ever since. Being the biggest club in Sweden, patronised by His Majesty the King and lumbered with fans of ill repute, AIK are the Stockholm club more disliked than any other in the provinces.

After a couple of poor decades, Djurgården are better known for their successful ice hockey team. But the club is an institution in Swedish football, too, with four titles since World War II and a large number of supporters, even if the residents of their wealthy and leafy district pay little attention to the goings on at the Olympic stadium.

Attracting punks, drunks and bohemians of every hue, Hammarby are deeply rooted in Södermalm, the southern part of the inner city. This used to be a solid working-class area but it now attracts a wide variety of people, including trendy youngsters. No other big club in Sweden has failed as often as Hammarby – nor been so easily forgiven.

The thrilling fields

 AIK

Råsunda Stadion, Solnavägen 51
Capacity 36,000 (all-seated)
Colours Black-and-yellow shirts, white shorts
League champions 1900–01, 1911, 1914, 1916, 1923, 1932, 1937, 1992, 1998
Cup winners 1949–50, 1976, 1985, 1995–97, 1999

As you will be pedantically told as soon as you mention 'AIK Stockholm', despite being the capital's most famous club and lying just a ten-minute tube ride from the city centre, AIK actually come from the nearby town of Solna. The club's full name is Allmänna Idrottsklubben ('General Sports Club'), but don't bother trying to master the pronunciation – only their patron, His Royal Majesty King Karl Gustaf, ever uses the full title.

AIK is the largest sports club in the country, with 12,000 members and several sections including a popular ice-hockey team. As the team of the royals and of the capital's elite, they enjoyed their best days before World War II, when Swedish sport was no more than amateur recreation. With professionalism sneaking its way in from the Fifties on, the strictly amateur AIK struggled to attract talent. By the late Seventies members began to realise that professionalism needed to be increased if the club was to stay competitive. One of

the rough guide   593   european football

the administrators who took up the call was Lennart Johansson, chairman of the club for 16 years prior to becoming UEFA president. Johansson is currently AIK's honorary chairman.

The effort has paid off. During the Nineties, AIK re-established themselves as one of the great powers in Swedish football. In 1992 they won their first title for 55 years, and after another lull, they won the cup three years in a row from 1995. In 1996/97, a run to the quarter-finals of the Cup-Winners' Cup (where they gave Ronaldo's Barcelona a run for their money) rekindled media interest in the club.

A calamitous defeat by Slovenia's Primorje Ajdovščina in the same competition in 1997 pompted the sacking of Erik Hamrén and the arrival of British-born Stuart Baxter as coach. Star sriker Pascal Simpson was sold to Norway's Vålerenga, but his natural replacement, the fans' favourite Johan Mjällby, stepped effortlessly into his boots, and AIK came up on the rails of a

A Scot in Solna – manager Stuart Baxter

three-way title race with Helsingborg and Hammarby to be crowned champions in November 1998. Mjällby was then sold to Celtic, while Baxter quit the club, apparently frustrated at management's inability, even now, to grasp the mettle of a fully professional outlook. Within weeks, however, he was persuaded to change his mind, and with Elfsborg striker Christer Mattiasson and international defender Pontus Kåmark among a string of new signings, AIK won the domestic cup again in 1999, before embarking on a first Champions' League campaign.

After again running Barcelona close at home in their first game, AIK played disappointingly, taking only one point – thanks to a goalless draw at home to Fiorentina – from their six games. But the team were now firmly on the European map, and Baxter, suitably encouraged by the board's intention to make AIK the first Swedish club to be floated on the stock market, signed a new two-year contract in the spring of 2000.

Here we go!

Take the blue tube from T-Centralen in the direction of Akalla, get off at **Solna Centrum** and follow signs for Råsunda. The tube journey takes around 10mins.

Swift half

There are two expat pubs outside the north end of the Råsunda, equally popular with fans. *Caffrey's*, Solnavägen 104, and *Dick Turpin*, at #55, are both within sight of the ground.

Club merchandise

There are two shops close to each other in Solna. One, *AIK-shopen*, is inside the mall in Solna Centrum (open Mon–Fri 10am–6pm, Sat 10am–4pm, Sun midday– 4pm) – turn right at the slope as you leave the underground. The other, *Råsunda-shopen*, is situated by the main entrance to the east stand on Solnavägen.

Ultra culture

The local lads are the *Black Army*. After years of tension, the club has re-established diplomatic relations with the Black Army committee, but this has not stopped the foundation of a new group, the **Allmänna Supportklubben**, who are opposed to the clumsy politics of the Black Army.

In print

Programmes (20kr) are produced for all home games and are of a decent standard, while the club also now produces an ambitious monthly, Smokingliraren (40kr), with interviews, stats and historical features. The Black Army fanzine **Gnagaren** ('Rat') is sold at the Råsunda's north end before and after matches, along with a new competitor, **Norra Stå**.

In the net

AIK's **official homepage** is at: www.aik.se. There are no fewer than ten language options (English included), which must be some sort of record for a European football site. That said, only the news, history and ticket information areas are in English – though there's plenty more for Swedish-speakers, plus areas dedicated to the club's other sports sections.

 # Djurgårdens IF

Olympiastadion, Lidingövägen 1
Capacity 14,200 (all-seated)
Colours Light and dark blue striped shirts, dark blue shorts
League champions 1912, 1915, 1917, 1920, 1955, 1959, 1964, 1966
Cup winners 1990

Even if Djurgården aren't at home, it's worth visiting their ground. The Olympia-stadion, known locally as the Stockholms or Klocktornet ('clock tower'), is one of the quaintest venues in Europe. A listed historical site, it maintains the romantic aura it had when built for the 1912 Stockholm Olympics, untouched by the whims of twentieth-century architecture. The perimeter walls are covered with ivy and the two towers at the east end evoke a medieval castle. The east end was knocked down in the Fifties and a terrace

block built in its place, but in 1991 this was bulldozed to make way for an exact replica of the original 1912 tribune. The result is a beautifully proportioned, refined little ground.

Djurgården moved here in 1936, having previously played at the Traneberg sta-dium. The team were at their best in the late Fifties and early Sixties, when they lifted four titles with sides skippered by Gösta Sandberg, the club's record scorer.

But after spending three seasons from 1988 playing at the Råsunda, while restora-tion work was carried out on the Olympiastadion, the club have bounced between the premier and first divisions. The football section of the sports club became independent in 1991, but in the face of declining attendances and financial problems, Djurgården have become a classic 'yo-yo' team, their last movement being down into the Superettan after a bottom-place finish in 1999.

Here we go!

It's a ten-minute tube ride on the red line from T-Centralen in direction of Mörby Centrum, getting off at **Stadion**. Follow signs for Stadion.

Swift half

Stay on the tube for one more stop beyond Sta-dion, getting off at Tekniska Högskolan. From here, follow the signs for Östra station, then go up to ground level and into the train station. On the first floor, the **Järnvägsrestaurangen** is a simple café, serving meat and two veg and pints of draught Pripps beer.

Ultra culture

Having prided themselves on a good relationship with their younger, more volatile supporters, **The Blue Saints**, Djurgården have now broken off contact with the group. The decision followed a game with Halmstad in 1995, when a Saint ran onto the pitch and karate-kicked the referee.

The Saints no longer get cheap tickets and coffees with the club president, but they still gather at the north end. Meanwhile, the club now bestows favours on a splinter group, the **Järnkaminerna**.

In print

Programmes (20kr) are produced for every home match. *Järnkaminen* is the main fan group's magazine for members, while *Bågspännaren* is a fanzine produced by a splinter group of fans.

In the net

The official website is at www.dif.se. There's no English but the 'temperature gauge' graphic on the homepage, showing how many tickets have or have not been sold for the next game, tells its own story in any language.

The club's main fan group run their own site at: www.jarnkaminerna.nu. Again, no English, but news and match reports which offer an alternative perspective to the official version.

Hammarby IF

Söderstadion, Arenavägen, Stockholm-Globen
Capacity 10,800
Colours Green-and-white shirts, green shorts

If AIK are the establishment of Swedish football, Hammarby are the underclass. Despite a history of total and utter failure, they remain the most popular team in Stockholm. Before the 1999 campaign, they sold almost 7,000 season tickets, filling three-quarters of the stadium. There are plans to increase the number of seats available, but until that happens, almost every game will be a sellout. Hammarby have a strange history and can boast a passionate

Stockholm essentials

Stockholm's **Arlanda airport** is 45km north of the city. A high-speed rail link runs to Central station (every 15mins, 5am–12.35am, journey time 20mins, 120kr). A cheaper alternative is to take the *Flygbussarna* bus to Cityterminalen (every 10mins, 6.30am–11.30pm, from town every 30mins 4.25am–10pm, journey time 40mins); from the airport, buy your 60kr ticket onboard; for the return journey, buy it in the Cityterminalen departure area. A **taxi** will cost around 350kr, but take one with prices clearly displayed in the back window, otherwise you may be ripped off.

Flights operated by *Malmö Aviation* arrive at the more centrally located **Bromma**, also served by *Flygbussarna*, from gate #23 (every 20mins, 40kr), and there are services running between each airport (7.15am–11.10pm, every 45mins, 60kr). *Ryanair* use **Skavista** airport, 100km south of Stockholm, near Nyköping – buses meet each flight (journey time 80mins, 60kr).

Trains arrive at Central station, where all three *Tunnelbana* metro lines also meet. Next-door is **Cityterminalen**, the city's main bus station. The main **ferry terminal** is the Vikingterminalen on Södermalm – take a bus from there to Slussen, with its *Tunnelbana* station, if you don't fancy a 30min walk into town.

City transport consists of a colour-coded (red, green and blue) metro system and buses (5am–midnight), with night buses Sun–Thur and the metro running all night Fri–Sat. Buying single tickets (16kr for one zone, 8kr for each additional zone) can be uneconomical. A strip of 20 (*rabattkuponger*) costs 110kr – the employee at the entrance will stamp two bars per zone. A one-day tourist ticket is 70kr, a three-day one 135kr – stamp them onboard buses or at metro stations. Tickets are sold at newsstands (*Pressbyrån*), found almost everywhere, or at barriers in the metro.

Taxis are rarely hailed from the street. Dial either *Taxi Stockholm*, ☎08/150 000, or *Taxi Kurir*, ☎08/300 000. The meter will already show around 25kr, after which count on another 100kr for a 15min journey across town.

The main **tourist office** is in the *Sverigehuset*, Hamngatan 27, on the corner with Kungsträdgården (June–Aug Mon–Fri 8am–7pm, Sat & Sun 9am–5pm; Sept–May Mon–Fri 10am–6pm, Sat & Sun 9am–3pm; ☎08/789 2495, fax 08/789 2491). There you'll find a copy of the free listings publication *Stockholm This Week*. The Swedish-language monthly *Nöjesguiden*, distributed free around town, is better for nightlife tips.

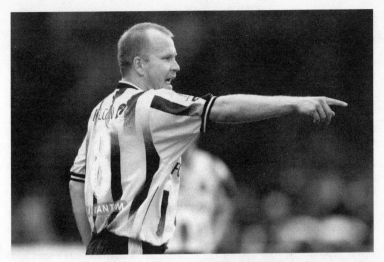

Back into the mire – Hammarby's Kaj Eskelinen points out a deficiency

support unlike any other in Sweden. The club's nickname is *Bajen* ('village') and the village of Hammarby was where they were formed. But the team have never played in Hammarby, having spent all of their life in Södermalm, the traditionally working-class south side of Stockholm.

In 1918, 21 years after their foundation, the club were involved in a curious merger with Stockholm side Johanneshofs IF. Hammarby kept their name, but in return the president of Johanneshofs made Hammarby sign an agreement that they would wear his club's yellow-and-black striped shirts for 60 years.

Despite the fact that their rivals AIK wore identical colours, Hammarby kept their side of the deal. In 1978 they reverted to their own green-and-white, but still wear the yellow as a change strip. Their stadium is dwarfed by a huge spherical ice-hockey and concert venue, the Globen, which was built on Hammarby's old training ground.

A record crowd of 14,221 turned out for Hammarby's biggest moment – a 1982 league play-off final defeat by IFK Gothenburg. Since then *Bajen* have bounced

between the premier and the first divisions. In 1997, Hammarby secured automatic promotion to the *Allsvenskan* by holding city rivals Djurgården to a 2–2 draw, then watched gleefully as Djurgården, who finished second, failed to get past Östers in the play-offs. The following year, coach Rolf Zetterlund led a largely unchanged side to the top of the *Allsvenskan*, where they stayed for a few weeks before falling off the championship pace just when it mattered most. Zetterlund was sacked during a much more mediocre 1999 season, when Hammarby escaped the play-off zone by only a point. His replacement, the experienced Sören Cratz, turned to some cheap Balkan imports to turn the tide in 2000.

Here we go!

Söderstadion is a 15min ride from T-Centralen on the green line tube in the direction of **Hagsätra**. Get off at **Globen**, turn right over the bridge, left at the dome, and you're there.

Swift half

Although the *Globen Star*, an ice-hockey theme bar next to the arena, is well placed for a pre-match pint, the **Kvarnen** at Tjärshovsgatan 4, close to the Medborgarplatsen tube station, has for decades been the Hammarby bar. It is one of the few working-class vodka and soup bars left in Stockholm. Two of the district's famous sons are framed on the walls: Joe Hill, who left Södermalm for America but took its radical politics with him and became a folk singer, and Lennart Nacka Skoglund, the local hero who left Hammarby for Serie A after World War II and died, a penniless alcoholic, on a Södermalm park bench.

Other places worth a look-in are the **Röda Kvarnen**, a basic bar/restaurant 50m from the ground at Arenavägen 33, and the **Gröne Jägeren**, Götgatan 64, where helmets are obligatory after 10pm.

Club merchandise

Hammarby-Shopen, Hornsgatan 96 (open Mon–Fri 10am–6pm, Sat 11am–3pm) is a high-street souvenir shop with plenty of merchandise on offer including children's clothes.

Ultra culture

Hammarby boast the best-humoured, loudest and probably most passionate supporters in all Sweden. The main organised group, **Bajen Fans**, enjoy a considerable reputation, even if their average age makes you wonder if there's no end to adolescence. Their weakness for the demon drink is well known. At derbies with AIK, the opposition crew's weakness for mineral water does not go unnoticed.

In print

Programmes (20kr) are produced for every home game. The club's official magazine is **Hammarbyiten** while the fans produce **Bajen Fanzine** – both are available at the club shop.

In the net

The official website now has an English-language introduction to the club, at: www.hammarby-if.se/fotboll. If you know your Swedish you'll be able to understand the plethora of news, debate and feature material which distinguish what is an unusually open official site.

The **Bajen Fans** now have their own site at: www.bajenfans.se. It's nicely designed, but in Swedish only for the time being.

Eat, drink, sleep…

Bars and clubs

There is no genuine tradition of bars or pubs in Stockholm, and the huge taxation on alcohol makes a night out here one of the most expensive in Europe. A pint will set you back anything from 30kr to 50kr. In the Eighties, mock English and Irish Pubs sprang up – even if your natural inclination is to avoid such places, you have little choice. Södermalm is the liveliest part of town; get off at Medborgarplatsen on the green metro line and there are bars in just about all directions.

G-Klubben, Kungsträdgården. If you're new in town and ask where to go and dance, this place, in the Dailys entertainment centre, is where you'll be directed to. Occasionally featuring guest DJs, always attracting the young and trendy. **Sturecompagniet**, Sturegatan 4, in Norrmalm, is in a similar vein, with three bar levels.

Melody, Kungsträdgården. Daytime café and restaurant, night-time two dance floors and a meeting point for the techno scene. Two minutes' walk from Kungsträdgården tube.

O'Leary's, Götgatan 11. American-style sports bar and restaurant. In addition to Sky Sports, the management have recently reached an agreement with Canal Plus to show all Allsvenskan, Premiership and Serie A games, otherwise strictly forbidden in Sweden. Green tube to Medborgarplatsen.

Pelikan, Blekingegatan 40. In the street where Greta Garbo lived is a bar/restaurant where many try to emulate her solitude. In the blue corner is Kristallen, playing acid jazz and stranger offshoots, in the red corner a shabby but atmospheric restaurant. Black clothes, deep thoughts. Very Södermalm. T-bana to Skanstull.

World Hockey Bar, Götgatan 93. Stockholm's first huge sports bar, done out like a classic American cinema, with a few odd touches like TV monitors in the toilets. Tex-Mex menu.

Despite the name, always shows the main football games. Short walk from T-bana Skanstull.

Tre Backar, Tegnérgatan 12–14. Cellar with live music and a cheap bar upstairs. Open 'til midnight. Green tube to Rådmansgatan.

Restaurants

Eating out is expensive. A main meal will cost upwards of 80kr, and three courses with a couple of drinks will top 300kr. As elsewhere in Sweden, the cheapest way to fill up is to take advantage of a lunchtime special. For around 50kr, you'll get a main meal, salad, bread, juice and unlimited amounts of coffee.

Anders LimpBar, Upplandsgatan 2. Salad bar owned by the former AIK, Arsenal and Everton winger. Team shirts and photos from USA '94 hang on the walls, above the counter which serves an acceptable 50kr lunch deal. Limp means 'loaf' in Swedish and when he got a break from the Goodison reserves, the man himself sometimes served up the salad.

Folkhemmet, Renstiernas Gata 30. A fine restaurant with two separate bars that has long attracted custom from all over the city. Charming interior and friendly service. Bus #3 or #46 from Slussen, Bondegatan stop.

Restaurant Pelé, Upplandsgatan 18. Opened in 1970, as a tribute to the man who dazzled Stockholm in '58. Italian owners keep the theme low-key with just one portrait behind the bar. Two big-screen TVs (used sparingly) and samba dancing. Reasonably priced Italian, Swedish and Brazilian food, outstanding Pelé T-shirts for 85kr. Visa accepted. Near T-Centralen.

Glenn Miller Café, Brunnsgatan 21a. Intimate, cosy restaurant with a jazz theme, a modest menu, and occasional live music. Friendly service. Short walk from T-bana Östermalmstorg.

Tre Indier, Åsögatan 92. One of many cheaper Indian restaurants in town, and certainly one of the best. No alcohol served. Tube to Medborgplatsen.

Accommodation

Finding somewhere to stay in Stockholm isn't normally a problem, but it almost certainly won't be cheap.

Hotellcentralen (Jun–Aug open daily 7am–9pm, May & Sep 8am–7pm, Oct–Apr 9am–6pm, ☎08/789 2425) is a booking agency at the Central station which charges a commission of 40kr per hotel room, 15kr per hostel bed if you call into the office. If you phone ahead, the service is free.

For private rooms contact *Hotelljänst* (☎08/104 467), who can normally find something for 300–400kr a night. The *Bed & Breakfast Center* (☎08/730 0003) offers single rooms at 250–350kr, doubles at 400–550kr.

Anno 1647, Mariagränd 3 (☎08/442 1680, fax 08/442 1647, e-mail info.anno@swedenhotels.se). In a 17th-century building (hence the name), this hotel also boasts period furniture. Around 750kr per person, close to the old town.

Bema, Upplandsgatan 13 (☎08/232 675, fax 08/205 338). A short walk from Central station, a small pension done out in the modern Swedish style. From 500kr for a single, 600kr a double.

City Backpackers, Upplandsgatan 2a (☎08/206 920, fax 08/100 464). New, clean youth hostel with kitchen, sauna, cable TV and laundry facilities. Six- or eight-bed rooms for 140–180kr per person. Five minutes from Cityterminalen – turn left up Vasagatan.

Lord Nelson, Västerlånggatan 22 (☎08/5064 0120, fax 08/5064 0130). A beautiful, upmarket hotel in the old town, with a marine theme. Singles from 800kr, doubles from 1,250kr.

Pensionat Oden, Odengatan 38 (☎08/612 4349, fax 08/612 4501). Around 500–750kr per person per night in this small, family-run pension. Book in advance. In Norrmalm, a 15min walk from Cityterminalen. Turn left up Vasagatan and continue straight ahead on Upplandsgatan until you reach Odengatan. Or take a taxi.

Gothenburg

IFK 600   Örgryte 603
GAIS 603

Fans in Gothenburg never tire of telling you that their city is the football capital of Sweden. In contrast to Stockholm, football grounds fit into the environment here, and the locals follow the game with passion and commitment. Perhaps not surprisingly, there were five clubs from the city and surrounding area in the 2000 *Allsvenskan,* as opposed to only two from Sweden's political capital.

As the industrial centre of Sweden in the late 19th century, Gothenburg naturally became the first city to take to football, and the early Swedish competitions were exclusively for Gothenburg clubs. Even when the Gothenburg-based Swedish FA allowed Stockholm clubs to compete, the local sides, in particular Örgryte IS and GAIS, dominated. Sweden's first international (an 11–3 win over the Norwegians in July 1908) took place at Gothenburg's Valhalla stadium.

After World War II, the city's grip on the game weakened. GAIS won their last title in 1954, while Örgryte had to wait until 1985 for their 14th championship. But the failures of the big two allowed IFK Gothenburg to emerge in the Eighties as a new force, not only in the city but in the country as a whole, and in Europe.

In the past couple of years, the revival of those two great old clubs, and the continued presence of nearby BK Häcken and Västra Frölunda in the top flight, has put pressure on IFK, who are no longer considered top dogs in their own city.

Meanwhile, trouble at the Euro 2000 qualifying match against England in September 1998 forced local authorities to review their position as international hosts in the future. All three of Gothenburg's main clubs, IFK, Örgryte and GAIS, play at the old Ullevi stadium (Gamla Ullevi). Next door is the new Ullevi (Nya Ullevi), built for the 1958 World Cup finals. The Nya Ullevi has hosted several internationals, was a venue for Euro '92 and is where IFK play their big European games.

The thrilling fields

🌐 IFK Gothenburg

Gamla Ullevi stadium, Ullevigatan
Capacity 18,000
Colours Blue-and-white striped shirts, blue shorts
League champions 1908, 1910, 1918, 1935, 1942, 1969, 1982–84, 1987, 1990–91, 1993–96
Cup winners 1979, 1982, 1983, 1992
UEFA Cup winners 1982, 1987

While the national team had been consistent performers, Swedish club sides were notoriously weak in European competition – that is, until IFK Gothenburg came along.

The man responsible for turning IFK from just another Swedish part-time outfit into a respected force in European football was Sven Göran Eriksson. He took over the reins in 1979, the year Malmö FF confirmed their status as the country's top club side by reaching the final of the European Cup. In his first season he led the side to a domestic cup win, but it was in 1982 that IFK made their big breakthrough.

After defeating Hamburg 1–0 at the Ullevi in the first leg of the UEFA Cup final, the *Blåvitt* ('*blue-and-whites*') hammered the Germans 3–0 away, with a classic display of counter-attacking football. It was the first time a Swedish side had won anything in Europe. Shortly after the victory, Eriksson joined Benfica, but IFK continued to progress under Gunder Bengtsson and Björn Westerberg.

In 1986 they made the semi-finals of the European Cup, where they lost on penalties to Barcelona. The disappointment didn't last long. In 1987, IFK won the UEFA Cup for the second time, with a victory over Dundee United.

In three Champions' League campaigns during the Nineties, IFK claimed the scalps of Manchester United, FC Porto and AC Milan among others Their success saw fan clubs being set up outside Gothenburg, and the blue-and-white shirt can now be seen in towns and villages all over Sweden.

Although IFK still have players who study or have some part-time work, they are edging closer to becoming a full-time professional club. Cash from the Champions' League has allowed the club to take more players on a full-time, professional basis, and IFK have even bought back some Swedish players from abroad, such as Stefan Pettersson, Stefan Lindqvist and Håkan Mild.

But the club remains incapable of keeping its younger talent. Following the victory over Milan in 1996, winger Jesper Blomqvist swapped shirts permanently, and since then, most of the main transfer activity has been outward. Thomas Ravelli, Niclas Alexandersson, Kennet Andersson, Stefan Rehn and Joachim Björklund, all title-winners with the club during the Nineties, have all now gone.

Perhaps predictably, IFK lost their title, to Halmstad, in 1997. Reine Almqvist replaced Mats Jingblad as coach, but the result was a desperate eighth-place finish in 1998. With the club's youth policy for once failing to come up with the goods, the

board looked to Norway for new signings while contemplating plans to float the club on the stock-exchange and renovate the Gamla Ullevi.

Both those latter projects remain on the drawing board, however, and IFK's change of playing-staff policy has been slow to pay dividends – sixth place was as good as the new-look team could manage in the 1999 *Allsvenskan*, and a penalty shoot-out defeat by Örgryte in the 1999/2000 cup semi-finals would see the club out of the European picture for at least one more season.

Here we go!

Both stadia are a well-signposted 5min walk from the city's Central station.

Just the ticket

Demand for tickets varies enormously depending on the opposition. For many league fixtures at the Galma Ullevi, simply turn up on the day. For bigger games, buy in advance from the box office at the *Scandinavium*, Valhallgatan 1, near the ground. In April 2000, IFK played a home league game at the Nya Ullevi as an experiment, and drew a crowd of 30,000 – the idea is likely to be repeated for some city derbies in the future.

Losing its shape – the Nya Ullevi is seeing progressively less European and international action

Swift half

The most popular meeting place for fans is the **supporters' club building** on Friggagatan 8 (open Tue–Thur midday–6pm and matchdays). There's a souvenir shop here as well as a bar, but after recent problems with their licence, the fans have had to make the place members only. You'll have to be signed in as a guest to get a drink.

Club merchandise

In addition to the supporters' club mentioned above, there is a **club shop** open on matchdays inside the main stand at the Gamla Ullevi.

Ultra culture

IFK's supporters' club is named *Änglarna* ('The Angels'). The group has around 3,500 members. IFK have had problems with hooligans and, following a series of unsavoury incidents, were forced to play their 1996 Champions' League qualifier against Ferencváros in Norrköping.

In print

The two local papers, *Goteborgs-Posten* (12kr) and *Goteborgs-Tidningen* (8kr), offer good coverage of all the Gothenburg clubs. *Rena Rama Blåvitt* fanzine is now no more and has been supplanted by *Milda Makter*.

In the net

The club's official site is at: www.ifkgoteborg.se. It's perhaps the most slick-looking of its kind in Sweden, with impressive graphics and sponsors' logos well to the fore, but in terms of pure content it's disappointing.

The *Änglarna* now have their own website at: www.anglarna.o.se.

Groundhopping

While IFK revitalised football in Gothenburg in the Nineties, the local clubs which dominated the early days of the Swedish league are enjoying something of a renaissance. Nonetheless, crowds of more than a few thousand are still rare unless the opponents are IFK...

Gothenburg essentials

Gothenburg's **Landvetter airport** is 25km east of town, connected to Drottningtorget, next to the central train station, by a *Flygbuss* (every 15–30mins, daily 5am–12.30am, from town 4.30am–11.40pm, journey time 35mins, 45kr). A taxi will cost around 200–250kr. **Ferries** from England arrive at Skandiahamn on Hisingen, connected by a special bus service (30kr) to Nils Ericssonplatsen behind the central train station, from where they depart, 90mins before sailing, from platform V. *Stena Line* ferries from Denmark come in a 20min walk from the city centre. Boats from Germany dock 3km away from town, connected by buses #3 and #86.

The main **train and bus stations** are centrally located next to each other. Although much of the centre – including the journey to the main Ullevi stadia – is pleasantly walkable, the city does have an efficient transport system consisting of eight colour-coded **tram lines** and **buses** (5am–midnight). Single tickets (16kr) are available from the driver, but *Tidpunkten* offices, *Pressbyrån* and *Ja* stands sell *Value Cards* (five rides 50kr, ten 100kr) – press 2 in the machine onboard for each journey, and when transferring press the *byte* button – and **day passes** (40kr, stamp once). Note that day passes are not valid on night transport, which runs Fri–Sat and costs 32kr per ticket from the driver, or four coupons from a Value Card. A *Tourist Card*, including access to tourist sites and museums (but not transport from the airport or Skandiahamn ferry terminal) is 75kr per day. The central **taxi** booking number is ☎031/650 000.

The main **tourist office** is by the canal on Kungsportplatsen 2 (June–Aug daily 9am–8pm; Sept–May Mon–Fri 9am–5pm, Sat & Sun 10am–2pm, ☎031/612 500, fax 031/612 501). There you can find a copy of the *Göteborg Guide*, with bars and restaurant **listings**.

Örgryte IS

Gamla Ullevi, see IFK above
Colours Red shirts, blue shorts
League champions 1896–99, 1902, 1904–07, 1909, 1913, 1926, 1928, 1985
Cup winners 2000

Riding a revival – Örgryte's Johan Anegrund takes off

ÖIS have won just one title since their prewar glory days. When they won the championship in 1985, it was the first time the team had finished in the top three since the Sixties. But there weren't many around to celebrate. The fan base shrank and the club failed to build on their title win – the best players were snapped up by wealthier teams and the side fell into the first-division south in 1991. In 1995, a promising young side won the first-division south title, but they have generally struggled in the premier, having to beat Umeå in the play-offs to retain their status in 1998. That same year, however, they did reach the cup final, losing to Helsingborg on penalties, and in 2000 star striker Marcus Allbäck was the inspiration behind another cup run which culminated in a 2–1 aggregate win over AIK in the final – the club's first silverware in 15 years.

The place to meet up with the ÖIS faithful is the **Berså Bar**, Kungsportsplatsen 5, a convivial bar/restaurant with a dancefloor, a 5min walk from the Gamla Ullevi.

GAIS

Gamla Ullevi, see IFK above
Colours Green-and-black striped shirts, white shorts
League champions 1919, 1922, 1931, 1954
Cup winners 1942

Gothenburg's other pre-war giant, Göteborg Atlet & Idrottsälskap, have won nothing at all since 1954. After spending much of the Eighties in the first division they returned to the top in 1987, and two years later finished third in the league, above IFK. But the 'Mackerels' went back down in 1992 and in 1996 were relegated to the regional league. They bounced back up in 1997, and in 1999 they beat Kalmar FF 3–2 on aggregate in the play-offs to rejoin the *Allsvenskan*. Near the Galma Ullevi, at Stureplatsen 2, is *GAIS City*, a café and souvenir shop where you can buy GAIS golfballs and women's underwear.

Eat, drink, sleep...

Bars and clubs

Like Stockholm, Gothenburg is a costly city in which to spend a night out. If you're feeling flush, the Avenyn and its surrounding streets are crowded with bars, cafés and restaurants. Gothenburg also has an abundance of attractive old coffee houses, tucked away all over the city, and you'll find some cheaper spots in the student areas of Vasaplan and Haga, west of Avenyn.

The local authorities are not currently granting licences to dance clubs, so the nightclub scene is centred on the kind of **discos** you find in hotels.

Babar, Avenyn 29. Huge sports pub, less pretentious than others on Avenyn, with a games section upstairs and a restaurant downstairs. The *Junggrens Café* at nearby #37 is a popular warm-up spot for a night on the town. Both are a 15min walk from Central station.

Kompaniet, Kungsgatan 19. Probably the best of Gothenburg's attempts at providing nightlife, with a well-stocked bar upstairs, a disco downstairs at weekends, and a relaxed crowd. Happy hours and late summer night openings.

O'Leary's, Östra Hamngatan 37. American-style bar with Tex-Mex kitchen and sport on TV. The *Auld Dubliner*, opposite, is the oldest of the city's Irish pubs, having been established in 1870.

Paddingtons, St Pauligatan 1. English pub with a large expat clientele glued to the Sky TV, and the occasional Swedish Liverpool fan. From the train station, take bus #34 or tram #1, #3 or #6 to the Retbergsplatsen.

Restaurants

You may be able to eat slightly more cheaply in Gothenburg than in Stockholm – but not much. As ever, lunchtime set menus are your best chance of tucking into local specialities such as smoked meats and fresh herring at an affordable price.

E.t.c., Vasaplatsen 4. Very sparse, very white, very Swedish, yet there's something homely about the reasonably priced set lunches and friendly service.

Golden Days, Södra Hamngatan 31. Pub and restaurant popular with sports fans due to its large TV screen and special meal deals on big matchdays.

Gyllene Prag, Sveagatan 25. Students hang out here for the cheap Czech food and fine draught Budweiser. From the Central train station, take tram #1 or #2 to Linnéplatsen.

Restaurant Frågetecken, Södra Vagan 20. Just off Götaplatsen, the 'Question Mark' features Balkan specialities served up in relaxed surroundings despite the constant bustle of visitors. A little pricy, but not prohibitively so.

Accommodation

The main **tourist office** (see *Essentials*) offers the Gothenburg Package, which includes a hotel, breakfast and the Gothenburg Card for around 400kr per person, daily June–Aug and weekends all year round. A cheaper alternative is to ask them to find you a **private room** – expect to pay around 200kr per person per night.

City Hotel, Lorensbergsgatan 6 (☎031/708 4000, fax 031/708 4002). Bang next to the Avenyn and similarly well-suited to a short stagger home from the nightlife. Between 250kr and 350kr per person.

Excelsior, Karl Gustavsgatan 7 (☎031/175 435, fax 031/175 439). Where Greta Garbo and Ingrid Bergman both stayed, and rarely touched since then. Around 1,300kr a double, 900kr a single, with a drop in rates at weekends. Near Avenyn.

Kvibergs Vandrarhem, Kvibergsvägen 5 (☎031/435 055, fax 031/432 650). Hostel open all year round, conveniently located in the old town, a short journey by tram #6 or #7 from Central Station. Four beds in each room at about 120kr each, plus sheet rental.

Switzerland

SFV/ASF, Haus des Fussballs, Postfach CH-3000 Berne 15
☎031/950 8111   Fax 031/950 8181   E-mail sfv.asf@football.ch

League champions St Gallen   **Cup winners** FC Zürich   **Promoted** FC Sion
Relegated Delémont

European participants 2000/01 St Gallen (UCL qualifiers); FC Basle, FC Zürich,
Lausanne-Sports (UEFA Cup); FC Lucerne, Neuchâtel Xamax (Intertoto Cup)

Switzerland is a country of foot-balling contradictions. Its position in the centre of Europe makes it home to the game's most powerful organisations, yet its national team have been permanent also-rans. It is the continent's most affluent country, yet even its leading football clubs play in shabby stadia, in front of a few thousand souls, rarely able to raise their game sufficiently to worry the European elite. A nation which appears to have everything it needs for a thriving football scene seems curiously uninterested in the world's most ardently followed professional sport.

On paper, it all looks great. Switzerland's stable economy means there are plenty of potential corporate sponsors for the game. A country sandwiched between a number of soccer hotbeds and made up of three of the continent's top footballing ethnic groups – Germans, Italians and French – should produce top-class players. The national team should be able to marry the discipline of the Germans with the tactical awareness of the Italians and the flair of the French. Yet somehow, it just doesn't happen.

Perhaps it is Switzerland's very stability – no wars, no revolutions, no economic hardship to escape from – which explain the bland character of the nation's football. The game here is not an outlet for frustrated passions as it is in so many countries, but simply one pastime among others – and one which, unlike winter sports, doesn't yield Olympic gold medals. The multi-ethnic state, rather than creating a delicious mix of playing and supporting styles, encourages fans in Zürich to tune into SAT1 to watch Borussia Dortmund rather than follow a local side, while down in the Italian-speaking region of Ticino, supporters nip across the border to Turin to watch Juventus.

Yet despite the absence of a popular football culture, Switzerland is, officially at least, the home of the game. FIFA, world football's governing body, are up in the hills overlooking their bank account in Zürich, while their European equivalents UEFA are on the shores of Lake Geneva in Nyon. It's not just the country's smooth, discreet banking system and the strength of the Swiss franc that persuaded these bodies to set up home in the confederation – Switzerland took an early and active role in the organisation of the game on the continent, and was one of the seven founding members of FIFA.

According to the historians, the first organised games of association football in continental Europe took place in Switzerland in the 1850s, between teams of English and Swiss students. FC St Gallen, the oldest Swiss club still in existence, were founded in 1879, and seven years later the country's most successful and best-known team, Grasshopper Club, were formed in Zürich. Indeed most of the teams currently in the top flight of Swiss football were formed before the turn of the century, and a national championship, played between the winners of three regional leagues, began in 1897, at a time when many European countries were still learning the rules from visiting English engineers. Three of the leading teams of the day – Zürich's

Basics

Citizens of many EU countries require only an identity card for entry into Switzerland, but Britons require a **full passport**, as do Americans, Canadians, Australians and New Zealanders.

The Swiss currency is the **Swiss Franc** (Sfr), divided into 100 centimes (c), the latter referred to as *Rappen* in some German-speaking areas. There are coins for 5c, 10c, 20c, 50c and Sfr1, Sfr2 and Sfr5, along with notes for Sfr10, Sfr20, Sfr50, Sfr100, Sfr500 and Sfr1000. Banks are generally open Mon–Fri 8.30am–4.30pm. Credit-card cash machines are widespread. Exchange rates tend to be best in banks but you'll also find exchange offices in major train stations and at post offices. The current rate is around Sfr2.25 to £1.

Public telephones are easy to find and accept 10c, 20c, 50c, Sfr1 and Sfr5 coins as well as phone cards, which are available at post offices and newsstands for Sfr10 and Sfr20. International calls can be made from almost all street phones – dial 00 and then the country code. Cheap rates apply 6am–8am, 5pm–7pm and 9pm–midnight, and even cheaper ones midnight–6am. From outside the country, the code for Switzerland is 41 – add 1 for Zürich, 22 for Geneva.

Switzerland has a superb **public transport** system – fast, integrated, clean and environmentally friendly. The state train company, SBB/CFF, covers all the main inter-city routes while private firms run mountain railways to smaller, rural destinations, and buses pick up the slack in the most remote areas. Fares are calculated per kilometre – a 100km journey costs Sfr30. A second-class return from Zürich to Geneva is Sfr128.

The *Swiss Pass*, available at all train stations, offers four-day, eight-day and 15-day options at Sfr200, Sfr250 and Sfr290 respectively. In addition to state railways, the Pass entitles you to travel free on lake steamers, most postbuses and bus/tram networks in major cities. A cheaper option, and more sensible if you'll be doing only a limited amount of travelling, is the *Half Fare Card*. This costs Sfr85, is valid for a month and gives a fifty percent discount on all trains, buses and lake ferries.Tourist information centres (*Verkehrsbüro* or *Office du Tourisme*) are often located close to stations.

Grasshopper, Servette of Geneva and Berne's Young Boys – would go on to take more than 50 titles between them, as Swiss neutrality ensured that the domestic league was played through both World Wars.

Internationally, the Swiss gained plenty of experience, if not success, in *ad hoc* friendlies – mostly against neighbouring Austria, Italy and Germany – from 1905. They made their competitive debut at the 1924 Paris Olympics, and won the silver medal, losing the final to Uruguay after beating Czechoslovakia, Italy and Sweden. In their semi-final over the Swedes, both goals were scored by Max Abegglen – who together with younger brother André would score more than 60 goals for Switzerland prior to World War II.

Yet the Swiss failed to build on this promising start. They took part in all six of the International Cup competitions between 1928 and 1960, finishing last in each of them. Swiss club sides had a similar lack of success in the Mitropa Cup.

After Austria had given them several lessons on the field, the Swiss FA decided to turn to an Austrian to coach their national team. In 1937, Karl Rappan took the reins for the first of four spells in charge which were to span four eventful decades. Rappan's approach was pragmatic – if the Swiss were to compete on the international stage, they would have to do so through strength of numbers in defence.

With its use of a sweeper and wingers who tracked back to defend, Rappan's so-called *verrou* ('Bolt') system was twenty years ahead of its time. The formation laid the groundwork for *catenaccio* and other sweeper systems, and also introduced the concept of the counter-attack. Up until the Bolt, most football tactics were concerned with the line-up of the attacking players; Rappan brought tactics to defensive and midfield play.

Rappan was not just a shrewd tactician, he was a great motivator, imbuing a side that had suffered a decade of defeats with new-found confidence. At the 1938 World Cup, Switzerland reached the quarter-finals with a 4–2 win over Germany, before losing 2–0 to Hungary.

Post-war Swiss football was given the ideal chance to make an impression when the country was awarded the 1954 World Cup finals. Stadia across the land were upgraded and two wins over Italy earned the hosts a quarter-final spot. Matched against their old rivals Austria, Switzerland took the field with their popular captain and centre-half Roger Bocquet unfit, but determined to play. They then went 3–0 up before the Alpine sun played havoc, Bocquet lost concentration, and Austria scored five in seven minutes – they went on to win 7–5.

The Swiss went on to qualify for the finals in 1962 and 1966, to make little impact, after which it would be 28 years before they returned to the World Cup stage. The Seventies and Eighties were a grim time for Swiss football, brightened only by a modest improvement in the form shown by the nation's clubs in European competition. FC Zürich repeated their 1959 run to the semi-finals of the European Cup when they reached the same stage in 1977. A year later their city rivals Grasshoppers reached the last four of the UEFA Cup.

Again, it took a foreign influence to put some pride back into Swiss football. In 1989, former West German international Uli Stielike took over as national-team

Friendly action – Switzerland outplay Germany, 2000

coach and, although he failed to take his team to either Italia '90 or Euro '92, he laid the foundations for the best postwar Swiss side, which reached the peak of its powers when Roy Hodgson took over from Stielike in 1991.

Hodgson, a former lower-division player in England, had enjoyed a successful spell as a coach in Sweden before taking charge of Swiss side Xamax Neuchâtel. Although unknown in his homeland he was respected in Switzerland and, after his appointment as national-team coach, he was to become a hero as crucial victories over Scotland and Italy earned the Swiss a place at USA '94.

The side included several players based in the German *Bundesliga*. Alain Sutter, the ponytailed midfield creator; Italian-born anchorman Ciriaco Sforza; and the formidable front pairing of Stéphane Chapuisat and Adrian Knup all brought their major-league experience to bear on a team that had previously lacked the conviction to turn its potential into achievement.

In the States, the Swiss survived a tough opener by drawing against the hosts, then mounted a stunning 4–1 win over Romania before bowing out in the second round to an effervescent Spain. Hodgson guided the same squad past Sweden and Hungary and on to Euro '96, but he was to miss out on a homecoming. Having accepted a coaching post at Internazionale, the Englishman felt he could combine his rôles at club and international levels. The Swiss FA thought otherwise, dismissed Hodgson, and replaced him with Artur Jorge, who immediately set about trying to turn a settled squad and strategy upside-down.

In England, drawn in a tough group with the hosts, Scotland and Holland, the Swiss finished bottom after scoring only once – from the penalty spot – in three matches.

Despite Jorge's post-tournament sacking and the appointment of the more sympathetic Rolf Fringer, Switzerland failed to qualify for France '98, defeats in Azerbaijan and at home to Finland proving fatal in a relatively easy group. The Swiss had plunged from third in the FIFA world rankings in 1994 to 73rd by 1997. Frenchman Gilbert Gress replaced Fringer, but failed to take Switzerland to Euro 2000, his team finishing level on points with Denmark behind Italy, but losing out on their head-to-head record. Gress turned down a contract extension, and his assistant Hans-Peter Zaugg, was appointed as a caretaker, doing well enough in friendly games – against Germany in particular – to be considered the logical man to take over.

But the Swiss FA, to the anger of local media and the surprise of the players, chose Argentine Enzo Trossero, who had taken Sion to the title in 1992 but then returned to his homeland, as the man to take on Yugoslavia, Russia and Slovenia in Switzerland's World Cup qualifying group. Meanwhile, the country's leading club,

Grasshoppers, continued to under-achieve, their latest coaching flop being Roy Hodgson who quit after nine months of poor performances and tabloid revelations about his personal life. But while the Swiss league seems incapable of providing quality football, it at least managed some romance in 2000, when St Gallen won their first title for 96 years. With an annual budget of only £1.5million and a stadium which holds just 11,300, they pipped Christian Gross' FC Basle to the title and finished well clear of Servette, despite the latter's cash injection from pay-TV company Canal Plus.

But with the few world-class players the country produces still turning their backs on their homeland and the national side failing to get close to the standards reached under Hodgson, Swiss fans continue to look enviously across their borders.

Essential vocabulary
French
Hello *Bonjour*
Goodbye *Au revoir*
Yes *Oui*
No *Non*
Two beers, please *Deux demis, s'il vous plaît*
Thank you *Merci*
Men's *Hommes*
Women's *Dames*
Where is the stadium? *Où est le stade?*
What is the score? *Où en sommes-nous?*
Referee *L'arbitre*
Offside *Hors jeu*

German
Hello *Guten Tag*
Goodbye *Auf wiedersehen*
Yes *Ja*
No *Nein*
Two beers, please *Zwei Bier, bitte*
Thank you *Danke*
Men's *Herren*
Women's *Damen*
Where is the stadium? *Wo ist das Stadion?*
What's the score? *Wie steht's?*
Referee *Schiedsrichter*
Offside *Abseits*

Match practice

A visit to a Swiss league game is a relaxing experience. Turning up two minutes before kick-off? Don't worry. You can still choose the best seat in the ground and, once ensconced there, munch on a sausage or casually sip a beer. You may well see local fans getting worked up about what's going on before them, but they are never abusive – a frustrated stamp of the feet or smack of hand on thigh is all the aggression you'll see. Swiss sports fans, it seems, save their energy for whooping and ringing cowbells on the piste.

The Swiss campaign runs from mid-July to early June the following year, finishing a month earlier if the Swiss national side is involved in the World Cup or European Championship finals. There is a lengthy winter break from early December to late February, when the Swiss can concentrate on their favourite sports: ice-hockey and skiing. There are indoor tournaments in January, and 'warm-up' friendlies for the spring season start in early February.

Games take place on Saturday evenings at 7.30pm (with a couple at 5.30pm), and switch to 2.30pm on Sunday afternoons either side of the winter break. Each weekend also sees a live TV game kicking-off at around 4pm on either Saturday or Sunday.

A different league

In the autumn half of the season, 12 teams compete in what's known as National League A, playing each other twice. The top eight sides at Christmas then have their points totals halved and play each other twice again in the second half of the season for the title and UEFA Cup places. This championship group is known as the *Finalrunde*. Meanwhile, the bottom four sides from the pre-Christmas NLA are 'relegated' to spend the spring season playing-off against the top four sides 'promoted' from the 12-team NLB; all pre-Christmas points are annulled, and the top four teams at the end of the campaign have the privilege of rejoining the NLA the following season.

Although this league structure means there is an exciting relegation dogfight in December, the title race only becomes interesting in spring, and demotion to the post-Christmas *Aufstiegsrunde* sounds the death-knell of any NLA team's season.

Every year the Swiss FA considers scrapping this heavily criticised league structure, which has been in place for more than a decade. Mid-ranking clubs complain that they must permanently live with the threat of relegation, while teams involved in Europe mutter darkly about having to play too many games.

Up for the cup

The Swiss cup final is a one-off affair, which as from 2001 will be played at the new national stadium being built in Basle to replace Berne's now-defunct Wankdorf. NLA clubs don't join until the last-32 stage. Ties are all single matches, which go to extra time at the end of 90 minutes, then penalties if the teams are still level.

No-one gets too excited about the cup until the final itself – it's not uncommon, even up to the quarter-final stage, to see ties on tiny provincial grounds (the lower-division side is always given home advantage up to the semi-finals) where fans are standing behind a rope with their dogs on leads.

Just the ticket

Admission prices are on the high side. The cheapest places are behind each goal at around Sfr15, the lower level being called an *Estrade* in German-speaking areas, *pelouse* in French ones. A seat in the stand will be in the range Sfr25–35.

Most clubs issue a matchday programme, either free of charge or for a (relatively) nominal fee.

Half-time

Along with the *bratwurst*, served with a *bürli*, or tooth-achingly crisp bread roll, the Swiss have their own, fatter sausage, the *servelat*. Chips with mayonnaise are preferred in French-speaking areas. Other popular match-time treats include sugary sweets and glazed almonds. Grills are often set up around grounds, and beer is normally available inside, where you will also usually find a pleasant bar/restaurant.

The back page

At one time, French- and German-speaking parts of Switzerland each had their own football publication. Now, sadly, the German *Sport* has folded due to lack of cash, leaving fans with the French *Match Mag* (Tuesdays, Sfr4.50), a glossy colour job, with reasonable foreign coverage and news from around the French-speaking region.

The Zürich daily papers *Tages Anzeiger* and *Neue Zürcher Zeitung* both have decent sports sections.

Action replay

German-based station SAT1 generally shows live league games at 4pm on Saturdays and 4.15pm on Sundays. State network DRS squeezes in around the edges with live reports from the Friday night game on its SF2 channel; *Sport Aktuell* highlights at 10–10.30pm on Saturdays on SF1; and the better-established highlights show *Sportpanorama* at 7.30pm on Sundays, also on SF1. The channel has added a Monday highlights show at 10.30pm on SF2, showing goals from around Europe.

Ultra culture

You might see the odd ultra-style banner proclaiming the presence of some *Blue Boys* gang or other, but those behind it will most likely be enthusiastic youngsters whose parents expect they will soon grow out of it. Friendly, multi-lingual Swiss fans pride themselves on their sporting behaviour and this is definitely one country where you can feel safe wherever you are sitting.

The lack of a visible fan culture can partly be blamed on the country's small Italian-speaking region not having a team of note (Lugano's last title win was in 1949) and the main city in the German-speaking region, Zürich, having the country's most successful club but an affluent, middle-class following.

Nearby St Gallen have more passion but nowhere near the numbers. One fan group challenging the status quo are those of FC Basle, whose various groups – the *Dragons, Bebbi, Mumpf* and *Orgesiss* – create the hottest atmosphere in the land. Whether this survives the club's move from its English-style St Jakob ('Joggeli') ground to the new all-purpose national arena in 2001 remains to be seen.

In the French-speaking alais region, FC Sion have their own peculiar following, cowbells and all, whose ringing may also be heard at Swiss national games. ('Hopp Schwiiz!' – as the saying goes.)

In the net

Switzerland's national FA has an official website at: www.football.ch. You've a choice of French and German language, and there are the latest stats and facts on the national team and domestic club competitions, but all in all it's not the greatest site of its type.

The unofficial site *SwissFoot* is a straightforward source of news and stats in French at: www.multimania.com/swissfoot. And there's an alternative links-and-stats site, with German and English options, at: www.vereine.ch/sport/fb/ch.

Zürich

Arriving at Zürich's main train station, you're soon hit by adverts promoting weekend travel offers for football fans – to see *Bundesliga* games in nearby Munich and Stuttgart. Meanwhile, crowds at the city's two clubs, Grasshoppers and FC Zürich, both with a century of tradition behind them, barely scrape five figures.

Yet this chic, wealthy city does have a strong footballing history, albeit an often well-concealed one. British students formed Grasshopper-Club back in 1886. Other local teams were soon set up, mainly with expat members, including the Anglo-American Football Club of Zürich, who won the second of the annual regional play-offs and provided most of the players for Switzerland's first unofficial match, against a South Germany XI in 1898.

The other three of the first four titles went to Grasshoppers, 'GC', who would become the country's most successful club. Their proud achievements and easy afflu-

ence contrast strongly with city rivals FC Zürich, formed from other local teams into a homely, working-class outfit that also won an early title in 1902.

By now Switzerland was firmly involved in developing the game on the continent, and its neutral position and central location persuaded the original seven members of the game's administrative body, FIFA, to base their office in Zürich. Stuck out in the hilly south-east suburb of Hirslanden (tram #3 or #15 from the station, or #8 from Paradeplatz, to the terminus at Klusplatz), FIFA's extensive library can be visited by appointment (☎01/384 9595), although most visitors remain firmly unimpressed by the drab nature of the building, given its global importance.

The heady political and cosmopolitan mix in Zürich either side of World War II allowed for a colourful football scene in the city. Young Fellows Zürich once boasted Vujadin Boskov and Sándor Kocsis

When the stars came out – Grasshoppers' nights of UCL action are a distant memory now

in their ranks – the club won the cup in 1936 – while Red Star Zürich, recently revived sufficiently to make a cup semi-final against Grasshoppers in 1999, also enjoyed their best period at this time.

A handful of games were played at the Hardturm when Switzerland hosted the 1954 World Cup – the Letzigrund was not suitable – but slowly the city settled down to the regular, gentle rivalry between GC and FCZ. The Swiss national team rarely deign to appear here these days, despite an excellent record at the Hardturm.

In the Nineties, a generation of fans grew up with GC's success and European progress, but the club still doesn't quite generate the kind of passions seen at Sion, or the kind of away support enjoyed by FC Basle. Meanwhile, FCZ have maintained a European presence of their own over the past couple of seasons, breathing fresh life into their eccentric home ground.

The thrilling fields

Grasshoppers

Hardturm stadium, Hardturmstrasse 321
Capacity 17,000 (16,000 seated)
Colours Blue-and-white halved shirts, white shorts
League champions 1900–01, 1905, 1921, 1927–28, 1931, 1937, 1939, 1942–43, 1945, 1952, 1956, 1971, 1978, 1982–84, 1990–91, 1995–96, 1998
Cup winners 1926, 1932, 1934, 1937–38, 1940–43, 1946, 1952, 1956, 1983, 1988–90, 1994

If one team are capable of making the leap from sleepy, Swiss semi-professionalism to the European soccer elite, then Grasshopper Club of Zürich are that team. Grasshoppers are the most popular club in the city and the most unpopular in the rest of the country, where they are seen as the epitome of Zürich's bourgeois wealth. They are the most successful club in Swiss history with 25 league titles and 18 cup wins to their credit. They have also been the only Swiss club to make a lasting impression in Europe. Their recent appearances in the Champions' League surprised many – although never looking likely to get near the final, the team impressed with their organisation and occasionally attractive football.

'GC' won the first Swiss championship final in 1898, and have been a near constant presence in the top rank ever since. Most of the key players in prewar Swiss national sides were Grasshoppers', among them the Abegglen brothers, Max and André. At European level, the club competed regularly in the tough Mitropa Cup competition, peaking with a quarter-final appearance in 1937.

After picking up Swiss titles at will in the early postwar period, GC hit a dry patch, failing to win a single domestic honour between 1957 and 1970. The suffering was made worse by the fact that across the city, FC Zürich were enjoying a revival.

A championship win in 1970 restored the faith of the fans, but it wasn't until 1978 that a superb UEFA Cup run laid the foundations for the revitalisation of the club. Inter Bratislava and Dynamo Tblisi were defeated to set up a quarter-final with Eintracht Frankfurt, at which Switzerland's traditional footballing inferiority complex *vis à vis* the Germans was swept aside, GC winning on away goals. In the semi-final they beat Bastia of France 3–2 in Zürich, but a 1–0 defeat in Corsica cost them a place in the final.

Four titles and three cup wins then followed in the Eighties, and the club's domination of the Swiss game stretched almost uninterrupted to the end of the Nineties. Grasshoppers' position was greatly enhanced by Champions' League qualification in 1995 and 1996, which brought Ajax and Real Madrid – as well as considerable amounts of cash – to the Hardturm. The team that coach Christian Gross built – Ciriaco Sforza, Alain Sutter and Giovane Elber among the stars – would

Zürich essentials

A train service connects **Zürich's aiport** at Kloten, 10km north of town, to the central Hauptbahnhof (every 15mins, 5.30am–midnight, journey time 10mins, Sfr6). At weekends, the 24-hour city transport pass (Sfr7.20) also includes the airport.

Zürich's **transport system** (5.30am-midnight) consists of S-Bahn trains, buses and trams – 24-hour passes and tickets for central zone 10, enough for most visitors' needs, are available from blue machines at stops or platforms. A journey of less than five stops, a *kurzstrecke*, is Sfr2.20, one within zone 10 is Sfr3.60 – punch tickets in the machine before boarding. **Night buses** run on major routes from the centre on Friday and Saturday nights, midnight–2am, pay Sfr6 onboard.

The two main taxi firms, *Taxi 2000* (☎01/444 4444) and *Züri Taxi* (☎01/222 2222), have a standing charge of Sfr6 plus Sfr3 per km, credit cards accepted.

The main **tourist office** is in the Hauptbahnhof (open Apr–Oct Mon–Fri 8.30am–8.30pm, Sat–Sun 8.30am–6.30pm, Nov–Mar Mon–Fri 8.30am–7pm, Sat–Sun 9am–6.30pm, ☎01/215 4000, fax 01/215 4044). There you'll find copies of the bi-monthly *Zürich Next* culture guide. The Friday edition of the *Tages Anzeiger* newspaper carries the *Züritipp* listings supplement, while *Toaster* (monthly, Sfr3) has club information for the whole country on two pages.

all flee the nest, as did Gross himself, for Tottenham, in November 1997. He was replaced by former national-team coach Rolf Fringer, and with the ever-prolific striker Kubi Türkyilmaz carrying on where Viorel Moldovan had left off, GC claimed their title back from Sion with a 16-point margin over the rest in 1998.

In 1998/99, the rebuilding of the Hardturm's west stand caused severe flooding on the pitch, and Grasshoppers were forced to play their home games in the autumn season at FCZ's Letzigrund. More crucially, the team were knocked out of the Champions' League qualifiers by Galatasaray, and although a decent UEFA Cup run – assisted by Fiorentina's expulsion after the Salerno firework-throwing incident – then ensued, the loss of Champions' League income prompted an unprecedented cashflow crisis.

While a group of directors set about engineering a management buyout to stave off insolvency, new coach Roger Hegi's side finished level with Servette at the top of the league, but lost their title on points earned during the autumn season. Then, after thrashing Red Star 7–0 in the semi-finals, they also lost the cup final, 2–0 to Lausanne-Sports.

In the close season, the new board appointed Roy Hodgson as coach for 1999/2000, but neither his experience nor a return to the club's own stadium was enough to lift the malaise, and Grasshoppers could manage no better than a meek fourth-place finish. Hodgson's former assistant, Walter Gruetes, assumed control before the campaign was over, but needs to act quickly if his charges are going to regain their status as Switzerland's natural born leaders.

Here we go!

The ground is a 15min ride on tram #4 from the Hauptbahnhof, direction Werdhölzli. Get off at the **Sportplatz Hardturm** stop.

Just the ticket

Average gates for domestic games are low, so there should be no problem turning up just before kick-off. The main **ticket offices** are on Hardturmstrasse, with entrances at each corner. The cheapest seats are behind each goal – with the GC fans in the *Tribüne Ost* (stand Sfr25, lower-level *estrade* Sfr15), or with the away fans through gates #3 and #4 opposite in the west stand. The *Estrade Süd* has covered (Sfr20) and uncovered (Sfr15) places, while the *Tribüne* with numbered seats at Sfr35; the *Nord* has seats at the same price. Note that prices increase dramatically for European ties.

Tickets go on sale at least a week in advance at the club office in the *Tribüne Süd* (open Mon–Fri 9am–midday, 2–6pm, most credit cards, ☎01/447 4646).

Swift half

As the stadium is bounded by a river, railway lines and an industrial zone, the only place for bars is the small stretch of Hardturmstrasse opposite the ground by the tram stop. The *Restaurant Neues Stadion* at #404 would do fine, except that it closes Saturday afternoons and Sundays, leaving just the *Hobo High Wayfood Number One* at #394, a small US-style diner with lovingly prepared sandwiches and beer, as the only pre-match option.

There is no alcohol on sale at the canteenstyle *Café Tribune Nord* under the Hardturm's north stand, nor at the stalls dotted around the ground. But look on the bright side. For European games, the club goes out of its way to offer fans some regional cuisine appropriate to the visiting side. The *paella* for Real Madrid in 1996 was a great success, but a year later Scots fans came to the Hardturm to find the local caterers obviously short of haggis and neeps, and were confronted instead with a 'Rangers Stew' strongly reminiscent of a British school dinner of the mid-Seventies.

Club merchandise

The main *Fan-Shop Kiosk* (open Mon–Fri 2–5pm and on matchdays) is under the *Tribüne Süd*, with a smaller one, open matchdays only, at the corner of the *Tribüne Nord* on Hardturmstrasse.

Ultra culture

The *Hardturm Front* in the east stand do make a noise, but it is often drowned out by the opposition chants of 'Can you see the Hoppers hop?' Official supporters' groups include *Die Heugümper*, the *Blue Lions* and the *Blue-White Hoppers*.

In print

GCZ Magazin (fortnightly, Sfr2) is a comprehensive review/programme available at the ground on matchdays.

In the net

The **official website** is at: www.gcz.ch. Its rather text-heavy homepage has all the latest news and match reports, and you can buy tickets and merchandise online, but while it is efficient enough, this is an unremarkable site overall.

For more verve, the *Blue-White Bulldogs* have a site at: sport.freepage.de/cgi-bin/feets/freepage_ext/41030x030A/rewrite/bulldogs/index.html. Like the official version, it's in German only for the time being.

🌐 FC Zürich

Letzigrund stadium, Herdenstrasse 47
Capacity 23,500 (11,500 seated)
Colours Blue-and-white striped shirts, blue shorts
League champions 1902, 1924, 1963, 1966, 1968, 1974–76, 1981
Cup winners 1966, 1970, 1972, 1973, 1976, 2000

FC Zürich are the club from the wrong side of the tracks – literally. Exactly a kilometre over the main Zürich-Basle railway line from Grasshoppers, FCZ have generally played second-fiddle to their more affluent neighbours, save for two short periods in the Sixties and Seventies.

They were formed in 1896 out of a merger of three local clubs, FC Turicum, FC Excelsior and FC Viktoria. The aim was to unite in order to challenge the dominance of Grasshoppers, but while the club remained true to their working-class roots, only two titles came their way in the seven decades that followed their foundation.

It was the arrival of wandering star forward Ladislav Kubala in the twilight of his career that instigated FCZ's post-war revival in the early Sixties. The club won the title in 1963, then reached the semifinals of the European Cup, where they were hammered 8–1 on aggregate by Real Madrid. Two young forwards, Roger Quentin and Köbi Kühn, led FCZ to a domestic double in 1966 before playing for Switzerland in that year's World Cup, and to another title two years later. Kühn, capped 63 times by his country, was still playing at the club when in 1976/77, when they reached another European Cup semi-final, losing 6–1 on aggregate to eventual winners Liverpool.

FCZ's last title came in 1981, when world athletics records were being set at the club's unusual Letzigrund stadium, with its fast running track and quirky, inwardly sloping roofing – while it may result in hindered views for some fans, the arena's design provides a handy summer money-spinner for the club.

For the past few years, FCZ have been propped up by construction millionaire Sven Hotz, whose smartest move was the hiring of former Grasshoppers star Raimondo Ponte as coach in 1995. Although originally unpopular with the fans, Ponte was able to galvanise talents like Sweden's Thomas Brolin, Nigeria's Rachidi Yekini and a prolific young striker from Burundi, Shabani Nonda. With Nonda scoring a hatful of goals, and Swiss international Marc Hodel keeping things steady at the back, FCZ enjoyed their best season for over a decade in 1997/98, finishing fourth.

Nonda was sold to Rennes in the following pre-season, but FCZ matched Grasshopper's achievements in the 1998/99 UEFA Cup, beating Celtic 5–3 on aggregate in the second round before going out to Roma after conceding a dubious injury-time penalty in Italy.

In the 1999/2000 version of the same competition, the two Zürich clubs again matched each other, and there was perhaps more honour in FCZ's second-round defeat by a resurgent Newcastle than in Grasshoppers' loss to Slavia Prague at the same stage. Domestically, however, the team suffered 'relegation' from the NLA in December, and Hotz lost patience with Ponte, signing former national-team coach Gilbert Gress to replace him. Under Gress the team finished third in the spring promotion group to regain their NLA place for 2000/01, and also reached the Swiss cup final, where goals from Georgian

Gocha Jamarauli and South Africa's Shaun Bartlett forced a 2–2 draw with Switzerland's cup specialists, Lausanne. FCZ then scored three penalties in the shoot-out, while goalkeeper Marco Pascolo saved two of Lausanne's – giving the Letzigrund its first silverware for 19 years.

Here we go!

Letzigraben has its own tram stop on the #2 route. From the train station, take tram #14 (direction Triemli) four stops to Stauffacher, then change onto the #2, coming from Paradeplatz in the direction Farbhof. If you've just missed a #14, then take a #6, #7, #11 or #13 from the station to Paradeplatz, and change there. Allow 25mins for the whole journey.

Just the ticket

You'll pay Sfr30 for a seat in either of the main east or west stands, Sfr15 for a place on those strange terraces. The main **ticket offices** are behind the two stands. The home end is the *Südtribüne*, accessed through entrances #3 and

Cup hero – Pascolo won the cup for FCZ

#4 along Badnerstrasse, while away fans go in the *Nordtribüne*, through entrance #2 on the corner of Herdernstrasse and Baslerstrasse. The *Osttribüne*, nearest the tram stop along Herdernstrasse, allows access to the *Klubraum*, while the *Westtribüne* has a lower *Estrade* section below the press and VIP area.

Note that plans are currently on the drawing board for FCZ and Grasshoppers to share a new stadium, but it will be at least two years before these come to fruition.

Swift half

The main pre-match bar is the **Restaurant Schlachthof**, by the slaughterhouse, on the corner of Herdernstrasse and Baslerstrasse. Football pennants and a strange collection of flags and hunting horns decorate this unpretentious bar/restaurant, with a grill outside. The **Zic-Zac Rock Garden**, diagonally opposite, is an ornate hostelry with a well-heeled clientele tucking into Sunday brunches, and a beer tent for the masses outside.

Inside the ground, under the *Westtribüne* you'll find the **Café Letzigrund**, a self-service bar/canteen with the stadium's history displayed on its walls. Alternatively, the **Klubraum**, between the *Süd*- and *Osttribüne*, is a pleasant bar with a charmingly dreadful painting of the 1973 cup-winning side.

Ultra culture

The **Zürcher Südkurve** and **FCZ Tigers** fill the east end of the *Stehplatz Süd*, producing a communal bark of '*Ef-Tse-Tsett!*' every ten minutes, and la-la-laing to the tune of *Brazil* whenever Brazilian striker Lima Francisco makes a run.

In print

The **FCZ Magazin** (Sfr2) is issued for every home game, on sale by the ticket offices. The official fan club produce a bimonthly fanzine, **Echo Vom Letzi** (Sfr2).

In the net

The club's **official site** is not as flashy as the GC equivalent, but has more in the way of meaningful content, at: www.fcz.ch. Elsewhere you can meet the **Südkurve** mob at their own site at: www.suedkurve.com. This is an excellent site with team news, a picture gallery, and match reports collated from all the local newspapers and magazines – German only, alas.

Eat, drink, sleep…

Bars and clubs

As if to celebrate the country's duality, the Swiss sink wine and beer in equal quantities, the latter generally the strong *Hürlimann* at Sfr6 a glass (*Stange*). Swiss nightlife centres on Zürich, where a recent relaxation of the **licensing laws** has seen a club culture spring up, mostly around Langstrasse, behind the station. For information, check the flyers in *Zap*, across the river at Zähringerstrasse 47, leading from the station bridge to Niederdorfstrasse, a haven of late bars.

Dörfli, Niederdorfstrasse 68. A classic nighthawks' bar, with a DJ spinning Fifties tunes to the regulars passed out on the counter – maybe it was the Hürlimann at Sfr4 a throw.

Nacht Café, Münstergasse 26. Former site of the *Cabaret Voltaire*, now a hip but welcoming designer bar with a dance club upstairs. The **Casa Bar** at #20 also attracts a cool crowd.

Oxa, Andreasstrasse 70. Just north of the centre at Oerlikon (regular quick train service from the main station) is Zürich's best dance club, from Fridays at 11pm through to Sundays at noon, entrance around Sfr20–25. Four floors of action including a chill-out garden at the top.

Rote Fabrik, Seestrasse 395. A converted squat still attracting an alternative crowd with its varied programme of DJ nights and live music. Decent cheap food and drink.

Züri Bar, Niederdorfstrasse 26. Bar with a beautiful interior, set off by framed shots of FCZ's first team and souvenir evidence of Celtic's recent visit. Next door to the tattooed, the pierced and the pounding of the two-floor **Kon-Tiki**, with its smoochy upstairs wine bar.

Restaurants

Swiss food is traditional **peasant fare** of cheese, meat and potatoes which has kept generations yomping up and down mountains. Staples include *rösti*, hash brown patties with cheese or bacon topping; *raclette*, cheese and jacket potato; and *geschnetzeltes*, veal in cream sauce.

Restaurants in Zürich can be expensive, so better to eat in a pub or beer-hall, or have your main meal at lunchtime – look out for a *Tagesmenü*, a set lunch for between Sfr15 and Sfr20, on offer in many central places.

Bar Bistrot Heugumper, Waaggasse 4. *Heugumper* is German for Grasshopper and this place is owned by the club. Upstairs is for officials only; downstairs is open to the public. Apart from the green grasshopper on the wall outside, there is no football theme to this rather expensive eaterie, and you're more likely to find bankers here than kids in blue-and-white halves. In the centre of town, just off the Bahnhofstrasse, opposite the Paradeplatz.

Johanntes Brasserie, Niederdorfstrasse 70. Large, wood-appointed *Stube* serving local dishes at Sfr20–25, with a separate bar area. Kitchen open 11am–3.30am.

Neue Waid, Waidbadstrasse 45. Panoramic restaurant high up in the Waidberg with breathtaking views of the city, the lake and the Alps beyond. Not cheap, but enough main dishes under Sfr25. Tram #11 or #15 from the station to Bucheggplatz, then bus #69 four stops to Waidbadstrasse.

Restaurant Raclette-Stube, Zähringerstrasse 16. All-you-can-manage fondues and *raclette* with humungous side-portions of *rösti*, all served by candlelight. Evenings only, closed Sun. On the edge of the old town, across from Rudolf-Brun-Brücke.

Zeughauskeller, Bahnhofstrasse 28a. By Paradeplatz, a traditional Zürich hostelry dating back centuries, with a beer garden in summer. Main courses around Sfr20, open daily 11.30am–11pm.

Accommodation

Many of Zürich's hotels are geared towards the business community, with prices to match. But the sheer size of the city makes it possible to track down a reasonably priced room, and it needn't be too far from the nightlife action, either.

The Hauptbahnhof tourist office (see *Essentials*) offers a separate free hotel reservation service (☎01/215 4040) for advance bookings. All the places listed below take credit cards.

City Backpacker, Niederdorfstrasse 5 (☎01/251 9015, fax 01/251 9024). Old town hostel with no curfew in the nightlife area. Dorm beds Sfr29, singles Sfr65, doubles Sfr88. Laundry, internet and kitchen facilities.

Hotel Splendid, Rosengrassen 5 (☎01/252 5850, fax 01/262 2559). Relatively inexpensive two-star hotel between Hirschenplatz and the river, with a downstairs bar. Singles at Sfr56–70, doubles Sfr93–110, showers in the corridor.

Marthahaus, Zähringerstrasse 36 (☎01/251 4550, fax 01/4540). Small hostel just across Bahnhofbrücke from the station, with dorm beds at Sfr34, singles Sfr68, doubles Sfr100, breakfast included.

Pension St Josef, Hirschengraben 64 (☎01/251 2757, fax 01/251 2808). Pleasant rooms in this cosy pension just across Bahnhofbrücke from the station, singles at Sfr70–120, doubles Sfr110–160, breakfast included, triples and quads also available. TV lounge.

Zic-Zac Rock-Hotel, Marktgasse 17, entrance in Niederdorfstrasse (☎01/261 2181, fax 01/261 2175). Themed hotel – you too can sleep with Bon Jovi – with a large bar downstairs. Clean rooms, all with TV. Singles from Sfr65, doubles from Sfr110, triples and quads also available. Airport shuttle service.

Lake views, Canal cash – the return of Servette

In football terms, **French-speaking Switzerland** has always trailed behind the German part of the country. Although Geneva staged the country's first football match in 1869, the city's main club, Servette, weren't founded until some 20 years later, after a local student was sent a rugby ball from England.

Servette continued to practise **both rugby and soccer** until the arrival of an ex-pro from England, Teddy 'Ducky' Duckworth, who introduced modern football training and tactics to the club in the Twenties. *Les Granats* duly won five championships in 11 years, followed by the first *Nationalliga* crown in 1934. By now, the half-back line was led by **Karl Rappan**, a new arrival from Vienna. Although Rappan left for better wages at Grasshoppers in 1935 – a familiar story – he returned to Geneva after World War II to coach Servette to another title.

Servette lost to Real Madrid in what was both clubs' first European Cup match in 1955, and **abject failure abroad** was to become a keynote of the post-war era. At home, Servette's last great side was winger **Jacky Fatton**'s in the early Sixties, twice title-winners. A brief revival led by goalscorer **Umberto Barberis** was cut short when a cash crisis led to the break-up of the 1979 title-winning team. Barberis would return three years later to lead Servette to a cup and championship win in the mid-Eighties.

A lengthy period of mediocrity then followed, the veil of gloom not lifted until the arrival of **Canal Plus** in January 1997. The European pay-TV giants, looking to repeat their success with Paris Saint-Germain, could neither re-generate public interest in the club nor, with a series of PSG hand-me-downs, bring about success on the pitch. Former president and benefactor Paul-Annicle Weiller had made the club a handsome profit from the sale of **Sonny Anderson** to Monaco and thence – thanks to a sell-on clause – to Barcelona, but it wasn't until the local knowledge of coach **Gérard Castella** came into play that Servette made a serious challenge for the title.

Having previously won promotion with Geneva's two other clubs, **Meyrin** and **Étoile Carouge**, Castella worked diligently with precocious ex-Meyrin midfielder Patrick Müller, and together they turned the 1997/98 season around, Servette finishing runners-up to Grasshoppers. Juventus quickly signed a pre-contract with Müller, but with Stefan Wolf and Johan Lonfat arriving from cash-strapped Sion, and with the goalscoring of Alexandre Rey still available, Servette made a bright start to the 1998/99 campaign. Castella encouraged the hiring of **Philippe Fargeon**, whom he coached at Étoile Carouge, as sports director, and Fargeon duly arranged the crucial signing of Bulgarian Martin Petrov, whose CSKA Sofia side had knocked Servette out of the 1998/99 UEFA Cup, to replace Müller.

Having been crowned 'autumn champions' of the *NLA*, Castella's side gifted the 1999 spring-season initiative to **Lausanne**, only to thrash their near-neighbours 5–2, with two goals from Petrov, on the campaign's final day. **Grasshoppers**, who beat Xamax 5–0 the same day, were condemned to second place despite finishing on the same points total as Servette, under Swiss rules which automatically give precedence to the team with the higher number of points earned during the autumn.

From Geneva's main Gare de Cornavin, take **bus #6** (tickets Sfr2.20, day passes Sfr5) six stops up Rue de Lyon to the Parc-des-Sports, or four stops to the nearest bars. *La Brasserie des Sports* at Rue de Lyon 75 is friendly, unpretentious, and sells match tickets. Some 300m nearer to Les Charmilles stadium is *La Boutique SFC*, where tickets are sold two hours before kick-off. The home end is the *Pelouses Ouest*, behind one goal, with the away end opposite at the *Pelouses Est* – entrance to the latter on the corner of Avenue de Châtelaine and Chemin des Sports. The *B tribune* has two *buvettes* – selling beer – under it.

Turkey

Türkiye Futbol Federasyonu Konaklar Mahallesi Ihlamurlu Sokak 9, 4 Levent
80620 Istanbul ☎212/282 7010   Fax 212/282 7015   E-mail tff@tff.org

League champions Galatasaray   **Cup winners** Galatasaray   **Promoted** Yimpas
Yozgatspor, Siirt Jet-PA, Çaykut Rizespor   **Relegated** Altay Izmir, Göztepe Izmir,
Vanspor

European participants 2000/01 Galatasaray, Beşiktaş (UCL qualifiers);
Antalyaspor, Gaziantep (UEFA Cup); Kocaelispor (Intertoto Cup)

Turkish football has arrived. After
a breakthrough had been threatened on several occasions during
the Nineties, Galatasaray became
the first Turkish team to win a European
club competition when they beat Arsenal in
the final of the UEFA Cup in 2000, while
the national team re-affirmed the country's
new-found status by reaching the quarter-
finals of Euro 2000.

A country which had for so long
imported foreign coaches to take charge
at its major clubs has now provided a coach
to *Serie A* – Galatasaray's Fatih Terim taking
over the very hot seat at Fiorentina as Giovanni Trapattoni's replacement. Clubs which

had for years bought mediocre foreign players to boost their squads are now selling
homegrown players for good money to
clubs outside Turkey. When Internazionale
sought a replacement for the injured
Ronaldo in the summer of 2000, they
signed a Turk, Hakan Sükür.

It's hard to believe that as recently as
the mid-Eighties, Turkey were considered
among the minnows of the European game,
twice hammered 8–0 by England. But while
Turkey became a fully-paid up member of
the European football elite in 2000, the
year will also be remembered for the
deaths of two Leeds United fans in Istanbul,
and the violent clashes involving Turkish

The English are coming – but you won't see this kind of security at an ordinary domestic game

Basics

In addition to a full **passport**, some EU nationals, including UK and Irish (but not French, German or Scandinavian) citizens, and Americans and Australians require a **visa** to enter Turkey. These are available on arrival, for varying amounts: £10 for UK nationals, £5 for Irish, $45 for Americans, $20 for Australians, and nominal fees for other EU nationals. Check with your local Turkish embassy for details.

The Turkish currency is the **lira**, indicated as TL. With **inflation** running at around 70% annually, prices fluctuate wildly from month to month; we've given rough sterling equivalents in this chapter where relevant. The exchange rate at press time was roughly 750,000TL to £1. Get rid of your spare lira before leaving, and don't bother buying any before you depart – you'll get a better rate in Turkey.

The best rates can be found at **exchange offices** located all over Istanbul. Banks (usually open 8.30am–midday and 1.30–5pm) are slow and charge varying levels of commission. Cash machines accepting Visa and Mastercard are widespread, and credit cards can also be used in many shops in the centre of Istanbul.

To call Turkey from outside the country, dial 90, then 212 for European Istanbul, 216 for its Asian side. Both city codes can be omitted in Istanbul itself. **Phonecards** for 30, 60 and 100 units (currently TL500,000, TL1,000,000 and TL1,500,000 respectively) are available from post offices (marked *PTT*) and street vendors. There are also privately run *kontürlü* phones, at which you pay in cash for the time used. *Jetons* for inland calls, available in three sizes, are also sold at post offices. The international access code is 00 – cheap rates apply 8pm–6am Mon–Sat and all day Sun.

Turkey's **train network** is pretty skeletal, so the best way to travel around the country is by **bus**. If you have visions of being squeezed into an overcrowded jalopy which will break down in the middle of a mountain pass, think again – long-distance coaches boast air-conditioning, chilled drinks and, in hot weather, free splashes of cologne from the conductor. Buy tickets from any of the dozens of **travel agencies** in central Istanbul, many of which have English-speaking staff – they'll tell you which of the city's **suburban bus stations** your service departs from.

and English supporters in Copenhagen before the UEFA Cup final. Turkish fans have become public enemy number one for England's hooligans, as Turkish immigrants in Belgium and Holland discovered at Euro 2000 – and it is unlikely that the ill feeling will dissipate swiftly.

And yet, for the football fan visiting Istanbul without a no-surrender, bulldog attitude, the city's passionate obsession with the game, which rarely spills over into violence at domestic matches, cannot fail to impress.

The three main clubs, Galatasaray, Fenerbahçe and Beşiktaş, were all founded at the turn of the century in Istanbul and have dominated the honours ever since. Initially, however, the game received a hostile reception from the last of the Ottoman empire's rulers, Sultan Abdülhamid. The sultan, sensing the loss of both empire and power, was suspicious of any foreign-influenced organisation and banned all clubs playing the 'British' game of football.

No coincidence, then, that the 'big three' all sprang up in areas of the city with large Christian and Jewish populations and famous foreign schools; non-Turkish citizens were exempted from the sultan's clampdown and local Turks took advantage of this by sneaking into expatriate sides. By the time the sultans had lost their power and the Turkish republic was established by Mustafa Kemal Atatürk (a Fenerbahçe fan) in 1923, local football had become organised with a thriving Istanbul league and, from 1937, a system of play-offs between Istanbul sides and those from the regions. But it wasn't until 1959 that a professional national league was instituted.

The national team had begun playing friendlies almost as soon as the republic was formed, and its encouraging early form, with wins over a string of Baltic and Balkan opponents, suggested a nation picking up the game quickly. Turkey qualified for the 1950 World Cup finals by beating Syria 7–0, then withdrew at the last minute. They actually turned up in 1954 but were knocked out at the group stage, after losing twice to the eventual winners, West Germany.

There then followed a long decline in which the Turks failed to qualify for any major tournament until Euro '96. The only player of any note to emerge before the Seventies was Lefter Kücükandonyadis, an ethnic Greek who played for Fenerbahçe in the Fifties and scored 21 goals in 46 appearances for the national team.

On the domestic club scene, the emergence of Trabzonspor, founded in 1967 and winners of a first title just nine years later, provided a long overdue challenge to Istanbul's dominance. The two sides from the Turkish capital Ankara, MKE Ankaragücü and Gençlerbirliği, have still mustered only three cup wins between them. Altay of İzmir's two cup wins and a run to the semifinals of the 1969 UEFA Cup have been the only other performances of note from the Asian part of the country, even though it represents some 97 percent of Turkey's land mass.

In a bid to boost performance at the European level, an increasing number of foreign coaches and players were brought into the Turkish game. Initially most of the players came from Yugoslavia and other parts of Eastern Europe, but coaches were imported from across the continent, many of them staying in their jobs for only short spells before quitting after rows with the clubs' famously impatient presidents.

The most successful foreign coaches were Englishmen Brian Birch and Gordon Milne. Birch, a former Busby Babe who debuted for Manchester United at the age of 17 but failed to establish himself at Old

Brussels party – Belgium are beaten, 2000

Trafford, led Galatasaray to three league titles and a cup win in the early Seventies. Two decades later, former Liverpool star Milne took Beşiktaş to three titles before leaving – of his own volition, unusually – for the Japanese J-League. (He has since returned to Turkey to coach Bursaspor and, subsequently, Trabzonspor.)

Yet it was a Turkish-born coach, Fatih Terim, who finally ended the national team's absence from elite competitions when he coaxed a young side past much-fancied Sweden and Hungary and on to Euro '96. There the Turks failed to win a match, notch up a point, or even score a goal – though how different it might have been had Croatia not poached the only goal of the two teams' opening game in the dying seconds at the City Ground, Nottingham.

After Euro '96, Terim returned to domestic football to take charge of

Galatasaray, and was replaced by Mustafa Denizli. His four-year reign was something of a rollercoaster ride – Turkey beat Holland 1–0 in Bursa, but still failed to qualify for the 1998 World Cup. They were then beaten 4–1 at home by Albania in a friendly, and Denizli only narrowly survived calls for his sacking. Then came another 1–0 win in Bursa, this time over Germany at the start of the Turks' Euro 2000 qualifying campaign. A goalless in Germany followed, and although Turkey allowed the Germans to top their section, a hard-fought play-off victory over Ireland earned them the right to be part of the show in the Low Countries.

In the run-up to the finals, Galatasaray's UEFA Cup triumph raised expectations of the national team to unprecedented levels, and the pressure was once more on Denizli to deliver. Yet had it not been for a penalty harshly awarded after Pippo Inzaghi had dived in the area, Turkey would have claimed a 1–1 draw from their opening encounter with Italy. A dire goalless draw with Sweden followed, leaving the Turks requiring an unlikely victory over the co-hosts, Belgium, to reach the quarter-finals. It was the Belgians who dictated the play for much of the game, but Denizli's side proved that they had mastered the art of the counter-attack, something the class of '96 had failed to do. Goals in each half from Hakan Sükür silenced the Brussels crowd – and prompted street parties in Istanbul.

A quarter-final against in-form Portugal was a test too far, not helped by the ill-deserved dismissal of defender Alpay Ozalan on the half-hour. Denizli departed just days after the 2–0 defeat, and Yenol Günes was swiftly named as his replacement. Yet for all the mixed press they'd received during the tournament, some of Denizli's players had shown enough to earn some key contracts abroad. As well as Hakan's move to Inter, Arif Erdem and Tayfun Korkut went to Real Sociedad, while defnder Alpay, who had an outstanding competition, was signed by Aston Villa.

Back home, Galatasaray's victory has given the bigger clubs the confidence to match their resources and ambition, and no Turkish team of any kind will be written off as minnows by Europe in the foreseeable future.

Essential vocabulary

Hello *Merhába*
Goodbye *Hoşçakal*
Yes *Evet*
No *Hayir*
Two beers, please *Iki bira lütfen*
Thank you *Teşekkürler*
Men's *Erkek*
Women's *Kadin*
Where is the stadium? *Stadyum nerede?*
What's the score? *Kaç kaç?*
Referee *Hakem*
Offside *Ofsayd*

Match practice

Forget your normal matchday routine. There is no tradition of drinking in a bar before the game in Turkey, and to arrive an hour before kick-off for a major match is cutting it fine. For the big derby games in Istanbul, fans begin to gather in the morning to discuss the prospects for the game. By the afternoon the area around the stadium will be buzzing with fans gathering to eat from *büfes* and talk tactics.

Most fans enter the stadium at least two hours before kick-off. An hour before kick-off the music starts – Turkish pop stars record football versions of their big hits, and the whole stadium sings and dances along for the full hour as the tracks are played over the PA. When the teams come out to warm up, they go through an elaborate ritual with the fans. The supporters shout out the name of each player and the word *buraya* – 'come here!' The player, always known by his first name, then runs to the fans and punches the air three times before blowing a kiss to the stands.

The most popular stars may have to do this several times before kick-off. Few players have ever refused to partake in this act of mutual appreciation, and the *buraya* is one of the first things explained to foreign players on arrival at a Turkish club.

The Turkish season runs from the middle of September to the end of December, then takes a three-week break in January. The second half of the season runs from the end of January until the end of May.

League games are played over the weekend and kick-off times vary. There is often a game on Friday evening, kicking off at 7pm. Saturday and Sunday games kick off at 1.30pm during autumn and winter, at 5pm or 7pm in spring and summer.

Live TV matches usually kick off at 7pm, as do midweek cup games and, barring TV interference, international games.

A different league

The *Türkiye Futbol Liga* has an 18-team top flight (*1.Lig*) with each side meeting home and away. The second tier consists of five regional leagues of 12 clubs, who play each other home and away before the winter break. Following the break, the top two teams from each of the regional leagues form a ten-team *Play Off Lig*, from which the top two are promoted at the end of the season.

In order to ensure that those who did not make the play-off group still have something to play for from January, the best of them face the third, fourth and fifth finishers from the *Play Off Lig* in an eight-team round robin, from which the winners are also promoted to the top flight.

Promotion and relegation between the second and third tiers is at least equally complicated, probably more so – not least since a number of minor clubs were given a 'year off' in 1999/2000 after the earthquakes which struck the outer Istanbul and Izmit areas. These teams were exempt from fulfilling their fixtures for the rest of the season, while their league status was preserved in their absence.

Up for the cup

Qualification rounds for regional league sides begin in mid-July, but the first round proper of the *Türkiye Kupa* is in November, and top-flight sides are not included until the fourth round. Until the sixth round games are decided on the night with extra-time and penalties. From then on games are two-legged, but the final itself has now reverted to a single-game format – the 2000 edition between Galatasaray and Antalyaspor being held in the southeastern city of Diyarbakir, as a goodwill gesture in an area blighted by 15 years of fighting between Kurdish rebels and government troops.

Just the ticket

Big derby matches *always* sell out, so buy a ticket in advance from the stadium. Even if a game has been designated as sold out, club officials may manage to rustle up a handful of tickets if you tell them you have travelled from afar to watch their team. If you still have no joy, there'll be touts operating around the stadium from breakfast time on matchdays.

Ticket prices vary according to the status of the match. For a normal league game at a small club such as İstanbulspor, you'll pay just over £1. Count on five times that for a big city derby, at which your ticket will be no guarantee of swift entry into the stadium – queues are chaotic, and watch out for pickpockets in the crush. For lesser games you can pay at the turnstile but you should still queue up for entrance at least half an hour before kick-off.

At the ground, the most expensive places will be in the covered (*Kapali*) area of numbered (*Numerali*) seats. Most will be full an hour before the game and seat numbers are generally ignored. The second dearest section will be an open (*Açik*) stand. The cheapest areas, behind the goals, are the *Kale Arkasi*. As a rule, a seated area will be indicated as *Oturulacak Yer*, while standing is shown as *Ayakta Duralacak Yer*.

Half-time

At big games you won't want to leave your seat at half-time and there is little reason to do so. The Turks don't like any distraction from their football and that includes eating and drinking. At smaller grounds, a wandering salesman may offer tiny, potent cups of tea (*çay*) or cartons of fruit juice (*meyva suyu*). You won't find beer or kebabs inside any ground, so fill up beforehand.

Action replay

Televised football in Turkey is a hot potato. Media magnate Cem Uzem's shock move in 1999 to buy live league rights for his Tele On channel (sister company of his Star TV which covers the Champions' League) had the more popular Cine 5 on the phone to their lawyers. Cine 5 had held these league rights prior to 1999, and part of the problem is that Tele On's agreement with the Turkish FA stipulates that no other company can show league highlights until 9pm the following day, by which time any match is old hat.

Whatever the outcome of the legal wrangling, Cine 5 does have live Premiership games – mainly Manchester United – at 5pm on Saturdays, while NTV screens Spanish, Italian and general European action lunchtimes and early evenings on Saturdays and Sundays.

The back page

You won't go short of football info in Turkey, and carrying one of the three daily sports papers under your arm has the added value of keeping Istanbul's tourist-baiting street traders off your back.

Fanatik, Fotomaç and *Spor* all cost around 10p and are similar in design and content – broadsheet size, tabloid style. They are packed with large colour photos, sound-bite quotes and snippets of gossip. All have two or three columnists dedicated to each club, who provide the talking points for your first cup of tea.

Fanatik, which devotes two pages each to Fenerbahçe and Galatasaray and a page each to Trabzonspor and Beşiktaş, is perhaps the pick of the bunch, but of late has been losing readers to the less analytical *Fotomaç*.

As an antidote to all this gloss, the major daily papers, *Sabah* and *Milliyet* among them, have sport on their back page, where you'll find fewer photos and more analytical writing, particularly on Tuesdays.

Ultra culture

Turkish fans were part of the two worst examples of football violence in the 1999/2000 European season: the UEFA Cup semi-final between Galatasaray and Leeds, when two Leeds fans were stabbed to death; and the final itself, when there were ugly scenes involving Arsenal fans in Copenhagen.

Problems between Turkishs and English fans began with the infamous clash between Galatasaray and Manchester United in 1993, and since then every visit by an English club to Istanbul has been a fiery one. With a reputation to live up to, Turkish fans – particularly Galatasaray ones – make a point of intimidating their opposition, whether it is the team flying into the airport or stepping out onto the pitch, or the visiting fans themselves.

The big Istanbul derbies are almost as ferocious. The relationship between players and fans is close – as demonstrated by the *buraya* – and the supporters see themselves not as passive spectators but as an active component in the whole event. Flags, smoke bombs and flares are accepted as being part of the atmosphere, but violence is not and the heavily armed (and often heavy-handed) police aren't there for show.

That said, trouble is rarely pre-arranged along the lines of West European *ultra* clashes, and violence is rare at most run-of-the-mill domestic fixtures.

In the net

The Turkish FA has a theoretical web presence at: www.tff.org. If this isn't accessible, try the online version of *Fanatik* at www.fanatic.com.tr. With separate areas for the big three in Istanbul and for Trabzonspor, this is a good, properly maintained source of the latest news, stats and gossip – assuming you can understand Turkish.

For an overall generic resource, *Serdar's Turkish Sports Site* is at: www.geocities.com/TheTropics/7223/turksport.htm.

Istanbul

Turkey's official capital may be Ankara, deep into Asia, but the nation's soccer city is Istanbul – a 24-hour, seven-day-a-week football madhouse. The traditional gold and leather merchants of the famed Grand Bazaar are today flanked by stalls dedicated to soccer souvenirs, and you'll see kids kicking a ball wherever they can find more than ten square metres of free space.

The thrilling fields

 ### Beşiktaş

İnönü Stadi, Kadirgalar Caddesi
Capacity 35,000
Colours Black-and-white striped shirts, white shorts
League champions 1960, 1966–67, 1982, 1986, 1990–92, 1995
Cup winners 1975, 1989–90, 1994, 1998

Try as they may, Beşiktaş Jimnastik Kulübü can never escape from being the third club in Istanbul. The club has a fine stadium, a good support base and a decent domestic record, particularly in recent years. Yet games between Beşiktaş and the 'big two' never have quite the same needle or significance as the Fener–Gala derby itself.

Pelé described the İnönü Stadi as 'one of the most beautiful football grounds in the world'. It's not the architecture that provokes such awe, but the stadium's setting. Nestled at the foot of the hills that lead up from the Bosphorus, it is surrounded by those rarest of commodities in Istanbul – grass and trees. From the east stand you can see the straits and just make out the roof of the Dolmabahçe palace on the shoreline.

The club's regal surroundings are a legacy of its first major benefactor, Osman Pasha, a member of Sultan Abdülhamid's government when the club was formed in 1903. The team earned their first nickname *The Car Men* from those early days when the Pasha provided his players with cars in which to travel to and from matches.

Today they're the Black Eagles and their best moments have come in the Nineties under imported coaches Gordon Milne and Christoph Daum. The former led the club to three titles, bringing over a certain Les Ferdinand, then struggling in QPR's reserve team, to boost his strikeforce. Since then the Beşiktaş line has been successfully led by the likes of German international Stefan Kuntz and Nigeria's former Everton striker Daniel Amokachi.

A second-place finish in 1996/97 saw coach John Toshack leading the club into the Champions' League for the first time the following season. There Beşiktaş gave a decent account of themselves against Bayern Munich, Paris Saint-Germain and IFK Gothenburg, often thanks to midfielder Mehmet and striker Oktay – and no thanks to the frequent disputes between Toshack and key members of the squad, including Amokachi, Bulgarian Yordan Lechkov and Croatian goalkeeper Marian Mrmić.

The Welshman's fiery tongue got the better of 19-year-old reserve goalkeeper Fevzi, whose plea for help included a pill-swallowing suicide attempt after one particular argument. All was forgiven by the end of the season when, after Mrmić had heavily criticised Toshack in a newspaper interview, Fevzi was recalled for the domestic cup final against Galatasaray. It would be Fevzi's push of a Hagi penalty onto the crossbar that would win the second-leg shoot-out at the Ali Sami Yen.

Alas, the side then contrived to pull out all the stops in defying their coach in the Cup-Winners' Cup of 1998/99. Three-up at half-time at home to Vålerenga in the second round second leg, they then committed a series of hilarious defensive errors that allowed the Norwegians to score three in ten minutes, and win the tie

'One of the most beautiful football grounds in the world' – BJK's Inönü

4–3 overall. By the spring, Toshack had gone to Real Madrid, and been replaced by German coach Karl-Heinz Feldkamp. He was unable to turn a mediocre league season around, and although a runners-up spot put the club in contention for a Champions' League return, that opportunity was lost with a qualifying-round defeat by Israel's Hapoel Haifa, and Feldkamp paid with his job.

Another German, Hans-Peter Briegel, was brought in, and a 13-game unbeaten run at least made Galatasaray sweat at the top of the table. Yet much of the progress made under Briegel was lost when he quit, bizarrely, after a row over his translator's salary. The team still finished second, however, and the appointment of Nevio Scala, formerly of Parma and Borussia Dortmund, as coach for 2000/01 was a sign that the club does not lack ambition.

Here we go!

Buses #30b, #71 and #76 make the short journey between **Taksim** and the Bosphorus suburb of Beşiktaş and all go past the stadium. If the traffic looks heavy, it's no more than a 15min walk.

Just the ticket

Tickets are only available at the stadium itself. The box office is open 2–5pm, and sells seats in three categories: TL12million, TL6million and TL2.5million. Home fans sit directly opposite the press box in the *Kapali Tribün*, or in one section of the *Yeni Açik*.

Swift half

Beşiktaş fans are nicknamed *Çarsi* or 'market boys', and sticking with tradition, many still meet in the **Kazan** beer hall, by the main local market, next to *Osmanli Bank* over the pedestrian footbridge from the bus station. There's a classic old shot of a BJK–Fener game over the cash till. At the stadium itself, there's the Durak Büfe in the coach park on Kadirgalar Cad, and another nameless one on Dolmabahçe Cad.

Club merchandise

The club shop is at **BJK Plaza**, 88 Spor Cad, a 10 min walk from Beşiktaş bus station (open Tue–Sat 10am–6pm).

There is a smaller one at the stadium, open on matchdays, plus any number of unofficial **souvenir stands** which spring up around the ground before every game.

In the net

A suitably puffed-up eagle sits proudly atop the Beşiktaş homepage at: www.bjk.com. Once an unofficial offering, this now has the backing of the club and remains one of the best one-club sites anywhere in Europe, with an amazing stats archive, match reports from a range of Turkish media, stills and animation from *Fanatik*, Quick-Time action movies in a *Beşiktaş TV* area, an interactive chat zone and much more besides. Most of the content is available in both English and Turkish, which is a bonus.

Elsewhere, the **Black Eagles** fan group run an unofficial site at: www.bjk1903.com. There's plenty more English content here, even if some of it is taken (with permission) from the official site.

 Fenerbahçe

Fenerbahçe Stadyum, Fener Caddesi, Kadıköy
Capacity 30,000
Colours Yellow-and-blue striped shirts, white shorts
League champions 1959, 1961, 1964–65, 1968, 1970, 1974–75, 1978, 1983, 1985, 1989, 1996
Cup winners 1968, 1974, 1979, 1983

While Galatasaray are probably the best-known club outside of Turkey, Fenerbahçe Spor Kulübü are the most popular within the country. The club claim to have 25 million supporters, and while that might be stretching it, there is no denying the strength of support for 'Fener' in the provinces as well as in their heartland: the Kadıköy district of Istanbul, on the Asian side of the Bosphorus.

The Canaries were the third team to be formed in Istanbul, out of the ranks of a French college, St Joseph's. The team competed in the Istanbul league but were overshadowed for much of that period by Galatasaray and Beşiktaş, despite winning nine of te 34 titles prior to the setting up of a national league. The team's popularity was earned away from competitive football, in friendly matches. With Turkey in chaos during the Balkan Wars, World War

I and subsequent war with Greece, Fenerbahçe played on, taking on sides from various enemies and occupiers in a series of exhibition games, the most famous of which came in 1923 when a British Army XI were humbled 2–1.

Since the setting up of the national league, Fener have been more or less regular contenders. After a lean spell in the early Nineties, they rose back to the top under the guidance of club president Ali Şen. A charismatic figure with fingers in many pies, Ali Şen is the Bernard Tapie of Turkish football – although he did his spell of porridge while Tapie was still playing for his school team in France. He was elected on a simple promise – to bring the title to Fenerbahçe for the first time since 1989. He achieved that in 1996, albeit not without a further, more controversial promise to take referees under his 'protection', which caused uproar on the other side of the Bosphorus. In Kadıköy, meanwhile, he was treated like royalty.

Fenerbahçe's domestic success has not been transferred to European competition. Nonetheless, visitors from Manchester will be constantly reminded of victories over City in 1968/69 and United in 1996, the latter during Fener's first appearance in the Champions' League.

Although unable to repeat their title-winning feat, the Canaries played attractive football under Croatian coach Otto Barić in 1997/98, but were criticised for their lack of scoring power. Meanwhile Ali Şen was voted out and replaced by Aziz Yıldırım, who duly sacked Barić and sold Jay-Jay Okocha to Paris Saint-Germain. Fire-power was now provided by Elvir Baljić – playing alongside his Bosnian compatriot and near-namesake Elvir Bolić, scorer of *that* goal against Manchester United – and Romanian Viorel Moldovan.

Under German coach Joachim Löw, at first the new-look Fener looked like putting in a serious bid to recapture the title. But they finished third, six points off the title pace, and a shortage of cash gave Yıldırım little choice but to accept Real Madrid's

£6million offer for Baljić, despite it falling well below his asking price. Low was predictably sacked, and after MTK of Hungary had put a premature end to the club's 1999/2000 UEFA Cup campaign, his replacement Ridvan Dilmen jumped before he was pushed.

In Dilmen's place came a much higher-profile figure, the controversial Czech coach Zdeněk Zeman, who'd spent the bulk of his career in Italy, working at both Rome clubs. Those who had seen Zeman in action in Italy were not surprised when he began to court trouble with his colourful comments to the press, and when results failed to go his way (Fener's fourth-place finish, behind provincial side Gaziantep, meant an absence from European competition in 2000/01), he too was shown the door.

Former national-team coach Mustafa Denizli was available after Euro 2000 and took over the reigs, but the loss of Alpay Ozalan to Aston Villa and Moldovan to Nantes badly weakened his squad. Moving in the other direction were Zoran Mirković from Juventus and towering Swedish striker Kennet Andersson from Bologna, signings that showed the club was capable of attracting established players. But, after four seasons of constant Galatasaray success, the pressure on Denizli and his squad during 2000/01 would be ferocious.

Here we go!

Take a boat to Kadıköy harbour from landing #2 at Eminönü (tokens L300,000, journey time 15mins). From the bus terminal the harbour, take either a #4 bus marked Bostanci or a #FBI to the Dere Agzi stop, just over the canal by the stadium.

Just the ticket

Tickets go on sale two weeks before each match at the **Fenerbahçe Marketi** store at the ground. Two days before the game, and also on matchday itself subject to availability, small kiosks around the other side of the ground also sell tickets: *Maraton Tribün* places at TL5million, *Numerali Bilet* at TL10million.

Swift half

Opposite the main stand you'll find three bars: the **Köşe Burger**, the **Stad Büfe** and the **Star Büfe**. Just inside is the modest **Dürüm Evi**, while the more upmarket **Sampiyon** bar/restaurant was sadly closed for refurbishment when this book was being researched.

Club merchandise

The **Fenerbahçe Marketi** underneath the main stand is surprisingly spartan but does offer a decent range of souvenirs. Next door is a better-stocked **Adidas shop** offering the full range of canary-coloured sportswear. Both are open daily 10.30am–5.30pm, later on matchdays.

In the net

The official website is at: www.fenerbahce.org. It's a good-looking site with deecent news and stats archives, though in Turkish only for the time being. For a busy, well-maintained unofficial site – with an English area promised for the future – try: www.antu.com.

Short-lived coach – Fener's Ridvan Dilmen

Galatasaray

Ali Sami Yen Stadyum, Büyükdere Caddesi, Mecidiyeköy
Capacity 25,000
Colours Yellow-and-red striped shirts, yellow shorts
League champions 1962–63, 1969, 1971–73, 1987–88, 1993–94, 1997–2000
Cup winners 1963–66, 1973, 1976, 1982, 1985, 1991, 1993, 1996, 1999–2000
UEFA Cup winners 2000

After a season of controversy and high drama, 2000 will go down in history as the year when Galatasaray truly joined the European footballing elite. After beating AC Milan, Borussia Dortmund, Real Mallorca, Leeds and Arsenal, they claimed the UEFA Cup, not just their first European honour but Turkey's first, too.

They also won a fourth successive league title and, just to complete a 'treble' every bit as memorable as Manchester United's a year earlier, beat Antalyaspor

Istanbul essentials

From across the arrivals car park at Istanbul's **Atatürk airport**, 25km west of town, a *havaş* bus (every 30mins, 5.30am–11pm), runs to various points in town, terminating at central Taksim square (about 500,000TL, pay onboard). A **taxi** through the busy traffic into town will cost around $15 – make sure the driver's metre is switched on – but a cheaper way is to ride as far as nearby Yeşilköy suburban train stop, then take a train to the main **Sirkeci station**, terminus for international trains from Europe.

Istanbul is split down the middle by the **Bosphorus strait**, which divides the European and Asian parts of the city. Most of the tourist sites, nightlife, hotels and all football stadia (except Fenerbahçe's) are on the European side. The two main **bus stations**, Esenler and Harem, are on either side – the former, on the European side, is on a *hizli tramvay*, a fast tram line, marked *metro* – which is scheduled to be extended to the airport by 2000.

Getting around the city is a cheap but frustrating exercise. There are three **tram lines** – the so-called *metro* between Aksaray and Yeni Bosna; another from Topkapi gate via the tourist centre of Sultanahmet to Eminönü; and the old one on the other side of the Galata bridge, which runs along İstiklâl Caddesi between the underground funicular *Tünel* station and Taksim. Tickets are bought at platform booths and deposited in the boxes onboard.

Most **buses** are orange – buy tickets for these rom *otogar* offices or newsstands, and deposit them in the metal box by driver. For buses of other colours, pay the conductor onboard. You'll also find old-style *dolmuş*, communal taxis which follow set routes displayed in the windscreen (tell the driver your destination and pay him accordingly) and *minibüs*, a faster option operating on the same principle. The best **taxis** are yellow. Make sure the metre is running (it should start at 200,000TL daytime), and beware that prices double after midnight, and that a small toll is charged for crossing the Bosphorus. Even so, cabs are a cheap means of getting around.

The fastest and most attractive journey across the Bosphorus is by **ferry-boat**, either from the main terminal at Eminönü, adjacent to Sirkeci station, or from Beşiktaş. Buy a token (*jeton*) at the entrance or pay the onboard collector. The main terminal on the other side of the water is at Kadıköy – ferries terminating there often call at Haydarpaşa **train station**, for rail services to Asia, along the way. **Catamarans** run between Karaköy and Kadıköy for a higher but still very reasonable fee.

The main **tourist offices** is in the Hippodrome in the tourist area of Sultanahmet (open Mon–Fri 9am–5pm, ☎212/518 1802). Detailed street maps are a rarity in Istanbul, so try to buy one before you go. The *Istanbul Guide* (updated bi-monthly, 1,500,000TL) has excellent practical tips, plus bar and restaurant **listings**.

5–3 after extra-time to add the domestic cup to the haul.

Critics might carp that the 1999/2000 restructuring of European club competition, which allowed Gala and their opponents in the UEFA Cup final, Arsenal, to enter the tournament after they'd been knocked out of the Champions' League, is iniquitous. That the club were fortunate not to have been thrown out at the semi-final stage after the murder of two Leeds fans in Istanbul. Or that the manner of their victory in Copenhagen, in a penalty shoot-out after a drab, goalless 120 minutes of football in which Gala's best player, Gheorghe Hagi, was sent off, was somehow unworthy.

None of that matters to the inhabitants of Mecidiyeköy, where tower blocks dominate the skyline and an inner-city motorway flies overhead, bringing extra noise and pollution to one of Istanbul's least attractive suburbs, and into which Gala's Ali Sami Yen stadium is cramped. This was their finest hour, and one entirely in keeping with their club's proud history.

Like their rivals, Galatasaray Spor Kulübü were formed from the efforts of a student team. After an early tour to Switzerland, the soccer-playing pupils of Galatasaray high school brought a Swiss football song, *Jim, Bom, Bom*, back with them. The song has stayed with the team to this day and earned them their nickname, *Cim Bom Bom*.

Today the club's influence spreads far beyond their ground, which the board wants to knock down and build an all-new, 42,000-capacity stadium more in keeping with Gala's status as the largest sports club in Turkey, with nearly 10,000 members participating in a wide range of pursuits. The club also own several businesses and one of the islands in the Bosphorus, complete with swimming pool, harbour, restaurant, disco and casino. In the autumn of 1999, Gala became the first Turkish football club to be floated on the stock exchange.

The Lions, as they are also commonly known, were the first Turkish team to play abroad when, during the Balkan Wars, they travelled to Transylvania to play Kalosvár (now Cluj-Napoca). In the modern era the team have been regular participants in European club competition, but only in recent years have they had any results to show for their endeavours.

In 1989 Gala had the best European run of any Turkish side thus far, reaching the semi-final of the Champions' Cup, defeating Rapid Vienna, Xamax Neuchâtel of Switzerland and AS Monaco before losing to Steaua Bucharest. Three years later they reached the quarter-finals of the Cup-Winners' Cup, and the following year they pulled off a major upset in knocking out Manchester United (after a thrilling 3–3 draw at Old Trafford and a tense, goalless stalemate in Istanbul) to qualify for the Champions' League. They made it to the League again in 1994/95 when, although they failed to make it out of the group stage, they beat Barcelona at home and again held United to a draw in Istanbul.

Galatasaray has also been the club to have produced the three major stars of modern Turkish football. In the Seventies, Metin Oktay bagged 608 league and cup goals for his club and was first-choice striker for the national team (he was tragically killed in a car accident in 1995), while in the Eighties, Tanju Çolak was the player whose pin-up was on every young Turkish boy's bedroom wall.

The most recent hero at the Ali Sami Yen was Hakan Sükür, 'the Bull of the Bosphorus' whose goals enabled Turkey to reach Euro '96, propelled his country into the quarter-finals of Euro 2000, and were instrumental in landing Gala their first European title. European adventures or not, Galatasaray's support has traditionally demanded nothing more than victory over Fenerbahçe. When that was achieved in the Turkish cup final of 1996, Gala's Scottish coach Graeme Souness planted a red-and-yellow flag on the Fenerbahçe field, provoking rioting in the stands. Though it received swift condemnation from Gala officials, the act made Souness a hero in

The history men – Galatasaray players and officials celebrate their UEFA Cup win in Copenhagen

Mecidiyeköy. Then again, as Souness discovered when Fener pipped his side to the title and he was fired, derby glory lasts only as long as the next game.

In 1996/97, former Turkish national-team coach Fatih Terim arrived at Gala and immediately set about constructing a title-winning side, adding the guile of Romanian midfielder Gheorghe Hagi to the goal-poaching of Hakan. It proved a combination no other Turkish side could live with.

The Hagi–Hakan partnership was just as lethal in 1997/98, when Gala came from behind to beat Fenerbahçe to the title, with Hakan 12 clear of his nearest rival in the league goalscoring stakes.

The following year, Gala again had to overhaul their nearest rivals, in this case Beşiktaş, to retain their domestic title. But earlier in the season they had been pre-occupied by their best-ever run in the Champions' League, when only lapses in their last two games against Juventus and Athletic Bilbao prevented them from reaching the knockout stage.

Ironically, Terim's side could do no more than match that achievement in 1999/2000. Drawn in a group with Chelsea, AC Milan and Hertha Berlin, they were 2–1 down and facing a bottom-place finish in

the dying minutes of their last game against Milan. Yet somehow, showing a resilience once rare in Turkish teams, they rustled up two late goals to claim the consolation prize of a berth in the UEFA Cup.

Two big away wins – 2–0 at Borussia Dortmund and 4–1 at Real Mallorca – then showed Europe that this side, their confidence growing all the time, were not as dependent on fearsome home support as some Gala teams of the past. And while the hard work against Leeds was done at home and with their opponents clearly in a state of shock, Terim's side did well to hold out for a draw in the return leg at Elland Road, where the atmosphere was charged with a vengeful hatred.

There was no way past a disciplined Arsenal side at the final in Copenhagen, but successful regrouping, after Hagi's red card four minutes into extra-time, showed yet another advance, a Turkish side capable of adjusting its gameplan on the hoof.

Istanbul had seen nothing like the reception given to the team on its return from Denmark, yet the celebrations were cut surprisingly short. Terim decided to quit while ahead, and accepted an offer to take over at Fiorentina, becoming the first Turkish coach to work at a big West European club. Hakan, despite a brief, disastrous spell at Torino in the mid-Nineties, decided to re-tread his footsteps to Italy and signed for Internazionale.

Perhaps fearful that Hagi and Popescu might follow suit, the club appointed Romanian Mircea Lucescu as coach, then splashed out £20million on prolific Brazilian striker Mário Jardel from Porto. That signing was final proof that Galatasaray are no longer underdogs in the European scheme of things, but a rise in status also means a rise in expectations – Lucescu will be aware that nothing but constant success will now keep the club satisfied.

Here we go!

Any bus to **Mecidiyeköy** – from Taksim take the #50 or #59a. The stadium is a 5min walk from the bus station, but allow plenty of time for monstrous traffic.

Just the ticket

Advance tickets are available a few days before kick-off from the **club offices** at Hasnan Galif Sok 11, near Taksim square, just along from the club shop (see below).

Swift half

The *Altin Fici*, next to the Shell petrol station opposite the ground, requires a sprint across a busy road running under the motorway. It's worth putting your life in the hands of Turkish drivers for, with real spit, sawdust and draught Efes beer.

Club merchandise

The official **club shop**, a short walk from Taksim off main İstiklâl Cad, is on the corner of Hasnan Galif Sok and Büyük Parmak Kazi Sok. There are several booths around the perimeter of the stadium which are open on matchdays.

In the net

The official Gala website resides at: www.galatasaray.net. Click on the 'About Galatasaray' link and you'll get a full Enligsh subsite with stadium information, a club history, roll of honour and other information, while the latest news and match reports are on the main site in Turkish.

Groundhopping

Two of the city's lesser lights, Sariyer and Zeytinburnuspor, were relgated in 1996/97 and have not returned to the top flight since, but a trip out to one of these smaller grounds can tell you more about the state of Turkish league football than the highly charged 'event' atmosphere of a major derby. Take your pick…

İstanbulspor

Bayrampaşa Stadi, Yolu Star Sokak, Ikitelli
Capacity 11,000
Colours Yellow-and-black shirts, white shorts

The resignation of the club's president and major benefactor, media magnate Cem Uzan, in the autumn of 1998 left İstanbulspor in turmoil. Having put in a creditable performance in the 1997 Intertoto Cup, achieved a best-ever league finish of fourth in 1997/98 and lost only on away goals to Arges Piteşti of Romania in the following year's UEFA Cup, coach Safet Susić's side suffered a loss of form midway through the 1998/99 domestic season. A 4–1 defeat by Ankaragücü at the club's decrepit old Bayrampaşa stadium (Beşiktaş wanted too much money to continue sharing theirs) was the final straw for Uzan, who had wanted a quicker return on his £30million investment.

Reserve-team and junior players filled the positions once occupied by experienced internationals, and İstanbulspor are slowly sliding – they finished ninth in 1998/99, 15th a year later, escaping relegation on goal difference.

The club are not without history – Istanbul champions in 1932, home of Cemil Turan, top international goalscorer in the Seventies – but whether they can survive without Cem's riches remains to be seen.

To find out how they're getting on, take the metro to Sagmalcilar, five stops from the Aksaray central terminus.

Sariyer

Yusuf Ziya Önis Stadi, Eski Sular Yolü 42, Sariyer
Capacity 12,000
Colours Blue-and-white shirts, white shorts

Despite never having finished in the top three or made it as far as the cup final, Sariyer Gençlik Kulübü had been a pretty constant mid-table presence in Turkey's top flight until recently. A trip to their scruffy ground, with a playing surface your local pub team would bitch about, is a refreshing escape from the city, and there can be few finer groundhops than the Bosphorus ferry journey from Eminönü, which leaves at 10.35am and arrives at Sariyer (one stop from the terminus on the Asian side) at 11.50am.

Once on dry land again, you're perfectly placed for a pre-match swiftie in the **Baba Necmi Nin Yeri** on Nalbant Çesme Sok, or in the **Stadiyum Cafe** opposite the main entrance, a 10 min walk from the harbour down Sular Cad. The ferry back at 3.20pm may be a little too early, so take bus #25e to Eminönü.

Zeytinburnu

Zeytinburnu Stadyumu, Zubeyde Hanim Caddesi 1, Zeytinburnu
Capacity 10,000
Colours All white with blue trim

If someone were to write a 'rags to riches' novel about a Turkish footballer, the 'rags' period would be set here. Surrounded by tower blocks and wasteland in one of Istanbul's poorest districts, huge chunks of concrete terracing are relieved only by a small stand on the halfway line. The directors' box is surrounded by a barbed-wire fence – given that Zeytinburnu have never won a thing, it is not there to protect board members from being mobbed by jubilant fans.

Which is not say there isn't plenty of footballing activity here – the backstreets

and patches of scrubland around the ground play host to scores of games any day of the week. Maybe the scouts would be better off looking there.

The ground is right across the street from **Kazliçesme** suburban train station, seven stops from main Sirkeci on the *banliyö* train line. By the station you,ll find a fine terrace fish restaurant, the **Balikçi Bilgin**. On two corners of the ground are the more modest **Stad Büfe** and **Durak Büfe**.

Eat, drink, sleep...

Bars and clubs

Istanbul is a fine night out. There are bars and restaurants all over the place, catering for all tastes. The local *bira* is **Efes Pilsen**, which is surprisingly good and has an almost 100% monopoly. The traditional watering hole is a *meyhane* where beer and raki – a powerful aniseed-flavoured spirit – are accompanied by plates of salad or cold snacks (*mezes*). A *birahane* is much the same thing. Unaccompanied women may feel ill at ease in some of the seedier joints. Western-style bars and clubs can be found in Taksim and Etiler. In summer, discos pop up spontaneously, mostly along the European side of the Bosphorus.

Dulcinea, Meşelik Sok 18/20. This area boasts designer bars a-plenty, and this is the best of them. DJs most evenings, trendy atmosphere, imaginative menu, good source of flyers.

Isis, Kadife Sok 26. Restored three-storey Kadıköy house, now a bar/dance venue (acid jazz, trip-hop) with a summer garden.

James Joyce, Taralabaşi Cad/Dernek Sok. Main Irish pub in the Taksim area, with live music and a separate bar for pool, darts and Sky TV. Happy hour early evenings.

Magma, karsu Sok 5, Galatasaray. The trendiest underground club since opening in 1998, with British DJs flying in for one-off spots.

Restaurants

Turkish food has far more going for it than the admittedly **ubiquitous kebab**. *Güveç*, a casserole of meat and vegetables, and *turlu*, a vegetable stew, are both good alternatives if you become bored with the range of spiced and grilled meats, though portions can be small for a main course.

Along the Bosphorus there is no shortage of fine fish (*balik*) on offer and in summer salads are excellent, as are soups (*çorba*). Turkish sweets and cakes are outstanding, if an acquired taste.

Bolkepçe, Muallin Naci Cad 49/9. Just off Ortaköy square, a lovely place serving up authentic Turkish cuisine, especially popular on Sundays. Open Mon–Thur 11am–1am, Fri–Sat 10am–2am, most major credit cards.

İzmirli Balikçi, Cebeciyan courtyard, Kapali Çarşi. Only seafood restaurant in old Istanbul's covered bazaar, and a good one, very popular at lunchtimes. Considering its touristy location, not overpriced.

Mediterrane, Çukurluçemse Sok 18. Charming family-run eaterie next to a second-hand store in İstiklâl Cad, serving eastern Anatolian cooking prepared with homemade olive oil and deliciously fresh produce. Open daily 8am–10.30pm. No alcohol served.

Olimpiyat 2, Neşet Ömer Sok 8a. Smart restaurant owned by former Fenerbahçe and Turkish international star Ahmet Erol. The walls are covered with black-and-white blowups of Fener and Olympic action. In the back there is a betting room with a fine collection of portraits. Full Turkish menu, licensed bar. Ferry-boat to Kadıköy, restaurant opposite harbour.

Accommodation

There is plenty of reasonably priced accommodation in Istanbul and during the football season you should have no problem finding a room. The hotels around Taksim are the most expensive but there are good options all over the city. Sultanahmet has some of the best *pansiyons*, but the area is a fair way from the nightlife action.

Gezi Hotel, Mete Cad 42 (☎212/251 7430, fax 212/251 7473). Right next to Taksim square. The terrace restaurant looks out over the busy streets, and the rooms are clean and comfortable. First three floors relatively old-fashioned, with lower prices – around $70 a double, $50 a single, with breakfast. Renovated floors above are $10 more expensive. Extra bed provided in doubles for $15.

Hotel Turkoman, Asmali Çeşme Sok, Adilye Yani 2 (☎212/516 2956, fax 212/516 2957). By the Hippodrome, a classy option at reasonable rates – about $80 a double – in this house converted into 19th-century style. Singles and triples also available, great views from the roof terrace.

Otel Avrupa, Topçu Cad 32 (☎212/250 9420, fax 212/250 7399). Conveniently situated near Taksim, this converted apartment house has rooms of varying sizes and prices – around $40 a double.

Terrace Guesthouse, Kutlugün Sok 39 (☎212/638 9733, fax 212/638 9734). Perfect budget option, a short walk from both the tramway and the *banliyö* lines – clean, friendly pension where the price includes a panoramic rooftop breakfast. About $50 a double.

Ukraine

Football Federation of Ukraine, Laboratornaya Str 1, PO Box 293, 252150 Kiev
☎044/252 8498   Fax 044/252 8513   E-mail em@ffu.Kiev.ua

League champions Dynamo Kiev   **Cup winners** Dynamo Kiev   **Promoted** Stal
Alchivsk   **Relegated** Prykparpattya I-F, Chornomorets Odessa, Zirka Kirovohrad

European participants 2000/01 Dynamo Kiev, Shakhtar Donetsk (UCL qualifiers);
Kryvbas Kryvyi Rih, Vorskla Poltava (UEFA Cup)

astern Europe's newest football force are old hands at the international game. Though their emerging nation has yet to appear at one, the Ukraine's leading players have already starred in half-a-dozen World Cups – wearing the bright red shirt of the USSR. As the second-largest republic in the old Soviet Union (the largest was Russia), the Ukraine provided the country's only European club trophies, their star player of the modern era, and the backbone of the side which impressed at the 1982 and 1986 World Cups.

It was the Ukraine's flagship team, Dynamo Kiev, who won the Cup-Winners' Cup in 1975 and 1986, both times with Oleg Blokhin, the player who heads the all-time Soviet caps and goalscoring lists. The club still represent the pride of the nation, as the bulk of the now-independent national team are from the Kiev side who set the Champions' League alight in 1998/99. After the club failed to make the final, however, many of its stars – including Milan-bound Andriy Shevchenko – are heading abroad, and the domestic league Dynamo dominate is rather more shambolic than its Russian counterpart.

After being part of Tsarist Russia when football first came to the region – there were local leagues in Kiev, Kharkhiv and Odessa by the turn of the century – the Ukraine was a separate entity only for a short period between the end of World War I and the end of the Civil War in 1920. From then on it was brutally subjugated, known as the 'bread basket' of Russia, with the Ukrainian language initially banned in

Following in vain – Ukrainians in Ljubljana

Soviet schools. In some parts, the Nazi invasion of World War II was greeted with open arms.

In the meantime, the Ukraine's leading football club, Dynamo Kiev, had been formed in 1927 – four years after Zarja in Lugansk, which was to house the republic's most famous sports school. By the Forties, the Ukraine's three other main clubs – Shakhtar Donetsk, Metalist Kharkhiv and Dnipro Dniepropetrovsk – had also been founded.

Basics

All visitors to the Ukraine require a **visa**. Those on package trips will be given a tourist voucher automatically. Individual travellers need either a tourist visa, valid for the number of days listed on the fax confirming their pre-booked accommodation, or a business visa, arranged through a Ukrainian company via a letter of invitation. Three-day visa processing costs $80, but check with your local **Ukrainian embassy** for the latest details. The UK office is at 78 Kensington Park Road, London W1 12PL (☎020/7727 6312, fax 020/7792 1708).

On arrival you will have to fill out a currency declaration form stating how much money you have with you. On leaving, you will have to fill out a similar form, declaring how much you are taking out. The Ukrainian currency is the **hryvny** (hr), in notes of 1, 2, 5, 10, 20, divided into 100 kopecks (k), in coins of 1, 2, 5, 10 and 50. At the time of writing there were about hr3.5 to £1, but local **exchange offices** – set up at almost every other shop in major cities – prefer dollars or Deutschmarks in cash. Take your currency declaration form to be stamped for each transaction. The *Bank of Ukraine* gives cash advances on Visa and Mastercard for a hefty commission. Credit-card payment is generally only accepted at upmarket hotels and restaurants.

Local calls from Soviet-style **telephones** require 60k *taksofon* tokens, available at post offices and metro stations. For international calls, buy a *Utel* **phonecard** (hr10, hr20 or hr40) from newsstands, and use the modern blue-and-silver public phones. There are no cheap international rates. From inside the country, the international access code is 8 (pause) 10. Remember that the Ukraine is an hour ahead of Central European Time. To call the Ukraine from abroad, dial 380, then 44 for Kiev, 572 for Kharkhiv or 482 for Odessa; put a 0 in front of the city code for calls inland.

Transport across Europe's **second biggest country** is corrupt and complicated. Trains are cheap, but buying a ticket can be a nightmare. Some long-distance departures require you to buy your tickets a couple of days in advance, while in other instances, tickets are only available on the day. An easier option might be to buy one from a tout at the station, or bribe the ticket inspector. All tickets should have the train time and seat clearly marked. There are four classes, from *lyux* to *obshchy*, the latter generally shared with farm animals.

Air Ukraine International (Kiev office ☎044/216 6730, fax 044/216 8225) serves Kiev, Odessa and Lviv; their prices increase considerably for Westerners.

The Soviet league was dominated by the Moscow giants until Dynamo Kiev broke the capital's stranglehold by winning the title in in 1961, with a side that featured the club's future coach, Valery Lobanovsky. Five years later, Dynamo won three in a row, and with Lobanovsky at the helm from the Seventies onwards, they would become the most-titled club in the Soviet game.

It was the Ukrainian game's infrastructure that allowed the republic to develop the biggest football powerbase in the Soviet Union. Nearly a thousand new stadia were built, and young players – with fewer distractions through the long, hot Ukrainian summer than their Russian counterparts – rose through fiercely competitive sports schools such as the one in Lugansk, then called Voroschilovgrad, from which would come the second Ukrainian team to win the Soviet title in 1972. Ten years later, after Dnipro Dniepropetrovsk had become the third, the school produced World Cup star Alexandr Zavarov.

Tactically, one man remoulded Ukrainian football and enabled it to escape the Soviet straightjacket – Valery Lobanovsky. From his coaching debut at Dnipro, he moved up to the most prestigious club in the land, Dynamo Kiev, with his assistant Oleg Basilevitch coming from Shakhtar

Donetsk. Their high work-rate, high-speed approach was far in advance of the cumbersome Russian game, though it had a tendency to wear players out – even fit, young, enthusiastic ones.

Loba inherited a good team at Kiev. Four players had been in the Soviet side which finished second in the 1972 European Championship, and the star was Oleg Blokhin, a bronze-medal winner with the Soviet Olympic squad later that summer. The side were champions of the USSR in 1974 and 1975, and won the Cup-Winners' Cup in the latter year. Before long the club's players formed the backbone of the Soviet national side, and Dynamo's coaching pair were put in charge of the 1976 Olympic soccer team. They flopped, partly because of refereeing decisions in the semi-final with East Germany, mainly through fatigue – for which Basilevitch blamed himself and resigned.

Dynamo's new-found European prestige, however, meant that kids from all over the republic were eager to join the club's ranks. Lobanovsky, back from national duty in Moscow, made sure he got the pick of the bunch, leaving the clubs in the capital to scrap for the rest. With Blokhin still leading the Dynamo line, the coach created a new side from the fastest players he could find. Zavarov was one, Igor Belanov from Chornomorets Odessa another.

Like the team of a decade earlier, this Kiev side would win the domestic double, then the Cup-Winners' Cup. But unlike their earlier counterparts, they would then also represent the Soviet Union at the World Cup. In Mexico in 1986, they started brilliantly, beating Hungary 6–0 and drawing with France to win their group. In the second round against unfancied Belgium, despite a Belanov hat-trick that included couple of outstanding strikes from long range, they were beaten 4–3. Though two of the Belgian goals looked offside, Lobanovsky refused to criticise the referee, instead blaming his own players for committing 'schoolboy errors' which had invited the officials to make mistakes.

As a decade earlier, the strains of fatigue from international and domestic duty were showing. Dynamo Kiev failed to qualify for Europe in 1987, and Belanov began to spend long periods injured. Two players then arrived, to bolster both squads, from the strong Dnipro team which had made good progress in Europe in the mid-Eighties: Gennady Litovchenko and Oleg Protasov. They would be the Soviet Union's goalscorers in a 1988 European Championship semi-final win over Italy. In the final, with Zavarov absent injured and a half-fit Belanov missing a penalty, the USSR were beaten 2–0 by a rampant Holland – although they had beaten the Dutch in an earlier group game.

Lobanovsky remained in charge of the national side, but the 1990 World Cup in Italy would be his last – and that of the country. Two years later, with the Soviet Union breaking up and qualifying for the 1994 World Cup getting underway, FIFA had to decide which republic best merited a qualifying berth. Even though the Soviet team had been stuffed full of Ukrainians for more than 20 years, pressure from powerful FIFA vice-president Vyacheslav Koloskov resulted in the place being awarded to Russia. As a compromise, Ukrainian stars – Andrei Kanchelskis and Viktor Onopko among them – were allowed to choose which republic to represent, and with Russia landing an easy qualifying group stripped of sanctions-struck Yugoslavia, most plumped for the bright lights of USA '94. (Ironically, many would then withdraw on the eve of the tournament in a dispute over tactics and money.)

It wasn't just the stars who defected. By the mid-Nineties, there were 300 Ukrainians playing in the Russian league or those of the emerging Baltic states. Back home, a modest league was formed, won by tiny Tavria Simferopol in 1992. Without any Muscovites to kick around, crowds and media interest were low. Practicalities such as travel – the distance between Lugansk and Lviv is nearly 1,400km, the same as

London to Prague – were a constant headache.

The national side's debut was equally low-key – a defeat by a Hungarian select XI in the sleepy railway border town of Uzhhorod. In the series of 13 friendlies against lowly opposition that followed, the Ukraine won only four. They fared little better in their first competitive fixture – a home defeat by Lithuania, who would finish above them in their qualifying group for Euro '96. Coach Josef Szabo, a team-mate of Lobanovsky's from the Sixties, had only one real star, the hot-headed Kiev forward Viktor Leonenko, in his squad.

Regardless of the Ukraine's newly independent status, some things remained unchanged from Soviet days. In particular, it was clear football could not thrive without state backing. Happily, in a strongly nationalist government that saw soccer as a matter of Ukrainian pride, the game found an enthusiastic saviour.

It was state intervention that saved Dynamo Kiev from bankruptcy in 1993, after which a new management team under businessman Hrihoriy Surkis, with close links to the government, assumed control. When the board were caught trying to bribe a referee before a Champions' League game (business practices differ between post-Communist Ukraine and the West) in 1995, it was a personal plea from state president Leonid Kravchuk that persuaded UEFA to reduce Dynamo's two-year ban.

After Surkis began to put the game on some kind of business footing – he became president of the 'professional' league in 1996 – Lobanovsky, who had spent much of the Nineties coaching in the Arab world, was persuaded to return to Dynamo. He would also be given a senior position above Szabo in the national setup.

The Ukrainians gave a much better account of themselves in their qualifying group for France '98, their side now including the young Kiev strike partnership of Shevchenko and Serhiy Rebrov. But two home draws, against Armenia and Germany, saw them slip to second place, forcing them into a play-off with Croatia. Even then, they were unfortunate not to win through. Having lost the away leg 2–0, the Ukraine had the eventual bronze-medal

A class apart – Rebrov outmanoeuvres Southgate, Wembley, May 2000

winners on the rack for much of the return in Kiev. They were a goal up in four minutes, but a second goal was wrongly ruled offside three minutes later. A deflected Croatian goal against the run of play before the half-hour took the wind out of the Ukrainians' sails, and the game finished 1–1.

Since then, money has begun pouring in from Dynamo's European campaigns, allowing new training facilities to be built and a complete overhaul of Kiev's second stadium, the 'Dynamo'. In the far southwest, businessman Rinat Ahmetov has matched Dynamo's efforts by building a new complex at his own club, Shakhtar Donetsk. The former miners' team have provided a serious and much-needed domestic challenge to Dynamo, whose progress to the semi-finals of the Champions' League in 1998/99 improved the country's ranking sufficiently to open up another qualifying spot for Ukrainian clubs.

From its disastrous state in 1992, Ukrainian football has been transformed, inspiring a nation and setting an example for other former Soviet republics to follow. The proof of the pudding came with the opening of the Euro 2000 qualifying campaign in September 1998, when the national side was pitted against a Russian team containing two of the players who had snubbed the Ukraine six years previously – Kanchelskis and Onopko. The home side tore at the opposition with a force demanded of them by a wild 80,000 crowd in the Respublikansky stadium. Their 3–2 victory, richly deserved, was followed by two more, and only some world-class goalkeeping from Fabien Barthez prevented the Ukraine from coming away from the Stade de France with more than a point against the World Cup holders in March 1999.

Six months later, and Ukrainian chances of appearing at Euro 2000 hinged on the outcome of the return match against the Russians in Moscow. With three minutes to go, Russia were 1–0 up and in the play-offs. Then Shevchenko's harmless-looking free-kick confused Russian 'keeper Alexan-

der Filimonov, who somehow managed to punch the ball into his own net and hand Ukraine the vital point which allowed them to leapfrog the Russians into second place in their section behind France.

Yet the chance of a first appearance in a major tournament, seemingly taken for granted by players and supporters, was dramatically lost when a 2–1 defeat to Slovenia in the first leg of the Euro 2000 play-off was followed only by a 1–1 draw in Kiev. In the shock that followed, poor old Szabo was forced to resign and, not surprisingly, the Ukrainian FA chose Lobanovsky as his replacement. It was a logical move, considering the level of Dynamo's influence on the national team, although some had called in vain for a younger man, such as Dynamo assistant coach and former Soviet international Alexei Mikhailichenko, to be given a chance.

In any event, it may not be long before Lobanovsky, who has increasingly struggled with his health, gives a chance to one of his protegés and, when that happens, it will be a real test of the strength of Ukranian football to see how well the nation's top players can fare without the influence of one of the modern game's truly great coaches.

Essential vocabulary

Hello *Dobry den'*
Goodbye *Do pobachennya*
Yes *Tak*
No *Ni*
Two beers, please *Dva pyva bud' laska*
Thank you *Diakuyu*
Men's *Cholovichyi*
Women's *Zhinochyi*
Where is the stadium? *De znahodyt'sia stadion?*
What is the score? *Yakyi rahunok?*
Referee *Suddia*
Offside *Poza groyu*

Match practice

Many fans miss the days of the old Soviet league, when top teams from Moscow, Georgia and the Baltic states would draw a six-figure full house to Kiev. Now the average crowd is less than 5,000, and interest is low, despite Dynamo's exploits in Europe.

Games generally kick-off on Saturdays or Sundays at 5pm. Note that fixtures involving Dynamo are often moved (usually back) when the club have an important upcoming fixture in Europe.

The Ukrainian season is divided into two halves, July to late October and March to June, with a four-month winter break in between.

A different league

The elite section of the Ukrainian league is a premier division (vishcha liga), reduced from 16 to 14 teams in 2000, playing each other home and away over the course of a season. At the end of the campaign, the two lowest-placed teams swap divisions with the top two of the first division (persha liga), which is composed of 20 teams. Among the first-division sides, the reserve teams of Dynamo Kiev (who won the championship in 1999), CSCA Kiev and Shakhtar Donetsk cannot be promoted.

The second division (druga liga) consists of four groups of 16 teams, each group winner going up to the first, which loses its bottom four clubs in return.

Up for the cup

All premier and first division clubs, the 30 best second division clubs from the previous season and the amateur cup holders enter the Kubok Ukraïni, which is staged over seven two-legged rounds in which away goals count double if the aggregate scores are level. The bottom half of the previous season's premier division enters at the third-round stage, the top half at the fourth round. The final is decided on one game at the Respublikanski stadium, on the last Sunday in May – Kiev Day.

Just the ticket

Ukrainian domestic football is as cheap as anywhere in Europe, with prices ranging from hr3 to hr9. For matches at the bigger stadia, your ticket will indicate the sektor, ryad (row), mistse (place) and, in the case of the Respublikanski, yarus, or level. In a hangover from the Soviet days, the matchday programme (programka) is a collectible item. Keep it in your attic.

Half-time

Beer is on sale around most grounds, along with the slightly alcoholic, yeasty kvas – a particular favourite on hot summer afternoons in Kiev, sold in communal glasses from large metal tankers. Sunflower seeds (nasinnia) are devoured by the coneload during the match.

Action replay

Lack of decent domestic TV coverage is one of the factors contributing to the domestic game's impoverished state. State channel UT1 shows international games and the occasional live Dynamo Kiev match, but that's about it. Domestic highlights are mainly confined to short sports items following the main news bulletin.

Satellite channel Inter and UT1 both offer European highlights, including English Premiership action, but these are often not screened until a fortnight after matches have taken place, and at wildly varying times.

The back page

The classic daily is the Ukrainian-language Sportivna Gazeta. Its main competition comes from the Russian-language pink 'un, Komanda, and from the more provincial daily Ukraïns'kiï Futbol. All cost between hr1 and hr1.50. They are supplemented by the colour Russian-language weekly Futbol (Mondays, hr2.50), and the monthly Inter Futbol (hr3).

Ultra culture

Domestic football having few fans, there is little fan culture to speak of. The situation is very much as it was in Russia before organised fan groups began re-emerging from the ruins of the old Soviet system. Travelling support is discouraged by the vast distances between venues, while the

Paying the price for failure – former coach Josef Szabo

lack of city – and ethnic – rivalries makes for a lukewarm atmosphere at many matches.

The Ukraine has no football madhouses near war zones, like Russia's Vladikavkaz, and if it is to develop any serious rivalries, they will have to come from Polish-influenced Lviv, the former mining stronghold of Donetsk, and Kiev itself.

In the net

The Ukrainian FA has an official website at: www.ffu.org.ua. Run by the same outfit responsible for the Russian FA site, it offers a decent amount of English-language content, including the latest league tables, official federation news, a photo gallery and match reports for all levels of the national team.

A much livelier site, meanwhile, resides at: ukrainiansoccer.net. A treasure trove of English-language gossip, rumours and chat, it is constantly updated, interestingly designed and leaves no stone unturned when it comes to match reports, news and relevant links.

Kiev

Columns and lights – few European stadia can match Kiev's Respublikanski for grandeur

Unknown to most football followers outside the former Soviet Union, Kiev is one of Europe's great football capitals. Ever since Ukrainian flagship club Dynamo won their first Soviet title in 1961, the city's streets have regularly shaken with the sound of the local populace out celebrating great victories.

In Soviet times, through Dynamo, Kiev was the rallying point for Ukrainian nationalist sentiment. Not as fierce, perhaps, as the Catalan credo in Barcelona, but anyone who went to a Dynamo Kiev–Spartak Moscow fixture would come away from the Respublikanski stadium with the noise of a hundred thousand roaring Ukrainians ringing in their ears.

Now capital of a freshly independent Ukraine, Kiev has assumed the role it once held by proxy, and the atmosphere at the Ukraine–Russia Euro 2000 qualifying game in September 1998 was remarkably similar to that in days of old.

Part of the early enthusiasm in Kiev was more than just football passion. The day the great Respublikanski stadium, 3km south of the town centre, was due to be inaugurated in 1941, the Nazis invaded and laid waste to it. Another Kiev stadium, Start, on Vul Marshala Ribalka between the Politekhnichnii Institut and Lykh'yanivska metro stops, is said to have played host to the infamous 'Match of Death' a year later, when a Kiev side beat a Nazi one, and were sent to their deaths days later. Although the Soviet authorities made great propaganda out of it, no proof remains of such an event having taken place. What is certain is that Kievites restored their football grounds with pride, and that a huge depth of feeling continued to be expressed against German teams for years.

The post-war Dynamo revival coincided with the city being slowly restored, often thanks to the influence of the club's biggest fan at the top in Moscow, Soviet premier

Kiev essentials

Kiev-Boryspil **airport** is 30km east of the city centre. Shuttle buses run on the hour, 1pm–9pm, from outside the terminal to anywhere in town for $10 in hryvny. Cheaper *Polit* buses leave roughly every hour, 5am–9.30pm, for a number of central stops including the *Rus Hotel* and *Universityet* metro, fare about hr8. Call ☎044/296 7564 to book your shuttle bus back from town; *Polit* buses (☎044/296 7367) leave from Peremohy Ploschad. Both buses take about under an hour. **Taxi** drivers will almost certainly fleece you, but hr100 should secure safe passage to your destination, which should be clearly written for the driver to read.

The main **train station**, Kiev-Passazhirsky, is centrally located and served by Vokzalna metro. City transport is cheap and efficient, running from 6am to past midnight. A ride on the three-line colour-coded **metro system** requires a 30k token from the ticket office – insert your token into the slot in the metal barrier before the escalators. Tickets for **trams, buses and trolleybuses** are 30k from newsstands (punch them onboard) or from the conductor immediately as you board. **Minibuses** (*marshryti*), follow the main routes, offer a little more and can stop anywhere along the way. They cost 50k – pass it to the driver and tell him where you want to go.

Checkered-signed state **taxis** can be ordered by dialling ☎058, but normally you can flag down a private car, a common practice in Kiev as in Moscow. No journey in town should cost more than hr5.

There is no **tourist office** in Kiev. The quarterly *Kiev Business Directory*, available at most newsstands, has a reasonable amount of tourist information. The Thursday edition of the *Kiev Post*, free in Western bars and hotels, offers a cursory **listings section**.

Nikita Khrushchev. The Respublikanski was even named after him for a short while.

With every tenement courtyard an improvised miniature football pitch throughout the long Ukrainian summer, and older players arriving from all over the republic to try to stake a place at Dynamo, Kiev has always been a hotbed of football. Even Dynamo's reserve games in their smaller, eponymously named stadium in the centre of town once attracted five-figure crowds. The stadium is still used, for Dynamo's junior fixtures and the Ukraine's Under-21 games.

Meanwhile Kiev's other club, the army team CSCA, continue to eke out a respectable existence at their modest ground, the other side of the tracks from the main train station.

With a population of three million, the city of Kiev could easily support two or three clubs in the Ukrainian top flight. The problem is that Kievites support only one: Dynamo.

The thrilling fields

 Dynamo Kiev

Club office Vul Grushevs'kovo 3
Stadium Respublikanski, Vul Chervonoarminska 55
Capacity 83,500 (all-seated)
Colours White shirts with blue trim
League champions (USSR) 1961, 1966–68, 1971, 1974–75, 1977, 1980–81, 1985–86, 1990
Cup winners (USSR) 1954, 1964, 1966, 1974, 1978, 1982, 1985, 1987, 1990
League champions (Ukraine) 1993–2000
Cup winners (Ukraine) 1993, 1998–2000
European Cup-Winners' Cup winners 1975, 1986

The most successful East European club of the modern era, Dynamo Kiev have built their considerable reputation on the back of three great sides from each of the last three decades, each of them coached by the most powerful man in the domestic game – Valery Lobanovsky. Having played in the club's first title-winning team in 1961, Lobanovsky turned an already successful domestic outfit into one capable of winning European honours, repeated the feat with his own group of youngsters ten years afterwards, then did it again ten years after that, this time creating a side capable of reaching the semi-finals of the Champions' League in 1999.

Founded as a branch of the Ukrainian Electrical Workers' Union under the old Communist setup in 1927, Dynamo Kiev were one of the inaugural members of the Soviet league in 1936, and would become one of three teams never to be relegated.

Apart from a solitary cup win in 1954, however, they never managed to challenge the dominance of the Moscow clubs until the Khrushchev era of the early Sixties. The Soviet leader who replaced Stalin was a Dynamo Kiev fan, and political favours which used to fall Moscow's way now went south.

In the late Fifties, club coach Oleg Ochenkov had brought in three youngsters who would have a huge bearing on the later development of the domestic game – Jozef Szabo, Oleg Basilevitch and a young winger and dead-ball specialist called Valery Lobanovsky. Under Ochenkov's replacement, Viatcheslav Soloviov, Basilevitch and Lobanovsky played a vital role in the attack which won the Soviet championship for Kiev in 1961. The arrival of Viktor Maslov three years later saw Dynamo step up a gear, but not in the way Lobanovsky wanted – he left to start his coaching career early in Odessa.

Meanwhile Maslov's team, with Anatoly Byshovets a formidable target man, became the best in the Soviet Union, winning four titles in six years. In continental competition, they knocked holders Celtic out of the European Cup in 1967 – revenge for a defeat by the same side the year before – but never progressed beyond the quarter-final stage.

Regardless of its lack of European impact, the team had huge potential which did not go unnoticed among the selectors for the USSR national side. The giant Rudakov in goal, Troshkin in defensive midfield, Kolotov in the middle and Onishenko upfront – all were in the Soviet side which lost to West Germany in the European Championship final of 1972.

By now, former Kiev coach Ochenko was head of football in the Ukranian republic. Impressed by Lobanovsky's training methods and results at Odessa and Dniepropetrovsk – and those of his former team-mate Basilevitch at Donetsk – he suggested the two work together at Dynamo. The duo duly arrived in the autumn of 1973, and set about their minor revolution. The gospel they preached was highly scientific, a marriage of Lobanovsky's strict tactics and Basilevitch's harsh physical training. Young striker Oleg Blokhin was one of the first to benefit, capable of running 100m in under 11 seconds once the trainer of Olympic champion sprinter Valery Borzov had arrived to build up the players' speed. The Dynamo game was one of total engagement and high energy, but it was given a soft midfield touch by Muntyan, Buryak, Fomenko and Veremeyev.

Unbeatable in the Soviet league, the formula would also bring success in Europe. In the 1974/75 Cup-Winners' Cup, the team's key fixture was a second-round tie with Eintracht Frankfurt, when Reshko and Maslov marked the dangerous Grabowski and Hölzenbein out of both legs. Goals from Onishenko and Blokhin then saw to Ferencváros in the final, 3–0, and Blokhin would be voted European Footballer of the Year in December.

The following season, Dynamo delivered Bayern Munich their first European Cup exit in four years. Yet achievement in the premier competition foundered at the feet of the two most adventurous sides of the day, Saint-Étienne in 1976 and Borussia Mönchengladbach in 1977. At least partly to blame was an overload of football – even though both ties were played before the

Soviet season had got going. As Dynamo were still officially attached to the Ministry of the Interior, Lobanovsky and Basilevitch had been ordered to take charge of the Soviet Olympic side of 1976, and filled it with Dynamo players. After the team failed to make the final, both were officially banned from the national team for life, and though the punishments were swiftly rescinded, Basilevitch quit Dynamo.

Kiev players – Baltacha and Demyanenko at the back, Buryak, Bessonov and Blokhin – formed a key part of the USSR's 1982 World Cup side, and Dynamo continued to dominate the Soviet domestic game. Lobanovsky, however, was looking to create a new team. He grouped together the best 20 youngsters from the Ukraine, among them a new forward duo of Alexandr Zavarov from Voroschilovgrad and Igor Belanov from Chornomorets Odessa, and worked with them tirelessly, encouraging their powers of acceleration and improvisation. Computerised training methods were brought in, with the aim of ensuring that players knew where to make each run and when.

Champions' League challenge – Nesta sits on Kossovskyi

With Zavarov, Belanov and the experienced but still rapid Blokhin, Kiev had the fastest forward line in the Soviet league, while Rats and Yakovenko provided vital movement off the ball in midfield. Double-winners at home, they swept all before them through the Cup-Winners' Cup of 1985/86 to the final, where they beat Atlético Madrid 3–0.

Once again, Lobanovksy was in charge of the Soviet side, and once again, key players were worn out by international duty. Zavarov, Belanov and others were sold to the West – where they would flop, Belanov leaving Mönchengladbach in shame after his wife was arrested for shoplifting – and the transfer revenue allowed Dynamo to wrest control of their affairs away from Soviet bureaucracy. But the trading angered Lobanovsky, who sought his own private fortune coaching in the Arab world.

In the new independent domestic setup, Dynamo foundered, and were almost bankrupt by 1992. It was a time of hyper-inflation, when colour photocopiers were banned in the Ukraine because of the *Monopoly* money design of the coupons that had replaced the Soviet rouble as currency. The club was considered a national treasure, however, and the government somehow found the money to rescue them. A new management team was set up under Hrihoriy Surkis, an entrepeneur who had made his money in America.

A new Kiev slowly rose from the ashes, winning the title in 1993 and every year thereafter. A first Champions' League campaign in 1994, in which a 3–2 home win over Spartak Moscow was the highlight, gave the new bosses a keen appetite for further European progress – perhaps a little too keen. Before a home fixture against Panathinaikos in September 1995, a delegation from Dynamo met the UEFA officials at Kiev-Boryspil airport, and immediately took them to the duty-free store to buy them fur coats. At an official dinner that evening, Spanish referee López Nieto was handed a note from Hrihoriy's brother Igor, reading '$30,000 for you – Dynamo victory'. López Nieto reported the events to UEFA, who banned the club from Europe for two years.

During this time, feelers were being put out to persuade Lobanovsky to return. The elements were all in place – a solid defence featuring Oleg Luzhny and Olexander Golovko, international Viktor Leonenko in attack, a squad of more than 40 behind them and plenty of cash to reinforce it if deemed necessary.

Lobanovsky finally decided to come back after seeing Kiev's successful display at the Moscow winter tournament in 1996. He rejected Leonenko, building his attack instead around Serhiy Rebrov, spotted by Dynamo scouts at Shakhtar Donetsk, and Andriy Shevchenko, who had come up through the ranks. Both were barely out of their teens, but they were skilful, hungry and lightning quick. With Vittaly Kossovsky and Yuri Kalintvintsev in the midfield, Lobanovsky created a system of seemingly perpetual motion, a team that was as well-orchestrated as it was self-confident.

The side exploded onto the scene in the 1997/98 Champions' League, beating PSV 3–1 in Eindhoven in their first game, unluckily being held 2–2 at home by Newcastle, then chalking up back-to-back thrashings of Louis van Gaal's Barcelona – 3–0 at home, 4–0 at the Nou Camp.

Now Lobanovsky had to persuade his players to stick around during the winter break. It proved a surprisingly easy task. With training facilities second to none and rich beyond their dreams – and perhaps warned off by Belanov's experience in the

Eighties – most of the stars chose to stay put, with only goalscoring midfielder Yuri Maximov leaving (Surkis dismissed his departure as irrelevant, though in truth it was a blow), for Werder Bremen.

The togetherness wasn't quite enough. Though they got a 1–1 draw against Juventus in Turin, Dynamo were humbled at home by a Pippo Inzaghi hat-trick and were out at the quarter-final stage.

The team needed a penalty shoot-out win over Sparta Prague to qualify for the group stage again in 1998/99, and once there they got off to a poor start, losing at Panathinaikos and drawing with Lens and Arsenal. Three wins in their last three games, however, showed the team had lost none of its confidence or counter-attacking verve.

In the quarter-finals against holders Real Madrid, the side again brought a 1–1 draw back to Kiev – but this time eased through thanks to two quick pieces of finishing from Shevchenko.

Black-market ticket prices hit the roof for the semi-final first leg against Bayern Munich in Kiev. Romantics everywhere yearned for Dynamo, a homegrown side who could score from any situation, to make the final, but it wasn't to be. Lobanovsky and his assistant Alexei Mikhailichenko, the former Sampdoria and Rangers midfielder who had become the coach's main communicator to the players, could only watch in horror as Kiev blew chances to add to a 3–1 lead, before being pegged back to 3–3. Bayern won the return 1–0 and, perhaps, a generation's best chance of European Cup glory had gone.

Shevchenko duly completed his long-arranged move to AC Milan, although Rebrov, once also wanted by the Italians, remained to spearhead another effort in 1999/2000. Some had suggested that without Shevchenko, Dynamo would lack the sharpness in attack to maintain their presence as a major force in the Champions' League. But Maxim Shatskikh proved to be a more then adequate replacement as Rebrov's partner, and Dynamo qualified for the second group phase ahead of Bayer Leverkusen and the Slovenians of Maribor. But a 2–1 home defeat by Real Madrid followed by an identical loss away to Bayern meant a quarter-final place required a miracle. In the final round of games Dynamo did their bit, exacting some revenge for the events of a year earlier by beating Bayern 2–0. But Real were too much for Rosenborg that same night, and took second place in the group thanks to a better head-to-head record against Dynamo.

Perhaps bored by the comfort of another yet domestic double, Rebrov surprisingly chose Tottenham as his dream move, over interest from some major European clubs. Without their two great strikers, and with Lobonovsky's health clearly deteriorating, Dynamo's European ambitions may be more modest in the coming seasons.

But the club's monolithic power at home is unlikely to be challenged, even if, in July 2000, they did sustain their first domestic defeat for two years.

Here we go!

The Respublikanski stadium has its own **metro station**, on the blue line, two stops from the Khreshchatik. The Palats Sportu metro stop, on the blue and black lines, is also within a short walk. The smaller Dynamo stadium is a 10min walk from Arsenal'na metro up Vul Grushevs'kovo.

Just the ticket

At the Respublikanski, there's a light-blue **ticket pagoda** on the concourse by the main entrance, with delicately drawn stadium plans posted up in the kiosk windows. There is also a ticket booth by the Palats Sportu entrance. If you want to avoid the queues, old ladies sell tickets on the steps of the metro station.

The Respublikanski is a two-tiered **open bowl**, with sectors numbered #1–40 in each. Sectors #7–15 are behind the north goal, favoured by the home crowd, sectors #26–34 behind the south goal. For international games, the away sector is on the upper level, #22 or

#23. The best seats are around the lodge and press area, sectors #1–3 and #36–38.

Swift half

Opposite the main entrance on the other side of Vul Chervonoarminska is the **Valentin**, an unpretentious sit-down beer tent. The concourse between the metro entrance and the stadium is swamped with stalls, some selling beer, and you'll find a bar in the amusement tent full of bouncy toy animals and ear-piercing facilities.

On the Palats Sportu side, the **Atlantik** at Vul Yesplanada 28 is proper bar, its ambience tailored to the aspirations of the modern Ukrainian businessman.

At the Dynamo stadium, the comfortable **Chet'man** bar, with tables outside, is by the entrance to the incline, and there is a small terrace bar by the main entrance and the adjacent ticket office.

Club merchandise

The new **Dynamo Store** (open Mon–Sat 10am–7pm, Sun 11am–5pm, no credit cards), a 5min walk from the stadium at Vul Chervonoarminska 88, is more of a small Adidas showroom than anything else. Replica Dynamo shirts can be had here for hr100–130.

Ultra culture

Gone are the days when visits from Spartak Moscow would provoke mayhem all day long on the streets of Kiev. For big games, thousands of Ukrainians would arrive from all over the region, killing the endless hours on the bus with vodka, to give it their best in the stadium – usually with chants in Russian.

Dynamo's current crews, **Ultras Kiev** and **Crazy Legion**, pale in comparison. Those young fans you do see at European games will invariably be wearing a blue-and-white neckerchief, the older ones naked from the waist up.

In the net

The main website, fan-run but apparently with some official backing, is at: www.dynamo.kiev.ua. It's exceptionally thorough, but sadly in Ukrainian only for the time being. For an **unofficial site** with some half-decent English content, try: www.dynamokiev.da.ru.

Groundhopping

CSCA Kiev

CSCA stadium, Povitroflotskii prospekt
Capacity 15,000
Colours Red and black

Kiev's second club, CSCA, are a classic former army team. Second-stringers in the old Soviet setup – their best performance was a cup semi-final place in 1952 – they are now pushing for honours in the weaker Ukrainian league, enjoying backing from both the army and the country's emerging private business sector, and poaching talent from their illustrious city rivals to establish themselves in the modern era.

With 1986 Cup-Winners' Cup winner Volodimir Bessonov on the coaching staff and another old Dynamo star, Viktor Leonenko, in the attack, CSCA lost a hard-fought Ukrainian cup final 2–1 to Dynamo in 1998. A late injury-time away goal at Cork City helped them to a 3–2 aggregate win in their subsequent Cup-Winners' Cup qualifying tie, but CSCA were easy meat for Lokomotiv Moscow in the next round.

The 1999/2000 season was one of disappointment, the team finishing tenth, six points clear of the expanded relegation zone needed to reduce Ukraine's top flight from 16 to 14 teams.

The home legs for those 1998/99 European ties were moved to the Dynamo stadium from CSCA's traditional ground, which lies across the mass of train tracks near the main train station – **metro Vokzal'na**. Before crossing the walkway over Povitroflotskii Prospekt, grab a beer in the old-style *Tetyana* bar at #3. Once at the stadium, the **ticket offices** are by the main entrance – sectors #1–4 are in the main stand, sectors #5–9 behind the goal.

Eat, drink, sleep…

Bars and clubs

The average featureless **Kiev bar** beeps loudly with Europop or fruit-machine noises and serves local *Obolon* beer at hr2.5, or imported *Bitburger* at hr4. Gone are the *shinoks*, the old stand-up vodka joints which once littered the city, while the new nightclubs are for those with more Western money than sense. No wonder so many drink out in the open, especially around Maïdan Nezalezhnosti, which adjoins a vague bar area, up the streets leading away from the main Khreshchatik towards Podil. For **DJ events**, ask around the Kinoclub, in the *Kievskaya Rus* cinema, or at the *Club Sofia* listed below.

Club Sofia, Vul Sofiivska 7. Decorated with local caricatures, an excellent cellar bar, the most popular of those run by the enterprising and friendly German landlord, Eric. His best, however, is the **Ukraïna** at Malaya Zhitomirska 15a, round the corner. Both metro Maïdan Nezalezhnosti.

Cowboy Bar, passage under Kreshchatik 15. It's gone midnight, you're off your face, some R&B act have just murdered the entire *Stax* back catalogue, everything's wooden, crowded and smoky. Next morning, someone tells you you were in the *Cowboy Bar*. Metro Kreshchatik.

Dab, Vul Chervonoarmiïska 23. One of several terrace bars in the courtyards tucked off Chervonoarmiïska, a blessed relief from the relentless summer heat and traffic fumes. Metro Ploscha Lva Tolstoho.

Guliver, Vozdivzhenskaya 60 (Andrivski Uzviz). Up a precarious metal staircase to a fine Podil bar offset with disco lights and a young clientele determined to enjoy them.

O'Briens, Vul Mykhaïlivska 17a. Decent Irish bar offering full breakfasts 8am–11am, pub grub otherwise, Sky Premiership football at 6pm Sundays, local beer at hr5, Czech or Irish at hr10.

Open 8am–2am daily, most major credit cards. Metro Maïdan Nezalezhnosti.

Restaurants

The mainstays of cheap hot food for the masses, the *stolovaya* and *yidalnya*, are dying out, and in their place are overpriced, **empty restaurants**, whose trade relies on the occasional business customer spending hr50 a head – a fortune for the average Ukrainian.

As an alternative, American and local fast-food joints abound, and most hotel restaurants and expat bars offer a reasonable menu.

Bombay Palace, Krutiy Uzviz 6. Quality Indian cuisine, popularly situated opposite the *British Council* office, with an extensive menu including vegetarian options. Open midday–midnight, most major credit cards, home delivery. Off Ploscha Bessarabska near metro Ploscha Lva Tolstoho.

Pantagruel, Vul Lysenko 1. Decent Italian food at hr12–20 a dish, with a terrace overlooking the gardens by Zoloti Vorota metro. Open Sun–Thur until 11pm, Fri–Sat until 2am. Avoid the live music 8pm–10pm. Most major credit cards.

Pilsner Bar, Vul Pushkinska 20. As well as a monument to the king of beers, whose history is documented around the walls, a decent restaurant with main dishes at hr25–35, starters at hr15–20. Most major credit cards. Metro Teatralna.

Stariy Podol, Vul Khoriva 19. One of many bars and restaurants near Kontraktova Ploscha metro, this one features a terrace garden with enough hidden corners for you to avoid the brightly dressed musicians. Fish a speciality, main courses at hr15–25. Perfect summer spot.

V Hostyakh u Bakhusa, Vul Sagaïdachnoho 29. That rare gem, a friendly bar featuring a cheap menu of domestic fare, with locals dancing, soft red curtains, big wooden tables and no loud beep-beep music. Open daily 9am–11pm. Metro Poshtova Ploscha.

Accommodation

Tourism has not yet come to Kiev. Hotels cater for the business traveller and what budget places there are triple their prices for Westerners. Student hostels are away from the centre of town, and if you're paying anything less than $100 a night anywhere, you cannot be assured of **hot water** or **toilet paper**.

To get your visa in the first place, you will have had to have faxed proof of booked accommodation, but you can get around much of the expense by staying one night, then arranging a **private room** for hr50–80 by heading down to the train station and dealing with one of the many grandmothers waiting for custom off the incoming international trains.

Druzhba, Bul'var Druzhby Narodiv 5 (☎044/268 3387, fax 044/268 3300). Soviet-era hotel near Lybidska metro whose swimming pool and fitness centre have been under construction since Ukrainian independence. Twin rooms at $25 a bed. No credit cards.

Grazhdanski Aviatski Institut, Vul Nyzhinska 29e (☎044/484 9059). The cheapest and most accessible student hostel – look out for the *Gostinitsa FPK* sign in the block of houses on Nyzhinska. Singles and doubles at under hr20, modest supplement if staying one night only. No credit cards. Take tram #3 to Harmatna from near Vokzalna metro.

Lybid', Ploschad' Peremohy (☎044/274 0063, fax 044/224 0578). Reasonable bet if there's a pair of you coming in on the train, as it's near the station and has a $110 deal on a twin room. The *Playoffs International* bar is a pick-up joint with little football talk. Most credit cards. Metro Vokzalna.

Hotel Rus, Vul Hospitalna 4 (☎044/220 5646, fax 044/220 4396). The cheaper end of the *Kievska Rus* complex overlooking the Respublikanski stadion, recently renovated, each room with bath and TV. Business facilities downstairs, swimming pool. Most credit cards, $160 a single, $250 a twin. Metro Palats Sportu/Klovska.

Yugoslavia

Fubdbalski Savez Jugoslavije (FSJ), Terazije 35, CP263, 11000 Belgrade
☎011/323 3447   Fax 011/323 3433   E-mail fsj@eunet.yu

League champions Red Star Belgrade   **Cup winners** Red Star Belgrade
Promoted Zeta Golubovci, Napredak Krusevac   **Relegated** Proleter Zrenjanin,
Hajduk Belgrade, Mogren Budva, Spartak Subotica, Borac Ćaćak

European participants 2000/01 Red Star Belgrade (UCL qualifiers); Partizan
Belgrade, Napredak Krusevac (UEFA Cup); FK Obilić (Intertoto Cup)

To add to ten years of being embroiled in bloody conflicts with its neighbours, what remained of Yugoslavia (at the time of writing, the republics of Serbia and Montenegro) suffered from the heaviest bombing campaign Europe had seen since World War II in 1999. Twelve months on, and with the prospect of civil war between supporers of the despot Slobodan Milošević and the opposition, not to mention an uprising in Montenegro, it is going to be some time before Yugoslavs can afford themselves the luxury of addressing the dire state of their domestic football. It will also be some time, alas, before visitors from NATO countries – Britain included – will be offered a beer and a friendly chat about the beautiful game, in what was once one of Europe's most instinctively hospitable nation states.

And yet, had history taken a different course, Yugoslavia might now be basking in the glow of a decade of unprecedented footballing success. For in 1990 the country seemed on the brink of becoming one of the giants of the European game. The national side had been desperately unlucky to bow out of Italia '90 at the quarter-final stage, losing a shoot-out after their ten men had played all the football against an ultra-defensive Argentina in Florence. At club level, Red Star Belgrade were assembling a

Support without frontiers – Bosnian Serbs were among Yugoslavia's fans at Euro 2000

Face of the fightback – Savo strikes against Slovenia

Even had the war-torn country been allowed to send a team to Sweden, that team would have been shorn of much of their attacking talent. Of the 24 goals the Slavs scored in their Euro '92 qualifying games, 19 came from Croats, Slovenes, Bosnians or Macedonians – all of whom had withdrawn from the national side by the time of the finals, their nationalities now those of independent states. Croatian and Slovenian clubs had pulled out of the Yugoslav league at the end of the 1990/91 season, the Bosnians and Macedonians a year later.

While independent Croatia, Slovenia and Macedonia all took part in the qualifiers for the 1996 European Championship, the ban on the Yugoslav national team was to last throughout the qualifying competitions for USA '94 and Euro '96, and clubs from what was left of the old federal league were barred from European competition until 1995/96.

bold young side capable of some of the finest counter-attacking the continent had seen in years. As Red Star glided effortlessly to a 1991 European Cup win over Marseille, the national side embarked on a similarly impressive run toward the Euro '92 finals in Sweden.

Then came war. The heart of the old Yugoslav federation was torn apart by Europe's most brutal conflict since 1945, and football, like so many aspects of normal life, would never be the same again. After some vacillating, UEFA decided it could not defy the logic of United Nations sanctions and at the last minute banned Yugoslavia from Euro '92. They were replaced by Denmark, whom the Slavs had already eliminated at the qualifying stage, and who went on to win the entire competition.

Today's Yugoslav league comprises teams from Serbia and the tiny republic of Montenegro. Of the giants of the old six-state league, only the Belgrade rivals, Red Star and Partizan, remain, with provincial opposition – of a sort – coming from Vojvodina Novi Sad and the biggest Montenegrin side, Budućnost Podgorica. Obilić Belgrade have emerged as a new force in the capital, but they have been beset by controversy ever since it emerged that their main benefactor was an indicted war criminal, Željko Ražnjatović, better-known as *Arkan*. The club were allowed back into Europe only in the summer of 2000, after their backer's assassination in Belgrade.

Faced with a dramatically lower standard of football, falling crowds and pitifully low salaries, the stars of Serbian soccer have left in droves. Today more than a thousand Yugoslav players are plying their trade in leagues around the world, along with scores of coaches whose tactical awareness bears testimony to the success of the old federation's national coaching programme.

Historically, socialist Yugoslavia's football mirrored the country's political development. In the years immediately after World War II the game was reorganised along classic Communist lines, 1945 seeing the formation of an army side, Partizan, and a police team, Red Star, as well as the two major Croatian clubs, Dinamo Zagreb and Hajduk Split. While the Belgrade duo were learning to hate each other, the national team strutted their stuff in the tournament 'amateur' socialist countries focused so much attention on – the Olympics. After a remarkable series of silver medals in 1948, 1952 and 1956, Yugoslavia defeated Denmark to win gold at the 1960 Games in Rome. In the same year they were runners-up in the first-ever European Championship, then called the Nations' Cup, losing to the Soviet Union in the final.

During the Sixties and Seventies, Yugoslav club sides featured seven times in the finals of European club competitions, and with big domestic clashes regularly attracting 60,000-plus crowds, pressure began to build for clubs to be freed from their Soviet-style structure.

Professionalism was gradually introduced in the Seventies, and by the early Eighties clubs had been given the right to run their own affairs, many developing commercial interests around their stadia, effectively turning their land into miniature business parks.

Yugoslavia's liberal (for a Communist country) travel policy allowed players to move abroad to Western clubs from the mid-Sixties, a development which intensified in the Eighties without having much detrimental effect on the domestic game.

It was members of the sanctions-inspired, Nineties exodus who found themselves unwittingly caught up in the aftermath of the latest, non-football crisis to hit the Yugoslav game – the Kosovo war. In March 1999, players such as Pedja Mijatović, Siniša Mihajlović and Dejan Savićević were in Belgrade preparing for a much-awaited Euro 2000 qualifier against Croatia when the air-raid sirens began wailing. NATO bombers were overhead and everyone – Yugoslavia's most celebrated footballers included – was forced to take cover. In the turmoil that followed, the Croatia game, along with a string of other qualifiers scheduled to be played in the area that month, was postponed by UEFA, while those players with family in Belgrade or elsewhere in Serbia or Montenegro did their best to ascertain their whereabouts.

When they returned to their clubs in France, Spain, Italy and Germany, the players did their best to rally support for the Serb cause, sporting *Stop The Bombing* T-shirts and giving a series of high-profile media interviews. From the other side of the argument, UEFA faced calls to ban the Yugoslavs from Euro 2000, just as it had banned them seven years earlier, unless Slobodan Milošević withdrew his troops from Kosovo.

At least the eventual withdrawal of said forces in the summer, followed by NATO's occupation of Kosovo, allowed Yugoslavia back into the footballing fold in time for the country's Euro 2000 qualifying programme to resume, albeit with an unenviable fixture backlog. The side would have a new coach, too, the veteran former Sampdoria boss Vujadin Boskov having replaced Milan Zivadinović, who in turn had been in the job for less than year, after stepping into the boots of Slobodan Santrac.

It was Santrac who had led Yugoslavia to their first major international tournament of the post-sanctions era – the 1998 World Cup. His team had qualified brilliantly, eliminating the Czechs and Slovaks at the group stage before putting 12 goals in two games past Hungary in the play-offs. They began brightly in France, too, crafting a carefully controlled 1–0 win over Iran, drawing 2–2 with Germany, and completing the job with another comfortable 1–0 victory, this time over the USA.

Yet they could surely have done better than the second-round elimination by Holland that followed. Having survived an early spell of pressure and pulled the game back to 1–1, Yugoslavia retreated into a defensive shell once Mijatović had missed the penalty that would have put them in front, and Dennis Bergkamp had escaped unpunished from stamping on Mihajlović. In the circumstances, there was a certain inevitability about Edgar Davids' deflected long-range winner in stoppage time.

After the 1999 ceasefire, Boskov's team beat Macedonia and drew 0–0 at home to Croatia, leaving themselves needing a point in Zagreb to secure first place in their Euro 2000 qualifying group, and deny their old enemies even so much as a play-off spot. Despite playing the bulk of the second half with ten men after Zoran Mirković was sent-off, and despite the intimidating atmosphere generated by the Zagreb crowd, goals from Mijatović and Dejan Stanković

Face of fatalism – former boss Vujadin Boskov

earned a 2–2 draw and a ticket to the Low Countries which had seemed utterly implausible less than six months earlier.

Once at the finals, Yugoslavia's progress was, perhaps predictably, haphazard. Three goals down to Slovenia in their opening game, they lost their defensive lynchpin Mihajlović to a second yellow card and were immediately inspired, Savo Milošević scoring twice to help the scores back to 3–3. In their next game against Norway they won few friends with their tough tackling and play-acting, yet also showed touches of deftness of a kind that were completely beyond their opponents, and were worth their 1–0 win.

With Norway expected to beat the Slovenes comfortably, Boskov's team needed only a point from their final game with Spain to progress to the quarter-finals. At the end of 90 entertaining minutes, the Yugoslavs were 3–2 up. Then, three minutes into injury time, the Spaniards were awarded a highly debatable penalty which Mendieta converted, and somehow there was still enough time for Alfonso to knock in a winner in the 95th minute. Heads were in hands, players lay on their backs in despair, and Yugoslavia's travelling support, which had earned praise for its noise and colour despite limited numbers, began to hurl objects onto the pitch in frustration. But then the score came through from Arnhem. In the richest of ironies, Slovenia, the country which had been the first to declare independence from the Yugoslav federation at the start of the Nineties, had held Norway to a goalless draw, enabling both Spain and Yugoslavia to qualify for the quarter-finals.

A more composed team, better prepared for the big occasion, might have reacted positively to the prospect of gaining revenge over Holland in the quarter-finals. Boskov's Yugoslavia were no such team, and with Mihajlović all over the place at the back, they were crushed, 6–1.

In the aftermath, Boskov resisted calls for his resignation, vowing to continue until the 2002 World Cup. But even his friends at the Yugoslav FA, the FSJ, could see it was time for a change. Their choice of former OFK Belgrade star and Servette coach Ilija Petković as new national boss was uninspiring, but many believe his is only a short-term appointment, and that Dragan Stojković will take up the reins once he has finished his playing career in Japan.

Whoever is in the hot seat, he will at least have a new generation of players experienced in European competition to choose from. UEFA had initially banned Yugoslav clubs from Europe in 1999/2000, but by the time of the draw for the Champions' League and UEFA Cup qualifiers, peace of a kind had descended on the region, and the teams were allowed back in at the last minute. Sadly, champions Partizan Belgrade were no match for Spartak Moscow in the Champions' League qualifiers, and then fell to Leeds in the UEFA Cup – having had to play their 'home' leg in Holland because of security fears. Likewise, cup winners Red Star and fourth-placed Vojvodina Novi Sad (who had replaced Obilić) were eliminated at the same first-round stage.

Whether Red Star, who won the domestic title after losing only once in 40 games, could do any better in Europe in 2000/01 was a moot point. The name and the heritage were there – the players, the facilities and the imperative sadly not.

A different league

After experimenting with championship and promotion groups, Yugoslavia reverted to a straightforward, 18-team first division in 1998. The simple life did not last long. The suspension of the league programme midway through the 1998/99 campaign left promotion and relegation issues unresolved, as well as championship ones, and after much bureaucratic indecision, the Yugoslav FA decided that no teams would drop down, but that the teams placed first and second in the two regional second divisions should be promoted.

With Kosovo's FK Priština withdrawing, this led to a 21-team top flight, from which five teams were relegated at the end of 1999/2000, while only two were promoted – resulting in a more manageable 18-club division for 2000/01.

Up for the cup

With the semi-finals and final of the 1998/99 cup competition having to be squeezed in during what would normally be the Yugoslav season's summer break, the FA departed from tradition and arranged a single-game final in Belgrade. The match was a success, so the experiment was repeated in 2000, when Red Star completed a domestic double by beating second-division Napredak Krusevac 4–0.

In the net

As those on both sides of the Kosovo conflict found, the internet can be a vital means of staying in touch when places become accessible and other lines of communication are broken. So it is, for the time being, with Yugoslav football.

The FA runs an official website at: www.fsj.yu. It's nice to look at and quick to navigate, with an English section that includes national-team match reports, news and a bit of history. For more detailed stats, try the *Former Yugoslavia Soccer* site at: www.fyusoccer.com.

You can also get the latest word from the two big Belgrade clubs online. Red Star's official site is under heavy construction but probably worth a look at: www.fcredstar.com. Otherwise, the club's *Delije* fan group run a superb site at: www.delije.net.

Likewise, the Partizan official site can be hard to access at: www.partizan.co.yu. But an excellent unofficial version provides a one-stop resource for all Partizan and related sites on the web, at: partizan.net.

ALSO AVAILABLE...

Stay in touch with us!

ROUGH*NEWS* **is Rough Guides' free newsletter. In four issues a year we give you news, travel issues, music reviews, readers' letters and the latest dispatches from authors on the road.**

I would like to receive ROUGH*NEWS*: please put me on your free mailing list.

NAME . . . .

ADDRESS . . . .

Please clip or photocopy and send to: Rough Guides, 62–70 Shorts Gardens, London WC2H 9AH, England or Rough Guides, 375 Hudson Street, New York, NY 10014, USA.

ROUGH GUIDES: Travel

Alaska
Amsterdam
Andalucia
Argentina
Australia
Austria

Bali & Lombok
Barcelona
Belgium &
  Luxembourg
Belize
Berlin
Brazil
Britain
Brittany &
  Normandy
Bulgaria
California
Canada
Central America
Chile
China
Corsica
Costa Rica
Crete
Croatia
Cuba
Cyprus
Czech & Slovak
  Republics

Dodecanese &
  the East Aegean
Devon &
  Cornwall
Dominican
  Republic
Dordogne & the
  Lot
Ecuador
Egypt
England
Europe
Florida
France
French Hotels &
  Restaurants
  1999
Germany
Goa
Greece
Greek Islands
Guatemala
Hawaii
Holland
Hong Kong &
  Macau
Hungary

Iceland
India
Indonesia
Ionian Islands
Ireland

Israel & the
  Palestinian
  Territories
Italy
Jamaica
Japan
Jordan
Kenya
Lake District
Languedoc &
  Roussillon
Laos
London
Los Angeles
Malaysia,
  Singapore &
  Brunei
Mallorca &
  Menorca
Maya World
Mexico
Morocco
Moscow
Nepal
New England
New York
New Zealand
Norway
Pacific
  Northwest
Paris
Peru
Poland
Portugal
Prague
Provence & the
  Côte d'Azur
The Pyrenees
Romania
St Petersburg
San Francisco

Sardinia
Scandinavia
Scotland
Scottish
  highlands and
  Islands
Sicily
Singapore
South Africa
South India
Southeast Asia
Southwest USA
Spain
Sweden
Switzerland
Syria

Thailand
Trinidad &
  Tobago
Tunisia
Turkey
Tuscany &
  Umbria
USA
Venice
Vienna
Vietnam
Wales
Washington DC
West Africa
Zimbabwe &
  Botswana

AVAILABLE AT ALL GOOD BOOKSHOPS

ROUGH GUIDES: Mini Guides, Travel Specials and Phrasebooks

MINI GUIDES

Antigua
Bangkok
Barbados
Beijing
Big Island of Hawaii
Boston
Brussels
Budapest
Cape Town
Copenhagen
Dublin
Edinburgh

Florence
Honolulu
Ibiza & Formentera
Jerusalem
Las Vegas
Lisbon
London Restaurants
Madeira
Madrid
Malta & Gozo
Maui
Melbourne
Menorca

Montreal
New Orleans

Paris
Rome
Seattle
St Lucia
Sydney
Tenerife
Tokyo
Toronto
Vancouver

TRAVEL SPECIALS

First-Time Asia
First-Time Europe
Women Travel

PHRASEBOOKS

Czech
Dutch
Egyptian Arabic
European
French
German
Greek

Hindi & Urdu
Hungarian
Indonesian
Italian
Japanese
Mandarin
  Chinese
Mexican
  Spanish
Polish
Portuguese
Russian
Spanish
Swahili
Thai
Turkish
Vietnamese

AVAILABLE AT ALL GOOD BOOKSHOPS